Lecture Notes in Computer Scie

Commenced Publication in 1973
Founding and Former Series Editors:
Gerhard Goos, Juris Hartmanis, and Jan van Leeuwen

Amit Sahai (Ed.)

Theory
of Cryptography

10th Theory of Cryptography Conference, TCC 2013
Tokyo, Japan, March 3-6, 2013
Proceedings

 Springer

Volume Editor

Amit Sahai
UCLA
3731E Boelter Hall
Los Angeles, CA 90095, USA
E-mail: sahai@cs.ucla.edu

ISSN 0302-9743   e-ISSN 1611-3349
ISBN 978-3-642-36593-5   e-ISBN 978-3-642-36594-2
DOI 10.1007/978-3-642-36594-2
Springer Heidelberg Dordrecht London New York

Library of Congress Control Number: 2013931230

CR Subject Classification (1998): E.3, D.4.6, K.6.5, F.1.1-2, C.2.0, F.2.1-2, G.2.2, I.1

LNCS Sublibrary: SL 4 – Security and Cryptology

Typesetting: Camera-ready by author, data conversion by Scientific Publishing Services, Chennai, India

Printed on acid-free paper

Springer is part of Springer Science+Business Media (www.springer.com)

Preface

These are the proceedings of TCC 2013, the 10th Theory of Cryptography Conference, held at the University of Tokyo, Japan, during March 3–6, 2013. The conference was sponsored by the International Association for Cryptologic Research (IACR). The General Chairs were Masayuki Abe and Tatsuaki Okamoto.

The Program Committee accepted 36 papers out of 98 submissions. The program included papers on a wide variety of topics, from secure computation to zero-knowledge PCPs, by authors from many different backgrounds: one paper, "On the Circular Security of Bit-Encryption," is solely authored by a PhD student, Ron D. Rothblum; another paper, "Characterizing the Cryptographic Properties of Reactive 2-Party Functionalities," is co-authored by R. Amzi Jeffs, who was a high-school student at the time the paper was written.

On behalf of the Program Committee (PC), I thank the authors of all submissions for contributing excellent manuscripts. These contributions are of course the lifeblood of TCC, providing the most essential ingredient for the conference. The high quality of the submissions made the PC's job both rewarding and challenging. Conflicts of interest were taken seriously by the PC. In particular, no PC member (including the PC chair) played any role in deciding the fate of submissions by authors that were current students, postdoctoral researchers, or colleagues in the same institution. The program also included three invited talks: by Craig Gentry, titled "Encrypted Messages from the Heights of Cryptomania"; by Tal Malkin, titled "Secure Computation for Big Data"; and by Benny Applebaum, titled "Cryptographic Hardness of Random Local Functions – A Survey." The conference featured a rump session for informal short presentations and announcements, chaired by abhi shelat.

There are many individuals to whom I am grateful in connection with this conference. But I begin by thanking Dan Boneh and Shai Halevi, who went above and beyond the call of duty in providing assistance to the success of the conference, despite having no official role in the organization of TCC 2013.

This year, to increase the quality of the reviewing process, I wanted to add an automated way for PC members to have ongoing anonymous interactive communication with authors throughout the review period: this would enable reviewers to obtain clarifications on any aspects of submissions in a timely manner – at the time when they are most engaged with any particular paper. (This is in contrast to a single response phase, where often the author responses arrive too late to help with crucial PC discussions.) However, no currently available software package for conference management supports such a feature, and communication via the PC Chair is too cumbersome to encourage such interactions. Dan Boneh volunteered to write a Web-based software system to enable such interactions, and was very responsive to my requests for additional features and changes. Shai Halevi generously agreed to incorporate Dan's system into his existing conference management software, and provided me with very helpful assistance for using his software throughout the review process. The PC used this new system throughout the TCC review process, and it greatly helped in clarifying issues about submissions. Despite this being a new experimental process, the PC used the new system to engage in interactions with over a quarter of submitted papers. This would not have been possible without the generous contributions of time and effort by Dan Boneh and Shai Halevi, and I am deeply grateful to them for their work.

The PC, which consisted of 20 top researchers in our field, worked very hard and I thank them for their dedication and effort. Special thanks are in order to Allison Lewko, Thomas Holenstien, and Mohammad Mahmoody, who agreed to serve as shepherds for certain accepted papers. I also thank all the external reviewers (listed in the following pages) for providing thoughtful reviews of submissions. For running the conference itself, I am very grateful to the General Chairs Masayuki Abe and Tatsuaki Okamoto, and all the members of the local Organizing Committee for their hard work: Takeshi Chikazawa, Masami Hagiya (Organizing Committee Chair), Noboru Kunihiro, Hirofumi Muratani, Ryo Nishimaki, Miyako Ohkubo, Yuji Suga, Koutarou Suzuki, Keisuke Tanaka, Shigenori Uchiyama, and Saho Uchida. I also wish to thank the two volunteers who managed the conference website: Shinichiro Matsuo and Hirokazu Hiruma. All of these individuals gave their time on a voluntary basis and their work was essential to the organization of the conference.

Finally, I am indebted to Oded Goldreich, the Chair of the TCC Steering Committee, and all the members of the TCC Steering Committee, Mihir Bellare, Ivan Dåmgard, Shafi Goldwasser, Shai Halevi, Russell Impagliazzo, Ueli Maurer, Silvio Micali, Moni Naor, and Tatsuaki Okamoto, for their advice and trust. I am also grateful to previous TCC Chairs Tal Rabin, Shai Halevi, Ran Canetti, Yuval Ishai, and Ronald Cramer for their generous advice.

January 2013   Amit Sahai

TCC 2013

The 10th Theory of Cryptography Conference

University of Tokyo, Tokyo, Japan
March 3–6, 2013

Sponsored by the International Association for Cryptologic Research (IACR).

General Chairs

Masayuki Abe	NTT, Japan
Tatsuaki Okamoto	NTT, Japan

Program Chair

Amit Sahai	UCLA, USA

Program Committee

Masayuki Abe	NTT, Japan
Boaz Barak	Microsoft Research New England, USA
Ivan Damgård	Aarhus University, Denmark
Rosario Gennaro	City University of New York, USA
Vipul Goyal	Microsoft Research, India
Thomas Holenstein	ETH Zurich, Switzerland
Yuval Ishai	Technion, Israel
Yael Kalai	Microsoft Research New England, USA
Allison Lewko	Microsoft Research New England, USA
Mohammad Mahmoody	Cornell University, USA
Hemanta Maji	UCLA, USA
Ilya Mironov	Microsoft Research Silicon Valley, USA
Steve Myers	Indiana University, USA
Krzysztof Pietrzak	IST Austria, Austria
Tal Rabin	IBM Research, USA
Alon Rosen	IDC Herzliya, Israel
Amit Sahai	UCLA, USA, Chair
abhi shelat	University of Virginia, USA
Stefano Tessaro	MIT, USA
Hoeteck Wee	George Washington University, USA

External Reviewers

Table of Contents

Overcoming Weak Expectations

Yevgeniy Dodis[1] and Yu Yu[2]

[1] New York University
dodis@cs.nyu.edu
[2] Institute for Interdisciplinary Information Sciences,
Tsinghua University
yuyu@yuyu.hk

Abstract. Recently, there has been renewed interest in basing cryptographic primitives on weak secrets, where the only information about
the secret is some non-trivial amount of (min-) entropy. From a formal
point of view, such results require to upper bound the expectation of
some function $f(X)$, where X is a weak source in question. We show an
elementary inequality which essentially upper bounds such 'weak expectation' by two terms, the first of which is independent of f, while the
second only depends on the 'variance' of f under uniform distribution.
Quite remarkably, as relatively simple corollaries of this elementary inequality, we obtain some 'unexpected' results, in several cases noticeably
simplifying/improving prior techniques for the same problem.

Examples include non-malleable extractors, leakage-resilient symmetric encryption, alternative to the dense model theorem, seed-dependent
condensers and improved entropy loss for the leftover hash lemma.

1 Introduction

Formal cryptographic models take for granted the availability of perfect randomness. However, in reality we may only obtain 'weak' random sources that are far
from uniform but only guaranteed with high unpredictability (formalized with
min-entropy), such as biometric data [11,4], physical sources [3,2], secrets with
partial leakage, and group elements from Diffie-Hellman key exchange [18,20].
We refer to the former as ideal model and the latter as real model.

From a formal point of view, the standard (T, ε)-security (in the ideal model)
of a cryptographic application P essentially requires that for any adversary A
with resource[1] T, the expectation of $f(U_m)$ is upper bounded by ε, where function $f(r)$ denotes A's advantage conditioned on secret key being r, and U_m
denotes uniform distribution over $\{0, 1\}^m$. In the real model, keys are sampled
from some non-uniform distribution R and thus the resulting security is the expected value of $f(R)$, which we call 'weak expectation'. We would hope that if
P is (T, ε)-secure in the ideal setting, then P is also (T', ε') in the real setting
by replacing U_m with R of sufficiently high min-entropy, where T' and ε' are not
much worse than T and ε respectively.

---

[1] We use the word "resource" to include all the efficiency measures we might care
about, such as running time, circuit size, number of oracle queries, etc.

A. Sahai (Ed.): TCC 2013, LNCS 7785, pp. 1–22, 2013.

In this paper, we present an elementary inequality that upper bounds the weak expectation of $f(R)$ by two terms: the first term only depends on the *entropy deficiency* (i.e. the difference between $m = length(R)$ and the amount of entropy it has), and the second is essentially the 'variance' of f under uniform distribution U_m. Quite surprisingly, some 'unexpected' results follow as simple corollaries of this inequality, such as non-malleable extractors [14,10,7,21], leakage-resilient symmetric encryptions [24], alternative to the dense model theorem [28,27,16,17], seed-dependent condensers [12] and improved entropy loss for the Leftover Hash Lemma (LHL) [1]. We provide a unified proof for these diversified problems and in many cases significantly simply and/or improve known techniques for the same problems.

OUR TECHNIQUE. Our main technique is heavily based on several tools introduced by Barak et al. [1] in the context of improving the "entropy loss" of the Leftover Hash Lemma [19]. This work concentrated on the setting of deriving (or extracting) a cryptographic key R from a weak source X, using public randomness S. The main observation of [1] in this context was the fact that, for a certain class of so called "square-friendly" applications P, — an informal notion later made more explicit by [12], and which we explain later — one can reduce the minimal entropy requirement on X by "borrowing" the security from P. The main insight of this work comes from "lifting" this important observation one level higher. Namely, "square-friendly" applications have the property of *directly tolerating weak keys* R. Informally, if P is "square-friendly" and (T, ε)-secure with uniform key U_m, then P is (T', ε')-secure with any weak key R having entropy deficiency (see above) d, where $T' \sim T$ and $\varepsilon' \sim 2^d \cdot \varepsilon$.[2]

DIRECT APPLICATIONS. As mentioned above, this "obvious-in-retrospect" observation leads to several interesting (and sometimes unexpected!) consequences. First, by considering simple applications, such as information-theoretic one-time MACs [22,9], we immediately obtain results which used to be proven directly, occasionally with elaborate analyses (essentially re-doing the elaborate analyses for the uniform case). Second, for some applications, such as weak pseudorandom functions and leakage-resilient symmetric-encryption, we obtain greatly improved results as compared to state-of-the-art [24] (and, again, with much simpler proofs). Third, we carefully design new "square-friendly" applications P, generally not studied in 'ideal' (uniform-key) setting — either because of their elementary analyses, or the lack of direct applications. However, by mechanically translating such 'uninteresting' applications P to the 'real' (weak-key) setting, we obtain natural and much more 'interesting' applications P'. Moreover, by 'blindly' applying our machinery, we get surprisingly non-trivial results about the 'real' security of such applications P'. For example, starting from a (carefully crafted) variant of pairwise independent hash functions, we get the definition of so called *non-malleable extractors* [14]! Using our machinery, we obtain an *elementary* construction of such non-malleable extractors from 4-wise independent hash functions, which beats a much more elaborate construction

---

[2] Precisely, $\varepsilon \cdot 2^d$ for unpredictability and $\sqrt{\varepsilon \cdot 2^d}$ for indistinguishability applications.

recently found by [10].[3] Using a simpler P, — essentially a "one-wise" independent hash function, — we also get a cute variant of the Leftover Hash Lemma.

APPLICATIONS TO KEY DERIVATION. Finally, we apply our improved understanding of 'real' security of "square-friendly" applications to the setting of key derivation, which was the original motivation of [1]. First, consider the case when the application P is "square-friendly". In this case, since P can directly tolerate keys R with small entropy deficiency d, our key derivation function h only needs to be a good *condenser* [25,26] instead of being an *extractor*. Namely, instead of guaranteeing that $R = h(X; S)$ is nearly uniform (i.e., has 0 entropy deficiency), we only require that R has small entropy deficiency. This observation was recently made by [12] in a (somewhat advanced) "seed-dependent" setting for key derivation, where the distribution of X could depend on the "seed" S used to derive the final key R, and where non-trivial extraction is *impossible* [12,29]. However, we observe that the same observation is true even in a more traditional "seed-independent" setting, where randomness extraction is possible (e.g., using LHL). In particular, since universal hash functions are good condensers for a wider range of parameters than extractors, we immediately get the same LHL improvements as [1]. Although this does not directly lead to further improvements, we believe our modular analysis better explains the results of [1], and also elegantly unifies the seed-independent [1] and the seed-dependent [12] settings. Indeed, the seed-dependent condenser from [12] is obtained from our construction by replacing a universal hash function by a collision-resistant hash function, and (literally!) changing one line in the proof (see Lemma 6 vs. Lemma 8).

More interestingly, we also look at the question of deriving keys for *all* (possibly "non-square-friendly") applications P. As follows from our results on seed-independent condensers (see Corollary 5), the question is the most challenging when the length of the source X is also m.[4] In this case, we use (appropriately long) public randomness S and a length-doubling pseudorandom generator (PRG) G on m-bit seed, to derive the following *"square-friendly" key derivation function* for P: compute $X' = G(X)$ and interpret the $2m$-bit value X' as the description of a pairwise independent hash function h from $|S|$ to m bits; then interpret S as the input to h; finally, set the final key $R = h(S) = h_{X'}(S)$.[5] Interestingly, this method is not only useful for "non-square-friendly" applications, but even for "square-friendly" applications with security $\varepsilon \gg \varepsilon_{\text{prg}}$ (where ε_{prg} is the security of G against the same resources T as P).

PRGs WITH WEAK SEEDS. However, the above result is especially interesting when applied to PRGs themselves (i.e., $P = G$)! Namely, instead of using $G(X)$

---

[3] The same final construction, with a direct proof, was independently discovered by Li [21]. As we explain later, our approach might have some advantages.

[4] Otherwise, one can apply a universal hash function to X with an m-bit output without affecting the "effective" entropy of the source.

[5] We mention that our result is similar in spirit to the works of [13,8], who showed that *public* pairwise independent hash functions can save on the amount of *secret* randomness in some applications.

directly as a pseudorandom string, which is not secure with weak seeds,[6] we evaluate a 'hash function' $h_{G(X)}$ on a public (random) input S, after which it is suddenly "safer" to start expanding the derived key R using G.

Prior to our work, the only alternative method of tolerating weak PRG seeds came from the "dense model theorem" [28,27,16,17], which roughly states that the $2m$-bit output $X' = G(X)$ of a $(T, \varepsilon_{\mathsf{prg}})$-secure PRG G is (T', ε')-computationally close to having the same entropy deficiency $d \ll m$ as X (despite being twice as long). This means, for example, that one can now apply an m-bit extractor (e.g., LHL) h' to X' to derive the final m-bit key $R = h'(G(X))$. Unfortunately, a closer look shows that not only ε' degrades by at least the (expected) factor 2^d as compared to $\varepsilon_{\mathsf{prg}}$, but also the time T' is much less than T: the most recent variant due to [17] has $T' \ll T^{1/3}$, while previous versions [16,27] had $T' = T \cdot \mathsf{poly}(\varepsilon)$. In contrast, by replacing any extractor h' by a "special" extractor — a pairwise independent hash function h — and also swapping the roles of the key and the input, we can maintain nearly the same resources $T' \approx T$, but at the cost of potentially[7] increasing ε' from roughly $\varepsilon_{\mathsf{prg}} \cdot 2^d + T^{-1/3}$ to $\sqrt{\varepsilon_{\mathsf{prg}} \cdot 2^d}$. We believe such a tradeoff is quite favorable for many natural settings. Additionally, our approach is likely to use fewer public random bits S: $\log(1/\varepsilon_{\mathsf{prg}})$ bits vs. the seed length for an extractor extracting a constant fraction of min-entropy.

2   Preliminaries

NOTATIONS AND DEFINITIONS. We use $s \leftarrow S$ to denote sampling an element s according to distribution S. The min-entropy of a random variable X is defined as $\mathbf{H}_\infty(X) \stackrel{\text{def}}{=} -\log(\max_x \Pr[X = x])$. We use $\mathsf{Col}(X)$ to denote the collision probability of X, i.e., $\mathsf{Col}(X) \stackrel{\text{def}}{=} \sum_x \Pr[X = x]^2 \leq 2^{-\mathbf{H}_\infty(X)}$, and collision entropy $\mathbf{H}_2(X) \stackrel{\text{def}}{=} -\log \mathsf{Col}(X) \geq \mathbf{H}_\infty(X)$. For $c \in \{2, \infty\}$, we say that a distribution X over $\{0,1\}^m$ has *entropy deficiency* d (for a given entropy $\mathbf{H}_c$) if $\mathbf{H}_c(X) \geq m - d$. We also refer to the value $D \stackrel{\text{def}}{=} 2^d$ as *security deficiency* of X (the reason for the name will be clear from our results).

We denote with $\Delta_C(X, Y)$ the advantage of a circuit C in distinguishing the random variables X, Y: $\Delta_C(X, Y) \stackrel{\text{def}}{=} |\Pr[C(X) = 1] - \Pr[C(Y) = 1]|$. The *statistical distance* between two random variables X, Y, denoted by $\mathsf{SD}(X, Y)$, is defined by

$$\frac{1}{2} \sum_x |\Pr[X = x] - \Pr[Y = x]| = \max_C \ \Delta_C(X, Y)$$

We write $\mathsf{SD}(X, Y | Z)$ (resp. $\Delta_C(X, Y | Z)$) as shorthand for $\mathsf{SD}((X, Z), (Y, Z))$ (resp. $\Delta_C((X, Z), (Y, Z))$).

---

[6] E.g., if 1st bit of source X is constant, and 1st bit of $G(X) = 1^{st}$ bit of X.

[7] Our security is slightly worse only when $T^{-2/3} \ll \varepsilon_{\mathsf{prg}} \cdot 2^d$, and is never worse by more than $T^{1/6}$ factor irrespective of $\varepsilon_{\mathsf{prg}}$ and d, since $\varepsilon_{\mathsf{prg}} \cdot 2^d + T^{-1/3} \geq \sqrt{\varepsilon_{\mathsf{prg}} \cdot 2^d} \cdot T^{-1/6}$.

ABSTRACT SECURITY GAMES. We first define the general type of applications where our technique applies. The security of an application P can be defined via an interactive game between a probabilistic attacker A and a probabilistic challenger $C(r)$, where C is fixed by the definition of P, and where the particular secret key r used by C is derived from U_m in the 'ideal' setting, and from some distribution R in the 'real' setting. The game can have an arbitrary structure, but at the end $C(r)$ should output a bit, with output 1 indicating that A 'won' the game and 0 otherwise.

Given a particular key r, we define the *advantage* $f_A(r)$ of A on r (against C fixed by P) as follows. For unpredictability games, $f_A(r)$ is the expected value of $C(r)$ taken over the internal coins of A and C, so that $f_A(r) \in [0;1]$; and for indistinguishability games, $f_A(r)$ is the expectation of $C(r) - 1/2$, so that $f_A(r) \in [-1/2;1/2]$. When A is clear from the context, we simply write $f(r)$.

We will refer to $|\mathbb{E}(f_A(U_m))|$ as the advantage of A (in the ideal model). Similarly, for $c \in \{2, \infty\}$, we will refer to $\max_R |\mathbb{E}(f_A(R))|$, taken over all R with $\mathbf{H}_c(R) \geq m - d$, as the advantage of A in the $(m - d)$-real$_c$ model.

Definition 1 (Security). *An application P is (T, ε)-secure (in the ideal model) if the advantage of any T-bounded A is at most ε.*

An application P is (T', ε')-secure in the $(m - d)$-real$_c$ model if the advantage of any T'-bounded A in the $(m - d)$-real$_c$ model is at most ε'.

We note that a security result in the real$_2$ model is more desirable than (and implies) that in the real$_\infty$ model.

3   Overcoming Weak Expectations

UNPREDICTABILITY APPLICATIONS. For unpredictability applications (with non-negative f), the following inequality implies that the security degrades at most by a factor of $D = 2^d$ compared with the ideal model (which is stated as Corollary 1), where d is the entropy deficiency.

Lemma 1. *For any (deterministic) real-valued function $f : \{0,1\}^m \to \mathbb{R}^+ \cup \{0\}$ and any random variable R with $\mathbf{H}_\infty(R) \geq m - d$, we have*

$$\mathbb{E}[f(R)] \leq 2^d \cdot \mathbb{E}[f(U_m)] \tag{1}$$

Proof. $\mathbb{E}[f(R)] = \sum_r \Pr[R = r] \cdot f(r) \leq 2^d \cdot \sum_r \frac{1}{2^m} \cdot f(r).$ □

Corollary 1. *If an unpredictability application P is (T, ε)-secure in the ideal model, then P is $(T, 2^d \cdot \varepsilon)$-secure in the $(m - d)$-real$_\infty$ model.*

The above only applies to all "unpredictability" applications such as one-way functions, MACs and digital signatures. In the full version [15] we give a simple concrete example, by applying this technique to one-time (information-theoretic) message authentication codes, and re-deriving the results of [22,9] in a simpler, more modular manner.

INDISTINGUISHABILITY APPLICATIONS. Unfortunately, Corollary 1 critically depends on the non-negativity of f, and is generally false when f can be negative, which happens for indistinguishability applications. In fact, for certain indistinguishability applications, such as one-time pad, pseudo-random- generators and functions (PRGs and PRFs), there exists R with $d = 1$ such that $\mathbb{E}[f(U_m)]$ is negligible (or even zero!) but $\mathbb{E}[f(R)] = 1/2$. For example, consider one-time pad encryption $e = x \oplus r$ of the message x using a key r, which has perfect security $\varepsilon = 0$ in the ideal model, when $r \leftarrow U_m$. However, imagine an imperfect key R, whose first bit is 0 and the remaining bits are uniform. Clearly, $\mathbf{H}_\infty(R) = m - 1$, but one can perfectly distinguish the encryptions of any two messages differing in the first bit, implying $(m - 1)$-real$_\infty$ security $\varepsilon' = 1/2$. Fortunately, below we give another inequality for general f, which will be useful for other indistinguishability applications.

Lemma 2. *For any (deterministic) real-valued function $f : \{0,1\}^m \to \mathbb{R}$ and any random variable R with $\mathbf{H}_2(R) \geq m - d$, we have*

$$| \mathbb{E}[f(R)] | \leq \sqrt{2^d} \cdot \sqrt{\mathbb{E}[f(U_m)^2]} \tag{2}$$

Proof. Denote $p(r) = \Pr[R = r]$, and also recall the Cauchy-Schwartz inequality $|\sum a_i b_i| \leq \sqrt{(\sum a_i^2) \cdot (\sum b_i^2)}$. We have

$$| \mathbb{E}[f(R)] | = \left| \sum_r p(r) \cdot f(r) \right| \leq \sqrt{2^m \cdot \sum_r p(r)^2} \cdot \sqrt{\frac{1}{2^m} \sum_r f(r)^2}$$
$$= \sqrt{2^d \cdot \mathbb{E}[f(U_m)^2]}$$

$\square$

Lemma 2 upper bounds the (squared) weak expectation by the product of "security deficiency" $D = 2^d$ of R and $\mathbb{E}[f(U_m)^2]$. As with unpredictability applications, the value D comes to play due to the entropy deficiency of R, independent of f. Also, the second term $\mathbb{E}[f(U_m)^2]$ only depends on the uniform distribution (and not on R). However, it no longer bounds the ideal model security $\mathbb{E}[f(U_m)]$ of our application in consideration, but rather the expected square of the attacker's advantage. This leads us to the notion of *square security*, which was implicitly introduced by [1] and later made explicit by [12] in a more restricted context of key derivation.

Definition 2 (Square Security). *An application P is (T, σ)-square secure if for any T-bounded adversary A we have $\mathbb{E}[f(U_m)^2] \leq \sigma$, where $f(r)$ denotes A's advantage conditioned on key being r.*

Applying this definition to Lemma 2, we get the following general result.

Corollary 2 (Square security implies real model security). *If P is (T, σ)-square secure, then P is $(T, \sqrt{2^d \cdot \sigma})$-secure in the $(m - d)$-real$_2$ model.*

WHAT APPLICATIONS HAVE SQUARE SECURITY? More precisely, for which applications P does a good bound on standard security ε also imply a good bound on their square security? Let us call such applications *square-friendly*. We start with a few simple observations. First, all (T, ε)-secure unpredictability applications P are (T, ε)-square secure, since for non-negative f we have $\mathbb{E}[f(U_m)^2] \leq \mathbb{E}[f(U_m)]$. Hence, we immediately get $\sqrt{2^d \cdot \varepsilon}$-security in $(m-d)$-real$_2$ model for such applications. Notice, this bound is weaker than the $2^d \varepsilon$ bound in Corollary 1, although it applies whenever $\mathbf{H}_2(R) \geq m-d$ (instead of only when $\mathbf{H}_\infty(R) \geq m-d$, which is more restrictive). Still, we will find the seemingly weaker bound from Lemma 2 useful even for unpredictability applications, when we talk about key derivation functions in Section 4. This will precisely use the fact that Renyi entropy is a weaker restriction than min-entropy, making it easier to construct an appropriate key derivation function.

Moving to indistinguishability applications, it is known that PRGs, PRFs and one-time pads cannot have good square security (see [1]). Indeed, given our earlier counter-example for the one-time pad, a different result would contradict the bound in Corollary 2. To see this explicitly, consider a 1-bit one time pad encryption $e = x \oplus r$, where $x, r, e \in \{0, 1\}$ are the message, the key and the ciphertext, respectively. Consider also the attacker A who guesses that $x = e$. When the key $r = 0$, A is right and $f(0) = 1 - \frac{1}{2} = \frac{1}{2}$. Similarly, when the key $r = 1$, A is wrong and $f(1) = 0 - \frac{1}{2} = -\frac{1}{2}$. This gives perfect $\varepsilon = \mathbb{E}[f(U_1)] = 0$, but $\sigma = \mathbb{E}[f(U_1)^2] = \frac{1}{4}$.

Fortunately, there are still many interesting indistinguishability applications which are square-friendly, such as stateless chosen plaintext attack (CPA) secure encryption and weak pseudo-random functions (weak PRFs), as shown by [1]. These examples are shown using an elegant "double run" technique from [1]. In the following we give a slightly cleaner exposition of this technique, by decomposing (until Section 4) the core of this technique from the specifics of the key derivation setting. We also mention the "multi-run" extension of this technique, and then derive several new, somewhat unexpected examples, using several variants of q-wise independent hash functions.

3.1   Square-Friendly Applications via the Double-Run Trick

To make the exposition more intuitive, we start with a nice example of CPA-secure symmetric-key encryption schemes from [1], and later abstract and generalize the resulting technique.

ILLUSTRATING EXAMPLE. Recall, for this application P the attacker "resources" $T = (t, q)$, where t is the running time of A and q is the total number of encryption queries made by A. More specifically, A is allowed to (adaptively) ask the challenger $\mathsf{C}(r)$ to produce (randomly generated) encryptions of $(q-1)$ arbitrary messages $s_1, \ldots, s_{q-1}$ under the secret key r, and (at any moment) one special "challenge" query (s_0^*, s_1^*). In response to this latter query, $\mathsf{C}(r)$ picks a random bit $b \in \{0, 1\}$ and returns the encryption of s_b^*. Eventually, A outputs a bit b' and 'wins' if $b' = b$. As with other indistinguishability applications, the advantage $f(r)$ of A on key r is $\Pr[b = b'] - 1/2$.

Lemma 3 ([1]). *Assume P is a symmetric-key encryption scheme which is $((2t, 2q), 2\varepsilon)$-CPA-secure (in the ideal model). Then P is $((t, q), \varepsilon)$-square secure. Hence, standard CPA-security implies essentially the same level "CPA-square-security" (formally, with all parameters halved).*

Proof. It suffices to show that for any r and any attacker A with running time t and q queries, there exists another attacker B with running time $2t$ and $2q$ queries, such that B's advantage on r is twice the squared advantage of A on r.

The strategy of B is to initialize two independent copies of A (with fresh randomness) — call them A_1 and A_2 — and run them one after another as follows. First, it first simulates a run of A_1 against the 'imaginary' challenger $C_1(r)$, using q regular encryption queries to its own 'real' challenger $C(r)$, to simulate both $(q-1)$ regular *and* 1 challenge queries of A_1 to $C_1(r)$. In particular, the knowledge of the first challenge bit b_1 (which B chose himself) allows B to know whether or not A_1 succeeded in this simulated run. After the first simulated run is over, B now runs a second fresh copy A_2 of A "for real", now using A_2's challenge query (s_0^*, s_1^*) to C_2 as its own challenge query with C. This uses a total of $2q$ queries for B to complete both runs. Finally, if A_1 wins the game in its first run (against simulated C_1), then B returns A_2's answer in the second run unmodified; otherwise, B reverses the answer of A_2, interpreting the mistake of A_1 in the first run as an indication of a likely mistake of A_2 in the second run as well. In particular, irrespective of the sign of A's advantage ε below, we have

$$\Pr[\text{B wins}] = \Pr[\text{A wins twice}] + \Pr[\text{A loses twice}]$$
$$= \left(\frac{1}{2} \pm \varepsilon\right)^2 + \left(\frac{1}{2} \mp \varepsilon\right)^2 = \frac{1}{2} + 2\varepsilon^2$$

□

The following theorem immediately follows from Corollary 2 and Lemma 3.

Theorem 1. *Assume P is a $((2t, 2q), 2\varepsilon)$-CPA secure symmetric-key encryption scheme in the ideal model. Then P is also $((t, q), \sqrt{2^d \cdot \varepsilon})$-secure in the $(m - d)$-$real_2$ model.*

DOUBLE-RUN TRICK. We now generalize this technique to any indistinguishability application P which we call (T', T, γ)-*simulatable*, slightly generalizing (and, in our opinion, simplifying) the related notion introduced by [1]. For syntactic convenience (and without loss of generality), we assume that in the security game for P the challenger $C(r)$ chooses a random bit b, and the attacker A wins by outputting a bit $b' = b$ *without violating some failure predicate F*, where F is efficiently checkable by both A and C. For example, for the CPA encryption example from above, this failure predicate F is empty. In contrast, for the related notion of chosen ciphertext (CCA) security, F will be true if A asked C to decrypt the actual challenge ciphertext. Notice, since any A can efficiently check F, we could have assumed that no such A will violate F (we call such A *legal*). However, we will find our small convention slightly more convenient in the future, including the following definition.

Definition 3. *We say that an indistinguishability application P is (T', T, γ)-simulatable, if for any secret key r and any legal, T-bounded attacker A, there exists a (possibly illegal!) T'-bounded attacker B (for some $T' \geq T$) such that:*

(1) The execution between B and 'real' $C(r)$ defines two independent executions between a copy A_i of A and a 'simulated' challenger $C_i(r)$, for $i = 1, 2$. In particular, except reusing the same r, $A_1, C_1(r), A_2, C_2(r)$ use fresh and independent randomness, including independent challenge bits b_1 and b_2.

(2) The challenge b used by 'real' $C(r)$ is equal to the challenge b_2 used by 'simulated' C_2.

(3) Before making its guess b' of the challenge bit b, B learns the values b_1, b_1' and b_2'.

(4) The probability of B violating the failure predicate F is at most γ.

For example, the proof of Theorem 1 showed that any CPA-secure encryption is $(T' = (2t, 2q), T = (t, q), \gamma = 0)$-simulatable, since B indeed simulated two runs of A satisfying conditions (1)-(4) above. In particular, a straightforward abstraction of our proof shows the following:

Lemma 4. *Assume P is a (T', ε)-secure and (T', T, γ)-simulatable, then P is (T, σ)-square secure, where $\sigma \leq (\varepsilon + \gamma)/2$. In particular, by Corollary 2 P is $(T, \sqrt{2^{d-1}(\varepsilon + \gamma)})$-secure in the $(m - d)$-real$_2$ model.*

MULTI-RUN EXTENSION. In the double-run game we use a test-run to estimate the sign of the advantage (whether it is positive or not), which advises attacker B whether or not to reverse A's answer in the real run. We can generalize this to a multi-run setting: the attacker B test-runs A for some odd $(2i + 1)$ times, and takes a majority vote before the actual run, which gives B more accurate estimate on the sign of the advantage of A. Interestingly, with a different motivation in mind, this precise question was studied by Brakerski and Goldreich [5]. Translated to our vocabulary, to gain a factor $\alpha > 1$ in the square security (i.e., to show that $\sigma \leq \varepsilon/\alpha$), one needs to run the original distinguisher A for $\Theta(\alpha^2)$ times. Going back to Corollary 2, to get 'real' security $\varepsilon' = \frac{1}{\alpha} \cdot \sqrt{2^d} \cdot \varepsilon$, one needs to run A for $O(\alpha^4)$ times, therefore losing this factor in the allowed resources T. Although theoretically interesting, it appears that the best practical tradeoff is already achieved using the "double-run" trick itself, a conclusion shared by [5].

3.2 Applications to Weak Pseudorandom Functions and Extractors

Recall, weak PRFs [23] are close relatives of CPA-secure symmetric encryption, and relax the notion of (regular) PRFs. For future applications, we give a precise definition below.

Definition 4 $(((t, q), \delta)$-weak PRFs). *A family $\mathcal{H}$ of functions $\{h_r : \{0,1\}^n \to \{0,1\}^l \mid r \in \{0,1\}^m\}$ is $((t, q), \delta)$-secure weak PRF, if for any t-bounded attacker A, and random $s, s_1, \ldots, s_{q-1} \leftarrow U_n$ and $r \leftarrow U_m$, we have*

$$\Delta_A(h_r(s), U_l \mid s, s_1, h_r(s_1), \cdots, s_{q-1}, h_r(s_{q-1})) \leq \delta$$

Notice, it is impossible to achieve $\delta = 0$ in this definition for $q > 1$, as there is always a small chance that $s \in \{s_1, \ldots, s_{q-1}\}$. Also, just like CPA-secure encryption, weak PRFs are easily seen to be $((2t, 2q), (t, q), 0)$-simulatable, since the 'outer' attacker B can choose its own bit b_1, and set the challenge value of the first run to be $h_r(s_q)$ if $b_1 = 0$, and uniform U_l otherwise. By Lemma 4, this means that

Theorem 2. *Assume P is a $((2t, 2q), \delta)$-secure weak PRF in the ideal model. Then P is $((t, q), \delta/2)$-square secure, as well as $((t, q), \sqrt{2^{d-1} \cdot \delta})$-secure in the $(m - d)$-$real_2$ model.*

Moreover, by applying the multi-run extension, if P is a $((O(\alpha^4 \cdot t), O(\alpha^4 \cdot q)), \delta)$-secure, then P is also $((t, q), \frac{1}{\alpha} \cdot \sqrt{2^d \cdot \delta})$-secure in the $(m - d)$-$real_2$ model. This results nicely improves (and simplifies!) a result of Pietrzak [24], who achieved security $\delta' \sim \delta \cdot 2^d$, but at a price of reducing the allowed running time t' and the number of queries q' by a *huge* factor $\mathsf{poly}(1/\delta') = \mathsf{poly}(2^d, 1/\delta)$. A comparable (actually, slightly better) result follows from our multi-run derivation above, by taking a very large value of $\alpha \sim 1/\sqrt{2^d\delta}$. Of course, such large α makes the resulting values t and q really low compared to the original t' and q'. Indeed, we believe the region of 'small' α, and especially the result of Theorem 2, is much more relevant for practical use.

While the security of weak PRFs with weak keys was already studied by [24,1] with large q in mind, we obtain some expected results by concentrating on the most basic case of $q = 1$.

APPLICATION TO EXTRACTORS. By looking at the k-$real_2$ security (where $k = m - d$) of weak PRFs for $q = 1$ and $t = \infty$, we essentially obtain the notion of extractors for Renyi entropy!

Definition 5 (Extractors). *We say that an efficient function $\mathsf{Ext} : \{0,1\}^m \times \{0,1\}^n \to \{0,1\}^l$ is a strong (k, ε)-extractor, if for all R (over $\{0,1\}^m$) with $\mathbf{H}_2(R) \geq k$ and for random S (uniform over $\{0,1\}^n$), we get*

$$\mathsf{SD}(\ \mathsf{Ext}(R; S)\ ,\ U_l \mid S) \leq \varepsilon$$

where coins $S \leftarrow U_n$ is the random seed of Ext. The value $L = k - l$ is called the entropy loss of Ext.

To apply Theorem 2 (with $q = 1$, $t = \infty$ and $k = m - d$) and obtain such extractors, all that remains is to build an $((\infty, 2), \delta)$-secure weak PRFs for a low value of δ, which is essentially a *pairwise independent* hash function on two random inputs:

$$\mathsf{SD}(\ h_r(s),\ U_l \mid s, s', h_r(s')\ ) \leq \delta \tag{3}$$

where $r \leftarrow U_m$ and $s, s' \leftarrow U_n$. For example, using any traditional pairwise independent hash function, which has the property that

$$\Pr_{r \leftarrow U_m}[h_r(s) = a\ \wedge\ h_r(s') = a'] = 2^{-2l} \tag{4}$$

for any $s \neq s'$ and any $a, a' \in \{0,1\}^l$, we achieve that the only case when one can distinguish $h_r(s)$ and $h_r(s')$ is when $s = s'$, which happens with probability 2^{-n}. In other words, pairwise independent hashing gives $\delta = 2^{-n}$, which, in turn, gives (by Theorem 2, with $q = 1$, $t = \infty$, $k = m - d$ and $\delta = 2^{-n}$):

Corollary 3 (Alternative LHL). *If* $\mathcal{H} \stackrel{\text{def}}{=} \{h_r : \{0,1\}^n \to \{0,1\}^l \mid r \in \{0,1\}^m\}$ *is pairwise independent (i.e., satisfies Equation (4)), then* $\mathsf{Ext}(r; s) \stackrel{\text{def}}{=} h_r(s)$ *is a strong* $(k, \sqrt{2^{m-k-n}})$-*extractor.*

To compare this result with the standard LHL [19], the optimal key length m for a family of pairwise independent hash functions from n to l bits (where $l \leq m/2$) is known to be $m = n + l$ (e.g., using Toeplitz matrices). Plugging this to our bound in ε above, we get the same bound $\varepsilon = \sqrt{2^{l-k}} = 2^{-L/2}$ as the leftover hash lemma, where in both cases l is output size and k is the entropy of the source. More detailed comparison can be found in the full version [15].

COMPUTATIONAL PAIRWISE INDEPENDENCE. Continuing our exploration of $q = 1$ (whose square security follows from regular security of $q = 2$), information-theoretic pairwise independence requires that the length m of the key r is at least twice the length l of the function output $h_r(s)$. Looking ahead at the key derivation setting in Section 4.3, m will be equal to the security parameter, and we will need to achieve output length $l \geq m$, which is impossible information-theoretically. Instead, we observe that the result can be easily achieved computationally, by applying a length-doubling pseudorandom generator (PRG) $G : \{0,1\}^m \to \{0,1\}^{2m}$ first. Namely, a weak computationally pairwise independent hash function with an m-bit key *and* output can be obtained by first expanding the key r to $r' = G(r)$, and then using r' as the $2m$-bit key of (no longer impossible) pairwise independent hash function $h_{r'}$ with an m-bit output. We postpone further exploration of this computationally $((t, 2), \delta)$-secure weak PRF, and its application to key derivation, till Section 4.3.

3.3 Application to Non-malleable Extractors

Having obtained randomness extractors for $q = 1$, we now continue our exploration for $q = 2$ (and larger values). First, however, we strengthen the security experiment for weak PRFs in order to obtain much stronger results. Indeed, while the "double-run" trick seems to require that the challenge input s is randomly chosen,[8] there seems to be no reason not to allow the attacker A to *choose* the input values $s_1, \ldots, s_{q-1}$, as long as all of them are different from the actual challenge s. In fact, we will even allow A to select $s_1, \ldots, s_{q-1}$ based on the challenge input s.[9]

The resulting notion, which we (for simplicity) only state for the information-theoretic case of $t = \infty$, is given below. Here the phrase that "$s_1 \ldots s_n$ can be

---

[8] Otherwise, we arrive at the notion of of PRFs, which we know are not square-friendly.
[9] As mentioned later, we could even allow A to see the challenge $h_r(s)/U_l$ *and* s before selecting $s_1, \ldots, s_{q-1}$, although we do not formally pursue this direction.

arbitrarily correlated to s" means that the unbounded attacker A (implicit in the definition below) chooses $s_1 \ldots s_{q-1}$ as a function of s.

Definition 6 (weak (q, δ)-wise independence). *A family $\mathcal{H}$ of functions $\{h_r : \{0,1\}^n \to \{0,1\}^l \mid r \in \{0,1\}^m\}$ is weakly (q, δ)-wise independent, if for $r \leftarrow U_m$, $s \leftarrow U_n$, and for $s_1, \cdots, s_{q-1} \in \{0,1\}^n$ that are distinct from and arbitrarily correlated to s, we have*

$$\mathsf{SD}(\ h_r(s),\ U_l \mid s, h_r(s_1), \cdots, h_r(s_{q-1})\ ) \leq \delta$$

The failure event F happens when one of the points $s_i = s$.

Notice that, unlike weak with PRFs, here ideal security $\delta = 0$ is possible, since we explicitly require that $s \notin \{s_1 \ldots s_{q-1}\}$. In fact, a (perfectly) q-wise independent hash function (where the analog of Equation (4) holds for larger q) is also weakly $(q, 0)$-wise independent.

Also observe that we can naturally view the above definition as a game between a challenger C and the attacker A, where $(q-1)$ measures the "resources" of A (distinct from s points where he learns the true value of h_r), and δ is the advantage of distinguishing $h_r(s)$ from random. In particular, we can naturally define the (q, σ_q)-square security of $\mathcal{H}$ (with random key $r \leftarrow U_m$) and then use Corollary 2 to bound the security of $\mathcal{H}$ in the $(m - d)$-real$_2$ model, when using a weak key R with $\mathbf{H}_2(R) \geq m - d$. In fact, we can successfully apply the double-run trick above to show that $\mathcal{H}$ is $(2q, q, \gamma)$-simulatable, where, for the first time we have a non-zero failure probability $\gamma = q/2^n$. Indeed, to simulate the first virtual run of A, B simply chooses its own random point s and asks its value $h_r(s)$. The subtlety comes from the fact that both s and the the $(q - 1)$-correlated values $s_1 \ldots s_{q-1}$ might accidentally collide with the second (fortunately) random challenge s', making the resulting 'outer' attacker B illegal. Luckily, the probability that a random s' collides with any of these q values is at most $\gamma \leq q/2^n$, indeed.

Theorem 3. *If function family $\mathcal{H}$ is weakly $(2q, \delta)$-wise independent, then $\mathcal{H}$ is $(q, (\delta + q/2^n)/2)$-square secure, as well as weakly (q, ε)-wise independent in the $(m - d)$-real$_2$ model, where $\varepsilon = \sqrt{(\delta + \frac{q}{2^n}) \cdot 2^{d-1}}$.*

NON-MALLEABLE EXTRACTORS. Next, we consider the case of $q = 2$, where the notion of $(2, \varepsilon)$-wise independence in the $k = (m - d)$-real$_2$ model becomes a *non-malleable extractor* [14] (for Renyi entropy; the case $q = 1$ collapses to the setting of weak PRF considered in the previous section).

Definition 7 (Non-Malleable Extractors). *We say that an efficient function nmExt : $\{0,1\}^m \times \{0,1\}^n \to \{0,1\}^l$ is a (k, ε)-non-malleable extractor, if for all R (over $\{0,1\}^m$) with $\mathbf{H}_2(R) \geq k$, for random S (uniform over $\{0,1\}^n$), and for all functions $g : \{0,1\}^n \to \{0,1\}^n$, s.t. $g(s) \neq s$ for all s, we get*

$$\mathsf{SD}(\ \mathsf{nmExt}(R; S)\ ,\ U_l \mid S, \mathsf{nmExt}(R; g(S))\ ) \leq \varepsilon$$

Applying Theorem 3 to (perfectly) 4-wise independent hash functions (i.e., $2q = 4$, $\delta = 0$, $k = m - d$), we get:

Corollary 4 (Non-Malleable Extractors). *If* $\mathcal{H} \overset{\text{def}}{=} \{h_r : \{0,1\}^n \to \{0,1\}^l \mid r \in \{0,1\}^m\}$ *is 4-wise independent, then* $\mathsf{nmExt}(r;s) \overset{\text{def}}{=} h_r(s)$ *is a* $(k, \sqrt{2^{m-k-n}})$-*non-malleable extractor.*

For a simple instantiation, let $\mathcal{H}$ be the following (optimal) 4-wise independent hash function with known parameters $n = m/2$ and $l = m/4$ (using BCH codes; see [21]). The key $r \in \{0,1\}^m$ is viewed as a tuple of 4 elements (r_1, r_2, r_3, r_4) in $GF[2^{m/4}] = GF[2^l]$, and a seed $s \in \{0,1\}^n \backslash 0^n$ is viewed as a non-zero point in $GF[2^n]$. Then, the m-bit value of $(s\|s^3)$ is viewed as 4 elements (s_1, s_2, s_3, s_4) in $GF[2^l]$, and the l-bit output of the function is set to $h_r(s) = r_1 \cdot s_1 + \ldots + r_4 \cdot s_4$. Using Corollary 4, this simple function is a $(k, \sqrt{2^{m/2-k}})$-non-malleable extractor with an output of size $l = m/4$. Quite surprisingly, this noticeably improves a much more complicated initial construction of non-malleable extractors of [10]. That result could only extract $l = k/2 - m/4 - \Omega(\log m) - \log(1/\varepsilon) \ll m/4$ bits, and relied on an unproved conjecture in number theory. In particular, even for one-bit output, it achieved slightly worse security $\varepsilon' = O(\text{poly}(n)) \cdot \sqrt{2^{m/2-k}}$.

As mentioned earlier, the same final construction was independently discovered by Li [21] with a different, more direct proof. We believe that our modular approach might have some advantages (beyond simplicity). For example, in addition to generalizing to larger values of q (an observation also made by Li [21]), it appears that our approach seamlessly tolerates more elaborate variants of non-malleable extractors, such as when the points $s_1, \ldots, s_{q-1}$ could also depend on the challenge $h_r(U_m)/U_l$. It is not immediately clear if the same easily holds for the proof of [21].

3.4 Side Information

So far we presented our results assuming $\mathbf{H}_c(R) \geq m - d$ from the perspective of our attacker A. In some settings, such as the key derivation setting in Section 4 below, R itself is derived using some procedure, at the end of which the attacker A gets some side information S about R. To deal with this natural generalization, we define average-case (aka conditional) collision entropy $\mathbf{H}_2(R|S) \overset{\text{def}}{=} -\log\left(\mathbb{E}_{s \leftarrow S}\left[\sum_r \Pr[R = r|S = s]^2\right]\right)$ and average-case min-entropy $\mathbf{H}_\infty(R|S) \overset{\text{def}}{=} -\log\left(\mathbb{E}_{s \leftarrow S}\left[\max_r \Pr[R = r|S = s]\right]\right)$, which then allows one to define the average-case $(m - d)$-real$_c$ model, after which one can easily generalize our basic Lemma 1 and Lemma 2 to the average-case setting. We defer these (rather straightforward) details to the full version [15], here only stating the required generalization of Lemma 1 and Lemma 2.

Lemma 5. *For any real-valued function $f(r,s)$ and any random variables (R, S), where $|R| = m$:*

(a) If $\mathbf{H}_\infty(R \mid S) \geq m - d$ and $f \geq 0$, then $\mathbb{E}[f(R,S)] \leq 2^d \cdot \max_s \mathbb{E}[f(U_m, s)]$.

(b) If $\mathbf{H}_2(R \mid S) \geq m - d$, then
$$|\mathbb{E}[f(R,S)]| \leq \sqrt{2^d \cdot \mathbb{E}[f(U_m, S)^2]} \leq \sqrt{2^d \cdot \max_s \mathbb{E}[f(U_m, s)^2]}.$$

4   Key Derivation Functions

So far we studied the security of various applications when their m-bit secret key is weak (i.e., has some entropy deficiency d). In many situations, one is given a source of randomness X of some, possibly different, length n and having some entropy k, and we need to first map it to the m-bit key R by means of some *key derivation function* (KDF) $h : \{0,1\}^n \to \{0,1\}^m$. As we will see, the source entropy k and the output length m play the most important role in this scenario, which leads to the following definition.

Definition 8. *We define (k,m)-real$_c$ model (for $c \in \{2, \infty\}$) as the key derivation setting, where a given KDF h with range $\{0,1\}^m$ is applied to any source X with $\mathbf{H}_c(X) \geq k$, to get a secret key $R = h(X)$ (for some application in question).*

As it turns out, in this level of generality deterministic key derivation is (essentially)[10] impossible for *all* sources of entropy k (see [12] for related discussion), so we will assume (and critically capitalize on) the existence of *public randomness S*. Depending on context, we will view such S either as a *seed* for $h(X; S)$, or as the description of h itself.

Having clarified the setting, we now turn to the question of designing such KDFs h for a given application P. First, when the source entropy $k \geq m + 2\log(1/\varepsilon)$, where ε is the desired security level for P, we can apply a good strong randomness extractor (e.g., by using LHL) to derive a key R which is (statistically) ε-close to U_m (even conditioned on the seed S). In practice, however, many sources do not have this much entropy, so we will consider the more challenging (and, often, more realistic) case when k is (noticeably) less than $m + 2\log(1/\varepsilon)$. We will divide our study intro three complementary approaches.

First, in Section 4.1 we will leverage the rich body results we obtained in Section 3 for dealing with "square-friendly" applications, and show that *randomness condensers* (instead of more demanding extractors) are precisely the right primitives to obtain improved key derivation results for all square-friendly applications. This will lead to the improved variant of LHL discovered by Barak et al. [1], but in a more modular and, arguably, intuitive manner. Interestingly, the parameters of standard extractors (i.e., standard LHL) will also "pop-up" to cover all (even non-square-friendly) applications when $k \geq m + 2\log(1/\varepsilon)$.

Second, in Section 4.2 we turn to a more challenging *seed-dependent* setting, considered by Dodis et al. [12], where the distribution on the source X could depend on the public seed S. This more or less follows the presentation of [12], and is included in this work mainly for completeness and modularity of exposition.

---

[10] Except maybe in the model of uniform adversaries, not considered here.

Finally, while the results of the previous subsections were interesting mainly from the perspective of the presentation, in Section 4.3 we consider the ("seed-independent") setting where the results of Section 4.1 lead to poor parameters. Namely, when the application P is either non-square-friendly, or has poor exact security ε to withstand the multiplicative 2^d loss incurred by our prior techniques. This will be done by capitalizing on our setting of public randomness to design a *square-friendly key derivation function* h. This has the advantage that the security of this key derivation step only needs to be analyzed with *uniform* X (i.e., in the ideal model), and our prior results will immediately imply the security of h in the real model. Moreover, instead of using the security of our final application P (which, as we said, leads to poor parameters), we will view the process of key derivation *as a new application P' of its own*! In particular, if the resulting key $R = h(X)$ will be pseudorandom, we can use it for any 'outer' P, irrespective of P's security or "square-friendliness".

We notice that a less optimized variant of this idea was already proposed by [1], who noticed that a weak PRF h_X— with public randomness S viewed as the input to h_X — is precisely the square-friendly primitive we are looking for. In this work we take this observation one step further, by capitalizing on the fact that h only needs to be secure for *two queries* in the ideal model (and, hence, one query in the real model). This leads to a simple (computationally-secure) construction of such a KDF h using length-doubling PRGs, already mentioned at the end of Section 3.2. As an unexpected consequence, also mentioned in the Introduction, our new KDF will give us an interesting (and often more favorable) alternative to the dense model theorem [28,27,16,17].

4.1   Condensers and Improved Leftover Hash Lemma

Recall, in the (k, m)-*real$_c$ model* we have an n-bit source X having $\mathbf{H}_c(X) \geq k$, and we wish to derive an m-bit key R from X. Moreover, the results on Section 3 — in particular Corollary 1 (for $c = \infty$) and Corollary 2 (for $c = 2$) — show that all we need from our KDF h is to ensure that $\mathbf{H}_c(R) \geq m - d$ to ensure security degradation of the order 2^d. Remembering the fact that our key derivation has a public seed S, which means that R should have entropy even given S. Fortunately, by the results of Section 3.4 all our results in Section 3 hold with respect to the side information S. Thus, we naturally arrive at the following definition.

Definition 9 (Condensers). *Let $c \in \{2, \infty\}$. We say that an efficient function* Cond $: \{0,1\}^n \times \{0,1\}^v \rightarrow \{0,1\}^m$ *is a $(\frac{k}{n} \rightarrow \frac{m-d}{m})_c$-condenser if for $\mathbf{H}_c(X) \geq k$ and uniformly random S we have $\mathbf{H}_c(\,\mathsf{Cond}(X; S) \mid S\,) \geq m - d$.*

Both $\mathbf{H}_\infty$- and $\mathbf{H}_2$- condensers are useful in cryptography. The former connects well with Lemma 1 (formally, its extension Lemma 5(a)) and Corollary 1, and the latter is more in line with Lemma 2 (formally, its extension Lemma 5(b)) and Corollary 2. In the sequel, though, we will only use $\mathbf{H}_2$ (and let $c = 2$ hereafter) since it seems to give stronger final bounds (even for unpredictability applications!), and applies to more cases (e.g. square-friendly indistinguishability applications). See [12] for more discussion.

We now recall the notion of universal hashing [6] and explicitly prove a well-known folklore[11] that universal hashing gives very good randomness condensers.

Definition 10 (Universal Hashing). *A family of functions* $\mathcal{G} \overset{\text{def}}{=} \{g_s : \{0,1\}^n \to \{0,1\}^m \mid s \in \{0,1\}^v\}$ *is universal, if for any distinct* $x_1, x_2 \in \{0,1\}^n$ *we have*

$$\Pr_{s \leftarrow U_v}[g_s(x_1) = g_s(x_2)] = 2^{-m}$$

Lemma 6. *Universal hash function family* $\mathcal{G} \overset{\text{def}}{=} \{g_s : \{0,1\}^n \to \{0,1\}^m \mid s \in \{0,1\}^v\}$ *defines a* $(\frac{k}{n} \to \frac{m-d}{m})_2$-*condenser* $\mathsf{Cond}(x;s) \overset{\text{def}}{=} g_s(x)$, *where* $2^d = 1 + 2^{m-k}$.

Proof. We directly analyze the collision probability by estimating the probability that two independent samples X_1 and X_2 of X collide under g_S. The latter is done by conditioning on whether X_1 and X_2 collide among themselves, and using the universality of $\mathcal{G}$ to tackle the case of no collision:

$$\Pr[g_S(X_1) = g_S(X_2)] \le \Pr[X_1 = X_2] + \Pr[\, g_S(X_1) = g_S(X_2) \ \wedge \ X_1 \neq X_2]$$
$$\le 2^{-k} + 2^{-m} \ = \ 2^{-m} \cdot (2^{m-k} + 1) \ = \ 2^{d-m}$$

Instead of composing this result with Lemma 2/Lemma 5(b), we use a slightly different version of these lemmas (whose proof is very similar as well, and is omitted) leading to improved final results.

Lemma 7 ([1]). *For any (deterministic) real-valued function* $f : \{0,1\}^m \to \mathbb{R}$ *and any random variable* R *with* $\mathbf{H}_2(R) \ge m - d$, *we have*

$$\mid \mathbb{E}[f(R)] - \mathbb{E}[f(U_m)] \mid \ \le \ \sqrt{2^d - 1} \cdot \sqrt{\mathbb{E}[f(U_m)^2]} \tag{5}$$

More generally, when side information S *is present, and* $\mathbf{H}_2(R \mid S) \ge m - d$, *we have:*

$$\mid \mathbb{E}[f(R,S)] - \mathbb{E}[f(U_m,S)] \mid \ \le \ \sqrt{2^d - 1} \cdot \sqrt{\mathbb{E}[f(U_m,S)^2]} \tag{6}$$

Corollary 5 (Using Universal Hashing as KDF). *If* P *is* (T, ε)-*secure and* (T, σ)-*square secure (in the ideal model), then using* $R = g_s(X)$ *makes* P (T, ε')-*secure in the* (k, m)-*real$_2$ model, where* $\varepsilon' \le \varepsilon + \sqrt{\sigma \cdot 2^{m-k}}$.

REDUCED ENTROPY LOSS FOR LEFTOVER HASH LEMMA. Recalling the notion of entropy loss $L \overset{\text{def}}{=} k - m$, used in the earlier study of extractors, the bound of Corollary 5 can be rewritten as $\varepsilon' \le \varepsilon + \sqrt{\sigma \cdot 2^{-L}}$. In particular, since any application has square-security $\sigma \le 1$, we get $\varepsilon' \le \varepsilon + \sqrt{2^{-L}}$. This implicitly recovers the traditional application of the LHL, which argues that entropy loss

---

[11] This argument is usually hidden inside the proof of the standard LHL, but here we find it worthy on its own.

$L \geq 2 \log(1/\varepsilon)$ is enough to ensure comparable security $\varepsilon' \leq 2\varepsilon$ for any application P. More interestingly, we saw in Section 3 that many "square-friendly" applications, including all unpredictability applications and many indistinguishability applications, achieve $\sigma \approx \varepsilon$, in which case we get a bound $\varepsilon' \leq \varepsilon + \sqrt{\varepsilon \cdot 2^{-L}}$. Thus, to achieve $\varepsilon' \approx \varepsilon$, we only need to set $L = \log(1/\varepsilon)$ for such applications, saving $\log(1/\varepsilon)$ in the entropy requirement on X. More surprisingly, the resulting bound is meaningful even for negative L, in which case we are extracting more bits than the entropy k we have.

Finally, one can interpret Corollary 5 as the indication that the most challenging setting for key derivation occurs when the source X has length $n = m$, a result we will use in Section 4.3. Indeed, when $n = m$, the value $m - k$ is simply the *entropy deficiency* d of our source X. In particular, applying any of the results in Section 3 directly to X (without doing the key derivation) would incur a factor $2^d = 2^{m-k}$ loss in security. Using Corollary 5, we see that by applying an m-bit universal hash to any n-bit source X, we get the *same* security degradation 2^{m-k} as if the derived m-bit key R had the *same* entropy k as the original n-bit source X!

4.2   Seed-Dependent Key Derivation

We now generalize the notion of a condenser to the seed-dependent setting, where the adversarial sampler A can depend on the seed S but is computationally bounded. This challenging setting was considered by [29] in the context of seed-dependent *extractors*, where the authors made a pessimistic conclusion that the complexity of the seed-dependent extractor must be larger than that of the sampler A, making this notion not very useful for key derivation in practical applications. In contrast, we follow the result work of [12] who showed that (strong enough) collision-resistant hash functions (CRHFs) must be seed-dependent *condensers*, and thus can be used as KDFs for all square secure applications, despite having much smaller complexity than the complexity of the sampler A. This partially explains the use of CRHFs as KDFs in practical applications.

Definition 11 (Seed-Dependent Condensers). *An efficient function* Cond: $\{0,1\}^n \times \{0,1\}^v \rightarrow \{0,1\}^m$ *is a* $(\frac{k}{n} \rightarrow \frac{m-d}{m}, t)_2$-*seed-dependent condenser if for all probabilistic adversaries* A *of size* t *who take a random seed* $s \leftarrow U_v$ *and output (using more coins) a sample* $X \leftarrow A(s)$ *of entropy* $\mathbf{H}_2(X|S) \geq k$, *we have* $\mathbf{H}_2(\ \mathsf{Cond}(X;S) \mid S\ ) \geq m - d$.

Definition 12 (CRHF). *A family of hash functions* $\mathcal{G} \stackrel{\text{def}}{=} \{g_s \ : \ \{0,1\}^n \rightarrow \{0,1\}^m \ \mid \ s \in \{0,1\}^v\}$ *is* (t,δ)-*collision-resistant if for any (non-uniform) attacker* B *of size* t, *we have*

$$\Pr[g_s(x_1) = g_s(x_2) \ \wedge \ x_1 \neq x_2] \leq \delta$$

where $s \leftarrow U_v$ *and* $(x_1, x_2) \leftarrow B(s)$.

Lemma 8 (CRHFs are seed-dependent condensers). *A family of* $(2t,$
$\frac{D(t)}{2^m})$*-collision-resistant hash functions* $\mathcal{G} \overset{\text{def}}{=} \{g_s : \{0,1\}^n \to \{0,1\}^m \mid s \in$
$\{0,1\}^v\}$ *defines a seed-dependent* $(\frac{k}{n} \to \frac{m-d}{m}, t)_2$*-condenser* $\mathsf{Cond}(x; s) = g_s(x),$
where $2^d = 2^{m-k} + D(t).$

Proof. We estimate the collision probability of $\mathsf{A}(S)$ given S, but letting $\mathsf{A}(S)$
sample $X_1, X_2 \leftarrow \mathsf{A}(S)$, and bounding the probability of collision as follows:

$$\Pr[g_S(X_1) = g_S(X_2)] \leq \Pr[X_1 = X_2] + \Pr[\ g_S(X_1) = g_S(X_2) \ \wedge \ X_1 {\neq} X_2\ ]$$
$$\leq 2^{-k} + D(t){\cdot}2^{-m} \ = \ 2^{-m} \cdot (2^{m-k} + D(t)) \ = \ 2^{d-m}$$

where $\Pr[\ g_S(X_1) = g_S(X_2) \ \wedge \ X_1 {\neq} X_2\ ] \leq D(t)/2^m$, since otherwise we can
define an efficient collision-finding adversary $\mathsf{B}(S)$, who simply runs the sampler
$\mathsf{A}(S)$ twice to get the collision (X_1, X_2).

In the above, the entropy deficiency d is essentially the logarithm of $D(t)$, which is
a function on the sampler's complexity t. We note $D(t) = \Omega(t^2)$ due to birthday
attacks, and this bound can be achieved in the random oracle model. In general,
it is reasonable to assume $D(t) = \mathsf{poly}(t)$ for strong enough CRHFs. Then, using
the definition of condensers and Corollary 2, we get the following surprising
result, which partially explains the prevalent use of CRHFs (which do not appear
to have any extraction properties based on their definition) for key derivation:

Corollary 6 (Using CRHFs as KDFs). *If P is (T, σ)-square secure, $\{g_s\}$ is
a family of $(2t, \frac{\mathsf{poly}(t)}{2^m})$-CRHFs, and X is a source produced by a sampler $\mathsf{A}(s)$
of complexity at most t and having $\mathbf{H}_2(X|S) \geq k \geq m - O(\log t)$, then using
$R = g_s(X)$ makes P (T, ε')-secure, where $\varepsilon' \leq O(\sqrt{\sigma{\cdot}\mathsf{poly}(t)})$.*

From an asymptotic point of view, for square-friendly applications (e.g. CPA-
secure encryptions, weak PRFs, unpredictability primitives) with negligible ideal
ε (and hence negligible $\sigma \approx \varepsilon$), and all source samplers running in polynomial
time t (all in the "security parameter"), we get negligible security
$\varepsilon'=O(\sqrt{\varepsilon{\cdot}\mathsf{poly}(t)})$ in the real model.

4.3   Generic, Square-Friendly Key Derivation

Finally, we return to the "seed-independent" setting and turn to the question of generic key derivation for all applications P, by viewing the process
of key derivation with public randomness as an application in itself! Indeed,
we can imagine a game between the challenger $\mathsf{C}(x)$ and an attacker A, where
$\mathsf{C}(x)$ sends the public randomness s in the first round, and then challenges
A to distinguish the value $r = h(x; s)$ from uniform. In fact, this is nothing
more than the weak PRF game for $q = 1$ considered in Section 3.2,[12] except
we (confusingly) "renamed" our secret r by x, and the derived key $h_r(s)$ by

---

[12] Alternatively, one can view this game as a *computational extractor*, where the extracted string r is only required to be pseudorandom.

$r = h(x; s)$ (the input s kept its letter)! In particular, we saw that the weak PRFs are square-friendly, which means that all we need to do (not counting letter translation) in order to apply Theorem 2 is to design a "good enough" $((t, 2), \delta)$-secure weak PRF *in the ideal model.*

To do so, let us examine the parameters we need. First, as explained at the end of Section 4.1, we will assume that our source length $n = m$ (since we can always apply Corollary 5 to more or less reduce to this case). Thus, we need a $((t, 2), \delta)$-secure weak PRF where both the key (now called x) and the output (now called r) are m-bit long. As explained at the end of Section 3.2, we cannot achieve this result information-theoretically. Instead, we return to the "computational pairwise independent" construction sketched at the end of Section 3.2, starting with a formal definition of a PRG.

Definition 13 (PRG). *We say that a function* $G : \{0, 1\}^m \to \{0, 1\}^{2m}$ *is a* $(2t, \varepsilon_{\mathsf{prg}})$-*secure PRG if for any* $2t$-*bounded attacker* A, $\Delta_{\mathsf{A}}(G(U_m), U_{2m}) \leq \varepsilon_{\mathsf{prg}}$.

We now compose such a PRG G with any pairwise independent hash function (see Equation (4)) $h_y : \{0, 1\}^p \to \{0, 1\}^m$, where key length $|y| = 2m$ (we will set the input length $p \leq m$ shortly). For example, viewing $y = (a, b)$, where $a, b \in GF[2^m]$ and $s \in \{0, 1\}^p \subseteq GF[2^m]$, we could set $h_{a,b}(s) = a \cdot s + b$. Recall, as discussed in Section 3.2, the resulting family $\mathcal{H}$ is clearly a $((\infty, 2), 2^{-p})$-secure weak PRF, except its key y is too long ($2m$ bits instead of m). Therefore, we define the composed function $h'_x : \{0, 1\}^p \to \{0, 1\}^m$, with key $x \in \{0, 1\}^m$, by $h'_x(s) = h_{G(x)}(s)$. A simple hybrid argument shows that the resulting hash family $\mathcal{H}'$ is a $((2t, 2), \varepsilon_{\mathsf{prg}} + 2^{-p})$-secure weak PRF. Combining this result with Theorem 2, we finally get our key derivation function from m-to-m bits:

Theorem 4. *If* G *is* $(2t, \varepsilon_{\mathsf{prg}})$-*secure and* $\mathcal{H}$ *is pairwise independent, then the* m-*to-*m-*bit key derivation function* $h'_x(s) = h_{G(x)}(s)$ *uses* p *bits of public randomness* s *and achieves* $(t, \sqrt{2^{d-1} \cdot (\varepsilon_{\mathsf{prg}} + 2^{-p})})$-*security in the* $(m - d, m)$-*real$_2$-model.*

In particular, if $p = \log(1/\varepsilon_{\mathsf{prg}})$, *then* $\mathcal{H}'$ *is* $(t, \sqrt{2^d \cdot \varepsilon_{\mathsf{prg}}})$-*secure in the* $(m - d, m)$-*real$_2$-model, and the derived key* R *can be used in any (even non-square-friendly)* (t, ε)-*secure application* P *needing an* m-*bit key, giving* $(t, \varepsilon + \sqrt{2^d \cdot \varepsilon_{\mathsf{prg}}})$-*security for* P *in the* $(m - d, m)$-*real$_2$-model.*

Notice, the latter bound might be beneficial not only for non-square-friendly applications, where no other options are available, but also for square-friendly applications where $\varepsilon \gg \varepsilon_{\mathsf{prg}}$. Also, the assumption $p \geq \log(1/\varepsilon_{\mathsf{prg}})$ is easy to achieve, since the standard "$a \cdot s + b$" pairwise independent hash function achieves $p = m$, and $m \gg \log(1/\varepsilon_{\mathsf{prg}})$ for any m-to-$2m$-bit PRG. Hence, we never need to use more than m bits of public randomness.

GENERIC KEY DERIVATION. We now combine Theorem 4 and Corollary 5 to tackle the case of a general n-to-m-bit key derivation function. As before, we take a $(2t, \varepsilon_{\mathsf{prg}})$-secure PRG $G : \{0, 1\}^m \to \{0, 1\}^{2m}$ and a pairwise independent family $\mathcal{H} = \{h_y : \{0, 1\}^p \to \{0, 1\}^m \mid y \in \{0, 1\}^{2m}\}$ with $p \geq \log(1/\varepsilon_{\mathsf{prg}})$, but now also use a universal family $\mathcal{G} = \{g_s : \{0, 1\}^n \to \{0, 1\}^m \mid s \in \{0, 1\}^v\}$. Define the new hash family $\mathcal{H}' = \{h'_{s,s'} : \{0,1\}^n \to \{0,1\}^m \mid s \in \{0,1\}^v, s' \in \{0,1\}^p\}$ by $h'_{s,s'}(x) = h_{G(g_s(x))}(s')$.

Before stating our final bound, we claim that we can instantiate $\mathcal{H}'$ so that the amount of public randomness $p + v$ it is at most $\max(m, n)$. Indeed, the size of s' can be made $p = \log(1/\varepsilon_{\mathsf{prg}}) \leq m$ bits. When $n \leq m$, $\mathcal{G}$ can be keyless and simply have the "never-colliding" identity function, so $m = m + 0 = \max(m, n)$ total bits is enough. When $n \geq m$, the optimal key size of a universal hash family from n bits to m bits is $v = n - m$ (by Toeplitz matrices construction, or, when n is a multiple of m, the "augmented" inner product construction discussed in Section 3.2). This gives total number of bits at most $m + (n - m) = n = \max(m, n)$.

Using Corollary 5 to analyze the 'inner' n-to-m-bit KDF with parameters of the 'outer' m-to-m-bit KDF given by Theorem 4, we get:

Corollary 7. *If G is $(2t, \varepsilon_{\mathsf{prg}})$-secure PRG, $\mathcal{H}$ is pairwise independent and $\mathcal{G}$ is universal, then the function family $\mathcal{H}'$ above defines an n-to-m-bit key derivation function that uses $p + v$ bits of public randomness and achieves $(t, \varepsilon_{\mathsf{prg}} + \sqrt{2^{m-k} \cdot \varepsilon_{\mathsf{prg}}})$-security in the (k, n)-real$_2$-model.*

In particular, the derived key R can be used in any (even non-square-friendly) (t, ε)-secure application P needing an m-bit key, giving $(t, \varepsilon + \varepsilon_{\mathsf{prg}} + \sqrt{2^{m-k} \cdot \varepsilon_{\mathsf{prg}}})$-security for P in the (k, n)-real$_2$-model.

Moreover, $\mathcal{H}$ and $\mathcal{G}$ can be instantiated so that the amount of public randomness $p + v \leq \max(m, n)$.

As before, the generic bound for P might be beneficial not only for non-square-friendly applications P, where no other options are available, but also for square-friendly applications where $\varepsilon \gg \varepsilon_{\mathsf{prg}}$.

ALTERNATIVE TO DENSE MODEL THEOREM. Finally, as mentioned in the Introduction, the most unexpected consequence occurs when we apply it to $P = G$ itself! In this case, while the initial value $Y = G(X)$ need not be pseudorandom at all when $\mathbf{H}_2(X) \geq m - d$, our result in Theorem 4 implies that $G(h_{G(X)}(S))$ is $(t, \varepsilon_{\mathsf{prg}} + \sqrt{2^d \cdot \varepsilon_{\mathsf{prg}}})$-pseudorandom, even conditioned on S.

Theorem 5 (Alternative to Dense Model Theorem). *Assume $G : \{0,1\}^m \to \{0,1\}^{2m}$ is a $(2t, \varepsilon_{\mathsf{prg}})$-secure PRG, $\mathcal{H} = \{h_y : \{0,1\}^p \to \{0,1\}^m \mid y \in \{0,1\}^{2m}\}$ is a pairwise independent family with $p \geq \log(1/\varepsilon_{\mathsf{prg}})$, X is any seed distribution over $\{0,1\}^m$ with $\mathbf{H}_2(X) \geq m - d$, and $S \leftarrow U_p$ is a public random string (independent of X). Then, for any t-bounded distinguishers A and B, we have*

$$\Delta_{\mathsf{A}}(\, h_{G(X)}(S) \,,\, U_m \mid S \,) \leq \sqrt{2^d \cdot \varepsilon_{\mathsf{prg}}}$$

$$\Delta_{\mathsf{B}}(\, G(h_{G(X)}(S)) \,,\, U_{2m} \mid S \,) \leq \varepsilon_{\mathsf{prg}} + \sqrt{2^d \cdot \varepsilon_{\mathsf{prg}}}$$

Thus, $G(h_{G(X)}(S))$ is $(t, \varepsilon_{\mathsf{prg}} + \sqrt{2^d \cdot \varepsilon_{\mathsf{prg}}})$-pseudorandom conditioned on S.

We defer the detailed comparison with the results obtained via the standard dense model theorem [28,27,16,17] to the full version [15] (but see the end of the

Introduction for some highlights), where we also give a simple concrete instantiation of our approach.

Acknowledgements. Yevgeniy Dodis was supported by the NSF CNS Grants 1065134, 1065288, 1017471, 0831299 and Google Faculty Award. Yu Yu was supported by the National Basic Research Program of China Grant 2011CBA00300, 2011CBA00301, the National Natural Science Foundation of China Grant 61033001, 61172085, 61061130540, 61073174, 61103221, 11061130539, 61021004 and 60703031.

References

1. Barak, B., Dodis, Y., Krawczyk, H., Pereira, O., Pietrzak, K., Standaert, F.-X., Yu, Y.: Leftover Hash Lemma, Revisited. In: Rogaway, P. (ed.) CRYPTO 2011. LNCS, vol. 6841, pp. 1–20. Springer, Heidelberg (2011)
2. Barak, B., Halevi, S.: A model and architecture for pseudo-random generation with applications to /dev/random. In: Proceedings of the 12th ACM Conference on Computer and Communication Security, pp. 203–212 (2005)
3. Barak, B., Shaltiel, R., Tromer, E.: True Random Number Generators Secure in a Changing Environment. In: Walter, C.D., Koç, Ç.K., Paar, C. (eds.) CHES 2003. LNCS, vol. 2779, pp. 166–180. Springer, Heidelberg (2003)
4. Boyen, X., Dodis, Y., Katz, J., Ostrovsky, R., Smith, A.: Secure Remote Authentication Using Biometric Data. In: Cramer, R. (ed.) EUROCRYPT 2005. LNCS, vol. 3494, pp. 147–163. Springer, Heidelberg (2005)
5. Brakerski, Z., Goldreich, O.: From absolute distinguishability to positive distinguishability. In: Electronic Colloquium on Computational Complexity (ECCC), vol. 16, p. 31 (2009)
6. Carter, J.L., Wegman, M.N.: Universal classes of hash functions. Journal of Computer and System Sciences 18, 143–154 (1979)
7. Cohen, G., Raz, R., Segev, G.: Non-malleable extractors with short seeds and applications to privacy amplification. In: Proceedings of the 27th Computational Complexity, pp. 110–124 (2012)
8. Dedić, N., Harnik, D., Reyzin, L.: Saving Private Randomness in One-Way Functions and Pseudorandom Generators. In: Canetti, R. (ed.) TCC 2008. LNCS, vol. 4948, pp. 607–625. Springer, Heidelberg (2008)
9. Dodis, Y., Katz, J., Reyzin, L., Smith, A.: Robust Fuzzy Extractors and Authenticated Key Agreement from Close Secrets. In: Dwork, C. (ed.) CRYPTO 2006. LNCS, vol. 4117, pp. 232–250. Springer, Heidelberg (2006)
10. Dodis, Y., Li, X., Wooley, T.D., Zuckerman, D.: Privacy amplification and non-malleable extractors via character sums. In: Proceedings of the 52nd IEEE Symposium on Foundation of Computer Science, pp. 668–677 (2011)
11. Dodis, Y., Ostrovsky, R., Reyzin, L., Smith, A.: Fuzzy extractors: How to generate strong keys from biometrics and other noisy data. SIAM Journal on Computing 38(1), 97–139 (2008)
12. Dodis, Y., Ristenpart, T., Vadhan, S.: Randomness Condensers for Efficiently Samplable, Seed-Dependent Sources. In: Cramer, R. (ed.) TCC 2012. LNCS, vol. 7194, pp. 618–635. Springer, Heidelberg (2012)

13. Dodis, Y., Smith, A.: Correcting errors without leaking partial information. In: Proceedings of the Thirty-Seventh Annual ACM Symposium on Theory of Computing, Baltimore, Maryland, May 22-24, pp. 654–663 (2005)

14. Dodis, Y., Wichs, D.: Non-malleable extractors and symmetric key cryptography from weak secrets. In: Mitzenmacher, M. (ed.) Proceedings of the 41st Annual ACM Symposium on Theory of Computing, Bethesda, MD, USA, pp. 601–610. ACM (2009)

15. Dodis, Y., Yu, Y.: Overcoming weak expectactions (2012), full version of this paper http://cs.nyu.edu/~dodis/ps/weak-expe.pdf

16. Dziembowski, S., Pietrzak, K.: Leakage-resilient cryptography. In: Proceedings of the 49th IEEE Symposium on Foundation of Computer Science, pp. 293–302 (2008)

17. Fuller, B., O'Neill, A., Reyzin, L.: A Unified Approach to Deterministic Encryption: New Constructions and a Connection to Computational Entropy. In: Cramer, R. (ed.) TCC 2012. LNCS, vol. 7194, pp. 582–599. Springer, Heidelberg (2012)

18. Gennaro, R., Krawczyk, H., Rabin, T.: Secure Hashed Diffie-Hellman over Non-DDH Groups. In: Cachin, C., Camenisch, J.L. (eds.) EUROCRYPT 2004. LNCS, vol. 3027, pp. 361–381. Springer, Heidelberg (2004)

19. Håstad, J., Impagliazzo, R., Levin, L.A., Luby, M.: Construction of pseudorandom generator from any one-way function. SIAM Journal on Computing 28(4), 1364–1396 (1999)

20. Krawczyk, H.: Cryptographic Extraction and Key Derivation: The HKDF Scheme. In: Rabin, T. (ed.) CRYPTO 2010. LNCS, vol. 6223, pp. 631–648. Springer, Heidelberg (2010)

21. Li, X.: Non-malleable extractors, two-source extractors and privacy amplification. In: Proceedings of the 53rd IEEE Symposium on Foundation of Computer Science, pp. 688–697 (2012)

22. Maurer, U.M., Wolf, S.: Privacy Amplification Secure against Active Adversaries. In: Kaliski Jr., B.S. (ed.) CRYPTO 1997. LNCS, vol. 1294, pp. 307–321. Springer, Heidelberg (1997)

23. Naor, M., Reingold, O.: Synthesizers and their application to the parallel construction of pseudo-random functions. J. Comput. Syst. Sci. 58(2), 336–375 (1999)

24. Pietrzak, K.: A Leakage-Resilient Mode of Operation. In: Joux, A. (ed.) EUROCRYPT 2009. LNCS, vol. 5479, pp. 462–482. Springer, Heidelberg (2009)

25. Raz, R., Reingold, O.: On recycling the randomness of states in space bounded computation. In: Proceedings of the 31st ACM Symposium on the Theory of Computing, pp. 159–168 (1999)

26. Reingold, O., Shaltiel, R., Wigderson, A.: Extracting randomness via repeated condensing. SIAM J. Comput. 35(5), 1185–1209 (2006)

27. Reingold, O., Trevisan, L., Tulsiani, M., Vadhan, S.P.: Dense subsets of pseudorandom sets. In: Proceedings of the 49th IEEE Symposium on Foundation of Computer Science, pp. 76–85 (2008)

28. Tao, T., Ziegler, T.: The primes contain arbitrarily long polynomial progressions (2006), http://arxiv.org/abs/math.NT/0610050

29. Trevisan, L., Vadhan, S.: Extracting randomness from samplable distributions. In: 41st Annual Symposium on Foundations of Computer Science, Redondo Beach, California, pp. 32–42. IEEE (November 2000)

A Counterexample to the Chain Rule
for Conditional HILL Entropy[*]
And What Deniable Encryption Has to Do with It

Stephan Krenn[1,**], Krzysztof Pietrzak[2], and Akshay Wadia[3,* * *]

[1] IBM Research – Zurich, Rüschlikon
stephan.krenn@ist.ac.at
[2] Institute of Science and Technology Austria
pietrzak@ist.ac.at
[3] University of California, Los Angeles
awadia@cs.ucla.edu

Abstract. A chain rule for an entropy notion $H(\cdot)$ states that the entropy $H(X)$ of a variable X decreases by at most ℓ if conditioned on an ℓ-bit string A, i.e., $H(X|A) \geq H(X) - \ell$. More generally, it satisfies a chain rule for *conditional* entropy if $H(X|Y, A) \geq H(X|Y) - \ell$.

All natural information theoretic entropy notions we are aware of (like Shannon or min-entropy) satisfy some kind of chain rule for conditional entropy. Moreover, many *computational* entropy notions (like Yao entropy, unpredictability entropy and several variants of HILL entropy) satisfy the chain rule for conditional entropy, though here not only the *quantity* decreases by ℓ, but also the *quality* of the entropy decreases exponentially in ℓ. However, for the standard notion of conditional HILL entropy (the computational equivalent of min-entropy) the existence of such a rule was unknown so far.

In this paper, we prove that for conditional HILL entropy no meaningful chain rule exists, assuming the existence of one-way permutations: there exist distributions X, Y, A, where A is a distribution over a *single* bit, but $H^{\mathsf{HILL}}(X|Y) \gg H^{\mathsf{HILL}}(X|Y, A)$, even if we simultaneously allow for a massive degradation in the quality of the entropy.

The idea underlying our construction is based on a surprising connection between the chain rule for HILL entropy and deniable encryption.

Keywords: Computational entropy, HILL entropy, Conditional chain rule.

1   Introduction

Various information theoretic entropy notions are used to quantify the amount of randomness of a probability distribution. The most common one is Shannon

---

[*] This work was partly funded by the European Research Council under an ERC Starting Grant (259668-PSPC).
[**] This work was done while the author was at IST Austria.
[* * *] This work was done while the author was visiting IST Austria.

A. Sahai (Ed.): TCC 2013, LNCS 7785, pp. 23–39, 2013.

entropy, which measures the incompressibility of a distribution. In cryptographic settings the notion of min-entropy, measuring the unpredictability of a random variable, is often more convenient to work with.

One of the most useful tools for manipulating and arguing about entropies are chain rules, which come in many different flavors for different entropy notions. Roughly, a chain rule captures the fact that the entropy of a variable X decreases by at most the entropy of another variable A if conditioned on A. For Shannon entropy, we have a particularly simple chain rule

$$H(X|A) = H(X, A) - H(A)$$

More generally, one can give chain rules for conditional entropies by considering the case where X has some entropy conditioned on Y, and bound by how much the entropy drops when given A. The chain rule for Shannon entropy naturally extends to this case

$$H(X|Y, A) = H(X|Y) - H(A)$$

For min-entropy (cf. Definition 2.1) an elegant chain rule holds if one uses the right notion of conditional min-entropy. The worst case definition $H_\infty(X|Y) = \min_y H_\infty(X|Y = y)$ is often too pessimistic. An average-case notion has been defined by [5] (cf. Definition 2.2), and they show it satisfies the following chain rules ($H_0(A)$ is the logarithm of the size of the support of A):

$$\tilde{H}_\infty(X|A) \geq H_\infty(X) - H_0(A) \quad \text{and} \quad \tilde{H}_\infty(X|Y, A) \geq \tilde{H}_\infty(X|Y) - H_0(A) \,.$$

1.1   Computational Entropy

The classical information theoretic notions anticipate computationally unbounded parties, e.g. no algorithm can compress a distribution below its Shannon entropy and no algorithm can predict it better than exponentially in its min-entropy. Under computational assumptions, in particular in cryptographic settings, one can talk about distribution that appear to have high entropy only for computationally bounded parties. The most basic example are pseudorandom distributions, where $X \in \{0, 1\}^n$ is said to be pseudorandom if it cannot be distinguished from the uniform distribution U_n by polynomial size distinguishers. So X appears to have n bits of Shannon and n bits of min-entropy.

Pseudorandomness is a very elegant and tremendously useful notion, but sometimes one has to deal with distributions which do not look uniform, but only seem to have some kind high entropy. Some of the most prominent such notions are HILL, Yao and unpredictability entropy. Informally, a distribution X has k bits of HILL-pseudoentropy [13] (conditioned on Z), if cannot be distinguished from some variable Y with k bits of min-entropy (given Z). X has k bits of Yao entropy [1,20] (conditioned on Z) if it cannot be compressed below k bits (given Z), and X has k bits of unpredictability entropy [14] conditioned on Z if no efficient adversary can guess X better than with probability 2^{-k} given Z.[1] When we talk about, say the HILL entropy of X, not only its *quantity k* is of

---

[1] Unlike HILL and Yao, unpredictability entropy is only interesting if the conditional part Z is not empty, otherwise it coincides with min-entropy.

interest, but also its *quality* which specifies against what kind of distinguishers X looks like having k bits of min-entropy. This is specified by giving two additional parameters (ε, s), and the meaning of $H^{\mathsf{HILL}}_{\varepsilon,s}(X) = k$ is that X cannot be distinguished from some Y with min-entropy k by distinguishers of size s with advantage greater than ε.

Chain rules for (conditional) entropy are easily seen to hold for some computational entropy notions (in particular for (conditional) Yao and unpredictability), albeit there are two caveats. First, one must typically assume that the part A we condition on comes from an efficiently samplable distribution, we will always set $A \in \{0,1\}^\ell$. Second, the quality of the entropy (the distinguishing advantage, circuit size, or both) typically degrades exponentially in ℓ. The chain rules for (conditional) computational entropy notions H we know state that for any distribution (X, Y, A) where $A \in \{0,1\}^\ell$ (X, Y, A) where $A \in \{0,1\}^\ell$

$$H_{\varepsilon',s'}(X|Y,A) \geq H_{\varepsilon,s}(X|Y) - \ell \qquad (1)$$

where $\varepsilon' = \mu(\varepsilon, 2^\ell)$, $s' = s/\nu(2^\ell, \varepsilon)$ for some polynomial functions μ, ν. For HILL entropy such a chain rule has only recently been found [7,15] (cf. Lemma 2.6), but only holds for the unconditional case, i.e., when Y in (1) is empty (or at least very short, cf. Theorem 3.7 [9]). Whether or not a chain rule holds for conditional HILL has been open up to now. In this paper we give a counterexample showing that the chain rule for conditional HILL entropy does not hold in a very strong sense.

We will not try to formally define what constitutes a chain rule for a computational entropy notion, not even for the special case of HILL entropy we consider here, as this would seem arbitrary. Instead, we will specify what it means that conditional HILL entropy does not satisfy a chain rule. This requirement is so demanding that it leaves little room for any kind of meaningful positive statement that could be considered as a chain rule.

We will say that an ensemble of distributions $\{(X_n, Y_n, A_n)\}_{n \in \mathbb{N}}$ forms a counterexample to the chain rule for conditional HILL entropy if

- X_n has a lot of high quality HILL entropy conditioned on Y_n : that is, $H^{\mathsf{HILL}}_{\varepsilon,s}(X_n|Y_n) = z_n$ where (high quantity) $z_n = n^\alpha$ for some $\alpha > 0$ (we will achieve any $\alpha < 1$) and (high quality) for every polynomial $s = s(n)$ we can set $\epsilon = \epsilon(n)$ to be negligible.
- The HILL entropy of X_n drops by a constant fraction conditioned additionally on a single bit $A_n \in \{0,1\}$, even if we only ask for very low quality entropy: (large quantitative gap) $H^{\mathsf{HILL}}_{\epsilon',s'}(X_n|Y_n, A_n) < \beta \cdot H^{\mathsf{HILL}}_{\epsilon,s}(X_n|Y_n)$ for $\beta < 1$ (we achieve $\beta < 0.6$) and (low quality) $\epsilon' > 0$ is constant (we achieve any $\epsilon' < 1$) and $s' = s'(n)$ is a fixed polynomial.

Assuming the existence of one-way permutations, we construct such an ensemble of distributions $\{(X_n, Y_n, A_n)\}_{n \in \mathbb{N}}$ over $\{0,1\}^{1.5n^2} \times \{0,1\}^{3n^2} \times \{0,1\}$.

$$H^{\mathsf{HILL}}_{\varepsilon',s'}(X_n|Y_n, A_n) < H^{\mathsf{HILL}}_{\varepsilon,s}(X_n|Y_n) - 1.25n$$

Moreover $H_{\varepsilon,s}^{\mathsf{HILL}}(X|Y) \approx 3n$, which gives a multiplicative gap of $(3n - 1.25n)/3n < 0.6$

$$H_{\varepsilon',s'}^{\mathsf{HILL}}(X_n|Y_n, A_n) \;<\; 0.6 \cdot H_{\varepsilon,s}^{\mathsf{HILL}}(X_n|Y_n)\,,$$

where $H_{\varepsilon,s}^{\mathsf{HILL}}$ is high-quality cryptographic-strength pseudoentropy (i.e., for any polynomial $s = s(n)$ we can choose $\varepsilon = \varepsilon(n)$ to be negligible) and (ε', s') is extremely low end where ε' can be any constant < 1 and s is a fixed polynomial (depending only the complexity of evaluating the one-way permutation). The entropy gap $1.25n$ we achieve is constant factor of entire HILL entropy $H_{\varepsilon,s}^{\mathsf{HILL}}(X_n|Y_n) \approx 3n$ in X. The gap is roughly the square root of the length $m = 4.5n^2$ of the variables (X_n, Y_n). This can be easily increased from $n \approx m^{1/2}$ to $n \approx m^{1-\gamma}$ for any $\gamma > 0$.

Interestingly, for several variants of conditional HILL entropy, chain rules in the conditional case do hold. In particular, this is the case for the so called *decomposable*, *relaxed* and *simulatable* versions of HILL entropy (cf. [9] and references therein).

1.2 Counterexamples from Deniable Encryption and One-Way Permutations

Deniable encryption has been proposed in 1997 by Canetti et al. [3], if such schemes actually exists has been an intriguing open problem ever since. The only known negative result is due to Bendlin et al. [2] who show that *receiver* deniable *non-interactive* public-key encryption is impossible. Informally, a *sender* deniable public-key encryption scheme (we will just consider bit-encryption) is a semantically secure public-key encryption scheme, which additionally provides some efficient way for the sender of a ciphertext C computed as $C := enc(pk, B, R)$ to come up with some *fake* randomness R' which explains C as a ciphertext for the opposite message $1 - B$. That is $C = enc(pk, 1 - B, R')$, and for a random B, (C, B, R) and $(C, 1 - B, R')$ are indistinguishable.

We show a close connection between deniable encryption and HILL entropy: any deniable encryption scheme provides a counterexample to the chain rule for conditional HILL entropy. This connection has been the starting point for the counterexample constructed in this paper. Unfortunately, this connection does not immediately prove the impossibility of a chain rule, as deniable encryption is not known to exist. Yet, a closer look shows that we do not need all the functionalities of deniable encryption to construct a counterexample. In particular, neither the faking algorithm nor decryption must be efficient. We will exploit this to get a counterexample from any one-way permutation.

1.3 Related Work

The concept of HILL entropy has first been introduced by Håstad et al. [13], and the conditional variant was suggested by Hsiao et al. [14]. Other notions of computational entropy include Yao entropy [1,20], unpredictability entropy [14], and metric entropy [1].

Chain rules for these entropy notions are known, e.g., Fuller et al. [8] for metric entropy, where they also show a connection between metric entropy and deterministic encryption. A chain rule for HILL entropy was proved independently by Reingold et al. [15] (it is a corollary of the more general dense model theorem proven in this work) and Dziembowski and Pietrzak [7] (as a tool for proving security of leakage-resilient cryptosystems). This chain rule only applies in the unconditional setting, but for some variants of HILL entropy, chain rules are known in the conditional setting as well. Chung et al. [4] proved a chain rule for *samplable* HILL entropy, a variant of HILL entropy where one requires the high min-entropy distribution Y as in Definition 2.5 to be efficiently samplable. Fuller et al. [8] give a chain rule for *decomposable* metric entropy (which implies HILL entropy). Reyzin [16] (cf. Theorem 2 and the paragraph following it in [16]) gives a chain rule for conditional *relaxed* HILL entropy, such a rule is implicit in the work of Gentry and Wichs [10].

A chain rule for normal conditional HILL entropy (citing [8]) "remains an interesting open problem". The intuition underlying the counterexample we construct (giving a negative answer to this open problem) borrows ideas from the deniable encryption scheme of Dürmuth and Freeman [6] presented at Eurocrypt 2011, which unfortunately later turned out to have a subtle flaw. In their protocol, after receiving the ciphertext, the receiver (knowing the secret key) helps the sender to evaluate a faking algorithm by sending some information the sender could not compute efficiently on its own. It is this interactive phase that is flawed. However, it turns out that for our counterexample to work, the faking algorithm does not need to be efficiently computable, and thus we can already use the first part of their protocol as a counterexample. Moreover, as we don't require an efficient decryption algorithm either, we can further weaken our assumptions and base our construction on any one-way permutation instead of trapdoor permutations.

1.4   Roadmap

This document in structured as follows: in Section 2 we recap the basic definitions required for paper. In Section 3 we then give the intuition underlying our results by deriving a counterexample to the chain rule for conditional HILL entropy from any sender-deniable bit-encryption scheme. The counterexample based on one-way permutations is then formally presented in Section 4.

2   Preliminaries

In this section we recap the basic definitions required for this document. We start by defining some standard notation, and then recapitulate the required background of entropy measures, hardcore predicates, and Stirling's formula.

We say that $f(n) = \mathcal{O}(g(n))$, if $f(n)$ is asymptotically bounded above by $g(n)$, i.e., there exists a $k \in \mathbb{N}$ such that $|f(n)| \leq k|g(n)|$ for all $n > k$. Similarly, $f(n) = \omega(g(n))$, if $f(n)$ asymptotically dominates $g(n)$, i.e., for every $k \in \mathbb{N}$, there exists $n_k \in \mathbb{N}$, such that for all $n > n_k$ we have that $kg(n) < f(n)$. A function $\nu(n)$ is called *negligible*, if it vanishes faster than every polynomial, i.e., for every integer k, there exists an integer n_k such that $\nu(n) < n^{-k}$ for all $n > n_k$, or alternatively, if $n^{-k} = \omega(\nu(n))$ for all k.

By $|\mathcal{S}|$ we denote the cardinality of some set $\mathcal{S}$. We further write $s \xleftarrow{\$} \mathcal{S}$ to denote that s is drawn uniformly at random from $\mathcal{S}$. The *support* of a probability distribution X, denoted by $\mathrm{supp}(X)$, is the set of elements to which X assigns non-zero probability mass, i.e., $\mathrm{supp}(X) = \{x \mid \Pr[X = x] > 0\}$. A distribution X is called *flat*, if it is uniform on its support, i.e., $\forall x \in \mathrm{supp}(X), \Pr[X = x] = 1/|\mathrm{supp}(X)|$. Finally, we use the notation $\Pr[\mathcal{E} : \Omega]$ to denote the probability of event $\mathcal{E}$ over the probability space Ω. For example, $\Pr\left[f(x) = 1 : x \xleftarrow{\$} \{0,1\}^n\right]$ is the probability that $f(x) = 1$ for a uniformly drawn x in $\{0,1\}^n$.

2.1   Entropy Measures

Informally, the entropy of a random variable X is a measure of the uncertainty of X. In the following we define those notions of entropy required for the rest of the paper.

Min-Entropy. Min-entropy is often useful in cryptography, as it ensures that the success probability of even a computationally unbounded adversary guessing the value of a sample from X is bounded above by $2^{-H_\infty(X)}$:

Definition 2.1 (Min-Entropy). *A random variable X has* min-entropy k, *denoted by $H_\infty(X) = k$, if*

$$\max_x \Pr[X = x] = 2^{-k} .$$

While a conditional version of min-entropy is straightforward to formulate, Dodis et al. [5] introduced the notion of *average min-entropy*, which is useful, if the adversary does not have control over the variable one is conditioning on.

Definition 2.2 (Average min-Entropy). *For a pair (X, Z) of random variables, the* average min-entropy *of X conditioned on Z is*

$$\widetilde{H}_\infty(X|Z) = -\log \mathop{\mathbb{E}}_{z \leftarrow Z} \max_x \Pr[X = x | Z = z] = -\log \mathop{\mathbb{E}}_{z \leftarrow Z} 2^{-H_\infty(X|Z=z)},$$

where the expectation is over all z with non-zero probability.

Similarly to min-entropy, an adversary learning Z can only predict X with probability $2^{-\widetilde{H}_\infty(X|Z)}$.

HILL Entropy. While min-entropy guarantees an information-theoretic bound on the probability of an adversary guessing a random variable, this bound might not be reached by any adversary of a limited size. For instance, this is the case for pseudorandom distributions. This fact is taken into account in computational variants of entropy.

Before formally defining HILL entropy, the computational equivalent of min-entropy, we recap what it means for two probability distributions to be close in a computational sense:

Definition 2.3 (Closeness of Distributions). *Two probability distributions X and Y are (ε, s)-close, denoted by $X \sim_{\varepsilon, s} Y$, if for every circuit D of size at most s the following holds:*

$$|\Pr[\mathsf{D}(X) = 1] - \Pr[\mathsf{D}(Y) = 1]| \leq \varepsilon.$$

We further say that two ensembles of distributions $\{X_n\}_{n \in \mathbb{N}}$ and $\{Y_n\}_{n \in \mathbb{N}}$ are $\varepsilon(n)$-computationally-indistinguishable if for every positive polynomial $\mathsf{poly}(n)$ there exists $n_0 \in \mathbb{N}$ such that for all $n > n_0$, it holds that $X_n \sim_{\varepsilon(n), \mathsf{poly}(n)} Y_n$.

Informally, a random variable X has a high HILL entropy, if it is computationally indistinguishable from a random variable with high min-entropy, cf. Håstad et al. [13]:

Definition 2.4 (HILL Entropy). *A distribution X has HILL entropy k, denoted by $H_{\varepsilon, s}^{\mathsf{HILL}}(X) \geq k$, if there exists a distribution Y satisfying $H_\infty(Y) \geq k$ and $X \sim_{\varepsilon, s} Y$.*

Intuitively, in the above definition, k can be thought of as the quantity of entropy in X, whereas ε and s specify its quality: the larger s and the smaller ε, the closer X is to a random variable Y with information-theoretic min-entropy k in a computational sense.

A conditional version of HILL entropy can be defined similarly as a computational analogue to average min-entropy [14]:

Definition 2.5 (Conditional HILL Entropy). *Let X, Z be random variables. X has conditional HILL entropy $H_{\varepsilon, s}^{\mathsf{HILL}}(X|Z) \geq k$ conditioned on Z, if there exists a collection of distributions $\{Y_z\}_{z \in Z}$ giving rise to a joint distribution (Y, Z) such that $\widetilde{H}_\infty(Y|Z) \geq k$, and $(X, Z) \sim_{\varepsilon, s} (Y, Z)$.*

It has been shown that conditioning X on a random variable of length at most ℓ reduces the HILL entropy by at most ℓ bits, if the quality may decrease exponentially in ℓ [7,15,8]:

Lemma 2.6 (Chain Rule for HILL Entropy). *For a random variable X and $A \in \{0, 1\}^\ell$ it holds that*

$$H_{\varepsilon', s'}^{\mathsf{HILL}}(X|A) \geq H_{\varepsilon, s}^{\mathsf{HILL}}(X) - \ell,$$

where $\varepsilon' \approx 2^\ell \varepsilon$ and $s' \approx s\varepsilon'^2$.

2.2   Hardcore Predicates

The counterexample we present in Section 4 is based on the existence of one-way permutations, which we define next. Intuitively, a permutation is one-way, if it is easy to compute but hard to invert. For an extensive discussion, see [11, Chapter 2]. The following definition is from [19]:

Definition 2.7 (One-Way Permutation). *A length-preserving function* $\pi :$ $\{0,1\}^* \to \{0,1\}^*$ *is called a* one-way permutation, *if* π *is computable in polynomial time, if for every* n, π *restricted to* $\{0,1\}^n$ *is a permutation, and if for every probabilistic polynomial-time algorithm* A *there is a negligible function* ν *such that the following holds:*

$$\Pr\left[\mathsf{A}(\pi(x)) = x \; : \; x \xleftarrow{\$} \{0,1\}^n\right] < \nu(n)\,.$$

While for a one-way permutation, given $\pi(x)$ it is hard to compute x in its entirety, it may be easy to efficiently compute a large fraction of x. However, for our construction we will need that some parts of x cannot be computed with better probability than by guessing. This is captured by the notion of a hardcore predicate [12]. We use the formalization from [18]:

Definition 2.8 (Hardcore Predicate). *We call* $p : \{0,1\}^* \to \{0,1\}$ *a* $(\sigma(n),$ $\nu(n))$-hardcore predicate *for a one-way permutation* π, *if it is efficiently computable, and if for every adversary running in at most* $\sigma(n)$ *steps, the following holds:*

$$\Pr\left[\mathsf{A}(\pi(x)) = p(x) \; : \; x \xleftarrow{\$} \{0,1\}^n\right] < \frac{1}{2} + \nu(n)\,.$$

It is well known that a one-way permutation π with a hardcore predicate p can be derived from any one-way permutation π' as follows [12]: for r of the same length as x, define $\pi(x,r) := (\pi'(x),r)$ and $p(x,r) := \langle x,r \rangle$, where $\langle \cdot, \cdot \rangle$ denotes the inner product modulo 2.

2.3   Stirling's Formula

Stirling's approximation [17] states that for any integer n it holds that:

$$\log n! = n \log n - \frac{n}{\ln 2} + \mathcal{O}(\log n)\,.$$

In our results we will make use of the following lemma, which directly follows from Stirling's formula.

Lemma 2.9. *For every integer* $a > 1$ *we have that*

$$\log \binom{an}{n} = an \log a - (a-1)n \log(a-1) + \mathcal{O}(\log n)\,. \tag{2}$$

3   A Counterexample from Sender Deniable Encryption

We start this section by defining sender deniable encryption schemes, and then show how such a scheme leads to a counterexample to the chain rule for conditional HILL entropy.

As the existence of sender deniable public key encryption schemes is an open problem, this implication does not directly falsify the chain rule. However, it shows up an interesting connection, and gives the idea underlying our result, as the proof given in Section 4 was strongly inspired by deniable encryption. We stress that the main purpose of this section is to give the reader some intuition, and thus we do not fully formalize all steps here.

3.1   Sender Deniable PKE

Deniable encryption, first introduced by Canetti et al. [3], is a cryptographic primitive offering protection against *coercion*. Consider therefore the following scenario: a sender sends an encrypted message to a receiver over a public channel. After the transmission, an adversary who wishes to learn the message sent, coerces one of the parties into revealing the secret information that was used to run the protocol (i.e., the secret message, the random tape used to generate keys, etc.). If the parties used a semantically secure but non-deniable encryption scheme, the adversary can check the consistency of the protocol transcript (which was carried over a public channel) and the secret information of the party, in particular learning whether the provided message was indeed the one being encrypted. A deniable encryption scheme tackles this problem by providing a *faking* algorithm. The faking algorithm allows a coerced party to come up with fake keys and random tapes that, while being consistent with the public transcript, correspond to an arbitrary message different from the real one. Deniable encryption schemes are classified as *sender deniable, receiver deniable* or *bi-deniable*, depending on which party can withstand coercion. For our purposes, we will focus only on sender deniable encryption schemes.

We will think of an encryption scheme as a two-party protocol between a sender S and a receiver R. The sender's input as well as the receiver's output are messages m from a message space M. For an encryption protocol ψ, we will denote by $tr_\psi(m, r_S, r_R)$ the (public) transcript of the protocol, where m is the sender's input, and r_S and r_R are the sender's and the receiver's random tapes, respectively. Let $tr_\psi(m)$ be the random variable distributed as $tr_\psi(m, r_S, r_R)$ where r_S and r_R are uniformly picked in their supports. A sender deniable encryption scheme is then defines as follows [3]:

Definition 3.1 (Sender Deniable PKE). *A protocol ψ with sender S and receiver R, and security parameter n, is a $\delta(n)$-sender-deniable encryption protocol if:*

Correctness: *The probability that R's output is different from S's input is negligible (as a function of n).*

Security: *For every $m_1, m_2 \in M$, the distributions $tr_\psi(m_1)$ and $tr_\psi(m_2)$ are computationally indistinguishable.*

Deniability: *There exists an efficient faking algorithm ϕ having the following property with respect to any $m_1, m_2 \in M$. Let r_S, r_R be uniformly chosen random tapes for S and R, respectively, let $c = tr_\psi(m_1, r_S, r_R)$, and let $\bar{r}_S = \phi(m_1, r_S, c, m_2)$. Then the random variables*

$$(m_2, \bar{r}_S, c) \text{ and } (m_2, r'_S, tr_\psi(m_2, r'_S, r'_R))$$

are $\delta(n)$-computationally-indistinguishable, where r'_S and r'_R are independent, uniformly chosen random tapes for S and R.

For notational convenience, when considering bit-encryption schemes (i.e., $M = \{0, 1\}$), we will ignore the last argument of the algorithm ϕ. Further, we will call a scheme negl-sender-deniable if $\delta(n)$ is some negligible function in n.

Canetti et al. [3] give a construction of sender deniable encryption with $\delta(n) = 1/\mathsf{poly}(n)$ for some polynomial $\mathsf{poly}(n)$. However, the problem of constructing a sender deniable scheme with a negligible $\delta(n)$ has remained open since (recently, Dürmuth and Freeman [6] proposed a construction of negl-sender-deniable encryption scheme, but their proof was found to be flawed, cf. the foreword of the full version of their paper).

3.2   A Counterexample from Deniable Encryption

In the following we explain how a non-interactive negl-sender-deniable encryption scheme for message space $M = \{0, 1\}$ would lead to a counterexample to the chain rule for conditional HILL entropy. Let ψ be the encryption algorithm of this scheme.

Let B be a uniformly random bit, and let R_S be the uniform distribution of appropriate length that serves as the random tape of the sender. Over this space, we now define the following random variables:

- Let C be a ciphertext, i.e., $C := \psi(B, R_S)$.
- Let R'_S be the *fake* random tapes for the sender, i.e.,

$$R'_S := \phi(B, R_S, C)$$

Fix now a transcript c, and let b_c be the bit that the receiver outputs for c. We then define the sets R_c and R'_c as follows:

$$R_c := \{r_S \mid c = \psi(b_c, r_S)\},$$
$$R'_c := \{\phi(b_c, r_S, c) \mid r_S \in R_c\}.$$

Note that for every $r'_S \in R'_c$, we have that $c = \psi(1 - b_c, r'_S)$.

In the following we will make two simplifying assumptions about the encryption scheme. We note that we make these assumptions only for the sake of presentation. The subsequent arguments can still be adapted to work without them:

(i) Firstly, for all public keys and all ciphertexts c_1, c_2, we have that $|R_{c_1}| = |R_{c_2}|$ and $|R'_{c_1}| = |R'_{c_2}|$. We will call these cardinalities $|R|$ and $|R'|$, respectively. Put differently, we assume that $|R|$ and $|R'|$ only depend on the security parameter n.

(ii) Secondly, we assume that ϕ induces a flat distribution on R'_c, i.e., if Z is the conditional distribution on R_c given c, then $\phi(b_c, Z)$ is flat on R'_c.

We now argue that the gap between $H^{\mathsf{HILL}}_{\varepsilon,s}(R'_S|C)$ and $H^{\mathsf{HILL}}_{\varepsilon',s'}(R'_S|C,B)$ is very large.[2]

1. The deniability property implies that no PPT adversary can distinguish between real and fake random tapes for the sender. Thus, the distributions (R_S, C) ad (R'_S, C) are computationally indistinguishable. Therefore,

$$H^{\mathsf{HILL}}_{\varepsilon,s}(R'_S|C) \geq \widetilde{H}_\infty(R_S|C) = \log(|R|).$$

2. Now consider $H^{\mathsf{HILL}}_{\varepsilon',s'}(R'_S|C,B)$. We argue that this value is bounded above by (roughly) $\widetilde{H}_\infty(R'_S|C,B)$. This is because given ciphertext c *and* bit b, there exists an efficient test to check if $r \in \mathrm{supp}(R'_S)$ or not. Indeed, given a random tape r, a transcript c and bit b, we can check if r is in the support of R'_S or not as follows: run the sender in ψ with input $1 - b$ and random tape r. The resulting ciphertext is equal to c, if and only if r lies in the support of R'_S. Thus, for any distribution Z such that (R'_S, C, B) and (Z, C, B) are computationally indistinguishable, it must be the case that the support of Z is (almost) a subset of the support of R'_S. Using further that R'_S is flat, we get that:

$$H^{\mathsf{HILL}}_{\varepsilon',s'}(R'_S|C,B) \approx \widetilde{H}_\infty(R'_S|C) = \log(|R'|).$$

3. To complete the argument, we need to show that the difference between $\log(|R|)$ and $\log(|R'|)$ is large. We do so by relating this difference to the decryption error of the encryption scheme. Consider a ciphertext c that decrypts to bit b. Consider the set of all random tapes that produce this ciphertext c. Out of these, $|R_c|$ of them encrypt bit b to c, while $|R'_c|$ of them encrypt bit $1 - b$ to c. Thus, an error will be made in decrypting c when the sender wanted to encrypt bit $1 - b$, but picked its random tape from the set R'_c. Combining this observation with the simplifying assumptions made earlier, we get that the decryption error of the encryption scheme is given by $\frac{|R'|}{|R|+|R'|}$. As the decryption error is negligible by Definition 3.1, we obtain that:

$$\log(|R|) - \log(|R'|) = \omega(\log(n)).$$

Combining the above arguments yields that the difference between $H^{\mathsf{HILL}}_{\varepsilon,s}(R_S|C)$ and $H^{\mathsf{HILL}}_{\varepsilon',s'}(R'_S|C,B)$ is at least super-logarithmic in the security parameter of the encryption scheme.

---

[2] For clarity of exposition, we will not detail the relation of the parameters ε, s and ε', s' in this section. The counterexample in Section 4 gives a formal treatment of all parameters, though. Furthermore, we do not make the public key explicit in the conditional entropies in the following.

4   Disproving the Conditional Chain Rule

In the previous section we showed that the existence of sender-deniable bit encryption schemes would disprove the chain rule for conditional HILL entropy. However, the existence of such schemes is currently unknown. Thus, in this section we give a counterexample which only relies on the existence of one-way permutations.

In the following we let $\pi : \{0,1\}^* \to \{0,1\}^*$ be a one-way permutation with hardcore predicate $p : \{0,1\}^* \to \{0,1\}$. Furthermore, we define the probabilistic algorithm C, taking a bit b and a parameter n in unary as inputs, as follows:

- C draws $3n$ distinct elements $x_1, \ldots, x_{3n} \xleftarrow{\$} \{0,1\}^n$ such that $p(x_i) = b$ for $1 \le i \le 2n$ and $p(x_j) = 1 - b$ for $2n < j \le 3n$.
- C outputs $\pi(x_1), \ldots, \pi(x_{3n})$ in lexicographical order.

We now define two random variables R and R' conditioned on a value $c = C(1^n, b)$ as $1.5n$-tuple in $\{0,1\}^n$ as follows:

R consists of	R' consists of
- a uniformly random subset of $x_1, \ldots, x_{2n}$ of cardinality n, and - a uniformly random subset of $x_{2n+1}, \ldots, x_{3n}$ of cardinality $n/2$,	- a uniformly random subset of $x_1, \ldots, x_{2n}$ of cardinality $n/2$, and - $x_{2n+1}, \ldots, x_{3n}$,
in lexicographical order.	in lexicographical order.

Having said this, we can now state the main result of this paper. Informally, it says that R' conditioned on C has high HILL entropy of high quality, while additionally conditioning on the single bit B decreases both, quantity *and* quality of the entropy by factors polynomial in n:

Theorem 4.1 (Counterexample for a Conditional Chain Rule). *Let p be a $(\sigma(n), \nu(n))$-hardcore predicate for π, and let $B \xleftarrow{\$} \{0,1\}$ and $C = C(1^n, B)$. Then for all sufficiently large n it holds that:*

$$H^{\mathsf{HILL}}_{\varepsilon,s}(R'|C) - H^{\mathsf{HILL}}_{\varepsilon',s'}(R'|C,B) > \frac{5}{4}n \, ,$$

where

$$\varepsilon(n) = n\nu(n), \qquad\qquad\qquad \varepsilon'(n) = 0.99,$$
$$s(n) = \sigma(n) - \mathcal{O}(n(\sigma_p(n) + \sigma_\pi(n))), \qquad s'(n) = 1.5n(\sigma_p(n) + \sigma_\pi(n)),$$

where $\sigma_p(n)$ and $\sigma_\pi(n)$ denote the required running times to evaluate p and π, respectively, on n-bit inputs.

We now briefly want to discuss what the theorem means for the potential loss of quality and quantity of conditional HILL entropy.

Loss in **Quality** *of Entropy.* Note that ε and s are roughly of the same size as the security parameters of p, while ε' and s' are completely independent thereof. This means that even if we have $(\sigma(n), \nu(n)) = (\mathsf{poly}_1(n), 1/\mathsf{poly}_2(n))$ for some polynomials $\mathsf{poly}_i(n)$, $i = 1, 2$, as is the case for cryptographic hardcore predicates, the loss of neither of the parameters can be bounded above by a constant, but is polynomial in n.

Loss in **Quantity** *of Entropy.* Despite this large tolerated loss in the quality of the entropy, Theorem 4.1 says that conditioning on a single bit of extra information can still decrease the conditional HILL entropy by arbitrarily large additive factors by choosing n sufficiently large.

Together this implies that in order to formulate a chain rule for conditional HILL entropy, neither the loss in quality nor in quantity could be bounded by a constant, as would be desirable for a reasonable such rule, but must also depend on the size of the random variable R' whose entropy one wants to compute.

4.1   Proof of Theorem 4.1

Before moving to the proof of the theorem, we prove that (R, C) and (R', C) are computationally indistinguishable.

Lemma 4.2. *Let $p : \{0,1\}^* \to \{0,1\}$ be a $(\sigma(n), \nu(n))$-hardcore predicate for π. Then, for R, R' and C as defined above it holds that:*

$$(R, C) \sim_{\varepsilon(n), s(n)} (R', C),$$

where $\varepsilon(n) = n\nu(n)$ and $s(n) = \sigma(n) - \mathcal{O}(n(\sigma_p(n) + \sigma_\pi(n)))$.

Proof. Assume that there exists an algorithm D running in $s(n)$ steps, for which

$$|\Pr[D(R, C) = 1] - \Pr[D(R', C) = 1]| > \varepsilon(n).$$

Consider the following series of hybrids. The distribution of $\mathcal{H}_0$ is given by $(R', C_0) = (R', C)$. Now, when moving from $\mathcal{H}_i$ to $\mathcal{H}_{i+1}$, C is modified as follows: one element $\pi(x_j)$ of C_i satisfying $p(x_j) = b$, for which x_j is not part of R', is substituted by a random $\pi(\bar{x}_j)$ satisfying $p(\bar{x}_j) = 1 - b$, and C_{i+1} is reordered lexicographically.

Then, by definition, we have that $(R', C_0) = (R', C)$. Furthermore, it can be seen that over the random choices of $B \overset{\$}{\leftarrow} \{0,1\}$, it holds that $(R', C_n) = (R, C)$. Furthermore, there exists an i such D can distinguish (R', C_i) and (R', C_{i+1}) with advantage at least $\varepsilon(n)/n$.

We now show how D (outputting either i or $i + 1$ for simplicity) can be turned into an algorithm A of roughly the same running time, which predicts $p(x)$ given $\pi(x)$ for a uniformly chosen x with probability at least $\frac{1}{2} + \frac{\varepsilon(n)}{n}$. On input $y = \pi(x)$, A proceeds as follows:

- A uniformly guesses a bit $b' \overset{\$}{\leftarrow} \{0,1\}$;

– it then computes $x_1, \ldots, x_{2n-i-1} \xleftarrow{\$} \{0,1\}^n$ satisfying $p(x_j) = b'$, as well as $x_{2n+1-i}, \ldots, x_{3n} \xleftarrow{\$} \{0,1\}$ for which $p(x_j) = 1 - b'$;
– A then calls D on $\pi(x_1), \ldots, \pi(x_{2n-i-1}), y, \pi(x_{2n+1-i}), \ldots, \pi(x_{3n})$, sorted lexicographically;
– finally, A outputs b' if D returned i, and $1 - b'$ otherwise.

It can be seen that A's input to D is a sample of (R', C_i), if the secret $p(x) = b'$, and a sample of (R', C_{i+1}) otherwise for a random b'. It thus follows that A guesses $p(x)$ correctly with the same probability as D is able to distinguish (R', C_i) and (R', C_{i+1}) for random bit b. The complexity of A is essentially that of D, plus that for drawing, on average, $6n$ random elements in $\{0,1\}^n$ and evaluating π and p on those, yielding a contradiction to p being a $(\sigma(n), \nu(n))$-hardcore predicate. □

Proof (of Theorem 4.1). The claim is proved in two steps.

A Lower Bound for $H^{\mathsf{HILL}}_{\varepsilon,s}(R'|C)$. By Lemma 4.2 we have that $(R, C) \sim_{\varepsilon,s} (R', C)$. We thus get that

$$H^{\mathsf{HILL}}_{\varepsilon,s}(R'|C) \geq \tilde{H}_\infty(R|C) = -\log\left(\binom{2n}{n}\binom{n}{n/2}\right)^{-1}$$

$$= \log\binom{2n}{n} + \log\binom{2\frac{n}{2}}{\frac{n}{2}} = 3n + \mathcal{O}(\log n),$$

where the first equality holds because R is uniformly distributed in its domain and $|R|$ does not depend on C, and the last one holds by (2). For sufficiently large n, this expression is lower bounded by $2.95n$.

An Upper Bound for $H^{\mathsf{HILL}}_{\varepsilon',s'}(R'|C, B)$. Recap that $H^{\mathsf{HILL}}_{\varepsilon',s'}(R'|C, B) \geq k$ if there exists a distribution X such that $(X, C, B) \sim_{\varepsilon',s'} (R', C, B)$, and $\tilde{H}_\infty(X|C, B) \geq k$. To prove our theorem we will now prove an upper bound on $H^{\mathsf{HILL}}_{\varepsilon',s'}(R'|C, B)$ by showing that the conditional average min-entropy of every X satisfying $(X, C, B) \sim_{\varepsilon',s'} (R', C, B)$, is not significantly larger than the conditional average min-entropy of R'.

Let now X be such that the joint distribution (R', C, B) and (X, C, B) are close. We then observe that:

$$\Pr\left[X \notin \mathrm{supp}(R'(c,b)) : b \xleftarrow{\$} \{0,1\}, c \xleftarrow{\$} \mathsf{C}(1^n, b)\right] < \varepsilon'.$$

This holds because given (x, c, b), we can efficiently verify if $x \in \mathrm{supp}(R')$ or not: simply check that for exactly n components of x, their hardcore predicate evaluates to $1 - b$, and secondly, that all components of x occur in c. Thus, if the probability X falling in the support of R' is more than ε', there exists an efficient distinguisher that tells the two distributions apart with advantage more than ε'.

Now, call a pair (c, b) *bad* if the above probability is larger than $\frac{1}{1.01}$, else, call it *good*. Then, by Markov's inequality, the fraction of bad (c, b) is at most $1.01\varepsilon'$. We then get that:

$$\widetilde{H}_\infty(X|C, B) = -\log \mathbb{E}_{c,b} \max_x \Pr[X = x|C = c \wedge B = b]$$

$$= -\log \left(\sum_{c,b} \Pr[C = c \wedge B = b] \max_x \Pr[X = x|C = c \wedge B = b] \right)$$

$$\leq -\log \left(\sum_{good\ (c,b)} \Pr[C = c \wedge B = b] \max_x \Pr[X = x|C = c \wedge B = b] \right.$$

$$\left. + \sum_{bad\ (c,b)} \Pr[C = c \wedge B = b] \max_x \Pr[X = x|C = c \wedge B = b] \right)$$

$$\leq -\log \left(\sum_{good\ (c,b)} \Pr[C = c \wedge B = b] \max_x \Pr[X = x|C = c \wedge B = b] \right)$$

Using that for each (c, b), R' is uniformly distributed in its support, and that for good pairs we have that $\Pr[X \in \text{supp}(R'(c, b))] > 1 - \frac{1}{1.01} = \frac{1}{101}$, we get that $\max_x \Pr[X = x|C = c \wedge B = b]$ is upper bounded by

$$\frac{1}{101} \max_r \Pr[R' = r|C = c \wedge B = b] = \frac{1}{101} \binom{2n}{n/2}^{-1},$$

which follows directly from the definition of R'. Using further that a fraction of at least $1 - 1.01\varepsilon'$ of all (b, c) is good, this now allows us to continue the above inequality chain by:

$$\leq -\log \left(\sum_{good(c,b)} \frac{\Pr[C = c \wedge B = b]}{101} \max_r \Pr[R' = r|C = c \wedge B = b] \right)$$

$$\leq -\log \left((1 - 1.01\varepsilon') \frac{1}{101} \binom{2n}{n/2}^{-1} \right)$$

$$= 4\frac{n}{2} \log 4 - 3\frac{n}{2} \log 3 + \mathcal{O}(\log n) - \log \left(\frac{1 - 1.01\varepsilon'}{101} \right)$$

$$< 1.65n + \mathcal{O}(\log n) + 20,$$

where the last two inequality follow from (2) and our choice of ε'.

Now, for sufficiently large n, we get that this term is upper bounded by $1.7n$, and the claim of the theorem follows. $\qquad\square$

5   Conclusion

Computational notions of entropy have found many applications in cryptography, and chain rules are a central tool in many security proofs. We showed that the chain rule for one (arguably the most) important such notion, namely HILL entropy, does not hold.

Given that the chain rule holds and has been used for several variants (like relaxed, decomposable or simulatable) of HILL entropy, the question arises whether the current standard notion of conditional HILL entropy is the natural one to work with. We don't have an answer to this, but our results indicate that it is the only right notion in at least one natural setting, namely when talking about deniable encryption.

We hope the connection between chain rules for HILL entropy and deniable encryption we show will open new venues towards constructing the first deniable encryption scheme.

Acknowledgment. The authors want to thank Sasha Rubin for insightful comments and discussions while working on this paper.

References

1. Barak, B., Shaltiel, R., Wigderson, A.: Computational Analogues of Entropy. In: Arora, S., Jansen, K., Rolim, J.D.P., Sahai, A. (eds.) RANDOM 2003 and APPROX 2003. LNCS, vol. 2764, pp. 200–215. Springer, Heidelberg (2003)
2. Bendlin, R., Nielsen, J.B., Nordholt, P.S., Orlandi, C.: Lower and Upper Bounds for Deniable Public-Key Encryption. In: Lee, D.H., Wang, X. (eds.) ASIACRYPT 2011. LNCS, vol. 7073, pp. 125–142. Springer, Heidelberg (2011)
3. Canetti, R., Dwork, C., Naor, M., Ostrovsky, R.: Deniable Encryption. In: Kaliski Jr., B.S. (ed.) CRYPTO 1997. LNCS, vol. 1294, pp. 90–104. Springer, Heidelberg (1997)
4. Chung, K.-M., Kalai, Y.T., Liu, F.-H., Raz, R.: Memory Delegation. In: Rogaway, P. (ed.) CRYPTO 2011. LNCS, vol. 6841, pp. 151–168. Springer, Heidelberg (2011)
5. Dodis, Y., Ostrovsky, R., Reyzin, L., Smith, A.: Fuzzy Extractors: How to Generate Strong Keys from Biometrics and Other Noisy Data. SIAM Journal on Computing 38(1), 97–139 (2008)
6. Dürmuth, M., Freeman, D.M.: Deniable Encryption with Negligible Detection Probability: An Interactive Construction. In: Paterson, K.G. (ed.) EUROCRYPT 2011. LNCS, vol. 6632, pp. 610–626. Springer, Heidelberg (2011), Full version including a description of the flaw available at http://eprint.iacr.org/2011/066.pdf
7. Dziembowski, S., Pietrzak, K.: Leakage-Resilient Cryptography. In: FOCS 2008, pp. 293–302. IEEE Computer Society (2008)
8. Fuller, B., O'Neill, A., Reyzin, L.: A Unified Approach to Deterministic Encryption: New Constructions and a Connection to Computational Entropy. In: Cramer, R. (ed.) TCC 2012. LNCS, vol. 7194, pp. 582–599. Springer, Heidelberg (2012)
9. Fuller, B., Reyzin, L.: Computational Entropy and Information Leakage. Cryptology ePrint Archive, Report 2012/466 (2012), http://eprint.iacr.org/
10. Gentry, C., Wichs, D.: Separating Succinct Non-Interactive Arguments from All Falsifiable Assumptions. In: STOC 2011, pp. 99–108 (2011)
11. Goldreich, O.: Foundations of Cryptography: Basic Tools. Cambridge University Press, New York (2000)

12. Goldreich, O., Levin, L.A.: A Hard-Core Predicate for all One-Way Functions. In: Johnson, D.S. (ed.) STOC 1989, pp. 25–32. ACM (1989)
13. Håstad, J., Impagliazzo, R., Levin, L.A., Luby, M.: A Pseudorandom Generator from any One-way Function. SIAM Journal on Computing 28(4), 1364–1396 (1999)
14. Hsiao, C.-Y., Lu, C.-J., Reyzin, L.: Conditional Computational Entropy, or Toward Separating Pseudoentropy from Compressibility. In: Naor, M. (ed.) EUROCRYPT 2007. LNCS, vol. 4515, pp. 169–186. Springer, Heidelberg (2007)
15. Reingold, O., Trevisan, L., Tulsiani, M., Vadhan, S.P.: Dense Subsets of Pseudo-random Sets. In: FOCS 2008, pp. 76–85. IEEE Computer Society (2008)
16. Reyzin, L.: Some Notions of Entropy for Cryptography. In: Fehr, S. (ed.) ICITS 2011. LNCS, vol. 6673, pp. 138–142. Springer, Heidelberg (2011)
17. Shoup, V.: A Computational Introduction to Number Theory and Algebra. Cambridge Press (2009)
18. Trevisan, L.: Cryptography. Lecture Notes from CS 276 (2009)
19. Wee, H.M.: One-Way Permutations, Interactive Hashing and Statistically Hiding Commitments. In: Vadhan, S.P. (ed.) TCC 2007. LNCS, vol. 4392, pp. 419–433. Springer, Heidelberg (2007)
20. Yao, A.C.: Theory and Applications of Trapdoor Functions (Extended Abstract). In: FOCS 1982, pp. 80–91. IEEE Computer Society (1982)

Hardness Preserving Reductions via Cuckoo Hashing

Itay Berman[1,*], Iftach Haitner[1,*], Ilan Komargodski[2,**], and Moni Naor[2,***]

[1] Tel Aviv University
{itayberm@post,iftachh@cs}.tau.ac.il
[2] Weizmann Institute of Science
{ilan.komargodski,moni.naor}@weizmann.ac.il

Abstract. A common method for increasing the usability and uplifting the security of pseudorandom function families (PRFs) is to "hash" the inputs into a smaller domain before applying the PRF. This approach, known as "Levin's trick", is used to achieve "PRF domain extension" (using a short, e.g., fixed, input length PRF to get a variable-length PRF), and more recently to transform non-adaptive PRFs to adaptive ones. Such reductions, however, are vulnerable to a "birthday attack": after $\sqrt{|\mathcal{U}|}$ queries to the resulting PRF, where $\mathcal{U}$ being the hash function range, a collision (i.e., two distinct inputs have the same hash value) happens with high probability. As a consequence, the resulting PRF is *insecure* against an attacker making this number of queries.

In this work we show how to go beyond the birthday attack barrier, by replacing the above simple hashing approach with a variant of *cuckoo hashing* — a hashing paradigm typically used for resolving hash collisions in a table, by using two hash functions and two tables, and cleverly assigning each element into one of the two tables. We use this approach to obtain: (i) A domain extension method that requires *just two calls* to the original PRF, can withstand as many queries as the original domain size and has a distinguishing probability that is exponentially small in the non cryptographic work. (ii) A *security-preserving* reduction from non-adaptive to adaptive PRFs.

1 Introduction

We study methods for strengthening pseudorandom functions; such methods transform functions that are somewhat weak (e.g., with a *small* domain, or withstands only non-adaptive (also known as static) attacks: the attacker choose its

---

[*] Research supported in part by Check Point Institute for Information Security and the Israeli Centers of Research Excellence (I-CORE) program (Center No. 4/11).

[**] Research supported in part by a grant from the I-CORE Program of the Planning and Budgeting Committee and the Israel Science Foundation.

[***] Incumbent of the Judith Kleeman Professorial Chair. Research supported in part by a grant from the Israel Science Foundation and in part by a grant from the I-CORE Program of the Planning and Budgeting Committee and the Israel Science Foundation.

A. Sahai (Ed.): TCC 2013, LNCS 7785, pp. 40–59, 2013.

query ahead of time, before seeing any of the answers) into 'stronger' functions, e.g., with a *large* domain, or secure against *adaptive* (dynamic) attacks: the attacker queries may be chosen as a function of all previous answers.

A common paradigm, first suggested by Levin [18, §5.4], for increasing the usability and uplifting the security of pseudorandom function families (PRFs), is to "hash" the inputs into a smaller domain before applying the PRF. This approach is used to achieve "PRF domain extension" (using a short, e.g., fixed, input length PRF to get a variable-length PRF), and more recently to transform non-adaptive PRFs to adaptive ones [6]. Such reductions, however, are vulnerable to the following "birthday attack": after $\sqrt{|\mathcal{U}|}$ queries to the resulting PRF, where $\mathcal{U}$ being the hash function range, a collision (i.e., two distinct inputs have the same hash value) happens with high probability. Such collisions are an obstacle for the indistinguishability of the PRF, since in a random function we either do not expect to see a collision at all (in case the range is large enough) or expect to see fewer collisions. Hence, the resulting PRF is *insecure* against an attacker making this number of queries.

In this work we study variants of the above hashing approach to go beyond the birthday attack barrier. Specifically, we consider constructions based on *cuckoo hashing*: a hashing paradigm typically used for resolving hash collisions in a table by using two hash functions and two tables, and assigning each element to one of the two tables (see Section 1.2). We use this paradigm to present a new PRF domain extension method that requires *just two calls* to the original PRF, can withstand as many queries as the original domain size and has a distinguishing probability that is exponentially small in the amount of non cryptographic work. A second implication is a *security-preserving reduction* from non-adaptive to adaptive PRFs, an improvement upon the recent result of [6].

Before stating our results, we discuss in more details the notions of pseudorandom functions and cuckoo hashing.

1.1   Pseudorandom Functions

Pseudorandom function families (PRFs), introduced by Goldreich, Goldwasser, and Micali [14], are function families that cannot be distinguished from a family of *truly* random functions, by an efficient distinguisher who is given an oracle access to a random member of the family. PRFs have an extremely important role in cryptography, allowing parties, which share a common secret key, to send secure messages, identify themselves and to authenticate messages [13, 19]. In addition, they have many other applications, essentially in any setting that requires random function provided as black-box [4, 7, 10, 12, 20, 26]. Different PRF constructions are known in the literature, whose security are based on different hardness assumptions. The construction that is most relevant to this work is the one of [14], hereafter the GGM construction, that uses a length-doubling pseudorandom generator (and thus can be based on the existence of one-way functions [15]).

We use the following definitions: an efficiently computable function family ensemble $\mathcal{F} = \{\mathcal{F}_n\}_{n \in \mathbb{N}}$ is a (q, t, ε)-PRF, if (for large enough n) a $q(n)$-query oracle-aided algorithm (distinguisher) of running time $t(n)$, getting access to a random function from the family, distinguishes between $\mathcal{F}_n$ and the family of all functions (with the same input/output domains), with probability at most $\varepsilon(n)$. $\mathcal{F}$ is *non-adaptive* (q, t, ε)-PRF, if it is only required to be secure against non-adaptive distinguishers (i.e., ones that prepare all their queries in advance). Finally, $\mathcal{F}$ is a t-PRF, in case q is only limited by t and $\varepsilon = 1/t$.

We note that the information-theoretic analog of a t-PRF is known as a t-wise independent family and is formally defined in Definition 5.

1.2   Cuckoo Hashing and Many-Wise Independent Hash Function

Cuckoo hashing, introduced by Pagh and Rodler [28], is an efficient technique for constructing dynamic dictionaries. Such data structures are used to maintain a set of elements, while supporting membership queries as well as insertions and deletions of elements. Cuckoo hashing maintains such a dynamic dictionary by keeping two tables of size only slightly larger than the number of elements to be inserted and two hash functions mapping the elements into cells of those tables, and applying a clever algorithm for placing at most a single element in each cell. Since its introduction, many variants of cuckoo hashing have been proposed and an extensive literature is devoted to its analysis.

Pagh and Pagh [27] used ideas in the spirit of cuckoo hashing to construct efficient many-wise independent hash functions. For that they introduce the following paradigm. Let $\mathcal{H}$, $\mathcal{G}$ and $\mathcal{F}$ be function families from $\mathcal{D}$ to $\mathcal{S}$, from $\mathcal{D}$ to $\mathcal{R}$ and from $\mathcal{S}$ to $\mathcal{R}$ respectively. Define the function family $\mathcal{PP}(\mathcal{H}, \mathcal{G}, \mathcal{F})$ from $\mathcal{D}$ to $\mathcal{R}$ as

$$\mathcal{PP}(\mathcal{H}, \mathcal{G}, \mathcal{F}) = (\mathcal{F} \circ \mathcal{H}) \oplus (\mathcal{F} \circ \mathcal{H}) \oplus \mathcal{G}, \tag{1}$$

where $\mathcal{F}_1 \circ \mathcal{F}_2$, for function families $\mathcal{F}_1$ and $\mathcal{F}_2$, is the function family whose members are the elements of $\mathcal{F}_1 \times \mathcal{F}_2$ and $(f_1, f_2)(x)$ is defined by $f_1(f_2(x))$ ($\mathcal{F}_1 \oplus \mathcal{F}_2$ is analogously defined). In other words, given $f_1, f_2 \in \mathcal{F}, h_1, h_2 \in \mathcal{H}$ and $g \in \mathcal{G}$, design a function $\mathcal{PP}_{f_1, f_2, h_1, h_2, g}(x) = f_1(h_1(x)) \oplus f_2(h_2(x)) \oplus g(x)$.

Pagh and Pagh [27] showed that when the families $\mathcal{H}$ and $\mathcal{G}$ are of "high enough" independence, roughly, both families are $(c \cdot \log |\mathcal{S}|)$-wise independent, then the family $\mathcal{PP}(\mathcal{H}, \mathcal{G}, \Pi)$ is $O(|\mathcal{S}|^{-c})$-indistinguishable from random by a $|\mathcal{S}|$-query, *non-adaptive* distinguisher, where Π being the set of all functions from $\mathcal{S}$ to $\mathcal{R}$. Note that the security of the resulting family goes well beyond the birthday attack barrier: it is indistinguishable from random by an attacker making $|\mathcal{S}| >> \sqrt{|\mathcal{S}|}$ queries.

Aumüller et al. [3] (building on the work of Dietzfelbinger and Woelfel [11]) were able to strengthen the result of Pagh and Pagh [27] by using more sophisticated hash functions $\mathcal{H}$ and $\mathcal{G}$ (rather than the $O(\log |\mathcal{S}|)$-wise independent that [27] used). Specifically, for a given $s \geq 0$, Aumüller et al. [3] constructed a function family $\mathcal{ADW}(\mathcal{H}, \mathcal{G}, \Pi)$ such that the family $\mathcal{ADW}(\mathcal{H}, \mathcal{G}, \Pi)$ is $O(|\mathcal{S}|^{-(s+1)})$-indistinguishable from random by a $|\mathcal{S}|$-query, *non-adaptive* distinguisher, where Π being the set of all functions from $\mathcal{S}$ to $\mathcal{R}$, as above. The idea to use more sophisticated hash functions, in the sense that they require less combinatorial work, has already appeared in previous works, e.g., the work of Arbitman et al. [2, §5.4].

In Section 3 we take the above results a step further, showing that they hold also for *adaptive* distinguishers. Furthermore, it turns out that by using the above function family with a pseudorandom function $\mathcal{F}$, namely the family $\mathcal{PP}(\mathcal{H}, \mathcal{G}, \mathcal{F})$ (or $\mathcal{ADW}(\mathcal{H}, \mathcal{G}, \mathcal{F})$), we get a pseudorandom function that is superior over $\mathcal{F}$ (the actual properties of $\mathcal{PP}(\mathcal{H}, \mathcal{G}, \mathcal{F})$ are determined by the choice of $\mathcal{F}$ and the choice of $\mathcal{H}$ and $\mathcal{G}$). This understanding is the main conceptual contribution of this paper, and the basis for the results presented below.

We note that the works of Pagh and Pagh [27], Dietzfelbinger and Woelfel [11] and Aumüller et al. [3] went almost unnoticed in the cryptography literature so far.[1] In this work we apply, in a black-box manner, the analysis of [27] and of [3] in cryptographic settings.

1.3 Our Results

We use a construction inspired by cuckoo hashing to improve upon two PRF reductions: PRF domain extension and non-adaptive to adaptive PRF.

PRF Domain Extension. PRF domain extensions use PRFs with "small" domain size, to construct PRFs with larger (or even unlimited) domain size. These extensions are used for reducing the cost of a single invocation of the PRF and increasing its usability. Domain extension methods are typically measured by the security of the resulting PRFs, and the amount of calls the resulting PRF makes to the underlying PRF.

A known domain extension technique is the MAC-based constructions, like CBC-MAC and PMAC (a survey on their security can be found in [24]). The number of calls made by these constructions to the underlying (small domain) PRF can be as small as two (for doubling the domain length). Assuming that the underlying PRF is a random function over $\{0,1\}^n$,[2] then the resulting family is $(q, \infty, O(q^2/2^n))$-PRF (i.e., the ∞ in the second parameter means that the distinguisher running time is unlimited). A second technique is using the Feistel or Benes transformations (e.g., [1, 29, 30], where a complete survey on can be found in [31]). The Benes based construction makes 8 calls to the underlying PRF and is $(q, \infty, O(q/2^n))$-PRF, where a 5-round Feistel based construction (that makes 5 calls to the underlying PRF) is $(q, \infty, O(q/2^n))$-PRF. Once you have a length doubling extension one can get any extension at the appropriate cost.

---

[1] Pagh and Pagh [27] did notice this connection, and in particular mentioned the connection of their work to that of Bellare et al. [5].

[2] Measuring the security of the resulting under this unrealistic random function assumption is a useful, and common, method for understanding the quality of the domain extension reduction itself.

Our cuckoo hashing based function family (see below) is $(q, \infty, O(q/2^n))$-PRF, makes only two calls to the underlying PRF and can extend the domain size to any poly(n) length.

Theorem 1 (informal). *Let $k \leq n$, let $\mathcal{H}$ and $\mathcal{G}$ be efficient k-wise independent function families mapping strings of length $\ell(n)$ to strings of length n, and let Π be the functions family of all functions from $\{0,1\}^n$ to $\{0,1\}^n$. Then the family $\mathcal{PP}(\mathcal{H}, \mathcal{G}, \Pi)$, mapping strings of length $\ell(n)$ to strings of length n, is a $(q, \infty, q/2^{\Omega(k)})$-PRF, for $q \leq 2^{n-2}$.*

Specifically, for $k = \Theta(n)$ Theorem 1 yields a domain extension that is $(q, \infty, q/2^n)$-PRF. The resulting PRF makes only two calls to the underlying PRF. Using larger k (i.e. higher independence in terms of combinatorial work) we can decrease the error to be arbitrarily small. We note that we actually get stronger result using the function family $\mathcal{ADW}(\mathcal{H}, \mathcal{G}, \Pi)$ (for different $\mathcal{H}$ and $\mathcal{G}$). See Theorem 7).

From PRG to PRF. Another application of the above technique is a hardness preserving construction of PRFs from pseudorandom generators (PRG). An efficiently computable function $G \colon \{0,1\}^n \mapsto \{0,1\}^{2n}$ is t-PRG, if any distinguisher of running time $t(n)$ can distinguish a random output of G from a truly random $2n$-bit string, with probability at most $1/t(n)$. We are interested in constructions of PRF using this PRG that preserve the security of G, more specifically, constructions that are $(2^{c'n})$-PRF for some $0 < c' < c$, assuming that G is a (2^{cn})-PRG.[3] The efficiency of such constructions is measured by the number of calls made to the underlying PRG as well as other parameters such as representation size.

The construction of Goldreich et al. [14] (i.e., GGM) is in fact such hardness preserving according to the above criterion. Their construction, however, makes n calls to the underlying PRG, which might be too expensive is some settings. In order to reduce the number of calls to the underlying PRG, Levin [18] suggested to first hash the input to a smaller domain, and only then apply GGM. The resulting construction, however, is not hardness preserving.

While the GGM construction seems optimal for the security it achieves (as shown in [16]), in some settings the number of queries the distinguisher can make is *strictly less* than its running time; for instance consider a distinguisher of running time 2^{cn} who can only make $2^{\sqrt{n}} \ll 2^{cn}$ queries. In such settings the security of the GGM seems like an overkill, and raises the question whether there exist more efficient reductions. Jain et al. [16] (who raised the above questions) gave the following partial answer, by designing a domain extension method tailored to the PRG to PRF reduction.

Theorem 2 ([16], informal). *Let $c > 0$ and $1/2 \leq \alpha < 1$. There exists an efficient oracle-aided function family JPT such that the following holds: assume*

---

[3] Considering this range of parameters is only for the sake of concreteness. Our actual result (see Section 4) handles a larger range of parameters.

that G is a length-doubling (2^{cn})-PRG, then JPT^G is a $(2^{n^\alpha}, 2^{c'n}, 2^{c'n})$-PRF, for every $0 < c' < c$. A function $f \in \mathsf{JPT}^G$ makes $O(n^\alpha)$ queries to G.

A restriction of Theorem 2 is that it dictates the resulting PRF family to use at least $\Omega(\sqrt{n})$ queries to the underlying PRG (since $1/2 \le \alpha < 1$). Here we use cuckoo hashing to give a more versatile version of their theorem, allowing α to be arbitrary, that also improves some of their parameters. Thus, our result implies hardness-preserving PRF reduction, which is useful to construct PRFs of low query complexity.

In the following we let GGM_m to be the variant of the GGM construction that on input of length $m(n)$, makes $m(n)$ calls to a length-doubling PRG on inputs of length n, and outputs a string of length n.[4]

Corollary 1 (informal). *Let $c > 0$ and $0 < \alpha < 1$, let $\mathcal{H} = \{\mathcal{H}_n \colon \{0,1\}^n \mapsto \{0,1\}^{m(n)}\}_{n \in \mathbb{N}}$ and $\mathcal{G} = \{\mathcal{G} \colon \{0,1\}^n \mapsto \{0,1\}^n\}_{n \in \mathbb{N}}$ be efficient $\Theta(n^\alpha + cn)$-wise independent function families. Assume that G is a length-doubling (2^{cn})-PRG, then $\mathcal{PP}(\mathcal{H}, \mathcal{G}, \mathsf{GGM}_m^G)$ is a $(2^{\Omega(n^\alpha)}, 2^{c'n}, 2^{c'n})$-PRF, for every $0 < c' < c$, and $m(n) = O(n^\alpha)$.*

Note that $f \in \mathcal{PP}(\mathcal{H}, \mathcal{G}, \mathsf{GGM}_m^G)$ makes $O(n^\alpha)$ queries to G. Again, using $\mathcal{ADW}(\mathcal{H}, \mathcal{G}, \mathsf{GGM}_m^G)$ (with different $\mathcal{H}$ and $\mathcal{G}$), we actually get stronger result (see Corollary 4). We refer to Corollary 4 for a more elaborate comparison between the construction of [16] and our construction.

Independently and concurrently with this work, Chandran and Garg [9] showed that a variant of the construction of [16] achieves similar security parameters to [16] and also works for 2^{n^α} queries for any $0 < \alpha < 1/2$. The construction of [9], however, outputs only $n^{2\alpha}$ bits, as opposed to n bits as in the construction of [16] and as in our construction.

From Non-adaptive to Adaptive PRF. Constructing adaptive PRFs from non-adaptive ones can be done using general techniques; for instance, using the PRG-based construction of Goldreich et al. [14] or the *synthesizers* based construction of Naor and Reingold [25]. These constructions, however, make (roughly) n calls to the underlying non-adaptive PRF (where n is the input length). Recently, Berman and Haitner [6] showed how to perform this security uplifting at a much lower price: the adaptive PRF makes only a *single* call to the non-adaptive PRF. The drawback of their construction, however, is a significant degradation in the security: assuming the underlying function is a non-adaptive t-PRF, then the resulting function is an (adaptive) $O(t^{1/3})$-PRF. The reason for this significant degradation in the security is the birthday attack we mentioned earlier.

We present a reduction from non-adaptive to adaptive PRFs that *preserves* the security of the non-adaptive PRF. The resulting adaptive PRF makes only two calls to the underlying non-adaptive PRF.

---

[4] GGM_m is a variant of the standard GGM function family, that on input of length $m(n)$ uses seed of length n for the underlying generator, rather than seed of length $m(n)$ (see Proposition 1 for the formal definition).

Theorem 3 (informal). *Let t be a polynomial-time computable integer function, let $\mathcal{H} = \{\mathcal{H}_n\colon \{0,1\}^n \mapsto [4t(n)]_{\{0,1\}^n}\}_{n\in\mathbb{N}}$ (where $[4t(n)]_{\{0,1\}^n}$ are the first $4t(n)$ elements of $\{0,1\}^n$) and $\mathcal{G} = \{\mathcal{G}_n\colon \{0,1\}^n \mapsto \{0,1\}^n\}_{n\in\mathbb{N}}$ be efficient $O(\log t(n))$-wise independent function families, and let $\mathcal{F}$ be a length-preserving non-adaptive $t(n)$-PRF. Then $\mathcal{PP}(\mathcal{H},\mathcal{G},\mathcal{F})$ is a length-preserving $(t(n)/4)$-PRF.*

As before, we actually get stronger result using $\mathcal{ADW}(\mathcal{H},\mathcal{G},\mathcal{F})$ (with different $\mathcal{H}$ and $\mathcal{G}$. See Theorem 9).

1.4   More Related Work

Bellare et al. [5] introduced a paradigm for using PRFs in the symmetric-key settings that, in retrospect, is similar to cuckoo hashing. Assume two parties, who share a secret function f, would like to use it for (shared-key) encryption. The 'textbook' (stateless) solution calls for the sender to choose r at random and send $(r, f(r) \oplus M)$ to the receiver, where M is the message to be encrypted. This proposal breaks down in case the sender chooses the same r twice (in two different sessions with different messages). Thus, the scheme is subject to the birthday attack and the length parameters should be chosen accordingly. This requires the underlying function to have large domain. Instead, [5] suggested choosing $t > 1$ values at random, and sending $(r_1,\ldots,r_t, f(r_1) \oplus \cdots \oplus f(r_t) \oplus M)$. They were able to show a much better security then the single r case. They also showed a similar result for message authentication. Our domain extension results (see Section 4) improve upon the results of [5].

The issue of transforming a scheme that is only resilient to non-adaptive attack into one that is resilient to adaptive attacks has received quite a lot of attention in the context of pseudorandom permutations (or block ciphers). Maurer and Pietrzak [22] showed that starting from a family of permutations that is information-theoretic secure against non-adaptive attacks,[5] if two independently chosen members of the family are composed, then the result is a permutation secure against adaptive attacks (see [22] for the exact formulation). On the other hand, Pietrzak [32] showed that this is not necessarily the case for permutations that are randomly looking under a computational assumption (see also [23, 33]) (reminding us that translating information theoretic results to the computational realm is a tricky business).

Paper Organization

Basic notations and formal definitions are given in Section 2. Section 3 is where we formally define the hashing paradigm of [27] and of [3], and show how to extend their results to hold against adaptive adversaries. Our domain extension is described in Section 4, and the improved non-adaptive to adaptive reduction is described in Section 5.

---

[5] That is, secure against (non-adaptive) unbounded attackers.

2 Preliminaries

2.1 Notations

All logarithms considered here are in base two. We use calligraphic letters to denote sets, uppercase for random variables, and lowercase for values. Let '$||$' denote string concatenation. For an integer t, let $[t] = \{1, \ldots, t\}$. For a set $\mathcal{S}$ and integer t, let $\mathcal{S}^{\leq t} = \{\bar{s} \in \mathcal{S}^* : |\bar{s}| \leq t \ \wedge \ \bar{s}[i] \neq \bar{s}[j] \ \forall 1 \leq i < j \leq |\bar{s}|\}$, and let $[t]_{\mathcal{S}}$ be the first t elements (in increasing lexicographic order) of $\mathcal{S}$ (equal to $\mathcal{S}$ in case $|\mathcal{S}| < t$). For integers n and ℓ, let $\Pi_{n,\ell}$ stands for the set of all functions from $\{0,1\}^n$ to $\{0,1\}^\ell$, and let $\Pi_n = \Pi_{n,n}$.

We let poly denote the set all polynomials, and let PPTM denote the set of probabilistic algorithms (i.e., Turing machines) that run in *strictly* polynomial time. Given a random variable X, we write $X(x)$ to denote $\Pr[X = x]$, and write $x \leftarrow X$ to indicate that x is selected according to X. Similarly, given a finite set $\mathcal{S}$, we let $s \leftarrow \mathcal{S}$ denote that s is selected according to the uniform distribution on $\mathcal{S}$. The *statistical distance* of two distributions P and Q over a finite set $\mathcal{U}$, denoted as $\mathrm{SD}(P, Q)$, is defined as $\max_{\mathcal{S} \subseteq \mathcal{U}} |P(\mathcal{S}) - Q(\mathcal{S})| = \frac{1}{2} \sum_{u \in \mathcal{U}} |P(u) - Q(u)|$.

2.2 Pseudorandom Generators

Definition 1 (Pseudorandom Generators). *A polynomial-time function* $G \colon \{0,1\}^n \mapsto \{0,1\}^{\ell(n)}$ *is* $(t(n), \varepsilon(n))$*-PRG, if* $\ell(n) > n$ *for every* $n \in \mathbb{N}$ *(G stretches the input), and*

$$\left| \Pr_{x \leftarrow \{0,1\}^n}[\mathsf{D}(G(x)) = 1] - \Pr_{y \leftarrow \{0,1\}^{\ell(n)}}[\mathsf{D}(y) = 1] \right| \leq \varepsilon(n)$$

for every algorithm (distinguisher) D of running time $t(n)$ and large enough n.

2.3 Function Families

Operating on Function Families. We consider two natural operation on function families.

Definition 2 (composition of function families). *Let* $\mathcal{F}^1 \colon \mathcal{D}^1 \mapsto \mathcal{R}^1$ *and* $\mathcal{F}^2 \colon \mathcal{D}^2 \mapsto \mathcal{R}^2$ *be two function families with* $\mathcal{R}^1 \subseteq \mathcal{D}^2$. *The* composition *of* $\mathcal{F}^1$ *with* $\mathcal{F}^2$, *denoted* $\mathcal{F}^2 \circ \mathcal{F}^1$, *is the function family* $\{(f_2, f_1) \in \mathcal{F}^2 \times \mathcal{F}^1\}$, *where* $(f_2, f_1)(x) := f_2(f_1(x))$.

Definition 3 (XOR of function families). *Let* $\mathcal{F}^1 \colon \mathcal{D} \mapsto \mathcal{R}^1$ *and* $\mathcal{F}^2 \colon \mathcal{D} \mapsto \mathcal{R}^2$ *be two function families with* $\mathcal{R}^1, \mathcal{R}^2 \subseteq \{0,1\}^\ell$. *The* XOR *of* $\mathcal{F}^1$ *with* $\mathcal{F}^2$, *denoted* $\mathcal{F}^2 \bigoplus \mathcal{F}^1$, *is the function family* $\{(f_2, f_1) \in \mathcal{F}^2 \times \mathcal{F}^1\}$, *where* $(f_2, f_1)(x) := f_2(x) \oplus f_1(x)$.

Function Family Ensembles. A function family ensemble is an infinite set of function families, whose elements (families) are typically indexed by the set of integers. Let $\mathcal{F} = \{\mathcal{F}_n \colon \mathcal{D}_n \mapsto \mathcal{R}_n\}_{n \in \mathbb{N}}$ stands for an ensemble of function families, where each $f \in \mathcal{F}_n$ has domain $\mathcal{D}_n$ and its range contained in $\mathcal{R}_n$. Such ensemble is *length preserving*, if $\mathcal{D}_n = \mathcal{R}_n = \{0,1\}^n$ for every n. We naturally extend Definitions 2 and 3 to function family ensembles.

For function family ensemble to be useful, it has to have an efficient sampling and evaluation algorithms.

Definition 4 (efficient function family ensembles). *A function family ensemble $\mathcal{F} = \{\mathcal{F}_n \colon \mathcal{D}_n \mapsto \mathcal{R}_n\}_{n \in \mathbb{N}}$ is* efficient, *if the following hold:*

Efficient sampling. *$\mathcal{F}$ is samplable in polynomial-time: there exists a* PPTM *that given 1^n, outputs (the description of) a uniform element in $\mathcal{F}_n$.*

Efficient evaluation. *There exists a deterministic algorithm that given $x \in \mathcal{D}_n$ and (a description of) $f \in \mathcal{F}_n$, runs in time $\mathrm{poly}(n, |x|)$ and outputs $f(x)$.*

Many-Wise Independent Hashing

Definition 5 (k-wise independent families). *A function family $\mathcal{H} = \{h \colon \mathcal{D} \mapsto \mathcal{R}\}$ is k-wise independent (with respect to $\mathcal{D}$ and $\mathcal{R}$), if*

$$\Pr_{h \leftarrow \mathcal{H}}[h(x_1) = y_1 \wedge h(x_2) = y_2 \wedge \ldots \wedge h(x_k) = y_k] = \frac{1}{|\mathcal{R}|^k},$$

for every distinct $x_1, x_2, \ldots, x_k \in \mathcal{D}$ and every $y_1, y_2, \ldots, y_k \in \mathcal{R}$.

For every $\ell, k \in \mathrm{poly}$, the existence of efficient $k(n)$-wise independent family ensembles mapping strings of length $\ell(n)$ to strings of length n is well known ([8, 35]). A simple and well known example of k-wise independent functions is the collection of all polynomials of degree $(k-1)$ over a finite field. This construction has small size, and each evaluation of a function at a given point requires k operations in the field. Starting with Siegel [34], there has been quite a lot of attention devoted to the question of whether it is possible to come up with constructions that require much less than k operations per evaluation (see Section 1.2).

As a side remark we mention that a k-wise independent families (as defined in Definition 5) look random for k-query distinguishers, *both* non-adaptive and adaptive ones. On the other hand, *almost* k-wise independent families[6] are only granted to be resistant against *non-adaptive* distinguishers. Yet, the result presented in Section 3 yields that, in some cases, the adaptive security of the latter families follows from their non-adaptive security.

---

[6] Formally, a function family $\mathcal{H} = \{h : \mathcal{D} \mapsto \mathcal{R}\}$ is (ε, k)-wise independent if for any $x_1, \ldots, x_k \in \mathcal{D}$ and for any $y_1, \ldots, y_k \in \mathcal{R}$ it holds that $\left|\Pr_{h \leftarrow \mathcal{H}}[h(x_1) = y_1 \wedge \cdots \wedge h(x_k) = y_k] - |\mathcal{R}|^{-k}\right| \leq \varepsilon$. We call a family of functions an almost k-wise independent family, if it is (ε, k)-wise independent for some small $\varepsilon > 0$.

2.4   Pseudorandom Functions

Definition 6 (Pseudorandom Functions). *An efficient function family ensemble* $\mathcal{F} = \{\mathcal{F}_n \colon \{0,1\}^n \mapsto \{0,1\}^{\ell(n)}\}_{n\in\mathbb{N}}$ *is an (adaptive)* $(q(n), t(n), \varepsilon(n))$*-PRF, if*

$$\left| \Pr_{f \leftarrow \mathcal{F}_n}[\mathsf{D}^f(1^n) = 1] - \Pr_{\pi \leftarrow \Pi_{n,\ell(n)}}[\mathsf{D}^\pi(1^n) = 1] \right| \leq \varepsilon(n)$$

for every $q(n)$*-query oracle-aided algorithm (distinguisher)* D *of running time* $t(n)$ *and large enough* n. *If* $q(n)$ *is only bounded by* $t(n)$, *then* $\mathcal{F}$ *is called* $(t(n), \varepsilon(n))$*-PRF. In addition, if we limit* D *above to be non-adaptive (i.e., it has to write all his oracle calls before making the first call), then* $\mathcal{F}$ *is called* non-adaptive $(t(n), \varepsilon(n))$*-PRF. Finally, The ensemble* $\mathcal{F}$ *is a* t*-PRF, if it is a* $(t, 1/t)$*-PRF according to the above definition (where the same conventions are also used for non-adaptive PRFs).*

3   From Non-adaptive to Adaptive Hashing

In this section we describe a general transformation of non-adaptive secure function families with a certain combinatorial property into adaptive secure ones. We note that the transformations defined in this section *cannot* be applied directly to (non-adaptive) PRFs, since we have no reason to assume that such families posses this property (alternatively, see Section 5 for the transformation from non-adaptive to adaptive PRFs).

Our framework can be used to prove that for certain function families, adaptive distinguishers are subject to the same distinguishing bound of non-adaptive ones. Specifically, it deals with constructions where the randomness can be partitioned into two (non empty) parts $\mathcal{U}$ and $\mathcal{V}$ and there exists some bad event that is defined only over the $\mathcal{U}$ part for a given subset of the domain (the queries). In addition, if the bad event does not happen, we require that the resulting output will be uniform over the subset of queries. We begin with a definition of *monotone sets*.

Definition 7 (monotone sets). *A set* $\mathcal{M} \subseteq \mathcal{S}^* \times \mathcal{T}$ *is* left-monotone, *if for every* $(\overline{s}_1, t) \in \mathcal{M}$ *and every* $\overline{s}_2 \in \mathcal{S}^*$ *that has* $\overline{s}_1$ *as a prefix, it holds that* $(\overline{s}_2, t) \in \mathcal{M}$.

Next, we formally state the lemma that is the basis of our framework. The lemma deals with a construction of a function family $\mathcal{F}$ that can be defined as $\mathcal{F} = \mathcal{F}(\mathcal{U}, \mathcal{V})$ where $\mathcal{U}$ and $\mathcal{V}$ are arbitrary non-empty sets. Intuitively, it states that assuming there exists a bad event BAD that can be defined over the inputs and the $\mathcal{U}$ part (i.e, independently of the $\mathcal{V}$ part) that happens with small probability, and conditioning on that BAD does not happen, we know that $\mathcal{F}$ is uniform over subsets of the range of size that is the number of queries, then we can say that the function family $\mathcal{F}$ is resistant against adaptive adversaries.

Lemma 1. *Let $\mathcal{F} = \mathcal{F}(\mathcal{U}, \mathcal{V})$ be a function family of the form $\{f_{u,v}\colon \mathcal{D} \mapsto \mathcal{R}\}_{(u,v)\in\mathcal{U}\times\mathcal{V}}$, where $\mathcal{U}$ and $\mathcal{V}$ are arbitrary non-empty sets, let $t \in \mathbb{N}$ and let $\mathrm{BAD} \subseteq \mathcal{D}^{\leq t} \times \mathcal{U}$ be a left-monotone set. Assume that for every $\bar{q} \in \mathcal{D}^{\leq t}$ it holds that*

1. $\left(f(\bar{q}_1), \ldots, f(\bar{q}_{|\bar{q}|})\right)_{f \leftarrow \{f_{u,v}\,:\, v\in\mathcal{V}\}}$ *is uniform over $\mathcal{R}^{|\bar{q}|}$ for every $u \in \mathcal{U}$ such that $(\bar{q}, u) \notin \mathrm{BAD}$, and*
2. $\Pr_{u\leftarrow\mathcal{U}}[(\bar{q}, u) \in \mathrm{BAD}] \leq \varepsilon$,

then for any t-query adaptive algorithm D, it holds that

$$\left|\Pr_{\substack{u\leftarrow\mathcal{U}\\v\leftarrow\mathcal{V}}}[\mathrm{D}^{f_{u,v}} = 1] - \Pr_{\pi\leftarrow\Pi}[\mathrm{D}^{\pi} = 1]\right| \leq \varepsilon$$

where Π is the set of all functions from $\mathcal{D}$ to $\mathcal{R}$.

Lemma 1 is a special case of a result given in [17, Theorem 12] (which closes a gap in the work of [21]), and its direct proof can be found in the full version of this paper.

3.1   Instantiation with the Pagh and Pagh [27] Function Family

In this section we instantiate the framework with the function family of Pagh and Pagh [27]. One advantage of this construction is the relative simplicity of description. We begin by describing their method of combining function families.

Definition 8 (The Pagh and Pagh [27] function family). *Let $\mathcal{H}$ be a function family from $\mathcal{D}$ to $\mathcal{S}$, let $\mathcal{G}$ be a function family from $\mathcal{D}$ to $\mathcal{R}$ and let $\mathcal{F}$ be a function family from $\mathcal{S}$ to $\mathcal{R}$. Define the function family $\mathcal{PP}(\mathcal{H}, \mathcal{G}, \mathcal{F})$ from $\mathcal{D}$ to $\mathcal{R}$ as*

$$\mathcal{PP}(\mathcal{H}, \mathcal{G}, \mathcal{F}) := (\mathcal{F} \circ \mathcal{H}) \oplus (\mathcal{F} \circ \mathcal{H}) \oplus \mathcal{G}.$$

For $h_1, h_2 \in \mathcal{H}$, let $\mathcal{PP}_{h_1,h_2}(\mathcal{G}, \mathcal{F}) := (\mathcal{F} \circ h_1) \oplus (\mathcal{F} \circ h_2) \oplus \mathcal{G}$.

Pagh and Pagh [27] showed that when instantiated with the proper function families, the above function family has the following properties:

Theorem 4 ([27]). *Let t be an integer, let $\mathcal{H} = \{h\colon \mathcal{D} \mapsto [4t]_{\mathcal{D}}\}$ and $\mathcal{G} = \{g\colon \mathcal{D} \mapsto \mathcal{R}\}$ be function families, and let Π be the all function family from $\mathcal{D}$ to $\mathcal{R}$. Then for every $k, t \in \mathbb{N}$ there exists left-monotone set $\mathrm{BAD} \subseteq \mathcal{D}^{\leq t} \times \mathcal{H}^2$, such that the following holds for every $\bar{q} \in \mathcal{D}^{\leq t}$:*

1. *Assuming that $\mathcal{G}$ is k-wise independent over the elements of $\bar{q}$, then $\left(f(\bar{q}_1), \ldots, f(\bar{q}_{|\bar{q}|})\right)_{f\leftarrow\mathcal{PP}_{h_1,h_2}(\mathcal{G},\Pi)}$ is uniform over $\mathcal{R}^{|\bar{q}|}$ for every $u \in \mathcal{U}$ such that $(\bar{q}, u) \notin \mathrm{BAD}$.*

2. *Assuming that $\mathcal{H}$ is k-wise independent over the elements of $\bar{q}$, then* $\mathrm{Pr}_{u \leftarrow \mathcal{H}^2}[(\bar{q}, u) \in \mathrm{BAD}] \leq t/2^{\Omega(k)}$.[7]

What Pagh and Pagh [27] concluded is that for (the many) applications where the analysis is applied to a static set it is safe to use this family. However, as we can see, the function family $\mathcal{PP}(\mathcal{H}, \mathcal{G}, \Pi)$ is not only closed to being uniform in the eyes of a non-adaptive distinguisher, but also allows us to apply Lemma 1 to deduce its security in the eyes of adaptive distinguishers. By plugging in Theorem 4 into the general framework lemma (Lemma 1), we get the following result:

Lemma 2. *Let $\mathcal{H}$, $\mathcal{G}$ and Π be as in Theorem 4, and let* D *be an adaptive, t-query oracle-aided algorithm. Then*

$$\left| \mathrm{Pr}_{f \leftarrow \mathcal{PP}(\mathcal{H}, \mathcal{G}, \Pi)}[\mathsf{D}^f = 1] - \mathrm{Pr}_{\pi \leftarrow \Pi}[\mathsf{D}^\pi = 1] \right| \leq t/2^{\Omega(k)}.$$

Proof. Let $\mathcal{U} = \mathcal{H} \times \mathcal{H}$, $\mathcal{V} = \Pi \times \Pi \times \mathcal{G}$. For $(h_1, h_2) \in \mathcal{U}$ and $(\pi_1, \pi_2, g) \in \mathcal{V}$, let $F_{(h_1, h_2),(\pi_1, \pi_2, g)} = \pi_1 \circ h_1 \oplus \pi_2 \circ h_2 \oplus g$, and let $\mathcal{F} = \{F_{u,v} : \mathcal{D} \mapsto \mathcal{R}\}_{(u,v) \in \mathcal{U} \times \mathcal{V}}$. Finally, let BAD be the set BAD of Theorem 4. We prove the lemma showing that the above sets meet the requirements stated in Lemma 1.

Item 1 of Theorem 4 assures that the first property of Lemma 1 is satisfied, and according to Item 2 of Theorem 4 we set ε of Lemma 1 to be $t/2^{\Omega(k)}$, and thus the second property is also satisfied. Hence, applying Lemma 1 with respect to the above sets, concludes the proof of the lemma. □

3.2   Instantiation with the Aumüller et al. [3] Function Family

We now explore instantiating the framework with the function families of Aumüller et al. [3]. The resulting families enjoy shorter description length and invoking them require less combinatorial work than [27] based families discussed above. On the other hand, describing them on paper is a bit more complicated. The function family of Aumüller et al. [3] (building upon Dietzfelbinger and Woelfel [11]) follows the same basic outline as the [27] function family, but uses more complex hash functions. Recall that the members of the Pagh and Pagh [27] function family $\mathcal{PP}(\mathcal{H}, \mathcal{G}, \mathcal{F})$ are of the form $(f_1 \circ h_1) \oplus (f_2 \circ h_2) \oplus g$, for $f_1, f_2 \in \mathcal{F}$, $h_1, h_1, \in \mathcal{H}$ and $g \in \mathcal{G}$. In the family $\mathcal{ADW}(\mathcal{H}, \mathcal{G}, \mathcal{F})$ described below, the role of h_1, h_2 and g is taken by some variant of *tabulation hashing* (and not taken from a relatively high k-wise independent family as in [27]). Specifically, at the heart of these functions lies a function of the form:

$$a_{h,\bar{g},M}(x) := \left(h(x) + \sum_{1 \leq j \leq z} M[\bar{g}_j(x), j] \right) \bmod m$$

---

[7] The function family we consider above (i.e., $\mathcal{PP}$) is slightly different than the one given in [27]. Their construction maps element $x \in \mathcal{D}$ to $F_1[h_1(x)] \oplus F_2[h_2(x)] \oplus g(x)$, where F_1 and F_2 are uniformly chosen vectors from $\mathcal{R}^t$, $h_1, h_2 : \mathcal{D} \mapsto [t]$ are uniformly chosen from a function family $\mathcal{H}$ and $g : \mathcal{D} \mapsto \mathcal{R}$ is chosen uniformly from a function family $\mathcal{G}$. Yet, the correctness of Theorem 4 follows in a straightforward manner from [27] original proof (specifically from Lemma 3.3 and 3.4).

where $M \in (\mathbb{Z}_m)_{\ell \times z}$ is a $\ell \times z$ matrix, $\bar{g} = (g_1, \cdots, g_z)$ is a list of z functions where $g_j \colon \mathcal{D} \mapsto \mathbb{Z}_\ell$ and $h \colon \mathcal{D} \mapsto \mathbb{Z}_m$. The matrix M will be chosen at random (sometimes actually pseudorandomly) and the g_j's and h from a relatively low independence family. In addition, unlike in Pagh and Pagh [27], the functions are chosen in a *correlated* manner (i.e., , sharing the *same* function vector $\bar{g}$).

In the rest of this section, we formally define the hash function family of Aumüller et al. [3], state their (non-adaptive) result, and apply Lemma 1 to get an adaptive variant of their result.

Definition 9 (The Aumüller et al. [3] function family). *For $z \in \mathbb{N}$, for functions $h_1, h_2, h_3 \colon \mathcal{D} \mapsto \mathbb{Z}_m$ and $f_1, f_2 \colon \mathcal{D} \mapsto \mathcal{R}$, a function vector $\bar{g} = (g_1, \cdots, g_z)$, where $g_j \colon \mathcal{D} \mapsto \mathbb{Z}_\ell$ for each $1 \leq j \leq z$, and matrices $M_1, M_2, M_3 \in (\mathbb{Z}_m)_{\ell \times z}$, define the function $\mathsf{adw}_{M_1,M_2,M_3,h_1,h_2,h_3,\bar{g},f_1,f_2}$ from $\mathcal{D}$ to $\mathcal{R}$ as*

$$\mathsf{adw}_{M_1,M_2,M_3,h_1,h_2,h_3,\bar{g},f_1,f_2} := (f_1 \circ a^{\mathcal{D}}_{h_1,\bar{g},M_1}) \oplus (f_2 \circ a^{\mathcal{D}}_{h_2,\bar{g},M_2}) \oplus a^{\mathcal{R}}_{h_3,\bar{g},M_3}, \quad (2)$$

where $a^{\mathcal{S}}_{h,\bar{g},M}(x)$, for a set $\mathcal{S}$, is the $(a_{h,\bar{g},M}(x))^{th}$ element of $\mathcal{S}$ (in lexicographic order), where $a_{h,\bar{g},M}(x) := \left(h(x) + \sum_{1 \leq j \leq z} M[\bar{g}_j(x), j] \right) \bmod m$.

For function families $\mathcal{H} = \{h \colon \mathcal{D} \mapsto \mathbb{Z}_m\}$ and $\mathcal{F} = \{f \colon \mathcal{D} \mapsto \mathcal{R}\}$, and $M_1, M_2, h_1, h_2, \bar{g}$ as above, let

$$\mathcal{ADW}_{M_1,M_2,h_1,h_2,\bar{g}}(\mathcal{H}, \mathcal{F}) := \{\mathsf{adw}_{M_1,M_2,M_3,h_1,h_2,h_3,\bar{g},f_1,f_2} : \quad (3)$$
$$M_3 \in (\mathbb{Z}_m)_{\ell \times z}, h_3 \in \mathcal{H}, f_1, f_2 \in \mathcal{F}\}$$

Finally, for function family $\mathcal{G} = \{g \colon \mathcal{D} \mapsto \mathbb{Z}_\ell\}$, and $\mathcal{H}, \mathcal{F}$ as above, let

$$\mathcal{ADW}_z(\mathcal{H}, \mathcal{G}, \mathcal{F}) := \{\mathsf{adw}_{M_1,M_2,M_3,h_1,h_2,h_3,\bar{g},f_1,f_2} : \quad (4)$$
$$M_1, M_2, M_3 \in (\mathbb{Z}_m)_{\ell \times z}, h_1, h_2, h_3 \in \mathcal{H}, \bar{g} \in \mathcal{G}^z, f_1, f_2 \in \mathcal{F}\}.$$

Aumüller et al. [3] proved the following result with respect to the above function family.

Theorem 5 ([3]). *The following holds for any $t, s \in \mathbb{N}$ and $\zeta, c_1, c_2 > 0$: let $m = (1 + \zeta)t$, $\delta = c_1/\log t$, $\ell = t^\delta$, $k = c_2 \cdot s \cdot \log t$ and $z = \lceil (s+2)/(c_1 \cdot c_2 \cdot s) \rceil$. Let $\mathcal{H} = \{h \colon \mathcal{D} \mapsto \mathbb{Z}_m\}$ and $\mathcal{G} : \{g : \mathcal{D} \mapsto \mathbb{Z}_\ell\}$ be $2k$-wise independent hash families, and let Π be the all function family from $\mathcal{D}$ to $\mathcal{R}$.*

Then for $t \in \mathbb{N}$ there exists a left-monotone set $\mathrm{BAD} \subseteq \mathcal{D}^{\leq t} \times ((\mathbb{Z}_m)^2_{\ell \times z} \times \mathcal{H}^2 \times \mathcal{G}^z)$, such that the following holds for every $\bar{q} \in \mathcal{D}^{\leq t}$:

1. $\left(f(\bar{q}_1), \ldots, f(\bar{q}_{|\bar{q}|}) \right)_{f \leftarrow \mathcal{ADW}_u(\mathcal{H}, \Pi)}$ *is uniform over $\mathcal{R}^{|\bar{q}|}$ for every $u \in (\mathbb{Z}_m)^2_{\ell \times z} \times \mathcal{H}^2 \times \mathcal{G}^z$ such that $(\bar{q}, u) \notin \mathrm{BAD}$, and*
2. $\Pr_{u \leftarrow (\mathbb{Z}_m)^2_{\ell \times z} \times \mathcal{H}^2 \times \mathcal{G}^z}[(\bar{q}, u) \in \mathrm{BAD}] \leq 1/t^{s+1}$.

That is, for the right choice of parameters, the function family $\mathcal{ADW}_z(\mathcal{H}, \mathcal{G}, \mathcal{F})$ is not only closed to being uniform in the eyes of a non-adaptive distinguisher, but also allows us to apply Lemma 1 to deduce its security in the eyes of adaptive distinguishers. Indeed, by plugging in Theorem 5 into the general framework lemma (Lemma 1), we get the following result:

Lemma 3. *Let* s, z, $\mathcal{H}$, $\mathcal{G}$ *and* Π *be as in Theorem 5 and let* D *be an* adaptive, *t-query oracle-aided algorithm. Then*

$$\left|\Pr_{f \leftarrow \mathcal{ADW}_z(\mathcal{H},\mathcal{G},\Pi)}[\mathsf{D}^f = 1] - \Pr_{\pi \leftarrow \Pi}[\mathsf{D}^\pi = 1]\right| \leq 1/t^{s+1}.$$

Proof. Let $\mathcal{U} = (\mathbb{Z}_m)_{\ell \times z} \times (\mathbb{Z}_m)_{\ell \times z} \times \mathcal{H} \times \mathcal{H} \times \mathcal{G}^z$, $\mathcal{V} = (\mathbb{Z}_m)_{\ell \times z} \times \Pi \times \Pi \times \mathcal{H}$. For $(M_1, M_2, h_1, h_2, \bar{g}) \in \mathcal{U}$ and $(M_3, \pi_1, \pi_2, h) \in \mathcal{V}$, let $F_{(M_1,M_2,h_1,h_2,\bar{g}),(M_3,\pi_1,\pi_2,h)} = (\pi_1 \circ a_{h_1,\bar{g},M_1}) \oplus (\pi_2 \circ a_{h_2,\bar{g},M_2}) \oplus a_{h,\bar{g},M_3}$, and let $\mathcal{F} = \{F_{u,v} \colon \mathcal{D} \mapsto \mathcal{R}\}_{(u,v) \in \mathcal{U} \times \mathcal{V}}$. Finally, let BAD be the set BAD of Theorem 5. We prove the lemma showing that the above sets meet the requirements stated in Lemma 1.

Item 1 of Theorem 5 assures that the first property of Lemma 1 is satisfied, and according to Item 2 of Theorem 5 we set ε of Lemma 1 to be $1/t^{s+1}$, and thus the second property is also satisfied. Hence, applying Lemma 1 concludes the proof of the lemma. $\qquad \square$

We note that for large enough t, in contrast to the function family using $\mathcal{PP}$, using $\mathcal{ADW}$ we get meaningful results even when using an underlying $k = O(\log t)$-wise independent family.

Remark 1. In the rest of the paper we mostly apply Lemma 3 with the parameters stated in Theorem 5. Different choice of parameters can be used to get different results. For example, using larger "random tables" (e.g., $\delta = 1/2$), we improve the result of Jain et al. [16] (see Section 4.1).

4   Extending the Domain of a PRF

In this section we show how to apply the constructions of Section 3, inspired by cuckoo hashing, in order to extend a domain of a given PRF $\mathcal{F}$ to an arbitrary size one.

Let $\mathcal{P}(\mathcal{U}, \mathcal{V}) = \{\mathcal{P}(\mathcal{U}_n, \mathcal{V}_n)\}_{n \in \mathbb{N}}$ be the ensemble of function families $\{P_{u,v} \colon \mathcal{D}_n \mapsto \mathcal{R}_n\}_{(u,v) \in \mathcal{U}_n \times \mathcal{V}_n}$, where $\mathcal{U}_n$ and $\mathcal{V}_n$ are some non-empty sets as described in Section 3. We begin by showing that $\mathcal{P}(\mathcal{U}, \mathcal{V}^{\mathcal{F}})$ is computationally indistinguishable from $\mathcal{P}(\mathcal{U}, \mathcal{V}^{\Pi})$, where $\mathcal{V}^{\mathcal{F}}$ denotes that $\mathcal{V}$ is implemented using pseudorandom functions and $\mathcal{V}^{\Pi}$ denotes that $\mathcal{V}$ is implemented using truly random functions.[8] In the sequel, we assume that $\mathcal{V}$ is implemented using 2 calls to the underlying functions (as this is the case in the actual constructions we work with).

Lemma 4. *Let* $\mathcal{P}(\mathcal{U}, \mathcal{V}) = \{\mathcal{P}(\mathcal{U}_n, \mathcal{V}_n)\}_{n \in \mathbb{N}}$ *be the ensemble of function families* $\{\Pi_{u,v} \colon \mathcal{D}_n \mapsto \mathcal{R}_n\}_{(u,v) \in \mathcal{U}_n \times \mathcal{V}_n}$, *where* $\mathcal{U}_n$ *and* $\mathcal{V}_n$ *are arbitrary sets,* $\Pi = \{\Pi_n \colon \mathcal{S}_n \mapsto \mathcal{R}_n\}_{n \in \mathbb{N}}$, *where* Π_n *is the set of all functions from* $\mathcal{S}_n$ *to* $\mathcal{R}_n$, *and*

---

[8] Namely, in case the implementation of $\mathcal{PP}$ is used, then $\mathcal{U} = \mathcal{H} \times \mathcal{H}$, $\mathcal{V}^{\mathcal{F}} = \mathcal{F} \times \mathcal{F} \times \mathcal{G}$ and $\mathcal{V}^{\Pi} = \Pi \times \Pi \times \mathcal{G}$. In case the implementation of $\mathcal{ADW}_z$ is used, then $\mathcal{U} = (\mathbb{Z}_m)_{\ell \times z} \times (\mathbb{Z}_m)_{\ell \times z} \times \mathcal{H} \times \mathcal{H} \times \mathcal{G}^z$, $\mathcal{V}^{\mathcal{F}} = (\mathbb{Z}_m)_{\ell \times z} \times \mathcal{F} \times \mathcal{F} \times \mathcal{H}$ and $\mathcal{V}^{\Pi} = (\mathbb{Z}_m)_{\ell \times z} \times \Pi \times \Pi \times \mathcal{H}$.

$\mathcal{F} = \{\mathcal{F}_n \colon \mathcal{S}_n \mapsto \mathcal{R}_n\}_{n \in \mathbb{N}}$ be an efficient function family. Then for every $q(n)$-query oracle-aided distinguisher D of running time $t(n)$, there exists $p \in$ poly and a $q(n)$-query distinguisher $\widehat{\mathsf{D}}$ of running time $t(n) + p(n)q(n)$, with

$$\left| \Pr_{f \leftarrow \mathcal{F}_n}[\widehat{\mathsf{D}}^f(1^n) = 1] - \Pr_{\pi \leftarrow \Pi_n}[\widehat{\mathsf{D}}^\pi(1^n) = 1] \right|$$
$$\geq \frac{1}{2} \cdot \left| \Pr_{f \leftarrow \mathcal{P}(\mathcal{U}_n, \mathcal{V}_n^{\mathcal{F}_n})}[\mathsf{D}^f(1^n) = 1] - \Pr_{f \leftarrow \mathcal{P}(\mathcal{U}_n, \mathcal{V}_n^{\Pi_n})}[\mathsf{D}^f(1^n) = 1] \right|,$$

for every $n \in \mathbb{N}$.

The proof of this lemma can be found in the full version of this paper.

Plugging in a specific function family $\mathcal{P}$ (e.g., $\mathcal{PP}$ or $\mathcal{ADW}$), we get domain extension for a PRF. Specifically, using Lemma 2 we get the following theorem.

Theorem 6 (Restating Theorem 1). Let $\mathcal{H} = \{\mathcal{H}_n \colon \{0,1\}^{\ell(n)} \mapsto \{0,1\}^{m(n)}\}_{n \in \mathbb{N}}$ and $\mathcal{G} = \{\mathcal{G}_n \colon \{0,1\}^{\ell(n)} \mapsto \{0,1\}^{s(n)}\}_{n \in \mathbb{N}}$ be efficient $k(n)$-wise independent function family ensembles, and let $\mathcal{F} = \{\mathcal{F}_n \colon \{0,1\}^{m(n)} \mapsto \{0,1\}^{s(n)}\}_{n \in \mathbb{N}}$ be a $(q(n), t(n), \varepsilon(n))$-PRF. Then $\mathcal{PP}(\mathcal{H}, \mathcal{G}, \mathcal{F}) = \{\mathcal{PP}(\mathcal{H}_n, \mathcal{G}_n, \mathcal{F}_n) \colon \{0,1\}^{\ell(n)} \mapsto \{0,1\}^{s(n)}\}_{n \in \mathbb{N}}$ is a $(q(n), t(n) - p(n)q(n), 2\varepsilon(n) + q(n)/2^{\Omega(k(n))})$-PRF, where $p \in$ poly is determined by the evaluation and sampling time of $\mathcal{H}$, $\mathcal{G}$ and $\mathcal{F}$ and $q(n) \leq 2^{m(n)-2}$.[9]

Notice that in order for Theorem 6 to be useful, we have to set $k(n) = \Omega(\log q(n))$. Plugging in Lemma 3 we get the following theorem.

Theorem 7. Let $s \geq 0$, z, $\mathcal{H} = \{\mathcal{H}_n \colon \{0,1\}^{\ell(n)} \mapsto \{0,1\}^{m(n)}\}_{n \in \mathbb{N}}$, $\mathcal{G} = \{\mathcal{G}_n \colon \{0,1\}^n \mapsto \{0,1\}^{\ell(n)}\}_{n \in \mathbb{N}}$ be as defined in Theorem 5, and let $\mathcal{F} = \{\mathcal{F}_n \colon \{0,1\}^{m(n)} \mapsto \{0,1\}^{s(n)}\}_{n \in \mathbb{N}}$ be a $(q(n), t(n), \varepsilon(n))$-PRF. Then $\mathcal{ADW}_z(\mathcal{H}, \mathcal{G}, \mathcal{F}) = \{\mathcal{ADW}_z(\mathcal{H}_n, \mathcal{G}_n, \mathcal{F}_n) \colon \{0,1\}^{\ell(n)} \mapsto \{0,1\}^{s(n)}\}_{n \in \mathbb{N}}$ is a $(q(n), t(n) - p(n)q(n), 2\varepsilon(n) + 1/q(n)^{s+1})$-PRF, where $p \in$ poly is determined by the evaluation and sampling time of $\mathcal{H}$, $\mathcal{G}$ and $\mathcal{F}$ and $q(n) \leq 2^{m(n)}/(1 + \zeta)$ where ζ is from Theorem 5.

Notice that we used the setting of parameters of Theorem 5. In particular, since the matrices that are sampled in the definition of $\mathcal{ADW}_z$ are of constant size, they can be embedded in the key of the PRF.

4.1   Hardness Preserving PRG to PRF Reductions

An important corollary of Theorem 6 is a security preserving reduction from pseudorandom generators to pseudorandom functions.

Definition 10 (PRG to PRF reductions). An oracle-aided function family ensemble $\mathcal{F}$ is a (v, q, t, ε)-PRG-to-PRF reduction, if the following holds:

1. For any oracle G and $n \in \mathbb{N}$, a function $f \in \mathcal{F}_n^G$ makes at most $v(n)$ oracle calls per invocation.

---

[9] The -2 factor is due to the definition of $\mathcal{H}$ is Theorem 4.

2. *Assuming that G is a length-doubling (t_G, ε_G)-PRG of evaluation time e_G, then $\mathcal{F}^G$ is a $(q(t_G, \varepsilon_G, e_G), t(t_G, \varepsilon_G, e_G), \varepsilon(t_G, \varepsilon_G, e_G))$-PRF.*

The following fact easily follows from [14].

Proposition 1 ([14]). *For any integer function m, there exists an efficient oracle-aided function family ensemble, denoted GGM_m, that maps strings of length $m(n)$ to strings of length n, and is a $(m(n), q(n), t_G(n) - m(n) \cdot q(n) \cdot e_G(n), m(n) \cdot q(n) \cdot \varepsilon_G(n))$-PRG-to-PRF reduction for any integer function q.*[10]

Combining Proposition 1 with Theorem 6 yields the following result.

Corollary 2. *Let $\mathcal{H} = \{\mathcal{H}_n \colon \{0,1\}^n \mapsto \{0,1\}^{m(n)}\}_{n \in \mathbb{N}}$ and $\mathcal{G} = \{\mathcal{G}_n \colon \{0,1\}^n \mapsto \{0,1\}^n\}_{n \in \mathbb{N}}$ be efficient $k(n)$-wise independent function family ensembles, then the oracle-aided function ensemble $\mathcal{PP}(\mathcal{H}, \mathcal{G}, \mathsf{GGM}_m^G)$ is a $(m(n), q(n), t_G(n) - p(n) \cdot m(n) \cdot q(n), 2m(n) \cdot q(n) \cdot \varepsilon_G(n) + q(n)/2^{\Omega(k(n))})$-PRG-to-PRF reduction, where $p \in \mathrm{poly}$ is determined by the evaluation and sampling time of $\mathcal{H}$, $\mathcal{G}$ and G, and $q(n) \leq 2^{m(n)-2}$.*

For settings of interest, Corollary 2 yields the following result.

Corollary 3 (Restating Corollary 1). *Let $c > 0$, $0 < \delta < 1$ and $0 < \alpha < \delta$, and let $\mathcal{H}$ and $\mathcal{G}$ be as in Corollary 2, with respect to $k(n) = \Theta(n^\alpha + cn^\delta)$ (the hidden constant is universal). Then $\mathcal{PP}(\mathcal{H}, \mathcal{G}, \mathsf{GGM}_m^G)$ is an $(O(n^\alpha), 2^{n^\alpha}, 2^{c'n^\delta}, 2^{-c'n^\delta})$-PRG-to-PRF reduction, for every $0 < c' < c$.*

Proof. Let $t(n) = t_G(n) - p(n) \cdot m(n) \cdot q(n)$ and $\varepsilon(n) = 2m(n) \cdot q(n) \cdot \varepsilon_G(n) + q(n)/2^{\Omega(k(n))}$. Set $k(n) = \Theta(n^\alpha + cn^\delta)$, with an appropriate constant, such that $\frac{q}{2^{\Omega(k)}} < 2^{-cn^\delta}$, and thus $\varepsilon(n) < 2^{1+\log(n^\alpha+2)+n^\alpha-cn^\delta} + 2^{-cn^\delta}$. Let $c'' \in \mathbb{N}$ such that $n^{c''} > p(n)$ for large enough n (where p is of Corollary 2), and thus it holds that $t(n) > 2^{cn^\delta} - n^{c''}2^{n^\alpha}(n^\alpha+2)$. Hence, for every $c' < c$, we have $\varepsilon(n) < 2^{-c'n^\delta}$ and $t(n) > 2^{c'n^\delta}$ for large enough n. $\square$

Combining Proposition 1 with Theorem 7 yields the following result.

Corollary 4. *Let $s \geq 0$, z, $\mathcal{H} = \{\mathcal{H}_n \colon \{0,1\}^n \mapsto \{0,1\}^{m(n)}\}_{n \in \mathbb{N}}$, $\mathcal{G} = \{\mathcal{G}_n \colon \{0,1\}^n \mapsto \{0,1\}^{\ell(n)}\}_{n \in \mathbb{N}}$ be as defined in Theorem 5, then the oracle-aided function ensemble $\mathcal{ADW}_z(\mathcal{H}, \mathcal{G}, \mathsf{GGM}_m^G)$ is a $(m(n), q(n), t_G(n) - p(n) \cdot m(n) \cdot q(n), 2m(n) \cdot q(n) \cdot \varepsilon_G(n) + 1/q(n)^{s+1})$-PRG-to-PRF reduction, where $p \in \mathrm{poly}$ is determined by the evaluation and sampling time of $\mathcal{H}$, $\mathcal{G}$ and G, and $q(n) \leq 2^{m(n)}/(1+\zeta)$ where ζ is from Theorem 5.*

---

[10] GGM_m is a variant of the standard GGM function family, that on input of length $m(n)$ uses seed of length n for the underlying generator, rather than seed of length $m(n)$. Formally, GGM_m is the function family ensemble $\{\mathsf{GGM}_{m(n)}\}_{n \in \mathbb{N}}$, where $\mathsf{GGM}_{m(n)} = \{f_r\}_{r \in \{0,1\}^n}$, and for $r \in \{0,1\}^n$, the oracle-aided function $f_r \colon \{0,1\}^{m(n)} \mapsto \{0,1\}^n$ is defined as follows: given oracle access to a length-doubling function G and input $x \in \{0,1\}^{m(n)}$, $f_r^G(x) = r_x$, where r_x is recursively defined by $r_\varepsilon = r$, and, for a string w, $r_{w\|0}\|r_{w\|1} = G(r_w)$.

Settling the Parameters. In the construction given in Corollary 3, assuming $2^{n^{1/2}} \leq q < 2^n$, we need to set k to be $\Theta(n)$. Higher independence means that we need to use a longer key and the evaluation time is larger. More accurately, the evaluation time of our construction is lower bounded by the evaluation time of the $\Theta(n)$-wise independent hash function (that may or may not be larger than $\Theta(\log(q) \cdot e_G)$). Moreover, the key length must be $\Theta(n^2)$, but this can be circumvented by extending a short key to a long one using GGM. This costs additional $\Theta(n \cdot e_G)$ time. As we have stated in Corollary 3, our construction gives a $(O(n^\alpha), 2^{n^\alpha}, 2^{c'n^\delta}, 2^{c'n^\delta})$-PRG-to-PRF reduction for every $0 < c' < c$, and works for any $0 < \alpha < \delta$, while the construction of JPT only works for $\delta/2 \leq \alpha < \delta$.

In the construction given in Corollary 4, assuming $2^{n^{1/2}} \leq q < 2^n$, we can get better results (that also improve upon Jain et al. [16]). Assume for simplicity of the exposition that $q = 2^{n^{1/2}}$. As opposed to the specification of parameters in Theorem 5, we can use long random tables of size $\Theta(\sqrt{q})$ (i.e., $\delta = 1/2$ in Theorem 5), $s = n/\log q$ and get that setting $k = \Theta(n^{1/2})$ is enough to get error $O(1/2^n)$. The point is that the creation of the (long) tables that we need in Theorem 5 (which so far were part of the key) can be done by applying GGM on a short input key. This only increases the evaluation time by an additional $\Theta(\log(q) \cdot e_G)$ term. In total, the evaluation time of our construction is $\Theta(\log(q) \cdot e_G)$.

5   From Non-adaptive to Adaptive PRF

In this section we show how to apply the Cuckoo Hashing based constructions of Section 3 in order to come up with a construction of an adaptive PRF from non-adaptive one in a security preserving manner. As in Section 4, let $\mathcal{P}(\mathcal{U}, \mathcal{V}) = \{\mathcal{P}(\mathcal{U}_n, \mathcal{V}_n)\}_{n \in \mathbb{N}}$ be the ensemble of function families $\{P_{u,v} : \mathcal{D}_n \mapsto \mathcal{R}_n\}_{(u,v) \in \mathcal{U}_n \times \mathcal{V}_n}$, where $\mathcal{U}_n$ and $\mathcal{V}_n$ are some non-empty sets as described in Section 3. We begin by showing that $\mathcal{P}(\mathcal{U}, \mathcal{V}^{\mathcal{F}})$ is computationally indistinguishable from $\mathcal{P}(\mathcal{U}, \mathcal{V}^{\Pi})$, where $\mathcal{V}^{\mathcal{F}}$ denotes that $\mathcal{V}$ is implemented using *non-adaptive* pseudorandom functions and $\mathcal{V}^{\Pi}$ denotes that $\mathcal{V}$ is implemented using truly random functions (see also Footnote 8). In the sequel, we assume that $\mathcal{V}$ is implemented using 2 calls to the underlying functions (as this is the case in the actual constructions we work with).

For ease of notation, in the following we assume $\ell(n) = n$ (i.e., $\mathcal{F}$ is length preserving).

Lemma 5. *Let $\mathcal{P}(\mathcal{U}, \mathcal{V}) = \{\mathcal{P}(\mathcal{U}_n, \mathcal{V}_n)\}_{n \in \mathbb{N}}$ be the ensemble of function families $\{P_{u,v} : \mathcal{D}_n \mapsto \mathcal{R}_n\}_{(u,v) \in \mathcal{U}_n \times \mathcal{V}_n}$, that is implementation of $\mathcal{PP}$ or $\mathcal{ADW}$, where $\mathcal{U}_n$ and $\mathcal{V}_n$ are arbitrary sets, $\Pi = \{\Pi_n : \mathcal{D}_n \mapsto \mathcal{R}_n\}_{n \in \mathbb{N}}$, where Π_n is the set of all functions from $\mathcal{D}_n$ to $\mathcal{R}_n$, and $\mathcal{F} = \{\mathcal{F}_n : \mathcal{D}_n \mapsto \mathcal{R}_n\}$ be an efficient function family. Let $\zeta > 0$ that depends on the instantiation of $\mathcal{P}$.[11] Then for*

---

[11] In case we use $\mathcal{PP}$ function family (Definition 8) then $\zeta = 3$, and in case we use $\mathcal{ADW}$ function family (Definition 9) then ζ is of Theorem 5.

every $q = q(n)$-*query, oracle-aided, adaptive distinguisher* D *of running time* $t = t(n)$, *there exists a* $(1 + \zeta)q$-*query, non-adaptive, oracle-aided distinguisher* $\widehat{\mathsf{D}}$ *of running time* $p(n)t(n)$, *with*

$$\left| \Pr_{f \leftarrow \mathcal{F}_n}[\widehat{\mathsf{D}}^f(1^n) = 1] - \Pr_{f \leftarrow \Pi_n}[\widehat{\mathsf{D}}^f(1^n) = 1] \right|$$

$$\geq \frac{1}{2} \cdot \left| \Pr_{f \leftarrow \mathcal{P}(\mathcal{U}_n, \mathcal{V}_n^{\mathcal{F}_n})}[\mathsf{D}^f(1^n) = 1] - \Pr_{f \leftarrow \mathcal{P}(\mathcal{U}_n, \mathcal{V}_n^{\Pi_n})}[\mathsf{D}^f(1^n) = 1] \right|,$$

for every $n \in \mathbb{N}$.

The proof of this lemma can be found in the full version of this paper.

Using Lemma 2 we immediately get the following theorem.

Theorem 8. *Let* q *be a polynomial-time computable integer function, let* $\mathcal{H} = \{\mathcal{H}_n : \{0,1\}^n \mapsto [4q(n)]_{\{0,1\}^n}\}_{n \in \mathbb{N}}$ *and* $\mathcal{G} = \{\mathcal{G}_n : \{0,1\}^n \mapsto \{0,1\}^n\}_{n \in \mathbb{N}}$ *be efficient* $(c \log(q(n)))$-*wise independent function family ensembles, where* $c > 0$ *is universal, and let* $\mathcal{F} = \{\mathcal{F}_n : \{0,1\}^n \mapsto \{0,1\}^{\ell(n)}\}_{n \in \mathbb{N}}$ *be a non-adaptive* $(4q(n), p(n)t(n), \varepsilon(n))$-*PRF, where* $p \in \text{poly}$ *is determined by the evaluation time of* $q, \mathcal{H}, \mathcal{G}$ *and* $\mathcal{F}$. *Then* $\mathcal{PP}(\mathcal{H}, \mathcal{G}, \mathcal{F})$ *is an adaptive* $(q(n), t(n), 2\varepsilon(n) + 1/q(n))$-*PRF.*

Proof. Recall that in this case $\varepsilon'(n) = q(n)/2^{\Omega(c \log(q(n)))}$. Setting c such that $q(n)/2^{\Omega(c \log(q(n)))} = 1/q(n)$ complete the proof.   □

Theorem 8 yields the following simpler corollary.

Corollary 5 (Restatement of Theorem 3). *Let* q, $\mathcal{H}$, $\mathcal{G}$ *and* p *be as in Theorem 8. Assuming* $\mathcal{F}$ *is a non-adaptive* $(p(n)t(n))$-*PRF, then* $\mathcal{PP}(\mathcal{H}, \mathcal{G}, \mathcal{F})$ *is an adaptive* $(t(n)/4)$-*PRF.*

Plugging in Lemma 3 we immediately get the following (similarly to Theorem 8):

Theorem 9. *Let* q *be a polynomial-time computable integer function, let* $s \geq 0$, z, $\mathcal{H} = \{\mathcal{H}_n : \{0,1\}^n \mapsto [(1 + \zeta)q(n)]\}$, $\mathcal{G} = \{\mathcal{G}_n : \{0,1\}^n \mapsto \{0,1\}^{\ell(n)}\}_{n \in \mathbb{N}}$ *be as defined in Theorem 5, and let* $\mathcal{F} = \{\mathcal{F}_n : \{0,1\}^n \mapsto \{0,1\}^{\ell(n)}\}_{n \in \mathbb{N}}$ *be a non-adaptive* $((1 + \zeta)q(n), p(n)t(n), \varepsilon(n))$-*PRF, where* $p \in \text{poly}$ *is determined by the evaluation time of* $q, \mathcal{H}, \mathcal{G}$ *and* $\mathcal{F}$. *Then* $\mathcal{ADW}_z(\mathcal{H}, \mathcal{G}, \mathcal{F})$ *is an adaptive* $(q(n), t(n), 2\varepsilon(n) + 1/q(n)^{s+1})$-*PRF.*

Notice that in Theorem 9 we used the setting of parameters of Theorem 5. In particular, since the matrices that are sampled in the definition of $\mathcal{ADW}_z$ are of constant size, we can embed them into the key of the PRF.

Acknowledgments. We thank Eylon Yogev and the anonymous referees for their helpful comments. The third author would like to thank his advisor Ran Raz for his support.

References

1. Aiello, W., Venkatesan, R.: Foiling Birthday Attacks in Length-Doubling Transformations - Benes: a non-reversible alternative to Feistel. In: Maurer, U.M. (ed.) EUROCRYPT 1996. LNCS, vol. 1070, pp. 307–320. Springer, Heidelberg (1996)
2. Arbitman, Y., Naor, M., Segev, G.: Backyard cuckoo hashing: Constant worst-case operations with a succinct representation. In: Proceedings of the 51th Annual Symposium on Foundations of Computer Science (FOCS), pp. 787–796 (2010)
3. Aumüller, M., Dietzfelbinger, M., Woelfel, P.: Explicit and Efficient Hash Families Suffice for Cuckoo Hashing with a Stash. In: Epstein, L., Ferragina, P. (eds.) ESA 2012. LNCS, vol. 7501, pp. 108–120. Springer, Heidelberg (2012)
4. Bellare, M., Goldwasser, S.: New Paradigms for Digital Signatures and Message Authentication Based on Non-interactive Zero Knowledge Proofs. In: Brassard, G. (ed.) CRYPTO 1989. LNCS, vol. 435, pp. 194–211. Springer, Heidelberg (1990)
5. Bellare, M., Goldreich, O., Krawczyk, H.: Stateless Evaluation of Pseudorandom Functions: Security beyond the Birthday Barrier. In: Wiener, M. (ed.) CRYPTO 1999. LNCS, vol. 1666, pp. 270–287. Springer, Heidelberg (1999)
6. Berman, I., Haitner, I.: From Non-adaptive to Adaptive Pseudorandom Functions. In: Cramer, R. (ed.) TCC 2012. LNCS, vol. 7194, pp. 357–368. Springer, Heidelberg (2012)
7. Blum, M., Evans, W.S., Gemmell, P., Kannan, S., Naor, M.: Checking the correctness of memories. Algorithmica 12(2/3), 225–244 (1994)
8. Carter, L.J., Wegman, M.N.: Universal classes of hash functions. Journal of Computer and System Sciences, 143–154 (1979)
9. Chandran, N., Garg, S.: Hardness preserving constructions of pseudorandom functions, revisited. IACR Cryptology ePrint Archive 2012:616 (2012)
10. Chor, B., Fiat, A., Naor, M., Pinkas, B.: Tracing traitors. IEEE Transactions on Information Theory 46(3), 893–910 (2000)
11. Dietzfelbinger, M., Woelfel, P.: Almost random graphs with simple hash functions. In: Proceedings of the 35th Annual ACM Symposium on Theory of Computing (STOC), pp. 629–638 (2003)
12. Goldreich, O.: Towards a Theory of Software Protection. In: Odlyzko, A.M. (ed.) CRYPTO 1986. LNCS, vol. 263, pp. 426–439. Springer, Heidelberg (1987)
13. Goldreich, O., Goldwasser, S., Micali, S.: On the Cryptographic Applications of Random Functions. In: Blakely, G.R., Chaum, D. (eds.) CRYPTO 1984. LNCS, vol. 196, pp. 276–288. Springer, Heidelberg (1985)
14. Goldreich, O., Goldwasser, S., Micali, S.: How to construct random functions. Journal of the ACM, 792–807 (1986)
15. Håstad, J., Impagliazzo, R., Levin, L.A., Luby, M.: A pseudorandom generator from any one-way function. SIAM Journal on Computing, 1364–1396 (1999)
16. Jain, A., Pietrzak, K., Tentes, A.: Hardness Preserving Constructions of Pseudorandom Functions. In: Cramer, R. (ed.) TCC 2012. LNCS, vol. 7194, pp. 369–382. Springer, Heidelberg (2012)
17. Jetchev, D., Özen, O., Stam, M.: Understanding Adaptivity: Random Systems Revisited. In: Wang, X., Sako, K. (eds.) ASIACRYPT 2012. LNCS, vol. 7658, pp. 313–330. Springer, Heidelberg (2012)
18. Levin, L.A.: One-way functions and pseudorandom generators. Combinatorica 7(4), 357–363 (1987)
19. Luby, M.: Pseudorandomness and cryptographic applications. Princeton computer science notes. Princeton University Press (1996)

20. Luby, M., Rackoff, C.: How to construct pseudorandom permutations from pseudorandom functions. SIAM Journal on Computing 17(2), 373–386 (1988)
21. Maurer, U.M.: Indistinguishability of Random Systems. In: Knudsen, L.R. (ed.) EUROCRYPT 2002. LNCS, vol. 2332, pp. 110–132. Springer, Heidelberg (2002)
22. Maurer, U.M., Pietrzak, K.: Composition of Random Systems: When Two Weak Make One Strong. In: Naor, M. (ed.) TCC 2004. LNCS, vol. 2951, pp. 410–427. Springer, Heidelberg (2004)
23. Myers, S.: Black-Box Composition Does Not Imply Adaptive Security. In: Cachin, C., Camenisch, J.L. (eds.) EUROCRYPT 2004. LNCS, vol. 3027, pp. 189–206. Springer, Heidelberg (2004)
24. Nandi, M.: A Unified Method for Improving PRF Bounds for a Class of Blockcipher Based MACs. In: Hong, S., Iwata, T. (eds.) FSE 2010. LNCS, vol. 6147, pp. 212–229. Springer, Heidelberg (2010)
25. Naor, M., Reingold, O.: Synthesizers and their application to the parallel construction of psuedo-random functions. In: Proceedings of the 36th Annual Symposium on Foundations of Computer Science (FOCS), pp. 170–181 (1995)
26. Ostrovsky, R.: An Efficient Software Protection Scheme. In: Brassard, G. (ed.) CRYPTO 1989. LNCS, vol. 435, pp. 610–611. Springer, Heidelberg (1990)
27. Pagh, A., Pagh, R.: Uniform hashing in constant time and optimal space. SIAM Journal on Computing 38(1), 85–96 (2008)
28. Pagh, R., Rodler, F.F.: Cuckoo hashing. J. Algorithms 51(2), 122–144 (2004)
29. Patarin, J.: Security of Random Feistel Schemes with 5 or More Rounds. In: Franklin, M. (ed.) CRYPTO 2004. LNCS, vol. 3152, pp. 106–122. Springer, Heidelberg (2004)
30. Patarin, J.: A Proof of Security in $O(2^n)$ for the Benes Scheme. In: Vaudenay, S. (ed.) AFRICACRYPT 2008. LNCS, vol. 5023, pp. 209–220. Springer, Heidelberg (2008)
31. Patarin, J.: Security of balanced and unbalanced feistel schemes with linear non equalities. IACR Cryptology ePrint Archive, 2010:293 (2010)
32. Pietrzak, K.: Composition Does Not Imply Adaptive Security. In: Shoup, V. (ed.) CRYPTO 2005. LNCS, vol. 3621, pp. 55–65. Springer, Heidelberg (2005)
33. Pietrzak, K.: Composition Implies Adaptive Security in Minicrypt. In: Vaudenay, S. (ed.) EUROCRYPT 2006. LNCS, vol. 4004, pp. 328–338. Springer, Heidelberg (2006)
34. Siegel, A.: On universal classes of extremely random constant-time hash functions. SIAM Journal on Computing 33(3), 505–543 (2004)
35. Wegman, M.N., Carter, L.: New hash functions and their use in authentication and set equality. J. Comput. Syst. Sci. 22(3), 265–279 (1981)

Concurrent Zero Knowledge in the Bounded Player Model

Vipul Goyal[1], Abhishek Jain[2], Rafail Ostrovsky[3],
Silas Richelson[4], and Ivan Visconti[5]

[1] Microsoft Research, India
vipul@microsoft.com
[2] MIT and Boston University, USA
abhishek@csail.mit.edu
[3] UCLA, USA
rafail@cs.ucla.edu
[4] UCLA, USA
sirichel@math.ucla.edu
[5] University of Salerno, Italy
visconti@dia.unisa.it

Abstract. In this paper we put forward the *Bounded Player Model* for secure computation. In this new model, the number of players that will ever
be involved in secure computations is bounded, but the number of computations is *not* a priori bounded. Indeed, while the number of devices and
people on this planet can be realistically estimated and bounded, the number of computations these devices will run can not be realistically bounded.
Further, we note that in the bounded player model, in addition to no a priori bound on the number of sessions, there is no synchronization barrier,
no trusted party, and simulation must be performed in polynomial time.

In this setting, we achieve concurrent Zero Knowledge (cZK) with
sub-logarithmic round complexity. Our security proof is (necessarily)
non-black-box, our simulator is "straight-line" and works as long as the
number of rounds is $\omega(1)$.

We further show that unlike previously studied relaxations of the
standard model (e.g., bounded number of sessions, timing assumptions,
super-polynomial simulation), concurrent-secure computation is still impossible to achieve in the Bounded Player model. This gives evidence
that our model is "closer" to the standard model than previously studied models, and study of this model might shed light on constructing
round efficient concurrent zero-knowledge in the standard model as well.

1 Introduction

Zero-knowledge proofs, introduced in the seminal work of Goldwasser, Micali and
Rackoff [21], are a fundamental building block in cryptography. Loosely speaking,
a zero-knowledge proof is an interactive proof between two parties — a prover
and a verifier — with the seemingly magical property that the verifier does not
learn anything beyond the validity of the statement being proved. Subsequent to
their introduction, zero-knowledge proofs have been the subject of a great deal
of research, and have found numerous applications in cryptography.

A. Sahai (Ed.): TCC 2013, LNCS 7785, pp. 60–79, 2013.

Concurrent Zero Knowledge. The original definition of zero knowledge is only relevant to the "stand-alone" setting where security holds only if the protocol runs in isolation. As such, unfortunately, it does not suffice if one wishes to run a zero-knowledge proof over a modern network environment, such as the Internet. Towards that end, Dwork, Naor and Sahai [16] initiated the study of cZK proofs that remain secure even if several instances of the protocol are executed concurrently under the control of an adversarial verifier. Subsequent to their work, cZK has been the subject of extensive research, with a large body of work devoted to studying its round-complexity. In the standard model, the round-complexity of cZK was improved from polynomial to slightly super-logarithmic [34,25,33]. In particular, the $\tilde{O}(\log k)$-round construction of [33] nearly matches the lower bound of $\tilde{\Omega}(\log k)$ w.r.t. black-box simulation [11].

Despite a decade of research, the $\tilde{O}(\log k)$-round construction of [33] is still the most round-efficient cZK protocol known. Indeed, the lower bound of [11] suggests that a breakthrough in non-black-box simulation techniques is required to achieve cZK with sub-logarithmic round complexity.[1]

Round-efficient cZK in Relaxed Models: Bounded Concurrency. While the round-complexity of cZK in the standard model still remains an intriguing open question, a long line of work has been dedicated towards constructing round-efficient cZK in various relaxations of the standard model.

An interesting relaxation of the standard model (and related to our setting) that has been previously studied is the bounded-concurrency model [2], where an *a priori bound* is assumed over the number of sessions that will ever take place (in particular, this bound is known to the protocol designer). It is known how to realize constant-round bounded cZK [2], and also constant-round bounded-concurrent secure two-party and multi-party computation [31].

Even though our model can be seen as related to (and a generalization of) the bounded concurrency model, the techniques used in designing round efficient bounded concurrent zero-knowledge do not seem to carry over to our setting. In particular, if there is even a single player that runs an unbounded number of sessions, the simulation strategies in [2,31] breakdown completely. This seems inherent because of the crucial difference this model has from our setting (which can understood by observing that general concurrent secure computation is possible in the bounded concurrent setting but impossible in our setting).

Bare Public Key and Other Preprocessing Models. The zero-knowledge preprocessing model was proposed in [24] in the stand-alone setting and in [13] in the context of cZK. In [13], interaction is needed between all the involved players in a preprocessing phase. Then, after a synchronization-barrier is passed, the preprocessing is over and actual proofs start. Interactions in each phase can take place concurrently, but the two phases can not overlap in time. An improved model was later proposed in [10] where the preprocessing is required to

---

[1] In this paper we only consider results based on standard complexity-theoretic and number-theoretic assumptions; in particular, we not consider "non-falsifiable" assumptions such as the knowledge of exponent assumption.

be non-interactive, and the model is called "Bare Public-Key" (BPK) model, since the non-interactive messages played in the preprocessing can be considered as public announcements of public keys. In this model it is known how to obtain constant-round concurrent zero knowledge with concurrent soundness under standard assumptions [14,15,37,36].

The crucial restriction of the BPK model is that all players who wish to ever participate in protocol executions must be fixed during the preprocessing phase, and new players cannot be added "on-the-fly" during the proof phase. We do *not* make such a restriction in our work and as such, the techniques useful in constructing secure protocols in the BPK model have limited relevance in our setting. In particular, constant round cZK is known to exist in the BPK model using only black-box simulation, while in our setting, non-black-box techniques are *necessary* to achieve sublogarithmic-round cZK.

Other Models. Round efficient concurrent zero-knowledge is known in a number of other models as well (which do not seem to be directly relevant to our setting). In the SPS model [30], the zero-knowledge simulator is allowed to run in super-polynomial time, as opposed to running in polynomial time (as per the standard definition of [21]). Indeed, this relaxation has yielded not only constant-round cZK [30], but also concurrent-secure computation [26,12,18]. This stands in contrast to the standard model, where concurrent-secure computation is known to be impossible to achieve [27] even with static input [5,1,19]. Other models where constant round cZK (as well as concurrently secure computation) is known include the timing model [16], the common reference string [7,8] model, etc.

Our Question. While the above relaxations of the standard model have their individual appeal, each of these models suffers from various drawbacks, either w.r.t. the security guarantees provided (e.g., as in the case of the SPS model), or w.r.t. the actual degree of concurrency tolerated (e.g., as in the case of the timing model). Indeed, despite extensive amount of research over the last decade, the round-complexity of cZK still remains open. In this work, we ask the question whether it is possible to construct cZK protocols with sub-logarithmic round-complexity in a natural model that does not suffer from the drawbacks of the previously studied models; namely, it does not require any preprocessing, assumes no trusted party or timing assumptions or an *a priori* bound on the number of protocol sessions, and requires standard polynomial-time simulation and standard complexity assumptions.

1.1   Our Results

In our work, we construct a concurrent (perfect) zero-knowledge argument system with sub-logarithmic round-complexity in a mild relaxation of the standard model; we refer to this as the *Bounded Player model*. In this model we only assume that there is an *a priori* (polynomial) upper-bound on the total number of players that may ever participate in protocol executions. We do not assume any synchronization barrier, or trusted party, and the simulation must be performed in polynomial time. In particular, we do *not* assume any *a priori* bound on the number of sessions, and achieve security under unbounded concurrency. As such, our model can be viewed as a strengthening of the bounded-concurrency model.[2] Below, we give an informal statement of our main result.

Theorem 1. *Assuming dense crypto systems and claw-free permutations, there exists an $\omega(1)$-round concurrent perfect zero-knowledge argument system with concurrent soundness in the Bounded Player model.*[3]

Our security proof is (necessarily) non-black-box, and the simulator of our protocol works in a "straight-line" manner. Our result is actually stronger since we only require a bound on the number of possible verifiers, while there is no restriction on the number of provers. We prove concurrent soundness since sequential and concurrent soundness are distinct notions in the Bounded Player model for the same reasons as shown by [29] in the context of the BPK model.

We stress that while our model bears some resemblance to the BPK model, known techniques from the BPK model are not applicable to our setting. Indeed, these techniques crucially rely upon the presence of the synchronization barrier between the pre-processing phase and the protocol phase, while such a barrier is not present in our model. As such, achieving full concurrency in our model is much harder and involves significantly different challenges. An important problem left open by our work is the existence of a constant round concurrent zero-knowledge protocol in the bounded player model. Our techniques (necessarily) require a super-constant number of rounds to keep the simulation time polynomial.

We further show that the impossibility results of Lindell for concurrent-secure computation [27] also hold in the Bounded Player model. This gives evidence that the Bounded Player model is much closer to the standard model than the previously studied models, and the study of this model might shed light towards the goal of constructing round efficient concurrent zero-knowledge in the standard model as well.

1.2 Our Techniques

Recall that in the Bounded Player model, the only assumption is that the total number of players that will ever be present in the system is *a priori* bounded. Then, an initial observation towards our goal of constructing sub-logarithmic round cZK protocols is that the black-box lower-bound of Canetti et al. [11] is applicable to our setting as well. Indeed, the impossibility result of [11] relies on

---

[2] Note that an upper-bound on the total number of concurrent executions implies an upper-bound on the total number of players as well.

[3] We note that if one only requires *statistical* (as opposed to perfect) zero knowledge, then the assumption on claw-free permutations can be replaced by collision-resistant hash functions. We further note that our assumption on dense cryptosystems can be further relaxed to trapdoor permutations by modifying our protocol to use the coin-tossing protocol of Barak and Lindell [4].

an adversarial verifier that opens a polynomial number $\ell(k)$ of sessions and plays adaptively at any point of time, depending upon the transcript generated "so far". The same analysis works in the Bounded Player model, by assuming that the adversarial verifier registers a new key each time a new session is played. In particular, consider an adversarial verifier that schedules a session s_i to be contained inside another session s_j. In this case, a black-box simulator does not gain any advantage in the Bounded Player model over the standard model. The reason is that since the adversarial verifier of [11] behaves adaptively on the transcript at any point, after a rewind the same session will be played with a fresh new key, thus rendering essentially useless the fact that the session was already solved before. Note that this is the same problem that occurs in the standard model, and stands in contrast to what happens in the BPK model (where identities are fixed in the preprocessing and therefore do not change over rewinds).

From the above observation, it is clear that we must resort to non-black-box techniques. Now, a natural approach to leverage the bound on the number of players is to associate with each verifier V_i a public key pk_i and then design an FLS-style protocol [17] that allows the ZK simulator to extract, in a non-black-box manner, the secret key sk_i of the verifier and then use it as a "trapdoor" for "easy" simulation. The key intuition is that once the simulator extracts the secret key sk_i of a verifier V_i, it can perform easy simulation of *all* the sessions associated with V_i. Then, since the total number of verifiers is bounded, the simulator will need to perform non-black-box extraction only an *a priori* bounded number of times (once for each verifier), which can be handled in a manner similar to the setting of bounded-concurrency [2].

Unfortunately, the above intuition is misleading. In order to understand the problem with the above approach, let us first consider a candidate protocol more concretely. In fact, it suffices to focus on a preamble phase that enables non-black-box extraction (by the simulator) of a verifier's secret key since the remainder of the protocol can be constructed in a straightforward manner following the FLS approach. Now, consider the following candidate preamble phase (using the non-black-box extraction technique of [4]): first, the prover and verifier engage in a coin-tossing protocol where the prover proves "honest behavior" using a Barak-style non-black-box ZK protocol [2]. Then, the verifier sends an encryption of its secret key under the public key that is determined from the output of the coin-tossing protocol.

In order to analyze this protocol, we will restrict our discussion to the simplified case where only one verifier is present in the system (but the total number of concurrent sessions are unbounded). At this point, one may immediately object that in the case of a single verifier identity, the problem is not interesting since the Bounded Player model is identical to the bare-public key model, where one can construct four-round cZK protocols using rewinding based techniques. However, simulation techniques involving rewinding do not "scale" well to the case of polynomially many identities (unless we use a large number of rounds) and fail[4]. Moreover the use of Barak's [2] straight-line simulation technique is also insufficient since it works only when the number of concurrent sessions is bounded (even when there is a single identity), but instead our goal is to obtain unbounded concurrent zero knowledge. In contrast, our simulation approach is "straight-line" for an unbounded number of sessions and scales well to a large bounded number of identities. Therefore, in the forthcoming discussion, we will restrict our analysis to straight-line simulation. In this case, we find it instructive to focus on the case of a single identity to explain our key ideas.

We now turn to analyze the candidate protocol. Now, following the intuition described earlier, one may think that the simulator can simply cheat in the coin-tossing protocol in the "inner-most" session in order to extract the secret key, following which all the sessions can be simulated in a straight-line manner, without performing any additional non-black-box simulation. Consider, however, the following adversarial verifier strategy: the verifier schedules an unbounded number of sessions in such a manner that the coin-tossing protocols in all of these sessions are executed in a "nested" manner. Furthermore, the verifier sends the ciphertext (containing its secret key) in each session only *after* all the coin-tossing protocols across all sessions are completed. Note that in such a scenario, the simulator would be forced to perform non-black-box simulation in an unbounded number of sessions. Unfortunately, this is a non-trivial problem that we do not know how to solve. More concretely, note that we cannot rely on techniques from the bounded-concurrency model since we cannot bound the total number of sessions (and thus, the total number of messages across all sessions). Further, all other natural approaches lead to a "blow-up" in the running time of the simulator. Indeed, if we were to solve this problem, then we would essentially construct a cZK protocol in the standard model, which remains an important open problem that we do not solve here.

In an effort to bypass the above problem, our first idea is to use multiple ($\omega(1)$, to be precise) preamble phases (instead of only one), such that the simulator is required to "cheat" in only one of these preambles. This, however, immediately raises a question: in which of the $\omega(1)$ preambles should the simulator cheat? This is a delicate question since if, for example, we let the simulator pick one of preambles uniformly at random, then with non-negligible probability, the simulator will end up choosing the first preamble phase. In this case, the adversary can simply perform the same attack as it did earlier playing only the first preamble phase, but for many different sessions so that the simulator will still have to cheat in many of them. Indeed, it would seem that any randomized oblivious simulation strategy can be attacked in a similar manner by simply identifying the first preamble phase where the simulator would cheat with a non-negligible probability.

Towards that end, our key idea is to use a specific probability distribution such that the simulator cheats in the first preamble phase with only negligible

---

[4] Indeed when the simulator rewinds the adversarial verifier, there is a different view and therefore the adversary will ask to play with new identities, making useless the work done with the old ones, as it happens in the standard model.

probability, while the probability of cheating in the later preambles increases gradually such that the "overall" probability of cheating is 1 (as required). Further, the distribution is such that the probability of cheating in the ith preamble is less than a fixed polynomial factor of the total probability of cheating in one of the previous $i - 1$ blocks. Very roughly speaking, this allows us to prevent the adversary from attacking the *first* preamble where the simulator cheats with non-negligible probability. More specifically, for any session, let us call the preamble where the simulator cheats the "special" preamble. Further, let us say that the adversary "wins" a session if he "stops" that session in the special preamble *before* sending the ciphertext containing the verifier's secret key. Otherwise, the adversary "loses" that session. Then, by using the properties of our probability distribution, we are able to show that the adversary's probability of losing a session is less than $1/n$ times the probability of winning. As a consequence, by careful choice of parameters, we are able to show that the probability of the adversary winning more than a given polynomially bounded number of sessions *without losing any sessions* w.r.t. any given verifier is negligible. Once we obtain this fixed bound, we are then able to rely on techniques from the bounded-concurrency model [2] to handle the bounded number of non-black-box simulations. For the sake of brevity, the above discussion is somewhat oversimplified. We refer the reader to the later sections for more details.

Impossibility of Concurrent-secure Computation. Once we have a cZK protocol (as discussed above) in the Bounded Player model, it may seem that it should be possible to obtain concurrent-secure computation as well by using techniques from [31]. Unfortunately, this turns out not to be the case, as we discuss below.

The key technical problem that arises in the setting of secure computation w.r.t. unbounded concurrency is the following. We cannot a priori bound the total number of "output delivery messages" (across all sessions) to the adversary; further, the session outputs cannot be "predicted" by the simulator before knowing the adversary's input. As such, known non-black-box simulation techniques cannot handle these unbounded number of messages and they inherently fail.[5] We remark that the same technical issue, in fact, arises in the standard model as well.

While the above argument only explains why known techniques fail, we can also obtain a formal impossibility result. Indeed, it is not difficult to see that the impossibility result of Lindell [27] also holds for the Bounded Player model. (See the full version [22] for details.)

2   Preliminaries and Definitions

2.1   Bounded Player Model

In this paper, we consider a new model of concurrent security, namely, the *bounded player model*, where we assume that there is an *a priori* (polynomial)

---

[5] We note that this problem does not occur in the case of zero knowledge because the adversary does not have any input, and the session outputs are fixed to be 1.

upper bound on the total number of player that will ever be present in the system. Specifically, let n denote the security parameter. Then, we will consider an upper bound $N = \text{poly}(n)$ on the total number of players that can engage in concurrent executions of a protocol at any time. We assume that each player P_i $(i \in N)$ has an associated unique identity id_i, and that there is an established mechanism to enforce that party P_i uses the same identity id_i in each protocol execution that it participates in. We stress that such identities, do not have to be established in advance. New players can join the system with their own (new) identities, as long as the number of players does not exceed N.

We note that this requirement is somewhat similar in spirit to the *bounded-concurrency model* [2,31], where it is assumed that the adversary cannot start more than an a priori fixed number of concurrent executions of a protocol. We stress, however, that in our model, there is *no* a priori bound on the total number of protocol sessions that may be executed concurrently. In this respect, one can view the Bounded Player model as a strengthening of the bounded-concurrency model. Indeed, one can argue that while the number of devices and people on this planet can be realistically estimated and bounded, the number of concurrent protocol executions on these devices can not.

Implementing the Bounded Player model. We formalize the Bounded Player model by means of a functionality F_{bp}^N that registers the identities of the player in the system. Specifically, a player P_i that wishes to participate in protocol executions can, at any time, register an identity id_i with the functionality F_{bp}^N. The registration functionality does not perform any checks on the identities that are registered, except that each party P_i can register at most one identity id_i, and that the total number of identity registrations are bounded by N. In other words, F_{bp}^N refuses to register any new identities once N number of identities have already been registered. The functionality F_{bp}^N is formally defined in Figure 1.

Functionality F_{bp}^N

F_{bp}^N initializes a variable *count* to 0 and proceeds as follows.

- **Register commands:** Upon receiving a message (**register**, sid, id_i) from some party P_i, the functionality checks that no pair (P_i, id_i') is already recorded and that *count* $< N$. If this is the case, it records the pair (P_i, id_i) and sets *count* = *count* + 1. Other wise, it ignores the received message.
- **Retrieve commands:** Upon receiving a message (retrieve, sid, P_i) from some party P_j or the adversary A, the functionality checks if some pair (P_i, id_i) is recorded. If this the case, it sends (sid, P_i, id_i) to P_j (or A). Otherwise, it returns $(sid, P_i, \bot)$.

Fig. 1. The Bounded Player Functionality F_{bp}^N

In our constructions we will only require that the identities correspond to values in the range of a one-way function. We note that in this particular case, the functionality F_{bp}^N bears much resemblance to the *bulletin-board certificate authority* functionality [23], which suffices for obtaining authenticated channels [9]. We finally remark that our model is also closely related to the *Bare Public-Key model*, introduced by Canetti et al. [10]. However, we stress that unlike the Bare Public-Key model, we do not assume any synchronization barrier between the registration phase and the protocol computation phase. In particular, we allow parties to register their identities even after the computation begins.

2.2   Concurrent Zero Knowledge in Bounded Player Model

In this section, we formally define concurrent zero knowledge in the Bounded Player model. Our definition, given below, is an adaptation of the one of [33] to the Bounded Player model, by also considering non-black-box simulation. Some of the text below is taken verbatim from [33].

Let PPT denote probabilistic-polynomial time. Let $\langle P, V \rangle$ be an interactive argument for a language L. Consider a concurrent adversarial verifier V^* that, given input $x \in L$, interacts with an unbounded number of independent copies of P (all on the same common input x and moreover equipped with a proper witness w), without any restriction over the scheduling of the messages in the different interactions with P. In particular, V^* has control over the scheduling of the messages in these interactions. Further, we say that V^* is an N-bounded concurrent adversary if it assumes at most N verifier identities during its (un-bounded) interactions with P.[6]

The transcript of a concurrent interaction consists of the common input x, followed by the sequence of prover and verifier messages exchanged during the interaction. We denote by $\mathsf{view}_{V^*}^P(x, z, N)$ the random variable describing the content of the random tape of the N-bounded concurrent adversary V^* with auxiliary input z and the transcript of the concurrent interaction between P and V^* on common input x.

Definition 1 (cZK in Bounded Player model). *Let $\langle P, V \rangle$ be an interactive argument system for a language L. We say that $\langle P, V \rangle$ is* concurrent zero knowledge *in the Bounded Player model if for every N-bounded concurrent non-uniform PPT adversary V^*, there exists a PPT algorithm $\mathcal{S}$, such that the following ensembles are computationally indistinguishable,*
$$\{\mathsf{view}_{V^*}^P(x, z, N)\}_{x \in L, z \in \{0,1\}^*, N \in poly(n)} \text{ and } \{\mathcal{S}(x, z, N)\}_{x \in L, z \in \{0,1\}^*, N \in poly(n)}.$$

2.3   Building Blocks

In this section, we discuss the main building blocks that we will use in our cZK construction.

---

[6] Thus, V^* can open multiple sessions with P for every unique verifier identity.

Perfectly Hiding Commitment Scheme. In our constructions, we will make use of a perfectly hiding string commitment scheme, denoted **Com**. For simplicity of exposition, we will make the simplifying assumption that **Com** is a non-interactive perfectly hiding commitment scheme (even though such a scheme cannot exist). In reality, **Com** would be taken to be a 2-round commitment scheme, which can be based on collections of claw-free permutations [20]. Unless stated otherwise, we will simply use the notation **Com**(x) to denote a commitment to a string x, and assume that the randomness (used to create the commitment) is implicit.

Perfect Witness Indistinguishable Argument of Knowledge. We will also make use of a perfect witness-indistinguishable argument of knowledge system for all of $\mathcal{NP}$ in our construction. Such a scheme can be constructed, for example, by parallel repetition of the 3-round Blum's protocol for Graph Hamiltonicity [6] instantiated with a perfectly hiding commitment scheme. We will denote such an argument system by $\langle P_{\mathsf{pWI}}, V_{\mathsf{pWI}} \rangle$.

Perfect Witness Indistinguishable Universal Argument. In our construction, we will use a perfect witness-indistinguishable universal argument system, denoted $\langle P_{\mathsf{pUA}}, V_{\mathsf{pUA}} \rangle$. Such an argument system can be constructed generically from a (computational) witness-indistinguishable universal argument pUA by using techniques of [32]. Specifically, in protocol $\langle P_{\mathsf{pUA}}, V_{\mathsf{pUA}} \rangle$, the prover P and verifier V first engage in an execution of pUA, where instead of sending its messages in the clear, P commits to each message using a perfectly hiding commitment scheme. Finally, P and V engage in an execution of a perfect zero knowledge argument of knowledge where P proves that the "decommitted" transcript of pUA is "accepting". The resulting protocol is still a "weak" argument of knowledge.

Perfect (Bounded-Concurrent) Zero-Knowledge. Our cZK argument crucially uses as a building block, a variant of the bounded cZK argument of Barak [2]. Similarly to [32], we modify the protocol appropriately such that it is *perfect* bounded cZK. Specifically, instead of a statistically binding commitment scheme, we will use a perfectly hiding commitment scheme. Instead of a computationally witness-indistinguishable universal argument (UARG), we will use a perfect witness indistinguishable UARG, denoted $\langle P_{\mathsf{pUA}}, V_{\mathsf{pUA}} \rangle$. Further, the length parameter $\ell(N)$ used in the modified protocol is a function of N, where N is the bound on the number of verifiers in the system. Protocol $\langle P_{\mathsf{pB}}, V_{\mathsf{pB}} \rangle_N$ is described in Figure 3 and can be based on claw-free permutations.

Resettable Witness Indistinguishable Proof System. We will further use a *resettable* witness-indistinguishable proof system [10] for all of $\mathcal{NP}$. Informally speaking, a proof system is resettable witness indistinguishable if it remains witness indistinguishable even against an adversarial verifier who can *reset* the prover and receive multiple proofs such that the prover uses the *same* random tape in each of the interactions. While the focus of this work is not on achieving security against reset attacks, such a proof system turns out to be useful when arguing concurrent soundness of our protocol (where our proof relies on a rewinding based argument). We will denote such a proof system by $\langle P_{\mathsf{rWI}}, V_{\mathsf{rWI}} \rangle$. It follows from [10] that such a proof system can be based on perfectly hiding commitments.

Dense Cryptosystems [35]. We will use a semantically secure public-key encryption scheme, denoted as $(\mathbf{Gen}, \mathbf{Enc}, \mathbf{Dec})$ that supports *oblivious* key generation (i.e., it should be possible to sample a public key without knowing the corresponding secret key). More precisely, there exists a deterministic algorithm $\mathbf{OGen}$ that takes as input the security parameter 1^n and a sufficiently long random string σ and outputs a public key $pk \leftarrow \mathbf{OGen}(1^n, \sigma)$, where pk is perfectly indistinguishable from a public key chosen by the normal key generation algorithm $\mathbf{Gen}$. For simplicity of exposition, we will assume that the $\mathbf{OGen}$ algorithm simply outputs the input randomness σ as the public key. Such schemes can be based on a variety of number-theoretic assumptions such as DDH [35].

3 Concurrent Zero Knowledge in Bounded Player Model

In this section, we describe our concurrent zero-knowledge protocol in the bounded player model.

Relation R_{sim}. We first recall a slight variant of Barak's [2] $\mathbf{NTIME}(T(n))$ relation R_{sim}, as used previously in [32]. Let $T : \mathbb{N} \to \mathbb{N}$ be a "nice" function that satisfies $T(n) = n^{\omega(1)}$. Let $\{\mathcal{H}_n\}_n$ be a family of collision-resistant hash functions where a function $h \in \mathcal{H}_n$ maps $\{0,1\}^*$ to $\{0,1\}^n$, and let $\mathbf{Com}$ be a perfectly hiding commitment scheme for strings of length n, where for any $\alpha \in \{0,1\}^n$, the length of $\mathbf{Com}(\alpha)$ is upper bounded by $2n$. The relation R_{sim} is described in Figure 2.

Instance: A triplet $\langle h, c, r \rangle \in \mathcal{H}_n \times \{0,1\}^n \times \{0,1\}^{\mathrm{poly}(n)}$.
Witness: A program $\Pi \in \{0,1\}^*$, a string $y \in \{0,1\}^*$ and a string $s \in \{0,1\}^{\mathrm{poly}(n)}$.
Relation: $R_{\mathsf{sim}}(\langle h, c, r \rangle, \langle \Pi, y, s \rangle) = 1$ if and only if: $|y| \leq |r| - n$, $c = \mathbf{Com}(h(\Pi); s)$ and $\Pi(y) = r$ within $T(n)$ steps.

Fig. 2. R_{sim} - A variant of Barak's relation [32]

Remark 1. The relation presented in Figure 2 is slightly oversimplified and will make Barak's protocol work only when $\{\mathcal{H}_n\}_n$ is collision-resistant against "slightly" super-polynomial sized circuits. For simplicity of exposition, in this manuscript, we will work with this assumption. We stress, however, that as discussed in prior works *[3,31]*, this assumption can be relaxed by using a "good" error-correcting code ECC (with constant distance and polynomial-time encoding and decoding procedures), and replacing the condition $c = \mathbf{Com}(h(\Pi); s)$ with $c = \mathbf{Com}(\mathsf{ECC}(h(\Pi)); s)$.

Parameters: Security parameter n, length parameter $\ell(N)$.
Common Input: $x \in \{0,1\}^{\mathrm{poly}(n)}$.
Private Input to P: A witness w such that $R_L(x, w) = 1$.

Stage 1 (Preamble Phase):
    $V \to P$: Send $h \xleftarrow{\text{R}} \mathcal{H}_n$.
    $P \to V$: Send $c = \mathbf{Com}(0^n)$.
    $V \to P$: Send $r \xleftarrow{\text{R}} \{0,1\}^{\ell(N)}$.
Stage 2 (Proof Phase):
    $P \leftrightarrow V$: A perfect WI UARG $\langle P_{\mathsf{pUA}}, V_{\mathsf{pUA}} \rangle$ proving the OR of the following statements:
        1. $\exists w \in \{0,1\}^{\mathrm{poly}(|x|)}$ s.t. $R_L(x, w) = 1$.
        2. $\exists \langle \Pi, y, s \rangle$ s.t. $R_{\mathsf{sim}}(\langle h, c, r \rangle, \langle \Pi, y, s \rangle) = 1$.

Fig. 3. Protocol $\langle P_{\mathsf{pB}}, V_{\mathsf{pB}} \rangle_N$

3.1 Our Protocol

We are now ready to present our concurrent zero knowledge protocol, denoted $\langle P, V \rangle$. Let P and V denote the prover and verifier respectively. Let N denote the bound on the number of verifiers present in the system. Let f_{owf} denote a one-way function, and $(\mathbf{Gen}, \mathbf{Enc}, \mathbf{Dec})$ denote a dense public key encryption scheme. Let $\langle P_{\mathsf{pB}}, V_{\mathsf{pB}} \rangle_N$ denote the perfect zero-knowledge argument system as described above. Further, let $\langle P_{\mathsf{pWI}}, V_{\mathsf{pWI}} \rangle$ denote a perfect witness indistinguishable argument of knowledge, and let $\langle P_{\mathsf{rWI}}, V_{\mathsf{rWI}} \rangle$ denote a resettable witness indistinguishable proof system.

The protocol $\langle P, V \rangle$ is described in Figure 4. For our purposes, we set the length parameter $\ell(N) = n^3 \cdot N \cdot P(n)$, where $P(n)$ is a polynomial upper bound on the total length of the prover messages in the protocol plus the length of the secret key of the verifier.

The completeness property of $\langle P, V \rangle$ follows immediately from the construction. Due to lack of space, we defer the proof of soundness to the full version [22]. We remark that, in fact, we prove *concurrent soundness* of $\langle P, V \rangle$, i.e., we show that a computationally-bounded adversarial prover who engages in multiple concurrent executions of $\langle P, V \rangle$ (where the scheduling across the sessions is controlled by the adversary) cannot prove a false statement in any of the executions, except with negligible probability. We note that similarly to the

Parameters: Security parameter n, $N = N(n)$, $t = \omega(1)$.
Common Input: $x \in \{0,1\}^{\text{poly}(n)}$.
Private Input to P: A witness w s.t. $R_L(x,w) = 1$.
Private Input to V: A public key $pk = (y_0, y_1)$ and secret key $sk = (b, x_b)$ s.t. $b \xleftarrow{R} \{0,1\}$, $y_b = f_{\text{owf}}(x_b)$.

Stage 1 (Preamble Phase): Repeat the following steps t times.
    $V \to P$: Send $pk = (y_0, y_1)$.
    $P \to V$: Choose $\sigma_p \xleftarrow{R} \{0,1\}^n$ and send $c_p = \mathbf{Com}(\sigma_p)$.
    $V \to P$: Send $\sigma_v \xleftarrow{R} \{0,1\}^n$.
    $P \to V$: Send σ_p. Let $\sigma = \sigma_p \oplus \sigma_v$.
    $P \leftrightarrow V$: An execution of $\langle P_{\text{pB}}, V_{\text{pB}} \rangle_N$ to prove the following statement: $\exists s$ s.t. $c = \mathbf{Com}(\sigma_p; s)$.
    $V \to P$: Send $e_1 = \mathbf{Enc}_\sigma(x_b)$, $e_2 = \mathbf{Enc}_\sigma(x_b)$.
    $V \leftrightarrow P$: An execution of resettable WI $\langle P_{\text{rWI}}, V_{\text{rWI}} \rangle$ to prove the following statement: $\exists \langle i, b, x_b, s \rangle$ s.t. $e_i = \mathbf{Enc}_\sigma(x_b; s)$ and $y_b = f_{\text{owf}}(x_b)$.

Stage 2 (Proof Phase):
    $P \leftrightarrow V$: An execution of perfect WIAOK $\langle P_{\text{pWI}}, V_{\text{pWI}} \rangle$ to prove the OR of the following statements:
        1. $\exists w \in \{0,1\}^{\text{poly}(|x|)}$ s.t. $R_L(x,w) = 1$.
        2. $\exists \langle b, x_b \rangle$ s.t. $y_b = f_{\text{owf}}(x_b)$.

Fig. 4. Protocol $\langle P, V \rangle$

Bare Public-Key model [10], "stand-alone" soundness does not imply concurrent soundness in our model. Informally speaking, this is because the standard approach of reducing concurrent soundness to stand-alone soundness by "internally" emulating all but one verifier does not work since the verifier's secret keys are private. Indeed, Micali and Reyzin [29] gave concrete counter-examples to show that stand-alone soundness does not imply concurrent soundness in the BPK model. We note that their results immediately extend to our model.

We now turn to prove that protocol $\langle P, V \rangle$ is concurrent zero-knowledge in the Bounded Player model.

3.2   Proof of Concurrent Zero Knowledge

In this section, we prove that the protocol $\langle P, V \rangle$ described in Section 3 is concurrent zero-knowledge in the bounded player model. Towards this end, we will construct a non-black-box (polynomial-time) simulator and then prove that the concurrent adversary's view output by the simulator is indistinguishable from the real view. We start by giving an overview of the proof and then proceed to give details.

Overview. Barak's argument system [2] is zero-knowledge in the bounded concurrency model where the concurrent adversary is allowed to open at most $m = m(n)$ concurrent sessions for a fixed polynomial m. Loosely speaking, Barak's simulator takes advantage of the fact that the total number of prover messages across all sessions is bounded; thus it can commit to a machine that takes only a bounded-length input y that is smaller than the challenge string r, and outputs the next message of the verifier, in any session. In our model, there is no bound on the total number of sessions, thus we cannot directly employ the same strategy. Towards this, an important observation in our setting is that once we are able to "solve" a verifier identity (i.e., learn secret key of a verifier), then the simulator does not need to do Barak-style simulation anymore for that identity. But what of the number of Barak-style simulations that the simulator needs to perform *before* it can learn any secret key? Indeed, if this number were unbounded, then we would run into the same problems that one encounters when trying to construct non-black-box cZK in the standard model. Fortunately, we are able to show that the simulator only needs to perform a bounded number of Barak-style simulations before it can learn a secret key. Thus, we obtain the following strategy: the simulator commits to an "augmented machine" that is able to simulate almost all of the simulator messages by itself; the remaining simulator messages are given as input to this machine. As discussed above, we are able to bound the total number of these messages, and thus by setting the challenge string r to be more than this bound, we ensure that the simulation is correct. More specifically, the input passed by the simulator to the machine consists of transcripts of concurrent sessions where again the simulator had to use Barak-style simulation[7] and the (discovered) secret keys of the verifiers to be used by the machine to carry on the simulation by itself (without performing Barak-style simulation).

The Simulator. We now proceed to describe our simulator. The simulator SIM consists of two main parts, namely, SIM_{easy} and $SIM_{extract}$. Loosely speaking, $SIM_{extract}$ is only used to cheat in a "special" preamble block of a session in order to learn the secret key of a verifier, while SIM_{easy} is used for the remainder of the simulation, which includes following honest prover strategy in preamble blocks and simulating the proof phase of each session using the verifier's secret key as the trapdoor witness. Specifically, $SIM_{extract}$ cheats in the $\langle P_{pB}, V_{pB} \rangle_N$ protocol by committing to an augmented verifier machine Π that contains the code of SIM_{easy}, allowing it to simulate all of the simulator messages except those generated by $SIM_{extract}$ (in different sessions). As we show below, these messages can be bounded to a fixed value. We now describe the simulator in more detail.

Setup and Inputs. Our simulator SIM interacts with an adversary $V^* = (V_1^*, \ldots, V_N^*)$ who controls verifiers $V_1, \ldots, V_N$. V^* interacts with SIM in m sessions, and

---

[7] The reason we pass this transcript as input is that in this way we can avoid the blow up of the running time of the simulator when nested Barak-style simulations are performed.

controls the scheduling of the messages. We give SIM non-black-box access to V^*. Throughout the interaction, SIM keeps track of a tuple $\boldsymbol{\beta} = (\beta_1, \ldots, \beta_N)$ representing the secret keys SIM has learned so far. At any point during the interaction either $\beta_i = \mathrm{sk}_i$ (more precisely, β_i is one of the coordinates of sk_i) or β_i is the symbol $\perp$. Initially, SIM sets each β_i to $\perp$, but it updates $\boldsymbol{\beta}$ throughout the interaction as it extracts secret keys. Additionally, SIM keeps a counter vector $\boldsymbol{a} = (a_1, \ldots, a_N)$, incrementing a_i each time it executes a preamble block using SIM_{extract} against V_i^*. We have SIM halt and output FAIL if any a_i ever surpasses n^3. Our technical lemma shows that this happens with negligible probability. Finally, we have SIM keep track of a set of tuples

$$\Psi = \left\{ \big((i,j,k)_\gamma; \phi_\gamma\big) : \gamma = 1, \ldots, n^3 N \right\}$$

where each $(i,j,k)_\gamma \in [N] \times [m] \times [t]$ and ϕ_γ is a string. The tuples $(i,j,k)_\gamma$ represent the preamble blocks played by SIM_{extract}; specifically, (i,j,k) corresponds to the k−th block of the j−th session against V_i^*. The string ϕ_γ is the collection of simulator messages sent in block $(i,j,k)_\gamma$. This set of tuples Ψ (along with β) will be the extra input given to the augmented machine. As we show below, the total size of Ψ will be a priori bounded by a polynomial in n.

Consider the interaction of SIM with some V^* impersonating V_i. Each time V^* opens a session on behalf of V_i, SIM chooses a random $k \in \{1, \ldots, t\}$ according to a distribution D_t which we define later. This will be the only preamble block of the session played by SIM_{extract} provided that $\beta_i = \perp$ when the block begins. If SIM has already learned the secret key sk_i, it does not need to call SIM_{extract}. We now describe the parts of SIM beginning with SIM_{easy}.

The sub-simulator SIM_{easy}. Recall that SIM_{easy} is run on input β and Ψ. When SIM_{easy} is called to execute the next message of a preamble block, it checks if the message is already in Ψ. If this is the case, SIM_{easy} just plays the message. Otherwise, SIM_{easy} plays fairly, choosing a random σ_p and sending $c_p = \mathrm{Com}(\sigma_p; s)$ for some s. Upon receiving σ_v, it returns σ_p and completes $\langle P_{\mathrm{pB}}, V_{\mathrm{pB}} \rangle$ using s as its witness. Its receipt of encryptions (e_1, e_2) and acceptance of $\langle P_{\mathrm{rWI}}, V_{\mathrm{rWI}} \rangle$ ends the preamble block. If SIM_{easy} does not accept V^*'s execution of $\langle P_{\mathrm{rWI}}, V_{\mathrm{rWI}} \rangle$ it aborts the interaction, as would an honest prover.

When SIM_{easy} is called to execute $\langle P_{\mathrm{pWI}}, V_{\mathrm{pWI}} \rangle$ then it checks if the secret key of the verifier is in β. If yes, SIM_{easy} completes $\langle P_{\mathrm{pWI}}, V_{\mathrm{pWI}} \rangle$ using sk_i as its witness. Otherwise, $\beta_i = \perp$ and SIM_{easy} halts outputting FAIL. Our technical lemma shows that the latter does not happen, except with negligible probability.

The sub-simulator $SIM_{extract}$. When SIM_{extract} is called to execute preamble block k of session j with verifier V_i^*, it receives Ψ, β and a as input. We assume $\beta_i = \perp$ since otherwise, SIM would not have called SIM_{extract}. Immediately upon being called, SIM_{extract} increments a_i and adds the tuple $\big((i,j,k); \phi\big)$ to Ψ. Initially, ϕ is the empty string, but each time SIM_{extract} sends a message, it appends the message to ϕ. By the end of the block, ϕ is a complete transcript of the simulator messages in preamble block (i,j,k).

The preamble block begins normally, with SIM_{extract} choosing a random string and sending c_p, a commitment to it. Upon receiving σ_v, however, SIM_{extract} runs **Gen** obtaining key pair (σ, τ) for the encryption scheme and returns $\sigma_p = \sigma \oplus \sigma_v$. Next, SIM_{extract} enters $\langle P_{\text{pB}}, V_{\text{pB}} \rangle$ which it completes using the already extracted secret key. Formally, when V^* sends h, beginning $\langle P_{\text{pB}}, V_{\text{pB}} \rangle$, SIM_{extract} chooses a random s and sends $\text{Com}(h(\Pi); s)$, where Π is the next message function of V^*, augmented with the ability to compute all the intermediate messages sent by SIM_{easy}. The machine Π takes input $y = (\Psi, \beta)$ and outputs the next verifier message in an interaction between V^* and a machine M who plays exactly like SIM_{easy} with the following exception. For each tuple $((i,j,k); \phi) \in \Psi$, M reads its messages of block (i,j,k) from the string y. In order to simulate SIM_{easy} in the subprotocols $\langle P_{\text{pWI}}, V_{\text{pWI}} \rangle$, M also uses the tuple $\beta = (\beta_1, \ldots, \beta_N)$ received as input, where each β_i is the secret key of the i'-th verifier (if available), and $\perp$ otherwise.

After committing to Π, and receiving r, SIM_{extract} completes $\langle P_{\text{pUA}}, V_{\text{pUA}} \rangle$ using witness $(\Pi, \Psi \| \beta, s)$ where Ψ and β might have been updated by other executions of SIM_{extract} occurring between the time SIM_{extract} sent $\text{Com}(h(\Pi); s)$ and received r. Our counter ensures that $|\Psi|$ is *a priori* bounded, while $|\beta|$ is bounded by definition. By construction, Π correctly predicts V^*'s message r, and so $(\Pi, \Psi \| \beta, s)$ is a valid witness for $\langle P_{\text{sUA}}, V_{\text{sUA}} \rangle$. Finally, SIM_{extract} receives encryptions e_1, e_2 and the proof of correctness in $\langle P_{\text{rWI}}, V_{\text{rWI}} \rangle$. It now decrypts the ciphertexts using τ thereby learning secret key sk_i of V_i^*. If the decrypted value is a valid secret key sk_i, then it updates β by setting $\beta_i = \text{sk}_i$. Otherwise, it outputs the abort symbol $\perp$ and stops. (It is easy to see that since the proof system $\langle P_{\text{rWI}}, V_{\text{rWI}} \rangle$ is sound, the probability of simulator outputting $\perp$ at this step is negligible.)

Analysis. There are two situations in which SIM outputs fail: if some counter a_i exceeds n^3, or if SIM_{easy} enters an execution $\langle P_{\text{pWI}}, V_{\text{pWI}} \rangle$ without knowledge of sk. Note that the latter will not happen, as to enter an execution of $\langle P_{\text{pWI}}, V_{\text{pWI}} \rangle$, all preamble blocks, in particular the one played by SIM_{extract}, must be complete, ensuring that SIM_{extract} will have learned sk. In our main technical lemma, we show that no counter will surpass n^3 by proving that after SIM has run SIM_{extract} n^3 times against each V_i controlled by V^* it has, with overwhelming probability, learned sk. Before stating the lemma, we introduce some terminology.

Now, focusing on a given verifier, we say that V^* has *stopped* session j in block k if the $k-$th preamble block of session j has begun, but the $(k+1)-$th has not. We say that V^* is playing *strategy* $\mathbf{k}' = (k_1', \ldots, k_m')$ if session j is stopped in block k_j' for all $j = 1, \ldots, m$. As the interaction takes polynomial time, V^* only gets to play polynomially many strategies over the course of the interaction. Let $k_j \in \{1, \ldots, t\}$ be the random number chosen by SIM at the beginning of session j as per distribution D_t. This gives us a tuple $\mathbf{k} = (k_1, \ldots, k_m)$ where the k_j are chosen independently according to the distribution D_t (defined below). At any time during the interaction, we say that V^* has *won* (resp. *lost, tied*) session j if $k_j' = k_j$ (resp. $k_j' > k_j$, $k_j' < k_j$). A win for V^* corresponds to SIM having run

SIM_{extract}, but not yet having learned sk. As SIM only gets to call SIM_{extract} n^3 times, a win for V^* means that SIM has used up one of its budget of n^3 without any payoff. A loss for V^* corresponds to SIM running SIM_{extract} and learning sk, thereby allowing SIM to call SIM_{easy} in all remaining sessions. A tie means that SIM has not yet called SIM_{extract} in the session, and therefore has not used any of its budget, but has not learned sk.

Notice that these wins and ties are "temporary" events. Indeed, by the end of each session, V^* will have lost, as he will have completed the preamble block run by SIM_{extract}. However, we choose to use this terminology to better convey the key intuition of our analysis: for SIM to output FAIL, it must be that at some point during the interaction, for some identity, V^* has won at least n^3 sessions and has not lost any. We will therefore focus precisely on proving that the probability that a PPT adversary V^* runs in the experiment m sessions so that the counter for one identity reaches the value n^3 is negligible.

For a verifier strategy $\boldsymbol{k'}$ and a polynomial m, let $P_{(\boldsymbol{k'},m)}(W, L)$ be the probability that in an $m-$session interaction between V^* and SIM that V^* wins for some identity exactly W sessions and loses exactly L, given that V^* plays strategy $\boldsymbol{k'}$. The probability is over SIM's choice of $\boldsymbol{k}$ with $k_j \in \{1, \ldots, t\}$ chosen independently according to D_t (defined below) for all $j = 1, \ldots, m$.

The Distribution D_t and the Main Technical Lemma. Define D_t to be the distribution on $\{1, \ldots, t\}$ such that $p_{k'} = \text{Prob}_{k \in D_t}(k = k') = \varepsilon n^{k'}$, where ε is such that $\sum p_{k'} = 1$. Note that ε is negligible in n.

Lemma 1 (Main Technical Lemma). *Let $\boldsymbol{k'}$ be a verifier strategy and $m = m(n)$ a polynomial. Then we have $P_{(\boldsymbol{k'},m)}(n^3, 0)$ is negligible in n.*

The above proves that any verifier strategy has a negligible chance of having n^3 wins and no losses. As V^* plays polynomially many (i.e., N) strategies throughout the course of the interaction, the union bound proves that V^* has a negligible chance of ever achieving n^3 wins and 0 losses. From this it follows that, with overwhelming probability, V^* will never have at least n^3 wins and no losses, which implies that SIM outputs FAIL with negligible probability as desired. The main idea of the proof is similar to the random tape switching technique of [33] and [28].

Proof. We fix a verifier strategy $\boldsymbol{k'}$ and a polynomial m and write $P(W, L)$ instead of $P_{(\boldsymbol{k'},m)}(W, L)$. Let $p_{k'}$ (resp. $q_{k'}$) be the probability that V^* wins (resp. loses) a session given that he stops the session in block k'. We chose the distribution D_t carefully to have the following two properties. First, since $p_1 = \varepsilon n$ is negligible, we may assume that V^* never stops in the first block of a session. And secondly, for $k' \geq 2$ we have,

$$q_{k'} = \sum_{i=1}^{k'-1} p_{k'} = \varepsilon \frac{n^{k'} - 1}{n - 1} \geq \frac{\varepsilon n^{k'}}{2n} = \frac{p_{k'}}{2n}.$$

It follows that no matter which block V^* stops a session in, it will hold that the probability he wins in that session is less then $2n$ times the probability that he looses that session. We will use this upper bound on the probability of V^* winning a single session to show that $P(n^3, 0)$ is negligible.

Let A be the event, $(W, L) = (n^3, 0)$, B be the event $W + L = n^3$ and $\neg B$ the event $W + L \neq n^3$. Since, $A \subset B$, and since $P(A|\neg B) = 0$, we have that

$$P(n^3, 0) = P(A) = P(A|B)P(B) + P(A|\neg B)P(\neg B) = P(A|B)P(B) \leq P(A|B),$$

and so it suffices to prove that $P(A|B)$ is negligible. We continue the proof for the case $W + L = n^3$ (and thus $m \geq n^3$).

If $W + L = n^3$ then V^* ties all but n^3 of the sessions. Let $\mathcal{C} = \{C \subset [m] : |C| = n^3\}$. Then $\mathcal{C}$ is the set of possible positions for the sessions which are not ties. We are looking to bound $P\big((W, L) = (n^3, 0)\big|W + L = n^3\big)$ and so we condition on the $C \in \mathcal{C}$. Once a fixed C is chosen, the position of each session which is not a tie is determined. Each such session must either be a win or a loss for V^*. Let p be the probability that some such session is a win. Since we proved already that the probability that V^* wins in a given session is less then $2n$ times the probability that V^* looses in that session, we have that $p \leq 2n(1 - p)$. Solving gives $p \leq \left(1 - \frac{1}{2n+1}\right)$. It follows that for any $C \in \mathcal{C}$, the probability that all sessions in C are wins is

$$\left(1 - \frac{1}{2n + 1}\right)^{n^3} \leq \left[\left(1 - \frac{1}{2n + 1}\right)^{2n+1}\right]^n \leq e^{-n}.$$

From the viewpoint of random tape switching, we have shown that for every random tape causing every session of C to be a win, there are exponentially many which cause a different outcome, we therefore have: $P(n^3, 0) \leq P\big((W, L) = (n^3, 0)\big|W + L = n^3\big) = \sum_{C \in \mathcal{C}} P\big((W, L) = (n^3, 0)\big|C\big)P(C) \leq e^{-n} \sum_{C \in \mathcal{C}} P(C) = e^{-n}$ as desired.

Bounding the length parameter $\ell(N)$. From the above lemma, it follows that the total length of the auxiliary input y to the machine Π committed by SIM_{extract} (at any time) is bounded by $n^3 \cdot N \cdot P(n)$, where $P(n)$ is a polynomial upper bound on the total length of prover messages in one protocol session plus the length of a secret. Thus, when $\ell(N) \geq n^3 \cdot N \cdot P(n)$, we have that $|y| \leq |r| - n$, as required.

In the full version [22] we show through a series of hybrid experiments that the simulation is perfectly indistinguishable from the real game.

Acknowledgments. Work supported in part by NSF grants 0830803, 09165174, 1065276, 1118126 and 1136174, US-Israel BSF grant 2008411, OKAWA Foundation Research Award, IBM Faculty Research Award, Xerox Faculty Research Award, B. John Garrick Foundation Award, Teradata Research Award, European Commission through the FP7 programme under contract 216676 ECRYPT II, MIUR Project PRIN "GenData 2020" and Lockheed-Martin Corporation Research Award. This material is based upon work supported by the Defense Advanced Research Projects Agency through the U.S. Office of Naval Research under Contract N00014 − 11 − 1 − 0392. The views expressed are those of the author and do not reflect the official policy or position of the Department of Defense or the U.S. Government.

References

1. Agrawal, S., Goyal, V., Jain, A., Prabhakaran, M., Sahai, A.: New Impossibility Results for Concurrent Composition and a Non-interactive Completeness Theorem for Secure Computation. In: Safavi-Naini, R. (ed.) CRYPTO 2012. LNCS, vol. 7417, pp. 443–460. Springer, Heidelberg (2012)
2. Barak, B.: How to go beyond the black-box simulation barrier. In: FOCS, pp. 106–115 (2001)
3. Barak, B., Goldreich, O.: Universal arguments and their applications. In: IEEE Conference on Computational Complexity, pp. 194–203 (2002)
4. Barak, B., Lindell, Y.: Strict polynomial-time in simulation and extraction. In: STOC, pp. 484–493 (2002)
5. Barak, B., Prabhakaran, M., Sahai, A.: Concurrent non-malleable zero knowledge. In: FOCS, pp. 345–354 (2006)
6. Blum, M.: How to prove a theorem so no one else can claim it. In: Proceedings of the International Congress of Mathematicians, pp. 1444–1451 (1987)
7. Blum, M., Santis, A.D., Micali, S., Persiano, G.: Noninteractive zero-knowledge. SIAM J. Comput. 20(6), 1084–1118 (1991)
8. Canetti, R., Lindell, Y., Ostrovsky, R., Sahai, A.: Universally composable two-party and multi-party secure computation. In: STOC, pp. 494–503 (2002)
9. Canetti, R.: Universally composable signature, certification, and authentication. In: CSFW (2004)
10. Canetti, R., Goldreich, O., Goldwasser, S., Micali, S.: Resettable zero-knowledge (extended abstract). In: STOC, pp. 235–244 (2000)
11. Canetti, R., Kilian, J., Petrank, E., Rosen, A.: Black-box concurrent zero-knowledge requires $\tilde{\Omega}(\log n)$ rounds. In: STOC, pp. 570–579 (2001)
12. Canetti, R., Lin, H., Pass, R.: Adaptive hardness and composable security in the plain model from standard assumptions. In: FOCS, pp. 541–550 (2010)
13. Di Crescenzo, G., Ostrovsky, R.: On Concurrent Zero-Knowledge with Pre-processing (Extended Abstract). In: Wiener, M. (ed.) CRYPTO 1999. LNCS, vol. 1666, pp. 485–502. Springer, Heidelberg (1999)
14. Di Crescenzo, G., Persiano, G., Visconti, I.: Constant-Round Resettable Zero Knowledge with Concurrent Soundness in the Bare Public-Key Model. In: Franklin, M. (ed.) CRYPTO 2004. LNCS, vol. 3152, pp. 237–253. Springer, Heidelberg (2004)
15. Di Crescenzo, G., Visconti, I.: Concurrent Zero Knowledge in the Public-Key Model. In: Caires, L., Italiano, G.F., Monteiro, L., Palamidessi, C., Yung, M. (eds.) ICALP 2005. LNCS, vol. 3580, pp. 816–827. Springer, Heidelberg (2005)
16. Dwork, C., Naor, M., Sahai, A.: Concurrent zero-knowledge. In: STOC, pp. 409–418 (1998)
17. Feige, U., Lapidot, D., Shamir, A.: Multiple non-interactive zero knowledge proofs based on a single random string (extended abstract). In: FOCS, pp. 308–317 (1990)
18. Garg, S., Goyal, V., Jain, A., Sahai, A.: Concurrently Secure Computation in Constant Rounds. In: Pointcheval, D., Johansson, T. (eds.) EUROCRYPT 2012. LNCS, vol. 7237, pp. 99–116. Springer, Heidelberg (2012)

19. Garg, S., Kumarasubramanian, A., Ostrovsky, R., Visconti, I.: Impossibility Results for Static Input Secure Computation. In: Safavi-Naini, R. (ed.) CRYPTO 2012. LNCS, vol. 7417, pp. 424–442. Springer, Heidelberg (2012)
20. Goldreich, O., Kahan, A.: How to construct constant-round zero-knowledge proof systems for np. J. Cryptology 9(3), 167–190 (1996)
21. Goldwasser, S., Micali, S., Rackoff, C.: The knowledge complexity of interactive proof-systems (extended abstract). In: STOC, pp. 291–304 (1985)
22. Goyal, V., Jain, A., Ostrovsky, R., Richelson, S., Visconti, I.: Concurrent zero knowledge in the bounded player model. IACR Cryptology ePrint Archive 2012, 279 (2012)
23. Kidron, D., Lindell, Y.: Impossibility results for universal composability in public-key models and with fixed inputs. J. Cryptology 24(3), 517–544 (2011)
24. Kilian, J., Micali, S., Ostrovsky, R.: Minimum resource zero-knowledge proofs (extended abstract). In: FOCS, pp. 474–479 (1989)
25. Kilian, J., Petrank, E.: Concurrent and resettable zero-knowledge in polyloalgorithm rounds. In: STOC, pp. 560–569 (2001)
26. Lin, H., Pass, R., Venkitasubramaniam, M.: A unified framework for concurrent security: universal composability from stand-alone non-malleability. In: STOC, pp. 179–188 (2009)
27. Lindell, Y.: Lower Bounds for Concurrent Self Composition. In: Naor, M. (ed.) TCC 2004. LNCS, vol. 2951, pp. 203–222. Springer, Heidelberg (2004)
28. Micali, S., Pass, R.: Precise zero knowledge (2007)
29. Micali, S., Reyzin, L.: Soundness in the Public-Key Model. In: Kilian, J. (ed.) CRYPTO 2001. LNCS, vol. 2139, pp. 542–565. Springer, Heidelberg (2001)
30. Pass, R.: Simulation in Quasi-Polynomial Time, and its Application to Protocol Composition. In: Biham, E. (ed.) EUROCRYPT 2003. LNCS, vol. 2656, pp. 160–176. Springer, Heidelberg (2003)
31. Pass, R.: Bounded-concurrent secure multi-party computation with a dishonest majority. In: STOC, pp. 232–241 (2004)
32. Pass, R., Rosen, A.: New and improved constructions of non-malleable cryptographic protocols. In: STOC, pp. 533–542 (2005)
33. Prabhakaran, M., Rosen, A., Sahai, A.: Concurrent zero knowledge with logarithmic round-complexity. In: FOCS, pp. 366–375 (2002)
34. Richardson, R., Kilian, J.: On the Concurrent Composition of Zero-Knowledge Proofs. In: Stern, J. (ed.) EUROCRYPT 1999. LNCS, vol. 1592, pp. 415–431. Springer, Heidelberg (1999)
35. Santis, A.D., Persiano, G.: Zero-knowledge proofs of knowledge without interaction. In: FOCS, pp. 427–436. IEEE Computer Society (1992)
36. Scafuro, A., Visconti, I.: On Round-Optimal Zero Knowledge in the Bare Public-Key Model. In: Pointcheval, D., Johansson, T. (eds.) EUROCRYPT 2012. LNCS, vol. 7237, pp. 153–171. Springer, Heidelberg (2012)
37. Visconti, I.: Efficient Zero Knowledge on the Internet. In: Bugliesi, M., Preneel, B., Sassone, V., Wegener, I. (eds.) ICALP 2006, Part II. LNCS, vol. 4052, pp. 22–33. Springer, Heidelberg (2006)

Public-Coin Concurrent Zero-Knowledge in the Global Hash Model[*]

Ran Canetti[1,2], Huijia Lin[1,3], and Omer Paneth[1]

[1] Boston University
[2] Tel Aviv University
[3] MIT

Abstract. *Public-coin zero-knowledge* and *concurrent zero-knowledge* *(cZK)* are two classes of zero knowledge protocols that guarantee some additional desirable properties. Still, to this date no protocol is known that is both public-coin and cZK for a language outside BPP. Furthermore, it is known that no such protocol can be black-box ZK [Pass et.al, Crypto 09].

We present a public-coin concurrent ZK protocol for any NP language. The protocol assumes that all verifiers have access to a globally specified function, drawn from a collision resistant hash function family. (This model, which we call the Global Hash Function, or GHF model, can be seen as a restricted case of the non-programmable reference string model.) We also show that the impossibility of black-box public-coin cZK extends also to the GHF model.

Our protocol assumes CRH functions against quasi-polynomial adversaries and takes $O(\log^{1+\epsilon} n)$ rounds for any $\epsilon > 0$, where n is the security parameter. Our techniques combine those for (non-public-coin) black-box cZK with Barak's non-black-box technique for public-coin constant-round ZK. As a corollary we obtain the first simultaneously resettable zero-knowledge protocol with $O(\log^{1+\epsilon} n)$ rounds, in the GHF model.

1 Introduction

Zero-knowledge (ZK) proofs and arguments are protocols that enable a prover to convince a verifier in the verity of a statement without revealing any information other than the fact that the statement is true. This is captured by requiring that for any efficient adversarial verifier there exists an efficient simulator that, knowing only whether the statement is correct, essentially recreates the adversary's view of the entire execution. ZK protocols are a fundamental building block in cryptographic protocols and applications; furthermore, the techniques used to construct ZK protocols often evolve and percolate to protocols for other cryptographic tasks.

[*] Supported by an ISF grant, NSF grant 1218461, the Check Point Institute for Information Security and the Center for Reliable Information Systems and Cyber-Security.

A. Sahai (Ed.): TCC 2013, LNCS 7785, pp. 80–99, 2013.

The first ZK protocols by [16, 15] and others have a very simple form, where the verifier's messages consist only of random strings with no additional structure. In the end of the protocol the verifier evaluates a deterministic predicate of the communication. The simplicity of this *public-coin*, or *Arthur-Merlin* structure is indeed attractive in of itself; in addition it has been shown over the years to have many other advantages, such as public verifiability, amenability to delegation, and better resilience to leakage [12, 4]. (In fact, we make use of some of these advantages in this work.)

However, it also soon became clear that obtaining stronger efficiency and security properties for ZK protocol while preserving the simple public-coin structure is challenging. One such parameter is the number of rounds: The basic protocols of [16, 15] take take super-logarithmic number of rounds — essentially, via sequential repetition of a basic building block that gives soundness error of one half. The first protocols that obtain a constant number of rounds have the verifier *commit* to its randomness ahead of time, thus losing the PC property [13]. Furthermore, [14] show that no constant rounds public-coin ZK protocol with negligible error probability can be proven secure via black-box simulation. A protocol public-coin ZK protocol with constant number of rounds came only years later and uses a completely new proof technique, which indeed involved non-black-box simulation [1].

Another security property that appears to stand at odds with public-coin ZK is parallel and concurrent ZK (cZK). Here we want the protocol to remain ZK even when the prover participates in many independent sessions for proving the same statement, and these sessions are scheduled in an adversarially controlled concurrent way. Also here known protocols are not public-coin ZK [23, 17, 22], and for a similar reason: an essential ingredient in these protocols is having the verifier commit to its randomness ahead of time. Furthermore, also here we know that no PC protocol can be proven to be concurrent (or even parallel) ZK via black-box simulation [21]. However, here we do not currently know of any way to get around this black-box impossibility result. In particular, the technique of [1] fails, at least in of itself. We are thus left with the question:

Do there exist public-coin concurrent zero-knowledge protocols?

A first indication that the answer might be positive was given by Pass, Rosen and Tseng [20], who construct a public-coin *parallel* ZK protocol. That is, their protocol (which is a relatively simple adapration of the [1] protocol) remains ZK even under parallel composition. However, their security analysis falls apart in the general concurrent setting.

We provide a positive answer to this question in the general concurrent setting, albeit with a caveat: We consider a setting where all verifiers have access to a single hash function h. In that setting, we design a public-coin protocol and show that this protocol is cZK, unless it is possible to efficiently find collisions in h. That is, we show how to efficiently construct a simulator, given an adversary, and then provide an *explicit efficient reduction* that turns an adversary that breaks the cZK property of the protocol w.r.t. the constructed simulator into an algorithm that finds collisions in h. We call this model the global hash function (GHF) model. See further discussion on the GHF model at the end of the Introduction. That is, we show:

Theorem (Informal): Assuming existence of collision resistant hash function families against quasipolynomial adversaries, there exist public-coin cZK protocols in the GHF model. In contrast, there exist no black-box public-coin cZK protocols in the GHF model.

Round Complexity. We present two public-coin cZK protocols. The first one has a polynomial number of rounds. The second one, which is considerably more involved, takes only $O(\log^{1+\epsilon} n)$ rounds for any $\epsilon > 0$, where n is the security parameter. This almost matches the best known round complexity for cZK, regardless of the public-coin property [22]. Recall that for black-box simulation this is the best possible [7]

Simultaneously Resettable ZK in Logarithmic Rounds. A question that is very related to public-coin cZK is the question of *simultaneously resettable* ZK. Such ZK protocols remain secure even if a cheating party (playing the role of either the prover or the verifier) has the ability to repeatedly reset the honest party to its initial state and random tape, and interact with it several times. The only known simultaneously resettable ZK protocol [10] in the plain model has polynomial number of rounds. (In the bare public key model, a protocol with constant number of rounds is known [9].)

As a corollary of our main result we get a new simultaneously resettable ZK protocol in the GHF model with only logarithmic number of rounds. The simultaneously resettable ZK protocol is obtained from our public-coin cZK protocol by applying two generic transformations: first we apply the transformation of [21] to go from a public-coin cZK to a resettably-sound cZK protocol that is also sound against resetting provers. Then we can apply the transformation of [10] to get simultaneously resettable ZK. Both transformations do not increase the round complexity of the protocol.

Our Techniques. In a nutshell, our protocols use the multiple-opportunity-slots simulation technique of the cZK protocols of [23, 17, 22] (which are inherently not public-coin) to make the public-coin protocol of [1] fully concurrent. In particular, in the context of the non-black-box simulator of [1], we generalize the concept of rewinding to re-running of certain portions of the simulation of the adversary's code.

The global hash function is used in the universal argument (UA) portion of the protocol of [1], allowing all instances of the UA in all concurrent sessions to the use the same hash function. This allows our simulator to amortize the work spent on preparing the universal arguments across multiple concurrent sessions.

On the Global Hash Function Model. We design and analyze our protocols in the global hash function (GHF) model, where all parties have access to a public hash function h, and the security of the protocol is argued by way of an efficient and explicit reduction from an adversary that breaks the security of the protocol to an adversary that finds collisions in h. Results in this model can be interpreted in several alternative ways. One interpretation, in the spirit of [24], is that the protocol indeed uses a single and fixed hash function h (say, SHA2) and the security (in our case, cZK) property "in practice" is based on the inability of Mankind to find explicit collisions in h — although such collisions exist in principle and can be found "in polynomial time". Note that this interpretation makes sense both when security is formalized in an asymptotic way *and* in terms of concrete, non-asymptotic security guarantees.

Another interpretation of results in this model is that they guarantee security against uniform-complexity polytime adversaries, as long as the (single) global hash function used by the protocol is collision resistant in an asymptotic way against such adversaries. We note however that this interpretation is relatively weak. In particular, it is not clear how to translate it into concrete, non-asymptotic security guarantees.

Yet another interpretation of results in this model is that they guarantee security in the "global reference string model", where the reference string is randomly chosen and consists of the description of a hash function h drawn from a collision resistant hash function family. Here the zero-knowledge simulator has to work with a given h rather than making up its own one. In fact, the simulation should succeed even when the function h is chosen adversarially.

The GHF model for zero knowledge protocols should be contrasted with the common reference string (CRS) model used elsewhere in cryptography (e.g. for non-interactive and universally composable zero knowledge [5, 6]). Indeed, the models are quite different: In the CRS model the public reference string is chosen as part of the protocol execution, and a distinguisher between a real execution and an ideal has no a-priori information on that string. In particular, the CRS model provides no guarantees whatsoever when the reference string is chosen adversarially, or even when the adversary is allowed to see trapdoor information related to the reference string.

Furthermore, the impossibility of public-coin black-box cZK protocols extends to the GHF model, whereas in the CRS model such protocols are known to exist (in fact, any NIZK protocol is such).

Organization. This extended abstract contains only high level descriptions of our results as well as our protocols and it's proof. Detailed definitions, constructions and analysis are given in the full version of this paper [8].

2   Overview of Our Public-Coin cZK Protocol

In the black-box simulation world, there has been a rich set of constructions [23, 17, 22] of fully concurrent ZK protocols; however, these constructions are not public-coin. In fact, as shown in [21], this is inherent: only languages in BPP have public-coin black-box parallel ZK protocols (that is, protocols that remain ZK under parallel composition). In contrast, in the non-black-box simulation world, known constructions [1, 20] are indeed public-coin; however, they are only ZK under composition with restricted concurrency (e.g., bounded concurrent composition, and parallel composition). Our construction can be viewed as "upgrading" the existing non-black-box simulation techniques to be fully concurrent, using the recursive the rewinding strategies from black-box cZK *while remaining public-coin*. We first a give quick overview of the current techniques and their limitations. Next, we present high-level ideas behind our construction.

2.1   Current Techniques

Public-coin ZK Protocols

BARAK'S PROTOCOL. We briefly recall the idea behind Barak's protocol. Roughly speaking, for language L and common input $x \in \{0,1\}^n$, the prover P and verifier V proceed in three stages.

- *Stage 1:* V starts by sending P a function h chosen randomly from a family of collision-resistant hash functions.
- *Stage 2:* P sends a commitment $c \in \{0,1\}^n$ to 0; V follows by sending a uniformly random "challenge" $r \leftarrow \{0,1\}^n$; we informally refer to the pair of messages (c, r) as a *slot*, for reasons that will become clear later.
- *Stage 3:* P proves that either $x \in L$ or c is a commitment to a hash of a program Π such that $\Pi(c) = r$.

The proof of Stage 3 proceeds via a public-coin witness indistinguishable universal argument (UA) [2]. This is the crux of the protocol, and where all the Difficulties lie. A UA system has the crucial property that the verification time and communication complexity are independent of the length of the witness. Still, the prover's complexity grows with the length of the witness.

Soundness follows from the fact that even if a malicious prover P tries to commit to some program Π (instead of committing to 0), with high probability, the V's challenge r will be different from $\Pi(c)$. To prove ZK, consider the non-black-box simulator that sets c to be a commitment to the hash of the code of the malicious verifier V^*; note that by definition it holds that $\Pi(c) = V^*(c) = r$, and the simulator can use Π as a "fake" witness in the final proof.

BOUNDED CONCURRENCY. Barak's protocol can be extended to a bounded concurrent ZK protocol by slightly changing the UA statement proven in State 3, and allowing Π to receive, other than c, some additional auxiliary input. Soundness holds as long as the length of the auxiliary input is significantly shorter than $|r|$. Now, the simulator can complete the UA by proving that V^* on input c, *and having received all messages from other sessions before generating its second message*, outputs r. As long as the total number of concurrent sessions is bounded, r can be chosen to be longer than the total length of messages V^* might receive inside any slot. Therefore, the simulation goes through. However, this approach is inherently limited to the bounded concurrency setting. In the unbounded concurrent setting, there is no a priori bound on the length of the messages that V^* receives. However, the protocol cannot allow the committed program Π to receive an arbitrarily long input, as otherwise soundness falls apart.

COMMITTING TO THE SIMULATOR'S CODE. One potential approach to circumvent the above limitation is having the simulator S commit to the code of *itself* (i.e., S) instead of commiting to the code of V^*. The intuition behind this idea is that, although in the unbounded concurrent setting the length of the messages that V^* receives is unbounded, these messages are generated by the simulator S, and thus can be shortly represented by the code of S. Therefore, if the simulator S commits to a machine Π that emulates its own execution until the message r is simulated, it can again prove in the UA argument that $\Pi() = r$, since all the messages V^* receives will be generated by Π in emulation of S. (Note that here we treat the simulator code as already including the code of V^* in some form.) Indeed, this idea is the main enabler in the public-coin parallel ZK protocol of Pass, Rosen and Tseng [20].

However, when moving to the concurrent setting, this technique runs into the problem that the running time of S grows exponentially with the number of "nested concurrent sessions". This problem is similar to the problem encountered by black-box simulation in the general, non-public-coin settings. In particular, this blow-up in simulation running time is demonstrated by the example of Dwork et. al [11]. To see the problem, consider a concurrent verifier V^* that starts two nested sessions, where session 1 is completely "enclosed" in the slot of session 2. In session 1, the simulator commits to a program Π_1 that emulates S until the challenge message in the first session r_1 is sent. S then completes the simulation of session 1 by proving that Π_1 outputs r_1. Similarly, in session 2, the simulator commits to a program Π_2 that emulates S until it simulates r_2. If Π_1 takes T steps to output r_1, then it takes S at least another T steps to give a UA argument that this is true. Therefore, in the second session, Π_2 takes at least $2T$ steps to output r_2 (since Π is emulating S, it needs to simulate the entire first session including its UA proof before V^* outputs r_2) and the time for giving the UA argument in session 2 is at least $2T$. Overall, the simulation time is at least $4T$. As in the case of [11], it is not hard to see that with d levels of nesting (i.e., d sessions, with session i entirely enclosed in the slot of session $i + 1$), the simulation time grows to at least $2^d T$. (In fact, the situation is even worse since the prover complexity in the best UAs is at least $O(T \log T)$.)

We remark that the idea described above, as well as the problem of exponential time simulation, were already described by Deng, Goyal and Sahai [10] in the context of simultaneously resettable ZK. In their protocol, the simulator commits to the code of the adversarial verifier together with some parts of the code and state of the simulator. The exponential time simulation problem is resolved using a combination of new black-box and non-black-box simulation techniques. However, the resulting concurrent ZK protocol is not public-coin.

cZK Protocols. The design of all existing cZK protocols follow the Feige-Lapidot-Shamir (FLS) paradigm: at the beginning of the protocol, the verifier sets up a "trapdoor" (e.g., by sending a commitment to a secret random value), followed by many invocations of a sub-protocol that hides the trapdoor, but allows a simulator to extract the trapdoor by rewinding some messages in the sub-protocol, referred to as a *slot*. Then, the prover proves, using a witness-indistinguishable proof, that either the statement is true or it knows the trapdoor. Roughly speaking, the protocol is ZK, since the simulator can extract the trapdoor via rewinding of any slot in the session and use it as a "fake" witness to "cheat" in simulation. The simulator will use a *rewinding strategy* to decide which slots to rewind in order to guarantee successful extraction of a trapdoor for each session in the concurrent setting.

THE "RECURSIVE REWINDING" PROBLEM. A good rewinding strategy of a cZK protocol needs to also guarantee that the time spent on rewinding is bounded. As observed already by [11], this turns out to be non-trivial and encounters a similar difficulty as the exponential-time simulation problem in the context of non-black-box simulation. To demonstrate the difficulty, consider a simplified protocol that has the structure describe above, but contains only one slot for rewinding, and a cheating verifier V^* that starts two nested sessions, where the first session is entirely enclosed in the slot of the second session. To simulate the second session, the simulator needs to rewind the slot in this session to extract a trapdoor; however, before V^* completes this slot, the simulator needs to first simulate messages in the first session for V^*, which requires it to recursively rewind the slot in the first session. This quickly leads to an exponential number of rewindings and the simulation time explodes.

Known black-box cZK protocols resolve this problem by having many sequential slots in the protocol, so that there are many extraction opportunities for the simulator. It is shown that when the number of slots is large enough, there are *recursive rewinding strategies* [23, 17, 22] that, by carefully choosing which parts of the execution to rewind, guarantee that the depth of nesting (i.e., the depth of recursive rewinding) is bounded and thus the simulation time is bounded. Below we recall the KP-PRS rewinding strategy, which will be useful for our construction later.

THE KP-PRS REWIDING STRATEGY. The simulator of [17, 22] simulates the view of the cheating verifier in a "main thread", using the trapdoors extracted via many recursive rewindings also called "lookahead threads". The KP-PRS rewinding strategy tells the simulator which parts of the execution to rewind based on the transcript simulated so far. The simulation strategy is recursive since rewindings are also used during the simulation of lookahead threads.

In KP-PRS, the rewinding strategy decides when to rewind the verifier *obliviously* of the content of the simulated messages, depending only on the number of simulated messages. More specifically, it divides messages in the main thread (resp. lookahead threads) into blocks of 2^i messages. Then, at the end of each block, it recursively rewinds the verifier from the beginning of the block once;

by rewinding an entire block, the simulator rewinds all the slots contained in that block "in one shot". It has been shown in [18] that the KP-PRS rewinding strategy can be generalized to consider blocks of length b^i for $b > 2$. Intuitively, the KP-PRS rewinding strategy is efficient since rewindings are performed only at selected points (i.e., the end of blocks) and the depth of nesting is bounded by $O(\log_b n)$. Furthermore, as long as the number of slots is $\omega(b \log_b n)$, it is guaranteed that at the end of every session, a trapdoor would be extracted successfully.

2.2 Our Approach

At a very high-level, the recursive rewinding problem in the context of black-box simulation and the exponential time simulation problem in the context of non-black-box simulation are similar: both are caused by the recursive execution of the simulator's code. In the context of black-box simulation the problem can be solved by providing more slots. We show how to solve the exponential time simulation problem in the context of public-coin non-black-box simulation. Towards this, we introduce a non-black-box analog of "rewinding slots" and use these slots to manage the complexity of the simulation. To illustrate the idea, consider the following overly simplified protocol (P_0, V_0) which is a k-slot variant of Barak's protocol. Our solution will require to replace the UA in State 3 of the protocol with a new type of interactive argument we call a "special proof". The properties of the special proof and its construction is the focus of the rest of this section.

An Overly Simplified Protocol (P_0, V_0):
- *Stage 1 (Hash Function Selection):* V sends P a randomly chose collision-resistant hash function $h \leftarrow \mathcal{H}$.
- *Stage 2 (k Slots):* This stage contains k sequential slots, where in the ith slot the prover sends a commitment c_i and the verifier replies with a challenge r_i.
- *Stage 3 (Proof Stage):* The prover proves using a *special proof* that either $x \in \mathcal{L}$, or there is a slot i, in which c_i is a commitment to a hash of a program Π that outputs r_i.

The idea of committing to the simulator's code can be adapted to work with this protocol as follows: on the main thread, the simulator simulates the view of V^* in a straight line. In every slot, the simulator commits to a program Π that mimics the simulation of the main thread. When the simulation of a session reaches Stage 3, the simulator proves that there is a slot i with transcript (c_i, r_i) such that c_i is a commitment to a program that "predicts" the challenge r_i.

With many slots, the simulator now gains the freedom to choose which slot to use as a witness for the special proof in each session. Similarly to the case of black-box simulation, the simulator will use a *proving strategy* to choose which slot to use in the proof of every session. The simulation might still recursively prove statements about its own computation, however, the proving strategy will control the recursion depth and thus also the complexity of the simulation. To do that, the proving strategy will reuse ideas from the black-box recursive rewinding strategies.

We start by spelling out the analogy between our situation and the case of black-box rewinding. At every slot, the simulator will commit to a program Π that mimics the execution of the main thread from the point in the simulation where the slot starts to the point where the slot ends. Now, the execution of Π can be thought of as analogous to the rewinding of the simulation in the slot. However, the non-black-box simulator does not directly execute Π. Instead, it generates a special proof about the execution of Π. Thus, the running time that is spent on the rewinding by the black-box simulator is spent by the non-black-box simulator on constructing a proof about the execution of Π. Similarly, constructing a UA proof for a program that recursively constructs proofs for other programs is analogous to recursive rewindings. Following this observation we will design a proving strategy based on the KP-PRS rewinding strategy.

A KP-PRS-Style Proving Strategy. Roughly speaking, the simulator divides the messages in the main thread into blocks of length b^i (where b is a parameter of the simulation); at the end of every block, the simulator constructs special proofs for slots contained in the block, this corresponds to rewinding the block[1]. After constructing the special proof at the end of the block, the simulator can use it to simulate the proof stage (Stage 3) of the corresponding session.

To turn the overly simplified version above into a working protocol we need to overcome a number of obstacles, mostly related to the special proof in use. Below, we proceed in two steps: first we construct a relatively simple public-coin cZK protocol with $O(n^\epsilon)$ rounds (for any constant ϵ), and then improve the round complexity to $O(\log^{1+\epsilon} n)$ to obtain our final protocol.

2.3 An $O(n^\epsilon)$-Round Protocol

To realize the proposed KP-PRS-style proving strategy, we need to construct a "special proof" as described above. In this section, we describe the challenges in constructing such a proof and how to resolve them to get a $O(n^\epsilon)$-round public-coin cZK protocol.

Using UA as a Special Proof. The KP-PRS rewinding strategy crucially relies on the fact that rewindings are only performed at the end of blocks to show that the depth of nesting and the simulation time are bounded. Similarly, we will require that the time spent by the simulator on constructing special proofs will be spent only in the end of blocks. This rules out using standard UA as special proofs, since constructing a UA requires the simulator to interact with the verifier and get its random challenges. However, the concurrent verifier might schedule the UA that corresponds to a session within a block only long after the end of the block.

---

[1] In fact, the simulator only constructs proofs for sessions that haven't been "solved", that is, sessions for which no previous proof was constructed.

ONLINE/OFFLINE UA. To resolve this problem, we observe that the construction of UA in [2] can be separated into an *expensive offline stage* and an *efficient online stage* as follows. Let x be a statement that can be proven by a UA where the prover runs in time t. The first verifier message specifies a hash function h and is independent of the statement x. After the first message is sent, the prover's work can be separated into an expensive offline stage that runs in time at most t, and an efficient online stage that runs in a fixed polynomial time in $|x|$. More precisely, we separate the prover in the construction of [2] into an "offline prover" $\mathcal{P}_{\mathsf{UA-OFF}}$ and an "online prover" $\mathcal{P}_{\mathsf{UA}}$ as follows: in the offline stage the verifier specifies a hash function h. Then, the offline prover $\mathcal{P}_{\mathsf{UA-OFF}}$ on input x, witness w and the hash h, constructs a PCP proof σ and a Merkle hash tree HT of σ using h. Finally, $\mathcal{P}_{\mathsf{UA-OFF}}$ outputs the string $\pi = \sigma \| HT$ which we refer to as the offline UA proof. In the online stage, the online prover $\mathcal{P}_{\mathsf{UA}}$ is given x and *oracle access* to π. $\mathcal{P}_{\mathsf{UA}}$ first sends the root of the hash tree to "commit" to the PCP proof. Then, the verifier sends its PCP queries and $\mathcal{P}_{\mathsf{UA}}$ produces answers by querying π. $\mathcal{P}_{\mathsf{UA}}$ obtains the relevant bits of the PCP proof from σ and the corresponding authentication paths from HT. See Protocol 1 for a description of the offline and online stages of the UA.

Pubic Coin Online/Offline UA Argument System

Building Blocks: A family of collision-resistant hash functions $\mathcal{H}$. A PCP proof system $(\mathcal{P}_{\mathsf{PCP}}, \mathcal{V}_{\mathsf{PCP}})$ with properties as defined in [2]).

Inputs: Common input $x \in \mathcal{L}$, and auxiliary input $w \in \mathcal{R}_{\mathcal{L}}(x)$ to $\mathcal{P}_{\mathsf{UA-OFF}}$.

OFFLINE STAGE

1st **Message:** *The verifier $\mathcal{V}_{\mathsf{UA}}$ sends a random hash function $h \leftarrow \mathcal{H}$.*

The offline prover $\mathcal{P}_{\mathsf{UA-OFF}}$ runs $\mathcal{P}_{\mathsf{PCP}}$ on input (x, w) to construct a PCP proof σ, and computes the Merkle hash tree HT of σ using h; let δ be the root of HT. We call $\pi = \sigma \| HT$ an offline UA proof string *.*

ONLINE STAGE*: The online prover $\mathcal{P}_{\mathsf{UA}}$ with oracle access to π and input x, interacts with $\mathcal{V}_{\mathsf{UA}}$ as follows:*

2nd **Message:** The prover $\mathcal{P}_{\mathsf{UA}}{}^{\pi}$ sends δ.

3rd **Message:** The verifier $\mathcal{V}_{\mathsf{UA}}$ sends a sufficiently long random string r.

4th **Message:** The prover $\mathcal{P}_{\mathsf{UA}}{}^{\pi}$ runs $\mathcal{V}_{\mathsf{PCP}}$ on input (x, r) to generate a set of queries Q; for each query $q \in Q$, it sends σ_q and an authentication path in the Merkle hash tree HT that leads to σ_q.

$\mathcal{V}_{\mathsf{UA}}$**'s decision:** $\mathcal{V}_{\mathsf{UA}}$ accepts if all the authentication paths verify, and $\mathcal{V}_{\mathsf{PCP}}$ on input $(x, r, \{\sigma_q\}_{q \in Q})$ accepts.

Fig. 1. The UA construction of [2] as an online/offline UA

USING THE ONLINE/OFFLINE UA IN OUR PROTOCOL. In our cZK protocol, the verifier specifies a hash function in Stage 1, which will be used as the offline verifier's message in the UA. Now the simulator can apply the KP-PRS-style proving strategy: at the end of a block, the simulator constructs an offline UA proof for each slot contained in that block. When a session enters the proof stage (Stage 3), the simulator uses a previously constructed offline proofs to generate messages in the online stage of the UA arguments.

However, the proof given in Stage 3 of the protocol cannot simply be the online stage of the UA. To see way, recall that following the FLS paradigm, the proof stage should consist of a witness-indistinguishable proof that $x \in \mathcal{L}$ or that the prover obtained a trapdoor for one of the slots in the session. The problem is that the proving the above statement (or even stating it) requires knowing the messages sent in all the slots of the session. However, it might be that at the end of the block, when to simulator needs to construct a proof, some of the slots of the session were not simulated yet. To fix the problem we use the online/offline UA to construct a *"special-purpose" witness-indistinguishable* UA similar to the one constructed in [19, 2]. Recall that at the end of the block the simulator constructs an (expensive) offline UA proof for some slot. We change the proof stage of the protocol as follows: the prover first provides an online proof that it has a trapdoor for some slot in the session (note that this statement involves only a single slot). To keep the proof witness-indistinguishable, the proof must not reveal which slot is used. Therefore, the online stage of this UA is executed in the following "oblivious" manner: the prover commits to the statement it proves as well as to all of its online UA messages instead of sending them in the clear, while the verifier simply sends random coins (here we use the fact that the online UA is public-coin). The honest prover (that does not have any trapdoor) will just commit to the all-zero string in every round. We refer to this as an *oblivious* UA execution. Then, the prover will provide a standard witness-indistinguishable proof of knowledge (for NP) to prove that $x \in \mathcal{L}$ or that the committed online UA messages form an accepting proof transcript for the statement defined by one of the slots.

The Problem of Exponential Size State. By separating the work of the UA prover into offline and online stages, the simulator has the freedom to construct a proof for a slot at any time and thus the KP-PRS-style proving strategy can be applied. However, here we encounter yet another difference between black-box and non-black-box simulation. In the former, after rewinding a slot successfully, the simulator extracts a *short* trapdoor of a fixed polynomial length, and thus can afford to remember all the trapdoors extracted so far and use them to complete the simulation of corresponding sessions in both the main and lookahead threads. In contrast, the non-black-box simulator does not obtain a short trapdoor; instead, it obtains *long* offline UA proofs (the length of which is not a priory bounded by some polynomial), of length proportional to the running time of the simulator when simulating the execution in a slot. Still, the simulator needs to remember all previously constructed offline proofs in order to simulate the online stage of the corresponding UAs in the main thread. This means that in each slot, when the simulator commits to its own code and state, it commits also to a record of all the offline proofs constructed so far. Thus, the offline proof arguing about the execution of the slot will be at least as long as all previously generated offline proofs. Again we encounter the problem of exponential blowup in the size of the proof. This time, however, it is due to the size of the state kept by the simulator rather than due to the computation time.[2] To resolve this problem, we first observe that though an offline proof can be arbitrarily long, only a few (fixed polynomial number of) bits of this proof are accessed when simulating the online stage of the UA. If the simulator knew which bits in an offline proof would be accessed later, it could have committed to a program Π containing only these bits instead of the whole offline proof. Then the space complexity of Π would have been bounded by a fixed polynomial (depending only on the size of the cheating verifier), and the size of the offline proofs would not have grown exponentially. However, this wishful thinking seems doomed, since at the time when the simulator needs to commit to Π (i.e., when a slot opens), it does not know which bits of the proof would be accessed, since these bits depend on the verifier's queries sent in the proof stage.

A potential alternative strategy is the following: when a slot opens, the simulator simply commits to a program Π that does not contain any information about previously constructed offline proofs. Only later, when the simulator needs to prove that Π predicts the verifier's random challenge, it does so by providing the appropriate bits of the proof as an auxiliary input to Π. The simulator can do so because at the time of constructing an offline proof about Π, the slot in which Π is committed to is already completely simulated and the simulator knows which bits of previous offline proofs are accessed during the simulation of that slot. However, this strategy fails again. This is because the number of bits accessed in a slot can be an arbitrary polynomial that depends on the number of concurrent sessions started by the cheating verifier. However, for soundness to hold, it is crucial that the committed program only receives auxiliary input much shorter than the length of the verifier's random challenge, which is bounded by an a priori fixed polynomial.

A "Hash-Inverting" Oracle. We finally resolve this problem by combining the ideas behind the above two failed approaches: when a slot opens, the simulator commits to a program Π containing *a root of a Merkle hash* of each offline proof; later, the simulator proves that Π, when given appropriate proof bits *that are consistent with the roots*, predicts the verifier's challenge in the slot. For soundness to hold, the proof bits must be given to the program via a carefully defined interface. The interface we describe next is inspired by the non-black-box simulation technique of [10]. The program Π will be given access to a "hash-inversion" oracle that can "invert" the hash tree. That is, when the program Π wants to access the bit j of the offline proof P, it will query the oracle with the root δ_P of the hash tree of P and the index j. The oracle will answer with the bit $P[j]$ together with the

---

[2] In fact, the time complexity for constructing a UA offline proof and the length of the proof is at least quasi-linear in the space complexity of the computation.

authentication path certifying that $P[j]$ is consistent with δ_P. The oracle will only respond to the query if the value of the root δ_P is contained in the initial state of Π committed in the beginning of the slot.

Giving the committed program Π access to such an oracle is different than just giving it the proof bit as auxiliary input. Even though the number of answer bits Π can obtain from its oracle is not bounded by any fixed polynomial, soundness still holds. The intuition is that all the oracle's answers are "computationally determined" by the starting state of Π. A bit more formally, we prove that no computationally bounded algorithm can produce two valid oracles that answer differently to one of Π's queries. This guarantees that the information that Π learns from its oracle is independent of the verifier's challenge r that is chosen after Π's code and the hash tree roots are committed to.

We modify the protocol correspondingly: in the proof stage (Stage 3), the prover proves that either the statement is true, or that, in one of the slots, it has committed to a program Π that predicts the verifier's challenge, given access to a valid hash-inverting oracle as described. When the simulation reaches the end of a block where the simulator needs to construct a proof for the computation of a committed program of some slot, the simulator has all the information about what proof bits were accessed during the simulation of the slot. Therefore, the simulator can construct the appropriate oracle that Π expects to access. The main difference between the oracle described above and the oracle used in [10] is that in [10], the oracle's answers are information-theoretically determined by the queries, whereas here, answers of the hash-inverting oracle are only computationally determined. However, as we show, in our settings this suffices for achieving soundness.

The Global Hash Model. In the description of the modified protocol above, the committed program is given access to a "hash-inverting" oracle. However, we did not specify how to choose the hash function inverted by the oracle. For soundness to hold, the hash function must not be specified by the prover, as otherwise, a cheating prover may specify a hash function with respect to which the hash tree roots are not binding. However, letting the verifier choose the hash function results in a problem with concurrent simulation: let h_i be the hash function specified by the cheating verifier in the ith session. Now, when the simulation commits to a program Π in a slot of the ith session, Π must contain the roots of Merkle hash trees using hash h_i for all previously constructed offline proofs. Otherwise, Π will not be able to query its oracle for bits of these proofs. It follows that whenever the cheating verifier starts a new session and sends a new hash function h_i, the simulator must recompute the hash tree on all previously constructed offline proofs using h_i. This operation may be as expensive as constructing all these offline proofs from scratch. Since we cannot guarantee that this expensive hash computations are performed only at the end block, we can no longer bound the running time of the simulation.

We resolve this problem by considering a global hash function h shared by all protocol executions. In this case, the simulator can construct Merkle hash trees of every offline proof using the same shared function h, and use the same hash tree roots in commitments given in all sessions. Now there is never a need to recompute a hash tree on a previously constructed proof and simulation running time is bounded. As explained above, soundness holds only if a cheating prover is unable to find collisions in h. Therefore we can prove the security of our protocol in the global hash model where the prover and all concurrent verifiers are given a single hash function that is assumed to be collision-resistent. The meaningfulness of this model is discussed in the introduction.

Tackling the Number of Rewindings per Block. To complete the description of the "special proofs" we need to address one more problem: unlike the KP-PRS rewinding strategy where the black-box simulator can rewind all slots contained in a block all at once, our non-black-box simulator creates a separate offline UA proof for each slot contained in the block. The result is that the time spent by the simulator on constructing proofs at the end of the block grows with the number of slots contained in the block. One consequence of this approach is that the running time of the simulation grows much faster as a function of the recursion depth. Unlike the case in [22] where the simulation can accommodate a logarithmic level of nesting, we can only tolerate a constant level of nesting. This can be ensured at the price of increasing the round-complexity of the protocol: if the simulator uses blocks of size b^i for a $b = n^\epsilon$ (ϵ is a constant), the level of nesting $O(\log_b n)$ becomes constant. However, to guarantee successful extraction of the trapdoor, the protocol must use $\omega(b \log_b n) = \omega(n^\epsilon)$ slots.

The Simulator's Randomness. So far we described how to construct "special proofs" that will allow realizing the KP-PRS-style proving strategy. Our starting point was the analogy between a simulator that commits to it own code and a rewinding black-box simulator. However, before we can implement this high-level idea, we need to introduce a final modification to the protocol that will enable the simulator to commit to its own code. The difficulty has to do with the way that the simulator generates its randomness. As described above, the simulator needs to use randomness to simulate the prover's messages. In particular, in every slot the simulator uses randomness to commit to a program Π that emulates the execution of the simulator itself, and in every session the simulator uses randomness to generate messages in the special proofs. Since the program Π must precisely emulate the simulation, it must use the same randomness as the simulator. This could be done, for example, by using a PRF: the simulator will choose a PRF seed s and use it to generate all the randomness needed. The committed program Π will use the same seed s to generate identical randomness. The problem is that the simulator commits to (a hash of) the code of Π that contains the seed s using randomness generated from s. Since the committed program is correlated with the randomness of the commitment, we cannot rely on the hiding property of the commitment.

This problem can be circumvented, as pointed out in [20], by committing to a program Π that does not contain s and instead receives s as a (short) auxiliary input. This allows us to use the hiding property of the commitment. However, we still encounter a similar problem when generating special proofs. In the special proof, the simulator proves that Π on input s (and given access to some oracle) predicts the verifier's random challenge. Thus, the witness of the special proof includes s and it is therefore correlated with the randomness used to generate the special proof. When this is the case we cannot rely on the witness-indistinguishability property of the special proof. We finally resolve this problem by letting the simulator use a list of PRF seeds $s_0, \ldots, s_m$, all generated from the last seed s_m in a "reverse chain" fashion, that is, $s_i = \mathsf{PRF}_{s_{i+1}}(\text{"NEXT"})$ (where "NEXT" is an arbitrary fixed value in the domain of the PRF). In simulation, the simulator orders all the special proofs simulated in the concurrent execution according to the order in which their first message is sent. The simulator starts by using the first seed s_0, and when the ith special proof starts, it switches to using seed s_i. Therefore, all the randomness used in the simulation before the ith special proof starts can be recovered using s_{i-1}. Let Π be the program used as a witness in the ith special proof. Since Π only emulates the main simulation until a point prior to the beginning of the ith special proof, Π only needs to receive the seed s_{i-1} in order to run correctly. Now, both the witness s_{i-1} for the ith special proof and the randomness used to generate the ith special proof are generated using PRF from seed s_i. In this setting, we can prove that the special proofs are witness-indistinguishable based on the properties of the PRF.

Putting All the Elements Together. We obtain a $O(n^\epsilon)$-round public-coin cZK protocol (P_1, V_1) as informally described below. As this protocol only serves as an intermediate step towards our final protocol, we omit the formal description.

An $O(n^\epsilon)$-round public-coin cZK protocol (P_1, V_1):
 - *Stage 1 (Global Hash):* P and V obtain the global hash function h.
 - *Stage 2 (k Slots):* P and V run k slots. In the ith slot the prover sends a commitment c_i and the verifier responds with a random challenge r_i.
 - *Stage 3 (Proof Stage):* the prover proves using a "special purpose" witness-indistinguishable UA that either $x \in \mathcal{L}$, or there is a slot i, in which c_i is a commitment to a hash of a program Π containing a set of hash tree roots, such that, Π on a short input s, and with access to some valid hash-inverting oracle, outputs r_i.

2.4 Improving the Round Complexity

In this section, we describe at a high-level how to improve the round complexity of the protocol (P_1, V_1) to obtain our final protocol with $O(\log^{1+\epsilon} n)$ rounds, for any constant ϵ. Towards this, recall that as discussed in Section 2.3, the reason that we set the number of slots in $(\mathcal{P}, \mathcal{V})$ to n^ϵ is to guarantee a constant nesting depth. This is required, since the simulation running time increases too fast as a function of the nesting depth. Thus, the key to improving the round complexity is to better control the growth of the simulation running time as a function of the nesting depth.

Let us first review the contributions to the simulation running time in the protocol (P_1, V_1). Recall that at the end of a block, the simulator needs to generate an offline UA proof for each slot that it contains. The time spent by the simulation on constructing proofs at the end of the block can therefore be attributed to two factors: first, if the simulation of a slot takes time T, the time for constructing an offline UA proof about that slot is $\text{poly}(T)$, where the specific polynomial depends on the underlying UA system. Second, since the simulator may potentially construct an offline UA proof for each slot contained in it, the number of offline proofs that needs to be constructed can be m, the number of concurrent sessions started by the verifier. Overall, the time spent at the end of a block can be $m \cdot \text{poly}(T)$. This implies a polynomial factor increase in the simulation running time for every level of nesting. To decrease the simulation time, we address both factors mentioned above:

- To improve the time complexity for constructing a single offline proof, we make use of a UA system where the offline prover's time complexity is quasi-linear; we can get such system by instantiating the construction of [2] with an underlying PCP system that has quasi-linear prover complexity [3].
- To decrease the number of proofs constructed at the end of each block, we modify the protocol and the simulation strategy so that essentially, only one offline proof needs to be constructed at the end of each block. This is harder to achieve and we describe the ideas in more details below.

As a result of the above modifications, the time spent by the simulation at the end of a block improves to $\tilde{O}(T)$, allowing the nesting depth to grow up to $O(\frac{\log n}{\log \log n})$ and leading to a protocol with $\log^{1+\epsilon} n$ slots, and $O(\log^{1+\epsilon} n)$ rounds.

The main idea behind achieving the second improvement described above is that instead of constructing an offline proof about the simulation of each slot, the simulator constructs a single "block-proof" arguing about the simulation of the *whole block* and then reuses the block-proof for the slots contained in the block. In the block-proof, the simulator proves that the committed program Π that mimics the execution of the main thread in the block outputs a transcript τ of the block (which includes the verifier's challenge messages of all the slots contained in this block). In order to use a block-proof to argue about one slot (c, r) contained in the block, the simulator creates, in addition to the block-proof, a second offline UA proof that r is contained in τ—we call this a "session-proof" (note that a UA is used since the transcript τ may be long). Informally speaking, putting the block-proof and the session-proof together, the simulator can now "cheat" by proving that c is a commitment to the hash of a program that outputs *a transcript containing the random challenge*. Intuitively, soundness still holds, as it is hard for a cheating prover to find a program that outputs any transcript of polynomial length that will contain the random challenge. To implement this idea, we need to make a few changes to the protocol as highlighted below.

- Let (c_i, r_i) be the ith slot in a session j, and let B be the block of minimal size that contains (c_i, r_i). As described above, at the end of block B, the simulator constructs a "block-proof" about the execution of Π that mimics the execution of the main thread in this block. For the simulator to be able to reuse this block-proof in the ith slot of session j, c_i must be a commitment to

Π. However, at the time the commitment c_i is generated, the simulator does not know when the message r_i will be scheduled and which block will be the minimal block containing this slot. Thus, the simulator does not know which program to commit to. To resolve this problem, we modify a slot to consist of n commitments $c_{i,1}, \ldots, c_{i,n}$ from the prover (and still one random challenge r_i from the verifier). Now, when a slot opens, the simulator can commit to all the programs that emulate the execution of the simulation in all the blocks that are currently open (that is, all blocks that may potentially contain this slot), and later generate a proof with respect to one of these commitments.

- We modify the special proof to consist of both the session-proof and the corresponding block-proof. The special proof will consist of two separate oblivious executions of the online stage of the UA standing for both proofs. Then, a witness-indistinguishable proof is given that either the statement is true or that the transcripts of UA hidden in the two oblivious executions are both accepting, and together form a trapdoor for one slot in the session.

Finally, we remark that now indeed only one block-proof is created after each block. However, it seems that we haven't gained anything as the simulator still needs to create a session-proof for each slot contained in it. However, since the length of τ is bounded by the running time of $\mathcal{V}^*$, the time complexity for constructing the session-proof is always bounded by a fixed polynomial in the running time of $\mathcal{V}^*$. Therefore, only the time complexity for constructing the block-proof grows with the nesting depth. This suffices for the purpose of controlling the simulation time from growing too fast.

3 The Final Protocol

In this section we give an informal description of our public-coin concurrent ZK protocol in the global hash model (Protocol 3). The number of rounds of the protocol depends on the parameter k. Next, we describe the notations used to describe Protocol 3.

Primitives. Protocol 3 makes use of a statistically binding commitment Com (described for simplicity as a non-interactive commitment), a witness indistinguishable argument of knowledge (WIAOK), and a hash function h sampled randomly from a family of collision-resistant hash functions and given to both parties as a common input. In the description of the language Λ_1 below we abuse notation and use h as a hash tree rather then a simple hash function. That is, $\delta = h(P)$ represents a root of a Merkle hash tree applied to a long string P. For an index j, we can compute the authentication path from δ to $P[j]$, certifying that the value of δ is consistent with $P[j]$.

Oblivious UA. Our protocol uses the online/offline public-coin UA protocol as given by Protocol 1, where the verifier's hash function sent in the offline stage is replaced by the global hash h. In Protocol 3 the online part of the online/offline

UA is executed twice in an oblivious way. That is, the online UA prover commits to the statement it wants to prove, and to all UA messages. The online UA verifier is only given the length of the proven statement (recall that the verifier messages in online UA are simply its random coins and therefore it can compute these messages without knowing the statement). For example, when proving any statement of the form $(h, h_\Pi, h_\tau, c, r) \in \Lambda_2$ (the language Λ_2 is described below) using an oblivious UA, the verifier is only given the length of the canonical statement $|\text{``}(h, 0^n, 0^n, c_{1,1}, r_1) \in \Lambda_2\text{''}|$. After the two oblivious executions of the online UA are completed, a WIAOK is used to prove that the transcript of each oblivious UA execution is consistent with valid online UA proof for the appropriate statements. That is, there exist openings for all the commitments sent by the prover in the oblivious UA executions into messages, such that these messages (together with the random messages sent by the verifier) form an accepting online UA proof for the statement of interest.

Block-Proofs and Session-Proofs. We refer to the first oblivious UA as a block-proof and the second as session-proof. Block-proofs are proofs of membership in the language Λ_1 defined as follows: $(h, h_\Pi, h_\tau) \in \Lambda_1$ if (h_Π, h_τ) are hashes of a program Π and a transcript τ respectively, such that program Π, given access to some valid oracle, and some short auxiliary input, produces the transcript τ. Session-proofs are proofs of membership in the language Λ_2 defined as follows: $(h, h_\Pi, h_\tau, c, r) \in \Lambda_2$ if c is a commitment to the hash h_Π and h_τ is the hash of a transcript τ that contains the message r. More formally, for the super-polynomial function $T(n) = n^{\log \log n}$ the languages Λ_1, Λ_2 are defined in Figure 2:

Block-proof: $(h, h_\Pi, h_\tau) \in \Lambda_1$ iff there exist:

- Π - description of a program such that $|\Pi| < T(n)$.
- τ - a transcript such that $|\tau| < T(n)$.
- O - description of an oracle such that $|O| < T(n)$.
- β - Auxiliary input Π such that $|\beta| < |r| - n$.

And the following conditions hold:

- $h_\Pi = h(\Pi)$, $h_\tau = h(\tau)$ and $\Pi^O(\beta)$ generates τ within $T(n)$ steps.
- O contains an answer to every query Π makes and only contains query-answer pairs of the form $((j, q), (b, a))$ such that:
  - The description of Π contains the variable δ_j.
  - There is a string P_j such that $\delta_j = h(P_j)$, $b = P_j[q]$ and a is the corresponding authentication path.

Session-proof: $(h, h_\Pi, h_\tau, c, r) \in \Lambda_2$ iff there exists randomness ρ for Com and a transcript $\tau, |\tau| < T(n)$ such that $c = \text{Com}(h_\Pi; \rho)$,$h_\tau = h(\tau)$, and τ contains r.

Fig. 2. Block-proof and session-proof

Common Input: $x \in \mathcal{L}$.
Auxiliary Input to $\mathcal{P}$: $w \in \mathcal{R}_{\mathcal{L}}(x)$.
Common Reference String: A hash function h.

1. $\mathcal{P}$ and $\mathcal{V}$ repeat the following for every $i \in [k]$:
   (a) $\mathcal{P}$ computes $c_{i,j} \leftarrow \mathsf{Com}(h(0^n), U_n)$ for $j \in [n]$ and sends $\{c_{i,j}\}_{j \in [n]}$ to $\mathcal{V}$.
   (b) $\mathcal{V}$ samples a random string $r_i \leftarrow U_{2n}$ and sends r_i to $\mathcal{P}$.
2. $\mathcal{P}$ and $\mathcal{V}$ run an oblivious UA for a statement of the same length as "$(h, 0^n, 0^n) \in \Lambda_1$". All commitments sent by $\mathcal{P}$ are to the all-zero string.
3. $\mathcal{P}$ and $\mathcal{V}$ run an oblivious UA for a statement of the same length as "$(h, 0^n, 0^n, c_{1,1}, r_1) \in \Lambda_2$". All commitments sent by $\mathcal{P}$ are to the all zero string.
4. $\mathcal{P}$ proves to $\mathcal{V}$ using a public-coin WIAOK that either $x \in \mathcal{L}$ or there exists $i \in [k]$, $j \in [n]$ and a hash values h_{Π}, h_{τ} such that both of the following hold:
   (a) The transcript of the first oblivious UA is consistent with an accepting proof for the statement: "$(h, h_{\Pi}, h_{\tau}) \in \Lambda_1$".
   (b) The transcript of the second oblivious UA is consistent with an accepting proof for the statement: "$(h, h_{\Pi}, h_{\tau}, c_{i,j}, r_i) \in \Lambda_2$".

Fig. 3. Pubic Coin cZK Protocol (Protocol 3)

References

[1] Barak, B.: How to go beyond the black-box simulation barrier. In: FOCS (2001)
[2] Barak, B., Goldreich, O.: Universal arguments and their applications. SIAM J. Comput. (2008)
[3] Ben-Sasson, E., Chiesa, A., Genkin, D., Tromer, E.: On the concrete-efficiency threshold of probabilistically-checkable proofs. In: Electronic Colloquium on Computational Complexity, ECCC (2012)
[4] Bitansky, N., Canetti, R., Halevi, S.: Leakage-Tolerant Interactive Protocols. In: Cramer, R. (ed.) TCC 2012. LNCS, vol. 7194, pp. 266–284. Springer, Heidelberg (2012)
[5] Blum, M., Feldman, P., Micali, S.: Non-interactive zero-knowledge and its applications (extended abstract). In: STOC (1988)
[6] Canetti, R., Fischlin, M.: Universally composable commitments. IACR Cryptology ePrint Archive (2001)
[7] Canetti, R., Kilian, J., Petrank, E., Rosen, A.: Black-box concurrent zero-knowledge requires (almost) logarithmically many rounds. SIAM J. Comput. (2002)
[8] Canetti, R., Lin, H., Paneth, O.: Public-coins concurrent zero-knowledge in the global hash model. IACR Cryptology ePrint Archive (2013)
[9] Deng, Y., Feng, D., Goyal, V., Lin, D., Sahai, A., Yung, M.: Resettable Cryptography in Constant Rounds – The Case of Zero Knowledge. In: Lee, D.H., Wang, X. (eds.) ASIACRYPT 2011. LNCS, vol. 7073, pp. 390–406. Springer, Heidelberg (2011)
[10] Deng, Y., Goyal, V., Sahai, A.: Resolving the simultaneous resettability conjecture and a new non-black-box simulation strategy. In: FOCS (2009)

[11] Dwork, C., Naor, M., Sahai, A.: Concurrent zero-knowledge. In: STOC (1998)
[12] Garg, S., Jain, A., Sahai, A.: Leakage-Resilient Zero Knowledge. In: Rogaway, P. (ed.) CRYPTO 2011. LNCS, vol. 6841, pp. 297–315. Springer, Heidelberg (2011)
[13] Goldreich, O., Kahan, A.: How to construct constant-round zero-knowledge proof systems for NP. Journal of Cryptology (1996)
[14] Goldreich, O., Krawczyk, H.: On the composition of zero-knowledge proof systems. SIAM J. Comput. (1996)
[15] Goldreich, O., Micali, S., Wigderson, A.: Proofs that yield nothing but their validity for all languages in np have zero-knowledge proof systems. J. ACM (1991)
[16] Goldwasser, S., Micali, S., Rackoff, C.: The knowledge complexity of interactive proof-systems (extended abstract). In: STOC (1985)
[17] Kilian, J., Petrank, E.: Concurrent and resettable zero-knowledge in polyloalgorithm rounds. In: STOC (2001)
[18] Pandey, O., Pass, R., Sahai, A., Tseng, W.-L.D., Venkitasubramaniam, M.: Precise Concurrent Zero Knowledge. In: Smart, N.P. (ed.) EUROCRYPT 2008. LNCS, vol. 4965, pp. 397–414. Springer, Heidelberg (2008)
[19] Pass, R., Rosen, A.: Concurrent non-malleable commitments. In: FOCS (2005)
[20] Pass, R., Rosen, A., Tseng, W.: Public-coin parallel zero-knowledge for np. Journal of Cryptology (2011)
[21] Pass, R., Tseng, W.-L.D., Wikström, D.: On the Composition of Public-Coin Zero-Knowledge Protocols. In: Halevi, S. (ed.) CRYPTO 2009. LNCS, vol. 5677, pp. 160–176. Springer, Heidelberg (2009)
[22] Prabhakaran, M., Rosen, A., Sahai, A.: Concurrent zero knowledge with logarithmic round-complexity. In: FOCS (2002)
[23] Richardson, R., Kilian, J.: On the Concurrent Composition of Zero-Knowledge Proofs. In: Stern, J. (ed.) EUROCRYPT 1999. LNCS, vol. 1592, pp. 415–431. Springer, Heidelberg (1999)
[24] Rogaway, P.: Formalizing Human Ignorance. In: Nguyên, P.Q. (ed.) VIETCRYPT 2006. LNCS, vol. 4341, pp. 211–228. Springer, Heidelberg (2006)

Succinct Malleable NIZKs and an Application to Compact Shuffles

Melissa Chase[1], Markulf Kohlweiss[2], Anna Lysyanskaya[3],
and Sarah Meiklejohn[4]

[1] Microsoft Research Redmond
melissac@microsoft.com
[2] Microsoft Research Cambridge
markulf@microsoft.com
[3] Brown University
anna@cs.brown.edu
[4] UC San Diego
smeiklej@cs.ucsd.edu

Abstract. Depending on the application, malleability in cryptography can be viewed as either a flaw or — especially if sufficiently understood and restricted — a feature. In this vein, Chase, Kohlweiss, Lysyanskaya, and Meiklejohn recently defined malleable zero-knowledge proofs, and showed how to *control* the set of allowable transformations on proofs. As an application, they construct the first *compact* verifiable shuffle, in which one such controlled-malleable proof suffices to prove the correctness of an entire multi-step shuffle.

Despite these initial steps, a number of natural problems remained: (1) their construction of controlled-malleable proofs relies on the inherent malleability of Groth-Sahai proofs and is thus not based on generic primitives; (2) the classes of allowable transformations they can support are somewhat restrictive.

In this paper, we address these issues by providing a generic construction of controlled-malleable proofs using succinct non-interactive arguments of knowledge, or SNARGs for short. Our construction can support very general classes of transformations, as we no longer rely on the transformations that Groth-Sahai proofs can support.

1 Introduction

Recently, malleability is increasingly being viewed more as a feature than as a bug [27,28,18,1,13,16,6]. In this vein, we (called CKLM in the sequel to disambiguate between our current and prior work) [7] introduced controlled-malleable non-interactive zero-knowledge proof systems (cm-NIZKs for short). At a high level, a cm-NIZK allows one, given a proof π for an instance $x \in L$, to compute a proof π' for the related instance $T(x) \in L$ for transformations T under which the language is closed. This malleability property can be additionally *controlled*, meaning there is some specified class of allowable transformations $\mathcal{T}$ such that, given the proof π for $x \in L$, a new proof π' for $T(x) \in L$ may be obtained only

A. Sahai (Ed.): TCC 2013, LNCS 7785, pp. 100–119, 2013.

for $T \in \mathcal{T}$. The notion of a cm-NIZK is non-trivial when the proof system also needs to be concise or *derivation-private*; i.e., in addition to π' being the same size as π, it should be impossible to tell whether π' was obtained using a witness or by mauling a proof for a previous statement.

The notion of a derivation-private cm-NIZK is well motivated: as one application, CKLM showed that it allows for the modular design of schemes that satisfy randomizable and homomorphic chosen-ciphertext security. Another application they presented is a *compactly verifiable shuffle* for an election, wherein a set of encrypted votes, submitted by N different voters, is shuffled (i.e. rerandomized and permuted), in turn, by L voting authorities. To ensure that the authorities are behaving honestly, each authority provides a non-interactive zero-knowledge proof that it has correctly shuffled the votes; if this is done using standard NIZKs, then in order to verify that the overall shuffling process was correct a verifier would need to access L separate proofs, each proving that an authority correctly performed the shuffling process. If each proof is of size $s(N)$, this means that the verifier's work is $\Theta(Ls(N))$ (here we ignore the security parameter). Using derivation-private cm-NIZKs, the verifier's workload can be reduced: each authority can, instead of producing a brand new proof, "maul" the proof of the previous authority; the proof produced by the last authority should then convince the verifier that the ciphertexts output at the end are a valid shuffling of the input ciphertexts. This makes vote shuffling a factor of L more efficient, as the verifier needs to verify a proof of size only $\Theta(s(N) + L)$. (The size of the proof is still dependent on L because each authority needs to, intuitively, add a "stamp of participation" in order for a verifier to ascertain that the shuffling process was performed correctly.)

CKLM then showed how to construct derivation-private cm-NIZK proof systems for a limited, but nevertheless expressive, class of transformations. Specifically, their approach builds heavily on the Groth-Sahai proof system [24]; this means that they can consider only relations on group elements in groups that admit bilinear pairings, and it might therefore seem as though controlled malleability were just a property of the Groth-Sahai proof system and not necessarily something that could be realized using more general building blocks. Interestingly, as a consequence of this limitation, CKLM did not fully deliver on the promise of a compactly verifiable shuffle: in order to prove that a given set of ciphertexts is a shuffle, they needed to represent everything, including the transformations applied to the set of ciphertexts, as a set of elements in the underlying group. The way they chose to do this was using a permutation matrix; since this permutation matrix needs to be extractable from the proof, the size of each proof in their construction was $\Theta(N^2 + L)$. For the usual voting scenario, in which the number of voters far exceeds the number of mix authorities, a vote shuffling scheme wherein each authority produces its own proof but the proofs are only of size $\Theta(N)$ (such as the verifiable shuffle of Groth and Lu [23]), therefore has a shorter proof overall.

Thus, the two important, and somewhat related open problems were: first, can a derivation-private controlled-malleable NIZK be realized in a modular fashion from general building blocks, without requiring the specific number-theoretic assumptions underlying the Groth-Sahai proof system? Second, can it be realized for general classes of languages and transformations, and not just those languages whose membership is expressible using pairing product equations over group elements as needed to invoke the Groth-Sahai proof system? In this paper, we give a positive answer to both.

Our Contributions. We first investigate how to construct a derivation-private cm-NIZK from succinct non-interactive arguments (SNARGs) [22,6]. We limit our attention to t-tiered languages and transformations; briefly, a language is t-tiered if each instance x can be efficiently labeled with an integer $i = \text{tier}(x)$, $1 \leq i \leq t$, and a transformation T for a t-tiered language L is t-tiered if $\text{tier}(T(x)) > \text{tier}(x)$ for all $x \in L$ where $\text{tier}(x) < t$, and $T(x) = \perp$ if $\text{tier}(x) = t$. Some transformations are naturally t-tiered: for example, a vote shuffling transformation carried out by authority i should output a set of ciphertexts and stamps of approval from each authority up to i; furthermore, all transformations can be made t-tiered if one is willing to reveal how many times a transformation has been applied.

Intuitively, our construction works as follows: given a proof π for an instance $x \in L$, to provide a proof for a new instance $x' = T(x) \in L$, a user can form a "proof of a proof;" i.e., prove knowledge of this previous instance x and its proof π, as well as the transformation T from x to x', and call this proof π'. By the succinctness property of SNARGs, this new proof π' can in fact be the same size as the previous proof π, and thus this "proof of a proof" approach can be continued without incurring any blowup in size.

Although the intuition is relatively simple, going from SNARGs to cm-NIZKs is in fact quite challenging. While the outline above describes how to build malleability into SNARGs, it is still the case that SNARGs satisfy only the non-black-box notion of adaptive knowledge extraction, whereas cm-NIZKs require a much stronger (black-box) version of extractability. (This stronger notion is crucially used in the CCA encryption and the shuffle applications in CKLM.) To therefore break all these requirements up into smaller pieces, we begin with SNARGs and then slowly work our way up to cm-NIZKs in three separate constructions, with each construction incorporating an additional requirement.

We begin in Section 3.1 with a construction of a malleable SNARG. This construction closely follows the intuition above (which is itself inspired by the "targeted malleability" construction of Boneh et al. [6]): malleability is achieved by proving knowledge of either a fresh witness or a previous instance and proof, and a transformation from that instance to the current one. As observed by Bitansky et al. [3,4], care must be taken with this kind of recursive composition of SNARGs, as the size of the extractor can quickly blow up as we continue to extract proofs from other proofs; we can therefore construct t-tiered malleable SNARGs (i.e., SNARGs malleable with respect to the class of all t-tiered transformations) for only constant t. Furthermore, a formal treatment of our particular recursive technique reveals that a stronger notion of extraction, in which the extractor gets to see not only the random tape but also the code for the adversary, is necessary for both our construction and the original one of Boneh et al.

With our construction in Section 3.1, we therefore added malleability to the SNARG while preserving succinctness. In Section 3.2, we next tackle the issue of extractability; in particular, we want to boost from the non-black-box notion of extractability supported by SNARGs to the standard black-box notion of a proof of knowledge (NIZKPoK). To do this, we in fact rely only on the soundness of the SNARG, and do not attempt to use the (non-black-box) extractor at all. Instead, we perform a sort of verifiable encryption, in which we encrypt the witness and then prove knowledge (using the malleable SNARG) of the value inside the ciphertext; in this our approach is perhaps most similar to that of Damgård et al. [11]. A black-box extractor is then simple to construct: it just decrypts the ciphertext and thus, provided the proof is sound, recovers the witness. In addition, to preserve the full generality of our t-tiered transformations one would instantiate the encryption scheme using fully homomorphic encryption, although we will also see in Section 4 that interesting classes of transformations can still be supported by more limited schemes (such as ones that are multiplicatively homomorphic).

With our construction in Section 3.2, we therefore achieved the same properties that the Groth-Sahai proof system already provided (namely, a malleable NIWIPoK), but with respect to a more general class of transformations. As such, to now construct cm-NIZKs in Section 3.3, we can follow approximately the same construction as CKLM, who also used malleable NIWIPoKs to construct their cm-NIZK. Once again, however, care must be taken in this step, as we would like to preserve the generality in the class of transformations that we supported in the previous two sections. We therefore modify the CKLM construction to allow for this, and thus achieve cm-NIZKs for all t-tiered transformations.

In summary, we show that if zero-knowledge SNARGs exist for all languages in NP and fully homomorphic encryption exists, then derivation-private cm-NIZK proof systems exist for all t-tiered classes of transformations, where t is a constant. We do this by constructing three distinct types of proofs, each of which may be of independent interest: first, a malleable SNARG, then a malleable NIZKPoK, and finally a cm-NIZK. While each of our constructions builds from the previous one, we stress that our constructions are all fully generic; e.g., any malleable SNARG can be used to construct a malleable NIZKPoK, not just the specific one we construct.

Finally, in Section 4, we show how to use our SNARG-based proofs for t-tiered transformation classes (using just multiplicatively homomorphic encryption rather than the heavyweight requirement of fully homomorphic encryption) to construct a compact verifiable shuffle with proof size $\Theta(N + L)$ under general assumptions. This enhances CKLM in two ways: (1) CKLM had proof size $\Theta(N^2 + L)$; (2) CKLM required Groth-Sahai proofs, rather than general assumptions. In a separate paper [9], we showed that, by making additional assumptions about groups that admit bilinear pairings (similar to those made by Groth and

Lu [23]), we can also obtain a compact verifiable shuffle with proofs of size $\Theta(N + L)$ using the Groth-Sahai proof system.

2   Definitions and Notation

We recall the main security notions we use. We begin with the recent definitions for malleability due to CKLM [7], as well as their definition for compactly verifiable shuffles; we then define succinct non-interactive zero-knowledge arguments (SNARGs), which form the basis for our construction of malleable proofs in Section 3.

2.1   Malleable Proofs

Let $R(\cdot, \cdot)$ be a relation such that the corresponding language $L_R = \{x \mid \exists w$ such that $(x, w) \in R\}$ is in NP. As defined by CKLM, the relation is *closed* with respect to a transformation $T = (T_{\text{inst}}, T_{\text{wit}})$ if, for every $(x, w) \in R$, $(T_{\text{inst}}(x), T_{\text{wit}}(w)) \in R$ as well. We define zero knowledge and related notions formally in the full version of the paper [8], but recall briefly here that a non-interactive zero-knowledge (NIZK) proof system [5,14,20] is a set of algorithms (CRSSetup, $\mathcal{P}, \mathcal{V}$) for which there exists an efficient simulator (S_1, S_2) such that no adversary can distinguish between proofs formed by the prover and proofs formed by the simulator, and an efficient extractor (E_1, E_2) that can produce a witness w such that $(x, w) \in R$ from any valid proof π for x. For zero knowledge, we discuss here two additional variants: the first, *composable* zero knowledge, says that the adversary should still be unable to distinguish even give the simulation trapdoor, and the second, *statistical* zero knowledge, says that the distribution of proofs formed by the simulator and prover are indistinguishable even to an unbounded adversary; composable zero knowledge is thus implied by statistical zero knowledge, as an unbounded adversary could produce the simulator trapdoor itself.

To incorporate malleability, CKLM extend a NIZK (CRSSetup, $\mathcal{P}, \mathcal{V}$) to add an additional algorithm, ZKEval, that given a transformation T, a previous instance x, and a previous proof π such that $\mathcal{V}(\text{crs}, x, \pi) = 1$, computes a valid proof for $T_{\text{inst}}(x)$; i.e., a proof π' such that $\mathcal{V}(\text{crs}, T_{\text{inst}}(x), \pi') = 1$. They then say that the proof system is *malleable* with respect to a set of transformations $\mathcal{T}$ if for every $T \in \mathcal{T}$, this computation can be performed efficiently. In terms of controlling malleability, the main definition of CKLM reconciles simulation soundness [29,12] and simulation-sound extractability [21] with malleability by requiring that, for a set of transformations $\mathcal{T}$, if an adversary can produce a proof π that $x \in L_R$ then the extractor can extract from π either a witness w or a transformation $T \in \mathcal{T}$ and previously proved instance x' such that $x = T_{\text{inst}}(x')$. This is defined more formally as:

Definition 2.1. [7] *Let* (CRSSetup, $\mathcal{P}, \mathcal{V}$, ZKEval) *be a NIZKPoK system for an efficient relation R, with a simulator (S_1, S_2) and an extractor (E_1, E_2). Let*

$\mathcal{T}$ be a set of unary transformations for the relation R such that membership in $\mathcal{T}$ is efficiently testable. Let SE_1 be an algorithm that, on input 1^k, outputs $(\mathsf{crs}, \tau_s, \tau_e)$ such that (crs, τ_s) is distributed identically to the output of S_1. Let $\mathcal{A}$ be given, let $Q := Q_{inst} \times Q_{proof}$ be a table for storing the instances queried to S_2 and the proofs given in response, and consider the following game:

- *Step 1.* $(\mathsf{crs}, \tau_s, \tau_e) \xleftarrow{\$} SE_1(1^k)$.
- *Step 2.* $(x, \pi) \xleftarrow{\$} \mathcal{A}^{S_2(\mathsf{crs}, \tau_s, \cdot)}(\mathsf{crs}, \tau_e)$.
- *Step 3.* $(w, x', T) \leftarrow E_2(\mathsf{crs}, \tau_e, x, \pi)$.
- *Step 4.* $b \leftarrow ((w \neq \bot \wedge (x, w) \notin R) \vee$

$$((x', T) \neq (\bot, \bot) \wedge (x' \notin Q_{inst} \vee x \neq T_{inst}(x') \vee T \notin \mathcal{T})) \vee$$
$$(w, x', T) = (\bot, \bot, \bot))$$

The NIZKPoK satisfies controlled-malleable simulation-sound extractability *(CM-SSE, for short) with respect to $\mathcal{T}$ if for all PPT algorithms $\mathcal{A}$ there exists a negligible function $\nu(\cdot)$ such that the probability (over the choices of SE_1, $\mathcal{A}$, and S_2) that $\mathcal{V}(\mathsf{crs}, x, \pi) = 1$ and $(x, \pi) \notin Q$ but $b = 1$ is at most $\nu(k)$.*

CKLM also defined the notion of *derivation privacy* for malleable proofs, which says that proofs should not reveal whether they were formed fresh or via transformation.

Definition 2.2. **[7]** *For a non-interactive proof* $(\mathsf{CRSSetup}, \mathcal{P}, \mathcal{V}, \mathsf{ZKEval})$, *an efficient relation R malleable with respect to $\mathcal{T}$, an adversary $\mathcal{A}$, and a bit b, let $p_b^{\mathcal{A}}(k)$ be the probability of the event that $b' = 0$ in the following game:*

- *Step 1.* $\mathsf{crs} \xleftarrow{\$} \mathsf{CRSSetup}(1^k)$.
- *Step 2.* $(\mathsf{state}, x_1, w_1, \pi_1, \ldots, x_q, w_q, \pi_q, T) \xleftarrow{\$} \mathcal{A}(\mathsf{crs})$.
- *Step 3.* If $\mathcal{V}(\mathsf{crs}, x_i, \pi_i) = 0$ for some i, $(x_i, w_i) \notin R$ for some i, or $T \notin \mathcal{T}$, abort and output $\bot$. Otherwise, form

$$\pi \xleftarrow{\$} \begin{cases} \mathcal{P}(\mathsf{crs}, T_{inst}(x_1, \ldots, x_q), T_{wit}(w_1, \ldots, w_q)) & \text{if } b = 0 \\ \mathsf{ZKEval}(\mathsf{crs}, T, \{x_i, \pi_i\}_{i=1}^q) & \text{if } b = 1. \end{cases}$$

- *Step 4.* $b' \xleftarrow{\$} \mathcal{A}(\mathsf{state}, \pi)$.

Then the proof system is derivation private *if for all PPT algorithms $\mathcal{A}$ there exists a negligible function $\nu(\cdot)$ such that $|p_0^{\mathcal{A}}(k) - p_1^{\mathcal{A}}(k)| < \nu(k)$.*

CKLM give a zero-knowledge variant of this definition called *strong* derivation privacy, in which proofs output by ZKEval should be indistinguishable from those output by the simulator. The security experiment is almost the same, with the only differences being that $\mathcal{A}$ is given the simulation trapdoor, $\mathcal{A}$ is not required to output any witnesses, and S_2 is used in place of $\mathcal{P}$. Putting these all together, if a proof system is zero knowledge, strongly derivation private, and CM-SSE, then CKLM call it a *cm-NIZK*.

2.2 Succinct Non-Interactive Arguments of Knowledge

Our cm-NIZK construction in Section 3 builds on succinct non-interactive arguments of knowledge, or SNARGs (also called SNARKs) for short. Proofs of this kind were first shown to exist by Micali in 2000 [26], who used the Fiat-Shamir heuristic [15] to eliminate the interaction in previous succinct arguments. More recently, Groth provided a construction using pairings [22] which was improved by Lipmaa [25], Bitansky et al. [3] constructed designated-verifier SNARGs using the new notion of extractable collision-resistant hash functions, and Gennaro et al. [17] constructed constant-sized SNARGs with a relatively short common reference string.

Our definition is based primarily on that of Boneh et al. [6], although for the succinctness property we incorporate the definition of Gentry and Wichs [19] as well. In addition, to perform our recursive composition in Section 3.1, we require a stronger notion of extraction than the original definition provided; essentially, we consider adversaries that take in advice strings as input. Although we present two formulations below, *strong* and *generative* adaptive knowledge extraction, we note that these notions are in fact equivalent; a more in-depth discussion can be found in the full version.

Definition 2.3. *Let $0 < \gamma < 1$ be a constant. A (strong) γ-succinct non-interactive argument of knowledge for a relation R is a tuple of probabilistic polynomial-time algorithms* $(\mathsf{CRSSetup}, \mathcal{P}, \mathcal{V})$ *with the following properties:*

1. *Perfect completeness. For all $k \in \mathbb{N}$, $(x, w) \in R$, $\mathsf{crs} \xleftarrow{\$} \mathsf{CRSSetup}(1^k)$, and $\pi \xleftarrow{\$} \mathcal{P}(\mathsf{crs}, x, w)$, the probability that $\mathcal{V}(\mathsf{crs}, x, \pi) = 1$ is 1.*

2. *Strong/generative adaptive knowledge extraction. For a PPT algorithm $\mathcal{A}$, let $E_{\mathcal{A}}$ be an associated PPT algorithm, and let z be a string whose size is polynomial in the security parameter. Then consider the following game:*
   - *Step 1. $\mathsf{crs} \xleftarrow{\$} \mathsf{CRSSetup}(1^k)$; $r \xleftarrow{\$} \{0,1\}^*$.*
   - *Step 2. $(x, \pi) \leftarrow \mathcal{A}(\mathsf{crs}, z; r)$.*
   - *Step 3. $w \leftarrow E_{\mathcal{A}}(\mathsf{crs}, z; r)$.*

   We say the argument system satisfies strong adaptive knowledge extraction if for all PPT $\mathcal{A}$ there exists an $E_{\mathcal{A}}$ and a negligible function $\nu(\cdot)$ such that for all z the probability (over the choices of $\mathsf{CRSSetup}$ and r) that $\mathcal{V}(\mathsf{crs}, x, \pi) = 1$ but $(x, w) \notin R$ is at most $\nu(k)$. This corresponds to previous definitions of adaptive knowledge extraction if we consider only $z = \bot$.

   In addition, it satisfies generative adaptive knowledge extraction if there exists a PPT algorithm $\mathcal{E}$ such that for all PPT $\mathcal{A}$ there exists a negligible function $\nu(\cdot)$ such that, on input the code of $\mathcal{A}$, $\mathcal{E}$ produces an extractor $E_{\mathcal{A}}$, running in time polynomial in that of $\mathcal{A}$, such that for all z the probability (over the choices of $\mathsf{CRSSetup}$ and r) that $\mathcal{V}(\mathsf{crs}, x, \pi) = 1$ but $(x, w) \notin R$ is at most $\nu(k)$.

3. *ϕ-succinct arguments. For all $k \in \mathbb{N}$, $(x, w) \in R$, and $\mathsf{crs} \xleftarrow{\$} \mathsf{CRSSetup}(1^k)$, it holds that $\mathcal{P}(\mathsf{crs}, x, w)$ produces a distribution over strings of length at most $\phi(k, |x|, |w|)$, where $\phi(k, |x|, |w|)$ is bounded by $poly(k)polylog(|x|) + \gamma|w|$ for some constant $0 < \gamma < 1$.*

While the succinctness property of SNARGs is quite attractive for applications, it comes with a price: all known SNARG constructions are based on so-called "knowledge of exponent" assumptions [10,2]; furthermore, a recent result due to Gentry and Wichs [19] that separates SNARGS from all falsifiable assumptions suggests that this dependence is perhaps inherent. In addition, to satisfy our stronger version of adaptive knowledge extraction (either strong or generative; again, they are equivalent), the knowledge of exponent assumption used to prove the security of existing SNARG constructions [22,17] would have to be potentially strengthened to consider an extractor that has access to the code of $\mathcal{A}$; for more details, we defer to the full version.

The final observation we make about SNARGs is that the definition of adaptive knowledge extraction requires the extractor to have non-black-box access to the malicious prover; as we will see in Section 3.2, this can make SNARGs difficult to integrate into protocol design. Fortunately, we can easily see that this notion relates to the standard notion of soundness for proofs [14] (as used implicitly in Groth's SNARG construction [22]):

Theorem 2.1. *If a proof system* (CRSSetup, $\mathcal{P}, \mathcal{V}$) *satisfies adaptive knowledge extraction then it also satisfies adaptive computational soundness.*

Proof. To show this, we take an adversary $\mathcal{A}$ that can break the soundness of the proof system with non-negligible probability ϵ and use it to construct an adversary $\mathcal{B}$ that breaks adaptive knowledge extraction with the same probability ϵ. The code for $\mathcal{B}$ is simple: on input (crs; r), it gives crs to $\mathcal{A}$ (and implicitly runs it on a random tape $r' \subseteq r$), and when $\mathcal{A}$ outputs a pair (x, π) $\mathcal{B}$ outputs the same. By the definition of soundness, $\mathcal{A}$ will win if $\mathcal{V}(\text{crs}, x, \pi) = 1$ but $x \notin L_R$; this implies that, for any w output by $E_{\mathcal{B}}$, it must be the case that $(x, w) \notin R$, as otherwise $x \in L_R$. $\mathcal{B}$ will therefore succeed whenever $\mathcal{A}$ does and thus succeeds with probability ϵ.

3   A Construction of cm-NIZKs from SNARGs

In this section, we construct cm-NIZK proofs from zero-knowledge SNARGs that are malleable with respect to a wide range of transformations, namely all t-*tiered* transformation classes. Intuitively, a relation is t-tiered if each instance x lives in some tier i. We would like transformations to move up through the tiers, and we would also like ensure that at most t transformations are applied. Formally, we say that a relation $R^{(t)}$ is t-tiered if there exists an efficiently computable function tier : $L_R^{(t)} \to [0, t]$ and $(\bot, \bot) \in R^{(t)}$, and that a transformation class $\mathcal{T}^{(t)}$ is t-tiered for $R^{(t)}$ if for all $T = (T_{\text{inst}}, T_{\text{wit}}) \in \mathcal{T}$ the following two conditions hold: (1) if $(x, w) \in R^{(t)}$ and tier$(x) < t$, then $(T_{\text{inst}}(x), T_{\text{wit}}(w)) \in R^{(t)}$ and tier$(T_{\text{inst}}(x)) > $ tier(x); and (2) if tier$(x) = t$ then $T_{\text{inst}}(x) = \bot$.

We summarize the contributions in this section in Figure 1. As discussed in the introduction, the construction in each subsection is used as a component in the next subsection's construction, with the end goal of constructing a cm-NIZK. In Section 3.1 we construct a SNARG, malleable with respect to a t-tiered transformation class, that we then use in Section 3.2 in combination with

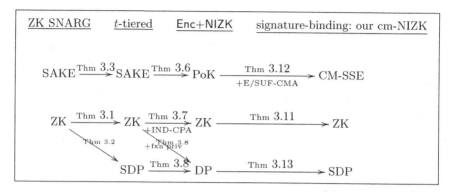

Fig. 1. The various relations among our constructions in this section. The arrows indicate which properties of the previous construction are used to obtain which properties of the next one, and are labeled on the top with the theorem number that proves the relation; the labels on the bottom indicate properties of additional primitives that are used as well. For example, we prove in Theorem 3.12 that our signature-binding construction of a cm-NIZK satisfies CM-SSE if our Enc+NIZK construction is a proof of knowledge, and the additional signature and one-time signature schemes we use are, respectively, unforgeable and strongly unforgeable; this is captured by the top rightmost arrow in the diagram. Strong adaptive knowledge extraction is written as SAKE, zero knowledge as ZK, proof of knowledge as PoK, and (strong) derivation privacy as (S)DP.

encryption to obtain a full NIZKPoK; this step seems necessary because SNARGs satisfy only the weak notion of adaptive knowledge extraction, which seems insufficient for constructing cm-NIZKs. Finally, using this NIZKPoK and a one-time and regular signature scheme, we construct in Section 3.3 a cm-NIZK that is malleable with respect to a broader class of transformations than could be supported by the construction of CKLM [7].

3.1   From SNARGs to Malleable but Weakly Extractable Proofs

We begin by constructing a derivation-private NIZK for a relation $R^{(t)}$, malleable with respect to a t-tiered transformation class $\mathcal{T}^{(t)}$, that achieves some degree of knowledge extraction. Our approach in this endeavor is inspired by that of Boneh et al. [6], who use SNARGs to construct a "targeted malleable" encryption scheme. To form a proof for an instance x_0 at the bottom level, one can use the SNARG directly to obtain a proof π_0. Now, suppose we would like to further form a proof for an instance $x_1 = T_{\mathrm{inst}}(x_0)$; one option is to use the witness $T_{\mathrm{wit}}(w_0)$ and form a fresh proof just as we did for x_0. Another option, however, is to "maul" the proof π_0: this can be accomplished by forming a new proof π_1 that proves knowledge of the old proof π_0 and instance x_0, as well as a transformation T such that $x_1 = T_{\mathrm{inst}}(x_0)$.

The reason why SNARGs are attractive for this application is that, because the extraction procedure is non-black-box and therefore the proofs can be succinct, the proof π_1 can in fact be the same size as the proof π_0. Continuing in this fashion, we can see that at the i-th level, a proof for x_i can be proved using either knowledge of a witness w_i for the relation $R^{(t)}$, or knowledge of a proof π_{i-1} for x_{i-1} and a transformation T such that $x_i = T_{\text{inst}}(x_{i-1})$.

It turns out that, if the SNARG proof system used is zero knowledge (or even just witness indistinguishable), then the resulting proof system is derivation private. As mentioned above, however, the notion of extractability we can satisfy is still only the weak notion of adaptive knowledge extraction that SNARGs provide. In the next section, we show how to bootstrap this construction to obtain a proof system that satisfies the standard notion of extractability for proofs of knowledge (and still satisfies all the malleability and derivation privacy requirements).

To begin our construction, we first formalize the intuition developed above by defining the languages we use: at the bottom level at $i = 0$ we have $L_0 := \{x \mid \exists \, w \text{ s.t. } (x, w) \in R^{(t)}\}$, and for i such that $1 \leq i \leq t$, we have

$$L_i := \left\{ (x, \text{crs}_{i-1}, \ldots, \text{crs}_0) \;\middle|\; \begin{array}{l} \exists \, (w, x', \pi', T) \text{ s.t } (x, w) \in R^{(t)} \text{ or} \\ \mathcal{V}_{i-1}(\text{crs}_{i-1}, (x', \text{crs}_{i-2}, \ldots, \text{crs}_0), \pi') = 1, \\ T_{\text{inst}}(x') = x, \text{ and } T \in \mathcal{T}^{(t)} \end{array} \right\}$$

Using these languages and $t + 1$ SNARG systems $(\text{CRSSetup}_i, \mathcal{P}_i, \mathcal{V}_i)$, we now define our malleable t-tiered construction for $R^{(t)}$.

- CRSSetup(1^k): Generate $\text{crs}_i \xleftarrow{\$} \text{CRSSetup}_i(1^k)$ for all i, $0 \leq i \leq t$. Output $\text{crs} := (\text{crs}_0, \ldots, \text{crs}_t)$.
- $\mathcal{P}(\text{crs}, x, w)$: Compute $i := \text{tier}(x)$; output $\pi \xleftarrow{\$} \mathcal{P}_i(\text{crs}_i, (x, \text{crs}_{i-1}, \ldots, \text{crs}_0), (w, \bot, \bot, \bot))$.
- $\mathcal{V}(\text{crs}, x, \pi)$: Compute $i := \text{tier}(x)$ and output $\mathcal{V}_i(\text{crs}_i, (x, \text{crs}_{i-1}, \ldots, \text{crs}_0), \pi)$.
- ZKEval(crs, T, x, π): Compute $i := \text{tier}(x)$, define $x' := T_{\text{inst}}(x)$, and output $\pi \xleftarrow{\$} \mathcal{P}_{i+1}(\text{crs}_{i+1}, (x', \text{crs}_i, \ldots, \text{crs}_0), (\bot, x, \pi, T))$.

Recall that there are three properties we would like this proof system to satisfy: (1) zero knowledge, (2) derivation privacy, and (3) strong adaptive knowledge extraction; we deal with each of these in turn. For the first, zero knowledge, if we assume that our underlying proof systems are zero knowledge then we get a proof of the following theorem for free:

Theorem 3.1. *If the SNARG systems* $(\text{CRSSetup}_i, \mathcal{P}_i, \mathcal{V}_i)$ *are zero knowledge for all* i, $0 \leq i \leq t$, *then the* t-*tiered construction is zero knowledge.*

We next turn to derivation privacy. At first glance, it would seem impossible that our construction could meet derivation privacy: after all, $\text{tier}(x)$ openly reveals exactly how many times a transformation has been applied! Looking at the definition of the prover $\mathcal{P}$, however, we see that for x such that $\text{tier}(x) = i$ it does in fact output a proof that "looks like" i transformations have been applied, even though it is using a fresh witness; as this is what the definition of derivation privacy requires (i.e., that the proof, rather than the instance, not reveal the transformation), we therefore use the witness indistinguishability of the SNARGs (which trivially follows from zero knowledge) to show that derivation privacy does hold. In addition, to show that strong derivation privacy holds, we require our SNARGs to be composable zero knowledge (as the adversary in the strong derivation privacy game gets to see the simulation trapdoor, and thus the zero knowledge adversary needs to as well); this requirement is met, for example, by the SNARG constructions of Groth [22] and Gennaro et al. [17], both of which actually satisfy the significantly stronger property of statistical zero knowledge. Due to space constraints, a proof of the following theorem can be found in the full version [8].

Theorem 3.2. *If the SNARG systems* $(\mathsf{CRSSetup}_i, \mathcal{P}_i, \mathcal{V}_i)$ *satisfy witness indistinguishability for all* i, *then the* t-*tiered construction satisfies derivation privacy for transformations in* $\mathcal{T}^{(t)}$. *Furthermore, if* $(\mathsf{CRSSetup}_i, \mathcal{P}_i, \mathcal{V}_i)$ *satisfy composable zero-knowledge for all* i, *then the* t-*tiered construction satisfies both derivation privacy and strong derivation privacy for transformations in* $\mathcal{T}^{(t)}$.

Next, we turn to adaptive knowledge extraction; here, we can show that if the number of times the "proof of a proof" method has been applied is constant, then the t-tiered construction is strongly adaptive knowledge extractable. As do Boneh et al. [6], we require t be constant so the runtime of the extractor does not blow up: if $\mathcal{A}$ runs in time τ, and we require the runtime of the extractor to be only polynomial in the runtime of $\mathcal{A}$, then the extraction of the t-th nested proof (i.e., if $\mathcal{A}$ has formed a proof of a proof t times) might take time $a^t \tau + tb$ for some constants a and b, which for arbitrary t could be exponential. To ensure that the time taken to extract from these nested proofs instead remains polynomial, we therefore require that t be constant. Furthermore, as we will see in the proof we rely on strong adaptive knowledge extraction to perform our recursive extraction (again, as do Boneh et al.). A proof of the following theorem can be found in the full version.

Theorem 3.3. *If the SNARG systems* $(\mathsf{CRSSetup}_i, \mathcal{P}_i, \mathcal{V}_i)$ *satisfy strong adaptive knowledge extraction (as defined in Definition 2.3) for all* i, *then the* t-*tiered construction satisfies strong adaptive knowledge extraction for constant* t.

Finally, we discuss the size of the proofs. Looking at the language L_i for some level, we see that an instance for the next language L_{i+1} consists of the same elements as an instance of L_i, with the addition of the CRS crs_i. If we consider, for example, the SNARG construction of Groth [22], then the size of crs_i is $O(|x^{(i)}|^2)$ for $x^{(i)} \in L_i$. Let f be the function that computes the size of the instance at level $i+1$ given the size of the instance x at level i. Then, because an element of size $|x|^2$ is added to obtain the instance for the next level up, we have that $f(f(|x|)) = |x|^4$, and, after t transformations, that $f^t(|x_0|) > |x_0|^{2^t}$. If t is constant, the fact that we require SNARGs to be of size $\mathrm{polylog}(|x|)$ accounts for every such polynomial factor. Considering next the witness, we observe that the size of the witness $w^{(i)}$ for $i > 0$ is $|w_i| + |x_{i-1}| + |\pi_{i-1}| + |T_i|$. In order for our proofs to be succinct, we require that $|\pi_i| \le |\pi_{i-1}|$. If we assume that $|w_i| \le |w_{i-1}|$, $|x_i| \le |x_{i-1}|$, and $|T_i| \le |T_{i-1}|$ and that $w^{(i)} = |w_i| + |x_{i-1}| +$

$|\pi_{i-1}| + |T_i| \leq 4|\pi_{i-1}|$, then a poly($k$)polylog($|x|$) $+ \gamma|w|$ succinct SNARG with $\gamma = 1/4$ is sufficient for our construction.

3.2 From Weak Malleable Proofs to Malleable Proofs of Knowledge

With our malleable NIZK in place, we might now try to use it to directly construct a cm-NIZK or, because we can satisfy only adaptive knowledge extraction, a weakened notion of cm-NIZK that accomodates this weaker extractability property. Looking back at the definition of controlled malleability (CM-SSE) in Definition 2.1, however, we can see that $\mathcal{A}$ is given access to a simulation oracle S_2. This oracle access seems to be fundamental to the definition: to achieve any kind of simulation soundness, in which we want $\mathcal{A}$ to be unable to produce its own proofs of false statements even after seeing many such proofs, we must give it an oracle that can produce false proofs. If we attempt to then use any non-black-box notion of extractability in conjunction with such an oracle, it is not clear how such an extractor would even be defined, as it cannot simply run the code for $\mathcal{A}$ (in particular, because the oracle's ability to produce false proofs must be presumably unavailable to $\mathcal{A}$ and therefore $E_{\mathcal{A}}$).

To avoid this obstacle altogether, we instead augment the construction from the previous section to achieve full extractability. To do this, our proofs consist of a ciphertext encrypting the witness, and a malleable zero-knowledge SNARG proving knowledge of the value inside of this ciphertext. Now, rather than require the use of the non-black-box extractor to prove any kind of extractability, we can instead give an extractor the secret key, and it can extract by decrypting the ciphertext. As we will see in our proof of Theorem 3.6, this means that all is required of the SNARG is soundness (which, we recall by Theorem 2.1, is implied by adaptive knowledge extraction).

In more detail, to construct a malleable NIZKPoK for a relation $R^{(pok)}$ and transformation class $\mathcal{T}^{(pok)}$, we use an encryption scheme and a proof system for the relation $R^{(t)}$ such that

$$((pk, x, c), (w, r)) \in R^{(t)} \iff c = \mathsf{Enc}(pk, w; r) \wedge (x, w) \in R^{(pok)}.$$

As for malleability, suppose we want to be able to transform the proofs for $R^{(pok)}$ with respect to some transformation class $\mathcal{T}^{(pok)}$. In order to implement ZKEval for a transformation $T = (T_{\text{inst}}, T_{\text{wit}}) \in \mathcal{T}^{(pok)}$, we will need to be able to transform the proof for $R^{(t)}$ and the ciphertext c. For the latter, this means we need to be able to apply a transformation T_c on the ciphertext that produces an encryption of $T_{\text{wit}}(w)$; i.e., the homomorphic property of the encryption scheme must be robust enough to allow us to apply T_{wit} to the encrypted message. For the proof, we also require a transformation T_r on the randomness r of the ciphertext, as we require a transformation that maps (pk, x, c) to $(pk, T_{\text{inst}}(x), T_c(c))$ and (w, r) to $(T_{\text{wit}}(w), T_r(r))$.

A bit more formally, for every $T = (T_{\text{inst}}, T_{\text{wit}}) \in \mathcal{T}^{(pok)}$ and r' from the randomness space $\mathcal{R}$, let T_c be the transformation that maps $c = \mathsf{Enc}(w; r)$ to $\mathsf{Eval}(c, T_{\text{wit}}; r') = \mathsf{Enc}(T_{\text{wit}}(w); r \circ r')$ (where $\circ$ denotes the operation that composes the randomness, and Eval denotes the homomorphic operation on ciphertexts), let T_r be the resulting transformation on the randomness, and let $\tau(T, r')$ be the transformation that maps instances (x, c) to new instances $(T_{\text{inst}}(x), T_c(c))$, and witnesses (w, r) to new witnesses $(T_{\text{wit}}(w), T_r(r))$ (i.e., the exact transformation we need for the proof). Finally, let $\mathcal{T}^{(t)}$ be the set of transformations that includes $\tau(T, r')$ for all $T \in \mathcal{T}^{(pok)}$, $r' \in \mathcal{R}$, and let $\mathcal{T}^{(E)}$ be the set of all T_{wit}.

To give our Enc+NIZK construction for $R^{(pok)}$, let (KeyGen, Enc, Dec, Eval) be a function-private homomorphic encryption schemewith randomness space $\mathcal{R}$ and let (CRSSetup', $\mathcal{P}'$, $\mathcal{V}'$, ZKEval') be a malleable zero-knowledge SNARG for the relation $R^{(t)}$ with transformation set $\mathcal{T}^{(t)}$. Our construction of a NIZKPoK is as follows:

- CRSSetup(1^k): Generate crs' $\xleftarrow{\$}$ CRSSetup'(1^k) and $(pk, sk) \xleftarrow{\$}$ KeyGen(1^k) and output crs := (crs', pk).
- $\mathcal{P}$(crs, x, w): Parse crs = (crs', pk) and pick randomness $r \xleftarrow{\$} \mathcal{R}$. Then compute $c \leftarrow$ Enc(pk, w; r) and $\pi' \xleftarrow{\$} \mathcal{P}'$(crs', (pk, x, c), (w, r)) and output $\pi := (\pi', c)$.
- $\mathcal{V}$(crs, x, π): Parse crs = (crs', pk) and $\pi = (\pi', c)$, and output $\mathcal{V}'$(crs', (pk, x, c), π').
- ZKEval(crs, T, x, π): Parse crs = (crs', pk), $\pi = (\pi', c)$, and $T = (T_{\text{inst}}, T_{\text{wit}})$. Then choose random $r' \xleftarrow{\$} \mathcal{R}$, compute $T' := \tau(T, r')$, and compute $\pi_T \xleftarrow{\$}$ ZKEval'(crs', T', (pk, x, c), π') and $c_T :=$ Eval(pk, T_{wit}, c; r'). Output (π_T, c_T).

We make the following requirements on the underlying SNARG to obtain the completeness and malleability properties; both of them follow directly from the Enc+NIZK construction:

Theorem 3.4. *Let $\mathbb{W}^{(E+N)}$ be the witness space for $R^{(pok)}$. If the SNARG is complete for $R^{(t)}$ and the encryption scheme has message space $\mathcal{M}$ such that $\mathbb{W}^{(E+N)} \subseteq \mathcal{M}$, then the Enc+NIZK construction is complete.*

Theorem 3.5. *The Enc+NIZK construction is malleable with respect to $\mathcal{T}^{(pok)}$ whenever the SNARG is malleable with respect to the corresponding set $\mathcal{T}^{(t)} = \tau(\mathcal{T}^{(pok)}, \mathcal{R})$ and the encryption scheme is malleable with respect to $\mathcal{T}^{(E)}$ (as defined above).*

If $\mathcal{T}^{(pok)}$ is a t-tiered class of transformations on $R^{(pok)}$, then $\tau(\mathcal{T}^{(pok)})$ will also be t-tiered on $R^{(t)}$. Thus, if we instantiate (KeyGen, Enc, Dec, Eval) using a fully homomorphic encryption scheme and we use the SNARGs constructed in the previous section, we can obtain a malleable proof system for any t-tiered $\mathcal{T}^{(pok)}$ with constant t. (On the other hand, we will see in Section 4 that there are interesting relations and transformation classes we can obtain without fully homomorphic encryption as well.) As for size efficiency, we know by the succinctness property of SNARGs that the size of π' will not grow through transformation. For the ciphertext c, if we assume that T_{wit} does not increase the size of the witness, then the size of c will stay the same as well and thus the proof will remain compact even as it is transformed.

We would now like to show that if the SNARG satisfies adaptive knowledge extraction then the Enc+NIZK construction satisfies extractability; i.e., is an argument of knowledge. We also must show that the construction retains the original zero knowledge and derivation privacy properties as well. Due to space constraints, proofs of the following three theorems can be found in the full version.

Theorem 3.6. *If the SNARG satisfies adaptive knowledge extraction with respect to $R^{(t)}$ then the Enc+NIZK construction is a proof of knowledge with respect to $R^{(pok)}$.*

Theorem 3.7. *If the SNARG is zero knowledge and the encryption scheme is IND-CPA secure, then the Enc+NIZK construction is zero knowledge.*

Theorem 3.8. *If the SNARG is zero knowledge and strongly derivation private with respect to the class of transformations $\mathcal{T}^{(t)}$ and the encryption scheme is function private with respect to $\mathcal{T}^{(E)}$ then the Enc+NIZK construction is derivation private with respect to $\mathcal{T}^{(pok)}$.*

3.3 From Malleable NIWIPoKs to cm-NIZKs

With our malleable NIZKPoK in place, we are finally ready to construct cm-NIZKs (although, as we will see, we require only witness indistinguishability rather than full zero knowledge). We first recall the construction of CKLM, who used a relation R' such that $((x, vk), (w, x', T, \sigma)) \in R'$ if $(x, w) \in R$ or $\mathsf{Verify}(vk, \sigma, x') = 1$, $x = T_{\mathrm{inst}}(x')$, and $T \in \mathcal{T}$, where σ was a signature for a secure signature scheme. We use the CKLM construction as a rough guideline for our own; the crucial alteration we make, however, is that CKLM were willing to retain the natural re-randomizability of Groth-Sahai proofs, whereas we want to consider classes of transformations that do not contain the identity (for example, the t-tiered transformation classes).

Suppose we want to construct a cm-NIZK for relation $R^{(cm)}$ and transformation class $\mathcal{T}^{(cm)}$. We use a NIWIPoK for an augmented relation $R^{(pok)}$ such that $((x, vk, vk_{\mathrm{ot}}), (w, x', vk'_{\mathrm{ot}}, T, \sigma)) \in R^{(pok)}$ if (1) $(x, w) \in R^{(cm)}$ or (2) $\mathsf{Verify}(vk, \sigma, (x', vk'_{\mathrm{ot}})) = 1$ and either (2a) $x = T_{\mathrm{inst}}(x')$ for $T = (T_{\mathrm{inst}}, T_{\mathrm{wit}}) \in \mathcal{T}^{(cm)}$, or (2b) $x' = x$ and $vk'_{\mathrm{ot}} = vk_{\mathrm{ot}}$, where vk_{ot} is a verification key for a one-time signature scheme.

Intuitively, to simulate proofs, we can use this last type of witness; i.e., on a query x, the simulator can use sk as a trapdoor to sign (x, vk_{ot}) and produce a signature σ, and then form a proof using $(\bot, x, vk_{\mathrm{ot}}, \bot, \sigma)$ as a witness. To ensure that an adversary cannot simply reuse this proof and claim it as its own (i.e., apply the identity transformation), proofs are accompanied by a one-time signature, on both the instance and the proof, to indicate that the proof was formed fresh for this instance. Because the one-time signature thus binds together the instance and the proof, we call this construction "signature binding."

Now, if we want to allow transformations $(\widehat{T}_{\text{inst}}, \widehat{T}_{\text{wit}}) \in \mathcal{T}^{(cm)}$ for our cm-NIZK, we will have to be able to transform the underlying NIWIPoK accordingly. To do this for any $\widehat{T} = (\widehat{T}_{\text{inst}}, \widehat{T}_{\text{wit}}) \in \mathcal{T}^{(cm)}$, and any $\widehat{vk}_{\text{ot}} \in VK_{\text{ot}}$ (where VK_{ot} is the set of all possible verification keys), let $\rho(\widehat{T}, \widehat{vk}_{\text{ot}})$ be a transformation that maps (x, vk, vk_{ot}) to $(\widehat{T}_{\text{inst}}(x), vk, \widehat{vk}_{\text{ot}})$ and $(w, x', vk'_{\text{ot}}, T, \sigma)$ to $(\widehat{T}_{\text{wit}}(w), x', vk'_{\text{ot}}, \widehat{T} \circ T, \sigma)$. We require the underlying NIWIPoK to be malleable with respect to this class $\mathcal{T}^{(pok)}$.

More formally, let (KeyGen, Sign, Verify) be an unforgeable signature scheme, (KeyGen$_{\text{ot}}$, Sign$_{\text{ot}}$, Verify$_{\text{ot}}$) be a strongly unforgeable one-time signature scheme, and let (CRSSetup$_{\text{WI}}$, $\mathcal{P}_{\text{WI}}$, $\mathcal{V}_{\text{WI}}$) be a malleable derivation-private NIWIPoK for $R^{(pok)}$. We give our construction of a cm-NIZK using these primitives as follows:

- CRSSetup(1^k): Generate $\text{crs}_{\text{WI}} \xleftarrow{\$} \text{CRSSetup}_{\text{WI}}(1^k)$; $(vk, sk) \xleftarrow{\$} \text{KeyGen}(1^k)$. Output $\text{crs} := (\text{crs}_{\text{WI}}, vk)$.
- $\mathcal{P}(\text{crs}, x, w)$: Parse $\text{crs} = (\text{crs}_{\text{WI}}, vk)$ and compute $\pi' \xleftarrow{\$} \mathcal{P}_{\text{WI}}(\text{crs}_{\text{WI}}, (x, vk, vk_{\text{ot}}), (w, \bot, \bot, \bot, \bot))$. Generate $(vk_{\text{ot}}, sk_{\text{ot}}) \xleftarrow{\$} \text{KeyGen}_{\text{ot}}(1^k)$, compute $\sigma_{\text{ot}} \xleftarrow{\$} \text{Sign}_{\text{ot}}(sk_{\text{ot}}, (x, \pi'))$, and output $\pi := (\pi', \sigma_{\text{ot}}, vk_{\text{ot}})$.
- $\mathcal{V}(\text{crs}, x, \pi)$: Parse $\pi = (\pi', \sigma_{\text{ot}}, vk_{\text{ot}})$ and check that $\text{Verify}_{\text{ot}}(vk_{\text{ot}}, \sigma_{\text{ot}}, (x, \pi')) = 1$; if this fails then output 0. Otherwise, parse $\text{crs} = (\text{crs}_{\text{WI}}, vk)$ and output $\mathcal{V}_{\text{WI}}(\text{crs}_{\text{WI}}, (x, vk, vk_{\text{ot}}), \pi')$.
- ZKEval(crs, T, x, π): Parse $\text{crs} = (\text{crs}_{\text{WI}}, vk)$ and $\pi = (\pi', \sigma_{\text{ot}}, vk_{\text{ot}})$. Generate $(\widehat{vk}_{\text{ot}}, \widehat{sk}_{\text{ot}}) \xleftarrow{\$} \text{KeyGen}_{\text{ot}}(1^k)$ and compute $\pi'' \xleftarrow{\$} \text{ZKEval}_{\text{WI}}(\text{crs}_{\text{WI}}, \rho(T, \widehat{vk}_{\text{ot}}), (x, vk, vk_{\text{ot}}), \pi')$ and $\sigma'_{\text{ot}} \xleftarrow{\$} \text{Sign}_{\text{ot}}(\widehat{sk}_{\text{ot}}, (x, \pi''))$. Output $(\pi'', \sigma'_{\text{ot}}, \widehat{vk}_{\text{ot}})$.

Although in using $\widehat{T} \circ T$ we require that $\mathcal{T}^{(cm)}$ be closed under composition, we note that this is not a strong restriction. Indeed, if $\mathcal{T}^{(cm)}$ is not closed under composition, then we can define the closure of $\mathcal{T}^{(cm)}$ to be the class of transformations $\mathcal{T}^{(cm)'}$ such that $T \in \mathcal{T}^{(cm)'}$ if and only if $T = T_1 \circ \ldots \circ T_j$ for $j < t$ and $T_1, \ldots, T_j \in \mathcal{T}^{(cm)}$. In this case, if we construct the NIWIPoK using our Enc+NIZK construction, our proofs have to increase in size by a factor of t. (The encryption scheme used will have to have message space large enough to represent $T_1 \circ \ldots \circ T_t$ as $(T_1, \ldots, T_t)$.) On the other hand, this size increase is unavoidable for general transformations if we want to obtain a definition (like CM-SSE) in which a non-interactive black-box extractor must be able to extract the entire transformation performed.

By construction, we directly obtain the following theorems:

Theorem 3.9. *If the proof system* (CRSSetup$_{\text{WI}}$, $\mathcal{P}_{\text{WI}}$, $\mathcal{V}_{\text{WI}}$, ZKEval$_{\text{WI}}$) *is complete for relation* $R^{(pok)}$, *and the one-time signature is correct, then the signature-binding construction is complete for relation* $R^{(cm)}$.

Theorem 3.10. *If the proof system* (CRSSetup$_{\text{WI}}$, $\mathcal{P}_{\text{WI}}$, $\mathcal{V}_{\text{WI}}$, ZKEval$_{\text{WI}}$) *is malleable with respect to the transformation class* $\mathcal{T}^{(pok)} = \rho(\mathcal{T}^{(cm)}, VK_{\text{ot}})$ *(as defined above), then the signature-binding construction is malleable for transformation class* $\mathcal{T}^{(cm)}$.

Now, if we want to instantiate the NIWIPoK using our Enc+NIZK construction from the previous section, we must first ensure that $R^{(pok)}$ and $\mathcal{T}^{(pok)}$ satisfy the constraints discussed therein. In particular, we required that $\mathcal{T}^{(pok)}$ be a t-tiered transformation class for $R^{(pok)}$, and that there is an encryption scheme whose message space contains the witness space for $R^{(pok)}$ that is homomorphic with respect to the class of transformations $\{T_{\text{wit}}\}$ for all $(T_{\text{inst}}, T_{\text{wit}}) \in \mathcal{T}^{(pok)}$.

Expanding on this last requirement, as our witnesses for $R^{(pok)}$ are of the form $(w, x', vk'_{\text{ot}}, T, \sigma)$, we need to use an encryption scheme in which the message space subsumes the space of all of these values; i.e., the witness, instance, and transformation spaces, as well as the space of possible one-time verification keys and signatures. We also need the encryption scheme to be homomorphic with respect to the set of transformations that map $(w, x', vk'_{\text{ot}}, T, \sigma)$ to $(\widehat{T}_{\text{wit}}(w), x', vk'_{\text{ot}}, \widehat{T} \circ T, \sigma)$ for any $(\widehat{T}_{\text{inst}}, \widehat{T}_{\text{wit}}) \in \mathcal{T}^{(cm)}$. Finally, we require that $\mathcal{T}^{(cm)}$ is t-tiered for $R^{(cm)}$, as this will guarantee that $\mathcal{T}^{(pok)}$ is t-tiered for $R^{(pok)}$. If we assume SNARGs for general languages and fully homomorphic encryption, then we can obtain a cm-NIZK for any t-tiered transformation class as long as t is constant; in Section 4, we will also see that we can construct cm-NIZKs for interesting relations using only multiplicatively homomorphic encryption. Moreover, if we continue our assumption from the previous section that T_{wit} does not increase the size of w, then the size of proofs will not grow by transformation here either.

Finally, in order to show that this is a cm-NIZK, we need to show that it satisfies zero knowledge, CM-SSE, and strong derivation privacy. Due to space constraints, proofs of the following three theorems can be found in the full version.

Theorem 3.11. *If the proof system* $(\mathsf{CRSSetup}_{\mathsf{WI}}, \mathcal{P}_{\mathsf{WI}}, \mathcal{V}_{\mathsf{WI}}, \mathsf{ZKEval}_{\mathsf{WI}})$ *is witness indistinguishable then the signature-binding construction is zero knowledge.*

Theorem 3.12. *If the signature scheme* $(\mathsf{KeyGen}, \mathsf{Sign}, \mathsf{Verify})$ *is unforgeable (i.e., EUF-CMA secure), the one-time signature* $(\mathsf{KeyGen}_{\text{ot}}, \mathsf{Sign}_{\text{ot}}, \mathsf{Verify}_{\text{ot}})$ *is strongly unforgeable (SUF-CMA secure), and the proof system* $(\mathsf{CRSSetup}_{\mathsf{WI}}, \mathcal{P}_{\mathsf{WI}}, \mathcal{V}_{\mathsf{WI}}, \mathsf{ZKEval}_{\mathsf{WI}})$ *is an argument of knowledge, the signature-binding construction satisfies the CM-SSE property.*

Theorem 3.13. *If the proof system* $(\mathsf{CRSSetup}_{\mathsf{WI}}, \mathcal{P}_{\mathsf{WI}}, \mathcal{V}_{\mathsf{WI}}, \mathsf{ZKEval}_{\mathsf{WI}})$ *is derivation private for* $\mathcal{T}^{(pok)}$ *then the signature-binding construction is strongly derivation private for* $\mathcal{T}^{(cm)}$.

4 A Compactly Verifiable Shuffle Using SNARGs

Now that we have just constructed our SNARG-based cm-NIZK, we consider how to use it to construct a compactly verifiable shuffle.

We start by defining formally the relation and transformations we want to use for shuffles. Abstractly, instances for the correctness of a shuffle are of the form $x = (pk, \{c_i\}_i, \{c'_i\}_i)$, where pk is a public key for a re-randomizable encryption scheme, $\{c_i\}_i$ are the original ciphertexts, and $\{c'_i\}_i$ are the shuffled ciphertexts. In addition, to allow each mix authority to prove that it participated in the shuffle, instances also contain a set $\{pk_j\}_j$ that consists of the public keys of the authorities that have participated thus far. Similarly, witnesses are of the form $w = (\varphi, \{R_i\}_i, \{sk_j\}_j)$, where φ is a permutation, $\{R_i\}_i$ are the re-randomization factors, and $\{sk_j\}_j$ are the secret keys corresponding to $\{pk_j\}_j$. The relation R is such that

$$((pk, \{c_i\}_i, \{c'_i\}_i, \{pk_j\}_j), (\varphi, \{R_i\}_i, \{sk_j\}_j)) \in R$$
$$\Leftrightarrow \{c'_i\}_i = \{\mathsf{ReRand}(pk, \varphi(c_i); R_i)\}_i \wedge (pk_j, sk_j) \in R_{pk} \; \forall j.$$

Briefly, valid transformations in $\mathcal{T}$ should be shuffles. Ignoring the authority keys for now (details can be found in the original CKLM paper and the full version of this paper), we define transformations on instances as

$$T_{\mathrm{inst}}(x) = T_{(\varphi', \{R'_i\}_i)}(pk, \{c_i\}_i, \{c'_i\}_i) := (pk, \{c_i\}_i, \{\mathsf{ReRand}(pk, \varphi'(c_i); R'_i)\}_i)$$

and on witnesses as

$$T_{\mathrm{wit}}(w) = T_{(\varphi', \{R'_i\}_i)}(\varphi, \{R_i\}_i) := (\varphi' \circ \varphi, \{\varphi'(R_i) * R'_i\}_i),$$

where $*$ is the operation used to compose the randomness (i.e., $\mathsf{ReRand}(pk, \mathsf{ReRand}(pk, c; R), R') = \mathsf{ReRand}(pk, c; R * R')$).

4.1   Our Construction

The shuffle construction of CKLM [7] used four building blocks: a hard relation R_{pk}, a re-randomizable encryption scheme ($\mathsf{KeyGen}, \mathsf{Enc}, \mathsf{Dec}, \mathsf{ReRand}$), a proof of knowledge ($\mathsf{CRSSetup}, \mathcal{P}, \mathcal{V}$), and a cm-NIZK ($\mathsf{CRSSetup}', \mathcal{P}', \mathcal{V}', \mathsf{ZKEval}'$). As we just constructed a cm-NIZK, we can simply plug it into this generic construction, which CKLM already proved secure. What it remains to show is that the requirements placed on transformations in Sections 3.2 and Section 3.3 are met by the shuffle transformations.

Recall the general requirement for transformations from Section 3.3: because we must encrypt values of the form $(w, x', vk'_{\mathrm{ot}}, T, \sigma)$, we need an encryption scheme ($\mathsf{KeyGen}, \mathsf{Enc}, \mathsf{Dec}, \mathsf{Eval}$) that is homomorphic with respect to the set of transformations that map $(w, x', vk'_{\mathrm{ot}}, T, \sigma)$ to $(\widehat{T}_{\mathrm{wit}}(w), x', vk'_{\mathrm{ot}}, \widehat{T} \circ T, \sigma)$ for any $(\widehat{T}_{\mathrm{inst}}, \widehat{T}_{\mathrm{wit}}) \in \mathcal{T}^{(cm)}$.

In order to meet this requirement for shuffles, we must therefore consider how to encrypt and appropriately transform all of these values. For all of the values except w and T, however, they are unchanged by the transformation; our only requirement here is therefore that they can be encrypted, meaning the spaces they live in are subsumed by the message space. As for the values that do get transformed, w and T, as they are defined for the shuffle we must consider how to transform the permutation φ, the re-randomization values $\{R_i\}_i$, and the secret keys $\{sk_j\}_j$. We deal with each of these in turn.

To encrypt a permutation $\varphi \in S_n$, we represent it as its component-wise action on indices. Formally, we first consider the collection $(c_1, \ldots, c_n)$ in which $c_i \xleftarrow{\$} \mathsf{Enc}(pk, i)$ for all i; i.e., the collection of ciphertexts encrypting their own index within the set. Now, to represent φ, we compute $c_i^{(\varphi)} \xleftarrow{\$} \mathsf{Enc}(pk, \varphi(i))$ for all i, $1 \leq i \leq n$; the set $\{c_i^{(\varphi)}\}_{i=1}^n$ is then equal to $\varphi(\{c_i\})_{i=1}^n$. When we need to compose this φ with a new permutation φ' (e.g., to compute $T_{\mathrm{wit}}(w)$), we can compute $\{c_i^{(\varphi' \circ \varphi)}\}_{i=1}^n = \varphi'(\{c_i^{(\varphi)}\}_{i=1}^n) = \varphi'(\varphi(\{c_i\}_{i=1}^n))$, which does represent the composed permutation $\varphi' \circ \varphi$ as desired.

Moving on to the re-randomization values $\{R_i\}_i$, we start in the same vein as with the permutations: for all i, we compute $c_i^{(r)} \xleftarrow{\$} \mathsf{Enc}(pk, R_i)$. We now place our only requirement on the encryption scheme $(\mathsf{KeyGen}, \mathsf{Enc}, \mathsf{Dec}, \mathsf{Eval})$, which is that it must be homomorphic with respect to the $*$ operation (i.e., the operation used to compose randomness); namely that there exist a corresponding operation $\circledast$ on ciphertexts such that if c_1 is an encryption of m_1 and c_2 is an encryption of m_2 then $c_1 \circledast c_2$ is an encryption of $m_1 * m_2$. With such an operation in place, when we want to permute using φ and add in new randomness $\{R_i'\}_i$, we can compute $c_i^{(r*r')} := \varphi(c_i^{(r)}) \circledast \mathsf{Enc}(pk, R_i')$. By the homomorphic properties of $\circledast$, $c_i^{(r*r')}$ will then be an encryption of $\varphi(R_i) * R_i'$.

Finally, for the keys, we note that as long as all values of sk_j lie in the message space then we are fine, as these values are simply appended to a list and thus do not need to be transformed.

As for the size of the resulting shuffle, we know that the CRS for the construction in Section 3.1 consists of t common references strings for the underlying SNARG. If we use the SNARG due to Gennaro et al. [17], in which the size of the CRS is linear in the circuit size, then the total size of the CRS is $O(\ell n)$. At the next level, in the Enc+NIZK construction, we add a public key pk, and at the next level, in the signature-binding construction, we add a verification key vk. If the size of each of these values is constant with respect to n (or even of size $O(n)$), then we obtain an overall shuffle parameter size of $O(\ell n)$. For the proofs, we know from our discussion in Section 3 that their size will depend on the representation of the witnesses w, instances x, and transformations T. As we've defined things here, the representations of φ and $\{R_i\}_i$ require n ciphertexts each, which means the representations of w and T are $O(n + \ell)$, as they each also contain ℓ secret keys. Similarly, the size of the instance x is $O(n + \ell)$, as it contains two sets of n ciphertexts and a set of ℓ public keys. The overall size of the proof is therefore $O(n + \ell)$.

Although the proof size is therefore smaller, having parameters of size $O(\ell n)$ means that the total number of bits read by the verifier is still $O(\ell n)$ and thus there is no benefit over previous shuffles. To get a parameter size of only $O(k\ell)$ (for the security parameter k), we assume we have a SNARG with a CRS of length $O(n)$ and proofs of length $O(n)$, and a collision-resistant hash function $H(\cdot)$ that produces k-bit strings. Then a straightforward transformation gives a SNARG where the verifier needs a CRS of length k and proofs are of length $O(n)$ as follows: first, CRSSetup generates a CRS crs for the underlying scheme, and outputs both crs and $H(\mathsf{crs})$. Then, the prover produces not only a proof π but also a CRS crs′ such that $H(\mathsf{crs'}) = H(\mathsf{crs})$; the proof must then verify under crs′. In order to verify such a proof, the verifier need only take as CRS input the value $H(\mathsf{crs})$. Knowledge extraction of this SNARG follows from collision resistance and knowledge extraction of the underlying SNARG: if the adversary produces a crs′ different from crs but such that $H(\mathsf{crs'}) = H(\mathsf{crs})$ then it breaks the collision resistance of the hash function, and if it produces a proof under crs then the underlying extractor will work. If we then use this modified SNARG in our construction in Section 3.1, we get a malleable SNARG where the verifier takes as input a CRS of length $O(k\ell)$ and proofs of length $O(n)$, meaning the elections monitor in our shuffle takes in parameters of size $O(k\ell)$ and proofs of size $O(n + \ell)$.

Acknowledgments. Anna Lysyanskaya was supported by NSF grants 1012060, 0964379, 0831293, and Sarah Meiklejohn was supported in part by a MURI grant administered by the Air Force Office of Scientific Research and in part by a graduate fellowship from the Charles Lee Powell Foundation.

References

1. Belenkiy, M., Camenisch, J., Chase, M., Kohlweiss, M., Lysyanskaya, A., Shacham, H.: Randomizable Proofs and Delegatable Anonymous Credentials. In: Halevi, S. (ed.) CRYPTO 2009. LNCS, vol. 5677, pp. 108–125. Springer, Heidelberg (2009)
2. Bellare, M., Palacio, A.: The Knowledge-of-Exponent Assumptions and 3-Round Zero-Knowledge Protocols. In: Franklin, M. (ed.) CRYPTO 2004. LNCS, vol. 3152, pp. 273–289. Springer, Heidelberg (2004)
3. Bitanksy, N., Canetti, R., Chiesa, A., Tromer, E.: From extractable collision resistance to succinct non-interactive arguments of knowledge, and back again. In: Proceedings of ITCS 2012 (2012)
4. Bitansky, N., Canetti, R., Chiesa, A., Tromer, E.: Recursive composition and bootstrapping for SNARKs and proof-carrying data. Cryptology ePrint Archive, Report 2012/095 (2012), http://eprint.iacr.org/2012/095
5. Blum, M., de Santis, A., Micali, S., Persiano, G.: Non-interactive zero-knowledge. SIAM Journal of Computing 20(6), 1084–1118 (1991)
6. Boneh, D., Segev, G., Waters, B.: Targeted malleability: homomorphic encryption for restricted computations. In: Proceedings of ITCS 2012 (2012)
7. Chase, M., Kohlweiss, M., Lysyanskaya, A., Meiklejohn, S.: Malleable Proof Systems and Applications. In: Pointcheval, D., Johansson, T. (eds.) EUROCRYPT 2012. LNCS, vol. 7237, pp. 281–300. Springer, Heidelberg (2012)
8. Chase, M., Kohlweiss, M., Lysyanskaya, A., Meiklejohn, S.: Succinct malleable NIZKs and an application to compact shuffles. Cryptology ePrint Archive, Report 2012/506 (2012), http://eprint.iacr.org/2012/506
9. Chase, M., Kohlweiss, M., Lysyanskaya, A., Meiklejohn, S.: Verifiable elections that scale for free. In: Proceedings of PKC 2013 (to appear, 2013)
10. Damgård, I.B.: Towards Practical Public Key Systems Secure against Chosen Ciphertext Attacks. In: Feigenbaum, J. (ed.) CRYPTO 1991. LNCS, vol. 576, pp. 445–456. Springer, Heidelberg (1992)

11. Damgård, I.B., Faust, S., Hazay, C.: Secure Two-Party Computation with Low Communication. In: Cramer, R. (ed.) TCC 2012. LNCS, vol. 7194, pp. 54–74. Springer, Heidelberg (2012)
12. De Santis, A., Di Crescenzo, G., Ostrovsky, R., Persiano, G., Sahai, A.: Robust Non-interactive Zero Knowledge. In: Kilian, J. (ed.) CRYPTO 2001. LNCS, vol. 2139, pp. 566–598. Springer, Heidelberg (2001)
13. Dodis, Y., Haralambiev, K., López-Alt, A., Wichs, D.: Cryptography against continuous memory attacks. In: Proceedings of FOCS 2010, pp. 511–520 (2010)
14. Feige, U., Lapidot, D., Shamir, A.: Multiple non-interactive zero knowledge proofs under general assumptions. SIAM Journal of Computing 29(1), 1–28 (1999)
15. Fiat, A., Shamir, A.: How to Prove Yourself: Practical Solutions to Identification and Signature Problems. In: Odlyzko, A.M. (ed.) CRYPTO 1986. LNCS, vol. 263, pp. 186–194. Springer, Heidelberg (1987)
16. Fuchsbauer, G.: Commuting Signatures and Verifiable Encryption. In: Paterson, K.G. (ed.) EUROCRYPT 2011. LNCS, vol. 6632, pp. 224–245. Springer, Heidelberg (2011)
17. Gennaro, R., Gentry, C., Parno, B., Raykova, M.: Quadratic span programs and succinct NIZKs without PCPs. Cryptology ePrint Archive, Report 2012/215 (2012), http://eprint.iacr.org/2012/215
18. Gentry, C.: Fully homomorphic encryption using ideal lattices. In: Proceedings of STOC 2009, pp. 169–178 (2009)
19. Gentry, C., Wichs, D.: Separating succinct non-interactive arguments from all falsifiable assumptions. In: Proceedings of STOC 2011, pp. 99–108 (2011)
20. Goldwasser, S., Micali, S., Rackoff, C.: The knowledge complexity of interactive proof systems. In: Proceedings of STOC 1985, pp. 186–208 (1985)
21. Groth, J.: Simulation-Sound NIZK Proofs for a Practical Language and Constant Size Group Signatures. In: Lai, X., Chen, K. (eds.) ASIACRYPT 2006. LNCS, vol. 4284, pp. 444–459. Springer, Heidelberg (2006)
22. Groth, J.: Short Pairing-Based Non-interactive Zero-Knowledge Arguments. In: Abe, M. (ed.) ASIACRYPT 2010. LNCS, vol. 6477, pp. 321–340. Springer, Heidelberg (2010)
23. Groth, J., Lu, S.: A Non-interactive Shuffle with Pairing Based Verifiability. In: Kurosawa, K. (ed.) ASIACRYPT 2007. LNCS, vol. 4833, pp. 51–67. Springer, Heidelberg (2007)
24. Groth, J., Sahai, A.: Efficient Non-interactive Proof Systems for Bilinear Groups. In: Smart, N.P. (ed.) EUROCRYPT 2008. LNCS, vol. 4965, pp. 415–432. Springer, Heidelberg (2008)
25. Lipmaa, H.: Progression-Free Sets and Sublinear Pairing-Based Non-Interactive Zero-Knowledge Arguments. In: Cramer, R. (ed.) TCC 2012. LNCS, vol. 7194, pp. 169–189. Springer, Heidelberg (2012)
26. Micali, S.: Computationally sound proofs. SIAM Journal of Computing 30(4), 1253–1298 (2000)
27. Prabhakaran, M., Rosulek, M.: Rerandomizable RCCA Encryption. In: Menezes, A. (ed.) CRYPTO 2007. LNCS, vol. 4622, pp. 517–534. Springer, Heidelberg (2007)
28. Prabhakaran, M., Rosulek, M.: Homomorphic Encryption with CCA Security. In: Aceto, L., Damgård, I.B., Goldberg, L.A., Halldórsson, M.M., Ingólfsdóttir, A., Walukiewicz, I. (eds.) ICALP 2008, Part II. LNCS, vol. 5126, pp. 667–678. Springer, Heidelberg (2008)
29. Sahai, A.: Non-malleable non-interactive zero knowledge and adaptive chosen-ciphertext security. In: Proceedings of FOCS 1999, pp. 543–553 (1999)

Encrypted Messages from the Heights of Cryptomania

Craig Gentry

IBM T.J. Watson Research Center,
Yorktown Heights, New York, USA

How flexible can encryption be? This question motivated the invention of public key encryption that began modern cryptography. A lot has happened since then. I will focus on two lines of research that I find especially interesting (mainly the second) and the mysterious gap between them.

The first line of research asks: how flexibly can encryption handle computation? The answer seems to be "very flexibly". We have fully homomorphic encryption (FHE) schemes [RAD78, Gen09, DGHV10, BV11b, GH11, BV11a] that allow a worker (non-interactively) to do arbitrary blind processing of encrypted data without obtaining access to the data. However, current FHE schemes do not handle access control flexibly; there is only one keyholder, and only it can decrypt.

The second line of research asks: how flexibly can encryption handle access control? Again, the answer seems to be "very flexibly". Building on Garg et al.'s [GGH12b] approximate multilinear maps, we now have attribute-based encryption (ABE) schemes for arbitrary circuits [SW12, GGH12a] that allow an encrypter (non-interactively) to embed an arbitrarily complex access policy into its ciphertext, such that only users whose keys are associated to a satisfying set of attributes can (non-interactively) decrypt. We can be even more flexible: Garg et al. [GGSW12] describe a "witness encryption" scheme where a user's decryption key is not really a key at all, but rather a witness for some arbitrary NP relation specified by the encrypter (the encrypter itself may not know a witness). However, current ABE and witness encryption schemes do not handle computation flexibly; the decrypter recovers the encrypter's message, unmodified.

In between, we have concepts like obfuscation and functional encryption that attempt to handle computation and access control simultaneously – in particular, by allowing the user to learn a prescribed function only of the user's input (similar to ABE), while hiding all intermediate values of the computation (similar to FHE). Here, it seems that we finally have reached the edge of Cryptomania, as we bump against impossibility results [BGI+01, vDJ10, BSW11, AGVW12]. However, the precise contours of the boundary between possible and impossible remain unknown.

In this talk, I will focus mostly on the recent positive results in the second line of research, showing how a somewhat homomorphic variant of the NTRU encryption scheme leads quite naturally to Garg et al.'s approximate multilinear maps, and describing how to use multilinear maps to construct witness encryption.

A. Sahai (Ed.): TCC 2013, LNCS 7785, pp. 120–121, 2013.

Regarding obfuscation, functional encryption, and the boundary between possible and impossible, I only promise to leave you with intriguing questions.

References

[AGVW12] Agrawal, S., Gorbunov, S., Vaikuntanathan, V., Wee, H.: Functional encryption: New perspectives and lower bounds. IACR Cryptology ePrint Archive, 2012:468 (2012)

[BGI+01] Barak, B., Goldreich, O., Impagliazzo, R., Rudich, S., Sahai, A., Vadhan, S.P., Yang, K.: On the (Im)possibility of Obfuscating Programs. In: Kilian, J. (ed.) CRYPTO 2001. LNCS, vol. 2139, pp. 1–18. Springer, Heidelberg (2001)

[BSW11] Boneh, D., Sahai, A., Waters, B.: Functional Encryption: Definitions and Challenges. In: Ishai, Y. (ed.) TCC 2011. LNCS, vol. 6597, pp. 253–273. Springer, Heidelberg (2011)

[BV11a] Brakerski, Z., Vaikuntanathan, V.: Efficient fully homomorphic encryption from (standard) LWE. In: FOCS 2011. IEEE Computer Society (2011)

[BV11b] Brakerski, Z., Vaikuntanathan, V.: Fully Homomorphic Encryption from Ring-LWE and Security for Key Dependent Messages. In: Rogaway, P. (ed.) CRYPTO 2011. LNCS, vol. 6841, pp. 505–524. Springer, Heidelberg (2011)

[DGHV10] van Dijk, M., Gentry, C., Halevi, S., Vaikuntanathan, V.: Fully Homomorphic Encryption over the Integers. In: Gilbert, H. (ed.) EUROCRYPT 2010. LNCS, vol. 6110, pp. 24–43. Springer, Heidelberg (2010), Full version available online from http://eprint.iacr.org/2009/616

[Gen09] Gentry, C.: Fully homomorphic encryption using ideal lattices. In: Mitzenmacher, M. (ed.) STOC, pp. 169–178. ACM (2009)

[GGH12a] Garg, S., Gentry, C., Halevi, S.: Attribute based encryption for general circuits (2012) (manuscript)

[GGH12b] Garg, S., Gentry, C., Halevi, S.: Candidate multilinear maps from ideal lattices and applications. Cryptology ePrint Archive, Report 2012/610 (2012), http://eprint.iacr.org/

[GGSW12] Garg, S., Gentry, C., Sahai, A., Waters, B.: Witness encryption and its applications (2012) (manuscript)

[GH11] Gentry, C., Halevi, S.: Implementing Gentry's Fully-Homomorphic Encryption Scheme. In: Paterson, K.G. (ed.) EUROCRYPT 2011. LNCS, vol. 6632, pp. 129–148. Springer, Heidelberg (2011)

[RAD78] Rivest, R., Adleman, L., Dertouzos, M.L.: On data banks and privacy homomorphisms. In: Foundations of Secure Computation, pp. 169–180 (1978)

[SW12] Sahai, A., Waters, B.: Attribute-based encryption for circuits from multilinear maps. Cryptology ePrint Archive, Report 2012/592 (2012), http://eprint.iacr.org/

[vDJ10] van Dijk, M., Juels, A.: On the impossibility of cryptography alone for privacy-preserving cloud computing. IACR Cryptology ePrint Archive, 2010:305 (2010)

Attribute-Based Functional Encryption on Lattices

Xavier Boyen

Abstract. We introduce a broad lattice manipulation technique for expressive cryptography, and use it to realize functional encryption for access structures from post-quantum hardness assumptions.

Specifically, we build an efficient key-policy attribute-based encryption scheme, and prove its security in the selective sense from learning-with-errors intractability in the standard model.

1 Introduction

Attribute-Based Encryption (ABE) is a very powerful notion of encryption, where ciphertexts are not decipherable according to the ownership of a specific key (as in public-key encryption), or a specific name (as in identity-based encryption), but according to the fulfillment of a functional condition expressed as a predicate that takes multiple attributes as input.

Attribute-based encryption was first coined in a paper by Goyal *et al.* [22], although the idea was already implicit in the Fuzzy IBE of Sahai and Waters [32], which for the first time permitted ciphertexts to be addressed on the basis of a condition that was strictly richer than a mere equality (of keys or identities). Since then, the notion of ABE has blossomed into an entire research program known as Functional Encryption [23,11], whereby rich functions driven by inputs from both the ciphertext and the key attempting to decrypt it, determine whether the message, or some function thereof, can be accessed. As an illustrative example of recent developments in this area, Waters very recently built a functional cryptosystem whose predicates are deterministic finite automata [33].

As impressive as these results may be, almost all of them appear to require the machinery of bilinear maps [27]—which leaves them completely vulnerable to quantum cryptanalysis, by virtue of hinging on the classically hard but quantumly easy Discrete Log problem. (Limited instances of construction from yet other techniques [16,10] do exist, but, with assumptions that hinge on Factoring, they are equally vulnerable to quantum attacks.) With quantum computers rapidly moving from a scientific to an engineering problem, it behooves us to have safe cryptographic alternatives ready before they become a reality— possibly with nary an advance warning. Lattices appear to be our best defense, for not only are they increasingly conjectured to thwart the quantum threat in a fundamental way, they also have a rich mathematical structure that makes them well suited for building "complex" and expressive cryptographic systems.

Lattices have made their apparition in cryptography with the work Ajtai [5], and have since been used to construct a vast variety of primitives, including one-way and collision-resistant hash functions [5,26], signatures [12,25], public-key

A. Sahai (Ed.): TCC 2013, LNCS 7785, pp. 122–142, 2013.

encryption [7,30,31], identity-based encryption schemes [21,15,1,2], lossy trap-door functions [29], and even a couple instances of functional encryption for inner-product [4] and threshold [3] functions. Lattices have also been very in-strumental in cracking the long-standing question of realizing fully homomorphic encryption [19,20,14].

Lattices are indeed rapidly emerging as a mathematical platform of choice for building increasingly powerful and efficient cryptographic primitives. In addition to lattice problems being generally conjectured to withstand quantum attacks, the mathematical properties of these objects make them both relatively efficient and flexible to enable the construction of powerful cryptosystems. Research in lattice-based cryptosystems that reduce from the "Learning With Errors" (LWE) hardness assumption has been particularly active, in no small part because the average-case LWE problem is itself reducible [31,28] from a slew of worst-case lattice problems, for a sound foundation.

Despite all of those incentives and successes, the reality is that functional en-cryption so far remains largely confined to the world of bilinear maps. In recent years, only a handful of such systems have been successfully realized using lat-tices, such as the already cited constructions of IBE [21,1], HIBE [15,2], IPE [4], and FuzzyIBE [3]. Further advances have remained elusive, despite the "pull" ex-erted by the faster pace of progress in that other world of bilinear maps. Rather disconcertingly indeed, as attempts are made to translate high-level principles of bilinear-map functional encryption into lattice analogues, serious difficulties tend to crop up in the most unexpected places when one tries to prove security. A pointed example, documented in [3], relates to the unresolved difficulties faced by those authors when trying to build ABE from LWE.

If anything, this brief history of functional encryption from lattices suggests that new ideas are in order for progress, beyond the field's classic paradigms.

1.1   Main Motivations

"Attribute-Based Encryption using Lattices" is by many authors' account an im-portant research question, having been posed and left unanswered in an number of recent works including [15,1,4,3]. Perhaps the best evidence of the problem's popularity is none other than a recent attempt by a large corporation to lay claim on its solution, in an eponymous patent application [17], even though the problem explicitly remained open to this day. [1] Why such eager enthusiasm?

First and foremost, functional encryption in general and ABE in particu-lar are extremely powerful cryptographic constructs that would seem almost incredible—e.g., by the standards of *circa* 2000. FE and ABE primarily give us unprecedented flexibility and expressiveness with which recipients can be desig-nated in a wholesale manner. Not only do there exist direct use cases for such

---

[1] The US patent application [17] appears to refer to a precursor of the "Fuzzy IBE using Lattices" subsequently published in [3], wherein a superset of the authors explicitly acknowledge that it did not extend to a proper ABE. We further opine on mathematical but not legal grounds that our ABE falls outside of the claims of [17].

power (we refer to the early literature on the subject for examples), but the prospects that it opens for protocol building are highly intriguing.

As already alluded to, such rewards would be for naught if the looming threat of a catastrophic quantum cryptanalysis kept relegating it to where damage would be contained. It would be foolish to believe that because quantum registers have only grown from 5 to 7 qubits during the last decade, that their size could not suddenly become cryptographically devastating during the next one. This is where lattices come into play.

Compounding their conjectured quantum robustness, lattices also have a number of rather unique efficiency and implementation advantages. For instance, while bilinear-map cryptosystems tend to be convenient to work with on paper thanks to the availability of clean abstractions, this view hides a rather complex elliptic-curve machinery that must be securely implemented in any physical implementation. In lattice-based cryptography, the situation is reversed: schemes and proofs tend to be more complex and mirred in details, but implementations require only small-number arithmetic and basic linear algebra.

Those are the reasons—from quantum peace of mind, to the sheer challenge of solving compelling theory with practical applications—why it is far from wasted effort to "reinvent" Attribute-Based Encryption, not from bilinear maps but from lattices. (And as a bonus, we introduce a new technique whose power likely reaches into FE far beyond mere ABE.)

1.2 Our Contributions

Our main result is the construction of a functional encryption scheme for monotone access structures, also known as (key-policy) attribute-based encryption, and reduce its security from LWE.

We achieve this result by way of a new lattice manipulation framework suited to the handling of complex access policies. Compared to earlier works on lattice-based IBE and FE, our framework has two distinguishing characteristics: the reliance on *ephemeral lattices* for all private-key extractions, and the subsequent application of a *basis splicing* technique which allows a recipient to convert an ephemeral lattice's basis into a basis for any lattice in a given family, as needed.

We introduce our framework in relation to a number of observations we make in our attempt to shed some light on the difficulties previously faced. This leads us to a (rather informal) discussion of FE with uniform and non-uniform policies, and how the latter appeared hard to tackle based on previous lattice techniques.

Here we focus solely on introducing our framework and building "key-policy" KP-ABE from it. We defer to future work the study of "ciphertext-policy" CP-ABE and even more ambitious FE.

2 Preliminaries

We refer to the Appendix—available in the eprint version of the paper [13]—for background on lattices in cryptography.

2.1 Attribute-Based Encryption

We follow the definition of the ABE functionality as given by Goyal et al. [22], albeit for security we consider the notion of ciphertext privacy which implies both semantic security and recipient anonymity.

Definition 1 (Key-Policy Attribute-Based Encryption). A Key-Policy Attribute-Based Encryption scheme consists of the following four algorithms:

Setup$(\lambda, \ell) \rightarrow$ (Pub, Msk): This algorithm is input a security parameter λ and an attribute number ℓ. It outputs a public key Pub and a master key Msk.

Extract(Pub, Msk, Policy) $\rightarrow$ Key: This algorithm takes a public key Pub, a master key Msk, and an access policy Policy. It outputs a decryption key Key.

Encrypt(Pub, Attrib, Msg) $\rightarrow$ Ctx: This algorithm is input a public key Pub, a list of attributes Attrib, and a message bit Msg. It outputs a ciphertext Ctx.

Decrypt(Pub, Key, Ctx) $\rightarrow b$: This algorithm takes a public key Pub, a decryption key Key, and a ciphertext Ctx. It outputs the bit b if the attributes Attrib used to create Ctx satisfy the policy Policy used in the creation of Key.

Definition 2 (Selective-Model KP-ABE Security). A KP-ABE scheme is ciphertext-private in the selective-attribute model of security if all probabilistic polynomial time (PPT) adversaries have at most a negligible advantage in this game:

Target: The adversary declares the challenge attributes, Attrib†, that it wishes to be challenged upon.

Setup: The challenger runs the Setup algorithm and gives the public key to the adversary.

Queries: The adversary is allowed to issue adaptive queries for private keys corresponding to policies Policy of its choice, as long as Attrib† does not satisfy Policy.

Challenge: The adversary signals its readiness to accept a challenge, and proposes a message to encrypt. The challenger encrypts the message for the challenge attributes Attrib†, and then flips a random coin r. If $r = 1$, the ciphertext is given to the adversary; if $r = 0$, a random element of the ciphertext space is returned.

Queries: This is a continuation of the earlier query phase.

Guess: The adversary outputs a guess r' of r. The advantage of an adversary A in this game is defined as $|\Pr[r' = r] - \frac{1}{2}|$

One also defines an adaptive-attribute version of the above game, where the adversary may defer the choice of target attributes until requesting the challenge.

2.2 Linear Secret Sharing

Definition 3 (LSSS over $\mathbb{Z}_q$). An LSSS Π over a set of parties $\mathcal{P}$ consists of an "index map" ρ and a "share-generating matrix" $\mathsf{L} \in \mathbb{Z}_q^{\ell \times \theta}$ with ℓ rows and θ columns, where ℓ is the number of shares specified by Π, and θ depends on the structure of Π. For all $i = 1, \ldots, \ell$, the function ρ maps the i-th row of L to its corresponding party. The matrix L maps an input θ-vector $\mathbf{v} = (s, r_2, \ldots, r_\theta)$, where $s \in \mathbb{Z}_q$ is the secret to be shared, and $r_2, \ldots, r_\theta \in \mathbb{Z}_q$ are random, into an output ℓ-vector $\mathsf{L}\,\mathbf{v} = (s_1, \ldots, s_\ell)$ containing the shares of the secret s according to Π. The share $s_i = (\mathsf{L}\,\mathbf{v})_i$ is assigned to party $\rho(i)$.

Every LSSS according to the above definition enjoys the linear reconstruction property. This means that if Π is an LSSS for the access structure $\mathbb{A}$, then the following is true. Let $S \in \mathbb{A}$ be any authorized set, and let $I \subset \{1, 2, \ldots, \ell\}$ be defined as $I = \{i : \rho(i) \in S\}$. Then, there exist constants $\{\kappa_i \in \mathbb{Z}_q\}$ for $i \in I$, such that, if the $\{\lambda_i = (\mathsf{L}\,\mathbf{v})_i\}$ are valid shares of any secret s according to Π, then $\sum_{i \in I} \kappa_i \lambda_i = s$. It was shown by Beimel [9], that these constants $\{\kappa_i\}$ can be found in time polynomial in the size of the share-generating matrix L.

Vector Secrets and Reconstruction over $\mathbb{Z}$. For the purpose of this paper, we will need a slightly modified notion of LSSS, where secrets and shares are ℓ-dimensional integer vectors in $\mathbb{Z}^\ell$, and share-generating matrices are defined over $\mathbb{Z}$ rather than over $\mathbb{Z}_q$. This creates a few issues:

1. Since secrets and shares are themselves vectors, the vector $\mathbf{v}$ of all such shares should be viewed as a tensor, and the product $(\mathsf{L} \cdot \mathbf{v})$ interpreted accordingly.
2. There is no notion of uniform share distribution over $\mathbb{Z}$: a benign issue here.
3. Reconstruction in $\mathbb{Z}$ may require fractional interpolation coefficients $\kappa_i \in \mathbb{Q}$. We alleviate this difficulty by relaxing our notion of reconstruction, allowing the reconstructed vector to be a non-zero multiple of the original vector (which is non-trivial only if the vector has dimension greater than one). Such reconstruction is possible using only integer coefficients $\kappa_i \in \mathbb{Z}$.

Low-Norm Share Generation. We will use the generic construction mechanism described in Appendix G of [24, eprint] to convert a monotone access structure into a deterministic LSSS matrix. For access formulas with AND ($\wedge$) and OR ($\vee$) gates only, it has the further advantage to build share-generating matrices $\mathsf{L} \in \{0, \pm 1\}^{\ell \times \theta}$ with ternary elements in $\{0, \pm 1\}$. For such formulas, the (unrelaxed) reconstruction coefficients κ_i will be binary in $\{0, 1\}$ by construction, even when working in $\mathbb{Z}$, hence already integer and low-norm without further relaxation.

Duplicated Attributes. For ease of exposition, we first restrict our attention to formulas where each attribute appears exactly once. Since ρ is then the identity function, we omit it from the notation altogether—until Section 4.5 and the Example Appendix of [13] where we handle missing and duplicated attributes.

3   Framework

3.1   Functional Encryption from Lattices

The Regev Cryptosystem. Recall that the Regev PKE scheme [31] makes use of an Ajtai lattice [5], defined as $\Lambda_q^\perp(\mathsf{A}) = \{\mathbf{x} : \mathsf{A}\,\mathbf{x} = \mathbf{0} \pmod{q}\} \subseteq \mathbb{Z}^m$, where

$q \in \mathbb{Z}^+$ and $A \in \mathbb{Z}_q^{n \times m}$ together specify the lattice (though not necessarily in a unique way). In Regev's PKE scheme, one assumes q fixed and $m > n \log q$. The private key is a vector $\mathbf{d} \in \mathbb{Z}^m$ with low euclidean norm $\|\mathbf{d}\| \ll q\sqrt{m}$. The public key is a pair $(A, \mathbf{u})$ such that $A\mathbf{d} = \mathbf{u} \pmod{q}$. To encrypt a bit $m \in \{0,1\}$, one selects a random ephemeral vector $\mathbf{s} \in \mathbb{Z}_q^n$, and output a pair $(c_0, \mathbf{c}_1)$, where $c_0 = \mathbf{s}^\top \mathbf{u} + \lfloor q/2 \rfloor m + \nu_0$ and $\mathbf{c}_1 = \mathbf{s}^\top A + \nu_1$, and where the additive terms ν_0 and ν_1 are low-norm independent discrete gaussian noise terms. To decrypt, the private-key holder computes the difference $\Delta = c_0 - \mathbf{c}_1 \mathbf{d}$ in $\mathbb{Z}_q$, and interprets it as "$m = 1$" if (the smallest non-negative representative of the coset) Δ lies in $\{\lceil q/4 \rceil, \lfloor 3\,q/4 \rfloor\}$, and as "$m = 0$" otherwise.

Preimage Sampling. The Regev system has served as a starting point for many "expressive" functional generalizations of public-key cryptography. The key turning point in this generalization has been the development, in [21], of a "preimage sampling" technique that, given A and $\mathbf{u}$, allow one to obtain a preimage $\mathbf{d}$ such that $A\mathbf{d} = \mathbf{u} \pmod{q}$ and such that $\mathbf{d}$ has the same conditional distribution given $\mathbf{u}$ as if it had been sampled first and its image computed from it. What makes the preimage-sampling approach cryptographically interesting, is that in order to sample a preimage of good quality (where the "quality" of a sample is an inverse measure of its norm), it is (conjectured) necessary to possess a good quality or low-norm basis B for the lattice $\Lambda_q^\perp(A)$. Furthermore, Ajtai's original result [5] does give us an efficient way to co-generate both a uniformly random matrix A and an associated short basis B for the lattice it induces; whereas it is a conjectured hard problem to find even a single short vector "after the fact" for a given random A. Together, these methods provide an effective way to obtain provably secure trapdoors from lattice hardness assumptions, that have been used in interesting ways to construct increasingly "expressive" functional cryptosystems: IBE [21,1], HIBE [15,2], IPE [4], FuzzyIBE [3], and now ABE.

More Expressive Predicates. The combination of the lattice/basis co-generation algorithm of [5], the basic public-key framework of [31], and the preimage sampling approach of [21], has led to the invention of several functional encryption schemes for various classes of functions, starting with the identity-based encryption scheme in the original paper [21]. A handful of other functional encryption schemes from lattices were later devised, including IBE in the standard model [15,1], hierarchical IBE [15,2], inner-product encryption [4], and fuzzy IBE [3]. At a high level, all of those schemes find their roots in the Regev PKE system, which they generalize in various ways following a common principle. The common principle is to extend Regev so that either or both the matrix A and/or the syndrome $\mathbf{u}$ depend on the functional decryption criterion, rather than being constant. In IBE, the decryption criterion is a match of identities, so we let A and/or $\mathbf{u}$ be function of the identity. In IPE and FuzzyIBE, the decryption criterion is an inner product equality or a threshold of equalities, obtained by splitting A and/or $\mathbf{u}$ into multiple shares A_i and/or $\mathbf{u}_i$, each of which depending on one of the attributes of the decryption predicate.

3.2   Complex Policies and Non-uniformity

In our quest to understand what differentiates successes from failures in earlier lattice-based FE construction attempts, we are drawn to observe the emergence of a pattern that we shall attempt to characterize informally (based on inductive rather than deductive reasoning).

Uniform Policies. The "successes" share a crucial simplifying characteristic: all attributes taken as formal arguments in the decryption policy are of equal importance; they play symmetrical roles.

- IBE and HIBE use trivial examples of uniform policies, because the decryption predicate is a mere equality test that treats a full identity string as a single atomic input (of variable length in the case of HIBE), comparing that of the ciphertext with that of the private key.
- IPE uses uniform policies, because none of the multiple attributes taken as inputs to the decryption predicate, plays a different role or is more important than the others. Indeed, the predicate is of the form, "$\langle \mathbf{k}, \mathbf{c} \rangle = 0 \pmod{q}$?" (where $\mathbf{k}$ and $\mathbf{c}$ are the key's and the ciphertext's attribute vectors). Now let us consider a permutation π. If we apply it to the components of $\mathbf{k}$ and also to the components of $\mathbf{c}$, one obtains the new predicate, "$\langle \pi(\mathbf{k}), \pi(\mathbf{c}) \rangle = 0 \pmod{q}$?", which is in fact unchanged and evaluates to the same value.
- FuzzyIBE uses uniform policies by same reasoning. The only difference is that here the predicate is a θ-out-of-ℓ threshold equality test between key and ciphertext attributes.

Non-Uniform Policies. To contrast, consider the following basic ABE decryption predicate: "$(A_k = A_c) \vee ((B_k = B_c) \wedge (C_k = C_c))$?" It falls within the scope of the ABE model; yet it is non-uniform since the atomic clause that takes attribute A as input, $(A_k = A_c)$, can by itself truthify the entire predicate, whereas neither the clause in B nor in C can do the same. The attributes are not symmetrical, since A carries more weight than either B or C. Per our earlier criterion, some permutations π of the attributes would not leave the predicate invariant.

Leakage from Non-Uniformity. The authors of [3] observe that the difficulty with extending existing lattice techniques into ABE stems from the conjunction of two risk factors: the necessity to prevent short-vector private keys from spilling a full basis; and the propensity of keys with asymmetrical components to do just that.

To be sure, there are examples of earlier "FE successes" that allow full-bases to be used as keys: all the HIBE schemes [15,1,2] fall in that category, since full bases are needed for key delegation. However, we contend that passing out full bases is not damaging in this case, because HIBE policies are trivially uniform, involving only a single attribute, so that either there is a full match or there is no match at all—no need to finesse the power of the decryption key in any way.

The other past "FE success" with multi-vector keys is the FuzzyIBE from [3]. There, a private key is a Regev key randomly secret-shared into a number of vectors function of the threshold—definitely not a full basis which would give too much power. Such sharing finesse led to an attack when one attempted to extend the scheme to ABE with non-uniform policies, because of dicrepancies in the relative importance of the private key components. *E.g.*, a key for $A \vee (B \wedge C)$ would be "heavier" at attribute A. In this situation, an adversary could, by making multiple key queries for related but distinct policies, obtain a collection of short vectors whose "heavy" coordinates together leak enough information to allow the adversary to reconstitute a "rogue" (sub-)basis. The uneven weight of the coordinates made it difficult to randomize the keys to prevent the "heavy" coordinates from leaking, without necessarily drowning the "light" coordinates in noise and render them useless.

3.3   Robust Embedding of Policies

Instead of trying to prevent the reconstitution of rogue bases from private-key vectors (which was the direction of future research envisioned in [3]), we shall make our private keys into full bases outright—albeit, bases of *ephemeral random lattices that vary with every invocation of key extraction.*

Ephemeral Lattices. Making keys from constantly changing, ephemeral lattices seems great for security—but how can such keys be useful for decryption in a Regev-like system, if the lattices used for encryption and key extraction are different? In a nutshell, the ephemeral lattices (or, rather, the Ajtai matrices defining them) will have a known structure, featuring both deterministic and randomized subcomponents. The ephemeral lattice is rather high-dimensional and its structure will encode the private-key policy attributes. The structure will allow the recipient to transform this "useless" random-lattice basis, into a basis for any target lattice, typically of a lower dimension, that belongs in a certain authorized set that corresponds to the policy encoded into the initial structure. Thus, if a private key is valid for a given ciphertext, meaning that the attributes of one satisfy the policy of the other, then the recipient is able to transform it into a basis for the lattice used in the ciphertext construction, and from there decryption à la Regev can proceed. Conversely, if a private key is invalid for a given ciphertext, the encryption lattice will be outside the authorized set, and the private key will be useless to derive a (short) basis for that lattice.

Basis Splicing. We refer as *basis splicing* the internal operations that let the recipient transform the given high-dimensional ephemeral-lattice basis, into a basis for any desired lower-dimensional lattice in the authorized set. In the case of ABE, the structure embedded in the ephemeral lattice will be obtained from an LSSS, and the basis splicing operations will amount to taking linear combinations of the basis vectors. Certain linear combinations will cause all the blinding randomness to vanish, transforming the initial *unknown* ephemeral lattice into a smaller *known* target lattice in the authorized set.

Security versus Functionality. At an intuitive level, the security benefits that we derive from our approach are twofold:

- *Private keys as full bases are more robust than single vectors.* In a system where private keys are mere vectors, there is an incentive to obtain more than one such vector, in a bid to reconctruct a rogue basis. If the key is a full basis, there is nothing to be gained in trying to obtain another, which can be generated from the first.
- *Ephemeral lattices make a very potent blinding and firewalling mechanism.* This is perhaps the most important aspect of the framework we propose: since the key-extraction mechanism involves an independently rerandomized lattice that changes upon each invocation, the private keys are in a very strong sense firewalled from one another and from the master secret.

These two properties should intuitively make it easy to construct a secure system, which should translate into easy-to-construct reductionist simulations.

4   Scheme

4.1   Intuition

Setup. The system setup is very straightforward. To each (binary) attribute Attrib_i named in the system, is associated a random Ajtai matrix A_i and a matching trapdoor B_i such that $\mathsf{A}_i\,\mathsf{B}_i = 0$ for small $\|\mathsf{B}_i\|$. The matrices A_i form the global public key. The trapdoors B_i form the keying authority's master key.

In KP-ABE, ciphertexts are created for sets of (binary) attributes, while private keys embed the decryption policies. To make it possible to encrypt for a set of attributes, a natural idea is, for each (binary) attribute in the system, to create an Ajtai matrix A_i and an associated trapdoor T_i. The matrices A_i will form the public key; the trapdoors T_i form the master key.

Encryption. To encrypt for an attribute set $\{\mathsf{Attrib}_i\}$, one creates a matrix F by concatenating the public matrices A_i designated by the Attrib_i, filling the gaps with the zero matrix 0; one then uses F as an "encryption matrix" à la Regev.[2]

Key Extraction. To create a private key for a given decryption policy represented as an LSSS, the key-extraction authority starts by constructing a (high-dimensional) ephemeral matrix $\mathsf{M} = [\mathsf{M}_{\mathrm{diag}}|\mathsf{M}_{\mathrm{lsss}}]$, where $\mathsf{M}_{\mathrm{diag}}$ is a block-diagonal assembly of all the A_i, and $\mathsf{M}_{\mathrm{lsss}}$ is a tensor product of the LSSS matrix and a secret ephemeral randomization matrix. Using its knowledge of the master-key bases B_i, the authority creates a short basis W for the lattice $\Lambda_q^\perp(\mathsf{M})$, randomizes it into a structure-less short basis K, and returns K as the private key. Notice that the basis K is that of a fresh random lattice whose defining Ajtai matrix M is not even revealed to the recipient.

---

[2] A Regev ciphertext $(\mathbf{c}_0, \mathbf{c}_1)$ is created in reference to an Ajtai lattice $\Lambda_q^\perp(\mathsf{F})$ defined by a known matrix F. We call the matrix F, the *Regev encryption matrix*. (It is usually denoted A but we use F to emphasize that it is a function of the encryption attributes; we reserve the notation A_i for the constant matrices in the public key.)

Decryption. Given a Regev ciphertext created from some encryption matrix F, the first step is to transform the private key K into a basis T for the lattice $\Lambda_q^\perp(F)$, using the basis-splicing technique.

The transformation requires the encryption matrix F to lie in the "span" of the (undisclosed!) ephemeral matrix M, *i.e.*, that there be a linear combination of the rows of M that yields $M \hookrightarrow [F|0]$. By the structure of $M = [M_{\text{diag}}|M_{\text{lsss}}]$, it follows that the i-th block-column of F is a multiple of the i-th block of M_{diag}, or, in other words, that F is the concatenation of $g_i A_i$ with computable coefficients g_i. Though K was orthogonal to M, it is not orthogonal to $[F|0]$. We can obtain orthogonality to $[F|0]$ by multiplying each row of K by an integer coefficient $\bar{g}_i \propto 1/g_i \pmod q$ inversely proportional modulo q to the coefficient g_i of the corresponding column of $[F|0]$ (taking $\bar{g}_i = 0$ when corresponding to the columns of 0 or those of F associated with a coefficient $g_i = 0$).

The basis K thus transformed is a matrix $[T^\top|0^\top]^\top$ where T has full rank and is orthogonal to F. The final observation is to take $\bar{g}_i = (\prod_{j:g_j \neq 0} g_j)/g_i$. Because those $\bar{g}_i$ are already in $\mathbb{Z}$, no modular reduction is necessary to ensure that $\bar{g}_i \propto 1/g_i \pmod q$. Hence the norm $\|T\|$ remains small when the g_i are binary or small enough. This makes of T a low-norm full-rank set, convertible into a basis suitable as a trapdoor for sampling low-norm vectors in $\Lambda_q^\perp(F)$.

We see that, by properly constructing M, it is possible for the recipient to know how its trapdoor K can be transformed into the desired trapdoor T, even though M itself is not revealed. Once the trapdoor T is obtained, it can be used to decrypt the ciphertext, *e.g.*, by finding a short preimage **d** of the encryption syndrome **u**, *i.e.*, such that $F\mathbf{d} = \mathbf{u} \pmod q$, and applying Regev.[3]

Issues. For this approach to work, it is necessary that the norm of the reconstructed trapdoor T be small in order to apply Regev. The only operation that can cause the norm of T to grow out of hand, is the LSSS-based derivation of T from K. In general, for circuits containing "proper" threshold gates—not just $\land$ nor $\lor$—with large fan-in, the coefficients g_i can become exponentially large, which would overwhelm the noise tolerance of the Regev decryption scheme unless the modulus q is itself chosen to be exponentially large.

The first good news is that, even in the pessimal case, the issue of the LSSS coefficients is somewhat mitigated by the fact that we only perform LSSS reconstruction "half-way", eschewing full-fledged Lagrange interpolation. Indeed, the worst way in which LSSS coefficients intervene in T is through simple products $\prod_j g_j$—and not as ratios of products that would further require denominator elimination as, say, in the Fuzzy IBE of [3]. Intuitively, the reason why we do not need to account for—and then eliminate—the common denominator in LSSS reconstruction, is because what needs to be reconstructed is not the secret decryption itself (such as a short pre image or basis), but merely a multiple of the (public) encryption matrix F; only a multiple is needed because F induces the same Ajtai lattice as all its multiples relatively prime to q.

---

[3] Because the private key is a full basis, it allows the recipient to find a preimage for any syndrome; hence the encryption syndrome **u** may change with each ciphertext.

The second and main good news is that, as long as the only gates present are $\wedge$ and $\vee$, regardless of their size or circuit complexity, the coefficients g_i can be made binary $\in \{0, 1\}$, thereby ensuring that $\|T\| \leq \|K\|$. This restriction is not as severe as it looks, as it should be emphasized that circuits of $\wedge$ and $\vee$ gates already capture most cases of practical interest for (monotone) access policies. Until now, it was not known how to realize ABE involving even the simplest non-uniform policies, $e.g.$, involving only one $\wedge$ and one $\vee$ gate.

4.2 Construction

We assume the existence of the following PPT algorithms for certain lattice sampling operations. See the Appendix in [13] for some background, and the rapidly evolving literature for the fastest and tightest instantiations, $e.g.$, [18].

– TrapGen for co-sampling a uniform Ajtai lattice and a short basis for it [5,6];
– SampleGaussian for discrete Gaussian sampling a point on a given Ajtai lattice;
– SamplePreimage for sampling a preimage of a given Ajtai syndrome, with a discrete Gaussian conditional density [21,8].
– ExtendRight for extending a trapdoor of an Ajtai matrix A into a trapdoor of any Ajtai matrix of the form $[A|Z]$, as long as A has full rank [15,1].

Remark. (Black-Box Sampling and Algorithm Parameters)
In the scheme description, we view all of the above sampling algorithms as (commodity, interchangeable) *black boxes*, without concern for their precise parameter requirements. For now, it suffices to know that the available sampling algorithms are both sufficiently fast and sufficiently tight, to make the entire system security reducible from the learning-with-error (LWE) hardness assumption with polynomially bounded parameters, so that is can in turn be further (quantumly [31], or for large moduli classically [28]) reduced from worst-case lattice assumptions.

The KP-ABE scheme consists of four algorithms specified as follows.

kpABE.Setup$(1^\lambda, 1^\ell)$: Given a security parameter λ, and an attribute bound ℓ:
1. Select a security dimension $n > \Omega(\lambda)$ and a base lattice dimension $m > 2\,n \log q$, together with a prime modulus $q > 2$. (See the Appendix for the constraints on q in function of the desired tightness α of LWE—the larger the modulus, the weaker the assumption.)
2. Use algorithm TrapGen(1^λ) to select, for each $i \in [\ell]$, a uniformly random $n \times m$-matrix $A_i \in \mathbb{Z}_q^{n \times m}$ with a full-rank m-vector set $B_i \subseteq \Lambda_q^\perp(A_i)$ that satisfies a low-norm condition.
3. Select a uniformly random $n \times m$-matrix $A_0 \in \mathbb{Z}_q^{n \times m}$.
4. Select a uniform random n-vector $\mathbf{u} \in \mathbb{Z}_q^n$.
5. Output the public key and master key,

$$ \mathsf{Pub} = \Big(\{A_i\}_{i \in [\ell]}, \; A_0, \; \mathbf{u} \Big) \quad ; \quad \mathsf{Msk} = \Big(\{B_i\}_{i \in [\ell]} \Big) $$

kpABE.Extract$(\mathsf{Pub}, \mathsf{Msk}, \mathsf{Policy})$: On input a public key denoted Pub, a master key denoted Msk, and an access structure denoted Policy, do:

1. Convert Policy into a (low-norm, and preferably deterministic) Linear Span Program matrix $L \in \mathbb{Z}^{\ell \times (1+\theta)}$, assigning the i-th row of L to the binary attribute of index $i \in [\ell]$. The columns $j \in [0, \theta]$ are numbered from 0 to θ, with $\theta \leq \ell$ being a function of Policy. The linear encoding rule we adopt for L is that, for a binary attribute list represented as Attrib $\in \{0,1\}^\ell$ or Attrib $\subseteq [\ell]$, the (monotone) access policy is satisfied iff the rows of L selected by Attrib contain in their span the row-vector $[1, 0, \ldots, 0] \in \mathbb{Z}^{1+\theta}$.

2. Select θ ephemeral uniform random $n \times m$-matrices $Z_j \in \mathbb{Z}_q^{n \times m}$ for $j \in [\theta]$.

3. Construct a "virtual encryption matrix" $M \in \mathbb{Z}_q^{\ell\, n \times (\ell+1+\theta)\, m}$, consisting of $\ell \times (\ell+1+\theta)$ blocks of $n \times m$-"sub-matrices", by translating the sharing matrix $L = \left(l_{i,j}\right)_{i \in [\ell], j \in [1+\theta]}$ as follows,

$$
M = \left[
\begin{array}{c|c|c}
\begin{array}{cccc}
\boxed{A_1} & & & \\
& \boxed{A_2} & & \\
& & \ddots & \\
& & & \boxed{A_\ell}
\end{array}
&
\begin{array}{c}
l_{1,0}\,\boxed{A_0} \\
l_{2,0}\,\boxed{A_0} \\
\vdots \\
l_{\ell,0}\,\boxed{A_0}
\end{array}
&
\begin{array}{ccc}
l_{1,1}\,\boxed{Z_1} & \ldots & l_{1,\theta}\,\boxed{Z_\theta} \\
l_{2,1}\,\boxed{Z_1} & \ldots & l_{2,\theta}\,\boxed{Z_\theta} \\
\vdots & & \vdots \\
l_{\ell,1}\,\boxed{Z_1} & \ldots & l_{\ell,\theta}\,\boxed{Z_\theta}
\end{array}
\end{array}
\right] \mod q
$$

$$
\underbrace{}_{\text{Public, constant, from Pub}} \quad \underbrace{}_{\text{From Pub}} \quad \underbrace{}_{\text{Secret, random, ephemerals}}
$$

Each row of L maps to a particular attribute according to the map ρ associated with the secret-sharing scheme. In this section, we are assuming for simplicity that each attribute (of index #i) appears exactly once (on the i-th row), making ρ the identity function. This restriction is lifted in Section 4.5, to handle missing and duplicated attributes.

4. Build a "structureless" random trapdoor K for $\Lambda_q^\perp(M)$, thus satisfying $M \cdot K = 0 \pmod{q}$. This can be done using ExtendRight, based on the fact that $M = [M_{\text{trapdoor}} | M_{\text{extension}}]$, where $M_{\text{trapdoor}} = Diag(A_1, \ldots, A_\ell)$ has full rank and a trivial trapdoor $Diag(B_1, \ldots, B_\ell)$.

   Unless ExtendRight is already guaranteed to produce an extended basis W whose vectors are idenpendently and identically distributed, it is necessary to rerandomize it to achieve this condition. Let K be the resulting "structureless" trapdoor for M.

5. A redundant form of the policy-based private key may be output, as,

$$
\text{Key} = \left(K, L \right)
$$

However, two optimizations can be made:

(a) If the sharing matrix L is deterministic in Policy, it may be omitted.

(b) It is not necessary to transmit all of K since the decryptor will only ever need the upper-left quadrant of dimension $(\ell+1)\, m \times (\ell+1)\, m$, which we denote by $K' \in \mathbb{Z}^{(\ell+1)\, m \times (\ell+1)\, m}$.

Hence, the private key for Policy may be given in compressed form, as,

$$
\text{Key} = \boxed{K'}
$$

kpABE.Encrypt(Pub, Attrib, Msg): On input a public key Pub, an attribute list Attrib $\subseteq [\ell]$, and a message bit Msg $\in \{0,1\}$, do:

1. Assemble an "encryption matrix" $F \in \mathbb{Z}_q^{n \times (\ell+1)\,m}$, obtained as the concatenation of, for each $i \in [\ell]$, either A_i if $i \in$ Attrib, or 0 if $i \notin$ Attrib, and A_0, as follows,

$$
F \;=\; \left[
\begin{array}{ccc|c}
F_1 \doteq & & F_\ell \doteq & F_0 \doteq \\[2pt]
\boxed{\begin{array}{c}A_1\\ \text{or }0\end{array}} & \cdots & \boxed{\begin{array}{c}A_\ell\\ \text{or }0\end{array}} & \boxed{A_0} \\[2pt]
\underbrace{\hphantom{\boxed{A_1}\cdots\boxed{A_\ell}}}_{A_i \text{ included iff } i \in \text{Attrib}} & & &
\end{array}
\right]
$$

2. Select a uniform random n-vector $\mathbf{s} \in \mathbb{Z}_q^n$.
3. Select a low-norm Gaussian noise scalar $\nu_0 \in \mathbb{Z}$ according to some parametric distribution Ψ_α (see Appendix), and compute the scalar,

$$
c_0 \;=\; \Big(\mathbf{s}^\top \cdot \mathbf{u} + \nu_0 + \lfloor \tfrac{q}{2} \rfloor \cdot \text{Msg} \Big) \bmod q
$$

4. Select a low-norm Gaussian noise vector $\nu_1 \in \mathbb{Z}^{(\ell+1)\,m}$ whose components are identically and independently distributed from Ψ_α, and compute the vector,

$$
\mathbf{c}_1 \;=\; \Big(\mathbf{s}^\top \cdot F + \nu_1 \Big) \bmod q
$$

5. Output the ciphertext,

$$
\text{Ctx} \;=\; \Big(c_0, \; \mathbf{c}_1 \Big)
$$

(It is not necessary to transmit the components of $\mathbf{c}_1$ that contain only added ν_1-noise, i.e., we only need to transmit the components of $\mathbf{c}_1$ at coordinates where $F_i \neq 0$.)

kpABE.Decrypt(Pub, Key, Ctx): Given a public key Pub, a policy-based key Key (for known policy Policy), and a ciphertext Ctx (for known attributes Attrib):

1. Find an as-short-as-feasible ℓ-vector $\mathbf{g} \in \mathbb{Z}^\ell$ satisfying the two conditions:

$$
\mathbf{g}^\top \cdot L = [d, 0, \ldots, 0] \propto [1, 0, \ldots, 0] \quad ; \quad \forall i \in [\ell] : (g_i = 0) \vee (i \in \text{Attrib})
$$

Namely, one finds a linear combination of the rows of L that yields some small d-multiple of $[1, 0, \ldots, 0]$ with $d \in \mathbb{Z} \setminus \{0\}$, using only rows corresponding to attributes in Attrib. This is possible iff Attrib satisfies Policy.

2. Notionally apply the linear combination $\mathbf{g}$ to the "block-rows" of M, to transform the "virtual" encryption matrix M into a "real" encryption matrix M' that matches the encryption matrix F of the given ciphertext (up to constant factors):

$$
M' \;=\; \left[
\begin{array}{ccc|c|ccc}
g_1 \boxed{\begin{array}{c}A_1\\ \text{or }0\end{array}} & g_2 \boxed{\begin{array}{c}A_2\\ \text{or }0\end{array}} & \cdots & g_\ell \boxed{\begin{array}{c}A_\ell\\ \text{or }0\end{array}} & d \cdot \boxed{A_0} & \underbrace{0 \cdot Z_1 \mid \cdots \mid 0 \cdot Z_\theta}_{0}
\end{array}
\right] \bmod q
$$

This is defined, even though the decryptor does not know the Z_i, for they all cancel out.

3. Let M'' be the matrix containing only the $|\mathsf{Attrib}| + 1$ non-zero "block-columns" of M' as shown above. Let K'' be the matrix obtained by removing from K the matching rows and columns—i.e., rows and columns with the same indices as the columns removed from M'. (Dimension-wise, we obtain $M'' \in \mathbb{Z}_q^{n \times (|\mathsf{Attrib}|+1)\, m}$ and $K'' \in \mathbb{Z}^{(|\mathsf{Attrib}|+1)\, m \times (|\mathsf{Attrib}|+1)\, m}$.) We have $M' \cdot K = 0$; therefore $M'' \cdot K'' = 0$, and K'' is a short basis of $\Lambda_q^\perp(M'')$.

4. Likewise, let F'' be the matrix retaining the $|\mathsf{Attrib}| + 1$ non-zero "block-columns" of F; and let $\mathbf{c}_1''$ be the ciphertext vector from which only the matching components of $\mathbf{c}_1$ remain.

5. We now build a trapdoor for the encryption matrix F, or, rather, its reduced form F''. Let 1 be the $m \times m$ identity matrix, and define the diagonal matrices,

$$
G = \begin{bmatrix} g_1 \cdot \boxed{1} & & & \\ & \ddots & & \\ & & g_\ell \cdot \boxed{1} & \\ & & & d \cdot \boxed{1} \end{bmatrix} \quad ; \quad G'' = \begin{bmatrix} \text{non-zero} \\ \text{diagonal} \\ \text{blocks} \\ \text{of } G \end{bmatrix} \begin{smallmatrix} (|\mathsf{Attrib}|+1)\, m\, \times \\ \in \mathbb{Z}^{(|\mathsf{Attrib}|+1)\, m} \end{smallmatrix}
$$

Notice $F'' \cdot G'' = M'' \pmod q$. Since $M'' \cdot K'' = 0 \pmod q$, we have $F'' \cdot G'' \cdot K'' = 0 \pmod q$. Compute $T'' = G'' \cdot K''$, whose norm is bounded as $\|T''\| \le \|G''\| \, \|K''\| \le \max\{g_i, d\} \, \|K\|$. The result T'' is our desired trapdoor for sampling short vectors in $\Lambda_q^\perp(F'')$.

6. Using SamplePreimage with trapdoor T'', find a short solution $\mathbf{f}''$ of $F'' \cdot \mathbf{f}'' = \mathbf{u} \pmod q$.

7. Compute $v = c_0 - (\mathbf{f}'')^\top \cdot \mathbf{c}_1'' \bmod q$, and represent its coset as an integer $v \in [-\lfloor \frac{q}{2} \rfloor, \lfloor \frac{q}{2} \rfloor]$.

8. Output the decrypted message bit as,

$$
b = \begin{cases} 0 & \text{if } \|v\| \le \lfloor \frac{q}{4} \rfloor \\ 1 & \text{if } \|v\| \ge \lceil \frac{q}{4} \rceil \end{cases}
$$

4.3 Correctness

Theorem 4. *For usual values of the lattice parameters in Regev-like encryption systems, the key-policy attribute-based encryption scheme of the previous section will correctly decrypt authorized ciphertexts with overwhelming probability.*

Proof. To see this, suppose that the "independent" initial bases and short vectors (namely, B_i, Y_i, $\mathbf{e}_{i,j}$, $\mathbf{d}_{i,j}$) are sampled with a suitable Gaussian parameter σ, for instance using the tools from [21,8]. Then, the norm of all "dependent" bases and vectors that are supposed to be short, will be bounded by multiples of σ to which certain "growth coefficients" will have applied. To bound those, we note that the only processes in the whole system that will induce "growth", are:

- in Extract: the randomized invocation of ExtendRight to obtain K, which merely multiplies the norm of the master-key trapdoors by a constant factor independent of the data;
- in Decrypt: the calculation of the trapdoor T″ from K″, which as we already noted multiplies the norm of K″ by a factor $\leq \max\{g_i, d\}$ that only depends on the linear-sharing reconstruction vector $\mathbf{g}$, itself function of the function Policy and its inputs Attrib.

Bounding $\max\{g_i, d\}$ for access-structure circuits with many gates can be tedious, but we note that $\max\{g_i, d\}$ will be dominated by the presence of large threshold gates. On the contrary, $\wedge$ and $\vee$ gates are essentially harmless, as shown below.

Claim. For a circuit consisting only of $\wedge$ and $\vee$ gates, $\max\{g_i, d\} = 1$.

Proof. There exists a deterministic construction of a linear sharing matrix L that guarantees binary reconstruction coefficients in this case (see Preliminaries). □

We defer to the full paper the exact quantification of the various norm and noise parameters. Of course, while the growing norm of supposedly short vectors can be compensated by commensurately increasing the modulus q, this is best avoided for efficiency reasons. □

4.4   Security

Theorem 5. *If there exists a probabilistic polynomial-time algorithm $\mathcal{A}$ with advantage $\epsilon > 0$ in a selective-security key-policy attack against the above scheme, then there exists a probabilistic polynomial-time algorithm $\mathcal{B}$ that decides the $(\mathbb{Z}_q, n, \bar{\Psi}_\alpha)$-LWE problem with advantage $\epsilon/2$, where $\alpha = O(poly(n))$.*

Proof. In the LWE problem, the decision algorithm is given access to a sampling oracle, $\mathcal{O}$, which is either a pseudo-random sampler $\mathcal{O}_s$ with embedded secret $s \in \mathbb{Z}_q^n$, or a truly random sampler $\mathcal{O}_\$$. Our decider algorithm $\mathcal{B}$ will simulate an attack environment for, and exploit the prowesses of $\mathcal{A}$, to decide which oracle it is given. The reduction proceeds as follows.

Instance. $\mathcal{B}$ requests from $\mathcal{O}$ and obtains $((1 + \ell) m + 1)$ LWE samples that we denote as,

$$\left[(\mathbf{w}_{-1}, v_{-1}) \right] \in (\mathbb{Z}_q^n \times \mathbb{Z}_q)$$
$$\left[(\mathbf{w}_0^1, v_0^1), \ldots, (\mathbf{w}_0^m, v_0^m) \right] \in (\mathbb{Z}_q^n \times \mathbb{Z}_q)^m$$
$$\left[(\mathbf{w}_1^1, v_1^1), \ldots, (\mathbf{w}_1^m, v_1^m) \right] \in (\mathbb{Z}_q^n \times \mathbb{Z}_q)^m$$
$$\vdots$$
$$\left[(\mathbf{w}_\ell^1, v_\ell^1), \ldots, (\mathbf{w}_\ell^m, v_\ell^m) \right] \in (\mathbb{Z}_q^n \times \mathbb{Z}_q)^m$$

Target. $\mathcal{A}$ announces a target attribute vector, denoted Attrib†, on which it wishes to be challenged.

Setup. $\mathcal{B}$ constructs the public key Pub as follows:

1. The vector $\mathbf{u} \in \mathbb{Z}_q^n$ is constructed from the LWE samples of index -1: simply set $\mathbf{u} = \mathbf{w}$.
2. The matrix $A_0 \in \mathbb{Z}_q^{n \times m}$ is built from the LWE samples of index 0: set $A_0 = [\mathbf{w}_0^1 | \ldots | \mathbf{w}_0^m]$.
3. For each $i \in [\ell]$ such that attribute $i \in \mathsf{Attrib}^\dagger$, the matrix A_i is constructed from the LWE samples of index i in a similar way as above: for $i \in \mathsf{Attrib}^\dagger$, set $A_i = [\mathbf{w}_i^1 | \ldots | \mathbf{w}_i^m]$.
4. For each $i \in [\ell]$ such that attribute $i \notin \mathsf{Attrib}^\dagger$, the matrix A_i is constructed as in the real scheme using TrapGen, which provides an associated low-norm full-rank matrix B_i such that $A_i \cdot B_i = 0$. (The LWE samples of all indices $i \notin \mathsf{Attrib}^\dagger$ will remain unused.)

The resulting public key Pub is given to $\mathcal{A}$.

Queries. $\mathcal{A}$ is allowed to make adaptive queries for keys Key for policies Policy that the target attribute list $\mathsf{Attrib}^\dagger$ does not satisfy. $\mathcal{B}$ constructs and returns a key Key for each query Policy, as follows.

1. As in the real scheme, derive from Policy a (low-norm) linear sharing matrix $L \in \mathbb{Z}^{\ell \times (1+\theta)}$.
2. Let $\phi = |\mathsf{Attrib}^\dagger|$. Make L' from L, keeping only the rows of index i such that $i \in \mathsf{Attrib}^\dagger$. Make L'' from L' by dropping the leftmost column of index $j = 0$ (keeping $j = 1, \ldots, \theta$).
3. W.l.o.g., suppose that $\mathsf{Attrib}^\dagger = \{i_1, i_2, \ldots, i_\phi\} = \{1, 2, \ldots, \phi\}$; i.e., the first ϕ attributes, from 1 to ϕ, are arbitrarily assumed to be the attacker's targets.
4. W.l.o.g., suppose that the ϕ left-most columns of L'' form a ϕ-dimensional square matrix of full rank. The columns of L from which L'' is derived can always be reordered to achieve this, since the order of its columns (other than that of index $j = 0$) is arbitrary. Notice that this step requires that the challenge $\mathsf{Attrib}^\dagger$ do *not* satisfy the query Policy. If it did, by definition some non-zero $[d, 0, \ldots, 0]^\top$ would be in the span of L, and thus $[0, \ldots, 0]^\top$ non-trivially in that of L''; therefore the ϕ left-most columns of L'' would not be full-rank.
5. Invoking TrapGen, sample ϕ random matrices $Z_i \in \mathbb{Z}_q^{n \times m}$ with short bases $Y_i \in \mathbb{Z}^{m \times m}$, for all $i \in \mathsf{Attrib}^\dagger$ (*i.e.*, w.l.o.g., $i = 1, \ldots, \phi$ are the indices of the Z_i with trapdoor Y_i).
6. Build a "virtual encryption matrix" M exactly as in the real scheme (see below about the boxes), as,

$$
M = \begin{bmatrix}
A_1 & & & & l_{1,0}\,A_0 & \boxed{l_{1,1}\,Z_1 \ldots l_{1,\phi}\,Z_\phi} & \ldots l_{1,\theta}\,Z_\theta \\
& \ddots & & & \vdots & \vdots \quad\quad \vdots & \vdots \\
& & A_\phi & & l_{\phi,0}\,A_0 & \boxed{l_{\phi,1}\,Z_1 \ldots l_{\phi,\phi}\,Z_\phi} & \ldots l_{\phi,\theta}\,Z_\theta \\
& & & \boxed{\ddots} & \vdots & \vdots \quad\quad \vdots & \vdots \\
& & & \boxed{A_\ell} & l_{\ell,0}\,A_0 & l_{\ell,1}\,Z_1 \ldots l_{\ell,\phi}\,Z_\phi & \ldots l_{\ell,\theta}\,Z_\theta
\end{bmatrix} \bmod q
$$

7. Denote by Z the $(\phi n \times \phi m)$-submatrix of M made of the blocks $l_{j,i}\,Z_i$ whose $i, j \in [\phi]$. Per Lemma 6, we can build (from the Y_i) a single trapdoor Y for Z as a whole.

Lemma 6. *For $i = 1, \ldots, \phi$, let $Z_i \in \mathbb{Z}_q^{n \times m}$ and $Y_i \in \mathbb{Z}^{m \times m}$ such that $Z_i Y_i = 0 \pmod q$. Suppose also that each Y_i is a basis of $\Lambda_q^{\perp}(Z_i)$ and has low norm $\|Y_i\| \le \beta \in \mathbb{R}$. Define,*

$$
Z = \begin{bmatrix} l_{1,1} Z_1 & \cdots & l_{1,\phi} Z_\phi \\ \vdots & \ddots & \vdots \\ l_{\phi,1} Z_1 & \cdots & l_{\phi,\phi} Z_\phi \end{bmatrix} \bmod q
$$

Then, for any full-rank integer matrix $(l_{i,j})$ with $i, j \in [\phi]$, the Ajtai lattice induced by $Z \in \mathbb{Z}_q^{\phi n \times \phi m}$ admits an efficiently computable (in fact constant) trapdoor $Y \in \mathbb{Z}^{\phi m \times \phi m}$ i.e., such that Y is a basis of $\Lambda_q^{\perp}(Z)$ with bounded norm $\|Y\| \le \beta$.

Proof. Take,

$$
Y = \begin{bmatrix} Y_1 & & 0 \\ & \ddots & \\ 0 & & Y_\phi \end{bmatrix}
$$

We have that $Z \cdot Y = 0 \pmod q$, that Y is a basis for $\Lambda_q^{\perp}(Z)$, and that $\|Y\| \le \max_i \|Y_i\|$. $\qquad\square$

8. Observe that we now have a trapdoor for every lattice defined by a submatrix of M encased in one of the boxes shown in Step 6. Let us notionally reorder the columns of M by swapping the ϕ left-most A_i-block-columns with the ϕ left-most Z_i-block-columns. We get a matrix $M' = [M'_{\text{trapdoor}} | M'_{\text{extension}}]$, where M'_{trapdoor} is full-rank, block-diagonal, and each of its blocks has an associated trapdoor. We can thus trivially build a trapdoor for all of M'_{trapdoor}. By invoking ExtendRight, we extend this into a trapdoor W' for all of M'. Reordering the rows of W' yields a trapdoor for the original M above: call it W.

9. Randomize W into a structure-less basis K whose norm matches that of the real scheme. (This step is only necessary if ExtendRight does not already produce a basis whose vectors all have the target discrete Gaussian distribution already; if they do, let $K = W$.)

This concludes the simulation of the private-key extraction. The adversary $\mathcal{A}$ is given the resulting $\mathsf{Key} = (K, L)$. Notice that it has exactly the same distribution as in the real scheme.

Challenge. $\mathcal{A}$ signals that it is ready to accept a challenge, and chooses a message bit $\mathsf{Msg}^\dagger \in \{0, 1\}$. $\mathcal{B}$ responds with a ciphertext $\mathsf{Ctx}^\dagger = (c_0^\dagger, c_1^\dagger)$ assembled from the LWE instance, as follows:

1. Let $c_0^\dagger = v_{-1} + \lfloor \frac{q}{2} \rfloor \cdot \mathsf{Msg}^\dagger$.

2. Let $c_1^\dagger = [\ \underbrace{v_1^1, \ldots v_1^m}_{\text{if } 1 \in \mathsf{Attrib}^\dagger}, \ldots, \underbrace{v_\ell^1, \ldots v_\ell^m}_{\text{if } \ell \in \mathsf{Attrib}^\dagger}, \underbrace{v_0^1, \ldots v_0^m}_{\text{always}}\ ]$

Observe that when the v_i come from a genuine LWE oracle, the foregoing is a well-formed Regev-like encryption of $\mathsf{Msg}^\dagger$ for the encryption matrix F

indicated by the challenge $\mathsf{Attrib}^\dagger$. On the contrary, when the v_i come from a random fake LWE oracle, the ciphertext is independent of the message bit since $c_0^\dagger$ in particular is uniformly and independently distributed.

Continuation. $\mathcal{A}$ is allowed to continue making further private-key extraction queries, after having obtained the challenge ciphertext.

Decision. $\mathcal{A}$ eventually emits a guess, whether $\mathsf{Ctx}^\dagger$ was actually a valid encryption of $\mathsf{Msg} \in \{0, 1\}$ as requested. $\mathcal{B}$ uses the guess to decide whether the LWE oracle $\mathcal{O}$ was genuine. If $\mathcal{A}$ says "valid", then $\mathcal{B}$ says "*genuine*"; if $\mathcal{A}$ says "invalid", then $\mathcal{B}$ says "*fake*".

If the adversary succeeds in guessing $\mathsf{Msg}^\dagger$ with probability at least $\frac{1}{2} + \epsilon$, then our decision algorithm $\mathcal{B}$ will correctly guess the nature of the LWE oracle with probability at least $\frac{1}{2} + \frac{\epsilon}{2}$. This concludes the proof of the security reduction. □

4.5 Extensions

So far we have assumed, merely for simplicity of notation, that policies will only encode monotone access structures given as formulas where each attribute appears as argument exactly once. We now show how to list such limitations.

Duplicated Attributes. Arbitrary monotone policies will generally be expressed as formulas where various attributes appear zero, once, or even multiple times. Accordingly, we show how to handle policies that can comport arbitrarily many $\wedge$ and $\vee$ gates, and an arbitrary wiring of the attribute inputs to feed them, including duplication.[4] The idea is very simple:

kpABE.Setup' is unchanged from the original version: to each attribute one continues to associate one Ajtai matrix A_i and its trapdoor B_i.

kpABE.Setup' also remains the same: the ciphertext is constructed as before, around a Regev encryption matrix F that either includes or excludes each submatrix A_i depending on whether or not the respective attribute $i \in \mathsf{Attrib}$.

kpABE.Extract' must be modified to allow for duplicate occurrences of the same attribute in the Boolean expression of Policy. This is done as follows:

1. Give each occurrence of some attribute $\#i$ in Policy a unique label, say $\#i.1$ and $\#i.2$, and accordingly rewrite the policy Policy into Policy' as a function of the augmented attributes. Policy' has the same topology (structure and size) as Policy, but its input literals are now unique. Keep track of the mapping from the augmented attributes i' to the original attributes i by means of a surjective map $\rho : i' \mapsto i$.

2. Construct the sharing matrix L in the regular way from the augmented-attribute formula Policy'. For each original attribute $\#i$, there will be as many rows in L as the number of occurrences of $\#i$ in the original Policy.

---

[4] We must however continue to caution on the use of t-out-of-n threshold gates $\geq_t$, because unless $t = 1$ or $t = n$ we cannot guarantee in general that the LSSS matrix L and the reconstruction coefficients will be small. Fortunately, as long as repeated attribute inputs are allowed, every possible monotone access structure can be expressed using only $\vee$ and $\wedge$ gates, in such a way that L is a binary or ternary matrix.

3. Construct the "virtual encryption matrix" M from L as before. Since the augmented attributes that emanate from the same original attribute, all refer to the same public matrix A_i, the key-extraction matrix M will thus contain multiple copies of A_i, albeit on different columns.

Once M has been constructed with possibly duplicated A_i on its left-side block-diagonal, key extraction both in the real scheme and in the simulation will proceed as usual. The only effect of the duplication is that, in the simulation, knowledge of trapdoors B_i will be linked to the presence of the original attributes—not the augmented ones—in $Attrib^\dagger$.

kpABE.Decrypt' requires a small adjustment to cope with duplicated attributes in the Policy encoded in the decryption key. Essentially, before applying the decryption algorithm, the decryptor needs to avail himself as many copies of the attribute as he will need. This is done by duplicating the various fragments of c_1 that correspond to the attributes that need to be duplicated, before using the result in the normal decryption process.

This construction is very efficient as the ciphertext size remains unchanged in |Attrib|, and the private key size has the same dependency on |Policy| as it did without attribute duplication (of course, |Policy| can now grow arbitrarily).

5   Conclusion

In this paper, we have introduced a new cryptographic framework for performing complex lattice basis manipulations, of the kind that seemingly can unlock the construction of very powerful and expressive cryptosystems such as functional encryption. We demonstrated its power and flexibility by building the first known attribute-based cryptosystem from "learning with errors", a (conjectured) quantum-resistant hardness assumption tied to many lattice problems.

Acknowledgments. The author would like to thank Dan Boneh for suggesting a simplification of the scheme and its proof by way of the ExtendRight abstraction, and to thank the TCC 2013 program committee for what appears to be a very thorough review.

References

1. Agrawal, S., Boneh, D., Boyen, X.: Efficient Lattice (H)IBE in the Standard Model. In: Gilbert, H. (ed.) EUROCRYPT 2010. LNCS, vol. 6110, pp. 553–572. Springer, Heidelberg (2010)
2. Agrawal, S., Boneh, D., Boyen, X.: Lattice Basis Delegation in Fixed Dimension and Shorter-Ciphertext Hierarchical IBE. In: Rabin, T. (ed.) CRYPTO 2010. LNCS, vol. 6223, pp. 98–115. Springer, Heidelberg (2010)
3. Agrawal, S., Boyen, X., Vaikuntanathan, V., Voulgaris, P., Wee, H.: Functional Encryption for Threshold Functions (or Fuzzy IBE) from Lattices. In: Fischlin, M., Buchmann, J., Manulis, M. (eds.) PKC 2012. LNCS, vol. 7293, pp. 280–297. Springer, Heidelberg (2012)

4. Agrawal, S., Freeman, D.M., Vaikuntanathan, V.: Functional Encryption for Inner Product Predicates from Learning with Errors. In: Lee, D.H., Wang, X. (eds.) ASIACRYPT 2011. LNCS, vol. 7073, pp. 21–40. Springer, Heidelberg (2011)
5. Ajtai, M.: Generating hard instances of lattice problems (extended abstract). In: STOC 1996 (1996)
6. Ajtai, M.: Generating Hard Instances of the Short Basis Problem. In: Wiedermann, J., Van Emde Boas, P., Nielsen, M. (eds.) ICALP 1999. LNCS, vol. 1644, pp. 1–9. Springer, Heidelberg (1999)
7. Ajtai, M., Dwork, C.: A public-key cryptosystem with worst-case/average-case equivalence. In: STOC 1997 (1997)
8. Alwen, J., Peikert, C.: Generating shorter bases for hard random lattices. In: STACS 2009 (2009)
9. Beimel, A.: Secure schemes for secret sharing and key distribution. PhD thesis, Department of Computer Science, Technion (1996)
10. Boneh, D., Gentry, C., Hamburg, M.: Space-efficient identity based encryption without pairings. In: FOCS 2007 (2007)
11. Boneh, D., Sahai, A., Waters, B.: Functional Encryption: Definitions and Challenges. In: Ishai, Y. (ed.) TCC 2011. LNCS, vol. 6597, pp. 253–273. Springer, Heidelberg (2011)
12. Boyen, X.: Lattice Mixing and Vanishing Trapdoors: A Framework for Fully Secure Short Signatures and More. In: Nguyen, P.Q., Pointcheval, D. (eds.) PKC 2010. LNCS, vol. 6056, pp. 499–517. Springer, Heidelberg (2010)
13. Boyen, X.: Attribute-based functional encryption on lattices. Cryptology ePrint Archive, Report 2012/??? (December 21, 2012), http://eprint.iacr.org/
14. Brakerski, Z., Vaikuntanathan, V.: Fully Homomorphic Encryption from Ring-LWE and Security for Key Dependent Messages. In: Rogaway, P. (ed.) CRYPTO 2011. LNCS, vol. 6841, pp. 505–524. Springer, Heidelberg (2011)
15. Cash, D., Hofheinz, D., Kiltz, E., Peikert, C.: Bonsai Trees, or How to Delegate a Lattice Basis. In: Gilbert, H. (ed.) EUROCRYPT 2010. LNCS, vol. 6110, pp. 523–552. Springer, Heidelberg (2010)
16. Cocks, C.: An Identity Based Encryption Scheme Based on Quadratic Residues. In: Honary, B. (ed.) Cryptography and Coding 2001. LNCS, vol. 2260, pp. 360–363. Springer, Heidelberg (2001)
17. Microsoft Corporation. Attribute based encryption using lattices. Application USPTO 20120155635 (December 17, 2010)
18. Ducas, L., Nguyen, P.Q.: Faster Gaussian Lattice Sampling Using Lazy Floating-Point Arithmetic. In: Wang, X., Sako, K. (eds.) ASIACRYPT 2012. LNCS, vol. 7658, pp. 415–432. Springer, Heidelberg (2012)
19. Gentry, C.: Fully homomorphic encryption using ideal lattices. In: STOC 2009 (2009)
20. Gentry, C.: Toward Basing Fully Homomorphic Encryption on Worst-Case Hardness. In: Rabin, T. (ed.) CRYPTO 2010. LNCS, vol. 6223, pp. 116–137. Springer, Heidelberg (2010)
21. Gentry, C., Peikert, C., Vaikuntanathan, V.: Trapdoors for hard lattices and new cryptographic constructions. In: STOC 2008 (2008)
22. Goyal, V., Pandey, O., Sahai, A., Waters, B.: Attribute-based encryption for fine-grained access control of encrypted data. In: CCS 2006 (2006)
23. Katz, J., Sahai, A., Waters, B.: Predicate Encryption Supporting Disjunctions, Polynomial Equations, and Inner Products. In: Smart, N.P. (ed.) EUROCRYPT 2008. LNCS, vol. 4965, pp. 146–162. Springer, Heidelberg (2008)

24. Lewko, A., Waters, B.: Decentralizing attribute-based encryption. Cryptology ePrint Archive, Report 2010/351 (2010), http://eprint.iacr.org/
25. Lyubashevsky, V.: Lattice Signatures without Trapdoors. In: Pointcheval, D., Johansson, T. (eds.) EUROCRYPT 2012. LNCS, vol. 7237, pp. 738–755. Springer, Heidelberg (2012)
26. Micciancio, D.: Generalized compact knapsacks, cyclic lattices, and efficient one-way functions from worst-case complexity assumptions. In: FOCS 2002 (2002)
27. Miller, V.: The Weil pairing, and its efficient calculation. J. Cryptology (2004)
28. Peikert, C.: Public-key cryptosystems from the worst-case shortest vector problem: extended abstract. In: STOC 2009 (2009)
29. Peikert, C., Waters, B.: Lossy trapdoor functions and their applications. SIAM J. Computing (2011)
30. Regev, O.: New lattice-based cryptographic constructions. J. ACM (2004)
31. Regev, O.: On lattices, learning with errors, random linear codes, and cryptography. In: STOC 2005 (2005)
32. Sahai, A., Waters, B.: Fuzzy Identity-Based Encryption. In: Cramer, R. (ed.) EUROCRYPT 2005. LNCS, vol. 3494, pp. 457–473. Springer, Heidelberg (2005)
33. Waters, B.: Functional Encryption for Regular Languages. In: Safavi-Naini, R. (ed.) CRYPTO 2012. LNCS, vol. 7417, pp. 218–235. Springer, Heidelberg (2012)

When Homomorphism Becomes a Liability

Zvika Brakerski[*]

Stanford University
zvika@stanford.edu

Abstract. We show that an encryption scheme cannot have a simple decryption function and be homomorphic at the same time, even with added noise. Specifically, if a scheme can homomorphically evaluate the majority function, then its decryption cannot be weakly-learnable (in particular, linear), even if the probability of decryption error is high. (In contrast, without homomorphism, such schemes do exist and are presumed secure, e.g. based on LPN.)

An immediate corollary is that known schemes that are based on the hardness of decoding in the presence of *low hamming-weight noise* cannot be fully homomorphic. This applies to known schemes such as LPN-based symmetric or public key encryption.

Using these techniques, we show that the recent candidate fully homomorphic encryption, suggested by Bogdanov and Lee (ePrint '11, henceforth BL), is insecure. In fact, we show two attacks on the BL scheme: One that uses homomorphism, and another that directly attacks a component of the scheme.

1 Introduction

An encryption scheme is called homomorphic if there is an efficient transformation that given $\mathsf{Enc}(m)$ for some message m, and a function f, produces $\mathsf{Enc}(f(m))$ using only public information. A scheme that is homomorphic w.r.t all efficient f is called fully homomorphic (FHE). Homomorphic encryption is a useful tool in both theory and practice and is extensively researched in recent years (see [20] for survey), and a few candidates for full homomorphism are known.

Most of these candidates [9, 10, 19, 6, 7, 11, 5, 12, 4] are based (either explicitly or implicitly) on *lattice assumptions* (the hardness of approximating short vectors in certain lattices). In particular, the learning with errors (LWE) assumption proved to be very useful in the design of such schemes. The one notable exception is [22], but even that could be thought of as working over an appropriately defined lattice over the integers.

An important open problem is, therefore, to diversify and base fully homomorphic encryption on different assumptions (so as to not put all the eggs in one basket). One appealing direction is to try to use the learning parity with noise (LPN) problem, which is very similar in syntax to LWE: Making a vast

[*] Supported by a Simons Postdoctoral Fellowship and by DARPA.

A. Sahai (Ed.): TCC 2013, LNCS 7785, pp. 143–161, 2013.

generalization, LWE can be interpreted as a decoding problem for a linear code, where the noise comes from a family of *low norm* vectors. Namely, each coordinate in the code suffers from noise, but this noise is relatively small (this requires that the code is defined over a large alphabet). The LPN assumption works over the binary alphabet and requires that the noise has low hamming weight, namely that only a small number of coordinates are noisy, but in these coordinates the noise amplitude can be large. While similar in syntax, a direct connection between these two types of assumptions is not known.

While an LPN-based construction is not known, recently Bogdanov and Lee [3] presented a candidate, denoted by BL throughout this manuscript, that is based on a different low hamming-weight decoding problem: They consider a carefully crafted code over a large alphabet and assume that decoding in the presence of low-hamming-weight noise is hard.

In this work, we show that not only that BL's construction is insecure, but rather the entire approach of constructing code based homomorphic encryption analogously to the LWE construction cannot work. We stress that we don't show that FHE cannot be based on LPN (or other code based assumptions), but rather that the decryption algorithm of such scheme cannot take the naïve form. (In particular this applies to the attempt to add homomorphism to schemes such as [1, 13, 2].)

1.1   Our Results

Our main result shows that encryption schemes with learnable decryption functions cannot be homomorphic, even if a high probability of decryption error is allowed. In particular, such schemes cannot evaluate the majority function. This extends the result of Kearns and Valiant [15] (slightly extended by Klivans and Sherstov [16]) that learnability breaks security for schemes with negligible decryption error. In other words, homomorphic capabilities can sometimes make noisy learning become no harder than noiseless learning.

We use a simplified notion of learning, which essentially requires that given polynomially many labeled samples (from an arbitrary distribution), the learner's hypothesis correctly computes the label for the next sample with probability, say, 0.9. We show that this notion, that we call *sc-learning*, is equivalent to *weak learning* defined in [15]. This allows us to prove the following theorem (in Section 3).

Theorem A. *An encryption scheme whose decryption function is sc- or weakly-learnable, and whose decryption error is $1/2 - 1/\text{poly}(n)$, cannot homomorphically evaluate the majority function.*

Since it is straightforward to show that linear functions are learnable (as well as, e.g., low degree polynomials), the theorem applies to known LPN based schemes such as [1, 13, 2]. This may not seem obvious at first: The decryption circuit of the aforementioned schemes is (commonly assumed to be) hard to learn, and their decryption error is negligible, so they seem to be out of the scope of our theorem. However, looking more closely, the decryption circuits consist of an inner product computation with the secret key, followed by additional post-processing. One can verify that if the post processing is not performed, then correct decryption is still achieved with probability $> 1/2 + 1/\text{poly}$. Thus we can apply our theorem and rule out majority-homomorphism.

Similar logic rules out the homomorphism of the BL candidate-FHE. While Theorem A does not apply directly (since the decryption of BL is not learnable out of the box), we show that it contains a sub-scheme which is linear (and thus learnable) and has sufficient homomorphic properties to render it insecure.

Theorem B. *There is a successful polynomial time CPA attack on the BL scheme.*

We further present a different attack on the BL scheme, targeting one of its building blocks. This allows us to not only distinguish between two messages like the successful CPA attack above, but rather decrypt any ciphertext with probability $1 - o(1)$.

Theorem C. *There is a polynomial time algorithm that decrypts the BL scheme.*

The BL scheme and the two breaking algorithms are presented in Section 4.

1.2   Our Techniques

Consider a simplified case of Theorem A, where the scheme's decryption function is learnable given t labeled samples, and the decryption error is (say) $1/(10(t + 1))$. The proof in this case is straightforward: Generate t labeled samples by just encrypting random messages, and feed them to the learner. Then use the learner's output hypothesis to decrypt the challenge ciphertext. We can only fail if either the learner fails (which happens with probability 0.1) or if one of the samples we draw (including the challenge) are not correctly decryptable, in which case our labeling is wrong and therefore the learner provides no guarantee (which again happens with at most 0.1 probability). The union bound implies that we can decrypt a random ciphertext with probability 0.8, which immediately breaks the scheme. Note that we did not use the homomorphism of the scheme at all, indeed this simplified version is universally true even without assuming homomorphism, and is very similar to the arguments in [15, 16]. (Some subtleties arise since we allow a non-negligible fraction of "dysfunctional" keys that induce a much higher error rate than others.)

The next step is to allow decryption error $1/2 - \epsilon$, which requires use of homomorphism. The idea is to use the homomorphism in order to reduce the decryption error and get back to the previous case (in other words, reducing the noise in a noisy learning problem). Consider a scheme that encrypts a message by generating many encryptions (say k) of that message, and then applying homomorphic majority on those ciphertexts and outputting the result. The security of this scheme directly reduces from that of the original scheme, and it has the same decryption function. However, now the decryption error drops exponentially with k. This is because in order to get an error in the new scheme, at least $k/2$ out of the k encryptions need to have errors. Since the expected number is $(1/2 - \epsilon)k$, the Chernoff bound implies the result by choosing k appropriately.

To derive Theorem B, we need to show that linear functions are learnable:[1] Assume that the decryption function is an inner product between the ciphertext and the secret key (both being n-dimensional vectors over a field $\mathbb{F}$). We will learn these functions by taking $O(n)$ labeled samples. Then, given the challenge, we will try to represent it as a linear combination of the samples we have. If we succeed, then the appropriate linear combination of the labels will be the value of the function on the challenge. We show that this process fails only with small constant probability (intuitively, since we take $O(n)$ sample vectors from a space of dimension at most n).

We then show that BL uses a sub-structure that is both linearly decryptable and allows for homomorphism of (some sort of) majority. Theorem B thus follows similarly to Theorem A.

For Theorem C, we need to dive into the guts of the BL scheme. We notice that BL use homomorphic majority evaluation in one of the lower abstraction levels of their scheme. This allows us to break this abstraction level using only linear algebra (in a sense, the homomorphic evaluation is already "built in"). A complete break of BL follows.

1.3   Other Related Work

An independent work by Gauthier, Otmani and Tillich [8] shows an interesting direct attack on BL's hardness assumption (we refer to it as the "GOT attack"). Their attack is very different from ours and takes advantage of the resemblance of BL's codes and Reed-Solomon codes as we explain below.

BL's construction relies on a special type of error correcting code. Essentially, they start with a Reed-Solomon code, and replace a small fraction of the rows of the generating matrix with a special structure. The homomorphic properties are only due to this small fraction of "significant" rows, and the secret key is chosen so as to nullify the effect of the other rows.

The GOT attack uses the fact that under some transformation (componentwise multiplication), the dimension of Reed-Solomon codes can grow by at most a factor of two. However, if a code contains "significant" rows, then the dimension can grow further. This allows to measure the number of significant rows in a given code. One can thus identify the significant rows by trying to remove one row at a time from the code and checking if the dimension drops. If yes then that row is significant. Once all significant rows have been identified, the secret key can be retrieved in a straightforward manner.

However, it is fairly easy to immunize BL's scheme against the GOT attack. As we explained above, the neutral rows do not change the properties of the

---

[1] We believe this was known before, but since we could not find an appropriate reference, we provide a proof.

encryption scheme, so they may as well be replaced by random rows. Since the dimension of random codes grows very rapidly under the GOT transformation, their attack will not work in such case.

Our attack, on the other hand, relies on certain functional properties that BL use to make their scheme homomorphic. Thus a change in the scheme that preserves these homomorphic properties cannot help to overcome our attack. In light of our attack, it is interesting to investigate whether the GOT attack can be extended to the more general case.

2   Preliminaries

We denote scalars using plain lowercase (x), vectors using bold lowercase ($\mathbf{x}$ for column vector, $\mathbf{x}^T$ for row vector), and matrices using bold uppercase ($\mathbf{X}$). We let $\mathbf{1}$ denote the all-one vector (the dimension will be clear from the context). We let $\mathbb{F}_q$ denote a finite field of cardinality $q \in \mathbb{N}$, with efficient operations (we usually don't care about any other property of the field).

2.1   Properties of Encryption Schemes

A public key encryption scheme is a tuple of algorithms ($\mathsf{Gen}, \mathsf{Enc}, \mathsf{Dec}$), such that: $\mathsf{Gen}(1^n)$ is the key generation algorithm that produces a pair of public and secret keys (pk, sk); $\mathsf{Enc}_{pk}(m)$ is a randomized encryption function that takes a message m and produces a ciphertext. In the context of this work, messages will only come from some predefined field $\mathbb{F}$; $\mathsf{Dec}_{sk}(c)$ is the decryption function that decrypts a ciphertext c and produces the message. Optimally, $\mathsf{Dec}_{sk}(\mathsf{Enc}_{pk}(\cdot))$ is the identity function, but in some schemes there are decryption errors.

The probability of decryption error is taken over the randomness used to generate the keys for the scheme, and over the randomness used in the encryption function (we assume the decryption is deterministic). Since in our case the error rates are high (approaching $1/2$), the effect of bad keys is different from that of bad encryption randomness, and we thus measure the two separately. We allow a small fraction of the keys (one percent, for the sake of convenience) to have arbitrarily large decryption error, and define the decryption error ϵ to be the maximal error over the 99% best keys. While the constant 1% is arbitrary and chosen so as to not over-clutter notation, we will discuss after presenting our results how they generalize to other values. The formal definition follows.

Definition 2.1. *An encryption scheme is said to have decryption error $< \epsilon$ if with probability at least 0.99 over the key generation it holds that*

$$\max_m \left\{ \Pr[\mathsf{Dec}_{sk}(\mathsf{Enc}_{pk}(m)) \neq m] \right\} < \epsilon \ ,$$

where the probability is taken over the random coins of the encryption function.

We use the standard definition of security against chosen plaintext attacks (CPA): The attacker receives a public key and chooses two values m_0, m_1. The attacker then receives a ciphertext $c = \mathsf{Enc}_{pk}(m_b)$, where $b \in \{0, 1\}$ is a random bit that is unknown to the attacker. The attacker needs to decide on a guess $b' \in \{0, 1\}$ as to the value of b. We say that the scheme is broken if there is a polynomial time attacker for which $\Pr[b' = b] \geq 1/2 + 1/\mathrm{poly}(n)$ (where n is the security parameter). Recall that this notion is equivalent to the notion of semantic security [14].

In addition, we will say that a scheme is *completely broken* if there exists an adversary that upon receiving the public key and $\mathsf{Enc}_{pk}(m)$ for *arbitrary value of* m, returns m with probability $1 - o(1)$.

While we discuss homomorphic properties of encryption schemes, we will only use homomorphism w.r.t the majority function. We define the notion of k-majority-homomorphism below.

Definition 2.2. *A public-key encryption scheme is k-majority-homomorphic (where k is a function of the security parameter) if there exists a function* $\mathsf{MajEval}$ *such that with probability 0.99 over the key generation, for any sequence of ciphertexts output by* $\mathsf{Enc}_{pk}(\cdot)$: $c_1, \ldots, c_k$, *it holds that*

$$\mathsf{Dec}_{sk}(\mathsf{MajEval}_{pk}(c_1, \ldots, c_k)) = \mathsf{Majority}(\mathsf{Dec}_{sk}(c_1), \ldots, \mathsf{Dec}_{sk}(c_k)) \ .$$

Again we allow some "slackness" by allowing some of the keys to not abide the homomorphism.

We note that Definition 2.2 above is a fairly strong notion of homomorphism in two aspects: First, it requires that homomorphism holds even for ciphertexts with decryption error. Second, we do not allow $\mathsf{MajEval}$ to introduce error for "good" key pairs. Indeed, known homomorphic encryption schemes have these properties, but it is interesting to try to bypass our negative results by finding schemes that do not have them.

Schemes with linear decryption, as defined below, have a special role in our attack on BL.

Definition 2.3. *An encryption scheme is n-linearly decryptable if its secret key is of the form $sk = \mathbf{s} \in \mathbb{F}^n$, for some field $\mathbb{F}$, and its decryption function is*

$$\mathsf{Dec}_{sk}(\mathbf{c}) = \langle \mathbf{s}, \mathbf{c} \rangle \ .$$

2.2 Spanning Distributions over Low Dimensional Spaces

We will use a lemma that shows that any distribution over a low dimensional space is easy to span in the following sense: Given sufficiently many samples from the distribution (a little more than the dimension of the support), we are guaranteed that any new vector falls in the span of previous samples. This lemma will allow us to derive a (distribution-free) learner for linear functions (see Section 2.3).

We speculate that this lemma is already known, since it is fairly general and very robust to the definition of dimension (e.g. it also applies to non-linear spaces).

Lemma 2.4. *Let $\mathcal{S}$ be a distribution over a linear space S of dimension s. For all k, define*

$$\delta_k \triangleq \Pr_{v_1,\ldots,v_k \xleftarrow{\$} \mathcal{S}} [v_k \notin \mathrm{Span}\{v_1,\ldots,v_{k-1}\}] \ .$$

Then $\delta_k \leq s/k$.

Proof. Notice that by symmetry $\delta_i \geq \delta_{i+1}$ for all i. Let D_i denote the (random variable) dimension of $\mathrm{Span}\{v_1,\ldots,v_i\}$. Note that always $D_i \leq s$.

Let E_i denote the event $v_i \notin \mathrm{Span}\{v_1,\ldots,v_{i-1}\}$ and let $\mathbb{1}_{E_i}$ denote the indicator random variable for this event. Then $\delta_i = \Pr[E_i] = \mathbb{E}[\mathbb{1}_{E_i}]$. By definition,

$$D_k = \sum_{i=1}^{k} \mathbb{1}_{E_i} \ .$$

Therefore

$$s \geq \mathbb{E}[D_k] = \mathbb{E}\left[\sum_{i=1}^{k} \mathbb{1}_{E_i}\right] = \sum_{i=1}^{k} \Pr[E_i] = \sum_{i=1}^{k} \delta_i \geq k \cdot \delta_k \ ,$$

and the lemma follows.

2.3   Learning

In this work we use two equivalent notions of learning: weak-learning as defined in [15], and an equivalent simplified notion that we call single-challenge-learning (sc-learning for short). The latter will be more convenient for our proofs, but we show that the two are equivalent. We will also show that linear functions are sc-learnable.

Notions of Learning. We start by introducing the notion of weak-learnability.

Definition 2.5 (weak-learning [15]). *Let $\mathcal{F} = \{\mathcal{F}_n\}_{n\in\mathbb{N}}$ be an ensemble of binary functions. A weak learner for $\mathcal{F}$ with parameters (t,ϵ,δ) is a polynomial time algorithm A such that for any function $f \in \mathcal{F}_n$ and for any distribution $\mathcal{D}$ over the inputs to f, the following holds. Let $x_1,\ldots,x_{t+1} \xleftarrow{\$} \mathcal{D}$, and let h ("the hypothesis") be the output of $A(1^n, (x_1, f(x_1)),\ldots,(x_t, f(x_t)))$. Then*

$$\Pr_{x_1,\ldots,x_t}\left[\Pr_{x_{t+1}}[h(x_{t+1}) \neq f(x_{t+1})] > \epsilon\right] \leq \delta \ .$$

We say that $\mathcal{F}$ is weakly learnable if there exists a weak learner for $\mathcal{F}$ with parameters $t = \mathrm{poly}(n)$, $\epsilon \leq 1/2 - 1/\mathrm{poly}(n)$, $\delta \leq 1 - 1/\mathrm{poly}(n)$. (We also require that the output hypothesis h is polynomial time computable.)

We next define our notion of (t,η)-sc-learning, which essentially corresponds to the ability to launch a t-query CPA attack on an (errorless) encryption scheme, and succeed with probability η. (The initials "sc" stand for "single challenge", reflecting the fact that a CPA attacker only receives a single challenge ciphertext.)

Definition 2.6 (sc-learning). *Let $\mathcal{F} = \{\mathcal{F}_n\}_{n \in \mathbb{N}}$ be an ensemble of functions. A (t, η)-sc-learner for $\mathcal{F}$ is a polynomial time algorithm A such that for any function $f \in \mathcal{F}_n$ and for any distribution $\mathcal{D}$ over the inputs to f, the following holds. Let $x_1, \ldots, x_{t+1} \overset{\$}{\leftarrow} \mathcal{D}$, and let h ("the hypothesis") be the output of $A(1^n, (x_1, f(x_1)), \ldots, (x_t, f(x_t)))$. Then $\Pr[h(x_{t+1}) \neq f(x_{t+1})] \leq \eta$, where the probability is taken over the entire experiment.*

We say that $\mathcal{F}$ is (t, η)-sc-learnable if it has a polynomial time (t, η)-sc-learner for it. We say that a binary $\mathcal{F}$ is sc-learnable if $t = \mathrm{poly}(n)$ and $\eta \leq 1/2 - 1/\mathrm{poly}(n)$. (We also require that the output hypothesis h is polynomial time computable.)

Since sc-learning only involves one challenge, we do not define the "confidence" and "accuracy" parameters (δ, ϵ) separately as in the definition of weak-learning.

We note that both definitions allow for *improper learning* (namely, the hypothesis h does not need to "look like" an actual decryption function).

Equivalence Between Notions. The equivalence of the two notions is fairly straightforward. Applying boosting [18] shows that sc-learning, like weak-learning, can be amplified.

Claim 1. *If $\mathcal{F}$ is sc-learnable then it is weak-learnable.*

Proof. This follows by a Markov argument: Consider a (t, η)-sc-learner for $\mathcal{F}$ (recall that $\eta \leq 1/2 - 1/\mathrm{poly}(n)$) and let $\delta = 1 - 1/\mathrm{poly}(n)$ be such that $\eta/\delta \leq 1/2 - \mathrm{poly}(n)$ (such δ must exist). Then letting $\epsilon \triangleq \eta/\delta$ finishes the argument.

The opposite direction will give us very strong amplification of learning by applying boosting [18]. The boosting algorithm can amplify the ϵ, δ values of a weak learner to arbitrarily small values, at the cost of increasing the number of required samples.

Claim 2. *If $\mathcal{F}$ is weak-learnable then it is $(\mathrm{poly}(n, 1/\eta), \eta)$-sc-learnable for all η.*

Proof. Let $\mathcal{F}$ be weak-learnable. Then by boosting [18] it is also PAC learnable [21]. Namely there is a learner with parameters $(\mathrm{poly}(n, 1/\epsilon, 1/\delta), \epsilon, \delta)$ for any inversely polynomial ϵ, δ. Setting $\epsilon = \delta = \eta/2$, the claim follows.

Learning Linear Functions. The following corollary (of Lemma 2.4) shows a simple direct construction of an sc-learner for the class of linear functions.[2]

Corollary 2.7. *Let $\mathcal{F}_n$ be a class of n-dimensional linear functions over a field $\mathbb{F}$. Then $\mathcal{F} = \{\mathcal{F}_n\}_n$ is $(10n, 1/10)$-sc-learnable.*

---

[2] The learner works even when the function class is not binary, which is only an advantage. The binary case follows by considering distributions supported only over the pre-images of $0, 1$.

Proof. We note that for any linear function $f : \mathbb{F}^n \to \mathbb{F}$, the set $\{(\mathbf{x}, f(\mathbf{x}))\}_{\mathbf{x} \in \mathbb{F}^n}$ is an n-dimensional linear subspace of $\mathbb{F}^{n+1}$.

The learner A works as follows. It is given $t = 10n$ samples $\mathbf{v}_i \triangleq (\mathbf{x}_i, f(\mathbf{x}_i)) \in \mathbb{F}^{n+1}$. Using Gaussian elimination, A will find $\mathbf{s} \in \mathbb{F}^n$ such that $(-\mathbf{s}, 1) \in \mathrm{Ker}\{\mathbf{v}_i\}_{i \in [t]}$ (note that such must exist). Finally A will output the hypothesis $h(\mathbf{x}) = \langle \mathbf{s}, \mathbf{x} \rangle$.

Correctness follows using Lemma 2.4. We let the distribution $\mathcal{S}$ be the distribution $(\mathbf{x}, f(\mathbf{x}))$ where $\mathbf{x} \xleftarrow{\$} \mathcal{D}$, and let $k = t + 1$. It follows that with probability $1 - 1/10$, it holds that $(\mathbf{x}_{t+1}, f(\mathbf{x}_{t+1})) \in \mathrm{Span}\{\mathbf{v}_i\}_{i \in [t]}$ which implies that $\langle (-\mathbf{s}, 1), (\mathbf{x}_{t+1}, f(\mathbf{x}_{t+1})) \rangle = 0$, or in other words $f(\mathbf{x}_{t+1}) = \langle \mathbf{s}, \mathbf{x}_{t+1} \rangle = h(\mathbf{x}_{t+1})$.

3   Homomorphism Is a Liability When Decryption Is Learnable

This section features our main result. We show that schemes with learnable decryption circuits are very limited in terms of their homomorphic properties, regardless of decryption error. This extends the previous results of [15, 16] showing that the decryption function cannot be learnable if the decryption error is negligible.

We start by showing that a scheme with $(t, 1/10)$-sc-learnable decryption function (i.e. efficient learning with probability $1/10$ using t samples, see Definition 2.6) cannot have decryption error smaller than $\Omega(1/t)$ and be secure (regardless of homomorphism). We proceed to show that if the scheme can homomorphically evaluate the majority function, then the above amplifies dramatically and security cannot be guaranteed for *any* reasonable decryption error ($1/2 - \epsilon$ error for any noticeable ϵ). Using Claim 2 (boosting), this implies that the above hold for any scheme with weakly-learnable (or sc-learnable) decryption. We then discuss the role of key generation error compared to encryption error.

For the sake of simplicity, we focus on the public key setting. However, our proofs easily extend also to symmetric encryption, since our attacks only use the public key in order to generate ciphertexts for known messages.

Learnable Decryption without Homomorphism. We start by showing that a scheme whose decryption circuit is $(t, 1/10)$-sc-learnable has to have decryption error $\epsilon = \Omega(1/t)$, otherwise it is insecure. This is a parameterized and slightly generalized version of the claims of [15, 16], geared towards schemes with high decryption error and possibly bad keys. The basic idea is straightforward: We use the public key to generate t ciphertexts to be used as labeled samples for our learner, and then use its output hypothesis to decrypt the challenge ciphertext. The above succeeds so long as all samples in the experiment decrypt correctly, which by the union bound is at least $1 - t \cdot \epsilon$. A formal statement and proof follows.

Lemma 3.1. *An encryption scheme whose decryption function is $(t, 1/10)$-sc-learnable for a polynomial t and whose decryption error $< 1/(10(t+1))$ is insecure.*

Proof. Consider a key pair (pk, sk) for the scheme, and consider the following CPA adversary. The adversary first generates t labeled samples of the form $(\mathsf{Enc}_{pk}(m), m)$, for random messages $m \xleftarrow{\$} \{0, 1\}$ (where $0, 1$ serve as generic names for an arbitrary pair of elements in the scheme's message space). These samples are fed into the aforementioned learner, let h denote the learner's output hypothesis. The adversary lets $m_0 = 0$, $m_1 = 1$, and given the challenge ciphertext $c = \mathsf{Enc}_{pk}(m_b)$, it outputs $b' = h(c)$.

To analyze, we consider the (inefficient) distribution $\mathcal{D}$ that first samples $m \xleftarrow{\$} \{0, 1\}$, and then outputs a random *correctly decryptable* encryption of m. More formally, $\mathcal{D}$ is the distribution $c = \mathsf{Enc}_{pk}(m) | (\mathsf{Dec}_{sk}(c) = m)$ for a randomly chosen $m \xleftarrow{\$} \{0, 1\}$. By Definition 2.6, if the learner gets t samples from this distribution, it outputs a hypothesis that correctly labels the $(t + 1)$ sample, with all but $1/10$ probability.

While we cannot efficiently sample from $\mathcal{D}$ (without the secret key), we show that the samples (and challenge) that we feed to our learner are in fact statistically close to samples from $\mathcal{D}$. Consider a case where (pk, sk) are such that the decryption error is indeed smaller than $\epsilon = 1/(10(t+1))$. In such case, our adversary samples from a distribution of statistical distance at most ϵ from $\mathcal{D}$, and the challenge ciphertext is drawn from the same distribution. It follows that the set of $(t+1)$ samples that we consider during the experiment (containing the labeled samples and the challenge), agree with $\mathcal{D}$ with all but $(t+1) \cdot \epsilon = 1/10$ probability.

Using the union bound on all aforementioned "bad" events (the key pair not conforming with decryption error as per Definition 2.1, the samples not agreeing with $\mathcal{D}$, and the learner failing), we get that $\Pr[b' = b] \geq 1 - 0.01 - 1/10 - 1/10 > 0.7$ and the lemma follows.

Using Claim 2, we derive the following corollary.

Corollary 3.2. *An encryption scheme whose decryption function is weakly-learnable must have decryption error $1/\mathrm{poly}(n)$ for some polynomial.*

We note that this corollary does not immediately follow from [15, 16] if a noticeable fraction of the keys can be "bad" (since they do not use boosting).

Plugging our learner for linear functions (Corollary 2.7) into Lemma 3.1 implies the following, which will be useful for the next section.

Corollary 3.3. *There exists a constant $\alpha > 0$ such that any n-linearly decryptable scheme with decryption error $< \alpha/n$ is insecure.*

Learnable Decryption with Majority Homomorphism. Lemma 3.1 and Corollary 3.2 by themselves are not very restrictive. Specifically, they are not directly applicable to attacking any known scheme. Indeed, known schemes with linear decryption (e.g. LPN based) have sufficiently high decryption error (or, viewed differently, adding the error makes the underlying decryption hard to learn). We now show that if homomorphism is required as a property of the scheme, then decryption error cannot save us.

The following theorem states that majority-homomorphic schemes (see Definition 2.2) cannot have learnable decryption for any reasonable decryption error.

Theorem 3.4. *An encryption scheme whose decryption circuit is $(t, 1/10)$-sc-learnable for a polynomial t and whose decryption error $< (1/2 - \epsilon)$ cannot be $O(\log t/\epsilon^2)$-majority-homomorphic.*

Let us first outline the proof of Theorem 3.4 before formalizing it. Our goal is the same as in the proof of Lemma 3.1, to generate t labeled samples, which will enable to break security. However, unlike above, taking t random encryptions will surely introduce decryption errors. We thus use the majority homomorphism: We generate a good encryption of m, i.e. one that is decryptable with high probability, by generating $O(\log t/\epsilon^2)$ random encryptions of m, and apply majority homomorphically. Chernoff's bound guarantees that with high probability, more than half of the ciphertexts are properly decryptable, and therefore the output of the majority evaluation is with high probability a decryptable encryption of m. At this point, we can apply the same argument as in the proof of Lemma 3.1. The formal proof follows.

Proof. Consider an encryption scheme (Gen, Enc, Dec) as in the theorem statement. We will construct a new scheme (Gen$'$ = Gen, Enc$'$, Dec$'$ = Dec) (with the same key generation and decryption algorithms) whose security relates to that of (Gen, Enc, Dec). Then we will use Lemma 3.1 to render the latter scheme insecure.

The new encryption algorithm $\mathsf{Enc}'_{pk}(m)$ works as follows: To encrypt a message m, invoke the original encryption $\mathsf{Enc}_{pk}(m)$ for (say) $k = 10(\ln(t+1) + \ln(10))/\epsilon^2$ times, thus generating k ciphertexts. Apply MajEval to those k ciphertexts and output the resulting ciphertext.

The security of the new scheme is related to that of the original by a straightforward hybrid argument. We will show that the new scheme has decryption error at most $1/(10(t+1))$, but in a slightly weaker sense then Definition 2.1: We will allow 2% of the keys to be "bad" instead of just 1% as before. One can easily verify that the proof of Lemma 3.1 works in this case as well.

Our set of good key pairs for Enc$'$ is those for which $\mathsf{Dec}_{sk}(\mathsf{Enc}_{pk}(\cdot))$ indeed have decryption error at most $1/2 - \epsilon$ and in addition MajEval is correct. By the union bound this happens with probability at least 0.98.

To bound the decryption error of $\mathsf{Dec}_{sk}(\mathsf{Enc}'_{pk}(\cdot))$, assume that we have a good key pair as described above. We will bound the probability that more than a $1/2 - \epsilon/2$ fraction of the k ciphertexts generated by Enc$'$ are decrypted incorrectly. Clearly if this bad event does not happen, then by the correctness of MajEval, the resulting ciphertext will decrypt correctly.

Recalling that the expected fraction of falsely decrypted ciphertexts is at most $1/2 - \epsilon$, the Chernoff bound implies that the aforementioned bad event happens with probability at most

$$e^{-2(\epsilon/2)^2 k} < 1/(10(t+1)) \,,$$

and the theorem follows.

From the proof it is obvious that even "approximate-majority homomorphism" is sufficient for the theorem to hold. Namely, even if MajEval only computes the majority function correctly if the fraction of identical inputs is more than $1/2 + \epsilon/2$. Even more generally, we can use any function FEval for which $\mathsf{Dec}_{sk}(\mathsf{FEval}(\mathsf{Enc}_{pk}(m), \ldots, \mathsf{Enc}_{pk}(m))) = m$ with high probability.

We can derive a general corollary for every weakly-learnable function using Claim 2. This applies, for example, to linear functions, low degree polynomials and shallow circuits.

Corollary 3.5. *An encryption scheme whose decryption function is weakly-learnable and whose decryption error is $1/2 - \epsilon$ cannot be $\omega(\log n/\epsilon^2)$-majority-homomorphic.*

The Role of Bad Keys. Recall that in Definitions 2.1 and 2.2 (decryption error and majority homomorphism) we allowed a constant fraction of keys to be useless for the purpose of decryption and homomorphic evaluation, respectively. In fact, it is this relaxation that makes our argument more involved than [15, 16].

As we mentioned above, the choice of constant 0.01 is arbitrary. Let us now explain how our results extend to the case of $1/2 - \kappa$ fraction of bad keys, where $\kappa = 1/\mathrm{poly}(n)$ (we now count the keys that are either bad for decryption or bad for homomorphism). In such case, the argument of Lemma 3.1 will work so long as we start with a (t, η)-sc-learner with $\eta < \kappa/3$ and so long as the decryption error for good keys is at most $\kappa/(3(t+1))$. If the scheme is furthermore $O(\log(t/\kappa)/\epsilon^2) = O(\log n/\epsilon^2)$-majority-homomorphic, the proof of Theorem 3.4 will also go through. Finally, using boosting, we can start with any weak learner and reduce η to $< \kappa/3$ at the cost of a polynomial increase in t, which is tolerable by our arguments (and swallowed by the asymptotic notation).

4   Attacks on the BL Scheme

In this section we use our tools from above to show that the BL scheme (outlined in Section 4.1 below) is broken. We present two attacks: the first, in Section 4.2, follows from Corollary 3.3 (and works in the spirit of Theorem 3.4); and the second, in Section 4.3, directly attacks a lower level subcomponent of the scheme and allows to decrypt any ciphertext. In fact, the latter attack also follows the same basic principles and exploits a "built-in" evaluation of majority that exists in that sub-component of BL.

4.1   Essentials of the BL Scheme

In this section we present the properties of the BL scheme. We concentrate on the properties that are required for our breaks. We refer the reader to [3] for further details.

The BL scheme has a number of layers of abstraction, which are all instantiated based on a global parameter $0 < \alpha < 0.25$ as explained below.

The Scheme $\mathbf{K}_q(n)$. BL introduce $\mathbf{K}_q(n)$, a public-key encryption scheme with imperfect correctness. For security parameter n, the public key is a matrix $\mathbf{P} \in \mathbb{F}_q^{n \times r}$, where $r = n^{1-\alpha/8}$, and the secret key is a vector $\mathbf{y} \in \mathbb{F}_q^n$ in the kernel of $\mathbf{P}^T$ (namely, $\mathbf{y}^T \cdot \mathbf{P} = 0$). The keys are generated in a highly structured manner in order to support homomorphism, but their structure is irrelevant to us. An encryption of a message $m \in \mathbb{F}_q$ is a vector $\mathbf{c} = \mathbf{P} \cdot \mathbf{x} + m \cdot \mathbf{1} + \mathbf{e}$, where $\mathbf{x} \in \mathbb{F}_q^r$ is some vector, and where $\mathbf{e} \in \mathbb{F}_q^n$ is a low hamming weight vector. Decryption is performed by taking the inner product $\langle \mathbf{y}, \mathbf{c} \rangle$, and succeeds so long as $\langle \mathbf{y}, \mathbf{e} \rangle = 0$ (the vector $\mathbf{y}$ is chosen such that $\langle \mathbf{y}, \mathbf{1} \rangle = 1$). It is shown how the structure of the keys implies that decryption succeeds with probability at least $\left(1 - n^{-(1-\alpha/2)}\right)$. Finally, BL show that $\mathbf{K}_q(n)$ is homomorphic with respect to a single addition or multiplication.[3]

Re-Encryption. In order to enable homomorphism, BL introduce the notion of re-encryption. Consider an instantiation of $\mathbf{K}_q(n)$, with keys $(\mathbf{P}, \mathbf{y})$, and an instantiation of $\mathbf{K}_q(n')$ with keys $(\mathbf{P}', \mathbf{y}')$, for $n' = n^{1+\alpha}$. Let $\mathbf{H}_{n':n} \in \mathbb{F}_q^{n' \times n}$ be an element-wise encryption of $\mathbf{y}$ using the public key $\mathbf{P}'$.[4] Namely $\mathbf{H}_{n':n} = \mathbf{P}' \cdot \mathbf{X}' + \mathbf{1} \cdot \mathbf{y}^T + \mathbf{E}'$. Due to the size difference between the schemes, it holds that with probability $\left(1 - n^{-\Omega(1)}\right)$, all of the columns of $\mathbf{H}_{n':n}$ are simultaneously decryptable and indeed $\mathbf{y}'^T \cdot \mathbf{H}_{n':n} = \mathbf{y}^T$. In such case, for any ciphertext $\mathbf{c}$ of $\mathbf{K}_q(n)$, we get $\langle \mathbf{y}', \mathbf{H}_{n':n}\mathbf{c} \rangle = \langle \mathbf{y}, \mathbf{c} \rangle$. The matrix $\mathbf{H}_{n':n}$ therefore re-encrypts ciphertexts of $\mathbf{K}_q(n)$ as ciphertexts of $\mathbf{K}_q(n')$.

The critical idea for our second break is that a re-encrypted ciphertext always belongs to an n-dimensional linear subspace (recall that $n \ll n'$), namely to the span of $\mathbf{H}_{n':n}$.

The Scheme **BASIC**. Using re-encryption, BL construct a ladder of schemes of increasing lengths that allow for homomorphic evaluation. They define the scheme **BASIC** which has an additional depth parameter $d = O(1)$ (BL suggest to use $d = 8$, but our attack works for any $d > 1$). They consider instantiations of $\mathbf{K}_q(n_i)$, where $n_i = n^{(1+\alpha)^{-(d-i)}}$, for $i = 0, \ldots, d$, so $n_d = n$. They generate

---

[3] Homomorphic operations (addition, multiplication) are performed element-wise on ciphertext vectors, and the structure of the key guarantees that correctness is preserved.

[4] A note on notation: In [3], the re-encryption parameters are denoted by I (as opposed to our $\mathbf{H}$). We feel that their notation ignores the important linear algebraic structure of the re-encryption parameters, and therefore we switched to matrix notation, which also dictated the change of letter.

all re-encryption matrices $\mathbf{H}_{n_{i+1}:n_i}$ (with success probability $\left(1 - n^{-\Omega(1)}\right)$) and can thus homomorphically evaluate depth d circuits.

The homomorphic evaluation works by performing a homomorphic operation at level i of the evaluated circuit (with i going from 0 to $d - 1$), and then using re-encryption with $\mathbf{H}_{n_{i+1}:n_i}$ to obtain a fresh ciphertext for the next level.

For the purposes of our (second) break, we notice that in the last step of this evaluation is re-encryption using $\mathbf{H}_{n_d:n_{d-1}}$. This means that homomorphically evaluated ciphertexts all come from a linear subspace of dimension $n_{d-1} = n^{1/(1+\alpha)}$.

Error Correction and the Matrix $\mathbf{H}_{n:n}$. Up to this point, BL only get homomorphism at the cost of increasing the input size (namely n). In order to get size-preserving homomorphism, BL show that given key-pairs $(\mathbf{P}, \mathbf{y})$, $(\mathbf{P}^*, \mathbf{y}^*)$ for $\mathbf{K}_q(n)$; they can generate, with probability $\left(1 - n^{-\Omega(1)}\right)$, a matrix $\mathbf{H}_{n:n}$ whose columns are encryptions of $\mathbf{y}$ under $\mathbf{y}^*$. Most importantly, $\mathbf{H}_{n:n}$ should not give an attacker any excess power. Such a matrix will allow a single size-preserving homomorphic operation.

The idea is to think about $(\mathbf{P}^*, \mathbf{y}^*)$ as the last step of the key ladder in **BASIC**, and generate encryptions of $\mathbf{y}$ under the first step of that ladder. Naturally, the probability that all of those encryptions are simultaneously correctly decryptable is very slim, but the depth d homomorphism of **BASIC** can then be used to homomorphically apply error correction on these ciphertexts. More details follow.

BL generate an instance of **BASIC**, with public keys $\mathbf{P}_0, \ldots, \mathbf{P}_d$, secret key $\mathbf{y}_d = \mathbf{y}^*$, and re-encryption matrices $\mathbf{H}_{n_{i+1}:n_i}$. An additional independent instance of $\mathbf{K}_q(n)$ is generated, whose keys we denote by $(\mathbf{P}, \mathbf{y})$. Then, a large number of encryptions of the elements of $\mathbf{y}$ under public key $\mathbf{P}_0$ are generated.[5] While some of these ciphertexts may have encryption error, BL show that homomorphically evaluating a depth-d correction circuit ($CORR$ in their notation), one can obtain a matrix $\mathbf{H}_{n:n}$, whose columns are encryptions of $\mathbf{y}$ that are decryptable under $\mathbf{y}^*$ without error. This process succeeds with probability $\left(1 - n^{-\Omega(1)}\right)$.

The resemblance to the learner of Corollary 2.7 is apparent. In a sense, the public key of **BASIC** is ready-for-use learner.

To conclude this part, BL generate a re-encryption matrix $\mathbf{H}_{n:n}$ that takes ciphertexts under $\mathbf{y}$ and produces ciphertexts under $\mathbf{y}^*$. Since $\mathbf{H}_{n:n}$ is produced using homomorphic evaluation, its rank is at most $n_{d-1} = n^{1/(1+\alpha)}$. We will capitalize on the fact that re-encryption using $\mathbf{H}_{n:n}$ produces ciphertexts that all reside in a low-dimensional space.

Achieving Full Homomorphism – The Scheme **HOM**. The basic idea is to generate a sequence of matrices $\mathbf{H}_{n:n}$, thus creating a chaining of the respective secret keys that will allow homomorphism of any depth. However, generating

---

[5] To be absolutely precise, BL encrypt a bit decomposition of $\mathbf{y}^*$, but this is immaterial to us.

an arbitrarily large number of such re-encryption matrices will eventually cause an error somewhere down the line. Therefore, a more sophisticated solution is required. BL suggest to encrypt each message a large number of times, and generate a large number of re-encryption matrices per level. Then, since the vast majority of matrices per level are guaranteed to be correct, one can use shallow approximate majority computation to guarantee that the fraction of erroneous ciphertexts per level does not increase with homomorphic evaluation.

Decryption is performed as follows: Each ciphertext is a set of ciphertexts $c_1, \ldots, c_k$ of $\mathbf{K}_q(n)$ (all with the same secret key). The decryption process first uses the $\mathbf{K}_q(n)$ key to decrypt the individual ciphertexts and obtain $m_1, \ldots, m_k$, and then outputs the majority between the values m_i. BL show that a majority of the ciphertexts (say more than $15/16$ fraction) are indeed correct, which guarantees correct decryption.

BL can thus achieve a (leveled) fully homomorphic scheme which they denote by **HOM**, which completes their construction.

4.2   An Attack on BL Using Homomorphism

We will show how to break the BL scheme using its homomorphic properties. We use Corollary 3.3 and our proof contains similar elements to the proof of Theorem 3.4. (The specifics of BL do not allow to use Corollary 3.5 directly.)

Theorem 4.1. *There is a polynomial time CPA attack on BL.*

Proof. Clearly we cannot apply our methods to the scheme **HOM** as is, since its decryption is not learnable. We thus describe a related scheme which is "embedded" in **HOM** and show how to distinguish encryptions of 0 from encryptions of 1, which will imply a break of **HOM**.

We recall that the public key of **HOM** contains "chains" of re-encryption matrices of the form $\mathbf{H}_{n:n}$. The length of the chains is related to the homomorphic depth of **HOM**. Our sub-scheme will only require a chain of constant length ℓ which will be determined later (such sub-chain therefore must exist for any instantiation of BL that allows for more than constant depth homomorphism). Granted that all links in the chain are successfully generated (which happens with probability $\ell \cdot n^{-\Omega(1)}$), such a chain allows homomorphic evaluation of any depth-ℓ function. Let us focus on the case where the chain is indeed properly generated.

Intuitively, we would have liked to use this structure to evaluate majority on 2^ℓ input ciphertexts. However, BL is defined over a large field $\mathbb{F}$, and it is not clear how to implement majority over $\mathbb{F}$ in depth that does not depend on $q = |\mathbb{F}|$. To solve this problem, we use BL's $CORR$ function. This function is just a NAND tree of depth ℓ (extended to $\mathbb{F}$ in the obvious way: $NAND(x, y) = 1 - xy$). BL show that given 2^ℓ inputs, each of which is 0 (respectively 1) with probability $1 - \epsilon$, the output of $CORR$ will be 0 (resp. 1) with probability $1 - O(\epsilon)^{2^{\ell/2}}$.

To encrypt a message $m \in \{0, 1\}$ using our sub-scheme, we will generate 2^ℓ ciphertexts. Each ciphertext will be an independent encryption of m using the public key of **HOM** (which essentially generates $\mathbf{K}_q(n)$ ciphertexts that correspond to the first link in all chains). We then apply $CORR$ homomorphically to the generated ciphertexts. Decryption in our subscheme will be standard $\mathbf{K}_q(n)$ decryption (which is a linear function) using the secret key that corresponds to the last link in the chain.[6]

We recall that the decryption error of $\mathbf{K}_q(n)$ is $\epsilon = n^{-\Omega(1)}$. By the properties of $CORR$, we can choose $\ell = O(1)$ such that the decryption error of our subscheme is at most (say) $o(1)/n$.

In conclusion, we get a sub-scheme of **HOM** such that with probability $1 - n^{-\Omega(1)} > 0.9$ over the key generation, the decryption error is at most $o(1)/n$. Furthermore, decryption is linear. Corollary 3.3 implies that such scheme must be insecure.

4.3 A Specific Attack on BL

We noticed that the scheme **BASIC**, which is a component of **HOM**, contains by design homomorphic evaluation of majority: this is how the matrix $\mathbf{H}_{n:n}$ is generated. We thus present an attack that only uses the matrix $\mathbf{H}_{n:n}$ and allows to completely decrypt BL ciphertexts (even non binary) with probability $1 - n^{-\Omega(1)}$. We recall that an attack *completely breaks* a scheme if it can decrypt any given ciphertext with probability $1 - o(1)$.

Theorem 4.2. *There exists a polynomial time attack that completely breaks* **BASIC***, and thus also BL.*

Proof. We consider the re-encryption matrix $\mathbf{H} = \mathbf{H}_{n:n} \in \mathbb{F}_q^{n \times n}$ described in Section 4.1, which re-encrypts ciphertexts under $\mathbf{y}$ into ciphertexts under $\mathbf{y}^*$. The probability that $\mathbf{H}$ was successfully generated is at least $1 - n^{-\Omega(1)}$, in which case it holds that

$$\mathbf{y}^{*T} \cdot \mathbf{H} = \mathbf{y}^T .$$

In addition, as we explained in Section 4.1, the rank of $\mathbf{H}$ is at most $h = n^{1/(1+\alpha)}$.

Our breaker will be given $\mathbf{H}$ and the public key $\mathbf{P}$ that corresponds to $\mathbf{y}$, and will be able to decrypt any vector $\mathbf{c} = \mathsf{Enc}_{\mathbf{P}}(m)$ with high probability, namely compute $\langle \mathbf{y}, \mathbf{c} \rangle$.

Breaker Code. As explained above, the input to the breaker is $\mathbf{H}, \mathbf{P}$ and challenge $\mathbf{c} = \mathsf{Enc}_{\mathbf{P}}(m)$. The breaker will execute as follows:

1. Generate $k = h^{1+\epsilon}$ encryptions of 0, denoted $\mathbf{v}_1, \ldots, \mathbf{v}_k$, for $\epsilon = \frac{\alpha(1-\alpha)}{4}$ (any positive number smaller than $\frac{\alpha(1-\alpha)}{2}$ will do).

---

[6] The secret key of the last link is not the same as the secret key of **HOM**, since we are only considering a sub-chain of a much longer chain. However, this is not a problem: Our arguments do not require that the secret key is known to anyone in order to break the scheme.

Note that this means that with probability $1 - n^{-\Omega(1)}$, all $\mathbf{v}_i$ are decryptable encryptions of 0. Intuitively, these vectors, once projected through $\mathbf{H}$, will span all decryptable encryptions of 0.

2. For all $i = 1, \ldots, k$, compute $\mathbf{v}_i^* = \mathbf{H} \cdot \mathbf{v}_i$ (the projections of the ciphertexts above through $\mathbf{H}$). Also compute $\mathbf{o}^* = \mathbf{H} \cdot \mathbf{1}$ (the projection of the all-one vector).

3. Find a vector $\tilde{\mathbf{y}}^* \in \mathbb{F}_q^n$ such that $\langle \tilde{\mathbf{y}}^*, \mathbf{v}_i^* \rangle = 0$ for all i, and such that $\langle \tilde{\mathbf{y}}^*, \mathbf{o}^* \rangle = 1$. Such a vector necessarily exists if all $\mathbf{v}_i$'s are decryptable, since $\mathbf{y}^*$ is an example of such a vector.

4. Given a challenge ciphertext $\mathbf{c}$, compute $\mathbf{c}^* = \mathbf{H} \cdot \mathbf{c}$ and output $m = \langle \tilde{\mathbf{y}}^*, \mathbf{c}^* \rangle$ (namely, $m = \tilde{\mathbf{y}}^{*T} \cdot \mathbf{H} \cdot \mathbf{c}$).

Correctness. To analyze the correctness of the breaker, we first notice that the space of ciphertexts that decrypt to 0 under $\mathbf{y}$ is linear (this is exactly the orthogonal space to $\mathbf{y}$). We denote this space by Z. Since $\mathbf{1} \notin Z$, we can define the cosets $Z_m = Z + m \cdot \mathbf{1}$. We note that all legal encryptions of m using $\mathbf{P}$ reside in Z_m.

We let Z^* denote the space $\mathbf{H} \cdot Z$ (all vectors of the form $\mathbf{H} \cdot \mathbf{z}$ such that $\mathbf{z} \in Z$). This is a linear space with dimension at most h. Similarly, define $Z_m^* = Z^* + m \cdot \mathbf{o}^*$.

Consider the challenge ciphertext $\mathbf{c} = \mathsf{Enc_P}(m)$. We can think of $\mathbf{c}$ as an encryption of 0 with an added term $m \cdot \mathbf{1}$. We therefore denote $\mathbf{c} = \mathbf{c}_0 + m \cdot \mathbf{1}$. Again this yields a $\mathbf{c}_0^*$ such that $\mathbf{c}^* = \mathbf{c}_0^* + m \cdot \mathbf{o}^*$.

Now consider the distribution $\mathcal{Z}$ over Z, which is the distribution of decryptable encryptions of 0 (i.e. the distribution $\mathbf{c} = \mathsf{Enc_P}(0)$, conditioned on $\langle \mathbf{y}, \mathbf{c} \rangle = 0$). The distribution $\mathcal{Z}^*$ is defined by projecting $\mathcal{Z}$ through $\mathbf{H}$. With probability $(1 - n^{-\Omega(1)})$, it holds that $\mathbf{v}_1^*, \ldots, \mathbf{v}_k^*$, and $\mathbf{c}_0^*$ are uniform samples from $\mathcal{Z}^*$.

By Lemma 2.4 below, it holds that $\mathbf{c}_0^* \in \mathrm{Span}\{\mathbf{v}_1^*, \ldots, \mathbf{v}_k^*\}$, with probability $(1 - n^{-\Omega(1)})$. In such case

$$\langle \tilde{\mathbf{y}}^*, \mathbf{c}^* \rangle = \langle \tilde{\mathbf{y}}^*, \mathbf{c}_0^* \rangle + m \cdot \langle \tilde{\mathbf{y}}^*, \mathbf{o}^* \rangle = m .$$

We conclude that with probability $1 - n^{-\Omega(1)}$, our breaker correctly decrypts $\mathbf{c}$ as required.

Acknowledgements. The author wishes to thank the MIT-BU cryptography reading group for introducing the BL scheme to him, and especially to Stefano Tessaro and Shafi Goldwasser for various discussions. We further thank Andrej Bogdanov for his comments on a preprint of this manuscript, and for the discussions that followed, leading to the general argument about homomorphic schemes. We thank Ron Rothblum for pointing out the learning-theory aspect of our argument. Lastly, we thank the anonymous reviewers of TCC 2013 for their helpful comments.

References

[1] Alekhnovich, M.: More on average case vs approximation complexity. In: FOCS, pp. 298–307. IEEE Computer Society (2003)

[2] Applebaum, B., Cash, D., Peikert, C., Sahai, A.: Fast Cryptographic Primitives and Circular-Secure Encryption Based on Hard Learning Problems. In: Halevi, S. (ed.) CRYPTO 2009. LNCS, vol. 5677, pp. 595–618. Springer, Heidelberg (2009)

[3] Bogdanov, A., Lee, C.H.: Homomorphic encryption from codes. Cryptology ePrint Archive, Report 2011/622 (2011), http://eprint.iacr.org/

[4] Brakerski, Z.: Fully Homomorphic Encryption without Modulus Switching from Classical GapSVP. In: Safavi-Naini, R., Canetti, R. (eds.) CRYPTO 2012. LNCS, vol. 7417, pp. 868–886. Springer, Heidelberg (2012), http://eprint.iacr.org/2012/078

[5] Brakerski, Z., Gentry, C., Vaikuntanathan, V.: (leveled) fully homomorphic encryption without bootstrapping. In: ITCS 2012 (2012), http://eprint.iacr.org/2011/277

[6] Brakerski, Z., Vaikuntanathan, V.: Fully Homomorphic Encryption from Ring-LWE and Security for Key Dependent Messages. In: Rogaway, P. (ed.) CRYPTO 2011. LNCS, vol. 6841, pp. 505–524. Springer, Heidelberg (2011)

[7] Brakerski, Z., Vaikuntanathan, V.: Efficient fully homomorphic encryption from (standard) LWE. In: Ostrovsky [17], pp. 97–106, References are to full version http://eprint.iacr.org/2011/344

[8] Gauthier, V., Otmani, A., Tillich, J.-P.: A distinguisher-based attack of a homomorphic encryption scheme relying on reed-solomon codes. Cryptology ePrint Archive, Report 2012/168 (2012), http://eprint.iacr.org/

[9] Gentry, C.: Fully homomorphic encryption using ideal lattices. In: STOC, pp. 169–178 (2009)

[10] Gentry, C.: Toward Basing Fully Homomorphic Encryption on Worst-Case Hardness. In: Rabin, T. (ed.) CRYPTO 2010. LNCS, vol. 6223, pp. 116–137. Springer, Heidelberg (2010)

[11] Gentry, C., Halevi, S.: Implementing Gentry's Fully-Homomorphic Encryption Scheme. In: Paterson, K.G. (ed.) EUROCRYPT 2011. LNCS, vol. 6632, pp. 129–148. Springer, Heidelberg (2011)

[12] Gentry, C., Halevi, S., Smart, N.P.: Fully Homomorphic Encryption with Polylog Overhead. In: Pointcheval, D., Johansson, T. (eds.) EUROCRYPT 2012. LNCS, vol. 7237, pp. 465–482. Springer, Heidelberg (2012)

[13] Gilbert, H., Robshaw, M.J.B., Seurin, Y.: How to Encrypt with the LPN Problem. In: Aceto, L., Damgård, I., Goldberg, L.A., Halldórsson, M.M., Ingólfsdóttir, A., Walukiewicz, I. (eds.) ICALP 2008, Part II. LNCS, vol. 5126, pp. 679–690. Springer, Heidelberg (2008)

[14] Goldwasser, S., Micali, S.: Probabilistic encryption and how to play mental poker keeping secret all partial information. In: Lewis, H.R., Simons, B.B., Burkhard, W.A., Landweber, L.H. (eds.) STOC, pp. 365–377. ACM (1982)

[15] Kearns, M.J., Valiant, L.G.: Cryptographic limitations on learning boolean formulae and finite automata. J. ACM 41(1), 67–95 (1994); Preliminary version in STOC 1989

[16] Klivans, A.R., Sherstov, A.A.: Cryptographic hardness for learning intersections of halfspaces. J. Comput. Syst. Sci. 75(1), 2–12 (2009); Preliminary version in FOCS 2006

[17] Ostrovsky, R. (ed.): IEEE 52nd Annual Symposium on Foundations of Computer Science, FOCS 2011, Palm Springs, CA, USA, October 22-25. IEEE (2011)

[18] Schapire, R.E.: The strength of weak learnability. Machine Learning 5, 197–227 (1990); Preliminary version in FOCS 1989

[19] Smart, N.P., Vercauteren, F.: Fully Homomorphic Encryption with Relatively Small Key and Ciphertext Sizes. In: Nguyen, P.Q., Pointcheval, D. (eds.) PKC 2010. LNCS, vol. 6056, pp. 420–443. Springer, Heidelberg (2010)

[20] Vaikuntanathan, V.: Computing blindfolded: New developments in fully homomorphic encryption. In: Ostrovsky [17], pp. 5–16

[21] Valiant, L.G.: A theory of the learnable. Commun. ACM 27(11), 1134–1142 (1984); Preliminary version in STOC 1984

[22] van Dijk, M., Gentry, C., Halevi, S., Vaikuntanathan, V.: Fully Homomorphic Encryption over the Integers. In: Gilbert, H. (ed.) EUROCRYPT 2010. LNCS, vol. 6110, pp. 24–43. Springer, Heidelberg (2010), Full Version in http://eprint.iacr.org/2009/616.pdf

Garbling XOR Gates "For Free" in the Standard Model

Benny Applebaum[*]

School of Electrical Engineering, Tel-Aviv University
bennyap@post.tau.ac.il

Abstract. Yao's Garbled Circuit (GC) technique is a powerful cryptographic tool which allows to "encrypt" a circuit C by another circuit $\hat{C}$ in a way that hides all information except for the final output. Yao's original construction incurs a constant overhead in both computation and communication per gate of the circuit C (proportional to the complexity of symmetric encryption). Kolesnikov and Schneider (ICALP 2008) introduced an optimized variant that garbles XOR gates "for free" in a way that involves no cryptographic operations and no communication. This variant has become very popular and has lead to notable performance improvements.

The security of the free-XOR optimization was originally proven in the random oracle model. Despite some partial progress (Choi et al., TCC 2012), the question of replacing the random oracle with a standard cryptographic assumption has remained open.

We resolve this question by showing that the free-XOR approach can be realized in the standard model under the *learning parity with noise* (LPN) assumption. Our result is obtained in two steps:
- We show that the random oracle can be replaced with a symmetric encryption which remains secure under a combined form of related-key (RK) and key-dependent message (KDM) attacks; and
- We show that such a symmetric encryption can be constructed based on the LPN assumption.

As an additional contribution, we prove that the combination of RK and KDM security is non-trivial: There exists an encryption scheme which achieves both RK security and KDM security but breaks completely at the presence of combined RK-KDM attacks.

1 Introduction

Yao's *garbled circuit* (GC) construction [42] is an efficient transformation which maps any boolean circuit $C : \{0,1\}^n \to \{0,1\}^m$ together with secret randomness into a "garbled circuit" $\hat{C}$ along with n pairs of short k-bit keys (W_i^0, W_i^1) such that, for any (unknown) input x, the garbled circuit $\hat{C}$ together with the n keys $W_x = (W_1^{x_1}, \ldots, W_n^{x_n})$ reveal $C(x)$ but give no additional information about

---
[*] Supported by Alon Fellowship, ISF grant 1155/11, Israel Ministry of Science and Technology (grant 3-9094), and GIF grant 1152/2011.

x. Yao's celebrated result shows that such a transformation can be based on the existence of any pseudorandom generator [12,41], or equivalently a one-way function [20].

The GC construction was originally motivated by the problem of secure multiparty computation [41,19]. Along the years, the GC construction has found a diverse range of other applications to problems such as computing on encrypted data, parallel cryptography, verifiable computation, software protection, functional encryption, and key-dependent message security (see [5] for references). Despite its theoretical importance, GC was typically considered to be impractical due to a large computational and communication overhead which is proportional to the circuit size. This belief was recently challenged by a fruitful line of works that optimizes the concrete efficiency of GC-based protocols up to a level that suits large-scale practical applications [36,33,30,29,38,37,21,22,40,23,28].

Among other things, all current implementations of GCs (e.g., [38,21,32,40,22]) employ the so-called *free-XOR* optimization of Kolesnikov and Schneider [27]. While in Yao's original construction every gate of the circuit C has a computational cost of few cryptographic operations (e.g., three or four applications of a symmetric primitive) and a communication cost of few ciphertexts, Kolesnikov and Schneider showed how to completely eliminate the communication and computational overhead of XOR-gates. Although this leads "only" to an efficiency improvement by a constant factor, the effect on the practical performance turns to be significant, especially for large or medium size circuits as demonstrated in [27,26,38].

As in many cases, this efficiency gain has a cost in terms of the underlying cryptographic assumptions. Unlike Yao's GC which can be based on the existence of standard symmetric-key cryptography, the free-XOR optimization relies on a hash function H which is modeled as a random oracle [9]. Due to the known limitations of the random oracle model [15], it is natural to ask:

Is it possible to realize the free-XOR optimization in the standard model?

This question was raised in the original work of Kolesnikov and Schneider [27] and was further studied in [3,16]. In [27] it was conjectured that the full power of the random oracle is not really needed, and that the function H can be instantiated with a *correlation-robust hash function* [24], a strong (yet seemingly realizable) version of a hash function which remains pseudorandom even when it is applied to linearly related inputs. Choi et al. [16] showed that the picture is actually more complex: correlation robustness alone does not suffice for security (as demonstrated by an explicit counter-example in the random-oracle model). Instead, one has to employ a stronger form of hash function which, in addition to being correlation-robust, also satisfies some form of circular security [14,10]. While the existence of circular correlation-robust hash functions (a new primitive introduced by Choi et al. [16]) seems to be a reasonable assumption (significantly weaker than the existence of a random oracle), it is still unknown how to realize it based on a standard cryptographic assumption. This leaves open the problem of implementing the free-XOR approach in the standard model.

1.1 Our Contribution

We resolve the above feasibility question by showing that the free-XOR approach can be realized in the standard model under the learning parity with noise (LPN) assumption [18,11]. This assumption, which can also be formulated as the intractability of decoding a random linear code, is widely studied by the coding and learning communities and was extensively employed in cryptographic constructions during the last two decades.

Specifically, we make the following contributions:

1. We introduce a new combined form of Related Key (RK) and Key Dependent Message (KDM) attacks. Roughly speaking, in such an attack the adversary is allowed to see ciphertexts of the form $\mathsf{Enc}_{\phi(K)}(\psi(K))$ where K is the secret key and the functions ϕ and ψ are chosen by the adversary from some predefined function families. This notion of security, referred to as *RK-KDM security*, generalizes the previous definitions of semantic security under related key attacks [3] and key-dependent message attacks [14,10]. In fact, as shown in Section 5, the RK-KDM security is strictly stronger than both RK-security and KDM-security.
2. We prove that the free-XOR construction is secure when instantiated with a semantically-secure symmetric encryption scheme whose security is preserved under linear RK-KDM attacks. (Essentially, $\phi(K) = K \oplus \Delta_1$ and $\psi(K) = K \oplus \Delta_2$ for any fixed shift vectors Δ_1 and Δ_2.)
3. We show that the LPN-based symmetric encryption of [17] and its generalization [2] satisfies RK-KDM security with respect to linear functions. In fact, our proof provides a general template for proving RK-KDM security based on pseudorandomness and joint key/message homomorphism. This is similar to previous results along these lines [13,2,6,3].

Altogether our proofs turn to be quite simple (which we consider as a virtue), short and modular. This is due to the following choices:

Encryption vs. Hashing. The key point in which we deviate from [27,16] is the use of (randomized) *symmetric encryption*, as opposed to deterministic *hash function* (or some other pseudorandom primitive). Indeed, the GC construction essentially employs the hash function only as a "computational one-time pad", namely, as a mean to achieve secrecy. Therefore, in terms of functionality it seems best (i.e., more general) to abstract the underlying primitive as an encryption scheme. While this is true in general for the standard GC (cf. [30,4] and the recent discussion in [7]), this distinction becomes even more important in the context of the free-XOR variant. In this case, the underlying primitive should satisfy stronger notions of security (RKA and KDM), and this turns to be much easier for randomized encryption than for pseudorandom objects such as hash functions. (See also [3].) As a secondary gain, the new security definition that arises for symmetric encryption (RKA-KDM semantic security) is natural and compatible with existing well-studied notions. In contrast, the analog definition of RKA-KDM security for hash functions (*circular correlation-robustness*) appears less natural as there is no obvious interpretation for the concepts of *message* and *key*.

GC as Randomized Encoding. It is important to distinguish between the garbled circuit transformation (i.e., the mapping from C to $\hat{C}$) and the secure function evaluation protocol which is based on it. The distinction between the two, which is sometimes blurred, can be formulated via the notion of *randomized encoding of functions* [25] as done in [4]. Our proofs follow this abstraction, and show that the free-XOR technique yields computationally private randomized encoding. At this point one can invoke, for example, the general theorem of [4] to derive a secure MPC protocol. Similarly, all other applications (cf. [1]) of randomized encoding can be obtained directly by invoking the reduction from RE to the desired task. This is the first modular treatment of the free XOR variant.

1.2   Discussion

The main goal of this work is to provide a solid theoretical justification for the free-XOR heuristic. This is part of an ongoing effort of the theory community to explain the security of "real world" protocols. Several such examples arise when trying to import random-oracle based protocols to the standard model. In this context, [15] suggested a two-step methodology: (1) "identify useful special-purpose properties of the random oracle" and (2) show that these properties "can be also provided by a fully specified function (or function ensemble)". In the context of the free-XOR optimization, the first step was essentially taken by [16] who identified the extra need of "circular security", while the current paper completes the second step which involves, in addition, some fine-tuning of step 1.

It should be emphasized that we do not suggest to replace the hash function with an LPN-based scheme in practical implementations (though we do not rule out such a possibility either). Still, we believe that the results of this work are useful even if one decides, due to efficiency considerations, to use a heuristic implementation. Specifically, viewing the primitive as an RKA-KDM secure encryption scheme allows to rely on other heuristic solutions such as block ciphers, for which RKA and KDM security are well studied.

Other Related Works. The notions of key-dependent message security (aka circular security) and related-key attacks were introduced by [14,10] and [8]. Both notions were extensively studied (separately) during the last decade. Most relevant to this paper is our joint work with Harnik and Ishai [3]. This work introduces the notion of semantic security under related-key attacks, describes several constructions, and shows that protocols employing correlation-robust hash functions and their relatives (e.g., [35,24]), can be securely instantiated with RKA-secure encryption schemes. In addition, [3] suggested to apply a similar modification to the free-XOR variant, which was believed to be secure when instantiated with correlation-robust hash functions [27]. As mentioned, the latter claim was found to be inaccurate, and therefore the results of [3] cannot be used in the context of the free-XOR approach. (The other applications mentioned in [3] remain valid.)

Organization. Following some preliminaries (Section 2), in Section 3 we define semantic security under RK-KDM attacks and describe an LPN-based implementation. Section 4 is devoted to the garbled circuit construction, including definitions (in terms of randomized encoding), a description of Yao's original construction and the free-XOR variant, and a proof of security that reduces the privacy of the free-XOR GC to the RK-KDM security of the underlying encryption. In Section 5, we describe an encryption scheme which is KDM secure and RKA secure but not RK-KDM secure, separating the latter notion from the formers. Finally, we end with a short conclusion in Section 6.

2   Preliminaries

We let $\circ$ denote string concatenation. Strings are often treated as vectors or matrices over the binary field $\mathbb{F}_2$, accordingly string *addition* is interpreted simply as bit-wise exclusive-or. When adding together two matrices $A_{n \times k}$ and $B_{N \times k}$ where $n < N$ we assume that the last $N - n$ missing rows of A are padded with zeroes. The same convention holds with respect to vectors (i.e., when $k = 1$).

2.1   Randomized Functions

We extensively use the abstraction of randomized functions which can be seen as a special case of Maurer's Random Systems [34]. A *randomized function* is a two argument function $f : X \times R \to Y$ whose first input x is referred to as the *deterministic input* and the second input is referred to as the *random input*. For every deterministic input x, we think of $f(x)$ as the random variable induced by sampling $r \xleftarrow{R} R$ and computing $f(x; r) \in Y$. When a (randomized) algorithm A gets an oracle access to a randomized function f, we assume that A has control only on the deterministic input; namely, if A queries f with x, it gets as a result a fresh sample from $f(x)$. Note that A^f itself defines a randomized function. We say that $\{f_s\}_{s \in \{0,1\}^*}$ is a *collection of randomized functions* if f_s is a randomized function for every key s. By default, all the collections are efficiently computable in the sense that $f_s(x)$ can be sampled in time $\text{poly}(|s| + |x|)$.

Indistinguishability. A pair of randomized functions f, g is *equivalent* $f \equiv g$ if for every input x the random variables $f(x)$ and $g(x)$ are identically distributed. A pair $f = \{f_s\}$ and $g = \{g_s\}$ of collections of randomized functions is *computationally indistinguishable*, denoted by $f \stackrel{c}{\equiv} g$, if for every efficient adversary $\mathcal{A}$ it holds that

$$\left| \Pr_{s \xleftarrow{R} \{0,1\}^k} [\mathcal{A}^{f_s}(1^k) = 1] - \Pr_{s \xleftarrow{R} \{0,1\}^k} [\mathcal{A}^{g_s}(1^k) = 1] \right| < \text{neg}(k).$$

We extend the above definition to the case of collections $f = \{f_{1^\kappa}\}$ and $g = \{g_{1^\kappa}\}$ which contain a single randomized function for every input length κ. In this case, we augment f (resp., g) by letting $f_s = f_{1^{|s|}}$ (resp., $g_s = g_{1^{|s|}}$) and use the previous definition.[1]

Let $\{f_s\}, \{g_s\}$ and $\{h_s\}$ be collections of randomized functions. We will need the following standard facts (cf. [34]).

Fact 1. *If for every* $k \in \mathbb{N}$, $\Pr_{s \xleftarrow{R} \{0,1\}^k}[f_s \equiv g_s] > 1 - \varepsilon(k)$ *for some negligible function* ε, *then* $\{f_s\} \overset{c}{\equiv} \{g_s\}$.

Fact 2. *If* $\{f_s\} \overset{c}{\equiv} \{g_s\}$ *and* A *is an efficient function then* $\{A^{f_s}\}_s \overset{c}{\equiv} \{A^{g_s}\}_s$.

Fact 3. *If* $\{f_s\} \overset{c}{\equiv} \{g_s\}$ *and* $\{g_s\} \overset{c}{\equiv} \{h_s\}$ *then* $\{f_s\} \overset{c}{\equiv} \{h_s\}$.

3   RK-KDM Security

A pair of efficient probabilistic algorithms (Enc, Dec) is a *symmetric encryption scheme* over the message-space $\{0,1\}^*$ and key-space $\{0,1\}^k$ (where k serves as the security parameter) if for every message $M \in \{0,1\}^*$

$$\Pr_{s \xleftarrow{R} \{0,1\}^k} [\mathsf{Dec}_s(\mathsf{Enc}_s(M)) = M] = 1.$$

We also assume (WLOG) length-regularity, i.e., that messages of equal length M, M' are always encrypted by ciphertexts of equal length $|\mathsf{Enc}_s(M)| = |\mathsf{Enc}_s(M')|$.

Our security definitions are parameterized by a family of key-derivation and key-dependent-message functions (which are also indexed by the security parameter k)

$$\Phi_{\mathsf{RKA}} = \left\{ \phi : \{0,1\}^k \to \{0,1\}^k \right\}, \qquad \Psi_{\mathsf{KDM}} = \left\{ \psi : \{0,1\}^k \to \{0,1\}^* \right\}.$$

These families determine the legal relations between the related-keys, and the key-related messages. RK-KDM Security is defined via the following pair of real/fake oracles Real_s and Fake_s which are indexed by a key $s \in \{0,1\}^k$. For a query $(\phi \in \Phi_{\mathsf{RKA}}, \psi \in \Psi_{\mathsf{KDM}})$, the oracle Real_s returns a sample from the distribution $\mathsf{Enc}_{\phi(s)}(\psi(s))$, whereas, the oracle Fake_s returns a sample from the distribution $\mathsf{Enc}_{\phi(s)}(0^{|\psi(s)|})$.

Definition 1 (RK-KDM-secure encryption). *A symmetric encryption scheme* (Enc, Dec) *is* semantically-secure under Related-Key and Key-Dependent Message Attacks *(in short, RK-KDM-secure) with respect to* $\Phi_{\mathsf{RKA}}, \Psi_{\mathsf{KDM}}$ *if* $\mathsf{Real}_s \overset{c}{\equiv} \mathsf{Fake}_s$ *where* $s \xleftarrow{R} \{0,1\}^k$.

---

[1] More generally, one can define computational indistinguishability with respect to a pair of key sampling algorithm $\mathsf{KeyGen}_f(1^\kappa)$ and $\mathsf{KeyGen}_g(1^\kappa)$ which induce, for every security parameter κ, a probability distribution over the ensembles f and g. However, for this paper the simpler definition suffices.

Remarks:

- **Relation to previous definitions.** We note that the above definition generalizes semantic security under related-key attacks [3] and semantic security under key-dependent message attacks [10]. Indeed, the former notion is obtained by restricting Ψ_{KDM} to contain only constant functions, and the latter is obtained by letting Φ_{RKA} contain only the identity function. If both restrictions are applied simultaneously, the definition becomes identical to standard semantic security under Chosen-Plaintext Attacks. On the other hand, as we show in Section 5, a scheme may satisfy both RKA security and KDM security without achieving the combined form of RKA-KDM security.
- **Non-Adaptivity.** Definition 1 allows the adversary to choose its queries in a fully adaptive way. One may define a seemingly weaker non-adaptive variant in which the adversary has to specify all its queries at the beginning of the game. We note that this weaker variant suffices for the free-XOR application.
- **LIN RK-KDM security.** We will be interested in linear functions over $\mathbb{F}_2$. Namely, both Φ_{RKA} and Ψ_{KDM} contain functions of the form $s \mapsto s + \Delta$ for every $\Delta \in \mathbb{F}_2^k$. To be compatible with standard semantic security, we require that Ψ_{KDM} also contains all fixed functions. Using a compact notation, we can describe each function in Ψ_{KDM} by a message M and a bit σ and let $g_{M,\sigma} : s \mapsto (M + (\sigma \cdot s))$. If the length of M is larger than k, we assume that $(\sigma \cdot s)$ is padded with zeroes at the end. Hence, the adversary may ask for an encryption of the shifted key concatenated with some fixed message. We refer to this notion as *LIN RK-KDM* security.[2]

3.1   LPN-Based Construction

The *learning parity with noise* problem is parameterized by positive integers k, t, and noise parameter $0 < \varepsilon < \frac{1}{2}$. The input to the problem is a random matrix $A \xleftarrow{R} \mathbb{F}_2^{t \times k}$ and a vector $y = As + e \in \mathbb{F}_2^t$ where $s \xleftarrow{R} \mathbb{F}_2^k$ and $e \xleftarrow{R} \mathsf{Ber}_\varepsilon^t$ is an "error" vector of t independent Bernoulli random variable which take the value 1 with probability ε. The goal is to recover the secret vector s. This can be considered to be a "decoding game" where A generates a random linear code and the goal is to recover a random information word s given a noisy codeword y. For polynomially bounded integer function $t = t(k)$ and a parameter ε, we say that the problem $\mathsf{LPN}_{t,\varepsilon}$ is *hard*, if there is no efficient adversary that can solve it with more than negligible success probability. We say that LPN_ε is *hard* if $\mathsf{LPN}_{t,\varepsilon}$ is hard for every polynomial $t(\cdot)$. We describe the symmetric encryption scheme of [2] which is a variant of the scheme of [17].

---

[2] A seemingly weaker definition of LIN RK-KDM security restricts the KDM family to functions $g_{M,\sigma} : s \mapsto (M + (\sigma \cdot s))$. If M is longer than k where M and s are of the same length. We note that a scheme that satisfies this notion can be trivially converted into a scheme that satisfies our definition (which supports M longer than s). This can be done by partitioning the long message M into t blocks $M_1, \ldots, M_t$ of length k each, and concatenating the encryptions of these two blocks. A query of the form $(f \in \Phi_{\mathsf{RKA}}, g_{M,\sigma})$ can then be emulated by a linear query $(f \in \Phi_{\mathsf{RKA}}, g_{M_1,1})$ and $t - 1$ fixed-message query $(f \in \Phi_{\mathsf{RKA}}, g_{M_i,0})$.

Parameters. Let $\ell = \ell(k)$ be a message-length parameter which is set to be an arbitrary polynomial in the security parameter k. (Shorter messages are padded with zeroes.) Let $\varepsilon < \frac{1}{2}$ and $0 < \delta < \frac{1}{2}$ be constants. We will use a family of linear binary error-correcting codes with information words of length $\ell(k)$ and block length $t = t(n)$, that has an efficient decoding algorithm D that can correct up to $(\varepsilon + \delta) \cdot t$ errors. We let $G = G_\ell$ be the $t \times \ell$ binary generator matrix of this family and we assume that it can be efficiently constructed (given 1^k).

Construction 4 (LPN-construction). *Let $N = N(k)$ be an arbitrary polynomial (which controls the tradeoff between the key-length and the time complexity of the scheme). The private key of the scheme is a matrix S which is chosen uniformly at random from $\mathbb{F}_2^{k \times N}$.*

- Encryption: *To encrypt a message $M \in \mathbb{F}_2^{\ell \times N}$, choose a random $A \xleftarrow{R} \mathbb{F}_2^{t \times k}$ and a random noise matrix $E \xleftarrow{R} \mathsf{Ber}_\varepsilon^{t \times N}$. Output the ciphertext*

$$(A, A \cdot S + E + G \cdot M).$$

- Decryption: *Given a ciphertext (A, Z) apply the decoding algorithm D to each of the columns of the matrix $Z - AS$ and output the result.*

Observe that the decryption algorithm errs only when there exists a column in E whose Hamming weight is larger than $(\varepsilon + \delta)m$, which, by Chernoff Bound, happens with negligible probability. (This error can be eliminated by rejecting noise vectors whose relative Hamming weight exceeds $(\varepsilon+\delta)$.) The scheme is also highly efficient. Encryption requires only cheap matrix operations and decryption requires in addition to decode the code G. It is shown in [2] that for proper choice of parameters both encryption and decryption can be done in quasilinear time in the message length (for sufficiently long message).

Construction 4 was proven to be semantically secure based on the intractability of the LPN_ε problem [2]. Security against KDM and RKA attacks with respect to linear functions was further proven in [2] and [3]. We now generalize these results and show that the scheme is LIN RK-KDM secure.

Theorem 5. *Assuming that LPN_ε is hard, the above construction is LIN RK-KDM secure.*

3.2   Proof of Theorem 5

Through this section we keep the convention that $S \in \mathbb{F}_2^{k \times N}$ is a key, $\Delta \in \mathbb{F}_2^{k \times N}$ is a key-shift vector, $M \in \mathbb{F}_2^{\ell \times N}$ is a message, $b \in \{0,1\}$ is a bit, and the pair $(A, Z) \in \mathbb{F}_2^{t \times k} \times \mathbb{F}_2^{t \times N}$ is a potential ciphertext. In addition, we let Enc denote the LPN encryption defined in Construction 4.

Recall that our goal is to prove that for a random key $S \xleftarrow{R} \mathbb{F}_2^{k \times N}$ the randomized functions

$$\mathsf{Real}_S : (\Delta, M, b) \mapsto \mathsf{Enc}_{S+\Delta}(M + bS)$$

$$\mathsf{Fake}_S : (\Delta, M, b) \mapsto \mathsf{Enc}_{S+\Delta}(0^{\ell \times N}),$$

are indistinguishable. This will be proven via a sequence of hybrids.

Let $\mathcal{R}_S$ be a randomized function which ignores the key S and the given input, and outputs a fresh uniformly chosen matrices $A \xleftarrow{R} \mathbb{F}_2^{t \times k}$ and $Z \xleftarrow{R} \mathbb{F}_2^{t \times N}$. (If $\mathcal{R}_S$ is applied to the same input more than once it responds with independent answers.)

The following lemma (which is implicit in [2]) shows that the LPN encryption scheme is not only semantically secure but also pseudorandom in the following sense:

Lemma 1. *Assuming that* LPN_ε *is hard,* $\{\mathsf{Enc}_S\} \overset{c}{\equiv} \{\mathcal{R}_S\}$, *where* $S \xleftarrow{R} \mathbb{F}_2^{k \times N}$.

We will need the following key observation:

Lemma 2. *There exists an efficient oracle machine* $F^{(\cdot)} : (\Delta, M, b) \mapsto (A, Z)$ *such that*

$$\mathsf{Real}_S \equiv F^{\mathsf{Enc}_S} \quad and \quad F^{\mathcal{R}_S} \equiv \mathcal{R}_S,$$

for every $S \in \mathbb{F}_2^{k \times N}$.

Proof. We define F as follows: Given a query (Δ, M, b) the machine F calls the oracle with input M, gets back the answer (A', Z'), and outputs the pair $A = A' + GH$ and $Z = Z' + A\Delta$ where G is the generating matrix used in Construction 4 and $H \in \mathbb{F}_2^{\ell \times k}$ is the matrix $\left(\begin{smallmatrix} b \cdot I_{k \times k} \\ 0^{\ell - k \times k} \end{smallmatrix} \right)$.

Fix a key S and a query (Δ, M, b), we will show that $F^{\mathsf{Enc}_S}(\Delta, M, b)$ is distributed identically to $\mathsf{Real}_S(\Delta, M, b)$. Let (A', Z') be a fresh sample from $\mathsf{Enc}_S(M)$. Clearly, $A = A' + GH$ is uniform in $\mathbb{F}_2^{t \times k}$ since A' is uniform. In addition, since $Z' = A' \cdot S + E + G \cdot M$ where $E \xleftarrow{R} \mathsf{Ber}_\varepsilon^{t \times N}$, and since $A' = A + GH$ we can write Z as

$$(A + GH) \cdot S + E + G \cdot M + A\Delta = A \cdot (S + \Delta) + E + G \cdot (M + HS)$$
$$= A \cdot (S + \Delta) + E + G \cdot (M + bS),$$

where the first equality is due to linearity, and the second equality follows from the definition of H. It follows that (A, Z) is a fresh sample from $\mathsf{Enc}_{S+\Delta}(M+bS)$.

To prove that $F^{\mathcal{R}_S} \equiv \mathcal{R}_S$, it suffices to show that for any fixed query (Δ, M, b) the transformation from (A', Z') to (A, Z) is an affine invertible mapping. This follows immediately from the definition of F. $\qquad\square$

We conclude that for $S \xleftarrow{R} \mathbb{F}_2^{k \times N}$,

$$\mathsf{Real}_S \equiv F^{\mathsf{Enc}_S} \overset{c}{\equiv} F^{\mathcal{R}_S} \equiv \mathcal{R}_S. \tag{1}$$

Indeed, the first and third transitions are due to Lemma 2, and the second transition is due to Lemma 1 and Fact 2.

To complete the argument we need two additional definitions. First we define an oracle machine which given an oracle $\mathcal{O}$ and an input (Δ, M, b) outputs a sample from $F^{\mathcal{O}}(\Delta, 0^{\ell \times N}, 0)$; namely, it replaces M, b with zeroes and proceeds as $F^{\mathcal{O}}$. By abuse of notation, we refer to this oracle as $F(\cdot, 0^{\ell \times N}, 0)$. Similarly, we let $\mathsf{Real}_S(\cdot, 0^{\ell \times N}, 0)$ denote the randomized function which maps (Δ, M, b)

to $\mathsf{Real}_S(\Delta, 0^{\ell \times N}, 0)$. Note that the latter is just an equivalent formulation of Fake_S. Moreover, we can write:

$$\mathcal{R}_S \equiv F(\cdot, 0^{\ell \times N}, 0)^{\mathcal{R}_S} \overset{c}{\equiv} F(\cdot, 0^{\ell \times N}, 0)^{\mathsf{Enc}_S(0^{\ell \times N})}$$

$$\equiv \mathsf{Real}_S(\cdot, 0^{\ell \times N}, 0) \equiv \mathsf{Fake}_S, \tag{2}$$

where the first and third transitions are due to Lemma 2, and the second transition is due to Lemma 1 and Fact 2. By combining Eq. 1 and Eq. 2 with Fact 3 we get that $\mathsf{Real}_S \overset{c}{\equiv} \mathsf{Fake}_S$, and Theorem 5 follows.   □

Remark 1 (Abstraction). The proof of Theorem 5 provides a general template for proving RKA-KDM security. Specifically, the properties needed are pseudorandomness (in the sense of Lemma 1) and key/message homomorphism (in the sense of Lemma 2). Indeed, observe that, apart from the proofs of Lemmas 1 and 2, the overall proof can be written in a fully generic form with no specific references to the LPN construction.

4   Yao's Garbled Circuit

4.1   Definition

Let $f = \{f_n\}_{n \in \mathbb{N}}$ be a polynomial-time computable function. In an abstract level, Yao's garbled circuit technique [42] constructs a randomized function $\hat{f} = \{\hat{f}_n\}_{n \in \mathbb{N}}$ which "encodes" f in the sense that for every x the distribution $\hat{f}(x)$ reveals the value of $f(x)$ but no other additional information. We formalize this via the notion of *computationally private randomized encoding* from [4], while adopting the original definition from a non-uniform adversarial setting to the uniform setting (i.e., adversaries are modeled by probabilistic polynomial-time Turing machines).

Definition 2 (Computational randomized encoding). *Let $f = \{f_n : \{0,1\}^n \to \{0,1\}^{\ell(n)}\}_{n \in \mathbb{N}}$ be an efficiently computable function and let $\hat{f} = \{\hat{f}_n : \{0,1\}^n \times \{0,1\}^{m(n)} \to \{0,1\}^{s(n)}\}_{n \in \mathbb{N}}$ be an efficiently computable randomized function. We say that $\hat{f}$ is a* computational randomized encoding *of f (or* encoding *for short), if there exist an efficient recovery algorithm* Rec *and an efficient probabilistic simulator algorithm* Sim *that satisfy the following:*

- **Perfect correctness.** *For any n and any input $x \in \{0,1\}^n$,*

$$\Pr[\mathsf{Rec}(1^n, \hat{f}_n(x)) \neq f_n(x)] = 0.$$

- **Computational privacy.** *The randomized function $\hat{f}_n(\cdot)$ is computationally indistinguishable from the randomized function* $\mathsf{Sim}(1^n, f_n(\cdot))$.

Remark 2. The above definition uses n both as an input length parameter and as a cryptographic "security parameter" quantifying computational privacy. When describing our construction, it will be convenient to use a separate parameter

k for the latter, where computational privacy will be guaranteed as long as $k \geq n^{\epsilon}$ for some constant $\epsilon > 0$. Furthermore, while it is convenient to define randomized encoding for a single function f, Yao's construction (as well as the free-XOR variant) actually provides a *compiler* that given a circuit C outputs the encoding $\hat{f}$, the recovery algorithm Rec and the simulator Sim, represented as circuits. (See [5] for formal definition.) In this sense the encoding is fully constructive.

4.2   Yao's Construction and the Free XOR Variant

Let $f = \{f_n : \{0,1\}^n \to \{0,1\}^{\ell(n)}\}_{n \in \mathbb{N}}$ be a polynomial-time computable function computed by the uniform circuit family $\{C_n\}_{n \in \mathbb{N}}$. In the following we describe Yao's construction and its free-XOR variant. Our notation and terminology borrow from previous presentations of Yao's construction in [39,36,31,4].

Double-keyed Encryption. Let $k = k(n)$ be a security parameter (by default, $k = n^{\varepsilon}$ for some constant $\varepsilon > 0$). We will employ a symmetric encryption scheme (E^2, D^2) which is keyed by a *pair* of k-bit keys K_1, K_2. Intuitively, this corresponds to a double-locked chest in the sense that decryption is possible only if one knows both keys. There are several ways to implement such an encryption scheme based on standard single-key symmetric encryption (Enc, Dec) and, for simplicity, we choose to use

$$E^2_{K_1,K_2}(M) := (\mathsf{Enc}_{K_1}(R), \mathsf{Enc}_{K_2}(R + M)),$$
$$D^2_{K_1,K_2}(C_1, C_2) := \mathsf{Dec}_{K_1}(C_1) + \mathsf{Dec}_{K_2}(C_2) \tag{3}$$

where R is a random string of length $|M|$. Other choices are also applicable under the LPN assumption.

The Original Construction. For each wire i of the circuit C_n we assign a pair of keys: a 0-key $W_i^0 \in \{0,1\}^k$ that represents the value 0 and a 1-key $W_i^1 \in \{0,1\}^k$ that represents the value 1. For each of these pairs we randomly "color" one key black and the other key white. This is done by choosing $r_i \xleftarrow{R} \{0,1\}$ and by letting $r_i + b$ be the color of W_i^b. Fix some input x for f_n, and let $b_i = b_i(x)$ be the value of the i-th wire induced by x. We refer to the key $W_i^{b_i}$ as the *active* key of the i-th wire.

The idea is to let the encoding $\hat{f}_n(x; (W, r))$ reveal only the value of the active keys $W_i^{b_i}$ and their colors c_i. This is done by traversing the circuit from inputs to outputs: first the encoding reveals the active keys of the inputs; in addition, for each gate, the encoding provides a mechanism that translates the active keys of the input wires into the active keys of the output wires. Specifically, for each Binary gate $g(\cdot, \cdot)$ (e.g., AND) the encoding outputs an encryption tables (or "gate labels") in which the keys of the outgoing wire W_ℓ^0, W_ℓ^1 are encrypted under the keys of the incoming wires i, j. Hence, one can propagate the values of $W_i^{b_i}$ from the inputs to the outputs. It is crucial to observe that the values of the active keys $W_i^{b_i}$ and their colors c_i reveal nothing on their semantics b_i. Only for the output wires, we reveal the coloring r_i, which makes it possible to recover the value of the i-th output wire b_i.

Free XOR-gates. The "free-XOR" optimization modifies the above construction by making sure that the key W_ℓ^0 and coloring r_ℓ of a wire which outgoes a XOR gate is just the sum of the keys and coloring of the incoming wires i and j, namely,

$$W_\ell^0 = W_i^0 + W_j^0, \qquad\qquad r_\ell = r_i + r_j.$$

In addition, all key pairs W_ℓ^0, W_ℓ^1 have a fixed global (secret) difference $s = W_\ell^0 + W_\ell^1$. As a result, for every pair of values $(\alpha, \beta) \in \{0,1\}^2$ for the input wires of a XOR gate, we have that

$$W_\ell^{\alpha+\beta} = W_i^\alpha + W_j^\beta.$$

Hence, one can derive the colored active key $(W_\ell^{b_\ell(x)}, r_\ell + b_\ell(x))$ of the output wire by XOR-ing the colored active keys $(W_i^{b_i(x)}, r_i + b_i(x))$, $(W_j^{b_j(x)}, r_j + b_j(x))$ of the input wires, and so gate labels are not needed. XOR gates have, therefore, no effect on the communication complexity of the encoding, and only a minor effect on the computational complexity. A formal description of the encoding is given in Figure 1.

Our main result shows that, assuming LIN RK-KDM security, the free XOR variant gives rise to a valid computational encoding:

Theorem 6 (Main). *If the underlying symmetric encryption scheme* (Enc, Dec) *is LIN RK-KDM secure, then the randomized function $\hat{f}$, as defined in Figure 1, is a randomized encoding of the function f.*

The proof of the theorem is deferred to Section 4.3 (correctness) and 4.4 (privacy).

4.3   Correctness

The following lemma shows that the encoding is correct.

Lemma 3 (Correctness). *There exists an efficient recovery algorithm* Rec *such that for every $x \in \{0,1\}^n$ it holds that*

$$\Pr[\mathsf{Rec}(1^n, \hat{f}_n(x; (r, W))) \neq f_n(x)] = 0.$$

Proof. Let $\alpha = \hat{f}_n(x; (r, W))$ for some $x \in \{0,1\}^n$ and $(r, W) \in \{0,1\}^{\mu(n)}$. It suffices to show that, given α, it is possible to recover the active key $W_i^{b_i}$ of every wire i together with its color $c_i = (b_i(x) + r_i)$. Indeed, once these values are known we can easily recover all the outputs of $f_n(x)$: For every output wire j, we recover b_j by XOR-ing c_j with the mask r_j which is given explicitly as part of α.

The Encoding $\hat{f}_n$

Input: $x \in \{0,1\}^n$.

Randomness: Choose a random global shift vector $s \xleftarrow{R} \{0,1\}^k$.
For a wire ℓ that is not an output of a XOR gate let

$$r_\ell \xleftarrow{R} \{0,1\}, \qquad W_\ell^0 \xleftarrow{R} \{0,1\}^k, \qquad W_\ell^1 := W_\ell^0 + s.$$

For a wire ℓ that is an output of a XOR gate with inputs i, j let

$$r_\ell := r_i + r_j, \qquad W_\ell^0 := W_i^0 + W_j^0, \qquad W_\ell^1 := W_i^0 + s.$$

Outputs: The encoding consists of the following outputs:

1. For an input wire i, labeled by a literal χ (either some variable x_u or its negation) output $W_i^{\chi(x)} \circ (\chi(x) + r_i)$. If i is an output wire i, output the mask of this wire r_i.

2. For a non-XOR gate t that computes some binary function $g : \{0,1\}^2 \to \{0,1\}$ with input wires i, j and output wire[a] y. We associate with this gate 4 ordered outputs ("gate labels"). For every $(a_i, a_j) \in \{0,1\}^2$ we output:

$$Q_t^{a_i, a_j} := E_{W_i^{a_i+r_i}, W_j^{a_j+r_j}}^2 \left(W_y^{g(a_i+r_i, a_j+r_j)} \circ (g(a_i + r_i, a_j + r_j) + r_y) \right), \tag{4}$$

where $\circ$ denotes concatenation, and E^2 is a double-encryption algorithm whose randomness is omitted for simplicity.

---

[a] If the fan-out is larger than 1, all outgoing wires are treated as a single wire, i.e., with the same key and the same color.

Fig. 1. The encoding $\hat{f}_n(x; (W, r, s))$ of the function $f_n(x)$. We assume that wires and gates of the circuit that computes f_n are numbered according to some topological order. The double-encryption algorithm $E_{K_1, K_2}^2(M)$ is defined based on a standard encryption $(\mathsf{Enc}, \mathsf{Dec})$ as in Eq. 3.

The active keys and their colors are computed by scanning the circuit from bottom to top as follows. For an input wire i the desired value, $W_i^{b_i} \circ c_i$, is given as part of α. Next, consider a wire y that goes out of a gate t, and assume that we have already computed the desired values of the input wires i and j of this gate. If t is a XOR gate then we let

$$W_y^{b_y} = W_y^{b_i + b_j} = W_i^{b_i} + W_i^{b_j}, \text{ and } c_y = (b_i + b_j) + r_y = (b_i + b_j) + (r_i + r_j) = c_i + c_j.$$

It t is not a XOR gate then we use the colors c_i, c_j of the active keys of the input wires to select the *active* label $Q_t^{c_i, c_j}$ of the gate t (and ignore the other 3 *inactive* labels of this gate). Consider this label as in Equation (4); recall that this cipher was "double-encrypted" under the key $W_i^{c_i - r_i} = W_i^{b_i}$ and the key $W_j^{c_j - r_j} = W_j^{b_j}$. Since we have already computed the values $c_i, c_j, W_i^{b_i}$ and $W_j^{b_j}$, we can decrypt the label $Q_t^{c_i, c_j}$ (by applying the decryption algorithm D^2) and recover the value

$$W_y^{g(b_i, b_j)} \circ (g(b_i, b_j) + r_y) = W_y^{b_y} \circ (c_y),$$

where g is the function that gate t, which satisfies, by definition, the equality $b_y = g(b_i, b_j)$.   □

4.4 Privacy

Computational privacy is slightly more subtle. The free-XOR optimization correlates the key pairs via the global shift s. This introduces two form of dependencies: (1) The four ciphertexts of every gate are encrypted under *related keys*; and (2) The keys (of the incoming wires) which are used to encrypt the gate-labels are correlated with the content of the labels (i.e., the keys of the outgoing wires). We show that if the underlying encryption (Enc, Dec) is RKA and KDM secure with respect to linear functions, then the encoding is indeed private.

Lemma 4 (Privacy). *There exists an efficient simulator* Sim *such that*

$$\hat{f}_n(\cdot) \overset{c}{\equiv} \mathsf{Sim}(1^n, f_n(\cdot)).$$

To prove the lemma we define an oracle-aided algorithm $H^{\mathcal{O}}(x)$ such that (1) when the oracle $\mathcal{O}$ is the real RK-KDM oracle (with respect to linear queries) the distribution of $H^{\mathcal{O}}(x)$ is identical to the distribution $\hat{f}_n(x)$, and (2) when the oracle $\mathcal{O}$ is the fake RK-KDM oracle, the distribution $H^{\mathcal{O}}(x)$ can be efficiently sampled based on the output $f_n(x)$, and therefore can be used as a simulator $\mathsf{Sim}(1^n, f_n(x))$. The indistinguishability of the two oracles implies that the simulator's output is computationally indistinguishable from the encoding's distribution $\hat{f}_n(x)$.

The Algorithm $H^{(\cdot)}(x)$. Let $k = k(n)$, $x \in \{0, 1\}^n$ be the input. We assume that H is given an oracle access to a randomized function $\mathcal{O}_s$ where $s \overset{R}{\leftarrow} \{0, 1\}^k$ will play the role of the secret global shifts. We will assume that $\mathcal{O}_s$ has the same interface as Real_s and Fake_s, namely, given a pair of linear functions (ϕ, ψ) the oracle outputs a ciphertext of $(\mathsf{Enc}, \mathsf{Dec})$. For every wire ℓ we define the following values:

1. If ℓ is not an output of a XOR gate, choose a random active key $W_\ell^{b_\ell} \xleftarrow{R} \{0,1\}^k$ and a random color bit $c_\ell \xleftarrow{R} \{0,1\}$.
2. If the wire ℓ is an output of a XOR gate, let $W_\ell^{b_\ell} := W_i^{b_i} + W_j^{b_j}$ and $c_\ell = c_i + c_j$ where i and j are the incoming wires.
3. If ℓ is an input wire output $W_\ell^{b_\ell} \circ c_\ell$; if it is an output wire output $r_\ell = c_\ell - b_\ell(x)$ (recall that x is known).
4. The inactive key $W_\ell^{b_\ell+1}$ is unknown, but it can be written as a linear function of the master-key s, i.e., $\phi_\ell : s \mapsto s + W_\ell^{b_\ell}$.

For every (non-XOR) gate t with input wires i, j and output wire y we do the following:

5. Output the active label

$$Q_t^{c_i, c_j} := E_{W_i^{b_i}, W_j^{b_j}}^2 (W_y^{b_y} \circ c_y) \tag{5}$$

6. Compute the inactive labels as follows. For every $(\alpha, \beta) \neq (0,0)$ choose $R_{\alpha,\beta} \xleftarrow{R} \{0,1\}^{k+1}$ and define the linear function $\psi_{\alpha,\beta}$ which maps s to the value

$$\left((W_y^{b_y} + s \cdot g(b_i + \alpha, b_j + \beta) + b_y) \circ (g(c_i + \alpha + r_i, c_j + \beta + r_j) + r_y) \right) + R_{\alpha,\beta},$$

where g is the function that the gate computes, and $b_i = b_i(x)$, $r_i = b_i + c_i$, $b_j = b_j(x)$, $r_j = b_j + c_j$ and $b_y = b_y(x)$, $r_y = b_y + c_y$. Now, output

$$Q_t^{c_i+1, c_j} := \left(\mathcal{O}(\phi_i, \psi_{1,0}), \mathsf{Enc}_{W_j^{b_j}}(R_{1,0}) \right)$$

$$Q_t^{c_i+1, c_j+1} := \left(\mathcal{O}(\phi_i, \psi_{1,1}), \mathcal{O}(\phi_j, R_{1,1}) \right) \tag{6}$$

$$Q_t^{c_i, c_j+1} := \left(\mathsf{Enc}_{W_i^{b_i}}(R_{0,1}), \mathcal{O}(\phi_j, \psi_{0,1}) \right),$$

where in the second equation, we let the string $R_{1,1}$ represent the constant function $s \mapsto R_{1,1}$.

Claim 7. *The randomized functions $\hat{f}_n$ and H^{Real_s} for $s \xleftarrow{R} \{0,1\}^k$ are identically distributed.*

Proof. We prove a stronger claim: for every $x \in \{0,1\}^n$ even if the encoding and the hybrid $H^{\mathsf{Real}_s}(x)$ output their internal coins (including the ones used by the oracle Real_s), the two experiments are identically distributed. First, it is not hard to verify that the values s, W_ℓ^0, r_ℓ and $W_\ell^1 = W_\ell^0 + s$ are identically distributed in both experiments. When these values are fixed, the active labels are also identically distributed. Finally, by substituting $\phi_i, \psi_{\alpha,\beta}$ in Eq. 6 it follows that the inactive labels are also distributed exactly as in $\hat{f}(x)$. $\square$

Let us move to the case where the oracle $\mathcal{O}$ is instantiated with the oracle Fake_s for $s \xleftarrow{R} \{0,1\}^k$. By the RK-KDM security of the scheme $(\mathsf{Enc}, \mathsf{Dec})$ and Fact 2, we get that

Claim 8. *The randomized functions $\{H^{\mathsf{Real}_s}\}_s$ and $\{H^{\mathsf{Fake}_s}\}_s$ are computationally indistinguishable.*

Finally, we define the simulator which is just an equivalent description of $H^{\mathsf{Fake}_s}(x)$:

The Simulator Sim. Given $z = f_n(x)$, for some $x \in \{0,1\}^n$, the simulator mimics the first three steps of H which can be computed based on the value of the output wires $f_n(x)$ (without knowing x itself). However, instead of virtually setting inactive keys in the forth step, the simulator chooses a random shift vector $s \xleftarrow{R} \{0,1\}^k$ and sets $W_\ell^{1+b_\ell} = W_\ell^{b_\ell} + s$ for every wire ℓ. Then, the simulator computes the active labels exactly as in Eq. 5. Note that all these computations can be done without knowing x (or $b_i(x)$). To compute the inactive labels the simulator mimics the distribution of $H^{\mathsf{Fake}_s}(x)$: It chooses $R_{1,0}, R_{1,1}, R_{0,1} \xleftarrow{R} \{0,1\}^{k+1}$ and computes

$$
\begin{aligned}
Q_t^{c_i+1,c_j} &:= \left(\mathsf{Enc}_{W_i^{b_i+1}}(0^{k+1}), \mathsf{Enc}_{W_j^{b_j}}(R_{1,0}) \right) \\
Q_t^{c_i+1,c_j+1} &:= \left(\mathsf{Enc}_{W_i^{b_i+1}}(0^{k+1}), \mathsf{Enc}_{W_j^{b_j+1}}(0^{k+1}) \right) \qquad (7) \\
Q_t^{c_i,c_j+1} &:= \left(\mathsf{Enc}_{W_i^{b_i}}(R_{0,1}), \mathsf{Enc}_{W_j^{b_j+1}}(0^{k+1}) \right).
\end{aligned}
$$

Indeed, all these ciphertexts can be computed directly since the inactive keys (and the global shift s) are known.

Claim 9. *The randomized functions $\mathsf{Sim}(f_n(\cdot))$ and $H^{\mathsf{Fake}_s}(\cdot)$ for $s \xleftarrow{R} \{0,1\}^k$ are identically distributed.*

Proof. Again, a stronger claim holds: for every $x \in \{0,1\}^n$ even if the simulator and the algorithm $H^{\mathsf{Fake}_s(\cdot)}(x)$ output their internal coins, the two experiments are identically distributed. First, it is not hard to verify that the values s, W_ℓ^0, r_ℓ and $W_\ell^1 = W_\ell^0 + s$ are identically distributed in both experiments. When these values are fixed, the active labels are also identically distributed. Finally, the inactive labels as defined by the simulator (Eq. 7) are computed exactly as they are computed by $H^{\mathsf{Fake}_s(\cdot)}(x)$ (i.e., as defined in Eq. 6 when the oracle $\mathsf{Fake}_s(\cdot)$ is being used). □

The proof of Lemma 4 follows from Claims 7–9 and Facts 1 and 3.

5 Separating RK-KDM from RKA and KDM

Recall that LIN RKA security corresponds to RK-KDM security with Φ_{RKA} taken to be the class of linear functions (over the binary field) and Ψ_{KDM} contains the identity function. Similarly, LIN KDM security corresponds to RK-KDM security with Ψ_{KDM} taken to be the class of all linear (and fixed) functions, and Φ_{RKA} contains the identity function.

We describe a symmetric encryption scheme $(\mathsf{Enc}, \mathsf{Dec})$ which is semantically security under linear related-key attacks and semantically-secure under linear key-dependent message attacks but does not achieve linear RK-KDM security. In fact, one can fully recover the secret key via a combined LIN RK-KDM attack. Our counter-example will be based on a pair of symmetric encryption schemes $(\mathsf{RE}, \mathsf{RD})$ and $(\mathsf{KE}, \mathsf{KD})$ as follows.

RKA-security+KDM-insecurity. We define the scheme $(\mathsf{RE}, \mathsf{RD})$ identically to the LPN construction (Construction 4) except that if the prefix of a plaintext M is *equal* to the key S, then the corresponding ciphertext will be M itself (unencrypted). It is not hard to prove that $(\mathsf{RE}, \mathsf{RD})$ is secure under linear related-key attacks, but is completely insecure at the presence of linear key-dependent message attacks. (See full version for a proof.)

KDM-security+RKA-insecurity. To define the scheme $(\mathsf{KE}, \mathsf{KD})$, we modify the LPN construction $(\mathsf{PE}, \mathsf{PD})$ as follows. The key $S \in \{0,1\}^{\kappa}$ is augmented with an index $i \in \{1, \ldots, \kappa\}$. A plaintext M will be encrypted by the triple $(\mathsf{PE}_S(M), i, S_i)$. In the full version we show that the scheme is LIN KDM secure. In fact, it will be useful to prove KDM security with respect to a slightly richer family of "extended linear functions" which contains functions of the form $\psi_{M,T} : S \to M + TS$ for every $M \in \mathbb{F}_2^{\ell}$ and matrix $T \in \mathbb{F}_2^{\ell \times \kappa}$.[3]

On the other hand, one can fully recover the key S via an RKA by shifting the index i through all possible indices in $\{1, \ldots, \kappa\}$. Note that this attack is oblivious to the messages encrypted; In particular, all the attacker needs is the ability to obtain, for any choice of Δ, a ciphertext $\mathsf{KE}_{(S,i)+\Delta}(M)$ where the message M may be arbitrary and possibly unknown (e.g., chosen by the oracle).

Counter Example. Our counter-example is defined via the following double-encryption:

$$\mathsf{Enc}_{S_1, S_2}(M) := \mathsf{KE}_{S_2}(\mathsf{RE}_{S_1}(M)), \qquad \mathsf{Dec}_{S_1, S_2}(C) := \mathsf{RD}_{S_1}(\mathsf{KD}_{S_2}(C)).$$

In the full version we will prove the following claim:

Claim 10. *Under the* LPN *assumption, the scheme* $(\mathsf{Enc}, \mathsf{Dec})$ *satisfies the followings:*

1. *Security under linear related-key attacks.*
2. *Security under linear key-dependent message attacks.*
3. *The secret key can be fully recovered via a LIN RK-KDM attack.*

---

[3] It is shown in [2] that the (non-modified) LPN encryption $(\mathsf{PE}, \mathsf{PD})$ satisfies this extended form of KDM security. To handle the single-bit leakage, we rely on additional "leakage resilience" properties of LPN. See full version.

The first and third items follow standard arguments. The proof of the second item is based on the observation that, when the key S_1 and the internal randomness of RE are fixed, the encryption $\mathsf{RE}_{S_1}(S_1, S_2)$ can be written as an (extended) linear function of S_2. Details are deferred to the full version.

6 Conclusion

We defined a new combined form of RKA-KDM security, proved that such an encryption scheme can be realized based on the LPN assumption, and showed that the free-XOR approach can be securely instantiated with it. Altogether, our results enable a realization of the free-XOR optimization in the standard model under a well-studied cryptographic assumption.

The new definition of RKA-KDM security further motivates the study of security under related-key and key-dependent attacks. Specifically, in light of our counter-example, it is is natural to ask whether LIN RKA-KDM security can be constructed based on some combination of an RKA-secure scheme and a KDM-secure scheme, or better yet, based on more general assumptions (e.g., CPA-secure encryption scheme). It will also be interesting to find additional applications of RKA/KDM secure primitives.

References

1. Applebaum, B.: Randomly Encoding Functions: A New Cryptographic Paradigm (Invited Talk). In: Fehr, S. (ed.) ICITS 2011. LNCS, vol. 6673, pp. 25–31. Springer, Heidelberg (2011)
2. Applebaum, B., Cash, D., Peikert, C., Sahai, A.: Fast Cryptographic Primitives and Circular-Secure Encryption Based on Hard Learning Problems. In: Halevi, S. (ed.) CRYPTO 2009. LNCS, vol. 5677, pp. 595–618. Springer, Heidelberg (2009)
3. Applebaum, B., Harnik, D., Ishai, Y.: Semantic security under related-key attacks and applications. In: ICS, pp. 45–60 (2011)
4. Applebaum, B., Ishai, Y., Kushilevitz, E.: Computationally private randomizing polynomials and their applications. Computional Complexity 15(2), 115–162 (2006); Preliminary version in Proc. 20th CCC (2005)
5. Applebaum, B., Ishai, Y., Kushilevitz, E.: How to garble arithmetic circuits. In: FOCS, pp. 120–129 (2011)
6. Bellare, M., Cash, D.: Pseudorandom Functions and Permutations Provably Secure against Related-Key Attacks. In: Rabin, T. (ed.) CRYPTO 2010. LNCS, vol. 6223, pp. 666–684. Springer, Heidelberg (2010)
7. Bellare, M., Hoang, V.T., Rogaway, P.: Garbling schemes. Cryptology ePrint Archive, Report 2012/265 (2012), http://eprint.iacr.org/
8. Bellare, M., Kohno, T.: A Theoretical Treatment of Related-Key Attacks: RKA-PRPs, RKA-PRFs, and Applications. In: Biham, E. (ed.) EUROCRYPT 2003. LNCS, vol. 2656, pp. 491–506. Springer, Heidelberg (2003)
9. Bellare, M., Rogaway, P.: Random oracles are practical: A paradigm for designing efficient protocols. In: First ACM Conference on Computer and Communications Security, pp. 62–73. ACM, Fairfax (1993)

10. Black, J., Rogaway, P., Shrimpton, T.: Encryption-scheme security in the presence of key-dependent messages. In: Nyberg, K., Heys, H.M. (eds.) SAC 2002. LNCS, vol. 2595, pp. 62–75. Springer, Heidelberg (2003)

11. Blum, A., Furst, M., Kearns, M., Lipton, R.J.: Cryptographic Primitives Based on Hard Learning Problems. In: Stinson, D.R. (ed.) CRYPTO 1993. LNCS, vol. 773, pp. 278–291. Springer, Heidelberg (1994), citeseer.nj.nec.com/blum94cryptographic.html

12. Blum, M., Micali, S.: How to generate cryptographically strong sequences of pseudo-random bits. SIAM J. Comput. 13, 850–864 (1984); preliminary version in Proc. 23rd FOCS (1982)

13. Boneh, D., Halevi, S., Hamburg, M., Ostrovsky, R.: Circular-Secure Encryption from Decision Diffie-Hellman. In: Wagner, D. (ed.) CRYPTO 2008. LNCS, vol. 5157, pp. 108–125. Springer, Heidelberg (2008)

14. Camenisch, J.L., Lysyanskaya, A.: An Efficient System for Non-transferable Anonymous Credentials with Optional Anonymity Revocation. In: Pfitzmann, B. (ed.) EUROCRYPT 2001. LNCS, vol. 2045, pp. 93–118. Springer, Heidelberg (2001)

15. Canetti, Goldreich, Halevi: The random oracle methodology, revisited. JACM: Journal of the ACM 51 (2004)

16. Choi, S.G., Katz, J., Kumaresan, R., Zhou, H.-S.: On the Security of the "Free-XOR" Technique. In: Cramer, R. (ed.) TCC 2012. LNCS, vol. 7194, pp. 39–53. Springer, Heidelberg (2012)

17. Gilbert, H., Robshaw, M.J.B., Seurin, Y.: How to Encrypt with the LPN Problem. In: Aceto, L., Damgård, I.B., Goldberg, L.A., Halldórsson, M.M., Ingólfsdóttir, A., Walukiewicz, I. (eds.) ICALP 2008, Part II. LNCS, vol. 5126, pp. 679–690. Springer, Heidelberg (2008)

18. Goldreich, O., Krawczyk, H., Luby, M.: On the existence of pseudorandom generators. SIAM J. Comput. 22(6), 1163–1175 (1993); preliminary version in Proc. 29th FOCS (1988)

19. Goldreich, O., Micali, S., Wigderson, A.: How to play ANY mental game. In: STOC, pp. 218–229 (1987)

20. Håstad, J., Impagliazzo, R., Levin, L.A., Luby, M.: A pseudorandom generator from any one-way function. SIAM J. Comput. 28(4), 1364–1396 (1999)

21. Henecka, W., Kögl, S., Sadeghi, A.R., Schneider, T., Wehrenberg, I.: TASTY: tool for automating secure two-party computations. In: CCS, pp. 451–462 (2010)

22. Huang, Y., Evans, D., Katz, J., Malka, L.: Faster secure two-party computation using garbled circuits. In: USENIX Security Symposium (2011)

23. Huang, Y., Shen, C.-H., Evans, D., Katz, J., Shelat, A.: Efficient Secure Computation with Garbled Circuits. In: Jajodia, S., Mazumdar, C. (eds.) ICISS 2011. LNCS, vol. 7093, pp. 28–48. Springer, Heidelberg (2011)

24. Ishai, Y., Kilian, J., Nissim, K., Petrank, E.: Extending Oblivious Transfers Efficiently. In: Boneh, D. (ed.) CRYPTO 2003. LNCS, vol. 2729, pp. 145–161. Springer, Heidelberg (2003)

25. Ishai, Y., Kushilevitz, E.: Randomizing polynomials: A new representation with applications to round-efficient secure computation. In: Proc. 41st FOCS, pp. 294–304 (2000), citeseer.nj.nec.com/ishai00randomizing.html

26. Kolesnikov, V., Sadeghi, A.-R., Schneider, T.: Improved Garbled Circuit Building Blocks and Applications to Auctions and Computing Minima. In: Garay, J.A., Miyaji, A., Otsuka, A. (eds.) CANS 2009. LNCS, vol. 5888, pp. 1–20. Springer, Heidelberg (2009)

27. Kolesnikov, V., Schneider, T.: Improved Garbled Circuit: Free XOR Gates and Applications. In: Aceto, L., Damgård, I., Goldberg, L.A., Halldórsson, M.M., Ingólfsdóttir, A., Walukiewicz, I. (eds.) ICALP 2008, Part II. LNCS, vol. 5126, pp. 486–498. Springer, Heidelberg (2008)
28. Kreuter, B., Shelat, A., Shen, C.H.: Towards billion-gate secure computation with malicious adversaries. IACR Cryptology ePrint Archive 2012, 179 (2012)
29. Lindell, Y., Pinkas, B., Smart, N.P.: Implementing Two-Party Computation Efficiently with Security Against Malicious Adversaries. In: Ostrovsky, R., De Prisco, R., Visconti, I. (eds.) SCN 2008. LNCS, vol. 5229, pp. 2–20. Springer, Heidelberg (2008)
30. Lindell, Y., Pinkas, B.: An Efficient Protocol for Secure Two-Party Computation in the Presence of Malicious Adversaries. In: Naor, M. (ed.) EUROCRYPT 2007. LNCS, vol. 4515, pp. 52–78. Springer, Heidelberg (2007)
31. Lindell, Y., Pinkas, B.: A proof of security of yao's protocol for two-party computation. J. Cryptology 22(2), 161–188 (2009)
32. Malka, L., Katz, J.: Vmcrypt - modular software architecture for scalable secure computation. Cryptology ePrint Archive, Report 2010/584 (2010), http://eprint.iacr.org/
33. Malkhi, D., Nisan, N., Pinkas, B., Sella, Y.: Fairplay — A secure two-party computation system. In: Proc. of 13th USENIX Security Symposium (2004)
34. Maurer, U.M.: Indistinguishability of Random Systems. In: Knudsen, L.R. (ed.) EUROCRYPT 2002. LNCS, vol. 2332, pp. 110–132. Springer, Heidelberg (2002)
35. Naor, M., Pinkas, B.: Oblivious Transfer with Adaptive Queries. In: Wiener, M. (ed.) CRYPTO 1999. LNCS, vol. 1666, pp. 573–590. Springer, Heidelberg (1999)
36. Naor, M., Pinkas, B., Sumner, R.: Privacy preserving auctions and mechanism design. In: Proc. 1st ACM Conference on Electronic Commerce, pp. 129–139 (1999)
37. Nielsen, J.B., Orlandi, C.: LEGO for Two-Party Secure Computation. In: Reingold, O. (ed.) TCC 2009. LNCS, vol. 5444, pp. 368–386. Springer, Heidelberg (2009)
38. Pinkas, B., Schneider, T., Smart, N.P., Williams, S.C.: Secure Two-Party Computation Is Practical. In: Matsui, M. (ed.) ASIACRYPT 2009. LNCS, vol. 5912, pp. 250–267. Springer, Heidelberg (2009)
39. Rogaway, P.: The Round Complexity of Secure Protocols. Ph.D. thesis, MIT (June 1991)
40. Shelat, A., Shen, C.-H.: Two-Output Secure Computation with Malicious Adversaries. In: Paterson, K.G. (ed.) EUROCRYPT 2011. LNCS, vol. 6632, pp. 386–405. Springer, Heidelberg (2011)
41. Yao, A.C.: Theory and application of trapdoor functions. In: Proc. 23rd FOCS, pp. 80–91 (1982)
42. Yao, A.C.: How to generate and exchange secrets. In: Proc. 27th FOCS, pp. 162–167 (1986)

Why "Fiat-Shamir for Proofs" Lacks a Proof*

Nir Bitansky[1,**], Dana Dachman-Soled[2], Sanjam Garg[3,***], Abhishek Jain[4,†],
Yael Tauman Kalai[2], Adriana López-Alt[5,‡], and Daniel Wichs[6]

[1] Tel Aviv University
[2] Microsoft Research New England
[3] UCLA
[4] MIT and BU
[5] NYU
[6] IBM Research, T.J. Watson

Abstract. The Fiat-Shamir heuristic [CRYPTO '86] is used to convert any 3-message public-coin proof or argument system into a non-interactive argument, by hashing the prover's first message to select the verifier's challenge. It is known that this heuristic is sound when the hash function is modeled as a random oracle. On the other hand, the surprising result of Goldwasser and Kalai [FOCS '03] shows that there exists a computationally sound *argument* on which the Fiat-Shamir heuristic is *never* sound, when instantiated with any *actual* efficient hash function.

This leaves us with the following interesting possibility: perhaps we can securely instantiates the Fiat-Shamir heuristic for all 3-message public-coin *statistically sound proofs*, even if we must fail for some computationally sound arguments. Indeed, this has been conjectured to be the case by Barak, Lindell and Vadhan [FOCS '03], but we do not have any provably secure instantiation under any "standard assumption". In this work, we give a broad black-box separation result showing that the security of the Fiat-Shamir heuristic for statistically sound proofs cannot be proved under virtually any *standard assumption* via a *black-box reduction*. More precisely:

- If we want to have a "universal" instantiation of the Fiat-Shamir heuristic that works for *all* 3-message public-coin proofs, then we cannot prove its security via a black-box reduction from any assumption that has the format of a "cryptographic game".
- For many concrete proof systems, if we want to have a "specific" instantiation of the Fiat-Shamir heuristic for that proof system, then we cannot prove its security via a black box reduction from any "falsifiable assumption" that has the format of a cryptographic game with an efficient challenger.

* This is an abridged merge of [BGW12] and [DJKL12]. See ePrint for full versions.
** Research was done while visiting IBM T.J., Watson Research Center. Supported by the Check Point Institute for Information Security, an ISF grant 20006317, and the Fulbright program.
*** Research conducted while at the IBM Research, T.J.Watson funded by NSF Grant No.1017660.
† Research conducted while at Microsoft Research New England.
‡ Research conducted while at Microsoft Research New England.

A. Sahai (Ed.): TCC 2013, LNCS 7785, pp. 182–201, 2013.

1   Introduction

The Fiat-Shamir (FS) heuristic [FS86] allows us to convert an interactive *public-coin* protocol between a *prover* P and a *verifier* V into a one-message (non-interactive) protocol. Recall that, in a public-coin protocol, the verifier sends a uniformly random *challenge* to the prover in each round. Under the FS heuristic, the prover executes the original interactive protocol "in his head", computing the verifier's challenge in each round by applying some *public hash function* to the transcript of the protocol so far. The prover then only sends the final protocol transcript to the actual verifier, who verifies its validity. The hash function can be initialized with some randomly chosen public seed, which we think of as a "common random string (CRS)", and therefore the compiled protocol is non-interactive in the CRS model. Alternatively, the seed can also be chosen by the verifier in an additional initial message, in which case the compiled protocol consists of two messages. This heuristic has numerous remarkable applications in cryptography, such as constructing practical *signature schemes* [Sch91, GQ90, Oka93], *non-interactive zero knowledge (NIZK)* [BR93], and non-interactive succinct arguments [Mic00].

Soundness of FS. Although the FS heuristic seems to produce secure cryptographic schemes in practice, its formal security properties remain elusive. Perhaps the most basic question is to understand the *soundness* of the heuristic when applied to a statistically sound *proof* or computationally sound *argument* for some NP language. We say that an instance of the FS-heuristic is sound if the resulting non-interactive protocol is a computationally sound argument, for the same language. We can ask what kind of protocols do we need to start with, and what kind of hash functions should we use, to make the FS-heuristic sound. Since we are interested in a negative result, we restrict our attention to *3-message public-coin (3PC)* protocols.

Applying FS to Arguments. On the positive side, if the FS heuristic uses a *random oracle* as its hash function, then it is known to be sound when applied to *any* 3PC argument [BR93, PS00, AABN02]. On the other hand, the work of Goldwasser and Kalai [GK03] shows a surprising negative result: the FS heuristic *cannot* be securely instantiated with any *actual* efficient hash function that would achieve the same result. In particular, there exists *some* 3PC argument on which the FS heuristic is *never* sound, no matter which efficient hash function we try to instantiate it with.

Applying FS to Proofs. The above negative result only applies to computationally sound arguments, and therefore we are still left with the following interesting possibility: perhaps the FS heuristic could be instantiated with some hash function that makes it sound for *all* 3PC statistically sound *proofs*, even if it can fail for some arguments. We call such a hash function *FS-universal*. When instantiated with an FS-universal hash function, the FS heuristic should successfully compile any 3PC proof into a non-interactive (computationally sound) argument.

Barak, Lindell, and Vadhan [BLV03] conjecture that such FS-universal hash functions should indeed exist, and define a plausible hash-function property called *entropy-preservation*, which they show to be sufficient. Variants of this entropy-preservation property were further studied by Dodis, Ristenpart and Vadhan [DRV12], who also showed that it is *necessary*. Nevertheless, despite the amazing possibility that such hash functions may exist, we do not have any candidate construction that is provably secure under some "standard" cryptographic hardness assumption.

Less ambitiously, we may hope to securely instantiate the Fiat-Shamir heuristic for many specific 3PC proof and argument systems. In particular, for some candidate 3PC proof or argument Π, we can hope to have a *FS(Π)-secure hash function* that preserves soundness when applying the FS heuristic specifically to the protocol Π. We do not know how to construct such FS(Π)-secure hash functions for essentially any "interesting" proof or argument system Π.

1.1 Our Results

In this work, we re-examine the possibility of having *FS-universal* hash functions, or *FS(Π)-secure* hash functions for specific proof systems Π. We prove broad black-box separation results showing that the security of such hash functions cannot be proved under virtually any *standard assumption* via a *black-box reduction* that treats the attacker as a black box. More specifically, we provide two main results:

FS-Universal Hash Functions. We show that one cannot prove the security of an FS-universal hash function via a black-box reduction from any "cryptographic game assumption" (see below). We leverage the connection of [BLV03, DRV12] between FS-universal and entropy preserving hash functions. Specifically, we first provide a separation for entropy preserving hash functions, and then use it to get a similar separation for FS-universal hash functions.

FS(Π)-Secure Hash Functions. For many specific proof and argument systems Π, we show that one cannot prove the FS(Π)-security of a hash function via a black-box reduction from any "falsifiable assumption" (see below). In particular, we first prove a black-box impossibility result for two-round zero knowledge w.r.t. super-poynomial simulation, extending the result of Goldreich and Oren [GO94]. Then, by relying on this result, we obtain a black-box impossibility result for any proof/argument system Π for a sub-exponentially hard language $\mathcal{L}$ if Π is also *honest-verifier zero-knowledge (HVZK)* against sub-exponential size distinguishers and has "short" challenges. The above includes many natural Σ-protocols.

As an additional application of our result on two-round zero knowledge, we show a black-box impossibility result for proving soundness of Micali's CS-proofs [Mic94] based on any falsifiable assumption. We note that unlike [GW11], this result also holds for *non-adaptive* cheating proves, who choose the instance before seeing the verifier's message.

We wish to emphasize that these results do *not* refute the highly believable conjecture that the FS heuristic can be securely instantiated for all proofs and many natural arguments. However, it shows that we will need to rely on new "non-standard" assumptions or develop new "non-black box" proof techniques if we ever hope to prove this conjecture.

Assumptions. To capture all "standard assumptions", we consider general classes of assumptions defined in terms of the syntactic format that the assumption takes. A *"cryptographic game assumption"* has the format of an interactive game between a (possibly inefficient) challenger who interacts in a black-box manner with some candidate attacker. The assumption states that every efficient attacker has at most negligible probability in winning this game. This notion is due to [DOP05, HH09]. A *"falsifiable assumption"* [Nao03] is a cryptographic game assumption where the challenger is also *efficient*. Note that these notions capture essentially all of the concrete assumptions we use in cryptography, such as the hardness of factoring, the RSA problem, the discrete logarithm problem, the computational/decisional Diffie-Hellman problem (CDH/DDH), learning with errors (LWE), etc. We stress that these notions are defined as liberally as possible so as to include essentially everything that could be considered a "standard assumption", and to make our negative result as strong as possible. Of course, it may also capture many non-standard (and false) assumptions, as well as trivially true and uninteresting assumptions.

FS-Universality. The assumption that a hash function is FS-universal does not have the format of a *cryptographic game*, since the assumption quantifies over all proof systems. In particular, an attack against "FS-universality" consists of two components: a 3PC proof system $\Pi = (P, V)$ for some language $\mathcal{L}$ and a breaker $\mathcal{A}$ that breaks the soundness of the Fiat-Shamir transform applied to Π. The challenger cannot test that Π is a 3PC proof system by interacting with P, V in a black-box manner. When we talk about *black-box reductions* for FS-universality, we naturally restrict the challenger to interact with $P, V, \mathcal{A}$ as a black box. In other words, the reduction is black-box in the code of the attacker, as well as the proof system Π.

FS(Π)-Security. For a particular proof system Π for a language $\mathcal{L}$, the assumption that a hash function is FS(Π)-secure *is* a cryptographic game assumption: the attacker wins if he can come up with a false statement x and an accepting proof π under the non-interactive argument that we get by applying the FS heuristic to Π. However, it does not have the format of a *falsifiable assumption* since the challenger cannot efficiently test whether x is false statement, and therefore, whether the attacker breaks soundness.

2   Preliminaries and Definitions

Let n denote the security parameter. We say that a function $f(n) = 1/n^{\omega(1)}$ *negligible* in the security parameter, and denote it by $\mathsf{negl}(n)$. We consider the class of efficient schemes to be ones that can be implemented by a probabilistic polynomial-time Turing machine, denoted by PPT. In contrast, we consider the class of efficient adversaries $\mathcal{A} = \{\mathcal{A}_n\}$ to be non-uniform families of polynomial-size circuits, denoted by polysize.

We start by describing the Fiat-Shamir heuristic for public-coin interactive proofs. Recall that an interactive proof system [GMR89] for a language L with corresponding relation R is a tuple of efficient algorithms $\Pi = (\mathcal{P}, \mathcal{V})$, where $\mathcal{P}$ and $\mathcal{V}$ denote the prover and the verifier algorithms respectively. We assume familiarity of the reader with the standard notions of *completeness* and *soundness* for an interactive proof system, and skip formal definitions.

The Fiat-Shamir Heuristic. Throughout the paper, we will mainly focus on the special case of applying the FS heuristic to a *3-message public-coin (3PC)* interactive proof system $\Pi = \langle P, V \rangle$ for an NP relation $\mathcal{R}$.[1] Denote the first message of the prover by α, the verifier's challenge by β, and the final message of the prover by γ. Also, let $\pi = (\alpha, \beta, \gamma)$ denote the transcript of the execution.

For security parameter n, let $m(n)$ and $k(n)$ denote the lengths of α and β, respectively. Let $\mathcal{H} = \{h_s : \{0,1\}^{m(n)} \to \{0,1\}^{k(n)}\}_{n \in \mathbb{N}, s \in \{0,1\}^{\ell(n)}}$ be a family of hash functions mapping m bits to k bits. The Fiat-Shamir collapse (or FS-collapse in short) of protocol $\Pi = \langle P, V \rangle$ using $\mathcal{H}$ is a two-message protocol $\Pi^{\mathsf{FS}} = \langle P_{\mathsf{FS}}, V_{\mathsf{FS}} \rangle$ defined as follows:

- In the first message, the FS verifier $V_{\mathsf{FS}}(1^n, x)$ selects a random seed $s \leftarrow \{0,1\}^{\ell(n)}$ for the hash function. (We can also skip this step by thinking of s as a common reference string).
- In the second message, the FS prover $P_{\mathsf{FS}}(1^n, x, w)$ runs $P(1^n, x, w)$ to derive its first message α. It then computes the challenge $\beta := h_s(\alpha)$ by hashing α, and passes β to P to get its third message γ. Finally, P_{FS} outputs the tuple (α, β, γ).
- The FS verifier $V_{\mathsf{FS}}(1^n, x)$ accepts the proof if $\beta = h_s(\alpha)$ *and* the original verifier $V(1^n, x)$ accepts the protocol (α, β, γ) when executed with random-coins β.

We say that the *FS-collapse is sound* if the resulting protocol Π^{FS} is a *computationally-sound argument system* as specified below.

Definition 1 (Fiat-Shamir soundness). *We say that Π^{FS} is computationally sound if, for any* polysize *prover $P^* = \{P_n^*\}$ and $x \notin \mathcal{L}(\mathcal{R})$*

$$\Pr_{s \xleftarrow{\$} \{0,1\}^{\ell(n)}} \left[V(1^n, x, \pi) = 1 \;\middle|\; \begin{array}{l} \pi \leftarrow P_n^*(x, s) \\ \pi = (\alpha, \beta, \gamma) \\ h_s(\alpha) = \beta \end{array} \right] \leq \mathsf{negl}(n) \ .$$

We call the above probability the advantage *of P^* in breaking computational soundness.*

---

[1] Indeed, this is the most common but also minimal case for which Fiat-Shamir is expected to work, and therefore restricting ourselves to this case gives us the strongest negative result.

Cryptographic Games and Falsifiable Assumptions. Cryptographic games present a general framework for defining cryptographic assumptions and security properties. A game is given by a protocol specified via a *challenger* who interacts with an arbitrary *attacker* – security mandates that no efficient attacker should be able to win the game with better than negligible probability.

Definition 2 (Cryptographic game [HH09]). *A cryptographic game* $\mathcal{G} = (\Gamma, c)$ *is defined by a (possibly inefficient) random system* Γ, *called the challenger, and a constant* $c \in [0, 1)$. *On security parameter* n, *the challenger* $\Gamma(1^n)$ *interacts with some attacker* $\mathcal{A}_n$ *and outputs a bit* b. *We denote the output of this interaction by* $b = (\mathcal{A}_n \leftrightarrows \Gamma(1^n))$. *The* advantage *of an attacker* $\mathcal{A}_n$ *in the game* $\mathcal{G}$ *is defined as*

$$\mathbf{Adv}_{\mathcal{G}}^{\mathcal{A}}(n) \overset{\text{def}}{=} \Pr[\, (\mathcal{A}_n \leftrightarrows \Gamma(1^n)) = 1 \,] - c \ .$$

A cryptographic game $\mathcal{G}$ *is* secure *if for all* polysize *attackers* $\mathcal{A} = \{\mathcal{A}_n\}$, *the advantage* $\mathbf{Adv}_{\mathcal{G}}^{\mathcal{A}}(n)$ *is negligible. The game is* $T(n)$-*secure if for all attackers running in time* $\mathsf{poly}(T(n))$ *the advantage* $\mathbf{Adv}_{\mathcal{G}}^{\mathcal{A}}(n)$ *is* $\mathsf{negl}(T(n)) = T(n)^{-\omega(1)}$.

When $c = 0$, the above definition of cryptographic games captures *search problems* such as factoring, the discrete logarithm problem, signature security etc. When $c = \frac{1}{2}$, it captures *decisional problems* such as DDH, encryption security etc. Note that cryptographic games may be highly interactive and may not even have any a-priori bound on the number of rounds of interaction between $\mathcal{A}$ and Γ. The work of [GW11] defined a more restricted notion of cryptographic games called "falsifiable assumptions" (following [Nao03]) where the challenger is also required to be efficient.

Definition 3 (Falsifiable Assumption). *We say that a cryptographic game* $\mathcal{G} = (\Gamma, c)$ *is a falsifiable assumption if the challenger* $\Gamma(1^n)$ *runs in time* $\mathsf{poly}(n)$.

3 Black-Box Impossibility of Entropy-Preserving Hashing and Fiat-Shamir Universality

In this section, we show a black-box separation between hash function that are *Fiat-Shamir-universal* and general cryptographic games. As explained in the introduction, an FS-universal hash function family guarantees the soundness of the Fiat-Shamir heuristic for *any* 3PC system with appropriate message and challenge length.

Definition 4 ((m, k)-FS-universal hash function). *We say that a hash-function family* $\mathcal{H} = \{h_s : \{0, 1\}^{m(n)} \to \{0, 1\}^{k(n)}\}_{s \in \{0,1\}^{\ell(n)}}$ *is* $(m(n), k(n))$-*FS-universal if for every 3PC (statistically sound) proof system* $\langle P, V \rangle$ *with first and second messages of respective lengths* $m = m(n)$ *and* $k = k(n)$, *the FS-collapse* Π^{FS} *is a (computationally sound) argument.*

As the main step towards this separation, we show a black-box separation between the notion of entropy-preserving hash-functions introduced by Barak et al. [BLV03] and general cryptographic games. We then leverage the connection between entropy-preserving hashing and FS-universal hashing as shown in [BLV03, DRV12] to prove a similar seperation for the latter.

3.1   Black-Box Impossibility for Entropy-Preserving Hashing

Barak et al. [BLV03] formulated a relatively simple entropy preservation property for hash functions, and showed that it is sufficient for FS-universality. Recall that the *(Shannon) entropy* of a random variable $\mathbf{x}$ is $\mathbf{H}(\mathbf{x}) = \mathbf{E}_{x \xleftarrow{\$} \mathbf{x}} [-\log(\Pr[\mathbf{x} = x])]$. For jointly distributed random variables $(\mathbf{x}, \mathbf{y})$, the *conditional entropy* of $\mathbf{x}$ given $\mathbf{y}$ is defined by

$$\mathbf{H}(\mathbf{x} \mid \mathbf{y}) = \mathop{\mathbf{E}}_{y \xleftarrow{\$} \mathbf{y}} [\mathbf{H}(\mathbf{x} \mid \mathbf{y} = y)],$$

where $\mathbf{x}|_{\mathbf{y}=y}$ is a random variable distributed according to $\mathbf{x}$ conditioned on $\mathbf{y} = y$.

Definition 5 (Definition 9.2 in [BLV03]). *We say that a hash function family* $\mathcal{H} = \{h_s : \{0,1\}^{m(n)} \to \{0,1\}^{k(n)}\}_{s \in \{0,1\}^{\ell(n)}}$ preserves $u(n)$-entropy, *if for any polysize* $\mathcal{A}$, *and all large enough values of the security parameter* $n \in \mathbb{N}$ *we have*

$$\mathbf{H}(h_\mathbf{s}(\mathbf{x}) \mid \mathbf{x}) > u(n) ,$$

where $\mathbf{s}, \mathbf{x}$ *are correlated random variables defined by choosing* $\mathbf{s}$ *uniformly at random over* $\{0,1\}^{\ell(n)}$, *and setting* $\mathbf{x}$ *to be the first* $m(n)$ *bits of the output of* $\mathcal{A}(1^n, \mathbf{s})$. *We say that the hash function (just plain)* preserves entropy *if it preserves* $u(n)$-entropy *for* $u(n) = 0$.

The work of [BLV03] shows that any hash function family that preserves $u(n) = k(n) - O(\log n)$ entropy is (m, k)-FS-universal. An alternative take on the notion of "entropy preserving" hash functions and a detailed exploration of the parameters is given by Dodis, Ristenpart, and Vadhan [DRV12]. The same work also shows an implication in the reverse direction: any (m, k)-FS-universal hash function family must also preserve entropy. We will thus focus on showing a black-box separation for entropy-preserving hash functions, and then adapt the [DRV12] result to our setting.

Black-Box Reductions. We now define the notion of a black-box reduction from entropy-preserving hashing to a cryptographic game.

Definition 6 (BB Reduction for Entropy Preserving Hash). *Let* $\mathcal{G} = (\Gamma, c)$ *be a cryptographic game and let* $\mathcal{H}$ *be a hash function family with input length* $m(n)$ *and output length* $k(n)$, *for some polynomials* m, k. *A black-box reduction showing that* $\mathcal{H}$ *is entropy-preserving from the security of the game* $\mathcal{G}$ *is an oracle-access PPT machine* $\mathcal{B}^{(\cdot)}$ *for which there exists some polynomial* p *such that the following holds. Let* $\mathcal{A} = \{\mathcal{A}_n\}$ *be any (possibly inefficient) attacker* *such that* $\mathbf{H}(h_{\mathbf{s}}(\mathbf{x}) \mid \mathbf{x}) = 0$, *where the random variable* $\mathbf{s}, \mathbf{x}$ *are defined the same way as in Definition 5, i.e.,* $\mathbf{s} \xleftarrow{\$} \{0,1\}^{\ell(n)}$, *and* $\mathbf{x} \leftarrow \mathcal{A}_n(\mathbf{s})$. *Then, the advantage of* $\mathcal{B}^{\mathcal{A}_n}(1^n)$ *in the game* $\mathcal{G}$ *is at least* $1/p(n)$.

Remark 1 (Reductions from $T(n)$-*security assumptions).* We can also consider a variant, where the black-box reduction is from the $T(n)$-security of the cryptographic game $\mathcal{G}$. In this case, we allow the reduction $\mathcal{B}^{(\cdot)}$ to run in time $\mathsf{poly}(T(n))$ and only insist that its advantage is $\geq 1/p(T(n))$.

For simplicity, we insist that the reduction itself has some *noticeable* advantage $1/p(n)$ rather than the standard requirement that its advantage is simply *non-negligible*. Furthermore, we also insist that the reduction is *security-parameter preserving* meaning that when it is called with security parameter 1^n it only accesses the oracle $\mathcal{A}_n$ on the *same* security parameter n. The above two requirements come with some loss of generality, but they hold for all of the natural reductions in cryptography.

BB Separation via Simulatable Attack. We now outline a general strategy for proving black-box separations via a technique called a *simulatable attack*. This strategy has been used in several prior works [BV98, Cor02, Bro05, PV05, GBL08] [DOP05, HH09, GW11, Pas11, Seu12, DHT12, Wic12]. The main idea of this paradigm is to construct a special *inefficient* attacker $\mathcal{A}$ that breaks the security of the target primitive (in our case, the entropy-preserving security of $\mathcal{H}$), but for which there is an *efficient* simulator Sim such that no distinguisher can tell the difference between "black-box" interaction with Sim and $\mathcal{A}$. This means that any efficient black-box reduction which can win some cryptographic game, given oracle access to the inefficient attacker $\mathcal{A}$, can also win the cryptographic game, given oracle access to the efficient simulator Sim. Hence, if we have a black-box reduction showing the entropy-preserving security of $\mathcal{H}$ under some cryptographic-game assumption, it implies that the reduction, together with the efficient simulator Sim, give us an efficient stand-alone attack against the assumption, and so it cannot be secure to begin with!

Aspects of this technique were recently formalized in [Wic12], and we will rely on the notation and the results from that work. However, for concreteness, we only restrict ourselves to describing this strategy for the specific case of *entropy preserving hash functions*.

Definition 7 (Simulatable Attack for Entropy-Preserving Hashing).
Let $\mathcal{H}$ *be some hash function family with input length* $m(n)$ *and output length* $k(n)$. *A* $\varepsilon(n)$-*simulatable attack on the entropy-preserving security of* $\mathcal{H}$ *consists of: (1) an ensemble of (possibly inefficient) stateless non-uniform attackers* $\{\mathcal{A}_{n,f}\}_{n\in\mathbb{N}, f\in\mathcal{F}_n}$ *where* $\{\mathcal{F}_n\}$ *is some ensemble of finite sets, and (2) a stateful* PPT *simulator* Sim. *We require that the following two properties hold:*

- *For each* $n \in \mathbb{N}, f \in \mathcal{F}_n$, *the (inefficient) attacker* $\mathcal{A}_{n,f}$ *successfully breaks the entropy-preserving security of* $\mathcal{H}$.

- *For every (possibly inefficient) oracle access machine* $\mathcal{M}^{(\cdot)}$, *making at most* $q = q(n)$ *queries to its oracle:*

$$\left| \Pr_{f \overset{\$}{\leftarrow} \mathcal{F}_n, \mathcal{M}} [\mathcal{M}^{\mathcal{A}_{n,r}}(1^n) = 1] - \Pr_{(\mathcal{M}, \mathsf{Sim})} [\mathcal{M}^{\mathsf{Sim}(1^n)}(1^n) = 1] \right| \le \mathsf{poly}(q(n)) \cdot \varepsilon(n).$$

namely, oracle access to $\mathcal{A}_{n,f}$ *for a random* $f \overset{\$}{\leftarrow} \mathcal{F}_n$ *is indistinguishable from that to* Sim.

We omit the $\varepsilon(n)$ and just say "*simulatable attack*" as shorthand for an $\varepsilon(n)$-simulatable attack with some negligible $\varepsilon(n) = \mathsf{negl}(n)$.

As discussed in the introduction, the existence of a simulatable attack against some scheme $\mathcal{H}$ ensures that one cannot prove the security of $\mathcal{H}$ using black-box reduction from cryptographic game assumption, unless the assumption is false. This is because a reduction must be able to use the simulatable attacker $\mathcal{A}$ against $\mathcal{H}$ to break the underlying assumption, but then this means that the reduction and the simulator together would give us an efficient stand-alone attack against the assumption to begin with. A general version of this theorem was given in [Wic12] and therefore we get the following as a special case.

Theorem 1 (Special case of [Wic12]). *If there exists a simulatable attack against the entropy preserving security of* $\mathcal{H}$, *and there is a black-box reduction showing the entropy preserving security of* $\mathcal{H}$ *from the security of some cryptographic game* $\mathcal{G}$, *then* $\mathcal{G}$ *is* not *secure.*

Furthermore, for any $T(n)$, *if there exists an* $\varepsilon(n) = T(n)^{-\omega(1)}$-*simulatable attack against* $\mathcal{H}$ *and there is a black-box reduction from the* $T(n)$-*security of* $\mathcal{G}$, *then* $\mathcal{G}$ *is* not $T(n)$-*secure.*

Constructing a Simulatable Attack. We now show that, for any family of hash functions $\mathcal{H}$, there is a simulatable attack against its entropy preserving security.

Theorem 2. *Let* $\mathcal{H} = \{h_s : \{0,1\}^{m(n)} \to \{0,1\}^{k(n)}\}_{n \in \mathbb{N}, s \in \{0,1\}^{\ell(n)}}$ *be any family of hash functions. Then there is a* $2^{-\Omega(m-k)}$-*simulatable attack against the entropy preserving security of* $\mathcal{H}$.

Proof outline. Let $\mathcal{F}_n$ be the set of functions $f : \{0,1\}^{m(n)} \to \{0,1\}^{k(n)}$, and let $\mathcal{F}_n^* \subseteq \mathcal{F}_n$ be a subset consisting of all the functions f such that for every $s \in \{0,1\}^{\ell(n)}$, there is some $x \in \{0,1\}^m$ on which $h_s(x) = f(x)$. We will define a family of inefficient attackers $\{\mathsf{Break}_f\}$, indexed by functions $f \in \mathcal{F}_n^*$, that break the entropy preserving security of $\mathcal{H}$. Before we do so, we first note that a simple counting argument shows that $\mathcal{F}_n^*$ is non-empty, and in fact forms a very dense subset of $\mathcal{F}_n$.

Claim. $\mathcal{F}_n^*$ *is dense in* $\mathcal{F}_n$ *with* $\frac{|\mathcal{F}_n^*|}{|\mathcal{F}_n|} = (1 - 2^{-\Omega(2^{m-k})})$-*fraction of* $\mathcal{F}_n$.

$$\text{Break}_f : f \in \mathcal{F}_n^*$$

Given input $s \in \{0,1\}^{\ell(n)}$, output a random x from the set of all values satisfying $h_s(x) = f(x)$.
(By the definition of $\mathcal{F}_n^*$, at least one such x always exists.)

Fig. 1.

Constructing an attack. Now, we are ready to define a family of inefficient attackers $\{\text{Break}_f\}$, indexed by functions $f \in \mathcal{F}_n^*$, that break the entropy preserving security of $\mathcal{H}$ as follows:

The attack is successful. For any fixed $f \in \mathcal{F}_n^*$, it is easy to see that the attacker Break_f breaks the entropy preserving security of $\mathcal{H}$. This is because, conditioned on seeing any output $x \leftarrow \text{Break}_f(s)$, we can completely determine the value $h_s(x)$ without knowing the seed s, via the relation $h_s(x) = f(x)$. Therefore, defining the random variables $\mathbf{s}$ to be uniform over $\{0,1\}^{\ell(n)}$ and $\mathbf{x} \leftarrow \text{Break}_f(\mathbf{s})$, we have $\mathbf{H}(h_\mathbf{s}(\mathbf{x}) \mid \mathbf{x}) = 0$ as desired.

The simulator for the attack. The more interesting part of the proof is showing that for random $f \leftarrow \mathcal{F}_n^*$, the attacker Break_f can be simulated very efficiently, with a small statistical error. Our (stateful) simulator is incredibly simple and, on each invocation, just outputs a fresh random value (which wasn't output previously).   It is easy to see that the simulator satisfies the efficiency requirements

---

$$\text{Sim}(1^n)$$

Initialize the set $X := \emptyset$.
On input $s \in \{0,1\}^{\ell(n)}$: Sample $x \leftarrow \{0,1\}^m \setminus X$, add x to the set X, and output x.

Fig. 2.

of the definition of a simulatable attack.

Indistinguishability of simulator. The next step is to show that a random attacker from the class $\{\text{Break}_f\}$ and the above simulator are statistically indistinguishable. In particular, for any (computationally unbounded) q-query distinguisher $\mathcal{M}$,

$$\left| \Pr_{f \xleftarrow{\$} \mathcal{F}_n^*} \left[\mathcal{M}^{\text{Break}_f}(1^n) = 1 \right] - \Pr_{\text{Sim}} \left[\mathcal{M}^{\text{Sim}(1^n)}(1^n) = 1 \right] \right| \leq q^2 \cdot 2^{-\Omega(m-k)} .$$

Theorem 1 and Theorem 2 allow us to conclude the following.

Corollary 1. *Let $\mathcal{G} = (\Gamma, c)$ be a cryptographic game assumption and let $\mathcal{H}$ be an (m, k)-hash function family for some polynomials $m = m(n), k = k(n)$ such that $m(n) - k(n) = \omega(\log(n))$. If there is a black-box reduction showing that*

$\mathcal{H}$ is entropy-preserving from the security of the game $\mathcal{G}$, then $\mathcal{G}$ is not secure. Furthermore, if $m(n) - k(n) = \omega(\log(T(n))$ and there is a black-box reduction showing that $\mathcal{H}$ is entropy preserving from the $T(n)$-security of $\mathcal{G}$, then $\mathcal{G}$ is not $T(n)$-secure.

3.2 Black-Box Impossibility of Fiat-Shamir Universality

As we have already mentioned, the work of Dodis, Ristenpart and Vadhan [DRV12], shows that any FS-universal hash function family $\mathcal{H}$ must also be entropy-preserving. Intuitively, this should imply that our negative result for entropy-preserving hashing from the previous section should yield a similar negative result for FS-universal hashing. Indeed, we do show a theorem along these lines. However, formalizing the above intuition requires some care. For example, it becomes important that our notion of black-box reductions for FS-universal hashing treats the 3PC proof-system as a black box. Intuitively, this is because the result of [DRV12] uses the attacker $\mathcal{A}$ against the entropy-preserving security of a hash family $\mathcal{H}$ to *construct* a 3PC proof system $\varPi^{\mathcal{A}} = \langle P^{\mathcal{A}}, V^{\mathcal{A}} \rangle$ as well as to *attacker* $\mathcal{D}^{\mathcal{A}}$ that breaks the soundness of the FS-collapse of $\varPi^{\mathcal{A}}$. Therefore, any black-box reduction that shows the FS-universality of $\mathcal{H}$ under some game assumption by treating the proof system $\varPi^{\mathcal{A}} = \langle P^{\mathcal{A}}, V^{\mathcal{A}} \rangle$ and the attacker $\mathcal{D}^{\mathcal{A}}$ as a black box, can also be used as a reduction showing the entropy-preserving security of $\mathcal{H}$ under the same assumption by treating the attacker $\mathcal{A}$ as a black box. Further details can be found in [BGW12].

4 Impossibility of Fiat-Shamir for Specific Proof Systems

In this section, we show that for many well-studied public-coin interactive proofs, the soundness of the Fiat-Shamir heuristic cannot be proven via a black-box reduction to any falsifiable assumption. Using similar techniques, we also show a black-box impossibility result for proving soundness of Micali's CS-proofs [Mic94] based on any falsifiable assumption. The main tool underlying both of these results is a black-box impossibility result for two-round zero-knowledge w.r.t. super-polynomial simulation.

We note that the connection between zero-knowledge and the (in)security of Fiat-Shamir heuristic was already made in prior works. In particular, Dwork et al. [DNRS99] showed that if a public-coin interactive protocol is "weakly" zero-knowledge (where the ZK property is weakened by changing the order of quantifiers in the standard ZK definition, but requiring the simulator and distinguisher to be polynomial time) then the Fiat-Shamir heuristic applied to this protocol is not sound. We note however, that known public-coin protocols where the FS-heuristic would typically be applied, are *not* known to satisfy their zero-knowledge property. In contrast, (as we discuss below) we only require the protocol to be honest-verifier zero-knowledge w.r.t. sub-exponential adversaries, and show that this property is satisfied by many well-known protocols (under some assumptions).

The rest of this section is organized as follows. In Section 4.1, we prove a general theorem on the black-box impossibility of 2-round zero-knowledge arguements. In Section 4.2 we apply this theorem to show that for many well-studied public-coin interactive *proofs*, the soundness of the Fiat-Shamir heuristic cannot be proven via a black-box reduction to any falsifiable assumption. Finally, in Section 4.3, we extend our techniques to show a black-box impossibility result for proving soundness of Micali's CS-proofs [Mic94].

4.1 Black-Box Impossibility for 2-Round Zero Knowledge

In this section, we give a black-box impossibility result for 2-round zero-knowledge arguments. Our theorem extends the negative result of Goldreich and Oren [GO94], and can be seen as essentially tight, in view of the positive result of Pass [Pas03]. We refer the reader to the full version [DJKL12] for a detailed comparison of our result with [GO94] and [Pas03].

We start with some preliminaries and then describe our result.

Hard Languages and Zero-Knowledge Proofs. We start by formally defining a hard NP language.

Definition 8 (T-Hard Language). *For any $T = T(n)$, an NP language L is said to be T-hard if there exist two distribution families $\mathcal{X} = \{\mathcal{X}_n\}_{n\in\mathbb{N}}$ and $\bar{\mathcal{X}} = \{\bar{\mathcal{X}}_n\}_{n\in\mathbb{N}}$, and a PPT sampling algorithm Samp such that:*

- *For every $n \in \mathbb{N}$ the support of $\mathcal{X}_n$ is in L and the support of $\bar{\mathcal{X}}_n$ is in $\bar{L}$.*
- *The distributions $\mathcal{X}$ and $\bar{\mathcal{X}}$ are $T(n)$-indistinguishable.*
- *The support of the sampling algorithm Samp consists of elements (x, w) such that $R(x, w) = 1$, and its projection to the first coordinate yields the distribution $\mathcal{X} = \{\mathcal{X}_n\}_{n\in\mathbb{N}}$.*
  Note that since Samp is efficient, the distribution family $\mathcal{X}$ is efficiently sampleable. There are no constraints on the size of the instances in $\mathcal{X}_n$ or $\bar{\mathcal{X}}_n$, however since $\mathcal{X}$ is efficiently sampleable each $x \leftarrow \mathcal{X}_n$ is of size at most $\mathrm{poly}(n)$.

An NP language is said to be sub-exponentially hard if it is 2^n-hard.[2]

We now define the zero-knowedge property for an interactive proof system [GMR89].

Definition 9 (T-Zero Knowledge). *For any $T = T(n)$, we say that an interactive proof system $\Pi = (\mathcal{P}, \mathcal{V})$ for an NP language L is (auxiliary-input) T-zero-knowledge if for every poly-size circuit $\mathcal{V}^*$ there exists a simulator $\mathcal{S}_{\mathcal{V}^*}(1^n)$ of size $\mathrm{poly}(T(n))$ such that for every $n \in \mathbb{N}$, every instance $x \in L$ of length*

---

[2] Note that it should be hard for a $\mathrm{poly}(2^n)$-time distinguisher to distinguish between elements in $\mathcal{X}_n$ and elements in $\bar{\mathcal{X}}_n$, where these elements can be much longer than n, and can be of length n^ϵ for any constant $\epsilon > 0$ (thus, capturing the sub-exponential hardness).

at most $\mathrm{poly}(n)$ *with a corresponding witness* w, *and every auxiliary input* $z \in \{0,1\}^{\mathrm{poly}(n)}$, *it holds that for every non-uniform distinguisher* $D = \{D_n\}$ *of size* $\mathrm{poly}(T(n))$

$$\big| \Pr[D\,((\mathcal{P}(w), \mathcal{V}^*(z))(1^n, x)) = 1] - \Pr[D\,(\mathcal{S}_{\mathcal{V}^*}(1^n, x, z)) = 1] \big| \leq \mathrm{negl}(T(n)),$$

where $(\mathcal{P}(w), \mathcal{V}^*(z))(1^n, x)$ *denotes the view of the verifier* $\mathcal{V}^*$ *after interacting with the honest prover on input security parameter* n, *statement* $x \in L$, *auxiliary input* z, *and* $\mathcal{S}_{\mathcal{V}^*}(1^n, x, z)$ *denotes the output of the simulator* $\mathcal{S}_{\mathcal{V}^*}$ *on input* $(1^n, x, z)$.

We now state our main technical theorem:

Theorem 3. *For any* $T(n)$ *and any* T-*hard language* L, *there does not exist a 2-round argument system* Π *for* L *such that:*

- Π *is (auxiliary-input)* T-*zero-knowledge, and*
- *the soundness of* Π *can be proven via a black-box reduction to a* T-*hard falsifiable assumption,*

unless the assumption is false.

Theorem 3, which we believe to be of independent interest, is also the starting point for our impossibility results for the Fiat-Shamir paradigm (see Section 4.2) and for CS proofs (see Section 4.3).

Proof Idea. Consider a 2-round argument system Π for a T-hard language L that is (auxiliary-input) T-zero-knowledge. We prove, by contradiction, that the soundness of Π cannot be proven via a black-box reduction to a T-hard falsifiable assumption. Let n be a security parameter and suppose that there exists a $\mathrm{poly}(T(n))$-time black-box reduction $\mathcal{R}$ such that given black-box oracle access to any cheating prover $\mathcal{P}^*$, uses this oracle to break a $T(n)$-hard falsifiable assumption. By the definitions of a $T(n)$-hard falsifiable assumption and a black-box reduction, we know the reduction $\mathcal{R}$ runs in time $\mathrm{poly}(T(n))$.

By naturally extending Goldreich and Oren's 2-round zero-knowledge impossibility result [GO94], we first prove that the T-zero-knowledge simulator $\mathcal{S}$ always produces an accepting transcript, even when given a statement $x \in \bar{L}$. Thus, we may view $\mathcal{S}$ as a cheating prover. This means that $\mathcal{R}$ breaks the assumption when given oracle access to $\mathcal{S}$ (and $\mathcal{S}$ is given $x \in \bar{L}$). For brevity, we say that $\mathcal{R}^{\mathcal{S}(x \in \bar{L})}$ breaks the assumption. However, we must be careful because the reduction $\mathcal{R}$ may "lie" about the security parameter and run $\mathcal{S}$ with security parameter $\kappa \neq n$. We denote by n the security parameter of the underlying falsifiable assumption, and denote by κ the security parameter that the reduction $\mathcal{R}$ uses when calling $\mathcal{S}$ (though the reduction $\mathcal{R}$ may call $\mathcal{S}$ many times with different security parameters). Note that the bound on the running time of $\mathcal{R}$ means $\kappa \leq T(n)$.

Our approach is to show that oracle access to $\mathcal{S}(x \in \bar{L}_\kappa)$ can be simulated in time $\mathrm{poly}(T(n))$ regardless of the value of κ. If $\kappa \leq n$ then $\mathcal{S}(x \in \bar{L}_\kappa)$ runs in time $\mathrm{poly}(T(\kappa)) \leq \mathrm{poly}(T(n))$ and we are done. However, if $\kappa > n$ then we show that if $\mathcal{R}^{\mathcal{S}(x \in \bar{L}_\kappa)}$ breaks the assumption then so does $\mathcal{R}^{\mathcal{P}(x \in L_\kappa, w)}$, where w is a valid witness for $x \in L_\kappa$ and $\mathcal{P}$ is the honest prover. Since $\mathcal{P}(x \in L_\kappa, w)$ runs in time $\mathrm{poly}(\kappa) \le \mathrm{poly}(T(n))$, this means we can simulate $\mathcal{S}(x \in \bar{L}_\kappa)$ in time $\mathrm{poly}(T(n))$.

4.2 Black-Box Impossibility for Fiat-Shamir Paradigm

For the sake of simplicity of notation, we present our results for the case of 3-round public-coin protocols. We note that although our techniques generalize to constant-round protocols, the case of 3-rounds already covers many interesting applications of the Fiat-Shamir paradigm.

We start by defining *special honest-verifier (auxiliary-input) T-zero-knowledge*. We will later show the black-box impossibility results for protocols which have this property.

Definition 10. *For any $T = T(n)$, we say that a 3-round public-coin proof (or argument) system $\Pi = (\mathcal{P}, \mathcal{V})$ for an NP language L is (auxiliary-input) special honest-verifier T-zero-knowledge if there exists a simulator $\mathcal{S}(1^n)$ of size $\mathrm{poly}(T(n))$ such that for every $n \in \mathbb{N}$, every instance $x \in L$ of length at most $\mathrm{poly}(n)$ with a corresponding witness w, every auxiliary input $z \in \{0,1\}^{\mathrm{poly}(n)}$, and every random tape β of the verifier it holds that for every non-uniform distinguisher $D = \{D_n\}$ of size $\mathrm{poly}(T(n))$*

$$\left| \Pr[D\left((\mathcal{P}(w), \mathcal{V}(z, \beta))(1^n, x)\right) = 1] - \Pr[D\left(\mathcal{S}(1^n, x, z, \beta)\right) = 1] \right| \le \mathrm{negl}(T(n)),$$

where $(\mathcal{P}(w), \mathcal{V}(z, \beta))(1^n, x)$ denotes the view of the honest verifier $\mathcal{V}$ after interacting with the honest prover on input security parameter n, statement $x \in L$, auxiliary input z, and random tape β, and $\mathcal{S}(1^n, x, z, \beta)$ denotes the output of the simulator $\mathcal{S}$ on the corresponding inputs.

We note that special honest verifier zero knowledge differs from honest verifier zero knowledge since the simulator must successfully simulate the view of the honest verifier for *every* given random tape β.

We now state the main theorem of this section:

Theorem 4. *For any $T(n)$ and any T-hard language L, let Π be a 3-round public-coin proof (or argument) system for $\mathcal{L}$ with $2^{|\beta|} \le T(n)$ which is special honest verifier (auxiliary input) T-zero knowledge. Then, the soundness of the FS-collapse of Π, namely, Π^{FS}, cannot be proven via a black-box reduction to a T-hard falsifiable assumption (unless the assumption is false).*

Note that many public-coin proof (or argument) systems (such as those discussed in Section 4.2) consist of ℓ parallel repetitions of a basic protocol where the length of the verifier's message is a constant number of bits (or may depend logarithmically on the size of the instance x). To save on communication, it is desirable to repeat the protocol only $\ell = \mathrm{poly}\log(n)$ times, since this already achieves negligible soundness error. For such protocols, Theorem 4 implies that if the language L is quasi-polyomially hard, then the Fiat-Shamir transformation applied to this protocol cannot be proven sound via a black-box reduction to a falsifiable assumption.

Given Theorem 4, one may hypothesize that the Fiat-Shamir transformation, when applied to protocols of the type discussed above, can in fact be proven secure (via a black-box reduction to a falsifiable assumption) when the number of parallel repetitions is increased to $\ell = \mathrm{poly}(n)$. However, we show that this is not the case; for many protocols of interest, the impossibility result holds even when the number of repetitions ℓ, is greater than the hardness of the language.

Corollary 2. *Let L be a sub-exponentially hard language and let Π be a 3-round public-coin proof (or argument) system for L with the following properties:*

- *The length of the second message, β, is polynomial in the security parameter, n, and is independent of the length of the instance, x.*
- *Π is special honest verifier (auxiliary input) $2^{|\beta|}$-zero knowledge.*

Then, the soundness of the FS-collapse of Π, namely, Π^{FS}, cannot be proven via a black-box reduction to a $2^{|\beta|}$-hard falsifiable assumption (unless the assumption is false).

Corollary 2 follows from Theorem 4, as follows. Recall that a language is said to be sub-exponentially hard if it is T-hard for $T(n) = 2^n$ (see Definition 8). Namely, if there exist distributions $\mathcal{X}_n$ and $\bar{\mathcal{X}}_n$ over strings of length $\mathrm{poly}(n)$ that are 2^n-indistinguishable, where $\mathcal{X}_n$ is a distribution over instances in the language and $\bar{\mathcal{X}}_n$ is a distribution over instances outside the language. Note that the length of these instances can be much larger than n, and can be of length $n^{1/\epsilon}$ for any constant $\epsilon > 0$.

We argue that any sub-exponentially hard language is also $2^{p(n)}$-hard, for any polynomial p. This follows by simply taking $\mathcal{X}'_n = \mathcal{X}_{p(n)}$ and by taking $\bar{\mathcal{X}}'_n = \bar{\mathcal{X}}_{p(n)}$. Using this observation, Corollary 2 follows immediately from Theorem 4 by choosing $T(n) = 2^{p(n)}$ such that $|\beta| = p(n)$.

Remark 2. It was first observed by Dwork et al. [DNRS99] that if Π is a 3-round public-coin proof (or argument) system for $\mathcal{L}$ that is T-zero-knowledge for $T = \mathrm{poly}(n)$, then the transformed protocol, Π^{FS}, cannot be not sound. In contrast, we prove our results for protocols Π that have *inefficient* zero-knowledge simulators; i.e., simulators that run in T-time, where T is superpolynomial in n. Note, however, that we only require *standard* soundness from Π^{FS}; i.e., we require that Π^{FS} is sound against *efficient*, polynomial-time, adversaries. Thus, our results do not follow from [DNRS99].

Applications of Theorem 4 and Corollary 2. Typically (or at least traditionally), the Fiat-Shamir paradigm is applied to 3-round identification schemes, or more generally to what are called Σ-protocols. All these protocols are special honest-verifier zero-knowledge (see Definition 10). Therefore, Theorem 4 and Corollary 2 imply (black-box) negative results for the Fiat-Shamir paradigm when applied to any such protocol. In what follows we give two specific examples, keeping in mind that there are many other natural examples that we do not mention.

Perfect Zero-Knowledge Protocol for Quadratic Residuosity. Recall the language L_{QR} of quadratic residues.

$$L_{\mathsf{QR}} = \{(N, y) \mid \exists x \in \mathbb{Z}_N^* \text{ s.t. } y = x^2 \mod N\}$$

This language is assumed to be hard w.r.t. distributions $\mathcal{X}_n$ and $\bar{\mathcal{X}}_n$, defined as follows. In both distributions, N is sampled by sampling two random n-bit primes p and q, and setting $N = pq$; in $\mathcal{X}_n$, the element y is a random quadratic residue, and in $\bar{\mathcal{X}}_n$ the element y is a random quadratic non-residue with Jacobi symbol 1.

Recall the well-known *perfect* zero-knowledge Σ-protocol for quadratic residuosity with soundness $1/2$ [Blu81]. We denote by $\Pi^{\ell\text{-QR}}$ the perfect special honest-verifier zero-knowledge protocol consisting of ℓ parallel executions of the basic Σ-protocol. We denote by $\Pi^{\mathsf{FS}(\ell\text{-QR})}$ the protocol obtained when applying the Fiat-Shamir paradigm to $\Pi^{\ell\text{-QR}}$. By applying Corollary 2, we obtain the following theorem:

Theorem 5. *For any* $\ell = \ell(n) = \mathrm{poly}(n)$, *if* L_{QR} *is sub-exponentially hard then the soundness of* $\Pi^{\mathsf{FS}(\ell\text{-QR})}$ *cannot be proven via a black-box reduction to a falsifiable assumption (unless the assumption is false).*

Blum's Zero-Knowledge Protocol for NP. Recall the well-known Σ-protocol for NP of Blum [Blu87], based on the NP-complete problem of Graph Hamiltonicity, with soundness $1/2$. We denote by $\Pi^{\ell\text{-Blum}}$ the special honest-verifier zero-knowledge protocol consisting of ℓ parallel executions of the basic Σ-protocol. Note that $\Pi^{\ell\text{-Blum}}$ is special honest-verifier 2^ℓ-zero-knowledge, if the hiding property of the commitment scheme holds against 2^ℓ-size adversaries.[3]

We denote by $\Pi^{\mathsf{FS}(\ell\text{-Blum})}$ the protocol obtained when applying the Fiat-Shamir paradigm to $\Pi^{\ell\text{-Blum}}$. By applying Corollary 2, we obtain the following theorem:

Theorem 6. *For any* $\ell = \ell(n) = \mathrm{poly}(n)$, *if there exist* NP *languages* L *which are sub-exponentially hard, and if* $\Pi^{\mathsf{FS}(\ell\text{-Blum})}$ *is instantiated with a commitment scheme whose hiding property holds against* 2^ℓ-*size adversaries, then the soundness of* $\Pi^{\mathsf{FS}(\ell\text{-Blum})}$ *cannot be proven via a black-box reduction to a falsifiable assumption (unless the assumption is false).*

As noted above, one can apply Theorem 4 or Corollary 2 to many other Σ protocols (such as the ones based on the DDH assumption or on the N'th residuosity assumption), and obtain (black-box) negative results for the soundness of the resulting protocols obtained by applying the Fiat-Shamir paradigm.

---

[3] Recall that for a protocol to be special honest-verifier 2^ℓ-zero knowledge, the simulated view needs to be 2^ℓ-indistinguishable from the real view (see Definition 10).

Proof Intuition for Theorem 4. Theorem 4 follows from the following lemma and from Theorem 3:

Lemma 1. *Let Π be a 3-round public-coin proof or argument system for a $T(n)$-hard language L with the following properties:*

- *The length of the second message, β, satisfies $2^{|\beta|} \leq T$.*
- *Π is special honest verifier (auxiliary input) T-zero knowledge.*

Then the FS-collapse of Π, namely, Π^{FS} is (auxiliary-input) T-zero-knowledge.

Proof Idea. In order to show that Π^{FS} is (auxiliary-input) T-zero knowledge, we must present a simulator $\mathcal{S}^{FS}$ that simulates the view of every poly-sized circuit $\mathcal{V}^*$. Informally, $\mathcal{S}^{FS}$ does the following:

- Begin an emulation of $\mathcal{V}^*$ and continue until $\mathcal{V}^*$ outputs h^{FS}.
- Choose T^2 random values $\beta_1, \ldots, \beta_{T^2}$
- Invoke $\mathcal{S}$, the special honest verifier T-zero-knowledge simulator for Π, T^2 times on $\beta_1, \ldots, \beta_{T^2}$, receiving transcripts $(\alpha_1, \beta_1, \gamma_1), \ldots, (\alpha_{T^2}, \beta_{T^2}, \gamma_{T^2})$.
- Return the first transcript $(\alpha_i, \beta_i, \gamma_i)$, such that $h^{FS}(\alpha_i) = \beta_i$. If no such transcript exists, return $\bot$.

We show that if there is a distinguisher D of size $\mathrm{poly}(T(n))$ that can distinguish between real and simulated transcripts outputted by $\mathcal{S}^{FS}$, then there is also a distinguisher D^* of size $\mathrm{poly}(T(n))$ that distinguishes between sequences of length T^2 of real and simulated transcripts ouputted by $\mathcal{S}$. This contradicts the special honest verifier (auxiliary-input) T-zero knowledge of Π.

Intuitively, D^* will emulate $\mathcal{S}^{FS}$, but will receive transcripts $(\alpha_i, \beta_i, \gamma_i)$, from an external challenger which are either sampled from the real distribution or which are sampled from $\mathcal{S}$. Then, D^* will run D on the view outputted by the emulation and will output whatever D outputs.

Now, in the case that $(\alpha_i, \beta_i, \gamma_i)$, are sampled from the real distribution, $\mathcal{S}^{FS}$ outputs $\bot$ with negligible (in T) probability. This is the case since in the real distribution, each β_i is independent of α_i and so the probability that $h^{FS}(\alpha_i) \neq \beta_i$ is $1 - 1/T$. Therefore, the probability that for all $1 \leq i \leq T^2$, $h^{FS}(\alpha_i) \neq \beta_i$, is at most $(1 - 1/T)^{T^2}$. Thus when $(\alpha_i, \beta_i, \gamma_i)$, are sampled from the real distribution, the output of D^* is statistically close to a real execution of Π^{FS}.

On the other hand, when $(\alpha_i, \beta_i, \gamma_i)$ are outputted by $\mathcal{S}$, then the output of D^* is identical to the output of $\mathcal{S}^{FS}$. Thus, D, and so also D^*, will distinguish between the two cases.

4.3   Separating CS Proofs from Falsifiable Assumptions

In this section we show that for sufficiently hard NP languages, there exist probabilistically checkable proofs (PCPs) such that Micali's CS proofs [Mic94] instantiated with such a PCP cannot be proven sound (even when the statement is chosen "non-adaptively") via a black-box reduction to any falsifiable assumption.

Let Π^{FS} denote Micali's 2-message CS proof system obtained by applying the Fiat-Shamir transformation to Kilian's succinct argument system [Kil92] Π using $h_s \leftarrow \mathcal{H}$. For any NP language L and any PCP, Π_{pcp}, for L, Micali proved that Π^{FS} is sound in the so called *random oracle model*, where the FS-hash h_s is modeled as a random oracle. We now prove that for every $2^{\ell(n)}$-hard language L, there exists an ℓ-query PCP such that the CS proof Π^{FS} for language L cannot be proven sound via a black-box reduction to any falsifiable assumption. More formally,

Theorem 7. *For all $\ell = \ell(n)$ and any $2^{\ell(n)}$-hard language L, there exists an ℓ-query PCP Π_{pcp} such that the soundness of CS proof Π^{FS} instantiated with Π_{pcp} for language L cannot be proven via a black-box reduction to a $2^{\ell(n)}$-hard falsifiable assumption (unless the assumption is false).*

The following corollary follows easily from Theorem 7.

Corollary 3. *For any sub-exponentially hard language L and for any $\ell = \text{poly}(n)$, there exists an ℓ-query PCP Π_{pcp} such that the soundness of CS proof Π^{FS} instantiated with Π_{pcp} for language L cannot be proven via a black-box reduction to a $2^{\ell(n)}$-hard falsifiable assumption (unless the assumption is false).*

Let L be a $2^{\ell(n)}$-hard language. Our main idea is to show that when Kilian's succinct argument Π is instantiated with a specific PCP (with some zero-knowledge properties), then it is a (special) honest verifier $2^{\ell(n)}$-zero knowledge argument for L, where the verifier's second message is of length at most ℓ. This, when combined with Theorem 4 immediately yields the proof of Theorem 7. Due to lack of space, we defer the proof to the full version [DJKL12].

References

[AABN02] Abdalla, M., An, J.H., Bellare, M., Namprempre, C.: From Identification to Signatures via the Fiat-Shamir Transform: Minimizing Assumptions for Security and Forward-Security. In: Knudsen, L.R. (ed.) EUROCRYPT 2002. LNCS, vol. 2332, pp. 418–433. Springer, Heidelberg (2002)

[BGW12] Bitansky, N., Garg, S., Wichs, D.: Why "fiat-shamir for proofs" lacks a proof. Cryptology ePrint Archive, Report 2012/705 (2012), http://eprint.iacr.org/

[Blu81] Blum, M.: Coin flipping by telephone. In: Proceedings of the 18th Annual International Cryptology Conference, CRYPTO 1981, pp. 11–15 (1981)

[Blu87] Blum, M.: How to prove a theorem so no one else can claim it. In: Proceedings of the International Congress of Mathematicians, pp. 1444–1451 (1987)

[BLV03] Barak, B., Lindell, Y., Vadhan, S.P.: Lower bounds for non-black-box zero knowledge. In: 44th Annual Symposium on Foundations of Computer Science, pp. 384–393. IEEE Computer Society Press (October 2003)

[BR93] Bellare, M., Rogaway, P.: Random oracles are practical: A paradigm for designing efficient protocols. In: Ashby, V. (ed.) ACM CCS 1993: 1st Conference on Computer and Communications Security, pp. 62–73. ACM Press (November 1993)

[Bro05]   Brown, D.R.L.: Breaking rsa may be as difficult as factoring. Cryptology ePrint Archive, Report 2005/380 (2005), http://eprint.iacr.org/

[BV98]   Boneh, D., Venkatesan, R.: Breaking RSA May Not Be Equivalent to Factoring. In: Nyberg, K. (ed.) EUROCRYPT 1998. LNCS, vol. 1403, pp. 59–71. Springer, Heidelberg (1998)

[Cor02]   Coron, J.-S.: Security Proof for Partial-Domain Hash Signature Schemes. In: Yung, M. (ed.) CRYPTO 2002. LNCS, vol. 2442, pp. 613–626. Springer, Heidelberg (2002)

[Cra12]   Cramer, R. (ed.): TCC 2012. LNCS, vol. 7194. Springer, Heidelberg (2012)

[DHT12]   Dodis, Y., Haitner, I., Tentes, A.: On the instantiability of hash-and-sign rsa signatures. In: Cramer [Cra12], pp. 112–132

[DJKL12]   Dachman-Soled, D., Jain, A., Kalai, Y.T., Lopez-Alt, A.: On the (in)security of the fiat-shamir paradigm, revisited. Cryptology ePrint Archive, Report 2012/706 (2012), http://eprint.iacr.org/

[DNRS99]   Dwork, C., Naor, M., Reingold, O., Stockmeyer, L.J.: Magic functions. In: FOCS, pp. 523–534 (1999)

[DOP05]   Dodis, Y., Oliveira, R., Pietrzak, K.: On the Generic Insecurity of the Full Domain Hash. In: Shoup, V. (ed.) CRYPTO 2005. LNCS, vol. 3621, pp. 449–466. Springer, Heidelberg (2005)

[DRV12]   Dodis, Y., Ristenpart, T., Vadhan, S.P.: Randomness condensers for efficiently samplable, seed-dependent sources. In: Cramer [Cra12], pp. 618–635

[FS86]   Fiat, A., Shamir, A.: How to Prove Yourself: Practical Solutions to Identification and Signature Problems. In: Odlyzko, A.M. (ed.) CRYPTO 1986. LNCS, vol. 263, pp. 186–194. Springer, Heidelberg (1987)

[GBL08]   Garg, S., Bhaskar, R., Lokam, S.V.: Improved Bounds on Security Reductions for Discrete Log Based Signatures. In: Wagner, D. (ed.) CRYPTO 2008. LNCS, vol. 5157, pp. 93–107. Springer, Heidelberg (2008)

[GK03]   Goldwasser, S., Kalai, Y.T.: On the (in)security of the Fiat-Shamir paradigm. In: 44th Annual Symposium on Foundations of Computer Science, pp. 102–115. IEEE Computer Society Press (October 2003)

[GMR89]   Goldwasser, S., Micali, S., Rackoff, C.: The knowledge complexity of interactive proof systems. SIAM Journal on Computing 18(1), 186–208 (1989); Preliminary version appeared in STOC 1985.

[GO94]   Goldreich, O., Oren, Y.: Definitions and properties of zero-knowledge proof systems. Journal of Cryptology 7(1), 1–32 (1994)

[GQ90]   Guillou, L.C., Quisquater, J.-J.: A "Paradoxical" Identity-Based Signature Scheme Resulting from Zero-Knowledge. In: Goldwasser, S. (ed.) CRYPTO 1988. LNCS, vol. 403, pp. 216–231. Springer, Heidelberg (1990)

[GW11]   Gentry, C., Wichs, D.: Separating succinct non-interactive arguments from all falsifiable assumptions. In: Fortnow, L., Vadhan, S.P. (eds.) 43rd Annual ACM Symposium on Theory of Computing, pp. 99–108. ACM Press (June 2011)

[HH09]   Haitner, I., Holenstein, T.: On the (Im)Possibility of Key Dependent Encryption. In: Reingold, O. (ed.) TCC 2009. LNCS, vol. 5444, pp. 202–219. Springer, Heidelberg (2009)

[Kil92]   Kilian, J.: A note on efficient zero-knowledge proofs and arguments. In: Proceedings of the 24th Annual ACM Symposium on Theory of Computing, STOC 1992, pp. 723–732 (1992)

[Mic94]   Micali, S.: A secure and efficient digital signature algorithm. Technical Memo MIT/LCS/TM-501b, Massachusetts Institute of Technology, Laboratory for Computer Science (April 1994)

[Mic00]   Micali, S.: Computationally sound proofs. SIAM Journal on Computing 30(4), 1253–1298 (2000); Preliminary version appeared in FOCS 1994

[Nao03]   Naor, M.: On Cryptographic Assumptions and Challenges. In: Boneh, D. (ed.) CRYPTO 2003. LNCS, vol. 2729, pp. 96–109. Springer, Heidelberg (2003)

[Oka93]   Okamoto, T.: Provably Secure and Practical Identification Schemes and Corresponding Signature Schemes. In: Brickell, E.F. (ed.) CRYPTO 1992. LNCS, vol. 740, pp. 31–53. Springer, Heidelberg (1993)

[Pas03]   Pass, R.: Simulation in Quasi-Polynomial Time, and Its Application to Protocol Composition. In: Biham, E. (ed.) EUROCRYPT 2003. LNCS, vol. 2656, pp. 160–176. Springer, Heidelberg (2003)

[Pas11]   Pass, R.: Limits of provable security from standard assumptions. In: Fortnow, L., Vadhan, S.P. (eds.) 43rd Annual ACM Symposium on Theory of Computing, pp. 109–118. ACM Press (June 2011)

[PS00]   Pointcheval, D., Stern, J.: Security arguments for digital signatures and blind signatures. Journal of Cryptology 13(3), 361–396 (2000)

[PV05]   Paillier, P., Vergnaud, D.: Discrete-Log-Based Signatures May Not Be Equivalent to Discrete Log. In: Roy, B. (ed.) ASIACRYPT 2005. LNCS, vol. 3788, pp. 1–20. Springer, Heidelberg (2005)

[Sch91]   Schnorr, C.-P.: Efficient signature generation by smart cards. Journal of Cryptology 4(3), 161–174 (1991)

[Seu12]   Seurin, Y.: On the Exact Security of Schnorr-Type Signatures in the Random Oracle Model. In: Pointcheval, D., Johansson, T. (eds.) EUROCRYPT 2012. LNCS, vol. 7237, pp. 554–571. Springer, Heidelberg (2012)

[Wic12]   Wichs, D.: Barriers in cryptography with weak, correlated and leaky sources. Cryptology ePrint Archive, Report 2012/459 (2012), http://eprint.iacr.org/

On the (In)security of Fischlin's Paradigm

Prabhanjan Ananth[1], Raghav Bhaskar[1], Vipul Goyal[1], and Vanishree Rao[2]

[1] Microsoft Research India
prabhanjan.va@gmail.com, {rbhaskar,vipul}@microsoft.com
[2] Department of Computer Science, UCLA
vanishri@cs.ucla.edu

Abstract. The Fiat-Shamir paradigm was proposed as a way to remove interaction from 3-round proof of knowledge protocols and derive secure signature schemes. This generic transformation leads to very efficient schemes and has thus grown quite popular. However, this transformation is proven secure only in the random oracle model. In FOCS 2003, Goldwasser and Kalai showed that this transformation is provably insecure in the standard model by presenting a counterexample of a 3-round protocol, the Fiat-Shamir transformation of which is (although provably secure in the random oracle model) insecure in the standard model, thus showing that the random oracle is uninstantiable. In particular, for every hash function that is used to replace the random oracle, the resulting signature scheme is existentially forgeable. This result was shown by relying on the non-black-box techniques of Barak (FOCS 2001).

An alternative to the Fiat-Shamir paradigm was proposed by Fischlin in Crypto 2005. Fischlin's transformation can be applied to any so called 3-round "Fiat-Shamir proof of knowledge" and can be used to derive non-interactive zero-knowledge proofs of knowledge as well as signature schemes. An attractive property of this transformation is that it provides online extractability (i.e., the extractor works without having to rewind the prover). Fischlin remarks that in comparison to the Fiat-Shamir transformation, his construction tries to "decouple the hash function from the protocol flow" and hence, the counterexample in the work of Goldwaaser and Kalai does not seem to carry over to this setting.

In this work, we show a counterexample to the Fischlin's transformation. In particular, we construct a 3-round Fiat-Shamir proof of knowledge (on which Fischlin's transformation is applicable), and then, present an adversary against both - the soundness of the resulting non-interactive zero-knowledge, as well as the unforegeability of the resulting signature scheme. Our attacks are successful except with negligible probability for any hash function, that is used to instantiate the random oracle, provided that there is an apriori (polynomial) bound on the running time of the hash function. By choosing the right bound, secure instantiation of Fischlin transformation with most practical cryptographic hash functions can be ruled out.

The techniques used in our work are quite unrelated to the ones used in the work of Goldwasser and Kalai. Our primary technique is to bind the protocol flow with the hash function if the code of the hash function is available. We believe that our ideas are of independent interest and maybe applicable in other related settings.

A. Sahai (Ed.): TCC 2013, LNCS 7785, pp. 202–221, 2013.

1   Introduction

The Fiat-Shamir paradigm [FS86] was proposed as a way to remove interaction from 3-round proof of knowledge protocols and derive secure signature schemes. It is a generic transformation which leads to quite efficient schemes thus making it quite popular. The security of this transformation was later analyzed under the ideal assumption that the hash function behaves as a random oracle [BR93, PS00]. Thus, the resulting non-interactive proofs and signature scheme are automatically secure in the random oracle model. Several signature schemes (with the best known ones being [Sch91, GQ88, Oka92]) were constructed following the Fiat-Shamir paradigm. It has also been useful in obtaining forward secure schemes and improving the tightness of security reductions [AABN02, MR02].

Random oracle model can be seen as a methodology to design secure cryptographic systems in two steps: first construct and analyze a scheme assuming only oracle access to the random function. Then, find a suitable hash function and instantiate the previous construction with that to get a real world secure cryptographic system.

For the Fiat-Shamir paradigm, Goldwasser and Kalai [GK03] showed that unfortunately the second step of the design methodology cannot be carried out. In particular, they show that the Fiat-Shamir transformation is uninstantiable in the real world: regardless of the choice of the hash function, the resulting signature scheme is insecure. To do this, they first gave a construction of a 3-round identification scheme based on the non-black-box simulation techniques of Barak [Bar01], and then showed that the resulting signature scheme is universally forgeable for any hash function.

An alternative to the Fiat-Shamir paradigm was proposed by Fischlin [Fis05]. Fischlin's transformation can be applied to any so called 3-round "Fiat-Shamir proof of knowledge" and can be used to derive non-interactive zero-knowledge proofs of knowledge as well as signature schemes. An attractive property of this transformation is that it provides online extractability. In other words, just by observing queries a (possibly malicious) prover makes to the random oracle, an extractor is guaranteed to be able to output the witness of the statement being proven (except with negligible probability). This is in contrast to Fiat-Shamir transformation where an extractor must work by rewinding the prover. This property is quite useful while using the resulting non-interactive schemes in larger systems. Fischlin also shows applications of his transformation in constructing group signature schemes [BBS04].

Even though the purpose of Fischlin's transformation is quite similar to that of Fiat-Shamir, the transformation itself is quite different. Fiat-Shamir transformation is applied on a 3 round public coin proof of knowledge protocol and works as follows. Prover sends a commitment to the verifier, the verifier sends back a random challenge, and, the prover finally responds to that challenge. In the transformed non-interactive protocol, the challenge of the verifier is generated by applying the random oracle to the first message (i.e., the commitment) of the prover. The non-interactive scheme is secure in the random oracle model since getting the challenge from the random oracle is similar to getting it from the external verifier; both challenges will be unpredictable to a malicious prover and trying again any polynomial number of times does not help.

Goldwasser and Kalai [GK03] showed insecurity of the Fiat-Shamir paradigm by relying the breakthrough work of Barak [Bar01]. Indeed it seems (in retrospect) that the non-black-box simulation techniques of Barak fits in quite well to show insecurity of the Fiat-Shamir paradigm:

- In the Fiat-Shamir paradigm, the verifier basically just acts as a hash function (i.e., the verifier message is computed by simply evaluating the hash function on the incoming prover message).
- Hence, having oracle access to the hash function is similar to having a black-box access to the verifier, while, having the code of the hash function directly translates to having non-black-box access to the verifier.
- Barak's techniques yield a zero-knowledge protocol which is secure given only black-box access to the verifier (in other words, a scheme which is *resettably-sound* [BGGL01]), but becomes insecure given non-black-box access to the verifier.

We remark that even though the above idea is the starting point towards showing insecurity of the Fiat-Shamir paradigm in [GK03], this by itself is not sufficient. This is because Barak's techniques do not yield a 3-round protocol. Goldwasser and Kalai make use of a number of additional tools and ideas; please refer to [GK03] for more details.

The above high level idea completely breaks down in the context of Fischlin's transformation. As Fischlin remarks [Fis05], "in comparison to the Fiat-Shamir transformation, this construction somewhat decouples the hash function from the protocol flow". In other words, the prover and the verifier messages of the underlying scheme are computed as specified in the underlying scheme; not by making use of the hash function in any way. The hash function is only used to make some final checks on the resulting transcript of interaction. Hence, as observed by Fischlin, the counterexample in [GK03] does not seem to carry over to this setting [Fis05]. This raises the following natural question.

"Is there a concrete hash function using which Fischlin transformation can be securely instantiated?"

Our Results. In this work, we give a partial answer to the above question. More specifically, we prove the following.

"There does not exist any hash function, whose running time is bounded by an apriori fixed polynomial, using which Fischlin transformation can be securely instantiated."

One can interpret the above result in two different ways. Firstly, the bound on the running time will typically be chosen to be a large polynomial in the security parameter. By choosing a large bound, we can rule out the instantiation of Fischlin transformation with widely used hash functions such as SHA-1. Another interpretation is that, given *any* hash function, we can construct a (3-round

Fiat-Shamir proof of knowledge) protocol such the the following holds. When Fischlin's transformation is applied on this protocol and instantiated using this hash function, the resulting signature scheme as well the non-interactive zero-knowledge scheme is completely insecure.

We note that the above does not invalidate the original security proof of Fischlin's transformation in any way (which are provided only in the random oracle model). No claims regarding the security of the transformation, once the hash function is instantiated are made in [Fis05]. Fischlin explicitly acknowledges the possibility of such a result in the introduction of his paper [Fis05].

1.1   Technical Overview

Before we discuss the techniques involved in our work, we briefly sketch Fischlin's transformation in the following.

Fischlin's Transformation. Fischlin [Fis05] proposed an approach to transform any Fiat-Shamir proof of knowledge (as defined in Section 2) to a non-interactive zero knowledge proof of knowledge in the random oracle model. The basic idea of his transformation is given in the following. The transformed prover (of the non-interactive zero-knowledge scheme) roughly works as follows.

- In the underlying Fiat-Shamir proof of knowledge, the challenge space is restricted to be of polynomial size (i.e., the challenge string of the verifier will be of logarithmic length). The protocol begins by executing a super-constant number of parallel copies of the honest prover of the underlying Fiat-Shamir proof of knowledge.
- For each parallel execution i, the prover computes the commitment α_i (i.e., the first message).
- For all possible (polynomially many) challenges β_i starting from 0 the prover performs the following test. It checks whether a fixed number (depending on the security parameter) of least significant bits of $\mathcal{O}((\alpha_1, \ldots, \alpha_r), i, \beta_i, \gamma_i)$ are all 0. Here γ_i is the prover's response to the challenge β_i and $\mathcal{O}$ denotes the random oracle. If the test passes, the prover fixes β_i to be the challenge for session i.
- Finally, the transcript $(\alpha_i, \beta_i, \gamma_i)$ corresponding to every execution i is output as the proof.
- Verifier accepts the proof only if: (a) the transcript for every execution is accepted by the verifier of the underlying Fiat-Shamir proof of knowledge, and, (b) for all executions, the least significant bits of the random oracle invocation come out to be all 0 (as described above). [1]

The above construction retains the completeness property: except with negligible probability, for each execution, there will be at least one challenge β_i for which the random oracle outputs 0 (in the relevant bits).

---

[1] This is actually the simplified version of the final construction in [Fis05]. Our results apply to both the variants.

The construction provides soundness for the following reasons. If the statement is false, for each α_i, there is a single challenge β_i for which a satisfying response γ_i can be given. Consider the vector of first messages chosen by the adversary $(\alpha_1, \ldots, \alpha_r)$. Except with negligible probability, there will exist at least one i such that $\mathcal{O}((\alpha_1, \ldots, \alpha_r), i, \beta_i, \gamma_i)$ does not have its required bits to be all 0. Once that happens, the adversary will have to change α_i (and hence the vector $(\alpha_1, \ldots, \alpha_r)$ changes). Thus, adversary has to essentially restart its effort to produce a false proof (and again it will only be successful with negligible probability).

Thus, it is crucial to have the entire vector $(\alpha_1, \ldots, \alpha_r)$ as part of the input to the random oracle. Even if the adversary fails to obtain the required 0's even in a single execution, it has to start again from scratch. See section 2 for more details.

Our Ideas. Recall that the verifier accepts the proof only if: (a) the transcript for every execution is accepted by the verifier of the underlying Fiat-Shamir proof of knowledge, and, (b) for all executions, the least significant bits of the random oracle invocation come out to be all 0. Normally, these two tests will be "independent and uncorrelated". This is because no random oracle invocations are involved in the first test (the underlying Fiat-Shamir proof of knowledge protocol does not make use of random oracles). However once the code of the hash function is available, it can be used in the underlying protocol *making the two tests correlated.* In fact, in our construction, the two tests will end up being *identical.* This would allow an adversarial prover to succeed (using the description of the hash function). Below we provide a very high level overview of our main idea.

- Observe that in the final transcript being output, for each session i, adversary needs to include an accepting response for just a single challenge β_i (for which the random oracle output has 0 in all required positions). What if somehow magically, adversary exactly has the capability to come up with an accepting response for just this β_i (note that adversary can have the capability of creating an accepting response just for a single challenge)?

- To achieve the following, we take any Fiat-Shamir proof of knowledge and then add another "mode of execution" to it. In this mode, the prover doesn't need the witness to execute the protocol. However the verifier's test is such that for each α_i, there is a single β_i for which verifier accepts. Hence, the protocol still maintains the special soundness property. This new protocol will be the underlying protocol on which Fischlin's transformation will be applied.

- Now we sketch the test the verifier performs in this second mode. The prover will be free to send any hash function to the verifier as part of α_i. Using this hash function, the verifier is instructed to compute the only acceptable β_i for this α_i. If that is the challenge he chose, the verifier is instructed to accept (and reject otherwise).

- The acceptable β_i is the first possible challenge (lexicographically) such that $H\big((\alpha_1, \ldots, \alpha_i, \ldots \alpha_r), i, \beta_i, \gamma_i\big)$ has 0 in all the required positions (where H is the hash function chosen by the prover).
- Now if the hash function H is the same as the random oracle, we have that the second test (by the verifier of the non-interactive proof) is satisfied for free. Hence, by running in the second mode, soundness of the non-interactive scheme can be violated.

There are several problems with this basic idea. To start with, the verifier of the (interactive) Fiat-Shamir protocol that we constructed is unaware of any other sessions. Whether or not it accepts should only be decided by the transcript of this session. However the test $H\big((\alpha_1, \ldots, \alpha_i, \ldots \alpha_r), i, \beta_i, \gamma_i\big)$ requires the knowledge of the first prover messages in all other sessions (we resolve this problem by having a construction in which a first prover message for one session can be used to compute first prover messages for the other sessions). Secondly, note that the random oracle instantiation could be done by any (possibly adversarial) hash function. Since the transcript of interaction in mode 1 and mode 2 may be easily distinguishable, the hash function may never give output having 0 in the relevant places for mode 2 messages (we solve this problem by employing encryption in a deterministic way using shared public randomness). The final construction is given in Section 3.

We note that once we have an adversary to violate soundness of the non-interactive zero-knowledge scheme, it is also easy to design a forger for the resulting signature scheme.

Further Comments. We note that Fischlin's transformation could still be secure in the following sense. For every protocol (on which Fischlin's transformation can be applied), there exists a hash function, whose running time depends upon the parameters of the protocol (in particular upon the running time of the parties in the protocol) such that the following happens. The signature scheme (and non-interactive zero-knowledge scheme) obtained by applying Fischlin's transformation on this protocol, when instantiated with this hash function, is secure in the plain model. However we note that the hash function used to instantiate the scheme has to be dependent on the protocol. In particular, one cannot use a fixed hash function (such as SHA-256) to instantiate the resulting schemes.

Furthermore, Fischlin's construction could still be instantiated if there are no shared public parameters between the prover and the verifier. As with the counterexample for the Fiat-Shamir transformation [GK03], our construction is in the setting where the prover and the verifier share some public parameters[2]. We also sketch an extension of our main construction to the setting where the prover and the verifier have no prior communication/setup in Section 4. In this setting, our results are only valid for the class of hash function whose output is pseudorandom. Indeed, it is natural to think of the random oracle being instantiated by a pseudorandom function. We leave getting an unrestricted result in this setting as an open problem.

---

[2] Note that none of the parties need to trust the public parameters for their security.

Related Works. A number of works have investigated the difference in the settings: where one only has oracle access to a primitive v/s having the full code of the primitive. These lines of research include ones on program obfuscation [BGI+01, GK05], non-black-box simulation techniques [Bar01, Pas04, DGS09], uninstantiabilty of constructions in the random oracle model [CGH04], etc.

2   Fischlin Transformation

In this section, we shall review the Fischlin transformation. We begin by stating the preliminaries. Throughout the paper, we denote the security parameter by k. A function $f : \mathbb{N} \to \mathbb{R}^+ \cup \{0\}$ is said to be negligible (in its input) if, for any constant $c > 0$, there exists a constant, $k_0 \in \mathbb{N}$, such that $f(k) < (1/k)^c$ for any $k > k_0$. We let $f(k) = negl(k)$ denote that $f(k)$ is a negligible function. We say that function is non-negligible if it is not negligible; namely, we say that $f(\cdot)$ is non-negligible in its input if there is constant c ¿ 0 such that for infinitely many k, it holds $f(k) \geq (1/k)^c$. For a probabilistic polynomial time algorithm $\mathcal{A}$, we use the notation $y \leftarrow \mathcal{A}(x)$ to denote $\mathcal{A}$ outputting y on input x. We use the notation $\Pr[E] \gtrsim 1$ to indicate that the probability of the event E is negligibly close to 1. Similarly, the notation $\Pr[E] \gtrsim 0$ is used to indicate that the probability of the event E is neglibly close to 0.

In this paper, we scrutinize the "real-world" security of protocols that are proven secure in the random oracle model. In the random oracle model, all the parties have access to a purely random function (i.e., a mapping that maps every input to an output that is distributed uniformly random in a range space whose size is dependent on the security parameter. We denote the random oracle by $\mathcal{O}$.

Fischlin transformation converts a 3-round zero-knowledge proof of knowledge, termed as Fiat-Shamir proof of knowledge, to a non-interactive zero-knowledge proof of knowledge proven secure in the random oracle model. In what follows we shall review the formal definitions for both Fiat-Shamir proof of knowledge as well as non-interactive zero-knowledge proof of knowledge as defined in [Fis05].

Definition 1. *A Fiat-Shamir proof of knowledge (with $O(\log(k))$-bit challenges) for a witness relation W is a pair (P, V) of probabilistic polynomial time algorithms $P = (P_0, P_1), V = (V_0, V_1)$ with the following properties.*

[Completeness]. For any parameter k, $(x, w) \in W_k$, $(\alpha, \beta, \gamma) \leftarrow (P(x, w), V_0(x))$ it holds $V_1(x, \alpha, \beta, \gamma) = \mathsf{Accept}$.

[Commitment Entropy]. For parameter k, for any $(x, w) \in W_k$, the min-entropy of $\alpha \leftarrow P_0(x, w)$ is superlogarithmic in k.

[Public Coin]. For any k, any $(x, w) \in W_k$, any $\alpha \leftarrow P_0(x, w)$, the challenge $\beta \leftarrow V_0(x, \alpha)$ is uniform on $\{0, 1\}^{l(k)}$.

[Unique responses]. For any probabilistic polynomial time algorithm A, for parameter k and $(x, \alpha, \beta, \gamma, \gamma') \leftarrow A(k)$, we have, as a function of k,

$$Pr[V_1(x, \alpha, \beta, \gamma) = V_1(x, \alpha, \beta, \gamma') = \mathsf{Accept} \wedge \gamma \neq \gamma'] \approx 0$$

[Special Soundness]. There exists a probabilistic polynomial time algorithm K, the knowledge extractor, such that for any k, any $(x, w) \in W_k$, any pairs (α, β, γ), $(\alpha, \beta', \gamma')$ with $V_1(x, \alpha, \beta, \gamma) = V_1(x, \alpha, \beta', \gamma') = \mathsf{Accept}$ and $\beta \neq \beta'$, for $w' \leftarrow K(x, \alpha, \beta, \gamma, \beta', \gamma')$ it holds $(x, w') \in W_k$.

[Honest-Verifier Zero-Knowledge]. There exists a probabilistic polynomial time algorithm Z, the zero-knowledge simulator, such that for any pair of probabilistic polynomial time algorithms $D = (D_0, D_1)$ the following distributions are computationally indistinguishable:

- Let $(x, w, \delta) \leftarrow D_0(k)$ and $(\alpha, \beta, \gamma) \leftarrow (P(x, w), V_0(x))$ if $(x, w) \in W_k$ and $(\alpha, \beta, \gamma) \leftarrow \perp$ otherwise. Output $D_1(\alpha, \beta, \gamma, \delta)$.
- Let $(x, w, \delta) \leftarrow D_0(k)$ and $(\alpha, \beta, \gamma) \leftarrow Z(x, \mathsf{YES})$ if $(x, w) \in W_k$ and $(\alpha, \beta, \gamma) \leftarrow Z(x, \mathsf{NO})$. Output $D_1(\alpha, \beta, \gamma, \delta)$.

Definition 2. *A pair (P, V) of probabilistic polynomial time algorithms is called a non-interactive zero-knowledge proof of knowledge for relation W with an online extractor (in the random oracle model) if the following holds.*
[Completeness] For any oracle $\mathcal{O}$, any $(x, w) \in W_k$ and any $\pi \leftarrow P^{\mathcal{O}}(x, w)$, we have $Pr[V^{\mathcal{O}}(x, \pi) = \mathsf{Accept}] \gtrsim 1$.
[Zero-knowledge] There exist a pair of probabilistic polynomial time algorithms $Z = (Z_0, Z_1)$, the zero-knowledge simulator, such that for any pair of probabilistic polynomial time algorithms $D = (D_0, D_1)$, the following distributions are computationally indistinguishable:

- Let $\mathcal{O}$ be a random oracle, $(x, w, \delta) \leftarrow D_0^{\mathcal{O}}(k)$, and $\pi \leftarrow P^{\mathcal{O}}(x, w)$ where $(x, w) \in W_k$. Output $D_1^{\mathcal{O}}(\pi, \delta)$.
- Let $(\mathcal{O}_0, \sigma) \leftarrow Z_0(k)$, $(x, w, \delta) \leftarrow D_0^{\mathcal{O}_0}(k)$ and $(\mathcal{O}_1, \pi) \leftarrow Z_1(\sigma, x)$. Output $D_1^{\mathcal{O}_1}(\pi, \delta)$.

[Online Extractor]. There exists a probabilistic polynomial time algorithm K, the online extractor, such that the following holds for any algorithm A. Let $\mathcal{O}$ be a random oracle, $(x, \pi) \leftarrow A^{\mathcal{O}}(k)$ and $Q_{\mathcal{O}}(A)$ be the sequence of queries of A to $\mathcal{O}$ and $\mathcal{O}$'s answers. Let $w \leftarrow K(x, \pi, Q_{\mathcal{O}}(A))$. Then, as a function of k,

$$Pr[(x, w) \notin W_k \wedge V^{\mathcal{O}}(x, \pi) = \mathsf{Accept}] \approx 0$$

We are now ready to give a formal description of the Fischlin transformation.

Fischlin Transformation. Let (P_{FS}, V_{FS}) be an interactive Fiat-Shamir proof of knowledge with challenges of $l = l(k) = O(\log(k))$ bits for a relation W. Define the parameters b, r, S, t as the number of test bits, repetitions, maximum sum and trial bits such that $br = \omega(\log(k))$, $t - b = \omega(\log(k))$, $b, r, t = O(\log(k))$, $S = O(r)$ and $b \le t \le l$. Define the following non-interactive proof system for relation W in the random oracle model where the random oracle maps to b bits.

Prover: The prover $P^{\mathcal{O}}$ on input (x, w), first runs the prover $P_{FS}(x, w)$ in r independent repetitions to obtain r commitments $(\alpha_1, \ldots, \alpha_r)$. Then $P^{\mathcal{O}}$ does the following, either sequentially or in parallel for each repetition i. For each $\beta_i = 0, 1, \ldots, 2^t - 1$ it lets P_{FS} compute the final responses γ_i by rewinding, until it finds the first one such that $\mathcal{O}(x, (\alpha_1, \ldots, \alpha_r), i, \beta_i, \gamma_i) = 0^b$, if no such tuple is found then $P^{\mathcal{O}}$ picks the first one for which the hash value is minimal among all 2^t hash values. The prover finally outputs $\pi = (\alpha_i, \beta_i, \gamma_i)_{i=1,\ldots,r}$.

Verifier: The verifier $V^{\mathcal{O}}$ on input x and $\pi = (\alpha_i, \beta_i, \gamma_i)_{i=1,\ldots,r}$ accepts if and only if $V_{1,FS}(x, \alpha_i, \beta_i, \gamma_i) = \mathsf{Accept}$ (*first test*) for each $i \in [r]$ and if $\sum_{i=1}^{r} \mathcal{O}(x, (\alpha_1, \ldots, \alpha_r), i, \beta_i, \gamma_i) \le S$ (*second test*).

We shall now briefly review the proof of security (in the random oracle model) of the Fischlin transformation. We shall begin by arguing completeness. We need to show that the (honest) prover fails to convince the verifier only with negligible probability. From the completeness property of the underlying Fiat-Shamir proof of knowledge, the proof produced by the honest prover passes the first test with probability 1. It can be shown that the probability that the proof passes the second test is negligibly close to 1 by the following two basic arguments:

- Probability that at least in one of the r repititions the smallest hash value that the prover obtains is $> S$ is negligible. Hence, with all but negligible probability the sum of the hash values $\le rS$.
- By a basic combinatorial argument, the sum of the hash values $> S$ and $\le rS$ only with negligible probability. Hence, the sum is $\le S$ with all but negligible probability.

From this, it can be seen that the honest prover passes the second test with probability negligibly close to 1.

We now prove that the protocol satisfies online extractability (which in turn implies soundness). Consider an adversarial prover who produces a proof given just the input instance. The claim is that except with negligible probability the proof is rejected by the verifier. Consider a particular commitment tuple $(\alpha_1, \ldots, \alpha_r)$. Observe that in the queries made by the adversarial prover to the random oracle there cannot be two accepting transcripts of the form $((\alpha_1, \ldots, \alpha_r), i, \beta, \gamma)$ and $((\alpha_1, \ldots, \alpha_r), i, \beta', \gamma')$ because then the special soundness property of the underlying Fiat-Shamir proof of knowledge would imply that the adversary has the witness for the input instance. Hence, corresponding to each repetition i and commitment tuple $(\alpha_1, \ldots, \alpha_r)$, the adversary can query the random oracle for at most one challenge β_i. Let s_i be the value output by the random oracle for this particular β_i. With negligible probability, the summation of s_i over all the repetitions is at most S. This is because, there are only polynomially many (in the security parameter) possible tuples $(s'_1, \ldots, s'_r)$ whose summation is at most S and since s_i is picked uniformly at random, the probability that the sum of s_i is at most S is $poly(k).negl(k)$ which is also negligible in k. This means that the adversary has negligible probability of succeeding for a given $(\alpha_1, \ldots, \alpha_r)$. Since, the adversary can try only polynomially many such commitment tuples, it is only with negligible probability that it can produce an accepting proof.

Fischlin showed that the non-interactive zero-knowledge proof of knowledge obtained from his construction can be used to construct signature schemes which are secure. The signature scheme derived from his construction was shown to be existentially unforgeable against adaptive chosen message attacks in the random oracle model.

In this paper, we give a construction of 3-round Fiat-Shamir proof of knowledge protocol such that the resulting protocol obtained after applying Fischlin transformation does not satisfy soundness in the real-world. And hence, note that the security of the signature scheme built over this non-interactive protocol (which is the output of Fischlin transformation) also breaks down.

3 Our Construction

Our goal is to construct a Fiat-Shamir proof of knowledge (P^*, V^*) for some witness relation such that the non-interactive protocol obtained after applying the Fischlin transformation to it is insecure when the random oracle is instantiated with a hash function ensemble containing functions whose running time is apriori bounded by some polynomial. We now give the intuition about the construction of proof of knowledge (P^*, V^*). We first consider a Fiat-Shamir proof of knowledge (P, V) from which we build (P^*, V^*). The verifier V^* is basically V with its verdict function extended so as to also accept in the case when the challenge equals the output of some pre-determined function, denoted by least (defined later). The function least takes the first message as input and returns a challenge. As the verifier chooses the challenge uniformly at random, it is only with low probability that the challenge equals the output of least of the first message. This, together with the fact that (P, V) is sound, implies that (P^*, V^*) satisfies soundness property. However, in the non-interactive protocol obtained by applying Fischlin transformation to (P^*, V^*), denoted by $(P^{\mathcal{O}}, V^{\mathcal{O}})$, the prover himself is supposed to compute the challenge messages. However, the probability that any adversarial prover succeeds in producing an accepting proof is negligible from the security proof of the Fischlin transformation. But when the random oracle $\mathcal{O}$ in $(P^{\mathcal{O}}, V^{\mathcal{O}})$ is instantiated by a hash function h drawn from a hash function ensemble to get (P_h, V_h) we can construct an adversary to violate the soundness of (P_h, V_h) as follows. The adversarial prover first makes the least function dependent on machine M, which implements the instantiated hash function h, in such a way that the first test and the second test become identical. The adversary then produces an accepting proof by setting the challenges in each repetition to be the output of the least function of the first message and thus succeeds in passing the first test and hence the second test too. We now give details of the construction below:

Let (P, V) be a Fiat-Shamir proof of knowledge for a relation W. We use two main tools for our construction, namely, a CPA symmetric encryption scheme $E = (\mathsf{KeyGen}, \mathsf{Enc}, \mathsf{Dec})$ and a pseudorandom function family $\mathcal{F}$. Before we describe the protocol, we make the following assumption: In all the executions of the protocol, the prover and the verifier have access to a string which is generated by a Setup algorithm. The Setup algorithm takes 1^k as input and executes KeyGen to obtain SK. It further chooses a key K uniformly at random to choose a function from the pseudorandom function family $\mathcal{F}$. Finally, $(\mathsf{SK}, \mathsf{K})$ is output by Setup.[3] The output of the Setup is used in the following way. Each time the prover or the verifier needs to encrypt a message m, they proceed as follows. Compute $f_\mathsf{K}(m)$ (where f_K is the function in $\mathcal{F}$ corresponding to key K) to obtain r. To encrypt m, execute the algorithm Enc with inputs m, SK and r. Unless explicitly mentioned, by $\mathsf{Enc}(m)$ we mean that m is encrypted using key SK and randomness $f_\mathsf{K}(m)$. This means that $\mathsf{Enc}(m)$ gives the same ciphertext every time it is executed. If we intend to use a different randomness, we use the notation $\mathsf{Enc}(m : R)$ to mean that m is encrypted using the randomness R. When the prover or the verifier wants to decrypt a message m they execute Dec with input m and key SK. Jumping ahead, we need to encrypt messages because the hash function used to instantiate the random oracle might have the code of the verifier V embedded in it. In this case the hash function may output values depending whether the input transcripts are accepting or rejecting. To make our security proof go through we need to make sure the hash function does not have the capability to distinguish the transcripts. We can ensure this by encrypting the messages of the prover (The Setup algorithm is considered to be a part of the interaction between a specific prover and a verifier; the hash function used to instantiate the random oracle is independent of the output of the Setup algorithm). We now proceed to describe the protocol.

As discussed before, we will first consider a Fiat-Shamir proof of knowledge (P, V). We assume that the prover P in (P, V) can be decomposed into P_0 and P_1, where $P_0(x, w)$ outputs the commitment α and $P_1(x, w, \alpha, \beta)$ outputs γ. Similarly, the verifier V can be decomposed into V_0 and V_1 such that V_0 interacts with P (by outputting β on input some (x, α)) to produce the transcript (α, β, γ) and then V accepts if and only if $V_1(\alpha, \beta, \gamma)$ accepts. We use the symbols r, b, t as defined in the Fischlin construction (c.f. Section 2). We denote the least significant l bits of $M(\mathbf{y})$ by $M(\mathbf{y})^{(l)}$.

Our protocol is parameterized by a polynomial p_{hash}. We are now ready to describe the protocol (P^*, V^*) for the relation W.

Protocol (P^*, V^*):

---

[3] We note that neither the prover nor the verifier needs to place any trust in the setup algorithm for their security. The reason to have $(\mathsf{SK}, \mathsf{K})$ as the public parameters (as opposed to the part of protocol messages) will become clear later on.

1. P^*: Run P_0 on (x, w) to obtain α. Define $\alpha^* = \mathsf{Enc}((\alpha, i, \mathsf{bit}, \mathsf{M}))$, where each of $i, \mathsf{bit}, \mathsf{M}$ is set to 0, with their lengths being $\log(r)$ bits, 1 bit, and $|x|$ bits, respectively[4]. Send α^* to V^*.
[Note: Looking ahead, in the protocol obtained by first applying Fischlin transformation to (P^*, V^*) and then instantiating it with the hash function, the adversary will set i to be the repetition number, bit to be 1 and M to be the hash function instantiating the random oracle.]

2. V^*: Execute $\mathsf{Dec}(\alpha^*)$ to obtain α_1 which is then parsed as $(\alpha, i, \mathsf{bit}, M)$. Run V_0 on input (x, α) to obtain β. Send β to P^*.

3. P^*: Run P_1 on input (x, w, α, β) to obtain γ. Send $\gamma^* = \mathsf{Enc}(\gamma)$ to V^*.

V^* then decides to accept or reject the transcript $(x, \alpha^*, \beta, \gamma^*)$ by executing the following.

   i. Let $\alpha_1 \leftarrow \mathsf{Dec}(\alpha^*)$ and $\gamma \leftarrow \mathsf{Dec}(\gamma^*)$.
   ii. Parse α_1 to be $(\alpha, i, \mathsf{bit}, M)$.
   iii. If $\mathsf{bit} = 0$ then Accept if and only if $V_0(x, \alpha, \beta, \gamma)$ accepts and $\gamma^* = \mathsf{Enc}(\gamma)$.
     [Note: Recall that $\mathsf{Enc}(m)$ is the encryption of m using the randomness $f_K(m)$. Hence, the check $\gamma^* = \mathsf{Enc}(\gamma)$ ensures that γ^* is indeed the encryption of γ using the randomness $f_K(\gamma)$. Looking ahead, this will be helpful to make the protocol satisfy the unique responses property.]
   iv. Else, do the following. If M is not a valid Turing machine then Reject. Otherwise, Accept if both the following conditions hold:
     • $\beta = \mathsf{least}(x, \alpha, i, M)$.
     • $\gamma^* = \mathsf{Enc}((i, \beta))$.

where the least procedure is defined below.

$\mathsf{least}(x, \alpha, i, M)$:

1. $\mathsf{min} \leftarrow 2^b + 1$
2. $\beta \leftarrow null$
3. For $j = 0$ to $2^t - 1$:
4. $y \leftarrow \Big(x, (\mathsf{Enc}((\alpha, 1, 1, M)), \ldots, \mathsf{Enc}((\alpha, r, 1, M)), i, j, \mathsf{Enc}((i, j))) \Big)$
5.   Execute $M(y)$ upto $p_{\mathsf{hash}}(|y|)$ steps
6.   If $M(y)$ terminates within $p_{\mathsf{hash}}(|y|)$ steps:
7. $\mathsf{hash} \leftarrow M(y)^{(b)}$
8.   If $\mathsf{min} > \mathsf{hash}$:
9. $\mathsf{min} \leftarrow \mathsf{hash}$
10. $\beta \leftarrow j$
11. Return β.

---

[4] Hereafter, unless specified otherwise, we maintain that the lengths of bit, i are specified above, and in every instance where we set M to 0, it is of length $|x|$.

The least algorithm does the following. It checks for what values of j from 0 to $2^t - 1$, the last b bits of $\mathsf{M}\Big(x, (\mathsf{Enc}((\alpha, 1, 1, \mathsf{M})), \ldots, \mathsf{Enc}((\alpha, r, 1, \mathsf{M})), i, j, \mathsf{Enc}((i, j))\Big)$ takes the minimum value among all possible 2^t values provided M terminates within $p_{\mathsf{hash}}\Big(\big|x, \mathsf{Enc}((\alpha, 1, 1, \mathsf{M})), \ldots, \mathsf{Enc}((\alpha, r, 1, \mathsf{M})), i, j, \mathsf{Enc}((i, j))\big|\Big)$ steps. If there are many values of j for which the hash function maps to the minimum then it picks the one which is the smallest. Observe that in the Fischlin construction, the non-interactive prover $P^{\mathcal{O}}$ would implicitly run the least algorithm as follows. It rewinds the prover in the Fiat-Shamir proof of knowledge until it finds the smallest β such that the hash value when applied on the entire transcript maps to a minimum. This observation was the main intuition behind our definition of the least algorithm.

We show that (P^*, V^*) satisfies all the properties of Fiat-Shamir proof of knowledge.

Lemma 1. *(P^*, V^*) is a Fiat-Shamir proof of knowledge for the relation W.*

Proof. Before we show that (P^*, V^*) satisfies all the properties of Fiat-Shamir proof of knowledge, we first make the observation that both the prover P^* and the verifier V^* run in polynomial time.

[Completeness]. For any $(\alpha^*, \beta, \gamma^*)$ resulting from the interaction between P^* and V^* on input x, we have that $\alpha^* = \mathsf{Enc}((\alpha, i, \mathsf{bit}, \mathsf{M}))$ and $\gamma^* = \mathsf{Enc}(\gamma)$ with each of $i, \mathsf{bit}, \mathsf{M}$ being 0. V^* accepts $(\alpha^*, \beta, \gamma^*)$ only if $V(x, \alpha, \beta, \gamma)$ accepts. Thus, the completeness of (P^*, V^*) follows from the completeness property of (P, V).

[Special Soundness]. Let K be a knowledge extractor for (P, V). We show that (P^*, V^*) satisfies special soundness by constructing a knowledge extractor K^* that uses K as follows. For any $(x, w) \in W$, on input $(x, \alpha^*, \beta_1, \gamma_1^*, \beta_2, \gamma_2^*)$ such that $V^*(x, \alpha^*, \beta_1, \gamma_1^*) = V^*(x, \alpha^*, \beta_2, \gamma_2^*) = \mathsf{Accept}$ and $\beta_1 \neq \beta_2$, K^* does the following. It decrypts α^* to obtain $(\alpha, i, \mathsf{bit}, \mathsf{M})$. Similarly it decrypts γ_1^* and γ_2^* to obtain γ_1 and γ_2 respectively. Then, K^* outputs whatever $K(x, \alpha, \beta_1, \gamma_1, \beta_2, \gamma_2)$ outputs. To see that K^* is indeed a knowledge extractor for (P^*, V^*), consider the following two cases.

- $\mathsf{bit} = 0$: Here, $V^*(x, \alpha^*, \beta_1, \gamma_1^*) = V^*(x, \alpha^*, \beta_2, \gamma_2^*) = \mathsf{Accept}$ only if $V(x, \alpha, \beta_1, \gamma_1) = V(x, \alpha, \beta_2, \gamma_2) = \mathsf{Accept}$. Hence the special soundness property is satisfied because the special soundness of (P, V) ensures that for such an input $(x, \alpha, \beta_1, \gamma_1, \beta_2, \gamma_2)$, K outputs w' such that $(x, w') \in W$.
- $\mathsf{bit} = 1$: In this case, V^* accepts both inputs $(\alpha^*, \beta_1, \gamma_1^*)$ and $(\alpha^*, \beta_2, \gamma_2^*)$ only if both β_1 and β_2 are equal to $\mathsf{least}(\alpha, i, 1, \mathsf{M})$. This contradicts the assumption that $\beta_1 \neq \beta_2$.

[Commitment entropy]. The first message of P^* contains α which has the same distribution as the first message of P and hence the commitment entropy property is satisfied.

[Public coin]. This follows from the description of V^*.

[Unique responses]. For any probabilistic polynomial-time algorithm $\mathcal{A}$ and $(x, \alpha^*, \beta, \gamma_1^*, \gamma_2^*) \leftarrow \mathcal{A}(1^k)$, where $\alpha^* = \mathsf{Enc}((\alpha, i, \mathsf{bit}, \mathsf{M}))$, $\mathsf{Enc}(\gamma_1) = \gamma_1^*$ and $\mathsf{Enc}(\gamma_2) = \gamma_2^*$. We claim that the following is negligible in k:

$$\Pr[V^*(\alpha^*, \beta, \gamma_1^*) = V^*(\alpha^*, \beta, \gamma_2^*) = \mathsf{Accept} \ \& \ \gamma_1^* \neq \gamma_2^*].$$

To prove this claim, consider the following cases.

- $\mathsf{bit} = 0$: Observe that in this case, $V^*(x, \alpha^*, \beta, \gamma_1^*) = \mathsf{Accept}$ only if $V(x, \alpha, \beta, \gamma_1) = \mathsf{Accept}$, and $V^*(x, \alpha^*, \beta, \gamma_2^*) = \mathsf{Accept}$ only if $V(x, \alpha, \beta, \gamma_2) = \mathsf{Accept}$. Also, γ_1 is equal to γ_2 only if γ_1^* is equal to γ_2^*. This is because of the following reason. γ_1^* is the encryption of γ_1 using the randomness $f_\mathsf{K}(\gamma_1)$ and γ_2^* is the encryption of γ_2 using the randomness $f_\mathsf{K}(\gamma_2)$. And hence if γ_1 were to be equal to γ_2 then this would imply that γ_1^* equals γ_2^*. Combining the above arguments we have the following. Conditioned on $\mathsf{bit} = 0$,

$$\Pr[V^*(\alpha^*, \beta, \gamma_1^*) = V^*(\alpha^*, \beta, \gamma_2^*) = \mathsf{Accept} \ \& \ \gamma_1^* \neq \gamma_2^*]$$

$$= \Pr[V(\alpha, \beta, \gamma_1) = V(\alpha, \beta, \gamma_2) = \mathsf{Accept} \ \& \ \gamma_1 \neq \gamma_2]$$

  Since (P, V) satisfies the unique responses property, the quantity $\Pr[V(\alpha, \beta, \gamma_1) = V(\alpha, \beta, \gamma_2) = \mathsf{Accept} \ \& \ \gamma_1 \neq \gamma_2]$ is negligible and hence the claim follows.
- $\mathsf{bit} = 1$: Note that in this case, one of the conditions that needs to be satisfied for V^* to accept $(\alpha^*, \beta, \gamma_1^*)$ (and $(\alpha^*, \beta, \gamma_2^*)$) is that $\gamma_1^* = \mathsf{Enc}((i, \beta))$ (resp., $\gamma_2^* = \mathsf{Enc}((i, \beta))$). This implies that $\gamma_1^* = \gamma_2^*$ and hence the following holds conditioned on $\mathsf{bit} = 1$.

$$\Pr[V^*(\alpha^*, \beta, \gamma_1^*) = V^*(\alpha^*, \beta, \gamma_2^*) = \mathsf{Accept} \ \& \ \gamma_1^* \neq \gamma_2^*] \ = \ 0$$

[Honest Verifier Zero-knowledge]. To prove that (P^*, V^*) satisfies honest verifier zero-knowledge property, we construct a zero-knowledge simulator Z^* for (P^*, V^*) as follows. Let Z be a zero-knowledge simulator for the protocol (P, V). On input $(x, \mathsf{membership})$, where $\mathsf{membership} \in \{\mathsf{yes}, \mathsf{no}\}$, Z^* runs $Z(x, \mathsf{membership})$ to obtain (α, β, γ). Z^* outputs $(\mathsf{Enc}((\alpha, i, \mathsf{bit}, \mathsf{M})), \beta, \mathsf{Enc}(\gamma))$, where i, bit and M are set to 0.

To prove that Z^* is a zero-knowledge simulator for (P^*, V^*), we first assume for contradiction that there exists a distinguisher $D^* = (D_0^*, D_1^*)$ such that the statistical distance between following two distributions is non-negligible.

- $\mathsf{Dist}_{\mathsf{real}}^*$: Let $(x, w, \mathsf{state}) \leftarrow D_0^*(1^k)$ and $(\alpha^*, \beta, \gamma^*) \leftarrow (P^*(w), V^*)(x)$ if $(x, w) \in W$, and $(\alpha^*, \beta, \gamma^*) \leftarrow \bot$ otherwise. Output $D_1^*(\alpha^*, \beta, \gamma^*, \mathsf{state})$.
- $\mathsf{Dist}_{\mathsf{sim}}^*$: Let $(x, w, \mathsf{state}) \leftarrow D_0^*(1^k)$ and $(\alpha^*, \beta, \gamma^*) \leftarrow Z^*(x, \mathsf{yes})$ if $(x, w) \in W$, and $(\alpha^*, \beta, \gamma^*) \leftarrow Z^*(x, \mathsf{no})$ otherwise. Output $D_1^*(\alpha^*, \beta, \gamma^*, \mathsf{state})$.

Then, we construct a distinguisher $D = (D_0, D_1)$ that contradicts the honest verifier zero-knowledge property of (P, V) as follows. $D_0(1^k)$ runs $D_0^*(1^k)$ to obtain (x, w, state) and outputs the same. Once D_1 receives (α, β, γ), if $(\alpha, \beta, \gamma) \neq \perp$ then it outputs $D_1^*(\text{Enc}((\alpha, i, \text{bit}, \text{M})), \beta, \text{Enc}(\gamma), \text{state})$, where i, bit and M are set to 0, else it outputs $D_1^*(\perp, \text{state})$. Now consider the following distributions.

- $\text{Dist}_{\text{real}}$: Let $(x, w, \text{state}) \leftarrow D_0(1^k)$ and $(\alpha, \beta, \gamma) \leftarrow (P(w), V)(x)$ if $(x, w) \in W$, and $(\alpha, \beta, \gamma) \leftarrow \perp$ otherwise. Output $D_1(\alpha, \beta, \gamma, \text{state})$.
- Dist_{sim}: Let $(x, w, \text{state}) \leftarrow D_0(1^k)$ and $(\alpha, \beta, \gamma) \leftarrow Z(x, \text{yes})$ if $(x, w) \in W$, and $(\alpha, \beta, \gamma) \leftarrow Z(x, \text{no})$ otherwise. Output $D_1(\alpha, \beta, \gamma, \text{state})$.

Now, from the way Z^* and D are constructed, the distribution $\text{Dist}_{\text{real}}$ is the same as $\text{Dist}_{\text{real}}^*$. Similarly, the distribution Dist_{sim} is the same as $\text{Dist}_{\text{sim}}^*$. This implies that the statistical distance between $\text{Dist}_{\text{real}}$ and Dist_{sim} is also non-negligible, a contradiction.

3.1   On the Insecurity of (P_h, V_h)

The non-interactive zero-knowledge proof of knowledge $(P^{*\mathcal{O}}, V^{*\mathcal{O}})$ obtained by applying the Fischlin transformation to (P^*, V^*) is sound in the random oracle model. This follows from the fact that (P^*, V^*) is Fiat-Shamir proof of knowledge (Theorem 3) and any protocol obtained by applying Fischlin transformation to a Fiat-Shamir proof of knowledge is secure in the random oracle model. In this section, we show that when the random oracle is instantiated by a hash function h, whose worst case running time is at most the polynomial p_{hash} in the size of its inputs, the protocol (P_h, V_h), which is obtained by instantiating the random oracle $\mathcal{O}$ in $(P^{*\mathcal{O}}, V^{*\mathcal{O}})$, is not sound. Typically, p_{hash} is chosen to be a polynomial of degree c, for a large constant c. The following theorem rules out the secure instantiation of the Fischlin construction with most of the practical hash functions.

Theorem 1. *Let (P^*, V^*) be the 3-round Fiat-Shamir proof of knowledge, for a witness relation W and the corresponding language $L = \{x : (x, w) \in W\}$, as described above. Let $(P^{*\mathcal{O}}, V^{*\mathcal{O}})$ be the non-interactive zero-knowledge proof of knowledge obtained by applying the Fischlin transformation to (P^*, V^*). Then, for any hash function h, that is used to instantiate the random oracle $\mathcal{O}$, and whose running time is at most $p_{\text{hash}}(|\boldsymbol{y}|)$ for any input $\boldsymbol{y} \in \{0, 1\}^*$, the resulting protocol (P_h, V_h) is not sound. In other words, there exists an adversary $\mathcal{A}$ such that $\Pr[(x, \pi) \leftarrow A(1^k) : V^h(x, \pi) = 1 \text{ and } x \notin L]$ is non-negligible.*

The proof of the above theorem can be found in the full version.

4   Simplified Construction for Pseudorandom Hash Functions

In this section, we present a simpler construction to demonstrate the insecurity of the Fischlin transformation with respect to hash functions which behave as pseudorandom functions (i.e., the output of such a hash function for any input is indistinguishable from random). As in the main construction, we restrict our attention to the case when the worst case running time of the hash function is at most some fixed polynomial in the size of the input. More formally, the insecurity arguments hold only for those hash functions whose running time is at most $p_{\mathsf{hash}}(|\boldsymbol{y}|)$ on input $\boldsymbol{y}$, where p_{hash} is a polynomial. Unlike the main construction, the construction presented below does not require any initial setup.

Let (P, V) be any 3-round Fiat-Shamir proof of knowledge for some witness relation W. We extend (P, V) to obtain a 3-round Fiat-Shamir proof of knowledge (P^*, V^*) as we shall describe shortly.

Let $P = (P_0, P_1)$ and $V = (V_0, V_1)$. On input (x, w), P_0 generates α, and on input (x, w, α, β) P_1 generates γ. Also, V_0 and V_1 are such that V_0 interacts with P to produce a transcript (α, β, γ) by generating β uniformly at random and then V accepts if and only if $V_1(x, \alpha, \beta, \gamma)$ accepts. The protocol (P^*, V^*) is described below.

1. P^*: Run P_0 on (x, w) to obtain α. Define $\alpha^* = (\alpha, i, \mathsf{bit}, \mathsf{M})$, where each of $i, \mathsf{bit}, \mathsf{M}$ is set to 0, with their lengths being $\log(r)$ bits, 1 bit, and and $|x|$ bits, respectively[5]. Send α^* to V^*.
2. V^*: Run V_0 to obtain β. Send β to P^*.
3. P^*: Run P_1 on input (x, w, α, β) to obtain γ. Send γ to V^*.
4. V^*: Parse α^* as $(\alpha, i, \mathsf{bit}, \mathsf{M})$. If $\mathsf{bit} = 0$ then Accept if $V_0(x, \alpha, \beta, \gamma)$ accepts. If $\mathsf{bit} = 1$ then check if M is a valid Turing Machine. If M is not a valid TM then Reject. Else, Accept if all the following conditions hold:
   - $\beta = \mathsf{least}(x, \alpha, i, 1, \mathsf{M})$
   - $\gamma = 0$

where the function least is defined as follows.

$\mathsf{least}(x, \alpha, i, \mathsf{M})$:

1. $\mathsf{min} \leftarrow 2^b + 1$
2. $\beta \leftarrow null$
3. For $j = 0$ to $2^t - 1$:
4. $\boldsymbol{y} \leftarrow \Big(x, ((\alpha, 1, 1, \mathsf{M}), \ldots, (\alpha, r, 1, \mathsf{M})), i, j, 0 \Big)$
5.   Execute $\mathsf{M}(\boldsymbol{y})$ upto $p_{\mathsf{hash}}(|\boldsymbol{y}|)$ steps
6.   If $\mathsf{M}(\boldsymbol{y})$ terminates within $p_{\mathsf{hash}}(|\boldsymbol{y}|)$ steps:
7. $\mathsf{hash} \leftarrow \mathsf{M}(\boldsymbol{y})^{(b)}$
8.   If $\mathsf{min} > \mathsf{hash}$:
9. $\mathsf{min} \leftarrow \mathsf{hash}$
10. $\beta \leftarrow j$
11. Return β.

---

[5] Hereafter, unless specified otherwise, we maintain that the lengths of $\mathsf{bit}, i, \mathsf{M}$ are as specified here.

The functionality of the least algorithm defined above is very similar to the one defined in the main construction with the main difference being that the first message and the last messages are not encrypted in the algorithm described above unlike the least algorithm defined in the main construction. Further, the symbols r, b, t are as described in the Fischlin construction (c.f. Section 2). We now show that (P^*, V^*) satisfies all the properties of Fiat-Shamir proof of knowledge.

4.1   On the Security of (P^*, V^*)

Theorem 2. (P^*, V^*) *is a Fiat-Shamir proof of knowledge for the relation* W.

Proof. [Completeness] For any $(\alpha^*, \beta, \gamma)$ resulting from the interaction between P^* and V^*, we have that $\alpha^* = (\alpha, i, \text{bit}, \text{M})$ with each of i, bit, M being 0 and with (α, β, γ) generated as per the description of (P, V). Since, if V accepts (α, β, γ) then V^* accepts $(\alpha^*, \beta, \gamma)$, completeness of (P, V) implies that of (P^*, V^*).

[Special Soundness]. Let K be a knowledge extractor for (P, V). We show that (P^*, V^*) satisfies special soundness by constructing a knowledge extractor K^* that uses K as follows: For any $(x, w) \in W_k$, on input $(x, \alpha^*, \beta, \gamma, \beta', \gamma')$, where $\alpha^* = (\alpha, i, \text{bit}, \text{M})$, $\beta \neq \beta'$, and $V^*(x, (\alpha, i, \text{bit}, \text{M}), \beta, \gamma) = V^*(x, (\alpha, i, \text{bit}, \text{M}), \beta', \gamma') = \text{Accept}$, K^* outputs $K(x, \alpha, \beta, \gamma, \beta', \gamma')$. To see that K^* is indeed a knowledge extractor for (P^*, V^*), consider the following two cases.

- bit = 0: Here, $V^*(x, (\alpha, i, \text{bit}, \text{M}), \beta, \gamma) = V^*(x, (\alpha, i, \text{bit}, \text{M}), \beta', \gamma') = \text{Accept}$ implies that $V(x, \alpha, \beta, \gamma) = V(x, \alpha, \beta', \gamma') = \text{Accept}$. Since special soundness of (P, V) ensures that for an input $(x, \alpha, \beta, \gamma, \beta', \gamma')$, K outputs w' such that $(x, w') \in W_k$, K^* also outputs a witness.
- bit = 1: In this case, V^* accepts on both inputs $((\alpha, i, \text{bit}, \text{M}), \beta, \gamma)$ and $((\alpha, i, \text{bit}, \text{M}), \beta', \gamma')$ only if both β and β' are equal to $\text{least}(\alpha, i, 1, \text{M})$ which leads to a contradiction to $\beta \neq \beta'$.

[Commitment entropy]. The first message of P^* contains α which has the same distribution as the first message of P and hence the commitment entropy property is satisfied.

[Public coin]. This follows directly from the description of V^*.

[Unique responses]. For any probabilistic polynomial-time algorithm $\mathcal{A}$, and $(x, (\alpha, i, \text{bit}, \text{M}), \beta, \gamma, \gamma') \leftarrow \mathcal{A}(1^k)$, we claim that the following is negligible in k:

$$\Pr[V^*((\alpha, i, \text{bit}, \text{M}), \beta, \gamma) = V^*((\alpha, i, \text{bit}, \text{M}), \beta, \gamma') = \text{Accept} \,\&\, \gamma \neq \gamma'].$$

We establish the claim under the following two cases.

- bit = 0: Note that, $V^*(x, (\alpha, i, \text{bit}, \text{M}), \beta, \gamma) = \text{Accept}$ implies that $V(x, \alpha, \beta, \gamma) = \text{Accept}$, and also, $V^*(x, (\alpha, i, \text{bit}, \text{M}), \beta, \gamma') = \text{Accept}$ implies that $V(x, \alpha, \beta, \gamma') = \text{Accept}$. Since $\Pr[V(\alpha, \beta, \gamma) = V(\alpha, \beta, \gamma') = \text{Accept} \,\&\, \gamma \neq \gamma']$ is negligibly close to 0, we have $\Pr[V^*((\alpha, i, \text{bit}, h), \beta, \gamma) = V^*((\alpha, i, \text{bit}, h), \beta, \gamma') = \text{Accept} \,\&\, \gamma \neq \gamma' | \text{bit} = 0]$ is negligibly close to 0.

- bit = 1: Observe that, $V^*(x, (\alpha, i, \text{bit}, \text{M}), \beta, \gamma) = \text{Accept}$ implies that $\gamma = 0$, and also, $V^*(x, (\alpha, i, \text{bit}, \text{M}), \beta, \gamma') = \text{Accept}$ implies that $\gamma = 0$, thus giving us $\gamma = \gamma'$.

[Honest Verifier Zero-knowledge]. To prove that (P^*, V^*) is an HVZK protocol, we construct a special zero-knowledge simulator Z^* for (P^*, V^*) as follows. Let Z be a special zero-knowledge simulator for the protocol (P, V). On input $(x, \beta, \text{memebership})$, where $\text{memebership} \in \{\text{yes}, \text{no}\}$, Z^* runs $Z(x, \beta, \text{memebership})$ to obtain (α, β, γ). If $(\alpha, \beta, \gamma) = \bot$, then Z^* also outputs $\bot$; otherwise, it outputs $((\alpha, i, \text{bit}, \text{M}), \beta, \gamma)$, where i, bit and M are set to 0.

To prove that Z^* is a special zero-knowledge simulator for (P^*, V^*), assume for contradiction that there exists a distinguisher $D^* = (D_0^*, D_1^*)$ such that the statistical distance, $\epsilon(k)$, between following two distributions is non-negligible.

- $\text{Dist}_{\text{real}}^*$: Let $(x, w, \text{state}) \leftarrow D_0^*(1^k)$ and $(\alpha^*, \beta, \gamma) \leftarrow (P^*(w), V^*)(x)$ if $(x, w) \in W_k$, and $(\alpha^*, \beta, \gamma) \leftarrow \bot$ otherwise. Output $D_1^*(\alpha^*, \beta, \gamma, \text{state})$.
- $\text{Dist}_{\text{sim}}^*$: Let $(x, w, \text{state}) \leftarrow D_0^*(1^k)$ and $(\alpha^*, \beta, \gamma) \leftarrow Z^*(x, \text{yes})$ if $(x, w) \in W_k$, and $(\alpha^*, \beta, \gamma) \leftarrow Z^*(x, \text{no})$ otherwise. Output $D_1^*(\alpha^*, \beta, \gamma, \text{state})$.

Then, we construct a distinguisher $D = (D_0, D_1)$ against the HVZK property of (P, V) as follows. $D_0(1^k)$ runs $D_0^*(1^k)$ to obtain (x, w, state) and outputs the same. Once D_1 receives (α, β, γ), if $(\alpha, \beta, \gamma) \neq \bot$ then it outputs $D_1^*((\alpha, i, \text{bit}, \text{M}), \beta, \gamma, \text{state})$, where i, bit and M are set to 0; otherwise, it sets $(\alpha^*, \beta, \gamma) \leftarrow \bot$ and outputs $D_1^*(\alpha^*, \beta, \gamma, \text{state})$. Now consider the following distributions.

- $\text{Dist}_{\text{real}}$: Let $(x, w, \text{state}) \leftarrow D_0(1^k)$ and $(\alpha, \beta, \gamma) \leftarrow (P(w), V)(x)$ if $(x, w) \in W_k$, and $(\alpha, \beta, \gamma) \leftarrow \bot$ otherwise. Output $D_1(\alpha, \beta, \gamma, \text{state})$.
- Dist_{sim}: Let $(x, w, \text{state}) \leftarrow D_0(1^k)$ and $(\alpha, \beta, \gamma) \leftarrow Z(x, \text{yes})$ if $(x, w) \in W_k$, and $(\alpha, \beta, \gamma) \leftarrow Z(x, \text{no})$ otherwise. Output $D_1(\alpha^*, \beta, \gamma, \text{state})$.

Now, from the way Z^* and D are constructed, the output of $\text{Dist}_{\text{real}}$ is the same as the output of $\text{Dist}_{\text{real}}^*$. Similarly, the output of Dist_{sim} is the same as the output of $\text{Dist}_{\text{sim}}^*$. This implies that the statistical distance between $\text{Dist}_{\text{real}}$ and Dist_{sim} is also $\epsilon(k)$, a contradiction.

4.2   On the Insecurity of (P_h, V_h)

Let $\mathcal{F}_{p_{\text{hash}}}$ be a pseudorandom function family such that each function in the family can be be evaluated on any input in time p_{hash} in the size of its inputs, where p_{hash} is a polynomial. Now we shall show that for every such hash function that is used to instantiate the random oracle in the non-interactive ZK PoK that is obtained by applying Fischlin transformation to (P^*, V^*), the resulting protocol does not satisfy the soundness.

In order to model a pseudorandom hash function family, one may look at the function to take a randomly chosen secret key also as an input. Thus, to instantiate the random oracle, first a key K is picked uniformly at random.

Let f_K be the pseudorandom hash function corresponding to K in $\mathcal{F}_{p_{hash}}$. Henceforth, we shall denote f_K by h for a simpler notation. Let (P_h, V_h) be the protocol obtained by applying Fischlin transformation to (P^*, V^*). The following theorem shows that the protocol (P_h, V_h) does not satisfy the soundness property.

Theorem 3. *Let (P^*, V^*) be the 3-round Fiat-Shamir proof of knowledge described above for a witness relation W with corresponding language L and let $(P^{\mathcal{O}}, V^{\mathcal{O}})$ be the non-interactive zero-knowledge proof of knowledge protocol obtained by applying Fischlin transformation to (P^*, V^*). Then for any pseudorandom hash function h in $\mathcal{F}_{p_{hash}}$ that is used to instantiate the random oracle $\mathcal{O}$, the resulting protocol (P_h, V_h) does not satisfy soundness. In other words, there exists an adversary $\mathcal{A}$ that outputs (x, π) such that $\Pr[V_h(x, \pi) = \mathsf{Accept}$ and $x \notin L]$ is non-negligible.*

The proof of the above theorem can be found in the full version.

References

[AABN02] Abdalla, M., An, J.H., Bellare, M., Namprempre, C.: From Identification to Signatures via the Fiat-Shamir Transform: Minimizing Assumptions for Security and Forward-Security. In: Knudsen, L.R. (ed.) EUROCRYPT 2002. LNCS, vol. 2332, pp. 418–433. Springer, Heidelberg (2002)

[Bar01] Barak, B.: How to go beyond the black-box simulation barrier. In: FOCS, pp. 106–115 (2001)

[BBS04] Boneh, D., Boyen, X., Shacham, H.: Short Group Signatures. In: Franklin, M. (ed.) CRYPTO 2004. LNCS, vol. 3152, pp. 41–55. Springer, Heidelberg (2004)

[BGGL01] Barak, B., Goldreich, O., Goldwasser, S., Lindell, Y.: Resettably-sound zero-knowledge and its applications. In: FOCS, pp. 116–125 (2001)

[BGI+01] Barak, B., Goldreich, O., Impagliazzo, R., Rudich, S., Sahai, A., Vadhan, S.P., Yang, K.: On the (Im)possibility of Obfuscating Programs. In: Kilian, J. (ed.) CRYPTO 2001. LNCS, vol. 2139, pp. 1–18. Springer, Heidelberg (2001)

[BR93] Bellare, M., Rogaway, P.: Random oracles are practical: A paradigm for designing efficient protocols. In: ACM Conference on Computer and Communications Security, pp. 62–73 (1993)

[CGH04] Canetti, R., Goldreich, O., Halevi, S.: The random oracle methodology, revisited. J. ACM 51, 557–594 (2004)

[DGS09] Deng, Y., Goyal, V., Sahai, A.: Resolving the simultaneous resettability conjecture and a new non-black-box simulation strategy. In: FOCS, pp. 251–260 (2009)

[Fis05] Fischlin, M.: Communication-Efficient Non-interactive Proofs of Knowledge with Online Extractors. In: Shoup, V. (ed.) CRYPTO 2005. LNCS, vol. 3621, pp. 152–168. Springer, Heidelberg (2005)

[FS86] Fiat, A., Shamir, A.: How to Prove Yourself: Practical Solutions to Identification and Signature Problems. In: Odlyzko, A.M. (ed.) CRYPTO 1986. LNCS, vol. 263, pp. 186–194. Springer, Heidelberg (1987)

[GK03] Goldwasser, S., Kalai, Y.T.: On the (in)security of the fiat-shamir paradigm. In: FOCS, pp. 102–113 (2003)

[GK05]   Goldwasser, S., Kalai, Y.T.: Yael Tauman Kalai. On the impossibility of obfuscation with auxiliary input. In: 46th Annual IEEE Symposium on Foundations of Computer Science, FOCS 2005, pp. 553–562 (October 2005)

[GQ88]   Guillou, L.C., Quisquater, J.-J.: A "Paradoxical" Identity-Based Signature Scheme Resulting from Zero-Knowledge. In: Goldwasser, S. (ed.) CRYPTO 1988. LNCS, vol. 403, pp. 216–231. Springer, Heidelberg (1990)

[MR02]   Micali, S., Reyzin, L.: Improving the exact security of digital signature schemes. J. Cryptology 15(1), 1–18 (2002)

[Oka92]   Okamoto, T.: Provably Secure and Practical Identification Schemes and Corresponding Signature Schemes. In: Brickell, E.F. (ed.) CRYPTO 1992. LNCS, vol. 740, pp. 31–53. Springer, Heidelberg (1993)

[Pas04]   Pass, R.: Bounded-concurrent secure multi-party computation with a dishonest majority, pp. 232–241 (2004)

[PS00]   Pointcheval, D., Stern, J.: Security arguments for digital signatures and blind signatures. J. Cryptology 13(3), 361–396 (2000)

[Sch91]   Schnorr, C.-P.: Efficient signature generation by smart cards. J. Cryptology 4(3), 161–174 (1991)

Signatures of Correct Computation

Charalampos Papamanthou[1], Elaine Shi[2], and Roberto Tamassia[3]

[1] UC Berkeley
cpap@cs.berkeley.edu
[2] University of Maryland
elaine@cs.umd.edu
[3] Brown University
rt@cs.brown.edu

Abstract. We introduce *Signatures of Correct Computation* (SCC), a new model for verifying dynamic computations in cloud settings. In the SCC model, a trusted *source* outsources a function f to an untrusted *server*, along with a public key for that function (to be used during verification). The server can then produce a succinct signature σ vouching for the correctness of the computation of f, i.e., that some result v is indeed the correct outcome of the function f evaluated on some point **a**. There are two crucial performance properties that we want to guarantee in an SCC construction: (1) verifying the signature should take asymptotically less time than evaluating the function f; and (2) the public key should be efficiently updated whenever the function changes.

We construct SCC schemes (satisfying the above two properties) supporting expressive manipulations over multivariate polynomials, such as polynomial evaluation and differentiation. Our constructions are adaptively secure in the random oracle model and achieve *optimal* updates, i.e., the function's public key can be updated in time proportional to the number of updated coefficients, without performing a linear-time computation (in the size of the polynomial).

We also show that signatures of correct computation imply *Publicly Verifiable Computation* (PVC), a model recently introduced in several concurrent and independent works. Roughly speaking, in the SCC model, *any client* can verify the signature σ and be convinced of some computation result, whereas in the PVC model only the client that issued a query (or anyone who trusts this client) can verify that the server returned a valid signature (proof) for the answer to the query. Our techniques can be readily adapted to construct PVC schemes with adaptive security, efficient updates and *without the random oracle model*.

1 Introduction

Given the emergence of the cloud computing paradigm in business and consumer applications, it has become increasingly important to provide integrity guarantees in third-party data management settings. Consider for example the following scenario: A company has developed some novel algorithm, e.g., for personalized medicine, or for stock trend prediction. To avoid investing in expensive IT infrastructure in-house, the company chooses to outsource the execution of this algorithm to an external, untrusted cloud provider (e.g., Amazon, Google). How could a user verify the correctness of the computation under the assumption that she *only* trusts the company that developed the

A. Sahai (Ed.): TCC 2013, LNCS 7785, pp. 222–242, 2013.

algorithm, but not the cloud provider? The above question poses two crucial requirements: (1) *efficiency*, meaning that the running time of the verification algorithms executed by the client should be asymptotically less than the time needed to execute the algorithm in the cloud; and (2) *public verifiability*, meaning that our verification mechanism should not be tied to a specific verifier's secret key so that any user can verify the computation. In addition, another desirable property is to *efficiently handle updates* to the outsourced algorithm, without computing public parameters from scratch.

In this paper, we propose a new paradigm for verifying dynamic computation in the cloud called *signatures of correct computation (SCC)*. SCC allows an untrusted worker to produce a signature vouching for the correctness of some computation over some input; any user can verify the signature using a public key (produced by an one-time preprocessing) published by a trusted source who outsourced the function in the cloud.

Signatures of correct computation are closely related to publicly verifiable computation (PVC), proposed by Parno *et al.* [31], Canetti *et al.* [9] and Fiore and Gennaro [12,13], in *concurrent and independent* works to ours. Specifically, *signatures of correct computation are stronger than publicly verifiable computation: given an SCC scheme, one can directly construct a PVC scheme*; while the other way around does not seem to be true. More specifically, in PVC, a "proof of correct computation" is tied to a specific challenge (generated by an algorithm ProbGen in [31]), and can only be verified by the client who has generated that challenge (or anyone who trusts this client). By contrast, a signature of correct computation is not tied to any challenge, and can be verified by anyone in the world, in much the same way as a traditional signature on a message. We provide a detailed comparison of PVC and SCC in Section 1.2.

1.1   Results and Contributions

We design SCC schemes for multivariate polynomial manipulations, including polynomial evaluation and differentiation. One of our technical highlights is a new method in this setting that allows us to *slightly modify our selectively secure schemes to achieve adaptive security*. Our SCC schemes achieve adaptive security under the random oracle model. We also show that under the weaker PVC model, our techniques can achieve adaptive security under the standard model without random oracles.

Our main results and contributions are summarized below:

Definition of New Paradigm. We are the first ones to formally define signatures of correct computation (SCC) and its security and to study its relation to PVC.

Novel Constructions for Polynomial Manipulations. We focus on deriving efficient and optimized constructions for *specific* functionalities rather than *generic* constructions, as the approach taken by Parno *et al.* [31] and Canetti *et al.* [9]. We present efficient SCC constructions for expressive polynomial manipulations, including multivariate polynomial evaluation and differentiation. Operations on polynomials represent a common building block in a wide range of applications, such as in statistical analysis, scientific computing, and machine learning. Fiore and Gennaro [13] point out many interesting applications of publicly verifiable computation on polynomials, including its use in proofs of retrievability, verifiable keyword search, discrete Fourier tranform, and linear transformations. Our constructions are based on bilinear groups. We prove the adaptive security of our constructions under the random oracle model.

Efficient Incremental Updates. Our constructions allow a trusted source to make *incremental updates* in time proportional to the number of the updated polynomial coefficients, and without performing a computation from scratch that would take linear time in the size of the polynomial.

Novel proof Techniques for Adaptive Security. Our constructions and proofs introduce several novel techniques. First, we observe key polynomial decomposition properties (Lemmas 1 and 3) that become the central idea underlying our constructions. Second, while achieving adaptive security appears relatively easy for univariate polynomial evaluation [23], achieving adaptive security in the multivariate case appears to be fundamentally more difficult. To this end, we present novel techniques that involve embedding randomness in the polynomial decomposition properties (Lemmas 2 and 4), such that our simulator can later manipulate these random numbers in the proof. We give a high-level technical overview in Section 1.3.

Contributions to Publicly Verifiable Computation. Our results also bring advances in the area of publicly verifiable computation. Specifically, our techniques can be readily applied to yield publicly verifiable computation schemes (for the same operations) with adaptive security (without the random oracle model) and with efficient updates. In comparison, existing PVC works [9,13,31], achieve adaptive security but do not support efficient updates. We give a more detailed comparison in Section 1.2.

1.2   Related Work

Authenticated Data Structures. The SCC model is directly related to the model of *authenticated data structures* (ADS) [33,35]. In some sense, SCC and ADS are dual problems to each other, sharing exactly the same security properties. In SCC, a trusted source outsources a function, and a client wishes to verify the outcome of the function at a given point. In ADS, a trusted source outsources the data or a data structure, and the client wishes to verify the correctness of the result of a data structure query, e.g., dictionaries [18,26], graphs [20,25] and hash tables [29,34]. Most authenticated data structures schemes incur logarithmic or linear overheads for verification costs, with some exceptions being authenticated range queries [2,19] and set operations [30], where verification takes time proportional to the size of the answer.

Verifiable Computation in the Secret Key Setting (SVC). Recent works on verifiable computation [1,10,14] achieve efficient verification of general boolean circuits, but in the secret key model. Therefore they are inherently inadequate for the setting of signatures, which are required to be publicly verifiable.

Verifiable Computation for Polynomials. Benabbas *et al.* [3] developed methods for efficient verification of multivariate polynomial evaluation by using algebraic one-way functions—however, in the SVC model. This work does not achieve efficient updates of polynomial coefficients (specifically, in order to update a coefficient, one has to re-randomize all the existing coefficients).[1] Kate *et al.* [23] give a publicly verifiable commitment scheme for univariate polynomials, which is essentially an SCC scheme for

---

[1] However, apart from verification of polynomial evaluation, their techniques can be applied to support very efficient dynamic verifiable databases (constant query and update complexity).

Table 1. Asymptotic cost on the client side. In the table below, n is the number of variables in the polynomial and d is the maximum degree. With **SVC** we denote a "secretly delegatable and verifiable scheme", with **PVC** we denote a "publicly delegatable and verifiable scheme", with **PVC*** we denote a "publicly verifiable but not publicly delegatable scheme" (see Section 1.2, Paragraph 5) and with **SCC** we denote a "signatures of correct computation scheme". Notice that an n-variate polynomial of degree d can have up to $\binom{n+d}{d}$ terms, requiring up to $\binom{n+d}{d}$ time to evaluate. Therefore, the verification costs here are smaller than the cost of evaluating the polynomial. For PVC schemes, the client cost includes both delegation and verification costs.

scheme	polynomial evaluation	polynomial differentiation	efficient updates	security	model
Benabbas *et al.* [3]	$n \log d$	N/A	no	adaptive	SVC
Parno *et al.* [31]	n	$n + \log d$	no	adaptive	PVC
Canetti *et al.* [9]	polylog $\left(\binom{n+d}{d}\right)$	polylog $\left(\binom{n+d}{d}\right)$	no	adaptive	PVC
Fiore and Gennaro [12,13]	$n \log d$	N/A	no	adaptive	PVC*
This paper	n	$n + d$	yes	selective	SCC
This paper	$n + d$	$n + d^2$	yes	adaptive	PVC
This paper	$n + d$	$n + d^2$	yes	adaptive (RO)	SCC

univariate polynomial evaluation. However, their scheme does not directly extend to multivariate polynomials. Also note that our construction is the first to support efficient verification of differentiation queries—even in the SVC setting.

Relation to CS Proofs and SNARGs. Our SCC model is strongly related to the model of *computationally-sound proofs*, introduced by Micali in 1994 [27], and to the subsequent works on *succinct non-interactive arguments* (SNARGs) by Groth [22], Bitansky *et al.* [4,5] and Gennaro *et al.* [15]. The main connection is that both SCC and SNARGs models are non-interactive and publicly verifiable (CS proofs can also be non-interactive in the random oracle model), i.e., a publicly verifiable proof can be computed independently from (and with no communication with) the verifier. We note here that all CS proofs and SNARGs constructions that have been presented in the literature are *generalized*, in that they can handle all of NP by using powerful tools such as the PCP theorem (with an exception of [15] that uses a different characterization of NP). Moreover, all of them (except for the work of Micali [27] that is secure in the random oracle model) are proved secure based on non-falsifiable assumptions [17], e.g., the works of Groth [22] and Gennaro *et al.* [15] use variants of the knowledge-based assumption introduced by Damgard [11]. Non-falsifiable assumptions are considered to be a lot stronger than all common assumptions used in cryptography (one-way functions, trapdoor permutations, DDH, RSA, LWE etc.). We note that the assumptions that we are using in our construction *do not belong* in this category—however, for verifying multivariate polynomials (not for univariate ones) we do use the random oracle, as the construction of Micali [27] does. The main difference (with [27]) however is that we do not use the PCP theorem, hence achieving more practical schemes.

Concurrent and Independent Works. Two closely related schemes are the ones by Parno *et al.* [31] and Cannetti *et al.* [9], which were developed concurrently with and independently from our work.

In the PVC formulation proposed by Parno *et al.* [31], any client can verify that an untrusted server correctly computes a function f on a specific input a. Their definition however requires an *input preparation* randomized algorithm (ProbGen), mapping user inputs a to server inputs σ_a and preparing an object VK_a to be used for verification, specific for σ_a. Therefore, as opposed to the SCC setting, only the client that issued a query for a (or anyone who trusts this client) can verify that the server returned a valid signature (proof) for $f(a)$. For otherwise, a client running the ProbGen algorithm can potentially collude with the server to forge a proof, convincing another party to accept the proof. Apart from defining PVC, Parno *et al.* [31] give a construction for generalized boolean functions (closed under complement) from attribute-based encryption (ABE). Their construction is asymptotically efficient—the proof size is proportional to the size of the answer. Moreover, due to recent advances in ABE schemes by Lewko and Waters [24], the PVC constructions of Parno *et al.* [31] can be proved adaptively secure, since they directly inherit the security of the underlying ABE scheme.

A PVC scheme having similar properties with the scheme of Parno *et al.* [31] was presented by Canetti *et al.* [9], where client verification is polylogarithmic in the size of the evaluated circuit. Canetti *et al.* achieve adaptive security under a slightly weaker model (as Parno *et al.* point out [31]), in which the client needs to keep certain secret state. Their scheme shares the same limitation with the scheme of Parno *et al.* [31] in that a client can verify only his queries unless extra assumptions are put into place.

The most closely related works are the recent works by Fiore and Gennaro [13], who presented a PVC scheme tailored for multivariate polynomials that is based on algebraic one-way functions. An improved version [12] uses less complex assumptions such as RSA to achieve the same goal. The works by Fiore and Gennaro differ from ours in the following sense. First, they consider a model (denoted with PVC* in Table 1) that is more *restrictive* than the PVC model proposed by Parno *et al.* [31]—and hence more restrictive than the SCC model. Specifically, there is an explicit delegation phase where a problem instance is generated based on an input (as in the PVC definition by Parno *et al.* [31]). However, in their constructions (and unlike the original PVC definition), only the party who ran the setup algorithm for a specific function can run the problem generation algorithm. Therefore, their schemes are *publicly verifiable, but not publicly delegatable*. As a result, their schemes would not work for the application scenario where a pharmaceutical company outsources a genomic algorithm, and each user submits their own genomic data for computation. Moreover, they do not consider efficient updates of the polynomial coefficients. In comparison, their scheme has more efficient verification and a delegation step of $O(n \log d)$ cost. A detailed comparison of our scheme against several related works in terms of verification cost and security model is presented in Table 1.

1.3   Highlights of Techniques

Multivariate Polynomial Evaluation. The polynomial commitment scheme by Kate *et al.* [23] can be employed to construct an SCC scheme of univariate polynomial evaluations. Specifically, Kate *et al.* [23] observe that to vouch for the outcome of a polynomial $f(x)$ in $\mathbb{Z}_p$ evaluated at the point $a \in \mathbb{Z}_p$, one can rely on the property that the polynomial $f(x) - f(a)$ is perfectly divisible by the degree-1 polynomial

$x - a$, where $a \in \mathbb{Z}_p$. In other words, one can find a polynomial $w(x)$ such that $f(x) - f(a) = (x - a)w(x)$. Using this property, they construct a witness from the term $w(x)$, and using the pairing operation in bilinear groups, they encode the above test $f(x) - f(a) = (x - a)w(x)$ in the exponents of group elements.

Unfortunately, the above test does not apply to the multivariate case. We therefore propose a novel technique based on the following observation. Let $f(\mathbf{x})$ be a multivariate polynomial in $\mathbb{Z}_p$ where $\mathbf{x} = [x_1, x_2, \ldots, x_n]$. Then, for $\mathbf{a} = [a_1, a_2, \ldots, a_n] \in \mathbb{Z}_p^n$, the polynomial $f(\mathbf{x}) - f(\mathbf{a})$ can be expressed as $f(\mathbf{x}) - f(\mathbf{a}) = \sum_{i=1}^{n}(x_i - a_i)w_i(\mathbf{x})$. The polynomials $w_i(\mathbf{x})$ will be used to construct witnesses in our scheme. Specifically, we encode their terms as exponents of bilinear group elements. The verification is a pairing product equation encoding the above test in the exponent.

From Selective to Adaptive Security. The test that holds for the polynomial evaluation contains a sum of terms, as opposed to a single term in the univariate case [23]. This gives rise to certain technicalities in the proof, allowing us to prove only the weaker notion of *selective security* (see Definition 6 in the Appendix).

Going from selective security to adaptive security turns out to be non-trivial. To achieve this, we devise a novel technique where we build randomness into the polynomial decompositions (Lemmas 2 and 4) which are central to our constructions. As an immediate corollary of our adaptively secure SCC construction with random oracles, we construct an adaptively secure PVC scheme in the plain model.

Derivative Evaluation. A naive method to support verifiable derivative evaluation is for the source to commit to nk polynomials during setup, corresponding to the 1st, 2nd, ..., k-th derivatives of each possible variable. However, as noted in Section 5, this scheme results in increased setup and update overhead.

Our techniques for verifying the evaluation of an arbitrary derivative are inspired by the following observation that holds for first derivatives of univariate polynomials: Given a univariate polynomial $f(x)$, the remainder of dividing the polynomial $f(x) - f'(a)x$ with the polynomial $(x - a)^2$ is always a *constant* polynomial, and not a degree-one polynomial, as would generally happen. In other words, $f(x) - f'(a)x = (x - a)^2 q(x) + b$ for some $q(x) \in \mathbb{Z}_p[x]$, and $b \in \mathbb{Z}_p$. A similar, slightly more involved, observation can be made for higher-order derivatives and multivariate polynomials. More details are provided in Section 5.

2   Preliminaries, Definitions and Assumptions

In this section, we give necessary definitions that are going to be used in the rest of the paper. The security parameter is denoted λ, PPT stands for *probabilistic polynomial-time* and $\text{neg}(\lambda)$ denotes the set of negligible functions, i.e., all the functions less than $1/p(\lambda)$, for all polynomials $p(\lambda)$. We also use bold letters for vector variables, i.e., $\mathbf{x} = [x_1, x_2, \ldots, x_n]$ denotes a vector of n entries $x_1, x_2, \ldots, x_n$.

2.1   Problem Definition

We now formally define signatures of correct computation (SCC).

Definition 1 (SCC scheme). *An* SCC *scheme (signatures of correct computation) for a function family $\mathcal{F}$ is a tuple* (KeyGen, Setup, Compute, Verify, Update) *of five PPT algorithms with the following specification:*

1. (PK, SK) ← KeyGen($\lambda, \mathcal{F}$): *Algorithm* KeyGen *takes as input the security parameter λ and a function family $\mathcal{F}$. It outputs a public/secret key pair* (PK, SK). KeyGen *is run only once at system initialization by a trusted source;*
2. FK(f) ← Setup(SK, PK, f): *Algorithm* Setup *(run by a trusted source) takes as input the secret key* SK, *the public key* PK, *and a function $f \in \mathcal{F}$. It outputs the function public key* FK(f) *for the function f;*
3. (v, w) ← Compute(PK, f, **a**): *Algorithm* Compute *(run by an untrusted server) takes as input the public key* PK, *a function $f \in \mathcal{F}$ and a value $\mathbf{a} \in$ domain(f). It outputs a pair (v, w), where $v = f(\mathbf{a})$ and w is a signature;*
4. {0, 1} ← Verify(PK, FK(f), **a**, v, w): *Algorithm* Verify *(run by any verifier) takes as input the public key* PK, *the function public key* FK(f), *value $\mathbf{a} \in$ domain(f), a claimed result v and a signature w. It outputs 0 or 1;*
5. FK(f') ← Update(SK, PK, FK(f), f'): *Algorithm* Update *(run by a trusted source) takes as input the secret key* SK, *the public key* PK, *the function public key* FK(f) *for the old function f and the updated function description f'. It outputs the updated function public key* FK(f').

The Update algorithm allows the source to update the function f to a new function f'. A naive way to implement Update is to simply run the Setup algorithm again for the new f'. However, in practice, one may wish to allow more efficient incremental updates (and this is what is achieved by our constructions).

2.2   Correctness and Security Definitions

We describe now the correctness and adaptive security definitions for SCC. Intuitively, an SCC scheme is correct if whenever its algorithms are executed honestly, it never rejects a correct signature. Also, it is secure if, after the setup/update algorithms have been executed, an adversary cannot convince a verifier to accept a wrong result on an input of his choice, except with negligible probability.

Definition 2 (Correctness of an SCC scheme). *Let λ be the security parameter and let $\mathcal{P}$ be an SCC scheme* (KeyGen, Setup, Compute, Verify, Update) *for a function family $\mathcal{F}$. Let* (PK, SK) ← KeyGen($\lambda, \mathcal{F}$). *For all $i = 1, \ldots, \text{poly}(\lambda)$, for any function $f_i \in \mathcal{F}$, suppose* FK(f_i) *is the output of* Update(SK, PK, FK(f_{i-1}), f_i), *where* FK(f_0) *is output by algorithm* Setup(SK, PK, f_0) *for some $f_0 \in \mathcal{F}$. We say that $\mathcal{P}$ is correct, if for any $i = 0, \ldots, \text{poly}(\lambda)$, for any $\mathbf{a} \in$ domain(f_i), it is 1 ← Verify(PK, FK(f_i), $\mathbf{a}$, v, w), where (v, w) ← Compute(PK, f_i, $\mathbf{a}$).*

Definition 3 (Adaptive security of an SCC scheme). *Let λ be the security parameter and let $\mathcal{P}$ be an SCC scheme* (KeyGen, Setup, Compute, Verify, Update) *for a function family $\mathcal{F}$. We say that $\mathcal{P}$ is adaptively secure if no PPT adversary $\mathcal{A}$ has more than negligible probability* neg(λ) *in winning the following security game, played between the adversary $\mathcal{A}$ and a challenger:*

1. *Initialization.* *The challenger runs algorithm* KeyGen *which outputs* $(\mathsf{PK}, \mathsf{SK})$ *and then gives* PK *to the adversary but maintains* SK *secret;*
2. *Setup and update.* *The adversary makes an oracle query to the* Setup$(\mathsf{SK}, \mathsf{PK}, f_0)$ *algorithm, specifying an initial function* $f_0 \in \mathcal{F}$, *outputting* FK(f_0). *Then, for* $i = 1, \ldots, k$, *where* $k = \mathsf{poly}(\lambda)$, *he makes a polynomial number of oracle queries to the* Update$(\mathsf{SK}, \mathsf{PK}, \mathsf{FK}(f_{i-1}), f_i)$ *algorithm, each time specifying* $f_i \in \mathcal{F}$. *The challenger answers the queries by returning the resulting* FK(f_i);
3. *Forgery.* *The adversary* $\mathcal{A}$ *outputs a point* $\mathbf{b} \in \mathsf{domain}(f_i)$ *for some* $0 \leq i \leq k$, *and the forgery* $(\mathbf{b}, v, w)$.

The adversary $\mathcal{A}$ *wins the game if* $1 \leftarrow$ Verify$(\mathsf{PK}, \mathsf{FK}(f_i), \mathbf{b}, v, w)$ *and* $f_i(\mathbf{b}) \neq v$.

2.3 SCC Implies PVC

As we highlighted in the introduction, signatures of correct computation (SCC) are stronger than the publicly verifiable computation (PVC) notions studied in concurrent but independent papers [9,12,13,31]. Specifically, a correct and secure SCC scheme implies a correct and secure PVC scheme, but not the other way around. To see that, one can implement algorithm $\sigma_{\mathbf{a}} \leftarrow$ ProbGen$(\mathsf{PK}, \mathbf{a})$ of the PVC scheme (e.g., [31]) to simply output $\mathbf{a}$ and all the other algorithms remain the same.

For completeness, in Definition 6 in the Appendix, we also provide the definition of publicly verifiable computation (PVC) . Our PVC definition is essentially equivalent to those proposed by Parno *et al.* [31] and Canetti *et al.* [9], with the exception that we augment it with an Update algorithm which a trusted source can employ to incrementally update the outsourced function (also, our ProbGen algorithm is called Challenge).

2.4 Multivariate Polynomials Notation

We now give some notation for multivariate polynomials. We use the notion of a *multiset* over some universe $\mathcal{U}$, a generalized set comprising elements from the universe $\mathcal{U}$, where each element can appear more than once; for example, $\{1, 1, 2, 3, 3, 3\}$ is a multiset. In this paper, we use the following notation to denote multisets. Formally, a multiset $S : \mathcal{U} \rightarrow \mathbb{Z}^{\geq 0}$ is a function mapping each element in a universe $\mathcal{U}$ to its *multiplicity*. For any $x \notin S$, $S(x) = 0$. E.g., for the multiset $\{a, a, b, c, c, c\}$, we have $S(a) = 2$, $S(b) = 1$, $S(c) = 3$; however, $S(e) = 0$ since e is not contained in the above multiset.

Let now S, T denote two multisets over universe $\mathcal{U}$. It is $S \subseteq T$, if $\forall a \in \mathcal{U}$, $S(a) \leq T(a)$. The *size* of S over universe $\mathcal{U}$, denoted $|S|$, is defined as the sum of the multiplicity of all elements in S, i.e., $|S| = \sum_{a \in \mathcal{U}} S(a)$. Finally, $\mathcal{S}_{d,n}$ denotes the set of multisets of size at most d over the universe $\{1, 2, \ldots, n\}$. Let now $f \in \mathbb{Z}_p[x_1, x_2, \ldots, x_n] = \mathbb{Z}_p[\mathbf{x}]$ be an n-variate polynomial over $\mathbb{Z}_p$ with maximum degree d. We can use the following generic notation to represent f, i.e.,

$$f(\mathbf{x}) = f(x_1, x_2, \ldots, x_n) = \sum_{S \in \mathcal{S}_{d,n}} c_S \cdot \prod_{i \in S} x_i^{S(i)}. \tag{2.1}$$

For example, the multiset $\{1, 1, 2, 2, 2, 5\}$ corresponds to the term for $x_1^2 x_2^3 x_5$ in the expanded form of the polynomial. The empty multiset $\emptyset$ corresponds to the constant term in the polynomial. Finally, the *degree* of a multivariate polynomial is the maximum total degree of any monomial contained in the polynomial. For example, the degree of the polynomial $3x_1x_2 + x_3^3x_4x_5$ is 5.

2.5   Bilinear Groups and Computational Assumption

We now review some background on bilinear groups of prime order. Let $\mathbb{G}$ be a cyclic multiplicative group of prime order p, generated by g. Let also $\mathbb{G}_T$ be a cyclic multiplicative group with the same order p and $e : \mathbb{G} \times \mathbb{G} \to \mathbb{G}_T$ be a bilinear pairing with the following properties: (1) Bilinearity: $e(P^a, Q^b) = e(P, Q)^{ab}$ for all $P, Q \in \mathbb{G}$ and $a, b \in \mathbb{Z}_p$; (2) Non-degeneracy: $e(g, g) \neq 1$; (3) Computability: There is an efficient algorithm to compute $e(P, Q)$ for all $P, Q \in \mathbb{G}$. We denote with $(p, \mathbb{G}, \mathbb{G}_T, e, g)$ the bilinear pairings parameters, output by a PPT algorithm on input 1^λ. We use the following computational assumption [6]:

Definition 4 (Bilinear ℓ-strong Diffie-Hellman assumption). *Suppose λ is the security parameter and let $(p, \mathbb{G}, \mathbb{G}_T, e, g)$ be a uniformly randomly generated tuple of bilinear pairings parameters. Given the elements $g, g^t, \ldots, g^{t^\ell} \in \mathbb{G}$ for some t chosen at random from $\mathbb{Z}_p^*$, for $\ell = \mathrm{poly}(\lambda)$, there is no PPT algorithm that can output the pair $(c, e(g, g)^{1/(t+c)}) \in \mathbb{Z}_p^* \backslash \{-t\} \times \mathbb{G}_T$ except with negligible probability $\mathrm{neg}(\lambda)$.*

3   Selectively Secure Multivariate Polynomial Evaluation

As a warm-up exercise, in this section we first present an SCC scheme for multivariate polynomial evaluation that is secure under a relaxed security model, namely, the *selective* security model. Then, in Section 4, we explain how to augment this selectively secure scheme and achieve adaptive security in the random oracle model.

Selective security is weaker than adaptive security, requiring the adversary to *commit ahead of time* to the challenge point **a**, which is analogous to the selective security notion often adopted in Identity-Based Encryption (IBE) [7], Attribute-Based Encryption (ABE) [21], Functional Encryption (FE) [32] and Predicate Encryption (PE) [8]. The detailed selective security definition is described in Definition 6 in the Appendix.

3.1   Intuition

Our construction relies on the following key observation.

Lemma 1 (Polynomial decomposition). *Let $f(\mathbf{x}) \in \mathbb{Z}_p[\mathbf{x}]$ be an n-variate polynomial. For all $\mathbf{a} \in \mathbb{Z}_p^n$, there exist polynomials $q_i(\mathbf{x}) \in \mathbb{Z}_p[\mathbf{x}]$ such that the polynomial $f(\mathbf{x}) - f(\mathbf{a})$ can be expressed as $f(\mathbf{x}) - f(\mathbf{a}) = \sum_{i=1}^{n}(x_i - a_i)q_i(\mathbf{x})$. Moreover, there exists a polynomial-time algorithm to find the above polynomials $q_i(\mathbf{x})$.*

The above lemma can be proved by explicit construction, dividing each time the polynomial $f(\mathbf{x}) - f(\mathbf{a})$ with $(x_i - a_i)$. Its proof is given in the full version of our paper [28].

Given now an n-variate polynomial $f(\mathbf{x})$, the trusted source runs algorithms KeyGen and Setup to create the function public key $\mathsf{FK}(f) = g^{f(\mathbf{t})}$ of the polynomial f

evaluated over a randomly chosen point t. Later in the computation stage, when a server wishes to prove that v is indeed the value $f(a)$, it will rely on the key observation stated in Lemma 1: It will compute n polynomials $q_1(x), q_2(x), \ldots, q_n(x)$ such that the relation of Lemma 1 holds, and the values $g^{q_i(t)}$ $(i = 1, \ldots, n)$ will be provided as the signature. To allow the server to evaluate the polynomials $q_i(x)$ at the commitment point t in the exponent, the public key must contain appropriate helper terms. If the claimed computation result v is correct, then the following must be true, where both sides of the equation are evaluated at the commitment point t, i.e., it should be $f(t) - v = \sum_{i \in [n]} (t_i - a_i) q_i(t)$. We note here that in the real construction, the terms in the above equation are encoded in the exponents of group elements, and therefore the verifier cannot directly check the above equation. However, the verifier can check the above condition using operations in the bilinear group, including the pairing operation which allows one to express one multiplication in the exponent. The bilinear group operations directly translate to checking the above condition in the exponent.

3.2 Detailed Construction

We now present our *selectively* secure SCC scheme supporting multivariate polynomial evaluation.

Algorithm $(\mathsf{PK}, \mathsf{SK}) \leftarrow \mathsf{KeyGen}(\lambda, \mathcal{F})$: Suppose that the function family $\mathcal{F} \subseteq \mathbb{Z}_p[x]$ represents all polynomials over $\mathbb{Z}_p$ with at most n variables and degree bounded by d. Namely, family $\mathcal{F}$ contains the polynomials represented by multisets in set $\mathcal{S}_{n,d}$ (see Equation 2.1). The KeyGen algorithm invokes the bilinear group generation algorithm to generate a bilinear group instance of prime order p (of λ bits), with a bilinear map function $e : \mathbb{G} \times \mathbb{G} \to \mathbb{G}_T$. Then it chooses a random generator $g \in \mathbb{G}$ and a random point $t = [t_1, t_2, \ldots, t_n] \in \mathbb{Z}_p^n$ and computes the *signature generation set* $\mathcal{W}_{n,d}$

$$\mathcal{W}_{n,d} = \left\{ g^{\prod_{i \in S} t_i^{S(i)}} : \forall S \in \mathcal{S}_{n,d} \right\}. \tag{3.2}$$

For example, $\mathcal{W}_{2,2}$ contains the elements $g, g^{t_1}, g^{t_2}, g^{t_1^2}, g^{t_2^2}, g^{t_1 t_2}, g^{t_1^2 t_2}, g^{t_1^2 t_2^2}$. The algorithm finally outputs the public key PK that contains $g, \mathcal{W}_{n,d}$ and the description of $\mathbb{G}, \mathbb{G}_T, e$. The secret key SK contains the commitment point t. We describe an optimization referring to reducing the number of group elements of $\mathcal{W}_{n,d}$ in the full version of the paper [28].

Algorithm $\mathsf{FK}(f) \leftarrow \mathsf{Setup}(\mathsf{SK}, \mathsf{PK}, f)$: Let $f(x) \in \mathbb{Z}_p[x]$ denote an n-variate polynomial of maximum degree d over $\mathbb{Z}_p$ that is represented by the multisets $S_1, S_2, \ldots, S_k \in \mathcal{S}_{n,d}$ and the respective coefficients $c_1, c_2, \ldots, c_k \in \mathbb{Z}_p$ (the polynomial has k terms), as defined in Equation 2.1. The setup algorithm, by using the signature generation set $\mathcal{W}_{n,d}$ contained in PK, computes the polynomial public key, i.e.,

$$\mathsf{FK}(f) = g^{f(t)} = \left(g^{\prod_{i \in S_1} t_i^{S_1(i)}} \right)^{c_1} \times \left(g^{\prod_{i \in S_2} t_i^{S_2(i)}} \right)^{c_2} \times \ldots \times \left(g^{\prod_{i \in S_k} t_i^{S_k(i)}} \right)^{c_k}. \tag{3.3}$$

The algorithm outputs the function public key $\mathsf{FK}(f)$.

Algorithm $(v, w) \leftarrow \mathsf{Compute}(\mathsf{PK}, f, a)$: This algorithm first computes $v = f(a)$. Using Lemma 1, it finds an appropriate set of polynomials $q_1(x), q_2(x), \ldots, q_n(x)$ to express polynomial $f(\mathbf{x}) - v$ as $f(\mathbf{x}) - v = \sum_{i=1}^{n}(x_i - a_i)q_i(\mathbf{x})$. The signature w is a vector of n witnesses $w_1, w_2, \ldots, w_n$, such that $w_i = g^{q_i(\mathbf{t})}$ for all $i \in [n]$. Note that w_i can easily be computed using the signature generation set $\mathcal{W}_{n,d}$, as is achieved for the function public key in Equation 3.3. It finally outputs the pair (v, w), where v is the outcome of the polynomial evaluated at $\mathbf{a}$, and w is the signature of correctness.

Algorithm Verify($\mathsf{PK}, \mathsf{FK}(f), \mathbf{a}, v, w$): Parse PK as the signature generation set $\mathcal{W}_{n,d}$. To verify that v is indeed $f(\mathbf{a})$, given a signature $w = [w_1, w_2, \ldots, w_n]$, algorithm Verify checks if the following equation holds:

$$\mathsf{e}\left(\mathsf{FK}(f)g^{-v}, g\right) \stackrel{?}{=} \prod_{i=1}^{n} \mathsf{e}\left(g^{t_i - a_i}, w_i\right) . \tag{3.4}$$

In the above, the terms g^{t_i} are contained in PK (specifically in $\mathcal{W}_{n,d}$) and the function public key $\mathsf{FK}(f)$ equals $g^{f(\mathbf{t})}$. The algorithm accepts the result v, and outputs 1 if the above equations hold; otherwise, it rejects and outputs 0.

Algorithm $\mathsf{FK}(f') \leftarrow$ Update($\mathsf{SK}, \mathsf{PK}, \mathsf{FK}(f), f'$): Let f denote the current polynomial and f' be the new polynomial that corresponds to the update. Assume f' and f differ in only one coefficient. Specifically, let S denote the multiset corresponding to that coefficient.[2] Suppose the current function public key is $\mathsf{FK}(f)$. The algorithm sets

$$\mathsf{FK}(f') = \mathsf{FK}(f) \cdot g^{(c'_S - c_S) \prod_{i \in S} t_i^{S(i)}},$$

updating $\mathsf{FK}(f)$ to $\mathsf{FK}(f')$, the new function public key. We now state our first theorem.

Theorem 1. *There exists an SCC scheme for polynomial evaluation such that (1) It is correct according to Definition 2; (2) For univariate polynomials, it is adaptively secure according to Definition 3 and under the ℓ-SBDH assumption; (3) For multivariate polynomials, it is selectively secure according to Definition 6 and under the ℓ-SBDH assumption.*

The correctness of our construction follows in a straightforward manner from Lemma 1, and the bilinear property of the pairing operation e. The asymptotic cost analysis of the scheme's algorithms are presented in Section 6. The security proofs are presented in the full version of the paper [28]. However, we give a proof sketch in the following.

3.3   Selective Security Proof Sketch

We briefly explain the selective security proof intuition of our scheme. The simulator obtains an ℓ-SBDH instance, $g, g^{\tau}, \ldots, g^{\tau^{\ell}} \in \mathbb{G}$ and it will construct a simulation such that if an adversary can break the selective security of the SCC scheme, the simulator can leverage it to break the ℓ-SBDH instance. Specifically, with knowledge of the challenge point $\mathbf{a} = [a_1, a_2, \ldots, a_n]$ that the adversary commits to at the beginning of the selective security game, the simulator can carefully craft the simulation such that

---

[2] I.e., the only difference between f and f' is that the coefficient c_S corresponding to term $\prod_{i \in S} x_i^{S(i)}$ is updated to c'_S in f'.

$t_i - a_i = \lambda_i(\tau + c)$, where $t = [t_1, t_2, \ldots, t_n]$ represents the committed point used to compute the polynomial digest, and λ_i and c are constants known to the simulator.

If an adversary can forge a signature for a wrong outcome of a polynomial, then the simulator is able to raise terms in Equation 3.4 to the $(\tau + c)^{-1}$ power and output $e(g, g)^{(\tau+c)^{-1}}$, breaking in this way the ℓ-SBDH assumption. Notice that in the selective security proof, the simulator's ability to take appropriate terms in Equation 3.4 to the $(\tau + c)^{-1}$ power relies on knowing the challenge point a in advance, and the ability to craft the simulation such that $t_i - a_i = \lambda_i(\tau + c)$.

4   Adaptively Secure Multivariate Polynomial Evaluation

In this section, we augment the above selectively secure SCC scheme to achieve adaptive security in the random oracle model. We also show that the same techniques can be applied to construct an adaptively secure PVC scheme under the formulation of Parno et al. [31] *without the random oracle model*.

4.1   Intuition

The intuition of the new construction is similar to the selectively secure construction. For technical reasons explained later, instead of relying on the polynomial decomposition method described in Lemma 1, we use a new decomposition that is *randomized*, so that it can later be manipulated by a simulator in the proof to achieve adaptive security. The decomposition we are using is the following:

Lemma 2 (Randomized decomposition). *Let $f(\mathbf{x}) \in \mathbb{Z}_p[\mathbf{x}]$ be an n-variate polynomial of degree at most d. For all $\mathbf{a} \in \mathbb{Z}_p^n$ and for all $r_1, \ldots, r_{n-1} \in \mathbb{Z}_p$ such that $r_1 r_2 \ldots r_{n-1} \neq 0$, there exist polynomials $q_i(\mathbf{x}) \in \mathbb{Z}_p[\mathbf{x}]$ such that the polynomial $f(\mathbf{x}) - f(\mathbf{a})$ can be expressed as*

$$f(\mathbf{x}) - f(\mathbf{a}) = \sum_{i=1}^{n-1} [r_i(x_i - a_i) + x_{i+1} - a_{i+1}] q_i(\mathbf{x}) + (x_n - a_n)q_n(x_n),$$

where $q_n(x_n)$ is a polynomial of degree at most d that contains only variable x_n. Moreover, there exists a polynomial-time algorithm to find the above polynomials $q_i(\mathbf{x})$.

The above lemma can be proved by explicit construction, each time dividing the polynomial by $r_i(x_i - a_i) + x_{i+1} - a_{i+1}$, for increasing values of i, in a way such that the remainder should not contain x_i. The full proof of Lemma 2 is provided in the full version of our paper [28]. We note here that in our construction explained below, the numbers $r_1, r_2, \ldots, r_{n-1}$ mentioned in Lemma 2 will be chosen "at random" by calling a hash function modelled as a random oracle (see Equation 4.5).

4.2   Detailed Construction

We now continue with the algorithms of our adaptively secure SCC scheme.

Algorithm $(\mathsf{PK}, \mathsf{SK}) \leftarrow \mathsf{KeyGen}(\lambda, \mathcal{F})$: Same as in Section 3.

Algorithm $\mathsf{FK}(f) \leftarrow \mathsf{Setup}(\mathsf{SK}, \mathsf{PK}, f)$: Same as in Section 3.

Algorithm $(v, w) \leftarrow \mathsf{Compute}(\mathsf{PK}, f, \mathbf{a})$: Parse $\mathbf{a}$ as $[a_1, a_2, \ldots, a_n]$. The algorithm first computes the outcome of the polynomial $v = f(\mathbf{a})$. Next, compute the following, where $\mathsf{H} : \{0, 1\}^* \to \mathbb{Z}_p$ is a hash function (later modelled as a random oracle):

$$\forall 1 \le i \le n - 1 : \quad r_i = \mathsf{H}(\mathbf{a}\|i) \, . \tag{4.5}$$

Now, using Lemma 2, find an appropriate set of polynomials $q_1(\mathbf{t}), q_2(\mathbf{t}), \ldots, q_n(t_n)$ to express polynomial $f(\mathbf{x}) - f(\mathbf{a})$ as $\sum_{i=1}^{n-1} [r_i(x_i - a_i) + x_{i+1} - a_{i+1}] q_i(\mathbf{x}) + (x_n - a_n)q_n(x_n)$. Next, leverage the signature generation set $\mathcal{W}_{n,d}$ (see Equation 3.2) to compute $w_i = g^{q_i(\mathbf{t})}$ for $1 \le i \le n - 1$. It is not hard to see that all w_i's can be computed from $\mathcal{W}_{n,d}$. The signature w is composed as $w = [w_1, w_2, \ldots, w_n,$ polynomial $q_n(x_n)]$, where the polynomial $q_n(x_n)$ contains the description of the polynomial, i.e., up to d coefficients $\beta_d, \ldots, \beta_0$, since it is a univariate polynomial in x_n of degree at most d.

The algorithm outputs the pair (v, w) denoting the outcome of the polynomial evaluated at $\mathbf{a}$, and a signature to vouch for the correctness of the computation.

Algorithm $\{0, 1\} \leftarrow \mathsf{Verify}(\mathsf{PK}, \mathsf{FK}(f), \mathbf{a}, v, w)$: Parse $\mathbf{a}$ as $[a_1, a_2, \ldots, a_n] \in \mathbb{Z}_p^n$; then parse the signature w as $[w_1, w_2, \ldots, w_{n-1},$ polynomial $q_n(x_n)]$. To verify that v is indeed the outcome of the correct polynomial evaluated at point $\mathbf{a} \in \mathbb{Z}_p^n$, algorithm Verify first computes $g^{q_n(t_n)}$ using the signature generation set $\mathcal{W}_{n,d}$ (Equation 3.2) which is part of the public key PK.

Next, it computes the r_i values in the same way as in Equation 4.5, namely, $r_i = \mathsf{H}(\mathbf{a}\|i)$ for $1 \le i \le n - 1$. Finally, it checks if the following equation holds:

$$\mathsf{e}\left(\mathsf{FK}(f) \cdot g^{-v}, g\right) \stackrel{?}{=} \prod_{i=1}^{n-1} \mathsf{e}\left(g^{r_i(t_i - a_i) + t_{i+1} - a_{i+1}}, w_i\right) \mathsf{e}\left(g^{t_n - a_n}, g^{q_n(t_n)}\right), \tag{4.6}$$

In the above, the terms g^{t_i} are contained in PK (specifically in $\mathcal{W}_{n,d}$) and $\mathsf{FK}(f)$ equals $g^{f(\mathbf{t})}$. The algorithm accepts if the above equation holds; otherwise, it rejects.

Algorithm $\mathsf{FK}(f') \leftarrow \mathsf{Update}(\mathsf{SK}, \mathsf{PK}, \mathsf{FK}(f), f')$: Same as in Section 3.

4.3   Adaptive Security Proof Sketch

The simulator obtains an ℓ-SBDH instance, $g, g^\tau, \ldots, g^{\tau^\ell} \in \mathbb{G}$ and it will construct a simulation such that if an adversary can break the adaptive security of the SCC scheme, the simulator can leverage it to break the ℓ-SBDH instance. Unlike in the selective security proof of Section 3.3, without the adversary committing to the challenge point in advance, the simulator cannot craft terms to satisfy conditions such as $t_i - a_i = \lambda_i(t + c)$—but this condition is crucial later for the simulator to compute $\mathsf{e}(g, g)^{(\tau + c)^{-1}}$ and break the hardness assumption.

To circumvent this barrier in the proof, we embed "randomness" into the verification equation, such that the simulator can manipulate these random numbers to satisfy a condition described below, without having to know the challenge point ahead of time:

$$r_i(t_i - a_i) + t_{i+1} - a_{i+1} = \lambda_i(\tau + c) \quad \text{for } i = 1, \ldots, n - 1, \tag{4.7}$$

where λ_i and c are constants known to the simulator.

Specifically, since these random numbers are outputs from a "random" hash function, under the random oracle model, the simulator can manipulate the answers to the random oracle queries in the simulation to achieve the above goal. Note that our SCC signature with adaptive security has size $O(n + d)$, as opposed to $O(n)$, which was the size of the signature in the selectively secure scheme (see Section 6). This is because it is essential the signature contain the polynomial $q_n(x_n)$ for the adaptive security proof to work, so that the simulator can divide both sides of Equation 4.6 with $\tau + c$. We can now state our main theorem (see detailed proof in the full version of our paper [28]).

Theorem 2. *There exists an SCC scheme for the evaluation of multivariate polynomials such that (1) It is correct according to Definition 2; (2) It is adaptively secure according to Definition 3, under the ℓ-SBDH assumption and in the random oracle model.*

4.4   An Adaptively Secure PVC Scheme without Random Oracles

Our techniques can be readily adapted to construct an adaptively secure PVC scheme for multivariate polynomial evaluation—see Section 2.3. Neverthelsess, if we were to use the observations of Section 2.3 as a black box, we would construct a PVC scheme that has the random oracle. However, we are able to remove the random oracle by taking advantage of the fact that PVC is weaker than SCC.

The resulting PVC scheme is very similar to our construction in this section—except that in the PVC scheme, the random numbers r_i's are directly chosen at random (as a challenge) by a client issuing a query to the untrusted server, instead of being the outputs of a hash function modeled as a random oracle. We provide the detailed PVC scheme with full security in the the full version of the paper [28].

Theorem 3. *There exists a PVC scheme for the evaluation of multivariate polynomials of total such that (1) It is correct according to Definition 8; (2) It is adaptively secure according to Definition 9 and under the ℓ-SBDH assumption.*

5   SCC Schemes for Polynomial Differentiation

In this section, we construct an SCC scheme for the verification of differentiation queries. Given a multivariate polynomial $f(\mathbf{x})$, we show how to construct signatures of correct computation for derivatives $\partial^k f(\mathbf{x}) / \partial x_j^k (\mathbf{a})$ evaluated at a chosen point $\mathbf{a}$.

One naive method to support verification of derivative computation is to commit to all nk polynomials corresponding to all the possible derivatives (k in total) of each possible variable. This would incur a setup cost of $O(nk\binom{n+d}{d})$. In contrast, our construction requires only $O(\binom{n+d}{d})$ setup cost (see Section 6), the same with the polynomial evaluation scheme. Another drawback of the naive method is increased update cost, since an update operation would now involve updating all nk polynomials. In contrast, our construction allows for efficient incremental updates.

5.1   Intuition

The intuition of supporting polynomial differentiation is similar to the evaluation case. In place of the decomposition lemmas (Lemmas 1 and 2) for polynomial evaluation, we have the following counterparts (Lemmas 3 and 4) for derivative computation:

Lemma 3 (Decomposition for derivatives). *For* $\mathbf{a} \in \mathbb{Z}_p^n$, *the n-variate polynomial* $f(\mathbf{x}) \in \mathbb{Z}_p[\mathbf{x}]$ *can be expressed as*

$$f(\mathbf{x}) = \sum_{i=1}^{n-1}(x_i - a_i)u_i(\mathbf{x}) + (x_n - a_n)^{k+1}q(x_n) + c_k x_n^k + \ldots + c_1 x_n + c_0 \, ,$$

Then, the k-th derivative of $f(\mathbf{x})$ *wrt* x_n *equals* $k! \cdot c_k$ *at point* $\mathbf{a}$, *i.e.,* $\partial^k f(\mathbf{x})/\partial x_n^k(\mathbf{a}) = k! \cdot c_k$. *A similar result holds for other variables* x_i *by variable renaming.*

Lemma 4 (Randomized decomposition for derivatives). *For* $\mathbf{a} \in \mathbb{Z}_p^n$ *and for all* $r_1, \ldots, r_{n-2} \in \mathbb{Z}_p$ *such that* $r_1 r_2 \ldots r_{n-2} \neq 0$, *the n-variate polynomial* $f(\mathbf{x}) \in \mathbb{Z}_p[\mathbf{x}]$ *can be expressed as*

$$f(\mathbf{x}) = \sum_{i=1}^{n-2}[r_i(x_i - a_i) + x_{i+1} - a_{i+1}]u_i(\mathbf{x}) + (x_{n-1} - a_{n-1})u_{n-1}(\mathbf{x})$$
$$+ (x_n - a_n)^{k+1}q(x_n) + c_k x_n^k + \sum_{i=0}^{k} c_i x_n^i \, ,$$

where $u_{n-1}(\mathbf{x})$ *is a polynomial containing only variables* x_{n-1} *and* x_n *and* $q(x_n)$ *is a polynomial containing only variable* x_n. *Then, the k-th derivative of* $f(\mathbf{x})$ *wrt* x_n *equals* $k! \cdot c_k$ *at point* $\mathbf{a}$, *i.e.,* $\partial^k f(\mathbf{x})/\partial x_n^k(\mathbf{a}) = k! \cdot c_k$. *A similar result holds for other variables* x_i *by variable renaming.*

Similar to the multivariate polynomial evaluation case, Lemmas 3 and 4 allow us to construct respectively: 1) an SCC scheme for polynomial differentiation with *selective security*; and 2) an SCC scheme for polynomial differentiation with *adaptive security in the random oracle model* and a PVC scheme for polynomial differentiation with *adaptive security without the random oracle model* .

5.2   Detailed Construction

We now present the *adaptively secure* SCC scheme for polynomial differentiation (based on Lemma 4). For completeness, we also present a selectively secure scheme for polynomial differentiation in the full version of the paper [28].

Algorithm $(\mathsf{PK}, \mathsf{SK}) \leftarrow \mathsf{KeyGen}(\lambda, \mathcal{F})$**:** Same as in Section 3.

Algorithm $\mathsf{FK}(f) \leftarrow \mathsf{Setup}(\mathsf{SK}, \mathsf{PK}, f)$**:** Same as in Section 3.

Algorithm $(v, w) \leftarrow \mathsf{Compute}(\mathsf{PK}, f, \mathbf{a}, k, \mathsf{ind})$**:** In addition to the point $\mathbf{a} \in \mathbb{Z}_p^n$, the Compute algorithm here takes in two additional parameters k and ind, indicating the evaluation of the k-th derivative of the polynomial with respect to variable x_{ind} at $\mathbf{a}$.

Without loss of generality, below we assume ind $= n$. In other words, the algorithm should evaluate the k-th partial derivative with respect to x_n at point a. First, the algorithm computes randomness r_i as

$$r_i = \mathsf{H}(\mathsf{a}||\mathrm{ind}||k||i) \ \forall 1 \leq i \leq n-2, \tag{5.8}$$

where $\mathsf{H} : \{0,1\}^* \to \mathbb{Z}_p$ is a hash function (later modeled as a random oracle). Due to Lemma 4, $f(\mathbf{x})$ can be expressed as $f(\mathbf{x}) = \sum_{i=1}^{n-2}[r_i(x_i - a_i) + x_{i+1} - a_{i+1}]u_i(\mathbf{x}) + (x_{n-1} - a_{n-1})u_{n-1}(\mathbf{x}) + (x_n - a_n)^{k+1}q(x_n) + \sum_{i=0}^{k} c_i x_n^i$. The signature w for correct derivative computation is the following tuple:

$$w = \left(g^{u_1(t)}, \ldots, g^{u_{n-2}(t)}, \ g^{q(t_n)}, \ c_{k-1}, \ldots, c_1, c_0, \ \text{polynomial } u_{n-1}(\mathbf{x}) \right),$$

where polynomial $u_{n-1}(\mathbf{x})$ is a description of the polynomial containing the corresponding coefficients. Note that by Lemma 4, polynomial $u_{n-1}(\mathbf{x})$ contains up to d^2 terms. Also, the signature does not contain the term c_k—this can be implicitly retrieved by the result v since $c_k = v/k!$. Finally, the result of the computation v is returned.

Algorithm Verify$(\mathsf{PK}, \mathsf{FK}(f), \mathsf{a}, k, \mathrm{ind}, v, w)$: Let $c_k = \frac{v}{k!}$. To verify that v is indeed the outcome of the k-th partial derivative on variable x_{ind} (ind $= n$) evaluated at point $\mathsf{a} \in \mathbb{Z}_p^n$, perform the following steps.

Parse w as $(w_1, \ldots, w_{n-2}, w_n, c_{k-1}, \ldots, c_1, c_0, \ \text{polynomial } u_{n-1}(\mathbf{x}))$.

Compute the r_i values in the same way as in Equation 5.8, i.e., $r_i = \mathsf{H}(\mathsf{a}||\mathrm{ind}||k||i)$ for $1 \leq i \leq n-2$.

Check if $\mathsf{e}\left(\mathsf{FK}(f), g\right)$ equals the following quantity (where $\mathsf{L} = \prod_{i=0}^{k} \mathsf{e}\left(g^{t_n^i}, g\right)^{c_i}$):

$$\prod_{i=1}^{n-2} \mathsf{e}\left(g^{r_i(t_i - a_i) + t_{i+1} - a_{i+1}}, w_i\right) \cdot \mathsf{e}\left(g^{t_{n-1} - a_{n-1}}, g^{u_{n-1}(t)}\right) \cdot \mathsf{e}\left(g^{(t_n - a_n)^{k+1}}, w_n\right) \cdot \mathsf{L},$$

The above quantity can be easily computed with the public keys in $O(n + d^2)$ time, since $u_{n-1}(\mathbf{x})$ is a polynomial containing d^2 terms and $k \leq d$ (see Section 6). The algorithm accepts v and outputs 1 if the above equation holds; otherwise, it rejects.

Algorithm $\mathsf{FK}(f') \leftarrow \mathsf{Update}(\mathsf{SK}, \mathsf{PK}, \mathsf{FK}(f), f')$: Same as in Section 3.

Theorem 4. *There exists an SCC scheme for the differentiation of multivariate polynomials such that (1) It is correct according to Definition 2; (2) It is adaptively secure according to Definition 3, under the ℓ-SBDH assumption and in the random oracle model.*

Corollary 1. *There exists a PVC scheme for the differentiation of multivariate polynomials such that (1) It is correct according to Definition 8; (2) It is adaptively secure according to Definition 9 and under the ℓ-SBDH assumption.*

6 Asymptotic Cost Analysis

In this section, we analyze the asymptotic cost of our schemes. Clearly, the worst-case complexity of KeyGen is $O\left(\binom{n+d}{d}\right)$, since the set $\mathcal{W}_{n,d}$ should contain one term for every possible term of the polynomial in n variables and total degree d. Similarly algorithm Setup takes $O(\binom{n+d}{d})$ time to execute in the worst case. In practice, both these complexities can be $O(m)$, where m is the number of the terms contained in the polynomial—see the full version of the paper [28] for minimizing the size of $\mathcal{W}_{n,d}$.

Also for our adaptive security schemes, the size of the signature is $O(n)$, and the client performs $O(n)$ amount of work to verify it using algorithm Verify (these costs are $O(n+d)$ for derivative computation). For our adaptive security schemes, the size of the signature increases to $O(n+d)$, and the client performs $O(n+d)$ amount of work to verify it (again, these costs $O(n+d^2)$ for derivative computation).

As for algorithm Compute, it needs to decompose the polynomial according to Lemmata 1, 2, 3, 4 (depending on which scheme we are using). This polynomial decomposition dominates the asymptotic performance. To perform the polynomial decomposition, the server performs n polynomial divisions. If we use the naive polynomial division algorithm, since each variable can have degree up to d, each polynomial division involves d steps, and each step takes time proportional to the number of terms in the polynomial, namely, $O(\binom{n+d}{d})$. Therefore, the polynomial decomposition (Lemma 1) can be achieved in $O(nd\binom{n+d}{d})$ time using the naive algorithm. However, in cases where $d > \log n$, one can use the FFT method to perform polynomial division, resulting in $O(n \log n \binom{n+d}{d})$ computation time. Finally, algorithm Update takes constant time to update a constant number of coefficients.

7   Extensions and Observations

7.1   I/O Privacy

In our constructions, the client's sensitive input is in plaintext, directly readable by the untrusted server. To offer input and output privacy, we could potentially use a *fully-homomorphic* public-key encryption scheme [16] (FHE scheme) so that algorithm Compute executed by the untrusted server could operate on encrypted points. In this way, everybody that knows pk could send queries to the server. After Compute executes on the encryption of some point $\bar{a}$, it outputs the encrypted signature w of the value $\bar{v} = f(\bar{a})$ under the public key pk, allowing only the owner of the secret key to decrypt and retrieve (and verify) the output of the computation. This could have various applications which we highlight in the Appendix of the full version of the paper [28].

7.2   Removing the Random Oracles Through Stronger Assumptions

We now observe that if we are willing to (i) use subexponential assumptions and (ii) restrict the size of the domain of the inputs of our polynomials to be subexponential (now it is exponential), we can remove the random oracle from our adaptively secure constructions. The subexponential assumption we use can be stated as follows:

Definition 5 (δ-**subexponential bilinear** ℓ-**strong Diffie-Hellman assumption**). *Suppose k is the security parameter, let $0 < \delta < \frac{\log k - 1}{\log k}$ and let $(p, \mathbb{G}, \mathbb{G}_T, e, g)$ be a uniformly randomly generated tuple of bilinear pairings parameters. Given the elements $g, g^t, \ldots, g^{t^\ell} \in \mathbb{G}$ for some t chosen at random from $\mathbb{Z}_p^*$, for $\ell = \mathsf{poly}(k)$, there is no* *algorithm running in time less than* 2^{2k^δ} *that can output the pair* $(c, \mathsf{e}(g,g)^{1/(t+c)}) \in$ $\mathbb{Z}_p^* \backslash \{-t\} \times \mathbb{G}_T$, *except with negligible probability* $\mathsf{neg}(k)$.

Note that in the above definition, we require $\delta < \frac{\log k - 1}{\log k}$ so that $2k^\delta < k$.

Theorem 5 (Adaptive security in the standard model). *Let* $\mathbf{x}$ *be the input to our polynomial. For* $\mathbf{x}$ *belonging to a domain of subexponential size, our selectively secure scheme (Section 3) is adaptively secure in the standard model and assuming the* δ*-subexponential bilinear* ℓ*-strong Diffie-Hellman assumption. Namely, for all PPT adversaries, we can build a simulator running in subexponential time that breaks the* δ*-subexponential bilinear* ℓ*-strong Diffie-Hellman assumption (see Definition 5).*

Proof. Suppose we have n variables $x_1, x_2, \ldots, x_n$, and each one of which can take values in $[0, 1, \ldots, m - 1]$. Assume that $m^n = 2^{k^\delta}$, yielding $n \log m = k^\delta$. To build the desired simulator, we modify the initialization phase of our selective security proof in Section 3.3: We do not require the adversary to commit to an initial point $\mathbf{a}$. Instead the simulator guesses the point $\mathbf{a}$ that the adversary is going to output later as a forgery—and the simulator aborts if the guess is wrong. Clearly, the guess is successful with probability 2^{-k^δ}. Therefore the simulation, in expectation, takes 2^{k^δ} time to succeed. Since the adversary runs in at most polynomial time (see our adaptive security definition), it follows that we have derived an algorithm that runs in $\mathsf{poly}(k)2^{k^\delta}$ time and breaks the assumption. Note that this is a contradiction since the function $\mathsf{poly}(k)2^{k^\delta} = o(2^{2k^\delta})$. This completes our proof. $\square$

The same technique was also described by Boneh and Boyen [7] to achieve adaptive security in their IBE scheme.

Acknowledgments. This work was supported by Intel through the ISTC for Secure Computing, by the National Science Foundation under grants CCF-0424422, 0842695, 0808617 and CNS-1228485, by the Air Force Office of Scientific Research (AFOSR) under MURI award FA9550-09-1-0539, by the MURI program under AFOSR grant FA9550-08-1-0352, by the Center for Geometric Computing at Brown University, and by a NetApp Faculty Fellowship. The authors thank Xavier Boyen, Basilis Gidas, Dawn Song and Nikos Triandopoulos for useful discussions, and the TCC 2013 reviewers for their feedback. Any opinions, findings, and conclusions or recommendations expressed in this material are those of the authors and do not necessarily reflect the views of the sponsors.

References

1. Applebaum, B., Ishai, Y., Kushilevitz, E.: From Secrecy to Soundness: Efficient Verification via Secure Computation. In: Abramsky, S., Gavoille, C., Kirchner, C., Meyer auf der Heide, F., Spirakis, P.G. (eds.) ICALP 2010. LNCS, vol. 6198, pp. 152–163. Springer, Heidelberg (2010)
2. Atallah, M.J., Cho, Y., Kundu, A.: Efficient data authentication in an environment of untrusted third-party distributors. In: ICDE, pp. 696–704 (2008)

3. Benabbas, S., Gennaro, R., Vahlis, Y.: Verifiable Delegation of Computation over Large Datasets. In: Rogaway, P. (ed.) CRYPTO 2011. LNCS, vol. 6841, pp. 111–131. Springer, Heidelberg (2011)

4. Bitansky, N., Canetti, R., Chiesa, A., Tromer, E.: From extractable collision resistance to succinct non-interactive arguments of knowledge, and back again. In: ITCS, pp. 326–349 (2012)

5. Bitansky, N., Canetti, R., Chiesa, A., Tromer, E.: Recursive composition and bootstrapping for snarks and proof-carrying data. IACR Cryptology ePrint Archive 2012:95 (2012)

6. Boneh, D., Boyen, X.: Short signatures without random oracles and the SDH assumption in bilinear groups. J. Cryptology 21(2), 149–177 (2008)

7. Boneh, D., Boyen, X.: Efficient selective identity-based encryption without random oracles. J. Cryptology 24(4), 659–693 (2011)

8. Boneh, D., Waters, B.: Conjunctive, Subset, and Range Queries on Encrypted Data. In: Vadhan, S.P. (ed.) TCC 2007. LNCS, vol. 4392, pp. 535–554. Springer, Heidelberg (2007)

9. Canetti, R., Riva, B., Rothblum, G.N.: Two 1-round protocols for delegation of computation. IACR Cryptology ePrint Archive 2011:518 (2011)

10. Chung, K.-M., Kalai, Y., Vadhan, S.: Improved Delegation of Computation Using Fully Homomorphic Encryption. In: Rabin, T. (ed.) CRYPTO 2010. LNCS, vol. 6223, pp. 483–501. Springer, Heidelberg (2010)

11. Damgård, I.B.: Towards Practical Public Key Systems Secure against Chosen Ciphertext Attacks. In: Feigenbaum, J. (ed.) CRYPTO 1991. LNCS, vol. 576, pp. 445–456. Springer, Heidelberg (1992)

12. Fiore, D., Gennaro, R.: Improved publicly verifiable delegation of large polynomials and matrix computations. IACR Cryptology ePrint Archive 2012:434 (2012)

13. Fiore, D., Gennaro, R.: Publicly verifiable delegation of large polynomials and matrix computations, with applications. In: CCS, pp. 501–512 (2012)

14. Gennaro, R., Gentry, C., Parno, B.: Non-interactive Verifiable Computing: Outsourcing Computation to Untrusted Workers. In: Rabin, T. (ed.) CRYPTO 2010. LNCS, vol. 6223, pp. 465–482. Springer, Heidelberg (2010)

15. Gennaro, R., Gentry, C., Parno, B., Raykova, M.: Quadratic span programs and succinct NIZKs without PCPs. IACR Cryptology ePrint Archive 2012:215 (2012)

16. Gentry, C.: Fully homomorphic encryption using ideal lattices. In: STOC, pp. 169–178 (2009)

17. Gentry, C., Wichs, D.: Separating succinct non-interactive arguments from all falsifiable assumptions. In: STOC, pp. 99–108 (2011)

18. Goodrich, M.T., Tamassia, R., Schwerin, A.: Implementation of an authenticated dictionary with skip lists and commutative hashing. In: DISCEX II, pp. 68–82 (2001)

19. Goodrich, M.T., Tamassia, R., Triandopoulos, N.: Super-Efficient Verification of Dynamic Outsourced Databases. In: Malkin, T. (ed.) CT-RSA 2008. LNCS, vol. 4964, pp. 407–424. Springer, Heidelberg (2008)

20. Goodrich, M.T., Tamassia, R., Triandopoulos, N.: Efficient authenticated data structures for graph connectivity and geometric search problems. Algorithmica 60(3), 505–552 (2011)

21. Goyal, V., Jain, A., Pandey, O., Sahai, A.: Bounded Ciphertext Policy Attribute Based Encryption. In: Aceto, L., Damgård, I., Goldberg, L.A., Halldórsson, M.M., Ingólfsdóttir, A., Walukiewicz, I. (eds.) ICALP 2008, Part II. LNCS, vol. 5126, pp. 579–591. Springer, Heidelberg (2008)

22. Groth, J.: Short Non-interactive Zero-Knowledge Proofs. In: Abe, M. (ed.) ASIACRYPT 2010. LNCS, vol. 6477, pp. 341–358. Springer, Heidelberg (2010)

23. Kate, A., Zaverucha, G.M., Goldberg, I.: Constant-Size Commitments to Polynomials and Their Applications. In: Abe, M. (ed.) ASIACRYPT 2010. LNCS, vol. 6477, pp. 177–194. Springer, Heidelberg (2010)

24. Lewko, A., Waters, B.: New Proof Methods for Attribute-Based Encryption: Achieving Full Security through Selective Techniques. In: Safavi-Naini, R. (ed.) CRYPTO 2012. LNCS, vol. 7417, pp. 180–198. Springer, Heidelberg (2012)
25. Yiu, M.L., Lin, Y., Mouratidis, K.: Efficient verification of shortest path search via authenticated hints. In: ICDE, pp. 237–248 (2010)
26. Merkle, R.C.: A Certified Digital Signature. In: Brassard, G. (ed.) CRYPTO 1989. LNCS, vol. 435, pp. 218–238. Springer, Heidelberg (1990)
27. Micali, S.: Computationally sound proofs. SIAM J. Comput. 30(4), 1253–1298 (2000)
28. Papamanthou, C., Shi, E., Tamassia, R.: Signatures of correct computation. IACR Cryptology ePrint Archive 2011: 587 (2011)
29. Papamanthou, C., Tamassia, R., Triandopoulos, N.: Authenticated hash tables. In: CCS, pp. 437–448 (2008)
30. Papamanthou, C., Tamassia, R., Triandopoulos, N.: Optimal Verification of Operations on Dynamic Sets. In: Rogaway, P. (ed.) CRYPTO 2011. LNCS, vol. 6841, pp. 91–110. Springer, Heidelberg (2011)
31. Parno, B., Raykova, M., Vaikuntanathan, V.: How to Delegate and Verify in Public: Verifiable Computation from Attribute-Based Encryption. In: Cramer, R. (ed.) TCC 2012. LNCS, vol. 7194, pp. 422–439. Springer, Heidelberg (2012)
32. Sahai, A., Waters, B.: Fuzzy Identity-Based Encryption. In: Cramer, R. (ed.) EUROCRYPT 2005. LNCS, vol. 3494, pp. 457–473. Springer, Heidelberg (2005)
33. Tamassia, R.: Authenticated Data Structures. In: Di Battista, G., Zwick, U. (eds.) ESA 2003. LNCS, vol. 2832, pp. 2–5. Springer, Heidelberg (2003)
34. Tamassia, R., Triandopoulos, N.: Efficient Content Authentication in Peer-to-Peer Networks. In: Katz, J., Yung, M. (eds.) ACNS 2007. LNCS, vol. 4521, pp. 354–372. Springer, Heidelberg (2007)
35. Tamassia, R., Triandopoulos, N.: Certification and authentication of data structures. In: Proc. Alberto Mendelzon Workshop on Foundations of Data Management (2010)

Appendix

Definition 6 (Selective security of an SCC scheme). *Let λ be the security parameter and let $\mathcal{P}$ be an SCC scheme* (KeyGen, Setup, Compute, Verify, Update) *for a function family $\mathcal{F}$. We say that $\mathcal{P}$ is selectively-secure if no PPT adversary $\mathcal{A}$ has more than negligible probability* neg(λ) *in winning the following game between $\mathcal{A}$ and a challenger:*

1. ***Initialization.*** *The adversary $\mathcal{A}$ commits to a point* b. *The challenger runs algorithm* KeyGen *which outputs* (PK, SK) *and gives* PK *to $\mathcal{A}$ but maintains* SK *secret;*
2. ***Setup and Update.*** *The adversary $\mathcal{A}$ initially makes an oracle query to algorithm* Setup(SK, PK, f_0), *specifying an initial function $f_0 \in \mathcal{F}$, outputting* FK(f_0). *Then, for $i = 1, \ldots, k$, where $k =$ poly(λ), he makes a polynomial number of oracle queries to the* Update(SK, PK, FK(f_{i-1}), f_i) *algorithm, each time specifying $f_i \in \mathcal{F}$. The challenger answers the queries by returning the resulting* FK(f_i);
3. ***Forgery.*** *The adversary $\mathcal{A}$ outputs a forgery* (b, v, w) *for point* b *that he committed in the initialization phase, for some function f_i previously queried where $0 \leq i \leq k$.*

The adversary $\mathcal{A}$ wins if $1 \leftarrow$ Verify(PK, FK(f_i), b, v, w) and $f_i(\mathbf{b}) \neq v$.

Definition 7 (PVC scheme). *We define a PVC scheme for a function family $\mathcal{F}$ to be a tuple of six PPT algorithms* (KeyGen, Setup, Challenge, Compute, Verify, Update) *with the following specification:*

1. $(PK, SK) \leftarrow KeyGen(\lambda, \mathcal{F})$: *Algorithm* KeyGen *takes as input the security parameter* λ *and a function family* $\mathcal{F}$. *It outputs a public/secret key pair* (PK, SK). KeyGen *is run only once at system initialization by a trusted source;*

2. $FK(f) \leftarrow Setup(SK, PK, f)$: *Algorithm* Setup *(run by a trusted source) takes as input the secret key* SK, *the public key* PK, *and a function* $f \in \mathcal{F}$. *It outputs the function public key* $FK(f)$ *for the function* f;

3. $chal(a) \leftarrow Challenge(PK, a)$: *Algorithm* Challenge *(run by the verifier) takes as input a value* $a \in domain(f)$. *It outputs a challenge* $chal(a)$ *corresponding to* a;

4. $(v, w) \leftarrow Compute(PK, f, a, chal(a))$: *Algorithm* Compute *(run by an untrusted server) takes as input the public key* PK, *a function* $f \in \mathcal{F}$ *and a value* $a \in domain(f)$. *It outputs a pair* (v, w), *where* $v = f(a)$ *and* w *is a signature;*

5. $\{0, 1\} \leftarrow Verify(PK, FK(f), a, chal(a), v, w)$: *Algorithm* Verify *(run by the verifier) takes as input the public key* PK, *function public key* $FK(f)$, *value* $a \in domain(f)$, *a claimed result* v *and a signature* w. *It outputs 0 or 1;*

6. $FK(f') \leftarrow Update(SK, PK, FK(f), f')$: *Algorithm* Update *(run by the trusted source) takes as input the secret key* SK, *the public key* PK, *the function public key* $FK(f)$ *for the old function* f *and the updated function description* f'. *It outputs the updated function public key* $FK(f')$.

Definition 8 (Correctness of a PVC scheme). *Let* λ *be the security parameter and let* $\mathcal{P}$ *be a PVC scheme* (KeyGen, Setup, Challenge, Compute, Verify, Update) *for a function family* $\mathcal{F}$. *Let* $(PK, SK) \leftarrow KeyGen(\lambda, \mathcal{F})$. *For all* $i = 1, \ldots, poly(\lambda)$, *for any function* $f_i \in \mathcal{F}$, *suppose* $FK(f_i)$ *is the output of* Update$(SK, PK, FK(f_{i-1}), f_i)$, *where* $FK(f_0)$ *is output by algorithm* Setup(SK, PK, f_0) *for some* $f_0 \in \mathcal{F}$. *We say that* $\mathcal{P}$ *is* correct, *if for any* $i = 0, \ldots, poly(\lambda)$, *for any* $a \in domain(f_i)$, *for any* $chal(a)$ *output by* Challenge(PK, a), *it is* $1 \leftarrow Verify(PK, FK(f_i), a, chal(a), v, w)$, *where* $(v, w) \leftarrow Compute(PK, f_i, a, chal(a)))$.

Definition 9 (Adaptive security of a PVC scheme). *Let* λ *be the security parameter and let* $\mathcal{P}$ *be a PVC scheme* (KeyGen, Setup, Challenge, Compute, Verify, Update) *for a function family* $\mathcal{F}$. *We say that* $\mathcal{P}$ *is* adaptively secure *if no PPT adversary* $\mathcal{A}$ *has more than negligible probability* $neg(\lambda)$ *in winning the following security game, played between the adversary* $\mathcal{A}$ *and a challenger:*

1. **Initialization.** *The challenger runs algorithm* KeyGen *which outputs* (PK, SK) *and then gives* PK *to the adversary but maintains* SK *secret;*

2. **Setup and Update.** *The adversary initially makes an oracle query to algorithm* Setup(SK, PK, f_0), *specifying an initial function* $f_0 \in \mathcal{F}$, *outputting* $FK(f_0)$. *Then, for* $i = 1, \ldots, k$, *where* $k = poly(\lambda)$, *he makes a polynomial number of oracle queries to the* Update$(SK, PK, FK(f_{i-1}), f_i)$ *algorithm, each time specifying* $f_i \in \mathcal{F}$. *The challenger answers the queries by returning the resulting* $FK(f_i)$;

3. **Challenge and Forgery.** *The adversary* $\mathcal{A}$ *outputs a point* b *and sends it to the challenger. The challenger returns* $chal(b)$ *output by* Challenge. *The adversary* $\mathcal{A}$ *outputs the forgery* $(b, chal(b), v, w)$ *for one of the functions* f_i $(0 \leq i \leq k)$ *that has been queried.*

The adversary $\mathcal{A}$ *wins if* $1 \leftarrow Verify(PK, FK(f_i), b, chal(b), v, w)$ *and* $f_i(b) \neq v$.

A Full Characterization of Functions that Imply Fair Coin Tossing and Ramifications to Fairness⋆

Gilad Asharov[1], Yehuda Lindell[1], and Tal Rabin[2]

[1] Department of Computer Science, Bar-Ilan University, Israel
[2] IBM T.J. Watson Research Center, New York
asharog@cs.biu.ac.il, lindell@biu.ac.il, talr@us.ibm.com

Abstract. It is well known that it is impossible for two parties to toss a coin fairly (Cleve, STOC 1986). This result implies that it is impossible to securely compute with fairness any function that can be used to toss a fair coin. In this paper, we focus on the class of deterministic Boolean functions with finite domain, and we ask for which functions in this class is it possible to information-theoretically toss an unbiased coin, given a protocol for securely computing the function with fairness. We provide a *complete characterization* of the functions in this class that imply and do not imply fair coin tossing. This characterization extends our knowledge of which functions cannot be securely computed with fairness. In addition, it provides a focus as to which functions may potentially be securely computed with fairness, since a function that cannot be used to fairly toss a coin is not ruled out by the impossibility result of Cleve (which is the *only* known impossibility result for fairness). In addition to the above, we draw corollaries to the feasibility of achieving fairness in two possible fail-stop models.

1 Introduction

1.1 Background

In the setting of secure multiparty computation, some mutually distrusting parties wish to compute some joint function of their inputs in the presence of adversarial behaviour. Loosely speaking, the security requirements from such a computation are that nothing is learned from the protocol other than the output (privacy), that the output is distributed according to the prescribed functionality (correctness), and that parties cannot choose their inputs as a function of the others' inputs (independence of inputs). Another important property is that of *fairness* which, intuitively, means that either *everyone* receives the output or *no one* does.

It is well known that when a majority of the parties are honest, it is possible to securely compute any functionality while guaranteeing all of the security properties mentioned above, including fairness [8,2,4,11]. Furthermore, when there is no

⋆ The first two authors were funded by the European Research Council under the European Union's Seventh Framework Programme (FP/2007-2013) / ERC Grant Agreement n. 239868, and by the ISRAEL SCIENCE FOUNDATION (grant No. 189/11). Much of this work was carried out while they were at the IBM T.J. Watson Research Center, New York.

A. Sahai (Ed.): TCC 2013, LNCS 7785, pp. 243–262, 2013.

honest majority, including the important case of two parties where one may be corrupted, it is possible to securely compute any functionality while guaranteeing all of the security properties mentioned above *except for fairness* [13,8,6]. The fact that fairness is not achieved in this latter case is inherent, as was shown in the seminal work of Cleve [5] who proved that there exist functions that cannot be computed by two parties with complete fairness. Specifically, Cleve showed that the very basic and natural functionality of coin-tossing, where two parties toss an unbiased coin, cannot be computed fairly. The impossibility result of Cleve implies that fairness cannot be achieved *in general*. That is, Cleve's result proves that it is impossible to securely compute with complete fairness any function that can be used to toss a fair coin (like the boolean XOR function).

Until recently, the accepted folklore from the time of Cleve's result was that *only trivial functions* can be securely computed with complete fairness without an honest majority. This changed recently with the surprising work of Gordon et al. [9] who showed that this folklore is incorrect and that there exist some non-trivial boolean functions that *can* be computed fairly, in the two party setting. They showed that *any* function that does not contain an embedded XOR (i.e., inputs x_1, x_2, y_1, y_2 such that $f(x_1, y_1) = f(x_2, y_2) \neq f(x_1, y_2) = f(x_2, y_1)$) can be computed fairly in the malicious settings. Examples of functions without an embedded XOR include the boolean OR and AND functions and Yao's millionaires problem [13] (i.e., the greater-than function). This possibility result changes our understanding regarding fairness, and re-opens the question of which functions can be computed with complete fairness. Given the possibility result mentioned above, and given the fact that Cleve's impossibility result rules out completely fair computation of boolean XOR, a natural conjecture is that the presence of an embedded XOR serves as a barrier to a fair computation of a given function. However, [9] showed that this is also incorrect: they give an example of a function that *does* contain an embedded XOR and construct a protocol that securely computes this function with fairness.

Since [9], there have been no other works that further our understanding regarding which (boolean) functions can be computed fairly without an honest majority in the two party setting. Specifically, Cleve's impossibility result is the only known function that cannot be computed fairly, and the class of functions for which [9] shows possibility are the only known possible functions. There is therefore a large class of functions for which we have no idea as to whether or not they can be securely computed with complete fairness.

1.2   Our Work

Motivated by the fundamental question of characterizing which functions can be computed with complete fairness, we analyze which functions *cannot* be computed fairly since they are already ruled out by Cleve's original result. That is, we show which boolean functions "imply" the coin-tossing functionality. We provide a simple property (criterion) on the truth table of a given boolean function. We then show that for every function that satisfies this property, it holds that the existence of a protocol that fairly computes the given function implies the existence of a protocol for fair coin-tossing in the presence of a fail-stop or malicious adversary, in contradiction to Cleve's impossibility result. This implies that the functions that satisfy the property cannot be computed fairly. The property is very simple, clean and general.

The more challenging and technically interesting part of our work is a proof that the property is *tight*. Namely, we show that a function f that does not satisfy the property *cannot* be used to construct a fair coin-tossing protocol (in the information theoretic setting). More precisely, we show that it is impossible to construct a fair two-party coin-tossing protocol, even if the parties are given access to a trusted party that computes f *fairly* for them. We prove this impossibility by showing the existence of an (inefficient) adversary that can bias the outcome with non-negligible probability. Thus, we prove that it is not possible to toss a coin with information-theoretic security, when given access to fair computations of f. We stress that this "impossibility" result is actually a source of optimism, since it *may* be possible to securely compute such functions with complete fairness. Indeed, the fair protocols presented in [9] are for functions for which the property does not hold.[1]

It is important to note that our proof that functions that do not satisfy the property do not imply coin tossing is very different from the proof of impossibility by Cleve. Specifically, the intuition behind the proof by Cleve is that since the parties exchange messages in turn, there must be a point where one party has more information than the other about the outcome of the coin-tossing protocol. If that party aborts at this point, then this results in bias. This argument holds since the parties cannot exchange information simultaneously. In contrast, in our setting, the parties *can* exchange information simultaneously via the computation of f. Thus, our proof is conceptually very different to that of Cleve, and in particular, is not a reduction to the proof by Cleve.

The Criterion. Intuitively, the property that we define over the function's truth table relates to the question of whether or not it is possible for one party to singlehandedly change the probability that the output of the function will be 1 (or 0) based on how it chooses its input. In order to explain the criterion, we give two examples of functions that imply coin-tossing, meaning that a fair secure protocol for computing the function implies a fair secure protocol for coin tossing. We discuss how each of the examples can be used to toss a coin fairly, and this in turn will help us to explain the criterion. The functions are given below:

(a)

	y_1	y_2	y_3
x_1	0	1	1
x_2	1	0	0
x_3	0	0	1

(b)

	y_1	y_2	y_3
x_1	1	0	0
x_2	0	1	0
x_3	0	0	1

---

[1] We remark that since our impossibility result is information theoretic, there is the possibility that some of the functions for which the property does not hold do imply coin tossing computationally. In such a case, the impossibility result of Cleve still applies to them. See more discussion in "open questions" below.

Consider function (a), and assume that there exists a fair protocol for this function. We show how to toss a fair coin using a single invocation of the protocol for f. Before doing so, we observe that the output of a single invocation of the function can be expressed by multiplying the truth-table matrix of the function by probability vectors.[2] Specifically, assume that party P_1 chooses input x_i with probability p_i, for $i = 1, 2, 3$ (thus $p_1 + p_2 + p_3 = 1$ since it must choose some input); likewise, assume that P_2 chooses input y_i with probability q_i. Now, let M_f be the "truth table" of the function, meaning that $M_f[i, j] = f(x_i, y_j)$. Then, the output of the invocation of f upon the inputs chosen by the parties equals 1 with probability exactly $(p_1, p_2, p_3) \cdot M_f \cdot (q_1, q_2, q_3)^T$.

We are now ready to show how to toss a coin using f. First, note that there are two complementary rows; these are the rows specified by inputs x_1 and x_2. This means that if P_1 chooses one of the inputs in $\{x_1, x_2\}$ uniformly at random, then no matter what distribution over the inputs (corrupted) P_2 uses, the result is a uniformly chosen coin. In order to see this, observe that when we multiply the vector $(\frac{1}{2}, \frac{1}{2}, 0)$ (the distribution over the input of P_1) with the matrix M_f, the result is the vector $(\frac{1}{2}, \frac{1}{2}, \frac{1}{2})$. This means that no matter what input P_2 will choose, or what distribution over the inputs it may use, the output is 1 with probability $1/2$ (formally, the output is 1 with probability $\frac{1}{2} \cdot q_1 + \frac{1}{2} \cdot q_2 + \frac{1}{2} \cdot q_3 = \frac{1}{2}$ because $q_1 + q_2 + q_3 = 1$). This means that if P_1 is honest, then a corrupted P_2 cannot bias the output. Likewise, there are also two complementary columns (y_1 and y_3), and thus, if P_2 chooses one of the inputs in $\{y_1, y_3\}$ uniformly at random, then no matter what distribution over the inputs (a possibly corrupted) P_1 uses, the result is a uniform coin.

In contrast, there are no two complementary rows or columns in the function (b). However, if P_1 chooses one of the inputs $\{x_1, x_2, x_3\}$ uniformly at random (i.e., each input with probability one third), then no matter what distribution P_2 will use, the output is 1 with probability $1/3$. Similarly, if P_2 chooses a uniformly random input, then no matter what P_1 does, the output is 1 with the same probability. Therefore, a single invocation of the function f in which the honest party chooses the uniform distribution over its inputs results in a coin that equals 1 with probability exactly $\frac{1}{3}$, irrespective of what the other party inputs. In order to obtain an unbiased coin that equals 1 with probability $\frac{1}{2}$ the method of von-Neumann [12] can be used. This method works by having the parties use the function f to toss two coins. If the resulting coins are different (i.e, 01 or 10), then they output the result of the first invocation. Otherwise, they run the protocol again. This yields a coin that equals 1 with probability $\frac{1}{2}$ since the probability of obtaining 01 equals the probability of obtaining 10. Thus, conditioned on the results being different, the probability of outputting 0 equals the probability of outputting 1.

The criterion is a direct generalization of the examples shown above. Let $f : \{x_1, \ldots, x_\ell\} \times \{y_1, \ldots, y_\ell\} \to \{0, 1\}$ be a function, and let M_f be the truth table representation as described above. We say that the function has the criterion if there exist two probability vectors, $\mathbf{p} = (p_1, \ldots, p_m)$, $\mathbf{q} = (q_1 \ldots, q_\ell)$

---

[2] $\mathbf{p} = (p_1, \ldots, p_m)$ is a **probability vector** if $p_i \geq 0$ for every $1 \leq i \leq m$, and $\sum_{i=1}^{m} p_i = 1$.

such that $\mathbf{p} \cdot M_f$ and $M_f \cdot \mathbf{q}^T$ are both vectors that equal δ everywhere, for some $0 < \delta < 1$. Observe that if such probability vectors exist, then the function implies the coin-tossing functionality as we described above. Specifically, P_1 chooses its input according to distribution $\mathbf{p}$, and P_2 chooses its inputs according to the distribution $\mathbf{q}$. The result is then a coin that equals 1 with probability δ. Using the method of von-Neumann, this can be used to obtain a uniformly distributed coin. We conclude:

Theorem 1.1 (informal). *Let $f : \{x_1, \ldots, x_m\} \times \{y_1, \ldots, y_\ell\} \to \{0,1\}$ be a function that satisfies the aforementioned criterion. Then, the existence of a protocol for securely computing f with complete fairness implies the existence of a fair coin tossing protocol.*

An immediate corollary of this theorem is that any such function cannot be securely computed with complete fairness, as this contradicts the impossibility result of Cleve [5].

As we have mentioned above, the more interesting and technically challenging part of our work is a proof that the criterion is tight. That is, we prove the following theorem:

Theorem 1.2 (informal). *Let $f : \{x_1, \ldots, x_m\} \times \{y_1, \ldots, y_\ell\} \to \{0,1\}$ be a function that does not satisfy the aforementioned criterion. Then, there exists an exponential-time adversary that can bias the outcome of every coin-tossing protocol that uses ideal and fair invocations of f.*

This result has a number of ramifications. Most notably, it helps focus our research on the question of fairness in two-party secure computation. Specifically, the only functions that can potentially be computed securely with fairness are those for which the property does not hold. In these functions one of the parties can partially influence the outcome of the result singlehandedly, a fact that is used inherently in the protocol of [9] for the function with an embedded XOR. This does not mean that all functions of this type can be fairly computed. However, it provides a good starting point. In addition, our results define the set of functions for which Cleve's impossibility result suffices for proving that they cannot be securely computed with fairness. Given that no function other than those implying coin tossing has been ruled out since Cleve's initial result, understanding exactly what is included in this impossibility is of importance.

On Fail-Stop Adversaries. Our main results above consider the case of malicious adversaries. In addition, we explore the fail-stop adversary model where the adversary follows the protocol like an honest party, but can halt early. This model is of interest since the impossibility result of Cleve [5] for achieving fair coin tossing holds also for fail-stop adversaries. In order to prove theorems regarding the fail-stop model, we first provide a definition of security with complete fairness for fail-stop adversaries that follows the real/ideal simulation paradigm. Surprisingly, this turns out not to be straightforward and we provide two natural formulations that are very different regarding feasibility. The formulations differ regarding the ideal-world adversary/simulator. The question that arises is whether or not the simulator is allowed to use a different input to the prescribed one. In the semi-honest model (which differs only in the fact that the adversary cannot halt early) the standard formulation is to not allow the simulator to change the prescribed input, whereas in the malicious model the simulator is always allowed to change the prescribed input. We therefore define two fail-stop models. In this first, called "fail-stop1", the simulator is allowed to either send the trusted party computing the function the prescribed input of the party or an abort symbol $\perp$, but nothing else. In the second, called "fail-stop2", the simulator may send any input that it wishes to the trusted party computing the function. Note, however, that if there was no early abort then the prescribed input must be used because such an execution is identical to an execution between two honest parties.

Observe that in the first model, the honest party is guaranteed to receive the output on the prescribed inputs, unless it receives abort. In addition, observe that any protocol that is secure in the presence of malicious adversaries is secure also in the fail-stop2 model. However, this is not true of the fail-stop1 model (this is due to the fact that the simulator in the ideal model for the case of malicious adversaries is more powerful than in the fail-stop1 ideal model since the former can send any input whereas the latter can only send the prescribed input or $\perp$).

We remark that Cleve's impossibility result holds in both models, since the parties do not have inputs in the coin-tossing functionality, and therefore there is no difference in the ideal-worlds of the models in this case. In addition, the protocols of [9] that are secure for malicious adversaries are secure for fail-stop2 (as mentioned above, this is immediate), but are *not* secure for fail-stop1.

We show that in the fail-stop1 model, it is impossible to securely compute with complete fairness any function containing an embedded XOR. We show this by constructing a coin-tossing protocol from any such function, that is secure in the fail-stop model. Thus, the only functions that can potentially be securely computed with fairness are those with no embedded XOR but with an embedded OR (if a function has neither, then it is trivial and can be computed unconditionally and fairly); we remark that there are very few functions with this property. We conclude that in the fail-stop1 model, fairness cannot be achieved for almost all non-trivial functions. We remark that [9] presents secure protocols that achieve complete fairness for functions that have no embedded XOR; however, they are not secure in the fail-stop1 model, as mentioned.

Regarding the fail-stop2 model, we prove an analogous result to Theorem 1.2. In the proof of Theorem 1.2, the adversary that we construct changes its input in one of the invocations of f and then continues honestly. Thus, it is malicious and not fail-stop2. Nevertheless, we show how the proof can be modified in order to hold for the fail-stop2 model as well.

These extensions for fail-stop adversaries deepen our understanding regarding the feasibility of obtaining fairness. Specifically, any protocol that achieves fairness for any non-trivial function (or at least any function that has an embedded XOR), must have the property that the simulator can send any input in the ideal model. Stated differently, the input that is effectively used by a corrupted party cannot be somehow committed, thereby preventing this behaviour. This also explains why the protocols of [9] have this property.

1.3 Open Questions

In this work we provide an almost complete characterization regarding what functions imply and do not imply coin tossing. Our characterisation is not completely tight since the impossibility result of Theorem 1.2 only holds in the information-theoretic setting; this is due to the fact that the adversary needs to carry out inefficient computations. Thus, it is conceivable that coin tossing can be achieved computationally from some such functions. It is important to note, however, that any function that does not fulfil our criterion implies oblivious transfer (OT). Thus, any protocol that uses such a function has access to OT and all that is implied by OT (e.g., commitments, zero knowledge, and so on). Thus, any such computational construction would have to be inherently nonblack-box in some sense. Our work also only considers finite functions (where the size of the domain is not dependent on the security parameter); extensions to other function classes, including non-Boolean functions, is also of interest.

The main open question left by our work is to characterize which functions for which the criterion does not hold can be securely computed with complete fairness. Our work is an important step to answering this question by providing a clearer focus than was previously known. Observe that in order to show that a function that does not fulfil the criterion cannot be securely computed with complete fairness, a new impossibility result must be proven. In particular, it will not be possible to reduce the impossibility to Cleve [5] since such a function does not imply coin tossing.

2 Definitions

The Coin-Tossing Functionality. We define the coin-tossing functionality simply by $f^{ct}(\lambda, \lambda) = (U_1, U_1)$, where λ denotes the empty input and U_1 denotes the uniform distribution over $\{0, 1\}$. That is, the functionality receives no input, chooses a uniformly chosen bit and gives both parties the same bit. This yields the following definition:

Definition 2.1 (Coin-Tossing by Simulation). *A protocol π is a* secure coin-tossing protocol via simulation *if it securely computes f^{ct} with complete fairness in the presence of malicious adversaries.*

The above definition provides very strong simulation-based guarantees, which is excellent for our positive results. However, when proving impossibility, it is preferable to rule out even weaker, non-simulation based definitions. We now present a weaker definition where the guarantee is that the honest party outputs an unbiased coin, irrespective of the cheating party's behaviour.

However, we stress that since our impossibility result only holds with respect to an all-powerful adversary (as discussed in the introduction), our definition is stronger than above since it requires security in the presence of any adversary, and not just polynomial-time adversaries.

Notations. Denote by $\langle P_1, P_2 \rangle$ a two party protocol where both parties act honestly. For $\ell \in \{1, 2\}$, let $\mathsf{out}_\ell \langle P_1^*, P_2^* \rangle$ denote the output of party P_ℓ^* in an execution of P_1^* with P_2^*. In some cases, we also specify the random coins that the parties use in the execution; $\langle P_1(r_1), P_2(r_2) \rangle$ denotes an execution where P_1 acts honestly and uses random tape r_1 and P_2 acts honestly and uses random tape r_2. Let $r(n)$ be a polynomial that bounds the number of rounds of the protocol π, and let $c(n)$ be an upper bound on the length of the random tape of the parties. Let Uni denote the uniform distribution over $\{0,1\}^{c(n)} \times \{0,1\}^{c(n)}$. We are now ready to define a coin-tossing protocol:

Definition 2.2 (Information-Theoretic Coin-Tossing). *A polynomial-time protocol $\pi = \langle P_1, P_2 \rangle$ is an* unbiased coin-tossing protocol, *if the following hold:*

1. **(agreement)** *There exists a negligible function $\mu(\cdot)$ such that for every n it holds that:*

$$\Pr_{r_1, r_2 \leftarrow \mathsf{Uni}} \left[\mathsf{out}_1 \langle P_1(r_1), P_2(r_2) \rangle \neq \mathsf{out}_2 \langle P_1(r_1), P_2(r_2) \rangle \right] \leq \mu(n) \ .$$

2. **(no bias)** *For every adversary $\mathcal{A}$ there exists a negligible function $\mu(\cdot)$ such that for every $b \in \{0, 1\}$ and every $n \in \mathbb{N}$:*

$$\Pr \left[\mathsf{out}_1 \langle P_1, \mathcal{A} \rangle = b \right] \leq \frac{1}{2} + \mu(n) \quad \text{and} \quad \Pr \left[\mathsf{out}_2 \langle \mathcal{A}, P_2 \rangle = b \right] \leq \frac{1}{2} + \mu(n) \ .$$

Observe that both requirements together guarantee that two honest parties will output the same uniformly distributed bit, except with negligible probability.

Function Implication. In the paper, we study whether or not a function f "implies" the coin-tossing functionality. We now formally define what we mean by "function implication". Our formulation uses the notion of a hybrid model, which is a combination of the ideal and real models (see [3,6]). Specifically, let f be a function. Then, an execution in the f-hybrid model consists of real interaction between the parties (like in the real model) and ideal invocations of f (like in the ideal model). The ideal invocations of f take place via a trusted party that receives inputs and sends the output of f on those inputs to both parties, exactly like in the ideal model. We stress that in our ideal model both parties receive the output of f simultaneously since we are considering fair secure computation. We are now ready for the definition.

Definition 2.3. *Let $f : X \times Y \to Z$ and $g : X' \times Y' \to Z'$ be functions. We say that* function f implies function g in the presence of malicious adversaries *if there exists a protocol that securely computes g in the f-hybrid model with complete fairness, in the presence of static malicious adversaries. We say that f* information-theoretically *implies g if the above holds with statistical security.*

Note that if g can be securely computed with fairness (under some assumption), then every function f computationally implies g. Thus, this is only of interest for functions g that either cannot be securely computed with fairness, or for which this fact is not known.

3   The Criterion

In this section we define the criterion, and explore its properties. We start with the definition of δ-balanced functions.

3.1 δ-Balanced Functions

A vector $\mathbf{p} = (p_1, \ldots, p_k)$ is a probability vector if $\sum_{i=1}^{k} p_i = 1$, and for every $1 \leq i \leq k$ it holds that $p_i \geq 0$. Let $\mathbf{1}_k$ be the all one vector of size k. In addition, for a given function $f : \{x_1, \ldots, x_m\} \times \{y_1, \ldots, y_\ell\} \to \{0, 1\}$, let M_f denote the matrix defined by the truth table of f. That is, for every $1 \leq i \leq m$, $1 \leq j \leq \ell$, it holds that $M_f[i, j] = f(x_i, y_j)$.

Informally, a function is balanced if there exist probabilities over the inputs for each party that determine the probability that the output equals 1, irrespective of what input the other party uses. Assume that P_1 chooses its input according to the probability vector $(p_1, \ldots, p_m)$, meaning that it uses input x_i with probability p_i, for every $i = 1, \ldots, m$, and assume that party P_2 uses the jth input y_j. Then, the probability that the output equals 1 is obtained by multiplying $(p_1, \ldots, p_m)$ with the jth column of M_f. Thus, a function is balanced on the left, or with respect to P_1, if when multiplying $(p_1, \ldots, p_m)$ with M_f the result is a vector with values that are all equal. Formally:

Definition 3.1. *Let* $f : \{x_1, \ldots, x_m\} \times \{y_1, \ldots, y_\ell\} \to \{0, 1\}$ *be a function, and let* $0 \leq \delta_1, \delta_2 \leq 1$ *be constants. We say that* f *is* δ_1-left-balanced *if there exists a probability vector* $\mathbf{p} = (p_1, \ldots, p_m)$ *such that:*

$$(p_1, \ldots, p_m) \cdot M_f = \delta_1 \cdot \mathbf{1}_\ell = (\delta_1, \ldots, \delta_1) \ .$$

Likewise, we say that the function f *is* δ_2-right-balanced *if there exists a probability vector* $\mathbf{q} = (q_1, \ldots, q_\ell)$ *such that:*

$$M_f \cdot (q_1, \ldots, q_\ell)^T = \delta_2 \cdot \mathbf{1}_m^T \ .$$

If f *is* δ_1-left-balanced *and* δ_2-right-balanced, *we say that* f *is* (δ_1, δ_2)-balanced. *If* $\delta_1 = \delta_2$, *then we say that* f *is* δ-balanced, *where* $\delta = \delta_1 = \delta_2$. *We say that* f *is strictly* δ-balanced *if* $\delta_1 = \delta_2$ *and* $0 < \delta < 1$.

Note that a function may be δ_2-right-balanced for some $0 \leq \delta_2 \leq 1$ but not left balanced. For example, consider the function defined by the truth table $M_f \stackrel{\text{def}}{=} \begin{bmatrix} 1 & 0 & 1 \\ 0 & 1 & 1 \end{bmatrix}$. This function is right balanced for $\delta_2 = \frac{1}{2}$ by taking $\mathbf{q} = (\frac{1}{2}, \frac{1}{2}, 0)$. However, it is not left-balanced for any δ_1 because for every probability vector

$(p_1, p_2) = (p, 1-p)$ it holds that $(p_1, p_2) \cdot M_{\widetilde{f}} = (p, 1-p, 1)$, which is not balanced for any p. Likewise, a function may be δ_2-right-balanced, but not left balanced.

We now prove a simple but somewhat surprising proposition, stating that if a function is (δ_1, δ_2)-balanced, then δ_1 and δ_2 must actually equal each other. Thus, any (δ_1, δ_2)-balanced function is actually δ-balanced.

Proposition 3.2. *Let* $f : \{x_1, \ldots, x_m\} \times \{y_1, \ldots, y_\ell\} \rightarrow \{0, 1\}$ *be a* (δ_1, δ_2)-*balanced function for some constants* $0 \le \delta_1, \delta_2 \le 1$. *Then,* $\delta_1 = \delta_2$, *and so* f *is* δ-*balanced.*

Proof: Under the assumption that f is (δ_1, δ_2)-balanced, we have that there exist probability vectors $\mathbf{p} = (p_1, \ldots, p_m)$ and $\mathbf{q} = (q_1, \ldots, q_\ell)$ such that $\mathbf{p} \cdot M_f = \delta_1 \cdot \mathbf{1}_\ell$ and $M_f \cdot \mathbf{q}^T = \delta_2 \cdot \mathbf{1}_m^T$. Observe that since $\mathbf{p}$ and $\mathbf{q}$ are probability vectors, it follows that for every constant c we have $\mathbf{p} \cdot (c \cdot \mathbf{1}_m^T) = c \cdot (\mathbf{p} \cdot \mathbf{1}_m^T) = c$; likewise $(c \cdot \mathbf{1}_\ell) \cdot \mathbf{q}^T = c$. Thus,

$$\mathbf{p} \cdot M_f \cdot \mathbf{q}^T = \mathbf{p} \cdot \left(M_f \cdot \mathbf{q}^T \right) = \mathbf{p} \cdot \left(\delta_2 \cdot \mathbf{1}_m^T \right) = \delta_2$$

and

$$\mathbf{p} \cdot M_f \cdot \mathbf{q}^T = \left(\mathbf{p} \cdot M_f \right) \cdot \mathbf{q}^T = \left(\delta_1 \cdot \mathbf{1}_\ell \right) \cdot \mathbf{q}^T = \delta_1,$$

implying that $\delta_1 = \delta_2$.   ■

Note that a function can be both δ_2-right-balanced and δ_2'-right-balanced for some $\delta_2 \ne \delta_2'$. For example, consider the function M_f, which was defined above. It is easy to see that the function is δ_2-right-balanced for every $1/2 \le \delta_2 \le 1$ (by multiplying with the probability vector $(1 - \delta_2, 1 - \delta_2, 2\delta_2 - 1)^T$ from the right). Nevertheless, in cases where a function is δ_2-right-balanced for multiple values, Proposition 3.2 implies that the function cannot be left-balanced for *any* δ_1. Likewise, if a function is δ_1-left balanced for more than one value of δ_1, it cannot be right-balanced.

3.2   The Criterion

The criterion for determining whether or not a function implies coin-tossing is simply the question of whether the function is *strictly* δ-balanced for some δ. Formally:

Property 3.3. *A function* $f : \{x_1, \ldots, x_m\} \times \{y_1, \ldots, y_\ell\} \rightarrow \{0, 1\}$ *is strictly balanced if it is* δ-*balanced for some* $0 < \delta < 1$.

Observe that if M_f has a monochromatic row (i.e., there exists an input x such that for all y_i, y_j it holds that $f(x, y_i) = f(x, y_j)$), then there exists a probability vector $\mathbf{p}$ such that $\mathbf{p} \cdot M_f = 0 \cdot \mathbf{1}_\ell$ or $\mathbf{p} \cdot M_f = 1 \cdot \mathbf{1}_\ell$; likewise for a monochromatic column. Nevertheless, we stress that the existence of such a row and column does not imply f is strictly balanced since it is required that δ be strictly between 0 and 1, and not equal to either.

3.3   Exploring the δ-Balanced Property

In this section we prove some technical lemmas regarding the property that we will need later in the proof. First, we show that if a function f is not left-balanced for any $0 \le \delta \le 1$ (resp. not right balanced), then it is *not close* to being balanced. More precisely, it seems possible that a function f can be not δ-balanced, but is only negligibly far from being balanced (i.e., there may exist some probability vector $\mathbf{p} = \mathbf{p}(n)$ (that depends on the security parameter n) such that all the values in the vector $\mathbf{p} \cdot M_f$ are at most negligibly far from δ, for some $0 \le \delta \le 1$). In the following claim, we show that this situation is impossible. Specifically, we show that if a function is not δ balanced, then there exists some constant $c > 0$, such that for any probability vector $\mathbf{p}$, there is a distance of at least c between two values in the vector $\mathbf{p} \cdot M_f$. This holds also for probability vectors that are functions of the security parameter n (as can be the case in our setting of secure protocols).

Lemma 3.4. *Let* $f : \{x_1, \ldots, x_m\} \times \{y_1, \ldots, y_\ell\} \to \{0, 1\}$ *be a function that is not left balanced for any* $0 \le \delta_1 \le 1$ *(including* $\delta_1 = 0, 1$*). Then, there exists a constant* $c > 0$*, such that for any probability vector* $\mathbf{p} = \mathbf{p}(n)$*, it holds that:*

$$\max_i(\delta_1, \ldots, \delta_\ell) - \min_i(\delta_1, \ldots, \delta_\ell) \ge c$$

where $(\delta_1, \ldots, \delta_\ell) = \mathbf{p} \cdot M_f$*, and* M_f *is the matrix representation of* f*.*

Proof: Let P^m be the set of all probability vectors of size m. That is, $\mathrm{P}^m \subseteq [0,1]^m$ (which itself is a subset of $\mathbb{R}^m$), and each vector sums up to one. P^m is a closed and bounded space. Therefore using the Heine-Borel theorem, P^m is a compact space.

We start by defining a function $\phi : \mathrm{P}^m \to [0, 1]$ as follows:

$$\phi(\mathbf{p}) = \max_i(\mathbf{p} \cdot M_f) - \min_i \cdot (\mathbf{p} \cdot M_f)$$

Clearly, the function $\mathbf{p} \cdot M_f$ (where M_f is fixed and $\mathbf{p}$ is the variable) is a continuous function. Moreover, the maximum (resp. minimum) of a continuous function is itself a continuous function. Therefore, from composition of continuous functions we have that the function ϕ is continuous. Using the extreme value theorem (a continuous function from a compact space to a subset of the real numbers attains its maximum and minimum), there exists some probability vector $\mathbf{p}_{\min}$ for which for all $\mathbf{p} \in \mathrm{P}^m$, $\phi(\mathbf{p}_{\min}) \le \phi(\mathbf{p})$. Since f is not δ-balanced, $\mathbf{p}_{\min} \cdot M_f \ne \delta \cdot \mathbf{1}_\ell$ for any $0 \le \delta \le 1$, and so $\phi(\mathbf{p}_{\min}) > 0$. Let $c \stackrel{\text{def}}{=} \phi(\mathbf{p}_{\min})$. This implies that for any probability vector $\mathbf{p}$, we have that $\phi(\mathbf{p}) \ge \phi(\mathbf{p}_{\min}) = c$. That is:

$$\max_i(\delta_1, \ldots, \delta_\ell) - \min_i(\delta_1, \ldots, \delta_\ell) \ge c \tag{1}$$

where $(\delta_1, \ldots, \delta_\ell) = \mathbf{p} \cdot M_f$. We have proven this for *all* probability vectors of size m. Thus, it holds also for every probability vector $\mathbf{p}(n)$ that is a function of n, and for all n's (this is true since for every n, $\mathbf{p}(n)$ defines a concrete probability vector for which Eq. (1) holds). ∎

A similar claim holds for the case where f is not right balanced.

4   Strictly-Balanced Functions Imply Coin Tossing

In this section, we show that any function f that is strictly balanced can be used to fairly toss a coin. Intuitively, this follows from the well known method of Von Neumann [12] for obtaining an unbiased coin toss from a biased one. Specifically, given a coin·that is heads with probability ϵ and tails with probability $1 - \epsilon$, Von Neumann showed that you can toss a coin that is heads with probability exactly $1/2$ by tossing the coin twice in each phase, and stopping the first time that the pair is either heads-tails or tails-heads. Then, the parties output heads if the pair is heads-tails, and otherwise they output tails. This gives an unbiased coin because the probability of heads-tails equals the probability of tails-heads (namely, both probabilities equal $\epsilon \cdot (1 - \epsilon)$). Now, since the function f is strictly δ-balanced it holds that if party P_1 chooses its input via the probability vector $(p_1, \ldots, p_m)$ then the output will equal 1 with probability δ, irrespective of what input is used by P_2; likewise if P_2 chooses its input via $(q_1, \ldots, q_\ell)$ then the output will be 1 with probability δ irrespective of what P_1 does. This yields a coin that equals 1 with probability δ and thus Von Neumann's method can be applied to achieve unbiased coin tossing. We stress that if one of the parties aborts early and refuses to participate, then the other party proceeds by itself (essentially, tossing a coin with probability δ until it concludes). We have the following theorem:

Theorem 4.1. Let $f : \{x_1, \ldots, x_m\} \times \{y_1, \ldots, y_\ell\} \to \{0, 1\}$ be a strictly-balanced function for some constant $0 < \delta < 1$, as in Property 3.3. Then, f information-theoretically and computationally implies the coin-tossing functionality f^{ct} with malicious adversaries.

Application to Fairness. Cleve [5] showed that there does not exist a protocol that securely computes the fair coin-tossing functionality in the plain model. Since any strictly-balanced function f implies the coin-tossing functionality, a protocol for f in the plain model implies the existence of a protocol for coin-tossing in the plain model. We therefore conclude:

Corollary 4.2. Let $f : \{x_1, \ldots, x_m\} \times \{y_1, \ldots, y_\ell\} \to \{0, 1\}$ be a strictly-balanced function. Then, f cannot be securely computed with fairness (with computational or information-theoretic security).

5   Unbalanced Functions Do Not Information-Theoretically Imply Coin Tossing

We now show that any function f that is *not* strictly-balanced (for all δ) does *not* information-theoretically imply the coin-tossing functionality. Stated differently, there does not exist a protocol for fairly tossing an unbiased coin in the f-hybrid model, with statistical security. Observe that in the f-hybrid model, it is possible for the parties to simultaneously exchange information, in some sense, since both parties receive output from calls to f at the same time. Thus, Cleve-type arguments [5] that are based on the fact that one party must know more than the other party at some point do not hold. We prove our result by showing that for every protocol there exists an unbounded malicious adversary that can bias the result. Our unbounded adversary needs to compute probabilities, which can actually be approximated given an $\mathcal{NP}$-oracle. Thus, it is possible to interpret our technical result also as a black-box separation, if desired.

As we have mentioned in the introduction, although we prove an "impossibility result" here, the implication is the opposite. Specifically, our proof that an unbalanced[3] f cannot be used to toss an unbiased coin implies that it may be possible to securely compute such functions with fairness. Indeed, the functions that were shown to be securely computable with fairness in [9] are unbalanced.

Recall that a function is not strictly balanced if is not δ-balanced for any $0 < \delta < 1$. We treat the case that the function is not δ-balanced at all separately from the case that it *is* δ-balanced but for $\delta = 0$ or $\delta = 1$. In the proof we show that in both of these cases, such a function cannot be used to construct a fair coin tossing protocol.

Theorem 5.1. *Let* $f : \{x_1, \ldots, x_m\} \times \{y_1, \ldots, y_\ell\} \to \{0, 1\}$ *be a function that is not left-balanced, for any* $0 \leq \delta_1 \leq 1$. *Then,* f *does not information-theoretically imply the coin-tossing functionality with malicious adversaries.*

Proof Idea: We begin by observing that if f does not contain an embedded OR (i.e., inputs x_0, x_1, y_0, y_1 such that $f(x_0, y_0) = f(x_1, y_0) = f(x_0, y_1) \neq f(x_1, y_1)$) or an embedded XOR (i.e., inputs x_0, x_1, y_0, y_1 such that $f(x_0, y_0) = f(x_1, y_1) \neq f(x_0, y_1) = f(x_1, y_0)$), then it is trivial and can be computed by simply having one party send the output to the other. This is because such a function depends only on the input of one party. Thus, by [5], it is impossible to fairly toss an unbiased coin in the f-hybrid model, since this is the same as fairly tossing an unbiased coin in the plain model. Thus, we consider only functions f that have an embedded OR or an embedded XOR.

In addition, we consider coin-tossing protocols that consist of calls to f only, and no other messages. This is due to the fact that we can assume that any protocol consists of rounds, where each round is either an invocation of f or a message consisting of a single bit being sent from one party to the other. Since f has an embedded OR or an embedded XOR, messages of a single bit can be sent by invoking f. This is due to the fact that in both cases there exist inputs x_0, x_1, y_0, y_1 such that $f(x_1, y_0) \neq f(x_1, y_1)$ and $f(x_0, y_1) \neq f(x_1, y_1)$. Thus, in order for P_2 to send P_1 a bit, the protocol can instruct the parties to invoke f where P_1 always inputs x_1, and P_2 inputs y_0 or y_1 depending on the bit that it wishes to send; similarly for P_1. Thus, any non-trivial function f enables "bit transmission" in the above sense. Observe that if one of the parties is malicious and uses an incorrect input, then this simply corresponds to sending an incorrect bit in the original protocol.

Intuition. The fact that f is not balanced implies that in any single invocation of f, one party is able to have some effect on the output by choosing its input

---

[3] Note, that the name unbalanced is a bit misleading as the complement of not being strictly balanced also includes being 1 or 0-balanced.

appropriately. That is, if the function is non-balanced on the left then the party on the right can use an input not according to the prescribed distribution in the protocol, and this will change the probability of the output of the invocation being 1 (for example). However, it may be possible that the ability to somewhat influence the output in individual invocations is not sufficient to bias the overall computation, due to the way that the function calls are composed. Thus, in the proof we need to show that an adversary is in fact capable of biasing the overall protocol. We demonstrate this by showing that there exist crucial invocations where the ability to bias the outcome in these invocation suffice for biasing the overall outcome. Then, we show that such invocations are always reached in any execution of the protocol, and that the adversary can (inefficiently) detect when such an invocation has been reached and can (inefficiently) compute which input it needs to use in that invocation in order to bias the output.

We prove the above by considering the execution tree of the protocol, which is comprised of calls to f and the flow of the computation based on the output of f in each invocation (i.e., the parties proceed left in the tree if the output of f in this invocation is 0; and right otherwise). Observe that a path from the root of the tree to a leaf-node represents a protocol execution. We show that in *every* path from the root to a leaf, there exists at least one node with the property that influencing the output of the single invocation of that node yields a bias in the final outcome. In addition, we describe the strategy of the adversary to detect such a node and choose its input for that node in order to obtain a bias.

In more detail, for every node v in the execution tree of the protocol, the adversary calculates (in an inefficient manner) the probability that the output of the computation equals 1, assuming that v is reached in the execution. Observe that the probability of obtaining 1 at the root node is at most negligibly far from $1/2$ (since it is a secure coin-tossing protocol), and that the probability of obtaining 1 at a leaf node is either 1 or 0, depending on whether the output at the given leaf is 1 or 0 (the way that we define the tree is such that the output is fully determined by the leaf). Using a pigeon-hole like argument, we show that on every path from the root to a leaf there must be at least one node where the probability of outputting 1 given that this node is reached is significantly different than the probability of outputting 1 given that the node's child on the path is reached. We further show that this difference implies that the two children of the given node yield significantly different probabilities of outputting 1 (since the probability of outputting 1 at a node v is the weighted-average of outputting 1 at the children, based on the probability of reaching each child according to the protocol). This implies that in every protocol execution, there exists an invocation of f where the probability of outputting 1 in the entire protocol is significantly different if the output of this invocation of f is 0 or 1. Since f is not balanced, it follows that for any distribution used by the honest party to choose its input for this invocation, there exist two inputs that the corrupted party can use that result in significantly different probabilities of obtaining 1. In particular, at least one of these probabilities is *significantly different from the probability of obtaining 1 in this call when both parties are honest and follow the protocol.*[4] Thus, the adversary can cause the output of the entire execution to equal 1 with probability significantly different than $1/2$, which is the probability when both parties play honestly.

The above description does not deal with question of whether the output will be biased towards 0 or 1. In fact we design two adversaries, one that tries to bias the output towards 0 and the other towards 1. Then we show that at least one of these adversaries will be successful (see Footnote 4 for an explanation as to why only one of the adversaries may be successful). The two adversaries are similar and very simple. They search for the node on the path of the execution where the bias can be created and there make their move. In all nodes until and after that node they behave honestly (i.e., choose inputs for the invocations of f according to the input distribution specified by the protocol). We analyze the success of the adversaries and show that at least one of them biases the output with noticeable probability. The full proof appears in [1]. ∎

The above theorem proves impossibility for the case that the function is not balanced. As we have mentioned, we must separately deal with the case that the function *is* balanced, but not *strictly* balanced; i.e., the function is either 0-balanced or 1-balanced. The main difference in this case is that not all nodes which have significantly different probabilities in their two children can be used by the adversary to bias the outcome. This is due to the fact that the protocol may specify an input distribution for the honest party at such a node that forces the output to be either 0 or 1 (except with negligible probability), and so the "different child" is only reached with negligible probability. This can happen since the function *is* balanced with $\delta = 0$ or $\delta = 1$. The proof therefore shows that this cannot happen too often, and the adversary can succeed enough to bias the output. The following is proven in [1]:

Theorem 5.2. *Let* $f : \{x_1, \ldots, x_m\} \times \{y_1, \ldots, y_\ell\} \to \{0, 1\}$ *be a 1-balanced or a 0-balanced function. Then, f does not information-theoretically imply the coin-tossing protocol.*

Conclusion: Combining Theorems 4.1, 5.1 and 5.2, we obtain the following:

Corollary 5.3. *Let* $f : \{x_1, \ldots, x_m\} \times \{y_1, \ldots, y_\ell\} \to \{0, 1\}$ *be a function.*

1. *If f is strictly-balanced, then f implies the coin-tossing functionality (computationally and information theoretically).*
2. *If f is not strictly-balanced, then f does not information-theoretically imply the coin-tossing functionality with malicious adversaries.*

Impossibility in the OT-Hybrid Model. Our proof of impossibility holds only in the information-theoretic setting since the adversary must carry out computations that do not seem to be computable in polynomial-time. It is natural

---

[4] Observe that one of these probabilities may be the same as the probability of obtaining 1 in an honest execution, in which case choosing that input will not result in any bias. Thus, the adversary may be able to bias the output of the entire protocol towards 1 or may be able to bias the output of the entire protocol towards 0, but not necessarily both.

to ask whether or not the impossibility result still holds in the computational setting. We do not have an answer to this question. However, as a step in this direction, we show that the impossibility still holds if the parties are given access to an ideal oblivious transfer (OT) primitive as well as to the function f. That is, we prove the following:

Theorem 5.4. *Let* $f : \{x_1, \ldots, x_m\} \times \{y_1, \ldots, y_\ell\} \to \{0, 1\}$ *be a function. If* f *is not strictly-balanced, then the pair of functions* (f, OT) *do not information-theoretically imply the coin tossing functionality with malicious adversaries.*

Proof: In order to see that this is the case, first observe that if f has an embedded-OR then it implies oblivious transfer [10]. Thus, f can be used to obtain OT, and so the question of whether f implies coin tossing or (f, OT) imply coin tossing is the same. It thus remains to consider the case that f does not have an embedded OR but does have an embedded XOR (if it has neither then it is trivial and so clearly cannot imply coin tossing, as we have mentioned). We now show that in such a case f must be strictly balanced, and so this case is not relevant. Let x_1, x_2, y_1, y_2 be an embedded XOR in f; i.e., $f(x_1, y_1) = f(x_2, y_2) \neq f(x_1, y_2) = f(x_2, y_1)$. Now, if there exists a y_3 such that $f(x_1, y_3) = f(x_2, y_3)$ then f has an embedded OR. Thus, x_1 and x_2 must be complementary rows (as in example function (a) in the Introduction). Likewise, if there exists an x_3 such that $f(x_3, y_1) = f(x_3, y_2)$ then f has an embedded OR. Thus, y_1 and y_2 must be complementary columns. We conclude that f has two complementary rows and columns, and as we have shown in the Introduction, this implies that f is strictly balanced with $\delta = \frac{1}{2}$.   ∎

6   Fairness in the Presence of Fail-Stop Adversaries

In order to study the feasibility of achieving fair secure computation in the fail-stop model, we must first present a definition of security for this model. To the best of our knowledge, there is no simulation-based security definition for the fail-stop model in the literature. As we have mentioned in the introduction, there are two natural ways of defining security in this model, and it is not clear which is the "correct one". We therefore define two models and study feasibility for both. In the first model, the ideal-model adversary/simulator must either send the party's prescribed input to the trusted party computing the function, or a special abort symbol $\perp$, but nothing else. This is similar to the semi-honest model, except that $\perp$ can be sent as well. We note that if $\perp$ is sent, then both parties obtain $\perp$ as output and thus fairness is preserved.[5] This is actually a very strong requirement from the protocol since both parties either learn the prescribed output, or they both output $\perp$. In the second model, the ideal adversary can send any input

---

[5] It is necessary to allow an explicit abort in this model since if the corrupted party does not participate at all then the output cannot be computed. The typical solution to this problem, which is to take some default input, is not appropriate here because this means that the simulator can change the input of the corrupted party. Thus, such an early abort must result in output $\perp$.

that it wishes to the trusted party, just like a malicious adversary. We remark that if the real adversary does not abort a real protocol execution, then the result is the same as an execution of two honest parties and thus the output is computed from the prescribed inputs. This implies that the ideal adversary can really only send a different input in the case that the real adversary halts before the protocol is completed. As we have mentioned in the Introduction, the impossibility result of Cleve [5] for coin-tossing holds in both models, since the parties have no input, and so for this functionality the models are identical.

6.1   Fail-Stop 1

In this section we define and explore the first fail-stop model.

Execution in the Ideal World. An ideal execution involves parties P_1 and P_2, an adversary $\mathcal{S}$ who has corrupted one of the parties, and the trusted party. An ideal execution for the computation of f proceeds as follows:

Inputs: P_1 and P_2 hold inputs $x \in X$, and $y \in Y$, respectively; the adversary $\mathcal{S}$ receives the security parameter 1^n and an auxiliary input z.

Send Inputs to Trusted Party: The honest party sends its input to the trusted party. The corrupted party controlled by $\mathcal{S}$ may send its prescribed input or $\perp$.

Trusted Party Sends Outputs: If an input $\perp$ was received, then the trusted party sends $\perp$ to both parties. Otherwise, it computes $f(x,y)$ and sends the result to both parties.

Outputs: The honest party outputs whatever it was sent by the trusted party, the corrupted party outputs nothing and $\mathcal{S}$ outputs an arbitrary function of its view.

We denote by $\mathrm{IDEAL}^{\text{f-stop-1}}_{f,\mathcal{S}(z)}(x,y,n)$ the random variable consisting of the output of the adversary and the output of the honest party following an execution in the ideal model as described above.

Security. The real model is the same as is defined in the standard definition of secure two-party computation [6], except that we consider adversaries that are fail-stop only. This means that the adversary must behave exactly like an honest party, except that it can halt whenever it wishes during the protocol. We stress that its decision to halt or not halt, and when, may depend on its view. We are now ready to present the security definition.

Definition 6.1 (Security – Fail-Stop1). *Protocol π securely computes f with complete fairness in the fail-stop1 model if for every non-uniform probabilistic polynomial-time fail-stop adversary $\mathcal{A}$ in the real model, there exists a non-uniform probabilistic polynomial-time adversary $\mathcal{S}$ in the ideal model such that:*

$$\left\{\mathrm{IDEAL}^{\text{f-stop-1}}_{f,\mathcal{S}(z)}(x,y,n)\right\} \overset{c}{\equiv} \left\{\mathrm{REAL}_{\pi,\mathcal{A}(z)}(x,y,n)\right\}$$

where $x \in X$, $y \in Y$, $z \in \{0,1\}^*$ and $n \in \mathbb{N}$.

Exploring Fairness in the Fail-stop-1 Model. We first observe that if a function contains an embedded XOR, then it cannot be computed fairly in this model.

Theorem 6.2. *Let* $f : \{x_1, \ldots, x_m\} \times \{y_1, \ldots, y_\ell\} \to \{0, 1\}$ *be a function that contains an embedded XOR. Then,* f *implies the coin-tossing functionality and thus cannot be computed fairly.*

Proof: Assume that f contains an embedded XOR; i.e., there exist inputs x_1, x_2, y_1, y_2 such that $f(x_1, y_1) = f(x_2, y_2) \neq f(x_1, y_2) = f(x_2, y_1)$. We can easily construct a protocol for coin-tossing using f that is secure in the fail-stop model. Party P_1 chooses input $x \in \{x_1, x_2\}$ uniformly at random, P_2 chooses $y \in \{y_1, y_2\}$ uniformly at random, and the parties invoke the function f where P_1 inputs x and P_2 inputs y. In case the result of the invocation is $\perp$, the other party chooses its output uniformly at random.

Since the adversary is fail-stop1, it must follow the protocol specification (including choosing its input in the invocation of f correctly until it aborts when it can input $\perp$). In both cases, it is easy to see that the honest party outputs an unbiased coin. Formally, for any given fail-stop adversary $\mathcal{A}$ we can construct a simulator $\mathcal{S}$: $\mathcal{S}$ receives from the coin tossing functionality f^{ct} the bit b, and invokes the adversary $\mathcal{A}$. If $\mathcal{A}$ sends the trusted party computing f the symbol $\perp$, then $\mathcal{S}$ responds with $\perp$. Otherwise, (if $\mathcal{A}$ sends some real value - either x_1, x_2 if it controls P_1, or y_1, y_2 if it controls P_2), then $\mathcal{S}$ responds with the bit b that it received from f^{ct} as if it is the output of the ideal call to f. It is easy to see that the ideal and real distributions are identical. ∎

As we have mentioned, if a function does not contain an embedded XOR or OR then it is trivial and can be computed fairly (because the output depends on only one of the parties' inputs). It therefore remains to consider the feasibility of fairly computing functions that have an embedded OR but no embedded XOR. Gordon et. al [9] present a protocol for securely computing any function of this type with complete fairness, in the presence of a malicious adversary. However, the security of their protocol relies inherently on the ability of the simulator to send the trusted party an input that is not the corrupted party's prescribed input. Thus, their protocol seems not to be secure in this model.

The problem of securely computing functions that have an embedded OR but no embedded XOR therefore remains open. We remark that there are very few functions of this type, and these functions have a very specific structure, as discussed in [9].

6.2   Fail-Stop 2

In this section we define and explore the second fail-stop model. In this case, the ideal adversary can send any value it wishes to the trusted party (and the output of the honest party is determined accordingly). It is easy to see that in executions where the real adversary does not abort the output is the same as between two honest parties. Thus, the ideal adversary is forced to send the prescribed input of the party in this case. Observe that the ideal model here is identical to the ideal model for the case of malicious adversaries. Thus, the only difference between this definition and the definition of security for malicious adversaries is the quantification over the real adversary; here we quantify only over fail-stop real adversaries. Otherwise, all is the same.

Definition 6.3 (Security – Fail-Stop2). *Protocol π securely computes f with complete fairness in the fail-stop2 model if for every non-uniform probabilistic polynomial-time fail-stop adversary $\mathcal{A}$ in the real world, there exists a non-uniform probabilistic polynomial-time adversary $\mathcal{S}$ in the ideal model such that:*

$$\left\{ \text{IDEAL}_{f,\mathcal{S}(z)}(x,y,n) \right\} \overset{c}{\equiv} \left\{ \text{REAL}_{\pi,\mathcal{A}(z)}(x,y,n) \right\}$$

where $x \in X$, $y \in Y$, $z \in \{0,1\}^*$ and $n \in \mathbb{N}$, and IDEAL denotes the standard ideal model for malicious adversaries.

In the g-hybrid-model for fail-stop2 adversaries, where the parties have access to a trusted party computing function g for them, a corrupted party may provide an incorrect input to an invocation of g as long as it halts at that point. This may seem arbitrary. However, it follows naturally from the definition since a secure fail-stop2 protocol is used to replace the invocations of g in the real model. Thus, if a fail-stop adversary can change its input as long as it aborts in the real model, then this capability is necessary also for invocations of g in the g-hybrid model.

Exploring Fairness in the Fail-Stop-2 Model. In the following we show that the malicious adversaries that we constructed in the proofs of Theorem 5.1 and Theorem 5.2 can be modified to be *fail-stop2*. We remark that the adversaries that we constructed did not abort during the protocol execution, but rather continued after providing a "different" input in one of the f invocations. Thus, they are not fail-stop2 adversaries. In order to prove the impossibility for this case, we need to modify the adversaries so that they *halt* at the node v for which they can bias the outcome of the invocation (i.e., a node v for which v's children in the execution tree have significantly different probabilities for the output of the entire execution equalling 1). Recall that in this fail-stop model, the adversary is allowed to send a different input than prescribed in the invocation at which it halts; thus, this is a valid attack strategy. In the full paper we prove:

Theorem 6.4. *Let $f : \{x_1, \ldots, x_m\} \times \{y_1, \ldots, y_\ell\} \to \{0,1\}$ be a function that is not δ-balanced, for any $0 < \delta < 1$. Then, f does not information-theoretically imply the coin-tossing protocol in the fail-stop2 model.*

We prove the above by considering two possible cases, relating to the potential difference between the honest party outputting 1 at a node when the other party aborts at that node but until then was fully honest, or when the other party continues honestly from that node (to be more exact, we consider the average of these differences over all nodes). First, assume that there is a noticeable difference between an abort after fully honest behavior and a fully honest execution.

In this case, we construct a fail-stop adversary who plays honestly until an appropriate node where such a difference occurs and then halts. (In fact, such an adversary is even of the fail-stop1 type). Next, assume that there is *no noticeable difference* between an abort after fully honest behavior and a fully honest execution. Intuitively, this means that continuing honestly or halting makes no difference. Thus, if we take the malicious adversaries from Section 5 and modify them so that they halt immediately after providing malicious input (as allowed in the fail-stop2 model), then we obtain that there is no noticeable difference between the original malicious adversary and the fail-stop2 modified adversary. We remark that this is not immediate since the difference in this case is between aborting and not aborting without giving any malicious input. However, as we show, if there is no difference when honest inputs are used throughout, then this is also no difference when a malicious input is used.

We conclude that one of the two types of fail-stop2 adversaries described above can bias any protocol.

Acknowledgements. We thank Gene S. Kopp and John D. Wiltshire-Gordon for helpful discussions.

References

1. Full version of this work. Cryptology ePrint Archive (2013)
2. Ben-Or, M., Goldwasser, S., Wigderson, A.: Completeness theorems for non-cryptographic fault-tolerant distributed computation. In: 20th STOC, pp. 1–10 (1988)
3. Canetti, R.: Security and composition of multiparty cryptographic protocols. Journal of Cryptology 13(1), 143–202 (2000)
4. Chaum, D., Crépeau, C., Damgård, I.: Multiparty unconditionally secure protocols. In: The 20th STOC, pp. 1–10 (1988)
5. Cleve, R.: Limits on the security of coin flips when half the processors are faulty (extended abstract). In: The 18th STOC, pp. 364–369 (1986)
6. Goldreich, O.: The Foundations of Cryptography. Basic Applications, vol. 2. Cambridge University Press (2004)
7. Goldreich, O., Micali, S., Wigderson, A.: Proofs that yield nothing but their validity or all languages in NP have zero-knowledge proof systems. JACM 38(1), 691–729 (1991)
8. Goldreich, O., Micali, S., Wigderson, A.: How to play any mental game or a completeness theorem for protocols with honest majority. In: The 19th STOC, pp. 218–229 (1987)
9. Gordon, S.D., Hazay, C., Katz, J., Lindell, Y.: Complete fairness in secure two-party computation. JACM 58(6), 24 (2011)
10. Kilian, J.: A general completeness theorem for two-party games. In: 23rd STOC, pp. 553–560 (1991)
11. Rabin, T., Ben-Or, M.: Verifiable secret sharing and multiparty protocols with honest majority. In: The 21st STOC, pp. 73–85 (1989)
12. von Neumann, J.: Various Techniques Used in Connection with Random Digits. Journal of Research of the National Bureau of Standards 12, 36–38 (1951)
13. Yao, A.: How to generate and exchange secrets (extended abstract). In: The 27th FOCS, pp. 162–167 (1986)

Characterizing the Cryptographic Properties of Reactive 2-Party Functionalities

R. Amzi Jeffs and Mike Rosulek*

1 Department of Computer Science, Harvey Mudd College
rjeffs@g.hmc.edu
2 Department of Computer Science, University of Montana
mikero@cs.umt.edu

Abstract. In secure multi-party computation, a reactive functionality is one which maintains persistent state, takes inputs, and gives outputs over many rounds of interaction with its parties. Reactive functionalities are fundamental and model many interesting and natural cryptographic tasks; yet their security properties are not nearly as well-understood as in the non-reactive case (known as secure function evaluation).

We present new combinatorial characterizations for 2-party reactive functionalities, which we model as finite automata. We characterize the functionalities that have passive-secure protocols, and those which are complete with respect to passive adversaries. Both characterizations are in the information-theoretic setting.

1 Introduction

Ever since Yao [17] introduced the concept of secure multi-party computation (SMPC) with his famous *Millionaire's Problem*, the majority of research in the area has focused on understanding **secure function evaluation (SFE)** tasks. In an SFE task, all parties provide inputs and then receive outputs according to a (typically) deterministic function, in a single round of interaction with the functionality. The functionality that carries out this task has no need for persistent memory — it simply receives inputs from the parties, computes outputs, and thereafter forgets everything.

Yet, SMPC security models (*e.g.*, [2]) allow for functionalities that maintain internal state across many rounds of interaction. We call such functionalities **reactive**. The most well-known example of an inherently reactive functionality is bit-commitment, the cryptographic equivalent of a locked box.

In a secure protocol, the parties must achieve the same effect as the functionality. Reactivity introduces new and unique challenges; in particular, there is a tension between the fact that the parties may *individually* have a great deal of uncertainty about the functionality's internal state, and the fact that the parties *collectively* must be able to maintain its internal state in order to correctly simulate its behavior.

---

* Supported by NSF grant CCF-1149647.

A. Sahai (Ed.): TCC 2013, LNCS 7785, pp. 263–280, 2013.

To understand reactive functionalities is, therefore, to understand how persistent information can be maintained, updated, kept secret, and computed upon. What's more, from a practical perspective, reactive tasks are fundamental — any task involving time-sensitive release of information or the ability for parties to adapt to new information learned from an interaction must be necessarily reactive.

Background & Related Work. The first security model for which SFE tasks were understood is the model of passive security against computationally unbounded adversaries. Beaver [1] & Kushilevitz [12] independently characterized secure realizability for 2-party SFE tasks in this model. These results characterized which functionalities have *perfectly* secure protocols; the same characterization was later extended to the case where negligible security error is allowed [13,11]. We strongly leverage this characterization in our own result for the reactive case.

A functionality $\mathcal{F}$ is said to be *complete* (with respect to some security notion for protocols) if every functionality has a secure protocol in which the parties are allowed to make use of ideal instances of $\mathcal{F}$. Kilian [6] was the first to characterize completeness for 2-party SFE functionalities. The result was later generalized to functionalities with possibly different outputs to the two parties [9]. As before, we strongly leverage the well-known characterization for the SFE case in our own result for the reactive case.

These characterizations, and many others for SFE tasks (*e.g.*, [4,7,8]) are exclusively *combinatorial* in nature. Each SFE is associated with its 2-dimensional input/output table and then classified based on whether this table has a certain structure — say, a forbidden kind of 2×2 submatrix.

In some security settings, there exist secure protocols for every SFE functionality (*e.g.*, standalone security in the computationally bounded setting); it is not hard to see that this also implies secure protocols for all reactive functionalities as well. However, *hardness* (infeasibility) results for reactive functionalities are much rarer in the literature. Some fundamental reactive functionalities like bit commitment have been studied in an *ad hoc* fashion [3]. To the best of our knowledge, large *classes* of reactive functionalities have been considered only in [15,14,16]. Of these, only one result of Maji, Prabhakaran, and Rosulek [14] involves a *combinatorial* (decidable) characterization. They characterize the 2-party reactive functionalities which have UC-secure protocols without any setup (the characterization is the same for both the computationally bounded and unbounded settings). They model functionalities as deterministic, finite-state transducers; our work uses the same automata model of reactive functionalities. We note that, while the SMPC paradigm allows one to consider reactive functionalities that cannot be represented as such finite automata, many important and natural functionalities can indeed be modeled in this way (*e.g.*, bit commitment).

1.1   Our Results

We derive combinatorial characterizations for the cryptographic properties of 2-party reactive functionalities. In particular, we characterize triviality (*i.e.*, feasibility) and completeness with respect to computationally unbounded, passive (a.k.a. semi-honest, or honest-but-curious) adversaries. Ours is the first work to classify properties of reactive functionalities in this fundamental setting. Following [14], we model reactive functionalities as finite automata.

For a reactive functionality $\mathcal{F}$, define a related *non-reactive* functionality $\mathcal{F}^{(k)}$ which takes a length-k sequence of inputs from each of Alice and Bob, then runs $\mathcal{F}$ for k rounds on these inputs and gives each party their corresponding length-k sequence of outputs. It is not difficult to see that:

- $\mathcal{F}$ is passive-trivial if and only if for all $k \in \mathbb{N}$, $\mathcal{F}^{(k)}$ is passive-trivial.
- $\mathcal{F}$ is passive-complete if and only if $\mathcal{F}^{(k)}$ is passive-complete for some $k \in \mathbb{N}$.

In this way it is possible to reduce the characterizations for reactive functionalities to the corresponding well-known ones for SFE functionalities.

However, the above characterizations are of limited use. Both conditions are infinitary in nature (requiring either the universe of all protocols to be enumerated, or an infinite number of values k to be checked). Our technical contribution is in our analyses showing that only a finite number of values k need to be checked. We obtain characterizations of the following form:

Main Theorem. *Let $\mathcal{F}$ be a reactive 2-party functionality. There exist constants K_t and K_c, which depend only on the number of states in $\mathcal{F}$, such that:*

1. *$\mathcal{F}$ is passive-trivial if and only if for all $k \leq K_t$, $\mathcal{F}^{(k)}$ is passive-trivial; and*
2. *$\mathcal{F}$ is passive-complete if and only if $\mathcal{F}^{(k)}$ is passive-complete for some $k \leq K_c$.*

Thus we obtain total decision procedures for determining triviality and completeness of reactive functionalities. The characterizations for SFE are combinatorial in nature, and thus ours also inherit that flavor. Also, the statement of the main theorem is valid even if protocols are allowed a negligible error (though the final characterization for passive-triviality is the same whether zero error or negligible error is required).

The bulk of our effort is devoted to proving the existence of the constant K_t above. The main technical challenge when dealing with reactive functionalities is accounting for the uncertainty both parties have about the (hidden) internal state of the functionality. For example, even if the behavior of the functionality is benign in every state, it may still be possible to elicit non-trivial behavior from the functionality when both parties have uncertainty about its internal state. To justify our somewhat complicated analysis, we show that simply inspecting the local behavior of each state does not suffice to characterize the security properties of reactive functionalities.

To properly deal with the complications of a functionality's hidden internal state, we develop a "normal form" for functionalities that explicitly captures the common knowledge both parties have about the internal state. The final characterization follows then by the requirements imposed by this normal form.

Our characterizations are for functionalities that give possibly different outputs to each party. Using the normal form described above, we show that, unless a functionality is passive-complete, it is isomorphic to one with symmetric output. This generalizes an analogous result of [9] for non-reactive functionalities.

2   Preliminaries

A probability $p(n)$ is negligible if for all $c > 0$, $p(n) < n^{-c}$ for all but finitely many n. We use bold symbols (e.g., $\boldsymbol{x}$, $\boldsymbol{y}$) to denote sequences over some finite alphabet (e.g., X or Y). We write $|\boldsymbol{x}|$ to denote the length of a sequence, and we use $\|$ to denote concatenation of sequences (e.g., $\boldsymbol{x}\|x$). When T is a 2-dimensional table, and a and b are appropriate indices, we use the notation $T[a, b]$ to denote the entry of T in row a, column b.

2.1   Passive Security

We use the standard real-ideal paradigm [5] to define protocol security. We exclusively consider security against passive (a.k.a. honest-but-curious, or semi-honest) and computationally unbounded adversaries, and we call protocols which achieve this standard **passive-secure** for short. We say that a protocol **uses** the functionality $\mathcal{G}$ if the parties are instructed to interact with ideal instances of the functionality $\mathcal{G}$ (i.e., the protocol is in the "$\mathcal{G}$-hybrid model").

We say that a functionality $\mathcal{F}$ is **passive-trivial** if there is a passive-secure protocol for $\mathcal{F}$ without any setups. We say that $\mathcal{F}$ is **passive-complete** if there is a passive-secure oblivious-transfer protocol that uses access to ideal instances of $\mathcal{F}$. In this work, we consider the information-theoretic setting exclusively, so adversaries are computationally unbounded. Unlike the first characterizations for SFE functionalities [1,12], we do not restrict our attention to protocols that achieve perfect security. Instead, we use the now-standard notion of passive security, which permits protocols to have a negligible simulation error.

Isomorphism. We call a protocol for $\mathcal{F}$ using $\mathcal{G}$ a *local* protocol if it uses just one instance of $\mathcal{G}$ to realize an instance of $\mathcal{F}$, does not use communication between the parties other than $\mathcal{G}$, and each round of outputs for $\mathcal{F}$ is realized in the protocol by the parties making a single call to $\mathcal{G}$. Then call two functionalities $\mathcal{F}$ and $\mathcal{G}$ **isomorphic** if there is a local, passive-secure protocol for $\mathcal{F}$ using $\mathcal{G}$ and vice-versa.

2.2   Notation and Characterizations for SFE

We briefly review known characterizations for passive-triviality and passive-completeness of SFE functionalities. We state the characterizations in terms of new notation, which cleanly unifies the cases of symmetric and non-symmetric output for the two parties. The terminology defined here is used throughout the work.

A **2-party SFE** $\mathcal{F}$ is specified by finite sets X and Y, and two deterministic functions $f_A : X \times Y \to \{0,1\}^*$ and $f_B : X \times Y \to \{0,1\}^*$. We use these default variable names throughout this work. As a cryptographic functionality, Alice and Bob provide inputs $x \in X$ and $y \in Y$ to $\mathcal{F}$, respectively, and receive outputs $f_A(x,y)$ and $f_B(x,y)$, respectively.[1]

---

[1] In this work we consider security only against passive adversaries. As such, issues of fairness in output delivery are not relevant.

Let restrict$(\mathcal{F}, A \times B)$ denote the restriction of $\mathcal{F}$ to the input domain $A \times B \subseteq X \times Y$. For $(x, y) \in X \times Y$, we define rectangle$(\mathcal{F}, x, y) = A_{x,y} \times B_{x,y}$ where $A_{x,y} = \{x' \mid f_B(x', y) = f_B(x, y)\}$ and $B_{x,y} = \{y' \mid f_A(x, y') = f_A(x, y)\}$. We say that $\mathcal{F}$ is **basic** on $\tilde{X} \times \tilde{Y}$ if: for all $y \in \tilde{Y}$, f_B is a constant function on $\tilde{X} \times \{y\}$, and for all $x \in \tilde{X}$, f_A is a constant function on $\{x\} \times \tilde{Y}$. Basic functions require no interaction to evaluate (a party's input has no influence on the other's output). Finally, an OR-**minor** in $\mathcal{F}$ is a tuple $(x, x', y, y') \in X^2 \times Y^2$ with:

$$f_A(x, y) = f_A(x, y'); \qquad f_B(x, y) = f_B(x', y);$$

$$\Big(f_A(x', y), f_B(x, y') \Big) \neq \Big(f_A(x', y'), f_B(x', y') \Big).$$

Passive-Completeness. OR-minors exactly characterize passive-completeness for SFE functionalities:

Lemma 1 ([9]). *The following are equivalent for a 2-party SFE $\mathcal{F}$:*

1. *$\mathcal{F}$ is passive-complete.*
2. *$\mathcal{F}$ has an OR-minor.*
3. *There exist inputs x, y such that $\mathcal{F}$ is **not** basic on rectangle$(\mathcal{F}, x, y)$.*

Proof. The equivalence of 1 & 2 was shown by Kraschewski & Müller-Quade [9], generalizing the analogous statement for symmetric-output functions by Kilian [6]. The equivalence of 2 & 3 follows straightforwardly from the definitions of OR-minor and rectangle$(\mathcal{F}, x, y)$.

The following useful lemma was also proven in [9]:

Lemma 2 (Symmetrization [9]). *Given an SFE $\mathcal{F}$, define the (symmetric) SFE functionality $\mathcal{F}_{sym}$, which on input x from Alice and y from Bob gives both parties output rectangle$(\mathcal{F}, x, y)$.*
If $\mathcal{F}$ has no OR-minor, then $\mathcal{F}$ is isomorphic to $\mathcal{F}_{sym}$.

Passive-Triviality. Passive-triviality for SFE functionalities is characterized by a combinatorial condition called *decomposability.*

Definition 1 ([1,12]). *An SFE $\mathcal{F}$ is **decomposable** if one of the following holds:*

1. *$\mathcal{F}$ is basic (defined above); or,*
2. *There is a partition $X = \tilde{X}_1 \cup \tilde{X}_2$ so that for all $x_1 \in \tilde{X}_1, x_2 \in \tilde{X}_2$ and $y \in Y$, $f_B(x_1, y) \neq f_B(x_2, y)$, and furthermore restrict$(\mathcal{F}, \tilde{X}_1 \times Y)$ and restrict$(\mathcal{F}, \tilde{X}_2 \times Y)$ are decomposable; or,*
3. *There is a partition $Y = \tilde{Y}_1 \cup \tilde{Y}_2$ so that for all $x \in X$, $y_1 \in \tilde{Y}_1$, and $y_2 \in \tilde{Y}_2$, $f_A(x, y_1) \neq f_A(x, y_2)$, and furthermore restrict$(\mathcal{F}, X \times \tilde{Y}_1)$ and restrict$(\mathcal{F}, X \times \tilde{Y}_2)$ are decomposable.*

Lemma 3 ([13,11]). *$\mathcal{F}$ is passive-trivial if and only if it is decomposable.*

This lemma was originally proved for the case of perfectly secure protocols by Beaver [1] & Kushilevitz [12] (independently); later it was extended for the standard notion of security (allowing negligible error) by Maji, Prabhakaran & Rosulek [13] and Künzler, Müller-Quade & Raub [11] (independently).

2.3   Model of Reactive Functionalities

We use the model of reactive functionalities from [14]:

Definition 2 ([14]). *A* **(2-party) deterministic finite functionality (DFF)** *is a tuple* $\mathcal{F} = (Q, X, Y, \delta, f_A, f_B, q_0)$, *where*

- Q *is a finite set of states,*
- X *and* Y *are finite input sets,*
- $\delta : Q \times X \times Y \to Q$ *is the state transition function,*
- $f_A, f_B : Q \times X \times Y \to \{0, 1\}^*$ *are two output functions, and*
- $q_0 \in Q$ *is the start state.*

The behavior of $\mathcal{F}$ as an ideal functionality is defined formally in Figure 1.[2] As before, we use these standard variable names throughout.

Set variable $q := q_0$. Then repeatedly do:

- Wait for input $x \in X$ from Alice and input $y \in Y$ from Bob. Give outputs $f_A(q, x, y)$ to Alice and $f_B(q, x, y)$ to Bob. Update $q := \delta(q, x, y)$ and repeat.

Fig. 1. Semantics of the DFF functionality $\mathcal{F} = (Q, X, Y, \delta, f_A, f_B, q_0)$

We extend the functions δ, f_A, and f_B to *sequences* of inputs in the natural way. Let $\boldsymbol{x} = (x_1, \ldots, x_k) \in X^k$ and $\boldsymbol{y} = (y_1, \ldots, y_k) \in Y^k$. We write $\delta(q, \boldsymbol{x}, \boldsymbol{y})$ to denote the state of $\mathcal{F}$ after receiving inputs $(x_1, y_1), \ldots, (x_k, y_k)$ starting in state q. We write $f_A(q, \boldsymbol{x}, \boldsymbol{y})$ to denote the *concatenation* of Alice's k outputs when $\mathcal{F}$ receives inputs $(x_1, y_1), \ldots, (x_k, y_k)$ starting in state q. We write $\mathcal{F}^{(k)}$ to denote the SFE functionality which on input $(\boldsymbol{x}, \boldsymbol{y})$ with $|\boldsymbol{x}| = |\boldsymbol{y}| = k$, gives output $f_A(q_0, \boldsymbol{x}, \boldsymbol{y})$ to Alice and $f_B(q_0, \boldsymbol{x}, \boldsymbol{y})$ to Bob. Then we have the following simple observations:

Proposition 1 *Let $\mathcal{F}$ be a DFF, and $\mathcal{F}^{(k)}$ defined above.*

1. *For all k, there is a passive-secure protocol for $\mathcal{F}^{(k)}$ using $\mathcal{F}$.*
2. *There is a passive-secure protocol for $\mathcal{F}$ using $\{\mathcal{F}^{(k)}\}_{k \in \mathbb{N}}$.*

Hence:

3. *$\mathcal{F}$ is passive-trivial if and only if, for all k, $\mathcal{F}^{(k)}$ is passive-trivial.*
4. *$\mathcal{F}$ is passive-complete if and only if $\mathcal{F}^{(k)}$ is passive-complete for some k.*

The secure protocol for $\mathcal{F}$ using (the infinite set of functionalities) $\{\mathcal{F}^{(k)}\}$ requires both parties to maintain their history of inputs $\boldsymbol{x}$ and $\boldsymbol{y}$. In the $(k+1)$th round with histories $\boldsymbol{x}$ and $\boldsymbol{y}$ and new inputs x and y, both parties call $\mathcal{F}^{(k+1)}$ with inputs $\boldsymbol{x}\|x$ and $\boldsymbol{y}\|y$.[3]

---

[2] As before, issues of fairness in output delivery are not relevant when considering only passive adversaries.

[3] Note that we use the fact that the parties honestly follow the protocol, as they must faithfully keep track of their history of inputs to simulate $\mathcal{F}$ using $\{\mathcal{F}^{(k)}\}$.

3   Limits of Local Conditions

When classifying a DFF for its cryptographic properties, one is tempted to examine the behaviors of each state, in isolation, for certain properties. We call such a test *local*, and in this section we describe the limitations of such local tests.

One way that local tests fail stems from the fact that local information is not enough to determine even whether two states have identical behavior. Given that, suppose some state has a transition function that contains an OR-minor involving states q, q'. How this OR-minor affects the triviality/completeness of the functionality depends crucially on whether q and q' have identical behavior. Still, we will show that, even when redundant states have been removed, local tests are insufficient to classify the cryptographic properties of DFFs.

We say that two states q and q' are **redundant** in $\mathcal{F}$ if for all x, y with $|x| = |y|$ we have $f_A(q, x, y) = f_A(q', x, y)$ and $f_B(q, x, y) = f_B(q', x, y)$. Redundant states can easily be collapsed in $\mathcal{F}$ using the classical Myhill-Nerode DFA minimization algorithm. Throughout this work we will generally assume without loss of generality that redundant states have been collapsed. Non-redundant state pairs (q, q') have a *distinguishing sequence* (x, y) satisfying

$$\big(f_A(q, x, y), f_B(q, x, y)\big) \neq \big(f_A(q', x, y), f_B(q', x, y)\big).$$

Local tests can give an indication of the complexity of some DFFs, but cannot give a complete characterization. We consider local tests which inspect the output and transition functions of each state. To formalize this, we define for a DFF $\mathcal{F}$ a related DFF $\mathcal{F}_{st}$ to be a modification to $\mathcal{F}$ which always announces its internal state to both parties. Then the output function of state q in $\mathcal{F}_{st}$ contains all the relevant information about both the output and transition functions of q in $\mathcal{F}$.

Lemma 4. *Let $\mathcal{F}$ be a DFF that contains no redundant states.*

1. *If any reachable state in $\mathcal{F}_{st}$ has an output function that is not decomposable, then $\mathcal{F}$ is not passive-trivial.*
2. *If any reachable state in $\mathcal{F}_{st}$ has an output function that contains an OR-minor, then $\mathcal{F}$ is passive-complete.*
3. *The converses of the above statements are false. In fact, there exist functionalities of arbitrary status (i.e., passive-trivial, passive-complete, neither) without redundant states whose output functions are constant and whose transition functions are decomposable in every state.*

Proof. For items (1) and (2), we can assume without loss of generality that it is the *start state* of $\mathcal{F}$ that has the offending transition/output functions. More formally, let $\mathcal{F}[q]$ denote $\mathcal{F}$ with its start state changed to q. If q is reachable in $\mathcal{F}$— say, via sequence (x, y) — then a passive-secure protocol for $\mathcal{F}[q]$ using $\mathcal{F}$ is to have both parties send an initial "preamble" of (x, y) to $\mathcal{F}$ and then proceed with the dummy protocol.

For items (1) and (2), if it is an output function in $\mathcal{F}$ (i.e., not in $\mathcal{F}_{st}$) that is non-decomposable (resp. contains an OR-minor), then the claim follows much more easily. There is a natural passive-secure protocol using $\mathcal{F}$ that realizes the start state's (SFE) output function – the parties simply interact with $\mathcal{F}$ for one round. The claims then follow from the complete characterizations for passive-triviality and passive-completeness of SFE (see Section 2.2).

(1) We fall into the case described above unless the start state's output function is decomposable. So, let $\mathcal{G} = (g_A, g_B)$ denote the SFE which evaluates the first round only of $\mathcal{F}_{st}$ and Let $\tilde{X} \times \tilde{Y}$ denote minimal subsets such that $\mathsf{restrict}(\mathcal{G}, \tilde{X} \times \tilde{Y})$ is not decomposable.

Next we show that the output function of the start state in $\mathcal{F}$ (not $\mathcal{F}_{st}$) is *basic* on $\tilde{X} \times \tilde{Y}$. If not, then since it is decomposable, it induces either a corresponding row- or column-decomposition step in $\mathcal{G}$ (which includes the $\mathcal{F}$-output as well as the state). This splits $\tilde{X} \times \tilde{Y}$ into at least two smaller subdomains, which by the minimality condition are decomposable. Thus $\mathcal{G}$ is decomposable on $\tilde{X} \times \tilde{Y}$, which we have assumed to be false. By this contradiction, we see that the output function of $\mathcal{F}$'s start state must be *basic* on $\tilde{X} \times \tilde{Y}$.

Let q, q' be two distinct states reachable from the start state by single transitions on $(x, y) \in \tilde{X} \times \tilde{Y}$. As these states are non-redundant, let $(\boldsymbol{x}, \boldsymbol{y})$ be a distinguishing sequence for them, with $|\boldsymbol{x}| = |\boldsymbol{y}| = k$. Now consider the SFE functionality $\mathcal{H} = (h_A, h_B)$ which on input $(x, y) \in \tilde{X} \times \tilde{Y}$ gives output $f_A(q_0, x\|\boldsymbol{x}, y\|\boldsymbol{y})$ to Alice and $f_B(q_0, x\|\boldsymbol{x}, y\|\boldsymbol{y})$ to Bob. There is a passive-secure protocol for $\mathcal{H}$ using $\mathcal{F}$ ($\mathcal{H}$ is a submatrix of $\mathcal{F}^{(k+1)}$). By Lemma 3 it suffices to show that $\mathcal{H}$ is not decomposable.

We have that $\mathsf{rectangle}(\mathcal{G}, x, y) \subseteq \mathsf{rectangle}(\mathcal{H}, x, y)$, since the first round of $\mathcal{F}$ gives *basic* output for inputs in $\tilde{X} \times \tilde{Y}$. Also, by our choice of $\boldsymbol{x}, \boldsymbol{y}$ as a distinguishing sequence we have that $\mathcal{H}$ itself is not basic. Consider any partition of $\tilde{X}$, say, $\tilde{X} = \tilde{X}_0 \cup \tilde{X}_1$. Since $\mathcal{G}$ is minimal and not decomposable, there exists $x_0 \in \tilde{X}_0$, $x_1 \in \tilde{X}_1$, $y \in \tilde{Y}$ such that $g_B(x_0, y) = g_B(x_1, y)$. Hence, $h_B(x_0, y) = h_B(x_1, y)$ so $\tilde{X} = \tilde{X}_0 \cup \tilde{X}_1$ does not satisfy the requirement for decomposability of $\mathcal{H}$. Symmetrically, no partition of $\tilde{Y}$ satisfies the requirement; hence $\mathcal{H}$ is not decomposable, as desired.

(2) Let (x_0, x_1, y_0, y_1) be the inputs of the relevant OR-minor in the start state of $\mathcal{F}_{st}$; as above, we may assume that the output function of q_0 in $\mathcal{F}$ is basic over $\{x_0, x_1\} \times \{y_0, y_1\}$. Hence, the OR-minor occurs entirely in the transition function of $\mathcal{F}$; i.e., $\delta(q_0, x_i, y_j) = r_{i \lor j}$ for some states $r_0 \neq r_1$. Let $(\boldsymbol{x}, \boldsymbol{y})$ be a distinguishing sequence for r_0, r_1, with $|\boldsymbol{x}| = |\boldsymbol{y}| = k$. Then it is straight-forward to verify that $(x_0\|\boldsymbol{x}, x_1\|\boldsymbol{x}, y_0\|\boldsymbol{y}, y_1\|\boldsymbol{y})$ is an OR-minor in $\mathcal{F}^{(k+1)}$. Note that we crucially use the fact that the output of $\mathcal{F}$ is basic in the first round for the chosen input sequences.

(3) Let $\mathcal{G}$ be an arbitrary *symmetric SFE* functionality to be chosen later, and define $\mathcal{F}$ to do the following: In the first round, $\mathcal{F}$ gives constant output (regardless of the input) and remembers Alice's input x in its states, ignoring Bob's input. In the second round, $\mathcal{F}$ gives constant output and transitions to state $r_{\mathcal{F}(x,y)}$, where y is the input of Bob in the second round (Alice's input in

this round is ignored). Here, states $\{r_i\}_i$ are a set of states distinct from those used to implement rounds 1 & 2. Finally, in state r_i, $\mathcal{F}$ gives constant output i and self-loops.

Note that the transition functions of $\mathcal{F}$ are all decomposable (in particular, at each round the transitions depend on at most one party's input), as are the output functions (they are constant functions in each state). A passive-secure protocol for $\mathcal{G}$ can be obtained from $\mathcal{F}$, and vice-versa, in the natural way. Thus, $\mathcal{F}$ and $\mathcal{G}$ have the same status (e.g., trivial, complete, neither). We complete the proof by taking $\mathcal{G}$ to be an appropriate passive-trivial, passive-complete, or intermediate SFE.

4   Characterizing Completeness

Theorem 2. *Let $\mathcal{F}$ be a DFF with n states. Then $\mathcal{F}$ is passive-complete if and only if there exists $k \le n^4$ such that $\mathcal{F}^{(k)}$ contains an OR-minor.*

Proof. The "$\Leftarrow$" direction follows trivially from Proposition 1 and the characterization of completeness for SFE functionalities based on OR-minors [6,9].

For the other direction, let π be a passive-secure protocol for 1-out-of-2 oblivious transfer (OT) using $\mathcal{F}$. For sake of contradiction, suppose that for every k, $\mathcal{F}^{(k)}$ has no OR-minor. Following Proposition 1, we can without loss of generality modify π to obtain a passive-secure OT protocol using the collection of SFE functions $\{\mathcal{F}^{(k)}\}_k$.

Consider an execution of the protocol in which input bits a_0, a_1 for Alice and b for Bob are chosen uniformly (i.e., Bob should learn a_b and Alice should learn nothing). Let V denote the messages exchanged in the protocol along with the list of rectangle($\mathcal{F}^{(k)}, x, y$) values for every time $\mathcal{F}^{(k)}$ is invoked with inputs (x, y) in the protocol. Define $P_{s,t} = \Pr[a_s = t \mid V]$ for $s, t \in \{0, 1\}$. Importantly, since no $\mathcal{F}^{(k)}$ contains an OR-minor, both parties can compute V (Lemma 2), and hence the $P_{s,t}$ values.

Suppose Bob guesses Alice's input a_s to be the value t that maximizes $P_{s,t}$. By a straight-forward argument, this guess will be correct with probability $P_{s,t}$. Hence, by the security of the protocol, $P_{1-b,0}$ and $P_{1-b,1}$ must be close to $1/2$ with high probability (recall that b is Bob's choice bit). However, by the correctness of the protocol we must also have P_{b,a_b} close to one and $P_{b,1-a_b}$ close to zero with high probability as well.[4] Since Alice can also compute these $P_{s,t}$ values, this gives her a way to determine Bob's choice bit b with high probability (i.e., guess the value b such that P_{b,a_b} is maximized). Hence, we contradict the passive-security of the protocol, as desired. We note that this part of the proof is essentially the same as Kilian's proof for the case of SFE functionalities [6].

---

[4] The correctness of the protocol implies that Bob's *entire view* determines a_b with high probability, whereas $P_{s,t}$ is computed using less information than Bob's view. In particular, V does not include Bob's inputs to the ideal functionality. However, every input for Bob from rectangle($\mathcal{F}^{(k)}, x, y$) would have had exactly the same effect on the interaction, in the absence of an OR-minor. In other words, an honest Bob only needs to remember his input with as much specificity as rectangle($\mathcal{F}^{(k)}, x, y$).

So far we have shown only that some $\mathcal{F}^{(k)}$ must have an OR-minor. Fix k to be minimal value such that $\mathcal{F}^{(k)}$ contains an OR-minor. If $k \leq n^4$ then we are done. Otherwise, let $d(\boldsymbol{x}, \boldsymbol{y}, i)$ denote the internal state of $\mathcal{F}$ after the first i rounds when the input sequence is $(\boldsymbol{x}, \boldsymbol{y})$, when $i \leq k = |\boldsymbol{x}| = |\boldsymbol{y}|$. Define

$$D(\boldsymbol{x}, \boldsymbol{y}, \boldsymbol{x}', \boldsymbol{y}', i) := \Big(d(\boldsymbol{x}, \boldsymbol{y}, i), d(\boldsymbol{x}, \boldsymbol{y}', i), d(\boldsymbol{x}', \boldsymbol{y}, i), d(\boldsymbol{x}', \boldsymbol{y}', i) \Big) \in Q^4.$$

Let $(\boldsymbol{x}, \boldsymbol{x}', \boldsymbol{y}, \boldsymbol{y}')$ be the OR-minor of $\mathcal{F}^{(k)}$. By the pigeonhole principle (since $k > n^4$) there are distinct indices $i, j \in \{0, \ldots, k\}$ such that $D(\boldsymbol{x}, \boldsymbol{y}, \boldsymbol{x}', \boldsymbol{y}', i) = D(\boldsymbol{x}, \boldsymbol{y}, \boldsymbol{x}', \boldsymbol{y}', j)$. Then removing positions i through $j-1$ in the input sequences $\boldsymbol{x}, \boldsymbol{y}, \boldsymbol{x}', \boldsymbol{y}'$ yields an OR-minor in $\mathcal{F}^{(k-j+i)}$. But this contradicts the minimality of k, so we must have originally had $k \leq n^4$.

5 Characterizing Passive Triviality

5.1 Overview

Our approach is to reduce our characterization of DFFs as much as possible to the known characterizations for SFE (given in Section 2.2). For intuition, suppose Alice & Bob have performed k rounds with $\mathcal{F}$, giving input sequences $\boldsymbol{x}$ and $\boldsymbol{y}$, respectively. When the functionality is passive-trivial, both parties can agree on $A \times B = \mathsf{rectangle}(\mathcal{F}^{(k)}, \boldsymbol{x}, \boldsymbol{y})$, knowing that $(\boldsymbol{x}, \boldsymbol{y}) \in A \times B$. Their uncertainty about the current *state* of $\mathcal{F}$ is then captured by $\mathsf{restrict}(\delta^{(k)}, A \times B)$, where $\delta^{(k)}$ is the extended transition function $\delta^{(k)}(\boldsymbol{x}, \boldsymbol{y}) = \delta(q_0, \boldsymbol{x}, \boldsymbol{y})$.

Intuitively, both parties can maintain the 2-dimensional table $C = \mathsf{restrict}(\delta^{(k)}, \mathsf{rectangle}(\mathcal{F}^{(k)}, \boldsymbol{x}, \boldsymbol{y}))$, along with their respective inputs $\boldsymbol{x}$ and $\boldsymbol{y}$ to this table. Furthermore, these three pieces of information ($\boldsymbol{x}$, $\boldsymbol{y}$, and C) are enough to determine all future behavior of $\mathcal{F}$. One could imagine a "canonical" protocol for $\mathcal{F}$ in which parties maintain such information (Alice maintaining $\boldsymbol{x}$ and C; Bob maintaining $\boldsymbol{y}$ and C).

With this as our starting point, we argue the following. First, duplicate rows & columns within C can be canonically removed. Second, the table C is a submatrix of $\delta^{(k)}$; as such, it can contain no OR-minor when $\mathcal{F}$ is passive-trivial. Finally, we prove a purely combinatorial lemma stating that any table that avoids duplicate rows, duplicate columns, and OR-minors must be bounded in its dimensions (the bound is a function of the number of allowed values in the cells of the table). Hence, when $\mathcal{F}$ is trivial, the table C described above has an a *priori*, finite bound in size.

Our combinatorial lemma reveals some structure of functions which avoid OR-minors. In that sense, our lemma is reminiscent of similar lemmas used in [4] and [10], for the n-party setting.

We prove our characterization by converting $\mathcal{F}$ into an equivalent "normal form" $\widehat{\mathcal{F}}$, which simulates $\mathcal{F}$ by keeping track of the information ($\boldsymbol{x}$, $\boldsymbol{y}$, and C) described above. In each state of $\widehat{\mathcal{F}}$, we use the internal state variable C to associate a related submatrix of $\mathcal{F}^{(k)}$ for some k. We then show that $\mathcal{F}$ is passive-trivial if and only if each of these submatrices of $\{\mathcal{F}^{(k)}\}_k$ is itself passive-trivial.

Importantly, there can be only a finite number of states — hence, a finite number of $\mathcal{F}^{(k)}$ submatrices — to inspect when deciding whether $\mathcal{F}$ is passive-trivial.

We highlight one important subtlety in the construction of $\widehat{\mathcal{F}}$. Our combinatorial lemma shows that the table C has bounded size, but we are also associating its rows & columns with $\mathcal{F}$-input sequences of length k. Thus, while the table itself has bounded size, conceivably the row- and column-"labels" become unbounded in length. Our construction of $\widehat{\mathcal{F}}$ implicitly shows that these row- and column-labels are not used meaningfully; that is, they can be renormalized to simply be numerical indices into the table. Hence, the entire state-space of $\widehat{\mathcal{F}}$ (which contains this table C as well as two labels indexing into the table) is indeed finite.

5.2 Combinatorial Lemma

Definition 3 (Grid colorings and their properties). A **k-coloring of an $m \times n$ grid** is a function $C : \{1, \ldots, m\} \times \{1, \ldots, n\} \to \{1, \ldots, k\}$. A row i is a **duplicate row** if $C(i, \cdot) \equiv C(i', \cdot)$ for some $i' \neq i$. Duplicate columns are defined analogously. A tuple (i, i', j, j') forms an OR-**minor** in C if $C(i, j) = C(i, j') = C(i', j) \neq C(i', j')$.

We will use the following lemma, which states that sufficiently large grid colorings cannot avoid duplicate rows, duplicate columns, and OR-minors.

Lemma 5 (Unavoidable structures of grid colorings). *There is a function $R : \mathbb{N} \to \mathbb{N}$ satisfying the following property. For every k-coloring C of an $m \times n$ grid, if $\max\{m, n\} \geq R(k)$, then C contains either a duplicate row, duplicate column, or an OR-minor.*

Proof. We prove the lemma for the bound $R(2) = 3$; $R(k) = k \cdot R(k-1)$. Thus $R(k) = \Theta(k!)$. In fact, we prove the two stronger statements that (1) if $m \geq R(k)$ then C contains either a duplicate row or an OR-minor; (2) if $n \geq R(k)$ then C contains either a duplicate column or an OR-minor. The two proofs are symmetric and we give the proof of (1) here. The case of $R(2) = 3$ can be verified by exhaustion.

For the inductive case, consider a k-coloring C with more than $R(k)$ rows. We assume that C has no OR-minors, and will show that there must be a duplicate row. By the pigeonhole principle, there must be some color (by symmetry, color #k) which appears more than $R(k)/k = R(k-1)$ times in the first column. The properties we seek are invariant under permuting rows and columns, so permute the rows and columns so that the north-west corner is colored #k, and the instances of color #k in the first row and first column are contiguous.

Since C contains no OR-minor, we have that C can be partitioned into four quadrants, NW, NE, SE, SW:

$$C = \left[\begin{array}{c|c} \text{NW} & \text{NE} \\ \hline \text{SW} & \text{SE} \end{array} \right],$$

where NW has more than $R(k-1)$ rows, NW contains only color #k, and NE and SW contain only colors $\{1, \ldots, k-1\}$. Thus, NE is a $(k-1)$-coloring with more than $R(k-1)$ rows and no OR-minors. As such it contains duplicate rows. When augmented to the left with identical sequences of k's, we obtain corresponding duplicate rows in C, as desired.

We proved the existence of such an R with $R(k) = \Theta(k!)$, which suffices for our purposes but which may or may not be optimal. We can obtain a lower bound of 2^{k-1} on the optimal value of $R(k)$, by considering the following recursively-defined k-colorings of a $2^{k-1} \times 2^{k-1}$ grid:

$$C_1 = [1]; \qquad C_k = \left[\begin{array}{c|c} U_k & C_{k-1} \\ \hline C_{k-1} & U_k \end{array} \right].$$

Here U_k denotes the $2^{k-2} \times 2^{k-2}$ grid filled uniformly with color k. The colorings $\{C_k\}_k$ avoid duplicate rows, duplicate columns, and OR-minors. We conjecture that $R(k) = 2^{k-1}$ is the optimal value for R as in the lemma statement.

5.3   Normal Form

Let T be a 2-dimensional table with row- and column-labels A and B, respectively. Define an equivalence relation, where $a \approx_A a'$ if for all $b \in B$, we have $T[a, b] = T[a', b]$ — that is, $a \approx_A a'$ if rows a and a' of T are identical. We define an equivalence relation $\approx_B$ analogously. Finally, let $[a]_A$ and $[b]_B$ denote equivalence classes under these relations, respectively.

Definition 4. *Let T, A, and B be as above. Let $e_1^A, \ldots, e_m^A$ denote the distinct equivalence classes of $\approx_A$, and let $e_1^B, \ldots, e_n^B$ denote the distinct equivalence classes of $\approx_B$.*

We define trim(i, j, T) *for $(i, j) \in A \times B$ to denote a tuple (i', j', T'), where:*

1. *T' is a table with row-labels $A' = \{1, \ldots, m\}$ and column-labels $B' = \{1, \ldots, n\}$. For each i^*, j^*, we have $T'[i^*, j^*] = T[a, b]$, where a is any representative of $e_{i^*}^A$ and b is any representative of $e_{j^*}^B$.*
2. *$e_{i'}^A = [i]_A$. That is, i' is the index of i's equivalence class.*
3. *$e_{j'}^B = [j]_B$. That is, j' is the index of j's equivalence class.*

By item (1) we see that T' has no duplicate columns or rows. Essentially, trim removes duplicate rows/columns and re-normalizes the row/column labels. Furthermore, the mapping $i \mapsto i'$ does not depend on j, the mapping $j \mapsto j'$ does not depend on i, and the mapping $T \mapsto T'$ does not depend on i or j.

Definition 5. *Let T be a 2-dimensional table with row- and column-labels A and B, respectively, and whose entries are states of a DFF $\mathcal{F}$. Then* explode(T) *is a 2-party SFE with input domain $(A \times X) \times (B \times Y)$. On input (a, x) from Alice and (b, y) from Bob, the output of* explode(T) *is $f_A(T[a, b], x, y)$ for Alice and $f_B(T[a, b], x, y)$ for Bob.*

Normal form $\widehat{\mathcal{F}}$. Let $\mathcal{F} = (Q, X, Y, \delta, f_A, f_B, q_0)$ be a DFF. Then define $\widehat{\mathcal{F}}$ to be a functionality given by Figure 2. Note that we define $\widehat{\mathcal{F}}$ without explicitly considering whether it is a DFF (that is, whether it has a finite number of states). Whether $\widehat{\mathcal{F}}$ has a finite number of states depends on $\mathcal{F}$ in a way that will be established later Lemma 8.

Maintain internal state (a, b, C), initialized to $a = b = 1$ and $C = [q_0]$ (that is, a 1×1 matrix), where q_0 is the start state of $\mathcal{F}$.

With internal state (a, b, C), and on input $x \in Y$ from Alice and $y \in Y$ from Bob:

1. Give output $f_A(C[a, b], x, y)$ to Alice and $f_B(C[a, b], x, y)$ to Bob.
2. Set $A' \times B' = \mathsf{rectangle}(\mathsf{explode}(C), (a, x), (b, y))$. Write A' and B' in some canonical ordering $A' = \{(a'_1, x'_1), \ldots, (a'_m, x'_m)\}$ and $B' = \{(b'_1, y'_1), \ldots (b'_n, y'_n)\}$. (Recall that inputs to $\mathsf{explode}(C)$ are tuples of this form.)
3. Define an $m \times n$ table C' via $C'[i, j] := \delta(C[a'_i, b'_j], x'_i, y'_j)$.
4. Set $a' := \mathsf{indexof}((a, x), A')$ and $b' := \mathsf{indexof}((b, y), B')$, where $\mathsf{indexof}(s, S = \{s_1, \ldots, s_n\})$ denotes the value i such that $s_i = s$.
5. Set $(a, b, C) := \mathsf{trim}(a', b', C')$.

Fig. 2. Functionality $\widehat{\mathcal{F}}$: the "normal-form" representation of $\mathcal{F}$

Lemma 6. *Let $\mathcal{F}$ and $\widehat{\mathcal{F}}$ be as above, and let $\delta^{(k)}$ denote the function $\delta^{(k)}(x, y) = \delta(q_0, x, y)$. Suppose that $\mathcal{F}$ is not passive-complete. Then, after reading inputs x and y (with $|x| = |y|$), $\widehat{\mathcal{F}}$ is in state*

$$(a, b, C) = \mathsf{trim}(x, y, \mathsf{restrict}(\delta^{(k)}, \mathsf{rectangle}(\mathcal{F}^{(k)}, x, y))).$$

It then follows that $\mathcal{F}$ and $\widehat{\mathcal{F}}$ have identical external behavior (since the above implies that $C[a, b] = \delta^{(k)}(x, y)$, and $\widehat{\mathcal{F}}$ gives outputs matching those of state $C[a, b]$ in $\mathcal{F}$).

Proof. The claims are true when x and y are empty sequences. Suppose $\widehat{\mathcal{F}}$ is in state (a, b, C) after receiving inputs (x, y), with $|x| = |y| = k$. Suppose that $\widehat{\mathcal{F}}$ receives inputs (x, y) at this point; we will prove the claims with respect to $x' = x \| x$, $y' = y \| y$. Denote the rows & columns of C as $A \times B$.

First, we prove the desired claims without the call to trim, for a variant of $\widehat{\mathcal{F}}$ that does not call trim. It is straight-forward to verify that it makes no difference to the end result to "postpone" all trim steps taken by $\widehat{\mathcal{F}}$ until the last step, at which point they are clearly idempotent.

By the inductive hypothesis, we have an isomorphism between $\mathsf{restrict}(\delta^{(k)}, \mathsf{rectangle}(\mathcal{F}^{(k)}, x, y))$ and C. Thus, we freely identify $A \times B$ with $\mathsf{rectangle}(\mathcal{F}^{(k)}, x, y)$, where a with is identified with x, and b is identified with y.

Since $A \times B = \mathsf{rectangle}(\mathcal{F}^{(k)}, x, y)$, and $\mathcal{F}^{(k)}$ has no OR-minor (recall we assume that $\mathcal{F}$ is not passive-complete), we have that $\mathcal{F}^{(k)}$ is *basic* on $A \times B$ (Lemma 1). As such, for any $x' \in A \times X$ and $y' \in B \times Y$ we have that

$$\mathsf{rectangle}(\mathsf{restrict}(\mathcal{F}^{(k+1)}, A \times X, B \times Y), x', y') = \mathsf{rectangle}(\mathcal{F}^{(k+1)}, x', y').$$

That is, within this domain of inputs, a party's input can influence the other's output only in the $k + 1$ round.

$\mathsf{explode}(C)$ is an SFE whose inputs are then $(A \times X) \times (B \times Y)$ — which we associate with input sequences of length $k + 1$ for Alice & Bob, respectively — and whose output is the corresponding output of $\mathcal{F}$ in the $(k+1)$-th round *only*. But again, when restricted to input domain $A \times B$, the first k rounds of output are *basic*, so

$$\mathsf{rectangle}(\mathsf{explode}(C), x', y') = \mathsf{rectangle}(\mathsf{restrict}(\mathcal{F}^{(k+1)}, A \times X, B \times Y), x', y').$$

Putting things together, from lines 3–4 of $\widehat{\mathcal{F}}$ it follows that C' is exactly $\mathsf{restrict}(\delta^{(k+1)}, \mathsf{rectangle}(\mathcal{F}^{(k+1)}, x', y'))$, a' is identified with x', and b' is identified with y', as desired.

Lemma 7. *If $\mathcal{F}$ is not passive-complete, then while interacting with $\widehat{\mathcal{F}}$, Alice has no uncertainty about (a, C) and Bob has no uncertainty about (b, C), where (a, b, C) is the internal state of $\widehat{\mathcal{F}}$.*

Proof. The claim is true for the initial configuration of $\widehat{\mathcal{F}}$. In round k, both parties inductively know C (and hence $\mathsf{explode}(C)$) from round $k - 1$. When $\mathcal{F}$ is not passive-complete, then each $\mathsf{explode}(C)$ contains no OR-minor. Hence, after giving inputs x and y respectively, and receiving their outputs (computed from $\mathsf{explode}(C)$), each party can deduce $R = \mathsf{rectangle}(\mathsf{explode}(C), x, y)$. In $\widehat{\mathcal{F}}$, the value C is updated based only on this common information R. The value a is updated based only on R and x; the value b is updated based only on R and y. Each party thus has enough information to update the values required for the lemma. ∎

Lemma 8. *Let $\mathcal{F}$ be a DFF. If $\mathcal{F}$ is not passive-complete, then in $\widehat{\mathcal{F}}$ the internal variable C is bounded in size by a constant that depends only on $\mathcal{F}$. Thus $\widehat{\mathcal{F}}$ has a finite number of states (at most $R(n)^2 \cdot n^{R(n)^2}$).*

Proof. It follows from the definition of $\widehat{\mathcal{F}}$ that, in every reachable state (a, b, C), the table C has no duplicate rows or columns. We will show that C also contains no OR-minor. Then it will follow from Lemma 5 that C has dimensions at most $R(n) \times R(n)$, where n is the number of states in $\mathcal{F}$. Since a and b are row and column indexes into C, there are at most $R(n)^2 n^{R(n)^2}$ states in $\widehat{\mathcal{F}}$.

Without loss of generality, assume that $\mathcal{F}$ contains no redundant states. Suppose for contradiction that C contains an OR-minor (a_0, a_1, b_0, b_1), so that $C(a_i, b_j) = r_{i \vee j}$ for distinct states r_0 and r_1. Let x^*, y^* be a distinguishing sequence for states r_0 and r_1, with $|x^*| = |y^*| = \ell$.

From Lemma 6, C is a submatrix of $\delta^{(k)}$ for some k, so there exist input sequences $\boldsymbol{x}_0, \boldsymbol{x}_1, \boldsymbol{y}_0, \boldsymbol{y}_1$ with $\delta^{(k)}(\boldsymbol{x}_i, \boldsymbol{y}_j) = C[a_i, b_j]$. Furthermore, $\{\boldsymbol{x}_0, \boldsymbol{x}_1\} \times \{\boldsymbol{y}_0, \boldsymbol{y}_1\} \subseteq \mathsf{rectangle}(\mathcal{F}^{(k)}, \boldsymbol{x}_i, \boldsymbol{y}_j)$, and so (since we are assuming that $\mathcal{F}$ is not passive-complete) $\mathcal{F}^{(k)}$ is *basic* restricted to $\{\boldsymbol{x}_0, \boldsymbol{x}_1\} \times \{\boldsymbol{y}_0, \boldsymbol{y}_1\}$.

But then $(\boldsymbol{x}_0 \| \boldsymbol{x}^*, \boldsymbol{x}_1 \| \boldsymbol{x}^*, \boldsymbol{y}_0 \| \boldsymbol{y}^*, \boldsymbol{y}_1 \| \boldsymbol{y}^*)$ is an OR-minor in $\mathcal{F}^{(k+\ell)}$, contradicting our assumption that $\mathcal{F}$ is not passive-complete. The reasoning is exactly the same as in the proof of Lemma 4. Importantly, Alice's input does not influence Bob's output (and vice-versa) for the first k rounds, and at least one party's total output depends only on whether r_0 or r_1 was reached in round k.

5.4   Deciding Passive-Triviality

The following theorem and its corollary provide total decision procedures for determining whether a given DFF is passive-trivial.

Theorem 3. *Let $\mathcal{F}$ be a DFF and $\widehat{\mathcal{F}}$ be as above. Suppose $\mathcal{F}$ is not passive-complete. Then $\mathcal{F}$ is passive-trivial if and only if, for every reachable state (a, b, C) in $\widehat{\mathcal{F}}$, $\mathsf{explode}(C)$ is decomposable.*

Proof. ($\Rightarrow$) Let (a, b, C) be a reachable state in $\widehat{\mathcal{F}}$. Then from Lemma 6 we have that C is a submatrix of $\delta^{(k)}$ for suitable k. As such, $\mathsf{explode}(C)$ is a submatrix of $\mathcal{F}^{(k+1)}$. By Proposition 1, $\mathcal{F}^{(k+1)}$, and hence all of its submatrices, is decomposable.

($\Leftarrow$) A passive-secure protocol for $\widehat{\mathcal{F}}$ (and hence $\mathcal{F}$, since they have identical external behavior — Lemma 6) is the following. Alice maintains (a, C) and Bob maintains (b, C) corresponding to the internal state of $\widehat{\mathcal{F}}$ at all times, as in Lemma 7. Inductively they will at each round compute the correct outputs and can thus update these (a, b, C) values. When Alice receives input x and Bob receives input y, both parties run a passive-secure protocol for evaluating $\mathsf{explode}(C)$ at inputs $a \| x$ and $b \| y$, respectively. Since $\mathsf{explode}(C)$ is decomposable, it follows that such a secure protocol exists; furthermore, both parties know a common C and can agree upon this protocol.

Corollary 4. *Let $\mathcal{F}$ be a DFF with n states, and let $K := R(n)^2 \cdot n^{R(n)^2}$, where R is the function from Lemma 5. Then $\mathcal{F}$ is passive-trivial if and only if, for all $k \leq K$, $\mathcal{F}^{(k)}$ is decomposable.*

Proof. The forward direction ($\Rightarrow$) follows trivially from Proposition 1.

For the other direction, if each of $\{\mathcal{F}^{(k)}\}_{k \leq K}$ is decomposable, then $\mathcal{F}$ is not passive-complete (Theorem 2). Then from Lemma 8, there are at most K distinct states in $\widehat{\mathcal{F}}$. Any reachable state in $\widehat{\mathcal{F}}$ is therefore reachable by an input sequence of length at most $K - 1$. If state (a, b, C) is reachable by an input sequence of length k, then $\mathsf{explode}(C)$ appears as a submatrix of $\mathcal{F}^{(k+1)}$; so if each of $\{\mathcal{F}^{(k)} \mid k \leq K\}$ is decomposable, then so is each $\mathsf{explode}(C)$. Hence, $\mathcal{F}$ is passive-trivial by Theorem 3.

5.5   Symmetrization

Theorem 5. *Let $\mathcal{F}$ be a DFF. If $\mathcal{F}$ is not passive-complete, then there exists a symmetric functionality (that is, one which gives identical output to each party in every round) $\mathcal{G}$ that is isomorphic to $\mathcal{F}$.*

This theorem is a generalization of an analogous theorem of Kraschewski and Müller-Quade [9] for the special case of SFE.

Proof. As described in the discussion after Lemma 1, when $\mathcal{F}$ is an **SFE**, we can take $\mathcal{G}$ to be the SFE that gives output $\mathsf{rectangle}(\mathcal{F}, x, y)$ to both parties on input x and y.

Now consider when $\mathcal{F}$ is a DFF, and recall its associated $\widehat{\mathcal{F}}$. If $\mathcal{F}$ is not passive-complete, then $\widehat{\mathcal{F}}$ is also a DFF (Lemma 8). In state (a, b, C) and on inputs (x, y) in $\widehat{\mathcal{F}}$, the parties are given the output of $\mathsf{explode}(C)$ on inputs (a, x) and (b, y). Define $\mathcal{G}$ to be the same as $\widehat{\mathcal{F}}$, except that both parties are given output $z = \mathsf{rectangle}(\mathsf{explode}(C), (a, x), (b, y))$. Since both parties know C, Alice without loss of generality knows (a, x), and Bob without loss of generality knows (b, y), the output z is enough for both parties to infer the corresponding output of $\widehat{\mathcal{F}}$. Similarly, both parties can infer z from their outputs from $\widehat{\mathcal{F}}$. Thus, $\mathcal{F}$ and $\mathcal{G}$ are isomorphic. $\qed$

6   Conclusion and Discussion

We presented two new characterizations for cryptographic properties of reactive functionalities, in the setting of computationally unbounded passive adversaries. We highlight several remaining areas of inquiry:

Active adversaries. While there is a characterization of triviality of reactive functionalities in the UC model [14], there is no such characterization for the stand-alone model. There is a characterization for completeness of DFFs as well [14], but it is in the polynomial-time setting. No characterization exists for completeness of reactive functionalities against active adversaries in the information-theoretic setting.

We conjecture that the characterization for active-completeness of DFFs will follow that of the SFE case [9]. That is, we expect there to be a suitable definition of *redundant inputs* for DFFs so that $\mathcal{F}$ is active-complete if and only if $\mathcal{F}$ is passive-complete after removing all redundant inputs. We note that [14] do in fact define a notion of redundant inputs for DFFs, but only for inputs in the first round. The characterization we seek would require the simultaneous removal of redundant inputs in all states.

A characterization of active (standalone) triviality for DFFs will require a significantly different approach than the one here for passive triviality. We highlight several fundamental aspects of our techniques that seem incompatible with active adversaries:

- We use the fact that $\mathcal{F}$ can be securely realized using $\{\mathcal{F}^{(k)}\}_k$ and vice-versa. Neither direction of this equivalence holds with respect to active security. When emulating the kth round of $\mathcal{F}$ using $\mathcal{F}^{(k)}$, we rely on the fact that parties *honestly* maintain their history of inputs and provide them as part of their input to $\mathcal{F}^{(k)}$. To emulate $\mathcal{F}^{(k)}$ using $\mathcal{F}$, the protocol invokes k rounds of $\mathcal{F}$. An active adversary could (depending on $\mathcal{F}$) violate security by adaptively changing its behavior based on the partial information it learns about the other party's input in the first $k-1$ rounds.
- In our proofs we use the fact that certain SFE functionalities appear as a submatrix of some $\mathcal{F}^{(k)}$, to demonstrate their triviality. In the passive security setting, every submatrix of an SFE inherits the triviality of the parent SFE. This property is not true in the active security setting; the characterization of standalone-triviality for SFE [13,11] is not closed under the submatrix relation.

Randomized functionalities. Compared to deterministic functionalities, our understanding of randomized functionalities is practically non-existent (an exception is for completeness of certain classes of SFE functionalities; cf. [7]). For example, there is still no analog of the Beaver-Kushilevitz characterization of passive-trivial SFE [1,12] in the randomized case (not even for perfectly-secure protocols).

Our characterization in this work reduces the reactive case to the non-reactive case in some sense. It may be that a similar approach would work even for DFFs with randomized output (even if the actual characterization for SFE is unknown). However, we expect that a randomized *transition function* would lead to complications that are not present in the deterministic case.

References

1. Beaver, D.: Perfect privacy for two-party protocols. In: Feigenbaum, J., Merritt, M. (eds.) Proceedings of DIMACS Workshop on Distributed Computing and Cryptography, vol. 2, pp. 65–77. American Mathematical Society (1989)
2. Canetti, R.: Universally composable security: A new paradigm for cryptographic protocols. In: Naor, M. (ed.) FOCS, pp. 136–145. IEEE Computer Society Press (2001); Revised version (2005) on Cryptology ePrint Archive, http://eprint.iacr.org/2000/067
3. Canetti, R., Fischlin, M.: Universally Composable Commitments. In: Kilian, J. (ed.) CRYPTO 2001. LNCS, vol. 2139, pp. 19–40. Springer, Heidelberg (2001)
4. Chor, B., Kushilevitz, E.: A zero-one law for boolean privacy. SIAM J. Discrete Math. 4(1), 36–47 (1991)
5. Goldreich, O., Micali, S., Wigderson, A.: How to play any mental game or a completeness theorem for protocols with honest majority. In: STOC, pp. 218–229. ACM (1987)
6. Kilian, J.: A general completeness theorem for two-party games. In: STOC, pp. 553–560. ACM (1991)
7. Kilian, J.: More general completeness theorems for secure two-party computation. In: STOC, pp. 316–324. ACM (2000)

8. Kilian, J., Kushilevitz, E., Micali, S., Ostrovsky, R.: Reducibility and completeness in private computations. SIAM J. Comput. 29(4), 1189–1208 (2000)

9. Kraschewski, D., Müller-Quade, J.: Completeness Theorems with Constructive Proofs for Finite Deterministic 2-Party Functions. In: Ishai, Y. (ed.) TCC 2011. LNCS, vol. 6597, pp. 364–381. Springer, Heidelberg (2011)

10. Kreitz, G.: A Zero-One Law for Secure Multi-party Computation with Ternary Outputs. In: Ishai, Y. (ed.) TCC 2011. LNCS, vol. 6597, pp. 382–399. Springer, Heidelberg (2011)

11. Künzler, R., Müller-Quade, J., Raub, D.: Secure Computability of Functions in the IT Setting with Dishonest Majority and Applications to Long-Term Security. In: Reingold, O. (ed.) TCC 2009. LNCS, vol. 5444, pp. 238–255. Springer, Heidelberg (2009)

12. Kushilevitz, E.: Privacy and communication complexity. In: FOCS, pp. 416–421. IEEE (1989)

13. Maji, H.K., Prabhakaran, M., Rosulek, M.: Complexity of Multi-party Computation Problems: The Case of 2-Party Symmetric Secure Function Evaluation. In: Reingold, O. (ed.) TCC 2009. LNCS, vol. 5444, pp. 256–273. Springer, Heidelberg (2009)

14. Maji, H.K., Prabhakaran, M., Rosulek, M.: A Zero-One Law for Cryptographic Complexity with Respect to Computational UC Security. In: Rabin, T. (ed.) CRYPTO 2010. LNCS, vol. 6223, pp. 595–612. Springer, Heidelberg (2010)

15. Prabhakaran, M., Rosulek, M.: Cryptographic Complexity of Multi-Party Computation Problems: Classifications and Separations. In: Wagner, D. (ed.) CRYPTO 2008. LNCS, vol. 5157, pp. 262–279. Springer, Heidelberg (2008)

16. Rosulek, M.: Universal Composability from Essentially Any Trusted Setup. In: Safavi-Naini, R., Canetti, R. (eds.) CRYPTO 2012. LNCS, vol. 7417, pp. 406–423. Springer, Heidelberg (2012)

17. Yao, A.C.: Protocols for secure computations (extended abstract). In: FOCS, pp. 160–164. IEEE (1982)

Feasibility and Completeness of Cryptographic Tasks in the Quantum World

Serge Fehr[1], Jonathan Katz[2,*],
Fang Song[3], Hong-Sheng Zhou[2,**], and Vassilis Zikas[4,***]

[1] Centrum Wiskunde & Informatica (CWI)
serge.fehr@cwi.nl
[2] University of Maryland
{jkatz,hszhou}@cs.umd.edu
[3] Pennsylvania State University
fus121@cse.psu.edu
[4] UCLA
vzikas@cs.ucla.edu

Abstract. It is known that cryptographic feasibility results can change by moving from the classical to the quantum world. With this in mind, we study the feasibility of realizing functionalities in the framework of universal composability, with respect to both computational and information-theoretic security. With respect to computational security, we show that existing feasibility results *carry over unchanged* from the classical to the quantum world; a functionality is "trivial" (i.e., can be realized without setup) in the quantum world if and only if it is trivial in the classical world. The same holds with regard to functionalities that are *complete* (i.e., can be used to realize arbitrary other functionalities).

In the information-theoretic setting, the quantum and classical worlds differ. In the quantum world, functionalities in the class we consider are either complete, trivial, or belong to a family of simultaneous-exchange functionalities (e.g., XOR). However, other results in the information-theoretic setting remain roughly unchanged.

1 Introduction

In a *classical* setting of cryptography, participants in a protocol (both the honest parties and the adversary), are modeled as being able to perform classical computation only. In the *quantum* setting, however, parties are able to send and receive quantum states and process quantum information. It is well known that cryptographic feasibility results in these two settings differ; for example, key exchange with information-theoretic security is possible in the quantum world, but not in the classical world. In this paper we focus on protocols for

---

* This work was supported by NSF awards #1111599 and #1223623.
** Supported by an NSF CI postdoctoral fellowship.
*** Work done while at the University of Maryland, and supported in part by a fellowship from the Swiss National Science Foundation (Project No. PBEZP2-134445).

A. Sahai (Ed.): TCC 2013, LNCS 7785, pp. 281–296, 2013.

universally composable two-party computation, and study the relationships between feasibility/impossibility results in the classical and quantum settings.

1.1 Universally Composable Computation in the Classical World

Our focus in on secure computation within the framework of universal composability [8], which provides strong composition guarantees when arbitrary protocols are executed concurrently. Soon after the introduction of this framework, Canetti and Fischlin [9] showed that, without honest majority, UC commitment is impossible to achieve. This was later extended to rule out protocols for securely achieving most other "interesting" tasks [10,32].

On the positive side, it is known that (under suitable cryptographic assumptions) any functionality can be securely computed, without honest majority, if we are willing to assume some form of trusted setup such as a common reference string [9,11]. Subsequent work has identified other *complete* setup assumptions [1,19,18,12]. Completeness results in the *information-theoretic* (or *statistical*) setting, where the adversary is computationally unbounded, have also been shown [21,18].

Maji et al. [28] proved a *zero/one law*: every two-party deterministic function with polynomial-size input domain is either *trivial*[1] (i.e, can be realized in the UC framework with no setup assumptions), or *complete* (i.e., sufficient for computing arbitrary other functions, under appropriate complexity assumptions). This characterization was extended by Katz et al. [20], who showed completeness for deterministic functions with exponential-size input domains, and by Rosulek [33], who showed completeness for randomized, reactive functions as well. In the setting of information-theoretic security, Kraschewski et al. [22] give a characterization of completeness for two-party deterministic functionalities, and show that a zero/one laws does not hold. In fact, Maji et al. [27] show there is an infinite hierarchy of function complexity in the statistical setting.

1.2 The Shift to a Quantum World

How do the results described in the previous section change when we move to the quantum world? The answer, *a priori*, is unclear. Feasibility results in the classical setting may not hold in the quantum setting since quantum adversaries are more powerful than classical ones. This is true even if "quantum-resistant" cryptographic assumptions are used, since techniques such as rewinding that are used to prove security against classical adversaries may not apply in the quantum setting. Even in the case of statistical security, feasibility results may not translate from the classical world to the quantum world [14].

In the other direction, impossibility results in the classical setting might potentially be circumvented in the quantum setting since honest parties can rely on quantum mechanics, too. As a notable example of this, statistically secure key exchange is possible in the quantum world [3] but not in the classical one.

---

[1] We use *trivial* and *feasible* exchangeably hereafter.

While several impossibility results for statistically secure two-party computation in the quantum setting are known [29,24,23,34,6], these results say nothing about the computational setting. They also say nothing about what might be possible given trusted setup. An example here, that also demonstrates the power of quantum protocols, arises in the context of building oblivious transfer (OT) from commitment. Classically, this is impossible [27]. However, there is a construction of OT from commitment in the quantum world [4,15,36,5]; as a consequence, commitment is complete for UC computation in that setting [36].

Given the above, the situation regarding triviality and completeness of functionalities within the *quantum* UC framework (see Section 2) is unclear, though partial answers are known. In the *statistical* setting, Unruh [36] gives a generic "lifting" theorem asserting that classically secure protocols remain (statistically) secure in the quantum world. So any functionalities that are classically trivial (in a statistical sense) are also trivial in a quantum setting. Moreover, any functionality that is classically *complete* in a statistical sense (and so in particular OT [36]) is complete with respect to the quantum UC framework as well. The situation is less clear with regard to computational security. A recent work by Hallgren et al. [17] "salvages" a few classically complete functionalities, showing that, for example, coin-flipping and zero-knowledge are still complete in the quantum world. But this does not rule out the possibility that some classically complete functionalities are no longer complete in the quantum setting.

1.3 Our Results

We study feasibility and completeness of an interesting class of two-party, deterministic functionalities on polynomial-size domains. We prove generic, *quantum-lifting* theorems and use them to show that feasibility in the quantum world is *equivalent* to classical feasibility, in both the computational and statistical settings. An important ingredient here is a quantum analogue of the Canetti-Fischlin result [9], showing that there is no quantum protocol realizing UC commitment against computationally bounded quantum adversaries in the plain model.[2] This result extends the known impossibility results mentioned earlier for statistically secure protocols in the quantum setting.

At the core of our quantum-lifting theorems is a quantum construction of statistically secure OT from the "2-bit cut-and-choose" functionality $\mathcal{F}_{2CC}$. (Note that $\mathcal{F}_{2CC}$ is not complete in the classical setting.) Our construction is a modification of the BBCS protocol [4], but existing techniques do not seem to apply for arguing its security. Instead, we introduce and analyze an *adaptive* version of the sampling technique from [5], and use this to prove the security of our OT protocol. The adaptive-sampling analysis may be of independent interest.

Our lifting theorems for the case of computational security, together with Unruh's lifting theorem for the statistical case [36], imply that any classically complete functionality remains complete in the quantum setting. On the other hand, we identify tasks that are statistically complete using quantum protocols but are incomplete classically. Our results show, roughly, that every functionality

---

[2] A similar result was stated in [31] with no proof.

in our class is either trivial or complete in the quantum computational setting; thus, the situation here is analogous to the classical case [28]. In the quantum *statistical* setting, however, functionalities fall into one of three different classes; this is in contrast with the (more complicated) classical picture [27,22].

1.4   Additional Related Work

Proving security of quantum protocols has been challenging and nontrivial. Indeed, it was only several years after the invention of quantum key-exchange protocols that rigorous proofs of security were given [30,25,35]. With regard to secure computation, the first broad feasibility results were in the setting of multi-party protocols with information-theoretic security, assuming honest majority [13,2]. Positive results for computational security in the quantum world, without honest majority, have only recently been shown [37,26,17,16].

1.5   Outline of the Paper

In Section 2, we describe the classical and the quantum UC models as well as our terminology. We prove our lifting theorems for completeness in Section 3, and for feasibility in Section 4. In Section 5, we apply our lifting theorems to classify the cryptographic complexity of functionalities in the class we consider.

2   The Model

In this section we describe the model and our terminology. We consider two types of security statements, namely classical and quantum. The classical statements are done in Canetti's (classical) UC framework [8]. For quantum statements we use the recently developed quantum-UC framework [36]. In this work, we assume *static*, i.e., non-adaptive corruption. Namely an adversary chooses the set of parties to corrupt before execution of the protocol.

The UC Framework. The security of protocols is argued via the simulation paradigm. Intuitively, a protocol *securely realizes* a given ideal functionality $\mathcal{F}$, if the adversary cannot gain more in the protocol (real-world) than what she could in an ideal-evaluation of $\mathcal{F}$ where a trusted party computes the function values and hand them to designated players (ideal-world). More formally, a protocol π securely realizes a functionality $\mathcal{F}$ if for every real-world adversary $\mathcal{A}$ there exists an ideal-world adversary $\mathcal{S}$, called the *simulator*, such that no environment can distinguish whether it is witnessing the real-world execution with adversary $\mathcal{A}$ or the ideal-world execution with simulator $\mathcal{S}$. The parties, the adversary, the simulator, the functionalities, and the environment, are modeled as interactive Turing-machines (ITMs). Depending on the assumed computing power of the adversaries and the environment we distinguish between *computational security*, where they are all considered to be polynomially bounded ITMs, and *information-theoretic (i.t.)*, also known as *statistical* security, where they are assumed to be computationally unbounded.

Universal Composability and the Hybrid Model. The most important feature of the simulation-based security definition is that it allows to argue about security of protocols in a composable way. In particular, let π be a protocol which securely realizes a functionality $\mathcal{F}$. If we can prove that a protocol π' securely realizes a functionality $\mathcal{F}'$ using invocations of $\mathcal{F}$ as in the ideal world, then it follows automatically that if we replace in π' the invocations of $\mathcal{F}$ by invocations of π, the resulting protocol also securely realizes $\mathcal{F}'$. Therefore we only need to prove the security of π' in the so-called $\mathcal{F}$-*hybrid* model, where the players run π' and are allowed to make invocations to $\mathcal{F}$.

Reductions and Cryptographic Complexity. For two ideal functionalities $\mathcal{F}$ and $\mathcal{F}'$, we say that $\mathcal{F}$ *computationally (classical) UC reduces to* $\mathcal{F}'$, denoted as $\mathcal{F} \sqsubseteq^{\text{CCOMP}} \mathcal{F}'$, if there exists a $\mathcal{F}'$-hybrid protocol $\pi^{\mathcal{F}'}$ which computationally securely realizes $\mathcal{F}$. If the protocol $\pi^{\mathcal{F}'}$ statistically securely realizes $\mathcal{F}$, then we say that $\mathcal{F}$ *statistically (classical) UC reduces to* $\mathcal{F}'$, denoted as $\mathcal{F} \sqsubseteq^{\text{CSTAT}} \mathcal{F}'$. As syntactic sugar, we say that $\mathcal{F}$ and $\mathcal{F}'$ are computationally (resp. statistically) UC equivalent, denoted as $\mathcal{F} \overset{\text{ccomp}}{\equiv} \mathcal{F}'$ (resp. $\mathcal{F} \overset{\text{cstat}}{\equiv} \mathcal{F}'$), if $\mathcal{F} \sqsubseteq^{\text{CCOMP}} \mathcal{F}'$ and $\mathcal{F}' \sqsubseteq^{\text{CCOMP}} \mathcal{F}$ (resp. $\mathcal{F} \sqsubseteq^{\text{CSTAT}} \mathcal{F}'$ and $\mathcal{F}' \sqsubseteq^{\text{CSTAT}} \mathcal{F}$).

The reduction-relation $\sqsubseteq$ is "transitive" in the sense that if $\mathcal{F}' \sqsubseteq \mathcal{F}$, then any task which is implementable in the $\mathcal{F}'$-hybrid world is also implementable in the $\mathcal{F}$-hybrid world. This implies a notion of cryptographic complexity for functions, where $\mathcal{F}' \sqsubseteq \mathcal{F}$ implies that $\mathcal{F}$ is at least as high in the hierarchy as $\mathcal{F}'$.

Feasibility and Completeness. Let $\mathcal{F}_{\text{SEC}}$ denote the secure channels functionality. We say that a functionality $\mathcal{F}$ is *computationally (resp. statistically) UC feasible* if $\mathcal{F} \sqsubseteq^{\text{CCOMP}} \mathcal{F}_{\text{SEC}}$ (resp. $\mathcal{F} \sqsubseteq^{\text{CSTAT}} \mathcal{F}_{\text{SEC}}$). Furthermore, we say that $\mathcal{F}$ is *computationally (resp. statistically) UC complete* if for any well-formed functionality $\mathcal{F}' : \mathcal{F}' \sqsubseteq^{\text{CCOMP}} \mathcal{F}$ (resp. $\mathcal{F}' \sqsubseteq^{\text{CSTAT}} \mathcal{F}$).

The Quantum UC Framework [36]. The quantum-UC framework generalizes the classical UC model, in which the players (including the adversaries and the environment) are quantum machines. A quantum universal composition theorem was proved in [36]. We point out that in this work we only consider ideal functionalities with classical inputs and outputs. For two ideal functionalities $\mathcal{F}$ and $\mathcal{F}'$, we say that $\mathcal{F}$ *computationally quantum-UC reduces to* $\mathcal{F}'$, denoted as $\mathcal{F} \sqsubseteq^{\text{QCOMP}} \mathcal{F}'$, if there exists a $\mathcal{F}'$-hybrid protocol $\pi^{\mathcal{F}'}$ which computationally securely realizes $\mathcal{F}$. If the protocol $\pi^{\mathcal{F}'}$ statistically securely realizes $\mathcal{F}$, then we say that $\mathcal{F}$ *statistically quantum-UC reduces to* $\mathcal{F}'$, denoted as $\mathcal{F} \sqsubseteq^{\text{QSTAT}} \mathcal{F}'$. We say that a functionality $\mathcal{F}$ is *computationally (resp. statistically) quantum-UC feasible* if $\mathcal{F}$ can be computationally (resp. statistically) quantum-UC realized in the plain quantum-UC model, i.e., without assuming any hybrids.[3] Furthermore, we say that $\mathcal{F}$ is *computationally (resp. statistically) quantum-UC complete* if for any well-formed (classical) functionality $\mathcal{F}' : \mathcal{F}' \sqsubseteq^{\text{QCOMP}} \mathcal{F}$ (resp. $\mathcal{F}' \sqsubseteq^{\text{QSTAT}} \mathcal{F}$).

---

[3] We point out that quantum secure channel is implied by authentication channel due to QKD protocols, which is by default provided in the quantum-UC framework, hence there is no need to assume quantum secure channels.

The definitions of computation and statistical quantum-UC equivalence is also analogous to the classical setting.

In [36] the so-called *(statistical) quantum lifting theorem* was proved which, roughly speaking shows that if a classical protocol is statistically UC secure then it is also statistically quantum-UC secure.

Fact 1 ([36, Theorem 15] – The Quantum Lifting Theorem). *If a protocol π statistically UC realizes a functionality $\mathcal{F}$, then π statistically quantum-UC realizes the functionality $\mathcal{F}$.*

Remark 1 (Polynomial Simulation). In all the security definitions considered in this work we explicitly require that the simulator's running time is polynomial to the running time of the adversary. We call this property *polynomial simulation*. The property ensures that when a protocol statistically realizes a functionality, then it also computationally realizes it [7,8]. We point out that the definition of statistical quantum-UC security in [36] explicitly requires *polynomial simulation*.

Ideal Functionalities and the Class $\mathcal{U}^-$. Ideally, we would like our statements to cover the whole class $\mathcal{U}$ of finite, deterministic, two-party functionalities, which is the central class studied in [27,28]. However, we were unable to prove or disprove (quantum-UC) neither completeness nor feasibility of the 1-bit cut-and-choose functionality $\mathcal{F}_{1\mathrm{cc}} \in \mathcal{U}$ (also denoted as $\mathcal{F}_{\mathrm{cc}}$). We were able to prove statistical quantum-UC completeness of its "closest sibling;" namely, the 2-bit cut-and-choose functionality $\mathcal{F}_{2\mathrm{cc}}$.[4] Therefore, our results are for the slightly smaller class $\mathcal{U}^-$ which is $\mathcal{U}$ excluding the small fraction of functionalities that are sufficient for (statistically classically) realizing $\mathcal{F}_{1\mathrm{cc}}$ but not for realizing $\mathcal{F}_{2\mathrm{cc}}$. Formally:

$$\mathcal{U}^- = \{\mathcal{F} \mid (\mathcal{F} \in \mathcal{U}) \wedge ((\mathcal{F}_{2\mathrm{cc}} \sqsubseteq^{\mathrm{CSTAT}} \mathcal{F}) \vee (\mathcal{F}_{1\mathrm{cc}} \not\sqsubseteq^{\mathrm{CSTAT}} \mathcal{F}))\}.$$

Note that, as demonstrated in [28], the missing fraction, i.e., $\mathcal{U} \setminus \mathcal{U}^-$, is indeed very small as, roughly, it corresponds to the lowest primitive of an infinite *strict* hierarchy of (statistically classically) incomplete "cut-and-choose" primitives.[5] Nevertheless, it remains an open problem to prove quantum-UC feasibility or completeness of $\mathcal{F}_{1\mathrm{cc}}$ (which would complete the characterization of $\mathcal{U}$) as it does not follow from any known classical or quantum results.

For completeness, we list a few two-party ideal functionalities that are used as setups in this work. Consistently with existing literature we use the names Alice and Bob for the parties:

• 1-out-of-2 Oblivious Transfer $\mathcal{F}_{\mathrm{OT}}$: Alice (the sender) inputs 2 bits (s_0, s_1) and Bob (the receiver) inputs a selection bit $c \in \{0, 1\}$. Bob receives s_c from $\mathcal{F}_{\mathrm{OT}}$.

---

[4] Our conjecture is that $\mathcal{F}_{1\mathrm{cc}}$ is also statistically quantum-UC complete. Recall that classically neither $\mathcal{F}_{\mathrm{cc}}$ nor $\mathcal{F}_{2\mathrm{cc}}$ is statistically UC complete [28].

[5] These are variations of $\mathcal{F}_{2\mathrm{cc}}$ parameterized by the size of Bob's input, i.e., $\mathcal{F}_{m\mathrm{cc}}$ behaves as $\mathcal{F}_{\mathrm{cc}}$ where Bob's input is a string of length m. ($\mathcal{F}_{1\mathrm{cc}}$ is the lowest and $\mathcal{F}_{2\mathrm{cc}}$ is the second lowest primitive in this hierarchy.) [28].

We also consider the more general string OT, where (s_0, s_1) are ℓ-bit strings. Our OT protocol in Sect. 3.1 realizes string OT.

- Commitment $\mathcal{F}_{\mathtt{COM}}$: Alice (the committer) inputs a bit b and Bob (the receiver) receives from $\mathcal{F}_{\mathtt{COM}}$ a notification that a bit was received. At a later point, Alice can input the command open to $\mathcal{F}_{\mathtt{COM}}$ in which case Bob receives b.

- XOR $\mathcal{F}_{\mathtt{XOR}}$: Alice and Bob input bits b_A and b_B, respectively. They both receive the output $y = b_A \oplus b_B$.

- 2-bit Cut-and-Choose $\mathcal{F}_{\mathtt{2CC}}$: Bob inputs a 2-bit string $b = (b_0, b_1)$, an Alice inputs a selection bit s_A; informally, s_A indicates whether or not Alice wishes to learn b. Bob receives output s_A and Alice receives output b if $s_A = 1$, and receives $\perp$ if $s_A = 0$.

- Coin Tossing $\mathcal{F}_{\mathtt{COIN}}$: Alice and Bob input a request to $\mathcal{F}_{\mathtt{COIN}}$, and $\mathcal{F}_{\mathtt{COIN}}$ randomly chooses a fair coin $r \in \{0, 1\}$ and it then sends delayed output r to both Alice and Bob.

Note that the functionalities $\mathcal{F}_{\mathtt{OT}}$, $\mathcal{F}_{\mathtt{XOR}}$, $\mathcal{F}_{\mathtt{2CC}}$, and $\mathcal{F}_{\mathtt{COM}}$ are in the set $\mathcal{U}^-$.

Notational Conventions. Throughout the paper we use small π to denote a classical protocol in classical UC model, while we use capital Π to denote a classical or quantum protocol in quantum UC model.

3   Quantum Lifting for Completeness

In this section we prove that statements about completeness of functionalities in the classical setting are preserved in the quantum setting. More precisely, we prove the following theorem:

Theorem 1. *For any $\mathcal{F} \in \mathcal{U}^-$ the following statements hold:*

1. *(Statistical Setting) If $\mathcal{F}$ is statistically classical-UC complete then $\mathcal{F}$ is statistically quantum-UC complete.*

2. *(Computational Setting) If $\mathcal{F}$ is computationally classical-UC complete under the semi-honest OT assumption shOT then $\mathcal{F}$ is computationally quantum-UC complete under the assumptions of existence of a quantum-secure pseudorandom generator and a dense encryption that is quantum IND-CPA.*

The statistical statement follows easily from Unruh's quantum lifting theorem (Fact 1) and the definition of completeness. In the remaining of this section we prove the computational statement. To this direction we follow a structure similar to that of [28]: First, in Section 3.1 we show that for any $\mathcal{F} \in \mathcal{U}^-$, either $\mathcal{F}$ is computationally quantum-UC feasible or for a functionality $\mathcal{F}' \in \{\mathcal{F}_{\mathtt{XOR}}, \mathcal{F}_{\mathtt{OT}}, \mathcal{F}_{\mathtt{2CC}}, \mathcal{F}_{\mathtt{COM}}\}$, there exists a statistically quantum-UC secure protocol which reduces $\mathcal{F}'$ to $\mathcal{F}$. Second, in Section 3.2, we show that $\mathcal{F}_{\mathtt{XOR}}$, $\mathcal{F}_{\mathtt{OT}}$, $\mathcal{F}_{\mathtt{2CC}}$, and $\mathcal{F}_{\mathtt{COM}}$ are computationally quantum-UC complete. Statement 2 of the theorem follows then immediately by combining the above steps and using the fact that any statistically quantum-UC secure protocol is also computationally quantum-UC secure.

3.1   Non-feasibility Implies $\mathcal{F}_{\text{XOR}}$, $\mathcal{F}_{\text{OT}}$, $\mathcal{F}_{\text{2CC}}$, or $\mathcal{F}_{\text{COM}}$

To show that every infeasible $\mathcal{F} \in \mathcal{U}^-$, there is some $\mathcal{F}' \in \{\mathcal{F}_{\text{XOR}}, \mathcal{F}_{\text{OT}}, \mathcal{F}_{\text{2CC}}, \mathcal{F}_{\text{COM}}\}$ such that $\mathcal{F}' \sqsubseteq^{\text{QCOMP}} \mathcal{F}$, we use the following result that is proved in [28, Theorems 1,4]: if $\mathcal{F} \in \mathcal{U}$ is not UC feasible, then for $\mathcal{F}' \sqsubseteq^{\text{CSTAT}} \mathcal{F}$. Using this result on $\mathcal{U}^-$ we obtain the following:

Fact 2 ([28]). *Let $\mathcal{F} \in \mathcal{U}^-$. If $\mathcal{F}$ is not computationally (UC) feasible, then for some $\mathcal{F}' \in \{\mathcal{F}_{\text{XOR}}, \mathcal{F}_{\text{OT}}, \mathcal{F}_{\text{2CC}}, \mathcal{F}_{\text{COM}}\}$ the following holds: $\mathcal{F}' \sqsubseteq^{\text{CSTAT}} \mathcal{F}$.*

Because the reductions in Fact 2 are information-theoretic (with polynomial-simulation), the statement can be translated to the quantum-UC setting by Fact 1. This proves the following lemma:

Lemma 1. *Let $\mathcal{F} \in \mathcal{U}^-$. If $\mathcal{F}$ is not statistically quantum-UC feasible , then for some $\mathcal{F}' \in \{\mathcal{F}_{\text{XOR}}, \mathcal{F}_{\text{OT}}, \mathcal{F}_{\text{2CC}}, \mathcal{F}_{\text{COM}}\}$ the following holds: $\mathcal{F}' \sqsubseteq^{\text{QSTAT}} \mathcal{F}$.*

Proof. First observe that $\mathcal{F}$ is not statistically classical-UC feasible, because otherwise the lifting lemma (Fact 1) will impy that $\mathcal{F}$ is also statistically quantum-UC feasible, contradicting the assumption. Then by our lifting theorem for feasibility in later section (Sect. 4, Theorem 2), statistical UC infeasibility of $\mathcal{F}$ implies that $\mathcal{F}$ is *not* computationally UC feasible. Then Fact 2 tells us that for some $\mathcal{F}' \in \{\mathcal{F}_{\text{XOR}}, \mathcal{F}_{\text{OT}}, \mathcal{F}_{\text{2CC}}, \mathcal{F}_{\text{COM}}\} : \mathcal{F}' \sqsubseteq^{\text{CSTAT}} \mathcal{F}$, which, in turns implies that $\mathcal{F}' \sqsubseteq^{\text{QSTAT}} \mathcal{F}$ by Fact 1.

3.2   Quantum-UC Completeness of $\mathcal{F}_{\text{XOR}}$, $\mathcal{F}_{\text{OT}}$, $\mathcal{F}_{\text{2CC}}$, and $\mathcal{F}_{\text{COM}}$

We next prove that each of the functionalities $\mathcal{F}_{\text{XOR}}$, $\mathcal{F}_{\text{OT}}$, $\mathcal{F}_{\text{2CC}}$ and $\mathcal{F}_{\text{COM}}$ is computationally quantum-UC complete[6]. The quantum-UC completeness of $\mathcal{F}_{\text{OT}}$ and $\mathcal{F}_{\text{COM}}$ was proved in [36]:

Lemma 2. *$\mathcal{F}_{\text{OT}}$ and $\mathcal{F}_{\text{COM}}$ are statistically quantum-UC complete.*

This immediately gives us the desired computational quantum-UC completeness of $\mathcal{F}_{\text{OT}}$ and $\mathcal{F}_{\text{COM}}$. Next, we show completeness for the XOR functionality. To this direction we use the following idea: first we use the straight-forward classical $\mathcal{F}_{\text{XOR}}$-hybrid coin-tossing protocol (each party chooses a random bit and sends it to $\mathcal{F}_{\text{XOR}}$; the output of every party is the value they receive from $\mathcal{F}_{\text{XOR}}$) to construct $\mathcal{F}_{\text{COIN}}$; subsequently, we apply the results of [17] who proved computationally quantum-UC completeness of $\mathcal{F}_{\text{COIN}}$ under proper assumptions.

Lemma 3. *Assuming existence of a quantum-secure pseudorandom generator and a dense encryption that is quantum IND-CPA, then $\mathcal{F}_{\text{XOR}}$ is computationally quantum-UC complete.*

---

[6] Actually, as will be shown, $\mathcal{F}_{\text{COM}}$, $\mathcal{F}_{\text{OT}}$, $\mathcal{F}_{\text{2CC}}$ are *statistically* quantum-UC complete.

The most involved completeness proof is the one concerning the cut-and-choose functionality $\mathcal{F}_{2CC}$. In [28], they constructed a classical protocol realizing $\mathcal{F}_{COM}$ from $\mathcal{F}_{1CC}$. However, their security proof involves rewinding, and it is unclear how to make it go through against quantum adversaries.[7]

Instead, we demonstrate completeness of $\mathcal{F}_{2CC}$ by constructing a *quantum* protocol that statistically quantum-UC realizes $\mathcal{F}_{OT}$ in $\mathcal{F}_{2CC}$-hybrid world (and then applying Lemma 2). The idea is motivated by the quantum OT construction in the $\mathcal{F}_{COM}$ hybrid world by Bennett et al [4]. In this protocol, roughly speaking, $\mathcal{F}_{COM}$ is used in a checking subroutine to ensure that malicious Bob measures his qubits upon arrival (and does not store them until Alice informs him about the bases used). More specifically, Alice sends several qubits encoded in random bases, and Bob measures all of them and commits, for each qubit, to the pair $(\tilde{x}_i^B, \tilde{\theta}_i^B)$, where $\tilde{x}_i^B$ is the outcome of the measurement of the ith qubit and $\tilde{\theta}_i^B$ is the corresponding basis Bob used. Alice then asks Bob to open a randomly chosen subset of the committed pairs, and she checks consistency with how she had prepared the qubits. Intuitively, this indeed ensures that Bob has measures most of the qubits, as otherwise he would not know what to commit to. Formally proving this intuition turned out to be non-trivial, with the first rigorous proofs given in [15,36,5].

Our protocol uses, instead of commitments, invocations to $\mathcal{F}_{2CC}$ to implement the checking step (see the protocol Π_{QOT} below). Intuitively, this should enforce Bob to measure all the qubits as in the original protocol based on commitments. Unfortunately, the formal proof does not carry over. The problem arises from the fact that in the original protocol, Bob has to commit to all the $\tilde{\theta}_i^B$ and $\tilde{x}_i^B$ *before* he gets to see the random subset that Alice chooses for testing consistency, whereas in our protocol based on $\mathcal{F}_{2CC}$, Bob can make his input $(\tilde{\theta}_i^B, \tilde{x}_i^B)$ to $\mathcal{F}_{2CC}$ *adaptively*, and *dependent* on which prior positions Alice has tested. Current proofs, like [15,5], cannot deal with that.

In order to deal with this issue, we introduce an *adaptive* version of the sampling framework of [5]. We then show, analogous to the static setting as in [5], that the security of the OT scheme reduces to the analysis of a quantum sampling problem in our adaptive sampling framework. Analyzing the quantum sampling problem can further be reduced to a classical probabilistic analysis, which can be handled by standard techniques (e.g., Azuma's inequality).

In the following, we describe the $\mathcal{F}_{2CC}$-hybrid OT protocol Π_{QOT} and state its security in Lemma 4. The formal proof can be found in the full version.

Lemma 4. *There exists an $\mathcal{F}_{2CC}$-hybrid protocol which statistically quantum-UC realizes $\mathcal{F}_{OT}$.*

The following corollary follows from Lemma 4 and the completeness of $\mathcal{F}_{OT}$ (Lemma 2), by applying the quantum-UC composition theorem.

---

[7] It is in general hard to clearly define what it means for a security proof to "not use rewinding". It is not enough for the protocol to have a straight-line simulator, which [28] actually satisfies. The subtlety is that the correctness of the simulator might still involve rewinding argument (e.g., in defining hybrid experiments).

Protocol Π_{QOT}

Parameters: A family $\mathbf{F} = \{f : \{0,1\}^n \to \{0,1\}^\ell\}$ of universal hash functions.
Parties: The sender Alice and the recipient Bob.
Inputs: Alice gets two ℓ-bit strings s_0 and s_1, Bob gets a bit c.

1. **(Initialization)**
   1.1 Alice chooses $\tilde{x}^A = (\tilde{x}_1^A, \ldots, \tilde{x}_n^A) \in_R \{0,1\}^n$ and $\tilde{\theta}^A = (\tilde{\theta}_1^A, \ldots, \tilde{\theta}_n^A) \in_R \{+, \times\}^n$ uniformly at random and sends $|\tilde{x}^A\rangle_{\tilde{\theta}^A}$ to Bob who denotes the received state by $|\psi\rangle$.
   2.2 Bob chooses $\tilde{\theta}^B = (\tilde{\theta}_1^B, \ldots, \tilde{\theta}_n^B) \in_R \{+, \times\}^n$ uniformly at random and measures the qubits of $|\psi\rangle$ in the bases $\tilde{\theta}^B$; denote the result by $\tilde{x}^B := (\tilde{x}_1^B, \ldots, \tilde{x}_n^B)$.

2. **(Checking)**
   2.1 For $i = 1, \ldots n$ the following steps are executed sequentially:
       (a) Alice chooses a bit $b_i \in_R \{0,1\}$ uniformly at random.
       (b) Alice and Bob invoke $\mathcal{F}_{\text{2CC}}$ with inputs b_i and $(\tilde{x}_i^B, \tilde{\theta}_i^B)$, respectively.
   2.2 If in some iteration i of Step 2.1 Alice receives $\tilde{\theta}_i^B = \tilde{\theta}_i^A$ but $\tilde{x}_i^B \neq \tilde{x}_i^A$, then Alice aborts. If in Step 2.1 Bob receives (as output of $\mathcal{F}_{\text{2CC}}$) the bit $b_i = 1$ more than $3n/5$ times then Bob aborts.
   2.3 Let $\hat{x}^A$ be the string resulting from removing in $\tilde{x}^A$ the bits at positions i with $b_i = 1$. Define $\hat{\theta}^A$, $\hat{x}^B$, $\hat{\theta}^B$ analogously.

3. **(Partition Index Set)** Alice sends $\hat{\theta}^A$ to Bob. Bob sets $I_c := \{i : \hat{\theta}_i^A = \hat{\theta}_i^B\}$ and $I_{1-c} := \{i : \hat{\theta}_i^A \neq \hat{\theta}_i^B\}$. Then Bob sends (I_0, I_1) to Alice.

4. **(Secret Transferring)**
   4.1 Alice picks a function $f \in_R \mathbf{F}$; for $i = 0, 1$: Alice computes $m_i := s_i \oplus f(x_i')$, where x_i' is the n-bit string that consists of $\hat{x}^A|_{I_i}$ padded with zeros, and sends (f, m_0, m_1) to Bob.
   4.2 Bob outputs $s := m_c \oplus f(x_B')$, where x_B' is the n-bit string that consists of $\hat{x}^B|_{I_c}$ padded with zeros.

Corollary 1. $\mathcal{F}_{\text{2CC}}$ *is statistically quantum-UC complete.*

The proof of Theorem 3 follows easily from Lemmas 1, 2, 3, and Corollary 1, by applying the quantum-UC composition theorem.

4   Quantum Lifting for Feasibility

In this section we show a bi-directional lifting theorem for feasibility statements. Informally, we show that if a functionality $\mathcal{F} \in \mathcal{U}^-$ is feasible in the classical UC setting, then $\mathcal{F}$ is also feasible in the quantum-UC setting and vise versa. In fact, we can even show a stronger statement, namely that the set of feasible functionalities in $\mathcal{U}^-$ is the same set *irrespective* of whether we are considering the classical or the quantum setting and independent of the level of security (i.e, computational or statistical). We point out that the computational statements in the following theorem are under that semi-honest OT assumption for the classical setting, and under the assumptions of existence of a quantum-secure pseudorandom generator and a dense encryption that is quantum IND-CPA, for the quantum setting.

Theorem 2. *Let $\mathcal{F} \in \mathcal{U}^-$. The following statements are equivalent*

1. *$\mathcal{F}$ is computationally (classical) UC feasible.*
2. *$\mathcal{F}$ is statistically (classical) UC feasible.*
3. *$\mathcal{F}$ is statistically quantum-UC feasible.*
4. *$\mathcal{F}$ is computationally quantum-UC feasible.*

Proof. $(1 \Rightarrow 2)$ is already implicit in [28]. For $\mathcal{F} \in \mathcal{U}^-$, if $\mathcal{F}$ is computationally feasible, then such $\mathcal{F}$ is splittable and we can construct a trivial protocol [32]. Then we can show the same trivial protocol can realize $\mathcal{F}$ information theoretically, which means $\mathcal{F}$ is statistically feasible.

$(2 \Rightarrow 3)$ is immediate from Unruh's quantum lifting lemma. $(3 \Rightarrow 4)$ follows because we require poly-time simulation in statistical UC model, and hence statistical UC security in particular implies computational UC security. We are left to show $(4 \Rightarrow 1)$.

Assume for contradiction that $\mathcal{F}$ is computationally quantum-UC feasible but classically not computationally classical-UC feasible. Invoke Fact 2 again, we have that for some $\mathcal{F}' \in \{\mathcal{F}_{\mathrm{OT}}, \mathcal{F}_{\mathrm{2CC}}, \mathcal{F}_{\mathrm{COM}}, \mathcal{F}_{\mathrm{XOR}}\} : \mathcal{F}' \sqsubseteq^{\mathrm{CSTAT}} \mathcal{F}$, which by Theorem 1, implies that $\mathcal{F}$ is computationally quantum-UC complete. This, combined with the assumption that $\mathcal{F}$ is computationally quantum-UC feasible, implies that every $\mathcal{F} \in \mathcal{U}^-$ is computationally quantum-UC feasible. This is a contradiction because one can prove that $\mathcal{F}_{\mathrm{COM}}$ is not computationally quantum-UC feasible, i.e., there exists no (quantum) protocol that realizes $\mathcal{F}_{\mathrm{COM}}$ with computational quantum-UC security. The argument is similar the classical impossibility proof of UC commitments [9], and the details can be found in the full version.

5 Putting it Together

In this section we bring the pieces together and describe the cryptographic-complexity landscape for $\mathcal{U}^-$ in the quantum world. In the case of computational quantum-UC security, we can derive a zero/one law in the flavor of [28]. For statistical quantum-UC security we show that, roughly speaking, every $\mathcal{F} \in \mathcal{U}^-$ is either statistically quantum-UC feasible, or $\mathcal{F}$ is statistically quantum-UC complete, or $\mathcal{F}_{\mathrm{XOR}}$ statistically quantum-UC reduces to $\mathcal{F}$.

5.1 Computational Security: A Zero/One Law

Our quantum lifting theorems for feasibility and completeness imply that all computational UC complete (resp. UC feasible) functionalities in $\mathcal{U}^-$ are also computational quantum-UC complete (resp. quantum-UC feasible). Using this fact along with the classical zero/one law, one can derive a zero-one law for the computational quantum-UC setting in a straight-forward manner (under the assumptions of existence of a quantum-secure pseudorandom generator and a dense encryption that is quantum IND-CPA). This proves the following theorem (see Figure 1a):

Theorem 3 (A Computational Zero/One Law). *Every functionality $\mathcal{F} \in \mathcal{U}^-$ is either computationally quantum-UC feasible or computationally quantum-UC complete.*

As a straightforward corollary of the above theorem we can conclude that the quantum lifting theorem for completeness can be made bi-directional in the computational setting. Theorem 1 already states that computational completeness of some $\mathcal{F} \in \mathcal{U}^-$ in the classical setting implies computational completeness of $\mathcal{F}$ in the quantum setting. In the other direction, if $\mathcal{F}$ is quantumly-UC complete, then Theorem 3 implies that it is not quantum-UC feasible, which implies (by Theorem 2) that it is not (classically) UC feasible; hence, the computational (classical) zero/one law implies that $\mathcal{F}$ is computationally (classically) UC complete. This proves the following:

Corollary 2. *Let $\mathcal{F} \in \mathcal{U}^-$ be a functionality. $\mathcal{F}$ is computationally UC complete under the semi-honest OT assumption* shOT *if and only if $\mathcal{F}$ is computationally quantum-UC complete under the assumptions of existence of a quantum-secure pseudorandom generator and a dense encryption that is quantum IND-CPA.*

5.2   Statistical Security: Three Classes

We next turn to the setting of statistical security. In the classical setting, the cryptographic-complexity landscape is complicated, as, apart from the complete/feasible functionalities, there is a partition of the set $\mathcal{U}^\top$ in clusters for which the exact relation is not known. In contrast we can show a "[zero/xor/one]-law" in the statistical quantum-UC setting. In other words we can divide the class $\mathcal{U}^-$ into functionalities that are either complete, or feasible, or we can reduce $\mathcal{F}_{\mathrm{XOR}}$ to them. This considerably simplifies the landscape of the classical statistical setting, as the hierarchy of functionalities that we can reduce $\mathcal{F}_{\mathrm{2CC}}$ to collapses at the second level (i.e, to $\mathcal{F}_{\mathrm{2CC}}$) which as it follows from Lemma 4 is in fact complete in the quantum setting. This illustrates, as [36] mentioned also, that the inverse of the Unruh's quantum lifting lemma is in general not true. Namely, *there exist classical well-formed infeasible functionalities $\mathcal{F}$ and $\mathcal{F}'$ such that there exist an $\mathcal{F}$-hybrid quantum protocol which statistically quantum-UC securely realizes $\mathcal{F}'$, but there exists no $\mathcal{F}$-hybrid classical protocol which statistically classical-UC realizes $\mathcal{F}'$.*

The following theorem states the aforementioned zero/xor/one-law:

Theorem 4 (A [Zero/Xor/One]-Law for the Information-Theoretic Setting). *Let $\mathcal{F} \in \mathcal{U}^-$. Then exactly one of the following statements holds: (1) $\mathcal{F}$ is quantum-UC feasible, (2) $\mathcal{F}$ is quantum-UC complete, and (3) $\mathcal{F}$ is neither*

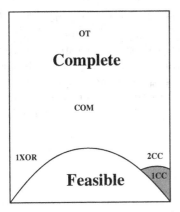
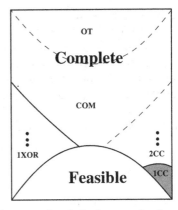

(a) Computational landscape: zero/one law. The picture is the same as in the classical-UC setting.

(b) Statistical landscape: zero/xor/one. The three dots represent an infinite hierarchy of functionalities.

Fig. 1. Cryptographic complexity in the quantum-UC framework: the box denotes the class of deterministic finite two-party functionalities. The set $\mathcal{U}^-$ corresponds to the white area. The solid lines represent separations between non-equivalent primitives. The dotted lines represent separations that exist only in the classical-UC setting.

quantum-UC complete nor quantum-UC feasible and $\mathcal{F}_{\text{XOR}} \sqsubseteq^{\text{QSTAT}} \mathcal{F}$. *Furthermore, for each of the three statements, there exists at least one* $\mathcal{F} \in \mathcal{U}^-$ *which satisfies it.*

Proof (Sketch). By Lemma 2 and because statistically, $\mathcal{F}_{\text{2CC}}$, $\mathcal{F}_{\text{COM}}$ and $\mathcal{F}_{\text{OT}}$ are quantum-UC complete and $\mathcal{F}_{\text{XOR}}$ is not quantum-UC feasible (since otherwise $\mathcal{F}_{\text{XOR}}$ is also classical-UC feasible, contradicting the classical impossibility result in [27]), we can see that that for any $\mathcal{F} \in \mathcal{U}^-$, either $\mathcal{F}$ is quantum-UC feasible, or at least one of the following two statements holds: (1) $\mathcal{F}$ is quantum-UC complete and (2) $\mathcal{F}_{\text{XOR}} \sqsubseteq^{\text{QSTAT}} \mathcal{F}$.

We then show that $\mathcal{F}_{\text{XOR}}$ is not quantum-UC complete by proving that there is *no* quantum protocol that UC realizes $\mathcal{F}_{\text{COM}}$ in the $\mathcal{F}_{\text{XOR}}$-hybrid world. Proof of this statement is reminiscence of Lo and Chau's proof that quantum protocols are impossible to implement commitment [24]. The essence there is a so called "purification" attack where a dishonest sender can purify the protocol in the commit phase which allows him to apply a transformation on his local system, by which he can open to a value other than what he committed to. In our case, the only difference is that a quantum protocol can use $\mathcal{F}_{\text{XOR}}$ as an extra setup. However, $\mathcal{F}_{\text{XOR}}$ is nothing but a classical fair-exchange channel. In particular, the classical information in the protocol is symmetric to both parties, and we can argue that a dishonest committer can make the overall quantum state pure conditioned on shared classical information at the end of commit phase, so that the purification attack still applies. We defer a formal proof to the full version.

Finally, [27] showed that classically the class of functionalities that $\mathcal{F}_{\text{XOR}}$ reduces to and are not complete, denoted $\mathcal{E}$, are exactly those of the form $\mathcal{F}_{\text{EXCH}}^{(\ell_1,\ell_2)}$: simultaneous exchange channels that trasmit ℓ_1 (resp. ℓ_2) bits from one party to the other. The above argument that $\mathcal{F}_{\text{XOR}}$ is not quantum-UC complete extends straightforwardly to all such $\mathcal{F}_{\text{EXCH}}$, thus we conclude that any functionality in the $\mathcal{F}_{\text{XOR}}$ family $\mathcal{E}$ are neither statistically quantum-UC complete nor statistically quantum-UC feasible. Thus we can derive the quantum-UC statistical landscape for $\mathcal{U}^-$ as in Figure 1b.

References

1. Barak, B., Canetti, R., Nielsen, J.B., Pass, R.: Universally composable protocols with relaxed set-up assumptions. In: 45th Annual Symposium on Foundations of Computer Science (FOCS), pp. 186–195. IEEE (October 2004)
2. Ben-Or, M., Crépeau, C., Gottesman, D., Hassidim, A., Smith, A.: Secure multiparty quantum computation with (only) a strict honest majority. In: 47th Annual Symposium on Foundations of Computer Science (FOCS), pp. 249–260. IEEE (October 2006)
3. Bennett, C., Brassard, G.: Quantum cryptography: Public key distribution and coin tossing. In: Proceedings of IEEE International Conference on Computers Systems and Signal Processing, Bangalore, India, pp. 175–179 (December 1984)
4. Bennett, C.H., Brassard, G., Crépeau, C., Skubiszewska, M.-H.: Practical Quantum Oblivious Transfer. In: Feigenbaum, J. (ed.) CRYPTO 1991. LNCS, vol. 576, pp. 351–366. Springer, Heidelberg (1992)
5. Bouman, N.J., Fehr, S.: Sampling in a Quantum Population, and Applications. In: Rabin, T. (ed.) CRYPTO 2010. LNCS, vol. 6223, pp. 724–741. Springer, Heidelberg (2010)
6. Buhrman, H., Christandl, M., Schaffner, C.: Complete insecurity of quantum protocols for classical two-party computation. Phys. Rev. Lett. 109, 160501 (2012)
7. Canetti, R.: Security and composition of multiparty cryptographic protocols. Journal of Cryptology 13(1), 143–202 (2000)
8. Canetti, R.: Universally composable security: A new paradigm for cryptographic protocols. In: 42nd Annual Symposium on Foundations of Computer Science (FOCS), pp. 136–145. IEEE (October 2001)
9. Canetti, R., Fischlin, M.: Universally Composable Commitments. In: Kilian, J. (ed.) CRYPTO 2001. LNCS, vol. 2139, pp. 19–40. Springer, Heidelberg (2001)
10. Canetti, R., Kushilevitz, E., Lindell, Y.: On the limitations of universally composable two-party computation without set-up assumptions. Journal of Cryptology 19(2), 135–167 (2006)
11. Canetti, R., Lindell, Y., Ostrovsky, R., Sahai, A.: Universally composable two-party and multi-party secure computation. In: 34th Annual ACM Symposium on Theory of Computing (STOC), pp. 494–503. ACM Press (May 2002)
12. Canetti, R., Pass, R., Shelat, A.: Cryptography from sunspots: How to use an imperfect reference string. In: 48th Annual Symposium on Foundations of Computer Science (FOCS), pp. 249–259. IEEE (October 2007)
13. Crépeau, C., Gottesman, D., Smith, A.: Secure multi-party quantum computation. In: 34th Annual ACM Symposium on Theory of Computing (STOC), pp. 643–652. ACM Press (May 2002)

14. Crépeau, C., Salvail, L., Simard, J.-R., Tapp, A.: Two Provers in Isolation. In: Lee, D.H., Wang, X. (eds.) ASIACRYPT 2011. LNCS, vol. 7073, pp. 407–430. Springer, Heidelberg (2011)

15. Damgård, I., Fehr, S., Lunemann, C., Salvail, L., Schaffner, C.: Improving the Security of Quantum Protocols via Commit-and-Open. In: Halevi, S. (ed.) CRYPTO 2009. LNCS, vol. 5677, pp. 408–427. Springer, Heidelberg (2009)

16. Dupuis, F., Nielsen, J.B., Salvail, L.: Actively Secure Two-Party Evaluation of Any Quantum Operation. In: Safavi-Naini, R. (ed.) CRYPTO 2012. LNCS, vol. 7417, pp. 794–811. Springer, Heidelberg (2012)

17. Hallgren, S., Smith, A., Song, F.: Classical Cryptographic Protocols in a Quantum World. In: Rogaway, P. (ed.) CRYPTO 2011. LNCS, vol. 6841, pp. 411–428. Springer, Heidelberg (2011)

18. Ishai, Y., Prabhakaran, M., Sahai, A.: Founding Cryptography on Oblivious Transfer – Efficiently. In: Wagner, D. (ed.) CRYPTO 2008. LNCS, vol. 5157, pp. 572–591. Springer, Heidelberg (2008)

19. Katz, J.: Universally Composable Multi-party Computation Using Tamper-Proof Hardware. In: Naor, M. (ed.) EUROCRYPT 2007. LNCS, vol. 4515, pp. 115–128. Springer, Heidelberg (2007)

20. Katz, J., Kiayias, A., Kumaresan, R., Shelat, A., Zhou, H.-S.: From impossibility to completeness for deterministic two-party SFE (2011) (manuscript)

21. Kilian, J.: Founding cryptography on oblivious transfer. In: STOC, pp. 20–31. ACM (1988)

22. Kraschewski, D., Müller-Quade, J.: Completeness Theorems with Constructive Proofs for Finite Deterministic 2-Party Functions. In: Ishai, Y. (ed.) TCC 2011. LNCS, vol. 6597, pp. 364–381. Springer, Heidelberg (2011)

23. Lo, H.-K.: Insecurity of quantum secure computations. Physical Review A 56(2), 1154–1162 (1997)

24. Lo, H.K., Chau, H.F.: Is quantum bit commitment really possible? Physical Review Letters 78, 3410–3413 (1997)

25. Lo, H.-K., Chau, H.F.: Unconditional security of quantum key distribution over arbitrarily long distances. Science 283(5410), 2050–2056 (1999)

26. Lunemann, C., Nielsen, J.B.: Fully Simulatable Quantum-Secure Coin-Flipping and Applications. In: Nitaj, A., Pointcheval, D. (eds.) AFRICACRYPT 2011. LNCS, vol. 6737, pp. 21–40. Springer, Heidelberg (2011)

27. Maji, H.K., Prabhakaran, M., Rosulek, M.: Complexity of Multi-party Computation Problems: The Case of 2-Party Symmetric Secure Function Evaluation. In: Reingold, O. (ed.) TCC 2009. LNCS, vol. 5444, pp. 256–273. Springer, Heidelberg (2009)

28. Maji, H.K., Prabhakaran, M., Rosulek, M.: A Zero-One Law for Cryptographic Complexity with Respect to Computational UC Security. In: Rabin, T. (ed.) CRYPTO 2010. LNCS, vol. 6223, pp. 595–612. Springer, Heidelberg (2010)

29. Mayers, D.: Unconditionally secure quantum bit commitment is impossible. Physical Review Letters 78, 3414–3417 (1997)

30. Mayers, D.: Unconditional security in quantum cryptography. J. ACM 48(3), 351–406 (2001)

31. Müller-Quade, J., Renner, R.: Composability in quantum cryptography. New J. Phys. 11, 085006 (2009)

32. Prabhakaran, M., Rosulek, M.: Cryptographic Complexity of Multi-Party Computation Problems: Classifications and Separations. In: Wagner, D. (ed.) CRYPTO 2008. LNCS, vol. 5157, pp. 262–279. Springer, Heidelberg (2008)
33. Rosulek, M.: Universal Composability from Essentially Any Trusted Setup. In: Safavi-Naini, R. (ed.) CRYPTO 2012. LNCS, vol. 7417, pp. 406–423. Springer, Heidelberg (2012)
34. Salvail, L., Schaffner, C., Sotáková, M.: On the Power of Two-Party Quantum Cryptography. In: Matsui, M. (ed.) ASIACRYPT 2009. LNCS, vol. 5912, pp. 70–87. Springer, Heidelberg (2009)
35. Shor, P.W., Preskill, J.: Simple proof of security of the BB84 quantum key distribution protocol. Phys. Rev. Lett. 85(2), 441–444 (2000)
36. Unruh, D.: Universally Composable Quantum Multi-party Computation. In: Gilbert, H. (ed.) EUROCRYPT 2010. LNCS, vol. 6110, pp. 486–505. Springer, Heidelberg (2010)
37. Watrous, J.: Zero-knowledge against quantum attacks. SIAM J. Comput. 39(1), 25–58 (2009); Preliminary version in STOC 2006

Languages with Efficient
Zero-Knowledge PCPs are in SZK

Mohammad Mahmoody[1],[*] and David Xiao[2],[**]

[1] Cornell University
mohammad@cs.cornell.edu
[2] LIAFA
CNRS, Université Paris Diderot - Paris 7
dxiao@liafa.univ-paris-diderot.fr

Abstract. A *Zero-Knowledge PCP* (ZK-PCP) is a randomized PCP such that the view of any (perhaps cheating) efficient verifier can be efficiently simulated up to small statistical distance. Kilian, Petrank, and Tardos (STOC '97) constructed ZK-PCPs for all languages in **NEXP**. Ishai, Mahmoody, and Sahai (TCC '12), motivated by cryptographic applications, revisited the possibility of *efficient* ZK-PCPs for all of **NP** where the PCP is encoded as a polynomial-size circuit that given a query i returns the ith symbol of the PCP. Ishai *et al.* showed that there is no efficient ZK-PCP for **NP** with a *non-adaptive* verifier, that prepares all of its PCP queries before seeing any answers, unless **NP** $\subseteq$ **coAM** and the polynomial-time hierarchy collapses. The question of whether *adaptive* verification can lead to efficient ZK-PCPs for **NP** remained open.

In this work, we resolve this question and show that any language or promise problem with efficient ZK-PCPs must be in **SZK** (the class of promise problems with a statistical zero-knowledge *single prover* proof system). Therefore, no **NP**-complete problem can have an efficient ZK-PCP unless **NP** $\subseteq$ **SZK** (which also implies **NP** $\subseteq$ **coAM** and the polynomial-time hierarchy collapses). We prove our result by reducing any promise problem with an efficient ZK-PCP to two instances of the CONDITIONAL ENTROPY APPROXIMATION problem defined and studied by Vadhan (FOCS'04) which is known to be complete for the class **SZK**.

Keywords: Probabilistically Checkable Proofs, Statistical Zero-Knowledge.

1 Introduction

Since their inception, interactive proofs [GMR89, BM88] have had a transformative effect on theoretical computer science in general and the foundations of

---

[*] Supported in part by NSF Awards CNS-1217821 and CCF-0746990, AFOSR Award FA9550-10-1-0093, and DARPA and AFRL under contract FA8750-11-2-0211. The views and conclusions contained in this document are those of the author and should not be interpreted as representing the official policies, either expressed or implied, of the Defense Advanced Research Projects Agency or the US government.

[**] Supported in part by the French ANR Blanc program under contract ANR-12-BS02-005 (RDAM) and the French ANR JCJC program under contract (ROMAnTIC).

A. Sahai (Ed.): TCC 2013, LNCS 7785, pp. 297–314, 2013.

cryptography in particular. In an interactive proof for a language L, a computationally bounded randomized verifier V and an all-powerful prover P are given a common input x, and P tries to convince V that $x \in L$. The proof must be *complete*: P successfully convinces V that $x \in L$; as well as *sound*: no cheating prover $\hat{P}$ should be able to convince V that $x \in L$ when $x \notin L$. [GMR89] showed that by allowing interaction and probabilistic verification, nontrivial languages outside of **BPP** can be proved while the verifier statistically "learns nothing" beyond the fact that $x \in L$. Thus in eyes of the verifier, the interaction remains "zero-knowledge". Shortly after, [GMW91] extend this fundamental result to *all* of **NP** based on computational assumptions and a computational variant of the notion of zero-knowledge.

The notion of zero-knowledge is formalized using the *simulation paradigm*: for each (possibly cheating) efficient verifier, there is an efficient simulator that generates a verifier view that is indistinguishable from the view the verifier would obtain by honestly interacting with the prover, and therefore anything the verifier could do using a transcript of his interaction with the prover, he could do by using the simulator (without talking to the prover). Throughout this paper by default we mean *statistical* indistinguishability and *statistical* zero knowledge, namely they must hold against any (possibly computationally inefficient) distinguisher. Any discussion about computational indistinguishability will be made explicit.

Motivated by the goal of *unconditional* security, Ben-Or et al. [BGKW88] showed that if a verifier V interacts with *multiple* interactive provers (MIPs) $P_1, P_2, \ldots$ who may coordinate on a strategy beforehand, but are unable to communicate once the interaction with V starts, then all languages in **NP** can be proved in a (statistical) zero-knowledge way *without* any computational assumption. Fortnow, Rompel, and Sipser [FRS94] showed that, the MIP model is essentially equivalent to having a (perhaps exponentially long) *proof*, whose answers to all possible queries are *fixed* before interaction begins (in contrast to the usual notion of a prover, who may choose to alter his answers based on the queries he has seen so far). Such proof systems are now known as *probabilistically checkable proofs* (PCPs for short) and have found applications throughout theoretical computer science, notably in the areas of hardness of approximation through the celebrated PCP theorem [BFL90, AS98, ALM$^+$98] and communication-efficient interactive proofs [Kil92].

The existence of of ZK proofs for **NP** in the MIP model [BGKW88] and the "equivalence" of MIP and PCP models (as a proof system) raised the following basic question: *Does **NP** have PCPs that remain zero-knowledge against malicious verifiers?*

The work of [BGKW88] does not resolve this question, because their protocol, when implemented in the PCP model, remains ZK only if cheating verifiers follow the protocol honestly. This highlights an important point: since we have no control over the cheating verifier (except that we assume it is efficient), if the proof is polynomial size then a cheating verifier may read the entire proof and this is not zero knowledge. Therefore, the proof π should be super-polynomially long, and we assume that an efficient (perhaps cheating) verifier $\hat{V}$ is only allowed black-box access to the proof. Since $\widehat{V}$ is polynomially bounded, having black-box access to such a proof π means that $\widehat{V}$ will be able to query only polynomially many symbols in the proof at will. Thus, by definition, ZK-PCPs are incomparable to standard (statistical) zero knowledge proofs in the single or multi-prover proof systems: (1) the zero knowledge property is harder to achieve in the PCP model because the proof is fixed and there is no control on which queries the verifier chooses to make, (2) but the soundness property may be easier to achieve in the PCP model because the soundness is required only against *fixed* cheating proofs (rather than cheating provers who may adaptively manipulate their answers).

Kilian, Petrank, and Tardos [KPT97] were the first to explicitly study the question above and (relying on the previous work of [DFK$^+$92] which in turn relied on the PCP theorem) showed that in fact every language in **NEXP** has a ZK-PCP. Their ZK-PCPs, however, were not *efficient* even when constructed for languages in **NP**, where by an efficient PCP for $L \in$ **NP**, we mean any PCP π whose answer $\pi(q)$ to any query q can be computed using a polynomial size circuit (which may depend on the common input $x \in L$, a witness w that $x \in L$, and an auxiliary random string r_π). This limitation is inherent in the approach of [KPT97], since in order to be ZK, their PCP requires more entropy than the number of queries made by any cheating verifier.

Motivated by the lack of progress for over 10 years towards giving ZK-PCPs for **NP** that are ZK with respect to all efficient cheating verifiers, Ishai, Mahmoody, and Sahai [IMS12] asked whether this may be inherently impossible. Namely, they asked the following question, which is also the main question studied in this work.

Main Question: *Are there* efficient *ZK-PCPs for* **NP***?*

Ishai *et al.* proved that any language or promise problem L with an efficient ZK-PCP *where the honest verifier's queries are non-adaptive* must satisfy $L \in$ **coAM**. Therefore, **NP** does not have such efficient ZK-PCPs unless the polynomial-time hierarchy collapses [BHZ87]. Thus, the main question above remained open whether there exist efficient ZK-PCPs for **NP** if we allow the verifier to be adaptive. In this paper we resolve this question in the negative; namely we prove:

Theorem 1 (Main Result). *Any promise problem L with an efficient ZK-PCP is in* **SZK**.

This strengthens the negative result of [IMS12] in two ways: (1) we lift the restriction that the verifier be non-adaptive, and (2) we can conclude that $L \in$ **SZK** which is stronger than $L \in$ **AM** $\cap$ **coAM**, since it is known that **SZK** $\subseteq$ **AM** $\cap$ **coAM** [For89, AH91]. On the other hand, [IMS12] only requires zero-knowledge to hold for non-adaptive malicious verifiers, while we assume that the zero-knowledge property holds for general (adaptive) malicious verifiers. (This is natural, since if the honest verifier is adaptive then even honest-verifier zero-knowledge would require zero-knowledge against an adaptive verifier, namely the honest one.) Finally, we emphasize that Theorem 1 does *not* assume that the simulation is black-box.

Relation to Resettable Zero-Knowledge. The notion of *resettable* zero-knowledge single prover proof systems introduced by Canetti *et al.* [CGGM00] is comparably stronger than the notion of ZK-PCPs. Essentially, a resettable-ZK proof is a ZK-PCP where soundness is required to hold even against adaptive cheating provers who may manipulate their answers based on the queries they see (rather than just fixed cheating proofs). Canetti *et al.* [CGGM00] showed how to obtain *efficient* PCPs that are *computational* zero-knowledge based on computational hardness assumptions. Thus, in the case of computational zero knowledge, the question is resolved in the positive direction (under believable computational assumptions). Similarly, it would be possible to get statistical zero-knowledge probabilistically checkable *arguments* (with soundness against computationally bounded stateful provers) if one can construct resettable statistical zero-knowledge arguments. The work of [GMOS07] shows the existence of a closely related object, namely *concurrent* statistical zero-knowledge arguments for all of **NP**. But recall that in this work, both the zero-knowledge and the soundness are statistical, and so these mentioned results do not resolve our main question.

Recently, Garg *et al.* [GOVW12] showed that *efficient* resettable *statistical* ZK proof systems exist for non-trivial languages (*e.g.* Quadratic Residuosity) based on computational assumptions. Therefore under the same assumptions, these languages also possess efficient ZK-PCPs. Garg *et al.* also showed that assuming the existence of exponentially hard one-way functions, statistical zero-knowledge proof systems can be made resettable. Unfortunately this transformation does not preserve the efficiency of the prover. Therefore, even though by the works of Micciancio, Ong, and Vadhan [MV03, OV08] we know that **SZK ∩ NP** has statistical zero-knowledge proofs with an efficient prover, the result of [GOVW12] does not necessarily preserve this efficiency.

Finally note that if one can transform any statistical ZK proof into a resettable statistical ZK proof without losing the efficiency of the prover, then together with our main result of Theorem 1 this would imply that the problems with efficient ZK-PCPs are exactly those in **SZK ∩ NP**.

Relation to Basing Cryptography on Tamper-Proof Hardware. A main motivation of [IMS12] to study the possibility of efficient ZK-PCPs for **NP** comes from a recent line of work on basing cryptography on tamper-proof hardware (*e.g.* [Kat07, MS08, CGS08, GKR08, GIS+10, Kol10, GIMS10]). In this model, the parties can exchange classical bits as well as *hardware tokens* that hide a stateful or stateless *efficient* algorithm. The receiver of a hardware token is only able to use it as a black-box and call it on polynomially many inputs. Using *stateless* hardware tokens makes the protocol secure against "resetting" attacks where the receiver of a token is able to reset the state of the token (say, by cutting its power). The work of Goyal *et al.* [GIMS10] focused on the power and limits of stateless tamper-proof hardware tokens in achieving *statistical* security and proved that statistical zero-knowledge for all of **NP** is possible using a single stateless token sent from the prover to the verifier followed by $O(1)$ rounds of classical interaction. A natural question remaining open after the work of [GIMS10] was whether the classical interaction can be eliminated and achieve statistical

ZK for **NP** using only a single stateless token. It is easy to see that this question is in fact equivalent to our main question above, and thus our Theorem 1 proves that a single (efficient) stateless token is not sufficient for achieving statistical ZK proofs for **NP**.

2   Our Techniques

In this section we describe the ideas and techniques behind the proof of Theorem 1. We then compare it to the approach of [IMS12], which is restricted to non-adaptive verifiers, and highlight why our technique bypasses this barrier. In the following let us assume for notational simplicity that L is a language; the idea is identical for general promise problems.

2.1   Our Approach

If L has a ZK-PCP, one naive approach to decide L using its simulator is to run the simulator to obtain a view $\nu = (r, (q_1, a_1), \ldots, (q_m, a_m))$, where r is the random seed of the verifier and the (q_i, a_i) are queries/answers to the ZK-PCP, and accept iff ν is an accepting view. This approach would obtain accepting views if $x \in L$ due to the zero-knowledge property, but there is no guarantee about the case $x \notin L$.

Our proof will show that if in addition to making sure that the view is accepting we do some extra tests on the distribution of the simulated view, then this will allow us to decide L. Suppose for a moment that the ZK-PCP is deterministic, *i.e.* on an input x the prover deterministically generates a proof π. (Of course it is known that ZK with deterministic provers cannot exist for non-trivial languages [GO94]. We make this simplification here only to make our proof sketch easier to describe, and we will argue below how one can do away with this simplification.)

We will show that when the ZK-PCP is deterministic, it suffices to run the simulator and check that the generated view is accepting and to check some entropy-related properties of the view which in our case happen to be a computational task in **SZK**. Let $(\mathbf{r}, (\mathbf{q_1}, \mathbf{a_1}), \ldots, (\mathbf{q}_m, \mathbf{a}_m))$ be the distribution of views generated when running the simulator for the honest verifier. By the ZK property, this is statistically close to the view of an honest verifier interacting with the honest prover on YES (*i.e.* $x \in L$) instances. Let $\mathbf{j}$ be uniform in $[m]$ and consider the distribution $(\mathbf{q_j}, \mathbf{a_j})$.

We argue that to decide the language it suffices to check first that the simulated transcript is accepting, and second that $H(\mathbf{a_j} \mid \mathbf{q_j})$ is small. On YES instances, the simulated transcript is almost surely accepting because of the ZK property, and furthermore $H(\mathbf{a_j}|\mathbf{q_j}) = 0$ because the simulated proof is deterministic. On the other hand, on NO (*i.e.* $x \notin L$) instances, we will show that if $H(\mathbf{a_j} \mid \mathbf{q_j})$ is sufficiently small, then the simulated transcript is statistically close to an interaction between an honest verifier and a proof sampled as follows: for each q, the corresponding answer bit of the proof is sampled according to $a_j \mid q_j = q$. By the soundness condition of the ZK-PCP, it follows that the transcript must be rejecting with high probability. It is clear that checking that the simulated transcript is accepting is in **BPP**, while checking that $H(a_j \mid q_j)$ is small is a conditional entropy approximation problem, which is in **SZK** [Vad06].

To generalize the above argument to the case of randomized ZK-PCPs, we use the following argument (which is a stronger version of an argument that first appeared in [IMS12]): Any efficiently computable PCP (as a random variable describing its truth table) has polynomial entropy. Therefore if we repeat the honest verifier ℓ times where ℓ is a polynomial sufficiently larger than the size of the circuit computing the PCP, we can essentially "exhaust" the entropy of the proof observed by the next independent verification över the same PCP. This allows us to prove that $H(a_j \mid q_j)$ is small *conditioned on* the PCP answers observed in the first ℓ verifications. Interestingly, this argument when applied to *a random* query index j (which is the index distribution we use—see Lemma 6) is rather delicate and heavily relies on the fact that PCPs are fixed; the statement is not true for interactive proofs, where the answers may depend on, say, the order of the queries.

Finally we note that even after making sure that the simulator is choosing its PCP answers close to some fixed oracle, it still might be the case that for NO instances it does not run an honest execution of the verifier against this PCP and somehow manages to generate accepting views for NO instances as well. To complete the proof, one final technicality that we check is that the random coins r generated by the simulator are indeed close to uniform conditioned on the ℓ previously sampled views. (They are guaranteed to be so on YES instances by ZK, but may not be on NO instances.) This latter task is also reducible to the conditional entropy approximation problem.

Approach of [IMS12]. At a high level, in our work we show that deciding the language using the simulator can be done in **SZK** by a direct reduction to a problem in **SZK**. In contrast, [IMS12] tried to "extract" a PCP from the simulator and then run the honest verifier against this extracted PCP. Since the extraction process requires sampling from inefficiently samplable distributions, this task is accomplished with the aid of an all-powerful yet untrusted prover (this is how they obtain the conclusion that the language is in **AM** ∩ **coAM**). This makes our approach conceptually different from the approach of [IMS12].

3   Preliminaries

Basic Terminology and Notation. We use bold letters to denote random variables (*e.g.* $\mathbf{X}$ or $\mathbf{x}$). By $x \leftarrow \mathbf{x}$ we mean that x is sampled according to the distribution of the random variable $\mathbf{x}$. We write $\mathbb{E}_x[\cdot]$ to denote $\mathbb{E}_{x \leftarrow \mathbf{x}}[\cdot]$, where any x appearing inside the expression in the expectation is fixed. For any finite set $\mathcal{S}$, $x \leftarrow \mathcal{S}$ denotes x sampled uniformly from $\mathcal{S}$. $\mathbf{U}_n$ denotes the uniform distribution over $\{0,1\}^n$, and $[n]$ denotes the set $\{1, 2, \ldots, n\}$. For jointly distributed random variables $(\mathbf{x}, \mathbf{y})$, and for a specific value $y \leftarrow \mathbf{y}$, by $(\mathbf{x} \mid y)$ we mean the random variable $\mathbf{x}$ conditioned on $\mathbf{y} = y$. When we say an event occurs with *negligible* probability denoted by negl(n), we mean it occurs with probability $n^{-\omega(1)}$. We call two random variables $\mathbf{x}, \mathbf{y}$ (or their corresponding distributions) over the support set $\mathcal{S}$ *ϵ-close* if their *statistical distance* $\Delta(\mathbf{x}, \mathbf{y}) = \frac{1}{2} \cdot \sum_{s \in S} |\Pr[\mathbf{x} = s] - \Pr[\mathbf{y} = s]|$ is at most ϵ. By an *ensemble* (of random variables) $\{\mathbf{y}_x\}_{x \in \mathcal{I}}$ we denote a set of random variables indexed by a set $\mathcal{I}$. We call two ensembles $\{\mathbf{y}_x\}_{x \in \mathcal{I}}$ and $\{\mathbf{z}_x\}_{x \in \mathcal{I}}$ with the same index set *statistically close* if $\Delta(\mathbf{y}_x, \mathbf{z}_x) = \text{negl}(|x|)$ for all $x \in \mathcal{I}$. We use the terms *efficient* and *PPT* to refer to any probabilistic polynomial time (perhaps oracle-aided) algorithm. For an oracle π and an (oracle-aided) algorithm V, by V^π we refer to an execution of V given access to π and by $\text{View}\langle \mathsf{V}^\pi \rangle$ we refer to the *view* of V in its execution given π which consists of its randomness r and the sequence of its oracle query-answer pairs $[(q_1, a_1), (q_2, a_2), \dots]$ (having only the oracle answers and r is sufficient to know $\text{View}\langle \mathsf{V}^\pi \rangle$). All logarithms are base 2. By $\mathrm{H}(\mathbf{X})$ we denote the Shannon entropy of $\mathbf{X}$ defined as $\mathrm{H}(\mathbf{X}) = \mathbb{E}_X \lg(1/\Pr[\mathbf{X} = X])$. By $\mathrm{H}(\mathbf{X} \mid \mathbf{Y})$, we denote the conditional entropy as $\mathbb{E}_Y[\mathrm{H}(\mathbf{X} \mid Y)]$, and we note the conditional mutual information as $\mathrm{I}(\mathbf{X}; \mathbf{Y} \mid \mathbf{Z}) = \mathrm{H}(\mathbf{X} \mid \mathbf{Z}) - (\mathbf{X} \mid \mathbf{YZ})$.

A language L is a *partition* of $\{0,1\}^*$ into $L^{\mathrm{Y}} = L$ and $L^{\mathrm{N}} = \{0,1\}^* \setminus L$.

A *promise* language (or problem) $L = (L^{\mathrm{Y}}, L^{\mathrm{N}})$ generalizes the notion of a language by only requiring that $L^{\mathrm{Y}} \cap L^{\mathrm{N}} = \varnothing$ (but there could be some $x \in \{0,1\}^* \setminus (L^{\mathrm{Y}} \cup L^{\mathrm{N}})$). For promise problems, we will sometimes use $x \in L$ to denote $x \in L^{\mathrm{Y}}$.

Definition 1 (Operations on Promise Languages). *We define the following three operations over promise languages.*

- *The* complement $\overline{L} = (\overline{L}^{\mathrm{Y}}, \overline{L}^{\mathrm{N}})$ *of a promise language* $L = (L^{\mathrm{Y}}, L^{\mathrm{N}})$ *is another promise language such that* $\overline{L}^{\mathrm{Y}} = L^{\mathrm{N}}$ *and* $\overline{L}^{\mathrm{N}} = L^{\mathrm{Y}}$.
- *Conjunction* $L = L_1 \wedge L_2$ *of promise languages* L_1 *and* L_2:
  - $x = (x_1, x_2) \in L^{\mathrm{Y}}$ *iff* $x_1 \in L_1^{\mathrm{Y}}$ *and* $x_2 \in L_2^{\mathrm{Y}}$,
  - $x = (x_1, x_2) \in L^{\mathrm{N}}$ *iff* $x_1 \in L_1^{\mathrm{N}}$ *or* $x_2 \in L_2^{\mathrm{N}}$.
- *Disjunction* $L = L_1 \vee L_2$ *of promise languages* L_1 *and* L_2:
  - $x = (x_1, x_2) \in L^{\mathrm{Y}}$ *iff* $x_1 \in L_1^{\mathrm{Y}}$ *or* $x_2 \in L_2^{\mathrm{Y}}$,
  - $x = (x_1, x_2) \in L^{\mathrm{N}}$ *iff* $x_1 \in L_1^{\mathrm{N}}$ *and* $x_2 \in L_2^{\mathrm{N}}$.

It is easy to see that $L_1 \vee L_2 = \overline{\overline{L_1} \wedge \overline{L_1}}$.

Definition 2 (Karp Reduction). *A Karp reduction* R *from a promise problem* L_1 *to another promise problem* L_2 *is a deterministic efficient algorithm such that* $R(x) \in L_2^{\mathrm{Y}}$ *for every* $x \in L_1^{\mathrm{Y}}$ *and* $R(x) \in L_2^{\mathrm{N}}$ *for every* $x \in L_1^{\mathrm{N}}$. ˙

Definition 3 (PCPs). *A (randomized) probabilistically checkable proof (PCP for short)* $\Pi = (\{\boldsymbol{\pi}_{x \in L}\}, \mathsf{V})$ *for a promise problem* L *consists of an ensemble of random variables* $\{\boldsymbol{\pi}_x\}$ *indexed by* $x \in L$ *whose values are oracles (also called proofs) and also a verifier* V *which is an oracle-aided PPT with randomness* r. *We require the following properties to hold.*

- **Completeness:** *For every* $x \in L^{\mathrm{Y}}$ *and every* $\pi \in \text{Supp}(\boldsymbol{\pi}_x)$ *it holds that* $\Pr_r[\mathsf{V}_r^\pi(x) = 1] \geq 2/3$.
- **Soundness:** *If* $x \in L^{\mathrm{N}}$, *then for every oracle* $\widehat{\pi}$: $\Pr_r[\mathsf{V}_r^{\widehat{\pi}}(x) = 0] \geq 2/3$.

We call a PCP for problem $L \in \mathbf{NP}$ efficient, if for all $x \in L$ and all $\pi \in \mathrm{Supp}(\pi_x)$, there exists a $\mathrm{poly}(n)$-sized circuit C_π such that for all queries q, $C_\pi(q) = \pi(q)$. Namely, C_π encodes π.

Notice that this definition of efficiency is non-uniform: the distribution of proofs C_π may depend non-uniformly on x. This only makes our negative results stronger than if we required C_π to depend uniformly on x. We also note that our negative result holds even using a weaker notion of completeness for PCPs in which $\Pr_r[\mathsf{V}_r^\pi(x) = 1] \geq 2/3$ holds over the randomness of the verifier and the randomness of sampling the oracle π. We use the above definition since the positive constructions of randomized PCPs do satisfy this stronger condition, and it is more convenient for amplifying the gap between the completeness and soundness errors.

Definition 4. *Let $\Pi = (\{\pi_{x \in L}\}, \mathsf{V})$ be a PCP for the problem L. Π is called zero-knowledge (ZK) if for every malicious $\mathrm{poly}(n)$-time verifier $\widehat{\mathsf{V}}$, there exists a simulator SIM which runs in (expected) $\mathrm{poly}(n)$-time and the following ensembles are statistically close:*

$$\{\mathrm{SIM}(x)\}_{x \in L} \quad , \quad \{\mathrm{View}\langle \widehat{\mathsf{V}}^{\pi_x}(x) \rangle\}_{x \in L}.$$

Note that $\widehat{\mathsf{V}}$ only has oracle access to $\pi \leftarrow \pi_x$, and the statistical indistinguishability should hold for large enough $|x|$. We call Π perfect ZK if the simulator's output distribution, conditioned on not aborting, is identically distributed to the view of the verifier $\widehat{\mathsf{V}}$ accessing $\pi \leftarrow \pi_{x \in L}$.

Non-uniformity vs. auxiliary input. By combining Definitions 3 and 4 one can obtain the definition of an *efficient ZK-PCP*. Note that, zero-knowledge with an "efficient prover" is typically defined using some auxiliary input given to the "prover", however, since here we prove a negative result using non-uniform efficiency (as in Definition 3) only makes our results stronger. In particular, if there exists an ensemble $\pi_{x,w}$ of efficiently computable proofs that is zero-knowledge and depends on both $x \in L$ and some witness w for $x \in L$, one can always obtain a non-uniformly computable efficient ZK-PCP (according to our Definitions 3 and 4) by hardwiring, for every $x \in L$, the lexicographically first witness w into the efficient algorithm computing π_x.

The definition of the complexity class **SZK** is indeed very similar to Definition 4 with the difference that the soundness holds against *provers* (which can be thought of as *stateful* oracles who could answer new queries depending on the previous queries asked.) Since we do not need the exact definition of the class **SZK**, here we only describe it at a high level.

Definition 5 (Complexity Class SZK). *The class **SZK** consists of promise problems which have an interactive (single prover) proof system with soundness error $\leq 1/3$ and the view of any malicious verifier can be simulated up to $\mathrm{negl}(n)$ statistical error.*

Lemma 1. *For a constant k, let $L_1, \ldots, L_k$ be a set of promise languages all in **SZK**, and let F be a constant-size k-input formula with operations: complement, conjunction, and disjunction as in Definition 1. Then $F(L_1, \ldots, L_K) \in \mathbf{SZK}$.*

See Section 4.5 and Corollary 6.5.1 of [Vad99] for a proof.

3.1   Shannon Entropy and Related Computational Problems

Fact 2 (Basic Facts about Entropy) *The following hold for any random variables* $\mathbf{X}, \mathbf{Y}, \mathbf{Z}$:

1. $H(\mathbf{X} \mid \mathbf{Y}) \leq H(\mathbf{X})$.
2. $I(\mathbf{X}; \mathbf{Y} \mid \mathbf{Z}) = H(\mathbf{X} \mid \mathbf{Z}) - H(\mathbf{X} \mid \mathbf{YZ}) = H(\mathbf{Y} \mid \mathbf{Z}) - H(\mathbf{Y} \mid \mathbf{XZ}) \geq 0$
3. *Data processing inequality: for any randomized function* $\mathbf{F}$ *(whose randomness is independent of* $\mathbf{X}, \mathbf{Y}, \mathbf{Z}$*), it holds that* $I(\mathbf{F}(\mathbf{X}); \mathbf{Y} \mid \mathbf{Z}) \leq I(\mathbf{X}; \mathbf{Y} \mid \mathbf{Z})$.

Definition 6 (Conditional Entropy Approximation). *The promise problem* CEA_ϵ *is defined as follows. Suppose* C *is a* poly(n)*-size circuit sampling a joint distribution* $(\mathbf{X}, \mathbf{Y})$*, i.e. this is the distribution of the output of* C *run over fresh randomness. Then given* (C, r) *we have:*

- $(\mathbf{X}, \mathbf{Y}, r) \in \mathrm{CEA}_\epsilon^{\mathrm{Y}}$ *iff* $H(\mathbf{X} \mid \mathbf{Y}) \geq r$.
- $(\mathbf{X}, \mathbf{Y}, r) \in \mathrm{CEA}_\epsilon^{\mathrm{N}}$ *iff* $H(\mathbf{X} \mid \mathbf{Y}) \leq r - \epsilon$.

Lemma 2. *For any* $\epsilon > 1/\mathrm{poly}(n)$, $\mathrm{CEA}_\epsilon \in$ **SZK**.

Proof. We give a reduction from CEA_ϵ to CEA_1, which is known to be **SZK**-complete [Vad06]. The reduction maps

$$(\mathbf{X}, \mathbf{Y}, r) \mapsto ((\mathbf{X}^1, \ldots, \mathbf{X}^{1/\epsilon}), (\mathbf{Y}^1, \ldots, \mathbf{Y}^{1/\epsilon}), r/\epsilon)$$

where for every $i \in [1/\epsilon]$, $(\mathbf{X}^i, \mathbf{Y}^i)$ is sampled identically to $(\mathbf{X}, \mathbf{Y})$ and independently of all other components (*i.e.* by an independent copy of the circuit C). It is easy to see that

$$H((\mathbf{X}^1, \ldots, \mathbf{X}^{1/\epsilon}) \mid (\mathbf{Y}^1, \ldots, \mathbf{Y}^{1/\epsilon})) = \frac{1}{\epsilon} \cdot H(\mathbf{X} \mid \mathbf{Y}).$$

In our main reduction, we will reduce problems to the following problem in **SZK**:

Definition 7 (Conditional Entropy Bound). $\mathrm{CEB}_{\alpha,\beta}$ *is the following promise problem where inputs are* poly(n)*-size circuits* C *sampling a joint distribution* $(\mathbf{X}, \mathbf{Y})$:

1. $(\mathbf{X}, \mathbf{Y}) \in \mathrm{CEB}_{\alpha,\beta}^{\mathrm{Y}}$ *iff* $H(\mathbf{X} \mid \mathbf{Y}) \geq \alpha$.
2. $(\mathbf{X}, \mathbf{Y}) \in \mathrm{CEB}_{\alpha,\beta}^{\mathrm{N}}$ *iff* $H(\mathbf{X} \mid \mathbf{Y}) \leq \beta$.

The following is immediate from Lemma 2:

Lemma 3. *For all functions* $\alpha(n), \beta(n)$ *uniformly computable in time* poly(n) *and satisfying* $\alpha(n) - \beta(n) > 1/\mathrm{poly}(n)$, $\mathrm{CEB}_{\alpha,\beta} \in$ **SZK**.

3.2 Statistical Distance vs Conditional Entropy

To prove our main result, we need to bound statistical distance using *conditional* (Shannon) entropy and vice versa. See the full version of the paper for proofs of the following two lemmas.

Lemma 4 (Conditional Entropy to Statistical Distance). *Suppose* $\text{Supp}(\mathbf{X}) = \{0,1\}^n$. *Then it holds that* $\mathbb{E}_{Y \leftarrow \mathbf{Y}} \Delta((\mathbf{X} \mid Y), \mathbf{U}_n) \leq \sqrt{n - H(\mathbf{X} \mid \mathbf{Y})}$.

Lemma 5 (Statistical Distance to Conditional Entropy). *For* $\epsilon \in [0,1]$ *let* $H(\epsilon) = \epsilon \lg(1/\epsilon) + (1 - \epsilon) \lg(1/1-\epsilon)$. *Suppose* $\Delta((\mathbf{X}, \mathbf{Y}), (\mathbf{X}', \mathbf{Y}')) \leq \epsilon$ *and* $\text{Supp}(\mathbf{X}) \cup \text{Supp}(\mathbf{X}') \subseteq \{0,1\}^n$. *Then it holds that* $|H(\mathbf{X} \mid \mathbf{Y}) - H(\mathbf{X}' \mid \mathbf{Y}')| \leq 4(H(\epsilon) + \epsilon \cdot n)$.

4   Proving the Main Result

Theorem 3. *Suppose the promise problem* $L = (L^Y, L^N)$ *has a ZK-PCP* $\Pi = (\{\boldsymbol{\pi}_{x \in L}\}, \mathsf{V})$ *of entropy at most* $H(\boldsymbol{\pi}_x) \leq \text{poly}(|x|)$. *Then* $L \in \mathbf{SZK}$.

(Note that the theorem extends beyond efficient ZK-PCP's and encompasses all ZK-PCP's where proofs have low entropy.) In the rest of this section we prove Theorem 3. Fix such a ZK-PCP for L and let $\eta = H(\boldsymbol{\pi}_x) \leq \text{poly}(n)$.

The first step of our proof is to define a verifier who can "exhaust" all of the entropy of the ZK-PCP so that the proof behaves essentially as if it were deterministic. We use the following verifier: let $\mathsf{V}^{[\ell]} = (\mathsf{V}^1, \ldots, \mathsf{V}^\ell)$ be a verifier who executes ℓ independent instances of V against the given oracle and let V^i be its ith verification. (We will fix a choice of $\ell = \text{poly}(n) \gg \eta$ later.) Let SIM be the simulator that simulates the view of $\mathsf{V}^{[\ell]}$ statistically well (*i.e.* SIM(x) is negl$(|x|)$-close to the view of $\mathsf{V}^{[\ell]}(x)$ when accessing $\pi \leftarrow \boldsymbol{\pi}_x$ for $x \in L$). The view of V^i can be represented as $\nu^i = (r^i, q_1^i, a_1^i, \ldots, q_m^i, a_m^i)$ where $r^i \in \{0,1\}^k$ is the randomness used by V^i, q_j^i is its jth oracle query and a_j^i is the answer to q_j^i. We use the notation $\overline{a}^i = (a_1^i, \ldots, a_m^i), \overline{q}^i = (q_1^i, \ldots, q_m^i)$. The view of $\mathsf{V}^{[\ell]}$ consists of $(\nu^1, \ldots, \nu^\ell)$.

In order to prove $L \in \mathbf{SZK}$, we show how to reduce L to a constant size formula over $\mathbf{SZK}$ languages. As we mentioned in the introduction, we need to check three conditions: the simulator generates an accepting view, the entropy of a random answer in the view has low entropy given the query, and the distribution of the random coins in the view is uniform.

To describe our reduction formally we first need to define a circuit C_x^{SIM} and a promise problem $D_{\alpha,\beta}$ as follows.

- The circuit C_x^{SIM} takes as input r_{SIM} (for input length $|x|$). The circuit C_x outputs SIM$(x; r_{\text{SIM}}) = (\nu^1, \ldots, \nu^\ell)$ where for each $i \in [\ell]$, $\nu^i = (r^i, q_1^i, a_1^i, \ldots, q_m^i, a_m^i)$.
- For $\alpha > \beta$, $D_{\alpha,\beta}$ is a promise problem whose inputs are Boolean circuits C of input length n and size $|C| = \text{poly}(n)$; then:
    1. $C \in D_{\alpha,\beta}^Y$ iff $\Pr[C(\mathbf{U}_n) = 1] \geq \alpha$, and
    2. $C \in D_{\alpha,\beta}^N$ iff $\Pr[C(\mathbf{U}_n) = 1] \leq \beta$.

The parameters α and β could be functions of n, and it is easy to see that for efficiently computable α, β (given n) it holds that $D_{\alpha,\beta} \in$ **BPP** if $\alpha - \beta > 1/\text{poly}(n)$.

Reduction 4 (Main Reduction). *Given a parameter ℓ, we map $x \mapsto (C_1, C_2, C_3)$ as follows.*

1. C_1 *checks the uniformity of the random coins in the view.* C_1 *is a circuit sampling the joint distribution* $(\mathbf{X}_1, \mathbf{Y}_1)$ *defined as follows. On input* (r_{SIM}, i), C_1 *executes the circuit* C_x^{SIM} *on* r_{SIM} *to get* $(\nu^1, \ldots, \nu^\ell) = C_x^{\text{SIM}}(r_{\text{SIM}})$ *and sets:* $X_1 = r^i$ *and* $Y_1 = (\nu^1, \ldots, \nu^{i-1})$.

2. C_2 *checks that the conditional entropy of a randomly chosen answer is low conditioned on the corresponding query.* C_2 *is a circuit sampling the joint distribution* $(\mathbf{X}_2, \mathbf{Y}_2)$ *defined as follows. On input* (r_{SIM}, i, j), C_2 *executes the circuit* C_x^{SIM} *on* r_{SIM} *to get* $(\nu^1, \ldots, \nu^\ell) = C_x^{\text{SIM}}(r_{\text{SIM}})$ *and sets:* $X_2 = a_j^i$ *and* $Y_2 = (\nu^1, \ldots, \nu^{i-1}, q_j^i)$. *We emphasize the fact that while* a_j^i, q_j^i *appear in the output of* C_2, *the actual index j itself does* not *appear in the output.*

3. C_3 *checks that the view is accepting.* C_3 *operates as follows: on input* (r_{SIM}, i), C_3 *executes the circuit* C_x^{SIM} *on* r_{SIM} *to obtain* $(\nu^1, \ldots, \nu^\ell) = C_x^{\text{SIM}}(r_{\text{SIM}})$, *and output 1 iff* ν^i *is an accepting view of* V.

Claim. Reduction 4 is a Karp reduction from L (specified in Theorem 3) to the promise language $Z = \text{CEB}_{k-1/200, k-1/100} \wedge \overline{\text{CEB}}_{2\eta/\ell, 1.1\eta/\ell} \wedge D_{0.66,\beta}$ for $\beta = 1/3 + 1/10 + 2m\eta/\ell$.

Proving Theorem 3 Using Claim 4. By taking $\ell = 40m\eta$, it holds that $2m \cdot \eta/\ell < 1/20$ in Lemma 7 and so $\beta < 1/2$, which implies that $D_{\alpha,\beta} \in$ **BPP**, $Z \in$ **SZK**, and so $L \in$ **SZK**.

In the following we prove Claim 4 by studying each case of $x \in L^Y$ and $x \in L^N$ separately. We begin with a lemma that will be useful for the case $x \in L^Y$.

The following lemma bounds the conditional entropy of a single answer to a single randomly chosen verifier query by the conditional entropy of the set of *all* answers to the set of *all* verifier queries. This is non-trivial because the verifier queries may be asked adaptively.

Lemma 6. *Let A be any randomized algorithm that (adaptively) queries a PCP π. Let $r \in \{0,1\}^k$ denote the random coins of A. Let $\bar{q} = (q_1, \ldots, q_m)$ be the queries that $A^\pi(r)$ makes and let $a_j = \pi(q_j)$ be the corresponding answers. Let π be an arbitrary distribution over proofs, and let $\bar{\mathbf{q}}$ and $\bar{\mathbf{a}}$ be the distribution over (the vectors of) queries and answers obtained by querying π using algorithm A on uniform random coins $\mathbf{r}$. Let also $\mathbf{j}$ be an arbitrary distribution over $[m]$. Then $\text{H}(\mathbf{a_j} \mid \mathbf{q_j}) \leq \text{H}(\bar{\mathbf{a}} \mid \mathbf{r})$ where in the notation $\mathbf{q_j}$ the value of $\mathbf{j}$ is not explicitly revealed.*

Proof. By the definition of conditional entropy and that $0 = \text{H}(\mathbf{a_j q_j} \mid \boldsymbol{\pi}) - \text{H}(\mathbf{a_j q_j} \mid \boldsymbol{\pi})$, we get $\text{H}(\mathbf{a_j} \mid \mathbf{q_j}) = \text{H}(\mathbf{a_j q_j}) - \text{H}(\mathbf{a_j q_j} \mid \boldsymbol{\pi}) - (\text{H}(\mathbf{q_j}) - \text{H}(\mathbf{a_j q_j} \mid \boldsymbol{\pi}))$. Since a proof π is *stateless* for any fixed π, given any query q asked at some point during the execution of A^π, the answer $a = \pi(q)$ is also fixed. Therefore it holds that $H(a_j q_j \mid \pi) = H(q_j \mid \pi)$, and by the definition of mutual information, we have $H(a_j \mid q_j) = I(a_j q_j; \pi) - I(q_j; \pi) \le I(a_j q_j; \pi)$. Since $I(a_j q_j; \pi) = H(\pi) - H(\pi \mid a_j q_j)$ and since π and $\mathbf{r}$ are independent, Item 1 of Fact 2 implies that

$$H(a_j \mid q_j) \le I(a_j q_j; \pi) = H(\pi) - H(\pi \mid a_j q_j)$$
$$\le H(\pi \mid \mathbf{r}) - H(\pi \mid a_j q_j \mathbf{r}) = I(a_j q_j; \pi \mid \mathbf{r})$$

Let $\mathbf{F}$ be the function that takes as input $(\overline{\mathbf{a}}, \overline{\mathbf{q}})$ and outputs (a_j, q_j) by sampling j. By the data processing inequality (Item 3 of Fact 2) it holds that

$$H(a_j \mid q_j) \le I(a_j q_j; \pi \mid \mathbf{r}) = I(\mathbf{F}(\overline{\mathbf{a}}\overline{\mathbf{q}}); \pi \mid \mathbf{r})$$
$$\le I(\overline{\mathbf{a}}\overline{\mathbf{q}}; \pi \mid \mathbf{r}) \le H(\overline{\mathbf{a}}\overline{\mathbf{q}} \mid \mathbf{r}) = H(\overline{\mathbf{a}} \mid \mathbf{r}) + H(\overline{\mathbf{q}} \mid \overline{\mathbf{a}}\mathbf{r})$$

Finally, since $H(\overline{\mathbf{q}} \mid \overline{\mathbf{a}}\mathbf{r}) = 0$, this implies the proposition.

Remark 1. We emphasize that if π was *stateful* (*i.e.* a "prover", rather than a "proof"), then Lemma 6 would be *false*. Even a deterministic prover can correlate his answers to the verifier's queries, and so it may be that $H(\overline{\mathbf{a}} \mid \overline{\mathbf{q}}) = 0$ but $H(a_j \mid q_j) > 0$. Namely, even given π (say for a stateful prover that π gives the random coins of the prover) and a query q, the answer to q may have entropy because π's answer to q may be different depending on whether q was asked as the first query or second query or third query, etc. In particular, the equality $H(a_j q_j \mid \pi) = H(q_j \mid \pi)$ used in the proof of Lemma 6 would not hold anymore. This is one place where we crucially use the fixed nature of a PCP.

Proof of Claim 4: The Case $x \in L^Y$. Here we would like to show that $(C_1 \in \mathrm{CEB}^Y_{k-1/200, k-1/100})$ and $(C_2 \in \overline{\mathrm{CEB}}^Y_{2\eta/\ell, 1.1\eta/\ell})$ and $(C_3 \in D^Y_{0.66, \beta})$. We study each of the generated instances C_i for $i \in [3]$. In all these cases, we first assume that the simulator's output is identically distributed to the view of $\mathsf{V}^{[\ell]}$ interacting with a prover and then will show how to remove this assumption.

The Instance C_1. If the simulator's outputs were identically distributed to the view of $\mathsf{V}^{[\ell]}$ interacting with a prover, then the simulated randomness $\mathbf{X}_1 = \mathbf{r}^i$ will be uniformly distributed over $\{0,1\}^k$ with entropy k *independently* of $\mathbf{Y}_1 = (\boldsymbol{\nu}^1, \ldots, \boldsymbol{\nu}^{i-1})$. Since the simulator generates a view that is statistically close to the honest interaction (and since $k = \mathrm{poly}(|x|)$ and $H(\mathrm{negl}(n)) = \mathrm{negl}(n)$) we may apply Lemma 5 to deduce that $H(\mathbf{X}_1 \mid \mathbf{Y}_1) \ge k - \mathrm{negl}(n) \ge k - 1/200$. Therefore, $C_1 \in \mathrm{CEB}^Y_{k-1/200, k-1/100}$.

The Instance C_2. Here we study the view of $\mathsf{V}^{[\ell]}$ while interacting with a proof generated according to the distribution π_x whose entropy is bounded by η. Suppose first that the simulator's outputs were identically distributed to the view of $\mathsf{V}^{[\ell]}$ interacting with π_x. In this case, by an argument similar to [IMS12], one can show that

Claim. $\mathbb{E}_{i \leftarrow [\ell]} H(\overline{\mathbf{a}}^i \mid \boldsymbol{\nu}^1, \ldots, \boldsymbol{\nu}^{i-1}, \mathbf{r}^i) \le \eta/\ell.$

Proof.

$$\eta + k\ell \geq H(\boldsymbol{\pi}_x) + H(\mathbf{r}^1, \ldots, \mathbf{r}^\ell)$$

$$(\boldsymbol{\pi}_x, \mathbf{r}^1, \ldots, \mathbf{r}^\ell \text{ independent}) \quad = H(\boldsymbol{\pi}_x, \mathbf{r}^1, \ldots, \mathbf{r}^\ell)$$

$$(\boldsymbol{\pi}_x, \mathbf{r}^1, \ldots, \mathbf{r}^\ell \text{ fix } \boldsymbol{\nu}^1, \ldots, \boldsymbol{\nu}^\ell) \quad \geq H(\boldsymbol{\nu}^1, \ldots, \boldsymbol{\nu}^\ell)$$

$$= \sum_{i \in [\ell]} H(\boldsymbol{\nu}^i \mid \boldsymbol{\nu}^1, \ldots, \boldsymbol{\nu}^{i-1})$$

$$(\mathbf{r}^i \text{ and } \overline{\mathbf{a}}^i \text{ determine } \overline{\mathbf{q}}^i) \quad = \sum_{i \in [\ell]} H(\mathbf{r}^i \mid \boldsymbol{\nu}^1, \ldots, \boldsymbol{\nu}^{i-1})$$

$$+ H(\overline{\mathbf{a}}^i \mid \boldsymbol{\nu}^1, \ldots, \boldsymbol{\nu}^{i-1}, \mathbf{r}^i)$$

$$= k\ell + \sum_{i \in [\ell]} H(\overline{\mathbf{a}}^i \mid \boldsymbol{\nu}^1, \ldots, \boldsymbol{\nu}^{i-1}, \mathbf{r}^i).$$

Thus, by averaging over i we have $\mathbb{E}_{i \leftarrow [\ell]} H(\overline{\mathbf{a}}^i \mid \boldsymbol{\nu}^1, \ldots, \boldsymbol{\nu}^{i-1}, \mathbf{r}^i) \leq \eta/\ell$.

The following claim is also based on the assumption that the simulation is perfect, and thus the distribution of $(\boldsymbol{\nu}^1, \ldots, \boldsymbol{\nu}^m)$ generated by the simulator is identical to the view of $\mathsf{V}^{[\ell]}$ run against $\pi \leftarrow \boldsymbol{\pi}_{x \in L, w}$.

Claim. For each fixed value of i and $(\boldsymbol{\nu}^1, \ldots, \boldsymbol{\nu}^{i-1})$, it holds that

$$H(\mathbf{a}_j^i \mid \mathbf{q}_j^i, \boldsymbol{\nu}^1, \ldots, \boldsymbol{\nu}^{i-1}) \leq H(\overline{\mathbf{a}}^i \mid \mathbf{r}^i, \boldsymbol{\nu}^1, \ldots, \boldsymbol{\nu}^{i-1}) \tag{1}$$

Namely, the entropy of the answers of the ith verification gives an upper-bound on the entropy of the answer to a randomly chosen query of the verifier *without* revealing its index.

Proof. Let $(\boldsymbol{\pi}_x, \boldsymbol{\nu}^1, \ldots, \boldsymbol{\nu}^{i-1})$ be the joint distribution of an honest proof $\boldsymbol{\pi}_x$ and $i-1$ executions of the honest verifier $\mathsf{V}^1, \ldots, \mathsf{V}^{i-1}$ using proof $\boldsymbol{\pi}_x$. Apply Lemma 6 using the distribution over proofs given by $(\boldsymbol{\pi}_x \mid \boldsymbol{\nu}^1, \ldots, \boldsymbol{\nu}^{i-1})$, and with the honest verifier algorithm V^i as the query algorithm accessing the proof.

Using Claims 4 and 4, we conclude that $H(\mathbf{X}_2 \mid \mathbf{Y}_2) \leq \eta/\ell$, *assuming that the simulator was perfect*. If we only assume that the simulator's output is statistically close to the view of $\mathsf{V}^{[\ell]}$ interacting with $\boldsymbol{\pi}_x$, then we can apply Lemma 5 and deduce that $H(\mathbf{X}_2 \mid \mathbf{Y}_2) \leq \eta/\ell + \mathrm{negl}(n) < 1.1\eta/\ell$ which implies that $C_2 \in \overline{\mathrm{CEB}}^{\mathrm{Y}}_{2\eta/\ell, 1.1\eta/\ell}$.

The Instance C_3. By the completeness of Π, when $\mathsf{V}^{[\ell]} = (\mathsf{V}^1, \ldots, \mathsf{V}^\ell)$ interacts with a proof, for all $i \in [\ell]$, V^i accepts with probability $\geq 2/3$. Since the simulation is statistically close to the real interaction, it holds that $\boldsymbol{\nu}^i$ is accepting with probability $2/3 - \mathrm{negl}(n) \geq 0.66$, and so $C_3 \in D^{\mathrm{Y}}_{0.66, \beta}$.

Proof of Claim 4: The Case $x \in L^N$. Here we would like to show that $C_1 \in \mathrm{CEB}^{\mathrm{N}}_{k-1/200, k-1/100}$ or $C_2 \in \overline{\mathrm{CEB}}^{\mathrm{N}}_{2\eta/\ell, 1.1\eta/\ell}$ or $C_3 \in D^{\mathrm{N}}_{0.66, \beta}$. This follows from the following lemma.

Lemma 7. *Suppose $x \in L^N$, $C_1 \notin \mathrm{CEB}^N_{k-1/200,k-1/100}$, and also that $C_2 \notin \overline{\mathrm{CEB}}^N_{2\eta/\ell,1.1\eta/\ell}$. Then $C_3 \in D^N_{0.66,\beta}$ for $\beta = 1/3 + 1/10 + 2m \cdot \eta/\ell$.*

Intuition. Since $C_2 \notin \overline{\mathrm{CEB}}^N_{2\eta/\ell,1.1\eta/\ell}$, therefore, the oracle answers returned to the verifier in the ith execution (for a random $i \leftarrow [\ell]$) all have very low entropy and thus close to a *fixed* proof. Moreover, due to $C_1 \notin \mathrm{CEB}^N_{k-1/200,k-1/100}$, the randomness of the verifier in this execution has almost full entropy, and therefore, the ith execution is close to an honest execution of the verifier against some oracle. Finally, since $x \in L^N$ by the soundness of the PCP, the verifier would accept with probability at most $\approx 1/3$. The formal argument goes through a hybrid argument as follows.

Experiments. The outputs of all experiments described below consist of a view of $\mathsf{V}^{[i]}$ (*i.e.* the first i executions of the verifier). The distribution of $(\nu^1, \ldots, \nu^{i-1})$ in all of these executions is the same and is sampled by $\mathrm{SIM}(x)$, and they only differ in the way they sample ν^i.

- **Experiment** Real. Choose $i \leftarrow [\ell]$, and take the output $(\nu^1, \ldots, \nu^i)$ by running $\mathrm{SIM}(x)$.
- **Experiment** Ideal. Choose $i \leftarrow [\ell]$, and take the output $(\nu^1, \ldots, \nu^{i-1})$ by running $\mathrm{SIM}(x)$. To sample $\boldsymbol{\nu}^i = (\mathbf{r}^i, \overline{\mathbf{q}}^i, \overline{\mathbf{a}}^i)$ we first sample $r^i \leftarrow \{0,1\}^k$ uniformly at random, and then using r^i we run the verifier against the oracle $\widehat{\pi}$ defined as follows.
  The Oracle $\widehat{\pi}$: Suppose we have fixed $(\nu^i, \ldots, \nu^{i-1})$. Recall the distribution $((\mathbf{q}^i_\mathbf{j}, \mathbf{a}^i_\mathbf{j}) \mid \nu^i, \ldots, \nu^{i-1})$ defined above when defining the instance C_2 (*i.e.*, $(\mathbf{a}^i_\mathbf{j}, \mathbf{q}^i_\mathbf{j})$ is a randomly chosen pair of query-answer pairs from the view ν^i without revealing the index j). For every query q, the oracle $\widehat{\pi}$ gets one sample according to $a \leftarrow (\mathbf{a}^i_\mathbf{j} \mid \nu^i, \ldots, \nu^{i-1}, \mathbf{q}^i_\mathbf{j} = q)$ and sets $\widehat{\pi}(q) = a$ forever. If $\Pr[\mathbf{q}^i_\mathbf{j} = q \mid \nu^i, \ldots, \nu^{i-1}] = 0$, we define $\widehat{\pi}(q) = \bot$.
- **Experiment** Hyb_j for $j \in [m+1]$. These experiments are in between Real and Ideal and for larger j they become closer to Real. Here we choose $i \leftarrow [\ell]$, and take the output $(\nu^1, \ldots, \nu^i)$ by running $\mathrm{SIM}(x)$. Then we will *re-sample* parts of ν^i as follows. We will keep $(r^i, (q^i_1, a^i_1), \ldots, (q^i_{j-1}, a^i_{j-1}))$ as sampled by $\mathrm{SIM}(x)$. For the remaining queries and answers we sample an oracle $\widehat{\pi}$ as described in Ideal, and we let $(q^i_j, a^i_j), \ldots, (q^i_m, a^i_m)$ be the result of continuing the execution of V^i using r^i and the oracle $\widehat{\pi}$. Note that $\mathsf{Hyb}_{m+1} \equiv$ Real.

Claim. If $x \in L^N$, then $\Pr_{\mathsf{Ideal}}[\nu^i$ accepts $] \leq 1/3$.

Claim. If $C_1 \notin \mathrm{CEB}^N_{k-1/200,k-1/100}$, then $\Delta(\mathsf{Ideal}, \mathsf{Hyb}_1) \leq 1/10$.

Claim. If $C_2 \notin \overline{\mathrm{CEB}}^N_{2\eta/\ell,1.1\eta/\ell}$, then $\mathbb{E}_{j \in [m]} \Delta(\mathsf{Hyb}_j, \mathsf{Hyb}_{j+1}) \leq 2\eta/\ell$.

Proving Lemma 7. Claims 4, 4, and 4 together imply that

$$\Pr_{\text{Real}}[\nu^i \text{ accepts }] \le \Pr_{\text{Ideal}}[\nu^i \text{ accepts }] + \Delta(\text{Ideal}, \text{Hyb}_1) + \sum_{j \in [m]} \Delta(\text{Hyb}_j, \text{Hyb}_{j+1})$$

$$\le 1/3 + 1/10 + 2m\eta/\ell$$

which proves that $C_3 \in D^{\text{N}}_{2/3,\beta}$. In the following we prove these claims.

Proof (Proof of Claim 4). Since the oracle $\hat{\pi}$ is sampled and fixed before choosing r^i and executing V^i, and because $x \in L^N$, by the soundness property of the PCP it holds that $\Pr_{\text{Ideal}}[\nu^i \text{ accepts }] \le 1/3$.

Proof (Proof of Claim 4). If $C_1 \notin \text{CEB}^{\text{N}}_{k-1/200, k-1/100}$, then we have $\mathbb{E}_{i \leftarrow [\ell]}[\mathsf{H}(\mathbf{r}^i \mid \nu^1, \ldots, \nu^{i-1})] \ge k - 1/100$. By Lemma 4 it holds that

$$\mathop{\mathbb{E}}_{i \leftarrow [\ell], \nu^1, \ldots, \nu^{i-1}}[\Delta((\mathbf{r}^i \mid \nu^1, \ldots, \nu^{i-1}), \mathsf{U}_k)] \le \sqrt{1/100} = 1/10.$$

But note that the only difference between Ideal and Hyb_1 is the way we sample r^i conditioned on the previously sampled parts (*i.e.* $\nu^1, \ldots, \nu^{i-1}$). Thus it holds that $\Delta(\text{Ideal}, \text{Hyb}_1) \le 1/10$.

Proof (Proof of Claim 4). The only difference between Hyb_j and Hyb_{j+1} is the way they answer q^i_j. In Hyb_{j+1} the original answer of the simulator is used, while in Hyb_j this answer is provided by the oracle $\hat{\pi}$. Thus, they are different only when the answer re-sampled by $\hat{\pi}$ differs from the original answer. Therefore, we have that:

$$\Delta(\text{Hyb}_j, \text{Hyb}_{j+1}) \le \mathop{\mathbb{E}}_{\nu^1, \ldots, \nu^{i-1}, i}\left[\mathop{\Pr}_{\bar{\mathbf{a}}^i, \bar{\mathbf{q}}^i, \hat{\pi}}[\mathbf{a}^i_j \ne \hat{\pi}(\mathbf{q}^i_j) \mid i, \nu^1, \ldots, \nu^{i-1}]\right]$$

Taking an expectation over all $j \leftarrow [\ell]$ we conclude Claim 4 as follows.

$$\mathop{\mathbb{E}}_{j}[\Delta(\text{Hyb}_j, \text{Hyb}_{j+1})] = \mathop{\mathbb{E}}_{j,i,\nu^1, \ldots, \nu^{i-1}}\left[\mathop{\Pr}_{\bar{\mathbf{a}}^i, \bar{\mathbf{q}}^i, \hat{\pi}}[\mathbf{a}^i_j \ne \hat{\pi}(\mathbf{q}^i_j) \mid i, \nu^1, \ldots, \nu^{i-1}]\right]$$

$$= \mathop{\mathbb{E}}_{i,\nu^1, \ldots, \nu^{i-1}}\left[\mathop{\Pr}_{j,\bar{\mathbf{a}}^i, \bar{\mathbf{q}}^i, \hat{\pi}}[\mathbf{a}^i_j \ne \hat{\pi}(\mathbf{q}^i_j) \mid i, \nu^1, \ldots, \nu^{i-1}]\right]$$

By combining the sampling of $\mathbf{a_j^i}, \mathbf{q_j^i}$ directly, we have that

$$\mathbb{E}_j[\Delta(\mathsf{Hyb}_j, \mathsf{Hyb}_{j+1})] = \mathop{\mathbb{E}}_{i,\nu^1,\dots,\nu^{i-1}} \left[\mathop{\Pr}_{\mathbf{a_j^i},\mathbf{q_j^i},\widehat{\pi}} [\mathbf{a_j^i} \neq \widehat{\pi}(\mathbf{q_j^i}) \mid i, \nu^1, \dots, \nu^{i-1}] \right]$$

$$= \mathop{\mathbb{E}}_{i,\nu^1,\dots,\nu^{i-1}} \left[1 - \mathop{\Pr}_{\mathbf{a_j^i},\mathbf{q_j^i},\widehat{\pi}} [\mathbf{a_j^i} = \widehat{\pi}(\mathbf{q_j^i}) \mid i, \nu^1, \dots, \nu^{i-1}] \right]$$

$$= \mathop{\mathbb{E}}_{i,\nu^1,\dots,\nu^{i-1},q_j^i,a_j^i} \left[1 - \mathop{\Pr}_{\widehat{\pi}}[a_j^i = \widehat{\pi}(q_j^i) \mid i, \nu^1, \dots, \nu^{i-1}] \right]$$

$$(1 - \alpha \leq \lg \tfrac{1}{\alpha} \ \forall \alpha \in [0,1]) \ \leq \mathop{\mathbb{E}}_{i,\nu^1,\dots,\nu^{i-1},q_j^i,a_j^i} \left[\lg \frac{1}{\Pr_{\widehat{\pi}}[a_j^i = \widehat{\pi}(q_j^i) \mid i, \nu^1, \dots, \nu^{i-1}]} \right]$$

$$(\text{by definition of } \widehat{\pi}) \ = \mathop{\mathbb{E}}_i \left[H(\mathbf{a_j^i} \mid \boldsymbol{\nu}^1, \dots, \boldsymbol{\nu}^{i-1}, \mathbf{q_j^i}) \right]$$

$$(C_2 \notin \overline{\mathrm{CEB}}^{\mathrm{N}}_{2\eta/\ell, 1.1\eta/\ell}) \ \leq 2\eta/\ell.$$

References

[AH91]   Aiello, W., Håstad, J.: Statistical zero-knowledge languages can be recognized in two rounds. Journal of Computer and System Sciences 42(3), 327–345 (1991); Preliminary version in FOCS 1987

[ALM+98]   Arora, S., Lund, C., Motwani, R., Sudan, M., Szegedy, M.: Proof verification and the hardness of approximation problems. Journal of the ACM 45(3), 501–555 (1998); Preliminary version in FOCS 1992

[AS98]   Arora, S., Safra, S.: Probabilistic checking of proofs: a new characterization of NP. Journal of the ACM 45(1), 70–122 (1998); Preliminary version in FOCS 1992

[BFL90]   Babai, L., Fortnow, L., Lund, C.: Non-deterministic exponential time has two-prover interactive protocols. In: FOCS, pp. 16–25 (1990)

[BGKW88]   Ben-Or, M., Goldwasser, S., Kilian, J., Wigderson, A.: Multi-prover interactive proofs: How to remove intractability assumptions. In: STOC, pp. 113–131 (1988)

[BHZ87]   Boppana, R.B., Håstad, J., Zachos, S.: Does co-NP have short interactive proofs? Information Processing Letters 25, 127–132 (1987)

[BM88]   Babai, L., Moran, S.: Arthur-merlin games: A randomized proof system, and a hierarchy of complexity classes. J. Comput. Syst. Sci. 36(2), 254–276 (1988)

[CGGM00]   Canetti, R., Goldreich, O., Goldwasser, S., Micali, S.: Resettable zero-knowledge (extended abstract). In: STOC, pp. 235–244 (2000)

[CGS08]   Chandran, N., Goyal, V., Sahai, A.: New Constructions for UC Secure Computation Using Tamper-Proof Hardware. In: Smart, N.P. (ed.) EUROCRYPT 2008. LNCS, vol. 4965, pp. 545–562. Springer, Heidelberg (2008)

[DFK+92]   Dwork, C., Feige, U., Kilian, J., Naor, M., Safra, M.: Low Communication 2-Prover Zero-Knowledge Proofs for NP. In: Brickell, E.F. (ed.) CRYPTO 1992. LNCS, vol. 740, pp. 215–227. Springer, Heidelberg (1993)

[For89]   Fortnow, L.: The complexity of perfect zero-knowledge. Advances in Computing Research: Randomness and Computation 5, 327–343 (1989)

[FRS94]   Fortnow, L., Rompel, J., Sipser, M.: On the power of multi-prover interactive protocols. Theoretical Computer Science 134(2), 545–557 (1994)

[GIMS10]   Goyal, V., Ishai, Y., Mahmoody, M., Sahai, A.: Interactive Locking, Zero-Knowledge PCPs, and Unconditional Cryptography. In: Rabin, T. (ed.) CRYPTO 2010. LNCS, vol. 6223, pp. 173–190. Springer, Heidelberg (2010)

[GIS⁺10]   Goyal, V., Ishai, Y., Sahai, A., Venkatesan, R., Wadia, A.: Founding Cryptography on Tamper-Proof Hardware Tokens. In: Micciancio, D. (ed.) TCC 2010. LNCS, vol. 5978, pp. 308–326. Springer, Heidelberg (2010)

[GKR08]   Goldwasser, S., Kalai, Y.T., Rothblum, G.N.: One-Time Programs. In: Wagner, D. (ed.) CRYPTO 2008. LNCS, vol. 5157, pp. 39–56. Springer, Heidelberg (2008)

[GMOS07]   Goyal, V., Moriarty, R., Ostrovsky, R., Sahai, A.: Concurrent Statistical Zero-Knowledge Arguments for NP from One Way Functions. In: Kurosawa, K. (ed.) ASIACRYPT 2007. LNCS, vol. 4833, pp. 444–459. Springer, Heidelberg (2007)

[GMR89]   Goldwasser, S., Micali, S., Rackoff, C.: The knowledge complexity of interactive proof systems. SIAM Journal on Computing 18(1), 186–208 (1989); Preliminary version in STOC 1985

[GMW91]   Goldreich, O., Micali, S., Wigderson, A.: Proofs that yield nothing but their validity or all languages in NP have zero-knowledge proof systems. Journal of the ACM 38(1), 691–729 (1991); Preliminary version in FOCS 1986

[GO94]   Goldreich, O., Oren, Y.: Definitions and properties of zero-knowledge proof systems. Journal of Cryptology 7(1), 1–32 (1994)

[GOVW12]   Garg, S., Ostrovsky, R., Visconti, I., Wadia, A.: Resettable Statistical Zero Knowledge. In: Cramer, R. (ed.) TCC 2012. LNCS, vol. 7194, pp. 494–511. Springer, Heidelberg (2012)

[IMS12]   Ishai, Y., Mahmoody, M., Sahai, A.: On Efficient Zero-Knowledge PCPs. In: Cramer, R. (ed.) TCC 2012. LNCS, vol. 7194, pp. 151–168. Springer, Heidelberg (2012)

[Kat07]   Katz, J.: Universally Composable Multi-party Computation Using Tamper-Proof Hardware. In: Naor, M. (ed.) EUROCRYPT 2007. LNCS, vol. 4515, pp. 115–128. Springer, Heidelberg (2007)

[Kil92]   Kilian, J.: A note on efficient zero-knowledge proofs and arguments (extended abstract). In: Proceedings of the 24th Annual ACM Symposium on Theory of Computing (STOC), pp. 723–732 (1992)

[Kol10]   Kolesnikov, V.: Truly Efficient String Oblivious Transfer Using Resettable Tamper-Proof Tokens. In: Micciancio, D. (ed.) TCC 2010. LNCS, vol. 5978, pp. 327–342. Springer, Heidelberg (2010)

[KPT97]   Kilian, J., Petrank, E., Tardos, G.: Probabilistically checkable proofs with zero knowledge. In: STOC: ACM Symposium on Theory of Computing (STOC) (1997)

[MS08]   Moran, T., Segev, G.: David and Goliath Commitments: UC Computation for Asymmetric Parties Using Tamper-Proof Hardware. In: Smart, N.P. (ed.) EUROCRYPT 2008. LNCS, vol. 4965, pp. 527–544. Springer, Heidelberg (2008)

[MV03]   Micciancio, D., Vadhan, S.P.: Statistical Zero-Knowledge Proofs with Efficient Provers: Lattice Problems and More. In: Boneh, D. (ed.) CRYPTO 2003. LNCS, vol. 2729, pp. 282–298. Springer, Heidelberg (2003)

[OV08]   Ong, S.J., Vadhan, S.P.: An Equivalence Between Zero Knowledge and Commitments. In: Canetti, R. (ed.) TCC 2008. LNCS, vol. 4948, pp. 482–500. Springer, Heidelberg (2008)

[Vad99]   Vadhan, S.P.: A Study of Statistical Zero-Knowledge Proofs. PhD thesis, Massachusetts Institute of Technology, Cambridge, MA, USA (1999)

[Vad06]   Vadhan, S.P.: An unconditional study of computational zero knowledge. SIAM Journal on Computing 36(4), 1160–1214 (2006); Preliminary version in FOCS 2004

Succinct Non-interactive Arguments via Linear Interactive Proofs*

Nir Bitansky[1,**], Alessandro Chiesa[2], Yuval Ishai[3,***],
Omer Paneth[4,†], and Rafail Ostrovsky[5,‡]

[1] Tel Aviv University
[2] MIT
[3] Technion
[4] Boston University
[5] UCLA

Abstract. *Succinct non-interactive arguments* (SNARGs) enable verifying NP statements with lower complexity than required for classical NP verification. Traditionally, the focus has been on minimizing the length of such arguments; nowadays researches have focused also on minimizing verification time, by drawing motivation from the problem of delegating computation.

A common relaxation is a *preprocessing* SNARG, which allows the verifier to conduct an expensive offline phase that is independent of the statement to be proven later. Recent constructions of preprocessing SNARGs have achieved attractive features: they are publicly-verifiable, proofs consist of only $O(1)$ encrypted (or encoded) field elements, and verification is via arithmetic circuits of size linear in the NP statement. Additionally, these constructions seem to have "escaped the hegemony" of probabilistically-checkable proofs (PCPs) as a basic building block of succinct arguments.

---

* The full version of this paper can be found on ePrint [BCI+12].

** This research was done while visiting Boston University and IBM T. J. Watson Research Center. Supported by the Check Point Institute for Information Security, an ISF grant 20006317, and the Fulbright program.

*** Supported by the European Research Council as part of the ERC project CaC (grant 259426), ISF grant 1361/10, and BSF grant 2008411. Research done in part while visiting UCLA and IBM T. J. Watson Research Center.

† Supported by an NSF grant 1218461.

‡ Department of Computer Science and Department of Mathematics, UCLA. Email: rafail@cs.ucla.edu. Research supported in part by NSF grants CNS-0830803; CCF-0916574; IIS-1065276; CCF-1016540; CNS-1118126; CNS-1136174; US-Israel BSF grant 2008411, OKAWA Foundation Research Award, IBM Faculty Research Award, Xerox Faculty Research Award, B. John Garrick Foundation Award, Teradata Research Award, and Lockheed-Martin Corporation Research Award. This material is also based upon work supported by the Defense Advanced Research Projects Agency through the U.S. Office of Naval Research under Contract N00014-11-1-0392. The views expressed are those of the author and do not reflect the official policy or position of the Department of Defense or the U.S. Government.

A. Sahai (Ed.): TCC 2013, LNCS 7785, pp. 315–333, 2013.

We present a general methodology for the construction of preprocessing SNARGs, as well as resulting concrete efficiency improvements. Our contribution is three-fold:

(1) We introduce and study a natural extension of the interactive proof model that considers *algebraically-bounded* provers; this new setting is analogous to the common study of algebraically-bounded "adversaries" in other fields, such as pseudorandomness and randomness extraction. More concretely, in this work we focus on linear (or affine) provers, and provide several constructions of (succinct two-message) *linear-interactive proofs* (LIPs) for NP. Our constructions are based on general transformations applied to both *linear* PCPs (LPCPs) and traditional "unstructured" PCPs.

(2) We give conceptually simple cryptographic transformations from LIPs to preprocessing SNARGs, whose security can be based on different forms of *linear targeted malleability* (implied by previous knowledge assumptions). Our transformations convert arbitrary (two-message) LIPs into designated-verifier SNARGs, and LIPs with degree-bounded verifiers into publicly-verifiable SNARGs. We also extend our methodology to obtain *zero-knowledge* LIPs and SNARGs. Our techniques yield SNARGs *of knowledge* and thus can benefit from known recursive composition and bootstrapping techniques.

(3) Following this methodology, we exhibit several constructions achieving new efficiency features, such as "single-ciphertext preprocessing SNARGs" and improved succinctness-soundness tradeoffs. We also offer a new perspective on existing constructions of preprocessing SNARGs, revealing a direct connection of these to LPCPs and LIPs.

1 Introduction

Interactive proofs [GMR89] are central to modern cryptography and complexity theory. One extensively studied aspect of interactive proofs is their expressibility, culminating with the result $\mathsf{IP} = \mathsf{PSPACE}$ [Sha92]. Another aspect, which is the focus of this work, is that proofs for NP statements can potentially be *much shorter* than an NP witness and be *verified much faster* than the time required for checking the NP witness.

1.1 Background

Succinct Interactive Arguments. In interactive proofs for NP with statistical soundness, significant savings in communication (let alone verification time) are unlikely [BHZ87, GH98, GVW02, Wee05]. If we settle for proof systems with *computational* soundness, known as *argument systems* [BCC88], then significant savings can be made. Using collision-resistant hashes (CRHs) and probabilistically-checkable proofs (PCPs) [BFLS91], Kilian [Kil92] showed a four-message interactive argument for NP where, to prove membership of an instance x in a given NP language L with NP machine M_L, communication and verification time are bounded by $\text{poly}(\lambda + |M_L| + |x| + \log t)$, and the prover's running time is $\text{poly}(\lambda + |M_L| + |x| + t)$. Here, t is the classical NP verification time of M_L for the instance x, λ is a security parameter, and poly is a *universal* polynomial (independent of λ, M_L, x, and t). We call such argument systems *succinct*.

Proof of Knowledge. A natural strengthening of computational soundness is (computational) *proof of knowledge*: it requires that, whenever the verifier is convinced by an efficient prover, not only can we conclude that a valid witness for the theorem *exists*, but also that such a witness can be *extracted efficiently* from the prover. This property is satisfied by most proof system constructions, including the aforementioned one of Kilian [BG08], and is useful in many applications of succinct arguments.

Removing Interaction. Kilian's protocol requires four messages. A challenge, which is of both theoretical and practical interest, is the construction of *non-interactive* succinct arguments. As a first step in this direction, Micali [Mic00] showed how to construct publicly-verifiable *one-message* succinct non-interactive arguments for NP, in the random oracle model, by applying the Fiat-Shamir heuristic [FS87] to Kilian's protocol. In the plain model, one-message solutions are impossible for hard-enough languages (against non-uniform provers), so one usually considers the weaker goal of two-message succinct arguments where the verifier message is generated *independently* of the statement to be proven. Following [GW11], we call such arguments *SNARGs*. More precisely, a SNARG for a language L is a triple of algorithms (G, P, V) where: the generator G, given the security parameter λ, samples a *reference string* σ and a corresponding *verification state* τ (G can be thought to be run during an offline phase, by the verifier, or by someone the verifier trusts); the (honest) prover $P(\sigma, x, w)$ produces a proof π for the statement "$x \in L$" given a witness w; then, $V(\tau, x, \pi)$ verifies the validity of π. Soundness should hold even if x is chosen depending on σ.

Gentry and Wichs [GW11] showed that no SNARG can be proven secure via a black-box reduction to a falsifiable assumption [Nao03]; this may justify using non-standard assumptions to construct SNARGs. (Note that [GW11] rule out SNARGs only for (hard-enough) NP languages. For the weaker goal of verifying deterministic polynomial-time computations in various models, there are beautiful constructions relying on standard assumptions, such as [GKR08, KR09, AIK10, CKV10, GGP10, BGV11, CRR11, CTY11, CMT12, FG12]. We focus on verifying *nondeterministic* polynomial-time computations.)

Extending earlier works [ABOR00, DLN+04, Mie08, DCL08], several works showed how to remove interaction in Kilian's PCP-based protocol and obtain SNARGs of knowledge (*SNARKs*) using *extractable collision-resistant hashing* [BCCT12a, DFH12, GLR11], or construct MIP-based SNARKs using fully-homomorphic encryption *with an extractable homomorphism property* [BC12].

The Preprocessing Model. A notion that is weaker than a SNARK is that of a *preprocessing* SNARK: here, the verifier is allowed to conduct an *expensive* offline phase. More precisely, the generator G takes as an additional input a time bound T, may run in time $\text{poly}(\lambda + T)$ (rather than $\text{poly}(\lambda + \log T)$), and generates σ and τ that can be used, respectively, to prove and verify correctness of computations of length at most T. Bitansky et al. [BCCT12b] showed that SNARKs can always be "algorithmically improved"; in particular, preprocessing SNARKs imply ones *without* preprocessing. (The result of [BCCT12b] crucially relies on the fast verification time and the adaptive proof-of-knowledge property of the SNARK.) Thus, "preprocessing can always be removed" at the expense of only a $\text{poly}(\lambda)$-loss in verification efficiency.

1.2 Motivation

The typical approach to construct succinct arguments (or, more generally, other forms of proof systems with nontrivial efficiency properties) conforms with the following methodology: first, give an information-theoretic construction, using some form of probabilistic checking to verify computations, in a model that enforces certain restrictions on provers (e.g., the PCP model [Kil92, Mic00, BG08, DCL08, BCCT12a, DFH12, GLR11] or other models of probabilistic checking [IKO07, KR08, SBW11, SMBW12, SVP+12, BC12, SBV+12]); next, use cryptographic tools to compile the information-theoretic construction into an argument system (where there are no restrictions on the prover other than it being an efficient algorithm).

Existing constructions of preprocessing SNARKs seem to diverge from this methodology, while at the same time offering several attractive features: such as public verification, proofs consisting of only $O(1)$ encrypted (or encoded) field elements, and verification via arithmetic circuits that are linear in the statement.

Groth [Gro10] and Lipmaa [Lip12] (who builds on Groth's approach) introduced clever techniques for constructing preprocessing SNARKs by leveraging knowledge-of-exponent assumptions [Dam92, HT98, BP04] in bilinear groups. At high level, Groth considered a simple reduction from circuit satisfaction problems to an algebraic satisfaction problem of quadratic equations, and then constructed a set of specific cryptographic tools to succinctly check satisfiability of this problem. Gennaro et al. [GGPR12] made a first step to better separate the "information-theoretic ingredient" from the "cryptographic ingredient" in preprocessing SNARKs. They formulated a new type of algebraic satisfaction problems, called *Quadratic Span Programs* (QSPs), which are expressive enough to allow for much simpler, and more efficient, cryptographic checking, essentially under the same assumptions used by Groth. In particular, they invested significant effort in obtaining an efficient reduction from circuit satisfiability to QSPs.

Comparing the latter to the probabilistic-checking-based approach described above, we note that a reduction to an algebraic satisfaction problem is a typical first step, because such satisfaction problems tend to be more amenable to probabilistic checking. As explained above, cryptographic tools are then usually invoked to enforce the relevant probabilistic-checking model (e.g., the PCP one). The aforementioned works [Gro10, Lip12, GGPR12], on the other hand, seem to somehow skip the probabilistic-checking step, and directly construct specific cryptographic tools for checking satisfiability of the algebraic problem itself. While this discrepancy may not be a problem per se, we believe that understanding it and formulating a clear methodology for the construction of preprocessing SNARKs are problems of great interest. Furthermore, a clear methodology may lead not only to a deeper conceptual understanding, but also to concrete improvements to different features of SNARKs (e.g., communication complexity, verifier complexity, prover complexity, and so on). Thus, we ask:

Is there a general methodology for the construction of preprocessing SNARKs?
Which improvements can it lead to?

1.3   Our Results

We present a general methodology for the construction of preprocessing SNARKs, as well as resulting concrete improvements. Our contribution is three-fold:

- We introduce a natural extension of the interactive proof model that considers *algebraically-bounded* provers. Concretely, we focus on *linear interactive proofs* (LIPs), where both honest and malicious provers are restricted to computing linear (or affine) functions of messages they receive over some finite field or ring. We then provide several (unconditional) constructions of succinct two-message LIPs for NP, obtained by applying simple and general transformations to two variants of PCPs.
- We give cryptographic transformations from (succinct two-message) LIPs to preprocessing SNARKs, based on different forms of *linear targeted malleability*, which can be instantiated based on existing knowledge assumptions. Our transformation is very intuitive: to force a prover to "act linearly" on the verifier message, simply encrypt (or encode) each field or ring element in the verifier message with an encryption scheme that only allows linear homomorphism.
- Following this methodology, we obtain several constructions that exhibit new efficiency features. These include "single-ciphertext preprocessing SNARKs" and improved succinctness-soundness tradeoffs. We also offer a new perspective on existing constructions of preprocessing SNARKs: namely, although existing constructions do not explicitly invoke PCPs, they can be reinterpreted as using *linear PCPs*, i.e., PCPs in which proof oracles (even malicious ones) are restricted to be a linear functions.[1]

We now discuss our results further, starting in Section 1.3 with the information-theoretic constructions of LIPs, followed in Section 1.3 by the cryptographic transformations to preprocessing SNARKs, and concluding in Section 1.3 with the new features we are able to obtain.

---

[1] A stronger notion of linear PCP has been used in other works [IKO07, SBW11, SMBW12, SVP+12, SBV+12] to obtain arguments for NP with nontrivial efficiency properties.

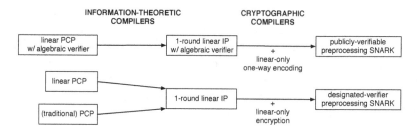

Fig. 1. High-level summary of our transformations

Linear Interactive Proofs. The LIP model modifies the traditional interactive proofs model in a way analogous to the way the common study of algebraically-bounded "adversaries" modifies other settings, such as pseudorandomness [NN90, BV07] and randomness extraction [GR05, DGW09]. In the LIP model both honest and malicious provers are restricted to apply linear (or affine) functions over a finite field $\mathbb{F}$ to messages they receive from the verifier. (The notion can be naturally generalized to apply over rings.) The choice of these linear functions can depend on auxiliary input to the prover (e.g., a witness), but not on the verifier's messages.

With the goal of non-interactive succinct verification in mind, we restrict our attention to (input-oblivious) *two-message* LIPs for boolean circuit satisfiability problems with the following template. To verify the relation $\mathcal{R}_C = \{(x, w) : C(x, w) = 1\}$ where C is a boolean circuit, the LIP verifier V_{LIP} sends to the LIP prover P_{LIP} a message $\mathbf{q}$ that is a vector of field elements, depending on C but not on x; V_{LIP} may also output a verification state $\mathbf{u}$. The LIP prover $P_{\mathsf{LIP}}(x, w)$ applies to $\mathbf{q}$ an affine transformation $\Pi = (\Pi', \boldsymbol{b})$, resulting in *only a constant number* of field elements. The prover's message $\mathbf{a} = \Pi' \cdot \mathbf{q} + \boldsymbol{b}$ can then be quickly verified (e.g., with $O(|x|)$ field operations) by V_{LIP}, and the soundness error is at most $O(1/|\mathbb{F}|)$. From here on, we shall use the term LIP to refer to LIPs that adhere to the above template.

LIP Complexity Measures. Our constructions provide different tradeoffs among several complexity measures of an LIP, which ultimately affect the features of the resulting preprocessing SNARKs. The two most basic complexity measures are the number of field elements sent by the verifier and the number of those sent by the prover. An additional measure that we consider in this work is the *algebraic complexity* of the verifier (when viewed as an $\mathbb{F}$-arithmetic circuit). Specifically, splitting the verifier into a query algorithm Q_{LIP} and a decision algorithm D_{LIP}, we say that it has *degree* (d_Q, d_D) if Q_{LIP} can be computed by a vector of multivariate polynomials of total degree d_Q each in the verifier's randomness, and D_{LIP} by a vector of multivariate polynomials of total degree d_D each in the LIP answers $\mathbf{a}$ and the verification state $\mathbf{u}$. Finally, of course, the running times of the query algorithm, decision algorithm, and prover algorithm are all complexity measures of interest.

As mentioned above, our LIP constructions are obtained by applying general transformations to two types of PCPs. We now describe each of these transformations and the features they achieve. Some of the parameters of the resulting constructions are summarized in Table 1.

LIPs from Linear PCPs. A *linear PCP* (LPCP) of length m is an oracle computing a linear function $\pi: \mathbb{F}^m \to \mathbb{F}$; namely, the answer to each oracle query $q_i \in \mathbb{F}^m$ is $a_i = \langle \pi, q_i \rangle$. Note that, unlike in an LIP where different affine functions, given by a matrix Π and shift b, are applied to a message q, in an LPCP there is one linear function π, which is applied to different queries. (An LPCP with a *single* query can be viewed as a special case of an LIP.) This difference prevents a direct use of an LPCP as an LIP.

Our first transformation converts any (multi-query) LPCP into an LIP with closely related parameters. Concretely, we transform any k-query LPCP of length m over $\mathbb{F}$ into an LIP with verifier message in $\mathbb{F}^{(k+1)m}$, prover message in $\mathbb{F}^{k+1}$, and the same soundness error up to an additive term of $1/|\mathbb{F}|$. The transformation preserves the key properties of the LPCP, including the algebraic complexity of the verifier. Our transformation is quite natural: the verifier sends $q = (q_1, \ldots, q_{k+1})$ where $q_1, \ldots, q_k$ are the LPCP queries and $q_{k+1} = \alpha_1 q_1 + \ldots + \alpha_k q_k$ is a random linear combination of these. The (honest) prover responds with $a_i = \langle \pi, q_i \rangle$, for $i = 1, \ldots, k+1$. To prevent a malicious prover from using inconsistent choices for π, the verifier checks that $a_{k+1} = \alpha_1 a_1 + \ldots + \alpha_k a_k$.

By relying on two different LPCP instantiations, we obtain two corresponding LIP constructions:

- A variant of the Hadamard-based PCP of Arora et al. [ALM+98] (ALMSS), extended to work over an arbitrary finite field $\mathbb{F}$, yields a very simple LPCP with three queries. After applying our transformation, for a circuit C of size s and input length n, the resulting LIP for $\mathcal{R}_C$ has verifier message in $\mathbb{F}^{O(s^2)}$, prover message in $\mathbb{F}^4$, and soundness error $O(1/|\mathbb{F}|)$. When viewed as $\mathbb{F}$-arithmetic circuits, the prover P_{LIP} and query algorithm Q_{LIP} are both of size $O(s^2)$, and the decision algorithm is of size $O(n)$. Furthermore, the degree of $(Q_{\mathsf{LIP}}, D_{\mathsf{LIP}})$ is $(2, 2)$.
- A (strong) quadratic span program (QSP), as defined by Gennaro et al. [GGPR12], directly yields a corresponding LPCP with three queries. For a circuit C of size s and input length n, the resulting LIP for $\mathcal{R}_C$ has verifier message in $\mathbb{F}^{O(s)}$, prover message in $\mathbb{F}^4$, and soundness error $O(s/|\mathbb{F}|)$. When viewed as $\mathbb{F}$-arithmetic circuits, the prover P_{LIP} is of size $\widetilde{O}(s)$, the query algorithm Q_{LIP} is of size $O(s)$, and the decision algorithm is of size $O(n)$. The degree of $(Q_{\mathsf{LIP}}, D_{\mathsf{LIP}})$ is $(O(s), 2)$.

A notable feature of the LIPs obtained above is the very low "online complexity" of verification: in both cases, the decision algorithm is an arithmetic circuit of size $O(n)$. Moreover, all the efficiency features mentioned above apply not only to satisfiability of boolean circuits C, but also to satisfiability of $\mathbb{F}$-arithmetic circuits.

In both the above constructions, the circuit to be verified is first represented as an appropriate algebraic satisfaction problem, and then probabilistic checking machinery is invoked. In the first case, the problem is a system of quadratic equations over $\mathbb{F}$, and, in the second case, it is a (strong) quadratic span program (QSP) over $\mathbb{F}$. These algebraic problems are the very same problems underlying [Gro10, Lip12] and [GGPR12].

As explained earlier, [GGPR12] invested much effort to show an efficient reduction from circuit satisfiability problems to QSPs. Our work does *not* subsume nor simplify the reduction to QSPs of [GGPR12], but instead reveals a simple LPCP to check a QSP, and this LPCP can be plugged into our general transformations. Reducing circuit satisfiability to a system of quadratic equations over $\mathbb{F}$ is much simpler, but generating proofs for the resulting problem is quadratically more expensive. (Concretely, both [Gro10] and [Lip12] require $O(s^2)$ computation already in the preprocessing phase).

LIPs from Traditional PCPs. Our second transformation relies on traditional "unstructured" PCPs. These PCPs are typically more difficult to construct than LPCPs; however, our second transformation has the advantage of requiring the prover to send only a *single* field element. Concretely, our transformation converts a traditional k-query PCP into a 1-query LPCP, over a sufficiently large field. Here the PCP oracle is represented via its truth table, which is assumed to be a binary string of polynomial size (unlike the LPCPs mentioned above, whose truth tables have size that is exponential in the circuit size). The transformation converts any k-query PCP of proof length m and soundness error ε into an LIP, with soundness error $O(\varepsilon)$ over a field of size $2^{O(k)}/\varepsilon$, in which the verifier sends m field elements and receives only a single field element in return. The high-level idea is to use a sparse linear combination of the PCP entries to pack the k answer bits into a single field element. The choice of this linear combination uses additional random noise to ensure that the prover's coefficients are restricted to binary values, and uses easy instances of subset-sum to enable an efficient decoding of the k answer bits.

Taking time complexity to an extreme, we can apply this transformation to the PCPs of Ben-Sasson et al. [BSCGT12] and get LIPs where the prover and verifier complexity are both optimal up to polylog(s) factors, but where the prover sends a single element in a field of size $|\mathbb{F}| = 2^{\lambda \cdot \mathrm{polylog}(s)}$. Taking succinctness to an extreme, we can apply our transformation to PCPs with soundness error $2^{-\lambda}$ and $O(\lambda)$ queries, obtaining an LIP with similar soundness error in which the prover sends a single element in a field of size $|\mathbb{F}| = 2^{\lambda \cdot O(1)}$. For instance, using the query-efficient PCPs of Håstad and Khot [HK05], the field size is only $|\mathbb{F}| = 2^{\lambda \cdot (3+o(1))}$.[2] (Jumping ahead, this means that a field element can be encrypted using a *single, normal-size* ciphertext of homomorphic encryption schemes such as Paillier or Elgamal even when $\lambda = 100$.) On the down side, the

---

[2] In the case of [HK05], we do not obtain an input-oblivious LIP, because the queries in their PCP depend on the input; while it is plausible to conjecture that the queries can be made input-oblivious, we did not check that.

degrees of the LIP verifiers obtained via this transformation are high; we give evidence that this is inherent when starting from "unstructured" PCPs.

Table 1. Summary of our LIP constructions

starting point of LIP construction	# field elements in verifier message	# field elements in prover message	algebraic properties of verifier	field size for $2^{-\lambda}$ knowledge error
Hadamard PCP	$O(s^2)$	4	$(d_Q, d_D) = (2,2)$	$2^\lambda \cdot O(1)$
QSPs of [GGPR12]	$O(s)$	4	$(d_Q, d_D) = (O(s), 2)$	$2^\lambda \cdot O(s)$
PCPs of [BSCGT12]	$\widetilde{O}(s)$	1	none	$2^{\lambda \cdot \mathrm{polylog}(s)}$
PCPs of [HK05]	poly(s)	1	none	$2^{\lambda \cdot (3 + o(1))}$

Honest-Verifier Zero-Knowledge LIPs. We also show how to make the above LIPs zero-knowledge against honest verifiers (HVZK). Looking ahead, using HVZK LIPs in our cryptographic transformations results in preprocessing SNARKs that are zero-knowledge (against malicious verifiers in the CRS model).

For the Hadamard-based LIP, an HVZK variant can be obtained directly with essentially no additional cost. More generally, we show how to transform *any* LPCP where the decision algorithm is of low degree to an HVZK LPCP with the same parameters up to constant factors; this HVZK LPCP can then be plugged into our first transformation to obtain an HVZK LIP. Both of the LPCP constructions mentioned earlier satisfy the requisite degree constraints.

For the second transformation, which applies to traditional PCPs (whose verifiers, as discussed above, must have high degree and thus cannot benefit from our general HVZK transformation), we show that if the PCP is HVZK (see [DFK+92] for efficient constructions), then so is the resulting LIP; in particular, the HVZK LIP answer still consists of a *single* field element.

Proof of Knowledge. In each of the above transformations, we ensure not only soundness for the LIP, but also a proof of knowledge property. Namely, it is possible to efficiently extract from a convincing affine function Π a witness for the underlying statement. The proof of knowledge property is then preserved in the subsequent cryptographic compilations, ultimately allowing to establish the proof of knowledge property for the preprocessing SNARK. As discussed in Section 1.1, proof of knowledge is a very desirable property for preprocessing SNARKs; for instance, it enables to remove the preprocessing phase, as well as to improve the complexity of the prover and verifier, via the result of [BCCT12b].

Preprocessing SNARKs from LIPs. We explain how to use cryptographic tools to transform an LIP into a corresponding preprocessing SNARK. At high level, the challenge is to ensure that an arbitrary (yet computationally-bounded) prover behaves as if it was a linear (or affine) function. The idea, which also implicitly appears in previous constructions, is to use an encryption scheme with targeted malleability [BSW12] for the class of affine functions: namely, an encryption scheme that "only allows affine homomorphic operations" on an encrypted plaintext (and these operations are independent of the underlying plaintexts). Intuitively, the verifier would simply encrypt each field element in the LIP message $\mathbf{q}$, send the resulting ciphertexts to the prover, and have the prover homomorphically evaluate the LIP affine function on the ciphertexts; targeted malleability ensures that malicious provers can only invoke (malicious) affine strategies.

We concretize the above approach in several ways, depending on the properties of the LIP and the exact flavor of targeted malleability; different choices will induce different properties for the resulting preprocessing SNARK. In particular, we identify natural sufficient properties that enable an LIP to be compiled into a *publicly-verifiable* SNARK. We also discuss possible instantiations of the cryptographic tools, based on existing knowledge assumptions. (Recall that, in light of the negative result of [GW11], the use of nonstandard cryptographic assumptions seems to be justified.)

Designated-Verifier Preprocessing SNARKs from Arbitrary LIPs. First, we show that *any* LIP can be compiled into a corresponding *designated-verifier* preprocessing SNARK with similar parameters. (Recall that "designated verifier" means that the verifier needs to maintain a secret verification state.) To do so, we rely on what we call *linear-only* encryption: an additively homomorphic encryption that is (a) semantically-secure, and (b) linear-only. The linear-only property essentially says that, given a public key pk and ciphertexts $\mathsf{Enc}_{\mathsf{pk}}(a_1), \ldots, \mathsf{Enc}_{\mathsf{pk}}(a_m)$, it is infeasible to compute a new ciphertext c' in the image of $\mathsf{Enc}_{\mathsf{pk}}$, except by "knowing" $\beta, \alpha_1, \ldots, \alpha_m$ such that $c' \in \mathsf{Enc}_{\mathsf{pk}}(\beta + \sum_{i=1}^{m} \alpha_i a_i)$. Formally, the property is captured by guaranteeing that, whenever $A(\mathsf{pk}, \mathsf{Enc}_{\mathsf{pk}}(a_1), \ldots, \mathsf{Enc}_{\mathsf{pk}}(a_m))$ produces valid ciphertexts $(c'_1, \ldots, c'_k)$, an efficient extractor E (non-uniformly depending on A) can extract a corresponding affine function Π "explaining" the ciphertexts. As a candidate for such an encryption scheme, we propose variants of Paillier encryption [Pai99] (as also considered in [GGPR12]) and of Elgamal encryption [EG85] (in those cases where the plaintext is guaranteed to belong to a polynomial-size set, so that decryption can be done efficiently). These variants are "sparsified" versions of their standard counterparts; concretely, a ciphertext does not only include $\mathsf{Enc}_{\mathsf{pk}}(a)$, but also $\mathsf{Enc}_{\mathsf{pk}}(\alpha \cdot a)$, for a secret field element α. (This "sparsification" follows a pattern found in many constructions conjectured to satisfy "knowledge-of-exponent" assumptions.) As for Paillier encryption, we have to consider LIPs over the ring $\mathbb{Z}_{\mathsf{pq}}$ (instead of a finite field $\mathbb{F}$); essentially, the same results also hold in this setting (except that soundness is $O(1/\min\{\mathsf{p}, \mathsf{q}\})$ instead of $O(1/|\mathbb{F}|)$).

We also consider a notion of targeted malleability, weaker than linear-only encryption, that is closer to the definition template of Boneh et al. [BSW12]. In such a notion, the extractor is replaced by a simulator. Relying on this weaker variant, we are only able to prove the security of our preprocessing SNARKs against *non-adaptive* choices of statements (and still prove soundness, though not proof of knowledge, if the simulator is allowed to be inefficient). Nonetheless, for natural instantiations, even adaptive security seems likely to hold for our construction, but we do not know how to prove it. One advantage of working with this weaker variant is that it seems to allow for more efficient candidates constructions. Concretely, the linear-only property rules out any encryption scheme where ciphertexts can be sampled obliviously; instead, the weaker notion does not, and thus allows for shorter ciphertexts. For example, we can consider a standard ("non-sparsified") version of Paillier encryption. We will get back to this point in Section 1.3.

Publicly-Verifiable Preprocessing SNARKs from LIPs with Low-Degree Verifiers. Next, we identify properties of LIPs that are sufficient for a transformation to *publicly-verifiable* preprocessing SNARKs. Note that, if we aim for public verifiability, we cannot use semantically-secure encryption to encode the message of the LIP verifier, because we need to "publicly test" (without decryption) certain properties of the plaintext underlying the prover's response. The idea, implicit in previous publicly-verifiable preprocessing SNARK constructions, is to use linear-only encodings (rather than encryption) that do allow such public tests, while still providing certain one-wayness properties. When using such encodings with an LIP, however, it must be the case that the public tests support evaluating the decision algorithm of the LIP and, moreover, the LIP remains secure despite some "leakage" on the queries. We show that LIPs with *low-degree verifiers* (which we call *algebraic* LIPs), combined with appropriate one-way encodings, suffice for this purpose.

More concretely, like [Gro10, Lip12, GGPR12], we consider candidate encodings in bilinear groups under similar knowledge-of-exponent and computational Diffie-Hellman assumptions; for such encoding instantiations, we must start with an LIP where the degree d_D of the decision algorithm D_{LIP} is at most quadratic. (If we had multilinear maps supporting higher-degree polynomials, we could support higher values of d_D.) In addition to $d_D \leq 2$, to ensure security even in the presence of certain one-way leakage, we need the query algorithm Q_{LIP} to be of polynomial degree.

Both of the LIP constructions from LPCPs described in Section 1.3 satisfy these requirements. When combined with the above transformation, these LIP constructions imply new constructions of publicly-verifiable preprocessing SNARKs, one of which can be seen as a simplification of the construction of [Gro10] and the other as a reinterpretation (and slight simplification) of the construction of [GGPR12].

Zero-Knowledge. In all aforementioned transformations to preprocessing SNARKs, if we start with an HVZK LIP (such as those mentioned in Section 1.3) and additionally require a rerandomization property for the linear-only encryption/encoding (which is available in all of the candidate instantiations we consider), we obtain preprocessing SNARKs that are (perfect) zero-knowledge in the CRS model. In addition, for the case of *publicly-verifiable* (perfect) zero-knowledge preprocessing SNARKs, the CRS can be tested, so that (similarly to previous works [Gro10, Lip12, GGPR12]) we also obtain succinct ZAPs.

New Efficiency Features for SNARKs. We obtain the following concrete improvements in communication complexity for preprocessing SNARKs.

"Single-Ciphertext Preprocessing SNARKs". If we combine the LIPs that we obtained from traditional PCPs (where the prover returns only a single field element) with "non-sparsified" Paillier encryption, we obtain (non-adaptive) preprocessing SNARKs that consist of *a single Paillier cipherext*. Moreover, when using the query-efficient PCP from [HK05] as the underlying PCP, even a standard-size Paillier ciphertext (with plaintext group $\mathbb{Z}_{pq}$ where p, q are 512-bit primes) suffices for achieving soundness error $2^{-\lambda}$ with $\lambda = 100$. (For the case of [HK05], due to the queries' dependence on the input, the reference string of the SNARK also depends on the input.) Alternatively, using the sparsified version of Paillier encryption, we can also get security against adaptively-chosen statements with only *two Paillier ciphertexts*.

Towards Optimal Succinctness. A fundamental question about succinct arguments is how low can we push communication complexity. More accurately: what is the optimal tradeoff between communication complexity and soundness? Ideally, we would want succinct arguments that are *optimally succinct*: to achieve $2^{-\Omega(\lambda)}$ soundness against $2^{O(\lambda)}$-bounded provers, the proof length is $O(\lambda)$ bits long.

In existing constructions of succinct arguments, interactive or not, to provide $2^{-\Omega(\lambda)}$ soundness against $2^{O(\lambda)}$-bounded provers, the prover has to communicate $\omega(\lambda)$ bits to the verifier. Concretely, PCP-based (and MIP-based) solutions require $\Omega(\lambda^3)$ bits of communication. This also holds for known preprocessing SNARKs, because previous work and the constructions discussed above are based on bilinear groups or Paillier encryption, both of which suffer from subexponential-time attacks.

If we had a candidate for (linear-only) homomorphic encryption that did not suffer from subexponential-time attacks, our approach could perhaps yield preprocessing SNARKs that are optimally succinct. The only known such candidate is Elgamal encryption (say, in appropriate elliptic curve groups) [PQ12]. However, the problem with using Elgamal decryption in our approach is that it requires, in general, to compute discrete logarithms.

One way to overcome this problem is to ensure that honest proofs are always decrypted to a known polynomial-size set. This can be done by taking the LIP to be over a field $\mathbb{F}_p$ of only polynomial size, and ensuring that any honest proof π has small ℓ_1-norm $\|\pi\|_1$, so that in particular, the prover's answer is taken from a set of size at most $\|\pi\|_1 \cdot p$. For example, in the two LPCP-based constructions described in Section 1.3, this norm is $O(s^2)$ and $O(s)$ respectively for a circuit of size s. This approach, however, has two caveats: the soundness of the underlying LIP is only $1/\text{poly}(\lambda)$ and moreover, the verifier's running time is proportional to s, and not independent of it, as we usually require.

A very interesting related question that may lead to a solution circumventing the aforementioned caveats is whether there exist LIPs where the decision algorithm has *linear* degree. With such an LIP, we would be able to directly use

Elgamal encryption because linear tests on the plaintexts can be carried out "in the exponent", without having to take discrete logarithms.

Finally, a rather generic approach for obtaining "almost-optimal succintness" is to use (linear-only) Elgamal encryption in conjunction with any linear homomorphic encryption scheme (perhaps not having the linear-only property) that is sufficiently secure. Concretely, the verifier sends his LIP message encrypted under both encryption schemes, and then the prover homomorphically evaluates the affine function on both. The additional ciphertext can be efficiently decrypted, and can assist in the decryption of the Elgamal ciphertext. For example, there are encryption schemes based on Ring-LWE [LPR10] that are conjectured to have quasiexponential security; by using these in the approach we just discussed, we can obtain $2^{-\Omega(\lambda)}$ soundness against $2^{O(\lambda)}$-bounded provers with $\widetilde{O}(\lambda)$ bits of communication.

Strong Knowledge and Reusability. Designated-verifier SNARKs typically suffer from a problem known as the *verifier rejection problem*: security is compromised if the prover can learn the verifier's responses to multiple adaptively-chosen statements and proofs. For example, the PCP-based (or MIP-based) SNARKs of [BCCT12a, GLR11, DFH12, BC12] suffer from the verifier rejection problem because a prover can adaptively learn the encrypted PCP (or MIP) queries, by feeding different statements and proofs to the verifier and learning his responses, and since the secrecy of these queries is crucial, security is lost.

Of course, one way to avoid the verifier rejection problem is to generate a new reference string for each statement and proof. Indeed, this is an attractive solution for the aforementioned SNARKs because generating a new reference string is very cheap: it costs $poly(\lambda)$. However, for a designated-verifier *preprocessing* SNARK, generating a new reference string is not cheap at all, and being able to *reuse* the same reference string across an unbounded number of adaptively-chosen statements and proofs is a very desirable property.

A property that is satisfied by all algebraic LIPs , which we call *strong knowledge*, is that such attacks are impossible. Specifically, for such LIPs, every prover either makes the verifier accept with probability 1 or with probability less than $O(poly(\lambda)/|\mathbb{F}|)$. (In the full version of this paper, we also show that traditional "unstructured" PCPs cannot satisfy this property.) Given LIPs with strong knowledge, it seems that designated-verifier SNARKs that have a reusable reference string can be constructed. Formalizing the connection between strong knowledge and reusable reference string actually requires notions of linear-only encryption that are somewhat more delicate than those we have considered so far.

1.4 Structured PCPs In Other Works

Ishai et al. [IKO07] proposed the idea of constructing argument systems with nontrivial efficiency properties by using "structured" PCPs and cryptographic primitives with homomorphic properties, rather than (as in previous approaches) "unstructured" polynomial-size PCPs and collision-resistant hashing. We have shown how to apply this basic approach in order to obtain succinct non-interactive arguments with preprocessing. We now compare our work to other works that have also followed the basic approach of [IKO07].

Strong vs. Weak Linear PCPs. Both in our work and in [IKO07], the notion of a "structured" PCP is taken to be a *linear PCP*. However, the notion of a linear PCP used in our work does not coincide with the one used in [IKO07]. Indeed there are two ways in which one can formalize the intuitive notion of a linear PCP. Specifically:

- A *strong* linear PCP is a PCP in which the honest proof oracle is guaranteed to be a linear function, and soundness is required to hold for *all* (including non-linear) proof oracles.
- A *weak* linear PCP is a PCP in which the honest proof oracle is guaranteed to be a linear function, and soundness is required to hold *only* for linear proof oracles.

In particular, a weak linear PCP assumes an algebraically-bounded prover, while a strong linear PCP does not. While Ishai et al. [IKO07] considered strong linear PCPs, in our work we are interested in studying algebraically-bounded provers, and thus consider weak linear PCPs.

Arguments from Strong Linear PCPs. Ishai et al. [IKO07] constructed a four-message argument system for NP in which the prover-to-verifier communication is short (i.e., an argument with a *laconic* prover [GVW02]) by combining a strong linear PCP and (standard) linear homomorphic encryption; they also showed how to extend their approach to "balance" the communication between the prover and verifier and obtain a $O(1/\varepsilon)$-message argument system for NP with $O(n^\varepsilon)$ communication complexity. Let us briefly compare their work with ours.

First, in this paper we focus on the non-interactive setting, while Ishai et al. focused on the interactive setting. In particular, in light of the negative result of Gentry and Wichs [GW11], this means that the use of non-standard assumptions in our setting (such as linear targeted malleability) may be justified; in contrast, Ishai et al. only relied on the standard semantic security of linear homomorphic encryption (and did not rely on linear targeted malleability properties). Second, we focus on constructing (non-interactive) succinct arguments, while Ishai et al. focus on constructing arguments with a laconic prover. Third, by relying on weak linear PCPs (instead of strong linear PCPs) we do not need to perform (explicitly or implicitly) linearity testing, while Ishai et al. do. Intuitively, this is because we rely on the assumption of linear targeted malleability, which ensures that a prover is algebraically bounded (in fact, in our case, linear); not having to perform proximity testing is crucial for preserving the algebraic properties of a linear PCP (and thus, e.g., obtain public verifiability) and obtaining $O(\mathrm{poly}(\lambda)/|\mathbb{F}|)$ soundness with only a constant number of encrypted/encoded group elements. (Recall that linearity testing only guarantees constant soundness with a constant number of queries.)

Turning to computational efficiency, while their basic protocol does not provide the verifier with any saving in computation, Ishai et al. noted that their protocol actually yields a *batching argument*: namely, an argument in which, in order to simultaneously verify the correct evaluation of ℓ circuits of size S, the verifier may run in time S (i.e., in time S/ℓ per circuit evaluation). In fact, a set of works [SBW11, SMBW12, SVP$^+$12, SBV$^+$12] has improved upon, optimized, and implemented the batching argument of Ishai et al. [IKO07] for the purpose of verifiable delegation of computation.

Finally, [SBV$^+$12] have also observed that QSPs can be used to construct weak linear PCPs; while we compile weak linear PCPs into LIPs, [SBV$^+$12] (as in previous work) compile weak linear PCPs into strong ones. Indeed, note that a weak linear PCP can always be compiled into a corresponding strong one, by letting the verifier additionally perform linearity testing and self-correction; this compilation does not affect proof length, increases query complexity by only a constant multiplicative factor, and guarantees constant soundness.

Remark 1.1. The notions of (strong or linear) PCP discussed above should not be confused with the (unrelated) notion of a *linear PCP of Proximity* (linear PCPP) [BSHLM09, Mei12], which we now recall for the purpose of comparison.

Given a field $\mathbb{F}$, an $\mathbb{F}$-*linear circuit* [Val77] is an $\mathbb{F}$-arithmetic circuit $C \colon \mathbb{F}^h \to \mathbb{F}^\ell$ in which every gate computes an $\mathbb{F}$-linear combination of its inputs; its *kernel*, denoted $\ker(C)$, is the set of all $w \in \mathbb{F}^h$ for which $C(w) = 0^\ell$. A *linear PCPP* for a field $\mathbb{F}$ is an oracle machine V with the following properties: (1) V takes as input an $\mathbb{F}$-linear circuit C and has oracle access to a vector $w \in \mathbb{F}^h$ and an auxiliary vector π of elements in $\mathbb{F}$, (2) if $w \in \ker(C)$ then there exists π so that $V^{w,\pi}(C)$ accepts with probability 1, and (3) if w is far from $\ker(C)$ then $V^{w,\pi}(C)$ rejects with high probability for every π.

Thus, a linear PCPP is a proximity tester for the kernels of linear circuits (which are not universal), while a (strong or weak) linear PCP is a PCP in which the proof oracle is a linear function.

References

[ABOR00]   Aiello, W., Bhatt, S., Ostrovsky, R., Rajagopalan, S.R.: Fast Verification of Any Remote Procedure Call: Short Witness-Indistinguishable One-Round Proofs for NP. In: Welzl, E., Montanari, U., Rolim, J.D.P. (eds.) ICALP 2000. LNCS, vol. 1853, pp. 463–474. Springer, Heidelberg (2000)

[AIK10]   Applebaum, B., Ishai, Y., Kushilevitz, E.: From Secrecy to Soundness: Efficient Verification via Secure Computation. In: Abramsky, S., Gavoille, C., Kirchner, C., Meyer auf der Heide, F., Spirakis, P.G. (eds.) ICALP 2010. LNCS, vol. 6198, pp. 152–163. Springer, Heidelberg (2010)

[ALM$^+$98] Arora, S., Lund, C., Motwani, R., Sudan, M., Szegedy, M.: Proof verification and the hardness of approximation problems. Journal of the ACM 45(3), 501–555 (1998); Preliminary version in FOCS 1992

[BC12]   Bitansky, N., Chiesa, A.: Succinct arguments from multi-prover interactive proofs and their efficiency benefits. In: Safavi-Naini, R. (ed.) CRYPTO 2012. LNCS, vol. 7417, pp. 255–272. Springer, Heidelberg (2012)

[BCC88]   Brassard, G., Chaum, D., Crépeau, C.: Minimum disclosure proofs of knowledge. Journal of Computer and System Sciences 37(2), 156–189 (1988)

[BCCT12a]   Bitansky, N., Canetti, R., Chiesa, A., Tromer, E.: From extractable collision resistance to succinct non-interactive arguments of knowledge, and back again. In: Proceedings of the 3rd Innovations in Theoretical Computer Science Conference (ITCS 2012), pp. 326–349 (2012)

[BCCT12b]   Bitansky, N., Canetti, R., Chiesa, A., Tromer, E.: Recursive composition and bootstrapping for SNARKs and proof-carrying data. Cryptology ePrint Archive, Report 2012/095 (2012)

[BCI⁺12]   Bitansky, N., Chiesa, A., Ishai, Y., Ostrovsky, R., Omer, P.: Succinct non-interactive arguments via linear interactive proofs. Cryptology ePrint Archive, Report 2012 (2012)

[BFLS91]   Babai, L., Fortnow, L., Levin, L.A., Szegedy, M.: Checking computations in polylogarithmic time. In: Proceedings of the 23rd Annual ACM Symposium on Theory of Computing (STOC 1991), pp. 21–32 (1991)

[BG08]   Barak, B., GoldreichUniversal, O.: arguments and their applications. SIAM Journal on Computing 38(5), 1661–1694 (2008); Preliminary version appeared in CCC 2002

[BGV11]   Benabbas, S., Gennaro, R., Vahlis, Y.: Verifiable Delegation of Computation over Large Datasets. In: Rogaway, P. (ed.) CRYPTO 2011. LNCS, vol. 6841, pp. 111–131. Springer, Heidelberg (2011)

[BHZ87]   Boppana, R.B., Håstad, J., Zachos, S.: Does co-NP have short interactive proofs? Information Processing Letters 25(2), 127–132 (1987)

[BP04]   Bellare, M., Palacio, A.: The Knowledge-of-Exponent Assumptions and 3-Round Zero-Knowledge Protocols. In: Franklin, M. (ed.) CRYPTO 2004. LNCS, vol. 3152, pp. 273–289. Springer, Heidelberg (2004)

[BSCGT12]   Ben-Sasson, E., Chiesa, A., Genkin, D., Tromer, E.: On the concrete-efficiency threshold of probabilistically-checkable proofs. Electronic Colloquium on Computational Complexity, TR12-045 (2012)

[BSHLM09]   Ben-Sasson, E., Harsha, P., Lachish, O., Matsliah, A.: Sound 3-Query PCPPs are Long. ACM Transactions on Computation Theory 1(2), 7:1–7:49 (2009); Preliminary version appeared in: Aceto, L., Damgård, I., Goldberg, L.A., Halldórsson, M.M., Ingólfsdóttir, A., Walukiewicz, I. (eds.) ICALP 2008, Part I. LNCS, vol. 5125, pp. 686–697. Springer, Heidelberg (2008)

[BSW12]   Boneh, D., Segev, G., Waters, B.: Targeted malleability: Homomorphic encryption for restricted computations. In: Proceedings of the 3rd Innovations in Theoretical Computer Science Conference (ITCS 1912), pp. 350–366 (2012)

[BV07]   Bogdanov, A., Viola, E.: Pseudorandom bits for polynomials. In: Proceedings of the 48th Annual IEEE Symposium on Foundations of Computer Science (FOCS 2007), pp. 41–51 (2007)

[CKV10]   Chung, K.-M., Kalai, Y., Vadhan, S.: Improved Delegation of Computation Using Fully Homomorphic Encryption. In: Rabin, T. (ed.) CRYPTO 2010. LNCS, vol. 6223, pp. 483–501. Springer, Heidelberg (2010)

[CMT12]   Cormode, G., Mitzenmacher, M., Thaler, J.: Practical verified computation with streaming interactive proofs. In: Proceedings of the 3rd Innovations in Theoretical Computer Science Conference (ITCS 2012), pp. 90–112 (2012)

[CRR11]   Canetti, R., Riva, B., Rothblum, G.N.: Two 1-round protocols for delega-
           tion of computation. Cryptology ePrint Archive, Report 2011/518 (2011)
[CTY11]   Cormode, G., Thaler, J., Yi, K.: Verifying computations with stream-
           ing interactive proofs. Proceedings of the VLDB Endowment 5(1), 25–36
           (2011)
[Dam92]   Damgård, I.B.: Towards Practical Public Key Systems Secure against
           Chosen Ciphertext Attacks. In: Feigenbaum, J. (ed.) CRYPTO 1991.
           LNCS, vol. 576, pp. 445–456. Springer, Heidelberg (1992)
[DCL08]   Di Crescenzo, G., Lipmaa, H.: Succinct NP Proofs from an Extractability
           Assumption. In: Beckmann, A., Dimitracopoulos, C., Löwe, B. (eds.) CiE
           2008. LNCS, vol. 5028, pp. 175–185. Springer, Heidelberg (2008)
[DFH12]   Damgård, I. B., Faust, S., Hazay, C.: Secure Two-Party Computation with
           Low Communication. In: Cramer, R. (ed.) TCC 2012. LNCS, vol. 7194,
           pp. 54–74. Springer, Heidelberg (2012)
[DFK+92]   Dwork, C., Feige, U., Kilian, J., Naor, M., Safra, M.: Low Communication
           2-Prover Zero-Knowledge Proofs for NP. In: Brickell, E.F. (ed.) CRYPTO
           1992. LNCS, vol. 740, pp. 215–227. Springer, Heidelberg (1993)
[DGW09]   Dvir, Z., Gabizon, A., Wigderson, A.: Extractors and rank extractors for
           polynomial sources. Computational Complexity 18(1), 1–58 (2009)
[DLN+04]   Dwork, C., Langberg, M., Naor, M., Nissim, K., Reingold, O.: Succinct
           NP proofs and spooky interactions (December 2004),
           www.openu.ac.il/home/mikel/papers/spooky.ps
[EG85]   El Gamal, T.: A public key cryptosystem and a signature scheme based
           on discrete logarithms. IEEE Transactions on Information Theory 31(4),
           469–472 (1985)
[FG12]   Fiore, D., Gennaro, R.: Publicly verifiable delegation of large polynomials
           and matrix computations, with applications. Cryptology ePrint Archive,
           Report 2012/281 (2012)
[FS87]   Fiat, A., Shamir, A.: How to Prove Yourself: Practical Solutions to Identi-
           fication and Signature Problems. In: Odlyzko, A.M. (ed.) CRYPTO 1986.
           LNCS, vol. 263, pp. 186–194. Springer, Heidelberg (1987)
[GGP10]   Gennaro, R., Gentry, C., Parno, B.: Non-interactive Verifiable Com-
           puting: Outsourcing Computation to Untrusted Workers. In: Rabin, T.
           (ed.) CRYPTO 2010. LNCS, vol. 6223, pp. 465–482. Springer, Heidelberg
           (2010)
[GGPR12]   Gennaro, R., Gentry, C., Parno, B., Raykova, M.: Quadratic span pro-
           grams and succinct NIZKs without PCPs. Cryptology ePrint Archive,
           Report 2012/215 (2012)
[GH98]   Goldreich, O., Håstad, J.: On the complexity of interactive proofs with
           bounded communication. Information Processing Letters 67(4), 205–214
           (1998)
[GKR08]   Goldwasser, S., Kalai, Y.T., Rothblum, G.N.: Delegating computation:
           Interactive proofs for Muggles. In: Proceedings of the 40th Annual ACM
           Symposium on Theory of Computing (STOC 2008), pp. 113–122 (2008)
[GLR11]   Goldwasser, S., Lin, H., Rubinstein, A.: Delegation of computation with-
           out rejection problem from designated verifier CS-proofs. Cryptology
           ePrint Archive, Report 2011/456 (2011)
[GMR89]   Goldwasser, S., Micali, S., Rackoff, C.: The knowledge complexity of inter-
           active proof systems. SIAM Journal on Computing 18(1), 186–208 (1989);
           Preliminary version appeared in STOC 1985

[GR05]   Gabizon, A., Raz, R.: Deterministic extractors for affine sources over large fields. In: Proceedings of the 46th Annual IEEE Symposium on Foundations of Computer Science (FOCS 2005), pp. 407–418 (2005)

[Gro10]   Groth, J.: Short Pairing-Based Non-interactive Zero-Knowledge Arguments. In: Abe, M. (ed.) ASIACRYPT 2010. LNCS, vol. 6477, pp. 321–340. Springer, Heidelberg (2010)

[GVW02]   Goldreich, O., Vadhan, S., Wigderson, A.: On interactive proofs with a laconic prover. Computational Complexity 11(1/2), 1–53 (2002)

[GW11]   Gentry, C., Wichs, D.: Separating succinct non-interactive arguments from all falsifiable assumptions. In: Proceedings of the 43rd Annual ACM Symposium on Theory of Computing (STOC 2011), pp. 99–108 (2011)

[HK05]   Håstad, J., Khot, S.: Query efficient PCPs with perfect completeness. Theory of Computing 1(1), 119–148 (2005)

[HT98]   Hada, S., Tanaka, T.: On the Existence of 3-Round Zero-Knowledge Protocols. In: Krawczyk, H. (ed.) CRYPTO 1998. LNCS, vol. 1462, pp. 408–423. Springer, Heidelberg (1998)

[IKO07]   Ishai, Y., Kushilevitz, E., Ostrovsky, R.: Efficient arguments without short PCPs. In: Proceedings of the Twenty-Second Annual IEEE Conference on Computational Complexity (CCC 2007), pp. 278–291 (2007)

[Kil92]   Kilian, J.: A note on efficient zero-knowledge proofs and arguments. In: Proceedings of the 24th Annual ACM Symposium on Theory of Computing (STOC 1992), pp. 723–732 (1992)

[KR08]   Kalai, Y.T., Raz, R.: Interactive PCP. In: Aceto, L., Damgård, I., Goldberg, L.A., Halldórsson, M.M., Ingólfsdóttir, A., Walukiewicz, I. (eds.) ICALP 2008, Part II. LNCS, vol. 5126, pp. 536–547. Springer, Heidelberg (2008)

[KR09]   Kalai, Y.T., Raz, R.: Probabilistically Checkable Arguments. In: Halevi, S. (ed.) CRYPTO 2009. LNCS, vol. 5677, pp. 143–159. Springer, Heidelberg (2009)

[Lip12]   Lipmaa, H.: Progression-Free Sets and Sublinear Pairing-Based Non-Interactive Zero-Knowledge Arguments. In: Cramer, R. (ed.) TCC 2012. LNCS, vol. 7194, pp. 169–189. Springer, Heidelberg (2012)

[LPR10]   Lyubashevsky, V., Peikert, C., Regev, O.: On Ideal Lattices and Learning with Errors over Rings. In: Gilbert, H. (ed.) EUROCRYPT 2010. LNCS, vol. 6110, pp. 1–23. Springer, Heidelberg (2010)

[Mei12]   Meir, O.: Combinatorial PCPs with short proofs. In: Proceedings of the 26th Annual IEEE Conference on Computational Complexity (CCC 2012) (2012)

[Mic00]   Micali, S.: Computationally sound proofs. SIAM Journal on Computing 30(4), 1253–1298 (2000); Preliminary version appeared in FOCS 1994

[Mie08]   Mie, T.: Polylogarithmic two-round argument systems. Journal of Mathematical Cryptology 2(4), 343–363 (2008)

[Nao03]   Naor, M.: On Cryptographic Assumptions and Challenges. In: Boneh, D. (ed.) CRYPTO 2003. LNCS, vol. 2729, pp. 96–109. Springer, Heidelberg (2003)

[NN90]   Naor, J., Naor, M.: Small-bias probability spaces: efficient constructions and applications. In: Proceedings of the 22nd Annual ACM Symposium on Theory of Computing (STOC 1990), pp. 213–223 (1990)

[Pai99]   Paillier, P.: Public-Key Cryptosystems Based on Composite Degree Residuosity Classes. In: Stern, J. (ed.) EUROCRYPT 1999. LNCS, vol. 1592, pp. 223–238. Springer, Heidelberg (1999)

[PQ12]   Petit, C., Quisquater, J.-J.: On Polynomial Systems Arising from a
              Weil Descent. In: Wang, X., Sako, K. (eds.) ASIACRYPT 2012. LNCS,
              vol. 7658, pp. 451–466. Springer, Heidelberg (2012)

[SBV⁺12]   Setty, S., Braun, B., Vu, V., Blumberg, A.J., Parno, B., Walfish, M.:
              Resolving the conflict between generality and plausibility in verified com-
              putation. Cryptology ePrint Archive, Report 2012/622 (2012)

[SBW11]   Setty, S., Blumberg, A.J., Walfish, M.: Toward practical and uncondi-
              tional verification of remote computations. In: Proceedings of the 13th
              USENIX Conference on Hot Topics in Operating Systems (HotOS 2013),
              p. 29 (2011)

[Sha92]   Shamir, A.: IP = PSPACE. Journal of the ACM 39(4), 869–877 (1992)

[SMBW12]   Setty, S., McPherson, M., Blumberg, A.J., Walfish, M.: Making argument
              systems for outsourced computation practical (sometimes). In: Proceed-
              ings of the 2012 Network and Distributed System Security Symposium
              (NDSS 2012) (2012)

[SVP⁺12]   Setty, S., Vu, V., Panpalia, N., Braun, B., Blumberg, A.J., Walfish, M.:
              Taking proof-based verified computation a few steps closer to practicality.
              In: Proceedings of the 21st USENIX Security Symposium (Security 2012)
              (2012)

[Val77]   Valiant, L.G.: Graph-Theoretic Arguments in Low-Level Complexity. In:
              Gruska, J. (ed.) MFCS 1977. LNCS, vol. 53, pp. 162–176. Springer,
              Heidelberg (1977)

[Wee05]   Wee, H.: On round-efficient argument systems. In: Caires, L., Italiano,
              G.F., Monteiro, L., Palamidessi, C., Yung, M. (eds.) ICALP 2005. LNCS,
              vol. 3580, pp. 140–152. Springer, Heidelberg (2005)

Unprovable Security of Perfect NIZK and Non-interactive Non-malleable Commitments

Rafael Pass*

Cornell University
rafael@cs.cornell.edu

Abstract. We present barriers to provable security of two fundamental (and well-studied) cryptographic primitives *perfect non-interactive zero knowledge (NIZK)*, and *non-malleable commitments*:

- Black-box reductions cannot be used to demonstrate *adaptive* soundness (i.e., that soundness holds even if the statement to be proven is chosen as a function of the common reference string) of any statistical (and thus also perfect) NIZK for $\mathcal{NP}$ based on any "standard" intractability assumptions.
- Black-box reductions cannot be used to demonstrate non-malleability of non-interactive, or even 2-message, commitment schemes based on any "standard" intractability assumptions.

We emphasize that the above separations apply even if the construction of the considered primitives makes a *non-black-box* use of the underlying assumption.

As an independent contribution, we suggest a taxonomy of game-based intractability assumption based on 1) the *security threshold*, 2) the number of *communication rounds* in the security game, 3) the *computational complexity* of the game challenger, 4) the *communication complexity* of the challenger, and 5) the *computational complexity of the security reduction*.

1 Introduction

Modern Cryptography relies on the principle that cryptographic schemes are proven secure based on mathematically precise assumptions; these can be *general*—such as the existence of one-way functions—or *specific*—such as the hardness of factoring products of large primes. The security proof is a *reduction*

---

* Pass is supported in part by a Alfred P. Sloan Fellowship, Microsoft New Faculty Fellowship, NSF Award CNS-1217821, NSF CAREER Award CCF-0746990, NSF Award CCF-1214844, AFOSR YIP Award FA9550-10-1-0093, and DARPA and AFRL under contract FA8750-11-2- 0211. The views and conclusions contained in this document are those of the authors and should not be interpreted as representing the official policies, either expressed or implied, of the Defense Advanced Research Projects Agency or the US Government.

A. Sahai (Ed.): TCC 2013, LNCS 7785, pp. 334–354, 2013.

that transforms any attacker A of the scheme into a machine that breaks the underlying assumption (e.g., inverts an alleged one-way function). This study has been extremely successful, and during the past three decades many cryptographic tasks have been put under rigorous treatment and numerous constructions realizing these tasks have been proposed under a number of well-studied complexity-theoretic hardness assumptions.

We here consider two fundamental cryptographic primitives—*perfect non-interactive zero-knowledge with adaptive statements* and *non-interactive non-malleable commitments*—for which security proofs based on well-studied intractability assumptions have remained elusive.

Perfect NIZK with Adaptive Inputs. A non-interactive zero-knowledge (NIZK) protocol [BFM88] is protocol between two parties, a Prover, and a Verifier, through which the Prover can non-interactively (i.e., by sending a single message π) convince the Verifier of the validity of a statement x, only if x is true (this is called the *soundness* property), while at the same time revealing nothing beyond the fact that x is true (this is called the *zero-knowledge* property). To make such constructs possible both parties are additionally assumed to have access to a "Common Reference String" (CRS) that has been ideally sampled according to some distribution. The original definition of [BFM88] only considered *non-adaptive* notions of soundness and zero-knowledge: Roughly speaking, the (non-adaptive) soundness condition requires that for every false statement $x \notin L$, with high probability over the choice of the CRS, any proof π output by a malicious prover will be rejected by the verifier. The (non-adaptive) zero-knowledge property, on the other hand, requires that for every true statement $x \in L$, the joint distribution consisting of the reference string, and an honestly generated proof, can be reconstructed by a simulator. In both of these properties, the statement x is required to be *fixed* before the reference string is known. Feige, Lapidot and Shamir [FLS90] introduced stronger *adaptive* notions of both soundness and zero-knowledge; roughly speaking, here soundness and zero-knowledge should hold even if the statement x is adversarially chosen *as a function of* the reference string.

As with traditional zero-knowledge protocols, NIZKs come in several flavors: *computational NIZK, statistical NIZK*, and *perfect NIZK*. In the computational notion, the simulator's output is only required to be computationally indistinguishable from an honestly generated view, whereas in the statistical (resp. perfect) variants, it is required to be statistically close (resp identical) to an honestly generated view. Computational NIZK with adaptive zero-knowledge and soundness were constructed early on based on standard cryptographic intractability assumptions [FLS90, BY96], but constructions of statistical and perfect NIZK were elusive.

Only recently, a breakthrough result by Groth, Ostrovsky and Sahai (GOS) [GOS06] provided a construction of a perfect NIZK for $\mathcal{NP}$ based on the hardness of a number theoretic assumption over bilinear groups. Their protocol satisfies the adaptive notion of zero-knowledge; however, it only satisfies the non-adaptive notion of soundness (that is, soundness is no longer guaranteed to hold if the attacker chooses a statement $x \notin L$ as a function of the common reference string). We here focus on whether there exists a perfect NIZK for $\mathcal{NP}$ with both adaptive soundness and zero-knowledge.

A step towards answering this question appears in the work of Abe and Fehr [AF07], which presented a perfect NIZK for $\mathcal{NP}$ with both adaptive soundness and zero-knowledge, using an "knowledge-extractaction" assumption (simular to the "knowledge-of-exponent" assumption of [Dam91]), as opposed to a computational-intractability assumption. Abe and Fehr also demonstrate that certain (arguably natural) types of proof techniques—which they refer to as "direct" black-box reductions—cannot be used to prove adaptive soundness of perfect NIZKs for $\mathcal{NP}$. Their notion of a "direct" proof, however, is quite restrictive (very roughly speaking, it requires the security reduction to "directly embedd" some hard instance into the CRS in a "structure preserving way").[1]

Non-interactive Non-malleable Commitments. Often described as the "digital" analogue of sealed envelopes, commitment schemes enable a *sender* to commit itself to a value while keeping it secret from the *receiver*. This property is called *hiding*. Furthermore, the commitment is *binding*, and thus in a later stage when the commitment is opened, it is guaranteed that the "opening" can yield only a single value determined in the committing stage. For many applications, however, the most basic security guarantees of commitments are not sufficient. For instance, the basic definition of commitments does not rule out an attack where an adversary, upon seeing a commitment to a specific value v, is able to commit to a related value (say, $v - 1$), even though it does not know the actual value of v. This kind of attack might have devastating consequences if the underlying application relies on the *independence* of committed values (e.g., consider a case in which the commitment scheme is used for securely implementing a contract bidding mechanism). In order to address the above concerns, Dolev, Dwork and Naor introduced the concept of *non-malleable commitments* [DDN00]. Loosely speaking, a commitment scheme is said to be non-malleable if it is infeasible for an adversary to "maul" a commitment to a value v into a commitment to a related value $\tilde{v}$.

More precisely, we consider a *man-in-the-middle* (MIM) attacker that participates in two concurrent executions of a commitment scheme Π; in the "left" execution it interacts with an honest committer; in the "right" execution it interacts with an honest receiver. Additionally, we assume that the players have n-bit identities (where n is polynomially related to the security parameter), and that the commitment protocol depends only on the identity of the committer; we sometimes refer to this as the identity of the interaction. Intuitively, Π being non-malleable means that if the identity of the right interaction is different

---

[1] Among other things, the structure preserving property requires that if the "hard instance" being directly embedded in the CRS is true, the CRS is valid, and if the hard instance is false, then the CRS is "invalid". This property can never hold when considering NIZK in the Uniform Reference String model (as every CRS is valid), and as such their result holds vacuosly when considering NIZK in the Uniform Reference String model.

than the identity of the left interaction (i.e., A does not use the same identity as the left committer), the value A commits to on the right does not depend on the value it receives a commitment to on the left; this is formalized by requiring that for any two values v_1, v_2, the value A commits to after receiving left commitments to v_1 or v_2 are indistinguishable.

The first non-malleable commitment protocol was constructed by Dolev, Dwork and Naor [DDN00] in 1991. The security of their protocol relies on the minimal assumption of one-way functions and requires $\Omega(\log n)$ rounds of interaction, where $k \in N$ is the length of party identities. The round-complexity of non-malleable commitments has since been extensively studied (see e.g., [Bar02, PR05b, PR05a, LPV08, LP09, PW10, Wee10]), leading up to constant round protocols based on one-way functions [LP11, Goy11].

The question of whether non-interactive, or even 2-round, non-malleable commitments exist, however, is wide open. (We note that in the Common Reference String model, constructions of non-interactive non-malleable commitments are known [CIO98]; we here focus on constructions in the plain model, without any set-up.) Some initial progress towards this question can be found in [PPV08] where a construction of non-interactive non-malleable commitments based on a new hardness assumption is given; this assumption, however, has a strong non-malleability flavor; as such, it provides little insight into the question of whether non-malleability can be obtained from a "pure" hardness assumptions (such as e.g., the hardness of factoring).

1.1 Our Results

The main result of this paper is showing that Turing (i.e., black-box) reductions cannot be used to base the security of the above-mentioned primitives, on a general class of intractability assumption.

More precisely, following Naor [Nao03] (see also [DOP05, HH09, RV10, Pas11, GW11]), we model an *intractability assumption* as an arbitrary game between a (potentially) unbounded challenger C, and an attacker A. A is said to break the assumption C with respect to the threshold t if it can make C output 1 with probability non-negligibly higher than the threshold t. All traditional cryptographic hardness assumptions (e.g., the hardness of factoring, the hardness of the discrete logarithm problem, the decisional Diffie-Hellman problem etc.) can be modeled as 2-round challengers C with the threshold t being either 0 (in case of the factoring or discrete logarithm problems) or 1/2 (in case of the decisional Diffie-Hellman problem). In all these examples C is polynomial-time; Naor [Nao03] and Gentry and Wichs [GW11] refer to such assumptions as "falsifiable". For generality, we here (following [Pas11]) refer to these as "efficient-challenger" assumptions. More generally, we refer to an assumption where the challenger can be implemented in time (resp. size) $T(\cdot)$ as a "$T(\cdot)$-time (resp. size) challenger assumption" Note that more "esoteric" assumptions such as the "one-more discrete logarithm assumption" [BNPS03, BP02], or "adaptive one-way functions" [PPV08], are not efficient-challenger assumptions, but they are exponential-time challenger assumptions.

Our first result rules out basing statistical (and thus also perfect) NIZK with adaptive soundness on efficient-challenger (a.k.a falsifiable) assumptions.

Theorem 1 (Main Theorem 1—Informally stated). *Assume the existence of (non-uniformly hard) one-way functions. Then there exists an $\mathcal{NP}$-language L such that the following holds. Let Π be a statistical non-interactive adaptively zero-knowledge argument for L. Assume there exists a polynomial-time Turing reduction R such that R^A breaks the efficient-challenger assumption C w.r.t. the threshold t for every A that breaks adaptive soundness of Π. Then C can be broken in polynomial-time with respect to the threshold t.*

We next show that if we additionally assume the existence of sub-exponential one-way functions, and consider the constructions of NIZK for proving *any* polynomial-length (in the security parameter) statement in $\mathcal{NP}$ based on a particular *exponential-time* challenger assumption (C, t), then the assumption can already be broken in polynomial time.

Moving on to non-interactive non-malleable commitments, we show that if non-malleability of a non-interactive, or two message, commitment scheme Π can be based on a efficient-challenger (resp. $T(\cdot)$-size) challenger assumption (C, t) using a polynomial-time (resp. $T(\cdot)$-sized) security reduction, then C can be broken in polynomial-time (resp. by a $\mathrm{poly}(T(\cdot))$-sized circuit).

Theorem 2 (Main Theorem 2—Informally stated). *Let Π be a two-message commitment scheme. Assume there exists a polynomial-time (resp. $T(\cdot)$-size) Turing reduction R such that R^A breaks the efficient-challenger (resp. $T(\cdot)$-size) assumption C w.r.t. the threshold t for every A that breaks non-malleability of Π. Then C can be broken in polynomial-time (resp. by a $\mathrm{poly}(T(\cdot))$-sized circuit) with respect to the threshold t.*

We emphasize that for all the above-mentioned results, the *construction* of the protocols Π need not make use of the underlying assumption in a black-box way; the only restriction we impose is that the security *reduction* is a Turing (i.e., black-box) reduction.

Let us also remark that although we see only superficial similarities between the primitives of non-interactive statistical NIZK and non-interactive non-malleable commitments (e.g., they both refer to non-interactive primitives), the techniques used to prove the above impossibility results have significant overlap.

Uniform v.s. Non-uniform Security Reductions. In this work we focus on ruling out *uniform* security reductions; that is, the security reduction is a Turing machine that gets no advice about the attacker. Nevertheless, a very recent work by Chung, Lin, Mahmoody and Pass [CLMP13] provides techniques for extending certain types of separation results for the uniform setting also to the *non-uniform* setting (where we consider reductions that may receive a polynomial-length advice about the attacker). These technique readily apply to our results, which thus also extend to rule out non-uniform security reductions.

A Taxonomy of Intractability Assumption. As an independent contribution, we slightly generalize the notion of an intractability assumption from [Pas11] (see also [Nao03, DOP05, HH09, RV10, GW11]) and provide an, in our eyes, natural taxonomy of intractability assumptions based on 1) the *security threshold*, 2) the number of *communication rounds* in the security game, 3) the *computational complexity* of the game challenger, 4) the *communication complexity* of the challenger, and 5) the *computational complexity of the security reduction*. Our results, combined with [Pas11, GW11], demonstrate several natural primitives that may be (trivially) based on assumption of a certain type (e.g., the soundness condition of a perfect NIZK can trivially be viewed as a bounded-round assumption), but cannot be based on a different type of assumption (e.g., an assumption where the challenger is efficient). Our results focus on understanding limitations in terms of items 1, 2, 3 and 5; we leave open an exploration of item 4, i.e., the communication complexity of the challenger. More generally, we are optimistic that cryptographic tasks may be classified in this taxonomy, based on whether they can be acheived—even using a *non-black-box construction*—based on a class of assumptions in this taxonomy, but not on another (much like the celebrated taxonomy of Impagliazzo [Imp95] in the context of *black-box constructions*.)

A Note on Random Oracles. Let us point out that in the Random Oracle model [BR93], both of the above-mentioned primitives are easy to construct. Perfect NIZK were construced in [BR93] (by relying on the "Fiat-Shamir heuristic" [FS87]) and non-interactive non-malleable commitments in [Pas03a]. Indeed, many practical protocols rely on the assumption that a "good" hashfunction behaves like a non-interactive non-malleable commitment, and on non-interactive zero-knowledge arguments constructed by applying the "Fiat-Shamir heuristic" [FS87] to a three-message perfect zero-knowledge protocol. Our results show that such commonly used sub-protocols cannot be proven secure based on standard hardness assumptions. Note that these results are incomparable to those of e.g., [CGH04, GK03] on the "uninstantiability of random oracles": the results of [CGH04, GK03] are stronger in the sense that any instantiation of their scheme with a concrete function can actually be *broken*, whereas we just show that the instantiated scheme cannot be *proven secure* using a Turing reduction based on standard assumptions. On the other hand, the separations of [CGH04, GK03] consider "artifical protocols", whereas the protocols we consider are natural (and commonly used in practice).

1.2   Related Separation Results

There is a large literature on separation results between cryptographic primitives/assumptions. We distinguish between two types of results.

Separations for Fully Black-box Constructions. The seminal work of Impagliazzo and Rudich [IR88] provides a framework for proving black-box separations between cryptographic primitives. We highlight that this framework considers so-called "fully-black-box constructions" (see [RTV04] for a taxonomy of various black-box separations); that is, the framework considers both black-box *constructions* (i.e., the higher-level primitive only uses the underlying primitive as a black-box), and black-box *reductions.*

Separations for Black-box Reductions. In recent years, new types of black-box separations have emerged. These types of separation apply even to non-black-box constructions, but still only rule out black-box proofs of security: Pass [Pas06] and Pass, Tseng and Venkitasubramaniam [PTV11] (relying on the works of Brassard [Bra83] and Akavia et al [AGGM06], demonstrating limitations of "NP-hard Cryptography"[2]) demonstrate that under certain (new) complexity theoretic assumptions, various cryptographic task cannot be based on *one-way functions* using a black-box security reduction, even if the protocol uses the one-way function in a non-black-box way. Very recently, two independent works demonstrate similar types of separation bounds, but this time ruling our security reductions to a *general* set of intractability assumptions: Pass [Pas11] demonstrates impossibility of using black-box reductions to prove the security of several primitives (e.g., Schnorr's identification scheme, commitment scheme secure under weak notions of selective opening, Chaum Blind signatures, etc) based on any "bounded-round" intractability assumption (where the challenger uses an a-priori bounded number of rounds, but is otherwise unbounded). Gentry and Wichs [GW11] demonstrate (assuming the existence of strong pseudorandom generators) impossibility of using black-box security reductions to prove soundness of "succinct non-interactive arguments" based on any "falsifiable" assumption (where the challenger is computationally bounded). Both of the above-mentioned work fall into the "meta-reduction" paradigm of Boneh and Venkatesan [BV98], which was earlier used to prove separations for restricted types of reductions (see e.g., [BMV08, HRS09, FS10]). Our separation results are in the vein of these two works, and follows some of their techniques.

1.3 Proof Overview: Perfect NIZK with Adaptive Inputs

Assume there exists a perfect NIZK (P, V) for a hard-on-the average language L; for simplicity, in this proof overview we focus on the case when the reference string is uniformly random (i.e., we consider only NIZK in the so-called Uniform Reference String (URS) Model). Assume further that there exists a Turing reduction R such that R^A breaks the assumption C (with respect to some thresholds t) whenever A breaks adaptive soundness of (P, V). Following the "meta-reduction" paradigm by Boneh and Venkatesan [BV98] (which is used in both [Pas11] and [GW11], and also [AF07]), we want to use R to directly break C.

More precisely (just as in [Pas11, GW11]) we exhibit a particular attacker A to the adaptive soundness of (P, V) and next show how to "emulate" this attacker for R without disturbing R's interaction with C. Whereas in [Pas11]

---

[2] See also the results of Feigenbaum and Fortnow [FF93] and the result of Bogdanov and Trevisan [BT03] that demonstrate limitations of NP-hard cryptography for *restricted* types of reductions.

the emulation was statistically close (and thus the separation could be applied also to unbounded challengers), in [GW11] the emulation was only *computationally indistinguishable*, but this still suffices for convincing C as long as C is computationally efficient. We here follow the approach of [GW11].

Let us turn to describing our attacker A, and next explain how to emulate it. Given a CRS ρ, A first attempts to recover the random coins r used by the simulator S when outputting the CRS ρ; since the simulation is perfect, such a string r exists (but finding r might require super-polynomial time). (Recall that since we are dealing with adaptive zero-knowledge, the zero-knowledge simulator needs to output a reference string ρ before knowing what statement it needs to simulate a proof of.) Next, A samples a false instance $x \notin L$ which is indistinguishable from a true instance (since L is hard-on-the average, this can be done efficiently). Finally, it runs the simulator S on the random coins r to generate ρ, and next feeds it the instance x, and lets π denote the proof output by S (again this final step is efficient).

Let us argue that the proof π of x is accepted by $V(\rho)$. Towards this, consider a hybrid attacker A' that performs exactly the same steps as A, but instead samples a *true* instance $x \in L$. It follows from the ZK property (combined with the completeness property) that V accepts the proofs output by A'. Now, intuitively, it should follow from the hard-on-the-average property of L that V also accepts the proofs output by A. But there is a catch: recall that A is *not efficient*. However, since it is only the first step of A that is inefficient, we can fix the random string r non-uniformly and still use the remaining steps of A and the efficient verifier V to contradict the hard-on-average property of L, as long as we assume that L is hard-on-average for non-uniform polynomial-time. Note that we here rely on the fact that A is allowed to choose the statement x *after* having seen the reference string ρ (i.e., we rely on A breaking *adaptive* soundness)—this is what allows us to non-uniformly choose r as a function of ρ, *before* sampling $x \in L$.

Now given this breaker A, let us see an attacker $\tilde{A}$ that efficiently simulates it (in a computationally indistinguishable way). $\tilde{A}(\rho)$ simply picks a random true statement x together with a witness w, and next runs the honest prover strategy $P(\rho, x, w)$ to produce a proof π (this strategy is similar to the one used in [GW11]). It follows by the ZK property that the output of C when communicating with $\tilde{A}$ and A' are indistinguishable, and we can then apply a similar argument as above (but more complicated) to argue that the output of C when communicating with A' and A are indistinguishable, and thus $R^{\tilde{A}}$ breaks C with roughly the same probability as R^A does.

Dealing with Exponential-time Challenger Assumptions. In case the running-time of the challenger C is super-polynomial in the security parameter k, the above approach seemingly fails: the fact that $\tilde{A}$ generates computationally indistinguishable messages does not suffice to argue that C still accepts in the interaction with $R^{\tilde{A}}$. However, if we assume that the language L is hard-on-the-average for non-uniform subexponential time, then the above approach still works, as long as C is subexponential time; in fact, it rules out also subexponential-time reductions. To deal with also exponential-time challenger assumptions, we proceed as follows. If the *same* assumption C can be used to prove *any* statement in $\mathcal{NP}$ of length polynomial in the security parameter, then if the language L is hard-on-the-average for non-uniform sub-exponential time, it suffices to pick statements x that are sufficiently long (but still of polynomial length) to ensure that $\tilde{A}$ generates messages that are indistinguishable from those sent by $\tilde{A}$, even by C.

1.4   Proof Overview: Non-interactive Non-malleable Commitments

Assume there exists a non-interactive commitment scheme Π; for simplicity of exposition we here focus only on non-interactive, as opposed to two-message, commitments. Assume further that there exists a Turing reduction R such that R^A breaks the assumption C (with respect to some thresholds t) whenever A breaks non-malleability of Π. Recall that an attacker A that breaks non-malleability of Π participates in two interactions—one on the "left" acting as a receiver, and one on the "right" acting as a committer. To be successful A needs to choose a different identity for the left and right interactions, and must commit to a value $\tilde{v}$ which is related to the value v it receives a commitment to on the left. Consider a strong attacker A that chooses identity 0 on the left, and 1 on the right, and upon receiving a commitment c recovers (using brute force) the unique value v that c is a commitment to (if the value is not unique v is set to $\perp$), and next honestly commits to v on the right. Clearly A breaks non-malleability of Π, and thus R^A also breaks C w.r.t. t.

Let us now see how to efficiently emulate A. We simply consider a "trivial" adversary $\tilde{A}$ that picks identity 0 on the left and 1 on the right (just as A), but instead of trying to commit to v on the right, it simply commits to 0 on the right. Now, intuitively, if the reduction R and the challenger C are polynomial-time, then it should follow by the hiding property of Π that $R^{\tilde{A}}$ still breaks C (w.r.t. t). Note, however, that R may be asking its oracle to break non-malleability of multiple commitments, and since A is not efficiently computable, we need to be a bit careful when doing the hybrid argument. Nevertheless, using a careful ordering of the hybrid (and as in the lower bound for statistical NIZK) relying on the *non-uniform* hiding property of Π we can show that $R^{\tilde{A}}$ still breaks C (w.r.t. t).

Note that the above proof idea applies to a very weak notion of "one-sided" non-malleability, where the attacker always uses identity 0 on the left and 1 on the right; Liskov et al [LLM+01] call commitments satisfying this weak notion of non-malleability, *mutually independent*. Interestingly, [LLM+01] shows a construction of a mutually independent commitment based on the existence of subexponentially hard one-way permutations. The idea is simple: Let Com_0 be a commitment scheme that is hard for subexponential time, and let Com_1 be a commitment scheme that can be fully broken in subexponential time. If a MIM upon receiving a commitment of v using Com_0 is able to output a commitment to a related value $\tilde{v}$ using Com_1, then we can violate the hiding of Com_0 by breaking Com_1 using brute-force. This security reduction, however, is super-polynomial (subexponential) time. A natural question is thus whether subexponential time/size reductions may be helpful for constructing "full-fledged" (as opposed to one-sided) non-interactive commitments.[3] We proceed to rule out such reductions (or rather to show that if there exists such a reduction, then the reduction itself must already break the assumption).

Consider a $T(k)$-sized reduction R, where $T(k)$ is super-polynomial, for basing non-malleability on an efficient challenger assumption C[4], and consider the algorithms A and $\tilde{A}$ described above. Note that if R has super-polynomial size, we have no guarantees that $R^{\tilde{A}}$ breaks C even if R^A does; since hiding of Π is only required to hold for polynomial-sized algorithms, $R^{\tilde{A}}$'s success probability may be very different from R^A success probability. But in this case, intuitively, R itself must be able to break the hiding of commitments using identity 1 (recall that A and $\tilde{A}$ use identity 1 on the right).

So, if $R^{\tilde{A}}$ does not already convince C, we can use R (in conjunction with C) to obtain a circuit D that distinguishes, say commitments to 0^k and 1^k using identity 1.[5] We may then use D to construct a man-in-the-middle attacker A' that chooses identity 1 on the *left* and 0 on the right (as opposed to 0 on the left and 1 on the right, as A and $\tilde{A}$ did) to break non-malleability of Π, and finally use R combined with A' to directly break C. So, summarizing, either $R^{\tilde{A}}$ works, or else, we use R in order to construct an MIM A' that breaks non-malleability, and then use $R^{A'}$ to convinve C—in essence, we use R "on itself" to convince C.

1.5 Overview of the Paper

We provide definitions of intractability assumptions and black-box reductions in Section 2; this section also contains our taxonomy of intractability assumptions. We formally state and prove our results about NIZK in Section 3. A formal treatment of our results about non-malleable commitments are found in the full version.

2   Intractability Assumptions and Black-box Reductions

Our definition of an intractability assumption closely follows [Pas11]. Following Naor [Nao03] (see also [DOP05, HH09, RV10]), we model an intractability assumption as an interaction (or game) between a probabilistic machine C—called

---

[3] Indeed, [PW10] rely on intuitions similar to those from mutually independent commitments to construct a "full-fledged" non-malleable commitment, but this construction requires multiple communication rounds.

[4] The assumption that C is an efficient challenger is only made here to simplify exposition; our actual proof also works when C is $T(k)$-sized.

[5] As in the previous proof, to obtain a machine that breaks the hiding of the commitment, we need to rely a polynomial-length non-uniform advice to deal with the above-mentioned inefficiency issue in the hybrid argument; this is why we work with circuits here.

the challenger—and an attacker A. Both parties get as input 1^k where k is the
security parameter. Any such challenger C, together with a threshold function
$t(\cdot)$ intuitively corresponds to the assumption:

> *For every polynomial-time adversary A, there exists a negligible function μ such that for all $k \in N$, the probability that C outputs 1 after interacting with A is bounded by $t(k) + \mu(k)$.*

We say that A *breaks* C *w.r.t* t *with probability* p *on common input* 1^k if
$\Pr\left[\langle A, C\rangle(1^k) = 1\right] \geq t(k) + p$.

If the challenger C is polynomial-time in the length of the messages it receives,
we say that the assumption is *efficient challenger*; such assumptions are referred
to as *falsifiable* assumptions by Naor [Nao03] and Gentry and Wichs [GW11].
More generally, we refer to an assumption as having a $T(\cdot, \cdot)$-time (resp. size)
challenger if C can be implemented in time (resp. size) $T(k, \ell)$ on input the security parameter 1^k, and when receiving messages of length ℓ. (C, t) is an efficient
challenger assumption iff C is a $T(\cdot, \cdot)$-assumption where $T(k, \ell)$ is polynomial
in both k and ℓ. For simplicity, we here consider either poly(k, ℓ)-time (or size)
challengers, or $T(k, \ell) = T(k)$-time (or size) challengers, where the running-time
of the challenger is bounded only as a function of the security parameter.

We can easily model all "traditional" cryptographic assumptions as efficient
challengers C and a threshold t. For instance, the assumption that a particular
function f is (strongly) one-way corresponds to the threshold $t(k) = 0$ and the 2-
round challenger C that on input 1^k pick a random input x of length k, sends $f(x)$
to the attacker, and finally outputs 1 iff the attacker returns an inverse to $f(x)$.
Decisional assumptions (such as, e.g., the decisional Diffie-Hellman problem, or
the assumption that a particular function g is a pseudorandom generator) can
also easily be modelled as 2-round challengers but now we have the threshold
$t(k) = 1/2$. More esoteric assumptions such as the "one-more discrete logarithm
assumption" [BNPS03, BP02], or "adaptive one-way functions" [PPV08], are not
efficient-challenger assumptions; however, they can be modeled as *exponential-
time* challenger assumptions.

We may also consider other restricted types of intractability assumptions. For
instance, [Pas11] considers challengers C that are computationally unbounded,
but for which there exists a polynomial upper bound in the terms of the security parameter k on the number of communications rounds by C; we refer to
these assumptions as *bounded round* intractability assumptions. Another interesting class of assumptions is obtained by further restricting the communication
complexity of C; for instance, we may require that there is a polynomial bound
(again in terms of the security parameter k) on the communication complexity of C; we refer to these assumptions as *bounded-communication intractability
assumption*.

In this work we focus on establishing impossibility results for reductions
from efficient-challenger (just as the results of [GW11]), and more generally
time/size $T(\cdot)$ challenger assumptions where $T(\cdot)$ is a super-polynomial function.
As mentioned, in [Pas11] impossibility results for reductions from bounded-round
assumptions are presented. Since both non-malleability of a protocol, and

adaptive soundness of a NIZK, is a bounded round assumption, we cannot hope to strengthen our result to rule out reductions also from bounded round assumptions. We leave open an exploration of bounded-communication intractability assumptions.

Finally, note that we can capture super-polynomial hardness of an assumption by allowing for super-polynomial-time reductions to the assumption.

A Taxonomy of Intractability Assumption. The above way of modeling assumptions, provides an, in our eyes, natural taxonomy of intractability assumptions based on 1) the *security threshold t*, 2) the number of *communication rounds* used by C, 3) the *computational complexity* of C, 4) the *communication complexity* of C, and 5) the *computational complexity of the security reduction*. We are optimistic that cryptographic tasks may classified in this taxonomy, based on whether they can be acheived—even using a *non-black-box construction*—based on class of assumptions in this taxonomy, but not on another (much like the celebrated taxonomy of Impagliazzo [Imp95] in the context of *black-box constructions.*)

Indeed, as mentioned above, the results of [Pas11, GW11] already yield some results in this direction, separating unbounded-round and bounded-round assumptions [Pas11] and unbounded-challenger and efficient-challenger assumptions [GW11]. The results in this paper further elucidate the landscape; among other things, separating unbounded challenger and exponential-time challenger assumptions, and exponential-time and efficient-challenger assumptions.

An interesting question for future work is obtaining separations for non-black-box constructions for more "structured" types of assumptions (such as the existence of one-way functions, one-way permutations). The results of [Pas06, PTV11] provide a first step in this direction, exhibiting separations from one-way functions for some natural cryptographic primitives, but rely on new complexity-theoretic assumptions.

Black-box Reductions. We consider probabilistic polynomial time Turing reductions—i.e., *black-box reductions*. A black-box reduction refers to a probabilistic polynomial-time oracle algorithm. Roughly speaking, a black-box reduction for basing the security of a primitive P on the hardness of an assumption C, is a probabilistic polynomial-time oracle machine R such that whenever the oracle O "breaks" P with respect to the security parameter k, then R^O "breaks" C with respect to a polynomially related security parameter k' such that k' can be efficiently computed given k. We restrict to the case when $k' = k$. This is without loss of generality: we can always redefine the assumption C so that it on input k acts as if its input actually was k' (since k' can be efficiently computed given k). To formalize this notion, we thus restrict to oracle machines R that on input 1^k always query their oracle on inputs $(1^k, \cdot)$.

Definition 1. *We say that R is a* valid *black-box reduction if R is an oracle machine such that $R(1^k)$ only queries its oracle with inputs of the form $(1^k, y)$, where $y \in \{0, 1\}^*$.*

The reason that we (and as it standard in the literature) restrict R to only query its oracle on a single "input length" k, is that standard cryptographic definitions require ruling out the existence of attackers that break some primitive even for *infinitely many* input lengths; as these inputs lengths can be very sparse, a *black-box* reduction must be successful even if it has access to an attacker that only succeeds on a single input length.[6]

3   Security of Perfect Adaptive NIZK

We recall the traditional definition of non-interactive proofs in the Common Reference String (CRS) model. For generality (and since we are proving a lower bound) we allow the CRS ρ be generated by an arbitrary polynomial-time distribution (as opposed to requiring it to be uniformly random). In the adaptively-sound notion of an non-interactive proof/argument, we require that soundness holds even if the attacker may adaptively pick a statement after having seen the CRS. We here focus only on proofs for languages in $\mathcal{NP}$ where the *prover is efficient* when given an $\mathcal{NP}$-witness.

Definition 2 (Non-Interactive Proofs/Arguments). *A triple of algorithms, $(\mathcal{D}, P, V)$, is called a **non-interactive proof system** (with non-adaptive soundness) for a language L if the algorithm $\mathcal{D}$ is probabilistic polynomial-time, the algorithm V is a deterministic polynomial-time, and P is probabilistic polynomial-time, such that the following two conditions hold:*

- Completeness: *There exists a negligible function μ such for every $x \in L$, every $w \in R_L(x)$ and every $k \in N$,*

$$\Pr\left[\rho \leftarrow \mathcal{D}(1^k, 1^{|x|}); \ \pi \leftarrow P(1^k, x, w, \rho) \ : \ V(1^k, x, \rho, \pi) = 1\right] \geq 1 - \mu(k)$$

- Soundness: *For every algorithm B and every polynomial q, there exists a negligible function μ such that for every $k \in N$ and every $x \notin L$ such that $|x| \leq q(k)$*

$$\Pr\left[\rho \leftarrow \mathcal{D}(1^k, 1^{|x|}); \ \pi' \leftarrow B(1^k, x, \rho) \ : \ V(1^k, x, \rho, \pi') = 1\right] \leq \mu(k)$$

If additionally the following condition holds, then we call $(\mathcal{D}, P, V)$ an adaptively-sound non-interactive proof system:

- Adaptive Soundness: *For every algorithm B and every polynomial q, there exists a negligible function μ such that for every $k \in N, n \in [q(k)]$*

$$\Pr\left[\begin{array}{l}\rho \leftarrow \mathcal{D}(1^k, 1^n); \ (x, \pi') \leftarrow B(1^k, 1^n, \rho) \ : \ V(1^k, x, \rho, \pi') = 1 \\ \wedge |x| = n \wedge x \notin L\end{array}\right] \leq \mu(k)$$

---

[6] For instance, consider an attacker that succeeds only on input lengths $2^c, 2^{2^c}, \ldots$ (and outputs $\bot$ on all other inputs); a black-box reduction that only accesses its oracle on a polynomially related security parameter can only access a single "non-$\bot$" input length

Finally, if the soundness (resp adaptive soundness) condition only holds w.r.t polynomial-time adversaries B, we call $(\mathcal{D}, P, V)$ a non-interactive argument *(resp. an adaptively-sound non-interactive argument))*.

Let us turn to defining zero-knowledge. Also here there is a non-adaptive and an adaptive version. In the *non-adaptive* definition of zero-knowledge from [BFM88], there is a single simulator, which, after seeing the statement to be proven, generates both the CRS and the proof at the same time. In the *adaptive* definition from [FLS90], there are two simulators—the first of which must output a string before seeing any theorems. The stronger adaptive definition guarantees zero-knowledge even when the statement to be proved is chosen as a function of the CRS. We here focus only on adaptive zero-knowledge.

Definition 3 (Non-Interactive Zero-Knowledge). *Let $(\mathcal{D}, P, V)$ be an non-interactive proof system for the language L. We say that $(\mathcal{D}, P, V)$ is (adaptively) zero-knowledge if there exists two probabilistic polynomial-time simulators S_1, S_2 such that for every polynomial q, every non-uniform polynomial-time statement-chosing algorithm $c(\cdot)$ that on input $(1^k, 1^n, \rho)$ outputs a n-bit statement $x \in L$, and every function $w(\cdot)$ such that $w(x) \in R_L(x)$, the following two ensembles are computationally indistinguishable*

$$\left\{ \rho \leftarrow \mathcal{D}(1^k, 1^n); \; x \leftarrow c(1^k, 1^n, \rho); w \leftarrow w(x); \pi \leftarrow P(1^k, x, w, \rho) \; : \; (\rho, x, \pi) \right\}_{k \in N, n \in [q(k)]}$$
$$\left\{ (\rho, \mathsf{aux}) \leftarrow S_1(1^k, 1^n); \; x \leftarrow c(1^k, 1^n, \rho); \pi' \leftarrow S_2(1^k, x, \mathsf{aux}) \; : \; (\rho, x, \pi') \right\}_{k \in N, n \in [q(k)]}$$

We furthermore say that $(\mathcal{D}, P, V)$ is perfect (resp. statistical) zero-knowledge if the above ensembles are identically distributed (resp. statistically close).

We use the (common) acronym "NIZK" to denote a non-interactive zero-knowledge proof or argument. Feige, Lapidot and Shamir and Bellare and Yung [FLS90, BY96] (building on [BFM88]) show that the existence of enhanced trap-door permutations implies that all of $\mathcal{NP}$ has a adaptively-sound NIZK, but the zero-knowledge property is only computational. As mentioned, Groth, Ostrovsky and Sahai [GOS06] show (under some number theoretic assumptions) that all of $\mathcal{NP}$ has a *perfect* NIZK with non-adaptive soundness. More recently, Abe and Fehr [AF07] present a perfect NIZK for $\mathcal{NP}$ also with adaptive soundness but based the soundness property on a "knowledge" assumption (rather than an intractability assumption).

We aim to prove limitations of basing even weak notions of adaptive soundness for perfect or statistical NIZK for $\mathcal{NP}$ on intractability assumptions. Let us first explicitly define what it means to break adaptive soundnessof a NIZK.

Definition 4 (Breaking Adaptive Soundness). *We say that A breaks adaptive soundness of $(\mathcal{D}, P, V)$ w.r.t the language L on input lengths $q(\cdot)$ with probability $\mu(\cdot)$ if for every $k \in N$,*

$$\Pr \left[\begin{array}{l} \rho \leftarrow \mathcal{D}(1^k, 1^{q(k)}); \; (x, \pi') \leftarrow A(1^k, \rho) \; : \; V(1^k, x, \rho, \pi') \wedge |x| \\ = q(k) \wedge x \notin L = 1 \end{array} \right] \geq \mu(k)$$

Let us turn to defining what it means to base adaptive soundness on an intractability assumption C.

Definition 5 (Basing Adaptive Soundness on the Hardness of C). *We say that R is a black-box reduction for basing adaptive soundness of $(\mathcal{D}, P, V)$ w.r.t. L and input lengths q, on the hardness of C w.r.t threshold $t(\cdot)$ if R is a valid black-box reduction and there exists a polynomial $p(\cdot, \cdot)$ such that for every probabilistic machine A that breaks adaptive soundness of $(\mathcal{D}, P, V)$ w.r.t L and inputs lengths $q(\cdot)$ with probability $\mu(\cdot)$, for every $k \in N$, R^A breaks C w.r.t t with probability $p(\mu(k), 1/k)$ on input 1^k.*

Note that we here require that R^O breaks the assumption C on the security parameter k by querying O on the *same* security parameter k. As previously mentioned, a seemingly more general definition would allow R^O to break C on a polynomially-related security parameter k' (which can be efficiently computed given k), but this extra generality does not buy us anything as we can always re-define C to on input k act as its input was k'.

We now have the following theorem:

Theorem 3. *Assume the existence of non-uniformly hard one-way functions. Then there exists an $\mathcal{NP}$-language L such that the following holds. Let $(\mathcal{D}, P, V)$ be a statistical non-interactive adaptively zero-knowledge argument for L, let $q(k)$ be polynomially related to k, and let (C, t) be any efficient-challenger assumption. If there exists a black-box reduction R for basing adaptive soundness of $(\mathcal{D}, P, V)$ w.r.t L and input lengths q on the hardness of C w.r.t threshold t, then there exists a probabilistic polynomial-time machine B and a polynomial $p'(\cdot)$ such that for infinitely many $k \in N$, B breaks C w.r.t t with probability $\frac{1}{p'(k)}$ on input 1^k. If furthermore assuming the existence of one-way functions secure against non-uniform subexponential-time algorithms, the above holds even if C is subexponential-time computable.*

Let us also remark that under the assumption of one-way functions secure against non-uniform subexponential-time algorithms, Theorem 3 directly extends also to a super-polynomial-time (SPS) [Pas03b] relaxation of the notion of a statistical NIZK, where the simulator may run in subexponential time. (Let us also briefly point our a very recent work by Chung, Lui, Mohammad and Pass [CLMP12] that presents barriers to *two-message* SPS zero-knowledge arguments.)

Note that in Theorem 3, we rule out statistical NIZK where adaptive soundness only needs to hold w.r.t. statements of a *particular* (polynomial) length $n = q(k)$.

Our next theorem rules out even *exponential-time* challenger assumptions C if the same assumption C can be used to prove adaptive soundness for *any polynomial length statement* (indeed, as far as we know, in all known NIZK constructions, the underlying intractability assumption depends only on the security parameter for the NIZK but not on the length of the statement to be proven).

Theorem 4. *Assume the existence of one-way functions secure against non-uniform subexponential-time algorithms. Then there exists an $\mathcal{NP}$-language L such that the following holds. Let $(\mathcal{D}, P, V)$ be a statistical non-interactive adaptively zero-knowledge argument for L, and let (C, t) be any exponential-time challenger assumption. If for every polynomial q, there exists a black-box reduction R*

for basing adaptive soundness of $(\mathcal{D}, P, V)$ *w.r.t* L *and the input length* q *on the hardness of* C *w.r.t threshold* t, *then there exists a probabilistic polynomial-time machine* B *and a polynomial* $p'(\cdot)$ *such that for infinitely many* $k \in N$, B *breaks* C *w.r.t* t *with probability* $\frac{1}{p'(k)}$ *on input* 1^k.

Note that Theorem 4 is weaker than Theorem 3 in that we require that the same assumption C can be used to prove any polynomial-length statement, whereas in Theorem 3 we rule out NIZK where the underlying hardness assumption may depend also on the length of the statement proved. This additional restriction is necessary: the assumption that a particular NIZK is adaptively sound for statements of length $q(k) = k$ can clearly be stated as an exponential-time challenger assumption.

We here only prove Theorem 3 and leave Theorem 4 for the full version.

3.1 Proof of Theorem 3

Proof. We here consider only a simplified case when the zero-knowledge property is *perfect* and the distribution sampled by $\mathcal{D}$ is uniform over $\{0,1\}^{poly(k)}$—i.e., we consider perfect NIZK in the so-called "Uniform Reference String" (URS) model. The remainder of the proof of Theorem can be found in the full version. Let $g : \{0,1\}^* \to \{0,1\}^*$ be a length-doubling PRG. Consider the language $L = \{g(s)|s \in \{0,1\}^*\}$. Assume there exists a perfect NIZK $(\mathcal{D}, P, V)$ for L in the URS model, where the reference string is of length $\ell(k)$ given the security parameter k, and assume there exists a black-box reduction R for basing adaptive soundness of $(\mathcal{D}, P, V)$ w.r.t L and input lengths $q(\cdot)$ on the hardness of C w.r.t threshold t. In particular, this means that for every A that breaks the adaptive soundness of $(\mathcal{D}, P, V)$ w.r.t L and input lengths $q(\cdot)$ *with overwhelming probability*, there exists a polynomial $p(\cdot)$ such that for infinitely many $k \in N$, R^A breaks C w.r.t t on common input 1^k with probability $\frac{1}{p(k)}$; i.e., $\Pr\left[\langle R^A, C\rangle(1^k) = 1\right] \geq t(k) + \frac{1}{p(k)}$

To be more concrete, R may feed $A(1^k)$ a reference string ρ, and will get in return a statement $x \in \{0,1\}^{q(k)}$—that with high probability is *false*—and a proof π of x—that with high probability is accepting; R may continue this process all throughout its interaction with C. Note that R is required to work even if A is probabilistic, and on each query made by R, A uses fresh random coins. (As we show in the full version, at the cost of a minor complication, the proof can be adapted to work also if only considering reductions that work as long as the attacker is deterministic.)

Our goal is to present a polynomial-time algorithm that directly breaks C without the help of A. Towards this goal, we will first define a particular *randomized* attacker A, and next present an efficient "simulator" $\tilde{A}$ for A, and show that $R^{\tilde{A}}$ still breaks C (w.r.t t).

Let us start by defining the attacker A. To simplify notation, let us assume that $q(k) = 2k$; it is easy to see that the same proof works as long as $q(k)$ is polynomially related to k. On input 1^k and a reference string ρ, A proceeds as follows:

- A first checks that $|\rho| = \ell(k)$; if not, it simply sends back $\bot$.
- Otherwise, it *uniformly* picks a random tape r such that $S_1(1^k, 1^n)$ outputs ρ, aux on input the random tape r. Since, by our assumption, the simulation is *perfect*, every string $\rho \in \{0,1\}^{\ell(k)}$ is output by $S_1(1^k, 1^n)$ with positive (and the same) probability, so A will succeed in this task. *Note, however, that this step is not necessarily efficient.*
- Next, A uniformly picks a string $x \in \{0,1\}^n$. Note that, except with probability 2^{-k}, $x \notin L$ (there are 2^{2k} strings, and at most 2^k can be in the range of the PRG g).
- Finally, A runs the simulator $S_2(1^k, 1^n, x, \text{aux})$ to produce the proof π, and outputs (x, π).

As noted above, with high probability, the statement x picked by A is false. But it remains to argue that the proof π of x output by A is accepting (for the reference string ρ). For now, let us simply assume that the proof is accepting with high probability, and let instead show how to emulate A in polynomial time (thus proving that C can be broken in polynomial time). We will then return to showing that A indeed is a "good" attacker, producing accepting proofs of false statements.

Consider the "simulator", $\tilde{A}$ that on input 1^k and a reference string ρ, proceeds as follows:

- Just as A, $\tilde{A}$ first check that $|\rho| = \ell(k)$; if not it simply sends back $\bot$.
- Next, $\tilde{A}$ uniformly picks a string $s \in \{0,1\}^k$, and lets $x = g(s)$. Note that by definition $x \in L$.
- Finally, $\tilde{A}$ runs the honest prover algorithm $P(1^k, \rho, x, w)$ to produce the proof π, and outputs (x, π).

The following claim shows that $\tilde{A}$ is a good simulator for A.

Claim 1. *For every efficient C and R, there exists a negligible function μ such that for every $k \in N$, $\left| \Pr\left[\langle R^{\tilde{A}}, C \rangle(1^k) = 1 \right] - \Pr\left[\langle R^A, C \rangle(1^k) = 1 \right] \right| \le \mu(k)$.*

Proof. As a first attempt to proving the claim, consider a hybrid attacker A' that performs exactly the same steps as A, but samples a *true* statement $x \in L$ in exactly the same way as $\tilde{A}$ (but otherwise runs the simulator, just as A). Note that the only difference between A' and $\tilde{A}$ is that A' provides "simulated" proofs (of true statements), whereas $\tilde{A}$ gives honestly generated proofs. Indeed, it follows from the perfect zero-knowledge property that A' perfectly emulates $\tilde{A}$. Furthermore, intuitively, it should follows from the fact that true and false statement are indistinguishable (by the pseudorandomness property of g) that A' correctly emulates A. But there is a problem: although, both C and R are efficient, A and A' are not, so *efficiently* contradicting the pseudorandomness property becomes problematic.

To circumvent this problem, we define a carefully ordered sequence of hybrid experiments, and rely on the fact that it is only the first step of A (and A') that is inefficient. With this careful ordering, the inefficient part of A can be dealt with using *non-uniformity* (and thus we finally contradict the pseudorandomness property of g w.r.t. non-uniform polynomial-time algorithms).

More precisely, assume for contradiction that the claim is false. That is, there exists a polynomial p' such that for infinitely many $k \in N$, $|\Pr\left[\langle R^{\tilde{A}}, C \rangle(1^k) = 1\right] - \Pr\left[\langle R^A, C \rangle(1^k) = 1\right]| \geq \frac{1}{p'(k)}$. Let $m(k)$ be an upper-bound on the number of oracle queries by R on input 1^k, and fix a canonical k for which the above happens. Consider a sequence of hybrid experiments $H_0, \ldots, H_{m(k)}$, where H_i is defined as the output of $C(1^k)$ after communicating with $R(1^k)$ where the first i oracle queries of R are answered by A, and the remaining ones are answered by the efficient $\tilde{A}$. Note that $H_0 = \langle R^{\tilde{A}}, C \rangle(1^k)$ and $H_{m(k)} = \langle R^A, C \rangle(1^k)$. It follows that there exists some j such that $|\Pr\left[H_{j+1} = 1\right] - \Pr\left[H_j = 1\right]| \geq \frac{1}{m(k)p'(k)}$. Define another hybrid H'_j which is identically defined to H_j, but where the statement x in the $j+1$ oracle query is selected as a true statement (just as in H_{j+1}) but we still run the simulation (just as in H_j). It follows directly by the perfect zero-knowledge property of $(\mathcal{D}, P, V)$ that the output of H'_j is identically distributed to the output of H_{j+1}. To reach a contradiction, let us finally argue that the output of H_j is indistinguishable to that of H'_j. Note that up until the point when R receives its $(j+1)$st proof back from the oracle, the two experiments proceed identically the same. Thus, if they are distinguishable, there exists some prefix τ of the execution of H_j[7], up until and including the $j+1$ query of R, such that conditioned on this prefix τ, H_j and H'_j are distinguishable. We may now simply extend τ to also include the string aux picked by A in the $j+1$ query, and conclude that there exists some extension τ' of τ such that even conditioned on τ', H_j and H'_j are distinguishable. But now, note that given the prefix τ', the continuations of H_j and H'_j (conditioned on τ') can be efficiently generated. And since the only difference between them is the choice of the statement x, if they can be distinguished, we violate the pseudorandomness property of g. Note that we here require that g is pseudorandom against non-uniform polynomial time (as we need the non-uniform advice τ'). This concludes the proof of Claim 1.   □

So conclude the proof of the theorem, it only remains to show that A is a good attacker. Note that by the completeness property of $(\mathcal{D}, P, V)$ it holds that, except with negligible probability, $\tilde{A}$ provides accepting proofs. It now follows as a corollary of Claim 1 that except with negligible probability, A also provides accepting proofs: simply let R be the reduction that picks an honestly generated reference string ρ, and upon receiving back the pair (x, π), outputs 1 iff $V(1^k, \rho, x, \pi)$ outputs 1, and let C be the algorithm that simply outputs whatever R outputs.

Ruling out Subexponential-time Challenger Assumptions. If the challenger C is not efficient, then in the above hybrid argument, when switching the statement $x = g(s)$ from being pseudorandom to being truly random, we can no longer

---

[7] Technically, the prefix includes the random tape of C and R and all the answers to the first j queries by R.

directly argue that the probability of C outputting 1 does not change by much. However, if use a PRG secure against subexponential time, then same proof goes through as long as C is subexponential-time computable. $\square$

Acknowledgements. I am extremely grateful to Kai-min Chung and Mohammad Mahmoody for many helpful comments and definitional discussions.

References

[AF07] Abe, M., Fehr, S.: Perfect NIZK with Adaptive Soundness. In: Vadhan, S.P. (ed.) TCC 2007. LNCS, vol. 4392, pp. 118–136. Springer, Heidelberg (2007)

[AGGM06] Akavia, A., Goldreich, O., Goldwasser, S., Moshkovitz, D.: On basing one-way functions on NP-hardness. In: STOC 2006, pp. 701–710 (2006)

[Bar02] Barak, B.: Constant-round coin-tossing with a man in the middle or realizing the shared random string model. In: FOCS 2002: Proceedings of the 43rd Symposium on Foundations of Computer Science, pp. 345–355. IEEE Computer Society, Washington, DC (2002)

[BFM88] Blum, M., Feldman, P., Micali, S.: Non-interactive zero-knowledge and its applications (extended abstract). In: STOC, pp. 103–112 (1988)

[BMV08] Bresson, E., Monnerat, J., Vergnaud, D.: Separation Results on the "One-More" Computational Problems. In: Malkin, T. (ed.) CT-RSA 2008. LNCS, vol. 4964, pp. 71–87. Springer, Heidelberg (2008)

[BNPS03] Bellare, M., Namprempre, C., Pointcheval, D., Semanko, M.: The one-more-rsa-inversion problems and the security of chaum's blind signature scheme. J. Cryptology 16(3), 185–215 (2003)

[BP02] Bellare, M., Palacio, A.: GQ and Schnorr Identification Schemes: Proofs of Security against Impersonation under Active and Concurrent Attacks. In: Yung, M. (ed.) CRYPTO 2002. LNCS, vol. 2442, pp. 162–177. Springer, Heidelberg (2002)

[BR93] Bellare, M., Rogaway, P.: Random oracles are practical: A paradigm for designing efficient protocols. In: ACM Conference on Computer and Communications Security, pp. 62–73 (1993)

[Bra83] Brassard, G.: Relativized cryptography. IEEE Transactions on Information Theory 29(6), 877–893 (1983)

[BT03] Bogdanov, A., Trevisan, L.: On worst-case to average-case reductions for np problems. In: FOCS, pp. 308–317 (2003)

[BV98] Boneh, D., Venkatesan, R.: Breaking RSA May Not Be Equivalent to Factoring. In: Nyberg, K. (ed.) EUROCRYPT 1998. LNCS, vol. 1403, pp. 59–71. Springer, Heidelberg (1998)

[BY96] Bellare, M., Yung, M.: Certifying permutations: Noninteractive zero-knowledge based on any trapdoor permutation. J. Cryptology 9(3), 149–166 (1996)

[CGH04] Canetti, R., Goldreich, O., Halevi, S.: The random oracle methodology, revisited. J. ACM 51(4), 557–594 (2004)

[CIO98] Di Crescenzo, G., Ishai, Y., Ostrovsky, R.: Non-interactive and non-malleable commitment. In: STOC, pp. 141–150 (1998)

[CLMP12] Chung, K.-M., Lui, E., Mahmoody, M., Pass, R.: Unprovable security of two-message zero-knowledge (2012)

[CLMP13] Chung, K.-M., Lin, H., Mahmoody, M., Pass, R.: On the power of non-uniform proof of security. In: ITCS 2013 (2013)

[Dam91] Damgård, I.B.: Towards Practical Public Key Systems Secure against Chosen Ciphertext Attacks. In: Feigenbaum, J. (ed.) CRYPTO 1991. LNCS, vol. 576, pp. 445–456. Springer, Heidelberg (1992)

[DDN00] Dolev, D., Dwork, C., Naor, M.: Nonmalleable cryptography. SIAM Journal on Computing 30(2), 391–437 (2000)

[DOP05] Dodis, Y., Oliveira, R., Pietrzak, K.: On the Generic Insecurity of the Full Domain Hash. In: Shoup, V. (ed.) CRYPTO 2005. LNCS, vol. 3621, pp. 449–466. Springer, Heidelberg (2005)

[FF93] Feigenbaum, J., Fortnow, L.: Random-self-reducibility of complete sets. SIAM Journal on Computing 22(5), 994–1005 (1993)

[FLS90] Feige, U., Lapidot, D., Shamir, A.: Multiple non-interactive zero knowledge proofs based on a single random string. In: FOCS 1990, pp. 308–317 (1990)

[FS87] Fiat, A., Shamir, A.: How to Prove Yourself: Practical Solutions to Identification and Signature Problems. In: Odlyzko, A.M. (ed.) CRYPTO 1986. LNCS, vol. 263, pp. 186–194. Springer, Heidelberg (1987)

[FS10] Fischlin, M., Schröder, D.: On the Impossibility of Three-Move Blind Signature Schemes. In: Gilbert, H. (ed.) EUROCRYPT 2010. LNCS, vol. 6110, pp. 197–215. Springer, Heidelberg (2010)

[GK03] Goldwasser, S., Kalai, Y.T.: On the (in)security of the fiat-shamir paradigm. In: FOCS 2003, pp. 102–111 (2003)

[GOS06] Groth, J., Ostrovsky, R., Sahai, A.: Perfect Non-interactive Zero Knowledge for NP. In: Vaudenay, S. (ed.) EUROCRYPT 2006. LNCS, vol. 4004, pp. 339–358. Springer, Heidelberg (2006)

[Goy11] Goyal, V.: Constant round non-malleable protocols using one way functions. In: STOC, pp. 695–704 (2011)

[GW11] Gentry, C., Wichs, D.: Separating succinct non-interactive arguments from all falsifiable assumptions. In: STOC, pp. 99–108 (2011)

[HH09] Haitner, I., Holenstein, T.: On the (Im)Possibility of Key Dependent Encryption. In: Reingold, O. (ed.) TCC 2009. LNCS, vol. 5444, pp. 202–219. Springer, Heidelberg (2009)

[HRS09] Haitner, I., Rosen, A., Shaltiel, R.: On the (Im)Possibility of Arthur-Merlin Witness Hiding Protocols. In: Reingold, O. (ed.) TCC 2009. LNCS, vol. 5444, pp. 220–237. Springer, Heidelberg (2009)

[Imp95] Impagliazzo, R.: A personal view of average-case complexity. In: Structure in Complexity Theory 1995, pp. 134–147 (1995)

[IR88] Impagliazzo, R., Rudich, S.: Limits on the Provable Consequences of One-Way Permutations. In: Goldwasser, S. (ed.) CRYPTO 1988. LNCS, vol. 403, pp. 8–26. Springer, Heidelberg (1990)

[LLM+01] Liskov, M., Lysyanskaya, A., Micali, S., Reyzin, L., Smith, A.: Mutually Independent Commitments. In: Boyd, C. (ed.) ASIACRYPT 2001. LNCS, vol. 2248, pp. 385–401. Springer, Heidelberg (2001)

[LP09] Lin, H., Pass, R.: Non-malleability amplification. In: STOC 2009, pp. 189–198 (2009)

[LP11] Lin, H., Pass, R.: Constant-round non-malleable commitments from any one-way function. In: STOC, pp. 705–714 (2011)

[LPV08] Lin, H., Pass, R., Venkitasubramaniam, M.: Concurrent Non-malleable Commitments from Any One-Way Function. In: Canetti, R. (ed.) TCC 2008. LNCS, vol. 4948, pp. 571–588. Springer, Heidelberg (2008)

[Nao03]   Naor, M.: On Cryptographic Assumptions and Challenges. In: Boneh, D. (ed.) CRYPTO 2003. LNCS, vol. 2729, pp. 96–109. Springer, Heidelberg (2003)

[Pas03a]   Pass, R.: On Deniability in the Common Reference String and Random Oracle Model. In: Boneh, D. (ed.) CRYPTO 2003. LNCS, vol. 2729, pp. 316–337. Springer, Heidelberg (2003)

[Pas03b]   Pass, R.: Simulation in Quasi-Polynomial Time, and its Application to Protocol Composition. In: Biham, E. (ed.) EUROCRYPT 2003. LNCS, vol. 2656, pp. 160–176. Springer, Heidelberg (2003)

[Pas06]   Pass, R.: Parallel repetition of zero-knowledge proofs and the possibility of basing cryptography on np-hardness. In: IEEE Conference on Computational Complexity, pp. 96–110 (2006)

[Pas11]   Pass, R.: Limits of provable security from standard assumptions. In: STOC, pp. 109–118 (2011)

[PPV08]   Pandey, O., Pass, R., Vaikuntanathan, V.: Adaptive One-Way Functions and Applications. In: Wagner, D. (ed.) CRYPTO 2008. LNCS, vol. 5157, pp. 57–74. Springer, Heidelberg (2008)

[PR05a]   Pass, R., Rosen, A.: Concurrent non-malleable commitments. In: FOCS 2005, pp. 563–572 (2005)

[PR05b]   Pass, R., Rosen, A.: New and improved constructions of non-malleable cryptographic protocols. In: STOC 2005, pp. 533–542 (2005)

[PTV11]   Pass, R., Tseng, W.-L.D., Venkitasubramaniam, M.: Towards Non-Black-Box Lower Bounds in Cryptography. In: Ishai, Y. (ed.) TCC 2011. LNCS, vol. 6597, pp. 579–596. Springer, Heidelberg (2011)

[PW10]   Pass, R., Wee, H.: Constant-Round Non-malleable Commitments from Sub-exponential One-Way Functions. In: Gilbert, H. (ed.) EUROCRYPT 2010. LNCS, vol. 6110, pp. 638–655. Springer, Heidelberg (2010)

[RTV04]   Reingold, O., Trevisan, L., Vadhan, S.P.: Notions of Reducibility between Cryptographic Primitives. In: Naor, M. (ed.) TCC 2004. LNCS, vol. 2951, pp. 1–20. Springer, Heidelberg (2004)

[RV10]   Rothblum, G.N., Vadhan, S.P.: Are pcps inherent in efficient arguments? Computational Complexity 19(2), 265–304 (2010)

[Wee10]   Wee, H.: Black-box, round-efficient secure computation via non-malleability amplification. In: FOCS 2010, pp. 531–540 (2010)

Secure Computation for Big Data

Tal Malkin

Columbia University, New York NY, USA
tal@cs.columbia.edu

Abstract. Secure computation has been a powerful and important research area in cryptography since the first breakthrough results in the 1980s. For many years this area was purely theoretical, as the feasibility results have not been considered even close to practical. Recently, it appears to have turned a corner, with several research efforts showing that secure computation for large classes of functions, and even generic secure computation, has the potential to become truly practical. This shift is brought on by algorithmic advancements and new cryptographic tools, alongside advancements in CPU speed, parallelism, and storage capabilities; it is further motivated by the explosion of new potential application domains for secure computation.

A compelling motivation for making secure computation practical is provided by the burgeoning field of *Big Data*, representing the deluge of data being generated, collected, and stored all around us. Protocols for secure computation on big data can provide critical value for many business, medical, legal, and personal applications. However, conventional approaches to secure computation are inherently insufficient in this setting, where even linear computation can be too prohibitive.

In this talk I discuss challenges and solutions related to secure computation for big data, following two thrusts:

- Overcoming inherent theoretical bounds of (in)efficiency; and
- Satisfying immediate practical needs in a theoretically sound way.

Both goals require the development of new models of secure computation, allowing for theoretically and practically meaningful relaxations of the standard model. In particular, I discuss a few works I have participated in over the last decade, which address the challenge of achieving efficient secure computation for massive data. I also share some experiences from the last few years working on secure search over massive data sets. This research has externally imposed practical constraints, such as strict performance requirements. I focus on my perspective as a theoretical cryptographer and discuss some open cryptographic challenges in this emerging domain.

A. Sahai (Ed.): TCC 2013, LNCS 7785, p. 355, 2013.

Communication Locality
in Secure Multi-party Computation
How to Run Sublinear Algorithms in a Distributed Setting

Elette Boyle[1], Shafi Goldwasser[2], and Stefano Tessaro[1,*]

[1] MIT CSAIL
eboyle@mit.edu, tessaro@csail.mit.edu
[2] MIT CSAIL and Weizmann
shafi@theory.csail.mit.edu

Abstract. We devise multi-party computation protocols for general secure function evaluation with the property that *each party is only required to communicate with a small number of dynamically chosen parties*. More explicitly, starting with n parties connected via a complete and synchronous network, our protocol requires each party to send messages to (and process messages from) at most $\mathsf{polylog}(n)$ other parties using $\mathsf{polylog}(n)$ rounds. It achieves secure computation of any polynomial-time computable randomized function f under cryptographic assumptions, and tolerates up to $(\frac{1}{3} - \epsilon) \cdot n$ statically scheduled Byzantine faults.

We then focus on the particularly interesting setting in which the function to be computed is a *sublinear algorithm*: An evaluation of f depends on the inputs of at most $q = o(n)$ of the parties, where the identity of these parties can be chosen randomly and possibly adaptively. Typically, $q = \mathsf{polylog}(n)$. While the sublinear query complexity of f makes it possible in principle to dramatically reduce the *communication complexity* of our general protocol, the challenge is to achieve this while maintaining security: in particular, while keeping the *identities* of the selected inputs completely hidden. We solve this challenge, and we provide a protocol for securely computing such sublinear f that runs in $\mathsf{polylog}(n) + O(q)$ rounds, has each party communicating with at most $q \cdot \mathsf{polylog}(n)$ other parties, and supports *message sizes* $\mathsf{polylog}(n) \cdot (\ell + n)$, where ℓ is the parties' input size.

Our optimized protocols rely on a multi-signature scheme, fully homomorphic encryption (FHE), and simulation-sound adaptive NIZK arguments. However, we remark that multi-signatures and FHE are used to obtain our bounds on message size and round complexity. Assuming only standard digital signatures and public-key encryption, one can still obtain the property that each party only communicates with $\mathsf{polylog}(n)$ other parties. We emphasize that the scheduling of faults can depend on the initial PKI setup of digital signatures and the NIZK parameters.

* This research was initiated and done in part while the authors were visiting the Isaac Newton Institute for Mathematical Sciences in Cambridge, UK.

A. Sahai (Ed.): TCC 2013, LNCS 7785, pp. 356–376, 2013.

1   Introduction

Multiparty computation (MPC) protocols for secure function evaluation (SFE) witnessed a significant body of work within the cryptography research community in the last 30 years.

These days, an emerging area of potential applications for secure MPC is to address privacy concerns in data aggregation and analysis, to match the explosive current growth of available data. Large data sets, such as medical data, transaction data, the web and web access logs, or network traffic data, are now in abundance. Much of the data is stored or made accessible in a distributed fashion. This necessitated the development of efficient distributed protocols to compute over such data. In order to address the privacy concerns associated with such protocols, cryptographic techniques such as MPC for SFE where *data items are equated with servers* can be utilized to prevent unnecessary leakage of information.

However, before MPC can be effectively used to address today's challenges, we need protocols whose efficiency and communication requirements scale practically to the modern regime of massive data. An important metric that has great effect on feasibility but has attracted surprisingly little attention thus far is the *number of other parties* that each party must communicate with during the course of the protocol. We refer to this as the communication *locality*. Indeed, if we consider a setting where potentially hundreds of thousands, or even millions of parties are participating in a computation over the internet, requiring coordination between each pair of parties will be unrealistic.

In this work, we work to optimize the communication locality for general secure function evaluation on data which is held distributively among n parties. These parties are connected via a complete synchronous communication network, of whom $(\frac{1}{3} - \epsilon)n$ may be statically scheduled, computationally bounded Byzantine faults. We do *not* assume the existence of broadcast channels.

We also focus on a particularly interesting setting in which the randomized function f to be computed is a *sublinear algorithm*: namely, a random execution of $f(x_1, ..., x_n)$ depends on at most $q = o(n)$ of the inputs x_i. We consider both non-adaptive and adaptive sublinear algorithms, in which the identities of the selected inputs may depend on the randomness r of execution, or on both r and the values of x_i queried thus far. Sublinear algorithms play an important role in efficiently testing properties and trends when computing on large data sets. The sublinear query complexity makes it possible in principle to dramatically reduce the *amount* of information that needs to be communicated within the protocol. However, the challenge is to achieve this while maintaining security—in particular, keeping the identities of the selected inputs completely hidden.

Straightforward application of known general MPC techniques results in protocols where each party sends and receives messages from all n parties, and where the overall communication complexity is $O(n^2)$, regardless of the complexity of the function to be computed. We remark that this is obviously the case for the classical general SFE protocols (beginning with [26,14,5]) in which every party first secret shares its input among all other parties (and exchanges messages between all n parties at the evaluation of every gate of the circuit of the function computed). Furthermore, although much progress was made in the MPC literature of the last two decades to make MPC protocols more efficient and suitable for practice, this is still the case both in works on scalable MPC [17,20,19,18] and more recent works utilizing the existence of fully homomorphic encryption schemes [35,3] for MPC. The latter achieve communication complexity that is independent of the circuit size, but not of the number of parties when broadcast channels are not available.

A recent notable exception to the need of each party to communicate with all other parties is the beautiful work of King, Saia, Sanwalani and Vee [34] on what they call scalable protocols for a relaxation of the Byzantine agreement and leader election problems. Their protocols require each honest party to send and process a $\mathsf{polylog}(n)$ number of bits. On the down side, the protocols of [34] do not guarantee that all honest parties will achieve agreement, but only guarantee that $1 - o(1)$ fraction of the good processors reach agreement—achieving only so-called *almost everywhere agreement*. In another work of King et al [32], it is shown how using $\tilde{O}(\sqrt{n})$ communication, full Byzantine agreement can be achieved. The technique of almost-everywhere leader election of [34] will be the technical starting point of our work.

1.1   Our Results

We provide multiparty computation protocols for general secure function evaluation with communication locality that is *polylogarithmic* in the number of parties. That is, starting with n parties connected via a complete and synchronous network, we prove the following main theorem:

Theorem 1. Let f be any polynomial-time randomized functionality on n inputs. Then, for every constant $\epsilon > 0$, there exists an n-party protocol Π_f that securely computes a random evaluation of f, tolerating $t < (1/3 - \epsilon)n$ statically scheduled active corruptions, with the following complexities:
(1) Communication locality: $\mathsf{polylog}(n)$.
(2) Round complexity: $\mathsf{polylog}(n)$.
(3) Message sizes: $O(n \cdot l \cdot \mathsf{polylog}(n))$, where $l = |x_i|$ is the individual input size.
(4) The protocol uses a setup consisting of $n \cdot \mathsf{polylog}(n)$ signing keys of size $\mathsf{polylog}(n)$, as well as a $\mathsf{polylog}(n)$-long additional common random string (CRS).[1]

The protocol assumes a secure multisignature scheme, a fully homomorphic encryption (FHE) scheme, simulation-sound NIZK arguments, as well as pseudorandom generators.

Assuming *only* a standard signature scheme and semantically secure public-key encryption, and setup as in (4), there exists a protocol for securely computing f with $\mathsf{polylog}(n)$ communication locality.

---

[1] Adversarial corruptions may be made as a function of this setup information.

Multisignatures [39,36] are digital signatures which enable the verification that a large number of signers have signed a given message, where the number of signers is not fixed in advance. The size of a multisignature is independent of the number of signers, but in order to determine their identities one must attach identifying information to the signature. Standard instantiations of such schemes exist under the bilinear computational Diffie-Hellman assumption [44,36].

The use of multisignatures rather than standard digital signatures enables us to bound the *size* of the messages sent in the protocol. Further, the use of FHE enables us to bound the *number* of messages sent, rather than depend on the time complexity of the function f to be computed and polynomially on the input size. However, we can obtain the most important feature of our complexity, the need of every party to send messages to (and process messages from) only polylog(n) parties in the network, solely under the assumption that digital signatures and public-key encryption exist.

In addition, we show how to convert an arbitrary sublinear algorithm with query complexity $q = $ polylog(n) into a multi-party protocol to evaluate a randomized run of the algorithm with polylog(n) communication locality and rounds, and where the *total communication complexity* sent by each party is only $O(\text{polylog}(n) \cdot (l + n))$ for $l = |x|$ an individual input size. We prove that participating in the MPC reveals no information beyond the output of the sublinear algorithm execution using a standard Ideal/Real simulation-based security definition.

For underlying query complexity q, our second main theorem is as follows:

Theorem 2. Let SLA be a sublinear algorithm which retrieves $q = q(n) = o(n)$ different inputs. Then, for all constant $\epsilon > 0$, there exists an n-party protocol Π_{SLA} that securely computes an execution of the sublinear algorithm SLA tolerating $t < (1/3 - \epsilon)n$ statically scheduled active corruptions, with the following complexities, where l is the size of the individual inputs held by the parties:

(1) Communication locality: $q \cdot$ polylog(n).
(2) Round complexity: $O(q) + $ polylog(n).
(3) Message sizes: $O((l + n) \cdot \text{polylog}(n))$.
(4) The protocol uses a setup consisting of $n \cdot$ polylog(n) signing keys of size polylog(n), as well as a polylog(n)-long additional CRS.

    The protocol assumes a secure multisignature scheme, an FHE scheme, simulation-sound NIZK arguments, and pseudorandom generators.

Techniques. We first describe how to achieve our second result, for the case when f is a sublinear algorithm. This setting requires additional techniques in order to attain the communication complexity gains. After this, we describe the appropriate modifications required to maintain polylog(n) communication locality for general functions f.

There are three main technical components to our protocol for sublinear algorithms. The first is to set up a committee structure constituted of a *supreme committee* C and n *input committees* $C_1, ..C_n$. These committees will all be of size polylog(n) and with high probability have a 2/3 majority of honest parties. Each committee C_i will (to begin with) hold shares of the input x_i whereas the role of the supreme committee will essentially be to govern the running of the protocol. A major challenge is to ensure that all parties in the network know the identity of parties in all the committees. The starting point to address this challenge is to utilize the communication-efficient *almost-everywhere* leader election protocol of [34]. We remark that [34] achieves better total communication complexity of polylog(n) bits and offers unconditional results, but only achieves an almost-everywhere agreement: there may be a $o(1)$ fraction of honest parties who will not reach agreement and, in our context, will not know the makeup of the committees. The main idea to remedy this situation is to add an iterated certification procedure using multi-signatures to the protocol of [34], while keeping the complexity of only polylog(n) messages sent and processed by any honest party. In the process, however, we move from unconditional to computational security and our message sizes grow, as they will be signed by multi-signatures. Whereas the size of the multi-signatures depends only on the security parameter, the messages should indicate the identities of the signers – this is cause for the increased size of messages.

The second component is to implement a randomly chosen secret reshuffling ρ of parties' inputs within the complexity restrictions we have alloted. At the end of the shuffling, committee $C_{\rho(i)}$ will hold the input of committee C_i. Informally, this will address the major privacy issue in executing a sublinear algorithm in a distributed setting, which is to ensure that the adversary does not learn which of the n inputs are used by the algorithm. We implement the shuffling via distributed evaluation of a switching network with very good mixing properties under random switching, all under central coordination by the supreme committee. We assume that a fixed switching network over n wires is given, with depth $d = $ polylog(n), and is known to everyone.

The third component, once the inputs will be thus permuted, is to actually run the execution of the sublinear algorithm. For lack of space, let us illustrate how this is done for the sub class of non-adaptive sublinear algorithms. This is a class of algorithms that proceed in two steps:

- First, a random subset I of size q of the indices $1, ..., n$ is selected.
- Second, an arbitrary polynomial-time algorithm is computed on inputs x_j for $j \in I$.

To run an execution of such an algorithm, the supreme committee: first selects a random and secret $q = $ polylog(n) size subset I of the inputs; and second, runs a secure function evaluation (SFE) protocol on the set of inputs in $\rho(I)$ with the assistance of parties in committees C_j for $j \in \rho(I)$. In the adaptive case, one essentially assumes queries are asked in sequence, and executes in a similar way the sublinear algorithm query after query, contacting committee $\rho(i)$ for each query i, instead of parallelizing the computation for all inputs from I. The price to pay is an additive factor q in the number of rounds of the protocol. However, note that in the common case $q = $ polylog(n), this does not affect the overall asymptotic complexity.

Now, consider the case when f is a general polynomial-time function, whose evaluation may depend on a large number of its inputs. In this case, we can skip the aforementioned shuffling procedure, and instead simply have *each party P_i* send his (encrypted) input up to the supreme committee C to run the evaluation of f. That is, each P_i gives an encryption of his input to the members of his input committee C_i, and each party in C_i sends the ciphertext up to C via a communication tree that is constructed during the process of electing committees (in Step 1). Then, the members of the supreme committee C (who collectively have the ability to decrypt ciphertexts) are able to evaluate the functionality f directly via a standard SFE.

Remarks. A few remarks are in order.

- *Flooding by faulty parties.* There is no limit (nor can there be) on how many messages are sent by faulty parties to honest parties, as is the case in the works mentioned above. To address this issue in [34,32,33,21], for example, it is (implicitly) assumed that the authenticated channels between parties can "recognize" messages from unwarranted senders which should not be processed and automatically drop them, whereas we will use a digital signature verification procedure to recognize and drop these messages which should not be processed.
- *Security definition for sublinear algorithms.* The security definition we achieve is the standard definition of secure multiparty computation (MPC). Informally, the parties will receive the output corresponding to a random execution of the sublinear algorithm but nothing else. Formally, we use the ideal/real simulation-based type definition. We note that in works of [29,23,31] on MPC for approximation algorithms for functions f, privacy is defined so as to mean that no information is revealed beyond the *exact* value of f, rather than beyond the approximate value of f computed by the protocol. One may ask for a similar privacy definition for sublinear algorithms, which are an approximation algorithm of sorts. However, this is an orthogonal concern to the one we address in this work.

1.2   Further Related Work

Work on MPC in partially connected networks, such as the recent work of Chandran, Garay and Ostrovsky [12,13], shows MPC protocols for network graphs of degree polylog(n) (thus each party is connected to no more than polylog(n) parties). They can only show how to achieve MPC amongst all but $o(n)$ honest parties. Indeed, in this setting it is unavoidable for some of the honest parties to be cut out from every other honest party. In contrast, in the present work, we assume that although the n parties are connected via a complete network and potentially any party can communicate with any other party, our protocols require each honest party to communicate with only at most polylog(n) parties whose identity is only determined during the course of the protocol execution.

The problem of sublinear communication in MPC has also been considered in the realm of *two-party* protocols, e.g. by [40] who provide communication-preserving protocols for secure function evaluation (but which require super-polynomial computational effort), and in a recent collection of works including [28] which achieve amortized sublinear time protocols, and the work of [31] which show polylogarithmic communication for specific functions.

An interesting point of comparison to our result is the work of Halevi, Lindell and Pinkas [30]. They design computationally secure MPC protocols for n parties in which one party is singled out as a server and all other parties communicate directly with the server in sequence (in one round of communication each). However, it is easy to see that protocols in this model can only provide a limited privacy guarantee: for example, as pointed out by the authors, if the last i parties collude with the server then they can always evaluate the function on as many input settings as they wish for variable positions $n - i, n - i + 1, \ldots, n$. No such limitations exist in our model.

In a recent and independent work to the current paper, King et al [21] extends [32] to show a protocol for unconditionally secure SFE for general f that requires every party to send at most $O(\frac{m}{n} + \sqrt{n})$ messages, where m is the size of a circuit representation of f. A cursory comparison to our work shows that in [21] each party sends messages to $\Omega(\sqrt{n})$ other parties.

Finally, let us point out that our approach to anonymize access patterns to parties is similar in spirit to problems arising in the context of Oblivious RAM [27], and uses similar ideas to the obfuscated secret shuffling protocols of Adida and Wilkström [2].

2   Preliminaries

We recall first the definitions of standard basic tools used throughout the paper, and then move to some important results on shuffling and our notation for sublinear algorithms.

2.1   Basic Tools

Non-interactive Zero Knowledge. We make use of a standard non-interactive zero knowledge (NIZK) argument system (Gen, Prove, Verify, $\mathcal{S} = (\mathcal{S}^{\mathsf{crs}}, \mathcal{S}^{\mathsf{Proof}})$) with unbounded adaptive simulation soundness, as defined in [22,6,7]. That is, soundness of the argument system holds even against PPT adversaries who are given access to an oracle that produces *simulated* proofs of (potentially false) statements. For a formal definition, we refer the reader to, e.g., [22,6,7].

Theorem 1. *[42] There exists an unbounded simulation-sound NIZK proof system for any* NP *language L, based on trapdoor one-way permutations, with proof length* $\mathsf{poly}(|x|, |w|)$, *where x is the statement and w is the witness.*

Fully Homomorphic Encryption. We make use of a fully homomorphic public-key encryption (FHE) scheme (Gen, Enc, Dec, Eval) as defined in, e.g., [25]. For our purposes, we require an FHE scheme with the additional property of *certifiability*. A certifiable FHE scheme is associated with a set R of "good" encryption randomness such that (repeated execution of) the Eval algorithm and the decryption algorithm Dec are correct on ciphertexts derived from those using randomness from R to encrypt. A formal definition follows.

Definition 1. *For a given subset $R \subseteq \{0,1\}^{poly(k)}$ of possible randomness values, we (recursively) define the class of R-evolved ciphertexts with respect to a public key pk to include all ciphertexts c of the form:*

- *$c = Enc_{pk}(m; r)$ for some m in the valid message space and randomness $r \in R$, and*
- *$c = Eval_{pk}((c_i)_{i \in I}, f)$ for some poly(k)-size collection of R-evolved ciphertexts $(c_i)_{i \in I}$ and some poly-size circuit f.*

Definition 2. *A FHE scheme is said to be* certifiable *if there exists a subset $R \subseteq \{0,1\}^{poly(k)}$ of possible randomness values for which the following hold.*

1. $\Pr[r \in R] = 1 - negl(k)$, *where the probability is over uniformly sampled $r \leftarrow \{0,1\}^{poly(k)}$.*
2. *There exists an efficient algorithm $\mathcal{A}_R$ such that $\mathcal{A}_R(r) = 1$ for $r \in R$ and 0 otherwise.*
3. *With overwhelming probability, Gen outputs a key pair (pk, sk) such that $Dec_{sk}(Eval_{pk}((c_i)_{1 \leq i \leq n}, f)) = f((x_i)_{1 \leq i \leq n})$ for all poly-sized circuits f and for all R-evolved ciphertexts $c_1, \ldots, c_n$, where $x_i = Dec_{sk}(c_i)$.*

Certifiable FHE schemes have been shown to exist based on the Learning with Errors assumption, together with a circular security assumption (e.g., Brakerski and Vaikuntanathan [10] and Brakerski, Gentry, and Vaikuntanathan [9]). For the readers who are familiar with these constructions, the set of "good" certifying randomness R corresponds to encrypting with sufficiently "small noise."

Multisignatures. A multisignature scheme is a digital signature scheme with the ability to combine signatures from multiple signers on the same message into a single short object (a *multisignature*).[2] The first formal treatment of multisignatures was given by Micali, Ohta, and Reyzin [39].

Definition 3. *A multisignature* scheme *is a tuple of PPT algorithms* (Gen, Sign, Verify, Combine, MultiVerify), *where syntactically* (Gen, Sign, Verify) *are as in a standard signature scheme, and* Combine, MultiVerify *are as follows:*

Combine($\{\{vk_j\}_{j \in J_i}, \sigma_i\}_{i=1}^{\ell}, m$): *For disjoint $J_1, \ldots, J_\ell \subseteq [n]$, takes as input a collection of signatures (or multisignatures) σ_i with respect to verification keys vk_j for $j \in J_i$, and outputs a combined multisignature, with respect to the union of verification keys.*

---

[2] Note that multisignatures are a special case of *aggregate* signatures [8], which in contrast allow combining signatures from n different parties on n *different* messages.

MultiVerify($\{\mathsf{vk}_i\}_{i \in I}, m, \sigma$): *Verifies multisignature σ with respect to the collection of verification keys $\{\mathsf{vk}_i\}_{i \in I}$. Outputs 0 or 1.*

All algorithms satisfy the standard natural correctness properties, except with negligible probability. Moreover, the scheme is secure if for any PPT adversary $\mathcal{A}$, the probability that the challenger outputs 1 in the following game is negligible in the security parameter k:

Setup. *The challenger samples n public key-secret key pairs, $(\mathsf{vk}_i, \mathsf{sk}_i) \leftarrow \mathsf{Gen}(1^k)$ for each $i \in [n]$, and gives $\mathcal{A}$ all verification keys $\{\mathsf{vk}_i\}_{i \in [n]}$. $\mathcal{A}$ selects a proper subset $M \subset [n]$ (corresponding to parties to corrupt) and receives the corresponding set of secret signing keys $\{\mathsf{sk}_i\}_{i \in M}$.*

Signing Queries. *$\mathcal{A}$ may issue multiple adaptive signature queries, of the form (m, i). For each such query, the challenger responds with a signature $\sigma \leftarrow \mathsf{Sign}_{\mathsf{sk}_i}(m)$ on message m with respect to the signing key sk_i.*

Output. *$\mathcal{A}$ outputs a triple $(\bar{\sigma}^*, m^*, I^*)$, where $\bar{\sigma}^*$ is an alleged forgery multisignature on message m^* with respect to a subset of verification keys $I^* \subset [n]$. The challenger outputs 1 if there exists $i \in I^* \setminus M$ such that the message m^* was not queried to the signature oracle with key sk_i, and $1 \leftarrow \mathsf{MultiVerify}(\{\mathsf{vk}_i\}_{i \in I^*}, m^*, \sigma^*)$.*

The following theorem follows from a combination of the (standard) signature scheme of Waters [44] together with a transformation from this scheme to a multisignature scheme due to Lu et. al. [36].

Theorem 2. *[44,36] There exists a secure multisignature scheme with signature size $\mathsf{poly}(k)$ (independent of message length and number of potential signers), based on the Bilinear Computational Diffie-Hellman assumption.*

Multi-party Protocols: Model and Security Definitions. We consider the setting of n parties $\mathcal{P} = \{P_1, ..., P_n\}$ within a synchronous network who wish to jointly compute any PPT function f over their private inputs. We allow up to t statically chosen Byzantine (malicious) faults and a rushing adversary. In our protocols below, we consider $t \leq (\frac{1}{3} - \epsilon)n$ for any constant $\epsilon > 0$. We assume that every pair of parties has the ability to initiate direct communication via a point-to-point private, authenticated channel. (However, we remark that in our protocol, each (honest) party will only ever send or process information along subset of only $\mathsf{polylog}(n)$ such channels.) We assume the existence of a public-key infrastructure, but allow the adversary's choice of corruptions to be made as a function of this public information.

The notion of security we consider is the standard simulation-based definition of secure multiparty computation (MPC), via the real/ideal world paradigm. Very loosely, we require that for any PPT adversary $\mathcal{A}$ in a real-world execution of the protocol, there exists another PPT adversary who can simulate the output of $\mathcal{A}$ given only access to an "ideal" world where he learns only the evaluated function output. We refer the reader to, e.g., [11] for a formal definition of (standalone) MPC security.

General secure function evaluation. The following theorem is well known and will be use throughout this paper. Let $\mathbb{C}$ be a circuit with n inputs, and let $F_\mathbb{C}$ the functionality that computes the circuit.

Theorem 3. *[5] For any $t < n/3$, there exists a protocol that securely computes the functionality $F_\mathbb{C}$ functionality, with perfect security. The protocol proceeds in $O(|\mathbb{C}|)$ rounds, and each party sends $\mathsf{poly}(n)$ messages of size $\mathsf{poly}(k, n)$ each.*

Verifiable Secret Sharing. A secret sharing scheme is a protocol that allows a dealer who holds a secret input s, to share his secret among n parties such that any t parties do not gain any information about the secret s, but any set of (at least) $t + 1$ parties can reconstruct s. A *verifiable secret sharing* (VSS) scheme, introduced by Chor et al. [15], is a secret sharing scheme with the additional guarantee that after the sharing phase, a dishonest dealer is either rejected, or is committed to a single secret s, that the honest parties can later reconstruct, even if dishonest parties do not provide their correct shares.

For concreteness, we consider a class of VSS constructions that takes advantage of reconstruction and secrecy properties of low-degree polynomials [43,38]. In particular, security of such a VSS protocol Share is formalized as emulating the ideal functionality F_{VSS}^t for parties $P_D, P_1, ..., P_n$ with distinguished dealer P_D such that $F_{\mathsf{VSS}}(q, (\emptyset, ..., \emptyset)) = (\emptyset, (q(\alpha_1), ..., q(\alpha_n)))$ for fixed evaluation points $\alpha_1, ..., \alpha_n$ if $\deg(q) \leq t$, and $F_{\mathsf{VSS}}(q, (\emptyset, ..., \emptyset)) = (\emptyset, (\perp, ..., \perp))$ otherwise. The party can also run a *reconstruction protocol* Reconst such that if honest parties input the correct shares output by the above functionality to them, then they recover the right value. The following result is well known.

Theorem 4. *[5,4] For any $t < n/3$, there exists a constant-round protocol Share that securely computes the F_{VSS}^t functionality, with perfect security. Each party sends $\mathsf{poly}(n)$ messages of size $O(l \log l)$, where $l = \max\{|x|, n\}$.*

Also, we will be interested in the case where the dealer D can be any of the n parties, and he sends shares to a subset P' of the n parties of size n' (e.g., $n' = \mathsf{polylog}(n)$), and we may not necessarily have $D \in P'$. The above functionality can be extended to this case naturally, and it is a folklore result that the protocols given by the above theorem also remain secure in this case as long as less than a fraction $1/3$ of the parties in P' are corrupted.

Broadcast. Another important functionality we need to implement is broadcast. To define, a broadcast protocol can be seen as an example of an MPC implementing a functionality F_{BC} for parties $P_D, P_1, ..., P_n$ with distinguished dealer P_D, defined as $F_{\mathsf{BC}}(m, (\emptyset, ..., \emptyset)) = (\emptyset, (m, ..., m)))$, where m is the message to be broadcast.

Theorem 5. *[24] For any $t < n/3$, there exists a constant-round protocol that securely computes the F_{BC} functionality, with perfect security. Each party sends $\mathsf{poly}(n)$ messages of size $O(|m|)$ each.*

2.2   Random Switching Networks and Random Permutations

Our protocol will employ what we call an *n-wire switching network*, which consists of a sequence of *layers*, each layer in turn consisting of one or more swapping gates which decide to swap the values of two wires depending on a bit. Formally, given an input vector $\boldsymbol{x} = (x_1, \ldots, x_n)$ (which we assume to be integers wlog), a swap gate operation $\mathsf{swap}(i, j, \boldsymbol{x}, b)$ returns $\boldsymbol{x}'$, where if $b = 0$ then $\boldsymbol{x} = \boldsymbol{x}'$, and if $b = 1$ then we have $x_i' = x_j$, $x_j' = x_i$, and $x_k' = x_k$ for all $k \neq i, j$. A switching layer is a set $L = \{(i_1, j_1), \ldots, (i_k, j_k)\}$ of pairwise-disjoint pairs of distinct indices of $[n]$. A d-depth switching network is a list $SN = (L_1, \ldots, L_d)$ of switching layers. Note that for each assignment of the bits of the gates in SN, the network defines a permutation from $[n]$ to $[n]$ by inputting the vector $\boldsymbol{x} = (1, 2, \ldots, n)$ to the network. The question we are asking is the following: If we set each bit in each swap gate uniformly and independently at random, how close to uniform is the resulting permutation? The following theorem guarantees the existence of a sufficiently shallow switching network giving rise to an almost-uniform random permutation.

Theorem 6. *For all $c > 1$, there exists an efficiently computable n-wire switching network of depth $d = O(\mathsf{polylog}(n) \cdot \log^c(k))$ (and size $O(n \cdot d)$) such that the permutation $\widehat{\pi} : [n] \to [n]$ implemented by the network when setting swaps randomly and independently has negligible statistical distance (in k) from a uniformly distributed random permutation on $[n]$.*

Proof. By Theorem 1.11 in [16], there exists such network SN of depth $d = O(\mathsf{polylog}(n))$ where the statistical distance is of the order $O(1/n)$. Consider now the switching network SN' obtained by cascading r copies of SN. Then, when setting switching gates at random, the resulting permutation $\widehat{\pi}$ equals $\widehat{\pi}_1 \circ \cdots \circ \widehat{\pi}_n$, where $\widehat{\pi}_i$ are independent permutations obtained each by setting the gates in SN uniformly at random. With π being a random permutation, a well-known property of the statistical distance $\Delta(\cdot, \cdot)$, combined with the fact permutation composition gives a group (see e.g. [37] for a proof) yields

$$\Delta(\widehat{\pi}, \pi) \leq 2^{r-1} \cdot \prod_{i=1}^{r} \Delta(\widehat{\pi}_i, \pi) \leq O\left(\left(\frac{2}{n}\right)^r\right) \leq O(2^{r(\log 2 - \log(n))}),$$

which is negligible in k for $r = \log^c(k)$. $\qquad\square$

Note that in particular this means that each wire is connected to at most $d = O(\mathsf{polylog}(n) \cdot \log^c(k))$ other wires via a switching gates, as each wire is part of at most one gate per layer.

2.3   Sublinear Algorithms

We consider a model where n inputs $x_1, \ldots, x_n$ are accessible to an algorithm SLA via individual queries for indices $i \in [n]$. Formally, a Q-*query algorithm* in the n-input model is a tuple of (randomized) polynomial time algorithms

SLA = (SLA.Sel$_1$, SLA.Sel$_2$, ..., SLA.Sel$_Q$, SLA.Exec). During an execution with inputs $(x_1, \ldots, x_n)$, SLA.Sel$_1$ takes no input and produces as output a state σ_1 and a query index $i_1 \in [n]$, and for $j = 2, \ldots, n$, SLA.Sel$_j$ takes as input a state σ_{j-1} and input $x_{i_{j-1}}$, and outputs a new state σ_j and a new query index i_j. Finally, SLA.Exec takes as input σ_Q and x_Q, and produces a final output y. We say that SLA is *sublinear* if $Q = o(n)$. We will also consider the special case of *non-adaptive* algorithms which consist without loss of generality of only two randomized algorithms SLA = (SLA.Sel, SLA.Exec), where SLA.Sel outputs a subset $I \subseteq [n]$ of indices of inputs to be queried, and the final output is obtained by running SLA.Exec on input $(x_i)_{i \in I}$.

Examples of sublinear algorithms, many of them non-adaptive, include algorithms for property testing such as testing sortedness of the inputs, linearity, approximate counting, and numerous graph properties, etc. Surveying this large area and the usefulness of these algorithms goes beyond the scope of this paper, and we refer the reader to the many available surveys [1].

3 Multi-party Computation for Sublinear Algorithms

We present a high-level overview geared at illustrating the techniques used within our sublinear algorithm compiler (Theorem 2), which is the more involved of our two results. For exposition, we focus on the case of non-adaptive algorithms. Given a Q-query non-adaptive sublinear algorithm SLA, we would like to evaluate it in a distributed fashion along the following lines. First, a small committee C consisting of polylog(n) parties is elected, with the property that at least two thirds of its members are honest. This committee then jointly decides on a random subset of Q parties I, output by SLA.Sel, from which inputs are obtained. The parties in $C \cup I$ jointly execute a multi-party computation among themselves to produce the output of the sublinear algorithm according to the algorithm SLA.Exec, which is then broadcasted to all parties.

But things will not be as simple. Interestingly, one main challenge is very unique to the setting of sublinear algorithms: An execution of the protocol needs to hide the subset I of parties whose inputs contribute to the output! More precisely, an ideal execution of the sublinear algorithm via the functionality $\mathcal{F}_{\mathsf{SLA}}$ only reveals the output of the sublinear algorithm. Therefore, we need to ensure that the adversary does not learn any additional information about the composition of I from a protocol execution beyond what leaked via the final output. Our protocol will indeed hide the set I completely. This will require modifying the above naive approach considerably.

The second challenge is complexity theoretic in nature. Enforcing low complexity of our protocol when implementing the above steps, while realizing our mechanism to hide the subset I, will turn out to be a delicate balance act.

In particular, at a high level our protocol will consist of the following components:

Committee Election Phase. The n parties jointly elect a supreme committee C, as well as individual committees $C_1, \ldots, C_n$ on which they *all agree*, sending each at most $\mathsf{polylog}(n)$ messages of size each $n \cdot \mathsf{poly}(\log n, \log k)$. All committees have size $\mathsf{polylog}(n)$ and at least a fraction $2/3$ of the parties in them are honest. As part of this process, the parties set up a communication structure that allows the supreme committee to communicate messages to all parties.

Commitment Phase. Each party P_i commits to its input so that C_i holds shares of these inputs.

Shuffling Phase. To hide the access pattern of the algorithm (i.e., which inputs are included in the computation), the committees will randomly shuffle the inputs they hold with respect to a random permutation ρ. This will happen by using a switching network with good shuffling properties. For each swap gate (i, j) in the switching network, committees C_i and C_j will swap at random the sharings they hold via a multi-party computation under a random decision taken by the supreme committee C. The supreme committee then holds a secret sharing of ρ.

Evaluation Phase. The parties in the supreme committee C sample a random query set I according to SLA.Sel via MPC and learn $\rho(I)$ only. They will then include the parties in committees C_i for $i \in \rho(I)$ in a multi-party computation to evaluate the sublinear algorithm on the inputs they hold. (Recall that C holds ρ in shared form.)

Output Phase. The supreme committee broadcasts the output of the computation to all parties, using the communication structure from the first stage.

In addition, we carefully implement sharings and multi-party computations using FHE to improve complexity, making the dependency of both the communication and round complexities linear in the input length $|x|$, rather than polynomial, and independent of the circuit sizes to implement the desired functionalities.

The following paragraphs provide a more detailed account of the techniques used within our protocol. In addition, a high-level description of the protocol procedure is given in Figure 1.

Committee Election Phase. The backbone behind this first phase is given by the construction of a *communication tree* using a technique of King et al [34]. Such tree is a sparse communication subnetwork which will ensure both the election of the supreme committee, as well as a basic form of communication between parties and the supreme committee where each party communicates only with $\mathsf{polylog}(n)$ other parties and only $\mathsf{polylog}(n)$ rounds of communication are required. Informally, the protocol setting up the tree assigns (possibly overlapping) subsets of parties of polylogarithmic size to the nodes of a tree with polylogarithmic height and logarithmic degree. The set of parties assigned to the root will take the role the supreme committee C. Communication from the root to the parties (or the other way round) occurs by communicating messages over paths from the root to the leaves of the tree, with an overall communication cost of $\mathsf{polylog}(n)$ messages per party. To elect the committees $C_1, \ldots, C_n$, we can have the supreme committee agree on the seed s of a PRF family $\mathcal{F} = \{F_s\}_s$ via a coin tossing protocol, where F_s maps elements of $[n]$ to subsets of $[n]$ of size $\mathsf{polylog}(n)$, and send s to all parties. We then let $C_i = F_s(i)$.

However, a closer look reveals that it is only possible for the protocol building the communication tree to enforce that a vast majority of the nodes of the tree are assigned to a set of parties for which a 2/3 majority is honest, but some nodes are unavoidably associated with too large a fraction of corrupted parties. Indeed, some parties may be connected to too many bad nodes and their communication ends up being essentially under adversarial control. As a consequence, the supreme committee is only able to correctly communicate with a $1 - o(1)$ fraction of the (honest) parties. Moreover, individual parties are not capable of determining whether the value they hold is correct or not. We refer to this situation as *almost-everywhere (ae) agreement*.

Our main contribution here is the use of cryptographic techniques to achieve *full agreement* on C and s in this stage, while maintaining $\mathsf{polylog}(n)$ communication locality; this improves on previous work in the information-theoretic setting [32,33,21] which requires each party to talk to $O(\sqrt{n} \cdot \mathsf{polylog}(n))$ other parties to reach agreement. We tackle these two issues in two separate ways.

1. *From ae agreement to ae certified agreement.* We first move to a stage where a large $1 - o(1)$ fraction of the parties learn the value sent by the supreme committee, together with a *proof* that the output is the one sent by the committee, whereas the remaining parties who do not know the output are also aware of this fact. We refer to this scenario as *almost-everywhere certified agreement*. Let us start with the basic idea using traditional signatures (we improve on this below using multisignatures). After having the supreme committee send a value m to all parties with almost-everywhere agreement, each party P_i receiving a value m_i will *sign* m_i with his own signing key, producing a signature σ_i. Then, P_i sends (m_i, σ_i) up the tree to the supreme committee, and each member will collect at least $n/2$ signatures on σ_i on some message m. Note that this will always be possible, as a fraction $1 - o(1) > n/2$ of the honest parties will receive the message $m_i = m$ and send a valid signature up the tree. Moreover, the adversary would need to forge signatures for honest parties in order to produce a valid certificate for a message which was not broadcast by the supreme committee.

2. *From ae certified agreement to full agreement.* We finally describe a transformation from ae certified agreement to full agreement. If a committee wants to broadcast m to all parties, the committee additionally generates a seed s for a PRF and broadcasts (m, s) in a certified way using the above transformations. Each party i receiving (m, s) with a valid certificate π forwards (m, s, π) to all parties in "his" committee $F_s(i)$. Whenever a party receives (m, s, π) with a valid certificate, it stops and outputs m. Note that no party sends more than $\mathsf{polylog}(n)$ additional messages in this transformation. Moreover, it is not hard to see that with very high probability every honest party will be in at least one of the $F_s(i)$ for a party i who receives (m, s) correctly with a certificate, by the pseudorandomness of $\mathcal{F}$. Note in particular that the same seed s can be used over multiple executions of this broadcast procedure from the committee to the parties, and can be used directly to generate the committees $C_1, \ldots, C_n$.

While we do guarantee that every party *sends* at most $\mathsf{polylog}(n)$ messages, a problem of the above approach is the potentially high complexity of processing incoming messages if dishonest parties flood an honest party by sending too many messages. Namely, the $t = \Theta(n)$ corrupted parties can always each send (m, s) with an invalid certificate to some honest party P_i, who needs to verify all signatures in the certificate to confirm that these messages are not valid. We propose a solution based on multisignatures that alleviates this problem by making certificates only consist of an individual *aggregate* signature (instead of of $\Theta(n)$), as well as of a description of the subset of parties whose signatures have been aggregated. The main idea is to have all parties initially sign the value they receive from the supreme committee with their own signing keys. However, when sending their values up the tree, parties assigned to inner nodes of the tree will aggregate valid signatures on the message which was previously sent down the tree, and keep track of which signatures have contributed.

Commitment Phase. Our instantiations of multi-party computations among subsets of parties will be based on fully homomorphic encryption (FHE). To this end, we want parties in each input committee C_i to store an FHE encryption $\mathsf{Enc}(\mathsf{pk}, x_i)$ of the input x_i that we want to be committing. The FHE public key pk is generated by the supreme committee (who holds secret shares of the matching secret key sk), and sent to all parties using the methods outlined above. A party i is committed to the value x_i if the honest parties in C_i all hold the *same* ciphertext encrypting x_i. This presents some challenges which we address and solve as follows:

1. First, a malicious party P_i must not be able to broadcast an invalid ciphertext to the members of the committee C_i. This is prevented by appending a simulation-sound NIZK argument π to the ciphertext c that there exists a message x and "good" randomness r such that $\mathsf{Enc}(\mathsf{pk}, x; r) = c$.

2. Second, for a security proof to be possible, it is well known that not only the encryption needs to be hiding and binding, but a simulator needs to be able to have some way to extract the corresponding plaintext from a valid ciphertext-proof pair (c, π). A major issue here is that the simulated setup must be independent of the corrupted set in our model. This prevents the use of NIZK arguments of knowledge. Moreover, we can expect the FHE encryption to be secure against chosen plaintext attacks only. We will solve this by means of *double encryption*, following Sahai's construction [41] of a CCA-secure encryption scheme from a CPA-secure one. Namely, we provide an additional encryption c_2 of x under a different public-key (for which no one needs to hold the secret key), together with an additional NIZK argument that c_1 and c_2 encrypt the same message. The ciphertext c_2 will not be necessary at any later point in time and serves only the purpose of verifying commitment validity (and permitting extraction in the proof).

3. Third, a final problem we have to face is due to rushing adversaries and the possibility of mauling commitments, in view of the use of the same public key pk for all commitments. This can be prevented in a black-box way by

letting every party P_i first (in parallel) VSS its commitment to the parties in C_i, and then in a second phase letting every committee C_i reconstruct the corresponding commitment. If the VSS protocol is perfectly secure, this ensures input-independence.

Another challenge is how to ensure that ciphertext sizes and the associated NIZK proof length are all of the order $|x| \cdot \mathsf{poly}(k)$, instead of $\mathsf{poly}(|x|, k)$. We achieve this by encrypting messages bit-by-bit using a bit-FHE scheme, whose ciphertexts are hence of length $\mathsf{poly}(k)$. The corresponding NIZK proof is obtained by sequentially concatenating individual proofs (each of length $\mathsf{poly}(k)$) for the encryptions of individual bits.

Shuffling Phase. The major privacy issue in executing a sublinear algorithm in a distributed setting is that the adversary must not learn which parties have contributed their inputs to the protocol evaluation, beyond any information that the algorithm's output itself reveals. Ideally, we would like parties to shuffle their inputs in a random (yet oblivious) fashion, so that at the end of such a protocol each party P_i holds the input of party $P_{\pi(i)}$ for a random permutation π, but such that the adversary has no information about the choice of π and for which party $\pi(i)$ he holds an input. At the same time, the supreme committee jointly holds information about the permutation π in a shared way. Unfortunately, this seems impossible to achieve: A disrupting adversary may always refuse to hold inputs for other parties. However, we can now exploit the fact that the inputs are held by *committees* $C_1, \ldots, C_n$ containing a majority of honest parties.

The actual shuffling is implemented via distributed evaluation of a switching network SN, under central coordination by the supreme committee. We assume that a switching network over n wires is given, with depth $d = \mathsf{polylog}(n)$, and is known to everyone, and with the property given by Theorem 6: i.e., it implements a nearly uniform permutation on $[n]$ under random switching. For each swap gate (i, j) in the network, the supreme committee members jointly produce an encryption $\hat{b}_{i,j}$ of an (unknown) random bit $b_{i,j}$, indicating whether the inputs x_i and x_j are to be swapped or not when evaluating the corresponding swapping gate. The value $\hat{b}_{i,j}$ is broadcast to all parties in C_i and C_j. At this point, each party in C_i broadcasts his copy of $\hat{x}_i$ to all parties in C_j, and each party in C_j does the same with $\hat{x}_j$ to all parties in C_i. (Each party then, given ciphertexts from the other committee, will choose the most frequent one as the right one.) Then, each party in C_i (or C_j) will update his encryption $\hat{x}_i$ to be an encryption of $\mathsf{Dec}(\mathsf{sk}, \hat{x}_j)$ or $\mathsf{Dec}(\mathsf{sk}, \hat{x}_i)$, depending on the value of $\hat{b}_{i,j}$, using homomorphic evaluation of the swap-or-not function. We note that this operation can be executed in parallel for all gates on the same layer, hence the swapping requires d rounds.

Evaluation Phase. Once the parties' inputs have been (obliviously) shuffled, we are ready to run the sublinear algorithm. The execution is controlled by the supreme committee C. First, the members of C will run an MPC to randomly select the subset of inputs $I \subset [n]$ to be used by the algorithm. The output of

---

Protocol for Non-adaptive Sublinear Algorithm Evaluation (Overview)

Committee Election Phase

1. Execute *almost-everywhere* committee election protocol of [34] to generate a communication tree together with a committee C at its root (where $(1 - o(1))$ fraction of honest parties agree on C).

2. Achieve *certified* almost-everywhere agreement on C and individual committees $\{C_i\}_{i \in [n]}$ as follows. Members of C collectively sample a PRF seed s and communicate it to (almost) all parties. Each C_i is defined by $F_s(i)$. Every party signs his believed value of (C, s) and passes it up the communication tree to C, where agreeing signatures are aggregated into a single multisignature at each inner node. The message and "certificate" multisignature that contains signatures from a majority of all parties is sent back down the tree.

3. Achieve *full* agreement on $C, \{C_i\}_{i \in [n]}$ as follows. Each party P_i possessing a valid certificate π on (C, s) sends (C, s, π) to each party in $C_i := F_s(i)$. Each party P_j who does *not* have a valid certificate listens for incoming messages and adopts the first properly certified tuple. (Note steps 2-3 enable C to broadcast messages).

Commitment Phase

4. Parties in the primary committee C run the (standard) MPC protocol of [5] amongst themselves to generate keys for the FHE scheme and a second standard PKE scheme. Parties in C receive the public keys $\mathsf{pk}, \mathsf{pk}'$ and a secret share of FHE key sk. They broadcast $\mathsf{pk}, \mathsf{pk}'$ to all parties.

5. In parallel, each party P_i acts as dealer to VSS the following values to his input committee C_i: (1) an FHE encryption of his input $\hat{x}_i \leftarrow \mathsf{Enc}_{\mathsf{pk}}(x_i)$, (2) a second encryption of x_i under the standard PKE with pk', and (3) NIZK proofs that $\hat{x}_i$ is a valid encryption and the two ciphertexts encrypt the same value.

Shuffling Phase

6. Parties in primary committee C run an MPC to generate a random permutation ρ, expressed as a sequence of random swap bits in the switching network SN. The output is an *FHE encryption* $\hat{\rho}$ of ρ, which they broadcast to all parties.

7. The committees C_i obliviously shuffle their stored input values, as follows. For each layer $L_1, ..., L_d$ in the sorting network SN,
   - Let $L_\ell = ((i_1, j_1), ..., (i_{n/2}, j_{n/2}))$ be the swapping pairs in the current layer ℓ.
   - In *parallel*, the corresponding pairs of committees $(C_{i_1}, C_{j_1}), ..., (C_{i_{n/2}}, C_{j_{n/2}})$ exchange their currently held input ciphertexts $\hat{x}_p, \hat{x}_q$ (using broadcast then majority vote) and homomorphically evaluate the swap-or-not function on $\hat{x}_p, \hat{x}_q$, and the appropriate encrypted swap bit $\hat{b}$ contained in $\hat{\rho}$.

   Outcome: each party in committee C_i holds encryption of input $x_{\rho(i)}$.

Evaluation Phase

8. Parties in primary committee C run an MPC to execute the input selection procedure $I \leftarrow \mathsf{SLA.Sel}$. The output of the MPC is the set of *permuted* indices $\rho(I) \subset [n]$.

9. Every party in C sends a message "Please send encrypted input ℓ" to every party P_j in C_ℓ for which $\ell \in \rho(I)$.

10. Each party $P_j \in C_\ell$ who receives consistent messages "Please send encrypted input ℓ" from a *majority* of the parties in C, broadcasts his currently held encrypted input $\hat{x}_p^j$ to all parties in C. (Recall that this allegedly corresponds to an encryption of the input x_p held by the committee $C_\ell = C_{\rho(p)}$ after the ρ-permutation shuffle).

11. The parties of C evaluate the second portion of the sublinear algorithm, $\mathsf{SLA.Exec}$ via an MPC. Each party of C broadcasts the resulting output answer to all parties.

Fig. 1. High-level overview of the protocol Π_{SLA} for secure distributed evaluation of a non-adaptive sublinear algorithm $\mathsf{SLA} = (\mathsf{SLA.Sel}, \mathsf{SLA.Exec})$

the MPC will be the set of *permuted* indices $\sigma(I) := \{\sigma(i) : i \in I\}$. The corresponding committees $\{C_j : j \in \sigma(I)\}$ are invited to join in a second MPC. Each member of C_j enters the MPC with input equal to his currently held encrypted secret share (of some unknown input x_i, for which $j = \sigma(i)$). Each member of C enters the MPC with input equal to his share of the secret decryption key sk. Collectively, the members of $C \cup (\bigcup_{j \in \sigma(I)} C_j)$ run an MPC which (1) recombines the shares of sk, (2) decrypts the secret shares held by each C_j, (3) reconstructs each of the relevant inputs x_i, $i \in I$, from the corresponding set of secret shares, (4) executes the sublinear algorithm on the reconstructed inputs, and (5) outputs *only* the output value dictated by the sublinear algorithm (e.g., for many algorithms, this will simply be YES/NO).

The main challenge is making the complexity of this stage such that only $\text{poly}(\log n, \log k)$ rounds are executed, and only messages of size $|x| \cdot \text{poly}(\log k, \log n)$ will be exchanged. This will be achieved by performing most of the computations locally via FHE by the parties in the supreme committee, and by generating the randomness to be used in SLA.Sel and SLA.Exec by first agreeing on a $\text{poly}(k)$-short seed of a PRG via coin-tossing, and then subsequently using the PRG output as the actual randomness.

Extension: Adaptive Algorithms. The above protocol can be modified to accommodate *adaptive* sublinear algorithms $\text{SLA} = (\text{SLA.Sel}_1, \ldots, \text{SLA.Sel}_q, \text{SLA.Exec})$ simply by modifying the evaluation phase such that an MPC is run for each next-query SLA.Sel_j to obtain the permuted index of the next query $\rho(i_j)$. Note that without loss of generality all queries are distinct. As a result of this modification, the number of rounds unavoidably increases: Namely, we need $O(q)$ additional rounds to obtain inputs from the committees $C_{\rho(i_j)}$ one by one. However, the proof and the protocol are otherwise quite similar, and we postpone a more detailed description to the final version of this paper.

Acknowledgments. This research was initiated and done in part while the authors were visiting the Isaac Newton Institute for Mathematical Sciences in Cambridge, UK. This work was partially supported by NSF contract CCF-1018064, a Simon Investigator award, and a Visiting Fellowship of the Isaac Newton Institute for Mathematical Sciences.

This material is based on research sponsored by DARPA under agreement number FA8750-11-2-0225. The U.S. Government is authorized to reproduce and distribute reprints for Governmental purposes notwithstanding any copyright notation thereon. The views and conclusions contained herein are those of the authors and should not be interpreted as necessarily representing the official policies or endorsements, either expressed or implied, of DARPA or the U.S. Government.

374   E. Boyle, S. Goldwasser, and S. Tessaro

References

1. Collection of surveys on sublinear algorithms,
   http://people.csail.mit.edu/ronitt/sublinear.html
2. Adida, B., Wikström, D.: How to Shuffle in Public. In: Vadhan, S.P. (ed.)
   TCC 2007. LNCS, vol. 4392, pp. 555–574. Springer, Heidelberg (2007)
3. Asharov, G., Jain, A., López-Alt, A., Tromer, E., Vaikuntanathan, V., Wichs, D.:
   Multiparty Computation with Low Communication, Computation and Interaction
   via Threshold FHE. In: Pointcheval, D., Johansson, T. (eds.) EUROCRYPT 2012.
   LNCS, vol. 7237, pp. 483–501. Springer, Heidelberg (2012)
4. Asharov, G., Lindell, Y.: A full proof of the bgw protocol for perfectly-secure
   multiparty computation. IACR Cryptology ePrint Archive, 2011:136 (2011)
5. Ben-Or, M., Goldwasser, S., Wigderson, A.: Completeness theorems for non-
   cryptographic fault-tolerant distributed computation. In: STOC, pp. 1–10 (1988)
6. Blum, M., Feldman, P., Micali, S.: Non-interactive zero-knowledge and its applications (extended abstract). In: STOC, pp. 103–112 (1988)
7. Blum, M., De Santis, A., Micali, S., Persiano, G.: Noninteractive zero-knowledge.
   SIAM J. Comput. 20(6), 1084–1118 (1991)
8. Boneh, D., Gentry, C., Lynn, B., Shacham, H.: Aggregate and Verifiably Encrypted
   Signatures from Bilinear Maps. In: Biham, E. (ed.) EUROCRYPT 2003. LNCS,
   vol. 2656, pp. 416–432. Springer, Heidelberg (2003)
9. Brakerski, Z., Gentry, C., Vaikuntanathan, V.: Fully homomorphic encryption
   without bootstrapping. In: ITCS, pp. 309–325 (2012)
10. Brakerski, Z., Vaikuntanathan, V.: Efficient fully homomorphic encryption from
    (standard) lwe. In: FOCS (2011)
11. Canetti, R.: Security and composition of cryptographic protocols: A tutorial. Cryp-
    tology ePrint Archive, Report 2006/465 (2006), http://eprint.iacr.org/
12. Chandran, N., Garay, J., Ostrovsky, R.: Improved Fault Tolerance and Secure
    Computation on Sparse Networks. In: Abramsky, S., Gavoille, C., Kirchner, C.,
    Meyer auf der Heide, F., Spirakis, P.G. (eds.) ICALP 2010. LNCS, vol. 6199, pp.
    249–260. Springer, Heidelberg (2010)
13. Chandran, N., Garay, J., Ostrovsky, R.: Edge Fault Tolerance on Sparse Networks.
    In: Czumaj, A., Mehlhorn, K., Pitts, A., Wattenhofer, R. (eds.) ICALP 2012, Part
    II. LNCS, vol. 7392, pp. 452–463. Springer, Heidelberg (2012)
14. Chaum, D., Crépeau, C., Damgård, I.: Multiparty Unconditionally Secure Proto-
    cols. In: Pomerance, C. (ed.) CRYPTO 1987. LNCS, vol. 293, p. 462. Springer,
    Heidelberg (1988)
15. Chor, B., Goldwasser, S., Micali, S., Awerbuch, B.: Verifiable secret sharing and
    achieving simultaneity in the presence of faults. In: FOCS, pp. 383–395 (1985)
16. Czumaj, A., Kanarek, P., Lorys, K., Kutylowski, M.: Switching networks for gen-
    erating random permutations. Manuscript (2001)
17. Damgård, I., Ishai, Y.: Scalable Secure Multiparty Computation. In: Dwork, C.
    (ed.) CRYPTO 2006. LNCS, vol. 4117, pp. 501–520. Springer, Heidelberg (2006)
18. Damgård, I., Ishai, Y., Krøigaard, M.: Perfectly Secure Multiparty Computa-
    tion and the Computational Overhead of Cryptography. In: Gilbert, H. (ed.)
    EUROCRYPT 2010. LNCS, vol. 6110, pp. 445–465. Springer, Heidelberg (2010)
19. Damgård, I., Ishai, Y., Krøigaard, M., Nielsen, J.B., Smith, A.: Scalable Multi-
    party Computation with Nearly Optimal Work and Resilience. In: Wagner, D.
    (ed.) CRYPTO 2008. LNCS, vol. 5157, pp. 241–261. Springer, Heidelberg (2008)

20. Damgård, I., Nielsen, J.B.: Scalable and Unconditionally Secure Multiparty Computation. In: Menezes, A. (ed.) CRYPTO 2007. LNCS, vol. 4622, pp. 572–590. Springer, Heidelberg (2007)
21. Dani, V., King, V., Movahedi, M., Saia, J.: Breaking the o(nm) bit barrier: Secure multiparty computation with a static adversary. CoRR, abs/1203.0289 (2012)
22. Feige, U., Lapidot, D., Shamir, A.: Multiple non-interactive zero knowledge proofs based on a single random string (extended abstract). In: FOCS, pp. 308–317 (1990)
23. Feigenbaum, J., Ishai, Y., Malkin, T., Nissim, K., Strauss, M.J., Wright, R.N.: Secure multiparty computation of approximations. ACM Transactions on Algorithms 2(3), 435–472 (2006)
24. Feldman, P., Micali, S.: Optimal algorithms for byzantine agreement. In: STOC, pp. 148–161 (1988)
25. Gentry, C.: Fully homomorphic encryption using ideal lattices. In: STOC, pp. 169–178 (2009)
26. Goldreich, O., Micali, S., Wigderson, A.: How to play any mental game or a completeness theorem for protocols with honest majority. In: STOC, pp. 218–229 (1987)
27. Goldreich, O., Ostrovsky, R.: Software protection and simulation on oblivious rams. J. ACM 43(3), 431–473 (1996)
28. Dov Gordon, S., Katz, J., Kolesnikov, V., Malkin, T., Raykova, M., Vahlis, Y.: Secure computation with sublinear amortized work. IACR Cryptology ePrint Archive, 2011:482 (2011)
29. Halevi, S., Krauthgamer, R., Kushilevitz, E., Nissim, K.: Private approximation of np-hard functions. In: STOC, pp. 550–559 (2001)
30. Halevi, S., Lindell, Y., Pinkas, B.: Secure Computation on the Web: Computing without Simultaneous Interaction. In: Rogaway, P. (ed.) CRYPTO 2011. LNCS, vol. 6841, pp. 132–150. Springer, Heidelberg (2011)
31. Indyk, P., Woodruff, D.P.: Polylogarithmic Private Approximations and Efficient Matching. In: Halevi, S., Rabin, T. (eds.) TCC 2006. LNCS, vol. 3876, pp. 245–264. Springer, Heidelberg (2006)
32. King, V., Lonargan, S., Saia, J., Trehan, A.: Load Balanced Scalable Byzantine Agreement through Quorum Building, with Full Information. In: Aguilera, M.K., Yu, H., Vaidya, N.H., Srinivasan, V., Choudhury, R.R. (eds.) ICDCN 2011. LNCS, vol. 6522, pp. 203–214. Springer, Heidelberg (2011)
33. King, V., Saia, J.: Breaking the $o(n^2)$ bit barrier: Scalable byzantine agreement with an adaptive adversary. J. ACM 58(4), 18 (2011)
34. King, V., Saia, J., Sanwalani, V., Vee, E.: Scalable leader election. In: SODA, pp. 990–999 (2006)
35. López-Alt, A., Tromer, E., Vaikuntanathan, V.: On-the-fly multiparty computation on the cloud via multikey fully homomorphic encryption. In: STOC, pp. 1219–1234 (2012)
36. Lu, S., Ostrovsky, R., Sahai, A., Shacham, H., Waters, B.: Sequential Aggregate Signatures and Multisignatures Without Random Oracles. In: Vaudenay, S. (ed.) EUROCRYPT 2006. LNCS, vol. 4004, pp. 465–485. Springer, Heidelberg (2006)
37. Maurer, U.M., Pietrzak, K., Renner, R.S.: Indistinguishability Amplification. In: Menezes, A. (ed.) CRYPTO 2007. LNCS, vol. 4622, pp. 130–149. Springer, Heidelberg (2007)
38. McEliece, R.J., Sarwate, D.V.: On sharing secrets and reed-solomon codes. Commun. ACM 24, 583–584 (1981)
39. Micali, S., Ohta, K., Reyzin, L.: Accountable-subgroup multisignatures: extended abstract. In: ACM Conference on Computer and Communications Security, pp. 245–254 (2001)

40. Naor, M., Nissim, K.: Communication preserving protocols for secure function evaluation. In: Proc. of 33rd STOC, pp. 590–599 (2001)
41. Sahai, A.: Non-malleable non-interactive zero knowledge and adaptive chosen-ciphertext security. In: FOCS, pp. 543–553 (1999)
42. De Santis, A., Di Crescenzo, G., Ostrovsky, R., Persiano, G., Sahai, A.: Robust Non-interactive Zero Knowledge. In: Kilian, J. (ed.) CRYPTO 2001. LNCS, vol. 2139, pp. 566–598. Springer, Heidelberg (2001)
43. Shamir, A.: How to share a secret. Communications of the ACM 22(11) (November 1979)
44. Waters, B.: Efficient Identity-Based Encryption Without Random Oracles. In: Cramer, R. (ed.) EUROCRYPT 2005. LNCS, vol. 3494, pp. 114–127. Springer, Heidelberg (2005)

Distributed Oblivious RAM for Secure Two-Party Computation[*]

Steve Lu[1] and Rafail Ostrovsky[2]

[1] Stealth Software Technologies, Inc., USA
steve@stealthsoftwareinc.com
[2] Department of Computer Science and Department of Mathematics, UCLA
Work done with consulting for Stealth Software Technologies, Inc.
rafail@cs.ucla.edu

Abstract. We present a new method for secure two-party Random Access Memory (RAM) *program* computation that does not require taking a program and first turning it into a circuit. The method achieves logarithmic overhead compared to an insecure program execution.

In the heart of our construction is a new Oblivious RAM construction where a client interacts with two non-communicating servers. Our two-server Oblivious RAM for n reads/writes requires $O(n)$ memory for the servers, $O(1)$ memory for the client, and $O(\log n)$ amortized read/write overhead for data access. The constants in the big-O notation are tiny, and we show that the storage and data access overhead of our solution concretely compares favorably to the state-of-the-art single-server schemes. Our protocol enjoys an important feature from a practical perspective as well. At the heart of almost all previous single-server Oblivious RAM solutions, a crucial but inefficient process known as oblivious sorting was required. In our two-server model, we describe a new technique to bypass oblivious sorting, and show how this can be carefully blended with existing techniques to attain a more practical Oblivious RAM protocol in comparison to all prior work.

As alluded above, our two-server Oblivious RAM protocol leads to a novel application in the realm of secure two-party RAM program computation. We observe that in the secure two-party computation, Alice and Bob can play the roles of two non-colluding servers. We show that our Oblivious RAM construction can be composed with an extended version of the Ostrovsky-Shoup compiler to obtain a new method for secure two-party *program* computation with lower overhead than all existing constructions.

Keywords: Oblivious RAM, Cloud Computing, Multi-Server Model, Software Protection, Secure Computation.

1 Introduction

While circuit-based secure two-party computation has a rich literature starting with Yao and Goldreich-Micali-Wigderson [42, 13] and has garnered recent interest due to fast

[*] Expanded version of this paper appears on ePrint [27]. Protected by patent application [30]. Supported in part by the Intelligence Advanced Research Projects Activity (IARPA) via Department of Interior National Business Center (DoI/NBC) contract number D11PC20199. The U.S. Government is authorized to reproduce and distribute reprints for Governmental purposes notwithstanding any copyright annotation therein. Disclaimer: The views and conclusions contained herein are those of the authors and should not be interpreted as necessarily representing the official policies or endorsement, either expressed or implied, of IARPA, DoI/NBC, or the U.S. Government.

A. Sahai (Ed.): TCC 2013, LNCS 7785, pp. 377–396, 2013.

implementations (e.g. [20], [24], etc.), modern algorithms are typically represented as Random Access Memory (RAM) programs rather than circuits, that contain multiple branches, recursion, while loops, etc. Unrolling these into circuits it often incredibly costly. The alternative was proposed by Ostrovsky and Shoup (in STOC 1997) [33]: to utilize Oblivious RAM machinery inside two party computation and "simulate" the client by two players. More specifically, Ostrovsky and Shoup [33] suggests simulating the CPU of an oblivious RAM machine using off-the-shelf secure computation to perform CPU execution steps with atomic instructions implemented by circuits (that are executed securely) to simulate a "virtual" client in the Oblivious RAM and rely on one of the players to implement encrypted memory of Oblivious RAM. The simulation of each CPU is done through circuit-based secure two-party computation, thus CPU size in the Oblivious RAM simulation must be minimized, as otherwise it impacts simulation of each step of the computation. Luckily, there are multiple Oblivious RAM solutions that require $O(1)$ CPU memory in the security parameter.

The Ostrovsky-Shoup compiler suffers from two drawbacks: (1) The best running time of Oblivious RAM simulation with $O(1)$ memory requires $O(\log^2 n / \log \log n)$ overhead for running programs of length n due to Kushilevitz, Lu, and Ostrovsky (in SODA 2012) [26] and (2) The most problematic part of this approach is that most Oblivious RAM simulations with small CPU size, starting with Goldreich and Ostrovsky require "Oblivious Sorting" that introduce a huge constant into Oblivious RAM simulation that essentially kills all practicality. In this paper we eliminate both drawbacks stated above.

At the heart of our construction is a model known as "Distributed (or two-Server) Oblivious RAM" where an Oblivious RAM client is allowed to interact with two or more **non-communicating** databases. This model is analogous to the multi-server Private Information Storage model introduced by Ostrovsky and Shoup [33]. The critical difference is that in [33], while using two servers, as a building block they use single-server Oblivious RAM solution as a building block. The principle difference in the current paper is to take a closer look that the Oblivious RAM technology itself and to show how two non-communicating servers can lead to significant efficiency improvements in the Oblivious RAM itself. Further, we argue that two-server model of the Oblivious RAM is very natural in multiple applications. For example, as already mentioned our Oblivious RAM construction critically uses the two servers in obtaining an efficient two-party computation (where two players naturally implement two servers) since we show how completely skip the expensive "oblivious sorting" step of Oblivious RAM. We then show how two players can act as two servers in distributed ORAM and sort directly on the pseudo-random keys. This contribution may also be of independent interest in the realm of practical Oblivious RAM, as well as theoretical constructions that use Oblivious RAM.

We highlight two practical and realistic scenarios in which our solution is especially important: as already mentioned, complicated programs with branching, loops, recursion, and multiple execution paths, and secondly, programs which access during runtime only a small number of bits from large public inputs. If the size of the random access program (which could be dramatically smaller than the corresponding circuit) and inputs are bounded by Λ and runs in time T, our solution is the first practical method with $O((T + \Lambda) \log(T + \Lambda))$ communication and computation complexity. We also remark that if we allow preprocessing on large inputs (such as on a large database, maps, graphs, networks, etc.), the online work can be reduced to $O((T + \varepsilon) \log(T + \Lambda))$, where ε bounds the size of online inputs (such as in a query). This precomputation model was used in the work of Gordon et al. [19] to achieve *polylogarithmic* online overhead, which we improve to *logarithmic* overhead. We now remind the reader of the motivation behind Oblivious RAM.

The concept of outsourcing data storage or computation is wide-spread in practice. This raises the issue of what happens to the privacy of the data when the outsourcing service is only semi-trusted or untrusted. Encryption can be employed to protect the *content* of the data, but it is apparent that information might be revealed based on how the data is accessed. Simply put, encryption by itself alone does not entirely address the issue of data privacy at hand.

The sequence of reads and writes a client makes to the remotely stored data is known as the *access pattern*. Even if the content of the data is protected by encryption, the server storing the data can deduce information about the encrypted data just by observing and analyzing the access pattern. For instance, the server can correlate this pattern with public information about the client's behavior, such as the purchase or sale of stock. Over time, the server may learn enough information to predict the behavior of the client or the underlying semantics of the data, thereby defeating the purpose of encrypting it in the first place.

A trivial solution would be for the client to access the entire stored database every single read or write. This clearly hides the access pattern, but the per-access overhead is linear in the size of stored data. The question remains:

Is it possible to hide the access pattern with less than linear overhead?

In the model where the client is a Random Access Machine (i.e. RAM model), Goldreich and Ostrovsky [11, 32, 31, 14] introduced the concept of hiding the access pattern in the context of software protection. A small protected CPU would run on a machine with large unprotected RAM. The goal was to obliviously simulate access to RAM, so that the set of instructions ran by the CPU would be protected against an outsider monitoring the RAM. In this manner, an adversary observing the RAM would learn nothing about what instructions were executed except the total number of instructions. The work of Goldreich [11] featured two solutions using constant client memory: a "square-root" solution and a "recursive square-root" solution. The amortized time overhead of executing a program in the former scheme was $O(\sqrt{n})$, and $O(2^{\sqrt{\log n \log \log n}})$ in the latter. Ostrovsky [32, 31] then discovered what is known as the "hierarchical solution" which had amortized overhead $O(\min\{\log^3 n, \log^3 t\})$, where t is the running time. The subsequent work of Goldreich and Ostrovsky [14] contains the merged results of [32, 31, 11] and featured a simpler method of reshuffling. The work described a way of simulating oblivious RAM with $O(\log^3 n)$ amortized overhead per access for n data items, using constant client storage[1] and $O(n \log n)$ server storage. A simple way to modify the solution to make it *worst-case* $O(\log^3 n)$ overhead per access was pointed out by Ostrovsky and Shoup in 1997 [33].

While the asymptotic behavior of $O(\log^3 n)$ overhead might seem efficient, this only gives a practical advantage over the trivial solution when $n > \log^3 n$ (without even considering the constants hidden in the O). A database of size $n = 2^{20}$ results in an overhead factor of roughly 8000, and such a large overhead would seem to cast oblivious RAM as outside the realm of practicality. Making oblivious RAM practical would be

---

[1] We count storage as the number of records or data items stored in memory. We do not count small variables such as counters or loop iterators toward this amount as these typically are tiny compared to the size of a data item, nor the private-key encryption/decryption cost.

of great impact, as it can be applied to software protection and several other important problems such as cloud computing, preventing cache attacks, etc. as we discuss later.

A highly interesting and powerful application of Oblivious RAM is in the problem of efficient, secure two-party *program* computation. While there are many ways to model computation, such as with Turing Machines, (Boolean) Circuits, Branching Programs, or Random Access Machines, one representation might be more natural than another, depending on the program. Nearly all secure two-party computation protocols require the program to be specified as a *circuit* between the two parties. Due to a classic result by Pippenger and Fischer [37], any Turing machine running in time T can be transformed into a circuit with only $O(\log T)$ blowup, but it is not known in the RAM model of computation whether there exists such an efficient transformation to circuits. Therefore, even using the most efficient secure two-party protocols for circuits (e.g. IKOS [21] or IPS [22] protocols), there is no clear path on how to apply these to efficiently perform secure RAM computation. We consider the question:

How can one efficiently perform secure two-party computation in the natural RAM model?

RELATED WORK. Subsequent to Goldreich and Ostrovsky [32, 31, 11, 14], works on Oblivious RAM [40, 41, 36, 16, 17, 38, 18, 26, 39] looked at improving the concrete and asymptotic parameters of oblivious RAM. We give a full summary of these schemes in Section 2. The major practical bottleneck of all these works on Oblivious RAMs is a primitive called *oblivious sorting* that is being called upon as a sub-protocol. Although the methods for oblivious sorting have improved, it still remains as both the critical step and the primary stumbling block of all these schemes. Even if new methods for oblivious RAM are discovered, there is an *inherent limit* to how much these schemes can be improved. It was shown in the original work of Goldreich and Ostrovsky [14] that there is a lower bound for oblivious RAM in this model.

([14], Theorem 6): *To obliviously perform n queries using only $O(1)$ client memory, there is a lower bound of $O(\log n)$ amortized overhead per access.*

We mention several results that are similar to Oblivious RAM but work in slightly different models. The works of Ajtai [1] and Damgård et al. [10] show how to construct oblivious RAM with information-theoretic security with poly-logarithmic overhead in the restricted model where the Adversary can not read memory contents. That is, these results work in a model where an adversary only sees the sequence of accesses and not the data. The work of Boneh, Mazieres and Popa [7] suggests ways to improve the efficiency of the "square-root" solution [11, 14] when memory contents are divided into larger blocks.

Finally, the notion of *Private Information Storage* introduced by Ostrovsky and Shoup [33] allows for private storage and retrieval of data. The work was primarily concentrated in the information theoretic setting. This model differs from Oblivious RAM in the sense that, while the communication complexity of the scheme is sub-linear, the server performs a *linear* amount of work on the database. The work of Ostrovsky and Shoup [33] gives a multi-server solution to this problem in both the computational and the information-theoretic setting and introduces the Ostrovsky-Shoup compiler of transforming Oblivious RAM into secure two-party computation. Directly quoting from their STOC 1997 [33] paper (with citations cross-referenced):

> *Both databases keep shares of the state of the CPU, and additionally one of the databases also keeps the contents of the Oblivious RAM memory. The main reason why we can allow one of the constituent databases to keep both the "share" of the CPU and the Oblivious RAM memory and still show that the view of this constituent database is*

computationally indistinguishable for all executions is that the Oblivious RAM memory component is kept in an encrypted (and tamper-resistant) form (see [14]), according to a distributed (between both databases) private-key stored in the CPU. For every step of the CPU computation, both databases execute secure two-party function evaluation of [42, 13] which can be implemented based on any one-way trapdoor permutation family (again communicating through the user) in order to both update their shares and output re-encrypted value stored in a tamper-resistant way in Oblivious RAM memory component.

The current work can be viewed as a generalization of the [33] model where servers must also perform sublinear work. The notion of single-server "PIR Writing" was subsequently formalized in Boneh, Kushilevitz, Ostrovsky and Skeith [6] where they provide a single-server solution. The case of amortized "PIR Writing" of multiple reads and writes was considered in [8].

Also along the lines of oblivious simulation of execution, the result of Pippenger and Fischer [37] shows that a single-tape Turing machine can be obliviously simulated by a two-tape Turing machine with logarithmic overhead.

With regard to secure computation for RAM programs, the implications of the Ostrovsky-Shoup compiler was explored in the work of Naor and Nissim [29] which shows how to convert RAM programs into so-called circuits with "lookup tables" (LUT). This transformation incurs a poly-logarithmic blowup, or more precisely, for a RAM running in time T using space S, there is a family of LUT circuits of size $T \cdot polylog(S)$ that performs the same computation. The work then describes a specific protocol that securely evaluates circuits with lookup tables. [29] also applies to the related model of securely computing branching programs.

The Ostrovsky-Shoup compiler was further explored in the work of Gordon et al. [19] in the case of amortized programs. Namely, consider a client that holds a small input x, and a server that holds a large database D, and the client wishes to repeatedly perform private queries $f(x, D)$. In this model, an expensive initialization (depending only on D) is first performed. Afterwards, if f can be computed in time T with space S with a RAM machine, then there is a secure two-party protocol computing f in time $O(T) \cdot polylog(S)$ with the client using $O(\log S)$ space and the server using $O(S \cdot polylog(S))$ space.

Efforts on making Oblivious RAM perform well in the worst case were initiated by Ostrovsky and Shoup [33] with follow-up works by Shi et. al [38] and Stefanov-Shi-Song [39]. These results independently discover a way to avoid oblivious sorting, though have worse asymptotics than our new scheme. Although these results asymptotically perform worse (such as having $O(\log^3 n)$ overhead), their focus was on reducing the worst-case overhead as well as minimizing actual constants and was effective for improving the running time for reasonably sized databases. Other works that considered worst-case overhead include Goodrich et. al [17] and Kushilevitz et. al [26].

OUR RESULTS. In this paper, we consider a model for oblivious RAM in which we can achieve far better parameters than existing single-server schemes. We mention that our model, like most existing schemes, focuses on computational rather than information-theoretic security, and we only make the mild assumption that one-way functions exist. Instead of having a single server store our data, similar to Ostrovsky-Shoup [33] we consider using multiple[2] servers to store client's data. These servers are assumed to not communicate or collude with each other, but only communicate with the client.

---

[2] In general, we can consider multiple servers. For our purposes, two servers suffice.

The main difference compared with [33] is that [33], while having several servers implemented virtual "off-the-shelf" Oblivious RAM that has a single server. We, in contrast, examine what two servers can bring to the Oblivious RAM world, where we allow these servers to perform simple computations such as hashing and sorting.

Note that although this Oblivious RAM model differs from the original model of the server only having read/write, we mention that it is still applicable in many of the interesting applications, such as cloud computing, tamper-proof CPUs interacting with other CPUs, and our main application, secure two-party computation. From a theoretical point of view, this model has been used in the past to much success such as in the seminal works in the areas of multi-prover Interactive Proof Systems [4] and multi-server Private Information Retrieval [9]. As already mentioned, this model is also directly applicable to the Ostrovsky-Shoup compiler for the construction of secure two-party RAM computation protocols.

In our two-server model, we introduce a new approach for Oblivious RAM **that completely bypasses oblivious sorting**, which was the inhibiting factor of practicality in most previous schemes (we give a comparison in Section 2.3). To perform a sequence of n reads or writes, our solution achieves $O(\log n)$ amortized overhead per access, $O(n)$ storage for the servers, and constant client memory. This matches the lower bound in the single-server model [14], and thus *no* single-server solution that uses constant client memory can asymptotically outperform our solution.

Theorem 1 (Informal). *Assume one-way functions exist. Then there exists an Oblivious RAM simulation in the* two-server *model with* $O(\log n)$ *overhead.*

In the work of [18], the notion of *Stateless* Oblivious RAM was introduced due to the fact that many Oblivious RAM solutions using super-constant client memory also required the client to maintain state between queries. All previous schemes with *constant* client memory were stateless and our new construction follows this trend.

As mentioned above, this new Oblivious RAM protocol leads to a novel application to secure *RAM program* computation. We then show how to perform secure two-party RAM computation by adapting our multi-server Oblivious RAM solution to fit the Ostrovsky-Shoup compiler [33]. This allows us (under cryptographic assumptions) to achieve the most efficient logarithmic communication complexity overhead for secure RAM computation as opposed to the *poly-logarithmic* overhead of all prior schemes [33, 29, 19, 28].

Theorem 2 (Informal). *Given any secure circuit computation protocol with $O(1)$ communication overhead, for any RAM program Π with upper bound T on its running time and Λ on its size (including $|\Pi|$) and length of inputs), there exists a two-party secure computation protocol for executing Π with $O((T + \Lambda) \cdot \log (T + \Lambda))$ communication and computation complexity. If large inputs are pre-processed and the online inputs sizes are bounded by ε, the online cost becomes $O((T + \varepsilon) \cdot \log (T + \Lambda))$.*

As an additional important remark, if players are willing to reveal to each other the actual running time on specific (private) inputs, we can replace in the above theorem T with the exact running on specific inputs, even though this may leak additional information. In some applications this information may be harmless, but in other applications with vastly different average-case/worst-case performance, this leads to a natural and interesting question on the tradeoff between efficiency and privacy.

1.1   Applications

SECURE TWO-PARTY AND MULTIPARTY COMPUTATION. In the case of MPC, we can apply oblivious RAM by letting the participants jointly simulate the client, and have the contents of the server be stored in a secret-shared manner. This application was originally described by Ostrovsky and Shoup [33] in the case of secure two-party computation. As described above, several other subsequent works [29, 10, 19] also investigated the application of Oblivious RAM to the area of secure computation. This can be beneficial in cases where the program we want to securely compute is more suitable to be modeled by a RAM program than a circuit. In particular, we demonstrate in this paper how our two-server ORAM construction can be applied to the case of secure two-party RAM program computation in the semi-honest model to obtain more efficient protocols for this purpose.

SOFTWARE PROTECTION. Original works of Goldreich [11] and Ostrovsky [32] envisioned protecting software using oblivious RAM. A small tamper-resistant CPU could be incorporated in a system with a large amount of unprotected RAM. A program could be run on this CPU by using oblivious RAM to access the large memory. Because this RAM could be monitored by an adversary, the benefit of oblivious RAM is that it hides the access pattern of the program that is running, thus revealing only the running time of the program to the adversary.

CLOUD COMPUTING. With the growing popularity of storing data remotely in the cloud, we want a way to do so privately when the data is sensitive. As mentioned before, simply encrypting all the data is insufficient, and by implementing oblivious RAM in the cloud, a client can privately store and access sensitive data on an untrusted server.

PREVENTING SIDE-CHANNEL ATTACKS. There are certain side-channel attacks that are based on measuring the RAM accesses that can be prevented by using oblivious RAM. For example, an adversary can mount a cache attack by observing the memory cache of a CPU. This poses a real threat as it can be used for cryptanalysis and has even been observed in practice in the work of Osvik-Shamir-Tromer [34].

PRIVATE DATA STRUCTURES. Rather than protecting an entire program, we can consider the middle ground of data structures. Data structures typically fit neatly into the RAM model, where each read or write is a sequence of accesses to memory. Performing these operations will leak information about the data, and we can use oblivious RAM to mitigate such issues. For example, commercial databases typically offer encryption to protect the data, but to protect the access pattern we can replace the data structures with oblivious ones.

2   Background

2.1   Model

We work in the RAM model, where there is a tiny machine that can run a program that performs a sequence of reads or writes to memory locations stored on a large memory. This machine, which we will refer to as the client, can be viewed as a stateful processor with a special data register v that can run a program Π. From a given state Σ of the client and the most recently read element x, $\Pi(\Sigma, x)$ acts as the next instruction function and outputs a read or write query and an updated state Σ'.

Because we wish to hide the type of access performed by the client, we unify both types of accesses into a operation known as a *query*. A sequence of n queries can be viewed as a list of (memory location, data) pairs $(v_1, x_1), \ldots, (v_n, x_n)$, along with a sequence of operations $op_1, \ldots, op_n$, where op_i is a READ or WRITE operation. In the case of READ operations, the corresponding x value is ignored. The sequence of queries, including both the memory location and the data, performed by a client is known as the *access pattern*.

In our model, we wish to obliviously simulate the RAM machine with a client, which can be viewed as having limited storage, that has access to multiple servers with large storage that do not communicate with one another. However, the servers are untrusted and assumed to only be, in the best case, *semi-honest*, i.e. each server follows the protocol but attempts to learn additional information by reviewing the transcript of execution. For our model, we assume that the servers can do slightly more than just I/O, in that they can do computations locally, such as shuffle arrays, as well as perform hashing and basic arithmetic and comparison operations.

An oblivious RAM is *secure* if for any two access patterns in the ideal RAM, the corresponding views in the execution of those access patterns of any individual server are computationally indistinguishable. Another way of putting it is that the view of a server can be simulated in a way that is indistinguishable from the view of the server during a real execution.

We also briefly state the model of secure two-party RAM computation which we work in (see, e.g. [12], for a more in-depth treatment of general models of secure computation). Let $f(A, B)$ be a function that can be efficiently computed by a RAM machine, that is to say, there exists a program Π that a client can execute starting with A and B stored in the appropriate input memory locations and halting with the result $f(A, B)$ in the appropriate output memory location on the server. We usually denote the running time $T(n)$ and the space used $S(n)$ which depend on the size of the input n.

We use an ideal/real simulation-based definition of security and also work in the setting of semi-honest adversaries. There are two parties, Alice and Bob that receive inputs A and B respectively and they wish to compute $f(A, B)$. In the ideal world, there is an ideal functionality $\mathcal{F}_f$ that on inputs A and B simply computes $f(A, B)$ and sends the output to Alice and Bob. In the real world, we can think of the Alice and Bob executing a protocol π_f that computes $f(A, B)$. Roughly speaking, we say that π_f *securely realizes* the functionality $\mathcal{F}_f$ if there exists an efficient simulator $\mathcal{S}$ playing the role of the corrupted party in the ideal world can produce an output that is computationally indistinguishable from the view of the corrupted party in the real world.

2.2 Tools

HASHING. In our scheme and in previous schemes, hashing is a central tool in storing the records. For our purposes, the hash functions used for hashing will be viewed as either a random function or a keyed pseudorandom function family F_k. Recall the standard hashing with buckets data structure: there is a table of m buckets, each of size b, and a hash function $h : \mathcal{V} \to \{1 \ldots m\}$. A record (v, x) is stored in bucket $h(v)$.

CUCKOO HASHING. A variant of standard hashing known as Cuckoo Hashing was introduced by Pagh and Rodler [35]. In this variant, the hash table does not have buckets, but now two hash functions h_1, h_2 are used. Each record (v, x) can only reside in one of two locations $h_1(v)$ or $h_2(v)$, and it is always inserted into $h_1(v)$. If there was a previous record stored in that location, the previous record is kicked out and sent to its other location, possibly resulting in a chain of kicks. If the chain grows too long or there is a cycle, new hash functions are chosen, and it was shown that this results in an amortized $O(1)$ insertion time. A version of cuckoo hashing with a stash was introduced by Kirsch et al. [23] where it was shown that the probability of having to reset drops exponentially in the size of the stash.

OBLIVIOUS SORTING. A key ingredient in most previous schemes is the notion of oblivious sorting. This is a sorting algorithm such that the sequence of comparisons it makes is independent of the data. For example, the schemes of Batcher [3] and Ajtai et al. [2] are based on sorting networks, and recently a randomized shell sort was introduced by Goodrich [15].

2.3   Comparison to Prior Work

We briefly overview the relevant key techniques used in previous schemes:

Table 1. Comparison of oblivious RAM schemes

Scheme	Comp. Overhead	Client Storage	Server Storage	# of Servers	Dist. Prob.[3]
[14]ORAM$_{GO1}$	$O(\sqrt{n}\log n)$	$O(1)$	$O(n + \sqrt{n})$	1	*negl*
[14]ORAM$_{GO2}$	$O(\log^4 n)$	$O(1)$	$O(n \log n)$	1	*negl*
[14]ORAM$_{GO3}$	$O(\log^3 n)$	$O(1)$	$O(n \log n)$	1	*negl*
[40]ORAM$_{WS}$	$O(\log^2 n)$	$O(\sqrt{n})$	$O(n \log n)$	1	*negl*
[41]ORAM$_{WSC}$	$O(\log n \log\log n)$	$O(\sqrt{n})$	$O(n)$	1	**poly**
[36]ORAM$_{PR}$	$O(\log^2 n)$	$O(1)$	$O(n)$	1	**poly**
[16]ORAM$_{GM1}$	$O(\log^2 n)$	$O(1)$	$O(n)$	1	*negl*
[16]ORAM$_{GM2}$	$O(\log n)$	$O(n^\nu)$	$O(n)$	1	*negl*
[18]ORAM$_{GMOT}$	$O(\log n)$	$O(n^\nu)$	$O(n)$	1	*negl*
[17]ORAM$_{GMOT2}$	$O(\log n)$	$O(n^\tau)$	$O(n)$	1	*negl*
[38]ORAM$_{SCSL}$	$O(\log^3 n)$	$O(1)$	$O(n \log n)$	1	*negl*
[39]ORAM$_{SSS}$	$O(\log n)$	$cn, c \ll 1$	$4n + o(n)$	1	*negl*
[26]ORAM$_{KLO}$	$O(\log^2 n / \log\log n)$	$O(1)$	$O(n)$	1	*negl*
Our Scheme	$O(\log n)$	$O(1)$	$O(n)$	2	*negl*

SQUARE ROOT SOLUTION. In the work of Goldreich [11] and subsequently Goldreich-Ostrovsky [14], a "square root" solution (which we label ORAM$_{GO1}$) was introduced for oblivious RAM. This solution was not hierarchical in nature, and instead had a permutation of the entire memory stored in a single array along with a cache of size $\sqrt{n}$ which was scanned in its entirety during every query. After every $\sqrt{n}$ queries, the entire array was obliviously sorted and a new permutation was chosen. This results in an amortized communication overhead of $O(\sqrt{n}\log n)$ per access.

---

[3] Due to flaws in the way hash functions are used, the security of these schemes could be only polynomially secure. For further discussion on the security analysis of these schemes, see [16, 26, 19].

HIERARCHICAL SOLUTION. In the work of Ostrovsky [32] and subsequently [14], a hierarchical solution was given for oblivious RAM. In this solution, the server holds a hierarchy of bucketed hash tables, growing geometrically in size. New records would be inserted at the smallest level, and as the levels fill up, they would be reshuffled down and re-hashed by using oblivious sorting. A query for v would scan bucket $h_i(v)$ in the hash table on level i. By using the oblivious sorting of Batcher [3], the scheme achieves an $O(\log^4 n)$ amortized query overhead (ORAM_{GO2}), and with AKS [2], an $O(\log^3 n)$ query overhead is achieved (ORAM_{GO3}).

BUCKET SORTING. In the work of Williams-Sion [40], the client was given $O(\sqrt{n})$ working memory instead of $O(1)$. By doing so, it was possible to achieve a more efficient oblivious sorting algorithm by sorting the data locally in chunks of size $\sqrt{n}$ and then sending it back to the server. This resulted in a solution (ORAM_{WS}) with $O(\log^2 n)$ query overhead. This idea of using the client to sort was continued in the work of Williams et al. [41] in which a Bloom filter [5] was introduced to check whether or not an element was stored in a level before querying upon it. This solution (ORAM_{WSC}) was suggested to have $O(\log n \log \log n)$ overhead, but the a more careful analysis of [36] shows that this depends on the number of hash functions used in the Bloom filter.

CUCKOO HASHING. Pinkas and Reinman [36] suggested a solution in which cuckoo hashing is used instead of standard bucketed hashing. The oblivious sorting algorithm used the more practical one of [15]. This resulted in a scheme (ORAM_{PR}) that only used constant client memory, $O(n)$ server storage, and only $O(\log^2 n)$ query overhead where the constant was empirically shown to be as small as 150. The work of Goodrich and Mitzenmacher [16] also made use of cuckoo hashing, although the stashed variant of cuckoo hashing was used for their scheme (ORAM_{GM1}), which resulted in similar parameters. They also suggested a solution where the client has $O(n^\nu)$ memory (ORAM_{GM2}) , in which case they are able to achieve $O(\log n)$ query overhead. A stateless version of this scheme is featured in [18] with similar asymptotic behavior. The best known overhead for schemes with constant client memory come from the work of Kushilevitz, Lu, and Ostrovsky [26] (full version appears on ePrint [25]), where they introduce a new balancing technique for their scheme (ORAM_{KLO}) to achieve an overhead of $O(\log^2 n / \log \log n)$.

WORST-CASE. Recent schemes considered also the worst-case overhead per client query. The first paper to address works-case overhead was [33] which showed a poly-log worst case overhead. Works such as Goodrich et. al [17] (which we label ORAM_{GMOT2}), Shi et. al [38] (ORAM_{SCSL}), Kushilevitz et. al [26], and Stefanov-Shi-Song [39] (ORAM_{SSS}) also featured schemes that provide worst-case guarantees. All these schemes additionally either bypass or amortize oblivious sorting, albeit in independent and different manners than our new construction in this paper.

3   Our Scheme

3.1   Overview

Our new scheme uses the hierarchical format of Ostrovsky [32]. The general principle behind protocols using this technique can be stated as: the data is encrypted (under semantically secure encryption) and stored in hierarchical levels that reshuffle and move into larger levels as they fill up. To keep track of the movement, for each level we logically divide different time periods into *epochs*, based on how many queries the client has already performed. All parties involved are aware of a counter t that indicates the number of queries performed by the client.

In hierarchical schemes, the reshuffling process is the main bottleneck in efficiency, specifically the need to perform "oblivious sorting" several times. We identify the purposes that oblivious sorting serves during reshuffling and describe methods on how to replace oblivious sorting in our two-server model.

The first purpose of oblivious sorting is to separate real items from "dummy" items. Dummy items are records stored in the levels to help the client hide the fact that it may have already found what it was looking for prior to reaching that level. For example, if the client was searching for virtual memory location v, and it was found on level 3, the client still needs to "go through the motions" and search on the remaining levels to hide the fact that v had already been found. On all subsequent levels in this example, the client would search for "*dummy*" $\circ$ t instead of v.

The second purpose of oblivious sorting is to identify old records being merged with new records. New records are always inserted at the topmost level, and as the levels are reshuffled down, there is the possibility that an old record will run into a new one on some lower level. Because they both have the same virtual memory location v, a collision will occur. To resolve this, when records are being reshuffled, an oblivious sort is performed to place old records next to new ones so that the old records can be effectively erased (re-encrypted as a dummy record).

Finally, oblivious sorting is used to apply a pseudorandom permutation to the records as they are being reshuffled. A permutation is necessary to prevent the server from being able to track entries as they get reshuffled into lower levels.

The key ingredient to our new techniques is the idea of "tagging" the records and letting the two servers do most of the work for the client. A typical record looks like (v, x) where v is the index of the record (virtual memory location), and x is the data stored at that index. In most previous schemes, a hash function was applied to v to determine where the record would be stored in the data structure. Because the client cannot reveal v to the servers, and yet we wish for the servers to do most of the work, the client needs to apply tags to the records. Later, when the client needs to retrieve index location v, the client first computes the tag and then looks up the tag instead of v in the data structure located on the servers.

Note that this tagging must be performed carefully. We want the client to use only $O(1)$ working memory, so it cannot simply keep a list of all the tags it has generated in the past. Instead, the tags must be deterministic so that the client is able to re-create the tag at a future point in time when needed. However, if the tags depend only on v, a server can immediately identify when two encrypted records have the same index location v.

To resolve the apparent tension between these two requirements, we use a pseudorandom function (PRF) applied to v, the level it is stored on, as well as the period of time which it is stored at that level, known as the *epoch*. We describe this in greater detail in our construction. In the expanded version [27] we first present a warm-up construction to demonstrate the utility of tagging and using two servers. For a sequence of client queries of length n, this *insecure* strawman construction will have the servers storing $O(n)$ data, the client having $O(1)$ working memory, and the amortized overhead of queries being $O(\log n)$.

3.2 Full Construction

A recent result [26] points out that hash overflows leads to an adversary distinguishing different access patterns. Plain cuckoo hashing and the variant of cuckoo hashing with a constant stash [16] yield a polynomial chance of this event occurring. The work of Goodrich-Mitzenmacher [16] shows that cuckoo hashing with *logarithmic* size stash yields a superpolynomially small chance (in n) of overflow, under the assumption that the size of the table is $\Omega(\log^7 n)$. Thus, as a starting point, we use the level layout of [16], where smaller levels are standard hash tables with buckets and larger levels are cuckoo hash tables with a stash of size $O(\log n)$. Furthermore, we use the idea of "caching the stash" that was previously used in [26] that can be viewed as an alternative to a "shared stash" [18]. We emphasize that this is where the similarities end with existing schemes and that significant modifications must be diligently balanced to yield a scheme with our desired parameters. Before we begin describing our full construction, we take a quick glance at the balancing dynamics involved in choosing the right parameters for our scheme. Our goal is to achieve $O(\log n)$ amortized overhead per query, while maintaining that the hash tables do not overflow with all but negligible probability.

Recall that the hybrid construction in [16] uses standard hashing with buckets for lower levels, up until the point where a level contains $\log^7 n$ elements, where it switches to cuckoo hashing with a stash of size $\log n$. For the probability of overflow to be negligible for standard hashing, the buckets must be of size $\log n$. To perform a read query, a bucket is scanned at each of the smaller levels, and the entire stash is scanned along with 2 elements of the cuckoo hash table at the larger levels. This operation already incurs a total of $O(\log n \log \log n)$ reads for the small levels and $O(\log^2 n)$ for the larger levels. We now summarize the series of modifications that need to be made to the structure of the scheme:

Reduce Bucket Size. The standard hash tables will now use buckets of size $3 \log n / \log \log n$. This causes the total amount of reads for the small levels to drop down to $O(\log n)$. This produces a negative side effect: a bucket will now overflow with $\frac{1}{n^2}$ probability.

Standard Hash with Stash. We introduce a stash of size $\log n$ to the standard hash tables to hold the overflows from the now reduced bucket sizes. We prove in expanded version [27] that the probability of overflowing the stash is negligible. This produces a negative side effect: each stash must be read at the smaller levels, bringing us back to $O(\log n \log \log n)$ reads for the smaller levels.

Cache the Stash.[18, 16, 26] For both the smaller levels and larger levels, the stash of size $\log n$ will not be stored at that level, but the entire stash is instead re-inserted into the hierarchy. In fact, by choosing the top level to be of size $O(\log n)$, we can fit the entire stash into the top level. We show how this step is done during a reshuffle. Now, because there is no longer a stash at any level, the total amount read from all the levels combined will be $O(\log n)$. This will cause the levels to be reshuffled more often, but we show that it is at most by a constant factor.

We now give the full details of our scheme.

Let $c = 2 \log n$, where c is taken to be the size of the top level ($i = 1$). We split the top level in half so that each server holds half of the top level, and for subsequent levels, server $\mathcal{S}_{i \mod 2}$ holds level i. Let ℓ_{cuckoo} be the level such that $c \cdot 2^{\ell_{cuckoo}-1}$ is $\Omega(\log^7 n)$, e.g. $7 \log \log n$. For levels $i = 2, \ldots, \ell_{cuckoo} - 1$, level i will be a standard hash table consisting of $c \cdot 2^{i-1}$ buckets, each of size $3 \log n / \log \log n$, along with a "mental"[4] stash of size $\log n$. For levels $i = \ell_{cuckoo}, \ldots, N$, level i will be a cuckoo hash table that can hold up to $c \cdot 2^{i-1}$ elements, which is of size $c \cdot 2^i$, along with a "mental" stash of size $\log n$.

The client keeps a local counter t of how many queries have been performed so far, as well as a counter s to indicate how many dummy stash elements were created. We describe how a query is performed in Figure 1. To reshuffle levels $1 \ldots i$ into level $i + 1$, suppose $\mathcal{S}_b$ holds level $i + 1$ and let $\mathcal{S}_a = \mathcal{S}_{1-b}$ be the other server. The steps in Figure 2 are performed.

---

1. The client allocates temporary storage m, large enough to hold a single record, initialized to a dummy value "*dummy*".
2. Read each entry of the entire top level from both servers one at a time. If v is found as some entry (v, x) then store x in m.
3. For small levels $i = 2 \ldots \ell_{cuckoo} - 1$, perform the following with the server holding level i:
   (a) If v has not already been found, compute the tag for v at this level as $z = F_s(i, e_i, v)$. Else, set $z = F_s(i, e_i, \text{"}dummy\text{"} \circ t)$.
   (b) Fetch into local memory the bucket corresponding to $h(z)$ one element at a time, i.e. fetch (v_j, x_j) for $j = 1, \ldots, 3 \log n / \log \log n$ from bucket $h(z)$ one element at a time.
   (c) If v is found in some record (v_i, x_i), then replace v_i with "*dummy*" $\circ t$ and store x_i in m.
   (d) Re-encrypt the fetched records and store them back to their original locations, releasing them from local client memory.
4. For large levels $i = \ell_{cuckoo} \ldots N$, perform the following with the server holding level i:
   (a) If v has not already been found, compute the tag for v at this level as $z = F_s(i, e_i, v)$. Else, set $z = F_s(i, e_i, \text{"}dummy\text{"} \circ t)$.
   (b) Fetch into local memory the records (v_0, x_0) and (v_1, x_1) from locations $h_0(z)$ and $h_1(z)$.
   (c) If v is found at one of these locations, i.e. $v = v_b$ for some $b = 0, 1$, then replace v_b with "*dummy*" $\circ t$ and store x_b in m.
   (d) Re-encrypt the fetched records and store them back to their original locations, releasing them from local client memory.
5. In the case of a write query, here we overwrite $m = y$.
6. Read each entry of the entire top level one at a time, and re-encrypt each record with the following exception: If the record is of the form (v, x), then overwrite it with (v, m) before re-encrypting it.
7. If (v, x) was not overwritten at the top level, write (v, m) in the first available empty spot (even if m is "*dummy*"), otherwise write a dummy value ("*dummy*" $\circ t$, "*dummy*").
8. The client increments the local query counter t. If t is a multiple of $c/2$, then a reshuffle step is performed as described below.

Fig. 1. Main Construction: Query

---

[4] There will be no physical stash at this level, but during reshuffles a temporary stash is created for the purpose of hashing which will subsequently be re-inserted back to the top level.

1. S_a allocates a temporary array and inserts every (encrypted) record it holds between levels 1 and i. S_a applies a random permutation to this temporary array and sends its contents one by one to the client.
2. The client re-encrypts each record and sends it to S_b. In this step, both empty and dummy records are treated as real records.
3. S_b allocates a temporary array and inserts every record it holds between levels 1 and i as well as the records it received from the client in the previous step. S_b applies a random permutation to this temporary array and sends its contents one by one to the client.
4. The client re-encrypts each record and sends it to S_a, announcing that it is empty if the record is empty, and tagging remaining records (v, x) with the output of the PRF $F_s(i+1, e_{i+1}, v)$, where e_{i+1} is the *new* epoch of level $i+1$. Note that v may be a virtual memory address, a dummy value, or a stash dummy value. In this step, dummy records are treated as real records and we are only concerned with eliminating empty records.
5. S_a now holds $c \cdot 2^{i-1}$ tagged records. It allocates a temporary hash table (standard or cuckoo, depending on the level), with a stash of size $\log n$ and it uses the hash functions corresponding to level $i+1$ and epoch e_{i+1} to hash these records into this temporary table. If the insertion fails, new hash functions are selected (we will show this happens with negligible probability). S_a then informs the client the number of elements inside the stash, σ, then sends both the temporary table and the stash one record at a time to the client.
6. As the client receives records from S_a one at a time, it re-encrypts each record and sends them to S_b without modifying the contents except:
   (a) The first σ empty records in the table the client receives from S_a are encrypted as ("*stashdummy*" $\circ$ s, "*empty*"), incrementing s each time. Note that a table is always more than half empty, and therefore we can always find σ empty slots.
   (b) Subsequent empty records from the table are encrypted as ("*empty*", "*empty*").
   (c) Every empty record in the stash is re-encrypted as ("*stashdummy*" $\circ$ s, "*empty*"), incrementing s each time.
7. S_b stores the table records in level $i+1$ in the order in which they were received, and stores the stash records at the top level.

Fig. 2. Main Construction: Reshuffle

3.3   Analysis of Main Construction

Theorem 1. *For a sequence of n queries, the main construction uses $O(n)$ memory for each server, $O(1)$ working memory for the client, and $O(\log n)$ amortized overhead for queries.*

Proof. Computing the sizes of the levels, level 1 is of size $c = 2 \log n$, split between the servers, levels $i = 2, \ldots, \ell_{cuckoo} - 1$ are of size $c \cdot 2^{i-1} \cdot 3 \log n / \log \log n$ each, giving a total of $O(\log^9 n)$ size, since $\ell_{cuckoo} = 7 \log \log n$. Levels $i = \ell_{cuckoo}, \ldots, N$ are of size $c \cdot 2^i$ each, where $c \cdot 2^N = n$, hence there is a total of $O(n)$ size. Note that the additional elements added in by the stash dummy elements can be counted as follows: every $c/2$ steps, we insert another $\log n$ stash dummy records into the hierarchy. Therefore, after n steps, at most $2n \log n / c = n$ stash dummy records have been inserted, and we can simply accommodate this by adding one extra level at the bottom.

Clearly, the client uses constant working memory as it only transmits records one at a time.

When the client performs the read operation, it reads $2 \log n$ records from the top level, $3 \log n / \log \log n$ elements from each level $i = 2, \ldots, \ell_{cuckoo} - 1$, and 2 elements from each level $i = \ell_{cuckoo}, \ldots, N$. Since $\ell_{cuckoo} = 7 \log \log n$ and $N = \log n - \log \log n - 1$, this gives a total of roughly $25 \log n$ elements read.

Because we re-insert the stash (which is half the size of the top level), we need to reshuffle twice as often. Note that each reshuffle only moves an element in the level at most 3 times. We sketch the analysis of the amortized overhead:

- For levels $2, \ldots, \ell_{cuckoo} - 1$, each level contains $c \cdot 2^{i-1} 3 \log n / \log \log n$ elements and needs to be reshuffled every $c \cdot 2^{i-1}/2$ steps. This incurs an amortized overhead of:

$$3 \sum_{i=2}^{7 \log \log n - 1} \frac{c \cdot 2^{i-1} 3 \log n / \log \log n}{c \cdot 2^{i-2}} = O(\log n)$$

  with a constant of roughly 125.
- For levels $\ell_{cuckoo}, \ldots, N$, each level contains $c \cdot 2^i$ elements and needs to be reshuffled every $c \cdot 2^{i-1}/2$ steps. This incurs an amortized overhead of:

$$3 \sum_{i=7 \log \log n}^{\log n - \log \log n - 1} \frac{c \cdot 2^i}{c \cdot 2^{i-2}} = O(\log n)$$

  with a constant of roughly 10.

Before we prove the security of our construction, we state a few important lemmas.

Lemma 1. *At all times during the execution of the scheme, any record of the form $(v, *)$ will appear at most once in the hierarchy unless $v = $ "empty".*

Proof. An index v must be either a virtual memory location, a dummy element, a stash dummy element, or empty. Virtual memory locations are only introduced into the hierarchy either from a read query that found v at a lower level and moved it to the top, or from a write query that did not find v in the hierarchy. A dummy element "$dummy$" $\circ t$ can only be introduced during query t, and it can be introduced at most once. Similarly, stash dummy elements can only be introduced once as s is incremented after every such entry.

Lemma 2. *The same v will not be queried upon twice between reshuffles at any level.*

Proof. Once v is queried upon at a level, i, either it is a "$dummy$" $\circ t$ value (in which case it will trivially never be queried again, as t is incremented at the next query), or it is some virtual memory location. In the latter case, v will be written to the top level after the query, and subsequent queries to v will find v before it reaches level i, and the only way v can reach a deeper level is if i is reshuffled.

Lemma 3. *Every level except the top will always be empty or half-full (a half-full standard hash contains a number of records equal to half the number of buckets) and this state depends only on t.*

Proof. The proof is straightforward and we refer the reader to the full version [27].

Lemma 4. *Any time a level i is reshuffled, its stash is included in the shuffle.*

Proof. We observe that the only way a level is shuffled is if all previous levels are shuffled as well and become empty. Because the stash of level i was stored in the hierarchy above level i, no elements of the stash will fall below level i unless caused by a reshuffle, in which case it will be shuffled with level i.

Theorem 2. *Under the assumption that one-way functions exists, the main construction is a secure two-server oblivious RAM.*

Proof. One-way functions allow private-key encryption and authentication. We use method of [31] to prevent tampering and thus must only show how to protect the access pattern.

We show how to simulate the view of a server's access pattern during the execution of the protocol upon any sequence of queries $q_1, \ldots, q_n$ knowing only the length n. We begin by first making the observation that every record is encrypted and will be re-encrypted whenever it is accessed. By the semantic security of the encryption, we can assume that all these data contents are computationally indistinguishable from the encryption of any other contents. We also replace both the hash functions (which are modeled as PRFs) and the tagging PRF by random functions.

We first consider the view of each server during a reshuffle. If the server is playing the role of S_a, after its initial message out, it sees a random sequence of encrypted records (real or dummy) with tags, and announced empty records. By Lemma 1, all the hidden records will contain elements with unique v's, and hence their tags will also be unique with overwhelming probability. The tags came from a random function that had not been previously used, and so the tags that the server sees are independent from its view. Furthermore, because of Lemmas 3 and 4, the number of empty records revealed will be deterministic and will not reveal any additional information. Thus, we can simulate this view by calculating the number of pre-determined items of each type, and use encryptions of 0 for all of them and tagging the appropriate records with completely random tags.

If the server is playing the role of S_b during a reshuffle, it will receive a sequence of encrypted records which reveals no information. Next, after it shuffles these records and sends them out, it receives back another sequence of encrypted records which also reveals no information. This view can be trivially simulated.

Finally, we argue that the sequence of reads can also be simulated. By the above arguments, we see that what each server holds at level i is nearly independent of its view, except for the fact that the tags of the records stored at that level are consistent with the hash function used at that level. By Lemma 2, between two reshuffles, the sequence of queries made to level i will all be distinct, but they may arbitrarily intersect the elements contained in level i. However, because only a negligible fraction of hash functions do not agree with the records in level i (i.e. would cause an overflow), the distribution of the outputs of the hash function applied to any sequence of distinct queries is statistically close to uniform[5]. Thus, we can simulate the probes to level i between reshuffles by a random sequence of probes.

4   Application to Secure Two-Party RAM Computation

In this section, we describe how our multi-party Oblivious RAM simulation can be applied to the setting of secure two-party computation on RAM programs. The idea of using Oblivious RAM for the purpose of secure computation has been suggested in the literature [33, 29, 10, 19] and we outline the high-level idea of its use.

Consider the setting of two (semi-honest) parties, Alice and Bob, who wish to securely compute some function f (computed as some RAM program Π that runs in time

---

[5] Note that this does not hold true for plain cuckoo hashing, where there is a noticeable difference between a uniform hash function and one that makes a consistent cuckoo hash table.

$T = T(n)$ and uses $S = S(n)$ space) on their inputs A and B. Observe that in an Oblivious RAM, the view of the server can be simulated, so the idea is to let Alice or Bob play the role of the server (or in the case of our construction, two servers). However, in the case of Oblivious RAM, the privacy of the data is not protected from the client, so in order to securely run Π, we need to somehow simulate the client as well. In order to do so, we let the state of the client be *shared* between Alice and Bob so that neither party learns what is going on until the end of the computation when their outputs are revealed. In order to compute on this shared state, each *fixed instruction* of Π is encoded as a circuit. We emphasize that rather than unrolling the entire program into a circuit, which may be quite inefficient, we are only representing each atomic instruction as a circuit.

Because the joint state secure computation occurs at each step in the program, we want to minimize the amount of computation and communication overhead incurred by this step. In particular, in order for Alice and Bob to jointly compute Π and simulate the state of the client efficiently, the client state should be as small as possible. This means that even if an ORAM solutions is efficient in terms of computation or communication overhead, we cannot use it if the footprint of the client is too large. In particular, works that require the memory of the client to be $O(\sqrt{n})$ (e.g. [40, 41]) or $O(n^\nu)$ (e.g. [16, 18]) will incur too much overhead per step of the program. The currently most efficient (single-server) ORAM protocol that is suitable for this purpose comes from the work of [26].

We point out that when modeling the client, we can either treat it as operating on bits or on "words". By this we mean the client may need, for example, pointers of $O(\log S)$ bits so that it can index into memory. The notion of a client having constant memory can implicitly mean that we are operating on words and these can each hold sufficiently many bits to perform the necessary instructions. However, when simulating the client steps using a circuit, we need to operate on bits rather than words.

Because of this, the client state may in fact be larger than a constant number of bits despite having only a constant number of words. In order not to gain any additional overhead when performing the simulation of the client state, we need to use an efficient MPC that has only *constant* overhead. For example, the protocols of IKOS [21] or IPS [22] suit this situation.

By using our two-server ORAM solution in the Ostrovsky-Shoup compiler, we are able to achieve lower overhead for secure RAM computation than any known single-server ORAM solution. We have:

Theorem 3. *Suppose there exists a symmetric-key encryption scheme and a hash function modeled as a random function or an efficient PRF (e.g. [21, 19]). Suppose there exists a two-party secure circuit computation protocol with constant overhead (e.g. [21, 22]). Then to securely compute a RAM program that runs in $T(n)$ time with access to $S(n)$ space with the size of the program (including inputs) bounded by $\Lambda(n)$, there exists a two-party secure RAM computation protocol in the semi-honest model with $O(\log(T + \Lambda))$ multiplicative overhead in communication and computational complexity, and an additive one-time cost of $O(\Lambda \log(\Lambda))$ for setup (that can be amortized over multiple secure evaluations on small online inputs). If the client computes on bits instead of words, there is an additional implicit $O(\log S)$ multiplicative overhead.*

Proof Sketch. We give a construction of such a scheme and argue that it is secure.

We follow the construction of the Ostrovsky-Shoup [33] compiler and let Alice and Bob hold inputs A and B respectively, and let Π be the program they wish to securely compute. Initialize the two-server ORAM as follows: let Alice play the role of one server and let Bob play the role of the other server. They jointly simulate the state of the client in our two-server ORAM protocol initialized to the secret sharing of the initial state. The parties then proceed by secret sharing A and B with each other. The two parties run the MPC protocol on the instructions that tells the client to obliviously insert (via ORAM) A and B into the locations inside the RAM where the program Π expects to read them as input. At the end of this process, Alice and Bob hold their respective encrypted server data as well as the shared state of the client.

Then, Alice and Bob begin to jointly execute the instructions of Π. Namely, they start with a shared state Σ and a shared value x and they perform the secure two-party computation on the circuit representing the step $\Pi(\Sigma, x)$ to receive a new shared state Σ' and a read or write operation op. The operation is converted into a sequence of oblivious instructions $op_1', \ldots, op_\ell'$ by running the MPC on the two-server ORAM protocol steps. When the operation involves reading or writing from the server Alice is holding, Bob sends Alice his share of that instruction and Alice reconstructs the instruction and executes it on her server before re-sharing the result. Similarly, Alice reveals her share to Bob when the operation involves reading or writing from his server. At the end of execution of Π, Alice and Bob recombine shares to retrieve the output.

We follow the (standard) proof technique of composition of simulation of CPU and simulation of Oblivious RAM in which we invoke the simulatability of both the underlying MPC and ORAM (see also [19]). To simulate the view of one party, say Alice, we begin by generating a uniformly random share of the initial state for her view. As her input and Bob's input are being stored on the servers obliviously, we simulate the intermediate state shares Σ as random shares as well. To simulate the instruction execution via $(\Sigma', op) \leftarrow \Pi(\Sigma, x)$, again we generate uniform random shares for the intermediate state as well as the values retrieved. In a real execution, the resulting operation op is then converted into a sequence of oblivious instructions $op_1', \ldots, op_\ell'$, and by the simulatability of the underlying oblivious RAM, we can in fact simulate the sequence by replacing op with a dummy operation. The simulator runs the sequence of oblivious instructions induced by this dummy operation and writes the sequences of Alice's memory probes to the simulated view.

Finally, when the output is about to be reconstructed, the simulator (which knows the result via interaction with the ideal functionality) sets the revealed share to be $r \oplus f(A, B)$ where r is the random share of the data for Alice during this final step.

5   Conclusion and Open Problems

In this paper, we introduced a new multi-server model for oblivious RAM and constructed a two-server scheme in this model. The scheme is secure against honest-but-curious servers assuming one-way functions exist. The parameters of the scheme – $O(1)$ client memory, $O(n)$ server memory, and $O(\log n)$ overhead – match the lower bound of single-server oblivious RAM. The natural open problem to ask is whether or not the same lower bound holds, or if a better scheme can be constructed in this new model.

Our scheme was constructed under the assumption of the existence of one-way functions. We ask the open question of whether or not information-theoretic multi-server oblivious RAM can be constructed with similar parameters. One naive way of doing so would be to duplicate each server and use information-theoretic secret sharing between each server and its duplicate in order to replace encryption. The interesting question is to ask whether one can do so with fewer servers or perhaps better performance.

In the follow-up paper we have shown how to make garble RAM programs non-interactive with poly-logarithmic communication overhead [28]. In this paper, we showed how to make the overhead logarithmic. This improves existing constructions [33, 29, 19, 28]. Notice, however, that unlike the non-interactive solution of [28], the solution presented in this paper is highly interactive. The task of achieving logarithmic overhead for non-interactive secure execution of RAM programs remains an interesting open question.

References

[1] Ajtai, M.: Oblivious RAMs without cryptogrpahic assumptions. In: STOC, pp. 181–190 (2010)

[2] Ajtai, M., Komlós, J., Szemerédi, E.: An $O(n \log n)$ sorting network. In: STOC, pp. 1–9 (1983)

[3] Batcher, K.E.: Sorting networks and their applications. In: AFIPS Spring Joint Computing Conference, pp. 307–314 (1968)

[4] Ben-Or, M., Goldwasser, S., Kilian, J., Wigderson, A.: Multi-prover interactive proofs: How to remove intractability assumptions. In: STOC, pp. 113–131 (1988)

[5] Bloom, B.H.: Space/time trade-offs in hash coding with allowable errors. Commun. ACM 13(7), 422–426 (1970)

[6] Boneh, D., Kushilevitz, E., Ostrovsky, R., Skeith III, W.E.: Public Key Encryption That Allows PIR Queries. In: Menezes, A. (ed.) CRYPTO 2007. LNCS, vol. 4622, pp. 50–67. Springer, Heidelberg (2007)

[7] Boneh, D., Mazieres, D., Popa, R.A.: Remote oblivious storage: Making oblivious RAM practical. CSAIL Technical Report, MIT-CSAIL-TR-2011-018 (2011)

[8] Chandran, N., Ostrovsky, R., Skeith III, W.E.: Public-Key Encryption with Efficient Amortized Updates. In: Garay, J.A., De Prisco, R. (eds.) SCN 2010. LNCS, vol. 6280, pp. 17–35. Springer, Heidelberg (2010)

[9] Chor, B., Goldreich, O., Kushilevitz, E., Sudan, M.: Private information retrieval. In: FOCS, pp. 41–50 (1995)

[10] Damgård, I., Meldgaard, S., Nielsen, J.B.: Perfectly Secure Oblivious RAM without Random Oracles. In: Ishai, Y. (ed.) TCC 2011. LNCS, vol. 6597, pp. 144–163. Springer, Heidelberg (2011)

[11] Goldreich, O.: Towards a theory of software protection and simulation by oblivious RAMs. In: STOC, pp. 182–194 (1987)

[12] Goldreich, O.: Foundations of Cryptography: Basic Tools. Cambridge University Press, Cambridge (2001)

[13] Goldreich, O., Micali, S., Wigderson, A.: How to play any mental game or a completeness theorem for protocols with honest majority. In: STOC, pp. 218–229 (1987)

[14] Goldreich, O., Ostrovsky, R.: Software protection and simulation on oblivious RAMs. J. ACM 43(3), 431–473 (1996)

[15] Goodrich, M.T.: Randomized shellsort: A simple oblivious sorting algorithm. In: SODA, pp. 1262–1277 (2010)

[16] Goodrich, M.T., Mitzenmacher, M.: Privacy-Preserving Access of Outsourced Data via Oblivious RAM Simulation. In: Aceto, L., Henzinger, M., Sgall, J. (eds.) ICALP 2011, Part II. LNCS, vol. 6756, pp. 576–587. Springer, Heidelberg (2011)

[17] Goodrich, M.T., Mitzenmacher, M., Ohrimenko, O., Tamassia, R.: Oblivious RAM simulation with efficient worst-case access overhead. In: CCSW, pp. 95–100 (2011)

[18] Goodrich, M.T., Mitzenmacher, M., Ohrimenko, O., Tamassia, R.: Privacy-preserving group data access via stateless oblivious RAM simulation. In: SODA, pp. 157–167 (2012)

[19] Gordon, D., Katz, J., Kolesnikov, V., Malkin, T., Raykova, M., Vahlis, Y.: Secure computation with sublinear amortized work. Cryptology ePrint Archive, Report 2011/482 (2011)

[20] Huang, Y., Evans, D., Katz, J., Malka, L.: Faster secure two-party computation using garbled circuits. In: USENIX Security Symposium (2011)

[21] Ishai, Y., Kushilevitz, E., Ostrovsky, R., Sahai, A.: Cryptography with constant computational overhead. In: STOC, pp. 433–442 (2008)

[22] Ishai, Y., Prabhakaran, M., Sahai, A.: Founding Cryptography on Oblivious Transfer – Efficiently. In: Wagner, D. (ed.) CRYPTO 2008. LNCS, vol. 5157, pp. 572–591. Springer, Heidelberg (2008)

[23] Kirsch, A., Mitzenmacher, M., Wieder, U.: More Robust Hashing: Cuckoo Hashing with a Stash. In: Halperin, D., Mehlhorn, K. (eds.) ESA 2008. LNCS, vol. 5193, pp. 611–622. Springer, Heidelberg (2008)

[24] Kreuter, B., Shelat, A., Shen, C.-H.: Towards billion-gate secure computation with malicious adversaries. Cryptology ePrint Archive, Report 2012/179 (2012)

[25] Kushilevitz, E., Lu, S., Ostrovsky, R.: On the (in)security of hash-based oblivious RAM and a new balancing scheme. Cryptology ePrint Archive, Report 2011/327 (2011)

[26] Kushilevitz, E., Lu, S., Ostrovsky, R.: On the (in)security of hash-based oblivious RAM and a new balancing scheme. In: SODA, pp. 143–156 (2012)

[27] Lu, S., Ostrovsky, R.: Multi-server oblivious RAM. IACR Cryptology ePrint Archive, 2011:384 (2011)

[28] Lu, S., Ostrovsky, R.: How to garble RAM programs. IACR Cryptology ePrint Archive, 2012:601 (2012)

[29] Naor, M., Nissim, K.: Communication preserving protocols for secure function evaluation. In: STOC, pp. 590–599 (2001)

[30] Ostrovsky, R.: Apparatus system and method to efficiently search and modify information stored on remote servers, while hiding the access pattern. U.S. Patent Application No. 12,768,617 (April 27, 2010)

[31] Ostrovsky, R.: Software Protection and Simulation On Oblivious RAMs. PhD thesis, Massachusetts Institute of Technology (1992)

[32] Ostrovsky, R.: Efficient computation on oblivious RAMs. In: STOC, pp. 514–523 (1990)

[33] Ostrovsky, R., Shoup, V.: Private information storage (extended abstract). In: STOC, pp. 294–303 (1997)

[34] Osvik, D.A., Shamir, A., Tromer, E.: Cache Attacks and Countermeasures: The Case of AES. In: Pointcheval, D. (ed.) CT-RSA 2006. LNCS, vol. 3860, pp. 1–20. Springer, Heidelberg (2006)

[35] Pagh, R., Rodler, F.F.: Cuckoo Hashing. In: Meyer auf der Heide, F. (ed.) ESA 2001. LNCS, vol. 2161, pp. 121–133. Springer, Heidelberg (2001)

[36] Pinkas, B., Reinman, T.: Oblivious RAM Revisited. In: Rabin, T. (ed.) CRYPTO 2010. LNCS, vol. 6223, pp. 502–519. Springer, Heidelberg (2010)

[37] Pippenger, N., Fischer, M.J.: Relations among complexity measures. J. ACM 26(2), 361–381 (1979)

[38] Shi, E., Chan, T.-H.H., Stefanov, E., Li, M.: Oblivious RAM with $O((\log N)^3)$ Worst-Case Cost. In: Lee, D.H., Wang, X. (eds.) ASIACRYPT 2011. LNCS, vol. 7073, pp. 197–214. Springer, Heidelberg (2011)

[39] Stefanov, E., Shi, E., Song, D.: Towards practical oblivious RAM. In: NDSS (2012)

[40] Williams, P., Sion, R.: Usable PIR. In: NDSS (2008)

[41] Williams, P., Sion, R., Carbunar, B.: Building castles out of mud: practical access pattern privacy and correctness on untrusted storage. In: ACM Conference on Computer and Communications Security, pp. 139–148 (2008)

[42] Yao, A.C.-C.: Protocols for secure computations (extended abstract). In: FOCS, pp. 160–164 (1982)

Black-Box Proof of Knowledge of Plaintext and Multiparty Computation with Low Communication Overhead

Steven Myers[1,*], Mona Sergi[2], and abhi shelat[2]

[1] Indiana University, Bloomington, IN, USA
[2] University of Virginia, Charlottesville, VA, USA

Abstract. We present a 2-round protocol to prove knowledge of a plaintext corresponding to a given ciphertext. Our protocol is black-box in the underlying cryptographic primitives and it can be instantiated with almost any fully homomorphic encryption scheme.

Since our protocol is only 2 rounds it cannot be zero-knowledge [GO94]; instead, we prove that our protocol ensures the semantic security of the underlying ciphertext.

To illustrate the merit of this relaxed proof of knowledge property, we use our result to construct a secure multi-party computation protocol for evaluating a function f in the standard model using only *black-box access* to a threshold fully homomorphic encryption scheme. This protocol requires communication that is *independent of $|f|$*; while Gentry [Gen09a] has previously shown how to construct secure multi-party protocols with similar communication rates, the use of our novel primitive (along with other new techniques) avoids the use of complicated generic white-box techniques (cf. PCP encodings [Gen09a] and generic zero-knowledge proofs [AJLA+12, LATV11].)

In this sense, our work demonstrates in principle that *practical* TFHE can lead to reasonably practical secure computation.

Keywords: Fully Homomorphic Encryption, Threshold Encryption, Secure Multi-Party Computation, Communication and Round Complexity, Proof Of Knowledge.

1 Introduction

The main technical contribution of this paper is a novel proof of knowledge of a plaintext protocol and its demonstrated use in the construction of a fully black-box multi-party computation protocol with low communication overhead. We briefly describe the motivation behind our work.

---

* This work, and the authors are sponsored by NSF Grant 0939718, and DARPA and Air Force Research Laboratory under Grant FA8750-11-2-0211. The views and conclusions contained in this document are those of the authors and should not be interpreted as representing the official policies, either expressed or implied, of the Defense Advanced Research Projects Agency or the US government.

A. Sahai (Ed.): TCC 2013, LNCS 7785, pp. 397–417, 2013.

Communication. Secure computation with an honest majority can be accomplished without any cryptographic assumptions, but the best such protocol requires the parties to communicate $|f| \log |f| + d^2 \cdot poly(n, \log |f|)$ bits [DIK10] and at least d rounds. Here $|f|$ is the size of the function being computed and d is the circuit depth of f, and thus the communication of the protocol is super-linearly related to the number of gates in f. Until recently, even the use of cryptographic assumptions for secure computation required $polylog(\lambda)$ communication overhead per gate [DIK10] where λ is a security parameter.

Gentry [Gen09a] circumvents per-gate overhead as follows: the honest-but-curious parities use secure multi-party computation to generate an FHE key, each party encrypts its input, and sends the resulting ciphertext and proof to other parties. Once all parties have encryptions of everyone's inputs, they compute the function of interest locally using the evaluation procedure of the FHE. Finally, to use the resulting ciphertexts as inputs to a secure multi-party computation which computes the decryption of the majority input. In order to be secure against malicious adversaries, the Naor and Nissim compiler [NN01], which makes use of the PCP theorem, can be applied. The use of the PCP theorem in the SMC steps makes the approach impractical, even when presented with a practical FHE scheme.

The motivation behind our work is to remove any use white-box techniques, such as the PCP theorem or generic ZK or NIZK, from the above framework for constructing communication-efficient secure protocols. These techniques have historically been inefficient. In other words, we seek a black-box transformation from TFHE to secure computation.

First Contribution. The main technical hurdle in devising a black-box transformation from TFHE to secure computation is to implement the requirement for each player to prove that they "know the plaintext" corresponding to the encrypted input that they have broadcast. This step is essential because it prevents one player from copying (or mauling via the homomorphism) the input of a player who has acted earlier. To handle this step, we show how to construct a two-round black-box proof of knowledge of an encrypted bit for any circuit private FHE scheme using only the encryption scheme. Since our protocol is only two rounds, it is not zero-knowledge (cf. [GO94]), but can provably keep the encrypted bit hidden. Our POK requires that the public-key contain a labeled encryption of 0 and 1, which given all known FHE schemes seems to be a natural modification. [1] For traditional FHE schemes, the POK can be used completely black-box, without even the need for the modification.

The basic idea of our proof of knowledge protocol is to first modify the encryption scheme so that the message is encoded using an error-correcting code (ECC) based verifiable secret sharing (VSS) scheme. To encrypt a message we

---

[1] Since all current schemes contain bit-wise encryptions of their own secret-keys which are random bit strings, and a natural extension of any protocol that provides encryptions of one's own secret-key can be used to derive a labeled encryption of 0 and 1 which we describe.

first generate its secret shares, and encrypt them independently using fresh randomness. A verifier now requests the Prover to reveal the randomness used to encrypt a sub-threshold number of the shares. The verifier then does a consistency check, based on the ECC underlying the scheme, to ensure that the shares were encoded properly. In particular, the error-correcting code we choose offers a property that allows one to check whether local parts of the codeword are error-free. The verifier accepts if everything appears to be properly coded. Since the number of shares revealed is less than the threshold, it does not leak any information about the original message. To show a proof of knowledge property, we argue that an extractor can rewind the Prover and ask for another set of shares to be opened. With high probability, this second transcript provides enough new shares to run the VSS recover algorithm, and recover the original message. The one issue with this approach is that the Prover must reveal the randomness used to encrypt some of the shares. The semantic security of an encryption scheme does not guarantee any security when these random bits are revealed—in particular, the security of the rest of the unopened encryptions are not guaranteed. Instead, we require the encryption scheme to be secure against a selective opening attack (SOA). Fortunately, a result of Hemenway et al. [HLOV11] can be generalized to show that any circuit private homomorphic encryption scheme can be made into an SOA-secure one.

We point out that our proof of knowledge requires the encryption scheme to be homomorphic and circuit-private. Recently, Damgård et al. [DPSZ12] demonstrates a three-round Σ-protocol for knowledge of plaintext, but their protocol *requires* the underlying encryption scheme to also be homomorphic on the random coins used to encrypt. Although many FHE schemes support this property on their random coins, it is certainly not specified in the definition of FHE. In contrast, circuit privacy has been independently defined and seems to be a naturally weaker property.[2] Moreover, their scheme requires the message space for the FHE to be over $\mathbb{Z}_N$ for N related to the security parameter. While in general, single-bit FHE implies many-bit FHE, we are not aware of any such transformation that *also* preserves the homomorphism over the random coins as required by their protocol. Thus, the requirement for large message space *and* homomorphism over the random coins seem to be extra assumption which our work can avoid (our protocol also works on single-bit FHE). Finally, the Σ-protocol from [DPSZ12] must be compiled into a full zero-knowledge protocol using standard techniques which add round complexity and/or setup assumptions; we show that our two-round protocol with its hidden-bit property suffices for our secure computation protocol.

Second Contribution. By combining our result with almost any TFHE scheme, we construct a secure multi-party protocol that avoids *both* per-gate communi-

---

[2] Even though current schemes achieve circuit privacy via randomness homomorphisms, it is certainly plausible for future constructions to achieve circuit privacy in other ways. Moreover, there do not seem to be any natural ways to transform a circuit private scheme to one with a randomness homomorphism, and thus we feel it is a weaker notion.

cation complexity *and* white-box techniques such as the PCP theorem or Zero-Knowledge. The communication complexity of our protocol is $O(\lambda^c \cdot n^2)$ where λ is a security parameter and c is a small constant for the TFHE scheme and is thus independent of $|f|$. Our black-box transformation is particularly important because if practical FHE (and TFHE) can be constructed, our transformations will result in practical SFE. Our work is in the standard model and does not require trust assumptions such as the common reference string, a random oracle or public-key setup.

Final Contribution. For completeness, we also construct a *threshold* fully homomorphic public-key encryption scheme (TFHE) based on the Approximate GCD problem and the fully homomorphic encryption scheme presented by van Dijk et al. [vDGHV10], and our result was the first to demonstrate the feasibility of directly achieving this threshold primitive for FHE. Since our original eprint submission, [AJLA+12] and [LATV11] present more efficient TFHE constructions based on LWE-style assumptions. The point of this construction is to demonstrate feasibility of TFHE under different complexity assumptions.[3]

We present our protocols in the information-theoretic model over secure point-to-point channels, and thus our protocols are secure in the presence of an honest majority. Thus, when used with our transformation, the resulting protocol is also only secure with an honest majority. By using another TFHE that tolerates a dishonest majority, our transformation results in an secure computation protocol that also tolerates the same.

The TFHE scheme provides a constant-round protocol for n players to generate a public-key and distribute private shares of the corresponding secret-key of a fully homomorphic encryption scheme. This step itself is non-trivial since the generation of the public-key for an FHE scheme (that is based on bootstrapping) requires encryption of the secret-key. Later, a majority of players can cooperatively decrypt a ciphertext by running a constant-round protocol on their private shares and a public ciphertext. We also provide methods for distributed encryption and for proving knowledge of an encrypted value.

We note that both our TFHE key generation and decryption protocols are more efficient than generically applying secure function evaluation techniques to the key generation or decryption algorithms of an FHE scheme. For example, with the right set of the parameters, our decryption protocol requires only a constant number of share multiplications, whereas generic techniques would require $O(poly(\lambda))$ such multiplications. We heavily exploit the linear nature of the operations involved in key generation, encryption and decryption for the particular FHE scheme of van Dijk et al. For key generation and decryption, we develop specific multiparty computation protocols that evaluates an arithmetic circuit using verifiable secret sharing techniques, that is more efficient than the application of generic techniques.

---

[3] We note that historically, threshold encryption has been presented where the key-generation algorithm and decryption algorithms are single algorithms, or they are multi-party protocols. We present multi-party protocols.

Comparison with Other FHE-Based Secure Computation Protocols. Gentry's [Gen09a] secure computation protocol was the first to achieve communication complexity that is independent of $|f|$ by using the PCP theorem in several steps.

Asharov, Jain and Wichs [AJLA+12] and López-Alt, Tromer, and Vaikuntanathan [LATV11] have constructed more efficient TFHE schemes based on LWE and the closely related RLWE assumption, which can be reduced to varying degrees to worst-case lattice problems. Their approaches rely on the ability to construct an FHE that also has a homomorphism on the secret-keys, and can also be used to achieve secure computation with communication that is independent of $|f|$. Together, our results demonstrate that the TFHE primitive can be developed from reductions to different classes of hardness assumptions, and therefore TFHE is not simply a consequence of a specific hardness property.

To achieve security against malicious adversaries, López-Alt et al. rely on a common reference string setup so that players can use a NIZK to prove to each other that their keys and their input ciphertexts are well-formed. The use of such NIZK also requires additional hardness assumptions, since (T)FHE is not known to imply NIZK. They can also instantiate their ideas in the standard model by replacing these NIZK proofs with traditional interactive ZK proofs; but in either case, the generic (NI)ZK techniques used require non-blackbox use of the underlying TFHE scheme.[4] By choosing the CRS model, the authors observed that by using a more expensive simulation-sound NIZK, their protocols can also achieve UC-security. Our protocols only claim standard security, but it has bee pointed out to us that it is likely that we can state some of ours results as UC in a TFHE-hybrid model.

Asharov et al. use efficient Σ-Protocol constructions to prove well-formedness; these make heavy use of the underlying mathematical structure of the LWE assumption. In order to have efficient NIZK proofs, they must rely on the use of the Random Oracle model, and the use of the Fiat-Shamir heuristic to transform the Σ-protocols into NIZK proofs. In any case, due to the black-box nature of our SMC construction, with simple modifications to the public-key to include labeled ciphertexts representing encryptions of 0 and 1, either of the López-Alt et al. or Asharov et al. TFHE schemes can be plugged in to our construction to achieve security against an arbitrary number of malicious adversaries, with abort. In contrast, with our scheme we are guaranteed output delivery, but need an honest majority of players.

The protocols of Damgård et al. [DPSZ12] and Bendlin et al. [BDOZ11] use a different approach to constructing secure computation protocols from traditional homomorphic encryption. Their schemes rely on the idea from Beaver [Bea91] for circuit randomization. First, they use an offline phase in which the parties use a somewhat homomorphic encryption primitive to create shares of triples (a, b, c) such that $a \cdot b = c$. One triple is required for each multiplication gate in f that is to be evaluated and requires approximately $O(n/s)$ "heavy" cryptographic

---

[4] In other words, the encryption algorithm of the TFHE will need to be expressed in terms of a graph-coloring instance (or Hamiltonicity, circuit-sat ,etc...). As far as we know, this transformation requires a high-order polynomial overhead.

operations to generate. Next, after such triples have been created, the parties use only information-theoretic methods to evaluate the circuit. This approach results in admirable communication parameters for small circuits (as they have also run practical examples); nonetheless, the approach requires linear communication for each gate in $|f|$, and thus does not achieve our main aim of eliminating this relationship.

Finally, these prior results are all in a model in which n parties are computing, and the protocols can tolerate up to $n - 1$ malicious parties. In contrast, our protocols require an honest majority. The relative incomparability of these models is well understood. In particular, in the model that tolerates up to $n - 1$ malicious adversaries, if any one party deviates form the protocol or fails, then all parties output $\perp$. Alternately, with an honest majority, all parties can output an effective output, as supported by our protocol. For a discussion of the relative merits of the two models, and the impossibility of having protocols that achieve the best of both worlds for general functionalities, see the work of Ishai et al. [IKK+11].

In summary, all of these recent works have advantages and disadvantages of their own; our major contribution is the black-box transformation and the independent hardness assumption.

Related work. Cramer, Damgård and Nielson [CDN01], along with Jakobbsson and Juels [JJ00] show how to use threshold cryptography to construct secure multiparty computation protocols. In more detail, we use many ideas from [CDN01] which shows how a homomorphic threshold cryptosystem can be used to achieve general multiparty computation protocols. The notion of using secret-sharing to encode encryptions, as we will do, was first seen in [CDSMW08] and has recently been extended in [GLOV12], although these works use the technique to ensure consistency, and not a proof-of-knowledge, as pursued here.

2   Preliminaries and Notation

A 4-tuple of protocols and algorithms (**Gen, Enc, Dec, Eval**) is a (t, n)-threshold fully homomorphic encryption scheme if the following hold:

Key Generation. An n-party protocol **Gen** that at each invocation returns a new public-key PK and the secret-key $(SK_1, \ldots, SK_n)$, where SK_i is the share of the secret-key for Player$_i$.

Encryption. A PPT algorithm $\mathbf{Enc}_{PK}(m, r)$ that returns the encryption of the plaintext m under the public-key PK with random coins r.

Decryption. There exists a PPT n-party protocol $\mathbf{Dec}(c, SK_1, \ldots, SK_n)$, which returns the plaintext m using the shares SK_i held by honest party Player$_i$, where $c = \mathbf{Enc}(m, r)$ for some random r.

f_{PK}-homomorphic. There exists a PPT algorithm **Eval** which given a polynomial f, ciphertexts $c_1 \in \mathbf{Enc}_{PK}(m_1), \ldots, c_k \in \mathbf{Enc}_{PK}(m_k)$ for some k and a public-key PK, outputs $c \in \mathbf{Enc}(f(m_1, \ldots, m_k))$.

The natural notion of chosen plaintext attack indistinguishability needs to be modified in the venue of threshold cryptography to take into account the fact that the adversary has access to shares of the secret-key. The appropriate corresponding and natural definition is given in [CDN01], and full version of our paper [MSas11]. Standard security notions for secure multi-party computation protocols can be used to define the security for the protocols **Gen** and **Dec** in any given instantiation of a TFHE (e.g., we can consider security in the real/ideal standalone paradigm, the UC framework, etc..)

Next, we present the notion of bootstrapping a ciphertext. Gentry developed the notion of Bootstrapping to reduce noise in a somewhat fully homomorphic encryption scheme, in order to achieve a fully homomorphic scheme. In contrast, we assume the existence of an FHE and simply use it to reduce noise produced in ciphertexts generated in our selective opening attack secure scheme that we introduce later.

Definition 1. *(Bootstrapping a Ciphertext) For a FHE scheme $\Pi = (G, E, D, \textbf{Eval})$ and the security parameter k, let D_Π be Π's decryption circuit, which takes a secret-key and s ciphertext as input. Given a ciphertext C encrypted with respect to a public-key PK and secret-key $SK = (SK_1, .., SK_\ell)$ we require that PK contains a bit-wise encryption of SK, denoted $s_1, ..., s_\ell$ where $s_i = E(PK, SK_i)$. Let $(C_1, .., C_n)$ denote the bits of C, and generate $c_i = E(PK, C_i)$. We say that the value $C^\dagger = \textbf{Eval}(PK, D_\pi, s_1, ..., s_\ell, c_1, .., c_n)$ (which homomorphically evaluates $D(SK, C)$) is the result of bootstrapping C.*

2.1 Selective Opening Security

In our construction, we will need to refer to encryption schemes where messages that are encrypted remain secure, even after the randomness used to encrypt related messages is revealed. This notion of security is called Selective Opening Security.

Definition 2 (IND-SO-SEC Encryption Security). *A public-key encryption scheme $\Pi = (G, E, D)$ is Indistinguishable Selective Opening secure if, for any message sampler M that supports efficient conditional resampling, and any ppt adversary $A = (A_1, A_2)$ there exists a negligible function μ such that for all sufficiently large k:*

$$\left| \Pr[A_\Pi^{\mathsf{Ind\text{-}SO\text{-}Real}}(1^k) = 1] - \Pr[A_\Pi^{\mathsf{Ind\text{-}SO\text{-}Ideal}}(1^k) = 1] \right| \leq \mu(k).$$

A message sampler M is a PPT algorithm that outputs a vector $\boldsymbol{m}$ of n messages from a given distribution. It is an efficient conditional resampler if, when given two auxiliary inputs, a set of indices $I \subseteq [n]$, and a vector of messages $\boldsymbol{m} = (m_1, ..., m_n)$, M samples another vector $\boldsymbol{m'} = (m'_1, \cdots, m'_n)$ conditioned on $m_i = m'_i$ for each $i \in I$. We define the experiments Ind-SO-Real and Ind-SO-Ideal as follows.

Ind-SO-Real(1^k, A)
  $(PK, SK) \leftarrow G(1^k)$
  $\boldsymbol{m} = (m_1, \ldots, m_n) \leftarrow M$
  $r_1, \ldots, r_n \leftarrow R$
  $(I, \sigma) \leftarrow A_1(PK, E_{PK}(m_1, r_1), \ldots, E_{PK}(m_n, r_n))$
  Output $A_2(\sigma, (m_i, r_i)_{i \in I}, \boldsymbol{m})$

Ind-SO-Ideal(1^k, A)
  $(PK, SK) \leftarrow G(1^k)$
  $\boldsymbol{m} = (m_1, \ldots, m_n) \leftarrow M$
  $(I, \sigma) \leftarrow A_1(PK, E_{PK}(m_1, r_1), \ldots, E_{PK}(m_n, r_n))$
  $\boldsymbol{m}' = (m_1', \ldots, m_n') \leftarrow M_{|I, m[I]}.$
  Output $A_2(\sigma, (m_i, r_i)_{i \in I}, \boldsymbol{m}')$

2.2   Circuit Privacy

Definition 3. *((Statistical) Circuit Private Homomorphic Encryption). A homomorphic encryption scheme $\varepsilon = (\boldsymbol{Gen}, \boldsymbol{Enc}, \boldsymbol{Dec})$ is circuit-private for circuits in a set C_ε if, for any key pair (PK, SK) output by $\boldsymbol{Gen}(\lambda)$, any circuit $C \in C_\varepsilon$, and any fixed ciphertext $\psi = \langle \psi_1, \ldots, \psi_t \rangle$ that are in the image of $\boldsymbol{Enc}$ for plaintexts $\pi_1, \ldots, \pi_t$, the following distributions (over the random coins in $\boldsymbol{Enc}, \boldsymbol{Eval}$) are (statistically) indistinguishable:*

$$\boldsymbol{Enc}_{PK}(C(\pi_1, \ldots, \pi_t)) \approx \boldsymbol{Eval}_{PK}(C, \psi)$$

In the original schemes first presented by both Dijk et al. [vDGHV10] and Gentry [Gen09a], the initial evaluation functions are deterministic and not circuit-private. In order to overcome this problem, both works introduce a method for adding random noise to encryptions, whether they are output from **Eval** or **Enc**, and thus in some sense rerandomizing them. This is done by adding an 'encryption' of 0 to the ciphertext in question, but where the 'encryption' has significantly more noise than would be generated by either the legitimate encryption or evaluation process. Specifically, they introduce ppt algorithms labeled CircuitPrivacy : $C_b \to C_b'$, where C consists of all the ciphertexts that are output from **Enc**$_{PK}(b)$ or a call to **Eval** with an encrypted output bit of b. It is the case that for any b and any $c_{b,0}, c_{b,1} \in C_b$.

$$\text{CircuitPrivacy}(c_{b,0}) \approx_s \text{CircuitPrivacy}(c_{b,1}).$$

3   Proof of Knowledge of an Encryption

As noted in the Introduction, the method of Cramer, Damgård, and Nielsen [CDN01] requires an honest-verifier zero-knowledge proof of knowledge of encrypted values for the threshold schemes that they employ. We provide a weaker 2-round solution to that requirement, which alas, is not zero-knowledge, but also does not release any information about the bit being discussed (we formalize this below). Moreover, our construction is black-box in the underlying circuit-private FHE scheme.

We construct this proof through a two-step process. At a high-level, instead of encrypting a bit b, we use a specific $(n, n/2 + 2)$ verifiable secret sharing scheme to generate n shares of b and encrypt those shares.[5] In order to give a proof of knowledge of the encryption of b, we allow a verifier to select $n/2 + 1$ of the encryptions of shares of b, and then direct the Prover to reveal the randomness used to encrypt those shares. To extract the bit, our extractor rewinds the proof and selects an alternate $n/2+1$ shares, so that with high probability, it can use $n/2+2$ shares to reconstruct b, and only b due to the verifiability of the secret sharing scheme. The problem with this approach is that revealing the randomness for an encryption raises selective decommitment issues. We use techniques from Hemenway et al. [HLOV11] to construct a bit-wise Indistinguishable Selective-Opening Secure encryption scheme from our threshold fully-homomorphic scheme. We can then use it to bitwise encrypt the VSS shares.

We note that the encryptions of the shares under the bit-wise Indistinguishable Selective-Opening Secure scheme, is not itself a homomorphic encryption scheme. For example, we cannot multiply directly two sets of shares encoding b_0 and b_1 and expect the result to encode $b_0 \cdot b_1$. However, the individual encrypted bits are still properly encoded ciphertexts under the FHE scheme that have a circuit-privacy evaluation function applied to them. Intuitively, therefore, we can homomorphically evaluate the reveal function of the secret sharing scheme to get a single encryption representing the reconstituted bit. This encryption can then be used to homomorphically evaluate the function as in Cramer et al. [CDN01]. There is however a snag: in principle, once the circuit-privacy function has been applied to a ciphertext, it may no longer be able to have homomorphic operations applied to it, as this is not guaranteed by the definition.[6] However, this problem is easily surmounted by applying Gentry's bootstrapping technique (cf. Defn 1) to re-encode the selective-opening secure schemes into ciphertexts which can have homomorphic operations applied to them, and thus the VSS's reveal algorithm can be applied to the individual bits of the shares, resulting in ciphertext of the encoded bit, which is in the ciphertext space of the TFHE scheme.

Using FHE to construct a Selective Opening Encryption Scheme. Hemenway et al. [HLOV11] show how any re-randomizable encryption scheme can be used to construct a natural lossy encryption scheme and thus, by the result of Bellare et al. [BHY09], is secure against indistinguishable selective opening attacks.

Since the Hemenway and Ostrovsky construction relies on re-randomization, they suggest that the distribution of a "fresh" encryption of a message should be

---

[5] We use a verifiable secret sharing scheme with a $n/2 + 2$ threshold to simplify the proof of the VSS, thus $|T| = n/2 + 1$ is chosen to be right under the threshold of the VSS, as one might expect.

[6] Further, in practice, with known schemes, these ciphertexts have too much noise in them to allow further homomorphic operations without sacrificing decryption correctness.

statistically close to a rerandomization of a fixed message. They point out that
all homomorphic encryption schemes up to that point achieved this property by
adding an encryption of 0 to the current message. While this property was true
of all schemes at the time, it is not actually true of the known fully homomorphic
encryption schemes, because each time we add an encrypted message to another
we increase the amount of noise that is embedded in the ciphertexts, and thus
fresh encryptions have less noise than encryptions that have had operations
(such as addition) applied to them. Fortunately, the property they state is overly
strong, and a simple observation shows that for their construction to go through
they only require that the distributions

$$\{r \leftarrow R : E_{pk}(,0,r) \boxplus E_{pk}(m,r_0)\} \approx_s \{r \leftarrow R : E_{pk}(0,r) \boxplus E_{pk}(m,r_1)\},$$

for all public-keys pk, messages m and random strings r_0 and r_1 where $\boxplus$ is the
homomorphic addition operation. However, it is simple to see that even these
two distributions are not statistically close for the fully homomorphic encryption
schemes that have been proposed. Fortunately, both schemes under consideration
have rerandomization functions built to ensure *Circuit-Privacy*, as is defined
in [Gen09b] and Def. 3.

Construction of a SOA from Lossy. We generate a public-key for the Lossy
scheme by generating a traditional public-key and secret-key for the TFHE,
and then we augment the public-key with two labeled ciphertexts c_0 and c_1,
representing encryptions of 0 and 1. Now, to encrypt a bit b, we take c_b, and
rerandomize it using the circuit-privacy function (In comparison, Hemenway and
Ostrovsky add an encryption of the bit 0). Decryption works as it does in the
FHE scheme. The lossy key generator simply has c_1 represent an encryption of
0 instead of 1. By the IND-CPA security of the TFHE scheme, the keys are
indistinguishable. The scheme is formally described below.

Key Generation $G'(1^k, b), b \in \{\mathsf{INJ}, \mathsf{LOSSY}\}$**:** Let $(\mathrm{PK}, \mathrm{SK}) \leftarrow G(1^k), c_0 \leftarrow E(\mathrm{PK}, 0)$, $c_1 \leftarrow E(\mathrm{PK}, 1)$ and $c_1' \leftarrow E(\mathrm{PK}, 0)$. If $b = \mathsf{INJ}$ Output $\mathrm{PK}' = (pk, c_0, c_1)$ and $\mathrm{SK}' = \mathrm{SK}$, else when $b = \mathsf{LOSSY}$ output $\mathrm{PK}' = (\mathrm{PK}, c_0, c_1')$ and $\mathrm{SK}' = \mathrm{SK}$.

Encryption $E'(\mathrm{PK}' = (\mathrm{PK}, c_0, c_1), b)$**:** Output $\mathsf{ReRand}(c_b)$.

Decryption $D'(\mathrm{SK}, c)$**:** Output $D(\mathrm{SK}, c)$.

Theorem 1. *If (G, E, D) is a circuit-private FHE, then the blackbox construction (G', E', D') described above is an IND-SO-SEC secure encryption scheme.*

Proof. Follows from [HLOV11] and [BHY09].

Modifying the SOA-secure Encryption Scheme to Support POKs. Again, in order
to be able to provide a proof of knowledge that a party has knowledge of the value
encrypted, we need to provide a POK. We will show a 2-round public-coin proof
of knowledge of the encrypted bit based on any selective opening secure scheme.
The protocol is neither zero-knowledge nor witness indistinguishable, but does

maintain secrecy of the encrypted bit. First, we encrypt bits using the following protocol. Let $\Pi' = (G', E', D')$ be the selective-opening attack secure scheme described in Thm. 1. We construct a new encryption scheme $\hat{\Pi} = (\hat{G}, \hat{E}, \hat{D})$ to encode bits as follows. We define $\hat{G} = G'$, and present the algorithms for $\hat{E}$ and $\hat{D}$ below. Refer to a full version of our work [MSas11] for the standard definitions of the Verifiable Secret Sharing algorithms.

$\hat{E}(\text{PK}, b, r)$

  $(s_1, ..., s_n) \leftarrow VSShare_{(n, n/2+2)}(b)$
  Let M be the $n \times n$ matrix
  representation of shares $(s_1, \ldots, s_n)$
  $c_{i,j} = E'(\text{PK}, M_{i,j}, r_{i,j})$
  Output $\mathbf{C} = \{c_{i,j}\}_{i,j \in n}$

$\hat{D}(\text{SK}, \mathbf{C})$

  $M = \{M_{i,j}\}_{i,j \in [n]} \leftarrow D'(\text{SK}, \mathbf{C})$
  Let $(s_1, \ldots, s_n)$ be the shares
  corresponding to matrix M.
  $T' = \{t | 1 \le t \le n$ share s_t
      is $n/2 + 2$ -consistent$\}$
  If $|T'| < n/2 + 2$ output $\perp$.
  Let $T \subseteq T'$ s.t. $|T| = n/2 + 2$.
  Output $VSReveal_{(n, n/2+2)}(\{s_{t_i}\})_{t_i \in T}$

Hidden Bit POK. Given a ciphertext $\mathbf{C} = \{c_{i,j}\}_{i,j \in n}$ output by encryption algorithm $\hat{E}$ and the random coins r used to generate it, we show how to perform a two-round proof of knowledge of the encrypted bit $\hat{D}(\text{SK}, \mathbf{C})$. P will prove that it has knowledge of the underlying shares of the verifiable secret-sharing scheme that have been encrypted. In order to do this, the verifier sends a random challenge of indices $T \subset [n]$, where $|T| = n/2 + 1$. The encryptor then decommits to these encryptions by providing the random-bits used to encrypt each share of the bit. If each bit decommits successfully, and the result is $n/2 + 1$ valid shares to the VSS, then the verifier accepts.

Prover$(\text{PK}, \mathbf{C} = \{c_{i,j}\}_{i,j \in [n]}$
  $= \hat{E}(\text{PK}, b, r), M, r)$

Let $c_{i,j} = E'(\text{PK}, M_{i,j}, r_{i,j})$

$\xleftarrow{\quad T \quad}$

$\xrightarrow{\{M_{i,x}, r_{i,x}, M_{x,i}, r_{x,i}\}_{\substack{i \in T \\ x \in [n]}}}$

Verifier$(\text{PK}, \mathbf{C} = \{c_{i,j}\}_{i,j \in [n]})$

$T \leftarrow \{S | S \subset [n] \wedge |S| = \frac{n}{2} + 1\}$

if $\exists i, j : c_{ij} \ne E'(\text{PK}, M_{i,j}, r_{i,j})$,
  output $\perp$.
Output 1.

Extractor$(\mathbf{C}, \text{PK}, U_1 = \{M_{i,x}, r_{i,x}, M_{x,i}, r_{x,i}\}_{\substack{i \in T_1 \\ x \in [n]}}, U_2 = \{M_{i,x}, r_{i,x}, M_{x,i}, r_{x,i}\}_{\substack{i \in T_2 \\ x \in [n]}})$

Let $T = T_1 \cup T_2$, $U = U_1 \cup U_2$
If $|T| < n/2$ output $\perp$.
If $\exists i \in T, x \in [n]$ s.t. $E'(\text{PK}, M_{i,x}, r_{i,x}) \ne c_{i,x}$ or $E'(\text{PK}, M_{x,i}, r_{x,i}) \ne c_{x,i}$ output $\perp$.
For each $i \in T$ reconstruct its corresponding share s_i.
Output $VSReveal_{(n, n/2+2)}(s_{r_1}, .., s_{r_{\frac{n}{2}}})$, where $r_1, .., r_{\frac{n}{2}}$ are the smallest indices in T.

Completeness. Follows by inspection.
Extractability (Soundness). Soundness follows from an extractor.

Theorem 2. *For all sufficiently large n, for all $d > 0$, for all $(SK, PK) \leftarrow \hat{G}$, for all 'ciphertext' inputs C, and provers P', if $(P', V)(C = \{c_{i,j}\}_{i,j \in [n]}, PK)$ accepts with probability $1/n^d$, then there exists a probabilistic polynomial time extractor that, with all but negligible probability, outputs a set of decommitments to all ciphertexts for a given set of indices $L = \{\ell_1, \cdots, \ell_{n/2+2}\} \subseteq [n]$ that constitute shares $S = \{s_{\ell_1}, ..., s_{\ell_{n/2+2}}\}$ such that $VSReveal_{(n,n/2+2)}(s_{\ell_1}, ..., s_{\ell_{n/2+2}}) = \hat{D}(SK, C)$.*

Definition 4. *We say an $n \times n$ matrix representation of shares has t-consistent indices if there is a set S of size t such that for each $i \in S$, each row i and column i is $n/2 + 2$ consistent.*

Proof. Given the ability to rewind the prover-verifier protocol, we can extract the encrypted bit by recovering enough shares of the VSS scheme. We continue to execute the prover/verifier protocol until we get two distinct separate accepting proofs. It is a simple observation that except with exponentially small probability, we will succeed in $O(n^{d+1})$ rewinds. Let (T_1, U_1) and (T_2, U_2) be the flows in the first and second accepting proofs, respectively. By the security of the commitment scheme (here we are using our encryption scheme as a simple commitment scheme), the probability that there is a ciphertext $c_{i,j}$ that is ever decommitted to in two distinct fashions is negligble.

We feed these inputs in to *Extractor*. If there is not a valid encryption of a bit (fewer than $n/2 + 2$ committed and consistent shares), then by Lemma 1, the probability that the verifier outputs anything other than $\perp$ is less than $\frac{1}{\binom{n}{n/2+2}}$ which grows exponentially small.

Given the decommitments of the shares $\{s_i\}_{i \in T_i}$ for different randomly chosen set of indices T_1 and T_2, note these sets are not the same by selection, and therefore there is no chance that $\perp$ is output by the extractor. Next the extractor executes a $VSReveal_{(n,n/2+2)}$ command. However, this is not necessarily over the same shares as would be revealed in a legitimate decryption. We need to ensure that no matter which of the rewound and newly played legitimate traces we receive, we are going to reveal the same encrypted bit, with all but negligible probability. That is, we need to ensure that $VSReveal_{(n,n/2+2)}(s_{r_1}, ..., s_{r_{n/2}}) = VSReveal_{(n,n/2+2)}(s_1, ..., s_{n/2})$. This is the case, as shown in Lemma 2 because of the verifiable properties of the secret sharing scheme ensures that even in the case of a corrupted dealer (improper ciphertext encoding of shares) then all honest players will reveal the same value, with all but negligible probability. Therefore, with all but negligible probability we have that the extractor outputs the same value as $D(SK, c)$.

Lemma 1. *Let M be an $n \times n$ matrix with at most $n/2 + 1$ consistent indices. The probability that any $n/2 + 1$ randomly selected indices (without replacement) choose a set of $n/2 + 1$ consistent indices is no more than*

$$1/\binom{n}{n/2+1}.$$

Proof. There can be at most 1 set of size $(n/2 + 1)$ that is $(n/2 + 1)$ consistent in an $n \times n$ matrix. The lemma follows by computing the probability of choosing this one set from a set of n objects.

Lemma 2. *Let M be $n \times n$ matrix representation of shares. Let $S, T \subseteq [n]$, $|S| = |T| = n/2 + 2$, $S \neq T$, and the rows $R_S = \{r_i\}_{i \in S}$, $R_T = \{r_i\}_{i \in T}$ and columns $C_S = \{c_i\}_{i \in S}$, $C_T = \{c_i\}_{i \in T}$ are all $n/2 + 2$-consistent. Let $s = (s_1, ..., s_{n/2+2})$ and $t = (t_1, ..., t_{n/2+2})$ be the shares drawn from M corresponding to the sets of indices S and T respectively. Then*

$$VSReveal_{(n,n/2+2)}(s_1, ..., s_{n/2+1}) = VSReveal_{(n,n/2+2)}(t_1, ..., t_{n/2+1})$$

Proof. Note that $VSReveal_{(n,n/2+2)}$ will never output $\bot$ under our conditions, so all that we need do is show that f will interpolate to the same value in both cases.

We know that the rows $R_T = \{r_i\}_{i \in T}$ and columns $C_R = \{c_i\}_{i \in T}$ are all $(n/2 + 2)$-consistent. Choose any $j \in S \setminus T$. Let $T = \{t_1, ..., t_{n/2+2}\}$. Consider $c_j = (c_{1,j}, c_{2,j}, ..., c_{n,j})^T$. Since c_j is $n/2 + 2$-consistent, the points $(c_{t_1,j}, t_1), ..., (c_{t_{n/2+1},j}, t_{n/2+2})$, interpolate to a unique univariate degree $n/2+1$ polynomial (i.e. $f(x, j)$). This defines $(c_{1,j}, c_{2,j}, ..., c_{n,j})^T$, so the column j must be consistent with T. Since the jth column was an arbitrary column in S different from those in T, all such columns must be consistent with the rows defined be T. A symmetric argument shows that rows selected by S must be consistent with the columns selected by T. Therefore, both sets are consistent in that they define the same polynomials. Therefore, interpolation in $VSReveal_{(n,n/2+2)}$ will result in the same output.

Hidden Bit. We show that no efficient cheating verifier can predict the bit b, when given $C = \hat{E}(PK, b, r)$ as a theorem for which we are engaging in a POK.

Theorem 3. *For every P.P.T. adversary $A = (A_1, A_2)$, there exists a negligible function μ such that $\Pr[HB_A(1^k) = 1] \leq 1/2 + \mu(k)$, where HB_A is defined below:*

$HB_A(1^k)$

$(PK, SK) \leftarrow \hat{G}(1^k)$
$b \in \{0, 1\}$
$C = \{c_{i,j}\}_{i,j \in [n]} = \hat{E}(PK, b)$ *where* $c_{i,j} = E'(PK, M_{i,j}, r_{i,j})$ *are SOA-sec.*
$(T, \sigma) \leftarrow A_1(PK, C)$ *where* $T \subset [n]$, $|T| = n/2 + 1$.
$b' \leftarrow A_2(\sigma, (M_{i,j}, r_{i,j})_{i,j \in T})$
Output 1 iff $b = b'$

Proof. This follows directly from the IND-SO-SEC security of $\Pi' = (G', E', D')$. Suppose an adversary $A = (A_1, A_2)$ breaks the hidden bit security of the protocol. That is for some $d > 0$ and infinitely many k: $\Pr[HB_A(1^k) = 1] \geq 1/2 + 1/k^d$. We use it to build an adversary $B = (B_1, B_2)$ and message selector M that breaks the IND-SO-SEC security (cf. Defn. in [BHY09] or [MSas11]) of $\Pi' = (G', E', D')$. The message selector M chooses a random* bit b, let

$(s_1, ..., s_n) \leftarrow VSShare_{(n,n/2+2)}(b)$, and let $\mathbf{M}$ be the $n \times n$ matrix that represents the shares $(s_1, \ldots, s_n)$ according to the ECC representation of the VSS. Output $\mathbf{M}$.

The adversary $B_1\left(\text{PK}, (E(\text{PK}, \mathbf{M_{i,j}}, \mathbf{r_{i,j}}))_{i,j \in n}\right)$ for the IND-SO-SEC experiment simulates $(T, \sigma) \leftarrow A_1(\text{PK}, C = (E(\text{PK}, \mathbf{M_{i,j}}, \mathbf{r_{i,j}})))$, and outputs $I = \{(i,j)|i, j \in n, i \in T \text{ or } j \in T\}$ and $\sigma' = (T, \sigma)$. Recall by the definition of A_1, $|T| = n/2 + 1$.

The conditional message selector $M_{I,m[I]}$ from the SOA security definition finds a random bi-variate polynomial of degree $n/2 + 1$ in each variable over the field F such that $f(0,0) \in \{0,1\}$ and for each $(i,j) \in I$, it holds that $f(i,j) = \mathbf{M}_{i,j}$. Since $|T| = n/2 + 1$, and thus we have effectively release $n/2 + 1$ shares for a VSS scheme that requires $n/2 + 2$ for reconstruction, the information secrecy property of the VSS guarantees there are exactly the same number of such selections for the case $f(0,0) = 0$ and $f(0,0) = 1$. $M_{I,m[I]}$ outputs $\{f(i,j)\}_{1 \leq, i,j \leq n}$.

The adversary $B_2(\sigma, (M_{i,j}, r_{i,j})_{(i,j) \in I}, \mathbf{M}^*)$ computes the shares $(s_1^*, ..., s_n^*)$ that correspond to $\mathbf{M}^*$, and runs $VSReveal_{(n,n/2+2)}(s_1^*, .., s_n^*) = b'$, it then executes $b \leftarrow A_2(\sigma, (m_{i,j}, r_{i,j})_{(i,j) \in I})$ and outputs 1 iff $b = b'$.

Now consider $\Pr[B_\Pi^{\text{Ind-SO-Real}}(1^k) = 1]$, this is a perfect simulation of $HB_A(1^k)$, and therefore by the assumption that A breaks the hidden-bit security, the term must exceed $1/2 + \epsilon$, where $\epsilon \geq 1/k^c$. In contrast, consider $\Pr[B_\Pi^{\text{Ind-SO-Ideal}}(1^k) = 1]$. In the case that $VSReveal_{(n,n/2+2)}(s_1^*, \ldots, s_n^*) = VSReveal_{(n,n/2+2)}(s_1, \ldots, s_n)$, which occurs with probability exactly $1/2$, it is again a perfect simulation of $HB_A(1^k)$, and so the experiment outputs 1 with probability $1/2 + \epsilon$. In contrast, when $VSReveal_{(n,n/2+2)}(s^*1..., s_n^*)) \neq VSReveal_{(n,n/2+2)}(s_1, ..., s_n)$, then we know that A_2 outputs $VSReveal_{(n,n/2+2)}(s_1, ..., s_n)$ with probability $1/2 + \epsilon$, and so B_2 outputs 1 with probability $1 - (1/2 + \epsilon) = 1/2 - \epsilon$. Therefore, $\Pr[B_\Pi^{\text{Ind-SO-Ideal}}(1^k) = 1] = (1/2)(1/2 + \epsilon + 1/2 - \epsilon) = 1/2$. Therefore, $\Pr[B_\Pi^{\text{Ind-SO-Real}}(1^k) = 1] - \Pr[B_\Pi^{\text{Ind-SO-Ideal}}(1^k) = 1] = 1/2 + \epsilon - 1/2 \geq 1/k^c$, breaking IND-SO-SEC security.

Using the SOA Ciphertexts in a Secure Multiparty Computation Protocol. In our SMC construction, we encode all users' inputs using the POK scheme above. The encrypted inputs are sent to the other parties. After each party's input has been confirmed with a proof of knowledge, the parties homomorphically evaluate the different ciphertexts to get an appropriate encrypted output. However, as explained before, the POK encryptions are not themselves homomorphic. To solve this problem we use Gentry's bootstrapping technique. Bootstrapping lets us take a ciphertext in an FHE scheme with any amount of noise that still allows for proper decryption (specially, this is potentially more noise than is permissible to perform any extra homomorphic operations without destroying the correctness of the ciphertext), and output a new ciphertext in the FHE scheme, of the same value, but with a small enough amount of noise that it can be properly computed on through the use of the FHE's evaluation function. Given a ciphertext $C = \{c_{i,j}\}_{i,j \in [n]}$ in the POK scheme, each $c_{i,j}$ is a ciphertext from a lossy encryption scheme. To convert C into a corresponding encryption $c^\dagger$ in the TFHE scheme we do the following: We bootstrap each $c_{i,j}$ which is simply a TFHE ciphertext that has had the circuit-privacy function applied to it—thus containing potentially too much noise to apply further homomorphic operations to, but not so much that it decrypts improperly— to receive the corresponding lower-noise TFHE ciphertext $c'_{i,j}$. The c' ciphertexts can now be evaluated in the THFE eval function, and in particular we can use the TFHE eval function, to evaluate $VSReveal_{(n, n/2+2)}$. The result of this evaluation is the ciphertext $C^\dagger$ corresponding to the output.

Protocols vs. Algorithms. We note that there is one technical issue that needs to be resolved, which is that in this section we have described the key generation and decryption algorithms as stand-alone algorithms, rather than protocols. For our purposes, we need a joint protocol for key generation and decryption. For this reason, we need to modify our key generation algorithm in the TFHE scheme to include an encryption of the bits 0 and 1 in the public-key. These values allow the parties to encrypt under the SOA secure encryption scheme $\hat{\Pi}$. The SOA secure scheme does not modify the decryption algorithm, so there is no need for modification to the decryption protocol.

4   Secure Multiparty Computation

We follow the Cramer et al. [CDN01] approach for constructing a multi-party computation protocol based on threshold cryptography. Our biggest changes are that we do not need a protocol for multiplication, we use a different approach for proving knowledge of encryption, and we explicitly describe a key generation phase whereas it is assumed as an external setup in [CDN01]. Since our solution requires less interaction among the parties, our simulation argument is simpler than the argument from [CDN01].

We use the standard simulation-based definition of stand-alone secure multi-party computation. We assume the existence of a standard n-party CoinFlipping protocol which guarantees soundness in the presence of $< n/2$ adversaries: namely, for any minority set of adversaries, the protocol guarantees that the distribution is still statistically close to uniform. Such a protocol can be easily constructed based on the existence of hiding commitments. (Unlike [CDN01], we do not need this coin flipping protocol to be simulatable.). See our full version [MSas11] for a definition of the real/ideal paradigm for secure multi-party computation from [CDN01] and [IKK+11]. In this section the TFHE scheme used is denoted $\tilde{\Pi} = (\tilde{G}, \tilde{E}, \tilde{D}, \mathbf{Eval})$.

We assume that the players can communicate via an authenticated broadcast channel and via point-to-point private and authenticated channels (which may in turn be implemented using signatures, public-key encryption, etc.)

Protocol 1. Each party holds private input x_i; the parties jointly compute $f(x_1, \ldots, x_n)$.

1: Party P_i receives as input $(1^k, n, x_i)$. (We assume the adversary receives as input $1^k, n$, a set of corrupted parties C and the inputs $\{x_c\}_{c \in X}$ for the corrupted parties, and auxiliary information.)

2: Players run the TFHE key generation subprotocol $\tilde{G}(\eta, \tau, \rho, \theta, \Theta, \kappa)$ to generate a public-key $\tilde{PK}$ and shares of the secret for the threshold scheme $\tilde{\Pi}$. At the end of this step, player p_i holds share SK_i of the secret-key SK. If the sub-protocol halts prematurely, then players halt and output $\perp$.

3: The players take sequential turns sharing their input using the encryption scheme $\hat{\Pi}$ that is constructed from Π (see §3). More specifically, for $i \in [n]$, player P_i broadcasts $c_{i,j} \leftarrow \hat{E}(\tilde{PK}, x_{i,j})$. Then all of the players run a standard CoinFlipping protocol to generate a random string r_i. Player P_i now interprets r_i as n strings $r_{i,1}, \ldots, r_{i,n}$ and uses coins $r_{i,j}$ as the random coins to run Verifier($PK, c_{i,j}$) (see §3) of the Hidden Bit POK protocol on input $c_{i,j}$ for each bit $j \in [n]$ of input x_i. Player P_i runs the corresponding Prover algorithm on $c_{i,j}$ using the random coins used to generate $c_{i,j}$ as the witness, and broadcasts the Prover message. The remaining players also execute the Verifier algorithm using the same random coins and verify that the first message is consistent and the second message is accepted. If player P_i fails the POK protocol, then P_i is excluded from the rest of the protocol, and the remaining players that have not been excluded use a canonical encryption of 0 as the input for P_i (e.g., they use $\tilde{E}(\tilde{PK}, 0; 0)$ as each input bit).

4: The players that have not been excluded locally run **Eval**($\tilde{PK}, c_{1,1}, \ldots, c_{n,n}, \tilde{f}$) where the function $\tilde{f}$ first transforms the input ciphertexts encrypted under $\hat{\Pi}$ into ones for scheme $\tilde{\Pi}$. This is done by homomorphically evaluating the decryption procedure described in §3 (i.e. bootstrapping, see Defn. 1).(Note: All of the ciphertexts in $c_{i,j}$ have a large degree of noise in them due to the circuit-privacy call that was used to rerandomize the ciphertexts. Therefore, the first thing that is done is that the ciphertexts are re-encoded with less noise using the same procedure as FHE bootstrapping.) Next, compute ciphertext z_i of the result $f(x_1, \ldots, x_n)$. Note that each player can complete this step using only local information (since the public-key for the FHE includes all the information needed for evaluation).

5: Each player P_i that has not been excluded broadcasts the ciphertext z_i computed in the previous step. Each player then locally computes the majority of the broadcasts as ciphertext z'. A majority is guaranteed to exist since the malicious players form a minority and **Eval** is deterministic. Any player whose broadcast differs from the majority is excluded from the remaining portion of the protocol.

6: Players p_i that have not been excluded run the distributed subprotocol $\tilde{D}(z', SK_1, \ldots, SK_n)$ using input z' and their local share SK_i. The output of the protocol is taken as the output.

Theorem 4. *Let π be Protocol 8 for a function f, and fix $s \in \{1, \ldots, n/2\}$. If Π is a circuit-private TFHE encryption scheme, then for any ppt adversary A, there exists a ppt adversary A' such that for every polynomial-size circuit family $Z = Z_k$ corrupting a minority of parties the following is negligible:*

$$|\Pr\left[\text{REAL}_{\pi,A,Z}(k) = 1\right] - \Pr\left[\text{IDEAL}_{f,A',Z}(k) = 1\right]|.$$

See full version for details.

5   Threshold FHE for the Integers

In this section we briefly highlight the construction of a TFHE scheme $\tilde{\Pi} = (\tilde{G}, \tilde{E}, \tilde{D}, \widetilde{\text{Eval}})$ from the FHE scheme $\Pi = (G, E, D, \text{Eval})$ based on the Approximate-GCD problem described by [vDGHV10]. The details are presented in our full version online. We point out that in any such transformation $\tilde{E} = E$ and $\widetilde{\text{Eval}} = \text{Eval}$, and thus we only need to describe protocols for computing $\tilde{G}$ and $\tilde{D}$.

Sharing the Public and Secret-Key. Recall the secret-key p for the "somewhat homomorphic encryption scheme" is an odd η-bit integer. To sample p in a distributed fashion, we notice that the bits p_0 and $p_{\eta-1}$ should be 1 whereas the rest of the bits $p_1, \ldots, p_{\eta-2}$ should be randomly shared. At the end, each player holds a share of p. We then extend techniques from [KLML05] to allow multiple parties who hold shares of p to compute shares of $1/p$ and $x_p = \lfloor 2^\kappa/p \rceil$.

Recall that the secret-key for Π consists of a Θ-bit vector s with Hamming weight θ. Our first modification to Π is to note that instead of θ, it suffices to select a vector with Hamming weight in the interval $\theta \pm \theta/4$. To verify this, note that the sparse subset-sum problem is assumed to be hard for $\theta = \Theta^\epsilon$ for $0 < \epsilon < 1$; our change does not violate this condition. Also, our new range of settings for θ does not increase the total degree of the decryption circuit by more than a factor of 2 and thus the condition that the decryption protocol is admissible is maintained (and thus the scheme is bootstrappable. See the computation on p.18 [vDGHV10].) Our approach for producing s is to securely generate a random number r_i in the range $[0, \Theta]$ for each s_i and setting $s_i = 1$ if $r_i \le \theta$ and 0 otherwise.

The public-key consists of the vectors x and u. Using s and x_p, we compute the vector u using the formula $u = \sum_i s_i \cdot u_i \mod 2^{\kappa+1}$. These shares can be used to compute the vector y.

Using bits of $1/p$ computed in previous steps, we generate the x_i's. Recall from the original public-key generation algorithm that we need to sample $x_i \leftarrow D_{\gamma,\rho}(p)$ for $i = 0, \ldots, \tau$. Intuitively, these x_i represent random encryptions of 0 that get added to our base encryption in the homomorphic scheme. Further, recall that

$$D_{\gamma,\rho}(p) = \{\text{choose } q \leftarrow Z \cap [0, 2^\gamma/p), r \leftarrow Z \cap (-2^\rho, 2^\rho) : \text{output } x \leftarrow pq + r\}.$$

After sampling, the list should be relabeled so that x_0 is the largest. The key-generation process requires that the process is restarted if either x_0 is even or $x_0 - \lfloor x_0/p \rceil \cdot p$ is odd. Since $x_0 = pq + r$ is generated as directed for some random q and r and since p is an odd number, the requirement that x_0 is odd can be checked by inspecting the least significant bits of the q and r: If $q_0 + r_0 = 1$, then x_0 satisfies the first condition. To check the second condition, that $x_0 - \lfloor x_0/p \rceil \cdot p$ is an odd number, we observe that because of the constraints $-2^\rho < r < 2^\rho$ and $2^{\eta-1} \le p < 2^\eta$, it follows that $-2^{\rho-\eta+1} < r/p < 2^{\rho-\eta+1}$.

Since $\rho = \lambda$ and $\eta = \tilde{O}(\lambda^2)$, therefore for all sufficiently large λ (if $\eta = \lambda^2$, then for $\lambda > 2$), $\lfloor r/p \rceil = 0$ and as a result r can be ignored. That is $\lfloor x_0/q \rceil = \lfloor pq + r/q \rceil = q + \lfloor r/q \rceil = q$. So $x_0 - \lfloor x_0/p \rceil \cdot p = x_0 - q \cdot p$. Because x_0 and p are both odd, q must be odd to make the term $x_0 - \lfloor x_0/p \rceil \cdot p$ even. These constraints imply that for x_0 to be odd and $x_0 - \lfloor x_0/p \rceil \cdot p$ to be even, then q must be even and r must be odd.

Computing encryptions of s. One step in Gentry's paradigm for FHE construction requires the public-key to contain an encryption of the secret-key. We assume circular security of the underlying encryption scheme, as do van Dijk et al. [vDGHV10] and Gentry [Gen09b]. Towards this goal, we design a protocol that enables players who hold private shares of the secret-key (as well as the entire public-key) to compute an encryption of the secret-key under the public-key. Note this *cannot* be done trivially with homomorphic evaluation because the encrypted secret-key is in fact necessary to homomorphically evaluate circuits of an arbitrary depth, resulting in a circular requirement.

Recall that in Dijk et al. [vDGHV10], the encryption of m under the public-key $\langle x_0, \ldots, x_\tau \rangle$ computes as $[m + 2r + 2\sum_{i \in S} x_i]_{x_0}$, where $r \in (-2^{\rho'}, 2^{\rho'})$ and $S \subseteq \{1, \ldots, \tau\}$ is a random subset. Since both the x_i's and r can take negative values (as integers) whereas the computation is in a finite field, we need to somehow make sure the computation in the finite field result in the same integer value of the encryption of m. To resolve this issue, we compute the value *min* which is a unique value that satisfies the following two properties: 1) *min* $= 0$ mod x_0, and 2) for an arbitrary S and for our set of x_i's and any value of r, it would make the summation $m + 2r + 2\sum_{i \in S} x_i$ positive. Because the range of values that r can take is public, all users can compute *min* locally and agree on respective shares. Next, to encrypt the secret-key, all users generate shares for a set S and the shares for a value r. All users then add their shares of r, use shares in S to add in appropriate x_i's, and add *min*. See the full version for details.

Computing encryptions of 0 and 1 for PK. The same techniques from the previous step can be used to produce encryptions of random bits. These encryptions can then be collaboratively decrypted until both an encryption of 0 and an encryption of 1 are identified. These two ciphertexts can then be adjoined to the public-key—they are guaranteed to be well-formed and have the right amount of noise.

References

[AJLA+12] Asharov, G., Jain, A., López-Alt, A., Tromer, E., Vaikuntanathan, V., Wichs, D.: Multiparty Computation with Low Communication, Computation and Interaction via Threshold FHE. In: Pointcheval, D., Johansson, T. (eds.) EUROCRYPT 2012. LNCS, vol. 7237, pp. 483–501. Springer, Heidelberg (2012)

[BDOZ11]   Bendlin, R., Damgård, I., Orlandi, C., Zakarias, S.: Semi-homomorphic Encryption and Multiparty Computation. In: Paterson, K.G. (ed.) EUROCRYPT 2011. LNCS, vol. 6632, pp. 169–188. Springer, Heidelberg (2011)

[Bea91]   Beaver, D.: Efficient Multiparty Protocols Using Circuit Randomization. In: Feigenbaum, J. (ed.) CRYPTO 1991. LNCS, vol. 576, pp. 420–432. Springer, Heidelberg (1992)

[BHY09]   Bellare, M., Hofheinz, D., Yilek, S.: Possibility and Impossibility Results for Encryption and Commitment Secure under Selective Opening. In: Joux, A. (ed.) EUROCRYPT 2009. LNCS, vol. 5479, pp. 1–35. Springer, Heidelberg (2009)

[CDD+99]   Cramer, R., Damgård, I., Dziembowski, S., Hirt, M., Rabin, T.: Efficient Multiparty Computations Secure against an Adaptive Adversary. In: Stern, J. (ed.) EUROCRYPT 1999. LNCS, vol. 1592, pp. 311–326. Springer, Heidelberg (1999)

[CDN01]   Cramer, R., Damgård, I.B., Nielsen, J.B.: Multiparty Computation from Threshold Homomorphic Encryption. In: Pfitzmann, B. (ed.) EUROCRYPT 2001. LNCS, vol. 2045, pp. 280–299. Springer, Heidelberg (2001)

[CDSMW08] Choi, S.G., Dachman-Soled, D., Malkin, T., Wee, H.: Black-Box Construction of a Non-malleable Encryption Scheme from Any Semantically Secure One. In: Canetti, R. (ed.) TCC 2008. LNCS, vol. 4948, pp. 427–444. Springer, Heidelberg (2008)

[DIK10]   Damgård, I., Ishai, Y., Krøigaard, M.: Perfectly Secure Multiparty Computation and the Computational Overhead of Cryptography. In: Gilbert, H. (ed.) EUROCRYPT 2010. LNCS, vol. 6110, pp. 445–465. Springer, Heidelberg (2010)

[Gen09a]   Craig Gentry. A fully homomorphic encryption scheme. PhD thesis, Stanford University (2009), http://crypto.stanford.edu/craig

[DPSZ12]   Damgård, I., Pastro, V., Smart, N.P., Zakarias, S.: Multiparty computation from somewhat homomorphic encryption. In: Safavi-Naini, R. (ed.) CRYPTO 2012. LNCS, vol. 7417, pp. 643–662. Springer, Heidelberg (2012)

[Gen09b]   Gentry, C.: Fully homomorphic encryption using ideal lattices. In: STOC, pp. 169–178 (2009)

[GLOV12]   Goyal, V., Lee, C.-K., Ostrovsky, R., Visconti, I.: Constructing non-malleable commitments: A black-box approach. In: FOCS, pp. 51–60 (2012)

[HLOV11]   Hemenway, B., Libert, B., Ostrovsky, R., Vergnaud, D.: Lossy Encryption: Constructions from General Assumptions and Efficient Selective Opening Chosen Ciphertext Security. In: Lee, D.H., Wang, X. (eds.) ASIACRYPT 2011. LNCS, vol. 7073, pp. 70–88. Springer, Heidelberg (2011)

[GO94]   Goldreich, O., Oren, Y.: Definitions and properties of zero-knowledge
            proof systems. J. Cryptology 7(1), 1–32 (1994)
[IKK+11]   Ishai, Y., Katz, J., Kushilevitz, E., Lindell, Y., Petrank, E.: On achiev-
            ing the "best of both worlds" in secure multiparty computation. SIAM
            J. Comput. 40(1), 122–141 (2011)
[JJ00]   Jakobsson, M., Juels, A.: Mix and Match: Secure Function Evalua-
            tion via Ciphertexts. In: Okamoto, T. (ed.) ASIACRYPT 2000. LNCS,
            vol. 1976, pp. 162–177. Springer, Heidelberg (2000)
[KLML05]   Kiltz, E., Leander, G., Malone-Lee, J.: Secure Computation of the Mean
            and Related Statistics. In: Kilian, J. (ed.) TCC 2005. LNCS, vol. 3378,
            pp. 283–302. Springer, Heidelberg (2005)
[LATV11]   López-Alt, A., Tromer, E., Vaikuntanathan, V.: Cloud-assisted multi-
            party computation from fully homomorphic encryption. IACR Cryptol-
            ogy ePrint Archive, 2011:663 (2011)
[MSas11]   Myers, S., Sergi, M., Shelat, A.: Threshold fully homomorphic en-
            cryption and secure computation. Cryptology ePrint Archive, Report
            2011/454 (2011), http://eprint.iacr.org/
[NN01]   Naor, M., Nissim, K.: Communication preserving protocols for secure
            function evaluation. In: STOC, pp. 590–599 (2001)
[vDGHV10]   van Dijk, M., Gentry, C., Halevi, S., Vaikuntanathan, V.: Fully Ho-
            momorphic Encryption over the Integers. In: Gilbert, H. (ed.) EURO-
            CRYPT 2010. LNCS, vol. 6110, pp. 24–43. Springer, Heidelberg (2010)

A   Verifiable Secret-Sharing Scheme

A $\binom{n}{n/2+2}$ Verifiable Secret-Sharing scheme consists of a sharing algorithm which takes as input a secret s and produces n-shares $s_1, ..., s_n$. These shares have the property that for any $T \subset \{1, \ldots n\}$, $|T| < n/2 + 2$ it is the case that $\{s_i\}_{i \in T}$ is information theoretically independent from s. However, for any $S \subseteq \{1, \ldots n\}$, $|S| \geq n/2 + 2$, it is the case that the reveal algorithm, when given $\{s_i\}_{i \in S}$, can reconstruct s. In a traditional interactive setting we require that all non-cheating parties agree on the reconstructed secret. We use a modification of the Cramer et al. [CDD+99] verifiable secret sharing scheme; we do not need to deal with interactive adversaries, nor players, so the scheme is significantly simplified. We present the sharing and revealing algorithms in our full version.

Definition 5. *A vector* $(e_1, ..., e_n) \in F_n$ *is* $n/2 + 2$*-consistent if there exists a polynomial* w *of degree at most* $n/2 + 1$ *such that* $w(i) = e_i$ *for* $0 \leq i < n$.

Definition 6. *Given two shares* $s_i = (i, a_i = (a_{i1}, \ldots, a_{in}), b_i = (b_{1i}, \ldots, b_{ni}))$ *and* $s_j = (j, a_j(a_{j1}, \ldots, a_{jn}), b_j = (b_{1j}, \ldots, b_{nj}))$, *we say that they are* pairwise consistent *if* $a_{ij} = b_{ij}$ *and* $a_{ji} = b_{ji}$.

Definition 7. *For our purposes it is useful to note that given the* $n \times n$ *matrix*

$$\begin{bmatrix} f(1,1) & f(1,2) & \dots & f(1,n) \\ f(2,1) & f(2,2) & \dots & f(2,n) \\ \vdots & \vdots & \ddots & \vdots \\ f(n,1) & f(n,2) & \dots & f(n,n) \end{bmatrix},$$

that a share s_i simply corresponds to the ith row and column of the matrix. We will call this the matrix representation of the shares. Notice that when given in the matrix representation, any two shares are necessarily pairwise consistent. Given a set of n pairwise consistent shares $s = (s_1, ..., s_n)$, we define M_s as the $n \times n$ matrix representation of the shares.

Testing the Lipschitz Property over Product Distributions with Applications to Data Privacy*

Kashyap Dixit, Madhav Jha, Sofya Raskhodnikova, and Abhradeep Thakurta**

Pennsylvania State University, USA
{mxj201,kashyap,sofya,azg161}@cse.psu.edu

Abstract. In the past few years, the focus of research in the area of statistical data privacy has been in designing algorithms for various problems which satisfy some rigorous notions of privacy. However, not much effort has gone into designing techniques to computationally verify if a given algorithm satisfies some predefined notion of privacy. In this work, we address the following question: *Can we design algorithms which tests if a given algorithm satisfies specific rigorous notion of privacy (e.g., differential privacy)?*

We design algorithms to test privacy guarantees of a given algorithm $\mathcal{A}$ when run on a dataset x containing potentially sensitive information about the individuals. More formally, we design a computationally efficient algorithm $\mathcal{T}_{priv}$ that verifies whether $\mathcal{A}$ satisfies *differential privacy on typical datasets* (DPTD) guarantee in time sublinear in the size of the domain of the datasets. DPTD, a similar notion to *generalized differential privacy* first proposed by [3], is a *distributional* relaxation of the popular notion of *differential privacy* [14].

To design algorithm $\mathcal{T}_{priv}$, we show a formal connection between the testing of privacy guarantee for an algorithm and the testing of the Lipschitz property of a related function. More specifically, we show that an efficient algorithm for testing of Lipschitz property can be used as a subroutine in $\mathcal{T}_{priv}$ that tests if an algorithm satisfies *differential privacy on typical datasets.*

Apart from formalizing the connection between the testing of privacy guarantee and testing of the Lipschitz property, we generalize the work of [21] to the setting of property testing under product distribution. More precisely, we design an efficient Lipschitz tester for the case where the domain points are drawn from hypercube according to some fixed but unknown product distribution instead of the uniform distribution.

1 Introduction

The trend towards data driven decision making has resulted in many commercial data sharing platforms like *BlueKai, TellApart* or *Criteo*. These platforms extensively collect and share user data with third-parties (e.g., advertisers) to enhance specific user experience (e.g., better behavioral targeting). Since the data which gets shared is extremely

---

* All omitted proofs appear in the full version [8].
** K.D. is supported in part by NSF Grant CCF-0964655. M.J. and S.R. are supported by NSF CAREER grant CCF-0845701 and NSF grant CDI-0941553. A.T. is supported in part by NSF Awards CCF-0747294, CDI-0941553 and US National Institutes of Health Clinical and Translational Science Award.

A. Sahai (Ed.): TCC 2013, LNCS 7785, pp. 418–436, 2013.

rich in user information, it poses serious privacy concerns about the users' information contained in the data [23,6]. A more cautious approach would be to require third-party clients to submit their algorithms (e.g. as binary executables or as programs) and run it "in-house" (i.e., within the data sharing platform itself) and only release the outputs of their algorithms. But what if the output of the algorithm itself reveals some private information? Fortunately, there are notions of privacy (e.g. *differential privacy* [14]) which impose strict *privacy requirements on the algorithm* computing on the data and guarantee that the output of the algorithm does not disclose too much information (provided the algorithm satisfies these requirements). There still remains the nagging question that these algorithms come from third-parties. How does one ensure that they have implemented their algorithms in a way which meet the specifications of the privacy-requirements?

One approach (e.g. [25,30,29]) that has been taken to address the above problem is to require clients to write their programs using a specific set of *trusted* built-in functions provided by the platform. The platform ensures (either statically or at run time) that the implementation complies by the rules of using only the built-in functions while operating on the private data. Another approach [21] based on *property reconstruction* allows *arbitrary* programs and uses the *global sensitivity* framework of [14] as the underlying privacy mechanism. However, this approach *provably* [1] requires prohibitively huge running time. Another approach [26] uses the algorithmic framework of [32,27] to allow arbitrary programs but the utility guarantees are limited by the guarantees of the framework.

In this work, we propose a new approach to the above problem which we call *privacy testing*. We do this by formulating the above problem in the well-studied framework of property testing [31,17]. Property testing is concerned with *approximately* deciding whether an input *object* (e.g. a graph or a function) satisfies a given property (e.g. connectivity or monotonicity). In the same spirit, we treat algorithm $\mathcal{A}$ as an object (e.g. as a family of functions) which is required to satisfy some fixed property, specifically, the property of being private under some well-defined notion of privacy. The goal is to design efficient algorithms which can test if $\mathcal{A}$ satisfies the privacy definition under consideration.

In this work, we design an algorithm $\mathcal{T}_{priv}$ to test if an untrusted algorithm $\mathcal{A}$ satisfies a *distributional relaxation* of the popular notion of *differential privacy* [10,14,11,12]. Roughly speaking, differential privacy guarantees that the output of an algorithm $\mathcal{A}$ does not depend "too much" on any particular record of the underlying dataset x. The distributional relaxation we adhere to in our work is called *differential privacy on typical datasets* (DPTD). DPTD ensures a similar guarantee as differential privacy, except that the guarantee is now only over *typical* data sets, namely, datasets with sufficiently high probability mass under a fixed data generating distribution. DPTD is a special case of *generalized differential privacy* from [3].

To test for DPTD, we show a new connection between differential privacy and the problem of testing the *Lipschitz property* of functions first studied by [21]. Informally, a function $f(x_1, \ldots, x_d)$ is Lipschitz if changing at most one input of f arbitrarily while keeping the other inputs fixed does not change the value of f drastically. For testing algorithm $\mathcal{A}$ for the property of being DPTD, we view $\mathcal{A}$ as a family of functions.

We show that testing DPTD reduces to testing the property that every function in the family is *simultaneously* Lipschitz. We allow $\mathcal{A}$ to be an arbitrary randomized algorithm (indeed, most privacy preserving algorithms are randomized) but, in this work, restrict it to have finite domain and range. While property testing algorithms usually only require black-box access to the object, in this exploratory work, we assume oracle access to values $\Pr[\mathcal{A}(x) = r]$ given arbitrary domain point x and range point r. (We discuss these assumptions in more detail in Section 7.)

Going beyond privacy testing, we show how to convert an arbitrary algorithm $\mathcal{A}$ into an algorithm which always satisfies DPTD. We test algorithm $\mathcal{A}$ for DPTD and only if the tester accepts, we allow it to be run on the private data. Details appear in Section 4.2.

Property testing of functions deals with algorithms which can distinguish between functions which satisfy a given property $\mathcal{P}$ (in our case, the Lipschitz property) from those which are *far* from the property. A function f is far from property $\mathcal{P}$ if the distance between f and every member of $\mathcal{P}$ (where we view $\mathcal{P}$ as the set of functions satisfying $\mathcal{P}$) is large under a suitable definition of distance between functions. In the standard property testing, the distance between functions f and g is given by $\Pr[f(x) \neq g(x)]$ where x is chosen uniformly from the domain. We refer to this as property testing under uniform distribution. While previous works [21,2,7] studied Lipschitz testing under uniform distribution, in this work we focus on the setting when the distribution on the underlying data set is an *unknown product* distribution. This is important to test the notion of DPTD for a large class of distributions (and not merely the uniform distribution). Property testing under unknown distribution is a well-studied area under the name of *distribution free testing* [19] with many positive and negative results [19,20]. In this work, we give the first Lipschitz tester which works for arbitrary unknown product distribution with nearly the same running time as the Lipschitz tester for the uniform distribution from [21].

1.1 Summary of Our Contributions

Formulate testing of data privacy property as Lipschitz property testing. In this paper we initiate the study of testing privacy properties of a given candidate algorithm $\mathcal{A}$. The specific privacy property that we test is *differential privacy on typical datasets* (DPTD) (see Definition 3.2). In order to design a tester for DPTD property, we cast the problem of testing DPTD property as a problem of testing the Lipschitz property. (See Theorem 4.1.) The problem of testing the Lipschitz property was initially proposed by [21].

Design a generic transformation to convert an algorithm $\mathcal{A}$ to its DPTD variant. We design a generic transformation to convert a candidate algorithm $\mathcal{A}$ to its DPTD variant. (See Theorem 4.2.)

Lipschitz testers over product distributions. In order to allow our privacy tester to be effective for a large class of data generating distributions, we extend the existing Lipschitz testers to work with product distributions. We give the first efficient tester for the Lipschitz property on the hypercube domain which works for arbitrary product distribution. (See Theorem 5.1.) Previous works [21,2,7] on Lipschitz testing focuses on the case of uniform distribution.

Concrete instantiation of privacy testers based on old and new Lipschitz testers. We instantiate privacy tester with the Lipschitz tester described in the previous item to get a concrete instantiation of the privacy tester. This also leads to a concrete instantiation of Item 2 mentioned above. We also instantiate privacy testers based on the state-of-the-art Lipschitz tester from [7] for the uniform distribution. This is summarized in Section 6.

1.2 Related Work

Recently, various notions of data privacy have been proposed such as k-anonymity [33], ℓ-diversity [24], differential privacy [14], noiseless privacy [4], generalized differential privacy [3] and natural differential privacy [5]. With known attacks (e.g. [15]) on k-anonymity and ℓ-diversity, privacy community has pretty much converged to theoretically sound notions of privacy like differential privacy. In this paper, we work with the definition of differential privacy on typical datasets (DPTD) (Definition 3.2). DPTD is a special case of generalized differential privacy (GDP), where we assume that the auxiliary information $\mathcal{A}ux$ in the GDP definition is all but one entry in the underlying dataset. The primary difference between GDP and the other related definitions is that it incorporates both the randomness in the underlying dataset x and the randomness of the algorithm $\mathcal{A}$, where as other notions (like noiseless privacy and differential privacy) consider either the randomness of the data or the algorithm.

[21] initiated the study of testing (and reconstruction) of the Lipschitz property. Subsequently, [2,7] gave Lipschitz testers with [7] being the current state-of-the-art for the Boolean hypercube domain. All these testers work for the uniform distribution on the domain. In our work, we allow arbitrary product distribution on the underlying domain. Thus, our work is closely related to the work done in the area of distribution free testing introduced by Goldreich et al [17]. (See also [19].) They noted that many graph properties have testers with query complexity independent of the input size when the points are drawn from the uniform distribution (e.g. bipartiteness, k-colorability etc.), but the distribution free testers for the same properties do not have query complexity independent of the input size. In contrast, Halevi and Kushilevitz gave a series of positive results for distribution-free testing in [20] and [19]. In particular, they proved that there are testers with time complexity independent of the domain size for the properties like sparse graph connectivity [19] and juntas, parities, low-degree polynomials and Boolean literals [20].

1.3 Organization of the Paper

In Section 2, we review the concepts of general property testing and provide the definition of the Lipschitz property testers that we use in our work. In Section 3, we show the connection between testing of differential privacy on typical datasets (DPTD) and Lipschitz property testing. Section 4 is dedicated to our main result giving the privacy tester (Section 4.1) and application of privacy tester in obtaining DPTD-algorithms (Section 4.2). In Section 5, we present our new Lipschitz property testers over product distributions on the hypercube domain. In Section 6, we instantiate privacy testers with Lipschitz testers. Lastly, in Section 7, we conclude with discussion about the limitations of our current approach and some open problems.

2 Preliminaries for Lipschitz Property Testing

Property testing [17,31] is concerned with distinguishing objects which satisfy a given property $\mathcal{P}$ from those which are *far* from satisfying it. When $\mathcal{P}$ is a property of functions $f : \mathcal{X}^d \to \mathbb{R}$ over a finite domain $\mathcal{X}^d$, distance to the property is usually measured in terms of the fraction of points in the domain $\mathcal{X}^d$ on which f must be modified in order to satisfy the property. A more general notion of distance is defined with respect to a probability distribution on the domain $\mathcal{X}^d$.

Definition 2.1 (Distance to a property). *Let $\mathcal{P}$ be a property (i.e., a set) of functions $f : \mathcal{X}^d \to \mathbb{R}$. Let Π be a distribution on $\mathcal{X}^d$. The distance $dist_\Pi(f, g)$ between functions $f, g : \mathcal{X}^d \to \mathbb{R}$ (with respect to the distribution Π) is $\Pr_{x \sim \Pi}[f(x) \neq g(x)]$. The distance $dist_\Pi(f, \mathcal{P})$ of a function f from the property $\mathcal{P}$ is $\min_{g \in \mathcal{P}} dist_\Pi(f, g)$. We say that f is ϵ-far from the property $\mathcal{P}$ if $dist_\Pi(f, \mathcal{P}) \geq \epsilon$.*

In this work, we study the Lipschitz property of functions, first considered in the context of property testing by [21].

Definition 2.2. *A real-valued function $f : \mathcal{X}^d \to \mathbb{R}$ is c-Lipschitz if $|f(x) - f(y)| \leq c \cdot d_H(x, y)$ where $d_H(x, y)$ is the Hamming distance between x and y, that is, the number of coordinates in which x an y differ. We say f is Lipschitz if f is 1-Lipschitz.*

Next we define a Lipschitz tester. Our definition differs from the standard definition of a property tester (e.g., as used in [21]) in two aspects: (i) we only require a Lipschitz tester to distinguish Lipschitz functions from functions which are ϵ-far from $(1 + \delta)$-Lipschitz for some fixed $\delta \geq 0$ and (ii) we measure the distance between functions with respect to a fixed probability distribution Π on the domain. The relaxation of Condition (i) has been considered earlier e.g. in [28] for the property of having small diameter and in [21] for the Lipschitz property. The generalization of Condition (ii) is well-studied in property testing under the name *distribution free testing*. See e.g. [19]. We remark that setting $(1 + \delta) = 1$, $\rho = 1/3$ and Π to be the uniform distribution on $\mathcal{X}^d$ in the definition below recovers the standard definition of property tester (in our case, the Lipschitz tester as defined in [21]).

Definition 2.3 (Approximate Lipschitz Tester). *A $(1+\delta)$-approximate Lipschitz tester $\mathcal{T}_{Lip}(\epsilon, \rho, \delta, d)$ is a randomized algorithm that gets as input: (i) oracle access to function $f : \mathcal{X}^d \to \mathbb{R}$; (ii) oracle access to independent samples from distribution Π on $\mathcal{X}^d$ and (iii) a few parameters, namely, the proximity parameter ϵ, the error probability parameter ρ, the approximation parameter δ and the parameter d. The tester provides the following guarantee. If f is Lipschitz, then the algorithm accepts. If f is ϵ-far from the $(1 + \delta)$-Lipschitz property with respect to distribution Π, then with probability at least $1 - \rho$, the algorithm rejects.*

We say the Lipschitz property can be tested with *one-sided* error if there exists a Lipschitz tester as defined above. Further, we say it can be tested *nonadaptively* if all the queries made by $\mathcal{T}_{Lip}$ to its oracles are made in advance without the knowledge of answers to the previous queries.

3   Differential Privacy and Its Connections to Testing the Lipschitz Property

Intuitively, the output of a differentially private algorithm is almost the same whether or not a specific person's data is present in the dataset. Datasets are modeled as fixed-length vectors from an arbitrary domain $\mathcal{X}^d$, where each coordinate represents one person's data. (For example, when $\mathcal{X}^d$ is $\{0, 1\}^d$, datasets consist of d-bit vectors and each person's data is a Boolean value.) An algorithm is differentially private if it has similar distribution on outputs when run on datasets which are close in Hamming distance. The Hamming distance between x and x', denoted $d_H(x, x')$, is the number of coordinates on which x and x' differ.

Definition 3.1 ((α, β)-Differential Privacy [14,13]). *A randomized algorithm $\mathcal{A}$ is (α, β)-differentially private if for any two datasets x and x' in $\mathcal{X}^d$, and for all measurable sets $\mathcal{Z} \subseteq Range(\mathcal{A})$, the following holds:*

$$\Pr[\mathcal{A}(x) \in \mathcal{Z}] \leq e^{\alpha \cdot d_H(x, x')} \Pr[\mathcal{A}(x') \in \mathcal{Z}] + \beta. \tag{1}$$

If $\beta = 0$, algorithm $\mathcal{A}$ is called α-differentially private.

In this work, we focus on differentially private algorithms which output values in a *finite* range space $\mathcal{Z}$. Such algorithms have a clean characterization in terms of the Lipschitz property. Specifically, define functions $f_z : x \to \mathbb{R}$ for every $z \in \mathcal{Z}$ by setting $f_z(x) = \log \Pr[\mathcal{A}(x) = z]$. We make the following simple but important observation.

Observation 3.1 (Differential Privacy as a Lipschitz Condition). Algorithm $\mathcal{A}$ is α-differentially private if and only if for every $z \in \mathcal{Z}$, function f_z is α-Lipschitz.

Therefore, one could check if an algorithm specified by functions f_z is differentially private, given oracle access to these functions, if one could design a procedure that decides if an input function is Lipschitz. However, as noted in [21], deciding if a given function is Lipschitz is NP-hard. Can we still efficiently check for some relaxation of differential privacy? Towards answering this question, we take motivation from relaxations of differential privacy considered in the literature based on *distributional* assumptions. Specifically, we adapt a particular relaxation from [3] and show that it can indeed be tested using a connection to testing the Lipschitz property. The relaxation we consider assumes that datasets come from some fixed distribution Π on the set of all datasets. The notion of privacy is relaxed from the worst case guarantee over all pairs of datasets (i.e., differential privacy) to a notion where the differential privacy condition is required to hold only on datasets which are more likely to occur (i.e., have high-probability mass under distribution Π). We refer to this notion as *differential privacy on typical datasets* (DPTD) (Definition 3.2). As mentioned earlier, DPTD is an adaptation of more general definition introduced in [3] under the name of *generalized differential privacy* (GDP). GDP was defined in the context of a related distributional notion of privacy called *noiseless privacy*, first introduced by [4]. A related notion called *natural differential privacy* has also been recently proposed by [5]. Since we focus on DPTD in this work, we do not discuss noiseless privacy (and its variants) further. Next we give a formal definition of

DPTD. The definition is parametrized by three parameters α, β and γ. The parameters α and β play the same role as in the differential privacy definition, while the parameter γ bounds the probability of the "bad" set B of databases on which the differential privacy condition fails to hold.

Definition 3.2 ((α, β, γ)-**Differential Privacy on Typical Datasets (DPTD)**). *Let Π be a fixed distribution on the domain $\mathcal{X}^d$ of datasets. A randomized algorithm $\mathcal{A}$ is (α, β, γ)-differentially private on typical datasets, if there exists a subset $B \subseteq \mathcal{X}^d$ satisfying $\mathrm{Pr}_{x \sim \Pi}[x \in B] \le \gamma$ such that condition (1) of Definition 3.1 holds for any two datasets $x, x' \in \mathcal{X}^d \setminus B$ and all measurable sets $\mathcal{Z} \subseteq Range(\mathcal{A})$. The probability in (1) is over the randomness of the algorithm $\mathcal{A}$.*

Our main observation is that for algorithms which output values in a finite range, testing DPTD can be reduced to testing the Lipschitz property (of a family of functions). Assume again that the output space of $\mathcal{A}$ is a finite set $\mathcal{Z}$ and define functions f_z as above.

Observation 3.2 (DPTD for Algorithms with Finite Range). Algorithm $\mathcal{A}$ is $(\alpha, 0, \gamma)$-differentially private if and only if the following two conditions hold: (i) there exists a subset $B \subseteq \mathcal{X}^d$ such that $\mathrm{Pr}_{x \sim \Pi}[x \in B] \le \gamma$; and (ii) for every $z \in \mathcal{Z}$, function f_z is α-Lipschitz on the set $\mathcal{X}^d \setminus B$.

Recall that a function f is ϵ-close to property $\mathcal{P}$ with respect to distribution Π if there is a function g which satisfies $\mathcal{P}$ and $\mathrm{Pr}_{x \sim \Pi}[f(x) \ne g(x)] \le \epsilon$. Observation 3.2, in particular, implies the following. If algorithm $\mathcal{A}$ satisfies $(\alpha, 0, \gamma)$-DPTD, then for every $z \in \mathcal{Z}$, function f_z is γ-close to the α-Lipschitz property with respect to the distribution Π. However, to apply a Lipschitz tester, we need a converse of this statement. The following lemma gives the converse.

Lemma 3.1 (Connection between DPTD and Testing the Lipschitz Property). *If for every $z \in R$, function f_z is ϵ_z-close to the α-Lipschitz property with respect to the distribution Π, then $\mathcal{A}$ is $(\alpha, 0, \sum_z \epsilon_z)$-DPTD. In particular, if $\mathcal{A}$ is not $(\alpha, 0, \gamma)$-DPTD, then there exists $z \in \mathcal{Z}$ such that f_z is $\gamma/|\mathcal{Z}|$-far from the α-Lipschitz property.*

Proof. Since every f_z is ϵ_z-close to the α-Lipschitz property with respect to the distribution Π, there exists B_z corresponding to each f_z such that (i) f_z is α-Lipschitz on $\mathcal{X}^d \setminus B_z$; and (ii) $Pr_{x \sim \Pi}[x \in B_z] \le \epsilon_z$. Let B be the union over all z of the sets B_z. Applying the union bound, we get $\mathrm{Pr}_{x \sim \Pi}[x \in B] \le \sum_z \epsilon_z$. Then the first part of the lemma follows from Observation 3.2 with B as the required set. The second part of the lemma follows from an averaging argument. □

3.1 Discussion of Differential Privacy on Typical Datasets

Differential privacy on typical datasets (DPTD) in Definition 3.2 is very similar to the definition of differential privacy, except in DPTD there exists a set of datasets B where the differential privacy condition (i.e., Equation 1 of Definition 3.1) does not hold. Moreover, the probability mass of B under the data generating distribution Π is at most γ. If we assume $\beta = 0$ for simplicity, then at a high-level DPTD implies that for any two datasets x and x' from the set $\mathcal{X}^d \setminus B$, which have sufficient probability mass under Π and differ in k-entries, the distribution of $\mathcal{A}(x)$ and $\mathcal{A}(x')$ have a statistical distance of $2k\alpha$ when $k\alpha$ is less than one.

In differential privacy, the scale of the parameters α and β are typically chosen as follows: α is chosen to be some small constant and β is chosen to be $O(1/d^2)$. With this choice of parameters, differential privacy ensures that *even in the presence of any auxiliary information, from the output of the algorithm $\mathcal{A}$, an adversary draws the same conclusions about any entry in the data set irrespective of its presence or absence.* (See [22] for more discussion.) Since α and β play the same role in DPTD, we think of α and β of the same order as discussed for differential privacy. Additionally, throughout this paper we think of γ and β to be of the same order.

In [3], a generalization of DPTD has been stated under the name of *generalized differential privacy* (GDP). Under suitable choice of auxiliary information (i.e., the random variable $\mathcal{A}ux$), the definition of [3] reduces to Definition 3.2. More precisely, for every data entry x_i, the auxiliary information in the GDP condition (of the definition of GDP) corresponds to all entries in the data set x except x_i.

4 Testing and Reconstruction of Differential Privacy on Typical Datasets

In this section we present an algorithm $\mathcal{T}_{priv}$ (Algorithm 1) which "tests" whether a given algorithm $\mathcal{A}$ is private. The guarantee of the testing algorithm $\mathcal{T}_{priv}$ is "asymmetric", i.e., if algorithm $\mathcal{A}$ is α-differentially private, then the tester accepts, and if the algorithm $\mathcal{A}$ is not $(\alpha, 0, \gamma)$-DPTD, then the tester rejects with high probability. It is worth highlighting that this style of utility guarantee deviates from the conventional utility guarantees in property testing literature (where the utility guarantee is symmetric over a particular property $\mathcal{P}$).

Next we use $\mathcal{T}_{priv}$ as a subroutine to design a "reconstruction" algorithm $\mathcal{A}_{privGen}$ (Algorithm 2). The algorithm $\mathcal{A}_{privGen}$ is guaranteed to be differential private on typical datasets under the data generating distribution Π. Moreover, if $\mathcal{A}$ is differentially private, then the output of $\mathcal{A}_{privGen}$ equals the output of $\mathcal{A}$. (See Theorem 4.2 for the exact parameters.)

4.1 Tester for Differential Privacy on Typical Datasets

In this section, we prove the following theorem.

Theorem 4.1 $((\alpha, \beta, \gamma, \delta)$**-Privacy testing**)**.** *Let $\mathcal{A}$ be a randomized algorithm which outputs values in the finite set $\mathcal{Z}$. Let Π be a data generating distribution. Let $\mathcal{T}_{Lip}$ be a δ-approximate Lipschitz tester. Suppose there is an oracle $\mathcal{O}_\mathcal{A}$ which for every value $z \in \mathcal{Z}$ and for every $x \in \mathcal{X}^d$ allows constant time access to the value $\Pr(\mathcal{A}(x) = z)$ (where the probability is only over the randomness of the algorithm $\mathcal{A}$). Then algorithm $\mathcal{T}_{priv}$ (Algorithm 1), given access to $\mathcal{O}_\mathcal{A}$, satisfies the following.*

- *If algorithm $\mathcal{A}$ is α-differentially private, then $\mathcal{T}_{priv}$ accepts.*
- *If algorithm $\mathcal{A}$ is not $(\alpha(1+\delta), 0, \gamma)$-DPTD, then the tester rejects with probability at least $1 - \beta$.*

The algorithm $\mathcal{T}_{priv}$ uses $\mathcal{T}_{Lip}$ as a subroutine and runs in time

$$O(|\mathcal{Z}| \cdot \textit{Run-time}\left(\mathcal{T}_{Lip}(\frac{\gamma}{|\mathcal{Z}|}, \beta, \delta, d)\right).$$

At high level, algorithm $\mathcal{T}_{priv}$ (Algorithm 1) does the following. For each possible output $z \in \mathcal{Z}$, it defines a function f_z (with the domain $\mathcal{X}^d$). It then invokes algorithm $\mathcal{T}_{Lip}$ to test f_z for the Lipschitz property. It accepts iff $\mathcal{T}_{Lip}$ accepts all f_z.

Algorithm 1 $\mathcal{T}_{priv}$: Tester of Differential Privacy on Typical Data Sets

---

Require: Algorithm $\mathcal{A}$, data generating distribution Π, data domain $\mathcal{X}^d$, output range $\mathcal{Z}$, privacy parameters $\alpha, \gamma \in (0, 1]$, failure probability $\beta \in (0, 1]$ and approximation parameter δ.
1: Let $\mathcal{T}_{Lip}$ be a δ-approximate Lipschitz tester defined in Definition 2.3.
2: **for all** values $z \in \mathcal{Z}$ **do**
3:     Define function $f_z : \mathcal{X}^d \to \mathbb{R}$ by setting $f_z(x) = \frac{1}{\alpha} \log \Pr(\mathcal{A}(x) = z)$.
4:     Run $\mathcal{T}_{Lip}$ on f_z with proximity parameter $\frac{\gamma}{|\mathcal{Z}|}$ and failure probability β.
5:     If $\mathcal{T}_{Lip}$ rejects, then **reject**.
6: **end for**
7: **Accept.**

Proof. We use Lemma 3.1 and Observation 3.1 to prove the theorem. To prove the first item, assume $\mathcal{A}$ is α-differentially private. Then Observation 3.1 implies that for every $z \in \mathcal{Z}$, function f_z (in Line 4 of Algorithm 1) is Lipschitz. Since $\mathcal{T}_{priv}$ always accepts a Lipschitz function, we get that $\mathcal{T}_{priv}$ accepts, as required. For the second item, assume $\mathcal{A}$ is *not* $(\alpha, 0, \gamma)$-DPTD. Then Lemma 3.1 implies that there exists z^* such that f_{z^*} is $\gamma/|\mathcal{Z}|$-far from being $(1 + \delta)$-Lipschitz. From definition of $\mathcal{T}_{Lip}$, it follows that $\mathcal{T}_{Lip}$ rejects f_{z^*} with probability at least $1 - \beta$, and therefore, so does $\mathcal{T}_{priv}$. The running time of $\mathcal{T}_{priv}$ follows from the fact that the tester $\mathcal{T}_{Lip}$ is invoked at most $|\mathcal{Z}|$ times. □

The proof above used the second part of Lemma 3.1 and used an *arbitrary* Lipschitz tester $\mathcal{T}_{Lip}$. It is possible to obtain faster privacy testers using the (stronger) statement given in the first part of Lemma 3.1. This requires making mild assumptions about the guarantees of the Lipschitz tester. We defer this analysis to the full version.

4.2 Application of DPTD Tester to Ensure Privacy of a Given Candidate Algorithm

In this section we will demonstrate how one can use algorithm $\mathcal{T}_{priv}$ (Algorithm 1) designed in the previous section to guarantee (α, β, γ)-differential privacy on typical datasets to the output produced by a candidate algorithm $\mathcal{A}$. The details are given in Algorithm 2.

Algorithm 2 $\mathcal{A}_{privGen}$: DPTD mechanism

Require: Dataset x, candidate algorithm $\mathcal{A}$, testing algorithm $\mathcal{T}_{priv}$, data generating distribution Π, data domain $\mathcal{X}^d$, output set $\mathcal{Z}$, privacy parameters α, β, γ

1: Run $\mathcal{T}_{priv}$ with parameters $\mathcal{A}, \Pi, \mathcal{X}^d, \mathcal{Z}$, privacy parameters α, γ, and failure parameter β
2: If $\mathcal{T}_{priv}$ accepts, then output $\mathcal{A}(x)$. Otherwise, output **FAIL**.

The guarantees for Algorithm 2 are given below.

Theorem 4.2 $(((1+\delta), \alpha, \beta, \gamma)$**-DPTD mechanism**$)$. *Let* $\mathcal{T}_{Lip}$ *be a* $(1+\delta)$-*approximate Lipschitz tester (see Definition 2.3) used in the testing algorithm* $\mathcal{T}_{priv}$ *(Algorithm 1). Under the assumptions of Theorem 4.1, algorithm* $\mathcal{A}_{privGen}$ *(Algorithm 2) satisfies:*

- *(**privacy**) Algorithm* $\mathcal{A}_{privGen}$ *(Algorithm 2) is* $(\alpha(1 + \delta), \beta, \gamma)$-*DPTD.*
- *(**utility**) If the candidate algorithm* $\mathcal{A}$ *is* α-*differentially private, then the output distributions of algorithm* $\mathcal{A}_{privGen}$ *(Algorithm 2) and* $\mathcal{A}$ *are identical.*

We defer the proof of this theorem to the full version.

5 Lipschitz Property Testing on the Hypercube under Product Distribution

In this section, we present a δ-approximate Lipschitz tester (see Definition 2.3) for functions defined on $\mathcal{X}^d = \{0, 1\}^d$ when the underlying distribution on $\{0, 1\}^d$ is an *unknown product* distribution. Specifically, the points in the dataset are distributed according to the product distribution $\Pi = Ber(p_1) \times Ber(p_2) \times ..., \times Ber(p_d)$ where $Ber(p)$ denotes the Bernoulli distribution with probability p. Namely, $Ber(p)$ is 1 with probability p and 0 with probability $1 - p$. Therefore, each vertex in $x \in \{0, 1\}^d$ has an associated probability mass $p_x = \prod_{i \in [d]} p_i^{x_i} (1 - p_i)^{1-x_i}$.

In this section, we view the domain $\{0, 1\}^d$ as vertices of the hypercube graph $\mathcal{H}_d = (\{0, 1\}^d, E)$. The edge set E consists of pairs $\{x, y\}$ of vertices $x, y \in \{0, 1\}^d$ which differ in exactly one coordinate (i.e., there exists $i \in [d]$ such that $x_i = y_i$ and for all $j \neq i, x_j = y_j$). Observe that f is Lipschitz on $\{0, 1\}^d$ if and only if for every edge $\{x, y\} \in E$, the following holds: $|f(x) - f(y)| \leq 1$. An edge which does not satisfy this condition is called a *violated edge*.

5.1 Algorithm for Testing the Lipschitz Property on the Hypercube

In this section, we prove the following theorem which gives a 1-approximate Lipschitz tester for $\delta\mathbb{Z}$-valued functions. A function is $\delta\mathbb{Z}$ valued if it produces outputs in integral multiples of δ. The running time of our tester is stated in terms of the *image diameter* of the input function f.

Definition 5.1 (Image Diameter). *The image diameter of a function* $f : \mathcal{X}^d \to \mathbb{R}$, *denoted by* $ImD(f)$, *is the difference between the maximum and the minimum values attained by* f, *i.e.,* $\max_{x \in \mathcal{X}^d} f(x) - \min_{x \in \mathcal{X}^d} f(x)$.

Theorem 5.1. *Let* $\{0, 1\}^d$ *be the domain from which the dataset are drawn according to a product probability distribution* $\Pi = Ber(p_1) \times Ber(p_2) \times ..., \times Ber(p_d)$. *The Lipschitz property of functions* $f : \{0, 1\}^d \to \delta\mathbb{Z}$ *on these datasets can be tested non-adaptively and with one sided error probability* ρ *in* $O(\frac{d \cdot \min\{d, ImD(f)\}}{\delta(\epsilon - d^2\delta)} \ln(\frac{2}{\rho}))$ *time for* $\delta \in (0, \frac{\epsilon}{d^2})$. *Here* ImD *is the image diameter defined in Definition 5.1.*

By discretizing, as in proof of Corollary 1.2 in [21], we obtain a $(1 + \delta)$-approximate Lipschitz tester for real-valued functions.

Corollary 5.1. *Let* $\{0, 1\}^d$ *be the domain from which the dataset are drawn according to a product probability distribution* $\Pi = Ber(p_1) \times Ber(p_2) \times ..., \times Ber(p_d)$. *There is an algorithm that on input parameters* $\delta \in (0, \frac{\epsilon}{d^2}), \epsilon \in (0, 1), d$ *and oracle access to a function* $f : \{0, 1\}^d \to \mathbb{R}$ *has the following behavior: It accepts if* f *is Lipschitz and rejects with probability at least* $1 - \rho$ *if* f *is* ϵ-far *(with respect to the distribution* Π) *from* $(1 + \delta)$-Lipschitz *and runs in* $O(\frac{d \cdot \min\{d, ImD(f)\}}{\delta(\epsilon - d^2\delta)} \ln(\frac{2}{\rho}))$ *time. Here* ImD *is the image diameter defined in Definition 5.1.*

Theorem 5.1 is proved in Section 5.2. To state the proof we need the following technical result stated in lemma 5.1.

We define a distribution D_E on edges of the hypercube where the probability mass of an edge $\{x, y\}$ is given by $\frac{p_x + p_y}{d}$. Note that $\sum_{(x,y) \in E(H_d)} \frac{(p_x + p_y)}{d} = 1$. Thus, D_E is well-defined. Our tester is based on detecting violated edges (that is, edges which violate the Lipschitz property) sampled from distribution D_E. Our main technical lemma (Lemma 5.1) gives a lower bound on the probability of sampling a violated edge according to distribution D_E for a function that is ϵ-far from Lipschitz. (Recall that ϵ-far is measured with respect to the distribution Π.)

Lemma 5.1. *Let function* $f : \{0, 1\}^d \to \delta\mathbb{Z}$ *be* ϵ-far *from Lipschitz. Let* $V(f)$ *denote the set of edges in* $\mathcal{H}_d$ *violated by* f. *Then*

$$\sum_{(x,y) \in V(f)} \frac{(p_x + p_y)}{d} \geq \frac{\delta(\epsilon - d^2\delta)}{d \cdot ImD(f)}$$

Here ImD *is the image diameter defined in Definition 5.1.*

We prove the above lemma in section 5.3.

5.2 Lipschitz Tester

In this section we prove Theorem 5.1 and Corollary 5.1. We first present the algorithm stated in Theorem 5.1.

Algorithm 3 Lipschitz Tester

Require: Data domain $\{0,1\}^d$, product distribution on dataset $\Pi = Ber(p_1) \times Ber(p_2) \times \dots \times Ber(p_d)$, failure probability ρ, proximity parameter ϵ', discretization parameter δ.

1: Set $\epsilon = \epsilon' - d^2\delta$.
2: Sample $t = \left\lceil \frac{2}{\epsilon} \ln(\frac{2}{\rho}) \right\rceil$ vertices $z_1, z_2, \dots, z_t$ independently from $\mathcal{H}_d$ according to the distribution Π.
3: Let $r = \max_{i=1}^{t} f(z_i) - \min_{i=1}^{t} f(z_i)$.
4: If $r > d$, **reject**.
5: Sample $\left\lceil \frac{dr}{\delta\epsilon} \ln(\frac{2}{\rho}) \right\rceil$ edges independently with each edge (x, y) picked with probability $\frac{(p_x + p_y)}{d}$ from the hypercube $\mathcal{H}_d$.
6: If any of the sampled edges is violated, then **reject**, else **accept**.

Proof (of Theorem 5.1). First observe that if input function f is Lipschitz then Algorithm 3 always accepts. This is because a Lipschitz function f has image diameter (see Definition 5.1) at most d and hence cannot be rejected in Step 4. Moreover, it does not have any violated edges and hence cannot be rejected in Step 6. Next consider the case when f is ϵ-far from Lipschitz. Towards this we first extend Claim 3.1 of [21] about sample diameter r to our setting where the distance (in particular, the notion of ϵ-far) is measured with respect to a product distribution.

Claim. Value r computed on Line 3 is at most $ImD(f)$ and with probability at least $1 - \frac{\rho}{2}$, f is ϵ-close to having diameter at most r.

Proof. Sort the points in $\{0,1\}^d$ according to their function values in non-decreasing order. Let L be the first ℓ-points such that their *probability mass* sums up to $\frac{\epsilon}{2}$ and R be the set of last ℓ' points such that their *probability mass* sums up to $\frac{\epsilon}{2}$. The rest of the proof is very similar to the proof of Claim 3.1 in [21], so we omit the details here.   □

Having established Claim 5.2, the rest of the proof of Theorem 5.1 is identical to [21]. We omit the details.   □

5.3 Repair Operator and Proof of Lemma 5.1

We show a transformation of an arbitrary function $f : \{0,1\}^d \to \delta\mathbb{Z}$ into a Lipschitz function by changing f on certain points, whose probability mass is related to the probability mass (with respect to D_E) of the violated edges of $\mathcal{H}_d$. This is achieved by repairing one dimension of $\mathcal{H}_d$ at a time as explained henceforth. To achieve this, we define an **asymmetric** version of the basic operator of [21]. The operator redefines function values so that it reduces the gap asymmetrically according to the Hamming weights (and probability masses in-turn) of the endpoints of the violated edge. This is the main difference from previous approaches ([21], [2]) which do not work if applied directly, because of the varying probability masses of the vertices with respect to the Hamming weight, defined as $|x|$ for a vertex x. We first define the building block of the repair operator which is called the asymmetric basic operator.

Definition 5.2 (Asymmetric basic operator). *Given* $f : \{0,1\}^d \to \delta\mathbb{Z}$, *for each violated edge* $\{x,y\}$ *along dimension* i, *where* $f(x) < f(y) - 1$, *define* B_i *as follows.*

1. *If* $|x| > |y|$, *then* $B_i[f](x) = f(x) + (1 - p_i)\delta$ *and* $B_i[f](y) = f(y) - p_i\delta$
2. *If* $|x| < |y|$, *then* $B_i[f](x) = f(x) + p_i\delta$ *and* $B_i[f](y) = f(y) - (1 - p_i)\delta$

Now we define the repair operator.

Definition 5.3 (Repair Operator). *Given* $f : \{0,1\}^d \to \delta\mathbb{Z}$, $A_i[f](x)$ *is obtained from* f *by several applications of the asymmetric basic operator (see Definition 5.2)* B_i *along dimension* i *followed by a single application of the rounding operator. Specifically, let* f' *be the function obtained from* f *by applying* B_i *repeatedly until there are no violated edges along the* i*-th dimension. Then,* $A_i[f]$ *is defined to be* $\mathbf{R}[f']$ *where the rounding operator* $\mathbf{R}$ *rounds the function values to the closest* $\delta\mathbb{Z}$*-valued function.*

In effect, we have the following picture for the repair operation.

$$f = f_0 \xrightarrow{A_1} f_1 \xrightarrow{A_2} f_2 \to \cdots \to f_{d-1} \xrightarrow{A_d} f_d.$$

Now we define a measure called violation score which will be used to show the progress of repair operation. As shown later, the violation score is approximately preserved along any dimension $j \neq i$ when we apply the repair operator to repair the edges along dimension i. Note that the violation score closely resembles the violation score in [21] except that it depends on the function value as well as the probability masses of the end-points of the edge.

Definition 5.4. *The violation score of an edge with respect to function* f, *denoted by* $vs(\{x,y\})$, *is* $\max(0, (p_x + p_y)(|f(x) - f(y)| - 1))$. *The violation score along dimension* i, *denoted by* $VS^i(f)$, *is the sum of violation scores of all edges along dimension* i

The violation score of an edge $\{x,y\}$ is positive iff it is violated and violation score of a $\delta\mathbb{Z}$ valued function is contained in the interval $[\delta(p_x + p_y), ImD(f)(p_x + p_y)]$. Let $V^i(f)$ denote be the set of edges along dimension i violated by f. Then

$$\delta \cdot \sum_{\{x,y\}\in V^i(f)} (p_x + p_y) \leq VS^i(f) \leq \sum_{\{x,y\}\in V^i(f)} (p_x + p_y) \cdot ImD(f) \tag{2}$$

Lemma 5.2 shows that A_i does not increase the violation score in dimensions other than i more than the additive value of δ.

Lemma 5.2. *For all* $i,j \in [d]$, *where* $i \neq j$, *and every function* $f : \{0,1\}^d \to \delta\mathbb{Z}$, *the following holds.*

- *(**progress**) Applying the repair operator* A_i *does not introduce new violated edges in dimension* j *if the dimension* j *is violation free, i.e.* $VS_j(f) = 0 \Rightarrow VS_j(A_i[f]) = 0$.
- *(**accounting**) Applying the repair operator* A_i *does not increase the violation score in dimension* j *by more than* δ, *i.e.* $VS_j(A_i[f]) \leq VS_j(f) + \delta$.

Application of the repair operator A_i entails several applications of the basic operator B_i followed by a single application of the rounding operator $\mathbf{R}$. In Lemma 5.3, we show that the applications of B_i does not increase the violation score along the remaining dimensions. In Claim 5.3, we show that the second step (rounding) is not too harmful for the remaining dimensions either. Finally, we use Lemma 5.3 and Claim 5.3 to prove Lemma 5.2.

Lemma 5.3. *Suppose* $f : \mathcal{H}_d \rightarrow \mathbb{R}$ *is such that for every edge* $\{x, y\}$ *in* $\mathcal{H}_d$*, the difference* $f(x) - f(y) \in \delta\mathbb{Z}$*. Let* f' *be the function obtained from* f *by applying* B_i *repeatedly until there are no violated edges along the i-th dimension. Then for every dimension* $j \neq i$*,* $VS_j(f') \leq VS_j(f)$*.*

Proof. First observe that it is sufficient to prove the lemma for a single application of the basic operator B_i. This is because for every edge $\{x, y\}$, the following holds: $f(x) - f(y) \in \delta\mathbb{Z} \Rightarrow B_i[f](x) - B_i[f](y) \in \delta\mathbb{Z}$. To see this observe that, by definition of the basic operator, $B_i[f](x) - B_i[f](y)$ is either $f(x) - f(y) + \delta$ or $f(x) - f(y) - \delta$ and we already started with the assumption that $f(x) - f(y) \in \delta\mathbb{Z}$. Note that before the application of repair operations, the function f has range in $\delta\mathbb{Z}$ and the assumption holds true. Also, it holds true for the further applications of B_i as shown above. Next we prove the lemma for one step of the basic operator.

Following the proof outline of a similar proof in [21], we show that application of the asymmetric basic operator in dimension i does not increase the violation score in dimension $j \neq i$. Standard arguments [16,9,21,2] show that it is enough to analyze the effect of applying B_i on one fixed disjoint square formed by adjacent edges that cross dimensions i and j. (This is because edges along dimensions i and j form disjoint squares in the hypercube. So proving the statement for one fixed square of the hypercube, the full claim follows by summing up the inequalities over all such squares.)

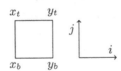

Fig. 1. Image courtesy [21]

Consider the two dimensional function $f : \{x_b, x_t, y_b, y_t\} \rightarrow \mathbb{R}$ where $\{x_b, x_t, y_b, y_t\}$ are as positioned in the figure. Assume that the basic operator is applied along the dimension i. We show that the violation score along dimension j does not increase. Assume that the violation score along edge $\{x_b, x_t\}$ increases. First, assume that the $B_i[f](x_t) > B_i[f](x_b)$. (The other case is very similar and we will prove it later.) Then B_i increases $f(x_t)$ and/or decreases $f(x_b)$. Assume that B_i increases $f(x_t)$. (The other case is symmetrical.) This implies that $\{x_t, y_t\}$ is violated and $f(x_t) < f(y_t)$. Recall that the repair operator is applied only if the edge is violated. Therefore $f(y_t) - f(x_t) > 1$. Since $f(y_t) - f(x_t) \in \delta\mathbb{Z}$ and $\frac{1}{\delta}$ is an integer, we have

$$f(y_t) \geq f(x_t) + 1 + \delta$$

The above inequality is crucial for the remaining proof of the lemma 5.1. Now consider the cases when either the bottom edge is also violated or is not violated.

If the bottom edge is not violated then we have $f(x_b) \geq f(y_b) - 1$ and $f(x_b)$ and $f(y_b)$ are not modified by the basic operator. Since $vs(\{x_t, x_b\})$ increases, $f(x_t) > f(x_b) + 1 - p_i\delta$. Combining the above inequalities, we get $f(y_t) \geq f(x_t) + 1 + \delta > f(x_b) + 2 + (1 - p_i)\delta \geq f(y_b) + 1 + (1 - p_i)\delta > f(y_b) + 1$. Thus the violation score increases along $\{x_t, x_b\}$ by $(p_{x_b} + p_{x_t})p_i\delta$ and decreases along $\{y_b, y_t\}$ by $(p_{y_b} + p_{y_t})(1 - p_i)\delta = (p_{x_b} + p_{x_t})\left(\frac{p_i}{1-p_i}\right)(1 - p_i)\delta$ which is same as $(p_{x_b} + p_{x_t})p_i\delta$, keeping the violation score along the dimension j unchanged.

If the bottom edge is violated, then the increase in $vs(\{x_b, x_t\})$ implies that $f(x_b)$ must decrease (after application of B_i) by $p_i\delta$ (since $|x_b| < |y_b|$) implying $f(y_b) + 1 < f(x_b)$). Therefore $f(x_t) + p_i\delta > f(x_b) + 1 - p_i\delta$ or $f(x_t) > f(y_t) + 1 - 2p_i\delta$. Therefore $f(y_t) > f(x_t) + 1 > f(x_b) + 2 - 2p_i\delta \geq f(y_b) + 3 - 2p_i\delta + \delta \geq f(y_b) + 1 + \delta$. The last inequality is true since $\delta \leq 1$ and $p_i \leq 1$. Thus, $vs(\{x_t, x_b\})$ increases by at most $(p_{x_b} + p_{x_t})2p_i\delta$ while $vs(\{y_t, y_b\})$ decreases by $(p_{y_t} + p_{y_b})2(1 - p_i)\delta = (p_{x_b} + p_{x_t})2p_i\delta$, ensuring that violation score along the vertical dimension does not increase.

Now we turn to the case when $B_i[f](x_t) < B_i[f](x_b)$. By the arguments very similar to the first case, it can be proved that $f(x_t) \geq f(y_t) + 1 + \delta$ and the application of basic operator decreases $f(x_t)$ by $p_i\delta$ and increases $f(y_t)$ by $(1 - p_i)\delta$.

If the bottom edge is not violated then $f(y_b) \geq f(x_b) - 1$ and $f(x_b)$ and $f(y_b)$ are not modified by the basic operator. Since $vs(\{x_t, x_b\})$ increases, $f(x_b) > f(x_t) + 1 - p_i\delta$. Combining the above inequalities, we get $f(y_b) \geq f(x_b) - 1 > f(x_t) - p_i\delta \geq f(y_t) + 1 + \delta(1 - p_i)$. Thus the violation score increases along $\{x_t, x_b\}$ by $(p_{x_b} + p_{x_t})p_i\delta$ and decreases along $\{y_b, y_t\}$ by $(p_{y_b} + p_{y_t})(1 - p_i)\delta = (p_{x_b} + p_{x_t})\left(\frac{p_i}{1-p_i}\right)(1 - p_i)\delta$ which is same as $(p_{x_b} + p_{x_t})p_i\delta$, keeping the violation score along the dimension j unchanged.

If the bottom edge is violated, then the increase in $vs(\{x_b, x_t\})$ implies that $f(x_b)$ must increase implying $f(y_b) > f(x_b) + 1$. Therefore, the increase in $vs\{x_b, x_t\}$ implies that $f(x_b) + p_i\delta > f(x_t) - p_i\delta + 1$ or $f(x_b) > f(x_t) - 2p_i\delta + 1$. Combining the above inequalities, we get $f(y_b) > f(x_b) + 1 > f(x_t) - 2p_i\delta + 2 \geq f(y_t) + 3 + \delta - 2p_i\delta \geq f(y_t) + 1 + \delta$. The last inequality is true since $\delta \leq 1$ and $p_i \leq 1$. Thus, $vs(\{x_t, x_b\})$ increases by at most $(p_{x_b} + p_{x_t})2p_i\delta$ while $vs(\{y_t, y_b\})$ decreases by $(p_{y_t} + p_{y_b})2(1 - p_i)\delta = (p_{x_b} + p_{x_t})2p_i\delta$, ensuring that violation score along the vertical dimension does not increase. □

Claim (Rounding is safe). Given $a, b \in \mathbb{R}$ satisfying $|a - b| \leq 1$, let a' (respectively, b') be the value obtained by rounding a (respectively, b) to the closest $\delta\mathbb{Z}$ integer. Then $|a' - b'| \leq 1$.

Proof. Assume without loss of generality $a \leq b$. For $x \in \mathbb{R}$, let $\lfloor x \rfloor_\delta$ be the largest value in $\delta\mathbb{Z}$ not greater than x. Observe that $a' \in \{\lfloor a \rfloor_\delta, \lfloor a \rfloor_\delta + \delta\}$. Using the fact that $\lfloor a \rfloor_\delta \leq b' \leq \lfloor a \rfloor_\delta + 1 + \delta$, we see that if $a' = \lfloor a \rfloor_\delta + \delta$ then $|b' - a'| \leq 1$ always holds. Therefore, assume $a' = \lfloor a \rfloor_\delta$. This can happen only if $a \leq \lfloor a \rfloor_\delta + \delta/2$. The latter implies $b \leq \lfloor a \rfloor_\delta + 1 + \delta/2$ (using the fact that $b - a \leq 1$). That is $b' \neq \lfloor a \rfloor_\delta + 1 + \delta$. In other words, $b' \leq \lfloor a \rfloor_\delta + 1$ again implying $b' - a' \leq 1$, as required. □

Proof (of Lemma 5.2). Let f' be the function from the statement of Lemma 5.3. Then function $A_i[f]$ is obtained by rounding the values of f' to the closest $\delta\mathbb{Z}$ values. Since rounding can never create new edge violations by Claim 5.3, we immediately get the first part of the lemma. The second part follows from the observation that the rounding step modifies each function value by at most $\delta/2$. Correspondingly, the violation score of an edge along the j-th dimension changes by at most $2 \cdot (\delta/2) \cdot (p_u + p_v)$ where the factor 2 comes because both endpoints of an edge may be rounded. Summing over all edges in the j-th dimension, we get, increase in violation score $\leq \sum_{\{u,v\}} \delta \cdot (p_u + p_v) = \delta$ where the last equality holds because edges along the j-th dimension form a perfect matching and therefore the probabilities $p_u + p_v$ sum to 1. □

Proof of Lemma 5.1. Using the arguments very similar to [21] as given below, we can get the following sequence of inequalities

$$Dist(f_{i-1}, f_i) = Dist(f_{i-1}, A_i(f_{i-1})) \leq \sum_{(x,y) \in V_i(f_{i-1})} (p_x + p_y)$$

$$\leq \frac{1}{\delta} VS^i(f_{i-1}) \leq \frac{1}{\delta} VS^i(f) + (d-i)\delta \leq \frac{1}{\delta} \sum_{(x,y) \in V^i(f)} (p_x + p_y) \cdot ImD(f) + (d-i)\delta$$

Here functions $\{f_i\}_{i=0}^{i=d}$ are defined in the same way as [21]. The first inequality holds because A_i modifies f only at the endpoints points x and y of violated edge (x, y) along dimension i, thus paying $p_x + p_y$. The second and fourth inequalities follow from Equation (2) and the third inequality holds because of Lemma 5.2. Therefore, by triangle inequality, we have

$$Dist(f, f_d) \leq \sum_{i \in [d]} Dist(f_{i-1}, f_i)$$

$$\leq \sum_{i \in [d]} \left(\sum_{(x,y) \in V^i f(H)} (p_x + p_y) \cdot \frac{ImD(f)}{\delta} \right) + (d-i)\delta$$

$$\leq \left(\sum_{(x,y) \in V(f))} (p_x + p_y) \cdot \frac{ImD(f)}{\delta} \right) + d^2\delta$$

For a function which is ϵ-far from Lipschitz, we have $Dist(f, f_d) \geq \epsilon$. Therefore, from the above inequality, we have

$$\sum_{(x,y) \in V(f)} \frac{(p_x + p_y)}{d} \geq \frac{\delta(\epsilon - d^2\delta)}{d \cdot ImD(f)}$$

6 Instantiation of Privacy Tester Using Lipschitz Testers

In this section, we instantiate the privacy tester of Section 4 with both known Lipschitz testers as well as the Lipschitz tester developed in this work. The table below compares the current state of art Lipschitz testers on the hypercube domain. The third column gives the "approximation factor" as defined in Definition 2.3 for the various testers. The last row gives the result of Lipschitz tester (Section 5) developed in this work. The discussion about the instantiations follows.

Reference	Functions	Approx. Factor	Distribution	Tester running time
[7]	$\{0,1\}^d \to \mathbb{R}$	1	Uniform	$O(\frac{d}{\epsilon})$
This work	$\{0,1\}^d \to \mathbb{R}$	$(1+\delta)$	**Product**	$O\left(\frac{d \cdot Im D(f)}{(\epsilon - d^2\delta)\delta}\right)$

First we analyze the result for the case when points are sampled from $\{0,1\}^d$ according to the uniform distribution. In this case, the running time for for $(\alpha, \beta, \gamma, \delta)$-privacy testing of $\mathcal{T}_{priv}$ (defined in theorem 4.1) is $O(\frac{|Z|^2 d}{\gamma})$. Let us now analyze the running time for the same when applied to the datasets coming from the hypercube domain according to some (possibly unknown) product distribution. We use the tester given in the algorithm 3. The running time in this case is given by $O(|Z| \cdot$ Run-time $\left(\mathcal{T}_{Lip}(\frac{\gamma}{|Z|}, \beta, \delta, d)\right)$. Choosing $\delta = \frac{\gamma}{4d^2|Z|}$, one gets the running time of the $\mathcal{T}_{priv}$ to be $O(\frac{d^4|Z|^3}{\gamma^2})$. In general, δ can be made smaller at the cost of higher running time of tester. This clearly shows the trade off between the privacy guarantee and running time of the tester.

7   Discussions and Open Problems

In this section we discuss some of the interesting implications of our current work and some of the new avenues it opens up. Also we state some of the open problems that remains unresolved in our work.

Privacy: In this work, we took the first step towards designing efficient testing algorithm for statistical data privacy. Our work indicates that it is indeed possible to design efficient testing algorithms for some existing notions of statistical data privacy (e.g., differential privacy on typical datasets). It is important that the current paper should be treated as an initial study of the problem and in no way should be interpreted as conclusive. It is interesting (and also important) to explore other rigorous notions of data privacy, their implications, and design testers for them.

In this paper, we test for differential privacy on typical datasets, which is a relaxation of differential privacy. It remains an open problem to design a privacy tester for *pure* (α, β)-differential privacy.

Lipschitz Testing: This work presents the first Lipschitz property tester for the setting where the domain points are sampled from a distribution that is not uniform. Because of possible applications to statistical data privacy, this work has motivated the design of such Lipschitz testers for other domains, e.g. hypergrid. Also, this paper mainly shows the tester for the product distribution over the hypercube domain, but it still remains open to design testers for other distributions that may be correlated in some way (e.g., pairwise correlation). In the current work, we have designed testers where the domain of the dataset is finite. A natural question that arises is that if we can extend the current results to design privacy testers when the datasets are drawn from continuous domain.

Other Limitations of our Approach: The current work on testing of privacy properties have several limitations which are worth highlighting. These limitations need to be addressed in order to allow our current testing algorithms to be used in practice. Firstly, our current testing algorithm works on discrete range space S. This significantly limits the applicability of our testing algorithm in various applications which are meaningful over continuous range spaces (e.g., various machine learning problems). Also the running time of our tester depends polynomially on the size of the range space S. Secondly, our testing algorithm needs oracle access to the probability measure induced on the range space of the untrusted algorithm $\mathcal{A}$. In general it is not clear how to come up with a computationally efficient oracle given just the algorithm $\mathcal{A}$. Thirdly, the current results are only for discrete domain of datasets $\mathcal{X}^d$. This restricts the applicability of our approach to many interesting applications (e.g., Gaussian process regression).

Acknowledgements. We would like to thank Adam Smith for suggesting the name Differential Privacy on Typical Datasets and for various other suggestions and comments.

References

1. Awasthi, P., Jha, M., Molinaro, M., Raskhodnikova, S.: Limitations of local filters of lipschitz and monotone functions. In: Gupta, et al.: [18], pp. 374–386
2. Awasthi, P., Jha, M., Molinaro, M., Raskhodnikova, S.: Testing lipschitz functions on hypergrid domains. In: Gupta, et al.: [18], pp. 387–398
3. Bhaskar, R., Bhowmick, A., Goyal, V., Laxman, S., Thakurta, A.: Noiseless database privacy. Cryptology ePrint Archive, Report 2011/487 (version: 20120524:110619) (2011), http://eprint.iacr.org/
4. Bhaskar, R., Bhowmick, A., Goyal, V., Laxman, S., Thakurta, A.: Noiseless Database Privacy. In: Lee, D.H., Wang, X. (eds.) ASIACRYPT 2011. LNCS, vol. 7073, pp. 215–232. Springer, Heidelberg (2011)
5. Bhowmick, A., Dwork, C.: Natural differential privacy. Personal Communication (2012)
6. Calandrino, J.A., Kilzer, A., Narayanan, A., Felten, E.W., Shmatikov, V.: "you might also like: " privacy risks of collaborative filtering. In: IEEE Symposium on Security and Privacy, pp. 231–246 (2011)
7. Chakrabarty, D., Seshadhri, C.: Optimal bounds for monotonicity and lipschitz testing over the hypercube. CoRR abs/1204.0849 (2012)
8. Dixit, K., Jha, M., Raskhodnikova, S., Thakurta, A.: Testing the lipschitz property over product distributions with applications to data privacy (2013), http://arxiv.org/abs/1209.4056
9. Dodis, Y., Goldreich, O., Lehman, E., Raskhodnikova, S., Ron, D., Samorodnitsky, A.: Improved Testing Algorithms for Monotonicity. In: Hochbaum, D.S., Jansen, K., Rolim, J.D.P., Sinclair, A. (eds.) RANDOM-APPROX 1999. LNCS, vol. 1671, pp. 97–108. Springer, Heidelberg (1999)

10. Dwork, C.: Differential Privacy. In: Bugliesi, M., Preneel, B., Sassone, V., Wegener, I. (eds.) ICALP 2006. LNCS, vol. 4052, pp. 1–12. Springer, Heidelberg (2006)
11. Dwork, C.: Differential Privacy: A Survey of Results. In: Agrawal, M., Du, D.-Z., Duan, Z., Li, A. (eds.) TAMC 2008. LNCS, vol. 4978, pp. 1–19. Springer, Heidelberg (2008)
12. Dwork, C.: The Differential Privacy Frontier (Extended Abstract). In: Reingold, O. (ed.) TCC 2009. LNCS, vol. 5444, pp. 496–502. Springer, Heidelberg (2009)
13. Dwork, C., Kenthapadi, K., McSherry, F., Mironov, I., Naor, M.: Our Data, Ourselves: Privacy Via Distributed Noise Generation. In: Vaudenay, S. (ed.) EUROCRYPT 2006. LNCS, vol. 4004, pp. 486–503. Springer, Heidelberg (2006)
14. Dwork, C., McSherry, F., Nissim, K., Smith, A.: Calibrating Noise to Sensitivity in Private Data Analysis. In: Halevi, S., Rabin, T. (eds.) TCC 2006. LNCS, vol. 3876, pp. 265–284. Springer, Heidelberg (2006)
15. Ganta, S.R., Kasiviswanathan, S.P., Smith, A.: Composition attacks and auxiliary information in data privacy. In: KDD, pp. 265–273 (2008)
16. Goldreich, O., Goldwasser, S., Lehman, E., Ron, D., Samorodnitsky, A.: Testing monotonicity. Combinatorica 20(3), 301–337 (2000)
17. Goldreich, O., Goldwasser, S., Ron, D.: Property testing and its connection to learning and approximation. J. ACM 45(4), 653–750 (1998)
18. Gupta, A., Jansen, K., Rolim, J., Servedio, R. (eds.): APPROX 2012 and RANDOM 2012. LNCS, vol. 7408. Springer, Cambridge (2012)
19. Halevy, S., Kushilevitz, E.: Distribution-free property-testing. SIAM J. Comput. 37(4), 1107–1138 (2007)
20. Halevy, S., Kushilevitz, E.: Distribution-free connectivity testing for sparse graphs. Algorithmica 51(1), 24–48 (2008)
21. Jha, M., Raskhodnikova, S.: Testing and reconstruction of lipschitz functions with applications to data privacy. In: Ostrovsky, R. (ed.) FOCS, pp. 433–442. IEEE (2011)
22. Kasiviswanathan, S.P., Smith, A.: A note on differential privacy: Defining resistance to arbitrary side information. CoRR abs/0803.3946 (2008)
23. Korolova, A.: Privacy violations using microtargeted ads: A case study. In: ICDMW, pp. 474–482 (2010)
24. Machanavajjhala, A., Gehrke, J., Kifer, D., Venkitasubramaniam, M.: l-diversity: Privacy beyond k-anonymity. In: ICDE, p. 24 (2006)
25. McSherry, F.D.: Privacy integrated queries: an extensible platform for privacy-preserving data analysis. In: SIGMOD, pp. 19–30 (2009)
26. Mohan, P., Thakurta, A., Shi, E., Song, D., Culler, D.: Gupt: privacy preserving data analysis made easy. In: SIGMOD, pp. 349–360 (2012)
27. Nissim, K., Raskhodnikova, S., Smith, A.: Smooth sensitivity and sampling in private data analysis. In: STOC, pp. 75–84 (2007)
28. Parnas, M., Ron, D.: Testing the diameter of graphs. Random Struct. Algorithms 20(2), 165–183 (2002)
29. Reed, J., Pierce, B.C.: Distance makes the types grow stronger: a calculus for differential privacy. In: ICFP, pp. 157–168 (2010)
30. Roy, I., Setty, S.T.V., Kilzer, A., Shmatikov, V., Witchel, E.: Airavat: Security and privacy for mapreduce. In: NSDI, pp. 297–312 (2010)
31. Rubinfeld, R., Sudan, M.: Robust characterization of polynomials with applications to program testing. SIAM J. Comput. 25(2), 252–271 (1996)
32. Smith, A.: Privacy-preserving statistical estimation with optimal convergence rates. In: STOC, pp. 813–822 (2011)
33. Sweeney, L.: k-anonymity: A model for protecting privacy. International Journal on Uncertainty, Fuzziness and Knowledge-based Systems 10(5), 557–570 (2002)

Limits on the Usefulness of Random Oracles

Iftach Haitner[1,*], Eran Omri[2,*,**,***], and Hila Zarosim[3,**,†]

[1] School of Computer Science, Tel Aviv University
iftachh@cs.tau.ac.il
[2] Dep. of Mathematics and Computer Science, Ariel University Center
omrier@gmail.com
[3] Dep. of Computer Science, Bar Ilan University
zarosih@cs.biu.ac.il

Abstract. In the *random oracle* model, parties are given oracle access to a random function (i.e., a uniformly chosen function from the set of all functions), and are assumed to have unbounded computational power (though they can only make a bounded number of oracle queries). This model provides powerful properties that allow proving the security of many protocols, even such that cannot be proved secure in the standard model (under any hardness assumptions). The random oracle model is also used for showing that a given cryptographic primitive cannot be used in a black-box way to construct another primitive; in their seminal work, Impagliazzo and Rudich [STOC '89] showed that no key-agreement protocol exists in the random oracle model, yielding that key-agreement cannot be black-box reduced to one-way functions. Their work has a long line of followup works (Simon [EC '98], Gertner et al. [STOC '00] and Gennaro et al. [SICOMP '05], to name a few), showing that given oracle access to a certain type of function family (e.g., the family that "implements" public-key encryption) is not sufficient for building a given cryptographic primitive (e.g., oblivious transfer). Yet, the following question remained open:

What is the exact power of the random oracle model?

We make progress towards answering this question, showing that essentially, any no private input, semi-honest two-party functionality that can be securely implemented in the random oracle model, can be securely implemented information theoretically (where parties are assumed to be all powerful, and no oracle is given). We further generalize the above result to function families that provide some natural combinatorial property.

Our result immediately yields that essentially the only no-input functionalities that can be securely realized in the random oracle model (in the sense of secure function evaluation), are the trivial ones (ones that can be securely realized information theoretically). In addition, we use the recent information theoretic impossibility result of McGregor et al. [FOCS '10], to show the existence of functionalities (e.g., inner product) that cannot

---

* Supported by the Israeli Centers of Research Excellence program (Center No. 4/11).
** Supported by the Israel Science Foundation (ISF) (Grant No. 189/11).
*** Research was done while Eran Omri was at Bar Ilan University.
† Hila Zarosim is grateful to the Azrieli Foundation for the Azrieli Fellowship.

A. Sahai (Ed.): TCC 2013, LNCS 7785, pp. 437–456, 2013.

be computed both accurately and in a differentially private manner in the random oracle model; yielding that protocols for computing these functionalities cannot be black-box reduced to one-way functions.

Keywords: random oracles, black-box separations, one-way functions, differential privacy, key agreement.

1   Introduction

In the *random-oracle* model, the parties are given oracle access to a random function (i.e., a uniformly chosen function from the set of all functions — the all-function family), and are assumed to have unbounded computational power (though they can only make a bounded number of oracle queries). Many cryptographic primitives are known to exist in this model, such as (exponentially hard) collision resistant hash functions. More importantly, in this model it is possible to implement secure protocols for tasks that are hard to implement in the standard model, and sometimes even completely unachievable; a well known example is the work of Fiat and Shamir [6], showing how to convert three-message identification schemes to a highly efficient (non interactive) signature scheme. In the random-oracle model, their methodology preserves the security of the original scheme [20], but (for some schemes) does not do so in the standard model [10, 3].

On a different route, the random-oracle model was used to show that one cryptographic primitive *cannot* be used in a black-box way to construct another primitive. In their seminal work, Impagliazzo and Rudich [13] showed that no key-agreement protocol exists in the random oracle model, yielding that key-agreement cannot be black-box reduced to one-way functions. Their work has initiated a long line of follow up works (Simon [22], Gertner et al. [9], and Gennaro et al. [8], to name a few) showing that given oracle access to a certain type of function family (e.g., the family that "implements" public-key encryption) is not sufficient for building a given cryptographic primitive (e.g., oblivious transfer). Yet, the following question remained open:

What is the exact power of the random-oracle model?

Apart from being aesthetic mathematically, answers to this question are very likely to enrich our understanding of (the limitations of) black-box reductions in cryptography.

It is well known that for malicious adversaries, there exist functionalities that cannot be achieved in the *information-theoretic model*, i.e., where all entities are assumed to be unbounded (with no oracle access), yet can be securely computed in the random-oracle model (e.g., commitment schemes, coin-tossing protocols and, non-trivial zero-knowledge proofs). All of these functionalities, however, are blatantly trivial when considering semi-honest adversaries, which are the focus of this work.

1.1   Our Result

We make progress towards answering the above question, showing that, essentially, *any* no private input, semi-honest, two-party computation that can be securely implemented in the random-oracle model, *can* be securely implemented in the *information-theoretic* model.

Theorem 1 (Main Theorem, Informal). *Let π be a no private-input, m-round, ℓ-query, oracle-aided two-party protocol. Then for any $\varepsilon > 0$ there exists an $O(\ell^2/\varepsilon^2)$-query oracle-aided function* Map, *and a stateless, no oracle, m-round protocol $\widetilde{\pi} = (\widetilde{\mathsf{A}}, \widetilde{\mathsf{B}})$ such that:*

$$\mathrm{SD}\left(\left(\mathsf{out}_\mathsf{A}, \mathsf{out}_\mathsf{B}, \mathsf{Map}^f(\bar{t})\right)_{f \leftarrow \mathcal{F}_{\mathrm{AF}}, (\mathsf{out}_\mathsf{A}, \mathsf{out}_\mathsf{B}, \bar{t}) \leftarrow \langle \mathsf{A}^f, \mathsf{B}^f \rangle}, \left\langle \widetilde{\mathsf{A}}, \widetilde{\mathsf{B}} \right\rangle\right) \in O(\varepsilon),$$

where $\mathcal{F}_{\mathrm{AF}}$ is the all functions family, and $\langle X, Y \rangle$ stands for a random execution of the protocol (X, Y), resulting in the parties' private outputs and the common transcript.

Furthermore, the projections of the above distributions to their first and third coordinates, or to their second and third coordinates are identically *distributed (i.e., the transcripts concatenated with the outputs of one of the parties, are identically distributed).*

Namely, the distributions induced by a random execution of π^f (for a random $f \leftarrow \mathcal{F}_{\mathrm{AF}}$) on the parties' private outputs and the common transcript, is almost the same as that induced by a random execution of the (no oracle) protocol $\widetilde{\pi}$, where the only difference is that one needs to apply an efficient procedure Map to π's transcript. Theorem 1 generalizes to all function families with the property that answers for *distinct* queries, induced by drawing a random member from the family, are independent.

A major ingredient in the proof of Theorem 1 is the *dependency finder* algorithm presented by Barak and Mahmoody [1], refining a similar algorithm by Impagliazzo and Rudich [13] (see Section 1.2). While we could have based the proof of Theorem 1 on a combination of several results from [1] (or alternatively, to get a somewhat weaker variant of the theorem by basing the proof on a followup result of Dachman-Soled et al. [5, Lemma 5] or of Mahmoody et al. [16, Lemma A.1]), we chose to give a new proof also for this part (modulo clearly marked parts taken from [1]). The new proof (given as part of the proof of Lemma 2) holds with respect to a larger set of function families. More significantly, it is more modular and introduces several simplifications comparing to the previous proofs.

Applications. We demonstrate the usefulness of Theorem 1 via the following three examples. The first example (reproving [13, 1]) concerns the existence of key-agreement protocols in the random-oracle model. Recall that key-agreement protocols cannot be realized in the information-theoretic model. Namely, for any (no oracle) protocol π, there exists a passive (i.e., semi-honest) adversary that extracts the key from the protocol's transcript. Hence, Theorem 1 yields that key-agreement protocols cannot be realized in the random-oracle model, and thus key-agreement protocols cannot be black-box reduced to one-way functions. The actual parameters achieved by applying Theorem 1, match the optimal bound given in Barak and Mahmoody [1].

As a second more detailed example, we prove that in the random-oracle model, it is impossible for two parties to accurately approximate the inner-product function in a *differentially private* manner. Namely, in a way that very little information is leaked about *any* single bit of the input of each party to the other party. A recent result of McGregor et al. [17] shows that in the information-theoretic model, it is impossible to approximately compute the inner product function in a differentially private manner. Combining their result with Theorem 1, we obtain the following fact.[1]

Theorem 2 (Informal). *Any ℓ-query, (ℓ^2, α, γ)-differentially private protocol, errs (with constant probability) with magnitude at least $\frac{\sqrt{n}}{\log(n) \cdot e^\alpha}$, in computing the inner product of two n-bits strings.*

Very informally, a protocol is (k, α, γ)-differentially private, if no party, making at most k queries to the oracle, learns more then ε information about one of the other party's input bits, except with some small probability γ.

The above result yields the impossibility of fully black-box reducing differentially private protocols for (well) approximating two-party inner-product to the existence of one-way functions. Roughly speaking, such a fully black-box reduction is a pair of efficient oracle-aided algorithms (Q, R) such that the following hold: (1) Q^f is a good approximation protocol of the inner-product for any function f, and (2) $R^{f,\mathcal{A}}$ inverts f, for any adversary $\mathcal{A}$ that learns too much about the input of one of the parties in Q^f. Since a random sample from the all-function family is hard to invert (cf., [13, 8]), the existence of such a reduction yields that Q^f is differentially-private with respect to poly-query adversaries, when f is chosen at random from the set of all functions.[2] Hence, Theorem 2 yields the following result.

Corollary 1 (Informal). *There exists no fully black-box reduction from (α, γ)-differentially private protocol computing the inner product of two n-bit strings with error magnitude less than $\frac{\sqrt{n}}{\log(n) \cdot e^\alpha}$, to one-way functions.*

We mention that, following an observation made by McGregor et al. [17], Theorem 2 and Corollary 1 imply similar results for two-party differentially private protocols for the Hamming distance functionality.[3]

The third (and last) example is with respect to no-input secure function evaluation. Let $G = (G_A, G_B)$ be a distribution over $\mathcal{A} \times \mathcal{B}$, where G_A and G_B denote

---

[1] We mention that the result of [17] is stated for protocol with inputs, where Theorem 1 is only applicable to no-input protocols. Indeed, a fair amount of work was needed to derive an impossibility result for no-input protocols, from the work of [17].

[2] Assume towards a contradiction the existence of a poly-query adversary $\mathcal{A}$ for Q^f, then the poly-query $R^{f,\mathcal{A}}$ would successfully invert a random f.

[3] The inner product between two bit strings x, y can be expressed as $\mathsf{IP}(x, y) = w(x) + w(y) + H_d(x, y)$, where the weight $w(z)$ is number of 1-bits in z. Thus, a differentially private protocol for estimating the Hamming distance $H_d(x, y)$ can be turned into one for the inner product by having the parties send differentially private approximations of the weights of their inputs.

its marginal distributions over $\mathcal{A}$ and $\mathcal{B}$ respectively. A protocol $\pi = (\mathsf{A}, \mathsf{B})$ is an *information-theoretically* δ-secure implementation of G, if it is a δ-correct (no-oracle) implementation of G (i.e., the local outputs of the parties induced by a random execution of π are δ-close to G), and is δ-private according to the simulation paradigm (against all-powerful distinguishers). Specifically, there exists an algorithm (a simulator) that on input $x \in \mathrm{Supp}(G_\mathsf{A})$, outputs a view for A that is δ-close to the distribution of A's view, conditioned on A's local output being x. Similarly, there exists a simulator for B's view. A protocol π is a (T, δ)-secure *random-oracle* implementation of G, if it is a correct random-model implementation of G, and it is δ-private according to the simulation paradigm, against T-query, all-powerful distinguishers. Finally, G is δ-*trivial*, if it has an information-theoretically δ-secure implementation. Theorem 1 yields the following result.

Theorem 3 (Informal). *Let π be an ℓ-query oracle-aided protocol that is an $(O(\ell^2/\delta^2), \delta)$-secure implementation of a distribution G in the random-oracle model. Then, G is $O(\delta)$-trivial.*

Applying Theorem 3 to a distribution G that has a $(\mathrm{poly}(n), 1/\mathrm{poly}(n))$-secure random-oracle model implementation, it follows that G has a $1/\mathrm{poly}(n)$-secure no-oracle implementation. We note that Theorem 3 does not seem to imply the previous two examples. Since, for instance, the notion of differential privacy cannot be realized via the real/ideal paradigm.

1.2   Our Technique

When using a no-oracle protocol to emulate an oracle-aided protocol π, having oracle access to a random member of the all-function family, the crucial issue is to find all *common* information the parties share at a given point. The clear obstacle are the oracle calls: the parties might share information without explicitly communicating it, say by making the same oracle call.

Here comes into play the *Dependency Finder* of Impagliazzo and Rudich [13], and Barak and Mahmoody [1] (algorithm *Eve*, in their terminology). This oracle-aided algorithm (Finder, hereafter) gets as input a communication transcript $\bar{t}$ of a random execution of π, and an oracle access to f, the "oracle" used by the parties in this execution. Algorithm Finder outputs a list of query/answer pairs to f that with high probability contains *all* oracle queries that are *common* to both parties (and possibly also additional ones). Moreover, with high probability Finder is guaranteed not to make "too many" oracle queries.

Equipped with Finder, we give the following definition for the mapping procedure Map and the stateless (no-oracle) protocol $\widetilde{\pi} = (\widetilde{\mathsf{A}}, \widetilde{\mathsf{B}})$: on a communication transcript $\bar{t}$, the oracle-aided algorithm Map^f outputs $\left((\bar{t}_1, \mathcal{I}_1 = \mathsf{Finder}^f(\bar{t}_1)), (\bar{t}_{1,2}, \mathcal{I}_2 = \mathsf{Finder}^f(\bar{t}_{1,2})) \ldots, (\bar{t}, \mathcal{I}_m = \mathsf{Finder}^f(\bar{t})) \right)$. Namely, Map invokes Finder on each prefix of the transcript, and outputs the result. The no-oracle protocol $\widetilde{\pi} = (\widetilde{\mathsf{A}}, \widetilde{\mathsf{B}})$ is defined as follows: assume that $\widetilde{\mathsf{A}}$ speaks in round $(i + 1)$, and that the i'th message is $((\bar{t}_1, \mathcal{I}_1), \ldots, (\bar{t}_{1,\ldots,i}, \mathcal{I}_i))$.

The stateless, no-oracle $\widetilde{\mathsf{A}}$ samples random values for $f \in \mathcal{F}_{\mathrm{AF}}$ and the random coins of A, conditioned on $(\bar{t}_{1,\ldots,i}, \mathcal{I}_i)$ being the protocol's transcript. It then lets t_{i+1} be the next message of A induced by the above choice of f and random coins, and sends $\left(\bar{t}' = (\bar{t}_{1,\ldots,i}, t_{i+1}), \mathsf{Finder}^f(\bar{t}')\right)$ back to $\widetilde{\mathsf{B}}$. In case this is the last round of interaction, $\widetilde{\mathsf{A}}$ locally outputs the (local) output of A induced by this choice of f and random coins. In other words, $\widetilde{\mathsf{A}}$ selects a random view (including the oracle itself) for A that is consistent with the information contained in the no-oracle protocol augmented transcript (i.e., the transcript of the oracle protocol and the oracle calls), and then acts as A would.

The fact that $\widetilde{\mathsf{A}}$ perfectly emulates A (and that $\widetilde{\mathsf{B}}$ perfectly emulates B) trivially holds for information theoretic reasons. For the same reason, it also holds that the transcript generated by applying Map^f to a random transcript of π^f, where $f \leftarrow \mathcal{F}_{\mathrm{AF}}$, generates *exactly* the same transcript as a random execution of $\widetilde{\pi}$ does (actually, the above facts hold for any reasonable definition of Finder^4 and for any function family). The interesting part is arguing that the *joint output* of the no-oracle protocol has similar distribution to that of the oracle-aided protocol. To see that this is not trivial, assume that in the last round both oracle parties make the *same* oracle query q and output the query/answer pair $(q, f(q))$. If it happens that $(q, \cdot) \notin \mathcal{I}$, where $\mathcal{I} = \mathsf{Finder}(\bar{t})$ is the query/answer pairs made by the final call to Finder on transcript $\bar{t}$, then the answer that each of the no-oracle parties compute for the query q might be different. In this case, the joint output of the no-oracle protocol does not look like the joint output of the oracle protocol. Luckily, the above scenario is unlikely to happen due to the guarantee of Finder; with high probability $\mathcal{I}$ contains *all* common queries that the two parties made, yielding that the joint output of the no-oracle protocol has similar distribution to that of the oracle protocol. It turns out that the above example generalizes to any possible protocol, yielding that the above mapping and no-oracle protocol are indeed the desired ones.

1.3 Related Work

In their seminal work, Impagliazzo and Rudich [13] showed that there are no key-agreement protocols in the random-oracle model, and deduce that key-agreement protocols cannot be black-box reduced to one-way functions. This result was later improved by Barak and Mahmoody [1], showing there are no ℓ-query key-agreement protocols in the random-oracle model, secure against adversary making $O(\ell^2)$ queries. Thus, matching the upper bound of Merkle [18].

In an independent work, Mahmoody et al. [16] show that the all-function family (and thus one-way functions) are useless for *secure function evaluation* of deterministic, polynomial input-domain, two-party functionalities. In other words, deterministic, bounded input domain functionalities that *can* be securely computed in the random-oracle model, are the *trivial* ones — functionalities that can be securely computed unconditionally. The comparison to the result stated here is that [16] handle *with input* functionalities, but *only deterministic with*

---

[4] Whose output contains all queries it made to the oracle.

polynomial input domain, where here we handle *input-less* functionalities, but *including randomized ones*. Putting the two results together, gives a partial characterization of the power of the random-oracle model for (semi-honest) two-party computation. It is still open, however, whether the random-oracle model is useful for securely computing randomized functionalities *with* inputs, or functionalities of super-polynomial input domain.

Additional Black-Box Separations. Following [13], the method of black-box separation was subsequently used in many other works: [21] shows that there does not exist a black-box reduction from a k-pass secret key agreements to $(k - 1)$-pass secret key agreements; [22] shows that there exist no black-box reductions from collision-free hash functions to one-way permutations; [14] shows that there exists no construction of one-way permutations based on one-way functions. Other works using this paradigm contain [4, 7, 8, 9, 11, 15, 23], to name a few.

Differential Privacy. Distributed differential privacy was considered by Beimel et al. [2], who studied the setting of multiparty differentially private computation (where an n-bit database is shared between n parties). They gave a separation between information theoretic and computational differential privacy in the distributed setting. The notion of computational differential privacy was considered in Mironov et al. [19]. They presented several definitions of computational differential privacy, studied the relationships between these definitions, and constructed efficient two-party computational differentially private protocols for approximating the Hamming-distance between two vectors. Two-party differential privacy (where an n-bit database is shared between two parties) was considered by McGregor et al. [17]. They prove a lower-bound on the accuracy of two party differentially private protocols, in the information theoretic model, for computing the inner-product between two n-bit strings (and, consequently for protocols for computing the Hamming distance). Hence, proving a separation between information theoretic and computational two-party differentially private computation. In this paper, we extend the lower-bound of [17] to the random-oracle model.

1.4 Open Problems

As mentioned above, the main open problem is the full characterization of the power of the random-oracle model with respect to semi-honest adversaries. Specifically, is it possible to come up with a similar mapping from any (also with inputs) oracle-aided protocol to an equivalent one in the no-oracle model? Another interesting problem is to use our mapping (or a variant of it) to show that the random-oracle model is also useless for protocols (say, input-less) that are secure against fail-stop adversaries. An immediate implication of such a result would be that optimally-fair coin tossing are impossible to achieve in the random function model.[5]

---

[5] We mention that Dachman-Soled et al. [5] showed such an impossibility result for $O(n/\log n)$-round protocols, where n being the random function input length.

Paper Organization

Formal definitions are given in Section 2. We state our main result in Section 3 where different applications of our main result are given in Section 4. For lack of space we omit most of the proofs, and they can be found in the full version of this paper [12].

2   Preliminaries

2.1   Interactive Protocols

The communication transcript (i.e., the "transcript") of a given execution of the protocol $\pi = (A, B)$, is the list of messages $\bar{t}$ exchanged between the parties in an execution of the protocol, where $\bar{t}_{1,\ldots,j}$ denotes the first j messages in $\bar{t}$. A view of a party contains its input, its random tape and the messages exchanged by the parties during the execution. Specifically, A's view is a tuple $v_A = (i_A, r_A, \bar{t})$, where i_A is A's input, r_A are A's coins, and $\bar{t}$ is the transcript of the execution. We let $(v_A)_j$ denote the partial view of A in the first j rounds of the execution described by v_A, namely, $(v_A)_j = (i_A, r_A, \bar{t}_{1,\ldots,j})$; we define v_B analogously. We call $v = (v_A, v_B)$ the *joint view* of A and B, and let $v_j = ((v_A)_j, (v_B)_j)$. Given a distribution (or a set) $\mathcal{D}$ on the joint views of A and B, we let $\mathcal{D}_A$ be the projection of $\mathcal{D}$ on A's view (i.e., $\Pr_{\mathcal{D}_A}[v_A] = \Pr_{(v_A, \cdot) \leftarrow \mathcal{D}}[v_A]$), and define $\mathcal{D}_B$ analogously. Finally, we sometimes refer to a well structured tuple v as a "view" of π, even though v happens with zero probability. When we wish to stress that we consider a view that has non-zero probability, we call it a *valid* view.

We call π an m-round protocol, if for *every* possible random tapes for the parties, the number of rounds is *exactly* m. Given a joint view v (containing the views of both parties) of an execution of (A, B) and $P \in \{A, B\}$, let v_P denote P's part in v and let $\text{trans}(v)$ denote the communication transcript in v. For $j \in [m]$, let $\text{out}_j^P(v) = \text{out}_j^P(v_P)$ denote the output of party P at the end of the j'th round of v (i.e., the string written on P's output tape), where $\text{out}_j^P(v) = \text{out}_{j-1}^P(v)$, in case P is inactive in the j'th round of v.

We sometimes consider *stateless* protocols – the parties hold no state, and in each round act on the message received in the previous round with freshly sampled random coins. Throughout this paper we almost solely consider *no-private input* protocols – the parties' only input is the common input (the only exception to that is in Section 4.2, additional required notations introduced therein). Given a no-input two-party protocol π, let $\langle \pi \rangle$ be the distribution over the joint views of the parties in a random execution of π.

Oracle-Aided Protocols. An oracle-aided, two-party protocol $\pi = (A, B)$ is a pair of interactive Turing machines, where each party has an additional tape called the *oracle tape*; the Turing machine can make a query to the oracle by writing a string q on its tape. It then receives a string ans (denoting the answer for this query) on the oracle tape.

For simplicity, we only consider function families whose inputs and outputs are binary strings. For an oracle-aided, no-input, two-party protocol $\pi = (\mathsf{A}, \mathsf{B})$ and a function family $\mathcal{F}$, we let $\Omega^{\mathcal{F}, \pi}$ be the set of all triplets $(r_\mathsf{A}, r_\mathsf{B}, f)$, where r_A and r_B are possible random coins for A and B, and $f \in \mathcal{F}$ (henceforth, we typically omit the superscript $(\mathcal{F}, \pi)$ from the notation, whenever their values are clear from the context). For $f \in \mathcal{F}$, the distribution $\langle \pi^f = (\mathsf{A}^f, \mathsf{B}^f) \rangle$, is defined analogously to $\langle \pi \rangle = \langle \mathsf{A}, \mathsf{B} \rangle$, i.e., it is the distribution over the joint views of parties in a random execution of π with access to f. Given some information inf about some element of Ω (e.g., a set of query/answer pairs, or a view), let $\mathrm{Pr}_\Omega[\mathrm{inf}] = \mathrm{Pr}_{\omega \leftarrow \Omega}[\omega$ is consistent with $\mathrm{inf}]$, and let $\mathrm{Pr}_{\Omega | \mathrm{inf}'}[\mathrm{inf}]$ be this probability conditioned that ω is consistent with inf' (set to zero in case $\mathrm{Pr}_\Omega[\mathrm{inf}'] = 0$).

Given a (possibly partial) execution of π^f, the views of the parties contain additional lists of query/answer pairs made to the oracle throughout the execution of the protocol. Specifically, A's view is a tuple $v_\mathsf{A} = (r_\mathsf{A}, \bar{t}, f_\mathsf{A})$, where r_A are A's coins, $\bar{t}$ is the transcript of the execution, and f_A are the oracle answers to A's queries. By convention, the active party in round j first makes all its queries to the oracle for this round, and then writes a value to its output tape and send a message to the other party. We denote by $(f_\mathsf{P})_j$ the oracle answers to the queries that party P makes during the first j rounds. As above, we let $(v_\mathsf{A})_j$ denote the partial view of A in the first j rounds of the execution described by v_A, namely, $(v_\mathsf{A})_j = (r_\mathsf{A}, \bar{t}_{1, \ldots, j}, (f_\mathsf{A})_j)$. We define v_B analogously.

For $\omega \in \Omega$, we let $\mathrm{view}(\omega)$ be the full view of the parties determined by ω. We say that a "view" v is consistent with $(\mathcal{F}, \pi)$, if $\mathrm{Pr}_{\Omega^{\mathcal{F}, \pi}}[v] > 0$.

We consider the following distributions.

Definition 1 ($\Omega(\bar{t}, \mathcal{I})$ and $\mathcal{VIEW}(\bar{t}, \mathcal{I})$). *Given a partial transcript $\bar{t}$ and a set of query/answer pairs $\mathcal{I}$, let $\Omega(\bar{t}, \mathcal{I}) = \Omega^{\mathcal{F}, \pi}(\bar{t}, \mathcal{I})$ be the set of all tuples $(r_\mathsf{A}, r_\mathsf{B}, f) \in \Omega = \Omega^{\mathcal{F}, \pi}$, in which f is consistent with $\mathcal{I}$, and $\bar{t}$ is a prefix of the transcript induced by $\langle \mathsf{A}^f(r_\mathsf{A}), \mathsf{B}^f(r_\mathsf{B}) \rangle$. Given a set $\mathcal{P} \subseteq \Omega$, let $\Omega_\mathcal{P}(\bar{t}, \mathcal{I}) = \Omega(\bar{t}, \mathcal{I}) \cap \mathcal{P}$.*

Let $\mathcal{VIEW}(\bar{t}, \mathcal{I}) = \mathcal{VIEW}^{\mathcal{F}, \pi}(\bar{t}, \mathcal{I})$ be the value of $\mathrm{view}(\omega)_{|\bar{t}|}$ for $\omega \leftarrow \Omega(\bar{t}, \mathcal{I})$, and define $\mathcal{VIEW}_\mathcal{P}^{\mathcal{F}, \pi}(\bar{t}, \mathcal{I})$ analogously.

We note that since we consider the uniform distribution over Ω, we have that for any partial transcript $\bar{t}$, set of query/answer pairs $\mathcal{I}$, set $\mathcal{P} \subseteq \Omega$, and information inf about some element of Ω it holds that $\mathrm{Pr}_{\Omega_\mathcal{P}(\bar{t}, \mathcal{I})}[\mathrm{inf}] = \mathrm{Pr}_{\Omega | \bar{t}, \mathcal{I}, \mathcal{P}}[\mathrm{inf}]$.

3 Mapping Oracle-Aided Protocols to No-Oracle Protocols

In this section we prove our main result, a mapping from protocols in the random-oracle model to (inefficient) no-oracle protocols.

3.1 Dependent Views

In the following we fix an m-round oracle-aided protocol π and a function family $\mathcal{F}$. We would like to restrict $\mathcal{VIEW}(\bar{t}, \mathcal{I})$ to those views for which $\mathcal{I}$ contains all the joint information of the parties about f. We start by formally defining what it means for $\mathcal{I}$ to contain all the joint information.

Definition 2. *Let v_A be a j_A-round view for A and v_B be a j_B-round view for B, for some $j_A, j_B \in [m]$. For $i \in [j_A]$, let $\mathcal{I}_A{}^i$ be the set of query/answer pairs that A makes in the i'th round of v_A (where $\mathcal{I}_A{}^i = \emptyset$, if A is idle in round i), and define $\mathcal{I}_B{}^i$ analogously. Given a set $\mathcal{I}$ of query/answer pairs, we define*

1. $\alpha_{v_A}^{\mathcal{I}} = \prod_{i \in [j_A]} \Pr_{\Omega \mid \mathcal{I}, \mathcal{I}_A{}^1 \dots, \mathcal{I}_A{}^{i-1}} \left[\mathcal{I}_A{}^i \right]$ *and*
2. $\alpha_{v_A \mid v_B}^{\mathcal{I}} = \prod_{i \in [j_A]} \Pr_{\Omega \mid \mathcal{I}, \mathcal{I}_A{}^1, \mathcal{I}_B{}^1, \dots, \mathcal{I}_A{}^{i-1}, \mathcal{I}_B{}^{i-1}} \left[\mathcal{I}_A{}^i \right]$,

and define $\alpha_{v_B \mid v_A}^{\mathcal{I}}$ and $\alpha_{v_B}^{\mathcal{I}}$ analogously.

Intuitively, $\alpha_{v_A}^{\mathcal{I}}$ is the probability of A's view of f given $\mathcal{I}$, and $\alpha_{v_A \mid v_B}^{\mathcal{I}}$ is this probability when conditioning also on B's view. We will focus on those views with $\alpha_{v_A}^{\mathcal{I}} = \alpha_{v_A \mid v_B}^{\mathcal{I}}$ and $\alpha_{v_B}^{\mathcal{I}} = \alpha_{v_B \mid v_A}^{\mathcal{I}}$.

Definition 3 (Dependent Views). *Let $v = (v_A, v_B)$ be a pair of (possibly partial) valid views.[6] We say that v_A and v_B are dependent with respect to a set of query/answer pairs $\mathcal{I}$ and a function family $\mathcal{F}$, denoted $\mathrm{Dependent}_{\mathcal{I}}^{\mathcal{F}}(v) = 1$, if $\alpha_{v_A}^{\mathcal{I}} \neq \alpha_{v_A \mid v_B}^{\mathcal{I}}$ or $\alpha_{v_B}^{\mathcal{I}} \neq \alpha_{v_B \mid v_A}^{\mathcal{I}}$.[7]*

A pair of views $v = (v_A, v_B)$ with $\mathrm{Dependent}_{\mathcal{I}}(v) = 0$ is called independent. We let $\mathrm{Ind}^{\mathcal{F}, \pi}(\bar{t}, \mathcal{I}) = \{ \omega \in \Omega(\bar{t}, \mathcal{I}) \colon \mathrm{Dependent}_{\mathcal{I}}^{\mathcal{F}}(\mathrm{view}(\omega)_{|\bar{t}|}) = 0 \}$ and let $\mathcal{VIEW}_{\mathrm{Ind}}^{\mathcal{F}, \pi}(y)$ stand for $\mathcal{VIEW}_{\mathrm{Ind}^{\mathcal{F}, \pi}(y)}^{\mathcal{F}, \pi}(y)$.

3.2 Intersecting Views

A special case of dependent views is when the two paries share a *common* oracle query not in $\mathcal{I}$.

Definition 4 (Intersecting Views). *A (possibly partial) pair of views $v = (v_A, v_B)$ are intersecting with respect to a set of query/answer pairs $\mathcal{I}$, denoted $\mathrm{Intersect}_{\mathcal{I}}(v) = 1$, if v_A and v_B share a common query q not in $\mathcal{I}$ (i.e., $(q, \cdot) \notin \mathcal{I}$).*

For most function families, an intersection implies being dependent (with respect to the same list of query/answer pairs). In this paper we limit our attention to "simple" function families for which also the other direction holds, namely dependency implies intersection.

---

[6] While properly defined for any pair of views (v_A, v_B), we will typically only consider the following notions for pairs with $\mathrm{trans}(v_A) = \mathrm{trans}(v_B)$ (i.e., both views induce the same transcript).

[7] One can verify that $\mathrm{Dependent}_{\mathcal{I}}^{\mathcal{F}}(v) = 1$, in case v is inconsistent with $\mathcal{F}$, namely, $\Pr_{\mathcal{F}}[\mathcal{I}_A, \mathcal{I}_B] = 0$, where $\mathcal{I}_A$ and $\mathcal{I}_B$, are the lists of query/answer pairs appear in v_A and v_B respectively.

Definition 5 (Simple Function Families). *A function family* $\mathcal{F}$ *is* simple, *if for any oracle-aided protocol* π, *list* $\mathcal{I}$ *of query/answer pairs that is consistent with some* $f \in \mathcal{F}$, *and a (possibly partial) pair of views* $v = (v_A, v_B)$ *consistent with* $\mathcal{I}$, *it holds that* Dependent$_{\mathcal{I}}^{\mathcal{F}}(v) = 1$ *iff* Intersect$_{\mathcal{I}}(v) = 1$.

It is not hard to verify that the all-function family is simple (see proof in [12]).

Definition 6 (the all-function family). *For* $n \in \mathbb{N}$, *let* $\mathcal{F}_{\mathrm{AF}n}$ *be the family of all functions from* n-*bit strings to* n-*bit strings.*

Lemma 1. *For every* $n \in \mathbb{N}$, *the family* $\mathcal{F}_{\mathrm{AF}n}$ *is simple.*

3.3   Oracle-Aided to No-Oracle Protocol Mapping

The following theorem shows that an execution of an oracle-aided protocol with oracle access to a random $f \in \mathcal{F}$, where $\mathcal{F}$ is a simple function family, can be mapped to an execution of a related protocol with no oracle access. In Section 4 we use this result to prove limitations on the power of oracle-aided protocols in achieving specific cryptographic tasks.

Definition 7 (Oracle-Aided to No-Oracle Mapping). *A pair of a function family* $\mathcal{F}$ *and a no-input,* m-*round, oracle-aided protocol* $\pi = (A, B)$, *has a* (T, ε)-*mapping, if there exists a deterministic, oracle-aided* T-query algorithm Map *and a stateless,* m-*round, no-input (and no-oracle) protocol* $(\widetilde{A}, \widetilde{B})$, *such that the following hold:*

1. SD $(\mathcal{D}_{\mathcal{F}}, \mathcal{D}_P) \leq \varepsilon$ *for every* $j \in [m]$, *where*

$$\mathcal{D}_{\mathcal{F}} = \left(\mathrm{out}_j^A(v), \mathrm{out}_j^B(v), \mathsf{Map}^f(\mathrm{trans}(v)_{1,\ldots,j}) \right)_{f \leftarrow \mathcal{F}, v \leftarrow \langle A^f, B^f \rangle} \quad and,$$

$$\mathcal{D}_P = \left(\mathrm{out}_j^{\widetilde{A}}(v), \mathrm{out}_j^{\widetilde{B}}(v), \mathrm{trans}(v)_{1,\ldots,j} \right)_{v \leftarrow \langle \widetilde{A}, \widetilde{B} \rangle} .^8$$

Furthermore, $\mathcal{D}_P[1, 3] \equiv \mathcal{D}_{\mathcal{F}}[1, 3]$ *and* $\mathcal{D}_P[2, 3] \equiv \mathcal{D}_{\mathcal{F}}[2, 3].^9$

2. *For every* $f \in \mathcal{F}$, *an* m-*round transcript* $\bar{t}$ *and* $j \in [m]$, *it holds that* $\mathsf{Map}^f(\bar{t}_{1,\ldots,j}) = \mathsf{Map}^f(\bar{t})_{1,\ldots,j}$. *Furthermore, the oracle calls made in* $\mathsf{Map}^f(\bar{t}_{1,\ldots,j})$ *are a subset of those made in* $\mathsf{Map}^f(\bar{t})$.

Theorem 4. *Let* $\mathcal{F}$ *be a simple function family and let* $\pi = (A, B)$ *be an* ℓ-*query, oracle-aided, no-input protocol, then* $(\mathcal{F}, \pi)$ *has an* $(256 \cdot \ell^2 / \varepsilon^2, \varepsilon)$-*mapping for any* $0 < \varepsilon \leq 1$.

Remark 1 (Round complexity of the no-oracle protocol). The proof of Theorem 4 can be easily modified to yield a one-message no-oracle protocol (in this case, $\mathcal{D}_{\mathcal{F}}$ and $\mathcal{D}_P$ should be modified to reflect the transcript and outputs at the end of the executions). The roles of $\widetilde{A}$ and $\widetilde{B}$ in the resulting protocol however, cannot reflect as closely the roles of A and B, as done in the many-round, no-oracle protocol stated above.

---

[9] I.e., the projections of $\mathcal{D}_P$ and $\mathcal{D}_{\mathcal{F}}$ to their transcript part and the output of one of the parties, are identically distributed.

The heart of the proof is the following lemma, proof given in [12] .[10]

Definition 8 (DependencyFinder). *Let $\mathcal{F}$ be a function family and let $\pi = (\mathsf{A}, \mathsf{B})$ be an m-round oracle-aided protocol. A deterministic oracle-aided algorithm Finder is a (T, ε)-DependencyFinder for $(\mathcal{F}, \pi)$ if the following holds for any $j \in [m]$: consider the following random process $\mathsf{CF} = \mathsf{CF}(\mathcal{F}, \pi, \mathsf{Finder})$:*

1. *Choose $(r_\mathsf{A}, r_\mathsf{B}, f) \leftarrow \Omega^{\mathcal{F}, \pi}$ and let $\bar{t}$ be the j-round transcript of π induced by $(r_\mathsf{A}, r_\mathsf{B}, f)$.*
2. *For $i = 1$ to j set $\mathcal{I}_i = \mathcal{I}_{i-1} \cup \mathsf{Finder}^f(\bar{t}_{1,...,i}, \mathcal{I}_{i-1})$ (letting $\mathcal{I}_0 = \emptyset$), where $\mathsf{Finder}^f(x)$ is the set of queries/answers made by $\mathsf{Finder}^f(x)$ to f.*
3. *Output $(\bar{t}, \mathcal{I}_j)$.*

Then

1. *$\mathrm{E}_{d \leftarrow \mathsf{CF}} \left[\mathrm{SD} \left(\mathcal{VIEW}^{\mathcal{F}, \pi}(d), (\mathcal{VIEW}^{\mathcal{F}, \pi}(d)_\mathsf{A}, \mathcal{VIEW}^{\mathcal{F}, \pi}(d)_\mathsf{B})) \right) \right] \leq \varepsilon$, and*
2. *$\Pr[\# \text{ of } f\text{-calls made in } \mathsf{CF} > T] \leq \varepsilon$.*

That is, conditioned on a random transcript of $\pi^{\mathcal{F}}$ and the oracle queries made by a (T, δ)-DependencyFinder, the parties' views are close to being in a product distribution.

Lemma 2. *Let $\mathcal{F}$ be a simple function family and let $\pi = (\mathsf{A}, \mathsf{B})$ be an ℓ-query oracle-aided protocol, then $(\mathcal{F}, \pi)$ has a $(64/\delta^2, \ell\delta)$-DependencyFinder for any $0 < \delta \leq 1/\ell$.*

We now use Lemma 2 to prove Theorem 4.

Proving Theorem 4. Fix a simple function family $\mathcal{F}$ and a no-input, m-round, ℓ-query oracle-aided protocol π. Fix $0 < \varepsilon \leq 1$ and let Finder be the $(T = 256 \cdot \ell^2/\varepsilon^2, \varepsilon/2)$-DependencyFinder guaranteed by Lemma 2 for $(\mathcal{F}, \pi)$ (taking $\delta = \varepsilon/2\ell$). We start by defining the mapping algorithm and then we define a protocol with no oracle access.

Algorithm 5 (Map)
Oracle: $f \in \mathcal{F}$.
Input: j-round transcript $\bar{t}$ of π.
Operation:

1. *For $i = 1$ to j set $\mathcal{I}_i = \mathcal{I}_{i-1} \cup \mathsf{Finder}^f(\bar{t}_{1,...,i}, \mathcal{I}_{i-1})$ (letting $\mathcal{I}_0 = \emptyset$).*
2. *If in some round i^* the overall number of f calls (made by Finder) is T, halt the above procedure and set $\mathcal{I}_{i^*}$ to be the set of T query/answer pairs obtained so far,[11] and set $\mathcal{I}_i = \mathcal{I}_{i^*}$ for all $i^* < i \leq j$.*
3. *Output $(\bar{t}_1, \mathcal{I}_1), (\bar{t}_{1,2}, \mathcal{I}_2), \ldots, (\bar{t}, \mathcal{I}_j)$.*

---

[10] As mentioned in the introduction, the proof of Lemma 2 could be essentially derived by combining several statements in [1]. Alternatively, a somewhat weaker variant of the lemma can be directly proved using the followup result of Dachman-Soled et al. [5, Lemma 5] or of Mahmoody et al. [16, Lemma A.1].

[11] I.e., augmenting $\mathcal{I}_{i^*-1}$ with the queries/answers made in round i^* before halting.

The no-oracle protocol. Our stateless, no-oracle protocol $\widetilde{\pi} = (\widetilde{\mathsf{A}}, \widetilde{\mathsf{B}})$, emulates the oracle-aided protocol π by keeping the "important" oracle queries as part of the transcript, and selecting the rest of the oracle at random (independently in each round). In particular, $\widetilde{\mathsf{A}}$ is active in $\widetilde{\pi}$ in the same rounds that A is in π (same for $\widetilde{\mathsf{B}}$ and B). The definition of $\widetilde{\mathsf{A}}$ is given below ($\widetilde{\mathsf{B}}$ is analogously defined).

Algorithm 6 ($\widetilde{\mathsf{A}}$)
Input: A pair $(\bar{t}, \mathcal{I})$, where $\bar{t}$ is a transcript of length j and $\mathcal{I}$ is a set of query/answer pairs.
Operation:

1. *Sample $(r_\mathsf{A}, r_\mathsf{B}, f) \leftarrow \Omega(\bar{t}, \mathcal{I})$, and let out_{j+1} and t_{j+1} denote A's output and message respectively, in the $(j+1)$ round of $\langle \mathsf{A}^f(r_\mathsf{A}), \mathsf{B}^f(r_\mathsf{B}) \rangle$.*
2. *Output out_{j+1}.*
3. *Compute the value of $\mathcal{I}_{j+1}$ output by $\mathsf{Map}^f(\overline{t_{j+1}})$ for $\overline{t_{j+1}} = (\bar{t}, t_{j+1})$.*
4. *Send $(\overline{t_{j+1}}, \mathcal{I}_{j+1})$ to $\widetilde{\mathsf{B}}$.*

Using Lemma 2, one can prove that above mapping function and no-oracle protocol, indeed establish mapping and protocol guaranteed in Theorem 4. For the formal proof, see the full version.

4   Applications

In this section we use our main result (i.e., the oracle-aided to no-oracle protocol mapping for simple function families) from Section 3 to derive the impossibility of realizing three cryptographic tasks, with respect to simple function families (implying the same result with respect to the all function family, which is simple). In Section 4.1 we re-establish the result of [13], showing that key-agreement protocols cannot be realized with respect to simple function families. Then, in Section 4.2, we extend the lower-bound of [17] on the accuracy of two-party differentially private no-oracle protocols, to show it also holds (with a slight loss in parameters) for oracle-aided differentially private protocols (with respect to this class of function families). Finally, in Section 4.3, we show that no-input functionalities that cannot be securely evaluated in the no-oracle model (even when allowing some small loss of security), cannot be securely evaluated (again, even with some small loss of security) by oracle-aided protocols that are given access to a random member of a simple function family.

Remark 2 (definitions for no-oracle primitives). Throughout this section we only give formal definitions (of the security and correctness) of primitives with respect to oracle-aided protocols. Deriving formal definitions for their no-oracle counterparts can be easily done by considering the trivial function family (i.e., a singleton family, whose only member returns $\perp$ on any query).

4.1 Key Agreement Protocols

In a key-agreement protocol two parties wish to agree on a common secret in a secure way — an observer (adversary) seeing the communication transcript, cannot find the secret. Below we prove that with respect to a certain class of function families, non-trivial key-agreement cannot be achieved. We start by formally defining the notion of key agreement. We then recall the known fact that in the no-oracle model, an adversary can reveal any secret agreement between two parties in the strongest possible sense (i.e., with the same probability that the parties themselves agree). Combining this fact with the mapping from oracle-aided to no-oracle protocols, described in Section 3, yields a similar result for oracle-aided protocols.

We remark that the results presented in this section yield very little conceptual added-value to what was already shown by [13, 1]. We do, however, present them here to demonstrate how they are easily derived from our main result (Theorem 4), and as a warm-up before moving on to the other applications of our main result, described in Sections 4.2 and 4.3.

Standard Definitions and Known Facts. Recall (see Section 2.1) that for a joint view $v \in \text{Supp}(\langle \pi^f \rangle)$, we let $\text{trans}(v)$ denote the communication transcript in v, and $\text{out}_i^\mathsf{P}(v)$ denote the output of the party P at the i'th round. In the following we let $\text{out}^\mathsf{P}(v) = \text{out}_m^\mathsf{P}(v)$, where m is the last round in v.

Definition 9 (Key Agreement Protocol). *Let $0 \leq \gamma$, $\alpha \leq 1$ and $k \in \mathbb{N}$. A two-party, oracle-aided protocol $\pi = (\mathsf{A}, \mathsf{B})$ is a (k, α, γ)-key-agreement protocol with respect to a function family $\mathcal{F}$, if the following hold:*

Consistency: *π is $(1-\alpha)$-consistent with respect to $\mathcal{F}$. Namely for every $f \in \mathcal{F}$,*

$$\Pr_{v \leftarrow \langle \pi^f \rangle} \left[\text{out}^\mathsf{A}(v) = \text{out}^\mathsf{B}(v) \right] \geq 1 - \alpha. \tag{1}$$

Security: *For every $\mathsf{P} \in \{\mathsf{A}, \mathsf{B}\}$ and any k-query adversary Eve,*

$$\Pr_{f \leftarrow \mathcal{F}, v \leftarrow \langle \pi^f \rangle} \left[\text{Eve}^f(\text{trans}(v)) = \text{out}^\mathsf{P}(v) \right] \leq \gamma. \tag{2}$$

A protocol π is an (α, γ)-key-agreement protocol, if it is a $(\cdot, \alpha, \gamma)$-key-agreement protocol with respect to the trivial function family.[12]

In the no-oracle model, all correlation between the parties is implied by the transcript. Hence, an adversary that on a given transcript $\bar{t}$ samples a random view for A that is consistent with $\bar{t}$ and outputs whatever A would upon this view, agrees with B with the same probability as does A. This simple argument yields the following fact.

---

[12] We remark that our impossibility result (as well the results of [13, 1]) would also hold with respesct to a weaker definition, requiring consistency to hold for a random f, rather than for every $f \in \mathcal{F}$.

Fact 7. *Let $0 \le \alpha \le 1$ and let $\pi = (\mathsf{A}, \mathsf{B})$ be a no-oracle, two-party, no-input protocol. Assume that the probability that in a random execution of π both parties output the same value is $1 - \alpha$. Then there exists an adversary that, given the transcript of a random execution of π, outputs the same value as does B with probability $1 - \alpha$.*

An immediate implication of Fact 7 is that there does not exist any no-oracle, two-party, (α, γ)-key-agreement protocol for any $0 \le \gamma < 1 - \alpha$. We next use our main result from Section 3 to prove a similar result for oracle-aided protocols.

Our Result. In the language of the above definition, our main result is stated as follows.

Theorem 8. *Let $\mathcal{F}$ be a function family and let π be an oracle-aided protocol. Assume that the pair $(\mathcal{F}, \pi)$ has a (T, ε)-mapping, then π is not a (T, α, γ)-key-agreement with respect to $\mathcal{F}$ for any $0 \le \gamma < 1 - (\alpha + \varepsilon)$.*

Proof. Assume to the contrary that π is a (T, α, γ)-key-agreement with respect to $\mathcal{F}$ for some $0 \le \gamma < 1 - (\alpha + \varepsilon)$. Let $\widetilde{\pi} = (\widetilde{\mathsf{A}}, \widetilde{\mathsf{B}})$ and Map be the no-input no-oracle protocol and oracle-aided algorithm, guaranteed by the assumption of the theorem. The first item in Definition 7 yields that

$$\mathrm{SD}\left(\left(\mathrm{out}^{\widetilde{\mathsf{A}}}(v), \mathrm{out}^{\widetilde{\mathsf{B}}}(v)\right)_{v \leftarrow \langle \widetilde{\pi} \rangle}, \left(\mathrm{out}^{\mathsf{A}}(v), \mathrm{out}^{\mathsf{B}}(v)\right)_{f \leftarrow \mathcal{F}, v \leftarrow \langle \pi^f \rangle} \right) \le \varepsilon \qquad (3)$$

Hence, the $(1 - \alpha)$-consistency of π yields that

$$\tau := \Pr_{v \leftarrow \langle \widetilde{\pi} \rangle} \left[\mathrm{out}^{\widetilde{\mathsf{A}}}(v) = \mathrm{out}^{\widetilde{\mathsf{B}}}(v) \right] \ge 1 - (\alpha + \varepsilon). \qquad (4)$$

Fact 7 yields an adversary $\widetilde{\mathsf{Eve}}$ that given the transcript of a random execution of $\widetilde{\pi}$, outputs the same value as does B with probability τ. Let Eve be an adversary for π that upon a transcript $\bar{t}$ (of an execution of π with access to f) applies $\widetilde{\mathsf{Eve}}$ to $\mathsf{Map}^f(\bar{t})$ and outputs whatever $\widetilde{\mathsf{Eve}}$ does. Note that by Definition 7, Eve makes at most T oracle calls. The definition of Eve yields that

$$\Pr_{f \leftarrow \mathcal{F}, v \leftarrow \langle \pi^f \rangle} \left[\mathsf{Eve}^f(\mathrm{trans}(v)) = \mathrm{out}^{\mathsf{B}}(v) \right] \qquad (5)$$

$$= \Pr_{f \leftarrow \mathcal{F}, v \leftarrow \langle \pi^f \rangle} \left[\widetilde{\mathsf{Eve}}\left(\mathsf{Map}^f(\mathrm{trans}(v)) \right) = \mathrm{out}^{\mathsf{B}}(v) \right]$$

$$= \Pr_{\tilde{v} \leftarrow \langle \widetilde{\pi} \rangle} \left[\widetilde{\mathsf{Eve}}(\mathrm{trans}(\tilde{v})) = \mathrm{out}^{\widetilde{\mathsf{B}}}(\tilde{v}) \right] = \tau \ge 1 - (\alpha + \varepsilon),$$

where the second equality follows from the furthermore statement of the first item in Definition 7, stating that $(\mathsf{Map}^f(\mathrm{trans}(v)), \mathrm{out}^{\mathsf{B}}(v))$ is identically distributed as $(\mathrm{trans}(\tilde{v}), \mathrm{out}^{\widetilde{\mathsf{B}}}(\tilde{v}))$, where f, v, and $\tilde{v}$ are sampled as in Equation (5). □

Combining Theorems 4 and 8 yields the following result.

Theorem 9. *Let $\mathcal{F}$ be a simple function family. For parameters $k, \ell \in \mathbb{N}$ and $\alpha, \gamma \in \mathbb{R}$ with $k \geq 2^{10} \cdot \left(\frac{\ell}{1-\alpha-\gamma} \right)^2$ and $1 - \alpha > \gamma \geq 0$, there exists no ℓ-query oracle-aided protocol, that is (k, α, γ)-key-agreement with respect to $\mathcal{F}$.*

4.2   Differentially Private Two-Party Computation

In this section we apply our main result to extend the lower-bound of McGregor et al. [17] to oracle-aided protocols equipped with simple function families. Specifically, we show that when given access to a random member of a simple function family (e.g., the all-function family), any two-party, differentially private, oracle-aided protocol computing the inner product of two s-bit strings, exhibits error magnitude of roughly $\Omega\left(\sqrt{s}/\log s\right)$.

Standard Definitions. For strings $x, x' \in \Sigma^s$, let $H_d(x, x') = |\{i \in [s] \colon x_i \neq x'_i\}|$ denote the Hamming distance between x and x'.

Definition 10 (Differential Privacy for Oracle-Aided Protocols). *Let $\mathcal{F}$ be a function family and let $\pi = (\mathsf{A}, \mathsf{B})$ be an s-bit input, oracle-aided protocol. The protocol π is (k, α, γ)-differentially private with respect to $\mathcal{F}$ and A, if for every k-query, oracle-aided distinguisher D and every $x, x', y \in \{0,1\}^s$ with $H_d(x, x') = 1$, it holds that*

$$\Pr_{f \leftarrow \mathcal{F}, v \leftarrow \langle \pi^f (x,y) \rangle} \left[\mathsf{D}^f \left(\mathrm{trans}(v) \right) = 1 \right] \leq e^\alpha \cdot \Pr_{f \leftarrow \mathcal{F}, v \leftarrow \langle \pi^f (x',y) \rangle} \left[\mathsf{D}^f \left(\mathrm{trans}(v) \right) = 1 \right] + \gamma.$$

Being (k, α, γ)-differentially private with respect to $\mathcal{F}$ and B, is analogously defined. If π is (k, α, γ)-differentially private with respect to $\mathcal{F}$ and both parties, then it is (k, α, γ)-differentially private with respect to $\mathcal{F}$.
Finally, π is (α, γ)-differentially private, if it is $(\cdot, \alpha, \gamma)$-differentially private with respect to the trivial function family.

Note that for no-oracle protocols, the above definition of (α, γ)-differentially private matches the standard (no-oracle) definition (slightly relaxed, as we only require the transcript to preserve the privacy of the parties). Our impossibility results, given below, apply to privacy parameter α being smaller than some constant.

Since differentially private mechanisms cannot be deterministic, for any deterministic (non-constant) function g of the input, one can only hope for the output of the mechanism being a good approximation for g. We next define a notion of accuracy for differentially private protocols.

Definition 11 (Good Approximations). *Let $g : \{0,1\}^s \times \{0,1\}^s \mapsto \mathbb{R}$ be a deterministic function and let $\pi = (\mathsf{A}, \mathsf{B})$ be an s-bit input, oracle-aided protocol. The protocol π is a (β, d)-approximation for g with respect to a function family $\mathcal{F}$, if for very $f \in \mathcal{F}$, for every $x, y \in \{0,1\}^s$ and $\mathsf{P} \in \{\mathsf{A}, \mathsf{B}\}$, it holds that*

$$\Pr_{v \leftarrow \langle \pi^f (x,y) \rangle} \left[\left| g(x, y) - \mathrm{out}^{\mathsf{P}}(v) \right| > d \right] < \beta. \tag{6}$$

Namely, we require that the output of both parties is within distance d from $g(x, y)$ with probability at least β.

For two s-bit strings x and y, let $\mathsf{IP}(x, y)$ denote the inner product of x and y; that is $\mathsf{IP}(x, y) = \sum_{i \in [s]} x_i \cdot y_i$.

Our Result. Combining Theorem 4 and the lower bounds of McGregor et al. [17] we get the following result (see proof in [12]) .

Definition 12 (The Sampled-Input Variant $\mu(\pi)$). *Given an s-bit input, (possibly, oracle-aided) protocol $\pi = (\mathsf{A}, \mathsf{B})$, let $\mu(\pi) = (\mu(\mathsf{A}), \mu(\mathsf{B}))$ denote the following s-bit sampled-input protocol: The parties $\mu(\mathsf{A})$ and $\mu(\mathsf{B})$ interact in an execution of $(\mathsf{A}(x_{\mathsf{A}}; r_{\mathsf{A}}), \mathsf{B}(x_{\mathsf{B}}; r_{\mathsf{B}}))$, taking the roles of A and B respectively, where x_{A} [resp., x_{B}] is the first s bits of $\mu(\mathsf{A})$'s [resp., $\mu(\mathsf{B})$'s] coins, and r_{A} [resp., r_{B}] is the rest of $\mu(\mathsf{A})$'s [resp., $\mu(\mathsf{B})$'s] coins. Let a and b be the outputs of A and B, respectively, in this execution, then the outputs of $\mu(\mathsf{A})$ and $\mu(\mathsf{B})$ will be (x_{A}, a) and (x_{B}, b), respectively.*

Theorem 10. *For numbers $\nu > 0$ and $\alpha \geq 0$, there exist numbers $\lambda > 0$ and $z \in \mathbb{N}$ such that the following holds. Let $\mathcal{F}$ be a function family and let $\pi = (\mathsf{A}, \mathsf{B})$ be an oracle-aided, s-bit input protocol.*

Assume that π is (T, α, γ)-differentially private with respect to $\mathcal{F}$, that the pair $(\mathcal{F}, \mu(\pi))$ has a (T, ε)-mapping (where $\mu(\pi)$ is sampled-input variant of π) and that $s \geq z$, then for some $f \in \mathcal{F}$,[13] and every $\mathsf{P} \in \{\mathsf{A}, \mathsf{B}\}$, there exist $x, y \in \{0, 1\}^s$ such that

$$\Pr_{v \leftarrow \langle \pi^f(x, y) \rangle} \left[\left| \mathrm{out}^{\mathsf{P}}(v) - \mathsf{IP}(x, y) \right| \leq \Delta := \lambda \cdot \frac{\sqrt{s}}{\log s} \cdot (\tau - \varepsilon) \right] \leq \tau \qquad (7)$$

for every $\tau \leq 1$ with $\tau - \varepsilon \geq \max\{48s\gamma, \nu\}$.[14]

Combining Theorems 4 and 10 yields the following result.

Theorem 11. *Let $\mathcal{F}$ be a simple function family. For numbers $0 < \nu < 1$ and $\alpha \geq 0$, there exist numbers $\lambda > 0$ and $z \in \mathbb{N}$ such that, for $s \geq z$, the following holds. Assume that π is an s-bit input, ℓ-query oracle-aided protocol that is (k, α, γ)-differentially private with respect to $\mathcal{F}$, with $k > 2^{10} \cdot \left(\frac{\ell}{1-\nu} \right)^2$ and $\gamma \leq \frac{\nu}{48 \cdot s}$. Then, π is not a (β, d)-approximation with respect to $\mathcal{F}$ for the inner-product function, with $\beta < \frac{1-\nu}{2}$ and $d \leq \lambda \cdot \nu \cdot \frac{\sqrt{s}}{\log s}$.*

4.3   Secure Function Evaluation

In this section we apply our main result to show that when given access to a random member of a simple function family (e.g., the all-function family),

---

[13] Actually, the following holds for *most* elements of $\mathcal{F}$.

[14] This constraint implies that γ should be smaller than the inverse of some polynomial in s, however, this is how we typically think of γ.

no oracle-aided protocol can securely compute any no-input functionality that cannot be (almost) securely computed by a no-oracle protocol.

In semi-honest no-input secure function evaluation, two parties A and B wish to compute some (randomized) functionality privately and correctly. Let $G = (G_A, G_B)$ be a distribution over $\mathcal{A} \times \mathcal{B}$, where G_A and G_B denote its marginal distributions over $\mathcal{A}$ and $\mathcal{B}$ respectively. The parties wish to perform a computation, where party A learns g_A and party B learns g_A for $g = (g_A, g_B) \leftarrow G$, but nothing else. Since the parties are semi-honest, they will always follow the prescribed protocol. A corrupted party, however, may try to use its view in the computation to infer additional information after the computation terminates.

Standard Definitions

Definition 13 (No-Input Secure Function Evaluation). *Let $G = (G_A, G_B)$ be a distribution over $\mathcal{A} \times \mathcal{B}$, where G_A and G_B denote its marginal distributions $\mathcal{A}$ and $\mathcal{B}$ respectively. A two-party, oracle-aided protocol $\pi = (A, B)$ is a (m, k, δ)-secure protocol for G with respect to a function family $\mathcal{F}$, for $\delta \in [0, 1]$ and $m, k \in \mathbb{N}$, if the following hold:*

Correctness: *π is a δ-correct implementation of G with respect to $\mathcal{F}$:*

$$\mathrm{SD}\left(\left(\mathrm{out}^A(v), \mathrm{out}^B(v) \right)_{v \leftarrow \langle \pi^f \rangle}, G \right) \leq \delta$$

for every $f \in \mathcal{F}$.

Privacy: *π is an (m, k, δ)-private implementation of G with respect to $\mathcal{F}$: for every $P \in \{A, B\}$ there exists an m-query algorithm (simulator) Sim_P such that*

$$\mathop{\mathrm{E}}_{f \leftarrow \mathcal{F}} \left[\left| \Pr\left[D\left(\left(\mathrm{Sim}_P^f(g), g \right)_{g \leftarrow G_P} \right) = 1 \right] - \Pr\left[D\left((v_P, \mathrm{out}^P(v))_{v \leftarrow \langle \pi^f \rangle} \right) = 1 \right] \right| \right] \leq \delta$$

for any k-query distinguisher D.

A protocol π is a δ-secure (no-oracle) implementation of G if it is a $(\cdot, \cdot, \delta)$-secure implementation of G with respect to the trivial (i.e., the empty) function family. A distribution G is δ-trivial, if G has a δ-secure no-oracle implementation.

Our Result. In the language of the above definitions, our main result is stated as follows (see proof in [12]) .

Theorem 12. *Let $\mathcal{F}$ be a function family, and let π be an oracle-aided protocol that is a $(\cdot, T, \delta)$-secure oracle-aided implementation of a distribution G with respect to $\mathcal{F}$. Assume that the pair $(\mathcal{F}, \pi)$ has a (T, δ)-mapping. Then, G is 2δ-trivial.*

Combining Theorems 4 and 12 yields the following result.

Theorem 13. *Let $\mathcal{F}$ be a simple function family. For parameters $k, \ell \in \mathbb{N}$ and $\delta \in \mathbb{R}$ with $k \geq 256 \cdot \left(\frac{\ell}{\delta} \right)^2$, and for a distribution G that is not 2δ-trivial, there exists no ℓ-query oracle-aided protocol that is a $(\cdot, k, \delta)$-secure oracle-aided implementation of G with respect to $\mathcal{F}$.*

References

1. Barak, B., Mahmoody-Ghidary, M.: Merkle Puzzles Are Optimal — An $O(n^2)$-Query Attack on Any Key Exchange from a Random Oracle. In: Halevi, S. (ed.) CRYPTO 2009. LNCS, vol. 5677, pp. 374–390. Springer, Heidelberg (2009)
2. Beimel, A., Nissim, K., Omri, E.: Distributed private data analysis: On simultaneously solving how and what. CoRR, abs/1103.2626 (2011)
3. Canetti, R., Goldreich, O., Halevi, S.: On the Random-Oracle Methodology as Applied to Length-Restricted Signature Schemes. In: Naor, M. (ed.) TCC 2004. LNCS, vol. 2951, pp. 40–57. Springer, Heidelberg (2004)
4. Chang, Y.-C., Hsiao, C.-Y., Lu, C.-J.: On the Impossibilities of Basing One-Way Permutations on Central Cryptographic Primitives. In: Zheng, Y. (ed.) ASIACRYPT 2002. LNCS, vol. 2501, pp. 110–124. Springer, Heidelberg (2002)
5. Dachman-Soled, D., Lindell, Y., Mahmoody, M., Malkin, T.: On the Black-Box Complexity of Optimally-Fair Coin Tossing. In: Ishai, Y. (ed.) TCC 2011. LNCS, vol. 6597, pp. 450–467. Springer, Heidelberg (2011)
6. Fiat, A., Shamir, A.: How to Prove Yourself: Practical Solutions to Identification and Signature Problems. In: Odlyzko, A.M. (ed.) CRYPTO 1986. LNCS, vol. 263, pp. 186–194. Springer, Heidelberg (1987)
7. Gennaro, R., Trevisan, L.: Lower bounds on the efficiency of generic cryptographic constructions. In: Proceedings of the 41st Annual Symposium on Foundations of Computer Science, pp. 305–313 (2000)
8. Gennaro, R., Gertner, Y., Katz, J., Trevisan, L.: Bounds on the efficiency of generic cryptographic constructions. SIAM Journal on Computing 35(1), 217–246 (2005)
9. Gertner, Y., Kannan, S., Malkin, T., Reingold, O., Viswanathan, M.: The relationship between public key encryption and oblivious transfer. In: Proceedings of the 32nd Annual ACM Symposium on Theory of Computing, STOC (2000)
10. Goldwasser, S., Tauman-Kalai, Y.: On the (in)security of the fiat-shamir paradigm. In: Proceedings of the 44th Annual Symposium on Foundations of Computer Science, FOCS (2003)
11. Haitner, I., Hoch, J.J., Reingold, O., Segev, G.: Finding collisions in interactive protocols – A tight lower bound on the round complexity of statistically-hiding commitments. In: Proceedings of the 48th Annual Symposium on Foundations of Computer Science, FOCS (2007)
12. Haitner, I., Omri, E., Zarosim, H.: Limits on the usefulness of random oracles. Technical Report 2012/573, Cryptology ePrint Archive (2012), http://eprint.iacr.org/2012/573
13. Impagliazzo, R., Rudich, S.: Limits on the provable consequences of one-way permutations. In: Proceedings of the 21st Annual ACM Symposium on Theory of Computing (STOC), pp. 44–61. ACM Press (1989)
14. Kahn, J., Saks, M., Smyth, C.: A dual version of reimer's inequality and a proof of rudich's conjecture. In: Proceedings of the 15th Annual IEEE Conference on Computational Complexity, 2000, pp. 98–103 (2000)
15. Kim, J.H., Simon, D., Tetali, P.: Limits on the efficiency of one-way permutation-based hash functions. In: 40th Annual Symposium on Foundations of Computer Science, 1999, pp. 535–542 (1999)
16. Mahmoody, M., Maji, H.K., Prabhakaran, M.: Limits of random oracles in secure computation. Technical Report, arXiv:1205.3554v1 (2012)

17. McGregor, A., Mironov, I., Pitassi, T., Reingold, O., Talwar, K., Vadhan, S.P.: The limits of two-party differential privacy. In: Electronic Colloquium on Computational Complexity (ECCC), p. 106 (2011); Preliminary version in FOCS 2010 (2010)
18. Merkle, R.C.: Secure communications over insecure channels. In: SIMMONS: Secure Communications and Asymmetric Cryptosystems (1982)
19. Mironov, I., Pandey, O., Reingold, O., Vadhan, S.: Computational Differential Privacy. In: Halevi, S. (ed.) CRYPTO 2009. LNCS, vol. 5677, pp. 126–142. Springer, Heidelberg (2009)
20. Pointcheval, D., Stern, J.: Security Proofs for Signature Schemes. In: Maurer, U.M. (ed.) EUROCRYPT 1996. LNCS, vol. 1070, pp. 387–398. Springer, Heidelberg (1996)
21. Rudich, S.: The Use of Interaction in Public Cryptosystems. In: Feigenbaum, J. (ed.) CRYPTO 1991. LNCS, vol. 576, pp. 242–251. Springer, Heidelberg (1992)
22. Simon, D.R.: Findings Collisions on a One-Way Street: Can Secure Hash Functions Be Based on General Assumptions? In: Nyberg, K. (ed.) EUROCRYPT 1998. LNCS, vol. 1403, pp. 334–345. Springer, Heidelberg (1998)
23. Wee, H.: One-Way Permutations, Interactive Hashing and Statistically Hiding Commitments. In: Vadhan, S.P. (ed.) TCC 2007. LNCS, vol. 4392, pp. 419–433. Springer, Heidelberg (2007)

Analyzing Graphs with Node Differential Privacy

Shiva Prasad Kasiviswanathan[1,*], Kobbi Nissim[2], Sofya Raskhodnikova[3,**],
and Adam Smith[3,***]

[1] General Electric Global Research, USA
kasivisw@gmail.com
[2] Ben-Gurion University, Israel
kobbi@cs.bgu.ac.il
[3] Pennsylvania State University, USA
{sofya,asmith}@cse.psu.edu

Abstract. We develop algorithms for the private analysis of network data that provide accurate analysis of realistic networks while satisfying stronger privacy guarantees than those of previous work. We present several techniques for designing *node* differentially private algorithms, that is, algorithms whose output distribution does not change significantly when a node and all its adjacent edges are added to a graph. We also develop methodology for analyzing the accuracy of such algorithms on realistic networks.

The main idea behind our techniques is to "project" (in one of several senses) the input graph onto the set of graphs with maximum degree below a certain threshold. We design projection operators, tailored to specific statistics that have low sensitivity and preserve information about the original statistic. These operators can be viewed as giving a fractional (low-degree) graph that is a solution to an optimization problem described as a maximum flow instance, linear program, or convex program. In addition, we derive a generic, efficient reduction that allows us to apply any differentially private algorithm for bounded-degree graphs to an arbitrary graph. This reduction is based on analyzing the smooth sensitivity of the "naive" truncation that simply discards nodes of high degree.

1 Introduction

Data from social and communication networks have become a rich source of insights in the social and information sciences. Gathering, sharing and analyzing these data is challenging, however, in part because they are often highly sensitive (your Facebook friends or the set of people you email reveal a tremendous amount of information about you, as in, e.g., Jernigan and Mistree [11]). This paper develops algorithms for the private analysis of network data that provide accurate analysis of realistic networks while satisfying stronger privacy guarantees than those of previous work.

---

* Part of this wok was done while the author was a postdoc at Los Alamos National Laboratory and IBM T.J. Watson Research Center.
** Supported by NSF CAREER grant CCF-0845701 and NSF grant CDI-0941553.
*** Supported by NSF Awards CCF-0747294 and CDI-0941553 as well as Penn State Clinical & Translational Research Institute, NIH/NCRR Award UL1RR033184.

A. Sahai (Ed.): TCC 2013, LNCS 7785, pp. 457–476, 2013.

A recent line of work, starting from Dinur and Nissim [4], investigates rigorous definitions of privacy for statistical data analysis. Differential privacy (Dwork *et al.* [8, 5]), which emerged from this line of work, has been successfully used in the context of "tabular", or "array" data. Roughly, differential privacy guarantees that changes to one person's data will not significantly affect the output distribution of an analysis procedure.

For tabular data, it is clear which data "belong" to a particular individual. In the context of graph data, two interpretations of this definition have been proposed: *edge* and *node* differential privacy. Intuitively, edge differential privacy ensures that an algorithm's output does not reveal the inclusion or removal of a particular edge in the graph, while node differential privacy hides the inclusion or removal of a node together with all its adjacent edges.

Node privacy is a strictly stronger guarantee, but until now there have been no node-private algorithms that can provide accurate analysis of the sparse networks that arise in practice. One challenge is that for many natural statistics, node privacy is impossible to achieve while getting accurate answers in the worst case. The problem, roughly, is that node-private algorithms must be robust to the insertion of a new node in the graph, but the properties of a sparse graph can be altered dramatically by the insertion of a well-connected node. For example, for common graph statistics – the number of edges, the frequency of a particular subgraph – the change can overwhelm the value of the statistic in sparse graphs.

In this paper we develop several techniques for designing differentially *node*-private algorithms, as well as a methodology for analyzing their accuracy on realistic networks. The main idea behind our techniques is to "project" (in one of several senses) the input graph onto the set of graphs with maximum degree below a certain threshold. The benefits of this approach are two-fold. First, node privacy is easier to achieve in bounded-degree graphs since the insertion of one node affects only a relatively small part of the graph. Technically, the *sensitivity* of a given query function may be much lower when the function is restricted to graphs of a given degree. Second, for realistic networks this transformation loses relatively little information when the degree threshold is chosen carefully.

The difficulty with this approach is that the projection itself may be very sensitive to a change of a single node in the original graph. We handle this difficulty via two different techniques. First, for a certain class of statistics, we design tailored projection operators that have low sensitivity and preserve information about a given statistic. These operators can be viewed as giving a fractional (low-degree) graph that is a solution to a convex optimization problem, typically given by a maximum flow instance or linear program. Using such projections we get algorithms for accurately releasing the number of edges in a graph, and counts of small subgraphs such as triangles, k-cycles, and k-stars (used as sufficient statistics for popular graph models) in a graph, and certain estimators for power law graphs (see Sections 4 and 5).

Our second technique is much more general: we analyze the "naive" projection that simply discards high-degree nodes in the graph. We give efficient algorithms for bounding the "local sensitivity" of this projection, which measures how sensitive it is to changes in a particular input graph. Using this, we derive a generic, efficient reduction that allows us to apply any differentially private algorithm for bounded-degree graphs to an arbitrary graph. The reduction's loss in accuracy depends on how far the input graph is from having low degree. We use this to design algorithms for releasing the entire degree distribution of a graph.

Because worst-case accuracy guarantees are problematic for node-private algorithms, we analyze the accuracy of our algorithms under a mild assumption on the degree distribution of the input graph. The simplest guarantees are for the case where a bound D on the maximum degree of the graph is known, and the guarantees typically relate the algorithms's accuracy to how quickly the query function can change when restricted to graphs of degree D (e.g., Corollary 6.1). However, real-world networks are not well-modeled by a graphs of a fixed degree, since they often exhibit influential, high-degree nodes. In our main results, we assume only that tail of the degree distribution decreases slightly more quickly than what trivially holds for all graphs. (If $\bar{d}$ is the average degree in a graph, Markov's inequality implies that the fraction of nodes with degree above $t \cdot \bar{d}$ is at most $1/t$. We assume that this fraction goes down as $1/t^{\alpha}$ for a constant $\alpha > 1$ or $\alpha > 2$, depending on the result.) Our assumption is satisfied by all the well-studied social network models we know of, including so-called *scale-free* graphs [3].

1.1   Related Work

The initial statements of differential privacy [8, 5] considered databases that are arrays or sets – each individual's information corresponds to an entry in the database, and this entry may be changed without affecting other entries. That paper also introduced the very basic technique for constructing differentially private function approximations, by the addition of Laplace noise calibrated to the *global sensitivity* of the function.[1] This notion naturally extends to the case of graph data, where each individual's information corresponds to an *edge* in the graph (edge privacy). The basic technique of Dwork *et al.* [8] continues to give a good estimate, e.g., for counting the number of edges in a graph, but it ceases to provide good analyses even for some of the most basic functions of graphs (diameter, counting the number of occurrences of a small specified subgraph) as these functions exhibit high global sensitivity.

The first differentially private computations over graph data appeared in Nissim *et al.* [15] where it was shown how to estimate, with differential edge privacy, the cost of the minimum spanning tree and the number of triangles in a graph. These computations employed a different noise addition technique, where noise is calibrated to a more local variant of sensitivity, called *smooth sensitivity*. These techniques and results were further extended by Karwa *et al.* [12]. Hay *et al.* [10] showed that the approach of [8] can still be useful when combined with a post-processing technique for removing some of the noise. They use this technique for constructing a differentially edge-private algorithm for releasing the degree distribution of a graph. They also proposed the notion of differential node privacy and highlighted some of the difficulties in achieving it.

A different approach to graph data was suggested by Rastogi *et al.* [16], where the privacy is weakened to a notion concerning a Bayesian adversary whose prior

---

[1] Informally, global sensitivity of a function measures the largest change in the function outcome than can result from changing one of its inputs.

distribution on the database comes from a specified family of distributions. Under this notion of privacy, and assuming that the adversary's prior admits mainly negative correlations between edges, they give an algorithm for counting the occurrences of a specified subgraph. The notion they use, though, is weaker than differential edge privacy. We refer the reader to [12] for a discussion on how the assumptions about an attacker's prior limit the applicability of the privacy definition.

The current work considers databases where nodes correspond to individuals, and edges correspond to relationships between these individuals. Edge privacy corresponds in this setting to a requirement that the properties of every relationship (such as its absence or presence) should be kept hidden, but the overall relationship pattern of an individual may be revealed. However, each individual's information corresponds to *all* edges adjacent to her node and a more natural extension of differential privacy for this setting would be that this entire information should be kept hidden. This is what we call *node privacy* (in contrast with *edge privacy* guaranteed in prior work). A crucial deviation from edge privacy is that a change in the information of one individual can affect the information of all other individuals. We give methods that provide node privacy for a variety of types of graphs, including very sparse graphs.

Finally, motivated by examples from social networks Gehrke *et al.* [9] suggest a stronger notion than differential node privacy – called *zero-knowledge privacy* – and demonstrate that this stronger notion can be achieved for several tasks in extremely dense graphs. Zero-knowledge privacy, as they employ it, can be used to release quantities that can be computed from small, random induced subgraphs of a larger graph. Their techniques are not directly applicable to sparse graphs (since a random induced subgraph will contain very few edges, with high probability).

We note that while node privacy gives a very strong guarantee, it may not answer all privacy concerns in a social network. Kifer and Machanavajjhala [13] criticize differential privacy in the context of social networks, noting that individuals can have a greater effect on a social network than just forming their own relationships (their criticism is directed at edge privacy, but it can also apply to node privacy).

Concurrent Work. In independent work, Blocki *et al.* [1] also consider node-level differential private algorithms for analyzing sparse graphs. Both our work and that of Blocki *et al.* are motivated by getting good accuracy on sparse graphs, and employ projections onto the set of low-degree graphs to do so. The two works differ substantially in the technical details. See Appendix A for a detailed comparison.

Organization. Section 2 defines the basic framework of node and edge privacy and gives background on sensitivity and noise addition that is needed in the remainder of the paper. Section 3 introduces a useful, basic class of queries that can be analyzed with node privacy, namely queries that are linear in the degree distribution. Section 4 gives our first projection technique based on maximum flow and applies it to privately estimate the number of edges in a graph (Section 4.2). Section 4.3 generalizes the flow technique to apply it to any concave function on degree. Section 5 provides a private (small) subgraph counting algorithm via linear programming. Finally, Section 6 describes our general reduction from privacy on all graphs to the design of algorithms that are private only on bounded-degree graphs, and applies it to privately release the (entire) degree distribution. Due to space constraints, all proofs are deferred to the full version of this paper.

2   Preliminaries

Notation. We use $[n]$ to denote the set $\{1, \ldots, n\}$. For a graph, (V, E), $\bar{d}(G) = 2|E|/|V|$ is the average degree of the graph G and $\deg_v(G)$ denotes the degree of node $v \in V$ in G. When the graph referenced is clear, we drop G in the notation. The asymptotic notation $O_n(\cdot), o_n(\cdot)$ is defined with respect to growing n. Other parameters are assumed to be functions independent of n unless specified otherwise.

Let $\mathcal{G}$ denote the set of unweighted, undirected finite *labeled* graphs, and let $\mathcal{G}_n$ denote the set of graphs on at most n nodes and $\mathcal{G}_{n,D}$ be the set of all graphs in $\mathcal{G}_n$ with maximum degree D.

2.1   Graphs Metrics and Differential Privacy

We consider two metrics on the set of labeled graphs: node and edge distance. The *node* distance $d_{\text{node}}(G, G')$ (also called *rewiring distance*) between graphs G and G' is the minimum number of nodes in G' that need to be changed ("rewired") to obtain G. Rewiring allows one to add a new node (with an arbitrary set of edges to existing nodes), remove it entirely, or change its adjacency lists arbitrarily. In particular, a rewiring can affect the adjacency lists of all other nodes. Equivalently, let k is the number of nodes in the largest induced subgraph of G which equals the corresponding induced subgraph of G'. The node distance is $d_{\text{node}}(G, G') = \max\{|V_G|, |V_{G'}|\} - k$. Graphs G, G' are node neighbors if their node distance is 1.

The *edge* distance $d_{\text{edge}}(G, G')$ is the minimum number of edges in G' that need to be changed (*i.e.*, added or deleted) to obtain G. We also count insertion or removal of an isolated node (to allow for graphs with different number of nodes). In this paper, distance between graphs refers to the node distance unless specified otherwise.

Definition 2.1 ((ϵ, δ)-differential Privacy [8, 5, 6]) *A randomized algorithm $\mathcal{A}$ is (ϵ, δ)-node-private (resp. edge-private) if for all events S in the output space of $\mathcal{A}$, and for all graphs G, G' at rewiring distance 1 (resp. edge-distance 1) we have:*

$$\Pr[\mathcal{A}(G) \in S] \leq \exp(\epsilon) \times \Pr[\mathcal{A}(G') \in S] + \delta.$$

When $\delta = 0$, the algorithm is ϵ-differentially private. In this paper, if node or edge privacy is not specified, we mean node privacy by default.

In this paper, for simplicity of presentation, we assume that $n = |V|$, the number of nodes of the input graph G, is publicly known. This assumption is justified since, as we will see, one can get a very accurate estimate of $|V|$ via a node-private query. Moreover, given a publicly known value n, one can force the input graph $G = (V, E)$ to have n nodes without sacrificing differential node privacy: one either pads the graph with isolated nodes (if $|V| < n$) or discards the $|V| - n$ "excess" nodes with the largest labels (if $|V| > n$) along with all their adjacent edges. Changing one node of G corresponds to a change of at most one node in the resulting n-node graph as long as the differentially private algorithms being run on the data do not depend on the labeling (i.e., they should be symmetric in the order of the labels).

Differential privacy "composes" well, in the sense that privacy is preserved (albeit with slowly degrading parameters) even when the adversary gets to see the outcome of multiple differentially private algorithms run on the same data set.

Lemma 2.1 (Composition, Post-processing [14, 7]). *If an algorithm $\mathcal{A}$ runs t randomized algorithms $\mathcal{A}_1, \ldots, \mathcal{A}_t$, each of which is (ϵ, δ)-differentially private, and applies an arbitrary (randomized) algorithm g to their results, i.e., $A(G) = g(\mathcal{A}_1(G), \ldots, \mathcal{A}_t(G))$, then $\mathcal{A}$ is $(t\epsilon, t\delta)$-differentially private.*

2.2 Calibrating Noise to Sensitivity

Output Perturbation. One common method for obtaining efficient differentially private algorithms for approximating real-valued functions is based on adding a small amount of random noise to the true answer. In this paper, we use two families of random distributions to add noise: Laplace and Cauchy. A *Laplace* random variable with mean 0 and standard deviation $\sqrt{2}\lambda$ has density $h(z) = (1/(2\lambda))e^{-|z|/\lambda}$. We denote it by $\mathrm{Lap}(\lambda)$. A *Cauchy* random variable with median 0 and median absolute deviation λ has density $h(z) = 1/(\lambda\pi(1 + (z/\lambda)^2))$. We denote it by $\mathrm{Cauchy}(\lambda)$.

Global Sensitivity. The most basic framework for achieving differential privacy, Laplace noise is scaled according to the *global sensitivity* of the desired statistic f. This technique extends directly to graphs as long as we measure sensitivity with respect to the same metric as differential privacy. Below, we define these (standard) notions in terms of node distance and node privacy. Recall that $\mathcal{G}_n$ is the set of all n-node graphs.

Definition 2.1 (Global Sensitivity [8]). *The ℓ_1-global node sensitivity of a function $f : \mathcal{G}_n \to \mathbb{R}^p$ is:*

$$\Delta f = \max_{\substack{G, G' \text{ node neighbors}}} \|f(G) - f(G')\|_1.$$

For example, the number of edges in a graph has node sensitivity n (when we restrict our attention to n-node graphs), since rewiring a node can add or remove at most n nodes. In contrast, the number of nodes in a graph has node sensitivity 1, even when we consider graphs of all sizes (not just a fixed size n).

Theorem 2.2 (Laplace Mechanism [8]). *The algorithm $\mathcal{A}(G) = f(G) + \mathrm{Lap}(\Delta f/\epsilon)^p$ (i.e., adds i.i.d. noise $\mathrm{Lap}(\Delta f/\epsilon)$ to each entry of f), is ϵ-node-private.*

Thus, we can release the number of nodes $|V|$ in a graph with noise of expected magnitude $1/\epsilon$ while satisfying node differential privacy. Given a public bound n on the number of nodes, we can release the number of edges $|E|$ with additive noise of expected magnitude $(n-1)/\epsilon$ (the global sensitivity for releasing edge count is $n-1$).

Local Sensitivity. The magnitude of noise added by the Laplace mechanism depends on Δf and the privacy parameter ϵ, but not on the database G. For many functions, this approach yields high noise, not reflecting the function's typical insensitivity to individual inputs. Nissim *et al.* [15] proposed a local measure of sensitivity, defined next.

Definition 2.2 (Local Sensitivity [15]). *For a function* $f : \mathcal{G}_n \to \mathbb{R}^p$ *and a graph* $G \in \mathcal{G}_n$, *the local sensitivity of* f *at* G *is* $LS_f(G) = \max_{G'} \|f(G) - f(G')\|_1$, *where the maximum is taken over all node neighbors* G' *of* G.

Note that, by Definitions 2.1 and 2.2, the global sensitivity $\Delta f = \max_G LS_f(G)$. One may think of the local sensitivity as a discrete analogue of the magnitude of the gradient of f.

A straightforward argument shows that every differentially private algorithm must add distortion at least as large as the local sensitivity on many inputs. However, finding algorithms whose error matches the local sensitivity is *not* straightforward: an algorithm that releases f with noise magnitude proportional to $LS_f(G)$ on input G is not, in general, differentially private [15], since the noise magnitude itself can leak information.

Smooth Bounds on LS. Nissim *et al.* [15] propose the following approach: instead of using the local sensitivity, select noise magnitude according to a *smooth* upper bound on the local sensitivity, namely, a function S that is an upper bound on LS_f at all points and such that $\ln(S(\cdot))$ has low global sensitivity. The level of smoothness is parameterized by a number β (where smaller numbers lead to a smoother bound) which depends on ϵ.

Definition 2.3 (Smooth Bounds [15]). *For* $\beta > 0$, *a function* $S : \mathcal{G}_n \to \mathbb{R}$ *is a* β-*smooth upper bound on the local sensitivity of* f *if it satisfies the following requirements:*

$$\text{for all } G \in \mathcal{G}_n : \qquad S(G) \geq LS_f(G);$$
$$\text{for all neighbors } G, G' \in \mathcal{G}_n : \qquad S(G) \leq e^{\beta} S(G').$$

One can add noise proportional to smooth bounds on the local sensitivity using a variety of distributions. We state here the version based on the Cauchy distribution.

Theorem 2.3 (Calibrating Noise to Smooth Bounds [15]). *Let* $f : \mathcal{G}_n \to \mathbb{R}^p$ *be a real-valued function and let* S *be a* β-*smooth bound on* LS_f. *If* $\beta \leq \epsilon/(\sqrt{2}p)$, *the algorithm* $\mathcal{A}(G) = f(G) + \text{Cauchy}(\sqrt{2}S(G)/\epsilon)^p$ *(adding i.i.d.* $\text{Cauchy}(\sqrt{2}S(G)/\epsilon)$ *to each coordinate of* f) *is* ϵ-*differentially private.*

From the properties of Cauchy distribution, the algorithm of the previous theorem has median absolute error $(\sqrt{2}S(G))/\epsilon$ (the median absolute error is the median of the random variable $|\mathcal{A}(G) - f(G)|$, where $\mathcal{A}(G)$ is the released value and $f(G)$ is the query answer). Note that the *expected* error of Cauchy noise is not defined. One can get a similar result with an upper bound on any finite moment of the error using different heavy-tailed probability distributions [15]. We use Cauchy noise here for simplicity.

To compute smooth bounds efficiently, it is convenient to break the expression defining it down into tractable components. For every distance t, consider the largest local sensitivity attained on graphs at distance at most t from G. The *local sensitivity of* f *at distance* t is:

$$LS^{(t)}(G) = \max_{G' \in \mathcal{G}_n : \, d_{\text{node}}(G, G') \leq t} LS_f(G') .$$

Now the smooth sensitivity is: $S^*_{f,\beta}(G) = \max_{t=0,\dots,n} e^{-t\beta} LS^{(t)}(G)$. Many smooth bounds on the local sensitivity have a similar form, with $LS^{(t)}$ being replaced by some other function $C^{(t)}(G)$ with the property that $C^{(t)}(G) \leq C^{(t+1)}(G')$ for all pairs of neighbors G, G'. For example, our bounds on the sensitivity of naive truncation have this form (Proposition 6.1, Section 6).

2.3 Sensitivity and Privacy on Bounded-Degree Graphs

A graph is D-bounded if it has maximum degree at most D. The degree bound D can be a function of the number of nodes in the graph. We can define a variant of differential privacy that constrains an algorithm only on these bounded-degree graphs.

Definition 2.4 (Bounded-degree (ϵ, δ)-differential Privacy) *A randomized algorithm $\mathcal{A}$ is $(\epsilon, \delta)_D$-node-private (resp. $(\epsilon, \delta)_D$-edge-private) if for all pairs of D-bounded graphs $G_1, G_2 \in \mathcal{G}_{n,D}$ that differ in one node (resp. edge), we have $\Pr[\mathcal{A}(G) \in \mathcal{S}] \leq e^{\epsilon} \Pr[\mathcal{A}(G') \in \mathcal{S}] + \delta$.*

In bounded-degree graphs, the difference between edge privacy and node privacy is relatively small. For example, an $(\epsilon, 0)_D$-edge-private algorithm is also $(\epsilon D, 0)_D$-node-private (and a similar statement can be made about (ϵ, δ) privacy, with a messier growth in δ).

The notion of global sensitivity defined above (from previous work) can also be refined to consider only how the function may change within $\mathcal{G}_{n,D}$, and we can adjust the Laplace mechanism correspondingly to add less noise while satisfying $(\epsilon, 0)_D$-differential privacy.

Definition 2.4 (Global Sensitivity on Bounded Graphs). *The ℓ_1-global node sensitivity on D-bounded graphs of a function $f : \mathcal{G}_n \to \mathbb{R}^p$ is:*

$$\Delta_D f = \max_{G, G' \in \mathcal{G}_{n,D}:\, d_{\text{node}}(G, G')=1} \|f(G) - f(G')\|_1.$$

Observation 2.5 (Laplace Mechanism on Bounded Graphs) *The algorithm $\mathcal{A}(G) = f(G) + \text{Lap}\,(\Delta_D f / \epsilon)^p$ is $(\epsilon, 0)_D$-node-private.*

2.4 Assumptions on Graph Structure

Let p_G denote the degree distribution of the graph G, i.e., $p_G(k) = |\{v : \deg_v(G) = k\}|/|V|$. Similarly, P_G denotes the *cumulative* degree distribution, i.e., $P_G(k) = |\{v : \deg_v(G) \geq k\}|/|V|$. Recall that $\bar{d}(G) = 2|E|/|V|$ is the average degree of G.

Assumption 2.6 (α-decay) *Fix $\alpha \geq 1$. A graph G satisfies α-decay if for all[2] real numbers $t > 1$, $P_G(t \cdot \bar{d}) \leq t^{-\alpha}$.*

Note that *all* graphs satisfy 1-decay (by Markov's inequality). The assumption is non-trivial for $\alpha > 1$, but it is nevertheless satisfied by almost all widely studied classes of

---

[2] Our results hold even when this condition is satisfied only for sufficiently large t. For simplicity, we use a stronger assumption in our presentation.

graphs. So-called "scale-free" networks (those that exhibit a heavy-tailed degree distribution) typically satisfy α-decay for $\alpha \in (1, 2)$. Random graphs satisfy α-decay for essentially arbitrarily large α since their degree distributions have tails that decay exponentially (more precisely, for any α we can find a constant c_α such that, with high probability, α-decay holds when $t > c_\alpha$). Regular graphs satisfy the assumption with $\alpha = \infty$. Next we consider an implication of α-decay.

Lemma 2.2. *Consider a graph G on n nodes that satisfies α-decay for $\alpha > 1$, and let $D > \bar{d}$. Then the number of edges in G adjacent to nodes of degree at least D is $O(\bar{d}^\alpha n / D^{\alpha-1})$.*

3   Linear Queries in the Degree Distribution

The first, and simplest, queries we consider are functions linear in the degree distribution. In many cases, these can be released directly with node privacy, though they also highlight why bounding the degree leads to such a drastic reduction in sensitivity. Suppose we are given a function $h : \mathbb{N} \to \mathbb{R}^{\geq 0}$ that takes nonnegative real values. We can extend it to a function on graphs as follows:

$$F_h(G) \stackrel{\text{def}}{=} \sum_{v \in G} h(\deg_v(G)),$$

where $\deg_v$ is the degree of the node v in G. We will drop the superscript in F_h when h is clear from the context. The query F_h can also be viewed as the inner product of $\boldsymbol{h} = (h(0), \ldots, h(n-1))$ with the degree distribution p_G, scaled up by n, i.e., $F_h(G) = n\langle \boldsymbol{h}, p_G \rangle$.

Several natural quantities can be expressed as linear queries. The number of edges in the graph, for example, corresponds to half the identity function, that is, $h(i) = i/2$ (since the sum of the degrees is twice the number of edges). The number of nodes in the graph is obtained by choosing the constant function $h(i) = 1$. The number of nodes with degrees in a certain range – say above a threshold D – also falls into this category. Less obviously, certain subgraph counting queries, namely, the number of k-stars for a given k, can be obtained by taking $h(i) = \binom{i}{k}$ for $i \geq k$ (and $h(i) = 0$ for $i < k$).

The sensitivity of these linear queries depends on the maximum value that h can take as well as the largest jump in h over the interval $\{0, \ldots, n-1\}$. Let

$$\|h'\|_\infty \stackrel{\text{def}}{=} \max_{0 \leq i < n-1} |h(i+1) - h(i)|.$$

We refer to $\|h'\|_\infty$ as the *maximum slope* of h. This quantity depends on n, though we leave n out of the notation for clarity. Let

$$\|h\|_\infty \stackrel{\text{def}}{=} \left(\max_{0 \leq i \leq n-1} |h(i)| \right).$$

Lemma 3.1. *The sensitivity of F_h on $\mathcal{G}_n$ is at most $\Delta F_h \leq \|h\|_\infty + (n-1) \cdot \|h'\|_\infty$. If there is a value $j \in \{0, \ldots, n-1\}$ such that $h(j) = 0$, then $\Delta F_h \leq 2(n-1)\|h'\|_\infty$.*

This simple rule immediately gives us tight bounds on the sensitivity of several natural functions, such as the number of nodes, number of edges and the number of k-stars for a given k). We mention here two functions that come up later in the paper.

(1) **Common Estimators for Power Law Coefficients:** Many real-world networks exhibit heavy-tailed degree distributions, and a common goal of analysts is to identify the coefficient of a power law that best fits the data (we note that power laws are not the only heavy-tailed distributions, but they are very popular). One well-studied approach to identifying the power law coefficient is to treat the degrees as n independent samples from a power law distribution (Clauset *et al.* [3]). In that case, the maximum likelihood estimator for the exponent is $1 + n/M(G)$ where $M(G) = \sum_{v \in V} \ln(\deg_v)$. Note that M is a linear function of the degree distribution (as $M(G) = F_h(G)$ with $h(i) = \ln(i)$ for $i \geq 1$ and $h(0) = 0$) with maximum slope $\ln(2) - \ln(1) = \ln(2)$ and maximum value $\ln(n - 1)$. The sensitivity of M is $\Theta(n)$. Therefore, applying the Laplace mechanism directly is problematic, since the noise (of magnitude $O(n/\epsilon)$) will swamp the value of the query. In Section 4.3, we propose a different approach (based on convex programming) for privately releasing these estimators.

(2) **Counting Nodes in an Interval:** If $f = \chi_{[a,b]}$ where $\chi_{[a,b]}(i) = 1$ if $a \leq i \leq b$, and 0 otherwise, then F_f counts the number of nodes of degree between thresholds a and b. However, the sensitivity $\Delta F_f = \Theta(n)$, making the answer to this query useless once Laplace noise has been added.

We can reduce the sensitivity of this query by *tapering* the characteristic function of the interval. Given an interval $[a, b]$, consider the tapered step function $f_{t,a,b}(i) = \max\{0, 1 - t \cdot dist(i, [a, b])\}$, where $dist(i, [a, b])$ denotes the distance from i to the nearest point in the interval $[a, b]$. The maximum slope of $f_{t,a,b}$ is t, so $\Delta F_{f_{t,a,b}} = 2tn$. Answers to this query may be meaningful for any $t = o(1)$ (since then the sensitivity will be $o(n)$). We will find this sort of "smoothed" counting query to be useful when estimating how many nodes of high degree there are in a graph (see Proposition 6.1, Section 6).

The linear queries already give us a toolkit for analyzing graphs with node privacy, much as linear queries (over the data points) give a powerful basic toolkit for the differentially private analysis of conventional data sets (as in the SuLQ framework of Blum *et al.* [2]). The difference, of course, is that we need to consider slowly varying functions in order to keep the sensitivity low.

Graphs of Bounded Degree. Notice that the techniques mentioned above for bounding the sensitivity of a linear query work better in bounded-degree graphs. Specifically, the sensitivity of F_h on D-bounded graphs is at most

$$\Delta F_h \leq \|h\|_\infty + D\|h'\|_\infty. \tag{1}$$

This motivates the approaches in the remainder of the paper, which seek to first bound the degree via a projection step.

4   Flow-Based Lipschitz Extensions

We now present our flow-based technique. In Section 4.1, we define a flow function and show that it has low global node sensitivity and, on bounded-degree graphs, it correctly computes the number of edges in the graph. In Section 4.2, we design a node-private algorithm for releasing the number of edges in a graph based on this flow function.

4.1   Flow Graph

Definition 4.1 (Flow graph). *Given an (undirected) graph $G = (V, E)$, let $V_\ell = \{v_\ell \mid v \in V\}$ and $V_r = \{v_r \mid v \in V\}$ be two copies of V, called the left and the right copies, respectively. Let D be a natural number less than n. The flow graph of G with parameter D, a source s and a sink t is a directed graph on nodes $V_\ell \cup V_r \cup \{s, t\}$ with the following capacitated edges: edges of capacity D from the source s to all nodes in V_ℓ and from all nodes in V_r to the sink t, and unit-capacity edges (u_ℓ, v_r) for all edges $\{u, v\}$ of G. Let $v_{fl}(G)$ denote the value of the maximum flow in the flow graph of G.*

Lemma 4.1. *The global node sensitivity $\Delta v_{fl} \leq 2D$.*

Lemma 4.2. *For all graphs G, the value $v_{fl}(G) \leq 2f_e(G)$. Moreover, if G is D-bounded then $v_{fl}(G) = 2f_e(G)$.*

4.2   Algorithm for Releasing the Number of Edges

In this section, we design a node-private algorithm for releasing the number of edges. The main challenge in applying the methodology from the previous section is that we need to select a good threshold D that balances two conflicting goals: keeping the sensitivity low and retaining as large a fraction of the graph as possible.

Given a graph G, let $f_e(G)$ be the number of edges in G. Observe that the global node sensitivity of the edge count, Δf_e, is at most n because rewiring (or adding/removing) a node can change this count by at most n. So releasing f_e with Laplace noise of the magnitude n/ϵ is ϵ-node-private. The resulting approximate count is accurate if the number of edges in the input graph G is large. The following algorithm allows us to release an accurate count even when this number is low, provided that G satisfies α-decay, a natural assumption discussed in Section 2.4.

Algorithm 1. ϵ-Node-Private Algorithm for Releasing $f_e(G)$

Input: parameters ϵ, D, n, and graph G on n nodes.
1: Let $\hat{e}_1 = f_e(G) + \mathrm{Lap}(\frac{2n}{\epsilon})$ and threshold $\tau = \frac{n \ln n}{\epsilon}$.
2: If $\hat{e}_1 \geq 3\tau$, **return** $\hat{e}_1$.
3: Else compute the flow value $v_{fl}(G)$ given in Definition 4.1 with D.
4: **return** $\hat{e}_2 = v_{fl}(G)/2 + \mathrm{Lap}(\frac{2D}{\epsilon})$.

Lemma 4.3. *Algorithm 1 is an ϵ-node-private algorithm that takes a graph G and parameters ϵ, n, D, and outputs an approximate count for $f_e(G)$ (number of edges in G).*

1. *If $f_e(G) \geq (5n \ln n)/\epsilon$, then with probability at least $1 - 1/\ln n$, Algorithm 1 outputs $\hat{e}_1$ with*

$$|\hat{e}_1 - f_e(G)| \leq (2n \ln \ln n)/\epsilon.$$

2. *If G satisfies α-decay for $\alpha > 1$, $D > \bar{d}$, and $f_e(G) < (n \ln n)/\epsilon$, then with probability at least $1 - 2/\ln n$, Algorithm 1 outputs $\hat{e}_2$ and*

$$|\hat{e}_2 - f_e(G)| = O\left(\frac{2D \ln \ln n}{\epsilon} + \frac{\bar{d}^\alpha}{D^{\alpha-1}}\right).$$

The algorithm runs in $O(n f_e(G))$ time.

Using this lemma, and setting $D = n^{1/\alpha}$, we get the following theorem about privately releasing edge counts.

Theorem 4.1 (Releasing Edge Counts Privately). *There is a node differentially private algorithm which, given constants $\alpha > 1$, $\epsilon > 0$, and a graph G on n nodes, computes with probability at least $1 - 2/(\ln n)$ an $(1 \pm o_n(1))$-approximation to $f_e(G)$ (the number of edges in G) if either of the following holds:*

1. *If $f_e(G) \geq (5n \ln n)/\epsilon$.*
2. *If G satisfies α-decay and $f_e(G) = \omega(n^{1/\alpha}(\ln n)^{\alpha+1})$.*

4.3   Extension to Concave Query Functions

The flow-based technique of the previous section can be generalized considerably. In this section, we look at linear queries in the degree distribution in which the function h specifying the query is itself concave, meaning that its increments $h(i + 1) - h(i)$ are non-increasing as i goes from 0 to $n - 2$. The number of edges in the graph is an example of such a query, since the increments of $h(i) = i/2$ are constant.[3]

For mathematical convenience, we assume that the function h is in fact defined on the real interval $[0, n - 1]$ and is increasing and concave on that set (meaning that for all $x, y \in [0, n - 1]$, we have $h((x + y)/2) \leq (h(x) + h(y))/2$. It is always possible to extend a (discrete) function on $\{0, \ldots, n - 1\}$ with nonincreasing increments to a concave function on $[0, n - 1]$ by interpolating linearly between each adjacent pair of values $h(i), h(i + 1)$. Note that the maximum of h is preserved by this transformation, and the largest increment $|h(i + 1) - h(i)|$ equals the Lipschitz constant of the new function (defined as $\sup_{x,y \in [0,n-1]} \frac{|h(x)-h(y)|}{|x-y|}$).

Given a graph G on at most n nodes, a concave function h on $[0, n - 1]$ and a threshold D, we define an optimization problem as follows: construct the flow graph (Definition 4.1) as before, but make the objective to maximize $obj_h(Fl) = \sum_{v \in V} h(Fl(v))$, where $Fl(v)$ is the units of flow passing from s to v_ℓ in the flow Fl. Let $opt_h(G)$ denote the maximum value of the objective function over all feasible flows. The constraints of this optimization problem are all linear.

---

[3] There is some possible confusion here: any query of the form F_h described in Section 3 is linear *in the degree distribution of the graph*. Our additional requirement here is that the "little" function h be concave *in the degree argument i*.

This new optimization problem is no longer a maximum flow problem (nor even a linear program), but the concavity of h ensures that it still a convex optimization problem and can be solved in polynomial time using convex programming techniques. Note that we need h be to concave only for computational efficiency purposes, and one could define the above flow graph and optimization problem for all h.

Proposition 4.1. *For every increasing function $h : [0, n - 1] \to \mathbb{R}$,*

1. *If G is D-bounded, then $opt_h = F_h(G)$ (that is, the value of the optimization problem equals the correct value of the query).*
2. *The optimum opt_h has global sensitivity at most $\|f\|_\infty + D\|f'\|_\infty$ on $\mathcal{G}_n$, where $\|f\|_\infty = \max_{0 \le x \le D} h(x)$ and $\|f'\|_\infty$ is the Lipschitz coefficient of h on $[0, D]$ (that is, the global sensitivity of the optimization problem's value is at most the sensitivity of F_h on D-bounded graphs).*
3. *If h is concave then $opt_h(G)$ can be computed to arbitrary accuracy in polynomial (in n) time.*

Thus, as with the number of edges, we can ask a query which matches F_h on D-bounded graphs but whose global sensitivity on the whole space is bounded by its sensitivity of the set of D-bounded graphs.

The MLE for power laws described in Section 3 is an interesting example where Proposition 4.1 could be used. There is a natural concave extension for the power law MLE: set $f(x) = x$ for $0 \le x < 1$ and $f(x) = 1 + \ln(x)$ for $x \ge 1$. The sensitivity of F_f on D-bounded graphs is $\Delta_D f \le 1 + \ln(D) + D$ (this follows from (1)). In graphs with few high-degree nodes of degree greater than D, this leads to a much better private approximation to the power-law MLE in low-degree graphs than suggested in Section 3.

5   LP-Based Lipschitz Extensions

In this section, we show how to privately release the number of (not necessarily induced copies) of a specified small template graph H in the input graph G. For example, H can be a triangle, a k-cycle, a length-k path, a k-star (k nodes connected to a single common neighbor), or a k-triangle (k nodes connected to a pair of common neighbors that share an edge). Let $f_H(G)$ denote the number of (not necessarily induced) copies of H in G, where H is a connected graph on k nodes.

5.1   LP-Based Function

Definition 5.1 (Function $v_{\mathrm{LP}}(G)$). *Given an (undirected) graph $G = ([n], E)$ and a number $D \in [n]$, consider the following LP. The LP has a variable x_C for every copy of the template graph H in G. Let $\Delta_D f$ denote the global node sensitivity of function f in D-bounded graphs. Then the LP corresponding to G is specified as follows:*

$$\text{maximize} \sum_{\text{copies } C \text{ of } H} x_C \text{ subject to:}$$

$$0 \le x_C \le 1 \text{ for all variables } x_C$$

$$S_v \le \Delta_D f_H \text{ for all nodes } v \in [n], \qquad \text{where } S_v = \sum_{C : v \in V(C)} x_C.$$

We denote the value that maximizes this linear program by $v_{\mathrm{LP}}(G)$.

When the variable x_C takes values 1 or 0, it signifies the presence or absence of the corresponding copy of H in G. The first type of constraints restricts these variables to $[0, 1]$. The second type of constraints says that every node can participate in at most $\Delta_D f_H$ copies of H. This is the largest number of copies of H in which a node can participate in a D-bounded graph.

Observation 5.1 $\Delta_D f_H \leq k \cdot D \cdot (D-1)^{k-2}$, *where k is the number of nodes in H.*

Lemma 5.1. *The global node sensitivity* $\Delta v_{\mathrm{LP}} \leq \Delta_D f_H \leq k \cdot D \cdot (D-1)^{k-2}$.

Lemma 5.2. *For all graphs G, the value* $v_{\mathrm{LP}}(G) \leq f_H(G)$. *Moreover, if G is D-bounded then* $v_{\mathrm{LP}}(G) = f_H(G)$.

5.2 Releasing Counts of Small Subgraphs

The LP-based function from the previous section can be used to privately release small subgraph counts. If $f_H(G)$ is relatively large then the Laplace mechanism will give an accurate estimate. Using the LP-based function, we can release $f_H(G)$ accurately when $f_H(G)$ is much smaller, provided that G satisfies α-decay. In this section, we work out the details of the algorithm for the special case when H has 3 nodes, i.e., is the triangle or the 2-star, but the underlying ideas apply even when H is some other small subgraph.

Algorithm 2. ϵ-Node-Private Algorithm for Releasing Subgraph Count $f_H(G)$

Input: parameters ϵ, D, n, template graph H on 3 nodes, and graph G on n nodes.
1: Let $\hat{f}_1 = f_H(G) + \mathrm{Lap}(\frac{6n^2}{\epsilon})$ and threshold $\zeta = \frac{n^2 \ln n}{\epsilon}$.
2: If $\hat{f}_1 \geq 7\zeta$, **return** $\hat{f}_1$.
3: Compute the value $v_{\mathrm{LP}}(G)$ given in Definition 5.1 using D.
4: **return** $\hat{f}_2 = v_{\mathrm{LP}}(G) + \mathrm{Lap}(\frac{6D^2}{\epsilon})$.

Lemma 5.3. *Algorithm 2 is an ϵ-node-private polynomial time algorithm that takes a graph G, parameters ϵ, D, n, and a connected template graph H on 3 nodes, and outputs an approximate count for $f_H(G)$ (the number of copies of H in G).*

1. *If $f_H(G) \geq (13n^2 \ln n)/\epsilon$, then with probability at least $1 - 1/\ln n$, Algorithm 2 outputs $\hat{f}_1$ and*
$$\left| \hat{f}_1 - f_H(G) \right| \leq (6n^2 \ln \ln n)/\epsilon.$$

2. *If G satisfies α-decay for $\alpha > 1$, $D > \bar{d}$, and $f_H(G) < (n^2 \ln n)/\epsilon$, then with probability at least $1 - 2/\ln n$, Algorithm 2 outputs $\hat{f}_2$ and*
$$|\hat{f}_2 - f_H(G)| \leq \frac{6D^2 \ln \ln n}{\epsilon} + t_h,$$
$$\text{where } t_h = \begin{cases} O\left(\bar{d}^\alpha n \cdot D^{2-\alpha}\right) & \text{if } \alpha > 2, \\ O\left(\bar{d}^\alpha n \cdot \ln n\right) & \text{if } \alpha = 2, \\ O\left(\bar{d}^\alpha n \cdot n^{2-\alpha}\right) & \text{if } 1 < \alpha < 2. \end{cases}$$

Lemma 5.4. *If H has 3 nodes and G satisfies α-decay for $\alpha > 1$ and $D \geq \bar{d}$ then $v_{\mathrm{LP}}(G) \geq f_H(G) - t_h$, where $t_h = O\left(\bar{d}^\alpha n D^{2-\alpha}\right)$ if $\alpha > 2$, $t_h = O\left(\bar{d}^2 n \ln n\right)$ if $\alpha = 2$, and $t_h = O\left(\bar{d}^\alpha n n^{2-\alpha}\right)$ if $1 < \alpha < 2$.*

Using Lemmas 5.3 and 5.4 with a carefully chosen threshold degree D, we get the following theorem about privately releasing counts of subgraphs on 3 nodes. A private value of $\bar{d}$ can be obtained using Theorem 4.1.

Theorem 5.2 (Releasing Subgraph Counts Privately). *There is a node differentially private algorithm which, given constants $\alpha > 1$, $\epsilon > 0$, a connected template graph H on 3 nodes, and a graph G on n nodes, computes with probability at least $1 - 2/(\ln n)$ an $(1 \pm o_n(1))$-approximation to $f_H(G)$ (the number of copies of H in G) if either of the following holds:*

1. *If $f_H(G) \geq (13n^2 \ln n)/\epsilon$.*
2. *If G satisfies α-decay, has average degree at most $\bar{d} > 1$, and either of the following holds: (a) $f_H(G) = \omega(\bar{d}^2 n^{2/\alpha} \ln n)$ if $\alpha > 2$, (b) $f_H(G) = \omega(\bar{d} n \ln^2 n)$ if $\alpha = 2$, or (c) $f_H(G) = \omega(\bar{d}^\alpha n^{3-\alpha} \ln n)$ if $1 < \alpha < 2$.*

6   Generic Reduction to Node Privacy in Bounded-Degree Graphs

We now turn to another, more general approach to getting more the accurate queries by looking at bounded degree graphs. Recall that if we had a promise that all degrees were at most D, then for many natural queries we could add less noise and still satisfy differential privacy. The question is, how can we enforce such a promise? Given an input graph G, possibly of large maximum degree, it is tempting to simply answer all queries with respect to a "truncated" version $T(G)$, in which nodes of very large degree have been removed. This is delicate, however, since the truncated graph $T(G)$ may change a lot when a single node of G is changed. That is, it could be that the *local sensitivity* of the "truncation" operator (viewed as a map from $\mathcal{G}_n$ to $\mathcal{G}_{n,D}$) is very high, making queries on the truncated graph also high-sensitivity.

More generally, consider a projection operator $T : \mathcal{G}_n \to \mathcal{G}_{n,D}$ which takes an arbitrary graph and outputs a D-bounded graph. We may define the (local, global, smooth) sensitivity of T in terms of the node distance $d_{\mathrm{node}}(T(G_1), T(G_2))$ where G_1 and G_2 differ in one node.

Given a query f defined on D-bounded graphs, it is easy to see that the local sensitivity of a *composed* query $f \circ T$ is bounded by the product $LS_T(G) \cdot \Delta_D f$ (one can see this as a discrete analogue of the chain rule from calculus). Our main lemma is that we can bound the smooth sensitivity similarly. We use the definition of β-smooth upper bound on local sensitivity from 2.3.

Lemma 6.1 (Smooth Bounds on Composed Functions). *Let $T : \mathcal{G}_n \to \mathcal{G}_{n,D}$. If $S_T(G)$ is a β-smooth upper bound on the local sensitivity of T (measured w.r.t. node distance), then $S_{f \circ T}(G) = S_T(G) \cdot \Delta_D F$ is a β-smooth bound on the local sensitivity of $f \circ T$.*

Given a smooth upper bound on the local sensitivity of $F_f \circ T$, we can use Theorem 2.3 to obtain a private algorithm for releasing F_f on all graphs in $\mathcal{G}_n$.

Instead of using smooth sensitivity, we can also use a differentially private upper bound on the local sensitivity, inspired by Dwork and Lei [7] and Karwa *et al.* [12]. This give a general technique to transform any algorithm that is private on D-bounded graphs to one which is private for all graphs.

Lemma 6.2 (Generic Reduction [12]). *Let $T : \mathcal{G}_n \to \mathcal{G}_{n,D}$. Suppose L_ϵ is an (ϵ, δ_1)-differentially private algorithm (on all graphs in $\mathcal{G}_n$) that outputs a real value such that $\Pr[L_\epsilon(G) > LS_T(G)] \geq 1 - \delta_2$ (where LS_T is measured w.r.t. node distance).*

Suppose that A is a $(\epsilon, 0)_D$-differentially private algorithm. Then the following algorithm is $(2\epsilon, e^\epsilon \delta_2 + \delta_1)$-differentially private: compute $\hat{L} = L_\epsilon(G)$, then run A on input $T(G)$ with privacy parameter $\epsilon' = \epsilon/\hat{L}$ and finally output the pair $\hat{L}, A(T(G))$.

Naive Truncation. This is the simplest truncation operator. Consider the operator T_{naive} that deletes all nodes of degree greater than D in $G = (V, E)$. This may have high local sensitivity (for example, rewiring one node may change the degrees of many nodes from D to $D+1$, resulting in a drastic increase in the number of nodes deleted by T_{naive}. This projector is computable in $O(n+m)$ time, where $n = |V|$ and $m = |E|$. The following simple lemma analyzes the sensitivity of this truncation operation.

Lemma 6.3. *Given a threshold D, the local sensitivity of naive truncation (w.r.t. node distance) is 1 plus the number of nodes with degree either D or $D + 1$.*

The following proposition bounds the local and smooth sensitivity of naive truncation. The last two parts of this proposition allow us to employ Lemmas 6.1 and 6.2, respectively.

Proposition 6.1 (Bounding the Sensitivity of Naive Truncation). *Given a graph G, let $N_k(G)$ denote the number of nodes in G with degrees in the range $[D-k, D+k+1]$. Let $C_k(G) = 1 + k + N_k(G)$. Then*

1. *$C_0(G)$ is the local sensitivity of naive truncation at G.*
2. *For any graph G' within rewiring distance $k + 1$ of G, the local sensitivity of naive truncation between G and G' is at most $C_k(G)$.*
3. *$S_{T_{\text{naive}}}(G) = \max_{k \geq 0} e^{-\beta k} C_k(G)$ is a smooth upper bound on the local sensitivity of naive truncation. Moreover, if $N_{\ln n/\beta}(G) \leq \ell$ (that is, if there are ℓ nodes in G with degrees in the range $D \pm \ln n/\beta$), then*

$$S_{T_{\text{naive}}}(G) \leq \ell + 1/\beta + 1.$$

4. *Consider the tapered interval query given by the function $f_{t,D,D+1}$ (defined in Section 3, Item (2)) for some $t \in (\frac{1}{n}, 1]$. The algorithm that returns*

$$L(G) = 1 + F_{f_{t,D,D+1}}(G) + \frac{2tn \log(1/\delta)}{\epsilon} + \text{Lap}\left(\frac{2tn}{\epsilon}\right)$$

is $(\epsilon, 0)$-node-private and returns a value larger than $LS_{T_{\text{naive}}}(G)$ with probability at least $1 - \delta$.

6.1   Using Naive Truncation: Deterministic and Randomized Cutoffs

The smooth sensitivity bound of Proposition 6.1 depends on the number of nodes immediately around the cutoff D. Thus, even if a graph G is D-bounded, truncating exactly at D may lead to a large smooth sensitivity bound. We get a much better bound on the noise by truncating slightly above the maximum degree. The following corollary follows by adding Cauchy noise as per Theorem 2.3.

Corollary 6.1. *For every $\epsilon > 0$, every threshold $D > \sqrt{2}(\ln n)/\epsilon$ and every real-valued function $f : \mathcal{G}_{n,D} \to \mathbb{R}$, there is a ϵ-node-private algorithm that outputs $f(G)$ with median error $O(\Delta_{\hat{D}} f/\epsilon^2)$, where $\hat{D} = D + 2\ln(n)/\epsilon \le 2D$.*

Randomizing the Degree Threshold One obvious problem with the truncation technique is that we may not know the maximum degree in the graph, or the maximum degree may be very large. Indeed, as have seen in the algorithms for counting subgraphs, it often makes sense to project to a degree threshold well below the maximum degree in a graph. In that case, the smooth sensitivity bound of Proposition 6.1 could be large.

One can get a substantially better bound by *randomizing* the cutoff. Given a target threshold D, consider an algorithm that picks a random threshold in a range of bounded by a constant multiple of D (say, between $2D$ and $3D$). We show that the smooth sensitivity of naive truncation is (likely to be) close to the *average* number of nodes of a random degree in the range, saving a factor of roughly D in the introduced noise.

Lemma 6.4 (Randomized Cutoff Lemma). *Fix $\beta > 0$, a graph G on n nodes, and an integer $D > 0$. Let $P_G(D)$ be the fraction of nodes in G of degree greater than D, and let $\hat{D}$ be uniformly random in the range $\{D + 1 + \ln n/\beta, \ldots, 2D + \ln n/\beta\}$. If T_{naive} is the naive truncation at degree $\hat{D}$, then*

$$\underset{\hat{D}}{\mathbb{E}}[S_{T_{naive}}(G)] \le 3\frac{nP_G(D)}{D} \cdot \frac{\ln n}{\beta} + \frac{1}{\beta} + 1.$$

6.2   Application of Naive Truncation for Releasing Degree Distribution

For concreteness, we work out one application of the naive truncation idea to releasing an approximation to the entire degree distribution (rather than releasing specific functions of that distribution). Our goal is to output a vector $\hat{p}$ that minimizes the ℓ_1-error $\|\hat{p} - p_G\|_1$, where p_G is the (true) degree distribution of the graph. If the error is $o(1)$, then $\hat{p}$ provides an estimate with vanishing error for all of the entries of degree distribution.

We use Lemma 6.1 to get a smooth bound on local sensitivity. The global sensitivity $\Delta_{\hat{D}}\|\hat{p} - p_G\|_1 \le 2\hat{D}$.

Theorem 6.1. *Algorithm 3 is an ϵ-node-private algorithm that takes a graph G and parameters n, D, ϵ, and outputs a vector $\hat{p}$ such that, if G satisfies α-decay for $\alpha > 1$ and $D > \frac{4}{\epsilon}\ln n$ and $D > \bar{d}$ where $\bar{d} = \bar{d}(G)$ is the average degree in G, then with probability at least $1/2$ we have*

Algorithm 3. ϵ-Node-Private Algorithm for Releasing Degree Distributions

Input: parameters ϵ, D, n, and a graph G on n nodes.

1: Pick $\hat{D} \in_R \{D + \frac{\ln n}{\beta} + 1, \ldots, 2D + \frac{\ln n}{\beta}\}$.

2: Compute the naive truncation $T_{\text{naive}}(G)$ with threshold $\hat{D}$ and the smooth bound $S_{T_{\text{naive}}}(G)$ with $\beta = \epsilon/(\sqrt{2}(\hat{D} + 1))$ (as in Proposition 6.1).

3: Output $\hat{p} = p_{T_{\text{naive}}(G)} + \text{Cauchy}\left(\frac{2\sqrt{2}\hat{D}}{\epsilon} S_{T_{\text{naive}}}(G)\right)^{\hat{D}+1}$ (that is, add i.i.d. Cauchy noise with median absolute deviation $\frac{2\sqrt{2}\hat{D}}{\epsilon} S_{T_{\text{naive}}}(G)$ to the entries of the degree distribution of $T_{\text{naive}}(G)$).

$$\|\hat{p} - p_G\|_1 = O\left(\frac{\bar{d}^\alpha \ln n \ln(D)}{\epsilon^2 D^{\alpha-2}} + \frac{D^3 \ln(D)}{n\,\epsilon^2}\right) = \tilde{O}\left(\frac{1}{\epsilon^2}\left(\frac{\bar{d}^\alpha}{D^{\alpha-2}} + \frac{D^3}{n}\right)\right),$$

and the $\tilde{O}$ notation hides constants depending on α and polylogarithmic factors in n.

We note that one can get slightly better bounds on the error by considering an algorithm that uses different noise distributions other than Cauchy. We stick to Cauchy noise here for simplicity. For the following corollary, we set $D = \bar{d}^{\frac{\alpha}{\alpha+1}} n^{\frac{1}{\alpha+1}}$ in the previous theorem.

Corollary 6.2 (Releasing Degree Distribution Privately). *There is a node differentially private algorithm running in $O(|E|)$ time which, given $\alpha > 1$, $\epsilon > 0$, and a graph $G = (V, E)$ on n nodes, computes an approximate degree distribution with ℓ_1 error (with probability at least $1/2$)*

$$\|\hat{p} - p_G\|_1 = \tilde{O}\left(\bar{d}^{\frac{3\alpha}{\alpha+1}} \Big/ \left(\epsilon^2 n^{\frac{\alpha-2}{\alpha+1}}\right)\right)$$

if G satisfies α-decay and has average degree at most $\bar{d} > 1$. In particular, this error goes to 0 for any constant $\alpha > 2$ when $\bar{d}$ is polylogarithmic in n.

Acknowledgments. We thank Madhav Jha for pointing out an error in an earlier version of the Randomized Cutoff Lemma.

References

[1] Blocki, J., Blum, A., Datta, A., Sheffet, O.: Differentially Private Data Analysis of Social Networks via Restricted Sensitivity. In: ITCS (to appear, 2013)

[2] Blum, A., Dwork, C., McSherry, F., Nissim, K.: Practical Privacy: The SuLQ Framework. In: PODS, pp. 128–138. ACM (2005)

[3] Clauset, A., Shalizi, C.R., Newman, M.E.J.: Power-Law Distributions in Empirical Data. SIAM Review 51(4), 661–703 (2009)

[4] Dinur, I., Nissim, K.: Revealing Information While Preserving Privacy. In: PODS, pp. 202–210. ACM (2003)

[5] Dwork, C.: Differential Privacy. In: Bugliesi, M., Preneel, B., Sassone, V., Wegener, I. (eds.) ICALP 2006. LNCS, vol. 4052, pp. 1–12. Springer, Heidelberg (2006)

[6] Dwork, C., Kenthapadi, K., McSherry, F., Mironov, I., Naor, M.: Our Data, Ourselves: Privacy Via Distributed Noise Generation. In: Vaudenay, S. (ed.) EUROCRYPT 2006. LNCS, vol. 4004, pp. 486–503. Springer, Heidelberg (2006)

[7] Dwork, C., Lei, J.: Differential Privacy and Robust Statistics. In: STOC, pp. 371–380 (2009)

[8] Dwork, C., McSherry, F., Nissim, K., Smith, A.: Calibrating Noise to Sensitivity in Private Data Analysis. In: Halevi, S., Rabin, T. (eds.) TCC 2006. LNCS, vol. 3876, pp. 265–284. Springer, Heidelberg (2006)

[9] Gehrke, J., Lui, E., Pass, R.: Towards Privacy for Social Networks: A Zero-Knowledge Based Definition of Privacy. In: Ishai, Y. (ed.) TCC 2011. LNCS, vol. 6597, pp. 432–449. Springer, Heidelberg (2011)

[10] Hay, M., Li, C., Miklau, G., Jensen, D.: Accurate Estimation of the Degree Distribution of Private Networks. In: ICDM, pp. 169–178 (2009)

[11] Jernigan, C., Mistree, B.F.T.: Gaydar: Facebook Friendships Expose Sexual Orientation. First Monday 14(10) (2009)

[12] Karwa, V., Raskhodnikova, S., Smith, A., Yaroslavtsev, G.: Private analysis of graph structure. PVLDB 4(11), 1146–1157 (2011)

[13] Kifer, D., Machanavajjhala, A.: No Free Lunch in Data Privacy. In: SIGMOD, pp. 193–204 (2011)

[14] McSherry, F., Mironov, I.: Differentially Private Recommender Systems: Building Privacy into the Net. In: KDD, pp. 627–636. ACM, New York (2009)

[15] Nissim, K., Raskhodnikova, S., Smith, A.: Smooth sensitivity and sampling in private data analysis. In: Symp. Theory of Computing (STOC), pp. 75–84. ACM (2007), full paper: http://www.cse.psu.edu/~asmith/pubs/NRS07

[16] Rastogi, V., Hay, M., Miklau, G., Suciu, D.: Relationship Privacy: Output Perturbation for Queries with Joins. In: PODS, pp. 107–116 (2009)

A   Comparison to Concurrent Work

Blocki *et al.* [1] provide algorithm for analyzing graph data with node-level differential privacy. They proceed from a similar intuition to ours, developing low-sensitivity projections onto the set of graphs of a given maximum degree. However, the results of the two papers are not directly comparable. This section discusses the differences between the two works.

Specifically, Blocki *et al.* have two main results on node privacy, both of which are incomparable to our corresponding results.

- First, Blocki *et al.* show that for every function $f : \mathcal{G}_{n,D} \to \mathbb{R}$, there exists an extension $g : \mathcal{G}_n \to \mathbb{R}$ that agrees with f on $\mathcal{G}_{n,D}$ and that has global sensitivity $\Delta g = \Delta_D f$. The resulting function need not be computable efficiently.

  In contrast, we give explicit, *efficient* constructions of such extensions for several families of functions (the number of edges, linear functions of the degree distribution defined by concave queries, and subgraph counting queries).
- Second, Blocki *et al.* give a specific projection from arbitrary graphs to graphs of a particular degree $\mu : \mathcal{G}_n \to \mathcal{G}_{n,D}$, along with a smooth upper bound on its local sensitivity. They propose to use this for answering queries which have low node sensitivity on $\mathcal{G}_{n,D}$.

We give a similar result for a different projection (naive truncation). As in their work, we propose to compose this projection with queries that have low sensitivity when restricted to graphs of bounded degree (Lemma 6.1), though we also observe that more general types of composition are also possible (Lemma 6.2).

The results for these different projections are similar in that both techniques have low smooth sensitivity (depending only on ϵ) when the input graph has degree less than the input threshold D.

To the best of our understanding, the accuracy results are nevertheless incomparable. The Blocki et al. projection has a bicriteria approximation guarantee: on input D and G, their projection function is guaranteed to output a graph of degree at most D such that the distance $d_{\mathrm{node}}(G, \mu(G)) \leq 4 d_{\mathrm{node}}(G, \mathcal{G}_{n, D/2})$. (No such guarantee is possible for naive truncation, which may be arbitrarily worse than the optimal projection even onto graphs of degree smaller than D.) Nonetheless, the sensitivity bound for μ can be quite a bit higher than the one we present for naive truncation, resulting in lower noise added for privacy (similarly, there are graphs for which the other projection is less sensitive).

Our approach has a considerable efficiency advantage: the naive truncation procedure we propose runs in $O(n + m)$ time for a graph with n vertices and m edges, whereas the projection of Blocki et al. seems to require solving a linear program with $n + \binom{n}{2}$ variables and $\Theta(n^2)$ constraints.

The final accuracy guarantees for our algorithms are stated for graphs that satisfy a mild tail bound on the degree distribution, called α-decay. In contrast, Blocki et al. only give accuracy guarantees for graphs with bounded degree.

Finally, Blocki et al. also consider *edge* privacy, and give a simple, elegant projection operator that has constant edge sensitivity. There is no analogue of that result in this paper, which focuses on node privacy.

Universally Composable
Synchronous Computation

Jonathan Katz[1], Ueli Maurer[2], Björn Tackmann[2], and Vassilis Zikas[3,*]

[1] Dept. of Computer Science, University of Maryland
jkatz@cs.umd.edu
[2] Dept. of Computer Science, ETH Zürich, Switzerland
{maurer,bjoernt}@inf.ethz.ch
[3] Dept. of Computer Science, UCLA
vzikas@cs.ucla.edu

Abstract. In synchronous networks, protocols can achieve security guarantees that are not possible in an asynchronous world: they can simultaneously achieve *input completeness* (all honest parties' inputs are included in the computation) and *guaranteed termination* (honest parties do not "hang" indefinitely). In practice truly synchronous networks rarely exist, but synchrony can be emulated if channels have (known) bounded latency and parties have loosely synchronized clocks.

The widely-used framework of universal composability (UC) is inherently asynchronous, but several approaches for adding synchrony to the framework have been proposed. However, we show that the existing proposals do *not* provide the expected guarantees. Given this, we propose a novel approach to defining synchrony in the UC framework by introducing functionalities exactly meant to model, respectively, bounded-delay networks and loosely synchronized clocks. We show that the expected guarantees of synchronous computation can be achieved given these functionalities, and that previous similar models can all be expressed within our new framework.

1 Introduction

In synchronous networks, protocols can achieve both *input completeness* (all honest parties' inputs are included in the computation) and *guaranteed termination* (honest parties do not "hang" indefinitely). In contrast, these properties cannot simultaneously be ensured in an asynchronous world [7,17].

The traditional model for synchronous computation assumes that protocols proceed in rounds: the current round is known to all parties, and messages sent in some round are delivered by the beginning of the next round. While this is a strong model that rarely corresponds to real-world networks, the model is still useful since it can be *emulated* under the relatively mild assumptions of a known bound on the network latency and loose synchronization of the (honest) parties'

---

* Work done while the author was at the University of Maryland.

A. Sahai (Ed.): TCC 2013, LNCS 7785, pp. 477–498, 2013.

clocks. In fact, it is fair to say that these two assumptions are exactly what is meant when speaking of "synchrony" in real-world networks.

The framework of *universal composability* (UC) [12] assumes, by default, completely asynchronous communication, where even eventual message delivery is not guaranteed. Protocol designers working in the UC setting are thus faced with two choices: either work in an asynchronous network and give up on input completeness [7] or guaranteed termination [29,15], or else modify the UC framework so as to incorporate synchronous communication somehow.

Several ideas for adding synchrony to the UC framework have been proposed. Canetti [10] introduced an ideal functionality $\mathcal{F}_{\text{SYN}}$ that was intended exactly to model synchronous communication in a general-purpose fashion. We prove in Section 5.1, however, that $\mathcal{F}_{\text{SYN}}$ does *not* provide the guarantees expected of a synchronous network. Nielsen [34] and Hofheinz and Müller-Quade [25] also propose ways of modeling synchrony with composition guarantees, but their approaches modify the foundations of the UC framework and are not sufficiently general to model, e.g., synchrony in an incomplete network, or the case when synchrony holds only in part of a network (say, because certain links do not have bounded delay while others do). It is fair to say that the proposed modifications to the UC framework are complex, and it is unclear whether they adequately capture the intuitive real-world notion of synchrony. The timing model considered in [20,23,26] extends the notion of interactive Turing machines by adding a "clock tape." It comes closer to capturing intuition, but (as we show in Section 5.2) this model also does not provide the guarantees expected from a synchronous network. A similar approach is taken in [4], which modifies the reactive-simulatability framework of [6] by adding an explicit "time port" to each automaton. Despite the different underlying framework, this work is most similar to the approach we follow here in that it also captures both guaranteed termination and incomplete networks. Their approach, however, inherently requires changing the underlying model and is based on restricting the class of adversaries (both of which we avoid). Such modifications result in (at least) a reformulation of the composition theorem and proof.

Our Approach and Results. We aim for an intuitively appealing model that faithfully embeds the actual real-world synchrony assumptions into the standard UC framework. The approach we take is to introduce functionalities specifically intended to (independently) model the two assumptions of bounded network delay and loose clock synchronization. An additional benefit of separating the assumptions in this way is that we can also study the case when only one of the assumptions holds.

We begin by formally defining a functionality corresponding to (authenticated) communication channels with *bounded delay*. Unfortunately, this alone is not sufficient for achieving guaranteed termination. (Throughout, we will always want input completeness to hold.) Intuitively, this is because bounded-delay channels alone—without any global clock—only provide the same "eventual message delivery" guarantee of classical asynchronous networks [7,9]. It thus becomes clear that what is missing when only bounded-delay channels are available is some notion of *time*. To rectify this, we further introduce a functionality $\mathcal{F}_{\text{CLOCK}}$ that directly corresponds to the presence of loosely synchronized clocks among the parties. We then show that $\mathcal{F}_{\text{CLOCK}}$ together with eventual-delivery channels is also not sufficient, but that standard protocols can indeed be used to securely realize any functionality with guaranteed termination in a hybrid world where both $\mathcal{F}_{\text{CLOCK}}$ and bounded-delay (instead of just eventual delivery) channels are available.

Overall, our results show that the two functionalities we propose—meant to model, independently, bounded-delay channels and loosely synchronized clocks—enable us to capture exactly the security guarantees provided by traditional synchronous networks. Moreover, this approach allows us to make use of the original UC framework and composition theorem.

Guaranteed Termination. We pursue an approach inspired by constructive cryptography [31,32] to model guaranteed termination. We describe the termination guarantee as a property of functionalities; this bridges the gap between the theoretical model and the realistic scenario where the synchronized clocks of the parties ensure that the adversary *cannot* stall the computation *even if he tries to (time will advance)*. Intuitively, such a functionality does not wait for the adversary *indefinitely*; rather, the environment—which represents (amongst others) the parties as well as higher level protocols—can provide the functionality with sufficiently many activations to make it proceed and eventually produce outputs, irrespective of the adversary's strategy. This design principle is applied to both the functionality that shall be realized and to the underlying functionalities formalizing the (bounded-delay) channels and the (loosely synchronized) clocks.

We then require from a protocol to realize a functionality with this guaranteed termination property, given as hybrids functionalities that have the same type of property. In more detail, following the real-world/ideal-world paradigm of the security definition, for any real-world adversary, there must be an ideal-world adversary (or simulator) such that whatever the adversary achieves in the real world can be mimicked by the simulator in the ideal world. As the functionality guarantees to terminate and produce output for any simulator, no (real-world) adversary can stall the execution of a secure protocol indefinitely.

The environment in the UC framework can, at any point in time, provide output and halt the entire protocol execution. Intuitively, however, this corresponds to the environment (which is the distinguisher) *ignoring the remainder of the random experiment*, not the adversary *stalling the protocol execution*. Any environment $\mathcal{Z}$ can be transformed into an environment $\mathcal{Z}'$ that completes the execution and achieves (at least) the same advantage as $\mathcal{Z}$.

A "Polling"-Based Notion of Time. The formalization of time we use in this work is different from previous approaches [20,23,26,33]; the necessity for the different approach stems from the inherently asynchronous scheduling scheme of the original UC model. In fact, the order in which protocols are activated in this model is determined by the communication; a party will only be activated during the execution whenever this party receives either an input or a message.

Given this model, we formalize a clock as an ideal functionality that is available to the parties running a protocol and provides a means of synchronization: the clock "waits" until all *honest* parties signal that they are finished with their tasks. This structure is justified by the following observation: the guarantees that are given to parties in synchronous models are that each party will be activated in every time interval, and will be able to perform its local actions fast enough to finish before the deadline (and then it might "sleep" until the next time interval begins). A party's confirmation that it is ready captures exactly this guarantee. As this model differentiates between honest and dishonest parties, we have to carefully design functionalities and protocols such that they do not allow *excessive* capabilities of detecting dishonest behavior. Still, the synchrony guarantee inherently *does* provide *some* form of such detections (e.g., usually by a time-out while waiting for messages, the synchrony of the clocks and the bounded delay of the channels guarantee that "honest" ones always arrive on time).

Our notion of time allows modeling both composition of protocols that run mutually asynchronously, by assuming that each protocol has its own independent clock, as well as mutually synchronous, e.g. lock-step, composition by assuming that all protocols use the same clock.

Organization of the Paper. In Section 2, we include a brief description of the UC model [12] and introduce the necessary notation and terminology. In Section 3, we review the model of completely asynchronous networks, describe its limitations, and introduce a functionality modeling bounded-delay channels. In Section 4, we introduce a functionality $\mathcal{F}_{\text{CLOCK}}$ meant to model loose clock synchronization and explore the guarantees it provides. Further, we define *computation with guaranteed termination* within the UC framework, and show how to achieve it using $\mathcal{F}_{\text{CLOCK}}$ and bounded-delay channels. In Section 5, we revisit previous models for synchronous computation. Many details and, in particular, proofs have been omitted from this version but they can be found in the full version of this paper [27].

2   Preliminaries

Simulation-Based Security. Most general security frameworks are based on the real-world/ideal-world paradigm: In the real world, the parties execute the protocol using channels as defined by the model. In the ideal world, the parties securely access an ideal functionality $\mathcal{F}$ that obtains inputs from the parties, runs the program that specifies the task to be achieved by the protocol, and returns the resulting outputs to the parties. Intuitively, a protocol *securely realizes* the functionality $\mathcal{F}$ if, for any real-world adversary $\mathcal{A}$ attacking the protocol execution, there is an ideal-world adversary $\mathcal{S}$, also called the *simulator*, that emulates $\mathcal{A}$'s attack. The simulation is good if no distinguisher $\mathcal{Z}$—often called the *environment*—which interacts, in a well defined manner, with the parties and the adversary/simulator, can distinguish between the two worlds.

The advantage of such security definitions is that they satisfy strong composability properties. Let π_1 be a protocol that securely realizes a functionality $\mathcal{F}_1$. If a protocol π_2, using the functionality $\mathcal{F}_1$ as a subroutine, securely realizes a functionality $\mathcal{F}_2$, then the protocol $\pi_2^{\pi_1/\mathcal{F}_1}$, where the calls to $\mathcal{F}_1$ are replaced by invocations of π_1, securely realizes $\mathcal{F}_2$ (without calls to $\mathcal{F}_1$). Therefore, it suffices to analyze the security of the simpler protocol π_2 in the $\mathcal{F}_1$-*hybrid* model, where the parties run π_2 with access to the ideal functionality $\mathcal{F}_1$. A detailed treatment of protocol composition appears in, e.g., [6,11,12,18,32].

Model of Computation. All security models discussed in this work are based on or inspired by the UC framework [12]. The definitions are based on the simulation paradigm, and the entities taking part in the execution (protocol machines, functionalities, adversary, and environment) are described as *interactive Turing machines* (ITMs). The execution is an interaction of *ITM instances* (ITIs) and is initiated by the environment that provides input to and obtains output from the protocol machines, and also communicates with the adversary. The adversary has access to the ideal functionalities in the hybrid models and also serves as a network among the protocol machines. During the execution, the ITIs are activated one-by-one, where the exact order of the activations depends on the considered model.

Notation, Conventions, and Specifics of UC '05. We consider protocols that are executed among a certain set of players $\mathcal{P}$, often referred to as the *player set*, where every $p_i \in \mathcal{P}$ formally denotes a unique party ID. A protocol execution involves the following types of ITMs: the environment $\mathcal{Z}$, the adversary $\mathcal{A}$, the protocol machine π, and (possibly) ideal functionalities $\mathcal{F}_1, \ldots, \mathcal{F}_m$. We say that a protocol π securely realizes $\mathcal{F}$ in the $\mathcal{F}'$-hybrid model if for each adversary $\mathcal{A}$ there exists a simulator $\mathcal{S}$ such that for all environments $\mathcal{Z}$, the contents of $\mathcal{Z}$'s output tape after an execution of π (using $\mathcal{F}'$) with $\mathcal{A}$ is indistinguishable from the contents of the tape after an execution of $\mathcal{F}$ with $\mathcal{S}$. For the details of the execution, we follow the description in [10].

As in [10], the statement "the functionality sends a *(private) delayed output* y to party i" describes the following process: the functionality requests the adversary's permission to output y to party i (without leaking the value y); as soon as the adversary agrees, the output y is delivered. The statement "the functionality sends a *public delayed output* y to party i" corresponds to the same process, where the permission request also includes the full message y.

All our functionalities $\mathcal{F}$ use *standard (adaptive) corruption* as defined in [10]. At any point in the execution, we denote by $\mathcal{H}$ the set of "honest" parties that have not (yet) been corrupted. Finally, all of our functionalities use a player set $\mathcal{P}$ that is fixed when the functionality is instantiated, and each functionality has a session ID which is of the form $sid = (\mathcal{P}, sid')$ with $sid' \in \{0,1\}^*$. We will usually omit the session ID from the description of our functionalities; different instances behave independently.

The functionalities in our model and their interpretation are specific to the model of [10] in that they exploit some of the mechanics introduced there, which we recall here. First, the order of activations is strictly defined by the model: whenever an ITI sends a message to some other ITI, the receiving ITI will immediately be activated and the sending ITI will halt. If some ITI halts without sending a message, the "master scheduler," the environment $\mathcal{Z}$, will become active. This scheme allows to model guaranteed termination since the adversary *cannot* prevent the invocation of protocol machines. Second, efficiency is defined as a "reactive" type of polynomial time: the number of steps that an ITI performs is bounded by a polynomial in the security parameter *and* (essentially) the length of the inputs obtained by this ITI. Consequently, the environment can continuously provide "run-time" to protocol machines to make them poll, e.g., at a bounded-delay or eventual-delivery channel. Our modeling of eventual delivery fundamentally relies on this fact.

3   Synchronous Protocols in an Asynchronous Network

Protocols in asynchronous networks cannot achieve input completeness and guaranteed termination simultaneously [7,17]. Intuitively, the reason is that honest parties cannot distinguish whether a message has been delayed—and to satisfy input completeness they should wait for this message—or whether the sender is corrupted and did not send the message—and for guaranteed termination they should proceed. In fact, there are two main network models for asynchronous protocols: on the one hand, there are fully asynchronous channels that do not at all guarantee delivery [10,15]; on the other hand, there are channels where delivery is guaranteed and the delay might be bounded by a publicly known constant or unknown [7]. In the following, we formalize the channels assumed in each of the two settings as functionalities in the UC framework and discuss how they can be used by round-based, i.e., synchronous, protocols. The results presented here formally confirm—in the UC framework—facts about synchrony assumptions that are known or folklore in the distributed computing literature.

3.1   Fully Asynchronous Network

The communication in a fully asynchronous network where messages are not guaranteed to be delivered is modeled by the functionality $\mathcal{F}_{\mathrm{SMT}}$ from [10], which involves a sender, a receiver, and the adversary. Messages input by the sender p_s are immediately given to the adversary, and delivered to the receiver p_r only after the adversary's approval. Different privacy guarantees are formulated by a so-called leakage function $\ell(\cdot)$ that determines the information leaked during the transmission if both p_s and p_r are honest. In particular, the authenticated channel $\mathcal{F}_{\mathrm{AUTH}}$ is modeled by $\mathcal{F}_{\mathrm{SMT}}$ parametrized by the identity function $\ell(m) = m$, and the ideally secure channel $\mathcal{F}_{\mathrm{SEC}}$ is modeled by $\mathcal{F}_{\mathrm{SMT}}$ with the constant function $\ell(m) = \perp$. (For realistic channels obtained by encryption one typically resorts to the length function $\ell(m) = |m|$, see [14].) An important property of $\mathcal{F}_{\mathrm{SMT}}$ is *adaptive message replacement*: the adversary can, depending on the leaked information, corrupt the sender and replace the sent message.

Canetti et al. [15] showed that, in this model and assuming a common reference string, any (well-formed) functionality can be realized, without guaranteed termination. Moreover, a combination of the results of Kushilevitz, Lindell, and Rabin [29] and Asharov and Lindell [1] show that appropriate modifications of the protocols from the seminal works of Ben-Or, Goldwasser, and Widgerson [8] and Chaum, Crépeau, and Damgård [16] (for unconditional security) or the work by Goldreich, Micali, and Widgerson [22] (for computational security)—all of which are designed for the synchronous setting—are sufficient to achieve general secure computation without termination in this asynchronous setting, under the same conditions on corruption-thresholds as stated in [8,16,22].

The following lemma formalizes the intuition that a fully asynchronous network is insufficient for terminating computation, i.e., computation which cannot be stalled by the adversary. For a functionality $\mathcal{F}$, denote by $[\mathcal{F}]^{\mathrm{NT}}$ the *non-terminating relaxation* of $\mathcal{F}$ defined as follows: $[\mathcal{F}]^{\mathrm{NT}}$ behaves as $\mathcal{F}$, but whenever $\mathcal{F}$ outputs a value to some honest party, $[\mathcal{F}]^{\mathrm{NT}}$ provides this output in a delayed manner (see Section 2). More formally, we show that there are functionalities $\mathcal{F}$ that are not realizable in the $\mathcal{F}_{\mathrm{SMT}}$-hybrid model, but their delayed relaxations $[\mathcal{F}]^{\mathrm{NT}}$ are. This statement holds even for stand-alone security, i.e., for environments that do not interact with the adversary during the protocol execution. Additionally, the impossibility applies to all *non-trivial*, i.e., not locally computable, functionalities (see [28]) with guaranteed termination as defined in Section 4. While the lemma is implied by the more general Lemma 5, we describe the proof idea for this simpler case below.

Lemma 1. *There are functionalities $\mathcal{F}$ such that $[\mathcal{F}]^{\mathrm{NT}}$ can be realized in the $\mathcal{F}_{\mathrm{SMT}}$-hybrid model, but $\mathcal{F}$ cannot be realized.*

Proof (idea). Consider the functionality $\mathcal{F}$ which behaves as $\mathcal{F}_{\mathrm{SMT}}$, but with the following add-on: upon receiving a special "fetch" message from the receiver p_r, outputs y to p_r, where $y = m$ if the sender has input the message m, and $y = \perp$ (i.e., a default value), otherwise. $[\mathcal{F}]^{\mathrm{NT}}$ is realized from $\mathcal{F}_{\mathrm{SMT}}$ channels by the dummy protocol, whereas realizing $\mathcal{F}$ is impossible.   □

3.2   Eventual-Delivery Channels

A stronger variant of asynchronous communication provides the guarantee that messages will be delivered *eventually*, independent of the adversary's strategy [7]. The functionality $\mathcal{F}_{\mathrm{ED\text{-}SMT}}$ captures this guarantee, following the principle described in Section 1: The receiver can enforce delivery of the message using "fetch" requests to the channel. The potential delay of the channel is modeled by ignoring a certain number D of such requests before delivering the actual message to p_r; to model the fact that the delay might be arbitrary, we allow the adversary to repeatedly increase the value of D during the computation. Yet, the delay that $\mathcal{A}$ can impose is bounded by $\mathcal{A}$'s running time.[1] The fact that this models eventual delivery utilizes the "reactive" definition of efficiency in [10]:

---

[1] This is enforced by accepting the delay-number only when given in unary notation.

after the adversary determined the delay D for a certain message, the environment can still provide the protocol machines of the honest parties with sufficiently many activations to retrieve the message from the channel. The eventual delivery channel $\mathcal{F}_{\text{ED-SMT}}$ is, like $\mathcal{F}_{\text{SMT}}$, parametrized by a leakage function $\ell(\cdot)$.

Functionality $\mathcal{F}_{\text{ED-SMT}}(p_s, p_r, \ell(\cdot))$

Initialize $M := \bot$ and $D := 0$.

- Upon receiving a message m from p_s, set $D := 1$ and $M := m$ and send $\ell(M)$ to the adversary.
- Upon receiving a message (fetch) from p_r:
  1. Set $D := D - 1$.
  2. If $D = 0$ then send M to p_r (otherwise no message is sent and, as defined in [10], $\mathcal{Z}$ is activated).
- Upon receiving a message (delay, T) from the adversary, if T encodes a natural number in unary notation, then set $D := D + T$; otherwise ignore the message.
- *(adaptive message replacement)*: Upon receiving (corrupt, p_s, m', T') from $\mathcal{A}$: if $D > 0$ and T' is a valid delay, then set $D := T'$ and set $M := m'$.

Channels with eventual delivery are strictly stronger than fully asynchronous communication in the sense of Section 3.1. Indeed, the proof of Lemma 1 extends to the case where $\mathcal{F}$ is the eventual-delivery channel $\mathcal{F}_{\text{ED-SMT}}$: the simulator can delay the delivery of the message only by a polynomial number of steps, and the environment can issue sufficiently many queries at the receiver's interface.

As with fully asynchronous channels, one can use channels with eventual delivery to achieve secure computation without termination. Additionally, however, eventual-delivery channels allow for protocols which are guaranteed to (eventually) terminate, at the cost of violating input completeness. For instance, the protocol of Ben-Or, Canetti, and Goldreich [7] securely realizes any functionality where the inputs of up to $\frac{n}{4}$ parties might be ignored. Yet, the eventual-delivery channels, by themselves, do not allow to compute functionalities with strong termination guarantees. In fact, the result of Lemma 1 holds even if we replace $\mathcal{F}_{\text{SMT}}$ by $\mathcal{F}_{\text{ED-SMT}}$. This is stated in the following lemma, which again translates to both stand-alone security and to arbitrary functionalities that are not locally computable, and is again implied by Lemma 5.

Lemma 2. *There are functionalities $\mathcal{F}$ such that $[\mathcal{F}]^{\text{NT}}$ can be realized in the $\mathcal{F}_{\text{ED-SMT}}$-hybrid model, but $\mathcal{F}$ cannot be realized.*

3.3   Bounded-Delay Channels with a Known Upper Bound

Bounded-delay channels are described by a functionality $\mathcal{F}_{\text{BD-SMT}}$ that is similar to $\mathcal{F}_{\text{ED-SMT}}$ but parametrized by a (strictly) positive constant δ bounding the delay that the adversary can impose. In more detail, the functionality $\mathcal{F}_{\text{BD-SMT}}$

works as $\mathcal{F}_{\text{ED-SMT}}$, but queries of the adversary that lead to an accumulated delay of $T > \delta$ are ignored. Furthermore, the sender/receiver can query the functionality to learn the value δ. A formal specification of $\mathcal{F}_{\text{BD-SMT}}$ is given in the following:

Functionality $\mathcal{F}^{\delta}_{\text{BD-SMT}}(p_s, p_r, \ell(\cdot))$

Initialize $M := \perp$ and $D := 1$, and $D_t := 1$.

- Upon receiving a message m from p_s, set $D := 1$ and $M := m$ and send $\ell(M)$ to the adversary.
- Upon receiving a message (LearnBound) from p_s, p_r, or $\mathcal{A}$, reply with δ.
- Upon receiving a message (fetch) from p_r:
    1. Set $D := D - 1$.
    2. If $D = 0$, then send M to p_r.
- Upon receiving (delay, T) from the adversary, if $D_t + T \leq \delta$, then set $D := D + T$ and $D_t := D_t + T$; otherwise ignore the message.
- Upon receiving (corrupt, p_s, m', T') from $\mathcal{A}$: if $D > 0$ and T' is a valid delay, then set $D := T'$ and $M := m'$.

In reality, a channel with latency δ' is at least as useful as one with latency $\delta > \delta'$. Our formulation of bounded-delay channels is consistent with this intuition: for any $0 < \delta' < \delta$, $\mathcal{F}^{\delta}_{\text{BD-SMT}}$ can be UC-realized in the $\mathcal{F}^{\delta'}_{\text{BD-SMT}}$-hybrid model. Indeed, the simple $\mathcal{F}^{\delta'}_{\text{BD-SMT}}$-hybrid protocol that drops $\delta - \delta'$ (fetch)-queries realizes $\mathcal{F}^{\delta}_{\text{BD-SMT}}$; the simulator also increases the delay appropriately. The converse is not true in general: channels with smaller upper bound on the delay are *strictly* stronger when termination is required. This is formalized in the following lemma, which again extends to both stand-alone security and to non-trivial functionalities with guaranteed termination as in Section 4.

Lemma 3. *For any $0 < \delta' < \delta$, the functionality $[\mathcal{F}^{\delta'}_{\text{BD-SMT}}]^{\text{NT}}$ can be realized in the $\mathcal{F}^{\delta}_{\text{BD-SMT}}$-hybrid model, but $\mathcal{F}^{\delta'}_{\text{BD-SMT}}$ cannot be realized.*

The proof of Lemma 3 follows the same idea as Lemma 2 and can be found in the full version of the paper. (The proof of Lemma 2 does not use the fact that no upper bound on the network latency is known.) The technique used in the proof already suggests that bounded-delay channels, without additional assumptions such as synchronized clocks, are not sufficient for terminating computation. While Lemma 3 only handles the case where the assumed channel has a strictly positive upper-bound on the delay, the (more general) impossibility in Lemma 5 holds even for *instant-delivery* channels, i.e., bounded-delay channels which become ready to deliver as soon as they get input from the sender.

In the remainder of this paper we use instant-delivery channels, i.e., $\mathcal{F}^{\delta}_{\text{BD-SMT}}$ with $\delta = 1$; however, our results easily extend to arbitrary values of δ. To simplify notation, we completely omit the delay parameter, i.e., we write $\mathcal{F}_{\text{BD-SMT}}$ instead of $\mathcal{F}^{1}_{\text{BD-SMT}}$. Furthermore, we use $\mathcal{F}_{\text{BD-SEC}}$ and $\mathcal{F}_{\text{BD-AUTH}}$ to denote the corresponding authenticated and secure bounded-delay channel with $\delta = 1$, respectively.

4   Computation with Guaranteed Termination

Assuming bounded-delay channels is not, by itself, sufficient for achieving both input completeness and termination. In this section, we introduce the functionality $\mathcal{F}_{\text{CLOCK}}$ that, together with the bounded-delay channels $\mathcal{F}_{\text{BD-SMT}}^{\delta}$, allows synchronous protocols to satisfy both properties simultaneously. In particular, we define what it means for a protocol to UC-realize a given multi-party function *with guaranteed termination*, and show how $\{\mathcal{F}_{\text{CLOCK}}, \mathcal{F}_{\text{BD-SMT}}^{\delta}\}$-protocols can satisfy this definition.

4.1   The Synchronization Functionality

To motivate the functionality $\mathcal{F}_{\text{CLOCK}}$, we examine how synchronous protocols in reality use the assumptions of bounded-delay (with a known upper bound) channels and synchronized clocks to satisfy the input-completeness and the termination properties simultaneously: they assign to each round a time-slot that is long enough to incorporate the time for computing and sending all next-round messages, plus the network delay. The fact that their clocks are (loosely) synchronized allows the parties to decide (without explicit communication) whether or not all honest parties have finished all their operations for some round. Note that it is sufficient, at the cost of having longer rounds, to assume that the clocks are not advancing in a fully synchronized manner but there is an known upper bound on the maximum clock-drift [23,26,33].

The purpose of $\mathcal{F}_{\text{CLOCK}}$ is to provide the described functionality to UC protocols. But as $\mathcal{F}_{\text{CLOCK}}$ is an ordinary UC functionality, it has no means of knowing whether or not a party has finished its intended operations for a certain round. This problem is resolved by having the parties signal their round status (i.e, whether or not they are "done" with the current round) to $\mathcal{F}_{\text{CLOCK}}$. In particular, $\mathcal{F}_{\text{CLOCK}}$ keeps track of the parties' status in a vector $(d_1, \ldots, d_n)$ of indicator bits, where $d_i = 1$ if p_i has signaled that it has finished all its actions for the current round and $d_i = 0$, otherwise. As soon as $d_i = 1$ for all $p_i \in \mathcal{H}$, $\mathcal{F}_{\text{CLOCK}}$ resets $d_i = 0$ for all $p_i \in \mathcal{P}$.[2] In addition to the notifications, any party p_i can send a synchronization request to $\mathcal{F}_{\text{CLOCK}}$, which is answered with d_i. A party p_i that observes that d_i has switched can conclude that all honest parties have completed their respective duties.[3] As $\mathcal{F}_{\text{CLOCK}}$ does *not* wait for signals from corrupted parties, $\mathcal{F}_{\text{CLOCK}}$ cannot be realized based on well-formed functionalities. Nevertheless, as discussed above, in reality time *does* offer this functionality to synchronous protocols.

---

[2] Whenever some party is corrupted, $\mathcal{F}_{\text{CLOCK}}$ is notified and updates $\mathcal{H}$ accordingly. This is consistent with models such as [10,34] (and, formally, requires a small change to the UC control function).

[3] For arbitrary protocols, the functionality offers too strong guarantees. Hence, we restrict ourselves to considering protocols that are either of the type described here or do not use the clock at all.

Functionality $\mathcal{F}_{\text{CLOCK}}(\mathcal{P})$

Initialize for each $p_i \in \mathcal{P}$ a bit $d_i := 0$.

- Upon receiving message (RoundOK) from party p_i set $d_i := 1$. If for all $p_j \in \mathcal{H} : d_j = 1$, then reset $d_j := 0$ for all $p_j \in \mathcal{P}$. In any case, send (switch, i) to $\mathcal{A}$.[a]
- Upon receiving (RequestRound) from p_i, send d_i to p_i.

---

[a] The adversary is notified in each such call to allow attacks at any point in time.

Synchronous Protocols as $\{\mathcal{F}_{\text{CLOCK}}, \mathcal{F}_{\text{BD-SMT}}\}$*-Hybrid Protocols.* The code of every party is a sequence of "send," "receive," and "compute" operations, where each operation is annotated by the index of the round in which it is to be executed. In each round r, each party first receives its messages from round $r - 1$, then computes and sends its messages for round r. The functionalities $\mathcal{F}_{\text{CLOCK}}$ and $\mathcal{F}_{\text{BD-SMT}}$ are used in the straightforward manner: At the onset of the protocol execution, each p_i sets its local round index to 1; whenever p_i receives a message from some entity other than $\mathcal{F}_{\text{CLOCK}}$ (i.e., from $\mathcal{Z}$, $\mathcal{A}$, or some other functionality), if a (RoundOK) messages has not yet been sent for the current round (i.e., the computation for the current round is not finished) the party proceeds with the computation of the current round (the last action of each round is sending (RoundOK) to $\mathcal{F}_{\text{CLOCK}}$); otherwise (i.e., if (RoundOK) has been sent for the current round), the party sends a (RequestRound) message to $\mathcal{F}_{\text{CLOCK}}$, which replies with the indicator bit d_i. The party p_i uses this bit d_i to detect whether or not every party is done with the current round and proceeds to the next round or waits for further activations accordingly.

In an immediate application of the above described protocol template, the resulting protocol would not necessarily be secure. Indeed, some party might start sending its round $r + 1$ messages before some other party has even received its round r messages, potentially sacrificing security. (Some models in the literature, e.g. [34], allow such an ordering, while others, e.g. [25], don't.) The slackness can be overcome by introducing a "re-synchronization" round between every two rounds, where all parties send empty messages.

Perfect vs. Imperfect Clock Synchronization. $\mathcal{F}_{\text{CLOCK}}$ models that once a single party observes that a round is completed, every party will immediately (upon activation) agree with this view. As a "real world" assumption, this means that all parties perform the round switch at exactly the same time, which means that the parties' clocks must be in perfect synchronization. A "relaxed" functionality that models more realistic synchrony assumptions, i.e., imperfectly synchronized clocks, can be obtained by incorporating "delays" as for the bounded-delay channel $\mathcal{F}_{\text{BD-SMT}}$. The high-level idea for this "relaxed" clock $\mathcal{F}_{\text{CLOCK}}^{-}$ is the following: for each party p_i, $\mathcal{F}_{\text{CLOCK}}^{-}$ maintains a value t_i that corresponds to the number of queries needed by p_i before learning that the round has switched. The adversary is allowed to choose (at the beginning of each round), for each party p_i a delay t_i up to some upper bound $\delta > 0$. A detailed description of the functionality $\mathcal{F}_{\text{CLOCK}}^{-}$ can be found in the full version [27].

4.2 Defining Guaranteed Termination

In formalizing what it means to UC-securely compute some specification *with guaranteed termination*, we follow the principle described in Section 1. For simplicity, we restrict ourselves to non-reactive functionalities (secure function evaluation, or SFE), but our treatment can be easily extended to reactive multi-party computation. We refer to the full version [27] for details on this extension.

Let $f : (\{0,1\}^*)^n \times R \longrightarrow (\{0,1\}^*)^n$ denote an n-party (randomized) function, where the i-th component of f's input (or output) corresponds to the input (or output) of p_i, and the $(n+1)$-th input $r \in R$ corresponds to the randomness used by f. In simulation-based frameworks like [10], the secure evaluation of such a function f is generally captured by an ideal functionality parametrized by f. For instance, the functionality $\mathcal{F}^f_{\mathrm{SFE}}$ described in [10] works as follows: Any honest party can either submit input to $\mathcal{F}^f_{\mathrm{SFE}}$ or request output. Upon input x_i from some party p_i, $\mathcal{F}^f_{\mathrm{SFE}}$ records x_i and notifies $\mathcal{A}$. When some party requests its output, $\mathcal{F}^f_{\mathrm{SFE}}$ checks if all honest parties have submitted inputs; if so, $\mathcal{F}^f_{\mathrm{SFE}}$ evaluates f on the received inputs (missing inputs of corrupted parties are replaced by default values), stops accepting further inputs, and outputs to p_i its output of the evaluation. We refer to [10,27] for a more detailed description of $\mathcal{F}^f_{\mathrm{SFE}}$.

As described in Section 1, an ideal functionality for evaluating a function f captures *guaranteed termination* if the honest parties (or higher level protocols, which are all encompassed by the environment in the UC framework) are able to make the functionality proceed and (eventually) produce outputs, irrespective of the adversary's strategy. (Technically, we allow the respective parties to "poll" for their outputs.) The functionality $\mathcal{F}^f_{\mathrm{SFE}}$ from [10] has this "terminating" property; yet, for most choices of the function f, there exists no synchronous protocol realizing $\mathcal{F}^f_{\mathrm{SFE}}$ from any "reasonable" network functionality. More precisely, we say that a network-functionality $\mathcal{F}_{\mathrm{NET}}$ provides *separable rounds* if for any synchronous $\mathcal{F}_{\mathrm{NET}}$-hybrid protocol which communicates exclusively through $\mathcal{F}_{\mathrm{NET}}$, $\mathcal{F}_{\mathrm{NET}}$ activates the adversary at least once in every round.[4] The following lemma then shows that for any function f which requires more than one synchronous round to be evaluated, $\mathcal{F}^f_{\mathrm{SFE}}$ cannot be securely realized by any synchronous protocol in the $\mathcal{F}_{\mathrm{NET}}$-hybrid model. Note that this includes many interesting functionalities such as broadcast, coin-tossing, etc.

Lemma 4. *For any function f and any network functionality $\mathcal{F}_{\mathrm{NET}}$ with separable rounds, every $\mathcal{F}_{\mathrm{NET}}$-hybrid protocol π that securely realizes $\mathcal{F}^f_{\mathrm{SFE}}$ computes its output in a single round.*

Proof (sketch). Assume, towards a contradiction, that π is a two-round protocol securely computing $\mathcal{F}^f_{\mathrm{SFE}}$. Consider the environment $\mathcal{Z}$ that provides input to all parties and immediately requests the output from some honest party. As $\mathcal{F}_{\mathrm{NET}}$ provides separable rounds, after all inputs have been submitted, the adversary

---

[4] In [10], this is not necessarily the case. A priori, if some ITI sends a message to some other ITI, the receiving ITI will be activated next. Only if an ITI halts without sending a message, the "master scheduler"—the environment—will be activated.

will be activated at least twice before the protocols first generate outputs. This is not the case for the simulator in the ideal evaluation of $\mathcal{F}_{\text{SFE}}^{f}$. Hence, the dummy adversary cannot be simulated, which contradicts the security of π.   □

To obtain an SFE functionality that matches the intuition of guaranteed termination, we need to circumvent the above impossibility by making the functionality activate the simulator during the computation. We parametrize $\mathcal{F}_{\text{SFE}}$ with a function $Rnd(k)$ of the security parameter which corresponds to the number of rounds required for evaluating f; one can easily verify that for any (polynomial) round-function $Rnd(\cdot)$ the functionality $\mathcal{F}_{\text{SFE}}^{f,Rnd}$ will terminate (if there are sufficiently many queries at the honest parties' interfaces) independently of the simulator's strategy. In each round, the functionality gives the simulator $|\mathcal{P}| + 1$ activations which will allow him to simulate the activations that the parties need for exchanging their protocol messages and notifying the clock $\mathcal{F}_{\text{CLOCK}}$.

Functionality $\mathcal{F}_{\text{SFE}}^{f,Rnd}(\mathcal{P})$

$\mathcal{F}_{\text{SFE}}^{f,Rnd}$ proceeds as follows, given a function $f : (\{0,1\}^* \cup \{\bot\})^n \times R \to (\{0,1\}^*)^n$, a round function Rnd, and a player set $\mathcal{P}$. For each $p_i \in \mathcal{P}$, initialize variables x_i and y_i to a default value $\bot$ and a current delay $t_i := |\mathcal{P}| + 1$. Moreover, initialize a global round counter $\ell := 1$.

- Upon receiving input (input, v) from some party $p_i \in \mathcal{P}$, set $x_i := v$ and send a message (input, i) to the adversary.
- Upon receiving input (output) from some party $p_i \in \mathcal{P}$, if $p_i \in \mathcal{H}$ and x_i has not yet been set then ignore p_i's message, else do:
  - If $t_i > 1$, then set $t_i := t_i - 1$. If (now) $t_j = 1$ for all $p_j \in \mathcal{H}$, then set $\ell := \ell + 1$ and $t_j := |\mathcal{P}| + 1$ for all $p_j \in \mathcal{P}$. Send (activated, i) to the adversary.
  - Else, if $t_i = 1$ but $\ell < Rnd$, then send (early) to p_i.
  - Else,
    * if x_j has been set for all $p_j \in \mathcal{H}$, and $y_1, \ldots, y_n$ have not yet been set, then choose $r \xleftarrow{R} R$ and set $(y_1, \ldots, y_n) := f(x_1, \ldots, x_n, r)$.
    * Output y_i to p_i.

Definition 1 (Guaranteed Termination). *A protocol π UC-securely evaluates a function f with guaranteed termination if it UC-realizes a functionality $\mathcal{F}_{\text{SFE}}^{f,Rnd}$ for some round function $Rnd(\cdot)$.*

Remark 1 (Lower Bounds). The above formulation offers a language for making UC-statements about (lower bounds on) the round complexity of certain problems in the synchronous setting. In particular, the question whether $\mathcal{F}_{\text{SFE}}^{f,Rnd}$ can be realized by a synchronous protocol corresponds to the question: "Does there exist a synchronous protocol π which securely evaluates f in $Rnd(k)$ rounds?", where k is the security parameter. As an example, the statement: "A function f needs at least r rounds to be evaluated." is (informally) translated to "There exists no synchronous protocol which UC securely realizes the functionality $\mathcal{F}_{\text{SFE}}^{f,r'}$, where $r' < r$."

The following theorem allows us to translate known results on feasibility of secure computation, e.g., [8,16,22,35], into our setting of UC with termination. (This follows from the theorem and the fact that these protocols are secure with respect to an efficient straight-line black-box simulator.) The only modification is that the protocols start with a void synchronization round where no honest party sends or receives any message. For a synchronous protocol ρ, we denote by $\hat{\rho}$ the protocol which is obtained by extending ρ with such a start-synchronization round. The proof is based on ideas from [29] and is included in the full version [27].

Theorem 1. *Let f be a function and let ρ be a protocol that, according to the notion of [11], realizes f with computational (or statistical or perfect) security in the stand-alone model, with an efficient straight-line black-box simulator. Then $\hat{\rho}$ UC-realizes f with computational (or statistical or perfect) security and guaranteed termination in the $\{\mathcal{F}_{\text{CLOCK}}, \mathcal{F}_{\text{BD-SEC}}\}$-hybrid model with a static adversary.*

4.3   The Need for Both Synchronization and Bounded-Delay

In this section, we formalize the intuition that each one of the two "standard" synchrony assumptions, i.e., bounded-delay channels and synchronized clocks, is *alone* not sufficient for computation with guaranteed termination. We first show in Lemma 5 that bounded-delay channels (even with instant delivery) are, by themselves, not sufficient; subsequently, we show in Lemma 6 that (even perfectly) synchronized clocks are also not sufficient, even in combination with eventual-delivery channels (with no known bound on the delay).

Lemma 5. *There are functions f such that for any (efficient) round-function Rnd and any $\delta > 0$: $[\mathcal{F}_{\text{SFE}}^{f,Rnd}]^{\text{NT}}$ can be realized in the $\mathcal{F}_{\text{BD-SMT}}^{\delta}$-hybrid model, but $\mathcal{F}_{\text{SFE}}^{f,Rnd}$ cannot.*

Proof (idea). Consider the two-party function f which, on input a bit $x_1 \in \{0,1\}$ from party p_1 (and nothing from p_2), outputs x_1 to p_2 (and nothing to p_1). The functionality $\mathcal{F}_{\text{SFE}}^{f,Rnd}$ guarantees that an honest p_1 will be able to provide input, independently of the adversary's behavior. On the other hand, a corrupted p_1 will not keep p_2 from advancing (potentially with a default input for p_1).[5] However, in the real world, the behavior of the bounded-delay channel in the above two cases is identical.

On the other hand, the functionality $[\mathcal{F}_{\text{SFE}}^{f,Rnd}]^{\text{NT}}$ can be realized from $\mathcal{F}_{\text{BD-SMT}}$: p_1 simply has to send the input to p_2 via the $\mathcal{F}_{\text{BD-SMT}}$-channel. The simulator makes sure that the output in the ideal model is delivered to the p_2 only after $\mathcal{Z}$ acknowledges the delivery. A detailed proof can be found in [27].   □

---

[5] This capability of distinguishing "honest" from "dishonest" behavior is key in synchronous models: as honest parties are guaranteed that they can send their messages on time, dishonest parties will blow their cover by not adhering to the deadline.

In reality, synchronous clocks alone are not sufficient for synchronous computation if there is no *known* upper bound on the delay of the channels (even with guaranteed *eventual* delivery); this statement is formalized using the clock functionality $\mathcal{F}_{\mathrm{CLOCK}}$ and the channels $\mathcal{F}_{\mathrm{ED\text{-}SMT}}$ in the following lemma. The proof is similar to the proof of Lemma 1 and can be found in [27].

Lemma 6. *There are functions f such that for any (efficient) round-function Rnd: $[\mathcal{F}_{\mathrm{SFE}}^{f,Rnd}]^{\mathtt{NT}}$ can be realized in the $\{\mathcal{F}_{\mathrm{ED\text{-}SMT}}, \mathcal{F}_{\mathrm{CLOCK}}\}$-hybrid model, but $\mathcal{F}_{\mathrm{SFE}}^{f,Rnd}$ cannot.*

4.4   Atomicity of Send/Receive Operations and Rushing

Hirt and Zikas [24] pointed out that the standard formulation of a "rushing" adversary [11] in the synchronous setting puts a restriction on the order of the send/receive operations within a synchronous round. The modularity of our framework allows to pinpoint this restriction by showing that the rushing assumption corresponds to a "simultaneous multi-send" functionality which cannot even be realized using $\mathcal{F}_{\mathrm{CLOCK}}$ and $\mathcal{F}_{\mathrm{BD\text{-}SMT}}$.

Intuitively, a rushing adversary [11] cannot preempt a party while this party is sending its messages of some round. This is explicitly stated in [11], where the notion of "synchronous computation with *rushing*" is defined (cf. [11, Page 30]). In reality, it is arguable whether we can obtain the above guarantee by just assuming bilateral bounded-delay channels and synchronized clocks. Indeed, sending multiple messages is typically not an atomic operation, as the messages are buffered on the network interface of the computer and sent one-by-one. Hence, to achieve the simultaneity, one has to assume that the total time it takes for the sender to put all the messages on the network minus the *minimum* latency of the network is not sufficient for a party to become corrupted.

The "simultaneous multi-send" guarantee is captured in the following UC-functionality, which is referred to as the *simultaneous multi-send* channel, and denoted by $\mathcal{F}_{\mathrm{MS}}$. On a high level, $\mathcal{F}_{\mathrm{MS}}$ can be described as a channel allowing a sender p_i to send a vector of messages $(x_1, \ldots, x_n)$ to the respective receivers $p_1, \ldots, p_n$ as an atomic operation. The formal description of $\mathcal{F}_{\mathrm{MS}}$ is similar to $\mathcal{F}_{\mathrm{BD\text{-}SMT}}$ with the following modifications: First, instead of a single receiver, there is a set $\mathcal{P}$ of receivers, and instead of a single message, the sender inputs a vector of $|\mathcal{P}|$ messages, one for each party in $\mathcal{P}$. As soon as some party receives its message, the adversary cannot replace any of the remaining messages that correspond to honest receivers, not even by corrupting the sender. As in the case of bounded-delay channels, we denote by $\mathcal{F}_{\mathrm{MS\text{-}AUTH}}$ the multi-send channel which leaks the transmitted vector to the adversary. The following lemma states that the delayed relaxation of $\mathcal{F}_{\mathrm{MS\text{-}AUTH}}$ cannot be realized from $\mathcal{F}_{\mathrm{BD\text{-}SEC}}$ and $\mathcal{F}_{\mathrm{CLOCK}}$ when arbitrary many parties can be corrupted. This implies that $\mathcal{F}_{\mathrm{MS\text{-}AUTH}}$ can also not be realized from $\mathcal{F}_{\mathrm{BD\text{-}SEC}}$ and $\mathcal{F}_{\mathrm{CLOCK}}$.

Functionality $\mathcal{F}_{\mathrm{MS}}(\ell, i, \mathcal{P})$

- Upon receiving a vector of messages $\boldsymbol{m} = (m_1, \ldots, m_n)$ from p_i, record $\boldsymbol{m}$ and send a message $(\mathtt{sent}, \ell(\boldsymbol{m}))$ to the adversary.
- Upon receiving $(\mathtt{fetch})$ from $p_j \in \mathcal{P}$, output m_j to p_j ($m_j = \bot$ if $\boldsymbol{m}$ has not been recorded).
- *(restricted response to* $\mathtt{replace}$ *)* Upon receiving a $(\mathtt{replace}, \boldsymbol{m}')$ request from the adversary for replacing p_i's input (after issuing a request for corrupting p_i), if no (honest or corrupted) p_j received m_j *before* p_i got corrupted, then replace $\boldsymbol{m}$ by $\boldsymbol{m}'$.

Lemma 7. *Let $\mathcal{P}$ be a player set with $|\mathcal{P}| > 3$. Then there exists no protocol which UC-realizes $[\mathcal{F}_{\mathrm{MS\text{-}AUTH}}]^{\mathrm{NT}}$ in the $\{\mathcal{F}_{\mathrm{CLOCK}}, \mathcal{F}_{\mathrm{BD\text{-}AUTH}}\}$-hybrid model and tolerates a corrupted majority.*

Proof (sketch). Garay et al. [21] showed that if atomic multi-send (along with a setup for digital signatures) is assumed, then the broadcast protocol from Dolev and Strong [19] UC-realizes broadcast (without guaranteed termination) in the presence of an adaptive adversary who corrupts any number of parties. Hence, if there exist a protocol for realizing $[\mathcal{F}_{\mathrm{MS\text{-}AUTH}}]^{\mathrm{NT}}$ in the synchronous model, i.e., in the $\{\mathcal{F}_{\mathrm{CLOCK}}, \mathcal{F}_{\mathrm{BD\text{-}AUTH}}\}$-hybrid world, with corrupted majority and adaptive adversary, then one could also realize broadcast in this model, contradicting the impossibility result from [24]. $\qquad\square$

The above lemma implies that the traditional notion of "synchronous computation with *rushing*" cannot be, in general, achieved in the UC model unless some non-trivial property is assumed on the communication channel. Yet, $[\mathcal{F}_{\mathrm{MS\text{-}AUTH}}]^{\mathrm{NT}}$ *can* be UC-realized from $\{[\mathcal{F}_{\mathrm{BD\text{-}AUTH}}]^{\mathrm{NT}}, [\mathcal{F}_{\mathrm{COM}}]^{\mathrm{NT}}\}$, where $\mathcal{F}_{\mathrm{COM}}$ denotes the standard UC-commitment functionality [13]. The idea is the following: In order to simultaneously multi-send a vector $(x_1, \ldots, x_n)$ to the parties $p_1, \ldots, p_n$, the sender sends an independent commitment on x_i to every recipient p_i, who acknowledges the receipt (using the channel $[\mathcal{F}_{\mathrm{BD\text{-}SEC}}]^{\mathrm{NT}}$). After receiving all such acknowledgments, the sender, in a second round, opens all commitments. The functionality $\mathcal{F}_{\mathrm{COM}}$ ensures that the adversary (unless the sender is corrupted in the first round) learns the committed messages x_i only after every party has received the respective commitment; but, from that point on, $\mathcal{A}$ can no longer change the committed message. For completeness we state the above in the following lemma.

Lemma 8. *There is a synchronous $\{[\mathcal{F}_{\mathrm{BD\text{-}AUTH}}]^{\mathrm{NT}}, [\mathcal{F}_{\mathrm{COM}}]^{\mathrm{NT}}\}$-hybrid protocol that UC-realizes $[\mathcal{F}_{\mathrm{MS\text{-}AUTH}}]^{\mathrm{NT}}$.*

Using Lemmas 7 and 8, and the fact that the delayed relaxation of any $\mathcal{F}$ can be realized in the $\mathcal{F}$-hybrid model, we can extend the result of [13] on impossibility of UC commitments to our synchronous setting.

Corollary 1. *There exists no protocol which UC-realizes the commitment functionality $\mathcal{F}_{\mathrm{COM}}$ in the $\{\mathcal{F}_{\mathrm{BD\text{-}AUTH}}, \mathcal{F}_{\mathrm{CLOCK}}\}$-hybrid model.*

5   Existing Synchronous Models as Special Cases

In this section, we revisit existing models for synchronous computation. We show that the $\mathcal{F}_{\text{SYN}}$-hybrid model as specified in [10] and the Timing Model from [26] are sufficient only for non-terminating computation (which can be achieved even in a fully asynchronous environment). We also show that the models of [34] and [25] can be expressed as special cases in our model. Many details are omitted; we refer to the full version of this paper [27] for a complete treatment.

5.1   The $\mathcal{F}_{\text{SYN}}$-Hybrid Model

In [10], a model for synchronous computation is specified by a *synchronous network* functionality $\mathcal{F}_{\text{SYN}}$. On a high-level, $\mathcal{F}_{\text{SYN}}$ corresponds to an authenticated network with storage, which proceeds in a round-based fashion; in each round r, every party associated to $\mathcal{F}_{\text{SYN}}$ inputs a vector of messages, where it is guaranteed that (1) the adversary cannot change the message sent by an honest party without corrupting this party, and (2) the round index is only increased after every honest party as well as the adversary have submitted their messages for that round. Furthermore, $\mathcal{F}_{\text{SYN}}$ allows the parties to query the current value of r along with the messages of that round r.

$\mathcal{F}_{\text{SYN}}$ requires the adversary to explicitly initiate the round switch; this allows the adversary to stall the protocol execution (by not switching rounds). Hence, $\mathcal{F}_{\text{SYN}}$ cannot be used for evaluating a non-trivial[6] function f with guaranteed termination: because we require termination, for every protocol which securely realizes $\mathcal{F}_{\text{SFE}}$ and for every adversary, the environment $\mathcal{Z}$ which gives inputs to all honest parties and issues sufficiently many fetch requests has to be able to make π generate its output from the evaluation. This must, in particular, hold when the adversary never commands $\mathcal{F}_{\text{SYN}}$ to switch rounds, which leads to a contradiction.

Lemma 9. *For every non-trivial n-party function f and for every round function Rnd there exists no $\mathcal{F}_{\text{SYN}}$-hybrid protocol which securely realizes $\mathcal{F}_{\text{SFE}}^{f,Rnd}$ with guaranteed termination.*

The only advantage that $\mathcal{F}_{\text{SYN}}$ offers on top of what can be achieved from (asynchronous) bounded-delay channels is that $\mathcal{F}_{\text{SYN}}$ defines a point in the computation (chosen by $\mathcal{A}$) in which the round index advances for all parties *simultaneously*. More precisely, denote by $\mathcal{F}_{\text{SYN}}^{-}$ the functionality that behaves as $\mathcal{F}_{\text{SYN}}$, except for a small modification upon receiving the (Advance-Round)-message: $\mathcal{F}_{\text{SYN}}^{-}$ advances the round, but, for each party, allows the adversary to further delay the output (initially, the (receive)-requests of p_i are still answered with the previous round messages). This is only a mild relaxation of the functionality: the adversary can delay the delivery of the new messages, but the important

---

[6] Recall that a non-trivial function is one that cannot be computed locally (cf. [28]).

property that the messages are "committed" by the time of the round switch is preserved.[7]

The functionality $\mathcal{F}_{\text{SYN}}^-$ can be realized by a protocol using asynchronous channels with eventual delivery. This protocol follows the ideas of [2,26]: In each round r, each party p_i sends a message to all other parties. After receiving messages from all p_j, p_i sends an acknowledgment to all p_j. Once all such acknowledgments have been received, p_i prepares the messages received in that round for local output (upon request) and starts the next round (as soon as messages have been provided as local input). This proves the following lemma.

Lemma 10. *There exist a protocol that UC-realizes the functionality $\mathcal{F}_{\text{SYN}}^-$ in the $\mathcal{F}_{\text{BD-SMT}}$-hybrid model.*

5.2   The Timing Model

The "Timing model" [23,26] integrates a notion of time into the protocol execution by extending the model of computation. Each party, in addition to its communication and computation tapes, has a *clock tape* that is writable for the adversary in a monotone and "bounded-drift"-preserving manner: The adversary can only increase the value of the clocks, and, for any two parties, the distance ϵ of their clocks' speed (drift) at any point in time is bounded by a known constant. The value of a party's clock-tape defines the local time of this party. Depending on this time, protocols delay sending messages or time-out if a message has not arrived as expected. We formalize this modeling of time in UC in the following straightforward manner: We introduce a functionality $\mathcal{F}_{\text{TIME}}$ that maintains a clock value for each party and allows the adversary to advance this clock in the same monotone and "bounded-drift"-preserving way. Instead of reading the local clock tape, $\mathcal{F}_{\text{TIME}}$-hybrid protocols obtain their local time value by querying $\mathcal{F}_{\text{TIME}}$.

Lemma 11 shows that $\mathcal{F}_{\text{TIME}}$ can be realized from fully asynchronous authenticated communication. The idea of the proof is the following: The protocol τ that realizes the functionality $\mathcal{F}_{\text{TIME}}$ from pairwise authenticated channels maintains, for each party p_i, a local integer variable t_i that corresponds to p_i's local time. Using the authenticated network, the parties ensure that the local time values increase with bounded drift. Together, Lemmas 11 and 12 demonstrate that "timed" protocols cannot UC-realize more functionalities than non-"timed" protocols, which is consistent with [26, Theorem 2] and implies that the Timing Model does not allow for computation with guaranteed termination.

Lemma 11. *Let $\mathcal{P}$ be a player set and $\epsilon \geq 1$. The functionality $\mathcal{F}_{\text{TIME}}(\mathcal{P}, \epsilon)$ can be UC-realized from pairwise authenticated channels $\mathcal{F}_{\text{AUTH}}$.*

In contrast to $\mathcal{F}_{\text{SYN}}$, which "lives" in the UC framework, security statements in the Timing Model cannot be automatically transferred to the UC setting. Indeed, there is a "type-mismatch" between functionalities/protocols in the two

---

[7] The delay can only be detected if the parties have access to a channel which delivers faster than the specified delay. The parties overcome this slackness by issuing (`receive`)-queries until they obtain the desired output.

frameworks, which we resolve by the following idea inspired by [3,30,32]: A functionality $\mathcal{F}$ in the timing model is compiled to a functionality in UC which behaves exactly as $\mathcal{F}$ but ensures that the interfaces are compatible with the UC model of computation. On a high-level, the functionality compiler $T_T(\cdot)$ works as follows: $T_T(\mathcal{F})$ behaves as $\mathcal{F}$, but on any input from an honest party it notifies the adversary (without leaking the contents). Whenever $\mathcal{F}$ outputs a value y to some party, $T_T(\mathcal{F})$ issues a (private) delayed output y instead.

Lemma 12 then shows that any security statement about a functionality $\mathcal{F}$ in the Timing Model can be translated into a statement about $T_T(\mathcal{F})$ in the $\{\mathcal{F}_{\text{TIME}}, \mathcal{F}_{\text{AUTH}}\}$-hybrid model (in UC). The translation is both constructive and uniform, i.e., we describe a protocol compiler $C_T(\cdot)$ that translates a protocol in the Timing Model into a corresponding one in the $\{\mathcal{F}_{\text{TIME}}, \mathcal{F}_{\text{AUTH}}\}$-hybrid model.

Lemma 12. *For an arbitrary functionality $\mathcal{F}$ and a protocol π in the Timing Model, π securely realizes $\mathcal{F}$ (in the Timing Model) if and only if the compiled protocol $C_T(\pi)$ UC-realizes $T_T(\mathcal{F})$ in the $\{\mathcal{F}_{\text{TIME}}, \mathcal{F}_{\text{AUTH}}\}$-hybrid model in the presence of a static adversary.*

5.3   Models with Explicit Round-Structure

Nielsen's Framework [34]. The framework described in [34] is an adaptation of the asynchronous framework of [12] to authenticated synchronous networks. While the general structure of the security definition is adopted, the definition of protocols and their executions differs considerably. For instance, the "subroutine" composition of two protocols is defined in a "lock-step" way: the round switches occur at the same time. Similarly to our bounded-delay channels, messages in transfer can be replaced if the sender becomes corrupted. Lemma 13 allows to translate, along the lines of Section 5.2, any security statement in the model of [34] into a security statement about a synchronous protocol in the $\{\mathcal{F}_{\text{CLOCK}}, \mathcal{F}_{\text{BD-AUTH}}\}$-hybrid model. As in the previous section, the translation is done by a functionality compiler $T_N(\cdot)$ that resolves the type-mismatch between the functionalities in UC and in [34], and a corresponding protocol compiler $C_N(\cdot)$. We emphasize that the converse statement of Lemma 13 does *not* hold, i.e., there are UC statements about synchronous protocols that cannot be modeled in the [34] framework. For instance, our synchronous UC model allows protocols to use further functionalities that run mutually asynchronously with the synchronous network, which cannot be modeled in [34].

Lemma 13. *For an arbitrary functionality $\mathcal{F}$ and a protocol π in [34], π securely realizes $\mathcal{F}$ (in [34]) if and only if the compiled protocol $C_N(\pi)$ UC-realizes $T_N(\mathcal{F})$ in the $\{\mathcal{F}_{\text{CLOCK}}, \mathcal{F}_{\text{BD-AUTH}}\}$-hybrid model.*

Hofheinz and Müller-Quade's Framework [25]. The framework of [25] also models authenticated synchronous networks based on the framework of [12], but the rules of the protocol execution differ considerably: The computation proceeds in rounds, and each round is split into three phases. In each phase, only a subset of the involved ITIs are activated, and the order of the activations follows a specific scheme. The adversary has a relaxed *rushing* property: while being the last to specify the messages for a round, he cannot corrupt parties within a round. This corresponds to a network with guarantees that are stronger than simultaneous multi-send: once the first message of an honest party is provided to the adversary, all messages of honest parties are guaranteed to be delivered correctly.[8] We model this relaxed rushing property in UC by the functionality $\mathcal{F}_{MS+}$ (cf. [27]), which is a modified version of $\mathcal{F}_{MS}$ and exactly captures this guarantee. As before, we translate the security statements of [25] to our model (where $\mathcal{F}_{MS+}$ is used instead of $\mathcal{F}_{AUTH}$) through a pair of compilers $(T_H(\cdot), C_H(\cdot))$.

Lemma 14. *For an arbitrary functionality $\mathcal{F}$ and a protocol π in [25], π securely realizes $\mathcal{F}$ (in [25]) if and only if the compiled protocol $C_H(\pi)$ UC-realizes $T_H(\mathcal{F})$ in the $\{\mathcal{F}_{CLOCK}, \mathcal{F}_{MS+}\}$-hybrid model.*

6 Conclusion

We described a modular security model for synchronous computation within the (otherwise inherently asynchronous) UC framework by specifying the real-world synchrony assumptions of bounded-delay channels and loosely synchronized clocks as functionalities. The design principle that underlies these functionalities allows us to treat guaranteed termination; previous approaches for synchronous computation within UC either required fundamental modifications of the framework (which also required re-proving fundamental statements) or did not allow to make such statements altogether. Given this model, we revisited basic results from the literature on synchronous protocols, formalizing and proving them within the UC framework. Finally, we showed that previous specialized frameworks can be cast as special cases of our model by introducing network functionalities that provide the guarantees formalized in those models.

Acknowledgments. We thank Ran Canetti for interesting discussions and comments on the comparison of our model with the $\mathcal{F}_{SYN}$-hybrid formulation. The first author was supported by NSF awards #0447075, #1111599, and #1223623. The second and third authors were supported by the Swiss National Science Foundation (SNF), project no. 200020-132794. The fourth author was partially supported by a fellowship from the SNF, project no. PBEZP2-134445.

References

1. Asharov, G., Lindell, Y., Rabin, T.: Perfectly-Secure Multiplication for Any $t < n/3$. In: Rogaway, P. (ed.) CRYPTO 2011. LNCS, vol. 6841, pp. 240–258. Springer, Heidelberg (2011)
2. Awerbuch, B.: Complexity of Network Synchronization. Journal of the ACM 32, 804–823 (1985)

---

[8] In the context of [25], this is an advantage as it strengthens the impossibility result.

3. Backes, M.: Unifying Simulatability Definitions in Cryptographic Systems under Different Timing Assumptions. In: Amadio, R.M., Lugiez, D. (eds.) CONCUR 2003. LNCS, vol. 2761, pp. 350–365. Springer, Heidelberg (2003)

4. Backes, M., Hofheinz, D., Müller-Quade, J., Unruh, D.: On Fairness in Simulatability-based Cryptographic Systems. In: Proceedings of FMSE, pp. 13–22. ACM (2005)

5. Backes, M., Pfitzmann, B., Steiner, M., Waidner, M.: Polynomial Fairness and Liveness. In: Proceedings of the 15th Annual IEEE Computer Security Foundations Workshop, pp. 160–174. IEEE (2002)

6. Backes, M., Pfitzmann, B., Waidner, M.: The Reactive Simulatability (RSIM) Framework for Asynchronous Systems. Information and Computation 205, 1685–1720 (2007)

7. Ben-Or, M., Canetti, R., Goldreich, O.: Asynchronous Secure Computation. In: Proceedings of the 25th Annual ACM Symposium on Theory of Computing, pp. 52–61. ACM (1993)

8. Ben-Or, M., Goldwasser, S., Widgerson, A.: Completeness Theorems for Non-Cryptographic Fault-Tolerant Distributed Computation. In: Proceedings of the 20th Annual ACM Symposium on Theory of Computing, pp. 1–10. ACM (1988)

9. Canetti, R.: Studies in Secure Multiparty Computation and Applications. PhD thesis, The Weizmann Institute of Science (1996)

10. Canetti, R.: Universally Composable Security: A New Paradigm for Cryptographic Protocols. In: Cryptology ePrint Archive, Report 2000/067 (2005)

11. Canetti, R.: Security and Composition of Multiparty Cryptographic Protocols. Journal of Cryptology 13, 143–202 (2000)

12. Canetti, R.: Universally Composable Security: A New Paradigm for Cryptographic Protocols. In: Proceedings of the 42nd Annual IEEE Symposium on Foundations of Computer Science, pp. 136–145. IEEE (2001)

13. Canetti, R., Fischlin, M.: Universally Composable Commitments. In: Kilian, J. (ed.) CRYPTO 2001. LNCS, vol. 2139, pp. 19–40. Springer, Heidelberg (2001)

14. Canetti, R., Krawczyk, H.: Universally Composable Notions of Key Exchange and Secure Channels. In: Knudsen, L.R. (ed.) EUROCRYPT 2002. LNCS, vol. 2332, pp. 337–351. Springer, Heidelberg (2002)

15. Canetti, R., Lindell, Y., Ostrovsky, R., Sahai, A.: Universally Composable Two-Party and Multi-Party Secure Computation. In: Proceedings of the 34th Annual ACM Symposium on Theory of Computing, pp. 494–503. ACM (2002)

16. Chaum, D., Crépeau, C., Damgård, I.: Multiparty Unconditionally Secure Protocols. In: Proceedings of the 20th Annual ACM Symposium on Theory of Computing, pp. 11–19. ACM (1988)

17. Chor, B., Moscovici, L.: Solvability in Asynchronous Environments. In: Proceedings of the 30th Annual IEEE Symposium on Foundations of Computer Science, pp. 422–427. IEEE (1989)

18. Dodis, Y., Micali, S.: Parallel Reducibility for Information-Theoretically Secure Computation. In: Bellare, M. (ed.) CRYPTO 2000. LNCS, vol. 1880, pp. 74–92. Springer, Heidelberg (2000)

19. Dolev, D., Strong, H.R.: Polynomial Algorithms for Multiple Processor Agreement. In: Proceedings of the 14th Annual ACM Symposium on Theory of Computing, pp. 401–407. ACM (1982)

20. Dwork, C., Naor, M., Sahai, A.: Concurrent Zero-Knowledge. In: Proceedings of the 30th Annual ACM Symposium on Theory of Computing, pp. 409–418. ACM (1998)

21. Garay, J.A., Katz, J., Kumersan, R., Zhou, H.-S.: Adaptively Secure Broadcast, Revisited. In: Proceedings of the 30th Annual ACM Symposium on Principles of Distributed Computing, pp. 179–186. ACM (2011)
22. Goldreich, O., Micali, S., Widgerson, A.: How to Play any Mental Game—A Completeness Theorem for Protocols with Honest Majority. In: Proceedings of the 19th Annual ACM Symposium on Theory of Computing, pp. 218–229. ACM (1987)
23. Goldreich, O.: Concurrent Zero-Knowledge with Timing, Revisited. In: Proceedings of the 34th Annual ACM Symposium on Theory of Computing, pp. 332–340. ACM (2002)
24. Hirt, M., Zikas, V.: Adaptively Secure Broadcast. In: Gilbert, H. (ed.) EURO-CRYPT 2010. LNCS, vol. 6110, pp. 466–485. Springer, Heidelberg (2010)
25. Hofheinz, D., Müller-Quade, J.: A Synchronous Model for Multi-Party Computation and the Incompleteness of Oblivious Transfer. In: Proceedings of Foundations of Computer Security — FCS 2004, pp. 117–130 (2004)
26. Kalai, Y.T., Lindell, Y., Prabhakaran, M.: Concurrent General Composition of Secure Protocols in the Timing Model. In: Proceedings of the 37th Annual ACM Symposium on Theory of Computing, pp. 644–653. ACM (2005)
27. Katz, J., Maurer, U., Tackmann, B., Zikas, V.: Universally Composable Synchronous Computation. In: Cryptology ePrint Archive, Report 2011/310 (2012)
28. Künzler, R., Müller-Quade, J., Raub, D.: Secure Computability of Functions in the IT Setting with Dishonest Majority and Applications to Long-Term Security. In: Reingold, O. (ed.) TCC 2009. LNCS, vol. 5444, pp. 238–255. Springer, Heidelberg (2009)
29. Kushilevitz, E., Lindell, Y., Rabin, T.: Information-theoretically Secure Protocols and Security under Composition. In: Proceedings of the 38th Annual ACM Symposium on Theory of Computing, pp. 109–118. ACM (2006)
30. Maji, H., Prabhakaran, M., Rosulek, M.: Cryptographic Complexity Classes and Computational Intractability Assumptions. In: Innovations in Computer Science. Tsinghua University Press (2010)
31. Maurer, U.: Constructive Cryptography – A New Paradigm for Security Definitions and Proofs. In: Mödersheim, S., Palamidessi, C. (eds.) TOSCA 2011. LNCS, vol. 6993, pp. 33–56. Springer, Heidelberg (2012)
32. Maurer, U., Renner, R.: Abstract Cryptography. In: Innovations in Computer Science. Tsinghua University Press (2011)
33. Maurer, U., Tackmann, B.: Synchrony Amplification. In: International Symposium on Information Theory Proceedings, pp. 1583–1587. IEEE (2012)
34. Nielsen, J.B.: On Protocol Security in the Cryptographic Model. PhD thesis, University of Aarhus (2003)
35. Rabin, T., Ben-Or, M.: Verifiable Secret Sharing and Multiparty Protocols with Honest Majority. In: Proceedings of the 21st Annual ACM Symposium on Theory of Computing, pp. 73–85. ACM (1989)

Multi-Client Non-interactive Verifiable Computation

Seung Geol Choi[1,*], Jonathan Katz[2],
Ranjit Kumaresan[3,*], and Carlos Cid[4]

[1] Department of Computer Science, Columbia University
sgchoi@cs.columbia.edu
[2] Department of Computer Science, University of Maryland
jkatz@cs.umd.edu
[3] Department of Computer Science, Technion
ranjit@cs.technion.ac.il
[4] Royal Holloway, University of London
carlos.cid@rhul.ac.uk

Abstract. Gennaro et al. (Crypto 2010) introduced the notion of *non-interactive verifiable computation*, which allows a computationally weak client to outsource the computation of a function f on a series of inputs $x^{(1)}, \ldots$ to a more powerful but untrusted server. Following a pre-processing phase (that is carried out only once), the client sends some representation of its current input $x^{(i)}$ to the server; the server returns an answer that allows the client to recover the correct result $f(x^{(i)})$, accompanied by a proof of correctness that ensures the client does not accept an incorrect result. The crucial property is that the work done by the client in preparing its input and verifying the server's proof is less than the time required for the client to compute f on its own.

We extend this notion to the *multi-client* setting, where n computationally weak clients wish to outsource to an untrusted server the computation of a function f over a series of *joint* inputs $(x_1^{(1)}, \ldots, x_n^{(1)}), \ldots$ without interacting with each other. We present a construction for this setting by combining the scheme of Gennaro et al. with a primitive called proxy oblivious transfer.

1 Introduction

There are many instances in which it is desirable to outsource computation from a relatively weak computational device (a *client*) to a more powerful entity or collection of entities (*servers*). Notable examples include:

- Distributed-computing projects (e.g., SETI@Home or distributed.net), in which idle processing time on thousands of computers is harnessed to solve a computational problem.

---

* Portions of this work were done while at the University of Maryland.

A. Sahai (Ed.): TCC 2013, LNCS 7785, pp. 499–518, 2013.

- Cloud computing, where individuals or businesses can purchase computing power as a service when it is needed to solve some difficult task.
- Outsourcing computationally intensive operations from weak mobile devices (e.g., smartphones, sensors) to a back-end server or some other third party.

In each of the above scenarios, there may be an incentive for the server to try to cheat and return an incorrect result to the client. This may be related to the nature of the computation being performed — e.g., if the server wants to convince the client of a particular result because it will have beneficial consequences for the server — or may simply be due to the server's desire to minimize the use of its own computational resources. Errors can also occur due to faulty algorithm implementation or system failures. In all these cases, the client needs some guarantee that the answer returned from the server is correct.

This problem of *verifiable (outsourced) computation* has attracted many researchers, and various protocols have been proposed (see Section 1.3). Recently, Gennaro et al. [13] formalized the problem of *non-interactive* verifiable computation in which there is only one round of interaction between the client and the server each time a computation is performed. Specifically, fix some function f that the client wants to compute. Following a pre-processing phase (that is carried out only once), the client can then repeatedly request the server to compute f on inputs $x^{(1)}, \ldots$ of its choice via the following steps:

Input Preparation: In time period i, the client processes its current input $x^{(i)}$ to obtain some representation of this input, which it sends to the server.
Output Computation: The server computes a response that encodes the correct answer $f(x^{(i)})$ along with a proof that it was computed correctly.
Output Verification: The client recovers $f(x^{(i)})$ from the response provided by the server, and verifies the proof that this result is correct.

The above is only interesting if the input-preparation and output-verification stages require less time (in total) than the time required for the client to compute f by itself. (The time required for pre-processing is ignored, as it is assumed to be amortized over several evaluations of f.) Less crucial, but still important, is that the time required for the output-computation phase should not be much larger than the time required to compute f (otherwise the cost to the server may be too burdensome). Gennaro et al. construct a non-interactive verifiable-computation scheme based on Yao's garbled-circuit protocol [25] and any fully homomorphic encryption scheme.

1.1   Our Results

The scheme presented in [13] is inherently *single-client*. There are, however, scenarios in which it would be desirable to extend this functionality to the *multi-client* setting, e.g., networks made up of several resource-constrained nodes (sensors) that collectively gather data to be used jointly as input to some computation. In this work we initiate consideration of this setting. We assume n

(semi-honest) clients wish to outsource the computation of some function f over a series of *joint* inputs $(x_1^{(1)}, \ldots, x_n^{(1)}), \ldots$ to an untrusted server.

A trivial solution to the problem would be for the last $n-1$ clients to send their inputs to the first client, who can then run a single-client verifiable-computation scheme and forward the result (assuming verification succeeded) to the other clients. This suffers from several drawbacks:

- This solution requires the clients to communicate *with each other*. There may be scenarios (e.g., sensors spread across a large geographical region) where clients can all communicate with a central server but are unable to communicate directly with each other.[1]
- This solution achieves no *privacy* since the first client sees the inputs of all the other clients.

Addressing the first drawback, we consider only *non-interactive* protocols in which each client communicates only with the server. A definition of soundness in the non-interactive setting is subtle, since without some additional assumptions (1) there is no way for one client to distinguish another legitimate client from a cheating server who tries to provide its own input x_i, and (2) there is nothing that "binds" the input of one client at one time period to the input of another client at that same time period (and thus the server could potentially "mix-and-match" the first-period input of the first client with the second-period input of the second client). We address these issues by assuming that (1) there is a public-key infrastructure (PKI), such that all clients have public keys known to each other, and (2) all clients maintain a counter indicating how many times they have interacted with the server (or, equivalently, there is some global notion of time). These assumptions are reasonable and (essentially) necessary to prevent the difficulties mentioned above.

Addressing the second drawback, we also define a notion of privacy of the clients' input from each other that we require any solution to satisfy. This is in addition to privacy of the clients' inputs from the server, as in [13].

In addition to defining the model, we also show a construction of a protocol for non-interactive, multi-client verifiable computation. We give an overview of our construction in the following section.

1.2   Overview of Our Scheme

Our construction is a generalization of the single-client solution by Gennaro et al., so we begin with a brief description of their scheme.

Single-Client Verifiable Computation. We first describe the basic idea. Let Alice be a client who wishes to outsource computation of a function f to a server. In the pre-processing phase, Alice creates a garbled circuit that corresponds to f,

---

[1] Note that having the clients communicate with each other by routing all their messages via the server (using end-to-end authenticated encryption, say) would require additional rounds of interaction.

and sends it to the server. Later, in the online phase, Alice computes input-wire keys for the garbled circuit that correspond to her actual input x, and sends these keys to the server. The server evaluates the garbled circuit using the input-wire keys provided by Alice to obtain the output keys of the garbled circuit; if the server behaves honestly, these output keys correspond to the correct output $f(x)$. The server returns these output keys to Alice, who then checks if the key received from the server on each output wire is a legitimate output key (i.e., one of the two possibilities) for that wire. If so, then Alice determines the actual output based on the keys received from the server. Loosely speaking, verifiability of this scheme follows from the fact that evaluation of a garbled circuit on input-wire keys corresponding to an input x does not reveal information about any output-wire keys other than those that correspond to $f(x)$. (See also [3].)

The scheme described above works only for a single evaluation of f. To accommodate multiple evaluations of f, Gennaro et al. propose the use of fully homomorphic encryption (FHE) in the following way. The pre-processing step is the same as before. However, in the online phase, Alice generates a fresh public/private key pair for an FHE scheme each time she wants the server to evaluate f. She then encrypts the input-wire keys that correspond to her input using this public key, and sends these encryptions (along with the public key) to the server. Using the homomorphic properties of the encryption scheme, the server now runs the previous scheme to obtain *encryptions* of the output-wire keys corresponding to the correct output. The server returns the resulting ciphertexts to Alice, who decrypts them and then verifies the result as before. Security of this scheme follows from the soundness of the one-time scheme described earlier and semantic security of the FHE scheme.

Multi-client Verifiable Computation. In the rest of the overview, we discuss how to adapt the solution of Gennaro et al. to the multi-client setting. In our discussion, we consider the case where only the first client gets output. (The more general case is handled by simply having the clients run several executions of the scheme in parallel, with each client playing the role of the first in one execution.) We discuss the case of two clients here for simplicity, but our solution extends naturally to the general case.

Suppose two clients Alice and Bob want to outsource a computation to a server. Applying a similar idea as before, say Alice creates a garbled circuit which it sends to the server in the pre-processing phase. During the online phase, Alice will be able to compute and send to the server input-wire keys that correspond to her input. However, it is unclear how the server can obtain the input-wire keys corresponding to Bob's input. Recall that we are interested in a *non-interactive* solution and Alice does not know the input of Bob; moreover, Alice cannot send two input-wire keys for any wire to the server or else soundness is violated.

We overcome this difficulty using a gadget called *proxy oblivious transfer* (proxy OT) [22]. In proxy OT, there is a *sender* that holds inputs (a_0, a_1), a *chooser* that holds input bit b, and a *proxy* that, at the end of the protocol, learns a_b and nothing else. Since we are ultimately interested in a non-interactive solution for multi-client verifiable computation, we will be interested only in non-interactive proxy-OT schemes. We show a construction of a non-interactive proxy OT from any non-interactive key-exchange protocol.

Coming back to the multi-client verifiable-computation scheme described earlier, we can use proxy OT to enable the server to learn the appropriate input-wire label for each wire that corresponds to Bob's input. In more detail, let $(\widetilde{w}_0, \widetilde{w}_1)$ denote the keys for input-wire w in the garbled circuit that was created by Alice in the pre-processing phase. Alice acts as the sender with inputs $(\widetilde{w}_0, \widetilde{w}_1)$ in a proxy OT protocol, and Bob acts as the chooser with his actual input bit b for that wire. The server is the proxy, and obtains output $\widetilde{w}_b$. The server learns nothing about $\widetilde{w}_{1-b}$ and so, informally, soundness is preserved. The rest of the protocol proceeds in the same way as the single-client protocol. The extension to accommodate multiple evaluations of f is done using fully homomorphic encryption as described earlier.

A Generic Approach to Multi-client Outsourcing. It is not hard to see that our techniques can be applied to any single-client, non-interactive, verifiable-computation scheme that is *projective* in the following (informal) sense: the input-preparation stage generates a vector of pairs $(w_{1,0}, w_{1,1}), \ldots, (w_{\ell,0}, w_{\ell,1})$, and the client sends $w_{1,x_1}, \ldots, w_{\ell,x_\ell}$ to the server.

1.3   Related Work

The problems of outsourcing and verifiable computation have been extensively studied. Works such as [9,16,17] have focused on outsourcing expensive cryptographic operations (e.g., modular exponentiations, one-way function inversion) to semi-trusted devices. Verifiable computation has been the focus of a long line of research starting from works on interactive proofs [2,15], and efficient argument systems [19,21,20]. In particular, Micali's work [21] gives a solution for non-interactive verifiable computation in the random oracle model. Goldwasser, Kalai, and Rothblum [14] give an interactive protocol to verify certain computations efficiently; their solution can be made non-interactive for a restricted class of functions.

Gennaro et al. [13] formally defined the notion of non-interactive verifiable computation for general functions and gave a construction achieving this notion. Subsequent schemes for non-interactive verifiable computation of general functions include [10,1]. Other works have focused on improving the efficiency of schemes for verifiable computation of specific functions [5,24,12,23], or in slightly different models [7,8,11,6]. To the best of our knowledge, our work is the first (in any setting) to consider verifiable computation for the case where multiple parties provide input. Kamara et al. [18] discuss the case of multi-client verifiable computation in the context of work on server-aided multi-party computation, but leave finding a solution as an open problem.

2   Multi-client Verifiable Computation

We start by introducing the notion of multi-client, non-interactive, verifiable computation ($\mathcal{MVC}$). Let κ denote the security parameter. Suppose there are

n clients that wish to evaluate a function f multiple times. Without loss of generality, we assume that each client P_j contributes an ℓ-bit input and that the output length of f is ℓ, that is, we have $f : \{0,1\}^{n\ell} \rightarrow \{0,1\}^\ell$. We abuse notation and let f also denote the representation of the function within some computational model (e.g., as a boolean circuit). Let $x_j^{(i)}$ denote client P_j's input in the ith execution. For simplicity, we assume that only one client (the first) learns the output; however, we can provide all clients with output by simply running an $\mathcal{MVC}$ scheme in parallel n times (at the cost of increasing the clients' computation by at most a factor of n).

Syntax. An n-party $\mathcal{MVC}$ scheme consists of the following algorithms:

- $(pk_j, sk_j) \leftarrow \mathsf{KeyGen}(1^\kappa, j)$. Each client P_j will run this *key generation algorithm* KeyGen and obtain a public/private key pair (pk_j, sk_j). Let $\overrightarrow{pk}$ denote the vector $(pk_1, \ldots, pk_n)$ of the public keys of all the clients.
- $(\phi, \xi) \leftarrow \mathsf{EnFunc}(1^\kappa, f)$. The client P_1 that is supposed to receive the output will run this *function-encoding algorithm* EnFunc with a representation of the target function f. The algorithm outputs an encoded function ϕ and the corresponding decoding secret ξ. The encoded function will be sent to the server. The decoding secret is kept private by the client.
- $(\chi_1^{(i)}, \tau^{(i)}) \leftarrow \mathsf{EnInput}_1(i, \overrightarrow{pk}, sk_1, \xi, x_1^{(i)})$. When outsourcing the ith computation to the server, the first client P_1 will run this *input-encoding algorithm* $\mathsf{EnInput}_1$ with time period i, the public keys $\overrightarrow{pk}$, its secret key sk_1, the secret ξ for the encoded function, and its input $x_1^{(i)}$. The output of this algorithm is an encoded input $\chi_1^{(i)}$, which will be sent to the server, and the input decoding secret $\tau^{(i)}$ which will be kept private by the client.
- $\chi_j^{(i)} \leftarrow \mathsf{EnInput}_j(i, \overrightarrow{pk}, sk_j, x_j^{(i)})$. When outsourcing the ith computation to the server, each client P_j (with $j \neq 1$) will run this *input-encoding algorithm* $\mathsf{EnInput}_j$ with time period i, the public keys $\overrightarrow{pk}$, its secret key sk_j, and its input $x_j^{(i)}$. The output of this algorithm is an encoded input $\chi_j^{(i)}$, which will be sent to the server. We let $\boldsymbol{\chi}^{(i)}$ denote the vector $(\chi_1^{(i)}, \ldots, \chi_n^{(i)})$ of encoded inputs from the clients.
- $\omega^{(i)} \leftarrow \mathsf{Compute}(i, \overrightarrow{pk}, \phi, \boldsymbol{\chi}^{(i)})$. Given the public keys $\overrightarrow{pk}$, the encoded function ϕ, and the encoded inputs $\boldsymbol{\chi}^{(i)}$, this *computation algorithm* computes an encoded output $\omega^{(i)}$.
- $y^{(i)} \cup \{\bot\} \leftarrow \mathsf{Verify}(i, \xi, \tau^{(i)}, \omega^{(i)})$. The first client P_1 runs this *verification algorithm* with the decoding secrets $(\xi, \tau^{(i)})$, and the encoded output $\omega^{(i)}$. The algorithm outputs either a value $y^{(i)}$ (that is supposed to be $f(x_1^{(i)}, \ldots, x_n^{(i)})$), or $\bot$ indicating that the server attempted to cheat.

Of course, to be interesting an $\mathcal{MVC}$ scheme should have the property that the time to encode the input and verify the output is smaller than the time to compute the function from scratch. Correctness of an $\mathcal{MVC}$ scheme can be defined naturally, that is, the key generation, function encoding, and input encoding algorithms allow the computation algorithm to output an encoded output that will successfully pass the verification algorithm.

2.1 Soundness

Intuitively, a verifiable computation scheme is sound if a malicious server cannot convince the honest clients to accept an incorrect output. In our definition, the adversary is given oracle access to generate multiple input encodings.

Definition 1 (Soundness). *For a multi-client verifiable-computation scheme* $\mathcal{MVC}$, *consider the following experiment with respect to an adversarial server* $\mathcal{A}$:

Experiment $\mathbf{Exp}_{\mathcal{A}}^{\text{sound}}[\mathcal{MVC}, f, \kappa, n]$ *Oracle* $\mathcal{IN}(x_1, \ldots, x_n)$:

For $j = 1, \ldots, n$: $i := i + 1$;

   $(pk_j, sk_j) \leftarrow \mathsf{KeyGen}(1^\kappa, j)$,   *Record* $(x_1^{(i)}, \ldots, x_n^{(i)}) := (x_1, \ldots, x_n)$.

$(\phi, \xi) \leftarrow \mathsf{EnFunc}(1^\kappa, f)$. $(\chi_1^{(i)}, \tau^{(i)}) \leftarrow \mathsf{EnInput}_1(i, \overrightarrow{pk}, sk_1, \xi, x_1^{(i)})$

Initialize counter $i := 0$ *For* $j = 2, \ldots, n$:

$\omega^* \leftarrow \mathcal{A}^{\mathcal{IN}(\cdot)}(\overrightarrow{pk}, \phi)$; $\chi_j^{(i)} \leftarrow \mathsf{EnInput}_j(i, \overrightarrow{pk}, sk_j, x_j^{(i)})$.

$y^* \leftarrow \mathsf{Verify}(i, \xi, \tau^{(i)}, \omega^*)$;   *Output* $(\chi_1^{(i)}, \ldots, \chi_n^{(i)})$.

If $y^* \notin \{\bot, f(x_1^{(i)}, \ldots, x_n^{(i)})\}$,

   output 1;

Else output 0;

A *multi-client verifiable computation scheme* $\mathcal{MVC}$ *is* sound *if for any* $n = \mathsf{poly}(\kappa)$, *any function* f, *and any PPT adversary* $\mathcal{A}$, *there is a negligible function* negl *such that:*

$$\Pr[\mathbf{Exp}_{\mathcal{A}}^{\text{sound}}[\mathcal{MVC}, f, \kappa, n] = 1] \leq \mathsf{negl}(\kappa).$$

Selective Aborts. Our $\mathcal{MVC}$ construction described in Section 5 inherits the "selective abort" issue from the single-client scheme of Gennaro et al. [13]; that is, the server may be able to violate soundness if it can send ill-formed responses to the first client and see when that client rejects. In our definition we deal with this issue as in [13] by assuming that the adversary cannot tell when the client rejects. In practice, this issue could be dealt with by having the first client refuse to interact with the server after receiving a single faulty response.

Adaptive Choice of Inputs. As in [13], we define a notion of *adaptive* soundness that allows the adversary to adaptively choose inputs for the clients after seeing the encoded function. (The weaker notion of non-adaptive soundness would require the adversary to fix the clients' inputs in advance, before seeing the encoded function.) Bellare et al. [3] noted that the proof of adaptive soundness in [13] is flawed; it appears to be non-trivial to resolve this issue since it amounts to proving some form of security against selective-opening attacks. Nevertheless, it is reasonable to simply make the assumption that Yao's garbled-circuit construction satisfies the necessary criterion (namely, aut!, as defined in [3]) needed to prove adaptive security. Similarly, we reduce the adaptive security of our scheme to adaptive authenticity (aut!) of the underlying garbling scheme. Alternately, we can prove non-adaptive soundness based on standard assumptions.

2.2 Privacy

We consider two notions of privacy.

Privacy against the First Client. In our schemes, clients other than the first client clearly do not learn anything about each others' inputs. We define the requirement that the first client not learn anything (beyond the output of the function), either. Namely, given any input vectors $\boldsymbol{x}_0 = (x_1, x_2, \ldots, x_n)$ and $\boldsymbol{x}_1 = (x_1, x'_2, \ldots, x'_n)$ with $f(x_1, x_2, \ldots, x_n) = f(x_1, x'_2, \ldots, x'_n)$, the view of the first client when running an execution of the protocol with clients holding inputs $\boldsymbol{x}_0$ should be indistinguishable from the view of the first client when running an execution with clients holding inputs $\boldsymbol{x}_1$.

Privacy against the Server. Next, we consider *privacy against the server*, that is, the encoded inputs from two distinct inputs should be indistinguishable to the server.

Definition 2 (Privacy against the Server). *For a multi-client verifiable computation scheme $\mathcal{MVC}$, consider the following experiment with respect to a stateful adversarial server $\mathcal{A}$:*

Experiment $\mathbf{Exp}_{\mathcal{A}}^{\mathrm{priv}}[\mathcal{MVC}, f, \kappa, n, b]$:
  $(pk_j, sk_j) \leftarrow \mathsf{KeyGen}(1^\kappa, j)$, *for* $j = 1, \ldots, n$.
  $(\phi, \xi) \leftarrow \mathsf{EnFunc}(1^\kappa, f)$.
  Initialize counter $i := 0$
  $((x_1^0, \ldots, x_n^0), (x_1^1, \ldots, x_n^1)) \leftarrow \mathcal{A}^{\mathcal{IN}(\cdot)}(\overrightarrow{pk}, \phi)$;
  Run $(\chi_1^{(i)}, \ldots, \chi_n^{(i)}) \leftarrow \mathcal{IN}(x_1^b, \ldots, x_n^b)$;
  Output $\mathcal{A}^{\mathcal{IN}(\cdot)}(\chi_1^{(i)}, \ldots, \chi_n^{(i)})$;

We define the advantage of an adversary $\mathcal{A}$ in the experiment above as:

$$\mathbf{Adv}_{\mathcal{A}}^{priv}(\mathcal{MVC}, f, \kappa, n) = \left| \begin{matrix} \Pr[\mathbf{Exp}_{\mathcal{A}}^{\mathrm{priv}}[\mathcal{MVC}, f, \kappa, n, 0] = 1] \\ - \Pr[\mathbf{Exp}_{\mathcal{A}}^{\mathrm{priv}}[\mathcal{MVC}, f, \kappa, n, 1] = 1] \end{matrix} \right|$$

$\mathcal{MVC}$ is private against the server if for any $n = \mathsf{poly}(\kappa)$, any function f, and any PPT adversary $\mathcal{A}$, there is a negligible function negl such that:

$$\mathbf{Adv}_{\mathcal{A}}^{priv}(\mathcal{MVC}, f, \kappa, n) \le \mathsf{negl}(\kappa).$$

3 Building Blocks for $\mathcal{MVC}$

3.1 (Projective) Garbling Schemes

Bellare et al. [4] recently formalized a notion of *garbling schemes* that is meant to abstract, e.g., Yao's garbled-circuit protocol [25]. We follow their definition, since it allows us to abstract the exact properties we need. For completeness, we present their definition below.

A *garbling scheme* [4] is a five-tuple of algorithms $\mathcal{G} = (\mathsf{Gb}, \mathsf{En}, \mathsf{De}, \mathsf{Ev}, \mathsf{ev})$ with the following properties:

- $y := \mathsf{ev}(f, x)$. Here, f is a bit string that represents a certain function mapping an ℓ-bit input to an m-bit output. (We require that ℓ and m be extracted from f in time linear in $|f|$.) For example, f may be a circuit description encoded as detailed in [4]. Hereafer, we abuse the notation and let f also denote the function that f represents. Given the description f and $x \in \{0, 1\}^\ell$ as input, $\mathsf{ev}(f, x)$ returns $f(x)$. A garbling scheme is called a *circuit garbling scheme* if $\mathsf{ev} = \mathsf{ev}_{\mathsf{circ}}$ is the canonical circuit-evaluation function.
- $(F, e, d) \leftarrow \mathsf{Gb}(1^\kappa, f)$. Given the description f as input, Gb outputs a garbled function F along with an encoding function e and a decoding function d.
- $X := \mathsf{En}(e, x)$. Given an encoding function e and $x \in \{0, 1\}^\ell$ as input, En maps x to a *garbled input* X. Our scheme will use a *projective garbling scheme*, i.e., the string e encodes a list of *tokens*, one pair for each bit in $x \in \{0, 1\}^\ell$. Formally, for all $f \in \{0, 1\}^*$, $\kappa \in \mathbb{N}$, $i \in [\ell]$, $x, x' \in \{0, 1\}^\ell$ s.t. $x_i = x'_i$, it holds that

$$\Pr \left[\begin{array}{l} (F, e, d) \leftarrow \mathsf{Gb}(1^\kappa, f), \\ (X_1, \ldots, X_\ell) := \mathsf{En}(e, x), \; : \; X_i = X'_i \\ (X'_1, \ldots, X'_\ell) := \mathsf{En}(e, x') \end{array} \right] = 1.$$

For a projective garbling scheme $\mathcal{G}$, it is possible to define an additional deterministic algorithm $\mathsf{En}_{\mathsf{proj}}$. Let $(X_1^0, \ldots, X_\ell^0) := \mathsf{En}(e, 0^\ell)$, and $(X_1^1, \ldots, X_\ell^1) := \mathsf{En}(e, 1^\ell)$. The output $\mathsf{En}_{\mathsf{proj}}(e, b, i)$ is defined as X_i^b. We refer to $\mathsf{En}_{\mathsf{proj}}$ as the projection algorithm.

- $Y := \mathsf{Ev}(F, X)$. Given a garbled function F and a garbled input X as input, Ev obtains the garbled output Y.
- $y := \mathsf{De}(d, Y)$. Given a decoding function d and a garbled output Y, De maps Y to a final output y.

Note that all algorithms except Gb are deterministic. A garbling scheme must satisfy the following:

1. *Length* condition: $|F|$, e, and d depend only on κ, ℓ, m, and $|f|$.
2. *Correctness* condition: for all $f \in \{0, 1\}^*$, $\kappa \in \mathbb{N}$, $x \in \{0, 1\}^\ell$, it holds that

$$\Pr[(F, e, d) \leftarrow \mathsf{Gb}(1^\kappa, f) \; : \; \mathsf{De}(d, \mathsf{Ev}(F, \mathsf{En}(e, x))) = \mathsf{ev}(f, x)] = 1.$$

3. *Non-degeneracy* condition: e and d depends only on κ, ℓ, m, $|f|$, and the random coins of Gb.

Authenticity. We will employ a garbling scheme that satisfies the *authenticity* property [4]. Loosely speaking, a garbling scheme is authentic if the adversary upon learning a set of tokens corresponding to some input x is unable to produce a set of tokens that correspond to an output different from $f(x)$. Different notions of authenticity are possible depending on whether the adversary chooses the input x adaptively (i.e., whether it sees the garbled function F before choosing x). We adopt the adaptive definition given in [3] because we want our $\mathcal{MVC}$ scheme to achieve adaptive soundness; alternately, we could use a non-adaptive definition of authenticity and achieve non-adaptive soundness.

Definition 3. *For a garbling scheme* $\mathcal{G} = (\mathsf{Gb}, \mathsf{En}, \mathsf{De}, \mathsf{Ev}, \mathsf{ev})$ *consider the following experiment with respect to an adversary* $\mathcal{A}$.

Experiment $\mathbf{Exp}_{\mathcal{A}}^{\mathsf{Aut!}\mathcal{G}}[\kappa]$:
$\quad f \leftarrow \mathcal{A}(1^\kappa)$.
$\quad (F, e, d) \leftarrow \mathsf{Gb}(1^\kappa, f)$.
$\quad x \leftarrow \mathcal{A}(1^\kappa, F)$.
$\quad X := \mathsf{En}(e, x)$.
$\quad Y \leftarrow \mathcal{A}(1^\kappa, F, X)$.
$\quad$ *If* $\mathsf{De}(d, Y) \neq \perp$ *and* $Y \neq \mathsf{Ev}(F, X)$, *output 1, else 0.*

A garbling scheme $\mathcal{G}$ *satisfies the authenticity property if for any PPT adversary* $\mathcal{A}$, *there is a negligible function* negl *such that*

$$\Pr[\mathbf{Exp}_{\mathcal{A}}^{\mathsf{Aut!}\mathcal{G}}[\kappa] = 1] \leq \mathsf{negl}(\kappa).$$

3.2 Fully Homomorphic Encryption

In a (compact) fully-homomorphic encryption scheme $\mathsf{FHE} = (\mathsf{Fgen}, \mathsf{Fenc}, \mathsf{Fdec}, \mathsf{Feval})$, the first three algorithms form a semantically secure public-key encryption scheme. Moreover, Feval takes a circuit C and a tuple of ciphertexts and outputs a ciphertext that decrypts to the result of applying C to the plaintexts; here, the length of the output ciphertext should be independent of the size of the circuit C. We will treat FHE as a black box.

4 Non-interactive Proxy OT

In this section, we introduce a new primitive called *non-interactive proxy oblivious transfer* (POT), which is a variant and generalization of proxy OT of the notion defined by Naor et al. [22]. In a POT protocol there are three parties: a sender, a chooser, and a proxy. The *sender* holds input (x_0, x_1), and the *chooser* holds choice bit b. At the end of the protocol, the *proxy* learns x_b (but not x_{1-b}); the sender and chooser learn nothing. Our definition requires the scheme to be non-interactive, so we omit the term 'non-interactive' from now on.

The generalization we define incorporates public keys for the sender and the chooser, and explicitly takes into account the fact that the protocol may be run repeatedly during multiple time periods. These are needed for the later application to our $\mathcal{MVC}$ construction.

Syntax. A proxy OT consists of the following sets of algorithms:

- $(pk_S, sk_S) \leftarrow \mathsf{SetupS}(1^\kappa)$. The sender runs this one-time setup algorithm to generate a public/private key pair (pk_S, sk_S).
- $(pk_C, sk_C) \leftarrow \mathsf{SetupC}(1^\kappa)$. The chooser runs this one-time setup algorithm to generate a public/private key pair (pk_C, sk_C).
- $\alpha \leftarrow \mathsf{Snd}(i, pk_C, sk_S, x_0, x_1)$. In the ith POT execution the sender, holding input $x_0, x_1 \in \{0,1\}^\kappa$, runs this algorithm to generate a single encoded message α to be sent to the proxy. We refer to α as the sender message.
- $\beta \leftarrow \mathsf{Chs}(i, pk_S, sk_C, b)$. In the ith POT protocol, the chooser, holding input $b \in \{0,1\}$, runs this algorithm to generate a single encoded message β to be sent to the server. We refer to β as the chooser message.
- $y := \mathsf{Prx}(i, pk_S, pk_C, \alpha, \beta)$. In the ith POT protocol, the proxy runs this algorithm using the sender message α and the chooser message β, and computes the value $y = x_b$.

A proxy OT is correct if the sender algorithm Snd and chooser algorithm Chs produce values that allow the proxy to compute one of two sender inputs based on the chooser's selection bit.

Sender Privacy. A proxy OT is sender private if the proxy learns only the value of the sender input that corresponds to the chooser's input bit. To serve our purpose, we define sender privacy over multiple executions. We stress that a *single* setup by each party is sufficient to run multiple executions (this is essential for our $\mathcal{MVC}$ construction).

Definition 4 (Sender Privacy). *For a proxy OT ($\mathsf{SetupS}, \mathsf{SetupC}, \mathsf{Snd}, \mathsf{Chs}, \mathsf{Prx}$), consider the following experiments with respect to an adversarial proxy $\mathcal{A}$.*

Experiment $\mathbf{Exp}_{\mathcal{A}}^{s\text{-}priv}[\text{POT}, \kappa, n, e]$:
$(pk_S, sk_S) \leftarrow \mathsf{SetupS}(1^\kappa)$.
For $j = 1, \ldots, n$:
  $(pk_{C,j}, sk_{C,j}) \leftarrow \mathsf{SetupC}(1^\kappa)$.
Output $\mathcal{A}^{\mathcal{POT}_e(\cdot)}(pk_S, pk_{C,1}, \ldots, pk_{C,n})$.

Oracle $\mathcal{POT}_e(i, j, x_0, x_1, b, x')$:
If a previous query
  used the same (i, j)
  output $\perp$ and terminate.
If $e = 0$, set $y_0 := x_0$, $y_1 := x_1$.
Else set $y_b := x_b$, $y_{1-b} := x'$.
  $\alpha \leftarrow \mathsf{Snd}(i, pk_{C,j}, sk_S, y_0, y_1)$.
  $\beta \leftarrow \mathsf{Chs}(i, pk_S, sk_{C,j}, b)$.
  Output (α, β).

Note that the sender messages α generated from oracle $\mathcal{POT}_0$ (resp., $\mathcal{POT}_1$) would encode the sender's input x_b and x_{1-b} (resp., x_b and x'). We define the advantage of an adversary $\mathcal{A}$ in the experiment above as:

$$\mathbf{Adv}_{\mathcal{A}}^{s\text{-}priv}(\text{POT}, \kappa, n) = \left| \begin{array}{l} \Pr[\mathbf{Exp}_{\mathcal{A}}^{s\text{-}priv}[\text{POT}, \kappa, n, 0] = 1] \\ \quad - \Pr[\mathbf{Exp}_{\mathcal{A}}^{s\text{-}priv}[\text{POT}, \kappa, n, 1] = 1] \end{array} \right|$$

A proxy OT ($\mathsf{SetupS}, \mathsf{SetupC}, \mathsf{Snd}, \mathsf{Chs}, \mathsf{Prx}$) is sender private, if for any $n = \mathsf{poly}(\kappa)$ and any PPT adversary $\mathcal{A}$, there is a negligible function negl such that:

$$\mathbf{Adv}_{\mathcal{A}}^{s\text{-}priv}(\text{POT}, \kappa, n) \leq \mathsf{negl}(\kappa).$$

Chooser Privacy. A proxy OT is chooser private if the proxy learns no information about the chooser's input bit. To serve our purpose, we define chooser privacy over multiple executions.

Definition 5 (Chooser Privacy). *For a proxy OT* (SetupS, SetupC, Snd, Chs, Prx), *consider the following experiments with respect to an adversarial proxy* $\mathcal{A}$.

$\textbf{\textit{Experiment }} \mathbf{Exp}_{\mathcal{A}}^{c\text{-}priv}[POT, \kappa, n, e]:$
  $(pk_S, sk_S) \leftarrow \mathsf{SetupS}(1^\kappa).$
  For $j = 1, \ldots, n:$
    $(pk_{C,j}, sk_{C,j}) \leftarrow \mathsf{SetupC}(1^\kappa).$
  Output $\mathcal{A}^{\mathcal{CHS}_e(\cdot)}(pk_S, pk_{C,1}, \ldots, pk_{C,n}).$

$\textbf{\textit{Oracle }} \mathcal{CHS}_e(i, j, b_0, b_1):$
  If a previous query
   used the same (i, j)
    output $\perp$ *and terminate.*
  $\beta \leftarrow \mathsf{Chs}(i, pk_S, sk_{C,j}, b_e).$
  Output $\beta.$

We define the advantage of an adversary $\mathcal{A}$ *in the experiment above as:*

$$\mathbf{Adv}_{\mathcal{A}}^{c\text{-}priv}(POT, \kappa, n) = \left| \begin{array}{l} \Pr[\mathbf{Exp}_{\mathcal{A}}^{c\text{-}priv}[POT, \kappa, n, 0] = 1] \\ \quad - \Pr[\mathbf{Exp}_{\mathcal{A}}^{c\text{-}priv}[POT, \kappa, n, 1] = 1] \end{array} \right|$$

A proxy OT (SetupS, SetupC, Snd, Chs, Prx) *is* chooser private, *if for any* $n = poly(\kappa)$ *and any PPT adversary* $\mathcal{A}$, *there is a negligible function* negl *such that:*

$$\mathbf{Adv}_{\mathcal{A}}^{c\text{-}priv}(POT, \kappa, n) \leq \mathsf{negl}(\kappa).$$

4.1 Proxy OT from Non-interactive Key Exchange

Non-interactive Key Exchange. A non-interactive key-exchange (NIKE) protocol allows two parties to generate a shared key based on their respective public keys (and without any direct interaction). That is, let $\mathsf{KEA}_1, \mathsf{KEB}_2$ be the algorithms used by the two parties to generate their public/private keys. (pk_a, sk_a) and (pk_b, sk_b), respectively. Then there are algorithms KEA_2 and KEB_2 such that $\mathsf{KEA}_2(pk_b, sk_a) = \mathsf{KEB}_2(pk_a, sk_b)$. An example is given by static/static Diffie-Hellman key exchange.

Regarding the security of NIKE, to the view of a passive eavesdropper the distribution of the key shared by the two parties should be indistinguishable from a uniform key.

Definition 6 (Security of NIKE). *A NIKE* $(\mathsf{KEA}_1, \mathsf{KEA}_2, \mathsf{KEB}_1, \mathsf{KEB}_2)$ *is secure if for any PPT* $\mathcal{A}$, *it holds that* $|p_1 - p_2|$ *is negligible in* κ, *where*

$$p_1 = \Pr \left[\begin{array}{l} (pk_a, sk_a) \leftarrow \mathsf{KEA}_1(1^\kappa); \\ (pk_b, sk_b) \leftarrow \mathsf{KEB}_1(1^\kappa) \end{array} : \mathcal{A}(pk_a, pk_b, \mathsf{KEA}_2(pk_b, sk_a)) = 1 \right]$$

$$p_2 = \Pr \left[\begin{array}{l} (pk_a, sk_a) \leftarrow \mathsf{KEA}_1(1^\kappa); \\ (pk_b, sk_b) \leftarrow \mathsf{KEB}_1(1^\kappa); \\ r \leftarrow \{0,1\}^\kappa \end{array} : \mathcal{A}(pk_a, pk_b, r) = 1 \right].$$

Proxy OT from NIKE. We define a protocol for proxy OT below. The main idea is that the sender and the chooser share randomness in the setup stage by using the key-exchange protocol. Then, using the shared randomness (which is unknown to the proxy), both parties can simply use a one-time pad encryption to transfer their inputs. Let Prf be a pseudorandom function.

- $(pk_S, sk_S) \leftarrow \mathsf{SetupS}(1^\kappa)$. Run a key exchange protocol on Alice's part, that is, $(pk_a, sk_a) \leftarrow \mathsf{KEA}_1(1^\kappa)$. Set $pk_S := pk_a$ and $sk_S := sk_a$.
- $(pk_C, sk_C) \leftarrow \mathsf{SetupC}(1^\kappa)$. Run a key exchange protocol on Bob's part, that is, $(pk_b, sk_b) \leftarrow \mathsf{KEB}_1(1^\kappa)$. Set $pk_C := pk_b$ and $sk_C := sk_b$.
- $\alpha \leftarrow \mathsf{Snd}(i, pk_C, sk_S, x_0, x_1)$. Let k be the output from the key-exchange protocol, i.e., $k := \mathsf{KEA}_2(pk_C, sk_S)$. Compute $(z_0, z_1, \pi) := \mathsf{Prf}_k(i)$ where $|z_0| = |z_1| = \kappa$ and $\pi \in \{0, 1\}$. Then, set $\alpha := (\alpha_0, \alpha_1)$, where

$$\alpha_\pi = z_0 \oplus x_0, \quad \alpha_{1 \oplus \pi} = z_1 \oplus x_1.$$

- $\beta \leftarrow \mathsf{Chs}(i, pk_S, sk_C, b)$. Let k be the output from the key exchange protocol, i.e., $k := \mathsf{KEB}_2(pk_S, sk_C)$. Compute $(z_0, z_1, \pi) := \mathsf{Prf}_k(i)$ where $|z_0| = |z_1| = \kappa$ and $\pi \in \{0, 1\}$. Then, reveal only the part associated with the choice bit b. That is, $\beta := (b \oplus \pi, z_b)$
- $y := \mathsf{Prx}(i, pk_S, pk_C, \alpha, \beta)$. Parse α as (α_0, α_1), and β as (b', z'). Compute $y := \alpha_{b'} \oplus z'$.

It is easy to see that the scheme satisfies the correctness property. Sender privacy over a single execution easily follows from the fact that the outputs from the key exchange and the pseudorandom function look random. Sender privacy over multiple pairs can also be shown with a hybrid argument. The scheme also hides the choice bit of the chooser from the proxy.

5   Construction of $\mathcal{MVC}$

In this section, we present our construction for $\mathcal{MVC}$. Our scheme uses proxy OT to extend the single-client scheme of Gennaro et al. [13] (see Section 1.2 for an overview of the scheme). In the pre-processing stage, the keys for proxy OT are set up, and the first client P_1, who will receive the function output, generates a garbled function F and gives it the server. Now delegating computation on input $(x_1, \ldots, x_n)$, where the client P_j holds $x_j \in \{0, 1\}^\ell$, is performed as follows:

1. For each $j \in [n]$ and $k \in [\ell]$, do the following in parallel:
   (a) Client P_1 computes the following pair for the potential garbled input.

   $$X_{jk}^0 := \mathsf{En}_{\mathrm{proj}}(e, 0, (j-1)\ell + k), \quad X_{jk}^1 := \mathsf{En}_{\mathrm{proj}}(e, 1, (j-1)\ell + k)$$

   (b) A proxy OT protocol is executed in which client P_1 plays as the sender with (X_{jk}^0, X_{jk}^1) as input, and the client P_j plays as the chooser with the kth bit of x_j as input; the server plays as the proxy.
2. Using the outputs from the proxy OT protocols, the server evaluates the garbled function F and sends the corresponding garbled output Y to P_1.
3. Client P_1 decodes Y to obtain the actual output y.

Protocol 1

Let $\mathcal{G}$ = (Gb, En, De, Ev, ev) be a projective garbling scheme, FHE = (Fgen, Fenc, Fdec, Feval) be a fully homomorphic encryption scheme, and (SetupS, SetupC, Snd, Chs, Prx) be a proxy OT scheme. Let $L_j := (j-1)\ell$ and $\mathrm{ID}_{ijk} := (i-1)n\ell + L_j + k$.

- $(pk_j, sk_j) \leftarrow \mathsf{KeyGen}(1^\kappa, j)$. The first client runs the algorithm $\mathsf{SetupS}(1^\kappa)$ to obtain (pk_1, sk_1). For each $2 \le j \le n$, client P_j runs $\mathsf{SetupC}(1^\kappa)$ to generate (pk_j, sk_j).

- $(\phi, \xi) \leftarrow \mathsf{EnFunc}(1^\kappa, f)$. The first client generates $(F, e, d) \leftarrow \mathsf{Gb}(1^\kappa, f)$, and sets $\phi := F$ and $\xi := (e, d)$.

- $(\chi_1^{(i)}, \tau^{(i)}) \leftarrow \mathsf{EnInput}_1(i, \overrightarrow{pk}, sk_1, \xi, x_1^{(i)})$. Let $a := x_1^{(i)}$ and parse a as $a_1 \ldots a_\ell$.
  1. Generate $(\mathrm{PK}_i, \mathrm{SK}_i) \leftarrow \mathsf{Fgen}(1^\kappa)$.
  2. For each $k \in [\ell]$, run $\tilde{X}_{i1k} \leftarrow \mathsf{Fenc}(\mathrm{PK}_i, \mathsf{En}_{\mathrm{proj}}(e, a_k, k))$. Set $\psi_{i1} := (\tilde{X}_{i11}, \ldots, \tilde{X}_{i1\ell})$.
  3. For $2 \le j \le n$, do the following:
     (a) For each $k \in [\ell]$, compute

     $$\tilde{X}_{ijk}^0 \leftarrow \mathsf{Fenc}(\mathrm{PK}_i, \mathsf{En}_{\mathrm{proj}}(e, 0, L_j + k)),$$
     $$\tilde{X}_{ijk}^1 \leftarrow \mathsf{Fenc}(\mathrm{PK}_i, \mathsf{En}_{\mathrm{proj}}(e, 1, L_j + k)),$$
     $$\alpha_{ijk} \leftarrow \mathsf{Snd}(\mathrm{ID}_{ijk}, pk_j, sk_1, \tilde{X}_{ijk}^0, \tilde{X}_{ijk}^1).$$

     (b) Set $\psi_{ij} := (\alpha_{ij1}, \ldots, \alpha_{ij\ell})$.
  4. Set $\chi_1^{(i)} := (\mathrm{PK}_i, \psi_{i1}, \ldots, \psi_{in})$ and $\tau^{(i)} := \mathrm{SK}_i$.

- $\chi_j^{(i)} \leftarrow \mathsf{EnInput}_j(i, \overrightarrow{pk}, sk_j, x_j^{(i)})$ for $j = 2, \ldots n$. Let $a := x_j^{(i)}$ and parse a as $a_1 \ldots a_\ell$.
  1. For each $k \in [\ell]$, compute $\beta_{ijk} \leftarrow \mathsf{Chs}(\mathrm{ID}_{ijk}, pk_1, sk_j, a_k)$.
  2. Set $\chi_j^{(i)} := (\beta_{ij1}, \ldots, \beta_{ij\ell})$.

- $\omega^{(i)} \leftarrow \mathsf{Compute}(i, \overrightarrow{pk}, \phi, (\chi_1^{(i)}, \ldots, \chi_n^{(i)}))$. Parse $\chi_1^{(i)}$ as $(\mathrm{PK}_i, \psi_{i1}, \ldots, \psi_{in})$, where $\psi_{i1} = (\tilde{X}_{i11}, \ldots, \tilde{X}_{i1\ell})$ and for $2 \le j \le n$, $\psi_{ij} = (\alpha_{ij1}, \ldots, \alpha_{ij\ell})$. In addition, for $2 \le j \le n$, parse $\chi_j^{(i)}$ as $(\beta_{ij1}, \ldots, \beta_{ij\ell})$. The server does the following:
  1. For $2 \le j \le n$ and for $1 \le k \le \ell$, compute $\tilde{X}_{ijk} := \mathsf{Prx}(\mathrm{ID}_{ijk}, pk_1, pk_j, \alpha_{ijk}, \beta_{ijk})$.
  2. Let C_F denote the circuit representation of $\mathsf{Ev}(F, \cdot)$. Then the server computes $\omega^{(i)} \leftarrow \mathsf{Feval}(\mathrm{PK}_i, C_F, \{\tilde{X}_{ijk}\}_{j \in [n], k \in [\ell]})$.

- $y^{(i)} \cup \{\bot\} \leftarrow \mathsf{Verify}(i, \xi, \tau^{(i)}, \omega^{(i)})$. Parse ξ as (e, d). Client P_1 obtains $Y^{(i)} \leftarrow \mathsf{Fdec}(\tau^{(i)}, \omega^{(i)})$, and outputs $y^{(i)} := \mathsf{De}(d, Y^{(i)})$.

Fig. 1. A scheme for multi-client non-interactive verifiable computation

The above scheme allows delegating the computation one-time; intuitively, the sender privacy of the underlying proxy OT makes the server learn the garbled inputs *only for the actual inputs* of all clients. Multiple inputs can be handled using fully-homomorphic encryption as with the single-client case. The detailed protocol (called Protocol 1) is described in Figure 1.

Correctness and Non-triviality. Correctness of our scheme follows from the correctness of the garbling scheme, the correctness of the fully homomorphic encryption scheme, and the correctness of the proxy OT. Non-triviality of our scheme follows from the fact that (1) the time required (by client P_1) for computing $\mathsf{En_{proj}}$, Fenc, and Snd is $O(\mathrm{poly}(\kappa)|x^{(i)}|)$, and is independent of the circuit size of f, and (2) the time required (by all clients P_j for $2 \leq j \leq n$) for computing Chs is $O(\mathrm{poly}(\kappa)|x^{(i)}|)$, and is independent of the circuit size of f.

Soundness. At a high level, the soundness of Protocol 1 follows from the sender security of proxy OT, the semantic security of FHE, and the authenticity property of the garbling scheme $\mathcal{G}$.

Theorem 1. *Suppose $\mathcal{G} = (\mathsf{Gb}, \mathsf{En}, \mathsf{De}, \mathsf{Ev}, \mathsf{ev})$ be a projective garbling scheme satisfying the authenticity property, FHE is a semantically secure FHE scheme, and $(\mathsf{SetupS}, \mathsf{SetupC}, \mathsf{Snd}, \mathsf{Chs}, \mathsf{Prx})$ is a proxy OT scheme that is sender private. Then Protocol 1 is a sound $\mathcal{MVC}$ scheme.*

A proof is given in the following section.

Privacy. It is easy to see that Protocol 1 is private against the first client, since the output of Compute algorithm is basically the encryption of the garbled output. For privacy against the server, we need a proxy OT that hides the chooser's input as well.

Theorem 2. *Suppose that FHE is a semantically secure fully homomorphic encryption scheme, and that $(\mathsf{SetupS}, \mathsf{SetupC}, \mathsf{Snd}, \mathsf{Chs}, \mathsf{Prx})$ is a proxy OT scheme that is chooser private. Then Protocol 1 is private against the server.*

5.1   Proof of Theorem 1

Suppose there exists an adversary $\mathcal{A}$ that breaks the soundness of Protocol 1 with respect to a function f.

Hybrid 0. Let p be an upper bound on the number of queries $\mathcal{A}$ makes. Consider the following experiment that is slightly different from $\mathbf{Exp}_{\mathcal{A}}^{\mathrm{sound}}[\mathcal{MVC}, f, \kappa, n]$:

Experiment $\mathbf{Exp}_{\mathcal{A}}^{\mathrm{r\text{-}sound}}[\mathcal{MVC}, f, \kappa, n]$:
  $(pk_j, sk_j) \leftarrow \mathsf{KeyGen}(1^\kappa, j)$, for $j = 1, \ldots, n$.
  $(\phi, \xi) \leftarrow \mathsf{EnFunc}(1^\kappa, f)$.
  Initialize counter $i := 0$
  $\boxed{\text{Choose } r \leftarrow [p].}$
  $(i^*, \omega^*) \leftarrow \mathcal{A}^{\mathcal{IN}(\cdot)}(\overrightarrow{pk}, \phi);$

> If $i^* \neq r$, output 0 and terminate.

$y^* \leftarrow \mathsf{Verify}(i^*, \xi, \tau^{(i^*)}, \omega^*)$;
If $y^* \neq \perp$ and $y^* \neq f(x_1^{(i^*)}, \ldots, x_n^{(i^*)})$, output 1;
Else output 0;

Since r is chosen uniformly at random, $\mathcal{A}$ would succeed in the above experiment with non-negligble probability (i.e., $\Pr[\mathbf{Exp}_{\mathcal{A}}^{\mathrm{sound}}[\mathcal{MVC}, f, \kappa, n] = 1]/p$).

Hybrid 1. In this hybrid, the oracle queries $\mathcal{IN}(x_1^{(i)}, \ldots, x_n^{(i)})$ are handled by the following instead of setting $\chi_1^{(i)} \leftarrow \mathsf{EnInput}_1(i, \vec{pk}, sk_1, \xi, x_1^{(i)})$

> $-$ Run $(\chi_1^{(i)}, \tau^{(i)}) \leftarrow \mathsf{EnInput}_1'(i, \vec{pk}, sk_1, \xi, (x_1^{(i)}, \ldots, x_n^{(i)}))$.

At a high level, $\mathsf{EnInput}_1'$ is identical to $\mathsf{EnInput}_1$ except it sets the inputs to the sender algorithm Snd of the proxy OT as follows: For all input bits, Snd obtains the correct token corresponding to the actual input bit, and a zero string in place of the token corresponding to the other bit. The explicit description of $\mathsf{EnInput}_1'$ is found in Figure 2.

$(\chi_1^{(i)}, \tau^{(i)}) \leftarrow \mathsf{EnInput}_1'(i, \vec{pk}, sk_1, \xi, (x_1^{(i)}, \ldots, x_n^{(i)}))$

Let $a_j := x_j^{(i)}$ for $j \in [n]$, and parse a_j as $a_{j1} \ldots a_{j\ell}$.

1. Generate $(\mathrm{PK}_i, \mathrm{SK}_i) \leftarrow \mathsf{Fgen}(1^\kappa)$.
2. For each $k \in [\ell]$, run $\tilde{X}_{i1k} \leftarrow \mathsf{Fenc}(\mathrm{PK}_i, \mathsf{En}_{\mathrm{proj}}(e, a_{1k}, k))$. Set $\psi_{i1} := (\tilde{X}_{i11}, \ldots, \tilde{X}_{i1\ell})$.
3. For $2 \leq j \leq n$, do the following:
   (a) For each $k \in [\ell]$, compute

   $$b := a_{jk}, \quad \tilde{X}_{ijk}^b \leftarrow \mathsf{Fenc}(\mathrm{PK}_i, \mathsf{En}_{\mathrm{proj}}(e, b, L_j + k)), \quad \boxed{\tilde{X}_{ijk}^{1-b} := 0^{|\tilde{X}_{ijk}^b|},}$$

   $$\alpha_{ijk} \leftarrow \mathsf{Snd}(\ell i + L_j + k, pk_j, sk_1, \tilde{X}_{ijk}^0, \tilde{X}_{ijk}^1).$$

   (b) Set $\psi_{ij} := (\alpha_{ij1}, \ldots, \alpha_{ij\ell})$.
4. Set $\chi_1^{(i)} := (\mathrm{PK}_i, \psi_{i1}, \ldots, \psi_{in})$ and $\tau^{(i)} := \mathrm{SK}_i$.

Fig. 2. Description of $\mathsf{EnInput}_1'$

It is easy to see that Hybrid 0 and Hybrid 1 are indistinguishable due to the sender privacy of the underlying proxy OT scheme. In the reduction, the adversary breaking sender privacy will simulate experiment $\mathbf{Exp}_{\mathcal{A}}^{\mathrm{r\text{-}sound}}[\mathcal{MVC}, f, \kappa, n]$ while invoking the oracle $\mathcal{POT}$ with queries $(i, j, \tilde{X}_{ijk}^0, \tilde{X}_{ijk}^1, x_{jk}^{(i)}, 0^{|\tilde{X}_{ijk}^0|})$ to generate the sender messages of the proxy OT, where $x_{jk}^{(i)}$ is the kth bit of $x_j^{(i)}$, and for $b \in \{0, 1\}$, the value $\tilde{X}_{ijk}^b$ is the output from $\mathsf{Fenc}(\mathrm{PK}_i, \mathsf{En}_{\mathrm{proj}}(e, b, L_j + k))$.

Hybrid 2. In this hybrid, the oracle queries $\mathcal{IN}(x_1^{(i)}, \ldots, x_n^{(i)})$ are handled using the following instead of running $\chi_1^{(i)} \leftarrow \mathsf{EnInput}_1'(i, \vec{pk}, sk_1, \xi, x_1^{(i)})$

1. If $i = r$, run $(\chi_1^{(i)}, \tau^{(i)}) \leftarrow \mathsf{EnInput}_1'(i, \vec{pk}, sk_1, \xi, (x_1^{(i)}, \ldots, x_n^{(i)}))$;

   $\boxed{\text{Otherwise, } (\chi_1^{(i)}, \tau^{(i)}) \leftarrow \mathsf{EnInput}_1''(i, \vec{pk}, sk_1, (x_1^{(i)}, \ldots, x_n^{(i)}))}$;

At a high level, $\mathsf{EnInput}_1''$ is identical to $\mathsf{EnInput}_1'$ except it replaces the token values to zero strings. The explicit description of $\mathsf{EnInput}_1''$ is found in Figure 3.

$$(\chi_1^{(i)}, \tau^{(i)}) \leftarrow \mathsf{EnInput}_1''(i, \vec{pk}, sk_1, (x_1^{(i)}, \ldots, x_n^{(i)}))$$

Let $a_j := x_j^{(i)}$ for $j \in [n]$, and parse a_j as $a_{j1} \ldots a_{j\ell}$. Let λ be the output length of the $\mathsf{En_{proj}}$ algorithm.

1. Generate $(PK_i, SK_i) \leftarrow \mathsf{Fgen}(1^\kappa)$.
2. For each $k \in [\ell]$, compute $\boxed{\tilde{X}_{i1k} \leftarrow \mathsf{Fenc}(PK_i, 0^\lambda)}$. Set $\psi_{i1} := (\tilde{X}_{i11}, \ldots, \tilde{X}_{i1\ell})$.
3. For $2 \leq j \leq n$, do the following:
   (a) For each $k \in [\ell]$, compute

   $$b := a_{jk}, \quad \boxed{\tilde{X}_{ijk}^b \leftarrow \mathsf{Fenc}(PK_i, 0^\lambda)}, \quad \tilde{X}_{ijk}^{1-b} := 0^{|X_{ijk}^b|},$$

   $$\alpha_{ijk} \leftarrow \mathsf{Snd}(\ell i + L_j + k, pk_j, sk_1, \tilde{X}_{ijk}^0, \tilde{X}_{ijk}^1).$$

   (b) Set $\psi_{ij} := (\alpha_{ij1}, \ldots, \alpha_{ij\ell})$.
4. Set $\chi_1^{(i)} := (PK_i, \psi_{i1}, \ldots, \psi_{in})$ and $\tau^{(i)} := SK_i$.

Fig. 3. Description of $\mathsf{EnInput}_1''$

Indistinguishability between Hybrid 1 and Hybrid 2 can be shown with a simple hybrid argument where indistinguishability between two adjacent hybrids holds from the semantic security of the underlying FHE scheme.

Final Step. As a final step, we reduce the security to the authenticity of the underlying garbling scheme. In particular, using the adversary $\mathcal{A}$ that succeeds in Hybrid 2 with non-negligible probability, we construct an adversary $\mathcal{B}$ that breaks the authenticity of the underlying garbling scheme. $\mathcal{B}$ works as follows:

$\mathcal{B}$ sends f to the challenger and receives F from it. Then, it simulates Hybrid 2 as follows:
1. Run $(pk_j, sk_j) \leftarrow \mathsf{KeyGen}(1^\kappa, j)$, for $j = 1, \ldots, n$.
2. Let p be the upper bound on the number of queries that $\mathcal{A}$ makes, and choose $r \leftarrow [p]$.
3. Run $(i^*, \omega^*) \leftarrow \mathcal{A}^{\mathcal{IN}(\cdot)}(\vec{pk}, \phi)$ while handling the query $\mathcal{IN}(x_1^{(i)}, \ldots, x_n^{(i)})$ as follows:

(a) For the input encoding of the first party, if $i = r$, then $\mathcal{B}$ sends $(x_1^{(i)}, \ldots, x_n^{(i)})$ to the challenger and receives the corresponding tokens $(X_1, \ldots, X_{n\ell})$. Using these tokens, $\mathcal{B}$ perfectly simulates $\mathsf{EnInput}_1'(i, \overrightarrow{pk}, sk_1, \xi, (x_1^{(i)}, \ldots, x_n^{(i)}))$ by replacing $\mathsf{En}_{\mathrm{proj}}(e, \cdot, k')$s with $X_{k'}$s. Otherwise, run $\mathsf{EnInput}_1''(i, \overrightarrow{pk}, sk_1, (x_1^{(i)}, \ldots, x_n^{(i)}))$.

(b) For $j = 2, \ldots, n$, run $\chi_j^{(i)} \leftarrow \mathsf{EnInput}(i, j, \overrightarrow{pk}, sk_j, x_j^{(i)})$.

4. If $i^* = r$, the adversary $\mathcal{B}$ runs $Y^* \leftarrow \mathsf{Fdec}(\mathrm{SK}_{i^*}, \omega^*)$ and outputs Y^* to the challenger. Otherwise, it outputs $\bot$.

The above simulation is perfect.

We show that $\mathcal{B}$ breaks the authenticity of the underlying garbling scheme with non-negligible probability. Let Succ be the event that $\mathcal{A}$ succeeds in Hybrid 2, that is, Y^* is a valid encoded output but different from $\mathsf{Ev}(F, X^r)$, where $X^{(r)}$ is the encoded input for $x^{(r)}$. This implies that

$$\Pr[\mathbf{Exp}_{\mathcal{B}}^{\mathsf{Aut!}_{\mathcal{G}}} = 1] \geq \Pr[\mathsf{Succ}].$$

Since by assumption, $\mathcal{G}$ satisfies the authenticity property, we conclude that $\Pr[\mathsf{Succ}]$ must be negligible in κ, contradiction. This concludes the proof of soundness of Protocol 1.

Acknowledgments. We thank the referees for their helpful feedback. This work was supported by the US Army Research Laboratory and the UK Ministry of Defence under Agreement Number W911NF-06-3-0001. The first author was also supported in part by the Intelligence Advanced Research Project Activity (IARPA) via DoI/NBC contract #D11PC20194. The views and conclusions contained here are those of the authors and should not be interpreted as representing the official policies, expressed or implied, of the US Army Research Laboratory, the US Government, IARPA, DoI/NBC, the UK Ministry of Defence, or the UK Government. The US and UK Governments are authorized to reproduce and distribute reprints for Government purposes notwithstanding any copyright notation herein.

References

1. Applebaum, B., Ishai, Y., Kushilevitz, E.: From Secrecy to Soundness: Efficient Verification via Secure Computation (Extended Abstract). In: Abramsky, S., Gavoille, C., Kirchner, C., Meyer auf der Heide, F., Spirakis, P.G. (eds.) ICALP 2010, Part I. LNCS, vol. 6198, pp. 152–163. Springer, Heidelberg (2010)
2. Babai, L.: Trading group theory for randomness. In: 17th Annual ACM Symposium on Theory of Computing (STOC), pp. 421–429. ACM Press (1985)
3. Bellare, M., Hoang, V.T., Rogaway, P.: Adaptively Secure Garbling with Applications to One-Time Programs and Secure Outsourcing. In: Wang, X., Sako, K. (eds.) ASIACRYPT 2012. LNCS, vol. 7658, pp. 134–153. Springer, Heidelberg (2012)

4. Bellare, M., Hoang, V.T., Rogaway, P.: Foundations of garbled circuits. In: 19th ACM Conf. on Computer and Communications Security (CCS), pp. 784–796. ACM Press (2012)

5. Benabbas, S., Gennaro, R., Vahlis, Y.: Verifiable Delegation of Computation over Large Datasets. In: Rogaway, P. (ed.) CRYPTO 2011. LNCS, vol. 6841, pp. 111–131. Springer, Heidelberg (2011)

6. Bitanksy, N., Canetti, R., Chiesa, A., Tromer, E.: Recursive composition and bootstrapping for SNARKs and proof-carrying data, http://eprint.iacr.org/2012/095

7. Canetti, R., Riva, B., Rothblum, G.: Practical delegation of computation using multiple servers. In: 18th ACM Conf. on Computer and Communications Security (CCS), pp. 445–454. ACM Press (2011)

8. Canetti, R., Riva, B., Rothblum, G.: Two Protocols for Delegation of Computation. In: Smith, A. (ed.) ICITS 2012. LNCS, vol. 7412, pp. 37–61. Springer, Heidelberg (2012)

9. Chaum, D., Pedersen, T.P.: Wallet Databases with Observers. In: Brickell, E.F. (ed.) CRYPTO 1992. LNCS, vol. 740, pp. 89–105. Springer, Heidelberg (1993)

10. Chung, K.-M., Kalai, Y., Vadhan, S.: Improved Delegation of Computation Using Fully Homomorphic Encryption. In: Rabin, T. (ed.) CRYPTO 2010. LNCS, vol. 6223, pp. 483–501. Springer, Heidelberg (2010)

11. Cormode, G., Mitzenmacher, M., Thaler, J.: Practical verified computation with streaming interactive proofs. In: Proc. 3rd Innovations in Theoretical Computer Science Conference (ITCS), pp. 90–112. ACM (2012)

12. Fiore, D., Gennaro, R.: Publicly verifiable delegation of large polynomials and matrix computations, with applications. In: 19th ACM Conf. on Computer and Communications Security (CCS), pp. 501–512. ACM Press (2012)

13. Gennaro, R., Gentry, C., Parno, B.: Non-interactive Verifiable Computing: Outsourcing Computation to Untrusted Workers. In: Rabin, T. (ed.) CRYPTO 2010. LNCS, vol. 6223, pp. 465–482. Springer, Heidelberg (2010)

14. Goldwasser, S., Kalai, Y.T., Rothblum, G.N.: Delegating computation: Interactive proofs for muggles. In: 40th Annual ACM Symposium on Theory of Computing (STOC), pp. 113–122. ACM Press (2008)

15. Goldwasser, S., Micali, S., Rackoff, C.: The knowledge complexity of interactive proof systems. SIAM Journal on Computing 18(1), 186–208 (1989)

16. Golle, P., Mironov, I.: Uncheatable Distributed Computations. In: Naccache, D. (ed.) CT-RSA 2001. LNCS, vol. 2020, pp. 425–440. Springer, Heidelberg (2001)

17. Hohenberger, S., Lysyanskaya, A.: How to Securely Outsource Cryptographic Computations. In: Kilian, J. (ed.) TCC 2005. LNCS, vol. 3378, pp. 264–282. Springer, Heidelberg (2005)

18. Kamara, S., Mohassel, P., Raykova, M.: Outsourcing multi-party computation, http://eprint.iacr.org/2011/272

19. Kilian, J.: A note on efficient zero-knowledge proofs and arguments. In: 24th Annual ACM Symposium on Theory of Computing (STOC), pp. 723–732. ACM Press (1992)

20. Kilian, J.: Improved Efficient Arguments. In: Coppersmith, D. (ed.) CRYPTO 1995. LNCS, vol. 963, pp. 311–324. Springer, Heidelberg (1995)

21. Micali, S.: Computationally sound proofs. SIAM Journal on Computing 30(4), 1253–1298 (2000)

22. Naor, M., Pinkas, B., Sumner, R.: Privacy preserving auctions and mechanism design. In: ACM Conf. Electronic Commerce, pp. 129–139 (1999)
23. Papamanthou, C., Shi, E., Tamassia, R.: Signatures of Correct Computation. In: Sahai, A. (ed.) TCC 2013. LNCS, vol. 7785, pp. 222–242. Springer, Heidelberg (2013)
24. Parno, B., Raykova, M., Vaikuntanathan, V.: How to Delegate and Verify in Public: Verifiable Computation from Attribute-Based Encryption. In: Cramer, R. (ed.) TCC 2012. LNCS, vol. 7194, pp. 422–439. Springer, Heidelberg (2012)
25. Yao, A.C.-C.: How to generate and exchange secrets. In: 27th Annual Symposium on Foundations of Computer Science (FOCS), pp. 162–167. IEEE (1986)

On the Feasibility of Extending Oblivious Transfer*

Yehuda Lindell and Hila Zarosim

Dept. of Computer Science
Bar-Ilan University, Israel
lindell@biu.ac.il, zarosih@cs.biu.ac.il

Abstract. Oblivious transfer is one of the most basic and important building blocks in cryptography. As such, understanding its cost is of prime importance. Beaver (STOC 1996) showed that it is possible to obtain $\mathsf{poly}(n)$ oblivious transfers given only n actual oblivious transfer calls and using one-way functions, where n is the security parameter. In addition, he showed that it is impossible to extend oblivious transfer information theoretically. The notion of extending oblivious transfer is important theoretically (to understand the complexity of computing this primitive) and practically (since oblivious transfers can be expensive and thus extending them using only one-way functions is very attractive).

Despite its importance, very little is known about the feasibility of extending oblivious transfer, beyond the fact that it is impossible information theoretically. Specifically, it is not known whether or not one-way functions are actually necessary for extending oblivious transfer, whether or not it is possible to extend oblivious transfers with adaptive security, and whether or not it is possible to extend oblivious transfers when starting with $O(\log n)$ oblivious transfers. In this paper, we address these questions and provide almost complete answers to all of them. We show that the existence of any oblivious transfer extension protocol with security for static semi-honest adversaries implies one-way functions, that an oblivious transfer extension protocol with adaptive security implies oblivious transfer with static security, and that the existence of an oblivious transfer extension protocol from only $O(\log n)$ oblivious transfers implies oblivious transfer itself.

1 Introduction

Background – Extending Oblivious Transfer. In the oblivious transfer problem [17,5], a sender holds a pair of input bits (b_0, b_1) and enables a receiver to obtain one of them at its choice. The security requirements are that the sender learns nothing about which input is obtained by the receiver, while the receiver learns only one bit.

---

* This research was supported by THE ISRAEL SCIENCE FOUNDATION (grant No. 189/11). Hila Zarosim is grateful to the Azrieli Foundation for the award of an Azrieli Fellowship.

Oblivious transfer is one of the most basic and important primitives in cryptography in general, and in secure computation in particular. Oblivious transfer is used in almost all general protocols for secure computation with no honest majority (e.g., see [20,7]), and has been shown to imply essentially all basic cryptographic tasks [13]. Due to its importance, the complexity of computing oblivious transfer is of great importance. Oblivious transfer can be constructed from enhanced trapdoor permutations [5,9] and from homomorphic encryption [1]. In addition, it is known that it is not possible to construct oblivious transfer from public-key encryption (or one-way functions and permutations) in a black-box manner [6]. Thus, oblivious transfer requires quite strong hardness assumptions (at least when considering black-box constructions, and no nonblack-box constructions from weaker assumptions are known).

Due to the importance of oblivious transfer and its cost, Beaver asked whether or not it is possible to use a small number of oblivious transfers and a weaker assumption like one-way functions in order to obtain many oblivious transfers [3]; such a construction is called an OT extension. Beaver answered this question in the affirmative and in a beautiful construction showed how to obtain $\mathsf{poly}(n)$ oblivious transfers given ideal calls to $O(n)$ oblivious transfers and using a pseudorandom generator and symmetric encryption, which can both be constructed from any one-way function. In addition, he showed that OT extensions cannot be achieved information theoretically. These results of [3] are of great importance theoretically since they deepen our understanding of the complexity of oblivious transfer. In addition, OT extensions are of interest practically, since oblivious transfer is much more expensive than symmetric primitives. Thus, OT extensions can potentially be used to speed up protocols that rely on many oblivious transfers. In this direction, efficient OT extensions (based on a stronger assumption than one-way functions) were presented in [11].

This Paper – A Feasibility Study of OT Extensions. In this paper, we ask the following questions:

1. *What is the minimal assumption required for constructing OT extensions?* It has been shown that one-way functions suffice, and that OT extensions cannot be carried out information theoretically [3]. However, it is theoretically possible that OT extensions can be achieved under a weaker assumption than that of the existence of one-way functions. Admittedly, it is hard to conceive of a cryptographic construction that is not information theoretic and does not require one-way functions. However, a proof that one-way functions really are necessary is highly desired.

2. *Can oblivious transfer be extended with adaptive security?* The known constructions of OT extensions maintain security only in the presence of static corruptions, where the set of corrupted parties is fixed before the protocol begins. This is because the messages sent by the sender in the constructions of [3,11] are binding with respect to the sender's input strings, and so an adaptive simulator cannot explain a transcript in multiple ways. Nothing is

known about whether or not adaptively secure OT extensions exist without assuming erasures[1].

3. *How many oblivious transfers are needed for extensions?* In the constructions of [3,11], one must start with $O(n)$ oblivious transfers where n is the security parameter. These constructions can also be made to work when a superlogarithmic number $\omega(\log n)$ of oblivious transfers are given. However, they completely break down if $O(\log n)$ oblivious transfers only are available. We ask whether or not it is possible to extend a logarithmic number of oblivious transfers.

We prove the following theorems:

Theorem 1.1. *If there exists an OT extension protocol from n to $n + 1$ (with security in the presence of static semi-honest adversaries), then there exist one-way functions.*

Thus, one-way functions are *necessary and sufficient* for OT extensions.

Theorem 1.2. *If there exists an OT extension protocol from n to $n + 1$ that is secure in the presence of adaptive semi-honest adversaries, then there exists an oblivious transfer protocol that is secure in the presence of static semi-honest adversaries.*

This means that the construction of an adaptive OT extension protocol involves constructing statically secure oblivious transfer from scratch. This can still be meaningful, since adaptive oblivious transfer cannot be constructed from static oblivious transfer in a black-box manner [15]. However, it does demonstrate that adaptive OT extensions based on weaker assumptions than those necessary for static oblivious transfer do not exist.

Theorem 1.3. *If there exists an OT extension protocol from $f(n) = \mathcal{O}(\log n)$ to $f(n) + 1$ that is secure in the presence of static malicious adversaries, then there exists an oblivious transfer protocol that is secure in the presence of static malicious adversaries.*

This demonstrates that in order to extend only a logarithmic number of oblivious transfers (with security for *malicious* adversaries), one has to construct an oblivious transfer protocol from scratch. Thus, meaningful OT extensions exist only if one starts with a superlogarithmic number of oblivious transfers.

We stress that all of our results are unconditional, and are not black-box separations. Rather, we construct concrete one-way functions and OT protocols in order to prove our results.

Our results provide quite a complete picture regarding the feasibility of constructing OT extensions. The construction of [3] is optimal in terms of the computational assumption, and the constructions of [3,11] are optimal in terms of

---

[1] Note that in the erasures model, an OT extension can be constructed from one-way functions using the original construction of Beaver and the two-party computation protocol of [14] that is adaptively secure with erasures and is based on Yao's protocol.

the number of oblivious transfers one starts with. Finally, the fact that no OT extensions are known for the setting of adaptive corruptions is somewhat explained by Theorem 2.

Open Questions. Theorem 2 shows that there do not exist adaptively secure OT extensions based on weaker assumptions than what is needed for *statically secure* OT. However, we do not know how to construct an adaptively secure OT extension even from statically secure OT. Thus, the question of whether or not it is possible to construct an adaptively secure OT extension from an assumption weaker than adaptive OT is still open.

Theorem 3 holds only with respect to OT-extensions that are secure against *malicious* adversaries. For the case of semi-honest adversaries, the question of whether one can construct an an OT-extension from $f(n) = \mathcal{O}(\log n)$ to $f(n) + 1$ from an assumption weaker than statically secure OT protocol is open.

In this paper, we have investigated OT extensions. However, the basic question of extending a cryptographic primitive using a weaker assumption than that needed for obtaining the primitive from scratch is of interest in other contexts as well. For example, hybrid encryption (where one encrypts a symmetric key using an asymmetric scheme, and then encrypts the message using a symmetric scheme) is actually an extension of public-key encryption that requires one-way functions only.

A primitive that could certainly benefit from a study such as this one is *key agreement*. In this context, the question is whether it is possible for two parties to agree on an $m + 1$-bit long key, given an m-bit key, under assumptions that are weaker than those required for constructing a secure key-agreement from scratch. In the basic case, it is clear that OWFs are necessary and sufficient for any nontrivial KA extension that starts with n bits (where n is the security parameter). A more interesting question regarding this problem relates to the adaptive setting. Specifically, since adaptive key agreement is very expensive, it would be very beneficial if one could extend this primitive more efficiently and/or under weaker assumptions.

2   Definitions and Notations

We denote the security parameter by n, and we denote by U_n a random variable uniformly distributed over $\{0, 1\}^n$. We say that a function $\mu : \mathbb{N} \to \mathbb{N}$ is negligible if for every positive polynomial $p(\cdot)$ and all sufficiently large n it holds that $\mu(n) < \frac{1}{p(n)}$. We use the abbreviation PPT to denote probabilistic polynomial-time. We denote the bits of a string $x \in \{0, 1\}^n$ by $x_1, \ldots, x_n$; for a subscripted string x_b, we denote the bits by $x_b^1, \ldots, x_b^n$. In addition, for strings $x_0, x_1, \sigma \in \{0, 1\}^n$ we denote by x_σ the string $x_{\sigma_1}^1, \ldots, x_{\sigma_n}^n$.

For two distribution ensembles $X = \{X(a, n)\}$ and $Y = \{Y(a, n)\}$ with $a \in \{0, 1\}^*$ and $n \in \mathbb{N}$, we write $X \overset{c}{\equiv} Y$ if they are computationally indistinguishable, and we write $X \overset{s}{\equiv} Y$ if they are statistically close. We also denote by $SD(X, Y)$ the statistical distance between X and Y.

Interactive Protocols. Let $\pi = \langle A, B \rangle$ be an interactive protocol for computing a functionality f. We denote $f = (f_A, f_B)$, where f_A is the first output of f (for party A) and f_B is the second output of f (for party B).

The random variable $\text{VIEW}_A^\pi(x_A, x_B)$ denotes the view of the party A in an execution of π with inputs x_A for A and x_B for B, where the random tapes of the parties are uniformly chosen. Note that a view of a party contains its input, randomness and the messages it has received during the execution.

The random variable $\text{OUTPUT}_A^\pi(x_A, x_B)$ denotes the output of the party A in an execution of π with inputs x_A for A and x_B for B, where the random tapes of the parties are uniformly chosen.

Definition 2.1. *Let $f(\cdot, \cdot)$ be a deterministic binary functionality, let $\pi = \langle A, B \rangle$ be an interactive protocol and let n be the security parameter. We say that π computes the functionality f if there exists a negligible function $\mathsf{negl}(\cdot)$ such that for all n, x_A and x_B:*

$$\Pr\left[\langle A(1^n, x_A), B(1^n, x_B) \rangle = (f_A(x_A, x_B), f_B(x_A, x_B)) \right] \geq 1 - \mathsf{negl}(n).$$

Definition 2.2. *Let $\pi = \langle A, b \rangle$ be a protocol that computes a deterministic functionality $f = (f_A, f_B)$. Protocol π securely computes f in the presence of static semi-honest adversaries if there exist two PPT algorithms $\mathcal{S}_A$ and $\mathcal{S}_B$ such that:*

$$\{\mathcal{S}_A(1^n, x_A, f_A(x_A, x_B))\} \stackrel{c}{\equiv} \{\text{VIEW}_A^\pi(1^n, x_A, x_B)\} \text{ and } \{\mathcal{S}_B(1^n, x_B, f_B(x_A, x_B))\}$$
$$\stackrel{c}{\equiv} \{\text{VIEW}_B^\pi(1^n, x_A, x_B)\} \text{ where } x_A, x_B \in \{0,1\}^* \text{ and } n \in \mathbb{N}.$$

Security in the Presence of Malicious Adversaries. To define security in the presence of malicious adversaries, we use the ideal/real framework as defined by Canetti in [4]. Loosely speaking, in this approach we formalize the real-life computation as a setting where the parties, given their private inputs, interact according to the protocol in the presence of a real-life adversary that controls a set of corrupted parties. The real-life adversary can be either static (where the set of corrupted parties is fixed before the protocol begins) or adaptive (where the adversary can choose to corrupt parties during the protocol execution based on what it sees). At the end of the computation, the honest parties output what is specified by the protocol and the adversary outputs some arbitrary function of its view. If the adversary is adaptive, there is an additional entity $\mathcal{Z}$, called the environment, who sees the output of all of the parties. In addition, there is a "postexecution phase", where $\mathcal{Z}$ can instruct the adversary to also corrupt parties after the execution of the protocol ends (and the transcript is fixed, implying that "rewinding" is no longer allowed). At the end of the postexecution phase, $\mathcal{Z}$ outputs some function of its view. .

Next we consider an ideal process, where an ideal-world adversary controls a set of corrupted parties. Then, in the computation phase, all parties send their inputs to some incorruptible trusted party. The ideal-world adversary sends inputs on behalf of the corrupted parties. The trusted party evaluates the function and hands each party its output. The honest parties then output whatever they received from the trusted party and the ideal-world adversary outputs some arbitrary value. Similarly to the real-life setting, in the case of adaptive security, there is an environment $\mathcal{Z}$ who sees all outputs and can instruct the adversary to also corrupt parties in the postexecution phase. At the end of the postexecution phase, $\mathcal{Z}$ outputs some function of its view.

Loosely speaking, a protocol π is secure in the presence of static malicious adversaries, if for every static malicious real-life adversary $\mathcal{A}$, there exists a static malicious ideal-world adversary $\mathcal{SIM}$ such that the distribution obtained in a real-life execution of π with adversary $\mathcal{A}$ is indistinguishable from the distribution obtained in a ideal-world with adversary $\mathcal{SIM}$. Likewise, a protocol π is secure in the presence of adaptive malicious adversaries, if for every adaptive malicious real-life adversary $\mathcal{A}$ and environment $\mathcal{Z}$, there exists an adaptive malicious ideal-world adversary $\mathcal{SIM}$ such that the output of $\mathcal{Z}$ in a real-life execution of π with adversary $\mathcal{A}$ is indistinguishable from its output in a ideal-world with adversary $\mathcal{SIM}$.

Security in the presence of adaptive semi-honest adversaries is defined in the same way as adaptive malicious adversaries, except that the adversary only sees the internal state of a corrupted party but cannot instruct it to deviate from the protocol specification. For full definitions see [4].

The Hybrid Model. Let ϕ be a functionality. The ϕ-hybrid model is defined as follows. The real-life model for protocol π is augmented with an incorruptible trusted party T for evaluating the functionality ϕ, and the parties are allowed to make calls to the ideal functionality ϕ by sending their ϕ-inputs to T. If we consider malicious adversaries, the adversary specifies the inputs of all parties under its control. If the adversary is semi-honest, then even the corrupted parties hand T inputs as specified by the protocol π. At each invocation of ϕ, the trusted party T sends the parties their respective outputs.

We stress that if π is in the ϕ-hybrid model, then a view of a party A contains also the inputs sent by A to the functionality ϕ and the outputs sent to A by T computing ϕ.

Oblivious Transfer and Extensions. We are now ready to define oblivious transfer and OT extensions.

Definition 2.3. *The* bit oblivious transfer functionality OT *is defined by* $OT((b_0, b_1), \sigma) = (\lambda, b_\sigma)$. *The* parallel oblivious transfer functionality $m \times OT$ *is defined for strings* $x_0, x_1, \sigma \in \{0, 1\}^m$ *as follows:* $m \times OT((x_0, x_1), \sigma) = (\lambda, (x_{\sigma_1}^1, \ldots, x_{\sigma_m}^m)) = (\lambda, x_\sigma)$ *(recall that* x_σ *denotes the string* $x_{\sigma_1}^1, \ldots, x_{\sigma_n}^n$*).*

We denote by OT^k the ideal functionality of k independent OT computations. We stress that OT^k is not the same as $k \times OT$, since in the latter all of the inputs are given at once whereas in OT^k the inputs can be chosen over time (in particular, the receiver can choose its inputs as a function of the previous outputs it received). Using this notation, we have that an OT extension protocol is a protocol that securely computes $m \times OT$ given access to OT^k, where $k < m$. Formally:

Definition 2.4 (OT-extension). *Let* π *be a protocol and let* $k, m : \mathbb{N} \to \mathbb{N}$ *be two functions where* $k(n) < m(n)$ *for all* n*. We say that* π *is an* OT-extension from $k = k(n)$ to $m = m(n)$ if π securely computes the $m \times OT$ functionality in the OT^k-hybrid model.

OT Extensions – Two Technical Propositions. We present two propositions that we use throughout the paper. Beaver showed that OT can be precomputed [2]. That is, it is possible to first compute OT on random inputs and then use the result to later compute an OT on any input. Stated formally:

Proposition 2.5 (Beaver [2]). *Let $m = m(n)$ be a polynomial. If there exists a protocol that securely computes the $m \times OT$ functionality, then there exists a protocol that securely computes the OT^m ideal functionality.*

Proposition 2.5 shows that Definition 2.4 could have been stated as a protocol that securely computes OT^m in the OT^k (or even the $k \times OT$) hybrid model.

The fact that a single extension implies many has been stated many times in the literature (e.g., [3]) and is well accepted folklore, but has not been formally proved. In the full version of this paper [16], we sketch a proof of this. We stress that this holds irrespectively of how many oblivious transfers you start with (even if only a *constant number*), as long as only a polynomial number of transfers are derived. We state the proposition for adaptive malicious adversaries and observe that it holds for all four combinations of static/adaptive and semi-honest/malicious adversaries.

Proposition 2.6. *Let $f : \mathbb{N} \to \mathbb{N}$ be any polynomially-bounded function, and let n be the security parameter. If there exists a protocol π that is an OT-extension from $f(n)$ to $f(n) + 1$ that is secure in the presence of adaptive malicious adversaries, then for every polynomial $p(\cdot)$ there exists an OT-extension protocol from $f(n)$ to $p(n)$ that is secure in the presence of adaptive malicious adversaries.*

3   OT Extensions Imply One-Way Functions

In this section we show that the existence of an OT extension protocol implies the existence of one-way functions. We prove the theorem for any OT extension that is secure in the presence of static semi-honest adversaries (thus the theorem also holds when the OT extension is secure in the presence of adaptive and/or malicious adversaries, since these variants all imply security for static semi-honest adversaries).

Theorem 3.1. *Let n be the security parameter. If there exists a protocol that is an OT-extension from n to $n + 1$ that is secure in the presence of static semi-honest adversaries, then there exist one-way functions.*

Proof Sketch: To prove this, we use an information-theoretic lower bound given in [18] to show that the existence of a protocol π that is an OT-extension from n to $n + 1$ implies the existence of two polynomial-time constructible probability ensembles that are computationally indistinguishable and yet their statistical distance is noticeable. The fact that this implies one-way functions was shown in [8].

We define two polynomial-time constructible probability ensembles $\mathsf{RL} = \{\mathsf{RL}_n\}_{n\in\mathbb{N}}$ and $\mathsf{SM} = \{\mathsf{SM}_n\}_{n\in\mathbb{N}}$ that are computationally indistinguishable, but have noticeable statistical distance. Let $\mathcal{S}_S$ and $\mathcal{S}_R$ be the two simulators that are guaranteed to exist for π by its semi-honest security. We begin by defining the probability ensembles RL and SM, that represent the real and the simulated transcripts, respectively.

RL_n: First, a party $P \in \{S, R\}$ is chosen at random. Then, inputs for both parties $x_0, x_1, \sigma \in \{0,1\}^n$ are chosen uniformly at random and the real protocol π is executed on inputs (x_0, x_1) for the sender and σ for the receiver. The output of RL_n is a pair (v, ω) where v is the view of party P in the execution described above and ω is the output of the other party.

SM_n: Similarly to the above, a party $P \in \{S, R\}$ and inputs $x_0, x_1, \sigma \in \{0,1\}^n$ are chosen uniformly at random. Then, the simulator $\mathcal{S}_P$ (that is, $\mathcal{S}_R$ is $P = R$ and $\mathcal{S}_S$ if $P = S$) is executed on the corresponding input and output of party P. The output of SM_n is a pair (v, ω) where v is the view generated by the simulator and ω is the output of the other party as defined by the functionality.

We now prove that the ensembles RL and SM are computationally indistinguishable but statistically far. The fact that they are computationally indistinguishable can be derived from the (computational) security of π. Specifically, for every $P \in \{S, R\}$, it holds that the view generated by the simulator $\mathcal{S}_P$ is computationally indistinguishable from a real view of P in an execution of π, and hence it can be easily shown that RL and SM are computationally indistinguishable. Intuitively, the fact that the two ensembles are statistically far apart follows from the fact that OT cannot be extended with statistical security [3] and so the ensembles cannot be statistically close. However, this argument is not sufficient, because it only implies that RL and SM are *not statistically close*, whereas what we need to show is that the two ensembles are *statistically far apart*. Specifically, the impossibility result of [3] only shows that there exists a polynomial $p(\cdot)$ such that *for infinitely many n's*, the statistical distance between RL_n and SM_n is $\frac{1}{p(n)}$, while the existence of one-way functions as proven in [8] only follows if there exists a polynomial $p(\cdot)$ such that *for all sufficiently large n's*, the statistical distance between RL_n and SM_n is $\frac{1}{p(n)}$. We therefore use the recent *non-asymptotic bound* on the statistical distance shown by [18], and use it to derive the following:

Claim 3.2. *There exists a polynomial $p(\cdot)$ such that for all sufficiently large n's the statistical distance between RL_n and SM_n is at least $1/p(n)$. Stated differently, the ensembles RL and SM have noticeable statistical distance.*

The proof of Claim 3.2 appears in [16]. Applying [8], as mentioned above, we conclude that one-way functions exist, and this concludes the proof sketch. ∎

4   Adaptive Security

In this section we consider the feasibility of constructing OT-extension protocols that are secure in the presence of adaptive adversaries. It is easy to see that the OT-extension protocols of Beaver [3] and Ishai et al. [11] are not secure when considering adaptive security. This is because the receiver's view is essentially a binding commitment to all of the sender's inputs.[2] This raises the question as to whether there exists an OT extension protocol at all in the presence of adaptive adversaries. Of course, if the existence of an OT extension protocol (that is secure for adaptive adversaries) implies OT that is secure for adaptive adversaries, then this means that only a trivial OT extension that constructs OT from scratch exists. We provide a partial answer to this question and show that a protocol for OT-extension that is secure in the presence of adaptive adversaries implies the existence of an OT protocol that is secure in the presence of *static* adversaries. Thus, any protocol for extending OT that maintains adaptive security needs to assume, at the very least, the existence of a statically secure protocol for OT. We state and prove this for semi-honest adversaries; an analogous theorem for malicious adversaries can be obtained by applying a GMW-type compiler. Formally, we prove the following theorem (the intuition appears immediately after Protocol 4.2 below):

Theorem 4.1. *Let n be the security parameter. If there exists an OT-extension protocol from n to $n + 1$ that is secure in the presence of adaptive semi-honest adversaries, then there exists an OT protocol that is secure in the presence of static semi-honest adversaries.*

Proof. We prove the theorem by building an OT protocol that is secure in the presence of static adversaries from any OT extension from n to $4n$ that is secure in the presence of adaptive adversaries. (Note that by Proposition 2.6, an OT extension from n to $4n$ exists if there exists an extension from n to $n + 1$.) We first present the construction of the OT protocol for static adversaries and then provide intuition as to why it is secure.

Let $\pi = \langle S, R \rangle$ be a protocol that securely computes the $4n \times OT$ functionality in the OT^n-hybrid model in the presence of adaptive semi-honest adversaries. We assume that all of the ideal calls to OT in π are such that S plays the sender and R plays the receiver. This is without loss of generality since the roles in OT can always be reversed [19]. We construct an OT protocol $\hat{\pi}$ in the plain model (i.e., with no calls to an ideal OT functionality), as follows:

Protocol 4.2 (OT protocol $\hat{\pi} = \langle \hat{S}, \hat{R} \rangle$ for Static Adversaries)

– **Inputs:** *Sender $\hat{S}$ has $b_0, b_1 \in \{0, 1\}$ and receiver $\hat{R}$ has $\sigma \in \{0, 1\}$.*

---

[2] In [3] a Yao garbled circuit is used which is binding when instantiated with known encryption methods. Likewise, [11] uses correlation-robust hash functions for which it is hard to find collisions, which is exactly what is needed in order to "explain the transcript" in different ways as is needed for proving adaptive security.

- **The protocol:**

  1. $\hat{S}$ *chooses two random strings* $\alpha_0, \alpha_1 \in \{0,1\}^{4n}$.
  2. $\hat{S}$ *and* $\hat{R}$ *run the extension protocol* π *as follows:*
     (a) $\hat{S}$ *plays the sender* S *in* π *with inputs* (α_0, α_1).
     (b) $\hat{R}$ *plays* R *in* π *with input* σ^{4n} *(i.e., the string of length $4n$ with all bits set to σ).*
     (c) *The parties follow the instructions of* π *exactly except that whenever π instructs them to make an ideal call to the OT functionality with input (β_0, β_1) for S and input τ for R, the sender $\hat{S}$ sends the pair (β_0, β_1) to $\hat{R}$, and $\hat{R}$ proceeds to run R with output β_τ from the simulated ideal call.*
     (d) *Let* $\gamma \in \{0,1\}^{4n}$ *denote the output of R in the execution of* π.
  3. $\hat{S}$ *chooses two random strings* $r_0, r_1 \in_R \{0,1\}^{4n}$ *and sets:*

  $$z_0 = \langle \alpha_0, r_0 \rangle \oplus b_0 \quad \text{and} \quad z_1 = \langle \alpha_1, r_1 \rangle \oplus b_1.$$

  $\hat{S}$ *sends* (r_0, z_0) *and* (r_1, z_1) *to* $\hat{R}$.

- **Output:** $\hat{R}$ *outputs* $z_\sigma \oplus \langle \gamma, r_\sigma \rangle$.

It is clear that $\hat{\pi}$ correctly computes the OT functionality. This is because by the correctness of the OT extension protocol, R will output $\gamma = \alpha_\sigma$ in Step 2d, except with negligible probability. Thus, $z_\sigma \oplus \langle \gamma, r_\sigma \rangle = z_\sigma \oplus \langle \alpha_\sigma, r_\sigma \rangle = b_\sigma$, as required.

We proceed to prove that π securely computes the OT functionality in the presence of semi-honest adversaries. We begin with the intuition. If $\hat{S}$ and $\hat{R}$ were to run the original extension protocol π with the ideal calls, then it is clear that $\hat{\pi}$ is a secure OT protocol. This is because $\hat{S}$ learns nothing about σ, and $\hat{R}$ learns α_σ but nothing about $\alpha_{1-\sigma}$. Thus, $\hat{R}$ learns b_σ but nothing about $b_{1-\sigma}$ (observe that $\langle \alpha_{1-\sigma}, r_{1-\sigma} \rangle$ hides $b_{1-\sigma}$ by the fact that $\alpha_{1-\sigma}$ is random). Now, in $\hat{\pi}$ the difference is that $\hat{S}$ sends both inputs to $\hat{R}$ in every ideal OT call within the execution of π. Clearly, $\hat{S}$'s view can be simulated since its view is identical to the case that π with the ideal OT calls is used. In contrast, $\hat{R}$ learns more information since it obtains both sender inputs in all ideal OT calls. Since the inputs to each ideal call are a single bit, we have that $\hat{R}$ obtains n more bits of information than in the original extension protocol using ideal OT calls. However, $\alpha_{1-\sigma}$ is $4n$ bits long and so still must have high entropy even given the n additional bits of information learned. This entropy is enough to hide $b_{1-\sigma}$ since $\langle \alpha_{1-\sigma}, r_{1-\sigma} \rangle$ is a perfect universal hash function, and so a good randomness extractor.

The above seems to have nothing to do with the fact that the extension protocol π is secure in the presence of *adaptive adversaries*. However, the argument that just n more bits of information are obtained is valid only in this case. Specifically, by the definition of security in the presence of adaptive adversaries, the simulator must be able to simulate in the case that the receiver is corrupted at the onset, and the sender is corrupted at the end after the protocol concludes (formally, in the "post-execution corruption phase"). This means that the simulator must first generate a receiver-view (given the receiver's input and output), and must then later generate a sender-view (given the sender's input) that is consistent with the *already fixed* receiver-view that it previously generated. This sender-view contains, amongst other things, the inputs that the sender uses in all of the n ideal calls to the OT functionality within the extension protocol π. Thus, it is possible to add these inputs of the sender to the previously generated receiver-view (we call this the extended receiver view) and the result is the receiver-view in the modified extension protocol used in Step 2 of $\hat{\pi}$; in particular, both sender's inputs to all ideal OT calls appear. Observe that only n bits of additional information are added to the receiver view in order to obtain the extended view, and so there are at most 2^n extended views for any given receiver view. However, there are 2^{4n} different possible strings $\alpha_{1-\sigma}$. The crucial point here is that the above implies that many different possible strings $\alpha_{1-\sigma}$ must be consistent with any given extended view (except with negligible probability). This relies critically on the fact that the receiver-view is fixed before the sender corruption and so the same extended receiver-view must be consistent with many different sender inputs to the ideal OT calls. Now, once we have that many different possible $\alpha_{1-\sigma}$ strings are consistent, we can use the fact that $\alpha_{1-\sigma}$ is randomly chosen to apply the leftover hash lemma and conclude that $\langle \alpha_{1-\sigma}, r_{1-\sigma} \rangle$ is a bit that is statistically close to uniform. We now proceed to the formal proof.

Corrupted Sender: The case of a corrupted sender is straightforward since the sender $\hat{S}$ receives no information in Step 2 of $\hat{\pi}$ beyond what it receives in a real execution of π with ideal OT calls. Thus the simulator that is assumed to exist for the sender S in π can be used to generate the exact view of $\hat{S}$ in Step 2 of $\hat{\pi}$. Since $\hat{S}$ receives no messages beyond in Step 2, there is nothing more to be added to the view of $\hat{S}$.

Corrupted Receiver: In order to construct our simulator $\mathcal{S}_{\hat{R}}$ for the corrupted receiver $\hat{R}$ in $\hat{\pi}$, we first define a specific simulator $\mathcal{SIM}$ for the extension protocol π for the adaptive setting. Let $\mathcal{A}$ and $\mathcal{Z}$ be the following real-life semi-honest adversary and environment for π; see Section 2 for a brief overview of the definition of adaptive security, and [4] for full definitions. At the beginning of the execution of π, the adversary $\mathcal{A}$ corrupts the receiver and learns its input $\sigma \in \{0,1\}^{4n}$. It then follows the honest strategy for R and at the end of the execution, outputs its entire view. In the post-execution phase, $\mathcal{Z}$ generates a "corrupt S" message, sends it to $\mathcal{A}$ who corrupts S and hands $\mathcal{Z}$ the internal view of S. $\mathcal{Z}$ then outputs its internal view (note that it contains views of both R and S). Let $\mathcal{SIM}$ be the ideal-process adversary that is guaranteed to exist for this $\mathcal{A}$ and $\mathcal{Z}$ by the security of π. We remark that $\mathcal{SIM}$ generates a view of an execution of π in the OT-hybrid model, where ideal calls are used for the n invocations of OT. We use $\mathcal{SIM}$ to construct the simulator $\mathcal{S}_{\hat{R}}$ for the case of a corrupted receiver in $\hat{\pi}$.

Construction 4.3 ($\mathcal{S}_{\hat{R}}$). $\mathcal{S}_{\hat{R}}$ *receives* σ *and* b_σ *as input and works in three stages as follows:*

1. Stage 1 – obtain simulated receiver-view in π:
    (a) *Choose a random string* $\alpha_\sigma \in_R \{0,1\}^{4n}$ *as the "output of* π*" and a random tape* $r_{\mathcal{SIM}}$ *for* $\mathcal{SIM}$ *of the appropriate length.*
    (b) *Start an execution of* $\mathcal{SIM}$ *with random-tape* $r_{\mathcal{SIM}}$*. When* $\mathcal{SIM}$ *corrupts the receiver, hand* σ^{4n} *to* $\mathcal{SIM}$ *as the input of* R*.*
    (c) *In the computation stage, play the role of the trusted party and send* α_σ *to* $\mathcal{SIM}$ *as the output of* R *from* $4n \times \mathcal{OT}$*. (Since we are in the semi-honest setting,* R *always sends its specified input* σ^{4n} *and so the output that it would receive is always* α_σ*.)*
    (d) *Let* v_R *be the output of* $\mathcal{SIM}$ *at the end of the execution phase (this consists of a view for the receiver). If* v_R *is not consistent with* σ^{4n} *and* $\alpha_\sigma,$[3] *return* $\perp$ *and abort. Otherwise, proceed to the next stage.*
2. Stage 2 – obtain extended receiver-view:
    (a) *Choose a random string* $\alpha_{1-\sigma} \in \{0,1\}^{4n}$*.*
    (b) *Send a "corrupt S" message to* $\mathcal{SIM}$ *on behalf of* $\mathcal{Z}$*. When* $\mathcal{SIM}$ *corrupts the sender, hand* (α_0, α_1) *to* $\mathcal{SIM}$ *as the input of* S*.*
    (c) *Let* v_S *be the view of the sender sent by* $\mathcal{SIM}$ *to* $\mathcal{Z}$*. If* v_S *is not consistent with* v_R *and the inputs, output* $\perp$ *and abort. If* v_S *is consistent with* v_R *and the inputs, then for each of the n calls for the ideal OT functionality, extend* v_R *by appending the other input used by the sender (as appear in* v_S*) into the view* v_R *(note that* v_R *already contains one of the inputs used by the sender in each call since the receiver receives one output in each ideal call). Let* v'_R *be the extended view.*
3. Stage 3 – complete simulation:
    (a) *Choose two random strings* $r_0, r_1 \in \{0,1\}^{4n}$*; let* $z_\sigma = \langle \alpha_\sigma, r_\sigma \rangle \oplus b_\sigma$ *(where* b_σ *is from the input of* $\mathcal{S}_{\hat{R}}$*) and let* $z_{1-\sigma}$ *be a random bit.*
    (b) *Output* v'_R, r_0, r_1, z_0, z_1*.*

We prove that:

$$\left\{ \mathcal{S}_{\hat{R}}(1^n, \sigma, b_\sigma) \right\}_{b_0,b_1,\sigma \in \{0,1\}, n \in \mathbb{N}} \overset{c}{\equiv} \left\{ \text{VIEW}_{\hat{R}}^{\hat{\pi}}(1^n, b_0, b_1, \sigma) \right\}_{b_0,b_1,\sigma \in \{0,1\}, n \in \mathbb{N}} \tag{1}$$

To prove Eq. (1), we consider a hybrid simulator $\mathcal{S}^h$ that receives as input $b_{1-\sigma}$ in addition to the input (σ, b_σ) of $\mathcal{S}_{\hat{R}}$. It then works exactly as $\mathcal{S}_{\hat{R}}$ except that in Stage 3 of the simulation it sets $z_{1-\sigma} = \langle \alpha_{1-\sigma}, r_{1-\sigma} \rangle \oplus b_{1-\sigma}$ (instead of setting $z_{1-\sigma}$ to a random bit as $\mathcal{S}_{\hat{R}}$ does).

We first prove that the output of the hybrid simulator is indistinguishable from the receiver view in a real execution. That is, we prove that:

$$\left\{ \mathcal{S}^h(1^n, \sigma, b_0, b_1) \right\} \overset{c}{\equiv} \left\{ \text{VIEW}_{\hat{R}}^{\hat{\pi}}(1^n, b_0, b_1, \sigma) \right\} \tag{2}$$

---

[3] We say that a view is **consistent** with inputs and outputs if when running the party on the given view and input, it outputs the correct output.

The only difference between the two distributions is that in $\text{VIEW}_{\hat{R}}^{\hat{\pi}}(1^n, b_0, b_1, \sigma)$, the "extended view of R" (including both inputs used by the sender in each ideal OT call) is generated in a real execution of π, whereas in $\mathcal{S}^h(1^n, \sigma, b_0, b_1)$ the extended view is generated by $\mathcal{SIM}$ after the corruption at the end. So intuitively the guarantee that $\mathcal{SIM}$ is a good simulator implies that the two ensembles are computationally indistinguishable. Formally, we define a machine $\mathcal{D}$ that receives the output of $\mathcal{Z}$ after an execution of π in the adaptive setting, and attempts to determine whether it obtained a pair of receiver/sender views from a real or ideal execution. $\mathcal{D}$ generates an extended receiver-view from the pair of receiver/sender views that it received, and in addition computes the messages $(r_0, z_0), (r_1, z_1)$ using the correct sender inputs b_0, b_1 (that it's given as auxiliary input) and using the strings α_0, α_1 that appear in $\mathcal{Z}$'s output. Finally, $\mathcal{D}$ outputs the extended receiver-view together with the last message; this constitutes a view of the receiver $\hat{R}$ in $\hat{\pi}$. It is immediate that if $\mathcal{D}$ received a pair of views from a real execution of π then it outputs a view which is *identical* to $\text{VIEW}_{\hat{R}}^{\hat{\pi}}(1^n, b_0, b_1, \sigma)$. In contrast, if $\mathcal{D}$ received a pair of views generated by $\mathcal{SIM}$ in an ideal execution, then it outputs a view which is *identical* to $\mathcal{S}^h(1^n, \sigma, b_0, b_1)$. Thus, Eq. (2) follows from the security of π with simulator $\mathcal{SIM}$.

We now proceed to prove that the output of $\mathcal{S}_{\hat{R}}$ is statistically close to the output of the hybrid simulator $\mathcal{S}^h$. That is:

$$\left\{\mathcal{S}_{\hat{R}}(1^n, \sigma, b_\sigma)\right\}_{b_0, b_1, \sigma \in \{0,1\}, n \in \mathbb{N}} \overset{\mathrm{s}}{\equiv} \left\{\mathcal{S}^h(1^n, \sigma, b_0, b_1)\right\}_{b_0, b_1, \sigma \in \{0,1\}, n \in \mathbb{N}} \quad (3)$$

First note that $\mathcal{S}_{\hat{R}}$ and $\mathcal{S}^h$ work identically in the first two stages of the simulation and differ only in how $z_{1-\sigma}$ is computed. In particular, the distributions over the extended views generated by $\mathcal{S}_{\hat{R}}$ and by $\mathcal{S}^h$ are identical; let $V_R'(1^n, \sigma)$ denote this distribution.

The first step is to show that with probability negligibly close to 1, there are exponentially many strings $\alpha_{1-\sigma}$ that are consistent with an extended view generated by $\mathcal{SIM}$ (as run by $\mathcal{S}^h$ or equivalently $\mathcal{S}_{\hat{R}}$). Fix $\sigma \in \{0,1\}$ and b_σ (the following holds for all σ, b_σ and we fix them here for clarity). For a given random tape $r_{\mathcal{SIM}}$ of $\mathcal{SIM}$ and a given α_σ, let v_R be the (regular, non-extended) view generated by $\mathcal{SIM}$ with random tape $r_{\mathcal{SIM}}$ and α_σ in the execution phase. Let $\Delta(r_{\mathcal{SIM}}, \alpha_\sigma)$ be the set of all strings $\alpha_{1-\sigma}$ of size $4n$ for which the views v_R, v_S generated by $\mathcal{SIM}$ with random tape $r_{\mathcal{SIM}}$ and inputs α_σ and $\alpha_{1-\sigma}$ in the computation and post-execution phases, respectively, are all *consistent* (we have already fixed σ and b_σ so consistency is also with respect to these values; see Footnote 3). Note that if $\mathcal{S}^h$ or $\mathcal{S}_{\hat{R}}$ would output $\perp$ in the first stage (i.e., if v_R is not consistent with the input and output) when choosing $r_{\mathcal{SIM}}, \alpha_\sigma$ then $\Delta(r_{\mathcal{SIM}}, \alpha_\sigma)$ is *empty*.

We now prove that for every $\sigma, b_\sigma \in \{0,1\}$, there exists a negligible function μ such that
$$\Pr_{r_{\mathcal{SIM}}, \alpha_\sigma}\left[|\Delta(r_{\mathcal{SIM}}, \alpha_\sigma)| \geq 2^{3n}\right] \geq 1 - \mu(n).$$

Intuitively, this holds because if $\Delta(r_{\mathcal{SIM}}, \alpha_\sigma)$ is "small", then $\mathcal{SIM}$ would fail with high probability. Formally, assume that $\Pr_{r_{\mathcal{SIM}}, \alpha_\sigma}[|\Delta(r_{\mathcal{SIM}}, \alpha_\sigma)| \geq 2^{3n}]$ is non-negligibly smaller than 1. We consider two cases:

1. With non-negligible probability, the view v_R generated by $\mathcal{SIM}$ with random tape $r_{\mathcal{SIM}}$ and α_σ cause $\mathcal{S}^h$ and $\mathcal{S}_{\hat{R}}$ to output $\bot$ (i.e., it is not consistent with the inputs/outputs): In this case, a distinguisher $\mathcal{Z}$ easily distinguishes the output of $\mathcal{SIM}$ from the views of v_R, v_S in a real execution of π since in a real execution the views are consistent except with negligible probability.

2. With non-negligible probability, v_R *is* consistent but $|\Delta(r_{\mathcal{SIM}}, \alpha_\sigma)| < 2^{3n}$: In this case, it is possible to distinguish a real execution of π from an ideal execution with $\mathcal{SIM}$ because the probability that a random $\alpha_{1-\sigma}$ is in $\Delta(r_{\mathcal{SIM}}, \alpha_\sigma)$ is less than $\frac{2^{3n}}{2^{4n}} = 2^{-n}$. Thus, the environment $\mathcal{Z}$ can just supply a random $\alpha_{1-\sigma}$ and see if in the post-execution corruption it receives a consistent view. In the real execution it will always receive a consistent view. However, in the ideal (simulated) execution, it will receive a consistent view with probability less than 2^{-n}. This is due to the fact that when $\alpha_{1-\sigma} \notin \Delta(r_{\mathcal{SIM}}, \alpha_\sigma)$ the view is *not* consistent. Thus, $\mathcal{Z}$ distinguishes with probability $(1 - 2^{-n})$ times the probability that this case occurs, which is non-negligible.

We stress that the calculation in the second case holds since the view of the receiver v_R is fixed before the post-execution phase and thus is fixed before $\alpha_{1-\sigma}$ is essentially chosen.

We now fix $r^*_{\mathcal{SIM}}$ and α^*_σ for which $|\Delta(r^*_{\mathcal{SIM}}, \alpha^*_\sigma)| \geq 2^{3n}$ and prove that the outputs of $\mathcal{S}^h$ and $\mathcal{S}_{\hat{R}}$ are statistically close for such $r^*_{\mathcal{SIM}}$ and α^*_σ. First, recall that an extended view v'_R is obtained by concatenating the other (previously not received) input of the sender in the n calls to the ideal OT to the view v_R. Since there are 2^n possible "other sender inputs" in the n ideal OT calls, it follows that for any given receiver-view v_R (which is fully determined by $r^*_{\mathcal{SIM}}$ and α^*_σ; recall that σ, b_σ are already fixed) there are at most 2^n possible associated extended views. (Again, this relies on the fact that the receiver-view is fixed before the post-execution corruption phase.)

Now, since there are 2^n possible extended views, we can partition the at least 2^{3n} consistent strings $\alpha_{1-\sigma} \in \Delta(r^*_{\mathcal{SIM}}, \alpha^*_\sigma)$ so that each partition contains the set of strings $\alpha_{1-\sigma}$ that yield the extended view v'_R. Equivalently, we associate $\alpha_{1-\sigma}$ with v'_R if $\mathcal{SIM}$ with $r^*_{\mathcal{SIM}}$ and α^*_σ outputs the extended view v'_R when given $\alpha_{1-\sigma}$ in the post-execution corruption phase. We denote by $\Gamma(v'_R, r^*_{\mathcal{SIM}}, \alpha^*_\sigma)$ the set of all strings $\alpha_{1-\sigma} \in \Delta(r^*_{\mathcal{SIM}}, \alpha^*_\sigma)$ which are associated with v'_R, as described above.

We argue that the probability of obtaining an extended view v'_R for which $|\Gamma(v'_R, r^*_{\mathcal{SIM}}, \alpha^*_\sigma)| < 2^n$ is at most 2^{-n} (i.e., an extended view for which the set of associated strings $\alpha_{1-\sigma}$ is small is obtained with probability at most 2^{-n}). We stress that the probability is over the choice of $\alpha_{1-\sigma}$ (all other randomness is fixed).

In order to see this, observe that the fact that $|\Delta(r^*_{\mathcal{SIM}}, \alpha^*_\sigma)| \geq 2^{3n}$ implies that there are at least 2^{3n} strings $\alpha_{1-\sigma}$ that are associated with *some* extended view v'_R. Now, for every v'_R for which $|\Gamma(v'_R, r^*_{\mathcal{SIM}}, \alpha^*_\sigma)| < 2^n$, we have that v'_R is generated by less than 2^n of those 2^{3n} strings. Thus, such a v'_R is obtained with probability less than $2^n/2^{3n} = 2^{-2n}$. By union bound over the 2^n possible extended views v'_R (which also bounds the number of extended views for which $|\Gamma(v'_R, r^*_{\mathcal{SIM}}, \alpha^*_\sigma)| < 2^n$) we conclude that

$$\Pr\left[\,|\Gamma(v'_R, r^*_{\mathcal{SIM}}, \alpha^*_\sigma)| < 2^n\right] < 2^n \cdot \frac{1}{2^{2n}} = \frac{1}{2^n} \tag{4}$$

where the probability is over the choice of $\alpha_{1-\sigma}$.

From Eq. (4), we know that when $\alpha_{1-\sigma}$ is random, the probability that we will obtain an extended view v'_R such that $\Gamma(v'_R, r^*_{\mathcal{SIM}}, \alpha^*_\sigma)$ is small (with less than 2^n strings $\alpha_{1-\sigma}$ associated with it) is less than 2^{-n}. We therefore proceed by conditioning further over views v'_R for which $|\Gamma(v'_R, r^*_{\mathcal{SIM}}, \alpha^*_\sigma)| \geq 2^n$. Specifically, we argue that the distributions generated by $\mathcal{S}_{\hat{R}}$ and $\mathcal{S}^h$ are statistically close, conditioned on $r^*_{\mathcal{SIM}}, \alpha^*_\sigma$ such that $|\Delta(r^*_{\mathcal{SIM}}, \alpha^*_\sigma)| \geq 2^{3n}$ and conditioned on the extended view being a specific v'^*_R for which $\left|\Gamma(v'^*_R, r^*_{\mathcal{SIM}}, \alpha^*_\sigma)\right| \geq 2^n$.

First, observe that since $\alpha_{1-\sigma}$ is chosen uniformly and independently of $r^*_{\mathcal{SIM}}, \alpha_\sigma$, it is uniformly distributed in $\Gamma(v'^*_R, r^*_{\mathcal{SIM}}, \alpha^*_\sigma)$, when conditioning on all of the above. (The conditioning over v'_R is equivalent to saying that $\alpha_{1-\sigma}$ is uniform in $\Gamma(v'^*_R, r^*_{\mathcal{SIM}}, \alpha^*_\sigma)$ instead of being uniform in $\{0,1\}^{4n}$.) Second, recall that $\Gamma(v'^*_R, r^*_{\mathcal{SIM}}, \alpha^*_\sigma)$ is a set of size at least 2^n. Third, note that $H_{r_{1-\sigma}}(x) = \langle r_{1-\sigma}, x\rangle)$ is a universal hash function from $\{0,1\}^{4n}$ to $\{0,1\}$. Thus, by the Leftover Hash Lemma (the version given in [12]), it holds that:

$$SD\left((r_{1-\sigma}, \langle r_{1-\sigma}, \alpha_{1-\sigma}\rangle), (r_{1-\sigma}, U_1)\right) \leq \frac{1}{2^{(n-1)/2}}$$

where SD denotes statistical distance and U_1 denotes the uniform distribution over $\{0,1\}$ (as above, this statistical distance is computed when conditioned over $v'^*_R, r^*_{\mathcal{SIM}}, \alpha^*_\sigma$). Thus, these random variables are statistically close, conditioned on $v'^*_R, r^*_{\mathcal{SIM}}, \alpha^*_\sigma$ as above. Noting that in the output of $\mathcal{S}_{\hat{R}}$ we have $(r_{1-\sigma}, z_{1-\sigma}) = (r_{1-\sigma}, U_1)$, and in the output of $\mathcal{S}^h$ we have that $(r_{1-\sigma}, z_{1-\sigma}) = (r_{1-\sigma}, \langle r_{1-\sigma}, \alpha_{1-\sigma}\rangle)$, we conclude that

$$\left\{\mathcal{S}_{\hat{R}}(1^n, \sigma, b_\sigma) \mid v'^*_R, r^*_{\mathcal{SIM}}, \alpha^*_\sigma\right\} \overset{s}{\equiv} \left\{\mathcal{S}^h(1^n, \sigma, b_0, b_1) \mid v'^*_R, r^*_{\mathcal{SIM}}, \alpha^*_\sigma\right\}$$

where the conditioning is as described above. We reiterate that this holds since the extended views and the pair (r_σ, z_σ) are generated in an identical way by $\mathcal{S}_{\hat{R}}$ and $\mathcal{S}^h$, and the only difference is with respect to $(r_{1-\sigma}, z_{1-\sigma})$. Eq. (3) follows from the fact that we condition here on events that occur with all but negligible probability (and the events have identical probability with $\mathcal{S}_{\hat{R}}$ and $\mathcal{S}^h$). Combining Eq. (2) with Eq. (3), we derive Eq. (1), thereby completing the proof of Theorem 4.1.

Corollary – Lengthening String OT. Observe that in our proof above the receiver always uses σ^{4n} for input. Thus, it follows that the theorem holds even if the receiver is interested in only obtaining the string of all of the "0 inputs" or the string of all of the "1 inputs". Stated differently, our proof holds also for the problem of lengthening string OT; i.e., for the problem of obtaining a *single string OT* for strings of length $n+1$ or more, given a *single string OT* for strings of length n.

5 OT Extensions Require Super-Logarithmic Calls

Theorem 5.1. *Let $f : \mathbb{N} \to \mathbb{N}$ be a function such that $f(n) \in \mathcal{O}(\log n)$, and let n be the security parameter. Then, if there exists a protocol π that is an OT-extension from $f(n)$ to $f(n) + 1$ that is secure in the presence of malicious adversaries, then there exists a protocol for the OT functionality that is secure in the presence of malicious adversaries.*

Proof. Intuitively, in an OT extension protocol using only $\mathcal{O}(\log n)$ ideal OT calls, it is possible for the receiver to guess the bits that it would receive as output from these calls instead of actually running them. Since there are only $\mathcal{O}(\log n)$ calls, the probability that the receiver guesses correctly is $2^{-\mathcal{O}(\log n)} = 1/\mathsf{poly}(n)$. This idea can be used to construct an OT protocol that is weak in the sense that full privacy is maintained, but correctness only holds with probability $1/2 + 1/\mathsf{poly}(n)$. We stress that a naive attempt to implement the above idea will not work since it is necessary to ensure that if the receiver's guesses are incorrect then it still outputs the correct output of the protocol with probability almost $1/2$. Otherwise, the "advantage" in obtaining the correct output when the receiver guesses correctly can be canceled out by the "disadvantage" when the receiver guesses incorrectly. We therefore use a similar technique as in the proof regarding adaptive adversaries above. Specifically, we use the fact that an extension from $f(n)$ to $f(n) + 1$ implies an extension from $f(n)$ to n, and then use this to obliviously transfer n random bits. The actual oblivious transfer is carried out by applying a universal hash function to the random strings and using the result to mask the actual bits being transferred. This ensures that we obtain correctness that is noticeable greater than $1/2$ and so can be amplified. However, in addition, we also have to claim that privacy is maintained. This is not immediate since the receiver does not follow the specified protocol (rather, it chooses the outputs from the ideal OT calls at random, and this may effect the other messages that it sends). By requiring that the extension protocol be secure for malicious adversaries, this ensures that the receiver cannot learn more by behaving in this way. In addition, we show that a malicious sender can also achieve the same affect by inputting a random bit (for both sender inputs) in each ideal OT call. This implies that a malicious sender can also not learn anything by the receiver behaving in this way. We now proceed to the formal proof.

Throughout the proof, we will construct protocols that are secure for *semi-honest adversaries* only. This suffices since semi-honest OT implies malicious OT [7,10]. Let $f : \mathbb{N} \to \mathbb{N}$ be a function such that $f(n) \in \mathcal{O}(\log n)$ and let $\pi = \langle S, R \rangle$ be a protocol such that on security parameter n and inputs $x_0, x_1 \in \{0,1\}^{f(n)+1}$ and $\sigma \in \{0,1\}^{f(n)+1}$ securely computes the $(f(n)+1) \times OT$ functionality in the $OT^{f(n)}$-hybrid model (that is, making at most $f(n)$ calls to an ideal OT). We assume that π is secure in the presence of malicious adversaries. We assume that in all of these calls, R is the one to receive output (this is without loss of generality since oblivious transfer is symmetric [19] and so the roles can be reversed by adding additional messages in π). We show how to construct a protocol for computing the OT functionality without any further assumptions other than the existence of an extension protocol π with the parameters in the theorem statement. This is achieved in two steps. First, we use the OT-extension from $f(n) = \mathcal{O}(\log n)$ to n to construct a protocol $\tilde{\pi}$ which is simulatable and therefore fully secure, but whose error might be large. Then we amplify the correctness of the protocol using multiple executions. As we show, this can be done once the basic protocol is fully secure.

Step 1 – Constructing a Weak-OT. We begin by formally defining weak-OT, which is an oblivious transfer for semi-honest adversaries that has weak correctness but full simulation security.[4] We then show how to construct a weak-OT protocol $\tilde{\pi} = \langle \tilde{S}, \tilde{R} \rangle$ from an OT-extension from $f(n)$ to n. Note that by Proposition 2.6, if there exists an extension protocol from $f(n)$ to $f(n)+1$, then there exists an extension protocol from $f(n)$ to n.

Definition 5.2 (Weak-OT). *A two-party protocol $\pi = \langle S, R \rangle$ is a* weak-OT *if the following hold:*

- **Weak-correctness:** *There exists a polynomial $p(\cdot)$ such that for all $b_0, b_1, \sigma \in \{0,1\}$ and all large enough n's, $\Pr[\text{OUTPUT}_R^\pi(1^n, b_0, b_1, \sigma) = b_\sigma] \geq \frac{1}{2} + \frac{1}{p(n)}$.*
- **Privacy:** *There exists PPT machines $\mathcal{S}_R$ and $\mathcal{S}_S$ such that*

$$\{\mathcal{S}_R(1^n, \sigma, b_\sigma)\}_{b_0, b_1, \sigma \in \{0,1\}, n \in \mathbb{N}} \overset{c}{\equiv} \{\text{VIEW}_R^\pi(1^n, b_0, b_1, \sigma)\}_{b_0, b_1, \sigma \in \{0,1\}, n \in \mathbb{N}}$$

$$\{\mathcal{S}_S(1^n, b_0, b_1)\}_{b_0, b_1, \sigma \in \{0,1\}, n \in \mathbb{N}} \overset{c}{\equiv} \{\text{VIEW}_S^\pi(1^n, b_0, b_1, \sigma)\}_{b_0, b_1, \sigma \in \{0,1\}, n \in \mathbb{N}}$$

Let $\alpha_0, \alpha_1, c \in \{0,1\}^n$ be n-bit strings. Let $\alpha_0 = \alpha_0^1, \ldots, \alpha_0^n$, $\alpha_1 = \alpha_1^1, \ldots, \alpha_1^n$, and $c = c_1, \ldots, c_n$. Recall that $\alpha_c = \alpha_{c_1}^1, \alpha_{c_2}^2, \ldots, \alpha_{c_n}^n$; that is, the ith bit of α_c is either α_0^i or α_1^i, depending on the value of c_i.

Let $\pi = \langle S, R \rangle$ be an OT-extension protocol from $f(n) = \mathcal{O}(\log n)$ to n. We construct a weak OT protocol $\tilde{\pi} = \langle \tilde{S}, \tilde{R} \rangle$ as follows:

Protocol 5.3 (A weak-OT with no ideal OT calls)

- **Inputs:** *Sender $\tilde{S}$ has two bits $b_0, b_1 \in \{0,1\}$, and receiver $\tilde{R}$ has $\sigma \in \{0,1\}$.*
- **The protocol:**
  1. *$\tilde{S}$ chooses two random strings $\alpha_0, \alpha_1 \in_R \{0,1\}^n$.*
  2. *$\tilde{R}$ chooses a random string $c \in_R \{0,1\}^n$.*
  3. *$\tilde{S}$ and $\tilde{R}$ simulate an execution of the extension protocol π, as follows:*
     (a) *$\tilde{S}$ plays the role of the sender S with input $\alpha_0, \alpha_1 \in \{0,1\}^n$ and $\tilde{R}$ plays the role of the receiver R with input $c \in \{0,1\}^n$.*
     (b) *Whenever π instructs the parties to make an OT call, the parties make no call and $\tilde{R}$ chooses a random bit as its output from the call. We denote by $\beta_1, \ldots, \beta_{f(n)}$ the random bits chosen by $\tilde{R}$ as the OT outputs.*
     (c) *Let $\gamma \in \{0,1\}^n$ denote the receiver-output of the simulation of π received by $\tilde{R}$.*

---

[4] Note that we cannot cast this as a special case of Definition 2.2 since full correctness is required there by stating that π computes f.

4. $\tilde{R}$ *chooses a random* $c' \in_R \{0,1\}^n$ *and sends* (c_0, c_1) *to* $\tilde{S}$, *where* $c_\sigma = c$ *and* $c_{1-\sigma} = c'$.
5. $\tilde{S}$ *chooses two random strings* $r_0, r_1 \in_R \{0,1\}^n$, *computes* $z_0 = \langle r_0, \alpha_{c_0} \rangle \oplus b_0$ *and* $z_1 = \langle r_1, \alpha_{c_1} \rangle \oplus b_1$, *and sends* $(r_0, z_0), (r_1, z_1)$ *to* $\tilde{R}$.

- **Output:** $\tilde{S}$ *outputs nothing and* $\tilde{R}$ *outputs* out $= z_\sigma \oplus \langle r_\sigma, \gamma \rangle$.

We now prove that Protocol 5.3, also denoted $\tilde{\pi}$, is a weak-OT protocol. Intuitively, weak correctness holds because $\tilde{R}$ correctly guesses the outputs of the OT calls with probability $1/2^{f(n)}$ in which case $\gamma = \alpha_c$ by the correctness of π (except with negligible probability), and thus $\langle r_\sigma, \gamma \rangle = \langle r_\sigma, \alpha_c \rangle$ and out $= b_\sigma$. In addition, when the guesses made by $\tilde{R}$ are not correct, it still outputs b_σ with probability $1/2$. This holds because when r is random, the function $\langle r, \cdot \rangle$ is a universal hash function, and so $\langle r_\sigma, \gamma \rangle$ is uniformly distributed and equals $\langle r_\sigma, \alpha_c \rangle$ with probability $1/2$. See [16] for the full proof.

We proceed to prove *privacy*, by constructing $\mathcal{S}_{\tilde{S}}$ and $\mathcal{S}_{\tilde{R}}$ as required. We start by constructing the simulator $\mathcal{S}_{\tilde{S}}$ for the case that the sender is corrupted. To prove this we use the fact that the original protocol π is secure in the presence of malicious adversaries. Consider a malicious adversary $\mathcal{A}$ for π that controls the sender and learns its input $\alpha_0, \alpha_1 \in \{0,1\}^n$. $\mathcal{A}$ follows the honest strategy for S except that it chooses random bits $\beta_1, \ldots, \beta_n$ and then in the jth call to the ideal OT functionality, it uses β_j as both sender inputs to the OT call (ensuring that R receives β_j). We stress that in the rest of the execution, it behaves as if it has used the correct inputs that were supposed to be sent to the OT calls. Observe that the view of $\mathcal{A}$ in an execution of π is *identically distributed* to the view of $\tilde{S}$ in the simulation of π run in Step 3 of Protocol 5.3. Let $\mathcal{SIM}$ be the simulator that is guaranteed to exist for $\mathcal{A}$ by the security of π. We construct the simulator $\mathcal{S}_{\tilde{S}}$ using $\mathcal{SIM}$:

Construction 5.4 ($\mathcal{S}_{\tilde{S}}$). : *Upon input* $b_0, b_1 \in \{0,1\}$, $\mathcal{S}_{\tilde{S}}$ *works as follows:*

1. $\mathcal{S}_{\tilde{S}}$ *chooses two random strings* $\alpha_0, \alpha_1 \in_R \{0,1\}^n$ *and runs* $\mathcal{SIM}$ *with sender-inputs* α_0, α_1. *Let* v_S *be the sender-view output by* $\mathcal{SIM}$ *at the end of its execution ($\mathcal{SIM}$ also sends input to the trusted party, but this is ignored by $\mathcal{S}_{\tilde{S}}$).*
2. $\mathcal{S}_{\tilde{S}}$ *chooses two random strings* $c_0, c_1 \in_R \{0,1\}^n$ *as the message received from* $\tilde{R}$ *in Step 4 of Protocol 5.3, and outputs* $v_{\tilde{S}} = (v_S, c_0, c_1)$.

The fact that $\mathcal{S}_{\tilde{S}}$ is a good simulator follows immediately from the fact that $\mathcal{SIM}$ generates a sender-view that is indistinguishable from what $\mathcal{A}$ would see in a real execution of π. Since we have already observed that the view of $\tilde{S}$ in Step 3 of Protocol 5.3 is identical to the view of $\mathcal{A}$ above in π, it follows that v_S is indistinguishable from $\tilde{S}$'s view in Step 3 of Protocol 5.3. Next observe that a distinguisher $\mathcal{D}$ for $\mathcal{SIM}$ and π obtains the input/output used (α_0, α_1, c) and thus can extend the view of the sender to include c_0, c_1 where $c_\sigma = c$, and c is the input of R into the execution of π with $\mathcal{A}$ (we can assume that $\mathcal{D}$ knows σ as auxiliary input). Thus, the view of $\tilde{S}$ in Protocol 5.3 (resp., as generated by simulator $\mathcal{S}_{\tilde{S}}$) can be perfectly constructed by $\mathcal{D}$ from the real view v_S of S in π

(resp., from a simulated view v_S of S as generated by $\mathcal{SIM}$). This implies that if the output of $\mathcal{S}_{\tilde{S}}$ can be distinguished from the view of $\tilde{S}$ in a real execution of Protocol 5.3, then the output of $\mathcal{SIM}$ can be distinguished from the view of $\mathcal{A}$ in a real execution of π, in contradiction to the security of π with simulator $\mathcal{SIM}$. The formal reduction is straightforward.

We now proceed to construct a simulator $\mathcal{S}_{\tilde{R}}$ for the case that the receiver is corrupted. As above, we consider a malicious adversary $\mathcal{A}$ for π as follows. $\mathcal{A}$ receives the receiver's input $c \in \{0,1\}^n$ and follows the honest receiver strategy except that in each of the calls to the ideal OT functionality, it chooses a random bit β_j and proceeds with β_j as the output of the ideal OT. Let $\mathcal{SIM}$ be the simulator that is guaranteed to exist for $\mathcal{A}$ by the security of π. We use it construct the simulator $\mathcal{S}_{\tilde{R}}$ (recall that $\mathcal{SIM}$ works in the setting for malicious adversaries and thus interacts with a trusted party and sends a receiver-input which is not necessarily the prescribed receiver-input):

Construction 5.5 ($\mathcal{S}_{\tilde{R}}$). : *Upon input $\sigma, b_\sigma \in \{0,1\}$, $\mathcal{S}_{\tilde{R}}$ works as follows:*

1. *$\mathcal{S}_{\tilde{R}}$ chooses three random strings $\alpha_0, \alpha_1, c \in_R \{0,1\}^n$.*
2. *$\mathcal{S}_{\tilde{R}}$ runs $\mathcal{SIM}$ with receiver input c.*
3. *When $\mathcal{SIM}$ sends some $c^* \in \{0,1\}^n$ to the trusted party, $\mathcal{S}_{\tilde{R}}$ hands α_{c^*} as the receiver-output to $\mathcal{SIM}$ from the trusted party. Let v_R be the output of $\mathcal{SIM}$.*
4. *$\mathcal{S}_{\tilde{R}}$ chooses random strings $c', r_0, r_1 \in_R \{0,1\}^n$, and sets $c_\sigma = c$ and $c_{1-\sigma} = c'$. Then, $\mathcal{S}_{\tilde{R}}$ computes $z_\sigma = \langle r_\sigma, \alpha_{c_\sigma} \rangle \oplus b_\sigma$ and sets $z_{1-\sigma} \in_R \{0,1\}$ to be a random bit.*
5. *$\mathcal{S}_{\tilde{R}}$ outputs a receiver view $(c_0, c_1, v_R, r_0, z_0, r_1, z_1)$. (Note that c_0, c_1 are actually part of $\tilde{R}$'s random tape, since they are chosen by $\tilde{R}$.)*

Intuitively, the two differences between the simulated and real executions are (a) the execution of π is simulated using $\mathcal{SIM}$ (which is indistinguishable by assumption), and (b) $z_{1-\sigma}$ is generated randomly instead of being computed as $z_{1-\sigma} = \langle r_{1-\sigma}, \alpha_{c_{1-\sigma}} \rangle \oplus b_{1-\sigma}$. However, since $c_{1-\sigma} = c'$ is chosen at random independently of the execution, and since $\mathcal{SIM}$ learns only the bits in the sender's input that correspond to c^*, with high probability there is enough uncertainty about $\langle \alpha_{c_{1-\sigma}}, r_{1-\sigma} \rangle$ and thus $z_{1-\sigma}$ is statistically close to a random bit. This is formally proven in [16]. We conclude that Protocol 5.3 is a weak-OT protocol.

Step 2 – full-OT from weak-OT. The last step to transform weak OT to full OT simply works by running multiple executions and taking the majority result. Since the weak OT is fully secure, and it is only the correctness that is weak, this preserves security and so achieves what is needed. This concludes the proof.

Acknowledgements. We thank Yuval Ishai for helpful discussions.

References

1. Aiello, W., Ishai, Y., Reingold, O.: Priced Oblivious Transfer: How to Sell Digital Goods. In: Pfitzmann, B. (ed.) EUROCRYPT 2001. LNCS, vol. 2045, pp. 119–135. Springer, Heidelberg (2001)
2. Beaver, D.: Precomputing Oblivious Transfer. In: Coppersmith, D. (ed.) CRYPTO 1995. LNCS, vol. 963, pp. 97–109. Springer, Heidelberg (1995)
3. Beaver, D.: Correlated Pseudorandomness and the Complexity of Private Computations. In: The 28th STOC, pp. 479–488 (1996)
4. Canetti, R.: Security and Composition of Multiparty Cryptographic Protocols. Journal of Cryptology 13(1), 143–202 (2000)
5. Even, S., Goldreich, O., Lempel, A.: A Randomized Protocol for Signing Contracts. Communications of the ACM 28(6), 637–647 (1985)
6. Gertner, Y., Kannan, S., Malkin, T., Reingold, O., Viswanathan, M.: The Relationship Between Public Key Encryption and Oblivious Transfer. In: The 41st FOCS, pp. 325–335 (2000)
7. Goldreich, O., Micali, S., Wigderson, A.: How to Play any Mental Game – A Completeness Theorem for Protocols with Honest Majority. In: 19th STOC, pp. 218–229 (1987) (For details see [9])
8. Goldreich, O.: A Note on Computational Indistinguishability. Information Processing Letters 34(6), 277–281 (1990)
9. Goldreich, O.: Foundations of Cryptography. Basic Applications, vol. 2. Cambridge University Press (2004)
10. Haitner, I., Ishai, Y., Kushilevitz, E., Lindell, Y., Petrank, E.: Black-Box Constructions of Protocols for Secure Computation. SIAM Journal on Computing 40(2), 225–266 (2011)
11. Ishai, Y., Kilian, J., Nissim, K., Petrank, E.: Extending Oblivious Transfers Efficiently. In: Boneh, D. (ed.) CRYPTO 2003. LNCS, vol. 2729, pp. 145–161. Springer, Heidelberg (2003)
12. Impagliazzo, R., Zuckerman, D.: How to Recycle Random Bits. In: The 30th FOCS, pp. 248–253 (1989)
13. Kilian, J.: Founding Cryptography on Oblivious Transfer. In: The 20th STOC, pp. 20–31 (1988)
14. Lindell, A.Y.: Adaptively Secure Two-Party Computation with Erasures. In: Fischlin, M. (ed.) CT-RSA 2009. LNCS, vol. 5473, pp. 117–132. Springer, Heidelberg (2009)
15. Lindell, Y., Zarosim, H.: Adaptive Zero-Knowledge Proofs and Adaptively Secure Oblivious Transfer. The Journal of Cryptology 24(4), 761–799 (2011)
16. Lindell, Y., Zarosim, H.: On the Feasibility of Extending Oblivious Transfer. Cryptology ePrint Archive: Report 2012/333 (2012)
17. Rabin, M.: How to Exchange Secrets by Oblivious Transfer. Tech. Memo TR-81. Aiken Computation Laboratory, Harvard University (1981)
18. Winkler, S., Wullschleger, J.: On the Efficiency of Classical and Quantum Oblivious Transfer Reductions. In: Rabin, T. (ed.) CRYPTO 2010. LNCS, vol. 6223, pp. 707–723. Springer, Heidelberg (2010)
19. Wolf, S., Wullschleger, J.: Oblivious Transfer Is Symmetric. In: Vaudenay, S. (ed.) EUROCRYPT 2006. LNCS, vol. 4004, pp. 222–232. Springer, Heidelberg (2006)
20. Yao, A.: How to Generate and Exchange Secrets. In: The 27th FOCS, pp. 162–167 (1986)

Computational Soundness of Coinductive Symbolic Security under Active Attacks

Mohammad Hajiabadi and Bruce M. Kapron

Dept. of Computer Science, University of Victoria, Victoria, CANADA V8W 3P6
{mhaji,bmkapron}@cs.uvic.ca

Abstract. In Eurocrypt 2010, Miccinacio initiated an investigation of cryptographically sound, symbolic security analysis with respect to *coinductive* adversarial knowledge, and showed that under an adversarially *passive* model, certain security criteria may be given a computationally sound symbolic characterization, without the assumption of *key acyclicity*. Left open in his work was the fundamental question of "the viability of extending the coinductive approach to prove computational soundness results in the presence of *active* adversaries." In this paper we make some initial steps toward this goal with respect to an extension of a *trace-based security model* (Micciancio and Warinschi, TCC 2004) including asymmetric and symmetric encryption; in particular we prove that a random *computational trace* can be *soundly abstracted* by a *coinductive symbolic trace* with overwhelming probability, provided that both the underlying encryption schemes provide IND-CCA2 security (plus ciphertext integrity for the symmetric scheme), and that the *diameter* of the underlying *coinductively-hidden subgraph* is constant in every symbolic trace. This result holds *even if* the protocol allows arbitrarily nested applications of symmetric/asymmetric encryption, unrestricted transmission of symmetric keys, and adversaries who *adaptively corrupt users*, along with other forms of active attack.

As part of our proof, we formulate a game-based definition of encryption security allowing *adaptive corruptions of keys* and certain forms of *adaptive key-dependent plaintext attack*, along with other common forms of CCA2 attack. We prove that (with assumptions similar to above) security under this game is implied by IND-CCA2 security. This also characterizes a *provably benign* form of *cyclic encryption* implied by standard security definitions, which may be of independent interest.

Keywords: Computational soundness, adaptive corruptions, coinduction, circular security, trace-based protocol security, active adversaries.

1 Introduction

Provable security, since its introduction in the early 1980s, has provided a rigorous foundation for the security analysis of cryptographic schemes. Typically, proving a cryptographic construction meets a given security goal within the provable security framework requires: (1) formally defining the security goal in

A. Sahai (Ed.): TCC 2013, LNCS 7785, pp. 539–558, 2013.

terms of what comprises a violation of the goal and what is assumed about the computational power of the adversary, and (2) giving a feasible method which transforms any attack against the construction to an attack against one of its underlying primitives [12,13]. This methodology provides strong security assurances against resource-bounded attackers, which is a fairly realistic assumption in real-world applications. However, doing computational security analysis, even for small-sized protocols, can be a gruelingly tedious task, and normally a small change in the protocol necessitates a new security proof. On the other hand, *formal* (logic-based) *methods* [24,15] greatly simplify security analysis using idealized abstractions of cryptographic primitives and limiting adversarial computation, even allowing for automated verification. While formal methods may help designers identify subtle flaws in their schemes, they do not necessarily provide guarantees of computational security. At the very least, a formally verified scheme may be computationally insecure if realized under "insufficiently strong" primitives (e.g. using *malleable* encryption in the case of active attacks). Motivated by the mismatch between these two approaches, a large body of work, starting from [1], attempts to give computational justifications for formal security proofs, in the form of *computational soundness* theorems. Generally speaking, a formal system for security proofs is computationally sound if whenever a scheme is proved secure in the system, it is guaranteed to also be secure in an appropriate computational security framework.

Background. Standard notions of secure encryption [26,38] ensure privacy of plaintexts chosen independently from the underlying secret key(s). It has long been known that a key encrypted under itself may no longer remain secret, and recent results [20,2] show that indeed for all $k \geq 1$, k-circular security is not implied by standard security. Moreover, currently known techniques for standard security fall short when trying to prove non-trivial security statements against more *adaptive* adversaries. As an example, assume in the standard multiple-key-based indistinguishability game [9] over keys $ck_1, \ldots, ck_n$, the adversary is additionally allowed to obtain the (nested) encryption of any ck_i under $\{ck_1, \ldots, ck_{i-1}\}$, giving rise to an acyclic *encryption ordering* between keys. One can use a standard hybrid argument to show that security in this setting is no stronger than standard security. However, this simple hybrid argument fails in the case that the (acyclic) encryption ordering is *a priori* unknown and formed adaptively by the adversary. (The naive approach of guessing the underlying ordering also trivially yields an exponential reduction factor.) In contrast, conventional Dolev-Yao style security analysis models adversarial knowledge *inductively* in an *all-or-nothing* fashion (i.e. the adversary either knows a secret piece of data, or it does not have any information about it). As a result, adversarial power is limited, essentially treating uniformly all symbolic ciphertexts whose encryption keys are *underivable* under so-called Dolev-Yao deduction rules. Consequently, Dolev-Yao models typically assume no difference between two symbolic encryptions $\{k\}_k$ and $\{k_1\}_k$. Also, the "adaptive problem" described above seems to not be a challenge within these models. For these reasons, most existing soundness results are restricted in their assumptions, which include excluding *key cycles* altogether in the case of *passive* adversaries [1,28], posing certain encryption orderings in the case of *passive-but-adaptive* adversaries [33], and disallowing symmetric encryption in the case of *active* adversaries [34,6,19].

As a resolution to the problems created by key cycles, Micciancio [32] proposes a *coinductive* method for modeling symbolic security, and obtains computational soundness in the setting of *message indistinguishability* for passive adversaries, while allowing key cycles and assuming only *semantic security* for the underlying encryption function. Coinductive symbolic security corresponds to a *greatest-fixedpoint*-based definition of adversarial knowledge, as opposed to the *least-fixedpoint*-based definition adopted by conventional inductive methods. From a cryptographic perspective, [32] implicitly characterizes a *provably benign* form of *circular encryption*, in particular the equivalence of standard security to secure encryption under a variant of the multiple-key-based game described above in which the adversary may obtain the (single or nested) encryption of any ck_i under arbitrary keys, provided at least one of them is in $\{ck_1, \ldots, ck_{i-1}\}$, resulting in a (possibly) cyclic encryption ordering. To obtain soundness, [32] shows that for an *a priori* known sequence of exchanged symbolic messages (which is the case in the passive setting), one may order all *coinductively irrecoverable* keys from this sequence as $k_1, \ldots, k_m$, such that each occurrence of k_i is encrypted under at least one of $\{k_1, \ldots, k_{i-1}\}$.

Our Results. In this paper we investigate the question left open in [32]; namely, whether a coinductive approach provides similar soundness guarantees when applied in the setting of *active* adversaries. We consider a symbolic/computational *trace-based execution model* [34], including asymmetric and symmetric encryption. In contrast to previous work, we allow *symmetric keys* to be *freely* included in protocol messages, symmetric and asymmetric encryptions to be arbitrarily *nested*, and adversaries to *adaptively corrupt users*, along with other forms of active attack. We first pose the following central question: to what extent can *any* encryption scheme with standard security withstand stronger types of attack including *adaptive corruptions of keys* and *key-dependent/circular encryption*? To formalize this, consider the following game over symmetric/asymmetric encryption schemes $\mathcal{E}^s = (G^s, E^s, D^s)$, $\mathcal{E}^a = (G^a, E^a, D^a)$, $\{ck_i\}_{1\leq i\leq n} \leftarrow G^s(1^\eta)$, and $\{(pk_i, sk_i)\}_{1\leq i\leq n} \leftarrow G^a(1^\eta)$, in which the adversary is allowed to adaptively corrupt keys (symmetric and asymmetric), obtain decryptions of *permissible* ciphertexts, and issue key-dependent encryption queries of the form $E^s(f(ck_1, \ldots, ck_n), ck_j)$ or $E^a(f(ck_1, \ldots, ck_n), pk_j)$, where f is any arbitrary composition of *constant, pairing, projection* $(P_i(ck_1, \ldots, ck_n) = ck_i)$, and *encryption* $(E^a_{pk_i}(\cdot), E^s_{ck_i}(\cdot))$ functions. We remark asymmetric decryption keys may not be used to form key-dependent messages, reflecting our assumption that such keys are not sent as plaintexts in protocol messages[1]. This function family allows one to describe encryption queries symbolically (e.g. $E^s(E^s(ck_1, ck_2), ck_1)$ is denoted $\{\{k_1\}_{k_2}\}_{k_1}$), and hence symbolically keep track of adversarial knowledge. Now we ask: if $\mathcal{E}^a$ and $\mathcal{E}^s$ provide IND-CCA2 security *only*, can we prove,

---

[1] Relaxing this requirement does not add to the technical difficulty of the proofs. We assumed this requirement as it seems to be the case for most protocols in practice.

at the end of the game, certain keys still maintain computational *secrecy*, in the sense they can securely be used in an encryption-based indistinguishability game[2]? Several negative results [20,2] show certain key cycles may compromise the secrecy of their component keys, but on the positive side this problem (in a generic sense involving circular encryption) has not been considered much. Motivating the discussion, the results of [32] in the context of the above game (but where only symmetric encryption is used,) imply if all queries are made at once (i.e. *nonadaptively*), then any ck_i, whose symbolic key k_i remains *coinductively irrecoverable* (*irrecoverable* for short), even if used in key cycles, maintains computational secrecy. Along these lines, we call $(\mathcal{E}^a, \mathcal{E}^s)$ *CI secure* if after the *adaptive* execution of the above game all keys whose symbolic keys remain irrecoverable maintain computational secrecy. We also consider *ACI security*, an extension of CI security which adds *ciphertext integrity* and obtain the following

Theorem (informal). If $(\mathcal{E}^a, \mathcal{E}^s)$ is ACI secure, it provides soundness for coinductive traces.

Next we ask if CI security may be based on IND-CCA2 security. Note that the CI attack model is ostensibly much stronger than the CCA2 one, allowing a CI adversary to adaptively corrupt keys and obtain circularly-encrypted ciphertexts. A naive reduction attempt would be to *a priori* guess all keys which remain irrecoverable during the game, together with their underlying encryption ordering, and then use a hybrid argument in the style of [32] to do the reduction. Such an idea clearly yields an infeasible reduction factor. Instead, we prove that if the *diameter* of the *coinductively-hidden subgraph* of the resulting *key graph* is constant, then CI security is implied by IND-CCA2 security. (It will soon be informally described why our reduction is dependent on this parameter.) Here, the key graph is the (random) multigraph G_k which has a node for every key in the game, and an edge $v_i \rightarrow v_j$ if v_i's associated key encrypts v_j's in an encryption query (e.g. the encryption query $\{\{k_1\}_{k_2}\}_{k_1}$ creates one self-loop and one normal edge,) and by "coinductively hidden subgraph" we mean the *induced subgraph* of G_k on *irrecoverable nodes* (nodes whose associated keys remain irrecoverable). We remark that as long as the above condition holds, the adversary may corrupt any number of keys, and create arbitrary key cycles and arbitrarily-long paths in the whole key graph.

Theorem (informal). If $\mathcal{E}^a$ and $\mathcal{E}^s$ are both IND-CCA2 secure, then for every adversary $\mathcal{A}$ where the diameter of the coinductively hidden subgraph of $G_k(\mathcal{A})$ is constant (i.e. independent of the security parameter), $\mathcal{A}$ has a negligible advantage in the CI game for $(\mathcal{E}^a, \mathcal{E}^s)$. Moreover, if $\mathcal{E}^s$ is also INT-CTXT secure, $\mathcal{A}$ has a negligible advantage in the ACI game.

The starting point of our proof is [36]'s positive results on security against adaptive corruptions (in an *authenticated* channel setting), showing that security

---

[2] Our definition of computational secrecy is close to the idea of *key usability*, developed in [23], for defining alternate, composition-amenable security criteria for key-exchange protocols.

in a setting over $\mathcal{E}^s$ and $\{ck_i\}_{1 \leq i \leq n} \leftarrow G^s(1^\eta)$, in which $\mathcal{A}$ may adaptively corrupt keys, and obtain *single encryptions* $E^s(ck_i, ck_j)$, for $1 \leq i, j \leq n$, subject to key *acyclicity*, is obtained via a reduction to the semantic security of $\mathcal{E}^s$, with a factor of $O(n^l)$ where l is the diameter of the resulting key graph. Although the results of [36] seem to extend, by its mere developed techniques, to an authenticated setting with *nested encryptions*, they crucially rely on acyclicity and break down if this latter is relaxed. Allowing *cyclic nested encryptions*, irrecoverable nodes may have self-loops or oppositely-directed edges between themselves (encryption queries $\{\{k_1\}_{k_2}\}_{k_3}$ and $\{k_2\}_{k_1}$ create such edges, while k_1, k_2 remain irrecoverable), and we still need to prove their computational secrecy. Central to our proof is a new notion of *coinductive continuability*, which for every irrecoverable node characterizes a special set of paths ending in that node, satisfying a property which enables a path-based reduction proof in the style of [36]. (Our reduction is based on guessing random coinductiely continuable paths with certain properties, making it depend on the diameter.) Also, allowing both nested encryptions and decryption queries creates a new complication; namely, to simulate a CI adversary $\mathcal{A}^{CI}$ by a CCA2 adversary $\mathcal{A}^{cca}$, nested encryptions may make an $\mathcal{A}^{cca}$'s *challenge ciphertext* a "legitimate" ciphertext for $\mathcal{A}^{CI}$ (e.g., when the ciphertext corresponding to $\{k_1\}_{k_2}$ in $\{\{k_1\}_{k_2}\}_{k_3}$ is created under $\mathcal{A}^{cca}$'s left-or-right oracle and k_3 remains irrecoverable), and if $\mathcal{A}^{CI}$ makes such a decryption query, our simulation fails. A large part of our proof, thus, involves showing $\mathcal{A}^{CI}$ may produce such ciphertexts only with negligible probability. Such a complication does not arise if one only deals with single encryptions, and in fact, the results of [36] immediately extend if decryption queries are also allowed.

Applications. Our reduction result implies for a protocol Π (which may contain symmetric keys and nonces as atomic messages) and a *trace-expressible* security property $\mathcal{P}$ (here, loosely speaking, by a trace we mean a sequence of states created during an execution of a protocol as a result of adversarial/honest-parties' actions. Formal definitions are given in Section 3), if the following two symbolic assertions hold, then the (CCA2, CCA2+CTXT)-based implementation of Π provably achieves $\mathcal{P}$ (in an *insecure* channel setting) with strong security guarantees against adaptive corruptions: (a) No symbolic coinductive adversary may create a trace containing an arbitrarily-long encryption chain (in the sense described above), and (b) Π is coinductively secure; namely, no coinductive symbolic adversary may produce a trace not satisfying the underlying symbolic property. We observe that all protocols in the Clark-Jacob library [21], in which the only primitives used are asymmetric/symmetric encryption, satisfy our soundness restriction (item (a) above), making it applicable to them. A number of these protocols are asymmetric encryption-based, and analyzable under previous soundness theorems (e.g. [34,6]). Using our techniques, we show that [27] the *Wide-Mouthed Frog authentication protocol*, which is not analyzable under the cryptographic library of [4] due to the classic *commitment problem* prevalent in simulation-based approaches, satisfies our soundness restriction. This advocates for the use of coinduction as a strong tool in yielding provably-sound security proofs, while circumventing issues involved with using induction-based methods.

Why Not KDM Security? It may be asked why we bother to investigate soundness of coinductive methods, when there are constructions in the standard model for secure encryption under *key-dependent messaging* [14,16]. We note that security against adaptive corruptions is a necessary requirement for any encryption scheme used in a protocol which is run in an environment with adversarially adaptive corruptions. In such situations, once a key is corrupted, the security of the protocol will depend on the preservation of secrecy for keys which are not trivially corrupted. Even in the idealized *static corruption* model, a key may dynamically be revealed by the exploitation of potential weaknesses of a protocol (e.g., consider a situation where the adversary gets to alter a communicated message by replacing an "honest" key with his own key, making an honest party then encrypt a secret key under the adversarial key.) To the best of our knowledge, there are no provable constructions of KDM-secure encryption in the standard model which also provide security against adaptive corruptions. Backes et al. [5] consider a limited case in which security is defined only in a left-or-right indistinguishability sense, not addressing the above problem. In subsequent work, [3] considers the problem in its full generality as described above, but their construction is in the random-oracle model. Moreover, they do not consider the question of whether generic constructions from KDM-secure encryption schemes exist (in the standard model) which also provide security against adaptive corruptions.

Related Work. Obtaining sound abstract security proofs for protocols involving symmetric encryption has also been considered following the ideal/real simulation paradigms of [17,37]. [4] shows that *secure realization* of *ideal* symmetric encryption (in the sense of *reactive simulatability*) is possible in their cryptographic library [6] if the *commitment problem* does not occur (i.e. any honest party's key, after it is used for encryption, never becomes "known" to the adversary), and the *used-order property* is satisfied. (i.e. Deployed keys admit an *a priori* encryption ordering.) The authors of [30], by extending the framework of [19] to allow symmetric encryption, show if a key-exchange protocol satisfies their symbolic criteria and if the above conditions hold, the protocol securely realizes a *key-exchange functionality* in the sense of *universal composability*. We comment the commitment problem may intrinsically occur as a direct result of security formalizations; adaptive corruptions, for instance, trivially enable this possibility. Also, the requirement that "a session-key loss in a key-exchange protocol should not affect the secrecy of other session keys" is formalized by allowing the adversary to adaptively learn session keys, leading, possibly, to the commitment problem. Thus the aforementioned frameworks do not consider the above two attack scenarios. We remark the commitment problem was known long before in the setting of *adaptively-secure multiparty computation*, with initial solutions given in [18]. The results of [22] are aimed at indistinguishability-based security properties (e.g., secrecy requirements for key-exchange protocols), by showing that *observational equivalence* between two processes implies computational indistinguishability under standard cryptographic assumptions. Although [22] allows symmetric encryption, it imposes the same restrictions as [4,30].

A very different approach which in principle supports reasoning about situations which include key-cyclic encryption and adaptive corruption for both symmetric and asymmetric encryption as well as other primitives is the use of what might be called *general-purpose security logics*. Here we include probabilistic process calculi [31,35], logics which axiomatize computational indistinguishability [29,8] and first-order logics augmented with axioms characterizing specific security properties [7]. The tradeoff involved in taking a more generic approach is the loss of structure in proofs, potentially undermining some of the benefits of the formal approach.

Basic Notation: For a review of the standard notions of encryption security, we refer to [10,11]. If D is a probability distribution, then $x \leftarrow D$ denotes choosing an element according to D, and if S is a set, $x \xleftarrow{\cdot} S$ denotes choosing an element uniformly at random from S. For a probability distribution D, $sup[D]$ denotes the *support set* of D, and we write $x \in D$ to mean $x \in sup[D]$. We call a function *negligible* if it grows more slowly than the inverse of any polynomial function. For ease of notation, we use $negl(\cdot)$ to refer to any negligible function.

2   Preliminaries

A Formal Language for Cryptographic Expressions. *Expressions* are built from four infinite sets of *basic symbols* – *identifiers*, ID, *public-key symbols*, $\mathcal{K}^{pub}$, *private-key symbols* $\mathcal{K}^{priv}$, and *nonces*, $\mathcal{X}$ – using *encryption*, $\{\diamond\}_\circ$, and *concatenation*, $(\cdot, \cdot)$, operators for building *compound* messages. We further partition $\mathcal{K}^{priv}$ into *asymmetric private keys*, $\mathcal{K}^{privasym}$, and *symmetric private keys* $\mathcal{K}^{privsym}$. We fix a bijective *key-inverse* operation $(.)^{-1} : \mathcal{K}^{pub} \cup \mathcal{K}^{privsym} \rightarrow \mathcal{K}^{priv}$, which induces the *identity* function on subdomain $\mathcal{K}^{privsym}$.

Whenever it is essential to distinguish between the adversary's and honest parties' basic symbols, we add a subscript A or H to basic symbols, and for every set S defined above, we further define $S = S_H \cup S_A$ (e.g. $\mathcal{K}_H^{priv}$ and $\mathcal{K}_A^{priv}$). Moreover, whenever it is necessary to distinguish between symmetric and asymmetric private-key symbols, we add a superscript sym to symmetric ones. (e.g. we have $(k_1^{sym})^{-1} = k_1^{sym}$.) The set of *formal expressions*, Exp, is:

$$Exp ::= Plain \mid Cipher \mid (Exp, Exp)$$

$$Plain ::= ID \mid \mathcal{X} \mid \mathcal{K}^{pub} \mid \mathcal{K}^{privsym}$$

$$Cipher ::= \{Plain\}_{k \in \mathcal{K}^{pub} \cup \mathcal{K}^{privsym}} \mid \{Cipher\}_{k \in \mathcal{K}^{pub} \cup \mathcal{K}^{privsym}}$$

Coniductive Modeling of Adversarial Knowledge. We take a coinductive approach to modeling adversarial attacks. To model *coinductive adversarial knowledge* [32], we define a *key-recovery function*, $\mathcal{F}$, which specifies given $e \in Exp$ and $T \subseteq \mathcal{K}_H^{priv}$, what keys can be deduced by "single-round" applications of Dolev-Yao rules. Defined naturally, $\mathcal{F}_s(T) = s \cap \mathcal{K}_H^{priv}$ for a basic symbol s, $\mathcal{F}_{(e_1,e_2)}(T) = \mathcal{F}_{e_1}(T) \cup \mathcal{F}_{e_2}(T)$, and $\mathcal{F}_{\{e\}_k}(T) = \mathcal{F}_e(T)$ if $k^{-1} \in T \cup \mathcal{K}_A^{priv}$ and $\mathcal{F}_{\{e\}_k}(T) = \emptyset$, otherwise. T is a *fixedpoint* of $\mathcal{F}_e$ if $\mathcal{F}_e(T) = T$, and is the *greatest* (resp. *least*) fixedpoint if T is the greatest (resp. least) solution of $\mathcal{F}_e(X) = X$

(according to $\subseteq$ ordering). Now T is *coinductively* (resp. *inductively*) defined by $\mathcal{F}_e$ if T is the greatest (resp. least) fixedpoint of $\mathcal{F}_e$. It is easy to see that $\mathcal{F}_e$ is a *monotone* function (i.e., $S_1 \subseteq S_2 \Rightarrow \mathcal{F}_e(S_1) \subseteq \mathcal{F}_e(S_2)$).

The Tarski-Knaster Theorem implies for every monotone function $F : \wp(D) \to \wp(D)$, where D is some set and $\wp(D)$ is its *powerset*, the least fixedpoint, $fix(F)$, and greatest fixedpoint, $FIX(F)$, of F exist and are obtained as follows

$$fix(F) = \bigcap_{S:F(S)\subseteq S} S \quad (1) \qquad\qquad FIX(F) = \bigcup_{S:S\subseteq F(S)} S \quad (2)$$

Note that if $T \subseteq \mathcal{F}_e(T)$, then $cl(T) \triangleq \cup_{i\geq 1}\mathcal{F}_e^i(T)$ is a fixedpoint, for which $T \subseteq cl(T)$, where $\mathcal{F}_e^i(T)$ denotes i successive applications of $\mathcal{F}_e$ on T. The latter follows from monotonicity of $\mathcal{F}_e$, and the former follows observing that $\mathcal{F}_e^k(T) = \mathcal{F}_e^{k+1}(T)$ for sufficiently large k's. (This is because the number of keys in e is finite.) Thus the following equivalent formulations follow:

$$fix(\mathcal{F}_e) = \bigcap_{\mathcal{F}_e(S)=S} S = \bigcup_{i\geq 1}\mathcal{F}_e^i(\emptyset) \quad (3)$$

$$FIX(\mathcal{F}_e) = \bigcup_{S=\mathcal{F}_e(S)} S = \bigcap_{i\geq 1}\mathcal{F}_e^i(\mathcal{K}_H^{priv}) \quad (4)$$

We show (4); the proof for (3) follows by a dual argument. The first equality for $FIX(\mathcal{F}_e)$ follows from (2) and the argument presented above. The second equality follows from the following three observations: (a) $\bigcap_{i\geq 1}\mathcal{F}_e^i(\mathcal{K}_H^{priv})$ is a fixedpoint of $\mathcal{F}_e$, (b) if T is a fixedpoint of $\mathcal{F}_e$, then $T = \bigcap_{i\geq 1}\mathcal{F}_e^i(T)$, and (c) by monotonicity, $\bigcap_{i\geq 1}\mathcal{F}_e^i(T) \subseteq \bigcap_{i\geq 1}\mathcal{F}_e^i(\mathcal{K}_H^{priv})$. Now the set of *coinductively recoverable keys* of e is the set coinductively defined by $\mathcal{F}_e$. For example for $e = k^{-1}, \{\{k_1^{sym}\}_{k_1^{sym}}, \{k_2^{sym}\}_{k_1^{sym}}\}_k$, its coinductively recoverable keys are $\{k^{-1}, k_1^{sym}, k_2^{sym}\}$. (As a convention, we omit parentheses in expressions and write e_1, e_2 for (e_1, e_2).) See [32] for more examples.

We define the *coinductive closure set* of $e \in Exp$, denoted $closure_c(e)$, to be the *smallest* set satisfying: (i) $closure_c(e)$ contains e, $FIX(\mathcal{F}_e)$, ID, $\mathcal{K}^{pub}$, and all the adversary's basic symbols, (ii) if $(e_1, e_2) \in closure_c(e)$ then $e_1, e_2 \in closure_c(e)$, (iii) if e' and e'' are both in $closure_c(e)$, so is (e', e''), (iv) if $\{m\}_k \in closure_c(e)$ and $k^{-1} \in closure_c(e)$ then $m \in closure_c(e)$, and (v) if $m \in closure_c(e)$ and $k \in closure_c(e)$ then $\{m\}_k \in closure_c(e)$. Although the above definition is a hybrid of inductive and coinductive definitions, an equivalent, (fully) coinductive definition is also possible; however, we adopt the above one as it is more natural. Now e_1 is *coinductively recoverable* from e if $e_1 \in closure_c(e)$. Note, if $e_1 \in closure_c(e)$ but $k^{sym} \notin closure_c(e)$, Rule (v) does not allow us to deduce $\{e_1\}_{k^{sym}} \in closure_c(e)$. This models the idealized symbolic assumption that if the adversary does not know an honest party's symmetric key, he cannot produce a ciphertext which decrypts to a meaningful plaintext under that key. To support this assumption in our computational model, we will assume the symmetric encryption scheme provides *ciphertext integrity*.

We say e' is a *subexp* of (or *occurs in*) e, denoted $e' \sqsubseteq e$, if $e = e'$, or $e = (e_1, e_2)$ and $e' \sqsubseteq e_1$ or $e' \sqsubseteq e_2$, or $e = \{e_1\}_k$ and $e' \sqsubseteq e_1$. We say k_1 encrypts k_2^{-1} in

e, denoted $k_1 \to^e k_2^{-1}$, if for some $\{e_1\}_{k_1}$ which occurs in e, $k_2^{-1} \sqsubseteq e_1$. An expression is *key cyclic* if it contains a *key cycle*, that is a sequence $k_0, k_1, \ldots k_{i-1}$ such that $k_j \to k_{(j+1 \bmod i)}^{-1}$ for all $j \geq 0$, and is called *key acyclic* if it is not key cyclic. It is known the inductive and coinductive definitions coincide for key-acyclic expressions[32]. The converse of this, however, does not hold true; it is possible some keys occur in certain key cycles but remain coinductively irrecoverable (e.g. consider $\{\{k_1^{-1}\}_{k_1}\}_{k_2}$). In fact, we will prove it is exactly such keys that remain "secure" under concrete implementations.

Computational Interpretation of Cryptographic Expressions. Under a pair of symmetric/asymmetric schemes $\mathcal{E}_p = (\mathcal{E}_{sym}, \mathcal{E}_{asy})$ with parameters (η_{sym}, η_{asy}), an invertible *pairing function*, and a mapping $\tau(\eta_{sym}, \eta_{asy}, \circ)$, which gives a *concrete value* to every basic symbol, every $e \in Exp$ induces a natural probability distribution, denoted $[\![e]\!]_\tau^{\mathcal{E}_p}$, which we call the *computational image of e with respect to $\mathcal{E}_p$ and τ*. If $E \in [\![e]\!]_\tau^{\mathcal{E}_p}$ and $e_1 \sqsubseteq e$, given τ, one may define the underlying value of e_1 in E in a natural way.

3 Symbolic and Computational Trace-Based Protocol Security

We will now introduce a protocol specification language and consider an extension of the model given in [34] for analyzing security protocols in the presence of active adversaries. For simplicity, we consider two-party protocols, and assume that each protocol runs in a constant number of rounds, and admits a symbolic specification. Under these assumptions, a *protocol* can be described as a sequence $\Pi = (M_1^I, M_1^R, M_2^I, M_2^R, \ldots M_r^I, M_r^R)$ of *messages* being sent alternately between two parties: *initiator* and *responder*. (Here having the responder send the last message is arbitrary.) We assume that each party has an associated *long-lived public key* which the other party may use to encrypt messages, and whose matching private key is never sent as a plaintext. The parties, however, may generate fresh symmetric keys, send them (encrypted) to each other, and later on use exchanged keys to encrypt future messages. Messages that we use to specify protocols are built upon four disjoint sets $Ids = \{I, R\}$, $nonces = \{X_1, X_2, \ldots\}$, $pubkeys = \{K_I, K_R\}$, and $symkeys = \{K_1^{sym}, K_2^{sym}, \ldots\}$, using encryption and concatenation for building compound messages, where K_I and K_R denote the parties' respective public keys. We further require protocols be *computationally executable*; in particular, a party should be able to fully decrypt (all encrypted parts of) a message she receives. (Our results seem to easily extend by relaxing this restriction, allowing, e.g., *ciphertext forwarding*, which allows a party to forward a message without decrypting it.) To summarize our assumptions, we call Π *valid* if: (1) for all $1 \leq i \leq r$ and $x \in \{I, R\}$; K_I^{-1} and K_R^{-1} do not occur in M_i^x, and (2) for all $1 \leq i \leq r$, $x \in \{I, R\}$, and $y = \{I, R\} - \{x\}$; if M_i^x has a subexp $\{M\}_K$, then K is *inductively* recoverable from $(K_y, M_1^x, \ldots, M_i^x)$. (We will use a coinductive approach for modeling adversarial attacks, and this condition is solely meant to specify our class of protocols. In particular, since we require parties be able to fully decrypt their received messages, and their roles be computationally executable, such a condition seems necessary.)

So far we have only described the "syntax" of protocols; this should not be confused with the formal execution semantics to be presented below. Treating Π as a tuple of messages, we denote its ith message by Π_i. We denote the set of protocol *users* (*participants*) by $U = \{u_1, u_2, ..., u_n\}$, where any two of whom may initiate an instance of the protocol together, in a manner controlled by an adversary. The adversary is not himself a protocol user, but may dynamically subvert users during the execution. We model adversarial power as an *oracle* with which he is *adaptively* interacting, by making the following types of query:

- *corrupt*(i): Corrupts user u_i. In response, the long-lived secret key of u_i (and all other u_i's internal information) is given to the adversary.
- *new-session*(i, j): Causes u_i and u_j to start a new session, with u_i as the initiator. The oracle assigns a unique *number*, sn, to their session and gives sn to the adversary plus the first message that u_i sends to u_j in this session.
- *send*(sn, m_1, I): Causes the oracle to send message m_1 to the initiator of session sn and give m_2, the message that the user produces in response, to the adversary. Here m_2 may be a valid message, an *error message* $\perp$ (indicating m_1 was not of the right format), or a *flag message* $*$ indicating that the user has received her last message, finishing her session.
- *send*(sn, m_1, R): Similar to above, but m_1 is sent to the responder of sn.

We now give formal and computational semantics for protocols. In the formal setting, we denote the long-lived public key of u_i by k_{u_i}, and for each session sn that u_i is a user of, we denote u_i's generated symmetric keys and nonces in sn, respectively, by $\mathbf{K}_{i,sn}^{sym} = \{k_{i,sn,j}^{sym} \mid j \in \mathbb{N}\} \subseteq \mathcal{K}_H^{privsym}$, $\mathbf{X}_{i,sn} = \{x_{i,sn,j} \mid j \in \mathbb{N}\} \subseteq \mathcal{X}_H$. The adversary may use his own basic symbols to build new messages; we denote the adversary's symmetric keys and nonces, respectively, by $\mathbf{K}_A^{sym} = \{k_{A,j}^{sym} \mid j \in \mathbb{N}\} \subseteq \mathcal{K}_A^{privsym}$, $\mathbf{X}_A = \{x_{A,j} \mid j \in \mathbb{N}\} \subseteq \mathcal{X}_A$. We let Exp_{basic} be the union of all $\mathbf{X}_A, \mathbf{K}_A^{sym}$, $\mathbf{K}_{i,sn}^{sym}$s, $\mathbf{X}_{i,sn}$'s.

The adversary initially knows only his own basic symbols and parties' IDs and public keys. If he corrupts u_i, he receives $k_{u_i}^{-1}$ as well as $\mathbf{K}_{i,sn}^{sym} \cup \mathbf{X}_{i,sn}$, for every sn that u_i has engaged in. A protocol *state* is characterized by the following components:

$$f : \{I, R\} \times BS(\Pi) \times SN \to Exp_{basic} \cup \{\perp\} \quad l : \{I, R\} \times SN \to \Pi_i \cup \{\sqrt{}\}$$
$$h : \{I, R\} \times SN \to U \qquad\qquad corr\text{-}users \subseteq \{u_1, \ldots, u_n\}$$

Here SN denotes the set of all session numbers, and, recall that, U is the set of all protocol users. Function f represents the symbolic values that the initiator and responder of each session of the protocol give to basic symbols in that session, and $\perp$ means that the party does not yet know the value of the corresponding basic message. Function l denotes the index of the next message in the protocol that the initiator and responder of each session expect to receive, and $\sqrt{}$ indicates that the party has finished her respective session. Finally function h indicates what protocol users take the roles of "initiator" and "responder" in each session.

We denote the initial state of the system by FS_0, where $corr\text{-}users = \emptyset$, and l, f, h map all their inputs to null values. An execution of a *formal adversary*, $\mathcal{A}_F$, can be described as a sequence of queries $E(\mathcal{A}_F) = (q_1, q_2, \ldots)$, with corresponding replies $(r_1, r_2, \ldots)$. We then call $\mathcal{A}_F$ *coinductively legitimate* if $m \in closure_c(r_1, r_2, \ldots, r_{i-1})$ for all i such that $q_i = send(sn, m, \{I, R\})$. Under $\mathcal{A}_F$'s execution, we denote the induced *formal trace* by $\mathcal{FT}(\mathcal{A}_F) = (FS_0, FS_1 \ldots)$, where state FS_i is obtained from FS_{i-1} as a result of query q_i.

Under the computational execution, elements of $BS(\Pi) \subseteq Ids \cup nonces \cup pubkeys \cup symkeys$ are replaced with random bitstrings, sampled w.r.t. a pair $\mathcal{E}_p = (\mathcal{E}_{asy}, \mathcal{E}_{sym})$, with w.l.o.g. a shared security parameter 1^η, and the coins tossed by both protocol users and the adversary during the protocol execution. Each (initially honest) u_i, before engaging in the protocol execution, samples her long-lived key pair, $(pk_i, sk_i) \leftarrow Gen_{asy}(\eta)$, and for each session sn that u_i participates in, u_i uses a (polynomially-long) uniformly-selected random string $\mathcal{R}_{i,sn}$ to sample her nonces and symmetric keys in that session, where symmetric keys are sampled according to Gen_{sym}, and nonces chosen uniformly at random from a fixed *nonce space*, $NS = \{0, 1\}^{poly(\eta)}$. The adversary, using random string $\mathcal{R}_A$, may choose his nonces and symmetric keys (to, e.g., replace those of corrupted parties, inject in messages on the network, etc.) in any arbitrary efficient manner; he may also initially corrupt a party and choose her public/private key pair in any arbitrary manner (not necessarily following Gen_{asy}).

Letting $C_\eta = NS \cup sup\,[Gen_{sym}(\eta)] \cup sup\,[Gen_{asy_1}(\eta)]$, a *computational state* of the protocol is given by $(F, L, H, Corr\text{-}Users)$, where $L, H, Corr\text{-}Users$ are defined analogously to their formal counterparts, and F is also defined similarly to f by replacing Exp_b with C_η. The adversary interacts with a *computational oracle* by issuing the four types of queries explained above, where the input/output of queries are probabilistic, depending on $\mathcal{R}_A$ and $\mathcal{R}_H$. (Here $\mathcal{R}_H$ is the concatenation of all random coins used by honest parties.) Among oracle queries, we only explain the effect of a **corruption** query (the others are fairly straightforward): if the adversary corrupts u_i, he is given (pk_i, sk_i), and for every session sn in which u_i takes the role $X \in \{I, R\}$, the adversary is given $F(X, bs, sn)$, for every $bs \in BS(\Pi)$. Finally, under fixed $\mathcal{R}_H$ and $\mathcal{R}_A$, the induced *computational trace* is deterministic and denoted by $CT(\mathcal{A}, \mathcal{R}_A, \mathcal{R}_H, \Pi_{\mathcal{E}_p})$.

Let $FT = \langle (f_1, l_1, h_1, corr\text{-}users_1), (f_2, h_2, l_2, corr\text{-}users_2), \ldots \rangle$ be a formal trace and let $\tau : Exp_{basic} \to C_\eta$ be a concrete mapping. We say a concrete trace

$$CT = \langle (F_1, L_1, H_1, Corr\text{-}Users_1), (F_2, L_2, H_2, Corr\text{-}Users_2), \ldots \rangle$$

is an *encoding* of FT under τ, written $FT \prec_\tau CT$, if $l_i = L_i$, $h_i = H_i$, $Corr\text{-}Users = corr\text{-}users$ and $F_i = \tau f_i$, for all $i \geq 1$. We say CT is the *computational image* of FT, written $FT \prec CT$, if there exists τ such that $FT \prec_\tau CT$. We are now ready give the computational soundness definition.

Definition 1. *A pair $\mathcal{E}_p = (\mathcal{E}_{asy}, \mathcal{E}_{sym})$ provides a computationally-sound interpretation of symbolic encryption with respect to coinductive Dolev-Yao traces (shortly, provides soundness) if for all valid protocols Π, adversaries $\mathcal{A}_c$, we have*

$$\Pr_{\mathcal{R}_A, \mathcal{R}_H} [\exists \{coind\text{-}legit \; \mathcal{A}_F\} : \mathcal{FT}(\mathcal{A}_F) \prec CT(\mathcal{A}_c, \mathcal{R}_A, \mathcal{R}_H, \Pi_{\mathcal{E}_p})] \geq 1 - negl(\eta)$$

4 Computational Realization of Coinductive Methods

We describe a joint notion of security for asymmetric/symmetric encryption which provides soundness for coinductive symbolic traces. We then explore how this notion may be achieved under standard complexity-theoretic assumptions. We begin with some motivation. Consider a single run of a protocol against a passive adversary, in which the whole sequence of exchanged messages is known *a priori*. We wish to formalize what it means for a piece of data (nonce or symmetric key) to remain *secure* in both the formal and computational settings. Under the formal approach, one would typically say the secrecy of a piece of data is retained if it cannot be deduced by applying Dolev-Yao rules. For a nonce X, for instance, if X is not formally deducible, it means all occurrences of X are encrypted under keys which cannot be obtained by a Dolev-Yao adversary. Thus, under the concrete instantiation, after the adversary has received the computational representations of the exchanged messages, the random nonce value underlying X should still be as computationally random as a freshly-generated random nonce, provided the encryption scheme is sufficiently strong. However, for the case of symmetric keys the situation is quite different: even if a symmetric key is not Dolev-Yao-style deducible, the key may leak significant information when it comes to a concrete implementation. For instance, a symmetric-key value may lose its original randomness if used for encryption. (i.e. The adversary will be able to tell it apart from a fixed key, causing it to not be as "random" as a freshly generated key.) Thus the definition of secrecy for symmetric keys in the computational model turns out to be more delicate.

Our ultimate goal is to establish a close correspondence between coinductive Dolev-Yao adversaries and computational adversaries, by showing that a computational adversary essentially cannot do anything (in terms of mounting successful attacks) which cannot already be performed by a simple Dolev-Yao adversary. We capture the essence of active-attack scenario within a *cryptographic game*, played between an adversary and a challenger, in which the adversary is faced with a number of unknown keys (both asymmetric and symmetric) and nonces, generated by the challenger, and his goal is to infer "non-trivial" information from the challenger's secret data, by exploiting active attacks such as corrupting arbitrary keys of the challenger, getting her to encrypt messages which depend on her own secret data, and getting her to decrypt "permissible" ciphertexts. Our goal is to show that, under sufficiently strong security requirements, the computational adversary cannot learn non-trivial information from a piece of data (nonce or private key) that cannot already be obtained by a coinductive Dolev-Yao adversary. The key point in our security definition is to formalize the idea of "computational secrecy" for private keys. As it is probably clear from the above discussion, "requiring the adversary not be able to distinguish the private key (used in the game) from a freshly generated key" would not work. We formalize it in the following standard way: a private key retains its computational secrecy if the adversary is unable to distinguish between the encryptions of real/random messages under that key. We will be able to show that security in our game provides computational soundness.

Our security notion is formalized via the following game which we call the *coinductive, key-dependent indistinguishability* game, or the *CI game* for short. Below, for $S = \{(s_1^1, s_1^2), \dots (s_n^1, s_n^2)\}$, we define $S^i \triangleq \{s_1^i, \dots, s_n^i\}$ for $i \in \{1, 2\}$.

4.1 Coinductive, Key-Dependent Indistinguishability (CI) Game

Assume $\mathcal{E}_{asy} = (Gen_{asy}, Enc_{asy}, Dec_{asy})$ and $\mathcal{E}_{sym} = (Gen_{sym}, Enc_{sym}, Dec_{sym})$ are asymmetric/symmetric encryption schemes whose joint security is to be defined, w.l.o.g., w.r.t. the shared *security parameter* 1^η. The game is played between an adversary, $\mathcal{A}$, and a challenger, $\mathcal{B}$, and is parameterized over a publicly-known, poly-bounded integer function $n(\eta)$ (we write n for $n(\eta)$). Suppose $\tau_B(\cdot)$ and $\tau_A(\cdot)$ are (dynamically growing) mappings which give bitstring values to, respectively, the basic symbols of $\mathcal{B}$ and $\mathcal{A}$ (we will see shortly what those symbols are), and let τ be a mapping defined to be τ_B on the domain of $\mathcal{B}$'s symbols and τ_A on $\mathcal{A}$'s. Here τ_A is publicly known, while access to τ_B and τ is restricted to $\mathcal{B}$. The game proceeds in three phases: **setup**, **interaction**, and **guessing**.

In the **setup** phase, $\mathcal{B}$ first picks $b \leftarrow \{0, 1\}$, generates $\{(pk_i, sk_i)\}_{1 \le i \le n} \leftarrow Gen_{asy}(\eta)$, symmetric keys $\{ck_i\}_{1 \le i \le n} \leftarrow Gen_{sym}(\eta)$, and nonces $\{nc_i\}_{1 \le i \le n} \leftarrow \{0, 1\}^{q(\eta)}$ (for some poly q), makes $\{pk_i\}_{1 \le i \le n}$ public, and keeps the rest secret. We introduce $\{(k_i, k_i^{-1})\}_{1 \le i \le n} \in \mathcal{K}_H^{pub} \times \mathcal{K}_H^{privasym}$, and $\{k_i^{sym}\}_{1 \le i \le n} \in \mathcal{K}_H^{privsym}$, and $\{x_i\}_{1 \le i \le n} \in \mathcal{X}_H$, and assign $\tau_B(k_i) = pk_i$, $\tau_B(k_i^{-1}) = sk_i$, $\tau_B(k_i^{sym}) = ck_i$ and $\tau_B(x_i) = nc_i$, for $1 \le i \le n$. We initialize *eval-exp* $= \emptyset$. During the **interaction** phase, $\mathcal{A}$ may dynamically update τ_A, mapping his newly-created basic symbols to arbitrary values. In the **interaction** phase $\mathcal{A}$ *adaptively* interacts with $\mathcal{B}$ by issuing queries of the following types:

1. *Corruption*: $\mathcal{A}$ may corrupt a $\mathcal{B}$'s key by issuing *corrupt*(s), where $s \in \{k_1^{-1}, \dots, k_n^{-1}, k_1^{sym}, \dots, k_n^{sym}\}$. In response $\mathcal{A}$ receives $\tau(s)$, and $(s, \tau(s))$ is added to *eval-exp*.

2. *Encryption*: $\mathcal{A}$ may issue a query *encrypt*(e, x), where $x \in \{k_1, \dots, k_n, k_1^{sym}, \dots, k_n^{sym}\}$, and e may not have any k_i^{-1}'s as a subexp. In response, $\mathcal{A}$ is given $c \leftarrow [\![\{e\}_x]\!]_\tau$ and $(\{e\}_x, c)$ is added to *eval-exp*. Here e may contain both the challenger's and adversary's basic symbols.

3. *Decryption*: $\mathcal{A}$ may issue *decrypt*(c, s'), where $s' \in \{k_1^{-1}, \dots, k_n^{-1}, k_1^{sym}, \dots, k_n^{sym}\}$. In response $\mathcal{A}$ receives $Dec_{asy}(c, sk_i)$ if $s' = k_i^{-1}$ and $Dec_{sym}(c, ck_i)$ if $s' = k_i^{sym}$, *unless* there exists $(\{e\}_{k_p}, c_p) \in$ *eval-exp* such that $\{e\}_{k_p}$ has a subexp $\{e'\}_s$ (where $s' = s^{-1}$) which in $\{e\}_{k_p}$ is encrypted only under keys whose decryption keys are in $closure_c(eval\text{-}exp^1)$, and that c corresponds to the computational image of $\{e'\}_s$ in c_p. In this case the answer is $\perp$.

After making a number of such queries, $\mathcal{A}$ proceeds to the final, **guessing** phase, in which he claims he is able to infer "non-trivial" information about irrecoverable secret data of $\mathcal{B}$. He does so by issuing a *challenge* query, which is either of the form *challenge*(s), where $s \in \{x_1, \dots, x_n\}$ (nonce challenge), or of the form *challenge*(s, bs), where $bs \in \{0, 1\}^*$ and $s \in \{k_1^{-1}, \dots, k_n^{-1}, k_1^{sym}, \dots, k_n^{sym}\}$ (secret key challenge.) The response to the query is decided as follows: if $s \in closure_c(eval\text{-}exp^1)$, then he is given $\perp$, otherwise:

- if $b = 0$, $\mathcal{A}$ is given nc_j if $s = x_j$, $Enc_{asy}(bs, pk_j)$ if $s = k_j^{-1}$, and otherwise $Enc_{sym}(bs, ck_j)$ if $s = k_j^{sym}$.
- if $b = 1$, $\mathcal{A}$ is given $nc'_j \leftarrow \{0,1\}^{q(\eta)}$ if $s = x_j$, $Enc_{asy}(r, pk_j)$ if $s = k_j^{-1}$, and $Enc_{sym}(r, ck_j)$ if $s = k_j^{sym}$, where $r \leftarrow \{0,1\}^{|bs|}$.

$\mathcal{A}$ finally outputs his guess for b. Denoting by $\mathcal{A}^{\mathrm{CI}_b^{\mathcal{E}_p}}$ the output of $\mathcal{A}$ when the secret bit is b, his *CI-advantage* is (below $\mathcal{E}_p$ refers to the pair of schemes):

$$Adv_{\mathcal{E}_p, \mathcal{A}}^{\mathrm{CI}}(\eta) = \left| \Pr[\mathcal{A}^{\mathrm{CI}_b^{\mathcal{E}_p}}(\eta) = 1 \mid b = 0] - \Pr[\mathcal{A}^{\mathrm{CI}_b^{\mathcal{E}_p}}(\eta) = 1 \mid b = 1] \right|.$$

Definition 2. *A pair of $\mathcal{E}_p = (\mathcal{E}_{sym}, \mathcal{E}_{asy})$ provides joint security under the CI game (shortly, is CI-secure) if for every $\mathcal{A}$, $Adv_{\mathcal{E}_p, \mathcal{A}}^{CI}(\eta)$ is negligible.*

We now explain the restrictions on *challenge* and *decryption* queries. For our discussion, assume that $\mathcal{E} = (Gen, Enc, Dec)$ is a symmetric encryption scheme wherein $Enc(ck, ck)$ leads to computation of ck. (This could happen although $\mathcal{E}$ is secure in any standard sense.) In the absence of the condition for *challenge* queries, $\mathcal{A}$ could simply win the game by doing the following: make two queries $encrypt(k_1^{sym}, k_1^{sym})$ and $encrypt(k_2^{sym}, k_2^{sym})$ to receive, respectively, c_1 and c_2, and then issue the *challenge* query $challenge(k_1^{sym}, 0^n)$; $\mathcal{A}$ may now obtain $\tau(k_1^{sym})$ from c_1 and $\tau(k_2^{sym})$ from c_2, trivially winning the game. Also in the absence of the condition for *decryption* queries, $\mathcal{A}$ could simply win as follows: (1) make two queries $encrypt(k_1^{sym}, k_1^{sym})$ and $encrypt(\{k_2^{sym}\}_{k_3^{sym}}, k_1^{sym})$ to receive, respectively, c_1 and c_2, (2) after computing $\tau(k_1^{sym})$ from c_1, issue the *decryption* query $decrypt(c_3, k_3^{sym})$, where $c_3 = Dec(c_2, \tau(k_1^{sym}))$, and (3) after obtaining $\tau(k_2^{sym})$ issue the *challenge* query $challenge(k_2^{sym}, 0^n)$, trivially winning the game. Finally we remark that the recent results of [20] show that there exists an IND-CCA2-secure symmetric encryption scheme such that ciphertexts $Enc(ck_1, ck_2), \ldots, Enc(ck_{n-1}, ck_n), Enc(ck_n, ck_1)$, for randomly-generated ck_i's, lead to revelation of all $ck_1, \ldots, ck_n$ (a weaker case than k-circular security). Therefore, the above attack methods extend to longer key cycles.

Note, $\mathcal{A}$ may use an *encrypt* query to obtain the encryption of any bitstring. For example, to encrypt m under ck_i, he may introduce a new basic symbol $x_{\mathcal{A}}$, set $\tau_{\mathcal{A}}(x_{\mathcal{A}}) = m$, and then issue $encrypt(x_{\mathcal{A}}, k_i^{sym})$. Also it is possible to define and extend results we present about CI security to a (seemingly) stronger notion in which $\mathcal{A}$ is allowed to make multiple *challenge* queries, possibly making them interleave with the other types of queries. Right now for applications that we consider, CI security suffices. CI security may be thought of as a variant of KDM security with the underlying function family consisting of any arbitrary composition of *constant*, *projection*, *pairing* and *encryption* functions. However, since we aim to prove generic implication results from standard security definitions, we have to restrict the set of keys for which we want to prove computational secrecy (i.e. those which remain coinductively irrecoverable). This differs from KDM security in which one wants to prove computational secrecy for all keys, regardless of what encryption queries were made. Finally we stress that a key $\mathcal{A}$ challenges in the **guessing** phase may have previously occurred in key cycles.

CI security is still insufficient for providing soundness as it does not provide *integrity of ciphertexts*. To account for this, we strengthen it to also provide ciphertext integrity and call the new notion *authenticated* CI (or ACI) security. We say $(\mathcal{E}_{asy}, \mathcal{E}_{sym})$ is *ACI secure* if it is CI secure and further any $\mathcal{A}$ has a negligible chance of winning in the ACI game defined as follows: the **setup** and **interaction** phases proceed exactly as in the CI game, while in the **guessing** phase, $\mathcal{A}$ outputs (c, i) and wins if: (1) $Dec_{sym}(c, ck_i) \neq \perp$, and (2) there does not exist $(\{e\}_{k_j}, c') \in eval\text{-}exp$ such that $\{e\}_{k_j}$ has a subexp $\{e'\}_{k_i}$ encrypted in $\{e\}_{k_j}$ only under keys whose decryption keys are in $closure_c(eval\text{-}exp^1)$, and that c is the corresponding image of $\{e'\}_{k_i}$ in c'.

As a step toward proving soundness with respect to ACI security, we formulate a new notion which characterizes security requirements capturing the basic Dolev-Yao assumptions made in protocol analysis, and prove that it provides soundness. Our notion, which we call *coinductive, key-dependent non-malleability* (shortly *CNM*) notion, is a generalization of the *Dolev-Yao non-malleability* notion of [28], which was defined for the passive setting.

4.2   Coinductive, Key-Dependent Non-Malleability (CNM) Game

The game is parameterized, again, over $\mathcal{E}_p = (\mathcal{E}_{asy}, \mathcal{E}_{sym})$, a shared security parameter η, and a computational mapping τ, and runs in three phases with the **setup** and **interaction** phases as in the CI game (except that no b is sampled). However, in the **guessing** phase, $\mathcal{A}$ claims he is able to construct the computational image of an expression which is not coinductively constructible from $eval\text{-}exp^1$. To this end, he outputs (e, E), where $e \in Exp$ (containing, possibly, both the adversary's and challenger's symbols) and $E \in \{0, 1\}^*$. The output of the game is 1, written as $\mathrm{CNM}_{\mathcal{E}_p, \eta}(\mathcal{A}) = 1$, if the following two conditions hold:

1. $e \notin closure_c(eval\text{-}exp^1)$; and
2. E is a possible mapping of e under τ and $\mathcal{E}_p$; namely, $E \in [\![e]\!]_{\tau}^{\mathcal{E}_p}$.

Note condition (2) is efficiently verifiable given access to τ. We define

$$Adv_{\mathcal{E}_p, \eta}^{CNM}(\mathcal{A}) = \Pr[\mathrm{CNM}_{\mathcal{E}_p, \eta}(\mathcal{A}) = 1].$$

Definition 3. *A pair $\mathcal{E}_p = (\mathcal{E}_{asy}, \mathcal{E}_{sym})$ provides security under the CNM game (shortly, is CNM-secure) if for every adversary $\mathcal{A}$, $Adv_{\mathcal{E}_p, \eta}^{CNM}(\mathcal{A})$ is negligible.*

Theorem 1. *1. CNM security $\Rightarrow$ soundness*
2. ACI security $\Rightarrow$ CNM security.

Proof (Outline): For (2) if $\mathcal{A}^{cnm}$ is able to output a CNM-valid (e, E), then $e \notin T$, where $T = closure_c(eval\text{-}exp^1)$ implies e has a subexp s such that s is either a nonce/private key, or $s = \{\cdot\}_{k_j^{sym}}$, and that any subexp of e which contains s is not in T. This implies the underlying value of s is recoverable from E (with the aid of the decryption oracle) through successive decryptions down along the path leading to s, which will then enable an attack either against CI security or ciphertext integrity depending on the type of s. The proof for (1) also follows using ideas similar to those of [34]. We give a full proof in [27]. □

For an adversary $\mathcal{A}$ in either of the above games, we define a *labeled key graph*, $G(\mathcal{A}) = (V_{\mathcal{A}}, E_{\mathcal{A}})$, as follows: $V_{\mathcal{A}} = \{v_1^{asy}, \ldots, v_n^{asy}, v_1^{sym}, \ldots, v_n^{sym}\}$, and $v_i^x \xrightarrow{a} v_j^y \in E_{\mathcal{A}}$, for $x, y \in \{asy, sym\}$ and $a \in \mathbb{N}$, if k_i^x encrypts the ath *occurrence* of $(k_j^y)^{-1}$ in the sequence of $\mathcal{A}$'s *encryption* queries. Here ath occurrence refers to an increasing numbering given to each decryption key as it appears in the sequence; for example, if $e_1 = \{k_1^{sym}, k_p^{sym}\}_{k_3}$, k_p^{sym} and $e_2 = k_2^{sym}, \{k_p^{sym}\}_{k_4}$ and the first two *encryption* queries are $encrypt(e_1, k_3)$ and $encrypt(e_2, k_5)$; the set of keys that encrypt the 3rd occurrence of k_p^{sym} is $\{k_4, k_5\}$. We call v_i^x *coinductively irrecoverable* (irrecoverable for short) if $k_i^{x-1} \notin closure_c(eval\text{-}exp^1)$, and we refer to the *induced* subgraph on irrecoverable nodes as the *hidden subgraph*. The *diameter* of a graph is the length of the longest path in the graph. We define $indeg(v_i^x)$ to be the maximum a for which we have an incoming edge with label a to v_i^x; this specifies the number of times k_i^{x-1} occurs in $\mathcal{A}$'s *encryption* queries. Note, $indeg(v_i^{asy}) = 0$, for every $1 \leq i \leq n$, and also both $G(\mathcal{A})$ and $indeg(v_i)$ are random variables depending on the coins tossed during the game.

If all *encryption* queries were of the form $encrypt(k_i^{sym}, k_j^x)$ (i.e. single encryptions) without cycle creation, then all nodes from which there was a path to an irrecoverable node would also be irrecoverable. However, in the case of nested encryptions with key cycles, the above appealing property no longer holds; namely, an irrecoverable node may occur in certain key cycles, and may have edges from nodes which are recoverable. For example, assuming $e_1 = \{k_1^{sym}\}_{k_2^{sym}}$ and $e_2 = \{k_3^{sym}\}_{k_4^{sym}}$, if $\mathcal{A}$ makes queries $encrypt(e_1, k_5^{sym})$, $encrypt(k_2^{sym}, k_1^{sym})$, $encrypt(e_2, k_6^{sym})$, and $corrupt(k_4^{sym})$, all keys except k_4^{sym} remain irrecoverable, and there exists, for instance, edges in both directions between v_1^{sym} and v_2^{sym} in $G(\mathcal{A})$.

However, in the case of cyclic nested encryption, we will base our hybrid arguments on a provable property, which we call *coinductive continuability*, of irrecoverable nodes. In $G(\mathcal{A})$, we say $v_{y_1}^x \xrightarrow{a_2} v_{y_2}^{sym} \xrightarrow{a_3} \ldots \xrightarrow{a_p} v_{y_p}^{sym}$, for $x \in \{sym, asy\}$, is a *coinductively continuable path* if the following conditions hold: (below for better clarity we drop the superscripts x and sym.)

1. Path validity: For all $2 \leq i \leq p$, $v_{y_{i-1}} \xrightarrow{a_i} v_{y_i} \in E_{\mathcal{A}}$, and if $1 \leq w < h \leq p$ then $v_{y_w} \neq v_{y_h}$,
2. For all $s \in \{k_{y_1}^{x-1}, k_{y_2}^{sym}, \ldots, k_{y_p}^{sym}\}$ it holds $s \notin closure_c(eval\text{-}exp^1)$, and
3. either $indeg(v_{y_1}) = 0$ or for *every* $1 \leq a_1 \leq indeg(v_{y_1})$ there exists v_i^w, with $w \in \{asy, sym\}$, such that $v_i^w \xrightarrow{a_1} v_{y_1} \xrightarrow{a_2} \ldots \xrightarrow{a_p} v_{y_p}$ is a coinductively continuable path.

We call v_i^x *coinductively continuable* if its associated path of length zero is so.

Lemma 1. *At any point, any irrecoverable node is coinductively continuable.*

Proof (Outline): We prove this by an induction over the length of the longest path ending in the irrecoverable node. A full proof is given in [27]. □

Definition 4. *We say that $\mathcal{E}_p = (\mathcal{E}_{asy}, \mathcal{E}_{sym})$ provides l-CI security if $Adv_{\mathcal{E},\mathcal{A}}^{CI}(\eta)$ is negligible for every $\mathcal{A}$ for whom the diameter of the hidden subgraph of $G(\mathcal{A})$ is always at most l. We say $\mathcal{E}_p$ provides l-ACI security if it is l-CI secure and any $\mathcal{A}$ (under the ACI game) for which the diameter of the resulting hidden subgraph is always at most l has a negligible advantage.*

Theorem 2. *If $\mathcal{E}_{asy}$ and $\mathcal{E}_{sym}$ are both IND-CCA2 secure, then $(\mathcal{E}_{asy}, \mathcal{E}_{sym})$ provides l-CI security, for every constant l.*

Proof (Outline): The central idea is to guess a "random", coinductively continuable path, with some associated parameters, which ends in the **challenge** key, give "fake" values to certain private keys occurring as plaintexts, and prove the adversary's advantage under this replying strategy is negligibly different from that under the standard game. A full proof is given in [27]. $\qquad\square$

Theorem 3. *If $\mathcal{E}_{asy}$ provides IND-CCA2 security, and $\mathcal{E}_{sym}$ provides both IND-CCA2 and INT-CTXT security, then $(\mathcal{E}_{asy}, \mathcal{E}_{sym})$ provides l-ACI security, for every constant l.*

Proof (Outline): We first show if $\mathcal{A}_{aci}$ is able to output an ACI-valid (c, i), then in a world, W_i, in which occurrences of k_i^{sym} as a plaintext and its occurrences as an encryption key are given two independent values, $\mathcal{A}_{aci}$ should have "the same" probability of producing a valid (c, i), or otherwise a CI-attack can be made. Next, we show if under W_i an adversary $\mathcal{A}$ is able to produce an ACI-valid (c, i) and c is already a plaintext of a ciphertext obtained under an *encryption* query (e.g. $\mathcal{A}$ has called $encrypt(\{x_1\}_{k_i^{sym}}, k_2^{sym})$ to obtain c_2, k_2^{sym} remains coinductively irrecoverably, and $c = Dec_{sym}(c_2, ck_2)$), then a CI attack follows, and otherwise an INT-CTXT attack follows. A full proof is given in [27]. $\qquad\square$

5   Conclusion

We investigated soundness of coinductive methods in a protocol model allowing arbitrary composition of symmetric/asymmetric encryption, as well as unrestricted transmission of secret keys. In such situations, an active adversary may selectively influence the encryption ordering between deployed keys, dynamically compromise them (naturally or under his corruption power), and potentially obtain encryption cycles. Any weakness in the underlying encryption schemes in the face of such an adversary may lead to insecure instantiations of protocols. Most previous work on computationally sound symbolic analysis of protocols either does not allow symmetric encryption, or imposes restrictions aimed at avoiding the above possibilities. Our soundness theorem, founded on coinduction, does not assume any such restrictions, while providing strong computational security guarantees against adaptive corruptions. Our results, however, rely on a property of protocols we call *boundedness* (formalized in [27]), which requires that no symbolic execution of the underlying protocol produce a coinductively-irrecoverable encryption chain of nonconstant length. We observe that almost all protocols from [21] (when run in *isolation*) admit (at most) 2-boundedness. (All of them are bounded.) In [27], we provide statements on how one can reason about boundedness of a protocol, and whether the boundedness property is retained when two (individually bounded) protocols are run concurrently.

While the main focus of this paper is on trace-based security, we believe similar results can also be proved for *key-exchange* (KE) security tasks. A central security requirement for key exchange is the *secrecy* condition, requiring a secret key exchanged by a KE protocol be *indistinguishable* from a freshly generated key. Our CI game is rich enough to encompass common features of a KE attack model, including adaptive corruptions of users and session keys, while guaranteeing that (under stated complexity assumptions) *coinducitve symbolic secrecy* under the game implies computational secrecy (*real-or-random indistinguishability* in the case of nonces and *key usability* [23] in the case of secret keys).

For simplicity we have assumed if a user is corrupted, the adversary obtains *only* her long-lived key and her past generated secret keys/nonces, but *not* her past *random coins*. In [27] we give partial results about this more general case.

As briefly explained in the introduction, current results about KDM security do not seem sufficient for (unrestricted) secure realizations of protocols with *inductive*, symbolic security proofs. It would be interesting to extend (and realize) KDM security definitions to support adaptive corruptions. As pointed out earlier, defining the extension in an entirely left-or-right indistinguishability sense, as in [5], would entail inherent limitations; for example, if a left-or-right encryption query is made under ck, then ck cannot be corrupted afterward.

Finally it would be interesting to improve the bounds imposed by our soundness theorem (and those of [36]), and investigate its extensions to more general cryptographic frameworks supporting *compositional reasoning* [6,19].

References

1. Abadi, M., Rogaway, P.: Reconciling Two Views of Cryptography (the computational soundness of formal encryption). In: Watanabe, O., Hagiya, M., Ito, T., van Leeuwen, J., Mosses, P.D. (eds.) TCS 2000. LNCS, vol. 1872, pp. 3–22. Springer, Heidelberg (2000)
2. Acar, T., Belenkiy, M., Bellare, M., Cash, D.: Cryptographic Agility and Its Relation to Circular Encryption. In: Gilbert, H. (ed.) EUROCRYPT 2010. LNCS, vol. 6110, pp. 403–422. Springer, Heidelberg (2010)
3. Backes, M., Dürmuth, M., Unruh, D.: OAEP Is Secure under Key-Dependent Messages. In: Pieprzyk, J. (ed.) ASIACRYPT 2008. LNCS, vol. 5350, pp. 506–523. Springer, Heidelberg (2008)
4. Backes, M., Pfitzmann, B.: Symmetric encryption in a simulatable dolev-yao style cryptographic library. In: CSFW, pp. 204–218. IEEE Computer Society (2004)
5. Backes, M., Pfitzmann, B., Scedrov, A.: Key-dependent message security under active attacks - brsim/uc-soundness of symbolic encryption with key cycles. In: CSF, pp. 112–124. IEEE Computer Society (2007)
6. Backes, M., Pfitzmann, B., Waidner, M.: A composable cryptographic library with nested operations. In: Jajodia, S., Atluri, V., Jaeger, T. (eds.) ACM Conference on Computer and Communications Security, pp. 220–230. ACM (2003)

7. Bana, G., Comon-Lundh, H.: Towards Unconditional Soundness: Computationally Complete Symbolic Attacker. In: Degano, P., Guttman, J.D. (eds.) POST 2012. LNCS, vol. 7215, pp. 189–208. Springer, Heidelberg (2012)

8. Barthe, G., Daubignard, M., Kapron, B.M., Lakhnech, Y.: Computational indistinguishability logic. In: Al-Shaer, E., Keromytis, A.D., Shmatikov, V. (eds.) ACM Conference on Computer and Communications Security, pp. 375–386. ACM (2010)

9. Bellare, M., Boldyreva, A., Micali, S.: Public-Key Encryption in a Multi-user Setting: Security Proofs and Improvements. In: Preneel, B. (ed.) EUROCRYPT 2000. LNCS, vol. 1807, pp. 259–274. Springer, Heidelberg (2000)

10. Bellare, M., Desai, A., Pointcheval, D., Rogaway, P.: Relations among Notions of Security for Public-Key Encryption Schemes. In: Krawczyk, H. (ed.) CRYPTO 1998. LNCS, vol. 1462, pp. 26–45. Springer, Heidelberg (1998)

11. Bellare, M., Namprempre, C.: Authenticated encryption: Relations among notions and analysis of the generic composition paradigm. J. Cryptology 21(4), 469–491 (2008)

12. Bellare, M., Rogaway, P.: Entity Authentication and Key Distribution. In: Stinson, D.R. (ed.) CRYPTO 1993. LNCS, vol. 773, pp. 232–249. Springer, Heidelberg (1994)

13. Bellare, M., Rogaway, P.: Provably secure session key distribution: the three party case. In: Leighton, F.T., Borodin, A. (eds.) STOC, pp. 57–66. ACM (1995)

14. Boneh, D., Halevi, S., Hamburg, M., Ostrovsky, R.: Circular-Secure Encryption from Decision Diffie-Hellman. In: Wagner, D. (ed.) CRYPTO 2008. LNCS, vol. 5157, pp. 108–125. Springer, Heidelberg (2008)

15. Burrows, M., Abadi, M., Needham, R.: A logic of authentication. ACM Trans. Comput. Syst. 8, 18–36 (1990)

16. Camenisch, J., Chandran, N., Shoup, V.: A Public Key Encryption Scheme Secure against Key Dependent Chosen Plaintext and Adaptive Chosen Ciphertext Attacks. In: Joux, A. (ed.) EUROCRYPT 2009. LNCS, vol. 5479, pp. 351–368. Springer, Heidelberg (2009)

17. Canetti, R.: Universally composable security: A new paradigm for cryptographic protocols. In: FOCS, pp. 136–145. IEEE Computer Society (2001)

18. Canetti, R., Feige, U., Goldreich, O., Naor, M.: Adaptively secure multi-party computation. In: Miller, G.L. (ed.) STOC, pp. 639–648. ACM (1996)

19. Canetti, R., Herzog, J.: Universally Composable Symbolic Analysis of Mutual Authentication and Key-Exchange Protocols. In: Halevi, S., Rabin, T. (eds.) TCC 2006. LNCS, vol. 3876, pp. 380–403. Springer, Heidelberg (2006)

20. Cash, D., Green, M., Hohenberger, S.: New Definitions and Separations for Circular Security. In: Fischlin, M., Buchmann, J., Manulis, M. (eds.) PKC 2012. LNCS, vol. 7293, pp. 540–557. Springer, Heidelberg (2012)

21. Clark, J., Jacob, J.: A survey of authentication protocol literature. Technical report (1997)

22. Comon-Lundh, H., Cortier, V.: Computational soundness of observational equivalence. In: Ning, P., Syverson, P.F., Jha, S. (eds.) ACM Conference on Computer and Communications Security, pp. 109–118. ACM (2008)

23. Datta, A., Derek, A., Mitchell, J.C., Warinschi, B.: Computationally sound compositional logic for key exchange protocols. In: CSFW, pp. 321–334. IEEE Computer Society (2006)

24. Dolev, D., Yao, A.C.: On the security of public key protocols. In: Annual IEEE Symposium on Foundations of Computer Science, pp. 350–357 (1981)

25. Gilbert, H. (ed.): EUROCRYPT 2010. LNCS, vol. 6110. Springer, Heidelberg (2010)

26. Goldwasser, S., Micali, S.: Probabilistic encryption. J. Comput. Syst. Sci. 28(2), 270–299 (1984)
27. Hajiabadi, M., Kapron, B.M.: Computational soundness of coinductive symbolic security under active attacks. IACR Cryptology ePrint Archive, 2012:560 (2012)
28. Herzog, J.: A computational interpretation of dolev-yao adversaries. Theor. Comput. Sci. 340(1), 57–81 (2005)
29. Impagliazzo, R., Kapron, B.M.: Logics for reasoning about cryptographic constructions. J. Comput. Syst. Sci. 72(2), 286–320 (2006)
30. Küsters, R., Tuengerthal, M.: Computational soundness for key exchange protocols with symmetric encryption. In: Al-Shaer, E., Jha, S., Keromytis, A.D. (eds.) ACM Conference on Computer and Communications Security, pp. 91–100. ACM (2009)
31. Lincoln, P., Mitchell, J.C., Mitchell, M., Scedrov, A.: A probabilistic poly-time framework for protocol analysis. In: Gong, L., Reiter, M.K. (eds.) ACM Conference on Computer and Communications Security, pp. 112–121. ACM (1998)
32. Micciancio, D.: Computational Soundness, Co-induction, and Encryption Cycles. In: Gilbert, H. (ed.) EUROCRYPT 2010. LNCS, vol. 6110, pp. 362–380. Springer, Heidelberg (2010)
33. Micciancio, D., Panjwani, S.: Adaptive Security of Symbolic Encryption. In: Kilian, J. (ed.) TCC 2005. LNCS, vol. 3378, pp. 169–187. Springer, Heidelberg (2005)
34. Micciancio, D., Warinschi, B.: Soundness of Formal Encryption in the Presence of Active Adversaries. In: Naor, M. (ed.) TCC 2004. LNCS, vol. 2951, pp. 133–151. Springer, Heidelberg (2004)
35. Mitchell, J.C., Ramanathan, A., Scedrov, A., Teague, V.: A probabilistic polynomial-time process calculus for the analysis of cryptographic protocols. Theor. Comput. Sci. 353(1-3), 118–164 (2006)
36. Panjwani, S.: Tackling Adaptive Corruptions in Multicast Encryption Protocols. In: Vadhan, S.P. (ed.) TCC 2007. LNCS, vol. 4392, pp. 21–40. Springer, Heidelberg (2007)
37. Pfitzmann, B., Waidner, M.: A model for asynchronous reactive systems and its application to secure message transmission. In: IEEE Symposium on Security and Privacy, pp. 184–200 (2001)
38. Rackoff, C., Simon, D.R.: Non-interactive Zero-Knowledge Proof of Knowledge and Chosen Ciphertext Attack. In: Feigenbaum, J. (ed.) CRYPTO 1991. LNCS, vol. 576, pp. 433–444. Springer, Heidelberg (1992)

Revisiting Lower and Upper Bounds for Selective Decommitments

Rafail Ostrovsky[1,2], Vanishree Rao[1], Alessandra Scafuro[3,*], and Ivan Visconti[3]

[1] Department of Computer Science, UCLA, USA
[2] Department of Mathematics, UCLA, USA
{rafail,vanishri}@cs.ucla.edu
[3] Dipartimento di Informatica, University of Salerno, Italy
{scafuro,visconti}@dia.unisa.it

Abstract. In [6,7], Dwork et al. posed the fundamental question of existence of commitment schemes that are secure against selective opening attacks (SOA, for short). In [2] Bellare, Hofheinz, and Yilek, and Hofheinz in [13] answered it affirmatively by presenting a scheme which is based solely on the non-black-box use of a one-way permutation needing a super-constant number of rounds. This result however opened other challenging questions about achieving a better round complexity and obtaining fully black-box schemes using underlying primitives and code of the adversary in a black-box manner.

Recently, in TCC 2011, Xiao ([23]) investigated on how to achieve (nearly) optimal SOA-secure commitment schemes where optimality is in the sense of both the round complexity and the black-box use of cryptographic primitives. The work of Xiao focuses on a simulation-based security notion of SOA. Moreover, the various results in [23] focus only on either parallel or concurrent SOA.

In this work we first point out various issues in the claims of [23] that actually re-open several of the questions left open in [2,13]. Then, we provide new lower bounds and concrete constructions that produce a very different state-of-the-art compared to the one claimed in [23].

1 Introduction

Commitment schemes are a fundamental building block in cryptographic protocols. By their usual notion, they satisfy two security properties, namely, hiding and binding. While the binding property guarantees that a committed message can not be opened to two distinct messages, the hiding property ensures that before the decommitment phase begins, no information about the committed message is revealed. Binding and hiding are preserved under concurrent composition, in the sense that even a concurrent malicious sender will not be able to open a committed message in two ways, and even a concurrent malicious receiver will not be able to detect any relevant information about committed messages as long as only commitment phases have been played so far.

---

* Work done while visiting UCLA.

A. Sahai (Ed.): TCC 2013, LNCS 7785, pp. 559–578, 2013.

In [6], Dwork et al. pointed out a more subtle definition of security for hiding where the malicious receiver is allowed to ask for the opening of only some of the committed messages, with the goal of breaking the hiding property of the remaining committed messages. This notion was captured in [6] via a simulation-based security definition, and is referred to as hiding in presence of selective opening attack (SOA, for short). [6] shows that, in a *trusted setup* setting, it is possible to construct a non-interactive SOA-secure commitment scheme from a trapdoor commitment scheme. Indeed, in the trusted setup the simulator sets the parameters of the trapdoor commitment, thus obviously it knows the trapdoor. However, the fundamental question of whether there exist SOA-secure commitment schemes in the *plain model*, is left open in [6]. We stress that the question is particularly important since commitments are often used in larger protocols, where often only some commitments are opened but the security of the whole scheme still relies on hiding the unopened commitments. For instance, the importance of SOA-secure commitments for constructing zero-knowledge sets is discussed in [10][1].

The SOA-security experiment put forth in [6] considers a one-shot commitment phase, in which the receiver gets all commitments in one-shot, picks adaptively a subset of them, and obtains the opening of such subset. Such definition implicitly considers non-interactive commitments and only parallel composition. Subsequent works have explored several extensions/variations of this definition showing possibility and impossibility results. Before proceeding to the discussion of the related work, it is useful to set up the dimensions that will be considered. One dimension is *composition*. As commitment is a two-phase functionality, other than parallel composition, one can consider two kinds of concurrent composition. Concurrent-with-barrier composition (considered in [2,13]), refers to the setting in which the adversarial receiver can interleave the execution of several commitments, and the execution of decommitments, with the restriction that all commitment phases are played before any decommitment phase begins. Thus, there is a barrier between commitment and decommitment stage. Fully-concurrent composition (considered in [23]) refers to the setting in which the adversary can arbitrarily interleave the execution of the commitment phase of one session with the decommitment of another session (and vice-versa).

Next dimension is the *access to primitive*, namely, if the construction uses a cryptographic primitive as a black-box (in short, BB), or in a non black-box way (in short, NBB).

Another dimension is *simulation*. In this discussion we consider always black-box simulators (if not otherwise specified).

The question of achieving SOA-secure commitments without any set-up was solved affirmatively in [2] by Bellare, Hofheinz, and Yilek, and by Hofheinz in [13], who presented an interactive SOA-secure scheme based on non-black-box use of any one-way permutation and with a commitment phase requiring a super-constant number of rounds. The security of such construction is proved in

---

[1] In [10] some forms of zero-knowledge sets were proposed, and their strongest definition required SOA-secure commitments.

the concurrent-with-barrier setting. [2,13] also show that non-interactive SOA-secure commitments which use cryptographic primitives in a black-box way do not exist. The same work introduces the notion of *indistinguishability* under selective opening attacks, that we do not consider in this work. The results of [2,13] left open several other questions on round optimality and black-box use of the underlying cryptographic primitives.

In TCC 2011 [23], Xiao addressed the above open questions and investigated on how to achieve nearly optimal schemes where optimality concerns both the round complexity and the black-box use of cryptographic primitives. In particular, Xiao addressed SOA-security of commitment schemes for both parallel composition and fully-concurrent composition and provided both possibility and impossibility results, sticking to the simulation-based definition. Concerning positive results, [23] shows a 4-round (resp., $(t + 3)$-round for a t-round statistically-hiding commitment) computationally binding (resp., statistically binding) SOA-secure scheme for parallel composition. Moreover, [23] provides a commitment scheme which is "strong" (the meaning of strong is explained later) SOA-secure in the fully-concurrent setting and requires a logarithmic number of rounds. All such constructions are fully black-box. Concerning impossibility results, [23] shows that 3-round (resp., 4-round) computationally binding (resp., statistically binding) parallel SOA-secure commitment schemes are impossible to achieve. As explained later, in this paper – among other things – we present issues in the proof of security of the constructions shown in [23]. We also show that, the strong security claimed for the construction suggested for the fully-concurrent setting, is actually impossible to achieve, regardless of the round complexity. We contradict the lower bounds claimed in [23] by providing a 3-round fully black-box commitment scheme which is SOA-secure under concurrent-with-barrier composition, which implies parallel composition.

In a subsequent work [25], after our results became publicly available, Xiao showed a black-box construction of 4-round statistically-binding commitment scheme which is SOA-secure under parallel composition. As we shall see later, our 3-round and 4-round schemes are only computationally binding, but are secure in the stronger setting of concurrent-with-barrier composition.

In [24], the same author provides an updated version of [23]. Concerning positive results, [24] includes the $(t + 3, 1)$-round construction of [23] and shows a new simulation strategy for it. Concerning impossibility results, [24] includes the lower bounds of [23] that are still valid for 2-round (resp., 3-round) computationally hiding and computationally (resp., statistically) binding, parallel, SOA-secure commitment schemes with black-box simulators. [24] contains also other contributions of [23] that are not contradicted by this work.

In [1], Bellare et al. proves that existence of CRHFs implies impossibility of non-interactive SOA-secure commitments (regardless of the black-box use of the cryptographic primitives). In fact, they show something even stronger; they show that this impossibility holds even if the simulator is non-black-box and knows the distribution of the message space. An implication of such results is that, standard security does not imply SOA-security. Previous results in [2,13] only showed the impossibility for the case of black-box reductions.

In [19], Pass and Wee provide several black-box constructions for two-party protocols. In particular, they provide constructions for look-ahead trapdoor commitments (in a look-ahead commitment, knowledge of the trapdoor is necessary already in the commitment phase in order for the commitment to be equivocal, in this paper we call such commitments "weak trapdoor commitments"), and trapdoor commitments. Such constructions have not been proved to be SOA-secure commitment schemes, as SOA-security is proven in presence of (at least) parallel composition, while security of the trapdoor commitment of [19] is proved only in the stand-alone setting. In the full version of this paper we discuss how the look-ahead thread of [19] can be plugged in our construction based on weak trapdoor commitments, to obtain a 6-round SOA-secure commitment scheme in the concurrent-with-barrier setting.

1.1   Our Contribution

In this work we focus on simulation-based SOA-secure commitment schemes, and we restrict our attention to black-box simulation, and (mainly) black-box access to cryptographic primitives (like in [23]). Firstly, we point out various issues in the claims of [23]. These issues essentially re-open some of the open questions that were claimed to be answered in [23]. We next show how to solve (in many cases in a nearly optimal way) all of them. Interestingly, our final claims render quite a different state-of-the-art from (and in some cases also in contrast to) the state-of-the-art set by the claims of [23].

In detail, by specifying as (x, y) the round complexity of a commitment scheme when the commitment phase takes x rounds and the decommitment phase takes y rounds, we revisit some claims of [23] and re-open some challenging open questions as follows.

1. The proof in [23] of the non-existence of $(3, 1)$-round schemes assumes implicitly that the sender sends the last message during the commitment phase. We show here that surprisingly this assumption is erroneous, and that one round might be saved in the commitment phase if the receiver goes last. This re-opens the question of the achievability of $(3, 1)$-round SOA-secure schemes, even for just parallel composition.
2. There are issues in the proof of binding and SOA-security of the $(4, 1)$-round scheme of [23] for parallel composition, and it is currently unknown whether the scheme is secure. The same issue in the SOA-security proof exists for the $(t + 3, 1)$-round statistically binding scheme of [23] which is based on any t-round statistically-hiding commitment. Indeed, for both constructions, SOA-security is claimed to follow from the simulation technique of Goldreich-Kahan [11]. The problem is that the simulator of [11] was built for a *stand-alone* zero-knowledge protocol, where an atomic sub-protocol is repeated several times in parallel, and the verifier cannot *selectively* abort one of the sub-protocols. Instead in the SOA-setting, the adversarial receiver interacts

with multiple senders and can decide to abort a subset of the sessions of its choice adaptively based on the commitment-phase transcript. We note that this implies that [23] contains no full proof of a constant round SOA-secure scheme (but we remark that, subsequent to our results, the same author presented a new proof of the $(t + 3, 1)$-round scheme based on statistically-hiding commitment in the work [25,24]).

3. There is an issue in the proof of security of the fully-concurrent SOA-secure commitment scheme proposed in [23]. The security of such construction is claimed even for the case in which the simulator cannot efficiently sample from the distribution of messages committed to by the honest sender (but needs to query an external party for it).[2] This notion is referred in [23] as "strong" security. This issue in [23] re-opens the possibility of achieving schemes that are strong SOA-secure under fully concurrent composition (for any round complexity).

In this paper we solve the above open problems (still sticking to the notion of black-box simulation as formalized in [23]) as follows.

1. We present a $(3, 1)$-round scheme based on BB use of any trapdoor commitment (TCom, for short), which contradicts the lower bound claimed in [23]. We also provide several constructions based on BB use of various weaker assumptions. We show: a $(3, 3)$-round scheme based on BB use of any OWP, a $(4, 1)$-round scheme based on BB use of any weak trapdoor commitment (wTCom, for short)[3], and a $(5, 1)$-round scheme based on BB use of any OWP.

2. We show that when the simulator does not know the distribution of the messages committed to by the honest sender, there exists no scheme that achieves fully concurrent SOA-security, regardless of the round complexity and of the BB use of cryptographic primitives. Thus contradicting the claimed security of the construction given in [23].

3. As a corollary of our $(3, 1)$-round scheme based on BB use of any TCom, there exists a $(3, 1)$-round scheme based on NBB use of any one-way function (OWF). This improves the round complexity in [2] from logarithmic in the security parameter to only 3 rounds and using minimal complexity-theoretic assumptions. Moreover, we observe that (as a direct consequence from proof techniques in [23]) a $(2, 1)$-round SOA-secure scheme is impossible regardless of the use of the underlying cryptographic primitive (for black-box simulation only). Thus, our $(3, 1)$-round scheme for black-box simulation is essentially round-optimal.

Notice that both our $(3, 1)$-round protocols – the one based on BB use of TCom and the other based on NBB use of OWFs – contradict the impossibility given

---

[2] For simplicity, we shall hereafter refer to this case as the simulator not knowing the distribution.

[3] This result indeed requires a relaxed definition of trapdoor commitment where the trapdoor is required to be known already during the commitment phase in order to later equivocate. We call it "weak" because any TCom is also a wTCom.

in [23], that was claimed to hold regardless of the access to the cryptographic primitives.

All the constructions shown in this paper are secure under concurrent-with-barrier composition, which obviously implies parallel composition. Our simulators work for any message distributions, and do not need to know the distribution of the messages committed to by the honest sender. In light of our impossibility for the fully concurrent composition (see Item 2 of the above list), the concurrency achieved by our schemes seems to be optimal for this setting.

As an additional application, we also show that our $(3, 1)$-round schemes can be used to obtain non-interactive (concurrent) zero knowledge [8] with 3 rounds of pre-processing. This improves upon [5] where (at least) 3 rounds of interactions are needed both in the pre-processing phase and in the proof phase. Moreover, the simulator of [5] works only with non-aborting verifiers, while our simulator does not have this limitation. This application also establishes usefulness of concurrency-with-barrier setting.

Comparison with Previous Work. For a better clarity we compare previous results and constructions with the contribution of this paper in Table 1. In the table, listings under "Impossible" column refer to the impossibility results in the papers heading the corresponding row. Similarly, the listings under "Constructions" column refer to the constructions in the papers heading the corresponding row. All such constructions are proved via black-box simulations. BB (resp., NBB) stands for black-box (resp., non black-box) access to cryptographic primitives. PAR, CwB, CC, refer respectively to parallel, concurrent-with-barrier, fully-concurrent composition. PB and SB are shorthands for perfectly binding and statistically binding, and TCom, wTCom, OWP are shorthands for Trapdoor Commitment, weak Trapdoor Commitment, One-Way Permutation. For instance, an entry like, "BB $(1, 1)$ (or PB) PAR" under Impossible column and for the row [2,13], says that [2,13] demonstrate that non-interactive, or perfectly-binding commitment schemes that are SOA-secure under parallel composition, are impossible to construct given only BB access to cryptographic primitives. The entry, "NBB $(\log n, 1)$ CwB OWP" under Constructions column and in the row headed by [2] says that [2] shows a $(\log n, 1)$-round scheme based on NBB use of OWPs that is SOA-secure under concurrent-with-barrier composition.

On Simulator not Knowing Message Distribution. All our protocols and impossibility results are in the setting where the simulator by itself cannot efficiently sample from the message distribution but needs to query an external oracle for the same. Positive results can only be stronger with this requirement.

Selective Opening, Adaptive Security, Trapdoor Commitments and Non-malleable Commitments. The concept of commitments secure in presence of selective opening attacks is very related to adaptively secure commitments[4], and trapdoor

---

[4] In such a notion, an adversary can corrupt a party anytime during the protocol execution, obtaining the party's internal state.

Table 1. This work in relation to the state-of-the-art

	Impossible	Constructions
[2,13]	BB (1,1) (or PB) PAR	NBB ($\log n$, 1) CwB OWP
[1]	NBB (1,1) PAR	
[6]		Set-up assumption: BB (1,1) CC TCom
This Paper on [19]		* BB (x,y) LA-TCom implies BB $(2+x,y)$ CwB
[23]	(3,1) PAR $(o(\log n/\log\log n), 1)$ CC BB SIM	BB (4,1) PAR OWP BB $(t+3,1)$ PAR $(t,1)$-SH BB $(\omega(t\log n),1)$ CC $(t,1)$-SH
This Paper on [23]	~~(3,1) PAR~~ BB SIM	~~BB (4,1) PAR OWP~~ ~~BB $(t+3,1)$ PAR $(t,1)$-SH~~ ~~BB $(\omega(t\log n),1)$ CC $(t,1)$-SH~~
This Paper	BB (any, any) CC BB SIM	BB (3,1) TCom; NBB (3,1) OWF BB (4,1) wTCom ; BB (3,3) OWP BB (5,1) OWP (all CwB)
[25]		BB SB $(t+2,1)$ PAR $(t,1)$-SH
[24]		BB $(t+3,1)$ PAR $(t,1)$-SH

commitments, – in which there exists a trapdoor that allows to open a commitment in many ways. However, they are three different settings.

First, trapdoor commitments are not necessarily SOA-secure (in the plain model). The reason is that trapdoor commitments only guarantee that *there exists* a trapdoor which would allow to equivocate a commitment, however, such trapdoor is clearly not available to a simulator. To achieve SOA-security from a trapdoor commitment scheme one should provide a mechanism for the simulator to get the trapdoor, still not violating binding. The converse moreover is not true, namely, a SOA-secure commitment is not necessarily also a trapdoor commitment. This comes from the fact that the simulator of a SOA-secure commitment could use rewinding capabilities instead of a trapdoor that might not exist at all.

Second, a commitment scheme that is adaptively secure in the parallel composition, is also parallel SOA-secure commitment. The converse is not necessarily true. Namely, a SOA-secure commitment scheme is not necessarily adaptively secure. The reason is that in a selective opening attack, a malicious receiver can "corrupt" the sender in the decommitment phase only, and by definition, it is allowed to see only the openings of the commitments instead of the *whole* state of the sender.

Finally, we stress that our adversary can play as sender only or as receiver only. An interesting question is which type of SOA security can be achieved also against man-in-the-middle attacks. The recent work of [12] gives hope towards a construction of a constant-round non-malleable SOA-secure protocol with black-box simulation and black-box use of any one-way function.

2   Preliminaries

Notation. We denote by $n \in \mathbb{N}$ the security parameter and by PPT the property of an algorithm of running in probabilistic polynomial-time. A function ϵ is negligible (negl., for short) in n (or just negligible) if for every polynomial $p(\cdot)$ there exists a value $n_0 \in \mathbb{N}$ such that for all $n > n_0$ it holds that $\epsilon(n) < 1/p(n)$. We denote by $[k]$ the set $\{1, \ldots, k\}$; $\mathtt{poly}(n)$ stands for polynomial in n. We denote by $x \leftarrow \mathcal{D}$ the sampling of an element x from the distribution $\mathcal{D}$. We also use $x \xleftarrow{\$} \mathsf{A}$ to indicate that the element x is uniformly sampled from set A. We denote by $(v_A, v_B) \leftarrow \langle A(), B() \rangle$ the pair of outputs of parties A and B, respectively, after the completion of their interaction. We use $v \xleftarrow{\$} A()$ when the algorithm A is randomized. Finally, let P_1 and P_2 be two parties running a protocol that uses protocol $\langle A, B \rangle$ as a sub-routine. When we say that party "P_1 runs $\langle A(\cdot), B(\cdot) \rangle$ with P_2" we always mean that P_1 executes the procedure of party A and P_2 executes the procedure of party B. In the paper we use the words decommitment and opening interchangeably.

2.1   Commitment Schemes

In the following definitions we assume that parties are stateful and that malicious parties obtain auxiliary inputs, although for better readability we omit them.

Definition 1 (Bit Commitment Scheme). *A commitment scheme is a tuple of PPT algorithms* $\mathsf{Com} = (\mathsf{Gen}, \mathsf{S}, \mathsf{R})$ *implementing the following two-phase functionality.* Gen *takes as input a random n-bit string r and outputs the public parameters pk. Given to S an input $b \in \{0,1\}$, in the first phase (*commitment phase*) S interacts with R to commit to the bit b; we denote this interaction as* $\langle \mathsf{S}(pk, \mathsf{com}, b), \mathsf{R}(\mathtt{rcv}) \rangle$. *In the second phase (*opening phase*) S interacts with R to reveal the bit b, we denote this interaction as* $\langle \mathsf{S}(\mathsf{open}), \mathsf{R}(\mathsf{open}) \rangle$ *and R finally outputs a bit b' or $\bot$. Consider the following two experiments:*

Experiment $\mathbf{Exp}_{\mathsf{Com}, \mathsf{S}^*}^{\mathrm{binding}}(n)$:	**Experiment $\mathbf{Exp}_{\mathsf{Com}, \mathsf{R}^*}^{\mathrm{hiding}\text{-}b}(n)$:**
R *runs* $(pk) \leftarrow \mathsf{Gen}(r)$ *and sends pk to S^*;*	$pk^* \leftarrow \mathsf{R}^*(1^n)$;
$\langle \mathsf{S}^*(pk, \mathsf{com}, b), \mathsf{R}(\mathtt{rcv}) \rangle$;	$(\cdot, b') \xleftarrow{\$} \langle \mathsf{S}(pk^*, \mathsf{com}, b), \mathsf{R}^*(\mathtt{rcv}) \rangle$;
$(\cdot, b_0) \xleftarrow{\$} \langle \mathsf{S}^*(\mathsf{open}, 0), \mathsf{R}(\mathsf{open}) \rangle$;	*output b'.*
rewind S^* and R back after the second step;	
$(\cdot, b_1) \xleftarrow{\$} \langle \mathsf{S}^*(\mathsf{open}, 1), \mathsf{R}(\mathsf{open}) \rangle$;	
output 1 iff $\bot \neq b_0 \neq b_1 \neq \bot$.	

$\mathsf{Com} = (\mathsf{Gen}, \mathsf{S}, \mathsf{R})$ *is a commitment scheme if the following conditions hold:*

Completeness. *If S and R are honest, for any S's input $b \in \{0,1\}$ the output of R in the opening phase is $b' = b$.*

Hiding. *For any PPT malicious receiver R^*, there exists a negligible function ϵ such that the following holds:*

$$\mathbf{Adv}_{\mathsf{Com}, \mathsf{R}^*}^{\mathrm{hiding}} = |\Pr[(\mathbf{Exp}_{\mathsf{Com}, \mathsf{R}^*}^{\mathrm{hiding}\text{-}0}(n) \to 1)] - \Pr[\mathbf{Exp}_{\mathsf{Com}, \mathsf{R}^*}^{\mathrm{hiding}\text{-}1}(n) \to 1)]| \leq \epsilon(n).$$

Binding. *For any PPT malicious sender S^* there exists a negl. function ϵ such that:* $\Pr[\mathbf{Exp}_{\mathsf{Com}, \mathsf{S}^*}^{\mathrm{binding}} \to 1] \leq \epsilon(n)$.

The above probabilities are taken over the choice of the randomness r for the algorithm Gen *and the random coins of the parties. A commitment scheme is statistically hiding (resp., binding) if hiding (resp., binding) condition holds even against an unbounded malicious Receiver (resp., Sender).*

The above definition is a slight modification of the one provided in [2,13], and is more general in the fact the it includes the algorithm Gen. Such a definition is convenient when one aims to use commitment schemes as sub-protocols in a black-box way. However, for better readability, when we construct or use as sub-protocol a commitment scheme that does not use public parameters, we refer to it only as Com = (S, R), omitting the algorithm Gen.

Definition 2 (Trapdoor Commitment). *A tuple of PPT algorithms* TC = (TGen, S, R, TFakeD) *is a trapdoor commitment scheme if* TGen, *on input a random n-bit string r, outputs a public key/secret key pair (pk, sk),* TGen_{pk} *is the related functionality that restricts the output of* TGen *to the public key,* $(\mathsf{TGen}_{pk}, \mathsf{S}, \mathsf{R})$ *is a commitment scheme, and* (S, TFakeD) *are such that:*

Trapdoor Property. *There exists* $b^\star \in \{0,1\}$, *such that for any* $b \in \{0,1\}$, *for all* $(pk, sk) \leftarrow \mathsf{TGen}(r)$, *and for any PPT malicious receiver* R* *there exists a negl. function* ϵ *such that the following holds:*

$$\mathbf{Adv}_{\mathsf{TC},\mathsf{R}^*}^{\mathsf{trapdoor}} = \Pr[\mathbf{Exp}_{\mathsf{TC}}^{\mathsf{Trap}}(n) \to 1] - \Pr[\mathbf{Exp}_{\mathsf{TC}}^{\mathsf{Com}}(n) \to 1] \leq \epsilon(n).$$

The probability is taken over the choice of r for the algorithm TGen *and the random coins of the players.*

$Experiment\ \mathbf{Exp}_{\mathsf{TC}}^{\mathsf{Com}}(n)$:	$Experiment\ \mathbf{Exp}_{\mathsf{TC}}^{\mathsf{Trap}}(n)$:
R* *chooses a bit b;*	R* *chooses a bit b;*
$\langle\mathsf{S}(pk,\mathrm{com},b),\mathsf{R}^*(pk,sk,b,\mathrm{rcv})\rangle;$	$(\xi,\cdot) \leftarrow \langle\mathsf{S}(pk,\mathrm{com},b^\star),\mathsf{R}^*(pk,sk,b,\mathrm{rcv})\rangle;$
$(\cdot,b') \xleftarrow{\$} \langle\mathsf{S}(\mathrm{open}),\mathsf{R}^*(\mathrm{open})\rangle;$	$(\cdot,b') \xleftarrow{\$} \langle\mathsf{TFakeD}(sk,\mathrm{open},b,\xi),\mathsf{R}^*(\mathrm{open})\rangle;$
output b';	*output b';*

In the experiment $\mathbf{Exp}_{\mathsf{TC}}^{\mathsf{Trap}}(n)$, S runs the procedure of the honest sender on input $b^\star$. The variable ξ contains the randomness used by S to compute the commitment phase and it is used by TFakeD to compute the decommitment. The knowledge of the trapdoor is required only in decommitment phase. In the trapdoor commitment of Pedersen [20], the trapdoor property holds for any $b^\star$, namely one can use the honest sender procedure to commit an arbitrary bit $b^\star$ and use the trapdoor to decommit to any $b \neq b^\star$. Instead, in the trapdoor commitment proposed by Feige and Shamir [9][5], the trapdoor property holds only if the honest procedure was used to commit to bit $b^\star = 0$. In both commitment schemes the trapdoor is used only in the decommitment phase.

---

[5] The commitment procedure consists of running the simulator of Blum's protocol [3] for Graph Hamiltonicity where the challenge is the bit to commit to. This commitment use OWFs in a NBB way.

Definition 3 (Hiding in the presence of Selective Opening Attacks (slight variation of [2,13])). *Let $k = \text{poly}(n)$, let $\mathcal{B}$ be a k-bit message distribution and $\mathbf{b} \xleftarrow{\$} \mathcal{B}$ be a k-bit vector, let $\mathcal{I} = \{\mathcal{I}_k\}_{k \in \mathbb{N}}$ be a family of sets, where each $\mathcal{I}_k$ is a set of subsets of $[k]$ denoting the set of legal subsets of (indexes of) commitments that the receiver (honest or malicious) is allowed to ask for the opening. A commitment scheme $\text{Com} = (\text{Gen}, \text{S}, \text{R})$ is secure against selective opening attacks if for all k, all sets $I \in \mathcal{I}$, all k-bit message distributions $\mathcal{B}$, all PPT relations $\mathcal{R}$, there exists an expected PPT machine Sim such that for any PPT malicious receiver R^* there exists a negl. function ϵ such that:*

$$\mathbf{Adv}^{\text{soa}}_{\text{Com}} = \left| \Pr[\mathbf{Exp}^{\text{real}}_{\text{Com},\text{S},\text{R}^*}(n) \to 1] - \Pr[\mathbf{Exp}^{\text{ideal}}_{\text{Com},\text{Sim},\text{R}^*}(n) \to 1] \right| \leq \epsilon(n).$$

The probability is taken over the choice of the random coins of the parties.

$\text{Experiment } \mathbf{Exp}^{\text{real}}_{\text{Com},\text{S},\text{R}^*}(n):$	$\text{Experiment } \mathbf{Exp}^{\text{ideal}}_{\text{Com},\text{Sim},\text{R}^*}(n):$
$pk \xleftarrow{\$} \text{R}^*(1^n);$	$pk \xleftarrow{\$} \text{R}^*(1^n);$
$\mathbf{b} \xleftarrow{\$} \mathcal{B};$	$\mathbf{b} \xleftarrow{\$} \mathcal{B};$
$I \xleftarrow{\$} \langle \text{S}_i(pk, \text{com}, \mathbf{b}[i])_{i \in [k]}, \text{R}^*(pk, \text{rcv}) \rangle;$	$I \xleftarrow{\$} \text{Sim}^{\text{R}^*}(pk);$
$(\cdot, ext) \xleftarrow{\$} \langle \text{S}_i(\text{open})_{i \in I}, \text{R}^*(\text{open}) \rangle;$	$ext \xleftarrow{\$} \text{Sim}^{\text{R}^*}(\mathbf{b}[i])_{i \in I};$
$\text{output } \mathcal{R}(I, \mathbf{b}, ext).$	$\text{output } \mathcal{R}(I, \mathbf{b}, ext).$

We denote by $(\cdot, ext) \xleftarrow{\$} \langle \text{S}_i(\cdot), \text{R}^*(\cdot) \rangle$ the output of R^* after having interacted concurrently with k instances of S each one denoted by S_i. In the paper an instance of the protocol is called session. A malicious receiver R^* can run many sessions in concurrency with the following limitation. R^* runs commitment phases concurrently for polynomially many sessions, but it can initiate the first decommitment phase only after the commitment phases of all the sessions have been completed (and therefore after the set of indexes has been requested). This means that the set of indexes I (i.e., the commitments asked to be opened), depends only of the transcript of the commitment phase. We call this definition **concurrent-with-barrier** (*CwB*, for short), meaning that many commitment phases (decommitment phases) can be run concurrently but the commitment phase of any session cannot be interleaved with the decommitment of any other session. Notice that as in [23], our definition assumes that the honest receiver chooses to open only a subset of the commitments, but this is done independently of the transcript (i.e., $I \xleftarrow{\$} \mathcal{I}$).

We now discuss the choices that we made to obtain the above definitions.

Concurrency-with-barrier Composition vs Parallel and Concurrent Composition. In [23] Xiao provides two main definitions: SOA-security under parallel (PAR) composition and SOA-security under "fully" concurrent composition (CC). In the fully concurrent definition there is no barrier between commitment and decommitment phase: R^* is allowed to interleave the commitment phase of one session with the decommitment phase of another, basically having the power of deciding which decommitment/commitment to execute, depending on the transcript of the commitment *and* decommitment of other sessions. This definition is pretty general, but unfortunately, as we show in this paper, achieving this result is impossible (under the assumption that the simulator does not know the distribution of the messages committed to by the honest sender); this is in contrast to [23] where it is claimed that this definition is achievable. The concurrent-with-barrier composition that we adopted (following [13]) implies security under parallel composition while due to the barrier between commitment and decommitment phase, it is weaker than the fully concurrent definition of [23].

Decommitment Phase can be Interactive. Following [13] our definition is more general than the one of [23] since it allows also the decommitment phase to be interactive.

Honest Party Behaviour. We follow [23] in defining the behaviour of the honest receiver, i.e, R chooses the subset of commitments to be opened according to some distribution $\mathcal{I}$. To see why this definition makes sense, think about extractable commitments where the sender and receiver engage in many commitments of pairs of shares of a message but finally only one share per pair is required to be opened in the commitment phase.

Concerning the honest sender, we assume that R* interacts with k independent senders, that are oblivious to each other, and play with input $\mathbf{b}[j]$, while [23] considers a single sender S^k who gets as input the complete k-bit string and plays k independent sessions with R*. This variation is cosmetic only.

Comparison with the Definitions of [2,13]. In [2,13] the behaviour of the honest receiver is not explicitly defined, implying that the honest receiver always obtains all the openings. In order to be more general and to make SOA-secure commitments useful in more general scenarios, we deviate from this definition allowing the honest receiver to ask for the opening of a subset of the commitments. Moreover, the set of indexes I chosen by the (possibly malicious) receiver is explicitly given as input to the relation $\mathcal{R}$.

Summing up, the definition that we adopt mainly follows the one of [2,13] and is more general than the one of [23] in the fact that it allows interaction also during the decommitment phase, and provides concurrency-with-barrier that implies the definition of security under parallel composition. Moreover, our definition is more general than the one of [13] since it allows also the honest receiver to choose the commitments to be opened. However, our definition is weaker than the concurrent definition of [23] that however we show to be impossible to achieve (when the distribution of the messages committed by S is unknown to Sim).

3   Upper Bounds

3.1   (3, 1)-Round Scheme from Trapdoor Commitments

We present a construction for round-optimal SOA-secure commitment scheme based on BB use of trapdoor commitments. In particular we show that if 2-round (where the first round only serves for the receiver to send the public parameters) trapdoor commitment schemes exist[6], then a 3-round SOA-secure commitment scheme exists.

Roughly, the main idea of the protocol is to require the sender to commit to its private bit using a trapdoor commitment scheme and to make the trapdoor extractable to a black-box simulator. The goal is to allow the simulator to cheat in the opening phase without changing the transcript of the commitment phase. This is inspired by the techniques used in [17]. The parameters of the trapdoor commitment are generated by the receiver (if this was not the case then a malicious sender can cheat in decommitment phase using the trapdoor), and are made extractable through cut-and-choose techniques.

In more details, the protocol goes as follows. R runs the generation algorithm of the trapdoor commitment scheme (TGen) to compute the pairs $(\mathsf{pk}_i, \mathsf{sk}_i)$ of public and trapdoor parameters, and sends the public parameters to the sender. To guarantee the extraction of the trapdoor, we require that R provides $2n$ public parameters to S. S will use half of them to commits to n shares of its secret bit, while for the other half, it will ask the receiver to reveal the trapdoors associated. Then in the decommitment phase S simply opens the n commitments, and R computes the xor of the opened values.

To argue hiding in presence of SOA adversaries, we show the following simulator. Recall that, the malicious receiver can open many sessions and run many commitment phases concurrently (CwB definition). For each session, the simulator honestly commits to n random bits, and obtains n trapdoors. This is the main tread. When all commitment phases are completed, the simulator obtains from the adversary, the indexes of the sessions to be opened, and from the experiments, the actual bits to open. Next, it starts a rewinding thread for each session that needs to be open. In each rewinding thread, the simulator runs as in the main thread, except that it asks the adversary to open a different subset of trapdoors. Therefore, after an expected polynomial number of rewindings, it will obtain at least one *new* trapdoor for each session. One trapdoor will suffice to equivocate one share, and therefore to successfully open to any bit for that session.

Binding follows straight-forwardly from the binding of the trapdoor commitment scheme used as sub-protocol.

In the full version of this paper [18] we additionally show a $(4, 1)$-round constructions that is based on weak trapdoor commitment schemes.

The formal description of the construction is provided in Protocol 1. We denote by $\mathsf{TC} = (\mathsf{TGen}, \mathsf{S_{TC}}, \mathsf{R_{TC}}, \mathsf{S}, \mathsf{TFakeD})$ a trapdoor commitment scheme. We denote by $\langle \mathsf{S_{TC}}_i^{\bar{d}_i}, \mathsf{R_{TC}}_i^{\bar{d}_i} \rangle$ the i-th invocation of sub-protocol TC run with public key $\mathsf{pk}_i^{\bar{d}_i}$. Here d_i denotes the ith challenge for the cut-and-choose, i.e., $\mathsf{S_{soa}}$ computes the trapdoor associated to the key pk^{d_i}, while it commits to the ith share of the input using key $\mathsf{pk}^{\bar{d}_i}$ (for which the trapdoor will not be revealed).

---

[6] [20] is an example of a trapdoor commitment scheme where the public parameters pk are generated by the receiver and sent to the sender in the first round. Given pk, the commitment procedure is non-interactive.

Protocol 1. *[(3,1)-round SOA-Commitment] [SOACom=$(\mathsf{S_{soa}}, \mathsf{R_{soa}})$]*
Commitment Phase

$\mathsf{R_{soa}}$: *For $i = 1, \ldots, n$:*
  1. $r_i^0, r_i^1 \xleftarrow{\$} \{0,1\}^n$; $(\mathsf{pk}_i^0, \mathsf{sk}_i^0) \leftarrow \mathsf{TGen}(r_i^0)$; $(\mathsf{pk}_i^1, \mathsf{sk}_i^1) \leftarrow \mathsf{TGen}(r_i^1)$;
  2. send $(\mathsf{pk}_i^0, \mathsf{pk}_i^1)$ to $\mathsf{S_{soa}}$;
$\mathsf{S_{soa}}$: *On input a bit b. Upon receiving $\{\mathsf{pk}_i^0, \mathsf{pk}_i^1\}_{i \in [n]}$:*
  1. secret share the bit b: for $i = 1, \ldots, n$: $b_i \xleftarrow{\$} \{0,1\}$, such that $b = (\bigoplus_{i=1}^n b_i)$;
  2. for $i = 1, \ldots, n$ do in parallel:
    – send $d_i \xleftarrow{\$} \{0,1\}$ to $\mathsf{R_{soa}}$;
    – run $\langle \mathsf{STC}_i^{\bar{d_i}}(\mathsf{pk}_i^{\bar{d_i}}, \mathsf{com}, b_i), \mathsf{RTC}_i^{\bar{d_i}}(\mathsf{pk}_i^{\bar{d_i}}, \mathsf{rcv}) \rangle$ with $\mathsf{R_{soa}}$;
$\mathsf{R_{soa}}$: *Upon receiving $d_1, \ldots, d_n$: if all commitment phases of protocol TC were successfully completed, send $\{r_i^{d_i}\}_{i \in [n]}$ to $\mathsf{S_{soa}}$;*
$\mathsf{S_{soa}}$: *Upon receiving $\{r_i^{d_i}\}_{i \in [n]}$ check consistency: for $i = 1, \ldots, n$: $(\mathsf{pk}_i'^{d_i}, \mathsf{sk}_i'^{d_i}) \leftarrow \mathsf{TGen}(r_i^{d_i})$; if $\mathsf{pk}_i'^{d_i} \neq \mathsf{pk}_i^{d_i}$ then abort.*

Decommitment Phase

$\mathsf{S_{soa}}$: *for $i = 1, \ldots, n$: run $(\cdot, b_i') \leftarrow \langle \mathsf{STC}_i^{\bar{d_i}}(\mathsf{open}), \mathsf{RTC}_i^{\bar{d_i}}(\mathsf{open}) \rangle$ with $\mathsf{R_{soa}}$;*
$\mathsf{R_{soa}}$: *If all opening phases were successful completed output $b' \leftarrow \bigoplus_{i=1}^n b_i'$. Otherwise, output $\perp$.*

The full proof of the following theorem can be found in the full version [18].

Theorem 1 (Protocol 1 is secure under selective opening attacks). *If TC = $(\mathsf{TGen}, \mathsf{STC}, \mathsf{RTC}, \mathsf{TFakeD})$ is a trapdoor commitment scheme, then Protocol 1 is a commitment scheme secure in presence of selective opening attacks.*

(3,1)-round SOA-secure Scheme based on NBB use of OWFs. We observe that, by instantiating Protocol 1 with the Feige-Shamir trapdoor commitment one can obtain a (3,1) SOA-secure scheme with non-black-box access to OWFs.

3.2 (3,3)-Round Scheme from One-Way Permutations

In this section we present a $(3, 3)$-round SOA-secure commitment scheme based on BB use of any OWP. As a main ingredient, we use a $(3, 1)$-round extractable commitment scheme, that we refer to as ExtCom. Very informally, extractable means that given black-box access to an adversarial sender, one can extract the bit played by the latter. A $(3, 1)$-round extractable commitment can be constructed from BB access to any OWP. Such construction is pretty standard, thus for further details we refer the reader to the full version [18].

The idea behind the protocol is as follows. The sender and the receiver first engage in a coin-flipping protocol where the receiver commits to its random-string, then the sender sends its random string in the clear, and finally the receiver reveals its random string. Simultaneously, the sender commits to its input bit b, n pairs of times (with the two commitments in each pair indexed by 0 and 1). In the decommitment phase, at the completion of the coin-flipping protocol, the sender opens only one of the commitments in each pair according to the outcome of the coin-flipping.

To allow for simulation (while arguing hiding), the commitment of the receiver in the coin-flipping protocol is implemented via extractable commitment scheme, so that the simulator can extract the receiver's string in the commitment phase itself. Furthermore, we require that the sender sends its random string for the coin-flipping only in the decommitment phase; by the beginning of the decommitment phase, the simulator will have received the bit b to open to, and this gives the simulator an opportunity to craft its random string to point to the commitments of b. To see why, first note that if the simulator somehow knows the receiver's random string before it sends its own, then it can easily open the commitment to either 0 or 1: in each pair, it just commits to 0 in one of the commitments and 1 in the other. Then, with the knowledge of the receiver's random string and the bit b, it can craft its own random string such that the xor with the string of R points to the commitments of b. Since the receiver commits via an extractable commitment scheme, the simulator is able to extract the receiver's random string and hence is able to equivocate in the opening phase. Furthermore, as it will appear more clearly in the protocol, since the sender would send its commitments (resp., decommitments) always *after* it receives commitments (resp., decommitments) from the receiver, we require that the sender's $2n$ commitments to its input bit are implemented via extractable commitment scheme so that we avoid malleability issues that may compromise the binding property.

We prove binding by reducing it to the binding property of ExtCom (due to the ExtCom commitments played by S_{soa}) and to the computational hiding property of ExtCom (due to the ExtCom commitments played by R_{soa}). At a high level, we show that if an adversarial sender breaks binding, then it should have been able to bias outcome of the coin-flipping by predicting the randomness committed to by the receiver using ExtCom, before the sender sends its own ExtCom commitments. Then in the reduction, we make use of this fact to break computational hiding of ExtCom.

We now provide formal specification of our protocol. Let ExtCom be a $(3,1)$-round extractable commitment scheme. In the following we denote by $\langle S_{ext}^{i}(\mathrm{com}, a_i), R_{ext}^{i}(\mathrm{rcv})\rangle$ the i-th of the n parallel executions of the extractable commitment scheme run by R_{soa} to commit to its random string for coin-flipping, while we denote by $\langle S_{ext}^{i,\sigma}(\mathrm{com}, b), R_{ext}^{i,\sigma}(\mathrm{rcv})\rangle$ the commitment in position σ of the i-th pair (among the n pairs) of parallel executions run by S_{soa} to commit to its input b.

Protocol 2. *[(3,3)-round SOA-Commitment] [SOACom$=(S_{soa}, R_{soa})$]*
Commitment Phase

R_{soa} : *For $i = 1, \dots, n$ do in parallel:*
    1. $a_i \xleftarrow{\$} \{0,1\}$;
    2. run $\langle S_{ext}^{i}(\mathrm{com}, a_i), R_{ext}^{i}(\mathrm{rcv})\rangle$ with S_{soa};

S_{soa} : *on input a bit b. For $i = 1, \ldots, n$ do in parallel:*

   1. run $\langle S_{ext}^{i,0}(com, b), R_{ext}^{i,0}(rcv) \rangle$ with R_{soa};

   2. run $\langle S_{ext}^{i,1}(com, b), R_{ext}^{i,1}(rcv) \rangle$ with R_{soa};

Decommitment Phase

S_{soa} : *If all extractable commitments played with R_{soa} are successfully completed,*
   send $d \xleftarrow{\$} \{0,1\}^n$ to R_{soa};

R_{soa} : *Open all commitments:*
   for $i = 1 \ldots, n$: run $\langle S_{ext}^i(open), R_{ext}^i(open) \rangle$ with S_{soa};

S_{soa} : *If all openings provided by R_{soa} are valid, for $i = 1, \ldots, n$:*

   1. $\sigma_i \leftarrow d_i \oplus a_i$;

   2. run $\langle S_{ext}^{i,\sigma_i}(open), R_{ext}^{i,\sigma_i}(open) \rangle$ with R_{soa};

R_{soa} : *If all the corresponding openings provided by S_{soa} open to the same bit b,*
   and if for every i, $\sigma_i = d_i \oplus a_i$, then output b. Otherwise, output $\perp$.

Theorem 2 (Protocol 2 is secure under selective opening attacks). *If* ExtCom *is an extractable commitment scheme, then Protocol 2 is a commitment scheme secure in presence of selective opening attacks.*

Details on the proof can be found in the full version of this paper [18]. In [18] we also show a variation of Protocol 2, which yield a 5-round commitment scheme with non-interactive decommitment, and is based on OWPs.

4   Issues in Some of the Claims of [23]

In this section we point out some issues regarding some of the main results in [23].

Revisiting Proof of Theorem 3.3 in [23]. Theorem 3.3 in [23] claims that their $(4,1)$-round protocol is SOA-secure under parallel composition with BB use of OWPs. The protocol recalls the equivocal commitment scheme of [5]. There is a preamble for coin flipping followed by Naor's commitment. In the preamble, the receiver commits to a random string α using a non-interactive (therefore computationally hiding only) commitment scheme; the sender sends a random string β in the clear; and finally, the receiver opens its commitment. Then the sender sends a Naor's commitment computed on the output of the coin flipping. Theorem 3.3 in [23] claims that the resulting protocol is computationally hiding, computationally binding and SOA-secure under parallel composition. We observe that this construction suffers of issues in the proof of binding and SOA-security. Concerning binding, [23] claims that it follows from the same arguments of Naor's commitment [16]. However this would be the case only if the commitment used by the receiver is at least statistically hiding (as in [5]), which is not the case in the $(4,1)$-round construction of [23]. SOA-security is claimed to follow from the simulation strategy of Goldreich and Kahan [11]. The issue here is that, such simulation strategy does not apply to the selective opening setting where multiple sessions are played in parallel with possibly different abort probabilities. Similar issues have been pointed out in [22] on previous work on round-optimal concurrent zero knowledge with bare public keys. The same issue on simulatability holds for the $(t + 3, 1)$-round scheme. We remark that although the $(t + 3, 1)$-round scheme of [23] is not simulatable directly via the Goldreich-Kahan's simulation strategy, the author of [23], elaborated an alternative simulation strategy for the same protocol. See [24] for details.

Revisiting Proof of Theorem 3.5 in [23]. Theorem 3.5 of [23] claims that if a coin-flipping preamble implemented via the $\omega(\log(n))$-round preamble of [21], is followed by Naor's commitment, then the resulting protocol is an $\omega(\log(n))$-round scheme that is SOA-secure under fully-concurrent composition with BB use of OWPs. Moreover, Theorem 3.5 also applies to the strong definition where the same simulator must work with respect to all distribution of messages, including the ones selected by the adversary and unknown to the simulator.

According to their proof, the simulatability of the protocol follows from the PRS's simulation strategy [21]. Specifically, if the coin-flipping is implemented with the PRS preamble, the claim of [23] is that the PRS's simulator obtains the random string committed to by the receiver, by the end of the coin-flipping, and this values can be used by the SOA-simulator to equivocate.

However the oblivious strategy of [21] cannot be applied in the SOA-setting (and, as we prove in Theorem 3 there exists no simulation strategy that can be applied if the black-box simulator has no access to the message distribution).

To see why, first recall that the proof of concurrent zero knowledge of [21] (used by [23]) critically relies on the fact that, the probability that the simulator aborts, namely, it reaches the end of a preamble without solving the session, is negligible. Second, observe that in the setting of fully-concurrent SOA, the adversarial receiver adaptively selects the sessions to be opened, and the opening of one session can be interleaved with the preamble of another session. In particular, during the rewinding threads needed by the PRS's simulator, the adversary can ask the opening of sessions that were not asked in the main thread. The simulator could handle such sessions in two possible ways. For one, it can query the external oracle to obtain the messages for the new sessions requested by the adversary[7], and then proceed to the completion of the rewinding thread. This would lead to a deviation in the distribution of the sessions queried to the external oracle, since the number of queries made in the simulation will be larger compared to the real game. On the other hand, the simulator can simply abort the rewinding threads that require the opening of new sessions (and thus additional queries to the external party). However, this will contradict the necessary condition (i.e., the simulator should abort with negligible probability only) for the PRS strategy [21] to be applicable. We stress that the above observations crucially rely on the fact that the protocol of [23] is claimed to be SOA-secure in the

---

[7] Note that here we are critically considering the case in which the distribution is not known to the simulator, and therefore the only way to answer consistently for it is to query the oracle. If instead the distribution is known, the simulator could sample from the distribution and therefore manage in some way the opening of new sessions started during rewinding thread.

strong sense, namely, the simulator cannot sample from the distribution of the messages committed by the honest sender.

Revisiting Proof of Theorem 4.4 in [23]. Theorem 4.4 in [23] states that, there exists no $(3, 1)$-round commitment scheme that is SOA-secure even under parallel composition, when security is proved using a black-box simulator. The proof essentially assumes that the structure of the commitment phase is such that the sender speaks first. However, we argue that this assumption loses generality. In fact, we present a $(3, 1)$-round commitment scheme (Protocol 1) in which the receiver speaks first, such that security in the concurrent-with-barrier setting (that is strictly stronger than the parallel composition setting of [23]) is proved using a black-box simulator. We observe that, the proof of Theorem 4.4. of [23], however, can be used to show impossibility of 2-round SOA-secure protocols (when security is proved via black-box simulation).

5 Impossibility of Strong Fully-Concurrent SOA-Security with Black-Box Simulation

The protocols presented in this paper achieve security under concurrent-with-barrier composition in the "strong" sense, that is, assuming that the simulator cannot sample from the distribution of the messages committed to by the sender. The last question to answer is whether there exist protocols that actually achieve the definition of security under strong fully-concurrent composition (as defined in [23]), or if the strong concurrent-with-barrier security definition is the best one can hope to achieve (when black-box simulation is taken into account). In this section we show that in contrast to the claim of Theorem 3.5 of [23], the strong fully-concurrent security definition of [23] is impossible to achieve. This holds regardless of the round complexity of the protocol [8] and of the black-box use of cryptographic primitives. Under the assumption that OWFs exist, the only requirements that we use for the impossibility is that the simulator is black-box and does not know the distribution of the messages committed by the sender. Both requirements are already specified in the strong fully concurrent security definition of [23].

Theorem 3. *If OWF exists, then no commitment scheme can be strong SOA-secure under fully-concurrent composition.*

Proof Idea. The proof consists in adapting a proof provided by Lindell in [15]. [15] shows that, there exist functionalities, for which proving that a protocol is secure under m-concurrent composition using a black-box simulator, requires that the protocol has at least m rounds. As corollary it holds that, for such functionalities, unbounded concurrency proved using a black-box simulator is impossible to achieve. Such a theorem cannot be directly applied to the case of SOA-secure

---

[8] This is therefore different from the case of concurrent zero knowledge [4,21].

commitments since it is provided only for two functionalities in which both parties have private inputs, such as, blind signatures and OT functionalities. In the setting of SOA-secure commitments the receiver has no private input and there is no ideal functionality involved. For our setting, we observe that, the fact that simulator cannot sample from the message distribution, means that it needs to access to an oracle for that. In our proof, we convert the role of the oracle into the role of the ideal functionality, and when deriving the contradiction we do not break the privacy of the receiver but the binding of the protocol.

The proof is based on the following two observations. First of all, since the simulator is black-box, the only advantage that it can exploit to carry out a successful simulation, is to rewind the adversary. Moreover, rewinds must be effective, in the sense that upon each rewind, the simulator must change the transcript in order to "extract" information from the adversary (obviously, if the transcript is not changed, then the rewind is useless). Second, in the strong SOA setting, the malicious receiver chooses the sessions to be opened, adaptively on the transcript seen so far, and the simulator can obtain the correct messages to be opened, only by querying the oracle. Changing the transcript in a rewinding attempt, may yield the adversary to change the sessions asked for opening (in particular to open sessions that were not asked in the main thread) and in turn, it may require the simulator to make additional queries to the oracle. Such additional queries are caused only by the rewinding attempts and they do not appear in the real-world execution. However, the distribution of the set of sessions' indexes asked by Sim in the ideal game, should not be distinguishable from the one asked by the adversary in the real game. Thus, the idea of the proof is to show that there exists an adversarial receiver, that makes the rewinding attempts of any black-box Sim ineffective, unless Sim makes additional queries the oracle, and hence the set of sessions asked in the ideal game is distinguishable from the set asked in the real game. Then, the next step is to show that, if nonetheless there exists a simulator that is able to deal with such an adversary (without rewinding), then such a simulator can be used by a malicious sender to break the binding of the protocol. The formal proof can be found in the full version of this paper [18].

6   Application to cZK with Pre-processing

We show how to use SOA-secure commitment schemes to construct concurrent zero-knowledge (cZK) protocol with pre-processing by using OWFs only, therefore improving a previous result of [5]. We combine our $(3, 1)$-round SOA-secure computationally binding scheme based on NBB use of OWFs with the use of the special $\mathcal{WIPoK}$ of [14]. The preprocessing takes 3 rounds and is composed by two subprotocols played in parallel. The first subprotocol is a coin-flipping protocol where the prover commits to a random string using the SOA commitment that ends with the 3rd round of the verifier. In the 3rd round the verifier also sends his random string and the xor of the two strings is the outcome of this subprotocol. The second subprotocol is a special $\mathcal{WIPoK}$ to prove that $x \in L$

or the output of the coin flipping is also the output of a PRG. Only two rounds of this subprotocol are played during the preprocessing.

At the end of the above preprocessing the prover knows the result of the coin flipping and later non-interactively can complete the proof by opening his SOA commitment and sending the last round of the special $\mathcal{WIPoK}$. The simulator will get advantage of the simulator of the SOA commitment to bias the outcome of all coin-flipping protocols, therefore being able to complete all proofs running the prover of the special $\mathcal{WIPoK}$ using the trapdoor witness. For more details the reader is referred to the full version of this paper [18].

Acknowledgments. Supported in part by NSF grants 0830803, 09165174,1065276, 1118126 and 1136174, US-Israel BSF grant 2008411, OKAWA Foundation Research Award, IBM Faculty Research Award, Xerox Faculty Research Award, B. John Garrick Foundation Award, Teradata Research Award, European Commission through the FP7 programme under contract 216676 ECRYPT II, MIUR Project PRIN "GenData 2020" and Lockheed-Martin Corporation Research Award. This material is also based upon work supported by the Defense Advanced Research Projects Agency through the U.S. Office of Naval Research under Contract N00014-11-1-0392. The views expressed are those of the author and do not reflect the official policy or position of the Department of Defense or the U.S. Government.

References

1. Bellare, M., Dowsley, R., Waters, B., Yilek, S.: Standard Security Does Not Imply Security against Selective-Opening. In: Pointcheval, D., Johansson, T. (eds.) EUROCRYPT 2012. LNCS, vol. 7237, pp. 645–662. Springer, Heidelberg (2012)
2. Bellare, M., Hofheinz, D., Yilek, S.: Possibility and Impossibility Results for Encryption and Commitment Secure under Selective Opening. In: Joux, A. (ed.) EUROCRYPT 2009. LNCS, vol. 5479, pp. 1–35. Springer, Heidelberg (2009)
3. Blum, M.: How to Prove a Theorem So No One Else Can Claim It. In: Proceedings of the International Congress of Mathematicians, pp. 1444–1451 (1986)
4. Canetti, R., Kilian, J., Petrank, E., Rosen, A.: Black-box concurrent zero-knowledge requires omega~(log n) rounds. In: STOC, pp. 570–579 (2001)
5. Di Crescenzo, G., Ostrovsky, R.: On Concurrent Zero-Knowledge with Preprocessing (Extended Abstract). In: Wiener, M. (ed.) CRYPTO 1999. LNCS, vol. 1666, pp. 485–502. Springer, Heidelberg (1999)
6. Dwork, C., Naor, M., Reingold, O., Stockmeyer, L.: Magic functions. In: 40th Annual Symposium on Foundations of Computer Science, FOCS 1999, pp. 523–534. IEEE Computer Society (1999)
7. Dwork, C., Naor, M., Reingold, O., Stockmeyer, L.: Magic functions. J. ACM 50(6), 852–921 (2003)
8. Dwork, C., Naor, M., Sahai, A.: Concurrent zero-knowledge. In: Proceedings of the Thirtieth Annual ACM Symposium on the Theory of Computing, STOC, pp. 409–418. ACM (1998)
9. Feige, U., Shamir, A.: Zero Knowledge Proofs of Knowledge in Two Rounds. In: Brassard, G. (ed.) CRYPTO 1989. LNCS, vol. 435, pp. 526–544. Springer, Heidelberg (1990)

10. Gennaro, R., Micali, S.: Independent Zero-Knowledge Sets. In: Bugliesi, M., Preneel, B., Sassone, V., Wegener, I. (eds.) ICALP 2006. LNCS, vol. 4052, pp. 34–45. Springer, Heidelberg (2006)
11. Goldreich, O., Kahan, A.: How to construct constant-round zero-knowledge proof systems for np. J. Cryptology 9(3), 167–190 (1996)
12. Goyal, V., Lee, C.K., Ostrovsky, R., Visconti, I.: Constructing non-malleable commitments: A black-box approach. In: 53rd Annual IEEE Symposium on Foundations of Computer Science, FOCS 2012, pp. 51–60. IEEE Computer Society (2012)
13. Hofheinz, D.: Possibility and impossibility results for selective decommitments. J. Cryptology 24(3), 470–516 (2011)
14. Lapidot, D., Shamir, A.: Publicly Verifiable Non-interactive Zero-Knowledge Proofs. In: Menezes, A., Vanstone, S.A. (eds.) CRYPTO 1990. LNCS, vol. 537, pp. 353–365. Springer, Heidelberg (1991)
15. Lindell, Y.: Bounded-concurrent secure two-party computation without setup assumptions. In: Proceedings of the 35th Annual ACM Symposium on Theory of Computing, STOC, pp. 683–692. ACM (2003)
16. Naor, M.: Bit commitment using pseudorandomness. J. Cryptology 4(2), 151–158 (1991)
17. Ostrovsky, R., Persiano, G., Visconti, I.: Simulation-Based Concurrent Non-malleable Commitments and Decommitments. In: Reingold, O. (ed.) TCC 2009. LNCS, vol. 5444, pp. 91–108. Springer, Heidelberg (2009)
18. Ostrovsky, R., Rao, V., Scafuro, A., Visconti, I.: Revisiting lower and upper bounds for selective decommitments. IACR Cryptology ePrint Archive 2011, 536 (2011)
19. Pass, R., Wee, H.: Black-Box Constructions of Two-Party Protocols from One-Way Functions. In: Reingold, O. (ed.) TCC 2009. LNCS, vol. 5444, pp. 403–418. Springer, Heidelberg (2009)
20. Pedersen, T.P.: Non-interactive and Information-Theoretic Secure Verifiable Secret Sharing. In: Feigenbaum, J. (ed.) CRYPTO 1991. LNCS, vol. 576, pp. 129–140. Springer, Heidelberg (1992),
http://portal.acm.org/citation.cfm?id=646756.705507
21. Prabhakaran, M., Rosen, A., Sahai, A.: Concurrent zero knowledge with logarithmic round-complexity. In: 43rd FOCS, pp. 366–375 (2002)
22. Scafuro, A., Visconti, I.: On Round-Optimal Zero Knowledge in the Bare Public-Key Model. In: Pointcheval, D., Johansson, T. (eds.) EUROCRYPT 2012. LNCS, vol. 7237, pp. 153–171. Springer, Heidelberg (2012)
23. Xiao, D.: (Nearly) Round-Optimal Black-Box Constructions of Commitments Secure against Selective Opening Attacks. In: Ishai, Y. (ed.) TCC 2011. LNCS, vol. 6597, pp. 541–558. Springer, Heidelberg (2011)
24. Xiao, D.: On the round complexity of black-box constructions of commitments secure against selective opening attacks. Cryptology ePrint Archive, Report 2009/513 - Revision May 29, 2012 (2012), http://eprint.iacr.org/
25. Xiao, D.: Round-Optimal Black-Box Statistically Binding Selective-Opening Secure Commitments. In: Mitrokotsa, A., Vaudenay, S. (eds.) AFRICACRYPT 2012. LNCS, vol. 7374, pp. 395–411. Springer, Heidelberg (2012)

On the Circular Security of Bit-Encryption

Ron D. Rothblum*

Weizmann Institute of Science
ron.rothblum@weizmann.ac.il

Abstract. Motivated by recent developments in fully homomorphic encryption, we consider the folklore conjecture that every semantically-secure bit-encryption scheme is circular secure, or in other words, that every bit-encryption scheme remains secure even when the adversary is given encryptions of the individual bits of the private-key. We show the following obstacles to proving this conjecture:

1. We construct a public-key bit-encryption scheme that is plausibly semantically secure, but is not circular secure. The circular security attack manages to fully recover the private-key.
   The construction is based on an extension of the Symmetric External Diffie-Hellman assumption (SXDH) from bilinear groups, to ℓ-multilinear groups of order p where $\ell \geq c \cdot \log p$ for some $c > 1$. While there do exist ℓ-multilinear groups (unconditionally), for $\ell \geq 3$ there are no known candidates for which the SXDH problem is believed to be hard. Nevertheless, there is also no evidence that such groups do not exist. Our result shows that in order to prove the folklore conjecture, one must rule out the possibility that there exist ℓ-multilinear groups for which SXDH is hard.
2. We show that the folklore conjecture cannot be proved using a black-box reduction. That is, there is no reduction of circular security of a bit-encryption scheme to semantic security of that very same scheme that uses both the encryption scheme and the adversary as black-boxes.

Both of our negative results extend also to the (seemingly) weaker conjecture that every CCA secure bit-encryption scheme is circular secure.

As a final contribution, we show an equivalence between three seemingly distinct notions of circular security for public-key bit-encryption schemes. In particular, we give a general search to decision reduction that shows that an adversary that distinguishes between encryptions of the bits of the private-key and encryptions of zeros can be used to actually recover the private-key.

1 Introduction

Modern cryptographic applications, both practical and theoretical, have led to the study of increasingly complex types of attacks on encryption schemes.

---

* This research was partially supported by the Israel Science Foundation (grant No. 1041/08). Parts of this research were conducted while the author was an intern at Microsoft Research, New England.

A. Sahai (Ed.): TCC 2013, LNCS 7785, pp. 579–598, 2013.

For example, chosen plaintext attacks (CPA) and chosen ciphertext attacks (CCA) extend the classical notion of semantic security [GM84] by allowing an attacker access to encryptions of arbitrary messages of its choice (in the CPA model) and to a decryption oracle (in the CCA model).

A different type of attack that has been recently considered is when the attacker manages to obtain encryptions of messages that are related to the (private) decryption-key. The notion of key dependent message (KDM) security was first considered by Camenisch and Lysyanskaya [CL01] and (independently) by Black et al.[BRS02]. Informally, an encryption scheme is KDM secure for a class of functions $\mathcal{F}$ if it is infeasible to distinguish between an oracle that on input $f \in \mathcal{F}$ outputs an encryption of f evaluated on the decryption-key and an oracle that just returns encryptions of zeros.

Perhaps the most basic type of KDM attack is one in which the attacker is just given an encryption of the entire decryption-key. Security with respect to such a KDM attack is also known as *"circular security"* since the key encrypts itself.[1]

While some encryption schemes have been proved to be circular secure under plausible cryptographic assumptions (e.g., [BHHO08, ACPS09]), it is natural to ask whether semantic security actually guarantees circular security. A folklore example shows that this is not the case: given any private-key encryption scheme we can slightly modify the encryption algorithm by checking if the input message is the (symmetric) key itself or not. If not, then the encryption proceeds as usual. But, if the input message equals the key, then the encryption algorithm is modified to output the key in the clear. The resulting scheme is still semantically secure[2] and yet it is not circular secure, since an adversary that gets an encryption of the key trivially breaks security. The counterexample can be easily extended to the public-key setting by having the encryption algorithm check whether a given input message functions as a "good" decryption-key.[3]

The foregoing counterexample shows that, in general, semantic security does not suffice for circular security. Motivated by recent developments in fully homomorphic encryption (see Section 1.2), we restrict our attention to a specific class of encryption schemes - those that encrypt their input bit-by-bit (also called bit-encryption schemes).[4] Thus, we ask whether every *bit-encryption* scheme that

---

[1] Circular security may also refer to larger key cycles were there are t keys arranged in a directed cycle and the adversary sees encryptions under every key of its next neighbor's key. We only consider the case $t = 1$.

[2] Semantic security follows from the fact that the probability that the message (which is selected before the keys) equals the key is negligible.

[3] The (public-key) encryption algorithm can do so by encrypting sufficiently many random messages and checking whether the given input message (used as a decryption-key) correctly decrypts these ciphertexts.

[4] We assume that the encryption algorithm does not maintain a state between executions. Note that the folklore counterexample for full fledged encryption can be adapted to *stateful* bit-encryption schemes by having the encryption algorithm record its last n (single-bit) messages in a buffer (where n is the length of the decryption-key), and outputting the decryption-key in the clear whenever the buffer equals the decryption-key.

is semantically secure is also circular secure. An alternative way to phrase the question is whether every semantically secure (either private-key or public-key) encryption scheme remains secure even if the adversary is given encryptions of the individual bits of the decryption-key (in order, of course).

At this point it is worthwhile to point out two ways in which the counterexample (for full fledged encryption schemes) uses the fact that the encryption algorithm is given the entire decryption-key as its message:

1. It is easy to identify when the decryption-key is given as the input message to the encryption algorithm (trivially in the private-key setting and almost as easily in the public-key setting); and
2. In the semantic security setting, the event that the message equals the decryption-key is sufficiently rare that we can modify the encryption algorithm to handle this event in a special way without jeopardizing security.

In the case of bit-encryption schemes both properties no longer hold and constructing a counterexample seems to be more difficult.[5] In fact, the above has led to a folklore conjecture, which we call the bit-encryption conjecture, that *every* secure bit-encryption scheme (either private-key or public-key) is in fact circular secure. Let us state this as:

Conjecture 1 (Bit-Encryption Conjecture). Every semantically secure public-key bit-encryption scheme is circular secure.

The focus of this work is to show obstacles to proving the validity of this conjecture. Focusing on the public-key case only strengthens our negative results since every public-key scheme is also a private-key scheme. (In Section 1.3 we also discuss the (seemingly) weaker conjecture that every CCA secure bit-encryption scheme is circular secure.)

1.1   Our Results

We address the question of circular security for bit-encryption schemes and show the following results:

A Circular Insecure Bit-encryption Scheme Based on ℓ-multilinear Maps. We construct a (plausibly) semantically secure public-key encryption scheme for which, given encryptions of the bits of the decryption-key, it is possible to fully recover the decryption-key (i.e., the strongest type of attack). The security of our construction is based on an extension of the Symmetric External Diffie-Hellman (SXDH) assumption (see, e.g., [ACHdM05, BGdMM05, ABBC10, CGH12]) to multilinear groups, which we describe next.

---

[5] In fact, for the very same reasons, even constructing an encryption scheme for logarithmically long messages that is semantically secure but circular *insecure* seems to be difficult. We note that our negative results extend also to this case but in this work we only discuss the single bit case.

An ℓ-multilinear map is a (non-degenerate) mapping $e : G_1 \times \cdots \times G_\ell \to G_T$ where $G_1, \ldots, G_\ell$ and G_T are cyclic groups of prime order p, such that for every $g_1 \in G_1, \ldots, g_\ell \in G_\ell$, every $i \in [\ell]$ and $a \in \mathbb{Z}_p$ it holds that

$$e(g_1, \ldots, g_i^a, \ldots, g_\ell) = e(g_1, \ldots, g_\ell)^a.$$

Recall that, informally, the Decisional Diffie Hellman (DDH) assumption is said to hold in the cyclic group G if it is infeasible to distinguish between g, g^a, g^b, g^{ab} and g, g^a, g^b, g^c where g is a generator of G and a, b and c are random exponents. The standard SXDH assumption extends the DDH assumption to 2-multilinear (a.k.a bilinear) groups by stating that there exist groups (G_1, G_2) equipped with a bilinear map for which the DDH assumption holds (separately) for each one of the groups G_1 and G_2. We further extend the SXDH assumption by assuming that there exist ℓ-multilinear groups for which DDH is hard in each one of the ℓ groups. For our result to hold we need $\ell \geq c \cdot \log p$ for some $c > 1$.

Since, for $\ell > 2$, we do not have candidate ℓ-multilinear groups for which we conjecture SXDH to be hard, we do not interpret our construction as a counterexample, but rather as an obstacle to proving the bit-encryption conjecture (Conjecture 1). Our construction shows that in order to prove that every semantically secure bit-encryption scheme is circular secure one would have to rule out the existence of ℓ-multilinear groups for which SXDH is hard.

The possibility of constructing ℓ-multilinear group schemes for which discrete log is hard was previously considered by Boneh and Silverberg [BS03], who showed cryptographic applications of multilinear maps as well as difficulties in constructing such group schemes based on known techniques in algebraic geometry. We note that [BS03] only considered the special case of $G_1 \equiv \ldots \equiv G_\ell$ and the hardness of discrete log for G_1 (in fact, if $G_1 \equiv \ldots \equiv G_\ell$ then SXDH becomes trivially easy[6]).

We also note that the *standard* SXDH assumption was previously used in the context of circular security by Acar *et al.*[ABBC10] and Cash *et al.*[CGH12]. Both Acar *et al.* and (independently) Cash *et al.* address the question of whether every encryption-scheme (not necessarily a bit-encryption scheme) is secure if the adversary gets a key-cycle of length 2. They show strong negative evidence by constructing an encryption scheme (that is not a bit-encryption scheme) that is semantically secure based on (standard) SXDH but is insecure if the adversary gets a key cycle of length 2. In contrast, we show a *bit-encryption* scheme (based on the aforementioned extension of SXDH to multilinear groups) that is insecure when the adversary gets a *cycle of length 1*, that is, an encryption of the secret key (see the discussion above for why bit-encryption is more interesting in this context).

Impossibility of Black-box Reductions. We show that a black-box reduction cannot be used to prove the bit-encryption conjecture. Our black-box impossibility

---

[6] Using the fact that the groups are equals, we can solve DDH in G_1. Specifically, given $g, g^a, g^b, g^c \in G_1$ just compare $e(g^a, g^b, g, \ldots, g)$ and $e(g^c, g, \ldots, g)$, where we use the fact that $g^b \in G_2 = G_1$. If $c = ab$ then equality holds but if c is random then the two values are different with overwhelming probability.

result differs from standard black-box impossibility results in that we do not consider the possibility of *constructing* a circular secure bit-encryption from any semantically-secure bit-encryption but rather the question of whether every semantically secure bit-encryption is *by itself* already circular secure.

In other words, we prove that there cannot exist a general black-box reduction that transforms any circular security attack into a semantic security attack. By black-box we mean that the reduction uses both the attack and the primitive (in our case the encryption scheme) in a black-box manner (for a discussion of different types of black-box separations, see [RTV04]).

We note that for the application to fully homomorphic encryption (see Section 1.2), a *construction* of a circular-secure scheme from any bit-encryption scheme would most likely not be helpful. Indeed, in order to be useful, such a construction would have to preserve both the homomorphic properties *and* the decryption depth (for the bootstrapping operation). Thus, we focus on the question of whether every bit-encryption scheme is by itself circular secure.

We mention that Haitner and Holenstein [HH09] also showed a (different) black-box impossibility result for KDM security. See the full version for a comparison of the results.

From Indistinguishability to Key-Recovery. We show an equivalence between three natural notions of circular security for public-key bit-encryption schemes. In all three scenarios we give the adversary access to an oracle that on input i returns an encryption of the i-th bit of the decryption-key. We refer to this oracle as the KDM oracle. The three security notions differ in the task that a hypothetical adversary, which has access to the KDM oracle, has to accomplish in order to be deemed successful (i.e., break security). We consider the following possible tasks:

1. The adversary needs to fully recover the decryption-key.
2. The adversary gets as input an encryption of a random bit and needs to guess the value of this bit.
3. The adversary is given access to either the KDM oracle or an oracle that always returns encryptions of 0 and needs to distinguish in which of the two cases it is. This is the standard notion of circular security as defined in [CL01, BRS02].

We show that the three foregoing notions are actually equivalent. In particular, this result implies a general search to decision reduction that transforms any circular security distinguisher into an adversary that, given access to the KDM oracle, can fully recover the decryption-key d. (In contrast, in the setting of semantic security, finding the key can be a much harder task than recovering the message from the ciphertext.)

1.2   Connection to Fully Homomorphic Encryption and Full KDM Security

Other than being an interesting and natural question on its own, the question of circular security for bit-encryption schemes is further motivated by recent breakthroughs in the construction of fully homomorphic encryption schemes (FHE) and fully KDM secure encryption schemes.

Fully Homomorphic Encryption. Informally, an FHE is an encryption scheme for which given an encryption of a message m and *any* circuit C, one can compute an encryption of $C(m)$ without knowing the decryption-key.

Gentry [Gen09] constructed the first FHE and gave a general technique called bootstrapping for the construction of FHE schemes. Gentry's idea is to first construct an encryption scheme that is somewhat homomorphic (that is, homomorphic with respect to some limited class of circuits), and then, using the bootstrapping technique, to transform it into an FHE. The bootstrapping technique inherently uses the assumption that the underlying somewhat homomorphic encryption is circular secure.[7] Since most of these schemes are bit encryption schemes and their circular security is only conjectured and not proved (based on their semantic security), the question of circular security for bit-encryption is especially important for the construction of secure FHE. In particular, proving the bit-encryption conjecture would establish the existence of an FHE based solely on (say) the hardness of the learning with errors (LWE) problem (see [BV11]).

Our KDM equivalence theorem for bit-encryption (see end of Section 1.1) is also of particular interest to the current candidate FHE schemes. As alluded to above, the theorem implies that a KDM distinguisher can be used to construct an attacker that *given access to the KDM oracle* actually finds the decryption-key. However, for the current candidate fully homomorphic bit-encryption schemes, the KDM oracle can actually be simulated using only the public-key.[8] Thus, the equivalence theorem gives a generic (and simple) search to decision reduction for these schemes that transforms any attack that breaks semantic security into an attack that finds the decryption-key (without using an external KDM oracle).

Full KDM Security from Semantic Security. An additional motivation for the study of the circular security of bit-encryption schemes arises from the recent

---

[7] Actually, there are two variants of the bootstrapping technique. The one that we refer to assumes circular security and constructs an FHE. The other variant does not assume circular security but only achieves *leveled* FHE (i.e., an encryption scheme that is homomorphic with respect to any circuit of some a priori fixed depth) and also increases the length of the public-key multiplicatively in the depth of supported circuits.

[8] This follows from the facts that (1) the public-key of these schemes actually contains encryptions of the bits of the decryption-key (for bootstrapping), and (2) ciphertexts can be re-randomized. An oracle query for the i-th bit of the decryption-key can be simulated by re-randomizing the ciphertext in the public-key that is an encryption of the i-th bit of the decryption-key.

work of Applebaum [App11] (following [BHHI10, BGK11]) who showed an amplification theorem for KDM security. Specifically, [App11] showed that an encryption scheme that is KDM secure for any fixed class of polynomial-size circuits, can be constructed from an encryption scheme that is KDM secure only with respect to the class of projections and negation of projections (i.e., any function f of the form $f(d) = d_i$ or $f(d) = 1 - d_i$). Thus, proving a slightly stronger variant of the bit-encryption conjecture would imply that semantic security is a sufficient assumption for the construction of a very strong form of KDM security.

1.3   Chosen Ciphertext Security vs. Circular Security

Recall that an encryption scheme is CCA-2 secure if it is semantically secure even when the attacker has access to a decryption oracle that decrypts any ciphertext other than the challenge ciphertext.

Since we show difficulties to proving that every semantically secure bit-encryption is circular secure, it is natural to ask whether a stronger notion of security, such as CCA security, might instead suffice. We first note that our black-box impossibility result extends also to this case. That is, we show that there is no blackbox reduction of circular-security even to CCA-2 security.

Actually, assuming the existence of doubly-enhanced trapdoor permutations, the conjecture that every CCA bit-encryption scheme is circular-secure is equivalent to the bit encryption conjecture. This equivalence follows from the fact that the Naor-Yung paradigm [NY90] transforms a semantically secure but circular insecure scheme into a CCA secure but circular *insecure* one.[9] Using this observation we can extend our construction of a circular-insecure bit-encryption scheme (based on multilinear SXDH, see Section 3) to a CCA-2 secure but circular-insecure bit-encryption scheme (assuming, in addition to multilinear SXDH, the existence of doubly-enhanced trapdoor permutations).[10]

Remark. We also mention that the converse direction that asks whether every circular secure bit-encryption scheme is also CCA secure is in fact false (assuming that there exist circular secure bit-encryption schemes at all). For example, taking any circular secure scheme and modifying it by adding to the public-key an encryption of the decryption-key, yields a scheme that is circular secure but is not even CCA-1 secure.

---

[9] Recall that the Naor-Yung paradigm consists of a double encryption of the plaintext using independent keys and a non-interactive zero-knowledge (NIZK) proof of consistency. A circular security attack on the underlying scheme immediately translates into a circular security attack on the constructed CCA secure scheme. Note that the Naor-Yung transformation can be made to achieve not only CCA-1 security but even CCA-2 security (see [Sah99] or [Lin06]).

[10] We note that this equivalence does not directly imply the extension of our black-box result to the CCA case because the Naor-Yung transformation makes non black-box use of the encryption scheme. Instead we prove the extension of the black-box result directly (without even assuming the existence of doubly-enhanced trapdoor permutations).

Organization

In Section 2 we define KDM security and the cryptographic assumptions that we will use. In Section 3 we present our "multilinear map" based circular insecure bit-encryption scheme. In Section 4 we prove the equivalence of three notions of KDM security. Finally, in Section 5, we present our black-box impossibility result.

2   Preliminaries

We denote by $x \in_R S$ a random variable x that is uniformly distributed in the set S.

Semantic Security and CCA Security. In this work we consider only bit-encryption schemes, that is, encryption schemes that encrypt only single bit messages. We use the standard definition of semantic-security and CCA security (as in [Gol04]) restricted to single-bit messages.

2.1   KDM and Circular Security for Bit-Encryption

To model KDM security we need to specify what information is given to the adversary and what it means for the adversary to break security. The former is the simpler of the two - we simply give the adversary access to an oracle (henceforth called the KDM oracle) that on input i returns a (random) encryption of the i-th bit of the decryption-key. Formally, for a pair (e, d) of encryption and decryption keys, we define an oracle $O_{e,d}(i)$ which on input $i \in [|d|]$ returns $Enc_e(d_i)$.

Turning to the second part of the definition, we consider three possible ways in which an adversary can break security. The strongest type of attack (which corresponds to the weakest definition of security) that we consider is full key recovery. Security against this type of attack means that no efficient adversary, which gets encryptions of the individual bits of the decryption-key, can find the entire decryption-key. Using the definition of the oracle $O_{e,d}$ we can define circular security of bit-encryption with respect to key-recovery:

Definition 2. *A public-key bit-encryption scheme ($KeyGen, Enc, Dec$) is* circular secure with respect to key recovery *if for every probabilistic polynomial-time oracle machine A it holds that*

$$\Pr_{(e,d) \leftarrow KeyGen(1^n)} \left[A^{O_{e,d}}(e) = d \right] < \mathrm{neg}(n).$$

It is worth noting that, in contrast to the semantic security setting, in the KDM setting the decryption-key is information theoretically determined and therefore there is at least some hope to recover the actual decryption-key used by the scheme.[11]

---

[11] In the semantic security model, there may be many decryption keys corresponding to the same encryption-key and a semantic security adversary (which only has access to functions of the encryption-key) cannot hope to always find the particular decryption-key being used.

Next, we consider an adversary that is given an encryption of a random bit, as well as access to the KDM oracle, and needs to guess the value of the bit:

Definition 3. *A public-key bit-encryption scheme is* circular secure with respect to message recovery *if for every probabilistic polynomial-time oracle machine A it holds that*

$$\Pr_{\substack{(e,d)\leftarrow KeyGen(1^n), \\ b\in_R\{0,1\}}} \left[A^{O_{e,d}}(e, Enc_e(b)) = b\right] < \frac{1}{2} + neg(n).$$

Lastly, we consider the standard definition of circular security as put forth by [CL01, BRS02]. Their definition requires that if be infeasible for an adversary to distinguish between the KDM oracle and an "all zeros" oracle that always returns encryptions of 0. Formally, for an encryption-key e, we define J_e to be an oracle that on input i just returns $Enc_e(0)$ (i.e., an encryption under e of the bit 0). In contrast to the two prior definitions, indistinguishability of oracles does not inherently imply semantic security and therefore we explicitly add this requirement.

Definition 4. *A semantically-secure public-key bit-encryption scheme is* circular secure with respect to indistinguishability of oracles *if for every probabilistic polynomial-time oracle machine A it holds that*

$$\left|\Pr_{(e,d)\leftarrow KeyGen(1^n)}\left[A^{O_{e,d}}(e)=1\right] - \Pr_{(e,d)\leftarrow KeyGen(1^n)}\left[A^{J_e}(e)=1\right]\right| < neg(n).$$

In Section 4 we show that the three notions of circular security presented above are actually equivalent.

2.2 Hardness Assumptions in Bilinear and ℓ-Multilinear Groups

We first define bilinear and ℓ-multilinear maps and then define the computational assumptions that we use.

An ℓ-multilinear map is a non-degenerate[12] function $e : G_1 \times \cdots \times G_\ell \to G_T$, where $G_1, \ldots, G_\ell, G_T$ are cyclic groups of prime order p such that for every $g_1 \in G_1, \ldots, g_\ell \in G_\ell$, every $i \in [\ell]$ and $a \in \mathbb{Z}_p$, it holds that:

$$e(g_1, \ldots, g_i^a, \ldots, g_\ell) = e(g_1, \ldots, g_\ell)^a.$$

An ℓ-multilinear group scheme is an algorithm that for every security parameter n produces a description of $\ell + 1$ groups of order p (where p is an n-bit prime) together with an efficiently computable ℓ-multilinear map that maps the first ℓ groups to the $(\ell + 1)$-th group:

---

[12] By degenerate we mean a function that maps all inputs to the identity element of G_T.

Definition 5. *Let $\ell = \ell(n)$ be a polynomially bounded function. An ℓ-multilinear group scheme is a probabilistic polynomial-time algorithm GS that on input 1^n outputs $params = (p, (G_1, \ldots, G_\ell, G_T), (g_1, \ldots, g_\ell, g_T), e)$ where $2^{n-1} < p < 2^n$ is an n-bit prime, $G_1, \ldots, G_\ell$ and G_T are concise descriptions of $\ell + 1$ groups of order p (that allow efficient evaluation of the group operation), with the respective generators $g_1, \ldots, g_\ell, g_T$ and $e : G_1 \times \cdots \times G_\ell \to G_T$ is a concise description of an efficiently computable ℓ-multilinear map.*

For every ℓ there exist trivial examples of ℓ-multilinear group schemes. However, our computational hardness assumptions do not hold for these trivial examples.[13] In fact, for $\ell \geq 3$ we do not know of a candidate ℓ-multilinear group scheme for which the discrete log problem is believed to be hard (in any of the groups). Nevertheless, there is also no negative evidence that such group schemes do not exist. For $\ell \leq 2$ there do exist candidate group schemes for which discrete log is conjectured to be hard (discussed next).

Computational Assumptions. Loosely speaking, the DDH assumption for a cyclic group G states that the distributions (g, g^a, g^b, g^{ab}) and (g, g^a, g^b, g^c) are computationally indistinguishable, where g is a generator of G and a, b and c are random exponents. The SXDH assumption extends DDH to 2-multilinear (a.k.a bilinear) groups by assuming that there exist groups G_1, G_2 equipped with a bilinear map such that the DDH assumption holds for both G_1 and G_2 (separately). We further extend SXDH to the ℓ-multilinear SXDH assumption which states that there exists an ℓ-multilinear group scheme for which DDH is hard for all ℓ groups $G_1, \ldots, G_\ell$. Note that 1-multilinear SXDH corresponds exactly to DDH and that 2-multilinear SXDH corresponds to the standard SXDH assumption. We emphasize that we only have candidate group schemes for which the ℓ-multilinear SXDH assumption is conjectured to hold for $\ell \leq 2$ (see, e.g., [ACHdM05, BGdMM05, ABBC10, CGH12]).

Definition 6. *The ℓ-multilinear SXDH assumption states that there exists an ℓ-multilinear group scheme GS such that for every function $i \colon \mathbb{N} \to \mathbb{N}$ for which $i(n) \in [\ell(n)]$, the following ensembles are computationally indistinguishable:*

1. *$\{params, i(n), g_{i(n)}^a, g_{i(n)}^b, g_{i(n)}^{ab}\}_{n \in \mathbb{N}}$; and*
2. *$\{params, i(n), g_{i(n)}^a, g_{i(n)}^b, g_{i(n)}^c\}_{n \in \mathbb{N}}$*

where $a, b, c \in_R \mathbb{Z}_p$ and $params \overset{\text{def}}{=} (p, (G_1, \ldots, G_\ell, G_T), (g_1, \ldots, g_\ell, g_T), e)$ is distributed as $GS(1^n)$.

---

[13] A trivial example of an ℓ-multilinear group scheme is when $G_1, \ldots, G_\ell$ are all the additive group mod p. Since exponentiation in the additive group corresponds to modular multiplication, being multilinear means that for every $a, z_1, \ldots, z_\ell \in \mathbb{Z}_p$ it holds that $e(z_1, \ldots, a \cdot z_i, \ldots, z_\ell) = a \cdot e(z_1, \ldots, z_\ell)$. Hence, the mapping $e(z_1, \ldots, z_\ell) = \prod_{i=1}^\ell z_i \bmod p$ is a multilinear map for these groups. Note however that discrete log in the additive group is equivalent to modular division and can be efficiently computed.

3   A Circular Insecure Bit-Encryption Scheme

In this section we show a construction of a bit-encryption scheme ($KeyGen$, Enc, Dec) that is (plausibly) semantically secure but is not circular secure. In Section 3.1 we present the construction and prove its correctness. See the full version for the proof of semantic security (based on the hardness of ℓ-multilinear SXDH, for $\ell \geq c \cdot \log p$ for some constant $c > 1$). In Section 3.2 we use the multilinear map to show a circular security attack on the scheme.

Notation. For a matrix X, we let $X[i, j]$ denote the (i, j)-th entry of X.

3.1   The Encryption Scheme

Let GS be any ℓ-multilinear group scheme (as in Definition 5).

Construction 7. *Consider the following public-key bit-encryption scheme* ($KeyGen$, Enc, Dec):

$\underline{KeyGen(1^n)}$
  1. *Invoke the group scheme algorithm to obtain params* $\leftarrow GS(1^n)$ *(where params equals* $(p, (G_1, \ldots, G_\ell, G_T), (g_1, \ldots, g_\ell, g_T), e))$.
  2. *Select* $X \in_R \mathbb{Z}_p^{2 \times \ell}$ *(i.e., a $2 \times \ell$ matrix with random entries in $\mathbb{Z}_p$).*
  3. *Set* $U = \begin{bmatrix} g_1^{X[0,1]} & g_2^{X[0,2]} & \cdots & g_\ell^{X[0,\ell]} \\ g_1^{X[1,1]} & g_2^{X[1,2]} & \cdots & g_\ell^{X[1,\ell]} \end{bmatrix}.$
  4. *Select* $s \in_R \{0,1\}^\ell$ *and set* $\alpha = \sum_{i=1}^{\ell} X[s_i, i] \bmod p$.
  5. *The (public) encryption-key is* ($params, U, \alpha$) *and the (private) decryption-key is* (X, s).

$\underline{Enc_{(params, U, \alpha)}(\sigma)}$ *(where $\sigma \in \{0,1\}$)*
  1. *Select at random* $r_1, \ldots, r_\ell \in_R \mathbb{Z}_p$.
  2. *Output* $(g_1^{r_1}, (U[\sigma, 1])^{r_1}), \ldots, (g_\ell^{r_\ell}, (U[\sigma, \ell])^{r_\ell})$.

$\underline{Dec_{(X,s)}((c_1, d_1), \ldots, (c_\ell, d_\ell))}$
  1. *If* $c_1^{X[0,1]} = d_1$ *output 0 and otherwise output 1.*

Before proceeding, we wish to highlight a few points. First, we note that both α and s are not used by the encryption or decryption algorithms and seem unneeded. Second, we note that (ignoring the presence of α in the public-key) even by setting $\ell = 1$ we obtain a secure encryption scheme (under DDH) and it is not clear why we need a larger ℓ (recall that we need $\ell >> \log p$).

The reason for the existence of α and s is (solely) to help the KDM attacker whereas the large value of ℓ helps maintain semantic security despite the fact that α is revealed in the public-key.[14] The key idea is that in the semantic

---

[14] Note that when using small values of ℓ (in particular using $\ell = 1$), the fact that α is revealed in the public-key makes the scheme totally insecure.

security setting, an attacker has essentially no information about s (because ℓ is sufficiently large that α looks random) whereas, in the KDM setting, the attacker can obtain additional information about s (specifically encryptions of the bits of s) and can use this additional information to verify that α is consistent with s.

The above gives us a way to distinguish between the KDM oracle and the all zeros oracle thereby breaking circular security with respect to indistinguishability of oracles. Using Theorem 8 this attack can be transformed into a full key-recovery attack.

We proceed to show that Construction 7 is indeed correct. See the full version for the proof that it is also semantically-secure (based on multilinear SXDH).

Correctness. Consider a pair of encryption and decryption keys $((params, U, \alpha), (X, s))$ and let $((c_1, d_1), \ldots, (c_\ell, d_\ell))$ be an encryption of a bit $\sigma \in \{0, 1\}$. If $\sigma = 0$ then $d_1 = c_1^{X[0,1]}$ and the ciphertext decrypts correctly to 0. If $\sigma = 1$ then $d_1 = c_1^{X[1,1]}$ and therefore, except with negligible probability, $d_1 \neq c_1^{X[0,1]}$. Hence, the ciphertext decrypts correctly to 1 (except with negligible probability).

Note that we can easily eliminate the negligible decryption error by sampling X from a statistically close distribution in which $X[0, 1] \neq X[1, 1]$.

3.2   The KDM Attack

We show a distinguisher that breaks the *circular security with respect to indistinguishability of oracles* (Definition 4) of Construction 7. Using Theorem 8, we can obtain a KDM attack that breaks *circular security with respect to key recovery* (Definition 2).

Our distinguisher gets as input a public-key and has access to either the KDM oracle that on input i returns an encryption of the i-th bit of the decryption-key or to the all-zeros oracle that always returns an encryption of 0. The goal of the distinguisher is to distinguish between the two cases.

Consider the following distinguisher which has access to an alleged KDM oracle and gets as input an encryption-key $(params, U, \alpha)$:

1. For $i = 1, \ldots, \ell$:

   (a) Query the oracle for an encryption $((c_1, d_1), \ldots, (c_\ell, d_\ell))$ of s_i (the i-th bit of s).

   (b) Set $y_i = c_i$ and $z_i = d_i$.

2. If $e(y_1, \ldots, y_\ell)^\alpha \equiv_p \prod_{i=1}^{\ell} e(y_1, \ldots, y_{i-1}, z_i, y_{i+1}, \ldots, y_\ell)$ then output 1 and otherwise output 0 (where $\equiv_p$ denotes congruence mod p).

We first show that when using the KDM oracle, the distinguisher always outputs 1. Indeed, in this case $y_i = g_i^{r_i}$ and $z_i = g_i^{r_i \cdot X[s_i, i]}$. Therefore,

$$\prod_{i=1}^{\ell} e(y_1, \ldots, y_{i-1}, z_i, y_{i+1}, \ldots, y_\ell) \equiv_p \prod_{i=1}^{\ell} e(g_1^{r_1}, \ldots, g_{i-1}^{r_{i-1}}, g_i^{r_i X[s_i, i]}, g_{i+1}^{r_{i+1}}, \ldots, g_\ell^{r_\ell})$$

$$\equiv_p \prod_{i=1}^{\ell} e(g_1^{r_1}, \ldots, g_\ell^{r_\ell})^{X[s_i, i]}$$

$$\equiv_p e(g_1^{r_1}, \ldots, g_\ell^{r_\ell})^{\sum_{i=1}^{\ell} X[s_i, i] \bmod p}$$

$$\equiv_p e(y_1, \ldots, y_\ell)^\alpha$$

and so the distinguisher outputs 1 in this case.

Next, consider the case that the distinguisher uses the all zeros oracle. In this case we yet again have $y_i = g_i^{r_i}$ but now $z_i = g_i^{r_i \cdot X[0,i]}$ and so we have:

$$\prod_{i=1}^{\ell} e(y_1, \ldots, y_{i-1}, z_i, y_{i+1}, \ldots, y_\ell) \equiv_p \prod_{i=1}^{\ell} e(g_1^{r_1}, \ldots, g_{i-1}^{r_{i-1}}, g_i^{r_i \cdot X[0,i]}, g_{i+1}^{r_{i+1}}, \ldots, g_\ell^{r_\ell})$$

$$\equiv_p \prod_{i=1}^{\ell} e(g_1^{r_1}, \ldots, g_\ell^{r_\ell})^{X[0,i]}$$

$$\equiv_p e(y_1, \ldots, y_\ell)^{\sum_{i=1}^{\ell} X[0,i] \bmod p}.$$

But, since the group G_T is cyclic, it holds that:

$$\Pr\left[e(y_1, \ldots, y_\ell)^\alpha \equiv_p e(y_1, \ldots, y_\ell)^{\sum_{i=1}^{\ell} X[0,i] \bmod p}\right]$$

$$= \Pr\left[\sum_{i=1}^{\ell} X[s_i, i] \equiv_p \sum_{i=1}^{\ell} X[0, i]\right] \leq 2^{-\ell} + \frac{1}{p}.$$

Hence, except with negligible probability, the distinguisher outputs 0 when given access to the all zeros oracle and we conclude that our distinguisher breaks the circular security of the scheme (with an overwhelming gap).

4   Equivalence of KDM Notions for Bit-Encryption

In this section, we establish an equivalence between the three notions of circular security for bit-encryption that were defined in Section 2.1.

Theorem 8. *For every public-key bit-encryption scheme the following are equivalent:*

1. *The scheme is circular secure with respect to key recovery.*
2. *The scheme is circular secure with respect to message recovery.*
3. *The scheme is circular secure with respect to indistinguishability of oracles.*

In particular, Theorem 8 implies that an adversary that merely distinguishes between a KDM oracle and an all zeroes oracle with a non-negligible gap can be used to fully recover the decryption-key.

We provide sketches of the proofs. See the full version for full proofs.

Lemma 9. *Every public-key bit-encryption scheme that is circular secure with respect to key recovery is also circular secure with respect to message recovery.*

Proof Sketch. Let $(KeyGen, Enc, Dec)$ be a public-key bit-encryption scheme, and suppose that there exists an adversary A that has access to the KDM oracle and is given as input an encryption-key e and an encryption of a random bit b and manages to guess b with non-negligible advantage. We use A to construct a key-recovery adversary (which also has access to the KDM oracle).

Intuitively, it seems as though in order to find d_i (the i-th bit of the decryption-key d), the key-recovery adversary can just invoke its KDM oracle on i to obtain $c_i = Enc_e(d_i)$ and then run A on input (e, c_i) (while answering A's oracle queries using its own KDM oracle). The intuition is that since A is a message recovery attacker, it should output the bit d_i. The problem with this intuition is that A is only guaranteed to work when given an encryption of a random bit that is *independent* of the decryption-key (which is obviously not the case for d_i).

We resolve this problem by restricting our attention to the set S of all keys (e', d') for which A manages to recover messages with non-negligible advantage. We make two simple observations:

1. The set S contains a polynomial fraction of the keys (this follows from the fact that A has a non-negligible advantage over all key pairs).
2. If a fixed key pair (e, d) is in S, then there should be a non-negligible gap between the distribution $A(e, Enc_e(0))$ and the distribution $A(e, Enc_e(1))$.

Note that for a fixed (e, d), the distribution $A(e, Enc_e(d_i))$ is exactly $A(e, Enc_e(0)$ if $d_i = 0$ and $A(e, Enc_e(1))$ if $d_i = 1$. Therefore, to find d_i we approximate the following probabilities:

- The probability μ_0 that A outputs 1 when given an encryption of 0.
- The probability μ_1 that A outputs 1 when given an encryption of 1.
- The probability ν that A outputs 1 when given an encryption of d_i. (To approximate this probability we use fresh calls to the KDM oracle.)

We guess that d_i is the bit b such that ν is closer to μ_b than to μ_{1-b} and we are correct with overwhelming probability (over the coins used for the approximations). By repeating this procedure for every $i \in [|d|]$ we obtain an overwhelming probability of finding d for every $(e, d) \in S$. Since S is sufficiently large, this gives us a non-negligible probability of finding D even for a random key-pair (e, d). □

Lemma 10. *Every public-key bit-encryption scheme that is circular secure with respect to message recovery is circular secure with respect to indistinguishability of oracles.*

Proof Sketch. Let $(KeyGen, Enc, Dec)$ be a public-key bit-encryption scheme that is circular insecure with respect to indistinguishability of oracles. That is, there exists an adversary A that gets as input an encryption-key e and access to an oracle that is either the KDM oracle or the all-zeros oracle and manages to distinguish between the two cases.[15] We use A to construct a circular security message recovery adversary A' for the scheme.

For simplicity, assume that A is just given an encryption-key e and a list of ciphertexts $c_1, \ldots, c_\ell$ (where ℓ is the length of the decryption-key d) and manages to distinguish between the case that for every i the ciphertext c_i is an encryption of the i-th bit of d and the case that for every i the ciphertext c_i is an encryption of 0.[16]

We use a hybrid argument to argue that there exists an $i \in [\ell]$ such that A, given input $e, (c_1, \ldots, c_\ell)$, distinguishes between the following two cases:

1. $c_1, \ldots, c_{i-1}$ are encryptions of the first $i - 1$ bits of d and $c_i, \ldots, c_\ell$ are encryptions of 0.
2. $c_1, \ldots, c_i$ are encryptions of the first i bits of d and $c_{i+1}, \ldots, c_\ell$ are encryptions of 0.

The hybrid argument only tells us that A distinguishes the two cases for a *random* pair of keys. The first step of our message-recovery adversary A' is to find i (this can be done by approximating the output distribution of A for every hybrid with respect to random key pair) and to check that A distinguishes between the two cases for the specific keys (e, d) (where A' uses the KDM oracle to generate the two neighboring distributions).

If A does not distinguish between the two cases then A' just outputs 0 and 1 with probability $\frac{1}{2}$. If on the other hand, A does distinguish (and by the hybrid argument there is a non-negligible probability for this event), then the i-th bit of d must be 1 (otherwise the two cases are identically distributed), and therefore A' can decrypt its challenge ciphertext c by running A on $c_1, \ldots, c_{i-1}, c, c_{i+1}, \ldots, c_\ell$ where $c_1, \ldots, c_{i-1}$ are encryptions of the first $i - 1$ bits of d and $c_{i+1}, \ldots, c_\ell$ are encryptions of 0. If c is an encryption of 0 then the input to A corresponds to the $(i - 1)$-th hybrid whereas if c is an encryption of 1 then the input corresponds to the i-th hybrid. The fact that A distinguishes between these two hybrids gives A' a non-negligible advantage in guessing the value of b. □

To complete the equivalence theorem, we also need to show the following:

Lemma 11. *Every public-key bit-encryption scheme that is circular secure with respect to indistinguishability of oracles is also circular secure with respect to key recovery.*

---

[15] Actually, since Definition 4 explicitly requires semantic security, we may instead have an adversary that directly breaks semantic security. The same adversary also breaks circular security with respect to message recovery.

[16] In the general case we need to handle an adversary that can ask for t encryptions of each bit of the decryption-key, where t is a bound on the running time of the adversary. To handle this case, we construct an intermediate adversary A' that distinguishes between t encryptions of 0 and t encryptions of 1. We use an additional hybrid argument to show how to convert A' to a single message adversary (see the full version for details).

Intuitively, given a key recovery adversary we can obtain an indistinguishability of oracles adversary by running the key-recovery adversary using the alleged KDM oracle. If the oracle is indeed the KDM oracle then with non-negligible probability the adversary finds the decryption-key whereas if the oracle is the all zeros oracle then it should be infeasible to find the decryption-key. Since it is easy to check whether the output of the key-recovery adversary is a "good" decryption-key or not, we obtain a non-negligible advantage in distinguishing between the two oracles. See the full version for the full proof.

5   A Black-Box Impossibility Result

In this section we show that the bit-encryption conjecture cannot be proved by a black-box reduction. Actually, as discussed in Section 1.3, we prove a stronger result, that the circular security of every CCA-2 secure bit-encryption cannot be proved using a black-box reduction.

We start off by defining what we mean by a black-box reduction of circular security of bit-encryption to semantic security and to CCA-2 security:

Definition 12. *A black-box reduction of circular security to semantic security for bit-encryption schemes is a probabilistic polynomial-time algorithm R such that for every encryption scheme (KeyGen, Enc, Dec) and every circular security adversary A for which there exists a polynomial p and infinitely many n such that:*

$$\left| \Pr_{(e,d) \leftarrow KeyGen(1^n)} [A^{O_{e,d}}(e) = 1] - \Pr_{(e,d) \leftarrow KeyGen(1^n)} [A^{J_e}(e) = 1] \right| > \frac{1}{2} + \frac{1}{p(n)}$$

there exists a polynomial p' such that for infinitely many n:

$$\Pr_{\substack{(e,d) \leftarrow KeyGen(1^n) \\ b \in_R \{0,1\}}} [R^{(KeyGen,Enc,Dec),A}(e, Enc_e(b)) = b] > \frac{1}{2} + \frac{1}{p'(n)}$$

where the probabilities are also over the coin tosses of all algorithms.

A black-box reduction of circular security to CCA-2 security is defined similarly except that the reduction R also has oracle access to the oracle Dec'_d that decrypts any message (using the decryption-key d) except for the challenge ciphertext.

We prove the following theorem:

Theorem 13. *There exists no black-box reduction of circular security to semantic security for bit-encryption schemes. Furthermore, there also exists no fully black-box reduction of circular security to CCA-2 security for bit-encryption schemes.*

Note that the furthermore clause actually implies the theorem since CCA-2 security implies semantic security. Therefore, to prove Theorem 13, it suffices to show a single encryption scheme and a successful circular security adversary for the scheme such that the scheme is CCA-2 secure even given access to the circular security adversary. Since we consider a reduction in which the circular security adversary is used in a black-box manner, we may even consider an *inefficient* circular security adversary.

For a given encryption-scheme, consider an inefficient circular security adversary A that given an encryption-key e first finds the corresponding decryption-key d (suppose that d is uniquely determined by e), then asks its oracle for encryptions of all the key bits, decrypts these ciphertexts to obtain $d'_1, \ldots, d'_n$ (where $n = |d|$) and outputs 1 if $d' \overset{\text{def}}{=} d'_1, \ldots, d'_n$ equals d and $\perp$ otherwise. Indeed, A breaks circular security and therefore to prove Theorem 13, it suffices to show a single encryption scheme for which it is infeasible to break semantic security even given oracle access to A.

Intuitively, we would like to argue that the adversary A specified above cannot be used to break the security of *any* CCA-2 secure encryption scheme (although to prove the theorem it suffices to show a single such scheme). The intuition is that for such schemes, it is infeasible, given only the encryption-key, to produce encryptions of all of the key bits.[17] Therefore, it seems as though the reduction cannot use the circular security adversary A in any meaningful way and that A can be simulated by always returning $\perp$. Thus, it seems as though the scheme remains CCA-2 secure even given oracle access to A.

The problem with the foregoing argument is that the reduction may decide to query A not on its own challenge encryption-key e but on some related key e'. In such a case we can no longer argue that A can be simulated by just returning $\perp$. While it seems strange for a *generic* reduction (which should work for any CCA-2 encryption-scheme) to run A on keys other than its own, we cannot rule out this possibility.

We overcome this difficulty by restricting our attention only to reductions that also use the encryption-scheme as a black-box. Such reductions should also work when given an *inefficient* encryption-scheme. We use this fact to construct a specific inefficient CCA-2 secure encryption scheme that has the additional important property that its encryption keys are totally unrelated. Therefore, intuitively, querying the adversary A on a key $e' \neq e$ cannot help the reduction break semantic security.

Proof (of Theorem 13).

We construct an *inefficient* encryption scheme $(KeyGen, Enc, Dec)$ and an inefficient circular security adversary A for $(KeyGen, Enc, Dec)$ such that no algorithm R that makes only polynomially many oracle calls to $(KeyGen, Enc, Dec)$ and A can break CCA-2 security. The encryption scheme that we construct has two main properties:

---

[17] If it were feasible to generate encryptions of all the key bits than a CCA attacker could use the decryption oracle on these encryptions to find the decryption-key and break the security of the scheme.

1. Given only the encryption-key it is infeasible to generate encryptions of all of the bits of the private-key.
2. Encryption keys of the scheme are totally unrelated.

As is usual in black-box separations, our construction is randomized. That is, we construct a family of encryption schemes and consider a random encryption scheme in the family. Specifically, consider a totally random length tripling injective function $\mathcal{G} : \{0,1\}^n \to \{0,1\}^{3n}$ and a collection of 2^n random injective functions $\mathcal{E} \stackrel{\text{def}}{=} \{\mathcal{E}_e : \{0,1\} \times \{0,1\}^n \to \{0,1\}^{3n}\}_{e \in \mathcal{G}(\{0,1\}^n)}$. We define the following family of encryption schemes (indexed by $\mathcal{G}, \mathcal{E}$):

$KeyGen(1^n)$: select at random $d \in \{0,1\}^n$ and output (e,d) such that $e = \mathcal{G}(d)$.
$Enc_e(\sigma)$: select at random $r \in \{0,1\}^n$ and output $\mathcal{E}_e(\sigma, r)$.
$Dec_d(c)$: output $b \in \{0,1\}$ if there exists an $r \in \{0,1\}^n$ such that $c = \mathcal{E}_e(b, r)$, where $e = \mathcal{G}(d)$. Otherwise output $\bot$.

Note that $(KeyGen, Enc, Dec)$ essentially form an idealized encryption scheme and that there is no correlation between different encryption keys. Additionally, note that both the set of encryption keys and the sets of ciphertexts are a random exponentially vanishing subset of $\{0,1\}^{3n}$ and therefore a polynomially bounded adversary only has probability $\frac{\text{poly}(n)}{2^{2n}} < 2^{-n}$ to produce a valid public-key or ciphertext without invoking the oracles $KeyGen$ and Enc.

Consider the following inefficient circular security adversary for $(KeyGen, Enc, Dec)$:

$A(e, (c_1, \ldots, c_n))$: output 1 if there exist $r_1, \ldots, r_n \in \{0,1\}^n$ and $d \in \{0,1\}^n$ such that $\mathcal{G}(d) = e$ and for every $i \in [n]$, it holds that $c_i = \mathcal{E}_e(d_i, r_i)$. Otherwise output $\bot$.

The attacker A indeed breaks the circular security (with respect to indistinguishability of oracles) of $(KeyGen, Enc, Dec)$ for every $\mathcal{G}, \mathcal{E}$. We proceed to show that the reduction cannot utilize A to break CCA-2. That is, we will show that for every probabilistic polynomial-time algorithm R and all sufficiently large n it holds that

$$\Pr_{\substack{\mathcal{G}, \mathcal{E} \\ (e,d) \leftarrow G(1^n) \\ b \in_R \{0,1\}}} [R^{(KeyGen, Enc, Dec), A, Dec'_d}(e, Enc_e(b)) = b] < \frac{1}{2} + 2 \cdot 2^{-n} \quad (1)$$

where the probability is also over the coin tosses of all the algorithms and Dec'_d is the aforementioned CCA-2 decryption oracle. The existence of a single $\mathcal{G}, \mathcal{E}$ that is semantically secure follows (from standard black-box techniques, see [IR89]).

Our main step is to show that R can essentially simulate A by itself (Proposition 14). Once we get rid of A, it is not hard to see that R cannot break semantic security (Proposition 15).

Proposition 14. *There exists a probabilistic polynomial-time algorithm R' such that for all sufficiently large n it holds that*

$$\left| \Pr_{\substack{\mathcal{G},\mathcal{E} \\ (e,d) \leftarrow G(1^n) \\ b \in_R \{0,1\}}} \left[R^{(KeyGen,Enc,Dec),A,Dec'_d} \left(e, Enc_e(b) \right) = b \right] \right.$$

$$\left. - \Pr_{\substack{\mathcal{G},\mathcal{E} \\ (e,d) \leftarrow G(1^n) \\ b \in_R \{0,1\}}} \left[R'^{(KeyGen,Enc,Dec),Dec'_d} \left(e, Enc_e(b) \right) = b \right] \right| < 2^{-n}.$$

Proposition 15. *For any (computationally unbounded) algorithm R' that makes at most polynomially many oracle queries and for all sufficiently large n, it holds that*

$$\Pr_{\mathcal{G},\mathcal{E},b \in_R \{0,1\}} [R'^{(KeyGen,Enc,Dec),Dec'_d}(e, Enc_e(b)) = b] < \frac{1}{2} + 2^{-n}$$

See the full version for the proofs of Proposition 14 and 15.

From Propositions 14 and 15 we obtain Eq. (1). Using standard techniques in black-box separations (specifically an application of Markov's inequality and the Borel-Cantelli lemma, see [IR89]), the latter implies that there exist specific oracles $\mathcal{G}$ and $\mathcal{E}$ for which the corresponding encryption scheme $(KeyGen, Enc, Dec)$ is CCA-2 secure. Thus, we have found an adversary A that breaks the circular security of $(KeyGen, Enc, Dec)$ but on the other hand $(KeyGen, Enc, Dec)$ is CCA-2 secure even given oracle access to A. □

Remark. Our black-box impossibility result only considers reductions that treat both the adversary *and the primitive* (in our case the encryption scheme) as black boxes. We note that the discussion preceding the proof of Theorem 13 shows that a reduction that uses *only the adversary* as a black-box must query the adversary on keys that are somehow related to the challenge encryption-key. Since such a reduction should work for *all* bit-encryption schemes, we view this as an additional obstacle to proving the bit-encryption conjecture.

Acknowledgments. I would like to thank Benny Applebaum, Oded Goldreich and Allison Lewko for very helpful conversations and comments.

References

[ABBC10]   Acar, T., Belenkiy, M., Bellare, M., Cash, D.: Cryptographic Agility and Its Relation to Circular Encryption. In: Gilbert, H. (ed.) EUROCRYPT 2010. LNCS, vol. 6110, pp. 403–422. Springer, Heidelberg (2010)

[ACHdM05]   Ateniese, G., Camenisch, J., Hohenberger, S., de Medeiros, B.: Practical group signatures without random oracles. Cryptology ePrint Archive, Report 2005/385 (2005), http://eprint.iacr.org/

[ACPS09]   Applebaum, B., Cash, D., Peikert, C., Sahai, A.: Fast Cryptographic Primitives and Circular-Secure Encryption Based on Hard Learning Problems. In: Halevi, S. (ed.) CRYPTO 2009. LNCS, vol. 5677, pp. 595–618. Springer, Heidelberg (2009)

[App11]   Applebaum, B.: Key-Dependent Message Security: Generic Amplification and Completeness. In: Paterson, K.G. (ed.) EUROCRYPT 2011. LNCS, vol. 6632, pp. 527–546. Springer, Heidelberg (2011)

[BGdMM05]   Ballard, L., Green, M., de Medeiros, B., Monrose, F.: Correlation-resistant storage via keyword-searchable encryption. Cryptology ePrint Archive, Report 2005/417 (2005), http://eprint.iacr.org/

[BGK11]   Brakerski, Z., Goldwasser, S., Kalai, Y.T.: Black-Box Circular-Secure Encryption beyond Affine Functions. In: Ishai, Y. (ed.) TCC 2011. LNCS, vol. 6597, pp. 201–218. Springer, Heidelberg (2011)

[BHHI10]   Barak, B., Haitner, I., Hofheinz, D., Ishai, Y.: Bounded Key-Dependent Message Security. In: Gilbert, H. (ed.) EUROCRYPT 2010. LNCS, vol. 6110, pp. 423–444. Springer, Heidelberg (2010)

[BHHO08]   Boneh, D., Halevi, S., Hamburg, M., Ostrovsky, R.: Circular-Secure Encryption from Decision Diffie-Hellman. In: Wagner, D. (ed.) CRYPTO 2008. LNCS, vol. 5157, pp. 108–125. Springer, Heidelberg (2008)

[BRS02]   Black, J., Rogaway, P., Shrimpton, T.: Encryption-scheme security in the presence of key-dependent messages. In: Selected Areas in Cryptography, pp. 62–75 (2002)

[BS03]   Boneh, D., Silverberg, A.: Applications of multilinear forms to cryptography. Contemporary Mathematics 324, 71–90 (2003)

[BV11]   Brakerski, Z., Vaikuntanathan, V.: Efficient fully homomorphic encryption from (standard) lwe. In: FOCS, pp. 97–106 (2011)

[CGH12]   Cash, D., Green, M., Hohenberger, S.: New Definitions and Separations for Circular Security. In: Fischlin, M., Buchmann, J., Manulis, M. (eds.) PKC 2012. LNCS, vol. 7293, pp. 540–557. Springer, Heidelberg (2012)

[CL01]   Camenisch, J.L., Lysyanskaya, A.: An Efficient System for Non-transferable Anonymous Credentials with Optional Anonymity Revocation. In: Pfitzmann, B. (ed.) EUROCRYPT 2001. LNCS, vol. 2045, pp. 93–118. Springer, Heidelberg (2001)

[Gen09]   Gentry, C.: Fully homomorphic encryption using ideal lattices. In: STOC, pp. 169–178 (2009)

[GM84]   Goldwasser, S., Micali, S.: Probabilistic encryption. Journal of Computer and System Sciences 28(2), 270–299 (1984)

[Gol04]   Goldreich, O.: Foundations of Cryptography: Basic Applications, vol. 2. Cambridge University Press (2004)

[HH09]   Haitner, I., Holenstein, T.: On the (Im)Possibility of Key Dependent Encryption. In: Reingold, O. (ed.) TCC 2009. LNCS, vol. 5444, pp. 202–219. Springer, Heidelberg (2009)

[IR89]   Impagliazzo, R., Rudich, S.: Limits on the provable consequences of one-way permutations. In: Proceedings of the 21st Annual ACM Symposium on Theory of Computing, STOC 1989, pp. 44–61. ACM (1989)

[Lin06]   Lindell, Y.: A simpler construction of cca2-secure public-key encryption under general assumptions. J. Cryptology 19(3), 359–377 (2006)

[NY90]   Naor, M., Yung, M.: Public-key cryptosystems provably secure against chosen ciphertext attacks. In: STOC, pp. 427–437 (1990)

[RTV04]   Reingold, O., Trevisan, L., Vadhan, S.P.: Notions of Reducibility between Cryptographic Primitives. In: Naor, M. (ed.) TCC 2004. LNCS, vol. 2951, pp. 1–20. Springer, Heidelberg (2004)

[Sah99]   Sahai, A.: Non-malleable non-interactive zero knowledge and adaptive chosen-ciphertext security. In: FOCS, pp. 543–553 (1999)

Cryptographic Hardness of Random Local Functions – Survey

Benny Applebaum*

School of Electrical Engineering, Tel-Aviv University
bennyap@post.tau.ac.il

Constant parallel-time cryptography allows performing complex cryptographic tasks at an ultimate level of parallelism, namely, by local functions that each of their output bits depend on a constant number of input bits. The feasibility of such highly efficient cryptographic constructions was widely studied in the last decade via two main research threads.

The first is an encoding-based approach, developed in [1,2], in which standard cryptographic computations are transformed into local computations via the use of special encoding schemes called *randomized encoding* of functions. The second approach, initiated by Goldreich [3], is more direct and it conjectures that almost all non-trivial local functions have some cryptographic properties.

In this survey we focus on the latter approach. We consider *random local functions* in which each output bit is computed by applying some fixed d-local predicate P to a randomly chosen d-size subset of the input bits. Formally, this can be viewed as selecting a random member from a collection $\mathcal{F}_{P,n,m}$ of d-local functions where each member $f_{G,P} : \{0,1\}^n \to \{0,1\}^m$ is specified by a d-uniform hypergraph G with n nodes and m hyperedges, and the i-th output of $f_{G,P}$ is computed by applying the predicate P to the d inputs that are indexed by the i-th hyperedge.

In this talk, we will investigate the cryptographic hardness of random local functions. In particular, we will survey known attacks and hardness results, discuss different flavors of hardness (one-wayness, pseudorandomness, collision resistance, public-key encryption), and mention applications to other problems in cryptography and computational complexity. We also present some open questions with the hope to develop a systematic study of the cryptographic hardness of local functions.

References

1. Applebaum, B., Ishai, Y., Kushilevitz, E.: Cryptography in NC⁰. SIAM Journal on Computing 36(4), 845–888 (2006)
2. Applebaum, B., Ishai, Y., Kushilevitz, E.: Computationally private randomizing polynomials and their applications. Journal of Computational Complexity 15(2), 115–162 (2006)
3. Goldreich, O.: Candidate one-way functions based on expander graphs. Electronic Colloquium on Computational Complexity (ECCC) 7(090) (2000)

* Supported by Alon Fellowship, ISF grant 1155/11, Israel Ministry of Science and Technology (grant 3-9094), and GIF grant 1152/2011.

A. Sahai (Ed.): TCC 2013, LNCS 7785, p. 599, 2013.

On the Power of Correlated Randomness in Secure Computation

Yuval Ishai[1,*], Eyal Kushilevitz[1,**], Sigurd Meldgaard[2,***],
Claudio Orlandi[2,†], and Anat Paskin-Cherniavsky[1,‡]

[1] Technion, Haifa, Israel
{yuvali,eyalk,anatp}@cs.technion.ac.il
[2] Aarhus University, Denmark
{stm,orlandi}@cs.au.dk

Abstract. We investigate the extent to which correlated secret randomness can help in secure computation with no honest majority. It is known that correlated randomness can be used to evaluate any circuit of size s with perfect security against semi-honest parties or statistical security against malicious parties, where the communication complexity grows linearly with s. This leaves open two natural questions: (1) Can the communication complexity be made independent of the circuit size? (2) Is it possible to obtain *perfect* security against malicious parties?

We settle the above questions, obtaining both positive and negative results on unconditionally secure computation with correlated randomness. Concretely, we obtain the following results.

MINIMIZING COMMUNICATION. Any multiparty functionality can be realized, with perfect security against semi-honest parties or statistical security against malicious parties, by a protocol in which the number of bits communicated by each party is linear in its input length. Our protocol uses an exponential number of correlated random bits. We give evidence that super-polynomial randomness complexity may be inherent.

PERFECT SECURITY AGAINST MALICIOUS PARTIES. Any finite "sender-receiver" functionality, which takes inputs from a sender and a receiver and delivers an output only to the receiver, can be *perfectly* realized given correlated randomness. In contrast, perfect security is generally impossible for functionalities which deliver outputs to both parties. We also show useful functionalities (such as string equality) for which there are *efficient* perfectly secure protocols in the correlated randomness model.

PERFECT CORRECTNESS IN THE PLAIN MODEL. We present a general approach for transforming perfectly secure protocols for sender-receiver

* Supported by the European Research Council as part of the ERC project CaC (grant 259426), ISF grant 1361/10, and BSF grant 2008411. Research done in part while visiting UCLA.
** Supported by ISF grant 1361/10 and BSF grant 2008411.
*** Supported by ERC grant 259426. Research mostly done while visiting the Technion.
† Supported by The Danish Council for Independent Research (DFF). Research done in part while visiting UCLA and Bar-Ilan University.
‡ Supported by ERC grant 259426.

A. Sahai (Ed.): TCC 2013, LNCS 7785, pp. 600–620, 2013.

functionalities in the correlated randomness model into secure protocols in the plain model which offer *perfect correctness* against a malicious sender. This should be contrasted with the impossibility of perfectly sound zero-knowledge proofs.

1   Introduction

Secure computation is a fundamental problem that has been extensively studied since the 1980s, originating from the seminal works of [35,20,6,11]. In this paper, we study the power of *correlated randomness* in secure two-party computation and multiparty computation with no honest majority. That is, we consider secure computation with a randomness distribution phase which takes place before the inputs are known. In this phase the parties receive a sample from a predetermined joint distribution. While each party only receives its own random string from this sample, these random strings are correlated as specified by the joint distribution.

From a theoretical point of view, the correlated randomness model is interesting because it can be used to circumvent impossibility results for the plain model such as the impossibility of information-theoretic security, analogously to the use of shared secret randomness for encryption. This model can also be of practical relevance, as it can be instantiated in the following ways:

- MPC WITH PREPROCESSING. It is often the case that parties can use idle time before they have any input to run a secure "offline protocol" for generating and storing correlated randomness. This correlated randomness is later consumed by an "online protocol" which is executed once the inputs become available. This paradigm for MPC is particularly useful when it is important that the outputs are known shortly after the inputs are (i.e., for low-latency computation). Note that if the online protocol is unconditionally secure, then it has the potential efficiency advantage of not requiring any "cryptographic" operations. If the online protocol is *perfectly secure*, then it has the additional potential advantage of a *finite* complexity that does not grow with a statistical security parameter. From here on we will refer to MPC with correlated randomness also as *MPC with preprocessing*.

- COMMODITY-BASED MPC. In the setting of commodity-based cryptography [4], the parties can "purchase" correlated randomness from one or more external servers. Security in this model is guaranteed as long as at most t of the servers are corrupted, for some specified threshold t, where corrupted servers may potentially collude with the parties. In contrast to the obvious solutions of employing a server as a trusted party or running an MPC protocol among the servers, the servers are only used during an offline phase before the inputs are known, and do not need to be aware of the existence of each other.

- HONEST-MAJORITY MPC. Recent large-scale practical uses of MPC [10,9] employed three servers and assumed that at most one of these servers is corrupted by a semi-honest adversary. Protocols in the correlated randomness model can be translated into protocols in this 3-server model by simply letting one server generate the correlated randomness for the other two.

A prime example of a cryptographic task that can benefit from having access to correlated randomness is oblivious transfer (OT) [30,16]. Beaver [3] shows that having access to the inputs and outputs of a random instance of OT can be used to realize OT on any inputs with unconditional security. This, together with the fact that OT is complete for secure computation [24,22], shows that every functionality can be securely computed given access to an appropriate source of correlated randomness and no additional assumptions.

While the OT protocol from [3] has both *perfect security* and *optimal communication complexity*, the protocols obtained using the compilers of [24,22] only achieve *statistical security* and their communication complexity grows linearly with the *circuit size* of the functionality. The same holds for more recent unconditionally secure MPC protocols in the preprocessing model [7,13]. This leaves open the following natural questions:

Question 1. What is the *communication complexity* of unconditionally secure computation in the preprocessing model? Can the communication be made independent of the circuit size?

Question 2. Are there general protocols in the preprocessing model that achieve *perfect security* against malicious parties?

While the first question is clearly motivated by the goal of (theoretical and practical) efficiency, we argue that this is also the case for the second question. Consider a scenario where two parties wish to securely evaluate a functionality $f(x,y)$ where x and y are taken from small input domains. Viewing the input size as constant, it can be shown that the asymptotic complexity of any statistically secure protocol with simulation error of $2^{-\sigma}$ must grow (at least) linearly with σ, whereas any perfectly secure protocol has constant complexity. Finally, the question of perfect security is conceptually interesting, as there are very few examples of perfectly secure cryptographic protocols with security against malicious parties.

Our Results: We essentially settle the above questions, obtaining both positive and negative results on unconditionally secure computation with correlated randomness. In doing so, we present a number of efficient protocols that can be useful in practice, especially when securely computing (many instances of) "unstructured" functions on small input domains. Concretely, we obtain the following results.

Communication Complexity. We show that any multiparty functionality can be realized, with perfect security against semi-honest parties or statistical security against malicious parties, by a protocol in which the number of bits communicated by each party is linear in its input length. A disadvantage of our protocols is that their storage complexity (i.e., the number of bits each party receives during preprocessing) grows exponentially with the input length. We give evidence that this disadvantage is inherent even when the honest parties are computationally unbounded. Concretely, if every two-party functionality had a protocol with polynomial storage complexity, this would imply an unexpected answer to a longstanding open question on the complexity of information-theoretic private information retrieval [12] (see Theorem 14).

We also prove a separation between the communication pattern required by unconditionally secure MPC in the preprocessing model and the communication with no security requirement. Concretely, for most functionalities (even ones with a short output) it is essential that the communication by *each party* grows linearly with its input length. In contrast, without security requirements it is always possible to make the communication by one of the parties comparable to the length of the output, independently of the input length. The same is true in the computational model of security under standard cryptographic assumptions. Concretely, such a communication pattern is possible either without preprocessing using fully homomorphic encryption [19], or with preprocessing by using garbled circuits [34] (provided that the inputs are chosen independently of the correlated randomness [5]).

Perfect Security. We show that any "sender-receiver" functionality, which takes inputs from both parties and delivers an output only to the receiver, can be *perfectly* realized in the preprocessing model. In contrast, we show that perfect security is generally impossible for functionalities which deliver outputs to both parties, even for non-reactive functionalities and even if one settles for "security with abort" without fairness (Thm. 4). A similar impossibility result for bit commitment (a reactive functionality) was obtained in [8].

The communication and storage complexity of our perfectly secure protocols are comparable to those of the statistical protocols, except for eliminating the dependence on a security parameter. In particular, the storage complexity grows exponentially with the bit-length of the inputs. We present storage-efficient protocols for several natural functionalities, including string equality (see Section 1.2 below), set intersection, and inner product (Appendix A). Our positive results for general functionalities are summarized in Table 1, and for specific sender-receiver functionalities in Table 2.

Table 1. Comparison of our positive results with previous work: s is the size of a boolean circuit computing the functionality, n is the length of the inputs, m is the output length, and σ is a statistical security parameter. In the asymptotic complexity expressions, the number of parties k is viewed as constant. The protocol of Theorem 3 applies only to sender-receiver two-party functionalities.

Protocol	Communication	Storage	Parties	Security
[20,3]	$O(s)$	$O(s)$	k	perfect, passive
[24,22]	$O(s) + \mathsf{poly}(\sigma)$	$O(s) + \mathsf{poly}(\sigma)$	k	statistical, active
Theorem 1	$O(n)$	$O(2^n m)$	k	perfect, passive
Theorem 2	$O(n + \sigma)$	$O(2^n(m + \sigma))$	k	statistical, active
Theorem 3	$O(n)$	$O(2^n(m + n))$	2	perfect, active

Table 2. Sender-receiver protocols for specific tasks. Two variants of set intersection are given: a perfectly secure with exponential computation, and a statistically secure with efficient computation.

Protocol	f	Communication	Storage	Computation	Security
Sec. 1.2	$x =_? y$	$2|x|$	$O(|x|)$	$\mathsf{poly}(|x|)$	perfect, active
Thm. 7	$x \cap y$	$\mathsf{poly}(|x|) + |y|$	$\mathsf{poly}(|x|)$	$\exp(|x|, |y|)$	perfect, active
Thm. 7	$x \cap y$	$\mathsf{poly}(|x|, k) + |y|$	$\mathsf{poly}(|x|, \sigma)$	$\mathsf{poly}(|x|, |y|, \sigma)$	statistical, active
Thm. 8	$\langle x, y \rangle$	$2|x|$	$O(|x|)$	$\mathsf{superpoly}(|x|)$	perfect, active

Perfect Correctness in the Plain Model. We present a somewhat unexpected application of our positive results in the preprocessing model to security in the plain model. Consider the goal of securely evaluating a sender-receiver functionality f. We say that a protocol for f is *perfectly correct* if the effect of any (unbounded) malicious sender strategy on the honest receiver's output can be perfectly simulated, via some distribution over the sender's inputs, in an ideal evaluation of f. For example, consider the string equality functionality $f(x, y)$ which receives an n-bit string from each party, and delivers 1 to the receiver if $x = y$ and 0 otherwise. A perfectly correct protocol for f should guarantee, for instance, that if the honest receiver picks its input at random, then the receiver should output 1 with *exactly* 2^{-n} probability, no matter which strategy the sender uses.

The impossibility of perfectly sound zero-knowledge proofs (which carries over to the preprocessing model, see Theorem 15) shows that perfect correctness cannot always be achieved when the honest parties are required to be efficient. We complement this by a positive result which applies to *all* functionalities on a small input domain as well as some natural functionalities on a large input domain (like string equality). Our result is based on a general approach for transforming perfectly secure protocols for sender-receiver functionalities in the preprocessing model into (computationally) secure protocols in the plain model which additionally offer perfect correctness against a malicious sender.

To summarize, we have the following *lower bounds:*

- We show limits to what functionalities can be implemented perfectly. Theorem 4 shows that not all two-party functionalities have protocols with perfect security and abort. This is generalized in Theorem 9 to show a function that requires $\Omega(\log \frac{1}{\epsilon})$ communication to compute with ϵ-security.
- We lower bound the amount of communication that a secure protocol for a non-trivial functionality must use. Theorem 11 for the perfect case and Theorems 12, 13 for the statistical case show that for general functionalities the communication complexity of our protocols is optimal. Another generalization (Theorem 10) shows that the negative results extends to the case of expected round complexity.
- We show that superpolynomial preprocessing is needed in general. Theorem 14 explains that improving on the preprocessing needed for sender-receiver functionalities will imply a breakthrough in information theoretic PIR.

On the positive side, we show in Theorem 5 and 6 how to use perfectly secure sender-receiver protocols in the preprocessing model to implement *perfectly
correct* protocols in the plain model (if the preprocessing is small enough).

1.1   Related Work

Beaver [3] showed that OT can be realized with perfect security given preprocessing. Later Beaver [4] generalized the above to the *commodity-based model*,
a setting where there are multiple servers providing precomputed randomness,
only a majority of which are honest (in the full version, we describe a general
approach for applying our results in the commodity-based model). Beaver also
notes that perfect security is not possible in general because commitment cannot
be realized perfectly, and a proof of this appeared in [8]. However, the question
was left open for standard (non-reactive) functionalities.

Since OT can be precomputed [3] and as it is complete for secure computation [24], it is possible to compute any function with statistical security. The
result of [22] improves the asymptotical complexity of [24], while [2,7,27] offer
efficient statistically secure protocols in the preprocessing model for arithmetic
and Boolean circuits respectively. A recent result [14] shows that this can be
done with no overhead during the online phase by giving a protocol with optimal communication complexity for the case of "generic preprocessing" (i.e., the
preprocessing does not depend on the function to be evaluated – only on its
size). Our results achieve better online communication complexity as we do not
rely on a circuit representation.

A protocol for computing secret shares of the inner product against malicious
adversaries was proposed in [15]. In Appendix A, we give a protocol for computing the inner product where one party learns the output. In the setting of
malicious corruptions, it is not trivial to reconstruct the results from the shares,
and therefore our protocol takes a substantially different approach than [15].

In [32], a perfectly secure protocol for oblivious polynomial evaluation in the
preprocessing model is presented. [32] also presents a protocol for equality which
is claimed to be perfectly secure but it is however not perfectly secure according to the standard simulation-based definition — see Section 1.2 below for a
perfectly secure protocol for equality.

The type of correlated randomness needed for realizing multiparty computation with unconditional security in the presence of an honest majority is studied
in [17,18]. Statistically secure commitment protocol from correlated randomness
are constructed in [31]. Finally [33] gives linear lower bounds on the storage
complexity of secure computation with correlated randomness.

1.2   Warmup: Equality Test

To introduce some of the notation and the techniques that we use later to prove
more general results, we describe the simple protocol in Figure 1 for equality
testing in the preprocessing model.

Functionality:
- The receiver has input $x \in X$, the sender input $y \in X$;
- The receiver learns 1 if $x = y$ or 0 otherwise. The sender learns nothing;

Preprocessing:
1. Sample a random 2-wise independent permutation $P : X \to X$, and a random string $r \in_R X$. Compute $s = P(r)$;
2. The preprocessing outputs (r, s) to the receiver and P to the sender;

Protocol:
1. The receiver computes $u = x + r$ and sends to sender;
2. The sender computes $v = P(u - y)$ and sends to the receiver;
3. The receiver outputs 1 if $v = s$, and 0 otherwise;

Fig. 1. A perfectly secure protocol for equality with preprocessing

We consider at the *sender-receiver* version of the functionality, where only the receiver gets output from the protocol. In this setting, we have a receiver and a sender holding respectively x, y in some group X. At the end of the protocol, the receiver learns whether $x = y$ or not. The protocol achieves perfect security against malicious adversaries and it is optimal in terms of communication complexity. Correctness follows from $v = P(u - y) = P(r + x - y)$, and this is equal to s iff $x = y$.

One can prove that the protocol is perfectly secure by a simulation argument: The simulator has access to all preprocessed information. In case of a corrupted *sender*, the simulator proceeds as follows: the simulator sends a random u to the adversary and, when the adversary replies v, the simulator computes $y = u - P^{-1}(v)$ and inputs it to the ideal functionality. In case of a corrupted *receiver*, the simulator extracts the input string x (using u, r) and inputs it to the ideal functionality for equality. If the ideal functionality outputs 1, the simulator sends $v = s$ to the corrupted receiver, but if it outputs 0, the simulator chooses $v \in_R X$ such that $v \neq s$. This simulation is perfect, as the adversary's view of the protocol is distributed identically both in the real execution and in the simulation. Note that it is enough for P to be drawn from a family of pairwise independent permutations, since the receiver only learns the permutation at two indices.

The protocol is also UC-secure (the simulation is straight line) and is *adaptively* secure. This is the case for all the protocols presented in this work.

2   Preliminaries

Notation. Let $[n]$ denote the set $\{1, 2, \ldots, n\}$. We use $Z^{X \times Y}$ to denote the set of matrices over Z whose rows are labeled by the elements of X and whose columns are labeled by the elements of Y.

Computational Model. We assume perfect uniform sampling from $[m]$, for any positive integer m, as an atomic computational step.

Network Model. We consider protocols involving n parties, denoted $P_1, \ldots, P_n$. The parties communicate over synchronous, secure and authenticated point-to-point channels. In some constructions we also use a broadcast channel. We note that, in the preprocessing model, all these channels can be implemented with unconditional security over insecure point-to-point channels. Specifically, secure channels can be perfectly implemented in the preprocessing model using a one-time pad, authentication (with statistical security) using a one-time message authentication code (MAC), and broadcast (with statistical security) using the protocol of [29].

Functionalities. We consider non-reactive secure computation tasks, defined by a deterministic or randomized *functionality* $f : X_1 \times \ldots \times X_n \to Z_1 \times \ldots \times Z_n$. The functionality specifies a mapping from n inputs to n outputs which the parties want to compute. We will often consider a special class of two-party functionalities referred to as *sender-receiver functionalities*. A sender-receiver functionality $f : X \times Y \to Z$ gets an input x from P_1 (the *receiver*), an input y from P_2 (the *sender*) and delivers the output z only to the receiver.

Protocols with Preprocessing. An n-party protocol can be formally defined by a *next message function*. This function, on input (i, x_i, r_i, j, m), specifies an n-tuple of messages sent by party P_i in round j, when x_i is its inputs, r_i is its randomness and m describes the messages it received in previous rounds. (If a broadcast channel is used, the next message function also outputs the message broadcasted by P_i in Round j.) The next message function may also instruct P_i to terminate the protocol, in which case it also specifies the output of P_i. In the *preprocessing model*, the specification of a protocol also includes a joint distribution $\mathcal{D}$ over $R_1 \times R_2 \ldots \times R_n$, where the R_i's are finite randomness domains. This distribution is used for sampling correlated random inputs $(r_1, \ldots, r_n)$ which the parties receive before the beginning of the protocol (in particular, the preprocessing is independent of the inputs). The next message function, in this case, may also depend on the private random input r_i received by P_i from $\mathcal{D}$. We assume that for every possible choice of inputs and random inputs, all parties eventually terminate.

Security Definition. We work in the standard ideal-world/real-world simulation paradigm. Our positive results hold for the strongest possible security model, namely UC-security with adaptive corruptions, while our negative results hold for the weaker model of standalone security against static corruptions. We consider both semi-honest (passive) corruptions and malicious (active) corruptions. Using the standard terminology of secure computation, the preprocessing model can be thought of as a *hybrid model* where the parties have a one-time access to an ideal randomized functionality $\mathcal{D}$ (with no inputs) providing them with correlated, private random inputs r_i. We consider by default *full security* (with guaranteed output delivery) for sender-receiver functionalities, and *security with abort* for general functionalities. We mainly focus on the cases of *statistical* or *perfect* security, though some of our results refer to computational security as well. We will sometimes refer separately to *correctness* and *privacy* – the former considers only the effect of the adversary on the outputs and the latter considers only the view of the adversary. The full security definition is omitted for lack of space.

3   Optimal Communication for General Functionalities

In this section, we settle the communication complexity of MPC in the preprocessing model. For simplicity, we restrict the attention to non-reactive functionalities, but the results of this section apply also to reactive functionalities.

3.1   Upper Bounds on Communication Complexity

The following is a summary of our upper bounds. These will follow from the Claims 1, 2 and 3 (some of which are in later sections) and by inspection of the protocols.

Theorem 1. *For any n-party functionality $f : X_1 \times \ldots \times X_n \to Z_1 \times \ldots \times Z_n$, there is a protocol π which realizes f, in the preprocessing model, and has the following features against semi-honest parties: (1) π is perfectly secure; (2) It uses two rounds of communication; (3) Let $\alpha = \sum_{i \in [n]} \log |X_i|$ be the total input length. Then, the total communication complexity is $O(\alpha)$ and the storage complexity is $O(\alpha 2^\alpha)$.*

Theorem 2. *For any n-party functionality $f : X_1 \times \ldots \times X_n \to Z_1 \times \ldots \times Z_n$ and $\epsilon > 0$, there is a protocol π which realizes f, in the preprocessing model against a malicious adversary, such that: (1) π is statistically ϵ-secure with abort; (2) It uses two rounds of communication (given broadcast); (3) The total communication complexity is $O(\alpha + n \log 1/\epsilon)$ and the storage complexity is $O(2^\alpha \cdot (\alpha + n \log 1/\epsilon))$, where α being the total input length, as above.*

Theorem 3. *For any 2-party sender-receiver functionality $f : X \times Y \to Z$, there is a protocol π which realizes f, in the preprocessing model against a malicious adversary, such that: (1) π is perfectly secure; (2) It uses two rounds of communication; (3) The total communication complexity is $\log |X| + \log |Y|$ and the storage complexity is $O(|X| \cdot |Y| \cdot \log |Y|)$.*

3.2   Semi-honest Two-Party Protocol, via One-Time Truth Table

For the sake of exposition, we focus on protocols where both parties P_1, P_2 receive the same output $f(x, y) \in Z$, for some function $f : X \times Y \to Z$. We view X, Y and Z as groups and use additive notation for the group operation, i.e., $(X, +), (Y, +), (Z, +)$.

In Figure 2 we present a simple protocol that is secure against a semi-honest adversary if the parties have access to a preprocessing functionality dealing correlated randomness. The protocol has communication complexity $\log |X| + \log |Y| + 2 \log |Z|$. A protocol with communication complexity $\log |X| + \log |Y| + \log |Z|$

follows from the protocol in Section 4.[1] We start by presenting this slightly less efficient protocol here, as this protocol is easier to generalize for security against malicious parties and for the multiparty case (see Figure 3 and the full version).

The protocol uses *one-time truth tables* (OTTT). Intuitively, OTTT can be seen as the one-time pad of secure function evaluation. The parties hold shares of a permuted truth-table, and each party knows also the permutation that was used for its input. In the two-party case, the truth-table can be seen as a matrix, where one party knows the permutation of the rows and the other knows the permutation of the columns. In fact, given that every truth table will be only used once, a random cyclic-shift can be used instead of a random permutation.

Functionality:
- P_1 has input $x \in X$, P_2 has input $y \in Y$.
- Both parties learn $z = f(x, y)$.

Preprocessing:
1. Sample random $r \in X, s \in Y$ and let A be the permuted truth table; i.e.,

$$A_{x+r, y+s} = f(x, y) \; ;$$

2. Sample a random matrix $M^1 \in Z^{X \times Y}$ and let $M^2 = A - M^1$;
3. Output (M^1, r) to P_1 and (M^2, s) to P_2;

Protocol:
1. P_1 sends $u = x + r$ to P_2;
2. P_2 sends $v = y + s$ and $z_2 = M^2_{u,v}$ to P_1;
3. P_1 sends to P_2 the value $z_1 = M^1_{u,v}$;
4. Both parties output $z = z_1 + z_2$;

Fig. 2. Semi-Honest Secure Protocol using One-Time Truth Table

Claim 1. The protocol in Figure 2 securely computes f with perfect security against semi-honest corruptions.

Proof. When both parties are honest, the protocol indeed outputs the correct value:

$$z = z_1 + z_2 = M^1_{u,v} + M^2_{u,v} = A_{u,v} = A_{x+r, y+s} = f(x, y).$$

Security against semi-honest parties can be argued as follows: the view of P_2 can be simulated by choosing a random $u \in X$ and defining $z_1 = z - M^2_{u,v}$. The view of P_1 can be simulated by choosing a random $v \in Y$ and defining $z_2 = z - M^1_{u,v}$. As both in the simulation and in the real protocol the values u, v, z_1, z_2 are distributed uniformly at random in the corresponding domains, the protocol achieves perfect security.

---

[1] The protocol of Section 4 has complexity $\log |X| + \log |Y|$ but only one party gets output; however, in the semi-honest case, this party may simply transfer the output ($\log |Z|$ bits) to the other party.

3.3   One-Time Truth Tables with Malicious Security

The above protocol is only secure against semi-honest adversaries, as a malicious party P_i could misreport its output share z_i and therefore change the output distribution. To fix this problem, we will enhance the OTTT protocol using information theoretic message authentication codes (MAC): the preprocessing phase will output keys for a one-time MAC to both parties, and will add shares of these MACs to the truth table. The resulting protocol is only statistically secure as an adversary will always have a (negligibly small) probability to output a fake share z_i together with a valid MAC. As we will see later (Section 4.1), this is inherent; i.e., it is impossible to securely compute every function with perfect security, even in the preprocessing model.

Definition 1 (One-Time MAC). *A pair of efficient algorithms* (Tag, Ver) *is a one-time ϵ-secure message authentication code scheme (MAC), with key space $\mathcal{K}$ and MAC space $\mathcal{M}$, if* $\text{Ver}_k(m, \text{Tag}_k(m)) = 1$ *with probability 1 and for every (possibly unbounded) adversary $\mathcal{A}$:*

$$\Pr[k \leftarrow \mathcal{K}, m \leftarrow \mathcal{A}, (m', t') \leftarrow \mathcal{A}(m, \text{Tag}_k(m)) : \text{Ver}_k(m', t') = 1 \wedge m \neq m'] < \epsilon \ .$$

The MAC can be instantiated with the standard "$am + b$" construction: Let $\mathbb{F}$ be a finite field of size $|\mathbb{F}| > \epsilon^{-1}$, and let $k = (a, b) \in \mathbb{F}^2$. To compute a MAC tag, let $\text{Tag}_k(m) = am + b$ and for verification compute $\text{Ver}_k(m, t) = 1$ iff $t = am + b$. Without loss of generality, the range of f, the function to be computed, is $Z = \mathbb{F}$. [2] For the purpose of this application, we will write the MAC space $\mathcal{M}$ as an additive group $(\mathcal{M}, +)$.

MAC Enhanced OTTT: In Figure 3, the protocol for general two-party computation in the preprocessing model using OTTT is presented. Note that, as all the MAC signatures are secret-shared and only one is reconstructed, we can use the same MAC key for all the entries in the matrix. We assume, for notational simplicity, that both parties obtain the same output z; the general case may be handled similarly.

Claim 2. The protocol in Figure 3 computes f with ϵ-security against a malicious adversary.

The proof of this claim is pretty straightforward and is therefore deferred to the full version of this paper. In the full version we also show how this protocol can be generalized to n parties. The main issue here is to have all the honest parties to output the same value (in particular, if one honest party outputs $\bot$ then all honest parties must output $\bot$). This is done using *unanimously identifiable commitments* from [21,28].

In the full version, we also prove negative results which complement the above positive results (see also Appendix B). In particular, we show that the communication complexity of the above protocols is optimal (for non-trivial functions) and give evidence that the exponential storage complexity (or randomness complexity) is inherent.

---

[2] Note that we still only need $\log_2 |\text{Im}(f)|$ bits to encode the output of the function.

Functionality:
- P_1 has input $x \in X$ and P_2 has input $y \in Y$.
- Both parties learn $f(x, y)$.

Preprocessing:
1. Sample random keys for an ϵ-secure MAC scheme $k_1, k_2 \in \mathcal{K}$;
2. Sample random $r \in X, s \in Y$ and let $A \in (Z \times \mathcal{M} \times \mathcal{M})^{X \times Y}$ be a matrix s.t.
$$A_{x+r, y+s} = \left(f(x, y), \mathsf{Tag}_{k_1}(f(x, y)), \mathsf{Tag}_{k_2}(f(x, y)) \right) ;$$
3. Sample a random matrix $M^1 \in (Z \times \mathcal{M} \times \mathcal{M})^{X \times Y}$ and let $M^2 = A - M^1$;
4. Output (M^1, r, k_1) to P_1 and (M^2, s, k_2) to P_2;

Protocol:
1. P_1 sends $u = x + r$ to P_2;
2. P_2 sends $v = y + s$ and $z_2 = M^2_{u,v}$ to P_1;
3. P_1 sends $z_1 = M^1_{u,v}$ to P_2;
4. Each party P_i parses $z_1 + z_2$ as (z, t_1, t_2);
5. If $\mathsf{Ver}_{k_i}(z, t_i) = 1$, party P_i outputs z, otherwise it outputs $\bot$;

Fig. 3. Malicious Secure Protocol using One-Time Truth Table

4 Perfect Security for Sender-Receiver Functionalities

In this section we show that, if only one party receives output, it is possible to achieve *perfect* security even against a *malicious* adversary. We will show, in Section 4.1, that this is not the case for general functionalities where all parties receive outputs.

The protocol is presented in Figure 4. The structure of the protocol is similar to previous constructions, in the sense that the preprocessing samples some random permutations, and then during the online phase the parties apply the random permutations on their inputs and exchange the results. However, the protocol uses the asymmetry between the sender and receiver: every row of the truth table (corresponding to each input of the receiver) is permuted using a different random permutation. The sender learns this set of permutations, permuted under a receiver permutation (implemented by a random circular shift, as in previous constructions). The receiver learns the truth table where each row is permuted according to the corresponding permutation.

In the online phase, the sender uses the first message of the receiver to determine which of the permutation to apply to his input. The receiver, using this value, can perform a look-up in the permuted truth table and output the correct result. The protocol is intuitively perfectly private as both parties only see each other's input through a random permutation. Perfect correctness is achieved because, in contrast to previous constructions, every message sent by the sender uniquely determines its input (together with the preprocessing information).

Claim 3. The protocol in Figure 4 securely computes the sender-receiver functionality f with perfect security and optimal communication complexity against malicious corruptions.

Functionality:
- R has input $x \in X$, S has input $y \in Y$.
- R learns $z = f(x, y)$;

Preprocessing:
1. Sample random $r \in X$;
2. Sample random permutations $\{P_x\}_{x \in X}$ with $P_x : Y \to Y$, and let $\{Q_i\}_{i \in X}$ be a "shifted" sequence of those permutations, where $Q_{x+r} = P_x$;
3. Compute the permuted truth table $A_{x, P_x(y)} = f(x, y)$;
4. Output (A, r) to R and $\{Q_i\}_{i \in X}$ to S;

Protocol:
1. R sends $u = x + r$ to S;
2. S sends $v = Q_u(y)$ to R;
3. R outputs $f(x, y) = A_{x,v}$ (if $v \notin Y$, then R outputs $f(x, y_0)$, for some fixed value y_0);

Fig. 4. Perfect Secure Protocol for Sender-Receiver Functionalities, Malicious Adversaries

Proof. When both parties are honest the output is correct:

$$A_{x,v} = A_{x,Q_u(y)} = A_{x,P_x(y)} = f(x, y).$$

If S^* is a corrupted sender, the simulator samples the preprocessing for S consisting of the permutations $\{Q_i\}_{i \in X}$. The simulator then picks a random message u, as the first message of the protocol. Then, it runs $v \leftarrow S^*(\{Q_i\}, y, u)$, and it extracts an effective input $y' = Q_u^{-1}(v)$ and inputs y' to the ideal functionality to get the ideal-world output $z = f(x, y')$. The simulator outputs the simulated view $(\{Q_i\}, v)$. Observe that u and $\{Q_i\}$ are distributed as in the real world and independently of x. The simulated view considered jointly with f's output on the effective input (i.e., z) is thus distributed identically to the view of S^* jointly with the receiver's output, in the real-world execution.

For a corrupted receiver R^*, the simulator samples $A, r, \{Q_i\}$, runs $u \leftarrow R^*(A, r, x)$, extracts $x' = u - r$, inputs it to the ideal functionality, receives $z = f(x', y)$, computes $u = A_{x,v}^{-1}(z)$ and outputs the simulated view (A, r, u). This is distributed identically to the real-world view of R^*.

Note that even for the case of semi-honest security, this protocol is more efficient than a protocol using 1-out-of-n OT, where the sender acts as the transmitter and offers $f(x_1, y), \ldots, f(x_m, y)$ for each possible $x_i \in X$ and the receiver acts as the chooser and selects x. Such protocol would have (online) communication complexity $O(|X| \log |Z|)$, while our protocol requires only $\log(|X|) + \log(|Y|)$ bits of communication.

4.1 Impossibility of Perfect Security for General Functionalities

The following theorem shows that the above positive result cannot be extended to general functionalities (see Appendix B and the full version for a tight tradeoff between communication and error probability).

Theorem 4. *Let $f(x_1, x_2) = (x_1 \oplus x_2, x_1 \oplus x_2)$. Then, there is no protocol for f, in the preprocessing model, which is* perfectly *secure with abort.*

Proof. Assume towards a contradiction that π perfectly realizes f with abort given preprocessing $\mathcal{D}$. Consider the experiment of running π on a uniformly random choice of inputs $(x_1, x_2) \in \{0,1\}^2$ and correlated random inputs (r_1, r_2) drawn from $\mathcal{D}$. Let i_1 be the *minimal* number such that, at the beginning of round i_1, the output of P_1 is always *determined* (over all choices of inputs and random inputs) regardless of subsequent messages (which may possibly be sent by a malicious P_2^*). That is, when running the above experiment, before round i_1, party P_1 may have an uncertainty about the output; but, at the beginning of round i_1, the view of P_1 always determines a unique output value $b \in \{0,1\}$ such that P_1 will either output b or $\perp$. The value i_2 is defined symmetrically. Note that i_1, i_2 are well defined, because the outputs are always determined at the end of the execution, and, moreover, they are distinct because only one party sends a message in each round.

Assume, without loss of generality, that $i_1 < i_2$ and, moreover, that in the above experiment there is an execution which terminates with P_2 outputting 0, but where in the beginning of round i_1 the output of P_2 is not yet determined (namely, there are messages of P_1^* that would make it output 1).

We can now describe a malicious strategy P_1^* that would make an honest P_2, on a random input x_2, output 1 with probability $p > 1/2$. Since this is impossible in the ideal model, we get the desired contradiction. The malicious P_1^* proceeds as follows.

- Run the protocol honestly on a random input x_1 until the beginning of round i_1. Let b be the output value determined at this point.
- If $b = 1$, continue running the protocol honestly.
- Otherwise, continue running the protocol by sending a uniformly random message in each round.

In the event that $b = 1$, which occurs with probability $1/2$, P_2 will always output 1. In the event that $b = 0$, by the above assumption there exist subsequent messages of P_1^* making P_2 output 1, and hence also in this case P_2 outputs 1 with nonzero probability. Overall P_2 outputs 1 with probability $p > 1/2$. $\square$

5   Perfect Correctness in the Plain Model

Theorem 15 shows that the impossibility of perfectly sound zero-knowledge proofs for NP carries over to the preprocessing model. This implies that some sender-receiver functionalities cannot be securely realized with perfect correctness in the plain model. In this section, we show that the class of functionalities that can be securely realized with perfect correctness is actually quite rich. To the best of our knowledge, this important fundamental question has been neglected in the literature so far.

We present a general transformation from perfect sender-receiver protocols in the preprocessing model, to protocols with perfect correctness in the plain model.

This is possible for functionalities for which the preprocessing can be realized in the plain model with perfect privacy (and computational correctness): the main conceptual contribution is to show how we can turn perfect privacy into perfect correctness by using an offline/online protocol.

The high level idea of this transformation is to use the "reversibility" of correlated randomness for turning perfect privacy in the plain model into perfect correctness in the plain model. Concretely, let π be a perfectly secure protocol for f in the preprocessing model. Using standard techniques (a combination of perfectly private OT protocols [26,1] with an information-theoretic variant of the garbled circuit technique [35,24]), one can get a *perfectly private* protocol π' (with unbounded simulation) for all sender-receiver functionalities in NC^1. We then use π', with the sender in π playing the role of the receiver in π', for generating the correlated randomness required by π. In this subprotocol the receiver picks its randomness r_x from the correct marginal distribution and the sender obtains as its output from π' a random input r_y sampled from the conditional distribution defined by r_x. This subprotocol prevents a malicious sender from learning *any* information about r_x other than what follows from r_y. Running π on top of the correlated randomness (r_x, r_y) generated by the subprotocol gives a perfectly correct protocol for f.

The approach described so far only guarantees security against semi-honest parties (in addition to perfect correctness against a malicious sender); however, using a GMW-style compiler we get (computational) security against malicious parties while maintaining perfect correctness against a malicious unbounded sender.

Formally, let $\mathcal{D}$ be a distribution over $R_1 \times R_2$ such that all probabilities in the support of $\mathcal{D}$ are rational. Let $\mathcal{D}_{r_1}$ be a family of distributions over R_2 such that the two distributions $\{(r_1, r_2) : (r_1, r_2) \leftarrow \mathcal{D}\}$ and $\{(r_1, r_2') : (r_1, r_2) \leftarrow \mathcal{D}, r_2' \leftarrow \mathcal{D}_{r_1}\}$ are identically distributed. Let $\mathsf{Pre}^{\mathcal{D}} : R_1 \to R_2$ be a randomized functionality[3] that, on input r_1 from party R outputs r_2, sampled according to $\mathcal{D}_{r_1}$ to S (if r_1 is not in the support of $\mathcal{D}$, the function outputs $\perp$). Applications and proofs of the following theorems are discussed in the full version.

Theorem 5. *Let f be a sender-receiver functionality that admits a perfectly secure protocol π_{online}, in the presence of preprocessing $\mathcal{D}$, where all probabilities in $\mathsf{support}(\mathcal{D})$ are rational. Let π_{pre} be a protocol that realizes $\mathsf{Pre}^{\mathcal{D}}$ which is semi-honest secure and perfectly private against malicious S.*

Then, it is possible to securely compute f with semi-honest security and perfect correctness.

Theorem 6. *Assuming one-way permutations exist, the result of Theorem 5 holds with security against malicious parties.*

---

[3] As discussed in Section 2, our computational model allows perfect sampling from the uniform distribution over $[m]$, for all integers m.

References

1. Aiello, W., Ishai, Y., Reingold, O.: Priced Oblivious Transfer: How to Sell Digital Goods. In: Pfitzmann, B. (ed.) EUROCRYPT 2001. LNCS, vol. 2045, pp. 119–135. Springer, Heidelberg (2001)

2. Beaver, D.: Efficient Multiparty Protocols Using Circuit Randomization. In: Feigenbaum, J. (ed.) CRYPTO 1991. LNCS, vol. 576, pp. 420–432. Springer, Heidelberg (1992)

3. Beaver, D.: Precomputing Oblivious Transfer. In: Coppersmith, D. (ed.) CRYPTO 1995. LNCS, vol. 963, pp. 97–109. Springer, Heidelberg (1995)

4. Beaver, D.: Commodity-based cryptography (extended abstract). In: STOC, pp. 446–455 (1997)

5. Bellare, M., Hoang, V.T., Rogaway, P.: Adaptively Secure Garbling with Applications to One-Time Programs and Secure Outsourcing. In: Wang, X., Sako, K. (eds.) ASIACRYPT 2012. LNCS, vol. 7658, pp. 134–153. Springer, Heidelberg (2012)

6. Ben-Or, M., Goldwasser, S., Wigderson, A.: Completeness theorems for non-cryptographic fault-tolerant distributed computation (extended abstract). In: STOC, pp. 1–10 (1988)

7. Bendlin, R., Damgård, I., Orlandi, C., Zakarias, S.: Semi-homomorphic Encryption and Multiparty Computation. In: Paterson, K.G. (ed.) EUROCRYPT 2011. LNCS, vol. 6632, pp. 169–188. Springer, Heidelberg (2011)

8. Blundo, C., Masucci, B., Stinson, D.R., Wei, R.: Constructions and bounds for unconditionally secure non-interactive commitment schemes. Des. Codes Cryptography 26(1-3), 97–110 (2002)

9. Bogdanov, D., Talviste, R., Willemson, J.: Deploying secure multi-party computation for financial data analysis - (short paper), pp. 57–64 (2012)

10. Bogetoft, P., Christensen, D.L., Damgård, I., Geisler, M., Jakobsen, T., Krøigaard, M., Nielsen, J.D., Nielsen, J.B., Nielsen, K., Pagter, J., Schwartzbach, M., Toft, T.: Secure Multiparty Computation Goes Live. In: Dingledine, R., Golle, P. (eds.) FC 2009. LNCS, vol. 5628, pp. 325–343. Springer, Heidelberg (2009)

11. Chaum, D., Crépeau, C., Damgård, I.: Multiparty unconditionally secure protocols (extended abstract). In: STOC, pp. 11–19 (1988)

12. Chor, B., Goldreich, O., Kushilevitz, E., Sudan, M.: Private information retrieval. In: FOCS, pp. 41–50 (1995)

13. Damgård, I., Pastro, V., Smart, N.P., Zakarias, S.: Multiparty Computation from Somewhat Homomorphic Encryption. In: Safavi-Naini, R., Canetti, R. (eds.) CRYPTO 2012. LNCS, vol. 7417, pp. 643–662. Springer, Heidelberg (2012)

14. Damgård, I., Zakarias, S.: Constant-Overhead Secure Computation of Boolean Circuits Using Preprocessing. In: Sahai, A. (ed.) TCC 2013. LNCS, vol. 7785, pp. 621–641. Springer, Heidelberg (2013)

15. Dowsley, R., van de Graaf, J., Marques, D., Nascimento, A.C.A.: A Two-Party Protocol with Trusted Initializer for Computing the Inner Product. In: Chung, Y., Yung, M. (eds.) WISA 2010. LNCS, vol. 6513, pp. 337–350. Springer, Heidelberg (2011)

16. Even, S., Goldreich, O., Lempel, A.: A randomized protocol for signing contracts. Commun. ACM 28(6), 637–647 (1985)

17. Fitzi, M., Gisin, N., Maurer, U.M., von Rotz, O.: Unconditional Byzantine Agreement and Multi-party Computation Secure against Dishonest Minorities from Scratch. In: Knudsen, L.R. (ed.) EUROCRYPT 2002. LNCS, vol. 2332, pp. 482–501. Springer, Heidelberg (2002)

18. Fitzi, M., Wolf, S., Wullschleger, J.: Pseudo-signatures, Broadcast, and Multi-party Computation from Correlated Randomness. In: Franklin, M. (ed.) CRYPTO 2004. LNCS, vol. 3152, pp. 562–578. Springer, Heidelberg (2004)
19. Gentry, C.: Fully homomorphic encryption using ideal lattices. In: STOC, pp. 169–178 (2009)
20. Goldreich, O., Micali, S., Wigderson, A.: How to play any mental game or a completeness theorem for protocols with honest majority. In: STOC, pp. 218–229 (1987)
21. Ishai, Y., Ostrovsky, R., Seyalioglu, H.: Identifying Cheaters without an Honest Majority. In: Cramer, R. (ed.) TCC 2012. LNCS, vol. 7194, pp. 21–38. Springer, Heidelberg (2012)
22. Ishai, Y., Prabhakaran, M., Sahai, A.: Founding Cryptography on Oblivious Transfer – Efficiently. In: Wagner, D. (ed.) CRYPTO 2008. LNCS, vol. 5157, pp. 572–591. Springer, Heidelberg (2008)
23. Kaplan, E., Naor, M., Reingold, O.: Derandomized constructions of k-wise (almost) independent permutations, vol. 55, pp. 113–133 (2009)
24. Kilian, J.: Founding cryptography on oblivious transfer. In: STOC, pp. 20–31 (1988)
25. Kuperberg, G., Lovett, S., Peled, R.: Probabilistic existence of rigid combinatorial structures, pp. 1091–1106 (2012)
26. Naor, M., Pinkas, B.: Efficient oblivious transfer protocols. In: SODA, pp. 448–457 (2001)
27. Nielsen, J.B., Nordholt, P.S., Orlandi, C., Burra, S.S.: A New Approach to Practical Active-Secure Two-Party Computation. In: Safavi-Naini, R., Canetti, R. (eds.) CRYPTO 2012. LNCS, vol. 7417, pp. 681–700. Springer, Heidelberg (2012)
28. Patra, A., Choudhary, A., Rangan, C.P.: Round Efficient Unconditionally Secure MPC and Multiparty Set Intersection with Optimal Resilience. In: Roy, B., Sendrier, N. (eds.) INDOCRYPT 2009. LNCS, vol. 5922, pp. 398–417. Springer, Heidelberg (2009)
29. Pfitzmann, B., Waidner, M.: Information-theoretic pseudosignatures and byzantine agreement for $t \geq n/3$. IBM Research Report RZ 2882 (#90830) (1996)
30. Rabin, M.: How to exchange secrets by oblivious transfer. Technical Report TR-81. Harvard Aiken Computation Laboratory (1981)
31. Rivest, R.: Unconditionally secure commitment and oblivious transfer schemes using private channels and a trusted initializer. Manuscript (1999)
32. Tonicelli, R., Dowsley, R., Hanaoka, G., Imai, H., Müller-Quade, J., Otsuka, A., Nascimento, A.C.A.: Information-theoretically secure oblivious polynomial evaluation in the commodity-based model. IACR Cryptology ePrint Archive, 2009: 270 (2009)
33. Winkler, S., Wullschleger, J.: On the Efficiency of Classical and Quantum Oblivious Transfer Reductions. In: Rabin, T. (ed.) CRYPTO 2010. LNCS, vol. 6223, pp. 707–723. Springer, Heidelberg (2010)
34. Yao, A.C.-C.: How to generate and exchange secrets, pp. 162–167 (1986)
35. Yao, A.C.-C.: Protocols for secure computations (extended abstract). In: FOCS, pp. 160–164 (1982)

A   Protocols for Specific Tasks

In this section, we present protocols for a number of specific sender-receiver tasks. We focus on the case of perfect security in the malicious model. All of these protocols have a 2-move structure: the receiver sends a message m_X, the sender replies with a message m_Y, and the receiver computes its output. Due to space limitations the proofs are deferred to the full version.

A.1 Set Intersection

Functionality:
- R has input x consisting of k distinct elements $x_1, \ldots, x_k \in U$; S has input y consisting of l distinct elements $y_1, \ldots, y_l \in U$;
- R learns the intersection $z = x \cap y$.

Preprocessing:
1. Pick a random permutation $P : U \to U$ and k distinct elements $r_1, \ldots, r_k \in_R U$;
2. S gets P and R gets $r_1, \ldots, r_k$ and $s_1 = P(r_1), \ldots, s_k = P(r_k)$;

Protocol:
1. R picks a random permutation $Q : U \to U$, under the constraint that $Q(x_i) = r_i$, for all $i \in [k]$. It sends Q to S;
2. S computes $\mathcal{M} = \{P(Q(y_j)) \mid j \in [l]\}$. It sends $\mathcal{M}$ (size-l sorted set) to R;
3. R outputs a set $\mathcal{I}$ consisting of all i such that $s_i \in \mathcal{M}$;

Fig. 5. Protocol for Set Intersection

In Figure 5, we present a protocol for computing the intersection of two sets x, y of fixed sizes (k, l, respectively) over some domain U.

Theorem 7. *The protocol in Figure 5 realizes the sender-receiver functionality set intersection with perfect security.*

Optimizing the protocol In the above protocol, both the randomness and the first message have size $O(|U| \log |U|)$ (the space it takes to describe a permutation). This may be super-exponential in the input size. Like for the equality protocol, we can optimize by taking advantage of k-wise independent families of permutations, as these may have smaller descriptions (the existence of small permutation families with this property was recently proven in [25], but this is only an existential result. Instead we can use the efficient explicit constructions of [23] but achieve only statistical security).

A.2 Inner Product

Let $\mathbb{F}_p$ be a finite field of size p, and let $t \geq 1$. The inner product functionality $\mathrm{IP}_{t,p}$ is as follows:

- S has input $y \in \mathbb{F}_p^t$ and R has a linear function $x : \mathbb{F}_p^t \to \mathbb{F}_p$, represented by a vector $x \in \mathbb{F}_p^t$, so that $x(y) = \langle x, y \rangle = \sum_{i \leq t} x_i y_i$.
- R outputs $x(y)$.

Some Algebraic Preliminaries. Let $e_i \in \mathbb{F}^t$ be the i-th unit vector of length t. Let $\mathbb{F}^*$ be the multiplicative group of a finite field $\mathbb{F}$. By default, vectors are column vectors. $\mathbb{F}^{m \times n}$ is the set of $m \times n$ matrices over $\mathbb{F}$. Let $GL(n, p)$ be the group (under matrix multiplication) of invertible matrices in $\mathbb{F}_p^{n \times n}$. M_i is the i'th row of a matrix M. Given vectors $v_1, \ldots, v_n \in \mathbb{F}^m$, let $(v_1; \ldots; v_n)$ denote the matrix $M \in \mathbb{F}^{n \times m}$ with rows $M_i = v_i^T$. We will also need the following algebraic primitive:

Definition 2 (Good exhaustive operator). *Let $L : \mathbb{F}_p^{\ t} \to \mathbb{F}_p^{\ t}$ be the linear, injective operator defined via $L(y) = y^T L$ (L represents both the operator and the matrix implementing it). Consider the (infinite) sequence $\mathrm{seq}_L = (v, L(v), \ldots, L^{(i)}(v), \ldots)$ generated by L for some v.*

We say that L is a g.e.o. for $v \in \mathbb{F}_p^{\ t}$ if:

1. *seq_L is periodic with period length $p^t - 1$ for v (i.e., all elements in $\mathbb{F}_p^t$, except 0, appear in seq_L).*
2. *The the first t elements in seq_L forms a basis for $\mathbb{F}_p^{\ t}$.*

Lemma 1 (instantiating good exhaustive operators). *Consider the operator L_x where $L_x(y) = x \cdot y$ where x, y are viewed as elements of $\mathbb{F}_{p^t}$ (the multiplication is over $\mathbb{F}_{p^t}$). Viewed as a linear function from $\mathbb{F}_p^{\ t}$ to $\mathbb{F}_p^{\ t}$, we have $L_x(y) = y^T L_x$. Let g be a generator of $\mathbb{F}_{p^t}^*$, then L_g is a g.e.o. for $v = e_t$ (could use any other vector v).*

Functionality:
  - Inputs: R gets $x \neq 0 \in \mathbb{F}_p^t$, and S gets $y \in \mathbb{F}_p^t$.
  - Output: R outputs $\langle x, y \rangle$.

Primitives: Let $L \in \mathbb{F}_p^{\ t \times t}$ be a *g.e.o.* for e_t. For $a \in \mathbb{F}_p^t \setminus \{0\}$, we let $ind(a)$ denote the index of the first appearance of a in seq_L.

Preprocessing:
  1. S gets a random vector $r_2 = y' \in \mathbb{F}_p^t$.
  2. R gets (x', p_2), where x' is randomly chosen at $\mathbb{F}_p^t \setminus \{0\}$ and $p_2 = \langle y', x' \rangle$.

Protocol:
  1. R sends $\delta = ind(x') - ind(x) \pmod{p^t - 1}$ to S.
  2. S sends the vector $m = (e_t^T L^0 (y + L^\delta y'), e_t^T L(y + L^\delta y'), \ldots, e_t^T L^{t-1}(y + L^\delta y'))$.
  3. R sets $M = (e_t^T; e_t^T L; \ldots; e_t^T L^{t-1})$, $r = x^T M^{-1}$. It outputs $rm - p_2$.

Fig. 6. A protocol for IP$+_{t,p}$

The Protocol. In Figure 6, we present a protocol for a slightly modified functionality, IP$+_{t,p}$, where x is restricted to be non-zero. This also implies a protocol for IP$_{t,p}$, as on input $x = 0$ the receiver can adopt any input $x' \neq 0$, and output 0 at the end, ignoring the communication.

Theorem 8. *The above protocol is a perfectly secure protocol, with preprocessing, for the functionality $IP+_{t,p}$, for all $t \geq 1$ and prime p. The communication complexity, randomness size and S's work are polynomial in $|x| = t \log p$, while R's computation is as hard as finding discrete log in $\mathbb{F}_{p^t}^*$.*

B   "Teasers" from the Full Version

The full version of this article contains several other results. Due to space limitation, we can only state the theorems here and invite the interested reader to look at the full version for further discussion, proofs and applications of the following theorems.

Theorem 9. *Every protocol with preprocessing Π that ϵ-securely computes the functionality $f(x_1, x_2) = (x_1 \oplus x_2, x_1 \oplus x_2)$ with abort, has communication complexity $\Omega(\log \frac{1}{\epsilon})$.*

Theorem 10. *Let $f(x_1, x_2) = (x_1 \oplus x_2, x_1 \oplus x_2)$. Then there is no protocol for f in the preprocessing model which is perfectly secure with abort, having expected communication complexity t, for any $t \in \mathbb{N}$.*

Theorem 11. *Given a perfectly secure protocol for some sender-receiver functionality $f : X \times Y \to Z$ in the semi-honest model, with sender message domain M_Y, and receiver message domain M_X. Then,*

- *If for all $y_1 \neq y_2 \in Y$, there exists $x \in X$ such that $f(x, y_1) \neq f(x, y_2)$, then $|M_Y| \geq |Y|$.*
- *If for every $z_1, z_2 \in Z$ and $x_1 \neq x_2 \in X$, we have $\{y | f(x_1, y) = z_1\} \neq \{y | f(x_2, y) = z_2\}$, then $|M_X| \geq |X|$.*

Theorem 12. *Let $c > 0$ be a constant, and consider a sender-receiver functionality $f : X \times Y \to \{0, 1\}$ where $\log |X| = n$, $\log |Y| = m$. Assume there exists a subset $X' \subseteq X$ of size $c \cdot m$, such that $\{(x', f(x', I_Y))\}_{x' \in X}$ determines I_Y, for all $I_Y \in Y$). Then, there exists $\epsilon > 0$, depending only on c, such that in any ϵ-secure protocol with preprocessing for f in the semi-honest model, the sender-side communication is $\Omega(m)$.*

Theorem 13. *Let $c_1, c_2, c_3 > 0$ be constants such that $(1 + c_3)(1 - c_2) < 1$. Consider a sender-receiver functionality $f : X \times Y \to \{0, 1\}$ where $\log |X| = n$, $\log |Y| = m$ satisfying*

- *For all $x \neq x' \in X$, we have $H(f(x', I_Y) | f(x, I_Y)) \geq c_1$, where I_Y is picked uniformly from Y.*
- *For all $y \neq y' \in Y$, we have $\Pr(f(I_X, y) = f(I_X, y')) \geq c_2$, where I_X is picked uniformly at random.*
- *There exists a subset $Y' \subseteq Y$ of size $(1 + c_3)n$, such that $\{y, f(I_X, y)\}_{y \in Y}$ determines I_X, for all $I_X \in X$).*

Then, there exists $\epsilon > 0$, depending only on the c_i's, such that in any ϵ-secure protocol with preprocessing for f, in the semi-honest model, the receiver-side communication is $\Omega(n)$.

Theorem 14. *Suppose there is a semi-honest statistically secure protocol in the preprocessing model for every sender-receiver functionality $f : \{0,1\}^n \times \{0,1\}^n \to \{0,1\}$ with correlated randomness complexity $r(n)$ (i.e., where $r_X, r_Y \in \{0,1\}^{r(n)}$) and communication complexity $c(n)$. Then, there is a 3-server statistical PIR protocol with communication complexity $O(r(\log N) + c(\log N) + \log N)$, where N is the database size.*

Theorem 15. *If $NP \not\subseteq BPP$, there exists a sender-receiver functionality that cannot be efficiently computed with semi-honest security and perfect correctness (even in the preprocessing model).*

Constant-Overhead Secure Computation of Boolean Circuits using Preprocessing

Ivan Damgård and Sarah Zakarias*

Dept. of Computer Science, Aarhus University

Abstract. We present a protocol for securely computing a Boolean circuit C in presence of a dishonest and malicious majority. The protocol is unconditionally secure, assuming a preprocessing functionality that is not given the inputs. For a large number of players the work for each player is the same as computing the circuit in the clear, up to a constant factor. Our protocol is the first to obtain these properties for Boolean circuits. On the technical side, we develop new homomorphic authentication schemes based on asymptotically good codes with an additional multiplication property. We also show a new algorithm for verifying the product of Boolean matrices in quadratic time with exponentially small error probability, where previous methods only achieved constant error.

1 Introduction

In multiparty computation, a set of players each holding a private input wish to compute an agreed function such that the intended result is the only new information that is revealed. This must hold also if some subset of the players are corrupted by an adversary. Even in the most difficult case where all but one player can be corrupt (aka. dishonest majority), it is known that any efficiently computable function can be computed securely, under appropriate complexity assumptions [CLOS02], also when asking for universal composable security [Can01]. This leads naturally to the question of what the price of security is, i.e., how much extra resources must we invest to compute the function securely, as opposed to just computing it?

The case of dishonest majority can be handled by different approaches. It is well known that using fully homomorphic encryption, the communication complexity can be made very small, and only needs to depend on the number of inputs and outputs of the function. Although the computational overhead is usually very large, for some cryptosystems even this can be made small, in fact poly-logarithmic in the security parameter, see [GHS12]. However, the exponent hidden in the poly-logarithmic notation is quite large because the approach requires so-called bootstrapping and currently does not yield practical

---

* The authors acknowledge support from the Danish National Research Foundation and The National Science Foundation of China (under the grant 61061130540) for the Sino-Danish Center for the Theory of Interactive Computation, within which part of this work was performed; and also from the CFEM research center (supported by the Danish Strategic Research Council) within which part of this work was performed.

A. Sahai (Ed.): TCC 2013, LNCS 7785, pp. 621–641, 2013.

protocols. The overhead can also be made small using "MPC-in-the-head" techniques [IKOS08], at least for a constant number of parties, but still using (somewhat non-standard) computational assumptions. Furthermore in these cases, only computational security can be obtained.

On the other hand, if we allow a preprocessing phase where the inputs to the function need not be known, then unconditional, active security can be obtained, and complexity can be reduced to a point where we get eminently practical protocols. This was first demonstrated by Bendlin et al. [BDOZ11], who showed that given a preprocessing functionality, an arithmetic circuit over a large field $\mathbb{F}_q$ can be computed with unconditional security and very efficiently: if the number of players is constant and $\log q \in \Omega(\kappa)$, where κ is the security parameter, then the total computational work invested by each player is a constant times the work one needs to compute the same circuit in the clear. More recently, Damgård et al.[DPSZ12] improved this result by showing the same for *any* number of players. In both cases, preprocessing works independently of the inputs, and simply produces 'raw material' for the computation phase. The preprocessing can be implemented by a general MPC protocol which can be run any time prior to the computation. However, [BDOZ11, DPSZ12] show particularly efficient preprocessing protocols based on public-key cryptosystems with special properties.

In this paper we are interested in computing *Boolean* circuits securely given preprocessing. Here, the techniques from the online phases of [BDOZ11] and [DPSZ12] also work, in particular Nielsen et al.[NNOB12] use the approach from [BDOZ11] for Boolean circuits. However, some efficiency is lost: for every AND-gate in the circuit, each player must do $\Omega(\kappa)$ bit operations, resulting in a computational overhead that is at least linear in κ. Getting constant overhead also for small fields was left as an open problem in [DPSZ12].

To be more precise about the cost of these protocols, we define three different types of overhead: the *data-overhead* is the total number of bits players must store from the preprocessing divided by $N \cdot |C|$, where $|C|$ is the size of the circuit to compute. The *communication-overhead* and the *computation-overhead* is the communication complexity and the computational complexity respectively (in bit operations) of the protocol divided by $N \cdot |C|$. For some protocols, these overheads turn out to be the same up to constant factors, and in such a case, we just speak of the overhead of the protocol. In a nutshell, the overhead represents the amount of resource each player needs to invest per gate in the circuit.

In this terminology, the protocol in [NNOB12] has overhead $\Omega(\kappa)$. It is nevertheless practical and has been implemented with promising results. On the other hand, Damgård et al. [DIK10] show that based on the "MPC in the head" technique one can obtain a protocol with overhead essentially $\log(|C|)polylog(\kappa)$. This is based on preprocessing of a large number of oblivious transfers and using them to convert a multiparty protocol for honest majority into a two-party protocol. The constants involved here are very large, however, and the protocol is in fact not practical. Both these protocols are for the two-party case. The one from [DIK10] generalizes to several players but then the overhead would be $\Omega(N \log(|C|)polylog(\kappa))$.

Before presenting our results, we consider how small overheads we can hope for. Here it is useful to distinguish between two cases: either the preprocessing is useful for computing any circuit, we call this *universal preprocessing* – or the preprocessing knows the circuit (but not the inputs) and only has to generate data for computing this circuit. We call this *dedicated preprocessing*.

In [DPSZ12] some lower bounds are shown for universal preprocessing, saying that data and computational overheads must be at least constant. For dedicated preprocessing, one can note that preprocessing targeted against a universal circuit is essentially universal preprocessing. Hence by the known bound, the data overhead cannot be sub-constant for all circuits even in the dedicated case. Moreover, it would be surprising if the computational overhead could be sub-constant, even for dedicated preprocessing. In such a case, each player would have to do substantially less work than it takes to compute the circuit in the clear. Since a single player has to rely on the work of other (corrupt) players, all players must prove correctness of their part. This should then be possible in complexity much smaller than the clear computation and with unconditional privacy and correctness for all parties. This is not something we know how to do, even with preprocessing.

Finally, for communication overhead, it follows from results in [IKM+13] that we only need communication linear in the size of the inputs, but this comes at the cost that the data overhead is exponential in the input size. Evidence is given in [IKM+13] that getting small communication *and* data overhead would lead to a major breakthrough in private information retrieval.

In conclusion, the results and evidence we know suggest that getting constant overhead is the goal we can realistically hope to achieve.

1.1   Our Contribution

In this paper we show a multiparty computation protocol in the preprocessing model, for computing Boolean circuits securely. It is information theoretically secure against an active adversary corrupting up to $N - 1$ players. We assume synchronous communication and secure point-to-point channels.

We focus on circuits that are not too "oddly shaped". Concretely, we assume that every layer of the circuit is $\Omega(\kappa)$ gates wide, where κ is the security parameter (except perhaps for a constant number of layers). Second, we want that the number of bits that are output from layer i in the circuit and used in layer j is either 0 or $\Omega(\kappa)$ for all $i < j$ (where again a constant number of exceptions are allowed). We call such circuits *well-formed*. In a nutshell, well-formed circuit are those that allow a modest amount of parallelization, namely a program computing the circuit can always execute $\Omega(\kappa)$ bit operations in parallel and when storing bits for later use or retrieving, it can always access $\Omega(\kappa)$ bits at a time.

Since our protocol has error probability $2^{-\kappa}$ and is unconditionally secure, the value of κ can be quite small, e.g., 80 and would not be affected by future advances in cryptanalysis. From a practical point of view one may therefore think of κ as being very small compared the the circuit size, and hence the requirement that the circuit be well-formed seems rather modest. We stress that our protocols work for arbitrary circuits, but the claims we can make on the overhead will be weaker.

Throughout, we think of the circuit size as being also much larger than the number of players. Our statements on overheads below therefore ignore additive terms that are $O(\kappa N/|C|)$.

Our protocols are based on families of codes with some specific nice properties that we explain in more detail below. The simplest construction follows from Reed-Solomon codes and from this we get:

Theorem 1. *There exists an N-party protocol for computing securely a well-formed Boolean circuit C in the dedicated preprocessing model, statistically secure against $N - 1$ active corruptions. For error probability $2^{-\kappa}$, the overhead is $O(polylog(\kappa))$, where κ is the security parameter.*

There also exists an N-party protocol for computing securely a well-formed Boolean circuit C in the universal preprocessing model, statistically secure against $N - 1$ active corruptions. For error probability $2^{-\kappa}$, the overhead is $O(\log(|C|) \cdot polylog(\kappa))$.

The second result applies a technique from [DIK10] to restructure C into a new circuit that has a more regular structure, but still computes the same function. The result from [DIK10] leads in general to circuits that have size $O(\log(|C|)|C| + d^2\kappa \log |C|)$, where d is the depth of C. However, in case of well-formed circuits the term depending on d disappears.

In comparison, the protocol one can construct from [DIK10] would have a larger overhead, namely $\Omega(\log(|C|) \cdot polylog(\kappa) \cdot N)$ in *both* the universal and dedicated preprocessing model[1]. In comparison to [NNOB12], we clearly do better asymptotically in the dedicated model. But also for concrete efficiency, our method can offer an improvement, particularly for the case where the circuit does a computation that is "born" parallel and hence lends itself easily to block-wise computation. In particular, using Reed-Solomon codes over the $\mathbb{F}_{256}$ and $n = 256$, then for 128 bit security we can obtain almost an 8-fold improvement in data overhead over [NNOB12], see more details in the full version [DZ12].

Using algebraic geometry codes and results on strongly multiplicative secret sharing from [CCX11] we obtain a result that is better than Theorem 1 when the number of players is large.

Theorem 2. *There exists an N-party protocol for computing securely a well-formed Boolean circuit C in the dedicated preprocessing model, statistically secure against $N - 1$ active corruptions. For an error probability of $2^{-\kappa}$, the data and communication overhead are $O(1)$ while the computation-overhead is $O(1 + \frac{\kappa}{N})$, where κ is the security parameter.*

---

[1] The reason why that protocol does not benefit from dedicated preprocessing is that it is based on processing bits in parallel in large blocks, and in between permuting bits inside these blocks. The efficiency, even in the online phase, crucially depends on the fact that only a logarithmic number of different permutations are needed. For this one needs to always transform C to a more regular form, leading to the $\log(|C|)$-factor.

There also exists an N-party protocol for computing securely a well-formed Boolean circuit C in the universal preprocessing model, statistically secure against $N - 1$ active corruptions. For error probability $2^{-\kappa}$, data and communication overheads are $O(\log(|C|))$, while computation overhead is $O(\log(|C|)(1 + \frac{\kappa}{N}))$.

If we are willing to assume that the layers in C are κ^2 gates wide, then we can get computational overhead $O(1 + \frac{\kappa^\epsilon}{N})$, Where ϵ is defined as the smallest value for which multiplication of n by n matrices can be done in time $O(n^{2+\epsilon})$. Based on the best known matrix multiplication algorithms, we can have $\epsilon \approx 0.3727$. It may even be that any $\epsilon > 0$ suffices, but this is an open problem.

Note that none of the overheads we obtain increase with N and in fact most of them do not depend on N. In particular our protocols have constant storage overhead and constant computation overhead for a large enough number of players. They are the first protocols in the preprocessing model for Boolean circuits with this property, and in fact, from the discussion in the introduction, the results seem close to optimal.

Techniques. We use the idea from [DPSZ12] of having the values we compute on be secret-shared among the players, where also a Message Authentication Code (MAC) on this value is secret-shared. Using precomputed values for multiplication, linear operations then suffice for executing the computation.

However, directly usage of the MACs from [DPSZ12] or any other previous construction would not be efficient enough here, since we would have to use values from a large field ($\mathbb{F}_{2^\kappa}$) to authenticate single bits. A naive approach where one groups κ bits together and authenticate them using a single MAC over $\mathbb{F}_{2^\kappa}$ fails: we will need to do bit-wise addition and multiplication on such κ-bit vectors, and since this does not commute with multiplication in $\mathbb{F}_{2^\kappa}$, we lose the homomorphic property of the MACs that is crucial for the protocol.

The key to our results consists of two technical contributions. First, we develop a new authentication scheme based on families of linear codes where each code as well as its so-called Schur-transform have minimum distance and dimension a constant times their length. This scheme has the homomorphic property we need, and is able to authenticate κ-bit vectors using MACs and keys of size $O(\kappa)$. We note that the idea of using small MACs on entries in an error correcting code appeared in a different context in [IKOS08]. However, that application did not use any homomorphic properties of the MACs, or the Schur transform.

The second technique is an efficient method for verifying membership in a linear binary code for a batch of purported codewords. We show how to do this with constant overhead per data bit. The underlying algorithm is of independent interest, as it is actually a general method for verifying multiplication of $\Theta(n)$ by $\Theta(n)$ binary matrices in time $O(n^2)$ with exponentially small error probability. The best previous methods give only constant error probability in the same time.

2   Linear Codes

In the following, we will consider a $[n, k, d]$ linear code C over a field $\mathbb{F} = \mathbb{F}_{2^u}$, i.e., C has length n, dimension k and minimum distance d. We will assume throughout that n, k, d are all $\Theta(\kappa)$, where κ is the security parameter. We will use boldface such as $\boldsymbol{x}$ to denote vectors, and when $\boldsymbol{x}, \boldsymbol{y}$ are vectors of the same length, we let $\boldsymbol{x} * \boldsymbol{y}$ denote the coordinate-wise product of $\boldsymbol{x}$ and $\boldsymbol{y}$.

For a vector $\boldsymbol{x} \in \{0, 1\}^k$, we let $C(\mathbf{x})$ be the encoding of $\boldsymbol{x}$ as a codeword in C. Without loss of generality, we assume throughout that the encoding is *systematic*, so that $\boldsymbol{x}$ itself appears as the first k entries in $C(\mathbf{x})$.

For a linear code C with parameters as above, the *Schur-transform* of C, written C^*, is a linear $[n, k^*, d^*]$-code, defined as the span of the set of vectors $\{\boldsymbol{x} * \boldsymbol{y} |\ \boldsymbol{x}, \boldsymbol{y} \in C\}$. It is easy to see that $k^* \geq k$ and $d^* \leq d$. However, we will assume that d^* is still large, namely $d^* \in \Theta(\kappa)$. This is by no means always the case, but can be obtained if C is properly constructed.

Let $\boldsymbol{x}, \boldsymbol{y}$ be k-bit strings. We define $C^*(\mathbf{x})$ to the set of codewords in C^* where $\boldsymbol{x}$ appears in the first k coordinates. This is indeed a set and not a single codeword: since k^* can be larger than k, $\boldsymbol{x}$ does not necessarily uniquely determine a codeword in C^*. Note that since $C(\mathbf{x}) * C(\mathbf{y}) \in C^*$, and since furthermore $\boldsymbol{x} * \boldsymbol{y}$ appears in the first k coordinates of this codeword, we have

$$C(\mathbf{x}) * C(\mathbf{y}) \in C^*(\mathbf{x} * \mathbf{y})$$

This also shows that $C^*(\mathbf{x})$ is always non-empty, by taking $\boldsymbol{y} = (1, 1, ..., 1)$.

Reed-Solomon Codes. As a first example, we give a simple construction showing that Reed-Solomon type codes have the right properties, if we assume that u is $\Theta(\log \kappa)$. Then we set $n = 3k$, and we may assume that $\mathbb{F}$ has at least n distinct elements $a_1, .., a_n$. Now define C to be the code consisting of vectors of form $(f(a_1), ..., f(a_n))$ where f is a polynomial over F of degree at most $k - 1$. Then C^* will be a code of the same form, but defined using polynomials of degree at most $2(k - 1)$.

It follows immediately from Lagrange interpolation that C and C^* have minimum distances as large as required. Note that we can put C in systematic form also using interpolation: given k field elements to encode, we interpolate a polynomial f such that $f(a_1), ..., f(a_k)$ equal these elements and then evaluate f in the remaining points to complete the codeword. Note also that in this case encoding and verifying membership in the codes is very efficient because it can be done by multiplication by Van der Monde matrices or their inverses. Using well-known algorithms based on the fast Fourier transform, this can be done in time $n \cdot polylog(n)$. In Section 4.1 we cover the complexity of our protocol when using Reed-Solomon codes.

Algebraic Geometry Codes. Using the work of Cascudo et al. [CCX11], one can do even better: based on Algebraic Geometry, they construct families of codes with properties as we require over *constant size fields*. In Section 4.2 we cover the complexity of our protocol when using Algebraic Geometry codes.

3   Authentication Schemes Based on Linear Codes

In this section we present a new authentication scheme that we will need in the following. We will assume that we have a code C as described above, of length n, dimension k and minimum distance d. In its most basic version there is a receiver who knows a key $\alpha \in \mathbb{F}^n$ chosen at random. The value to authenticate is a k-vector x and the message authentication code (MAC) is $m = C(\mathbf{x}) * \alpha$.

Note that we use coordinate-wise multiplication by α, and therefore the scheme is actually doing a standard MAC over the field $\mathbb{F}$ for every coordinate of $C(\mathbf{x})$. Since $\mathbb{F}$ has constant size, this would normally not be good enough since one can forge such a MAC with constant probability $1/|\mathbb{F}|$, namely by guessing the corresponding entry in α. But in our case, the coding saves the day: to forge a MAC, one would need to change to a different codeword and therefore forge not 1, but d MACs. Of course, if both x and m were known, information on α would leak and other MACs might be forged. But in the protocol to follow, m will be unknown to the adversary (since it is secret shared). It therefore turns out that the following basic result on security for these MACs is what we need:

Lemma 1. *Using the above notation, suppose the adversary is given x and then outputs x' and a "MAC-error" Δ. We say the adversary wins if $C(\mathbf{x}') * \alpha = m + \Delta$ and $x \neq x'$. The probability that the adversary wins is at most 2^{-d}.*

Proof. Assuming the adversary wins, we know $C(\mathbf{x}')*\alpha = m+\Delta$ holds. Plugging in $m = C(\mathbf{x}) * \alpha$, we obtain $\alpha * (C(\mathbf{x}) - C(\mathbf{x}')) = \Delta$. Since the adversary wins, $C(\mathbf{x}) - C(\mathbf{x}')$ is a non-zero codeword, so it is non-zero in at least d coordinates. The equation therefore determines α in at least d positions so we see that the adversary must guess at least d coordinates of the key to win.

Next, we consider a different way to use these MACs that turns out to be more efficient when many messages are authenticated. In this variant the scheme will use a single global key α that will be secret shared so it is unknown to the adversary. The MAC on a value x is defined as before as $m = \alpha * C(\mathbf{x})$. In the protocol we make sure to reveal nothing about α nor about any of the MACs until the end of the protocol where it will be too late for corrupted players to forge any values. The way we prove security is thus to design the following security game modeling the way this scheme is used in the protocol.

1. The challenger generates the secret key α and MACs $m_i \leftarrow \alpha * w_i$ and sends the messages $w_1, \ldots, w_T$ to the adversary. Note that here messages are codewords.
2. The adversary sends back messages $w'_1, \ldots, w'_T$.
3. The challenger generates random values $e_1, \ldots, e_T \leftarrow \mathbb{F}^n$ and sends them to the adversary.
4. The adversary provides an error Δ.
5. Set $w \leftarrow \sum_{i=1}^{T} e_i * w'_i, m \leftarrow \sum_{i=1}^{T} e_i * m_i$. Now, the challenger checks that all w'_i's are valid codewords and that $\alpha * w = m + \Delta$.

The adversary wins if there is an i for which $w'_i \neq w_i$ and the final checks pass.

Generating the e's. We will show below that the adversary can only win this game with negligible probability if the e_j's are uniformly random. However implementing such a (trusted) random choice in our protocol turns out to be expensive, so we consider instead a way to choose them pseudorandomly using a smaller number of random bits. What we will require is a way to generate (pseudo) random strings $\mathbf{v} = (v_1, ..., v_T) \in \mathbb{F}^T$ that are *linearly ϵ-biased*. By this we mean that for any fixed non-zero vector $\mathbf{u}$, we have $Pr[\mathbf{u} \cdot \mathbf{v} \neq 0] \geq \epsilon$ for some constant ϵ.

In [NN93], Naor and Naor present a construction (attributed there to Bruck) that does exactly this, based on codes with good properties, namely the same as we use here: both the dimension and the minimum distance of the code are a constant time the length of the code. Let G be the generator matrix of the code, where the rows of G form a basis of the code. Say that G has m columns where m is in $\Theta(T)$, and that the minimum distance of the code is ϵm for a constant ϵ.

Now the idea is to simply let $\mathbf{v}$ be a random column of G. To see why this works, fix any $\mathbf{u}$ and consider two random experiments: 1) compute the codeword $\mathbf{u}G$ and output a random entry from the result. 2) choose a random column $\mathbf{v}$ from G and output $\mathbf{u} \cdot \mathbf{v}$.

The first experiment clearly gives a non-zero result with probability ϵ, but on the other hand, it is equivalent to the second one since the entries in $\mathbf{u}G$ are the inner products of $\mathbf{u}$ with each column in G. We therefore get $Pr(\mathbf{u} \cdot \mathbf{v} \neq 0) \geq \epsilon$ as desired. To connect this to the above security game, let $\mathbf{e}_i = (e_i^1, ..., e_i^n)$ and define $\mathbf{e}^j := (e_1^j, \ldots, e_T^j)$. We can now choose the $\mathbf{e}^j$'s to be linearly ϵ-biased instead of choosing them at random. Note that for this we need a seed consisting of $\log m \in O(\log T)$ random bits for each $\mathbf{e}^j$, i.e, a total of $O(n \log T)$ random bits. We then have the following:

Lemma 2. *The adversary wins the above security game with probability at most $2^{-\Theta(n)}$. This holds, even if the $\mathbf{e}^j$ are not random but only linearly ϵ-biased.*

Proof. Let us start by assuming that the $\mathbf{e}_i$'s are completely random and look at the adversary's probability of winning. If the checks hold then we have the following equality $\boldsymbol{\alpha} * \sum_{i=1}^{T} \mathbf{e}_i * \mathbf{v}_i = \Delta$ where $\mathbf{v}_i := \mathbf{w}_i' - \mathbf{w}_i$ for $i = 1, \ldots, T$ are codewords and there exists at least one j for which $\mathbf{v}_j \neq \mathbf{0}$. Note that since $\mathbf{v}_j$ is a codeword it contains at least d entries that are 1.

Consider the sum $\sum_{i=1}^{T} \mathbf{e}_i * \mathbf{v}_i$. Let v_i^j be the j'th entry in $\mathbf{v}_i$, then we define $\mathbf{v}^j := (v_1^j, \ldots, v_T^j)$. Finally we define the function $f_{\mathbf{v}^j}(\mathbf{e}^j) := \sum_{i=1}^{T} e_i^j v_i^j$ which is a linear mapping, that is not the $\mathbf{0}$-mapping for at least d number of j's since at least one $\mathbf{v}_i \neq \mathbf{0}$ and hence has at least d entries which are nonzero. From linear algebra we then have the rank-nullity theorem telling us that $\dim(\ker(f_{\mathbf{v}^j})) = T - 1$. Furthermore, since $\mathbf{e}^j$ is random and the adversary does not know $\mathbf{e}^j$ when choosing the $\mathbf{w}_i'$'s, the probability of $\mathbf{e}^j \in \ker(f_{\mathbf{v}^j})$ is $|\mathbb{F}^{T-1}|/|\mathbb{F}^T| = 1/|\mathbb{F}| \leq 1/2$. In the following we assume for simplicity the worst case $|\mathbb{F}| = 2$. So we expect $d/2$ of the $f_{\mathbf{v}^j}(\mathbf{e}^j)$'s in question to be 1. We can use Hoeffding's inequality [Hoe63] to bound the probability that we are far from the expectation: define random variables $X_1, ..., X_d$ that take the value of the d non-trivial instances of

$f_{v^j}(e^j)$ when e^j is chosen at random. We can view the values as the result of d independent experiments where the expected value $E[X_i]$ is $1/2$. Then from Hoeffding's inequality we get that $\Pr[|\frac{\sum X_i}{d} - 1/2| \geq t] \leq e^{-2t^2 d}$, for any $t > 0$. This shows that except with exponentially small probability (as a function of d) we can guarantee to deviate with at most a small constant fraction, that is, we can guarantee at least $d/2 - td = cd$ number of nonzero entries in $\sum_{i=1}^{T} e_i * v_i$ for any $c < 1/2$.

Assume we have this many non-zero entries. Then going back to the equality $\alpha * \sum_{i=1}^{T} e_i * v_i = \Delta$, this implies that satisfying it is equivalent to guessing at least cd entries of α. However, since the adversary has no information about α, guessing can be done with probability at most 2^{-cd}. It follows that the probability the adversary wins is at most the probability that $\sum_{i=1}^{T} e_i * v_i$ has less than cd non-zero entries, plus 2^{-cd}. This is exponentially small in d and hence also in n since d is assumed to be $\Theta(n)$.

If the e_i's are instead chosen such that the e^j's are pseudorandom but independent and linearly ϵ-biased, then we can show the same result using a similar argument. The only difference will be that we expect to see at least ϵd non-zero entries in $\sum_{i=1}^{T} e_i * v_i$. By independence we can still use Hoeffding to guarantee we are close to this number of non-zero entries, and the adversary will now have to guess ϵd entries of α.

Note that the above security game and lemma work exactly the same way if we replace the code C by C^*, since we have assumed that the minimum distance of C^* is also $\Theta(n)$. We may even have codewords from both C and C^* in the game, as long as it is agreed in advance which words are supposed to be in C and C^* respectively. This is because the proof only depends on the fact that the non-zero vector v_j we construct has $\Theta(n)$ non-zero coordinates.

4   Protocol for Secure Computation

We are now ready to present our protocol. In structure it is much like the online protocol from [DPSZ12], but with the big difference that we are working with blocks of bits and doing parallel block-wise operations. Therefore, our protocol has an extra operation: Between two layers in the circuit we need to be able to reorganize the output bits so that they match up with the gates where they should be input. Here we assume a dedicated preprocessing phase where we know the circuit to be computed so we will know exactly how we need to move the bits around. However, as mentioned earlier, we will also show a solution which is general, i.e. it does not depend on a preprocessing where the circuit is known.

We assume synchronous communication and secure point-to-point channels. We also assume for simplicity that broadcast is available at unit cost. This assumption can be removed without affecting the complexity using a method from [DPSZ12] which also works for our protocol since it has a similar structure. Also for simplicity we assume there is only one input from each player and one public output. It is straightforward to remove these restrictions without affecting the complexity.

Representation of Values. Values in our computation will be bits which are grouped in vectors of length k, i.e. we have $\boldsymbol{x} \in \mathbb{F}^k$ so that we will be doing parallel operations on blocks of k bits. Each value will be secret shared among the players along with a MAC on the value. More concretely, player i will hold the encoding of a share $C(\boldsymbol{x}_i)$, where C is a linear code as described in the previous sections. There is also a public codeword $\boldsymbol{d}_{\boldsymbol{x}} = C(\boldsymbol{v})$ such that $\boldsymbol{x} = \boldsymbol{x}_1 + \cdots + \boldsymbol{x}_N + \boldsymbol{v}$. Moreover, the MAC $\boldsymbol{m}(\boldsymbol{x}) = \boldsymbol{\alpha} * C(\mathbf{x})$ will also be additively shared such that player i holds $\boldsymbol{m}(\boldsymbol{x})_i$. This MAC is based on C and computed using a global key $\boldsymbol{\alpha}$. The public codeword $\boldsymbol{d}_{\boldsymbol{x}}$ is necessary to easily add public values to our representation. Summing up we have the following representation for a shared value $\boldsymbol{x}$

$$\langle \boldsymbol{x} \rangle := \Big(\boldsymbol{d}_{\boldsymbol{x}}, \big(C(\boldsymbol{x}_1), \dots, C(\boldsymbol{x}_N) \big), \big(\boldsymbol{m}(\boldsymbol{x})_1, \dots, \boldsymbol{m}(\boldsymbol{x})_N \big) \Big).$$

Note that while the additive shares that represent $\boldsymbol{x}$ are codewords, the shares of the MAC are taken from the entire space $\mathbb{F}^n$. This is necessary as the MAC itself is not in general a codeword.

We will also need to work with another kind of representation, denoted $\langle \cdot \rangle^*$, which is exactly like the $\langle \cdot \rangle$-representation except that in $\langle \boldsymbol{x} \rangle^*$, the additive shares representing $\boldsymbol{x}$ are taken from C^* and add up to a codeword in $C^*(\boldsymbol{x})$. The MAC is still shared with shares from $\mathbb{F}^n$, but its security is now based on the minimum distance of C^*. The $\langle \cdot \rangle^*$-representation comes up when we multiply a $\langle \cdot \rangle$-representation with a public constant.

It is straight forward with $\langle \cdot \rangle$ to do linear operations. For adding two representations, and multiplying a public constant $\boldsymbol{u}$ encoded in $C(\boldsymbol{u})$ we simply compute component-wise. For adding the public constant we modify the first share and the public codeword. We write as follows:

$$\langle \boldsymbol{x} \rangle + \langle \boldsymbol{y} \rangle = \Big(\boldsymbol{d}_{\boldsymbol{x}} + \boldsymbol{d}_{\boldsymbol{y}}, \big(C(\boldsymbol{x}_1) + C(\boldsymbol{y}_1), \dots \big), \big(\boldsymbol{m}(\boldsymbol{x})_1 + \boldsymbol{m}(\boldsymbol{y})_1, \dots \big) \Big)$$
$$= \langle \boldsymbol{x} + \boldsymbol{y} \rangle .$$
$$C(\boldsymbol{u}) * \langle \boldsymbol{x} \rangle = \Big(C(\boldsymbol{u}) * \boldsymbol{d}_{\boldsymbol{x}}, \big(C(\boldsymbol{u}) * C(\boldsymbol{x}_1), \dots \big), \big(C(\boldsymbol{u}) * \boldsymbol{m}(\boldsymbol{x})_1, \dots \big) \Big)$$
$$= \langle \boldsymbol{u} + \boldsymbol{x} \rangle^* .$$
$$C(\boldsymbol{u}) + \langle \boldsymbol{x} \rangle = \Big(\boldsymbol{d}_{\boldsymbol{x}} - C(\boldsymbol{u}), \big(C(\boldsymbol{x}_1) + C(\boldsymbol{u}), \dots C(\boldsymbol{x}_N) \big), \big(\boldsymbol{m}(\boldsymbol{x})_1, \dots, \boldsymbol{m}(\boldsymbol{x})_N \big) \Big)$$
$$= \langle \boldsymbol{u} + \boldsymbol{x} \rangle .$$

With $\langle \cdot \rangle^*$ we cannot do multiplications since multiplying two codewords in C^* is not guaranteed to give a result in C^*. We solve this in the protocol, by converting $\langle \cdot \rangle^*$ back into a $\langle \cdot \rangle$-representation immediately after a multiplication. We convert $\langle \boldsymbol{w} \rangle^*$ into $\langle \boldsymbol{w} \rangle$ by taking a pair of random values ($\langle \boldsymbol{s} \rangle^*, \langle \boldsymbol{s} \rangle$) and open $\langle \boldsymbol{w} \rangle^* - \langle \boldsymbol{s} \rangle^*$ to get $\boldsymbol{\sigma}^* \in C^*(\boldsymbol{w} - \boldsymbol{s})$. From $\boldsymbol{\sigma}^*$, $\boldsymbol{w} - \boldsymbol{s}$ can be read on the first k coordinates. A single player, say P_1 then computes $\boldsymbol{\sigma} = C(\boldsymbol{w} - \boldsymbol{s})$ and broadcasts $\boldsymbol{\sigma}$. The rest of the players check that $\boldsymbol{\sigma}^*$ and $\boldsymbol{\sigma}^*$ are valid codewords encoding the same value and compute $\langle \boldsymbol{w} \rangle = \boldsymbol{\sigma} + \langle \boldsymbol{s} \rangle$.

To compute the mutiplication $\langle x \rangle * \langle y \rangle$ we need to use the preprocessing which will output random triples $\langle a \rangle, \langle b \rangle, \langle c \rangle^*$, where $c = a * b$. Given such a triple, we can do multiplication in the following standard way: To compute $\langle x * y \rangle$ we first open $\langle x \rangle - \langle a \rangle$ to get $\epsilon = C(x - a)$, and $\langle y \rangle - \langle b \rangle$ to get $\delta = C(y - b)$. Then, since $x * y = (a + (x - a)) * (b + (y - b)) = c + (x - a) * b + (y - b) * a + (x - a) * (y - b)$, a new representation of $x * y$ can be computed as

$$\langle x \rangle * \langle y \rangle = \langle c \rangle^* + \epsilon * \langle b \rangle + \delta * \langle a \rangle + \epsilon * \delta = \langle x * y \rangle^*.$$

A final operation we need is reorganizing of bits between layers s.t. the output bits become input bits to the intended gates. This may involve permuting bits, duplicating bits and/or leaving out some bits. Clearly this reorganizing can be expressed as a linear function F that takes as input all the output bits of a given layer, which in our representation will be a vector of blocks of bits $B = (b_1, \ldots, b_l)$. The output of F is a new vector of blocks $F(B) = B' = (b'_1, \ldots, b'_{l'})$. For this purpose we extend our notation of $\langle \cdot \rangle$ to also include a vector of blocks instead of only one single block. We will write this as $\langle B \rangle := \langle b_1 \rangle, \ldots, \langle b_l \rangle$. In general we will have that capital letters in $\langle \cdot \rangle$ denotes a vector of blocks. With this representation we still maintain the linear properties, simply by doing the operations coordinate-wise, i.e. $\langle A \rangle + \langle B \rangle := \langle a_1 \rangle + \langle b_1 \rangle, \ldots, \langle a_l \rangle + \langle b_l \rangle$ and so on. This means that we can compute $F(\langle B \rangle)$ and obtain $\langle F(B) \rangle$ for any linear function F. If we assume that we know in advance the circuit to be computed, then we also know exactly which reorganizing functions we need between the circuit layers. Thus, for each needed reorganizing function F, we will preprocess pairs of representations $\langle R \rangle, \langle F(R) \rangle$, where R is random and of appropriate length. As shown later, these pairs will then be used in the protocol to reorganize the actual bits.

An important note is that during our protocol we are actually not guaranteed that we are working with the correct results, since we do not immediately check the MACs of the opened values. During the first part of the protocol, parties only do what we define as a *partial opening*, meaning that each party P_i sends his share $C(a_i)$ to one chosen party, say P_1. Then, P_1 computes and broadcasts $C(a)$ and the other parties verify that $C(a)$ is a valid codeword. We assume here for simplicity that we always go via P_1, whereas in practice, one would balance the workload over the players.

The checking is postponed to the end of the protocol in the output phase. To check the MACs the global key α is needed. This key is provided by the preprocessing but in a slightly different representation:

$$[\alpha] := \left(\left(C(\alpha_1), \ldots, C(\alpha_N) \right), \left(\beta_i, m(\alpha)^i_1, \ldots, m(\alpha)^i_N \right)_{i=1,\ldots N} \right),$$

where $\alpha = \sum_{i=1}^N \alpha_i$ and $\sum_{j=1}^N m(\alpha)^j_i = C(\alpha) * \beta_i$. Player P_i holds $C(\alpha_i), \beta_i$, $m(\alpha)^i_1, \ldots, m(\alpha)^i_N$. The idea is that $m(\alpha)_i \leftarrow \sum_{j=1}^N m(\alpha)^j_i$ is the MAC authenticating α under P_i's private key β_i. To open $[\alpha]$, each P_j sends to each P_i his share $C(\alpha_j)$ of α and his share $m(\alpha)^j_i$ of the MAC on α made with P_i's private key and then P_i checks that $\sum_{j=1}^N m(\alpha)^j_i = C(\alpha) * \beta_i$. (To open the value to only one party P_i, the other parties will simply send shares only to P_i, who will do the checking.)

The protocol assumes access to a commitment functionality $\mathcal{F}_{\text{COM}}$ for commitments. A player commits by calling it with a secret value s as input. The functionality stores the value until the committer calls open, in which case the value is revealed to all players. This can be implemented based only on $\mathcal{F}_{\text{PREP}}$: We open a random $[\![r]\!]$ only to the committer, who then broadcasts $r + s$. When opening, we open $[\![r]\!]$ to all players so s can be computed.

The Protocol. We assume an ideal preprocessing functionality[2] $\mathcal{F}_{\text{PREP}}$, shown in Figure 6. Given $\mathcal{F}_{\text{PREP}}$ and the techniques described earlier we can construct a protocol that securely implements the ideal functionality in Figure 4. The protocol is presented in Figure 1 where we for brevity drop explicit mentioning of variable identifiers. We assume here that the circuit to be computed is structured such that there is only one type of gate per layer. This can be done without loss of generality since any function to be computed can be expressed by NAND-gates only, which then can be expressed by AND and XOR which are the operations we support. We can now state the theorem on security of the online protocol.

Theorem 3. *In the $\mathcal{F}_{\text{PREP}}, \mathcal{F}_{\text{COM}}$-hybrid model, the protocol Π_{MPC} implements $\mathcal{F}_{\text{MPC}}$ with statistical security against any static active adversary corrupting up to $N - 1$ parties.*

Proof (Theorem 3).

We construct a simulator $\mathcal{S}_{\text{MPC}}$ such that a poly-time environment $\mathcal{Z}$ cannot distinguish between the real protocol system $\mathcal{F}_{\text{PREP}}, \mathcal{F}_{\text{COM}}$ composed with Π_{MPC} and $\mathcal{F}_{\text{MPC}}$ composed with $\mathcal{S}_{\text{MPC}}$. We assume static, active corruption. The simulator will internally run a copy of $\mathcal{F}_{\text{PREP}}$ composed with Π_{MPC} where it corrupts the parties specified by $\mathcal{Z}$. The simulator relays messages between parties/$\mathcal{F}_{\text{PREP}}$ and $\mathcal{Z}$, such that $\mathcal{Z}$ will see the same interface as when interacting with a real protocol. The specification of the simulator $\mathcal{S}_{\text{MPC}}$ is presented in Figure 2.

To see that the simulated and real processes cannot be distinguished, we show that the view of the environment in the ideal process is statistically indistinguishable from the view in the real process. This view consists of the corrupt players' view of the protocol execution as well as inputs/outputs of honest players.

We first argue that the view up to the point where the output value is opened (step 5 of the 'output' stage) has exactly the same distribution in the real and in the simulated case: First, the value broadcast by honest players in the input stage are always uniformly random. Second, when a value is partially opened in a secure multiplication or a reorganize step, fresh shares of a random value

---

[2] Note that we don't show a specific implementation of $\mathcal{F}_{\text{PREP}}$, since that is not the core of our result. An implementation can always be done by a general MPC protocol. However, in [DPSZ12] an efficient preprocessing protocol is shown which works on vectors of values with coordinate-wise operations just as we need in our case. Furthermore, since our online protocol in structure resembles theirs, we can use the same kind of preprocessing. We will elaborate on this in the full version, [DZ12].

Protocol Π_{MPC}

Initialize: The parties first invoke the preprocessing to get the shared secret key $[\![\alpha]\!]$, a sufficient number of multiplication triples $(\langle a\rangle, \langle b\rangle, \langle c\rangle^*)$, pairs of random values and single values $(\langle r\rangle, [\![r]\!])$, $(\langle s\rangle, \langle s\rangle^*)$, $\langle t\rangle$, $[\![t']\!]$, and pairs $(\langle R\rangle, \langle F(R)\rangle)$ of representations for random blocks R and linear function F.

Rand: The parties take an available single $\langle t\rangle$.

Input: To share P_i's input x_i, take an available pair $\langle r\rangle, [\![r]\!]$ and do the following:
1. $[\![r]\!]$ is opened to P_i.
2. P_i broadcasts $\epsilon \leftarrow C(\mathsf{x_i}) - C(\mathsf{r})$.
3. The parties verify that ϵ is a codeword and if so, compute $\langle x_i\rangle \leftarrow \langle r\rangle + \epsilon$.

Add: To add representations $\langle x\rangle, \langle y\rangle$, parties locally compute $\langle x + y\rangle \leftarrow \langle x\rangle + \langle y\rangle$.

Multiply: To multiply $\langle x\rangle, \langle y\rangle$, parties take a triple $(\langle a\rangle, \langle b\rangle, \langle c\rangle^*)$ and a pair of random values $\langle s\rangle, \langle s\rangle^*$ from the set of the available ones and do:
1. Partially open $\langle x\rangle - \langle a\rangle$ to get ϵ and $\langle y\rangle - \langle b\rangle$ to get δ
2. Compute $\langle x * y\rangle^* \leftarrow \langle c\rangle^* + \epsilon * \langle b\rangle + \delta * \langle a\rangle + \epsilon * \delta$.
3. Partially open $\langle x * y\rangle^* - \langle s\rangle^*$ to get $\sigma^* \in C^*$. P_1 extracts $x * y - s$ and encodes this value into a codeword $\sigma \in C$ which he broadcasts.
4. All players check that σ^*, σ are codewords for the same value and then compute $\langle x * y\rangle \leftarrow \sigma + \langle s\rangle$.

Reorganize Let $B = (b_1, \ldots, b_l)$ be the vector of blocks containing the output bits of a given layer in the circuit. To reorganize these bits as inputs for the next layer the parties first identify the F matching this reorganizing and take preprocessed $(\langle R\rangle, \langle F(R)\rangle)$ for R with same length as B. The parties then do:
1. Partially open $\langle B\rangle - \langle R\rangle$, so a set of codewords $C(B - R)$ becomes public.
2. P_1 extracts $B - R$, computes $F(B - R)$ and broadcasts $C(F(B - R))$.
3. All players verify that $C(B - R)$, $C(F(B - R))$ are sets of valid codewords and that the encoded bits are related via F. Then compute $\langle F(R)\rangle \leftarrow C(F(B - R)) + \langle F(R)\rangle$.

Output: This stage is entered when the players have $\langle y\rangle$ for (possibly incorrect) but not opened output value y. They do the following:
1. Let $C(a_j), \ldots, C(a_{T'+1})$, be all partially opened values so far, where $\langle a_j\rangle = (\delta_j, (C(a_{j,1}), \ldots, C(a_{j,N})), (m(a_j)_1, \ldots, m(a_j)_N))$. Similarly let $C^*(a_{T'+1}), \ldots, C^*(a_T)$ be opened values encoded in C^*. Open $\lceil c \cdot N \log(T)/k\rceil$ random values $[\![t]\!]$ and use them as seeds to get $e_1, \ldots, e_T$ as described in Section 3. Compute $a \leftarrow \sum_{j=1}^{T} e_j * C(a)_j + \sum_{j=T'+1}^{T} e_j * C^*(a)_j$.
2. Each P_i calls $\mathcal{F}_{\text{COM}}$ to commit to $m_i \leftarrow \sum_{j=1}^{T} e_j * m(a_j)_i$. For output value $\langle y\rangle$, P_i also commits to his share y_i, and his share $m(y)_i$ in the MAC.
3. $[\![\alpha]\!]$ is opened.
4. Each P_i asks $\mathcal{F}_{\text{COM}}$ to open m_i, and all check that $\alpha * (a + \sum_{j=1}^{T} e_j * \delta_j) = \sum_{i=1}^{N} m_i$. If a check fails, the protocol aborts. Otherwise the players conclude that the output value is correctly computed.
5. The commitments to $y_i, m(y)_i$ are opened. Define y as $y := \sum_{i=1}^{N} y_i$ and check that $\alpha * (y + \delta) = \sum_{i=1}^{N} m(y)_i$, if so, y is the output.

Fig. 1. The online protocol

are subtracted, so the honest players will always send a set of uniformly random and independent values. Third, the honest players hold shares in MACs on the opened values, these are random sharings of a correct MAC. Therefore, also the MAC and shares revealed in step 4 of 'output' have the same distribution in the simulated as in the the real process. Finally note that if the simulated protocol aborts, the simulator makes the ideal functionality fail, so the environment will see that honest players generate no output, just as when the real process aborts.

Now, if the real or simulated protocol proceeds to the last step, the only new data the environment sees is output value y, plus some shares of honest players. These are random shares that are consistent with y and its MAC in both the simulated and real case. In other words, the environments' view of the last step has the same distribution in real and simulated case as long as y is the same.

In the simulation, y is of course the correct evaluation on the inputs matching the shares that were read from the corrupted parties in the beginning. To finish the proof, it is therefore sufficient to show that the same happens in the real process with overwhelming probability. In other words, we show that the event that the real protocol terminates but the output is not correct occurs with negligible probability. Incorrect outputs result if corrupted parties during the protocol successfully cheat with their shares. We have two kinds of checks on shares corresponding to the two kinds of representations $[\cdot]$ and $\langle \cdot \rangle$. The checks related to the openings of $[\cdot]$-values are done during 'Input and in steps 1 and 3 of 'Output'. We get from Lemma 1 that the probability of cheating in each of these openings is at most 2^{-d}.

For the check in step 5 (which is for all the opened $\langle \cdot \rangle$ and $\langle \cdot \rangle^*$ values) we turn to the security game of Lemma 2 in Section 3. It is not difficult to see this game indeed models 'Output'(up to step 5): The second step in the game where the adversary sends the w_i''s models the fact that corrupted players can choose to lie about their shares of values opened during the protocol execution. Δ models the fact that the adversary may modify the shares of MACs held by corrupt players. Finally, since α and m_i are secret shared in the protocol, the adversary has no information on α and m ahead of time in the protocol, just as in the security game. Therefore, we get from Lemma 2 that the probability of a party being able to cheat in step 5 is at most $2^{-\Theta(n)}$. Finally, for the check in step 6, only one MAC is checked for each output, so here the probability of cheating is 2^{-d}, again by Lemma 1.

Since the protocol aborts as soon as a check fails, the probability that it terminates with an incorrect output is the maximum probability with which any single check can be cheated. Since n and d are assumed to be $\Theta(\kappa)$, all these probabilities are $2^{-\Theta(\kappa)}$, and hence the maximum is also exponentially small.   □

Having shown the construction of the protocol and proved security, the only thing left is to argue about the complexities depending on the concrete linear codes and preprocessing model. In the following two sections we argue the complexities using Reed-Solomon and Algebraic Geometry codes respectively with both dedicated and universal preprocessing, and thereby completing the proofs of Theorem 1 and Theorem 2.

Simulator $\mathcal{S}_{\text{MPC}}$

Initialize: The simulator runs the "Initialize" step honestly on the copy. This involves initializing and creating the desired number of preprocessed values by doing the steps in $\mathcal{F}_{\text{PREP}}$. Note that here the simulator will read all data (shares, keys, errors) of the corrupted parties specified to the $\mathcal{F}_{\text{PREP}}$ copy.

Rand: The simulator runs the copy protocol honestly and calls *rand* on the ideal functionality $\mathcal{F}_{\text{MPC}}$.

Input: If P_i is not corrupted the copy is run honestly with dummy input, for example **0**. If in Step 1 during input, the MACs are not correct, the protocol is aborted.

If P_i is corrupted the input step is done honestly and then the simulator waits for P_i to broadcast $\boldsymbol{\epsilon}$. Given this, the simulator can compute $\boldsymbol{x}_i' = \boldsymbol{r} + \boldsymbol{\epsilon}$ since it knows (all the shares of) $\boldsymbol{r}$. This is the supposed input of P_i, which the simulator now gives to the ideal functionality $\mathcal{F}_{\text{MPC}}$.

Add: The simulator runs the protocol honestly and calls *add* on the ideal functionality $\mathcal{F}_{\text{MPC}}$.

Multiply: The simulator runs the protocol honestly and, as before, aborts if some codeword is not valid. Otherwise it calls *multiply* on the ideal functionality $\mathcal{F}_{\text{MPC}}$.

Reorganize The simulator runs the protocol honestly and, as before, aborts if some codeword is not valid. Otherwise it calls *reorganize* on the ideal functionality $\mathcal{F}_{\text{MPC}}$.

Output: The output step is run and the protocol is aborted if some MAC is not correct. Otherwise the simulator calls *output* on $\mathcal{F}_{\text{MPC}}$ and gets P_i's output $\boldsymbol{y}$ back. Now it has to simulate shares $\boldsymbol{y}_j$ of honest parties such that they are consistent with $\boldsymbol{y}$. Note that the simulator already has shares of an output value $\boldsymbol{y}'$ that was computed using the dummy inputs, as well as shares of the MAC for $\boldsymbol{y}'$.

The simulator now selects an honest party, say P_k and adds $\boldsymbol{y} - \boldsymbol{y}'$ to his share of $\boldsymbol{y}$ and compute its new encoding. Similarly it adds $\boldsymbol{\alpha} * C(\boldsymbol{y} - \boldsymbol{y}')$ to his share of the MAC. Note that the simulator can compute $\boldsymbol{\alpha} * C(\boldsymbol{y} - \boldsymbol{y}')$ since it knows from the beginning (all the shares of) $\boldsymbol{\alpha}$. Now it simulates the openings of shares of $\boldsymbol{y}$ towards the environment according to the protocol. If the environment lets this terminate correctly, send "OK" to $\mathcal{F}_{\text{MPC}}$.

Fig. 2. The simulator for $\mathcal{F}_{\text{MPC}}$

4.1 Using the Protocol with Reed-Solomon Codes

Dedicated Preprocessing. First, we note that by our assumptions on the code C, a codeword contains $k \in \Theta(n)$ data bits. Moreover, in the $\langle \cdot \rangle$-representation, each player stores only two n-bit vectors as his share of each encoded block, namely a codeword of the additive share of the value itself and a share of the MAC. It follows that each player stores $O(n)$ field elements per $\langle \cdot \rangle$-representation.

We then define a block operation to be an addition, a multiplication, or an opening of $\langle\cdot\rangle$-representations. Since the circuit is well formed and each $\langle\cdot\rangle$-representation "contains" $\Theta(n)$ data bits, it is not hard to see that the number of block operations we need to compute a circuit of size S is $O(S/n)$.

Now, the storage and communication overheads follow because we use at most a constant number of $\langle\cdot\rangle$- representations from the preprocessing for each block operation, and the communication needed is a most Nn field elements for each such operation. So $O(S/n \cdot Nn) = O(SN)$ field elements need to be stored from the preprocessing and this is also the communication complexity. The field has to have at least n elements for the Reed-Solomon construction to work, hence each field element has size $O(\log n) = O(\log \kappa)$ bits. Putting all this together, we see that the storage and communication overheads are both $O(SN \log \kappa/(SN)) = O(\log \kappa)$. It should be noted that we also use some of the more expensive $[\![\cdot]\!]$-representations, these cost $O(N^2 n)$ field elements in storage and communication when they are opened. However, we only need $\lceil c \cdot n \log(T)/k \rceil$ of these, which is $O(\log(T))$. Since T is linear in the circuit size S, the storage and communication overhead for this part will be $O(N^2 n \log(\kappa) \cdot \log(S)/(SN)) = O(N\kappa \log(\kappa) \log(S)/S)$. As explained in the introduction, we assume S is much larger than $N\kappa$, so this term can be ignored when we compute the overhead.

As for computation, the most expensive operation done on a block is the re-encoding and membership verification we need for every layer and every multiplication. This costs $O(n \cdot polylog(n))$ bit operations per block, because we are working with Van der Monde matrices, as explained in Section 2. This means the total computational complexity is $O(S/n \cdot N \cdot n \cdot polylog(n))$, so the overhead is $O(polylog(n)) = O(polylog(\kappa))$.

Universal Preprocessing. Here we use the restructuring of the circuit as described [DIK10]. This makes the circuit somewhat larger, namely by a factor of $O(log(S))$ as mentioned in Section 1.1. Now the reorganization of bits between layers can be done simply by permuting inside one block at a time. Moreover, the permutations we need are the same, independently of the circuit we want to compute. Hence a number of random pairs $\langle r \rangle, \langle \pi(r) \rangle$ can be prepared in advance, where π ranges over the permutations needed. This implies the second part of Theorem 1 if we again use Reed-Solomon codes. The only change compared to dedicated preprocessing is that overheads have to be multiplied by the factor by which the circuit gets larger when we apply the restructuring from [DIK10].

4.2   Using the Protocol with Algebraic Geometry Codes

Before going into depth with the argument for complexity using Algebraic Geometry codes, we look at the problem of batch verification of membership in binary codes.

Verifying Membership in (Binary) Codes with Amortized Efficiency. We will need a solution to the following problem: Suppose we are given a set of vectors of length n and it is claimed that they are all in the linear binary code C, of dimension k and length n. Say there are $\Theta(n)$ input vectors. We want to verify that every vector is indeed in C, possibly with an error probability that is negligible in n, and without making any assumptions on C.

Let H be the parity check matrix for C, so H has n columns and $n - k$ rows. We then put the input vectors as columns in a matrix M, where we assume for simplicity that there are $n - k$ input words so M has $n - k$ columns. Now, an obvious method is to just compute $U = HM$ and check this result is the all-0 matrix. Using good matrix multiplication algorithms, this does save time over the naive approach of just multiplying H on every input vector, namely we go from cubic time to $O(n^{2+v})$ where $v > 0$ depends on the matrix algorithm used. We could also use the algorithm of Freiwalds for verifying a matrix product [Fre77], but it has constant error probability for a constant-size field and is therefore not good enough for us even though it runs in time $O(n^2)$. We now explain how to do better.

Let G be a generator matrix for a linear time encodable code, of dimension $n - k$ and length m. From the results of Spielman [Spi96], it follows that families of such codes exist, that also have constant information and error rate. We can therefore assume that m is in $\Theta(n)$ and the minimum distance of the code generated by G is also in $\Theta(n)$. Using the standard convention that the rows of G form a basis of the code, We assume that G has m columns and $n - k$ rows. Let $G^\dagger$ be the transposed of G.

By linear time encodability, we can multiply a row vector with G in linear time (or multiply $G^\dagger$ by a column), and hence compute $G^\dagger H$ and MG in time $O(n^2)$. This leads to the algorithm in Figure 3, which is actually a general method for checking whether the product of two matrices is 0.

Algorithm *CheckZeroProduct*

1. On input H, M, compute $G^\dagger H$ and MG.
2. Select at random n pairs of indices $(i_\ell, j_\ell) \in \{1, \ldots, m\}^2$ for $\ell = 1, \ldots, n$.
3. For $\ell = 1, \ldots, n$, compute inner product of row i_ℓ of $G^\dagger H$ and column j_ℓ of MG.
4. If all inner products are 0, output "accept", else "reject".

Fig. 3. Algorithm for checking zero product of matrices

Theorem 4. *The algorithm CheckZeroProduct runs in time $O(n^2)$. If $HM = 0$ it always accepts, and if not, it accepts with probability in $2^{-\Theta(n)}$.*

Proof. Recall that $U = HM$ and note that

$$(G^\dagger H)(MG) = G^\dagger U G = (G^\dagger U)G.$$

Now, if $U = 0$, then $GUG^\dagger = 0$ and the algorithm accepts. Otherwise, at least one entry in U is not 0. We can think of the expression $(G^\dagger U)G$ as first encoding each column of U using $G^\dagger$ and then encoding each row of the result using G. Since the code generated by G has minimum weight/distance in $\Theta(n)$, it follows that a constant fraction of the entries in $(G^\dagger U)G$ are non-zero. The algorithm effectively probes n random entries in $(G^\dagger U)G$ and will therefore accept in this case with probability at most $2^{-\Theta(n)}$. We already argued that we can compute $G^\dagger H$ and MG in time $O(n^2)$ and the inner products clearly also take time $O(n^2)$.

Now we return to our protocol and derive the overheads we get if we use algebraic geometry codes and exploit the fast verification of codewords. This will establish the results claimed in Theorem 2.

For the storage and communication overhead, exactly the same arguments as for Reed-Solomon codes apply, with the only difference that the field size is now constant, so this immediately gives us that the storage and communication overheads are constant when we do dedicated preprocessing. For universal preprocessing we have to multiply by the "expansion factor" from [DIK10].

As for the computation overhead, again the re-encoding done for multiplication and reordering of bits is the bottleneck, in fact the overhead from other computation is constant. Note that in the protocol only a single player encodes data, while the other players only verify membership in the codes, and the overhead from verification can be made constant using the above algorithm. We therefore just need to compute the overhead coming from a single player doing $O(S/n)$ encodings, where S is the size of the circuit computed. Doing encoding by simply multiplying by the generator matrix costs $O(n^2)$ operations, so we get an overhead of $O(nS/(NS)) = O(\kappa/N)$.

If the circuit is wide enough that encoding can always be done in batches of size $\Omega(n)$, it can be done by matrix multiplication in time $O(n^{2+\epsilon})$ for a batch, or $O(n^{1+\epsilon})$ per encoded word. This gives computation overhead $O(\kappa^\epsilon/N)$ by the same argument as for Reed-Solomon.

Acknowledgment We thank Yuval Ishai for inspiring discussions leading to the *CheckZeroProduct* algorithm.

References

[BDOZ11]   Bendlin, R., Damgård, I., Orlandi, C., Zakarias, S.: Semi-homomorphic Encryption and Multiparty Computation. In: Paterson, K.G. (ed.) EURO-CRYPT 2011. LNCS, vol. 6632, pp. 169–188. Springer, Heidelberg (2011)

[Can01]   Canetti, R.: Universally composable security: A new paradigm for cryptographic protocols. In: FOCS, pp. 136–145 (2001)

[CCX11]   Cascudo, I., Cramer, R., Xing, C.: The Torsion-Limit for Algebraic Function Fields and Its Application to Arithmetic Secret Sharing. In: Rogaway, P. (ed.) CRYPTO 2011. LNCS, vol. 6841, pp. 685–705. Springer, Heidelberg (2011)

[CLOS02]   Canetti, R., Lindell, Y., Ostrovsky, R., Sahai, A.: Universally composable two-party and multi-party secure computation. In: STOC, pp. 494–503 (2002)

[DIK10]   Damgård, I., Ishai, Y., Krøigaard, M.: Perfectly Secure Multiparty Computation and the Computational Overhead of Cryptography. In: Gilbert, H. (ed.) EUROCRYPT 2010. LNCS, vol. 6110, pp. 445–465. Springer, Heidelberg (2010)

[DPSZ12]   Damgård, I., Pastro, V., Smart, N.P., Zakarias, S.: Multiparty Computation from Somewhat Homomorphic Encryption. In: Safavi-Naini, R., Canetti, R. (eds.) CRYPTO 2012. LNCS, vol. 7417, pp. 643–662. Springer, Heidelberg (2012)

[DZ12]   Damgård, I., Zakarias, S.: Constant-overhead secure computation for boolean circuits in the preprocessing model. Cryptology ePrint Archive, Report 2012/512, full version (2012), http://eprint.iacr.org/

[Fre77]   Freivalds, R.: Probabilistic machines can use less running time. In: IFIP Congress, pp. 839–842 (1977)

[GHS12]   Gentry, C., Halevi, S., Smart, N.P.: Fully Homomorphic Encryption with Polylog Overhead. In: Pointcheval, D., Johansson, T. (eds.) EUROCRYPT 2012. LNCS, vol. 7237, pp. 465–482. Springer, Heidelberg (2012)

[Hoe63]   Hoeffding, W.: Probability inequalities for sums of bounded random variables. Journal of the American Statistical Association 58(301), 13–30 (1963)

[IKM+13]   Ishai, Y., Kushilevitz, E., Meldgaard, S., Orlandi, C., Paskin-Cherniavsky, A.: On the Power of Correlated Randomness in Secure Computation. In: Sahai, A. (ed.) TCC 2013. LNCS, vol. 7785, pp. 600–620. Springer, Heidelberg (2013)

[IKOS08]   Ishai, Y., Kushilevitz, E., Ostrovsky, R., Sahai, A.: Cryptography with constant computational overhead. In: Dwork, C. (ed.) STOC, pp. 433–442. ACM (2008)

[NN93]   Naor, J., Naor, M.: Small-bias probability spaces: Efficient constructions and applications. SIAM J. Comput. 22(4), 838–856 (1993)

[NNOB12]   Nielsen, J.B., Nordholt, P.S., Orlandi, C., Burra, S.S.: A New Approach to Practical Active-Secure Two-Party Computation. In: Safavi-Naini, R., Canetti, R. (eds.) CRYPTO 2012. LNCS, vol. 7417, pp. 681–700. Springer, Heidelberg (2012)

[Spi96]   Spielman, D.A.: Linear-time encodable and decodable error-correcting codes. IEEE Transactions on Information Theory 42(6), 1723–1731 (1996)

A   Functionalities

Functionality $\mathcal{F}_{\text{MPC}}$

Initialize: On input $(init, k)$ from all parties, the store the block length k.

Rand: On input $(rand, P_i, vid)$ from all parties P_i, with vid a fresh identifier, the pick $r \leftarrow \mathbb{F}_2^k$ and store (vid, r).

Input: On input $(input, P_i, vid, x)$ from P_i and $(input, P_i, vid, ?)$ from all other parties, with vid a fresh identifier, store (vid, x).

Add: On command $(add, vid_1, vid_2, vid_3)$ from all parties (if vid_1, vid_2 are present in memory and vid_3 is not), retrieve (vid_1, x), (vid_2, y) and store $(vid_3, x + y)$.

Multiply: On input $(mult, vid_1, vid_2, vid_3)$ from all parties (if vid_1, vid_2 are present in memory and vid_3 is not), retrieve (vid_1, x), (vid_2, y) and store $(vid_3, x * y)$.

Reorganize: On input $(reorg, F, vid_1, \ldots, vid_l, vid'_1, \ldots, vid'_{l'})$ from all parties (if $vid_1, \ldots vid_l$ are present in memory and $vid'_1, \ldots, vid'_{l'}$ are not), retrieve $(vid_1, x_1), \ldots, (vid_l, x_l)$. Apply the function F (if the number of parameters match) to get $F(x_1, \ldots, x_l) = (x'_1, \ldots, x'_{l'})$ and store $(vid'_1, x'_1), \ldots, (vid''_l, x'_{l'})$.

Output: On input $(output, vid)$ from all honest parties (if vid is present in memory), retrieve (vid, x) and output it to the environment. If the environment returns "OK", then output (vid, x) to all players, else output $\perp$ to all players.

Fig. 4. The ideal functionality for MPC

$\mathcal{F}_{\text{PREP}}$ Macros

Usage: We describe two macros, one to produce $[\![v]\!]$ representations and one to produce $\langle v \rangle$ representations. We denote by A the set of corrupted players.

Bracket$(v_1, \ldots, v_N, \beta_1, \ldots, \beta_N)$, where $v_i, \beta_i \in \mathbb{F}^n$ and v_i's are codewords in C.
1. Let $v = \sum_{i=1}^{N} v_i$ and then for $i = 1, \ldots, N$:
   (a) Compute the MAC $m(v)_i \leftarrow v * \beta_i$.
   (b) For every corrupt P_j, $j \in A$ the environment specifies a share $m(v)_i^j$.
   (c) Set each share $m(v)_i^j$, $j \notin A$, uniformly st. $\sum_{j=1}^{N} m(v)_i^j = m(v)_i$.
2. Send $(v_i, (\beta_i, m(v)_i^1, \ldots, m(v)_i^N))$ to each honest player P_i.

Angle$(v_1, \ldots, v_N, \alpha)$, where $v_i, \alpha \in \mathbb{F}^n$ and v_i's are codewords, all in C or C^*.
1. Let $v = \sum_{i=1}^{N} v_i$, and compute the MAC $m(v) \leftarrow v * \alpha$.
2. For every corrupt player P_i, $i \in A$ the environment specifies a share $m(v)_i$.
3. The functionality sets each share $m(v)_i$ $i \notin A$ uniformly such that $\sum_{i=1}^{N} m(v)_i = m(v)$.
4. It send $(0, v_i, m(v)_i)$ to each honest player P_i.

Fig. 5. Macros for use in $\mathcal{F}_{\text{PREP}}$

Functionality $\mathcal{F}_{\text{PREP}}$

Usage: The functionality uses two macros described in Figure 5, to produce $[\![v]\!]$ and $\langle v \rangle$ representations. We denote by A the set of players controlled by the adversary. When any of the commands below are called, the environment may send "stop", in which case the functionality sends "fail" to all parties and stops.

Initialize: On input $(init, n, k, d, u, G)$ from all players, store integers n, k, d, u and generator matrix G for a linear $[n, k, d]$-code C over the field $\mathbb{F} = \mathbb{F}_{2^u}$.

1. For each corrupt player P_i, $i \in A$, get codeword $C(\alpha_i)$ of a share α_i from the environment.
2. Set each share α_i, $i \notin A$ uniformly.
3. For each corrupt player P_i, $i \in A$, the environment specifies a key β_i.
4. The functionality sets each key β_i $i \notin A$ uniformly.
5. It runs the macro $\mathsf{Bracket}(C(\alpha_1), \dots C(\alpha_n), \beta_1, \dots, \beta_n)$.

Pairs($\langle r \rangle$, $[\![r]\!]$): On input $(pair)$ from all players, do:

1. For each corrupt player P_i, $i \in A$, the environment specifies a codeword $C(r_i)$ of the share r_i.
2. Set each share r_i, $i \notin A$ uniformly.
3. Run $\mathsf{Bracket}(C(r_1), \dots, C(r_n), \beta_1, \dots, \beta_n)$, $\mathsf{Angle}(C(r_1), \dots, C(r_n), \alpha)$.

Pairs($\langle r \rangle$, $\langle r \rangle^*$): On input $(pair, *)$ from all players

1. For each corrupt player P_i, $i \in A$, the environment specifies codewords $C(r_i), C^*(r_i)$ of the share r_i.
2. Set each share r_i, $i \notin A$ uniformly.
3. Run $\mathsf{Angle}(C(r_1), \dots, C(r_n), \alpha), \mathsf{Angle}(C^*(r_1), \dots, C(r_n), \alpha)$.

Pairs($\langle R \rangle$, $\langle F(R) \rangle$)): On input $(pair, F(X))$ from all players

1. For each corrupt player P_i, $i \in A$, the environment specifies a vector of codewords $(C(r_{i1}), \dots, C(r_{il}))$ representing the vector $R_i = (r_{i1}, \dots, r_{il})$ of length l according to F.
2. Set each R_i, $i \notin A$ uniformly. (Now $R := \sum_i R_i = (r_1, \dots, r_l)$, where $r_j := \sum_i r_{ij}$.)
3. To get the shared representation of each entry in R and $F(R)$, run for $j = 1, \dots, l$ the macros $\mathsf{Angle}(C(r_{1j}), \dots, C(r_{nj}), \alpha)$ and $\mathsf{Angle}(F(r_{1j}), \dots, F(r_{nj}), \alpha)$, where we abuse the notation slightly to let $F(r_{ij})$ denote the jth entry of the vector $F(R_i)$.

Triples: On input $(triple)$ from all players

1. For each corrupt player P_i, $i \in A$, the environment specifies codewords $C(a_i), C(b_i)$ of shares a_i, b_i .
2. Set each share a_i, b_i, $i \notin A$ uniformly. Let $a := \sum_{i=1}^n a_i$, $b := \sum_{i=1}^n b_i$.
3. Set $c \leftarrow a * b$.
4. For each corrupt player P_i, $i \in A$, the environment specifies a codeword $C(c_i)$ of the share c_i .
5. Set each share c_i, $i \notin A$ uniformly with the constraint $\sum_{i=1}^n c_i = c$.
6. Run $\mathsf{Angle}(C(a_1), \dots, C(a_n), \alpha)$, $\mathsf{Angle}(C(b_1), \dots, C(b_n), \alpha)$, and $\mathsf{Angle}(C(c_1), \dots, C(c_n), \alpha)$.

Fig. 6. The ideal functionality for preprocessing

Implementing Resettable UC-Functionalities with Untrusted Tamper-Proof Hardware-Tokens

Nico Döttling, Thilo Mie, Jörn Müller-Quade, and Tobias Nilges

Karlsruhe Institute of Technology, Karlsruhe, Germany
{doettling,mueller-quade,nilges}@kit.edu,mie@ira.uka.de

Abstract. Resettable hardware tokens, usually in the form of smart cards, are used for a variety of security-critical tasks in open environments. Many of these tasks require trusted hardware tokens. With the complexity of hardware, however, it is not feasible to check if the hardware contains an internal state or gives away information over side channels. This inspires the question of the cryptographic strength of untrusted resettable hardware tokens in the universal composability framework.

In this work, we consider the problem of realizing general UC-functionalities from untrusted resettable hardware-tokens, with the goal of minimizing both the amount of interaction and the number of tokens employed. Our main result consists of two protocols, realizing functionalities that are sufficient to UC-realize any resettable two-party functionality.

The first protocol requires two rounds of interaction in an initialization phase and only a single hardware-token. The second protocol is fully non-interactive and requires two tokens. One of these relaxations, allowing either communication with the issuer of the token or issuing two tokens, is necessary. We show that even a simple functionality cannot be realized non-interactively using a single token.

Keywords: Resettably secure computation, Tamper-Proof hardware, Universal Composability.

1 Introduction

In this paper we investigate the cryptographic strength of tamper-proof resettable hardware tokens in the universal composability model. This setting is motivated by smart cards. Smart cards are tamper-proof and resettable. Our aim is to obtain non-interactive protocols where a sender can issue tamper-proof hardware which is not necessarily trusted by the receiver. Non-interactive protocols allow communication only in one direction from the sender to the receiver. We will, however, differentiate two types of non-interactive protocols. In the first type we allow an exchange of hardware tokens and interactive communication between sender and receiver in an initialization phase before the input is given. After the input is given the only communication allowed is one message sent from the sender to the receiver. The second and more strict type allows (even in

A. Sahai (Ed.): TCC 2013, LNCS 7785, pp. 642–661, 2013.

an initialization phase) communication and sending of hardware tokens in one direction only.

Of course, using resettable hardware and non-interactive protocols one cannot expect to realize any non-resettable ideal functionality. The real adversary could always reset the token and start the protocol all over again. Hence this unavoidable attack must be reflected in the ideal functionality. Note that this poses a limitation on the usefulness of some ideal functionalities. E.g. a coin-toss of a single bit becomes useless as an attacker could reset the protocol until his desired result occurs. Resettable functionalities resemble an ideal, i.e. black-box, code obfuscation which is impossible without secure hardware [1].

Our Contribution. In the following we prove that there exist simple resettable ideal functionalities, namely point-functions, which cannot securely be realized by a strictly non-interactive protocol using one single resettable hardware token. We prove the impossibility of realizing a point-function with a single resettable token in a strictly non-interactive protocol along the lines of [2]. Any successful simulator for a corrupted token would already yield a cheating strategy for the token in the real model.

If we were given a common-reference-string (CRS), however, non-interactive protocols can be realized via secure two party computations between the receiver and the hardware token. Note that the secure two-party computation must be adapted to be used with a resettable token. A general construction can be found in [3]. For each message m which is sent to the token in the secure two-party computation one sends the complete previous transcript plus the message m. The token then verifies the transcript and answers according to the protocol. Any UC-compiler for secure two-party computation in the CRS-hybrid-model (e.g. [4]) can be used to implement the underlying two-party protocol.

So the problem of non-interactive secure computation boils down to securely computing a CRS in an initialization phase of the protocol. As our main contribution we provide two constructions for securely realizing the CRS functionality with resettable tamper-proof hardware tokens. The first protocol-construction obtains a CRS using a single resettable hardware-token and a 4-move interactive initialization-phase. The second protocol-construction obtains a *resettable* CRS using two resettable hardware tokens and no further interaction with the sender.

Our Techniques. At the core of our first construction, which allows interaction with the sender in an initialization phase, is a Blum coin-toss protocol. In this protocol the hardware token is used like a UC-commitment which is opened via the possession of a secret which is sent by the sender in the unveil phase. This secret is not directly given to the token to avoid communication between the sender and the token, instead a zero-knowledge proof is used. Note that this ZK proof must be resettably-sound and therefore can only be achieved using non-black-box techniques.

Our second construction uses two hardware tokens which are both issued by the sender and works in the strictly non-interactive setting where nothing may ever be sent by the receiver. In the strictly non-interactive setting one cannot use one of the two tokens like a UC-commitment which is unveiled via the possession of a secret value, because both tokens are resettable and the receiver could learn the committed value, reset, and force the coin-toss to some malicious value. The basic idea behind our solution is a Blum coin-toss where the receiver commits to a random value x and sends x together with the commitment c to the first token. The token answers with a value y which is deterministically derived from the commitment by a pseudorandom function. The second token is then used to check if the value y is indeed deterministically derived. The second token is given the commitment c and must answer with the same y. In this case $x \oplus y$ is the result of the coin-toss. For the security proof in case of a corrupted receiver it is crucial that the communication with the two tokens takes place in this order. The second token must not reveal the value y too early, because the simulator must choose y depending on x which is not possible if he must choose y too early. To cope with that, the first token signs the commitment and the second token accepts a commitment only together with a proof of possession of a valid signature. For the simulation of a corrupted sender, however, it is necessary to obtain y before one is actually committed to x. To do so the simulator executes the protocol out of order. He is able to forge the proof of possession of a valid signature. To the best of our knowledge this simulation technique is novel and an interesting result on its own.

As an application of our non-interactive protocols we propose a *conditional decrypt* for a fully homomorphic encryption scheme. The condition for decryption being that a universal argument is provided to the token that a specific computation has been performed. This allows offloading computations from the token. The actual computation can be performed using fully homomorphic encryption and only the conditional decrypt has to be realized as a two-party computation. This construction can be used to achieve obfuscation.

Further Related and Concurrent Work. The notion of resettability has gained considerable attention, especially in the context of zero-knowledge. The results range from a resettable prover [3, 5, 6], to a resettable verifier [6, 7] and simultaneously resettable prover and verifier [8–10]. These works spawned a line of work realizing compilers for resettable and stateless secure multi-party computation. Goyal and Sahai [11] presented a compiler which enables multi-party computation of arbitrary PPT-functionalities either with honest majority where any party can be resettable, or no honest majority is required and only one predetermined party may be resettable. Surpassing the honest majority requirement, Goyal and Maji [12] introduced a compiler that transforms most PPT-functionalities (except a certain class of pseudorandom generators) into a stateless variant. Goyal et al. [13] present an unconditionally secure zero-knowledge protocol for $\mathcal{NP}$. They show that statistically secure commitments with one stateless token are only possible when interaction between the parties is allowed, but impossible in the non-interactive setting. This is due to the fact that in the non-interactive case the token needs to contain superpolynomial entropy since both sender and receiver are unbounded. In contrast, we consider computational UC-security [14], so their impossibility result does not apply to us.

There are several results concerning multi-party computation in the UC-framework. [14] showed that under the assumption of an honest majority, any multi-party protocol is realizable in the UC-framework. Since it is known to be impossible to construct large classes of UC-secure two-party protocols in the plain model [14–16], the result of Canetti et al. [4] was a breakthrough. In their work, a common reference string is needed as a setup assumption to overcome the impossibility results and realize arbitrary multi-party protocols in the UC-framework. Further work based on tamper-proof hardware includes [17, 18].

In a work independent and concurrent to ours, [19] investigated how stateless tamper-proof hardware tokens can serve as a minimal UC-setup assumption. They present a black-box protocol realizing OT with two stateless tokens and show that OT from one stateless token is not possible if only black-box techniques are used. This is similar to our impossibility result, but we cover any amount of resettable tokens in the non-interactive setting. Further, they construct a coin-toss protocol with a single hardware token using similar techniques to our first protocol. However, they do not consider a non-interactive coin-toss protocol.

2   Preliminaries

Let in the following k denote a security parameter. We use the cryptographic standard notions of negligible functions, as well as computational/statistical/perfect indistinguishability.

2.1   Framework

We state and prove our results in the UniversalComposability (UC)-framework of [14]. In this framework security is defined by comparison of a *real model* and an *ideal model*. The protocol of interest Π is running in the latter, where an adversary $\mathcal{A}$ coordinates the behavior of all corrupted parties. We assume static corruption, i.e. the adversary $\mathcal{A}$ cannot adaptively change corruption during a protocol-run. In the ideal model, which is secure by definition, an ideal functionality $\mathcal{F}$ implements the desired protocol task and a simulator $\mathcal{S}$ tries to mimic the actions of $\mathcal{A}$. An environment $\mathcal{Z}$ is plugged either to the ideal or the real model and has to guess which model it is actually plugged to. Denote the random variable representing the output of $\mathcal{Z}$ when interacting with the real model by $\mathsf{Real}_{\Pi}^{\mathcal{A}}(\mathcal{Z})$ and when interacting with the ideal model by $\mathsf{Ideal}_{\mathcal{F}}^{\mathcal{S}}(\mathcal{Z})$. Protocol Π is said to be UC-secure if for any environment $\mathcal{Z}$ the distributions $\mathsf{Real}_{\Pi}^{\mathcal{A}}(\mathcal{Z})$ and $\mathsf{Ideal}_{\mathcal{F}}^{\mathcal{S}}(\mathcal{Z})$ are (computationally, statistically or perfectly) indistinguishable.

2.2   Strongly Unforgeable Signatures

As our scheme requires the use of signatures, we shall briefly review the standard notion of strongly unforgeable signature schemes. A signature scheme SIG consists of three PPT-algorithms KeyGen, Sign and Verify.

- Keygen(1^k) generates a public verification key vk and a private signature key sgk.
- Sign$_{sgk}(m)$ takes a signature key sgk and a message $m \in \{0,1\}^*$ and returns a signature σ.
- Verify$_{vk}(m, \sigma)$ takes as input a verification key vk, a message $m \in \sigma^*$ and a signature σ and outputs 1 if σ is a valid signature for m and 0 otherwise.

In the EUF-CMA-experiment an adversary $\mathcal{A}$ is given a verification key vk and access to a signature-oracle. $\mathcal{A}$ wins the experiment if it manages to forge a valid signature σ for a message of its choice m, without having queried its signature-oracle with m. A signature scheme SIG is called EUF-CMA-secure, if no PPT-adversary $\mathcal{A}$ wins the EUF-CMA-experiment better than with negligible probability. For the sake of simplicity, we require signature schemes with a deterministic verification procedure and succinct signature length (i.e. the length of σ does not depend on m). Standard hash-and-sign [20, 21] constructions suffice these requirements.

Additionally, we require the signing procedure to be deterministic. However, this is no restriction since the random coins used for signing can be chosen by a pseudorandom function, which is seeded by a part of the signing key.

2.3   Resettably-Sound Zero-Knowledge Arguments of Knowledge

For the construction of our protocols we use resettably-sound zero-knowledge (rsZK) arguments of knowledge [7]. We briefly define the notions.

Definition 1. *A resettably-sound zero-knowledge argument of knowledge system for a language $L \in \mathcal{NP}$ (with witness-relation $\mathcal{R}_L$ and witness-set $w_L(x) = \{w : (x, w) \in R_L\}$) consists of a pair of PPT-machines (P, V), where the verifier V is stateless, such that there exist two PPT-machines Sim and Ext and the following conditions hold.*

- *Completeness. For every $(x, w) \in \mathcal{R}_L$ it holds that $\Pr[\langle \mathsf{P}(w), \mathsf{V} \rangle(x) = 1] = 1$.*
- *Computational Soundness. For every $x \notin L$ and every PPT-machine P^* it holds that $\Pr[\langle \mathsf{P}^*, \mathsf{V} \rangle(x) = 1] < \mathsf{negl}(|x|)$.*
- *Computational Zero-Knowledge. For every $(x, w) \in \mathcal{R}_L$ and every stateful or stateless PPT V^* it holds the distributions $\mathsf{Real} = \{\langle \mathsf{P}(w), \mathsf{V}^* \rangle(x)\}$ and $\mathsf{Ideal} = \{\mathsf{Sim}(x, \mathsf{V}^*)\}$ are computationally indistinguishable.*
- *Proof of Knowledge. For every $x \in L$ and every PPT-machine P^* there exists a negligible ν such that $\Pr[\mathsf{Ext}(x, \mathsf{P}^*)] \in w_L(x)] > \Pr[\langle \mathsf{P}^*, \mathsf{V} \rangle(x) = 1] - \nu$.*

2.4   Perfectly Binding Commitments

Another tool we need is a non-interactive perfectly binding commitment scheme. Generally, a commitment scheme consists of two phases: the *commit phase* in which a sender commits to a value v without revealing it, and the *reveal phase* where the sender reveals his private coins r together with v such that a receiver can verify the correctness of the commitment. The value v has to be hidden from the receiver while the commitment has to be binding for the sender. For our application, a standard computationally hiding and perfectly binding commitment scheme is sufficient, e.g. a construction based on a one-way permutation [22]. Perfectly binding means that there is exactly one randomness to unveil correctly.

3   Resettable Hardware in the UC-Framework

In this section, we will introduce resettable UC-functionalities and the ideal functionalities for resettable hardware tokens. We first provide the definition of resettable two-party UC-functionalities. Let M be a Turing machine. The resettable functionality $\mathcal{F}_\mathsf{M}$ specified by M is defined as follows. For the sake of readability, we omit session and message identifiers.

Functionality $\mathcal{F}_\mathsf{M}$ (parametrized by a security parameter k).

- Sender Input Upon receiving (`sender`, $init$) from S, store $init$, write $init$ on M's input tape and run M until it halts. Store the state of M. Accept no further inputs by $\mathcal{S}$
- Receiver Input Upon receiving (`receiver`, msg) from R, write msg on M's input tape and run M starting from most recent state until it halts. Store the state of M. Read a message out from M's output tape and send out to R.
- Reset (Adversarial receiver only) Upon receiving `reset` from R, reset the Turing machine M to its initial state. Write $init$ on M's input tape and run M until it halts. Store the state of M.

We use a definition of wrapper-functionalities very similar to [17, 18]. For simplicity, we state the functionality in the two-party case where only a sender-machine S and a receiver-machine R are present. This definition allows the sender S to wrap a program T in a hardware token, and send this token to the receiver R who can query it an arbitrary (polynomial) number of times. Additionally, we allow an adversarial receiver to reset the program T to its initial state.

Functionality $\mathcal{F}_{wrap}$ (parametrized by a security parameter k and a polynomial runtime bound $p(\cdot)$).

- Create Upon receiving (`create`, T, $p(\cdot)$) from S, where T is a Turing machine, send `create` to R and store T.
- Execute Upon receiving (`run`, w) from R, check if a `create`-message has already been sent by S, if not output $\perp$. Run T(w) for at most $p(k)$ steps, and let m be the output. Save the current state of T. Output m to R
- Reset (Adversarial Receiver only) Upon receiving `reset` from R, reset the Turing machine T to its initial state.

The messages between $\mathcal{F}_{wrap}$ and R are delivered immediately without scheduling by the adversary. In the sequel, we will use the notation T for programs (given as code, Turing-machine etc.) and $\mathcal{T}$ for the instance of the wrapper-functionality $\mathcal{F}_{wrap}$ in which T runs.

We will introduce two new hybrid functionalities as an intermediate building block between $\mathcal{F}_{wrap}$ and general resettable UC-functionalities. Both functionalities are enhanced wrapper-functionalities where both the receiver of the token and the wrapped program are given access to a trusted common reference string. The two different flavors of this functionality we consider here differ in that the common reference string is either resettable by a corrupted receiver or non-resettable.

Functionality $\mathcal{F}_{wrap}^{hybrid1}$ (parametrized by a security parameter k and a polynomial runtime bound $p(\cdot)$).

- Create Upon receiving $(\texttt{create}, \mathsf{T}, p(\cdot))$ from S, where T is a Turing machine, store T, choose the common reference string crs uniformly at random of length ℓ and give T read-access to crs. Send $(\texttt{create}, \mathsf{crs})$ to R and S.
- Execute Upon receiving $(\texttt{run}, w)$ from R, check if a create-message has already been sent by S, if not output $\bot$. Run $\mathsf{T}(w)$ for at most $p(k)$ steps, and let m be the output. Save the current state of T. Output m to R
- Reset (Adversarial Receiver only) Upon receiving $\texttt{reset}$ from R, reset the Turing machine T to its initial state.

Remark. By having the functionality $\mathcal{F}_{wrap}^{hybrid1}$ send the common reference string crs to the sender S we model an artifact that arises in our protocol.

Functionality $\mathcal{F}_{wrap}^{hybrid2}$ (parametrized by a security parameter k and a polynomial runtime bound $p(\cdot)$). Let H be a random oracle that maps to strings of length ℓ.

- Create Upon receiving $(\texttt{create}, \mathsf{T}, p(\cdot))$ from S, where T is a Turing machine, store T, set the common reference string to be $\mathsf{crs} = H(1)$ and give T read-access to crs. Send $(\texttt{create}, \mathsf{crs})$ to R.
- Execute Upon receiving $(\texttt{run}, w)$ from R, check if a create-message has already been sent by S, if not output $\bot$. Run $\mathsf{T}(w)$ for at most $p(k)$ steps, and let m be the output. Save the current state of T. Output m to R
- Reset (Adversarial Receiver only) Upon receiving $(\texttt{reset}, j)$ from R, reset Turing machine T to its initial state and set the common reference string to $\mathsf{crs} = H(j)$.

We will briefly sketch how general-purpose UC-compilers in the CRS-hybrid-model, like for instance the compiler of [4], can be used to implement arbitrary resettable two-party UC-functionalities in the $\mathcal{F}_{wrap}^{hybrid1}$ and $\mathcal{F}_{wrap}^{hybrid2}$ hybrid model. Recall that these functionalities provide both the receiver and the encapsulated program access to an encapsulated common reference string. The basic idea is to assign the receiver the role of one protocol-party and the encapsulated program the role of the other protocol-party. The case of a malicious sender is trivial, as any UC-simulator against a corrupted sender can also serve as a simulator against a malicious token. The case of a malicious receiver needs to take reset-attacks against the token into account. However, this can be dealt with by applying a transformation due to [3]. This transformation replaces random coins used by the token with pseudorandom coins, which deterministically depend on all the messages received by the token at each point in time. This transformation merely requires a pseudorandom function.

4   Limitations

In this section, we will sketch two limitations regarding the implementation of resettable UC-functionalities using untrusted resettable hardware tokens. For simplicity, we consider protocols realizing the point-function functionality $\mathcal{F}_{\mathsf{PF}}$. This functionality is initialized by an input $\hat{x} \in \{0,1\}^n$ from the sender. The receiver can query $\mathcal{F}_{\mathsf{PF}}$ an arbitrary (polynomial) amount of times with inputs x, receiving output $\mathsf{PF}_{\hat{x}}(x)$, where $\mathsf{PF}_{\hat{x}}(x) = 1$ if $x = \hat{x}$ and $\mathsf{PF}_{\hat{x}}(x) = 0$ otherwise.

Lemma 1. *There exists no protocol which (computationally) UC-realizes the $\mathcal{F}_{\mathsf{PF}}$-functionality using only a single hardware token and no further communication. Moreover, any protocol UC-realizing the $\mathcal{F}_{\mathsf{PF}}$-functionality using any amount of resettable hardware tokens (issued from S to R) must make use of non-black-box techniques in its security proof.*

Proof. First assume there exists a protocol Π_{PF} that UC-implements $\mathcal{F}_{\mathsf{PF}}$ using a single (resettable) hardware token and no interaction (w.l.o.g. we can assume that messages from S to R are sent together with the token). Let $\tilde{A}_{\mathsf{R}}$ be the dummy-adversary for the receiver R. Since Π_{PF} is UC-secure, there exists a simulator $\mathcal{S}_{\mathsf{R}}$ such that it holds for any PPT-environment $\mathcal{Z}$ that $\mathsf{Real}_{\Pi_{\mathsf{PF}}}^{\tilde{A}_{\mathsf{R}}}(\mathcal{Z}) \approx_c \mathsf{Ideal}_{\mathcal{F}_{\mathsf{PF}}}^{\mathcal{S}_{\mathsf{R}}}(\mathcal{Z})$. We will now show that for every sender-simulator $\mathcal{S}_{\mathsf{S}}$ there exists a PPT-environment $\mathcal{Z}^*$ such that the distributions $\mathsf{Real}_{\Pi_{\mathsf{PF}}}^{\tilde{A}}(\mathcal{Z}^*)$ and $\mathsf{Ideal}_{\mathcal{F}_{\mathsf{PF}}}^{\mathcal{S}_{\mathsf{S}}}(\mathcal{Z}^*)$ are efficiently distinguishable, contradicting the UC-security of Π_{PF}. This $\mathcal{Z}^*$ creates a malicious token $\mathcal{T}^*$ which behaves adaptively in the following sense. The token $\mathcal{T}^*$ internally simulates the simulator $\mathcal{S}_{\mathsf{R}}$ together with a malicious functionality $\mathcal{F}^*$, providing its interface with R to $\mathcal{S}_{\mathsf{R}}$. The malicious functionality $\mathcal{F}^*$ behaves as follows. Once it receives an input x for the first time, it checks whether x is equal to a secret random $\hat{x}_0$. If so, it will behave like the point function $\mathsf{PF}_{\hat{x}_0}$ in this call and all successive calls. If not, it will behave like a point function $\mathsf{PF}_{\hat{x}_1}$ (for a secret random $\hat{x}_1$) in this call and all successive calls. Observe now that from the view of R, the protocol Π_{PF} always implements a proper point function. However, a simulator $\mathcal{S}_{\mathsf{S}}$ must decide if it inputs $\hat{x}_0$ or $\hat{x}_1$ into the ideal functionality $\mathcal{F}_{\mathsf{PF}}$ without knowing the first input x of R. The environment $\mathcal{Z}$ can now distinguish between real and ideal as follows. It first flips an unbiased coin. If the outcome is 0, it provides input $x = \hat{x}_0$ to R, otherwise it provides input $x = \hat{x}_1$ to R. If $\mathcal{Z}^*$ is connected to the real experiment, then the output of R behaves according to the specification of $\mathcal{F}^*$.

In the ideal experiment however, the output of R behaves either like $PF_{\hat{x}_0}$ or $PF_{\hat{x}_1}$ (or completely different). Thus, with probability at least $1/2$ $\mathcal{Z}^*$ notices a difference. This contradicts the UC-security of Π_{PF}.

For the second statement of the lemma, assume there exists a protocol Π_{PF} UC-realizing $\mathcal{F}_{PF}$ and that there exists a black-box simulator $\mathcal{S}_S$ against a corrupted sender $\tilde{\mathcal{A}}_S$ such that it holds for all PPT-environments $\mathcal{Z}$ that $\mathsf{Real}^{\tilde{\mathcal{A}}_S}_{\Pi_{PF}}(\mathcal{Z}) \approx_c \mathsf{Ideal}^{\mathcal{S}_S}_{\mathcal{F}_{PF}}(\mathcal{Z})$. Such a simulator must be able to extract a point $\hat{x}$ from the malicious tokens $\mathcal{T}_1^*, \ldots, \mathcal{T}_n^*$ using only black-box techniques (i.e. rewinding). We will now construct an environment $\mathcal{Z}^*$ and a malicious receiver $\mathcal{A}_R$ that extracts the secret $\hat{x}$ from the tokens $\mathcal{T}_1, \ldots, \mathcal{T}_n$. $\mathcal{A}_R$ internally simulates $\mathcal{S}_S$ and provides his interface with $\mathcal{T}_1, \ldots, \mathcal{T}_n$ to $\mathcal{S}_S$. $\mathcal{A}_R$ then outputs to $\mathcal{Z}$ whatever $\mathcal{S}_S$ outputs. From the view of $\mathcal{S}_S$, the simulation of $\mathcal{A}_R$ is identically distributed to $\mathsf{Ideal}^{\mathcal{S}_S}_{\mathcal{F}_{PF}}(\mathcal{Z})$. Thus, $\mathcal{A}_R$ outputs the secret point $\hat{x}$ with overwhelming probability. On the other hand, any simulator $\mathcal{S}_R$ has only black-box access to the point function $PF_{\hat{x}}$ via $\mathcal{F}_{PF}$. Thus $\mathcal{S}_R$ succeeds to learn $\hat{x}$ only with negligible probability. Therefore $\mathcal{Z}^*$ can efficiently distinguish $\mathsf{Real}^{\mathcal{A}_R}_{\Pi_{PF}}(\mathcal{Z})$ and $\mathsf{Ideal}^{\mathcal{S}_R}_{\mathcal{F}_{PF}}(\mathcal{Z})$ for any PPT-simulator $\mathcal{S}_R$, contradicting the UC-security of Π_{PF}.

5 Resettable UC-Functionalities from Untrusted Hardware

In this section, we present the main result of this work. We provide two UC-secure protocols implementing the $\mathcal{F}_{wrap}^{hybrid1}$ and $\mathcal{F}_{wrap}^{hybrid2}$ UC-functionalities in the $\mathcal{F}_{wrap}$-hybrid model. The protocol for $\mathcal{F}_{wrap}^{hybrid1}$ requires only a single $\mathcal{F}_{wrap}$-instance, i.e. a single untrusted hardware token. However, the protocol requires an interactive initialization phase with the issuer of the token. The protocol $\mathcal{F}_{wrap}^{hybrid2}$ requires two $\mathcal{F}_{wrap}$-instances, but is on the other hand completely non-interactive. The blueprint for both protocols is the same. In a setup-phase, a common random reference string is negotiated via a variant of the Blum coin-tossing protocol tailored for the respective setting. In the second phase, a program M encapsulated in the wrapper-functionality (that has access to the common reference string) can be queried by the receiver.

We will start outlining the ideas behind the first protocol $\Pi^{hybrid1}$. On an intuitive level, the token is locked with a password. The receiver first needs to obtain the password a to use the token. The receiver obtains a after performing a Blum coin-toss with the sender which results in a common reference string. For this coin-toss, the issuer uses the token itself to commit to a random string y. More specifically, the sender programs the token to release y, after the token is convinced the the receiver is in possession of a. First the sender sends the token to the receiver to commit himself to the random string y. In the second step, the receiver sends a random x to the sender, who replies with y and the password a (which serves as unveil-information). The receiver now proves to the token that he is in possession of a, thereby obtaining (y', a') from the token. If it holds that $y = y'$, the receiver is convinced that the sender was a-priori committed to y

and a. If the receiver accepts, sender and receiver set $\mathsf{crs} = x \oplus y$ and the sender signs crs, so that the receiver can use it with the token.

One issue we did not address yet is how the receiver proves to the token that he is in possession of the password a. For that purpose, we first make the password a verifiable. We do this by choosing the string a uniformly at random and having the sender publish the image $b = \mathsf{F}(a)$ of a under a one-way function F. As the token is resettable, we will use a resettably-sound zero-knowledge argument of knowledge system for the receiver to prove to the token that he is in possession of the password a, i.e. he possesses an a such that $\mathsf{F}(a) = b$.

In our second protocol $\Pi^{hybrid2}$, where the sender issues two stateless tokens to the receiver and no communication between the sender and receiver is allowed, the above protocol fails. The reason for this is that once the receiver knows a, it can learn the string y, reset the second token (which acts in the role of the sender) and force the crs to a value of his liking by choosing his input x adaptively.

We now give an outline of our second protocol. In order to prohibit the receiver to choose his input x adaptively, he is now required to commit to x using a non-interactive perfectly binding commitment-scheme com. The protocol proceeds as follows. First, R computes $c = \mathsf{com}(x; r)$ (for random coins r). R then sends (x, c) to the first token $\mathcal{T}_1$ and proves that c is a proper commitment of x. Again, we use a resettably-sound zero-knowledge argument system, as $\mathcal{T}_1$ is resettable. If $\mathcal{T}_1$ accepts, it computes y pseudorandomly by $y = \mathsf{prf}(c)$, where prf is a pseudorandom function. Notice that a corrupted sender may choose prf maliciously, it is therefore essential that prf remains oblivious of x. Instead of releasing a password, $\mathcal{T}_1$ now computes a signature σ of c. This σ will now serve as a witness to unlock the second token $\mathcal{T}_2$ for a run with the commitment c. More specifically, R sends c to $\mathcal{T}_2$ and proves to $\mathcal{T}_2$, using a resettably-sound zero-knowledge argument system of knowledge, that it knows a valid signature of c under the verification key vk, i.e. it knows a σ such that verification succeeds. Once $\mathcal{T}_2$ is convinced that R knows such a σ, it computes $y' = \mathsf{prf}(c)$ and outputs y' to R. R now checks if $y = y'$ holds, if so it sets $\mathsf{crs} = x \oplus y$ and uses crs as common random reference string in a two-party computation with $\mathcal{T}_1$.

5.1 A Single Resettable Token

We now provide a formal statement of protocol $\Pi^{hybrid1}$ that UC-emulates $\mathcal{F}_{wrap}^{hybrid1}$. Let k be a security-parameter. Let $\mathcal{T} = \mathcal{F}_{wrap}$ be a resettable hardware wrapper-functionality, let $\mathsf{F} : \{0,1\}^k \rightarrow \{0,1\}^m$ be a one-way function and (P, V) be a resettably-sound zero-knowledge argument system of knowledge for the language $L = \{b : \exists a \in \{0,1\}^k \text{ s.t. } b = F(a)\}$. Further let SIG be an EUF-CMA-secure signature scheme.

Let $\ell = \mathsf{poly}(k)$ be the desired length of the output common reference string.

Protocol $\Pi^{hybrid1}$

1. Sender S (setup step 1): The input of S is a program M
   – Choose $a \leftarrow \{0,1\}^k$ uniformly at random. Set $b = F(a)$.

- Choose $y \leftarrow \{0,1\}^{\ell}$ uniformly at random.
- Generate a key pair $(vk, sgk) = \mathsf{SIG.KeyGen}()$
- Program a stateless token T with the following functionality.
  - Upon receiving a message unveil from R, run the verifier V with input b. Forward the messages between R and V. If V rejects, output $\perp$.
  - If V accepts, send y to R.
  - Upon receiving a message (crs, σ), check if $\mathsf{SIG.Verify}_{vk}(\mathsf{crs}, \sigma) = 1$, if not abort.
  - Upon receiving input $(\mathbf{run}, w)$ from R, run M on input w starting from its most recent state, output whatever M outputs and save the new state of M and wait for the next message $(\mathbf{run}, w)$.
- Input T into $\mathcal{T}$ and send (vk, b) to R
2. Receiver R (setup step 2):
   - Wait for the ready message from $\mathcal{T}$ and a message (vk, b) from S.
   - Choose $x \leftarrow \{0,1\}^{\ell}$ uniformly at random.
   - Send x to S.
3. Sender S (setup step 3):
   - Upon receiving a message x from R, set $\mathsf{crs} = x \oplus y$, compute $\sigma = \mathsf{SIG.Sign}_{sgk}(\mathsf{crs})$. Send (y, a, σ) to R. Output crs.
4. Receiver R (setup step 4):
   - Wait for a message (y, a, σ) from S.
   - Check if $\mathsf{F}(a) = b$, if not abort.
   - Run the prover P with input b and witness-input a. Forward the messages between P and $\mathcal{T}$. Let y' be the output of $\mathcal{T}$.
   - If $y \neq y'$, abort.
   - Set $\mathsf{crs} = x \oplus y$.
   - Send (crs, σ) to $\mathcal{T}$
5. Receiver R (Execute Phase): Upon receiving input $(\mathbf{run}, w)$, send $(\mathbf{run}, w)$ to $\mathcal{T}$ and output whatever $\mathcal{T}$ outputs.

5.2   Proof of Security

We will prove computational UC-security against both corrupted sender and receiver.

Corrupted Receiver. We will start with a corrupted receiver. Let $\mathcal{A}_{\mathsf{R}}$ be the dummy-adversary for a corrupted receiver. Let Ext be the knowledge-extractor for the argument of knowledge-system (P, V). We will first state the simulator $\mathcal{S}_{\mathsf{R}}$.

Simulator $\mathcal{S}_{\mathsf{R}}$

- Simulate the first round of a sender S, forward the message (vk, b) to $\mathcal{A}_{\mathsf{R}}$ and store the signature key sgk. Use the token-code T output by S to simulate the token $\mathcal{T}$ for $\mathcal{A}_{\mathsf{R}}$. Let a be the preimage of b under the one-way function F.

- When the simulated S receives a message x from $\mathcal{A}_R$ do the following. Let crs be the common reference string output by $\mathcal{F}^{hybrid1}_{wrap}$. Set $y = \mathsf{crs} \oplus x$ and $\sigma = \mathsf{SIG.Sign}_{sgk}(\mathsf{crs})$. Output (y, a, σ) to $\mathcal{A}_R$.
- If $\mathcal{A}_R$ sends an unveil-message to $\mathcal{T}$ do the following. If $\mathcal{A}_R$ has not yet sent x to S, output $\bot$, regardless if V would accept. Otherwise output the same y as S.
- If $\mathcal{A}_R$ sends a tuple (crs', σ') to $\mathcal{T}$ do the following. If it holds that $\mathcal{A}_R$ has not yet sent an x to S or $\mathsf{SIG.Verify}_{vk}(\mathsf{crs}', \sigma') = 0$ output $\bot$.
- If $\mathcal{A}_R$ sends a tuple $(\mathbf{run}, w)$ to $\mathcal{T}$ do the following. If $\mathcal{A}_R$ has not yet sent a tuple (crs, σ) to $\mathcal{T}_1$ with $\mathsf{SIG.Verify}_{vk}(\mathsf{crs}, \sigma) = 1$, output $\bot$. Otherwise forward $(\mathbf{run}, w)$ to $\mathcal{F}^{hybrid1}_{wrap}$ and output whatever $\mathcal{F}^{hybrid1}_{wrap}$ outputs.
- Whenever $\mathcal{A}_R$ sends a message $\mathbf{reset}$ to $\mathcal{T}$ send $\mathbf{reset}$ to $\mathcal{F}^{hybrid1}_{wrap}$ and reset the state of $\mathcal{T}$.

Theorem 1. *For every PPT-environment $\mathcal{Z}$, it holds that the random variables* $\mathsf{Real}^{\mathcal{A}_R}_{\Pi^{hybrid1}}(\mathcal{Z})$ *and* $\mathsf{Ideal}^{S_R}_{\mathcal{F}^{hybrid1}_{wrap}}(\mathcal{Z})$ *are computationally indistinguishable.*

To prove the theorem, we will show indistinguishability of the following experiments.

Experiment 1. Simulator $\mathcal{S}_1$ simulates the real protocol $\Pi^{hybrid1}$.

Experiment 2. Identical to experiment 1, except that $\mathcal{T}$ outputs $\bot$ if $\mathcal{A}_R$ sends an unveil-query for which the verifier V accepts before $\mathcal{A}_R$ has sent his coins x to S.

Experiment 3. Identical to experiment 2, except that S's coins y are computed by $y = \mathsf{crs} \oplus y$, where crs is a common random reference string chosen uniformly at random.

Experiment 4. Identical to experiment 3, except that $\mathcal{T}$ aborts if $\mathcal{A}_R$ sends a a tuple (crs, σ), where it holds that $\mathsf{SIG.Verify}_{vk}(\mathsf{crs}, \sigma) = 1$ and crs has not been signed by S. This is the ideal experiment.

Remarks. Experiment 1 and experiment 2 are computationally indistinguishable, given that the one-way function F is strongly one way. Experiment 2 and experiment 3 are identically distributed, as both x and crs are uniformly and independently distributed. The indistinguishability of experiment 3 and experiment 4 follows easily from the EUF-CMA-security of SIG.

Lemma 2. *From $\mathcal{Z}$'s view, experiment 1 and experiment 2 are computationally indistinguishable, given that F is a one-way function and the argument system* (P, V) *suffices the proof of knowledge property.*

Proof. From $\mathcal{Z}$'s view, experiment 1 and experiment 2 are identically distributed conditioned to the event that $\mathcal{A}_R$ does not convince V that it possesses an a such that $\mathsf{F}(a) = b$ before sending his own coins x to S. Thus, a $\mathcal{Z}$ distinguishing between experiment 1 and experiment 2 must succeed in making $\mathcal{A}_R$ convince $\mathcal{T}$ of this before receiving such a value a from S.

Assume that $\mathcal{Z}$ causes this event with non-negligible probability ϵ. We will construct an adversary B that inverts the one-way function F with non-negligible probability. Let $m = \mathsf{poly}(k)$ be an upper bound on the number of unveil calls that $\mathcal{A}_R$ sends to $\mathcal{T}$. Let b' be the image on which $\mathcal{B}$ is supposed to invert F. $\mathcal{B}$ first chooses an index $i \in \{1, \ldots, m\}$ uniformly at random.

Let $\mathcal{S}_1'$ be a simulator the behaves exactly like $\mathcal{S}_1$, except for one modification. $\mathcal{S}_1'$ sets $b = b'$ instead of generating b by $b = \mathsf{F}(a)$. $\mathcal{B}$ then simulates the interaction between $\mathcal{Z}$ and $\mathcal{S}_1'$ until $\mathcal{A}_R$ makes the i'th unveil-call. $\mathcal{B}$ now halts the computation of $\mathcal{Z}$. If the computation of $\mathcal{Z}$ continued after this point, the subsequent messages passed by $\mathcal{A}_R$ correspond to the messages of a malicious prover P* for the argument system (P, V). Thus, $\mathcal{B}$ can construct P* from the state of the halted $\mathcal{Z}$ which basically continues the simulation of $\mathcal{Z}$ at its current state and forwards messages between $\mathcal{A}_R$ and an external verifier V. $\mathcal{B}$ can now take the code of P* and run the extractor $\mathsf{Ext}(b, \mathsf{P}^*)$. Let a be the output of Ext. $\mathcal{B}$ outputs a and terminates.

First notice, that from $\mathcal{Z}$'s view, this simulation is identically distributed to experiment 1. Thus, the event that $\mathcal{A}_R$ succeeds in convincing $\mathcal{T}$ that it possesses a preimage a of b happens with probability at least ϵ. With probability at least $1/m$, the index i chosen by $\mathcal{B}$ matches the index of the proof where this event happens. Therefore, it holds that $\Pr[\langle \mathsf{P}^*, \mathsf{V}(c) \rangle = 1] \geq \epsilon/m$. Due to the proof of knowledge property of the argument system (P, V) it holds that $\Pr[\mathsf{Ext}(b, \mathsf{P}^*) \in w_{L_1}(b)] > \Pr[\langle \mathsf{P}^*, \mathsf{V}(c) \rangle = 1] - \nu \geq \epsilon - \nu$ for some negligible ν. Thus, with probability $\epsilon - \nu$, which is non-negligible, $\mathcal{B}$ outputs a preimage a of b' under F, thus breaking the one-wayness property of F.

Corrupted Sender. Next, we will prove computational UC-security for the case of a corrupted sender. Let $\mathcal{A}_S$ be the dummy-adversary for a corrupted sender and let Sim be the non-black-box simulator for the argument system (P, V), that takes as input a statement (k, b) and the code V* of a malicious verifier. The simulator $\mathcal{S}_S$ is given as follows.

Simulator $\mathcal{S}_S$

- Let T* be the token sent by $\mathcal{A}_S$ and (vk, b) be the message sent by $\mathcal{A}_S$.
- Simulate $\mathcal{T}$ using T*.
- Construct a malicious verifier V* for the argument system (P, V) that basically simulates the zero-knowledge step of T* and outputs the state of T* after the zero-knowledge step is over.
- Run the non-black-box simulator Sim on input b and auxiliary input V*. The output of Sim is the state of T* after the zero-knowledge protocol. Continue the simulation of $\mathcal{T}$ from this state until it outputs y.
- Let crs be the common reference string sent by $\mathcal{F}_{wrap}^{hybrid1}$. Set $x = \mathsf{crs} \oplus y$.
- Send x to S. Let (y', a, σ) be the response of S.
- If $y \neq y'$ or $\mathsf{F}(a) \neq b$ abort. Otherwise run $\mathcal{T}$ on input (crs, σ).

- Input T* with the most recent state taken from $\mathcal{T}$ hardwired into $\mathcal{F}_{wrap}^{hybrid1}$ and output crs to S.

Let $\mathcal{Z}$ be a PPT environment. We will now prove computational indistinguishability between $\mathsf{Real}_{\Pi_{CRS}^{AR}}^{A_R}(\mathcal{Z})$ and $\mathsf{Ideal}_{\mathcal{F}_{CRS}}^{S_R}(\mathcal{Z})$ directly, given that the argument system (P, V) is zero-knowledge.

Theorem 2. $\mathsf{Real}_{\Pi^{hybrid1}}^{A_S}(\mathcal{Z})$ and $\mathsf{Ideal}_{\mathcal{F}_{wrap}^{hybrid1}}^{S_S}(\mathcal{Z})$ are computationally indistinguishable.

To prove the theorem, we will show indistinguishability of the following experiments.

Experiment 1. Simulator S_1 simulates the protocol $\Pi^{hybrid1}$

Experiment 2. Identical to experiment 1, except that when R sends an unveil-message to T*, S_2 runs the non-black-box simulator Sim on the verifier V* (as constructed in the description of the simulator S_S) instead of letting the prover P interact with T*. S_2 then uses the output of Sim as most recent state to continue the computation of T*.

Experiment 3. Identical to experiment 2, except that S_3 runs the unveil-phase of $\mathcal{T}$ before interacting with A_S, thereby obtaining y. Set $x = \mathsf{crs} \oplus y$, where crs is a uniformly random common reference string. This is the ideal experiment.

Remarks. The indistinguishability of experiment 1 and experiment 2 follows from the computational zero-knowledge property of the argument system (P, V). Experiment 2 and experiment 3 are identically distributed, as the interactions of R with $\mathcal{T}$ and A_S are independent of one another in both experiments and thus exchangeable.

Lemma 3. *From $\mathcal{Z}$'s view, experiment 1 and experiment 2 are computationally indistinguishable, provided that the argument system (P, V) is computational zero-knowledge.*

Proof. Fix a PPT-environment $\mathcal{Z}$. Assume for contradiction that $\mathcal{Z}$ distinguishes experiment 1 and experiment 2 with non-negligible advantage ϵ. We will construct a malicious verifier V* and a distinguisher $\mathcal{D}$, such that $\mathcal{D}$ distinguishes the random variables $\langle P(a), V^* \rangle(b)$ and $\mathsf{Sim}(b, V^*)$ with advantage ϵ, for some a and b. Fix the random tape of $\mathcal{Z}$ such that $\mathcal{Z}$ with these fixed coins distinguishes between experiment 1 and experiment 2 with advantage ϵ. By a simple averaging argument, such coins must exist. Let (a, b) with $F(a) = b$ be the fixed tuple that corresponds with this $\mathcal{Z}$. The malicious verifier V* is constructed as in the description of the simulator. The distinguisher $\mathcal{D}$ is obtained by plugging the machine $\mathcal{Z}$ and S_2 together, with modification to the simulator S_2 that it does not obtain the state of $\mathcal{T}$ by running Sim on b and V*, but using its own input as state of $\mathcal{T}$. Clearly, if $\mathcal{D}$'s input is distributed by $\langle P(a), V^* \rangle(b)$, then $\mathcal{Z}$'s view is distributed identical as in experiment 1. If, on the other hand, $\mathcal{D}$'s input is distributed according to $\mathsf{Sim}(b, V^*)$, then $\mathcal{Z}$'s view is distributed identical to experiment 2. Thus $\mathcal{D}$ and V* contradict the zero-knowledge property of (P, V).

5.3   Two Resettable Tokens

In this section we will describe our protocol $\Pi^{hybrid2}$ that implements $\mathcal{F}_{wrap}^{hybrid2}$. Let {PRF} be a family of pseudorandom functions, $\mathsf{com}(\cdot, \cdot)$ be a non-interactive perfectly binding commitment scheme and $\mathsf{SIG} = (\mathsf{KeyGen}, \mathsf{Sign}, \mathsf{Verify})$ be an EUF-CMA-secure signature scheme with deterministic signing algorithm. We further need two resettably-sound zero-knowledge argument of knowledge systems. Let $(\mathsf{P}_1, \mathsf{V}_1)$ be such a system for the language $L_1 = \{(x, c) | \exists r : c = \mathsf{com}(x; r)\}$ and $(\mathsf{P}_2, \mathsf{V}_2)$ be such a system for the language $L_2 = \{(vk, c) | \exists \sigma : \mathsf{Verify}(c, \sigma) = 1\}$. Let $\mathcal{T}_1$ and $\mathcal{T}_2$ be two $\mathcal{F}_{wrap}$ functionalities.

Protocol $\Pi^{hybrid2}$

1. Sender S (setup step 1): The input of S is a program M
   - Sample a pseudorandom function $\mathsf{prf} \leftarrow \{\mathsf{PRF}\}$, generate signature and verification keys $(sgk, vk) = \mathsf{SIG.KeyGen}()$.
   - Choose a random tape for the token T_1 and program T_1 as follows.
     - Set flag $\mathtt{ready} = 0$.
     - Upon receiving input (x, c) from R, run the verifier V_1 with input (x, c). Forward the messages between R and V_1. If V_1 rejects, output $\perp$.
     - If V_1 accepts, compute $y = \mathsf{prf}(c)$ and $\sigma = \mathsf{SIG.Sign}_{sgk}(c)$. Set flag $\mathtt{ready} = 1$ and output (y, σ).
     - Upon receiving input $(\mathbf{run}, w)$ from R, run M on input w starting from its most recent state, output whatever M outputs and save the new state of M and wait for the next message $(\mathbf{run}, w)$.
   - Choose a random tape for the token T_2 and program T_2 as follows.
     - Upon receiving input c from R, run the verifier V_2 with input (vk, c). Forward the messages between R and V_2. If V_2 rejects, output $\perp$.
     - If V_1 accepts, compute $y = \mathsf{prf}(c)$ and output y.
   - Input T_1 into $\mathcal{T}_1$ and T_2 into $\mathcal{T}_2$. Send vk to R.
2. Receiver R (setup step 2):
   - Choose $x \leftarrow \{0, 1\}^k$ uniformly at random.
   - Compute $c = \mathsf{com}(x; r)$ with a uniformly random chosen r.
   - Send (x, c) to $\mathcal{T}_1$ and run the prover P_1 with input (x, c) and witness-input r. Forward the messages between P_1 and $\mathcal{T}_1$. Let (y, σ) be the output of $\mathcal{T}_1$.
   - Check if $\mathsf{SIG.Verify}_{vk}(c, \sigma) = 1$, if not abort.
   - Send c to $\mathcal{T}_2$ and run the prover P_2 with input (vk, c) and witness-input σ. Let y' be the output of $\mathcal{T}_2$.
   - Check whether $y = y'$, if not abort. Otherwise set $\mathsf{crs} = x \oplus y$.
3. Receiver R (Execute Phase): Upon receiving input $(\mathbf{run}, w)$, send $(\mathbf{run}, w)$ to $\mathcal{T}_1$ and output whatever $\mathcal{T}_1$ outputs.

Corrupted Receiver. We will prove computational UC-security against a corrupted receiver R. We therefore first provide the simulator $\mathcal{S}_\mathsf{R}$.

Simulator $\mathcal{S}_{\mathsf{R}}$

- Simulate the first round of a sender S and forward the message vk to $\mathcal{A}_{\mathsf{R}}$ and store sgk. Use the token-codes T_1 and T_2 output by S to simulate $\mathcal{T}_1$ and $\mathcal{T}_2$ for $\mathcal{A}_{\mathsf{R}}$. Setup a counter $j = 1$.
- If $\mathcal{A}_{\mathsf{R}}$ sends a message (x, c) to $\mathcal{T}_1$ do the following. Continue the simulation of $\mathcal{T}_1$ until the verifier V_1 either accepts or rejects. If it accepts, even though a tuple (x', y', c', j') has been stored, for some $x' \neq x$ and $c' = c$, output $\perp$. Otherwise, if V_1 accepts, compute $\sigma = \mathsf{SIG.Sign}_{sgk}(c)$ and output (y, σ), for which a tuple (x, y, c, j') has been stored. Send $(\mathtt{reset}, j')$ to $\mathcal{F}_{wrap}^{hybrid2}$. If no such tuple has been stored before, increment j by 1, send $(\mathtt{reset}, j')$ to the $\mathcal{F}_{wrap}^{hybrid2}$ functionality to get a string crs, set $y = x \oplus \mathsf{crs}$, compute $\sigma = \mathsf{SIG.Sign}_{sgk}(c)$, store the tuple (x, y, c, j) and output (y, σ).
- If $\mathcal{A}_{\mathsf{R}}$ sends a message c to $\mathcal{T}_2$ do the following. Continue the simulation of $\mathcal{T}_2$ until the verifier V_2 either accepts or rejects. If it accepts, check if a tuple (x', y', c', j') with $c' = c$ has been stored. If not, output $\perp$. Otherwise output y'.
- Whenever $\mathcal{A}_{\mathsf{R}}$ sends a message $\mathtt{reset}$ to $\mathcal{T}_2$, reset $\mathcal{T}_2$.

Theorem 3. *For every PPT-environment $\mathcal{Z}$, it holds that the random variables* $\mathsf{Real}_{\Pi^{hybrid2}}^{\mathcal{A}_{\mathsf{R}}}(\mathcal{Z})$ *and* $\mathsf{Ideal}_{\mathcal{F}_{wrap}^{hybrid2}}^{\mathcal{S}_{\mathsf{R}}}(\mathcal{Z})$ *are computationally indistinguishable.*

Again, to prove the theorem, we will show indistinguishability of the following experiments.

Experiment 1. Simulator $\mathcal{S}_1$ simulates the protocol $\Pi^{hybrid2}$. This is the real experiment.

Experiment 2. Identical to experiment 1, except that y is not computed as $y = \mathsf{prf}(c)$ but as follows. If a tuple (x', y', c', j') has been stored with $c' = c$, set $y = y'$. Otherwise, choose crs uniformly at random and set $y = x \oplus \mathsf{crs}$. Also store the tuple (x, y, c).

Experiment 3. Identical to experiment 2, except that $\mathcal{T}_1$ outputs $\perp$ if V_1 accepts, even though a tuple (x', y', c', j') has been stored, with $x' \neq x$ and $c' = c$.

Experiment 4. Identical to experiment 3, except that $\mathcal{T}_2$ outputs $\perp$ if V_2 accepts, even though no tuple (x', y', c', j') with $c' = c$ has been stored. This is the ideal experiment.

Remarks. Given that prf is a pseudorandom function, we can replace the outputs of prf with truly random values, thus experiment 1 and experiment 2 are indistinguishable. The indistinguishability of experiment 2 and experiment 3 follows from the binding property of the commitment scheme com. The event that $\mathcal{T}_1$ outputs $\perp$ even though V_1 accepts happens only when $\mathcal{A}_{\mathsf{R}}$ manages to convince $\mathcal{T}_1$ that c is a commitment to two different values x and x'. The proof of knowledge property of the argument system $(\mathsf{P}_1, \mathsf{V}_1)$ guarantees that the corresponding unveils r and r' can be extracted with high probability. The indistinguishability of experiment 3 and experiment 4 follows from the EUF-CMA-property of the signature scheme SIG. If $\mathcal{T}_2$ outputs $\perp$, even though the verifier V_2 accepts, then $\mathcal{A}_R$ has convinced V_2 that it possesses a signature on a commitment c for which it never received a signature σ from $\mathcal{T}_1$. The proof of knowledge property enables us to extract such a forged signature, contradicting the EUF-CMA-security of SIG. For the complete proof refer to the full version of this paper.

Corrupted Sender. We will prove computational UC-security against a corrupted sender S. Let therefore $\mathcal{A}_S$ be the dummy-adversary and $\mathcal{Z}$ be a PPT-environment. We first state the sender-simulator $\mathcal{S}_S$. This simulator programs a simulator-token T_S and sends this token to $\mathcal{F}_{wrap}^{hybrid2}$.

Simulator $\mathcal{S}_S$.

- Let T_1 and T_2 be the inputs of $\mathcal{A}_S$.
- Simulate $\mathcal{T}_2$ with the code T_2.
- Set $c = \mathsf{com}(0; r)$ for a randomly chosen r.
- Use the code T_2 to construct the code V_2^* of a verifier that runs the verifier-stage of $\mathcal{T}_2$ when its input is c. The output of V_2^* is the the same output that T_2 would provide to R.
- Run Sim_2 with input (vk, c) and witness-input V^*. Let y' be the output of Sim_2
- Program a token T_S as follows.
  - Read the common reference string crs provided by the $\mathcal{F}_{wrap}^{hybrid2}$ functionality. Set $x = \mathsf{crs} \oplus y'$.
  - Use the code T_1 to construct the code V_1^* of a verifier that runs the verifier stage of T_1 when its input is (x, c). The output of V_1^* is the the same output that T_1 would provide to R.
  - Run Sim_1 with input (x, c) and witness-input V_1^*. Let (y, σ) be the output of Sim_1.
  - Check whether $y = y'$. If not abort.
  - Upon receiving input $(\mathbf{run}, w)$ from R, run M on input w starting from its most recent state, output whatever M outputs and save the new state of M and wait for the next message $(\mathbf{run}, w)$.
- Input T_S into $\mathcal{F}_{wrap}^{hybrid2}$

Theorem 4. *For every PPT-environment $\mathcal{Z}$, it holds that the random variables* $\mathsf{Real}_{\Pi^{hybrid2}}^{\mathcal{A}_S}(\mathcal{Z})$ *and* $\mathsf{Ideal}_{\mathcal{F}_{wrap}^{hybrid2}}^{\mathcal{S}_S}(\mathcal{Z})$ *are computationally indistinguishable.*

To prove the theorem, we will show indistinguishability of the following experiments.

Experiment 1. Simulator $\mathcal{S}_1$ simulates the protocol $\Pi^{hybrid2}$. This is the real experiment.

Experiment 2. Identical to experiment 1, except that $\mathcal{S}_2$ does the following. Instead of running P_2 with input (vk, c) and witness-input σ, it runs Sim_2 with input (vk, c) and witness-input V_2^* (where V_2^* is as defined in the description of simulator $\mathcal{S}_\mathcal{S}$).

Experiment 3. Identical to experiment 2, except that S_3 does the following. Instead of running P_1 with input (x, c) and witness-input r, it runs Sim_1 with input (x, c) and witness-input V_1^* (where V_1^* is as defined in the description of simulator $\mathcal{S}_\mathcal{S}$).

Experiment 4. Identical to experiment 3, except that the commitment c is computed as $c = \mathsf{com}(0; r)$ instead of $c = \mathsf{com}(x; r)$.

Experiment 5. Identical to experiment 4, except that $\mathcal{S}_5$ first interacts with $\mathcal{T}_2$ and then with $\mathcal{T}_1$, instead of vice versa. Moreover, it sets $x = \mathsf{crs} \oplus y'$ instead of choosing x uniformly at random. This is the ideal experiment.

Remarks. Experiment 1 and experiment 2 are indistinguishable given that the argument system $(\mathsf{P}_1, \mathsf{V}_1)$ is zero-knowledge. Similarly, experiment 2 and experiment 3 are indistinguishable given that $(\mathsf{P}_2, \mathsf{V}_2)$ is zero-knowledge. Both indistinguishability proofs are almost identical to the proof of Lemma 3 and thus omitted. The indistinguishability of experiment 3 and experiment 4 follows straightforwardly from the hiding property of the commitment scheme com. Experiment 4 and experiment 5 are identically distributed, as in both experiments y is independently uniformly distributed.

6   Applications

One application for our protocols is implementing a UC-secure functionality we call conditional decryption, $\mathcal{F}_{\mathsf{CONDEC}}$. In essence, what can be achieved through the conditional decryption functionality is that the computational workload is transfered from the hardware token to the user of the protocol, similar in concept to delegation of computation [23, 24].

The $\mathcal{F}_{\mathsf{CONDEC}}$-functionality takes as sender-input a private key sk for a fully homomorphic encryption scheme FHE. The receiver can send decryption-queries c to $\mathcal{F}_{\mathsf{CONDEC}}$. Before $\mathcal{F}_{\mathsf{CONDEC}}$ decrypts such queries, the receiver must prove that the query is well-formed. This proof is implemented using a universal argument system [25]. Such a conditional decryption has a straightforward application in the context of obfuscation. Given $\mathcal{F}_{\mathsf{CONDEC}}$, a sender initializes the conditional decryption functionality. He can then encrypt an arbitrary program and send it to the receiver. All the receiver has to do is to homomorphically evaluate the encrypted program and send the result together with a proof to the token. If the homomorphic evaluation was carried out correctly, the token will decrypt the result and send it to the receiver. The advantage of this approach is that the sender can obfuscate programs arbitrarily without having to send a new token each time. A similar construction can be found in [26]. Due to space limitations, the above high level description omits several important details which are necessary for a UC-proof. A detailed description of the protocols and a full proof can be found in a preliminary version of this paper [27].

7 Conclusion

In this work, we investigated the cryptographic strength of untrusted resettable hardware tokens in the UC-framework. We devised two protocols that use resettable hardware tokens to realize intermediate functionalities that are sufficient to UC-emulate arbitrary resettable functionalities. The first protocol uses one resettable token and two rounds of interaction in an initialization phase, after which no further interaction takes place. In the second protocol, messages and hardware tokens are only passed from the sender to the receiver. However, this protocol requires two resettable token. Given these protocols, it is possible to UC-realize any resettable two-party computation. We showed that a completely non-interactive coin-toss with only one resettable token is impossible. Thus, both our protocols are optimal if one of the conditions (no interaction or just a single token) is dropped.

References

1. Barak, B., Goldreich, O., Impagliazzo, R., Rudich, S., Sahai, A., Vadhan, S.P., Yang, K.: On the (Im)possibility of Obfuscating Programs. In: Kilian, J. (ed.) CRYPTO 2001. LNCS, vol. 2139, pp. 1–18. Springer, Heidelberg (2001)
2. Canetti, R., Fischlin, M.: Universally Composable Commitments. In: Kilian, J. (ed.) CRYPTO 2001. LNCS, vol. 2139, pp. 19–40. Springer, Heidelberg (2001)
3. Canetti, R., Goldreich, O., Goldwasser, S., Micali, S.: Resettable zero-knowledge (extended abstract). In: STOC, pp. 235–244 (2000)
4. Canetti, R., Lindell, Y., Ostrovsky, R., Sahai, A.: Universally composable two-party and multi-party secure computation. In: STOC, pp. 494–503 (2002)
5. Barak, B., Lindell, Y., Vadhan, S.P.: Lower bounds for non-black-box zero knowledge. In: FOCS (2003)
6. Deng, Y., Lin, D.: Instance-Dependent Verifiable Random Functions and Their Application to Simultaneous Resettability. In: Naor, M. (ed.) EUROCRYPT 2007. LNCS, vol. 4515, pp. 148–168. Springer, Heidelberg (2007)
7. Barak, B., Goldreich, O., Goldwasser, S., Lindell, Y.: Resettably-sound zero-knowledge and its applications. In: FOCS, pp. 116–125 (2001)
8. Deng, Y., Goyal, V., Sahai, A.: Resolving the simultaneous resettability conjecture and a new non-black-box simulation strategy. In: FOCS, pp. 251–260 (2009)
9. Deng, Y., Feng, D., Goyal, V., Lin, D., Sahai, A., Yung, M.: Resettable Cryptography in Constant Rounds – The Case of Zero Knowledge. In: Lee, D.H., Wang, X. (eds.) ASIACRYPT 2011. LNCS, vol. 7073, pp. 390–406. Springer, Heidelberg (2011)
10. Cho, C., Ostrovsky, R., Scafuro, A., Visconti, I.: Simultaneously Resettable Arguments of Knowledge. In: Cramer, R. (ed.) TCC 2012. LNCS, vol. 7194, pp. 530–547. Springer, Heidelberg (2012)

11. Goyal, V., Sahai, A.: Resettably Secure Computation. In: Joux, A. (ed.) EURO-CRYPT 2009. LNCS, vol. 5479, pp. 54–71. Springer, Heidelberg (2009)

12. Goyal, V., Maji, H.K.: Stateless cryptographic protocols. In: FOCS, pp. 678–687 (2011)

13. Goyal, V., Ishai, Y., Mahmoody, M., Sahai, A.: Interactive Locking, Zero-Knowledge PCPs, and Unconditional Cryptography. In: Rabin, T. (ed.) CRYPTO 2010. LNCS, vol. 6223, pp. 173–190. Springer, Heidelberg (2010)

14. Canetti, R.: Universally composable security: A new paradigm for cryptographic protocols. In: FOCS, pp. 136–145 (2001)

15. Canetti, R., Kushilevitz, E., Lindell, Y.: On the limitations of universally composable two-party computation without set-up assumptions. J. Cryptology 19(2), 135–167 (2006)

16. Fischlin, M.: Universally Composable Oblivious Transfer in the Multi-party Setting. In: Pointcheval, D. (ed.) CT-RSA 2006. LNCS, vol. 3860, pp. 332–349. Springer, Heidelberg (2006)

17. Goyal, V., Ishai, Y., Sahai, A., Venkatesan, R., Wadia, A.: Founding Cryptography on Tamper-Proof Hardware Tokens. In: Micciancio, D. (ed.) TCC 2010. LNCS, vol. 5978, pp. 308–326. Springer, Heidelberg (2010)

18. Katz, J.: Universally Composable Multi-party Computation Using Tamper-Proof Hardware. In: Naor, M. (ed.) EUROCRYPT 2007. LNCS, vol. 4515, pp. 115–128. Springer, Heidelberg (2007)

19. Choi, S.G., Katz, J., Schröder, D., Yerukhimovich, A., Zhou, H.S.: (Efficient) universally composable two-party computation using a minimal number of stateless tokens. IACR Cryptology ePrint Archive 2011, 689 (2011)

20. Naor, M., Yung, M.: Universal one-way hash functions and their cryptographic applications. In: STOC, pp. 33–43 (1989)

21. Rompel, J.: One-way functions are necessary and sufficient for secure signatures. In: STOC, pp. 387–394 (1990)

22. Goldreich, O.: Foundations of Cryptography. Cambridge University Press (2001)

23. Gennaro, R., Gentry, C., Parno, B.: Non-interactive Verifiable Computing: Outsourcing Computation to Untrusted Workers. In: Rabin, T. (ed.) CRYPTO 2010. LNCS, vol. 6223, pp. 465–482. Springer, Heidelberg (2010)

24. Chung, K.-M., Kalai, Y., Vadhan, S.: Improved Delegation of Computation Using Fully Homomorphic Encryption. In: Rabin, T. (ed.) CRYPTO 2010. LNCS, vol. 6223, pp. 483–501. Springer, Heidelberg (2010)

25. Barak, B., Goldreich, O.: Universal arguments and their applications. In: IEEE Conference on Computational Complexity, pp. 194–203 (2002)

26. Bitansky, N., Canetti, R., Goldwasser, S., Halevi, S., Kalai, Y.T., Rothblum, G.N.: Program Obfuscation with Leaky Hardware. In: Lee, D.H., Wang, X. (eds.) ASIACRYPT 2011. LNCS, vol. 7073, pp. 722–739. Springer, Heidelberg (2011)

27. Döttling, N., Mie, T., Müller-Quade, J., Nilges, T.: Basing obfuscation on simple tamper-proof hardware assumptions. IACR Cryptology ePrint Archive 2011, 675 (2011)

A Cookbook for Black-Box Separations and a Recipe for UOWHFs

Kfir Barhum and Thomas Holenstein

Department of Computer Science,
ETH Zurich, 8092 Zurich, Switzerland

Abstract. We present a new framework for proving fully black-box separations and lower bounds. We prove a general theorem that facilitates the proofs of fully black-box lower bounds from a one-way function (OWF).

Loosely speaking, our theorem says that in order to prove that a fully black-box construction does not securely construct a cryptographic primitive **Q** (e.g., a pseudo-random generator or a universal one-way hash function) from a OWF, it is enough to come up with a large enough set of functions $\mathcal{F}$ and a parameterized oracle (i.e., an oracle that is defined for every $f \in \{0,1\}^n \to \{0,1\}^n$) such that $\mathcal{O}_f$ breaks the security of the construction when instantiated with f and the oracle satisfies two local properties.

Our main application of the theorem is a lower bound of $\Omega(n/\log(n))$ on the number of calls made by any fully black-box construction of a universal one-way hash function (UOWHF) from a general one-way function. The bound holds even when the OWF is regular, in which case it matches to a recent construction of Barhum and Maurer [4].

Keywords: Complexity-Based Cryptography, One-Way Functions, Universal One-Way Hash Functions, Black-Box Constructions, Lower Bounds.

1 Introduction

1.1 Cryptographic Primitives and Black-Box Constructions

An important question in complexity-based cryptography is understanding which cryptographic primitives (e.g., one-way functions, pseudo-random generators) are implied by others. In principle, an implication between two primitives can be proved as a logical statement (e.g., the existence of one-way functions implies the existence of pseudo-random generators). However, most proofs of such implications (with very few exceptions, e.g., [2]) are in fact so-called fully black-box constructions.

Informally, a black-box construction of a primitive **Q** from a primitive **P** is a pair of algorithms, called *construction* and *reduction*, such that the construction, using only the functionality of **P**, implements **Q** and the reduction, using only the functionality of **P** and the one of a potential breaker algorithm, breaks

A. Sahai (Ed.): TCC 2013, LNCS 7785, pp. 662–679, 2013.

P whenever the breaker algorithm breaks **Q**. As a corollary, such a black-box construction establishes that the existence of **P** implies the existence of **Q**. One of many such examples is the construction of a one-way function from a weak one-way function [18].

After futile attempts to prove that the existence of one-way functions implies that of key agreement, Impagliazzo and Rudich [10] proved the first black-box separation result: They showed that there is no fully black-box construction of key agreement from one-way functions. Their seminal work inspired a plethora of similar results and nowadays one identifies two main types of black-box separation results: black-box separations of a primitive **Q** from a primitive **P** and lower bounds on some complexity parameter (e.g., seed length, number of calls to the underlying primitive, etc.) in the construction of **Q** from **P**. Besides [10], the work of Simon [17], where he shows that there is no fully black-box construction of a collision-resistant hash function from a one-way function, is an example of the former. As an example of the latter, Kim *et. al.* [11] established a lower bound of $\Omega(\sqrt{k/\log(n)})$ on the number of queries of any construction of a universal one-way hash function that compresses k bits from a one-way permutation on n bits. This was later improved by Gennaro *et. al.* [5] to $\Omega(k/\log(n))$.

Reingold *et. al.* [13] were the first to formalize a model for and study the relations between different notions of "black-boxness" of cryptographic constructions.

A key property of a fully black-box construction of **Q** from **P** is the requirement that it constructs **Q** efficiently even when given black-box access to a non-efficient implementation of **P**. A proof technique utilizing this property, which is implicit in many black-box separations, involves an (inefficient) oracle instantiation of the primitive **P** and an appropriate (inefficient) breaker oracle B. The separation is usually proved by showing that B breaks the security of the candidate construction for **Q**, but at the same time no efficient oracle algorithm that has black-box oracle access to both the breaker and the primitive (in particular, the potential reduction) breaks the security property of the underlying instantiation of **P**.

1.2   Our Contribution

In constructions based on one-way functions (or permutations), i.e., when **P = OWF**, the oracle that implements **OWF** is usually set to be a random permutation, which is one-way with very high probability even in the presence of a non-uniform algorithm. On the other hand, the proof that the breaker algorithm for the constructed primitive **Q** does not help invert the permutation is repeated in an "ad-hoc" manner in many separation proofs, e.g., in [17,6] and also in a recent result on lower bounds on the number of calls made by any construction of a pseudo-random generator from a one-way function [9].

Thus, while in many separation proofs the task of finding the right breaker oracle is different (this is inherent, as each time it is required to break the security of a different primitive), we observe that the proof that it does not help in inverting the underlying one-way function can be facilitated and unified to a large extent. To that end, we prove a general theorem that facilitates the proof of black-box separations (Theorem 1). In particular, we show that any circuit with access to an oracle that satisfies two local properties, does not help to invert many functions.

Our framework allows proving separation results that exclude the existence of reductions with very weak security requirements. In this work we focus on the important case where the black-box construction is so-called fixed-parameter. That is, for a security parameter ρ, both the construction algorithm and the reduction access the primitive and breaker of security ρ only. All black-box constructions found in the literature are in fact fixed-parameter constructions. We believe that adapting the approach of [9], it is possible to extend our results to the most general case.

Our proof uses the encoding technique from [5], which was already adapted to the special cases in [6] and [9]. We also use the bending technique that originated in [17] and was subsequently used in [7] and [9].

As an application, in Section 4 we prove a lower bound of $\Omega(n/\log^3(n))$ on the number of calls made by any fully black-box construction of a universal one-way hash function (UOWHF) from a one-way function $f : \{0,1\}^n \to \{0,1\}^n$. This can be further improved to $\Omega(n/\log(n))$ (see Section 5 in [3]).

UOWHFs are a fundamental cryptographic primitive, most notably used for obtaining digital signatures. They were studied extensively since their introduction by Naor and Yung [12], who showed a simple construction that makes only one call to the underlying one-way function whenever, additionally, the function is a permutation. Rompel [14] showed a construction based on any one-way function, and the most efficient construction based on general one-way functions is due to Haitner $et.$ $al.$ [8]. Their construction makes $\tilde{O}(n^6)$ calls to a one-way function $f : \{0,1\}^n \to \{0,1\}^n$. Note that the bound given in [5] does not say anything for the mere construction of a UOWHF (e.g., for a function which compresses one bit), and prior to our work it would have been possible to conjecture that there exists a construction of a UOWHF from a general one-way function that makes only one call to the underlying one-way function. Our bound matches exactly and up to a log-factor the number of calls made by the constructions of [4] and [1], respectively.

Our result can be understood as an analog to that of Holenstein and Sinha, who show a bound of $\Omega(n/\log(n))$ on the number of calls to a one-way function that are made by a construction of a pseudo-random generator. We observe (details are omitted) that the recent result of [9] can be explained in our framework. Our characterization of UOWHFs (presented in Section 4.1) is inspired by their characterization of pseudo-random generators. For some candidate constructions, our proof also utilizes their BreakOW oracle. Our main technical contribution in Section 4.2 is the oracle BreakPI and the proof that it satisfies the conditions of our theorem from Section 3.

2   Preliminaries

2.1   The Computational Model

A function $p = p(\rho)$ is polynomial if there exists a value c such that $p(\rho) = \rho^c$. A machine M is efficient if there exists a polynomial p such that on every input $x \in \{0,1\}^*$, $M(x)$ halts after at most $p(|x|)$ steps. A function $s : \mathbb{N}^+ \to \mathbb{N}^+$ is a security function if for every $\rho \in \mathbb{N}^+$ it holds that $s(\rho + 1) \geq s(\rho)$, and s is efficiently computable (i.e., there exists an efficient machine M that on input 1^ρ outputs $s(\rho)$). For a security function s we define $\frac{1}{s} : \mathbb{N}^+ \to \mathbb{R}^+$ as $\frac{1}{s}(\rho) \overset{\text{def}}{=} \frac{1}{s(\rho)}$. A function $f : \mathbb{N}^+ \to \mathbb{R}^+$ is negligible if for all polynomial security functions p it holds that $f(\rho) < \frac{1}{p(\rho)}$ for all large enough ρ.

An (n, n')-oracle circuit $C^{(?)}$ is a circuit that contains special oracle gates of input length n and output length n'. An (n_1, n'_1, n_2, n'_2)-oracle circuit $C^{(?)}$ is a circuit that contains two types of oracle gates, where the ith type contains n_i input gates and n'_i output gates.

A family of functions $f = \{f_\rho\}_{\rho \in \mathbb{N}^+}$ is uniformly efficiently computable if there exists an efficient machine M such that for every $\rho \in \mathbb{N}^+$ it holds that $M(1^{(\rho)})$ outputs a circuit that implements f_ρ. A non-uniform algorithm $A = \{A_\rho\}_{\rho \in \mathbb{N}^+}$ is a parameterized family of circuits A_ρ. A non-uniform algorithm A implements the parametrized functions family $f = \{f_\rho\}_{\rho \in \mathbb{N}^+}$, if each A_ρ implements f_ρ.

A non-uniform oracle algorithm $A^{(?)} = \{A^{(?)}{}_\rho\}_{\rho \in \mathbb{N}^+}$ is a parameterized family of oracle circuits. Let $A^{(?)}$ be an oracle algorithm. A parametrized family of functions $f = \{f_\rho\}_{\rho \in \mathbb{N}^+}$ (resp., an algorithm $B = \{B_\rho\}_{\rho \in \mathbb{N}^+}$) is compatible with $A^{(?)}$ if for all $\rho > 0$ it holds that f_ρ (resp., B_ρ) is compatible with A_ρ. In this case we define the algorithm $A^{(f)} \overset{\text{def}}{=} \{A_\rho^{f_\rho}\}$ (resp., $A^{(B)} \overset{\text{def}}{=} \{A_\rho^{B_\rho}\}$).

Uniform Generation of Oracle Algorithms. The construction and reduction algorithms in fully black-box constructions are assumed to work for any[1] input/output lengths of the primitive and breaker functionalities, and therefore are modeled in the following way: In addition to the security parameter ρ, both the construction and the reduction algorithms take as input information about the input/output lengths of the underlying primitive f_ρ and the breaker algorithm B_ρ.

A uniform oracle algorithm is a machine M that on input $M(1^\rho, n(\rho), n'(\rho))$ outputs an $(n(\rho), n'(\rho))$-oracle circuit $A_\rho^{(?)}$. For a uniform oracle algorithm M and a parameterized family of functions $f = \{f_\rho : \{0,1\}^{n(\rho)} \to \{0,1\}^{n'(\rho)}\}_{\rho \in \mathbb{N}^+}$, define $M^{(f)} \overset{\text{def}}{=} \{A_\rho^{(f_\rho)}\}_{\rho \in \mathbb{N}^+}$, where $A_\rho^{(?)} \overset{\text{def}}{=} M(1^\rho, n(\rho), n'(\rho))$. For a non-uniform algorithm A, the family $M^{(A)}$ is defined analogously.

Let $s = s(\rho)$ be a security function. An s-non-uniform two oracle algorithm is a machine M such that for every $\rho, n_1, n'_1, n_2, n'_2 \in \mathbb{N}^+$ and every $a \in \{0,1\}^{s(\rho)}$,

---

[1] A-priori, for a fixed security parameter ρ there is no bound on the input length the construction is expected to work, as long as the series of the input-output lengths is bounded by *some* polynomial.

it holds that $M(1^\rho, n_1, n_1', n_2, n_2', a)$ outputs an (n_1, n_1', n_2, n_2')-two oracle circuit $A_{\rho,a}^{(?,?)}$ with at most $s(\rho)$ oracle gates. Note that the last requirement is essential and is implicit in the case of an efficient uniform oracle algorithm, where the number of oracle gates is bounded by the polynomial that bounds the running time of the algorithm. For an s-non-uniform two oracle algorithm M, a non-uniform algorithm B and a family of functions f, we formally define $M^{[B,f]} \overset{\text{def}}{=} (M, B, f)$.

2.2   Modeling Cryptographic Primitives

In order to state our results in their full generality, and in particular to exclude reductions that are allowed to use non-uniformity and are considered successful in inverting the one-way function even if they invert only a negligible fraction of the inputs of the function, the following two definitions are very general, and extend Definitions 2.1 and 2.3 from [13]. The example of modeling a one-way function follows the definition.

Definition 1 (Cryptographic Primitive). *A primitive* $\mathbf{Q}$ *is a pair* $\langle F_{\mathbf{Q}}, R_{\mathbf{Q}} \rangle$, *where* $F_{\mathbf{Q}}$ *is a set of parametrized families of functions* $f = \{f_\rho\}_{\rho \in \mathbb{N}^+}$ *and* $R_{\mathbf{Q}}$ *is a relation over triplets* $\langle f_\rho, C, \epsilon \rangle$ *of a function* $f_\rho \in f$ *(for some* $f \in F_{\mathbf{Q}}$*), a circuit* C *and a number* $\epsilon > 0$. *We define that* C ($\mathbf{Q}, \epsilon$)-*breaks* f_ρ *if and only if* $\langle f_\rho, C, \epsilon \rangle \in R_{\mathbf{Q}}$.

The set $F_{\mathbf{Q}}$ specifies all the correct implementations (not necessarily efficient) of $\mathbf{Q}$ and the relation $R_{\mathbf{Q}}$ captures the security property of $\mathbf{Q}$, that is, it specifies for every concrete security parameter implementation, how well a breaker algorithm performs with respect to the security property of the primitive.

Finally, let $s = s(\rho)$ be a security function, $B = \{B_\rho\}_{\rho \in \mathbb{N}^+}$ be a non-uniform algorithm, and $f \in F_{\mathbf{Q}}$. We say that B ($\mathbf{Q}, \frac{1}{s}$)-breaks f if $\langle f_\rho, B_\rho, \frac{1}{s(\rho)} \rangle \in R_{\mathbf{Q}}$ for infinitely many values ρ. Let us fix an s-non-uniform two oracle algorithm R. We say that $R^{[B,f]}$ ($\mathbf{Q}, \frac{1}{s}$)-breaks f if for infinitely many values ρ there exists an $a \in \{0,1\}^{s(\rho)}$ (called advice) such that $\langle f_\rho, R_{\rho,a}^{(B_\rho, f_\rho)}, \frac{1}{s(\rho)} \rangle \in R_{\mathbf{Q}}$, where $R_{\rho,a}^{(?,?)} = R(1^\rho, n, n', b, b', a)$.

The usual notion of polynomial security of a primitive is captured by the following definition: B $\mathbf{Q}$-breaks f if there exists a polynomial $p = p(\rho)$ such that B ($\mathbf{Q}, \frac{1}{p}$)-breaks f.

A primitive $\mathbf{Q}$ exists if there exists an efficient uniform algorithm M that implements an $f \in F_{\mathbf{Q}}$, and for every efficient uniform algorithm M' that, on input 1^ρ outputs a circuit, it holds that $\{M'(1^\rho)\}_{\rho \in \mathbb{N}^+}$ does not $\mathbf{Q}$-break f.

Observe that the requirement that M' outputs a circuit is made without loss of generality and captures the standard definition of an efficient randomized machine M' that breaks a primitive. Given such an M' that tosses at most $r = r(\rho)$ random coins, there exists[2] a (now deterministic) efficient uniform

---

[2] For example, by the canonical encoding of an efficient machine as in the Cook-Levin Theorem.

machine M'' that on input 1^ρ outputs a circuit C_ρ with $m(\rho) + r(\rho)$ input gates and $n(\rho)$ output gates that computes the output of M for all strings of length $m(\rho)$, and therefore $\mathbf{Q}$-breaks the primitive.

2.3   One-Way Functions

Our model for describing a primitive is very general and captures the security properties of many cryptographic primitives. As an example, we bring a standard definition of a one-way function and then explain how it can be described in our model.

Definition 2 (One-Way Function). *A one-way function* $f = \{f_\rho\}_{\rho \in \mathbb{N}^+}$ *is an efficiently uniformly computable family of functions* $f_\rho : \{0,1\}^{n(\rho)} \to \{0,1\}^{m(\rho)}$, *such that for every efficient randomized machine A, the function that maps ρ to*

$$\Pr_{x \xleftarrow{r} \{0,1\}^{m(\rho)}} \left[A(1^\rho, f_\rho(x)) \in f_\rho^{-1}(f_\rho(v)) \right] \text{ is negligible.}$$

In order to model a one-way function (OWF), we set $f = \{f_\rho\}_{\rho \in \mathbb{N}^+} \in F_{\mathbf{OWF}}$, where $f_\rho : \{0,1\}^{n(\rho)} \to \{0,1\}^{m(\rho)}$, if and only if $n = n(\rho)$ and $m = m(\rho)$ are polynomial security functions. We say that $F_{\mathbf{OWF}}$ contains a collection of sets of functions $\mathcal{F} = \{\mathcal{F}_\rho\}_{\rho \in \mathbb{N}^+}$, if for every family $f' = \{f'_\rho\}_{\rho \in \mathbb{N}^+}$, where $f'_\rho \in \mathcal{F}_\rho$ for every ρ, it holds that $f' \in F_{\mathbf{OWF}}$.

In this case, for a function $f_\rho \in f \in F_{\mathbf{OWF}}$, a circuit C that inverts f_ρ on an ϵ-fraction of its inputs, and $\epsilon' > 0$, set $\langle f, C, \epsilon' \rangle \in R_{\mathbf{OWF}}$ if and only if $\epsilon \geq \epsilon'$. The definition is general, and allows for the circuit C to implicitly use randomness. In such a case, for f_ρ as before, a circuit with C with $m(\rho) + r(\rho)$ input bits that computes an output $x \in \{0,1\}^{n(\rho)}$, and a value $\epsilon' > 0$, define $\langle f_\rho, C, \epsilon' \rangle \in R_{\mathbf{OWF}}$ if and only if $\epsilon \geq \epsilon'$, where ϵ is the probability over uniform $z \in \{0,1\}^{r(\rho)}$ and $x \in \{0,1\}^{n(\rho)}$ that $C(f_\rho(x), z)$ outputs an $x' \in f_\rho^{-1}(f_\rho(x))$.

2.4   Fully Black-Box Cryptographic Constructions

Finally, we bring the standard definition of a fixed-parameter fully black-box construction of a primitive $\mathbf{Q}$ from a primitive $\mathbf{P}$, which is usually implicit in the literature. The construction algorithm G is an efficient uniform oracle algorithm and the security reduction R is an efficient uniform two-oracle algorithm. For every security parameter ρ and a function $f_\rho : \{0,1\}^{n(\rho)} \to \{0,1\}^{n'(\rho)}$, G's output on $(1^\rho, n, n')$ is an (n, n')-oracle circuit $g_\rho^{(?)}$ such that $\{g_\rho^{(f_\rho)}\}_{\rho \in \mathbb{N}^+}$ implements $\mathbf{Q}$. The reduction algorithm works as follows: For a security parameter ρ and f as before, and additionally a breaker circuit $B : \{0,1\}^{b(\rho)} \to \{0,1\}^{b'(\rho)}$, the reduction R on input $(1^\rho, n, n', b, b')$ outputs an (n, n', b, b')-two-oracle circuit $R_\rho^{(?,?)}$. The security property property requires that indeed the series of circuits $\{R_\rho^{(B_\rho, f_\rho)}\}_{\rho \in \mathbb{N}^+}$ $\mathbf{P}$-breaks f. We emphasize that the vast majority (if not all) of the constructions of primitives from a one-way function found in the literature are in fact fixed-parameter fully black-box constructions. Formally:

Definition 3 (fixed-parameter fully black-box construction of Q from P). *An efficient uniform oracle algorithm G and an efficient uniform two oracle algorithm R are a* fixed-parameter fully-BB *construction of a primitive $\mathbf{Q} = \langle F_{\mathbf{Q}}, R_{\mathbf{Q}} \rangle$ from a primitive $\mathbf{P} = \langle F_{\mathbf{P}}, R_{\mathbf{P}} \rangle$ if for every $f \in F_{\mathbf{P}}$:*

1. **(correctness)** $G^{(f)}$ *implements* $f' \in F_{\mathbf{Q}}$.
2. **(security)** *For every algorithm B: If B $\mathbf{Q}$-breaks $G^{(f)}$ then $R^{(B,f)}$ $\mathbf{P}$-breaks f.*

For a super-polynomial security function $s = s(\rho)$ (e.g., $s(\rho) = 2^{\sqrt{\rho}}$), the following definition of a fully black-box construction is significantly weaker than the standard one in the following three aspects: First, it requires that reduction only mildly breaks the one-way property of the function f (whenever the breaker breaks the constructed primitive in the standard polynomial sense). Second, the reduction algorithm does not have to be efficient or uniform (but the non-uniformity is limited to an advice of length s). Lastly, it allows the reduction to make s calls to its oracles[3].

Definition 4 (s-weak fixed-parameter fully black-box construction of Q from P).
A uniform oracle algorithm G and an s-non-uniform two oracle algorithm R are an s-weak fixed-parameter fully-BB *construction of a primitive $\mathbf{Q} = \langle F_{\mathbf{Q}}, R_{\mathbf{Q}} \rangle$ from a primitive $\mathbf{P} = \langle F_{\mathbf{P}}, R_{\mathbf{P}} \rangle$ if for every $f \in F_{\mathbf{P}}$:*

1. **(correctness)** $G^{(f)}$ *implements an* $f' \in F_{\mathbf{Q}}$.
2. **(security)** *For every non-uniform algorithm B: If B $\mathbf{Q}$-breaks $G^{(f)}$ then $R^{[B,f]}$ $(\mathbf{P}, 1/s)$-breaks f.*

2.5 Random Permutations and Regular Functions

Let n and i be two integers such that $0 \le i \le n$. We denote the set of all permutations on $\{0,1\}^n$ by $\mathcal{P}_n$. Let $\mathcal{X}, \mathcal{Y}$ be sets. We denote by $(\mathcal{X} \to \mathcal{Y})$ the set of all functions from $\mathcal{X}$ to $\mathcal{Y}$. A function $f : \mathcal{X} \to \mathcal{Y}$ is regular if $|\{x' : f(x) = f(x')\}|$ is constant for all $x \in \mathcal{X}$. A family of functions $f = \{f_\rho\}_{\rho \in \mathbb{N}^+}$ is a regular function if for every ρ the function f_ρ is regular. We denote by $\mathcal{R}_{n,i}$ the set of all regular functions from $\{0,1\}^n$ to itself such that the image of f contains 2^i values. E.g., $\mathcal{R}_{n,n} = \mathcal{P}_n$ is the set of all permutations, and $\mathcal{R}_{n,0}$ is the set of all constant functions.

2.6 Bending a Function and Image Adaptation

It will be useful for us to compare the run of a circuit with oracle access to a function f to a run that is identical except that the output of one specific value is altered.

---

[3] In Definition 3 the limitation on the number of queries made to the oracles is implicit as R is an efficient algorithm, and so its output circuit has at most a polynomially number of oracle gates.

For a fixed function $f : \{0,1\}^n \to \{0,1\}^n$ and $y', y'' \in \{0,1\}^n$, set

$$f_{(y',y'')}(x) \stackrel{\text{def}}{=} \begin{cases} y'' & \text{if } f(x) = y' \\ f(x) & \text{otherwise.} \end{cases}$$

Similarly, for two fixed functions $f, f' : \{0,1\}^n \to \{0,1\}^n$ and a set $S \subset \{0,1\}^n$, we define the image adaptation[4] of f to f' on S to be the function

$$f_{(S,f')}(x) \stackrel{\text{def}}{=} \begin{cases} f'(x) & \text{if } x \in f^{-1}(f(S)) \\ f(x) & \text{otherwise.} \end{cases}$$

3   A General Theorem for Proving Strong Black-Box Separations

3.1   Deterministic Parametrized Oracles and Local Sets

The following definition allows to model general parameterized oracles, that is, oracles that, for any function f from some set of functions and any q from some query domain, return a value a from some answer set. We observe that many of the oracles used for black-box separations found in the literature could be described in such a way.

Let $\mathcal{X}, \mathcal{Y}, \mathcal{D}$ and $\mathcal{R}$ be sets. A deterministic parametrized oracle for a class of functions $(\mathcal{X} \to \mathcal{Y})$ is an indexed collection $\mathcal{O} = \{\mathcal{O}_f\}_{f \in \mathcal{X} \to \mathcal{Y}}$, where $\mathcal{O}_f : \mathcal{D} \to \mathcal{R}$. We call f, $\mathcal{D}$, and $\mathcal{R}$ the function parameter, the domain, and the range of the oracle, respectively.

Our first example of a deterministic parametrized oracle is the evaluation oracle $\mathcal{E}$ for functions on $\{0,1\}^n$, which on a query q returns the evaluation of f on q. In this case we have that $\mathcal{X} = \mathcal{Y} = \mathcal{D} = \mathcal{R} = \{0,1\}^n$ and $\mathcal{E}_f(q) \stackrel{\text{def}}{=} f(q)$.

The next two definitions capture two important local properties of parametrized oracles. We believe that they are natural and observe that many of the oracles devised for separation results satisfy them.

Intuitively, a determining set is an indexed collection of sets that determine the output of the oracle for every function f and query q in the following sense: If for two functions f and f' it holds that their corresponding oracle outputs differ for some q, then for one of them (f or f') it holds that the local change of an image adaptation of one of the functions to agree with that of the other on its determining set changes the output of the oracle. Formally:

Definition 5. *Let $\mathcal{O}$ be a deterministic parametrized oracle. A* determining set *$\mathcal{I}^{\mathcal{O}}$ for a class of functions $\mathcal{F} \subset (\mathcal{X} \to \mathcal{Y})$ is an indexed collection $\{\mathcal{I}^{\mathcal{O}}_{f,q}\}_{f \in \mathcal{F}, q \in \mathcal{D}}$ of subsets of $\mathcal{X}$, such that for every $f, f' \in \mathcal{F}$ and every query $q \in \mathcal{D}$: If $\mathcal{O}_f(q) \neq$*

---

[4] We mention that if f is a permutation, the condition $f(x) = y$ can be replaced by $x = f^{-1}(y)$, and similarly for $f_{(S,f')}$ check whether $x \in S$, which is what one may expect initially from such a definition.

$\mathcal{O}_{f'}(q)$, then it holds that either the image adaptation of f to f' on $\mathcal{I}^{\mathcal{O}}_{f',q}$ changes $\mathcal{O}_f(q)$ (i.e., $\mathcal{O}_{f_{\left(\mathcal{I}^{\mathcal{O}}_{f',q},f'\right)}}(q) \neq \mathcal{O}_f(q)$), or the image adaptation of f' to f on $\mathcal{I}^{\mathcal{O}}_{f,q}$ changes $\mathcal{O}_{f'}(q)$. $\mathcal{I}^{\mathcal{O}}$ is a t-determining set if for every function $f \in \mathcal{F}$ and query $q \in \mathcal{D}$ it holds that $\left|\mathcal{I}^{\mathcal{O}}_{f,q}\right| \leq t$.

In the example of the evaluation oracle, we observe that it has a 1-determining set. Indeed, setting $\mathcal{I}^{\mathcal{E}}_{f,q} \overset{\text{def}}{=} \{q\}$ satisfies the required definition, since if for any $f, f' \in \{0,1\}^n \to \{0,1\}^n$ and $x \in \{0,1\}^n$ for which $f(x) \neq f'(x)$ it holds that $f_{(\{x\},f')}(x) = f'(x) \neq f(x)$.

Consider an oracle $\mathcal{O}$ with a determining set $\mathcal{I}^{\mathcal{O}}$ for some class of permutations $\mathcal{F}$. Fix $f, f' \in \mathcal{F}$ and $q \in \mathcal{D}$. The following two propositions are immediate from the definition of determining sets:

Proposition 1. *If $\mathcal{O}_f(q) \neq \mathcal{O}_{f'}(q)$ and $f(x) = f'(x)$ for all $x \in \mathcal{I}^{\mathcal{O}}_{f',q}$ (in this case we say that f agrees with f' on $\mathcal{I}^{\mathcal{O}}_{f',q}$), then adapting f' to agree with f on $\mathcal{I}^{\mathcal{O}}_{f,q}$ changes $\mathcal{O}_{f'}(q)$.*

Proposition 2. *If for all $x \in \mathcal{I}^{\mathcal{O}}_{f,q} \cup \mathcal{I}^{\mathcal{O}}_{f',q}$ it holds that $f(x) = f'(x)$ (in this case we say that the functions agree on their determining sets), then $\mathcal{O}_f(q) = \mathcal{O}_{f'}(q)$.*

Proposition 2 establishes that determining sets indeed determine the output of the oracle in the following sense: If we know the value $\mathcal{O}_f(q)$ for a query q and a function f, and, moreover, we know that functions f', f agree on their determining sets for q, then this information already determines for us the value $\mathcal{O}_{f'}(q)$.

The next local property of an oracle captures the fact that it is in some sense "stable". For a function f and query q as before, and a value y in the image set of f, a bending set for f, q, and y is a set of all potentially "sensitive" y' values: For any value y which is not in the image of f on its determining set, and for any value y' which is not in the bending set, the oracle's answer to query q does not change for the local adaptations of f from y' to y. That is, it holds that $\mathcal{O}_{f_{(y',y)}}(q) = \mathcal{O}_f(q)$. Formally:

Definition 6. *Let $\mathcal{O}$ be a deterministic parametrized oracle. A bending set $\mathcal{B}^{\mathcal{O}}$ for $\mathcal{F}$ is an indexed collection $\{\mathcal{B}^{\mathcal{O}}_{f,q,y}\}_{f \in \mathcal{F}, q \in \mathcal{D}, y \in \mathcal{Y}}$ of subsets of $\mathcal{Y}$, such that for every function $f \in \mathcal{F}$, query $q \in \mathcal{D}$, for every target image $y \in \mathcal{Y}$, and for every source image $y' \notin \mathcal{B}^{\mathcal{O}}_{f,q,y}$, it holds that $\mathcal{O}_f(q) = \mathcal{O}_{f_{(y',y)}}(q)$. We say that $\mathcal{B}^{\mathcal{O}}$ is a t-bending set if for every function $f \in \mathcal{F}$, query $q \in \mathcal{D}$ and $y \in \mathcal{Y}$ it holds that $\left|\mathcal{B}^{\mathcal{O}}_{f,q,y}\right| \leq t$.*

For the example of the evaluation oracle, we observe that it also has a 1-bending set. Setting $\mathcal{B}^{\mathcal{E}}_{f,q,y} \overset{\text{def}}{=} \{f(q)\}$ (for the relevant f, q and y) satisfies the required definition. Indeed, for any $y' \neq f(q)$ and $y'' \in \mathcal{Y}$, it holds that $\mathcal{E}_{f_{(y',y'')}}(q) = f_{(y',y'')}(q) = f(q) = \mathcal{E}_f(q)$.

Finally, a deterministic parametrized algorithm $\mathcal{O}$ is t-stable for a class of functions $\mathcal{F}$ if there exist $(\mathcal{I}^{\mathcal{O}}, \mathcal{B}^{\mathcal{O}})$ that are a t-determining set and a t-bending set for $\mathcal{F}$, respectively, and at least one of them is not empty.

We note that determining and bending sets always exist unconditionally (just choose the entire domain and range of f, for every determining and bending set, respectively). The challange is finding an oracle that allows to break a primitive and at the same time is t-stable.

3.2   A t-Stable Oracle $\mathcal{O}_f$ Inverts Only a Few Functions

The next lemma, which first appeared in [5] and was subsequently adapted to many other separation results, e.g., [6,15,9], establishes an information-theoretic bound on the number of functions an oracle-aided algorithm can invert from a set $\mathcal{F}$ if the oracle is t-stable for $\mathcal{F}$. Essentially, it shows that given an oracle circuit $A^{(?)}$ with access to such an oracle $\mathcal{O}$, it is possible to encode a function $f \in \mathcal{F}$ that A inverts well using significantly fewer bits than $\log(|\mathcal{F}|)$, such that f can still be fully reconstructed, or equivallently, that the encoding is injective.

Lemma 1 (Encoding Lemma). *Let* $A^{(?)}$ *be an oracle circuit making at most* c *calls to its oracle, and let* $\mathcal{O} = \{\mathcal{O}_f\}_{f \in \{0,1\}^n \to \{0,1\}^n}$ *be a deterministic parameterized oracle such that for a class of permutations* $\mathcal{F} \subseteq \mathcal{P}_n$ *it is t-stable with sets* $(\mathcal{I}^{\mathcal{O}}, \mathcal{B}^{\mathcal{O}})$. *Then, for at most* $d_n = d_n(c,t) = \left(\binom{2^n}{b}\right)^2 \cdot ((2^n - b)!)$, *where* $b \overset{\text{def}}{=} \frac{2^n}{3 \cdot c^2 \cdot t}$, *of the permutations* f *in* $\mathcal{F}$, *it holds that* $\Pr_{x \xleftarrow{r} \{0,1\}^n}\left[A^{\mathcal{O}_f}(f(x)) = x\right] > \frac{1}{c}$.

The proof is a generalized version of the encoding technique of [5].

The next theorem is proved by means of a reduction to Lemma 1 and expressing canonically a regular function using premutations. Detailed proofs of the lemma and the theorem are available in [3].

Theorem 1 (Black-Box Separation Factory). *Let* $s = s(\rho)$ *be a security function, and* $p = p(\rho)$ *be a polynomial function. Let* $(G, A) = (G^{(?)}, A^{(?,?)})$ *be a uniform oracle algorithm and an s-non-uniform two-oracle algorithm, respectively. Let* $\mathcal{F} = \{\mathcal{F}_\rho\}_{\rho>0}$, *where* $\mathcal{F}_\rho \subset \mathcal{R}_{n(\rho),i(\rho)}(P_\rho, I_\rho)$, *be contained in* $\mathbf{F_{OWF}}$, *and* $\mathcal{O} = \{\mathcal{O}_\rho\}_{\rho>0}$, *where* $\mathcal{O}_\rho = \{\mathcal{O}_{\rho,f}\}_{f \in \mathcal{F}_{n(\rho),i(\rho)}(P_\rho,I_\rho)}$, *such that for all large enough* ρ:

1. $\mathcal{O}_{\rho,f}$ $(\mathbf{Q}, \frac{1}{p(\rho)})$-*breaks* $g_\rho^{(f)}$ *for every* $f \in \mathcal{F}_\rho$, *where* $g_\rho^{(?)} \overset{\text{def}}{=} G(1^\rho, n, n')$.
2. $\mathcal{O}_\rho$ *is t-stable with sets* $(\mathcal{I}^{\mathcal{O}}, \mathcal{B}^{\mathcal{O}})$ *for* $\mathcal{F}_\rho$ *such that* $2^{s(\rho)} \cdot d_i(s(\rho), t) < |\mathcal{F}_\rho|$ *holds, where* d_i *is as in Lemma 1.*

Then (G, A) *is not an s-weak fixed-parameter fully black-box construction of* $\mathbf{Q}$ *from* $\mathbf{OWF}$.

4   A Lower Bound on the Number of Calls for a Fixed-Parameter Fully Black-Box Construction of UOWHF from OWF

In this section we prove our second main result, namely a lower bound on the number of calls made by the construction algorithm G in any fully black-box construction (G, R) of **UOWHF** from **OWF**. Our bound is achieved by showing a sequence of efficient fixed-parameter fully black-box constructions, where each primitive is constructed from the one that precedes it, and by proving the lower bound on the number of calls a construction makes on the last primitive. A diagram of the reduction sequence is depicted in Figure 1.

4.1   A Characterization of Universal One-Way Hash Functions

Loosely speaking, a universal one-way hash function is a keyed compressing function for which the probability that an adversary wins the following game is very small: First the adversary chooses a preimage v. Then a random key for the UOWHF is chosen. Finally, the adversary "wins" the game he finds a different preimage v' that maps to the same value under the chosen key. Formally:

Definition 7 (UOWHF). *A universal one-way hash function* $h = \{h_\rho\}_{\rho \in \mathbb{N}^+}$ *is a family of uniformly efficiently computable keyed functions* $h_\rho : \{0,1\}^{\kappa(\rho)} \times \{0,1\}^{m(\rho)} \to \{0,1\}^{m'(\rho)}$ *with* $m'(\rho) < m(\rho)$ *such that for any pair of efficient randomized algorithms* (B_1, B_2) *the function mapping* ρ *to*

$$\Pr_{\substack{(v,\sigma) \xleftarrow{r} B_1(\rho) \\ k \xleftarrow{r} \{0,1\}^{\kappa(\rho)} \\ v' \xleftarrow{r} B_2(k,v,\sigma)}} [h_\rho(k,v) = h_\rho(k,v') \wedge v \neq v']$$

is negligible. The family h *is an* ℓ-bit compressing UOWHF, where $\ell = \ell(\rho)$, if $m(\rho) - m'(\rho) \geq \ell(\rho)$ for all large enough ρ.

The primitive **UOWHF** $= (F_{\mathbf{UOWHF}}, R_{\mathbf{UOWHF}})$ is defined implicitly analogously to the way **OWF** was defined for one-way functions

Domain Extension of a UOWHF. The definition of a UOWHF only guarantees that h_ρ is compressing (i.e., it is possible that $\ell(\rho) = 1$). The first reduction we use is a domain extension of a UOWHF, that allows to construct an ℓ-bit compressing UOWHF from a UOWHF. Shoup [16] shows a fully-black box construction of a ℓ-bit compressing UOWHF from one that compresses only one bit, which is the minimal requirement from any UOWHF.

Lemma 2 (UOWHF domain extension). *There exists a fixed-parameter fully black-box construction of an ℓ-bit compressing UOWHF h'_ρ :* $\{0,1\}^{\log(\ell) \cdot \kappa(\rho)} \times \{0,1\}^{m+\ell} \to \{0,1\}^m$ *from a one-bit compressing UOWHF $h_\rho : \{0,1\}^{\kappa(\rho)} \times \{0,1\}^{m+1} \to \{0,1\}^m$. In order to evaluate h'_ρ the construction makes exactly $\ell(\rho)$ calls to h_ρ. The security reduction $R_\rho^{h_\rho, B}$ makes ℓ calls to its h_ρ oracle, and exactly one call to the breaker $B_\rho = (B_1, B_2)_\rho$ oracle. Furthermore, if B_ρ (ℓ-UOWHF, ϵ)-breaks h'_ρ, then the reduction (UOWHF, $\frac{\epsilon}{\ell}$)-breaks h_ρ.*

We observe that the security definition for UOWHFs involves an interaction, and allows the adversary to save its state using σ. It will be more convenient for us to work with an equivalent non-interactive version. The following definition of collision resistance is tightly related to that of a UOWHF by the lemma that follows it, where we denote by $a\|b$ the concatenation of a and b.

Definition 8 (RP-CRHF). *A random preimage collision resistance hash function is an efficiently uniformly computable family of functions $h_\rho : \{0,1\}^{m(\rho)} \to \{0,1\}^{m'(\rho)}$ with $m'(\rho) < m(\rho)$, such that for every efficient randomized machine B the function mapping ρ to*

$$\Pr_{\substack{v \xleftarrow{r} \{0,1\}^{m(\rho)} \\ v' \xleftarrow{r} B(\rho,v)}} [h_\rho(v) = h_\rho(v') \wedge v \neq v'] \text{ is negligible.}$$

The family h is an ℓ-bit compressing RP-CRHF, where $\ell = \ell(\rho)$, if additionally it holds that $m(\rho) - m'(\rho) \geq \ell(\rho)$ for all large enough ρ.

The primitives **RP-CRHF** and $\log^2(\rho)$-**RP-CRHF** are defined analogously.

Lemma 3 (UOWHF to RP-CRHF, folklore). *Let $h = \{h_\rho\}_{\rho \in \mathbb{N}^+}$ be a UOWHF. Then the family $h'_\rho : \{0,1\}^{\kappa(\rho)+m(\rho)} \to \{0,1\}^{\kappa(\rho)+m'(\rho)}$ given by $h'_\rho(k\|v) \stackrel{\text{def}}{=} (k\|h_\rho(k,v))$ is an RP-CRHF.*

Pseudo-injective Functions. Our last reduction establishes that padding the output of a $\log^2(\rho)$-**RP-CRHF** yields a primitive that is both a one-way function, and behaves like an injective function. A pseudo-injective function is an efficiently uniformly computable family $g = \{g_\rho\}_{\rho \in \mathbb{N}^+}$ of length preserving functions $g_\rho : \{0,1\}^{m(\rho)} \to \{0,1\}^{m(\rho)}$ such that for a uniformly chosen input $v \in \{0,1\}^{m(\rho)}$ it is impossible to find another input $v' \neq v$ such that both map to the same value under g_ρ. We stress that pseudo-injective functions exists unconditionally: Any permutation is a pseudo-injective function. Formally:

Definition 9 (Pseudo-Injectivity). *A pseudo-injective function $g = \{g_\rho\}_{\rho \in \mathbb{N}^+}$ is a uniformly efficiently computable family of functions $g_\rho : \{0,1\}^{m(\rho)} \to \{0,1\}^{m(\rho)}$, such that for all uniform efficient algorithms A the function mapping ρ to*

$$\Pr_{\substack{v \xleftarrow{r} \{0,1\}^{m(\rho)} \\ v' \xleftarrow{r} A(1^\rho,v)}} [g_\rho(v') = g_\rho(v) \wedge v' \neq v] \text{ is negligible.}$$

Similarly to before, the primitive $\mathbf{PI} = \langle F_{\mathbf{PI}}, R_{\mathbf{PI}} \rangle$ corresponds to a pseudo-injective function. Next, we consider the primitive $\mathbf{OWF} \wedge \mathbf{PI}$ that corresponds to all functions which are both a one-way function and a pseudo-injective function. Formally, it holds that $f \in F_{\mathbf{OWF} \wedge \mathbf{PI}}$ if and only if $f \in F_{\mathbf{OWF}}$ *and* $f \in F_{\mathbf{PI}}$. For a breaker circuit C, a function $f_\rho \in f \in F_{\mathbf{OWF} \wedge \mathbf{PI}}$, and a number

ϵ it holds that $\langle f_\rho, C, \epsilon \rangle \in R_{\mathbf{OWF \wedge PI}}$ if and only if $\langle f_\rho, C, \epsilon \rangle \in R_{\mathbf{OWF}}$ or $\langle f_\rho, C, \epsilon \rangle \in R_{\mathbf{PI}}$. It turns out that padding any $\log^2(n)$-**RP-CRHF** to a length-preserving function, yields a function which is both a one-way function and a pseudo-injective function.

Lemma 4 ($\log^2(\rho)$-**RP-CRHF** to **OWF∧PI**). *Let* $h = \{h_\rho\}_{\rho \in \mathbb{N}^+}$ *be an RP-CRHF that compresses* $\ell(\rho) \overset{\text{def}}{=} m(\rho) - m'(\rho)$ *bits, where* $\ell(\rho) \geq \log^2(\rho)$. *Then the family* $\{h'_\rho\}_{\rho \in \mathbb{N}^+}$, *where* $h'_\rho(v) \overset{\text{def}}{=} h_\rho(v)\|0^{\ell(\rho)}$, *is a one-way function and a pseudo-injective function.*

Due to limitations of space the proof is omitted. The composition of the constructions depicted in Lemmas 2, 3 and 4 establishes a fixed-parameter fully black-box construction of an $h' \in F_{\mathbf{OWF \wedge PI}}$ from any $h \in F_{\mathbf{UOWHF}}$ that makes $\log^2(\rho)$ calls to the underlying UOWHF. The security reduction makes $\log^2(\rho)$ calls (to both its oracles) in order to break the security of the underlying UOWHF, and if B (**OWF∧PI**, $\frac{1}{p}$)-breaks the constructed h for some polynomial p and breaker B, then the reduction (**UOWHF**, $\frac{1}{p'}$)-breaks h, where p' is a different polynomial such that $p'(\rho) > 4 \cdot p(\rho) \cdot \log^2(\rho)$. Thus we obtain:

Corollary 1. *Suppose that* (G, R) *is an* s'-*weak fixed-parameter fully black-box construction of* **UOWHF** *from* **OWF** *that makes at most* $r' = r'(\rho)$ *queries to* **OWF**. *Then there exists an* s-*weak fixed-parameter fully black-box construction of* **OWF∧PI** *from* **OWF** *that makes* $r'(\rho) \cdot \log^2(\rho)$ *calls to the underlying one-way function, where* $s(\rho) \overset{\text{def}}{=} s'(\rho) \cdot \log^2(\rho)$.

Therefore, in order to show that there is no s'-weak fixed-parameter fully black-box construction of **UOWHF** from **OWF**, where the construction makes r' calls to the one-way functions, it is sufficient to show that there is no s-weak fixed-parameter fully black-box construction of **OWF∧PI** from **OWF** that makes r calls, where $s(\rho) \overset{\text{def}}{=} s'(\rho) \cdot \log^2(\rho)$ and $r(\rho) \overset{\text{def}}{=} r'(\rho) \cdot \log^2(\rho)$. This is the goal of the next section.

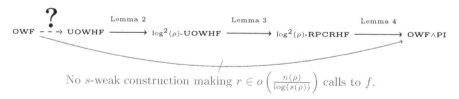

Fig. 1. Fully Black-Box Constructions Diagram

4.2 A Lower Bound on the Number of Calls for an s-Weak Fixed-Parameter Fully Black-Box Construction of OWF∧PI from OWF

As explained, a lower bound on a construction of **OWF∧PI** from **OWF** yields a very good (up to a $\log^2$-factor) bound on the construction of **UOWHF**.

Our proof utilizes the machinery from Section 3. Let us introduce some notation. For an (n, n)-oracle circuit $g^{(?)} : \{0,1\}^m \to \{0,1\}^m$, a function $f : \{0,1\}^n \to \{0,1\}^n$ and a value $v \in \{0,1\}^m$, denote by $X_g(f, v)$ and $Y_g(f, v)$ the sets of queries and answers made to and received from f during the evaluation of $g^{(f)}(v)$, respectively.

For any potential construction (G, R) denote by $r = r(\rho)$ the number of queries g_ρ makes when instantiated for security parameter ρ with a one-way function $f_\rho : \{0,1\}^\rho \to \{0,1\}^\rho$, that is we set $n(\rho) \stackrel{\text{def}}{=} n'(\rho) \stackrel{\text{def}}{=} \rho$. Additionally, let $s = s(\rho)$ be a super-polynomial security function smaller than $2^{\frac{\rho}{10}}$. I.e., for all polynomials p and all large enough ρ it holds that $p(\rho) < s(\rho) < 2^{\frac{\rho}{10}}$. We prove that if $r(\rho) < \frac{n(\rho)}{2000 \cdot \log(s(\rho)))}$ holds for all large enough ρ, then (G, R) is not an s-weak fixed-parameter fully black-box construction of **OWF∧PI** from **OWF**.

Theorem 2. *For all super-polynomial security functions $s = s(\rho) < 2^{\frac{\rho}{10}}$ and $r = r(\rho)$ there is no s-weak fixed-parameter fully black-box construction of* **OWF∧PI** *from* **OWF** *such that $g_\rho^{(?)} : \{0,1\}^{m(\rho)} \to \{0,1\}^{m(\rho)}$ makes at most $r(\rho)$ calls to the underlying one-way function, where $n(\rho) \stackrel{\text{def}}{=} n'(\rho) \stackrel{\text{def}}{=} \rho$ and $g_\rho^{(?)} \stackrel{\text{def}}{=} G(1^\rho, n, n')$, and $r(\rho) \leq \frac{n(\rho)}{2000 \cdot \log(s(\rho))}$ holds for all large enough ρ.*

Proof. Without loss of generality, we assume that the construction g makes exactly $r(\rho) \stackrel{\text{def}}{=} \frac{n(\rho)}{2000 \cdot \log(s(\rho))}$ different queries. Whenever this is not the case, it is always possible to amend G so that it behaves exactly as before, but on input $(1^\rho, n, n')$ it outputs an (n, n')-oracle circuit with $r(\rho)$ oracle gates, and additionally, all queries are different.

Let s and r be a pair of security functions such that s is super-polynomial, that is, for every polynomial p and large enough ρ it holds that $s(\rho) > p(\rho)$, and that $r(\rho) = \frac{n(\rho)}{2000 \cdot \log(s(\rho))}$ holds for all sufficiently large ρ.

We now explain how to construct the oracle $\mathcal{O} = \{\mathcal{O}_\rho\}_{\rho \in \mathbb{N}^+}$ and the collection of sets of functions $\mathcal{F} = \{\mathcal{F}_\rho\}_{\rho \in \mathbb{N}^+}$. For each security paramter ρ we define the oracle $\mathcal{O}_\rho$ and the set $\mathcal{F}_\rho$ *independently* of the oracles and function sets chosen for other security parameters. It will always hold that $\mathcal{F}_\rho \subset \{0,1\}^n \to \{0,1\}^n$, and so the constructed $\mathcal{F}$ is contained in $F_{\textbf{OWF}}$.

Therefore, from now on we omit the security parameter in our notation, but formally all our parameters depend on the security parameter ρ. In particular, $g^{(?)}$ is the construction that the uniform construction algorithm G outputs for security parameter $\rho = n = n'$ with a function $f_\rho : \{0,1\}^\rho \to \{0,1\}^\rho$.

Analogously to [9], for every security parameter we break either the one-wayness property of the constructed function, or its pseudo-injectivity. For the oracle circuit $g^{(?)} : \{0,1\}^m \to \{0,1\}^m$, we check whether when g is evaluated with a random permutation $f \xleftarrow{\text{r}} \mathcal{P}_n$ and a random input $v \xleftarrow{\text{r}} \{0,1\}^m$, the output $g^f(v)$ is significantly correlated with any subset of the set of oracle answers returned by f on the calls made to it during the evaluation of $g^f(v)$

(recall that these are denoted by $Y_g(f, v)$). To this end, we bring the procedure STA (for safe to answer), which returns true if and only if there is no such correlation:

Procedure $\mathrm{STA}(w, Q)$ (on $w \in \{0,1\}^m$ and $Q \subset \{0,1\}^n$ of size r)

---

for all $B \subseteq Q$ **do**

. **if** $\Pr_{f' \xleftarrow{\mathrm{r}} \mathcal{P}_n, v' \xleftarrow{\mathrm{r}} \{0,1\}^m} \left[g^{(f')}(v') = w \,\middle|\, B \subseteq Y_g(f', v') \right] \geq 2^{-m + \frac{n}{30}}$

.   **return false**

return true

We set $p(g)$, the probability that for a random permutation f and a random input v, the output $g^f(v)$ is correlated with some subset of the answers $Y_g(f, v)$. Define

$$p(g) \stackrel{\text{def}}{=} \Pr_{f \xleftarrow{\mathrm{r}} \mathcal{P}_n, v \xleftarrow{\mathrm{r}} \{0,1\}^m} \left[\mathrm{STA}(g^{(f)}(v), Y_g(f, v)) \right] . \tag{1}$$

We stress that both the output of STA (for any value y and a set Q), and the value $p(g)$ do not depend on any specific permutation, but rather on a combinatorial property of the construction as a whole, which averages over all permutations.

As explained, we set the oracle $\mathcal{O}$ and the set $\mathcal{F}$ based on the value $p(g)$. In case that $p(g) > \frac{1}{2}$ we set the oracle $\mathcal{O} \stackrel{\text{def}}{=} \mathrm{BreakOW}_g \stackrel{\text{def}}{=} \{\mathrm{BreakOW}_{g,f}\}_{f \in \{0,1\}^n \to \{0,1\}^n}$, where we use the oracle $\mathrm{BreakOW}_g$ from [9], which is described next. In [9] it is implicitly proved that there exists a set $\mathcal{F} \subset \mathcal{P}_n$ of size $|\mathcal{F}| > \frac{|\mathcal{P}_n|}{5}$, such that $\mathrm{BreakOW}_{g,f}$ $(\mathbf{OWF}, \frac{1}{4})$-breaks g^f for all $f \in \mathcal{F}$, and that $\mathrm{BreakOW}_g$ is $2^{\frac{n}{5}}$-stable for $\mathcal{F}$, in which case condition (2) in Theorem 1 is satisfied.

Algorithm $\mathrm{BreakOW}_{g,f}(w)$ (on input $w \in \{0,1\}^m$)

---

for all $v \in \{0,1\}^m$ **do**

. **if** $g^{(f)}(v) = w$ **then**

.   **if** $\mathrm{STA}(w, Y_g(f, v))$ **then**

.   **return** v

return $\perp$

In the case $p(g) \leq \frac{1}{2}$ we show that when f is chosen uniformly at random from a set of regular degenerate functions, it is often the case that the construction $g^{(f)}$ is not injective, and therefore there exists an oracle which breaks the pseudo-injectivity of $g^{(f)}$. The challenge is to find a breaker oracle that is t-stable. The next lemmas establish that the oracle BreakPI satisfies the required conditions in this case.

Formally, for a construction circuit g we define the oracle $\text{BreakPI}_g = \{\text{BreakPI}_{g,f}\}_{f \in \{0,1\}^n \to \{0,1\}^n}$ that for a function f is given by:

Algorithm $\text{BreakPI}_{g,f}(v)$ (on input $v \in \{0,1\}^m$)

---

for all $v' \in \{0,1\}^m$ **do**
. **if** $g^{(f)}(v) = g^{(f)}(v')$ **and** $v' \neq v$ **then**
.   **if** $Y_g(f,v) = Y_g(f,v')$ **then**
.   **return** v'
return $\perp$

Now, we fix $i \stackrel{\text{def}}{=} \frac{n}{200 \cdot r} = 10 \cdot \log(s)$. We show that for a $\frac{1}{6}$-fraction of the functions f in $\mathcal{R}_{n,i}$ it holds that $\text{BreakPI}_{g,f}$ breaks the pseudo-injectivity of $g^{(f)}$.

Lemma 5. *Let* $g : \{0,1\}^m \to \{0,1\}^m$ *be an r-query oracle construction with* $p(g) \leq \frac{1}{2}$. *Then for a $\frac{1}{6}$-fraction of the functions in $\mathcal{R}_{n,\frac{n}{200 \cdot r}}$ it holds that*

$$\Pr_{v \stackrel{r}{\leftarrow} \{0,1\}^m} \left[\text{BreakPI}_{g,f}(v) \text{ outputs } v' \text{ s.t. } v \neq v' \wedge g^{(f)}(v) = g^{(f)}(v') \right] \geq \frac{1}{24}. \quad (2)$$

The proof of the Lemma appears in [3]. We conclude from Lemma 5 that if $p(g) \leq \frac{1}{2}$, there exists a partition P of $\{0,1\}^n$ to sets of size 2^{n-i} and an image-set I of size 2^i, such that (2) holds for at least a $\frac{1}{6}$-fraction of the functions $f \in \mathcal{R}_{n,i}(P,I)$. Set $\mathcal{F} \subset \mathcal{R}_{n,i}(P,I)$ to be the set of all functions for which (2) holds. It follows that $|\mathcal{F}| \geq \frac{1}{6} \cdot 2^i$, as $|\mathcal{R}_{n,i}(P,I)| = |\mathcal{P}_i|$.

We next show that for the class of functions $\mathcal{R}_{n,i}(P,I)$ the oracle can be implemented such that it is stable.

Lemma 6. *Let* $i \in \mathbb{N}^+$ *and* $I \subset \{0,1\}^n$ *of size 2^i and P a partition of $\{0,1\}^n$ to sets of size 2^{n-i}. Then there exists an implementation of the oracle BreakPI_g that is n-stable for $\mathcal{R}_{n,i}(P,I)$.*

The proof of the Lemma appears in [3]. It is left to check (the simple calculation is omitted) that $2^s \cdot d_i(s,n) < |\mathcal{F}|$.

We have shown that the conditions of Theorem 1 hold, and therefore we conclude that there is no s-weak fixed-parameter fully black-box construction of **OWF∧PI** from **OWF**. The theorem is proved. $\square$

4.3   Deriving the Lower Bound

We are now ready to derive our lower bound for constructions of a universal one-way hash function from a one-way function:

Corollary 2. *Let s' be a security function such that $s(n) \stackrel{\text{def}}{=} s'(n) \cdot \log^2(n)$ is a super-polynomial security function for which $s(n) < 2^{\frac{n}{10}}$ holds. Then there is no s-weak fixed-parameter fully black-box construction of **UOWHF** from **OWF**,* *where the construction makes at most* $r'(n) = \frac{n}{2000 \cdot \log(s(n)) \cdot \log^2(n)}$ *calls to a one-way function* $f = \{f_n : \{0,1\}^n \to \{0,1\}^n\}_{n \in \mathbb{N}^+}$.

Proof. We apply Corollary 1 with Theorem 2.   □

Corollary 3. *There is no fixed-parameter fully black-box construction of* **UOWHF** *from* **OWF***, where the construction makes at most* $r = r(n)$ *calls to a OWF* $f = \{f_n : \{0,1\}^n \to \{0,1\}^n\}_{n \in \mathbb{N}^+}$, *where* $r \in o\left(\frac{n}{\log^3(n)}\right)$.

Proof. Let $r \in o\left(\frac{n}{\log^3(n)}\right)$. Then there exists a super-constant function $\alpha = \alpha(n)$, such that the function $r'(n)$ given by $r'(n) \stackrel{\text{def}}{=} r(n) \cdot \alpha(n)$ is still in $o\left(\frac{n}{\log^3(n)}\right)$. The bound follows immediately from Corollary 2 applied with $s(n) \stackrel{\text{def}}{=} 2^{\alpha(n) \cdot \log(n)}$.   □

Acknowledgments. We thank the anonymous reviewers for their helpful comments.

References

1. Ames, S., Gennaro, R., Venkitasubramaniam, M.: *The Generalized Randomized Iterate* and Its Application to New Efficient Constructions of UOWHFs from Regular One-Way Functions. In: Wang, X., Sako, K. (eds.) ASIACRYPT 2012. LNCS, vol. 7658, pp. 154–171. Springer, Heidelberg (2012)
2. Barak, B.: How to go beyond the black-box simulation barrier. In: FOCS, pp. 106–115. IEEE Computer Society (2001)
3. Barhum, K., Holenstein, T.: A Cookbook for Black-Box Separations and a Recipe for UOWHFs. Full version available as ECCC report TR12-173
4. Barhum, K., Maurer, U.: UOWHFs from OWFs: Trading Regularity for Efficiency. In: Hevia, A., Neven, G. (eds.) LATINCRYPT 2012. LNCS, vol. 7533, pp. 234–253. Springer, Heidelberg (2012)
5. Gennaro, R., Gertner, Y., Katz, J., Trevisan, L.: Bounds on the efficiency of generic cryptographic constructions. SIAM J. Comput. 35(1), 217–246 (2005)
6. Haitner, I., Hoch, J.J., Reingold, O., Segev, G.: Finding collisions in interactive protocols - a tight lower bound on the round complexity of statistically-hiding commitments. In: FOCS, pp. 669–679. IEEE Computer Society (2007)
7. Haitner, I., Holenstein, T.: On the (Im)Possibility of Key Dependent Encryption. In: Reingold, O. (ed.) TCC 2009. LNCS, vol. 5444, pp. 202–219. Springer, Heidelberg (2009)
8. Haitner, I., Holenstein, T., Reingold, O., Vadhan, S., Wee, H.: Universal One-Way Hash Functions via Inaccessible Entropy. In: Gilbert, H. (ed.) EUROCRYPT 2010. LNCS, vol. 6110, pp. 616–637. Springer, Heidelberg (2010)
9. Holenstein, T., Sinha, M.: Constructing a pseudorandom generator requires an almost linear number of calls. CoRR, abs/1205.4576 (2012)
10. Impagliazzo, R., Rudich, S.: Limits on the provable consequences of one-way permutations. In: STOC, pp. 44–61. ACM (1989)

11. Kim, J.H., Simon, D.R., Tetali, P.: Limits on the efficiency of one-way permutation-based hash functions. In: FOCS, pp. 535–542. IEEE Computer Society (1999)
12. Naor, M., Yung, M.: Universal one-way hash functions and their cryptographic applications. In: STOC, pp. 33–43. ACM (1989)
13. Reingold, O., Trevisan, L., Vadhan, S.P.: Notions of Reducibility between Cryptographic Primitives. In: Naor, M. (ed.) TCC 2004. LNCS, vol. 2951, pp. 1–20. Springer, Heidelberg (2004)
14. Rompel, J.: One-way functions are necessary and sufficient for secure signatures. In: STOC, pp. 387–394. ACM (1990)
15. Rosen, A., Segev, G.: Chosen-ciphertext security via correlated products. SIAM J. Comput. 39(7), 3058–3088 (2010)
16. Shoup, V.: A Composition Theorem for Universal One-Way Hash Functions. In: Preneel, B. (ed.) EUROCRYPT 2000. LNCS, vol. 1807, pp. 445–452. Springer, Heidelberg (2000)
17. Simon, D.R.: Findings Collisions on a One-Way Street: Can Secure Hash Functions Be Based on General Assumptions? In: Nyberg, K. (ed.) EUROCRYPT 1998. LNCS, vol. 1403, pp. 334–345. Springer, Heidelberg (1998)
18. Yao, A.C.-C.: Theory and applications of trapdoor functions (extended abstract). In: FOCS, pp. 80–91. IEEE Computer Society (1982)

Algebraic (Trapdoor) One-Way Functions and Their Applications

Dario Catalano[1], Dario Fiore[2,*], Rosario Gennaro[3], and Konstantinos Vamvourellis[4]

[1] Dipartimento di Matematica e Informatica, Università di Catania, Italy
catalano@dmi.unict.it
[2] Max Planck Institute for Software Systems (MPI-SWS), Germany
fiore@mpi-sws.org
[3] City College of New York, USA
rosario@cs.ccny.cuny.edu
[4] New York University, USA
kv472@nyu.edu

Abstract. In this paper we introduce the notion of *Algebraic (Trapdoor) One Way Functions*, which, roughly speaking, captures and formalizes many of the properties of number-theoretic one-way functions. Informally, a (trapdoor) one way function $F : X \to Y$ is said to be algebraic if X and Y are (finite) abelian cyclic groups, the function is *homomorphic* i.e. $F(x) \cdot F(y) = F(x \cdot y)$, and is *ring-homomorphic*, meaning that it is possible to compute linear operations "in the exponent" over some ring (which may be different from $\mathbb{Z}_p$ where p is the order of the underlying group X) without knowing the bases. Moreover, algebraic OWFs must be *flexibly one-way* in the sense that given $y = F(x)$, it must be infeasible to compute (x', d) such that $F(x') = y^d$ (for $d \neq 0$). Interestingly, algebraic one way functions can be constructed from a variety of *standard* number theoretic assumptions, such as RSA, Factoring and CDH over bilinear groups.

As a second contribution of this paper, we show several applications where algebraic (trapdoor) OWFs turn out to be useful. These include publicly verifiable secure outsourcing of polynomials, linearly homomorphic signatures and batch execution of Sigma protocols.

1 Introduction

ALGEBRAIC ONE-WAY FUNCTIONS. This paper introduces the notion of *Algebraic One-Way Function*, which aims to capture and formalize many of the properties enjoyed by number-theoretic based one-way functions. Intuitively, an Algebraic One-Way Function (OWF) $F : \mathcal{X}_\kappa \to \mathcal{Y}_\kappa$ is defined over abelian cyclic groups $\mathcal{X}_\kappa, \mathcal{Y}_\kappa$, and it satisfies the following properties:

- *Homomorphic:* the classical property that says that group operations are preserved by the OWF.

---

* Work entirely done while at NYU.

A. Sahai (Ed.): TCC 2013, LNCS 7785, pp. 680–699, 2013.

– *Ring-Homomorphic:* this is a new property saying, intuitively, that it is possible to efficiently perform linear operations "in the exponent" over some ring $\mathbb{K}$. While this property turns out to be equivalent to the homomorphic property for groups of known order n and the ring $\mathbb{K} = \mathbb{Z}_n$, it might not hold for groups of unknown order. Yet for the case of RSA Moduli we show that this property holds, and more interestingly it holds for *any* finite ring.
– *Flexibly One-Way:* We strengthen the usual notion of one-wayness in the following way: given $y = F(x)$ is should be unfeasible to compute (x', d) such that $F(x') = y^d$ and $d \in \mathbb{K}_{\neq 0}$ (in contrast with the traditional definition of one-wayness where d is fixed as 1).

In our work we also consider natural refinements of this notion to the cases when the function is a permutation and when there exists a trapdoor that allows to efficiently invert the function.

We demonstrate the existence of Algebraic OWFs with three instantiations, the security of which is deduced from the hardness of the Diffie-Hellman problem in groups with bilinear maps and the RSA/Factoring assumptions respectively.

APPLICATIONS. As a second contribution of this paper, we turn our attention to three separate practical problems: outsourcing of polynomial computations, linearly homomorphic signatures and batch executions of identification protocols. In all three separate problems, we show that Algebraic OWFs can be used for building truly efficient schemes that improve in several ways on the "state-of-the-art". In particular, we propose solutions for:

– *Publicly Verifiable Secure Outsourcing of Polynomials* which works over rings of *arbitrary* size and characteristic and does not necessarily use bilinear maps.
– *Linearly Homomorphic Signature Schemes* also over *arbitrary* rings, and in particular even small fields such as $\mathbb{F}_2$. The only known constructions for the latter case require assumptions over lattices [8] while we can use any of the assumptions above obtaining more efficient algorithms.
– *Batch Executions of Identification Protocols:* we construct a Sigma-protocol based on algebraic one-way functions and then we show that it is possible to construct a "batch" version of it where many statements are proven basically at the cost of a single one. A similar batch version for the Schnorr's Sigma protocol has been proposed in [20] and we generalize it to any of the assumptions above. In particular for the instantiation based on RSA we obtain a batch version of the Guillou-Quisquater protocol [25] which yields, to the best of our knowledge, the first batch verifiable Sigma protocol for groups of unknown order, a problem left open in [20].

The application to batch executions of identification protocols is deferred to the full version of this paper [11]. Below, we elaborate in detail about the improvements of our solutions to the remaining two applications.

1.1 Secure Outsourcing of Polynomials

Starting from work by Benabbas *et al.* [6], several papers have been investigating the problem of securely outsourcing the computation of large polynomials.

The problem can be described as follows: a computationally weak client stores a large polynomial (say in m variables, of degree d) with a powerful server. Later, the client will request the server to evaluate the polynomial at a certain input x and the server must provide such result together with a "proof" of its correctness. In particular, it is crucial that verifying such a proof must require substantially less resources than computing the polynomial from scratch. Furthermore, the client must store only a "small" amount of secret information, e.g. not the entire polynomial.

Following [6], several other papers (e.g. [33,34,16]) have investigated this problem, focusing specifically on the feature of *public verification*, i.e. the proof of correctness of the result provided by the server can be verified by *anyone*. This comes in contrast with the original solution in [6] which obtained only private verification, i.e. the proof of correctness of the result provided by the server can be verified only by the client who initially stored the polynomial.

The popularity of this research problem can be explained by its numerous practical applications including, as discussed in [6], *Proofs of Retrievability* (the client stores a large file F with the server and later wants a short proof that the entire file can be retrieved) and *Verifiable Keyword Search* (given a text file $T = \{w_1, \ldots, w_\ell\}$ and a word w, the server tells the client if $w \in T$ or not).

Limitation of Previous Solutions. The solutions for outsourcing of polynomial computations mentioned above suffer from two main drawbacks:

- *Large Field Size.* The schemes presented in [6,33,16] work only for polynomials computed over fields of prime characteristic p, which is the same p as the order of the underlying cryptographic group that is used to prove security. That means that for the schemes to be secure, p must be large. Therefore up to now, none of the existing schemes could handle small field sizes. The solution recently proposed in [34] can support polynomials over $\mathbb{Z}_2$, and thus, by working in a "bit-by-bit" fashion, over any field. However, to work over other fields of any characteristic p, it incurs a $O(\log p)$ computational overhead since $O(\log p)$ parallel instances of the scheme must be run. It would be therefore nice to have a scheme that works for polynomials over arbitrary fields, without a "bit-by-bit" encoding, so that the same scheme would scale well when working over larger field sizes.
- *Public Verifiability via Bilinear Maps.* All previous solutions that achieve public verifiability [33,34,16] do so by means of groups with bilinear maps as the underlying cryptographic tool. Since pairing computations may be expensive compared to simpler operations such as exponentiations, and given that bilinear maps are the only known algebraic structure under which we can currently build publicly verifiable computation, it is an interesting question to investigate whether we can have solutions that use alternative algebraic tools and cryptographic assumptions (e.g. RSA moduli) to achieve public verifiability.

Our new solution removes these two problems. As discussed above, we can instantiate our protocols over RSA moduli, and prove their security under the

DDH/RSA/Factoring Assumptions over such groups, therefore avoiding the use of bilinear maps. Perhaps more interestingly, our protocols can handle finite rings of any size and any characteristic, thus allowing for much more flexibility and efficiency. Moreover, the schemes in [34] are based on specific Attribute-Based Encryption schemes (e.g. [28]) whose security relies on "q-type" assumptions, whereas our solution can do so based on the well known RSA/Factoring assumptions.

As in the case of [16] our techniques extend for building a protocol for *Matrix Multiplication*. In this problem (also studied in [30]) the client stores a large $(n \times d)$ matrix M with the server and then provides d-dimensional vectors $\boldsymbol{x}$ and obtains $\boldsymbol{y} = M \cdot \boldsymbol{x}$ together with a proof of correctness.

Other Comparisons with Related Work. The subject of verifiable outsourced computation has a large body of prior work, both on the theoretical front (e.g. [4,24,27,29,23]) and on the more applied arena (e.g. [31,5,37,38]).

Our work follows the "amortized" paradigm introduced in [18] (also adopted in [14,2]) where a one-time expensive preprocessing phase is allowed. The protocols described in those papers allow a client to outsource the computation of an arbitrary function (encoded as a Boolean circuit) and use fully homomorphic encryption (i.e. [21]) resulting in solutions of limited practical relevance. Instead, we follow [6] by considering a very limited class of computations (polynomial evaluation and matrix multiplication) in order to obtain better efficiency.

As discussed above, we improve on [33] by providing a solution that works for finite rings of arbitrary characteristic (even small fields) and by avoiding the use of bilinear maps. Given that our solution is a generalization of [16] we also inherit all the improvements of that paper. In particular, compared to [33]:

- we get security under constant-size assumptions (i.e. assumptions that do not asymptotically depend on the degree of the polynomial), while their scheme uses a variation of the CDH Assumption that grows with the degree.
- we handle a larger class of polynomial functions: their scheme supports polynomials in m variables and total degree d (which we also support) but we additionally consider also polynomials of degree d in each variable.
- For the case we both support, we enjoy a much faster verification protocol: a constant amount of work (a couple of exponentiations over an RSA modulus) while they require $O(m)$ pairings[1].

1.2   Linearly Homomorphic Signatures

Imagine a user Alice owns some data set $m_1, \ldots, m_n \in \mathcal{M}$ that she keeps (signed) in some database stored at a, not necessarily trusted, server. Imagine also that

---

[1] In contrast the delegation phase is basically free in their case, while our delegation step requires $O(md)$ work – note however that in a publicly verifiable scheme, the verification algorithm might be run several times and therefore its efficiency is more important.

some other user, Bob, is allowed to query the database to perform some basic computation (such as the mean or other statistics) over Alice's data set. The simplest way to do this in a reliable manner (for Bob) is to download the full data set from the server, check all the signatures and compute the desired statistic. This solution, however, has two drawbacks. First, it is inefficient in terms of bandwidth. Second, even though Alice allows Bob to access some statistics over her data, she might not want this data to be explicitly revealed. Homomorphic signatures allow to overcome both these issues in a very elegant fashion [8]. Indeed, using a homomorphic signature scheme, Alice can sign $m_1, \ldots, m_n$, thus producing the signatures $\sigma_1, \ldots, \sigma_n$, which can be verified exactly as ordinary signatures. The homomorphic property provides the extra feature that given $\sigma_1, \ldots, \sigma_n$ and some function $f : \mathcal{M}^n \to \mathcal{M}$, one can compute a signature σ_f on the value $f(m_1, \ldots, m_n)$ *without* knowledge of the secret signing key SK. In other words, for a fixed set of original signed messages, it is possible to provide any $y = f(m_1, \ldots, m_n)$ with a proof of correctness σ_f. In particular the creation and the verification of σ_f does not require SK. The security definition is a relaxation over the classical security notion for signatures: it should be impossible to create a signature σ_f for $m \neq f(m_1, \ldots, m_n)$ without knowing SK.

The notion of homomorphic signature was introduced by Johnson *et al.* [26] and later refined by Boneh *et al.* [7]. Its main motivation was realizing a linear network coding scheme [1,35] secure against pollution attacks. The construction from [7] uses bilinear groups as the underlying tool and authenticates linear functions on vectors defined over large prime fields. Subsequent works considered different settings as well. In particular, the constructions in [19,12,13] are based on RSA, while [9,8] rely on lattices and can support linear functions on vectors over small fields. A general framework for building homomorphic signatures in the standard model, was recently provided by Freeman [17].

Our Contribution. In this paper we show that algebraic trapdoor one way permutations, *directly* allow for a very simple and elegant extension of Full Domain Hash (FDH) to the case of linearly homomorphic signatures. Similarly to standard FDH signatures our construction is secure in the random oracle model and allows for very efficient instantiations. Our framework allows for great flexibility when choosing a homomorphic signature scheme and the underlying message space. Indeed our constructions support messages and homomorphic operations over *arbitrary* finite rings. While it was already known how to realize linearly homomorphic signatures over small fields [9,8], ours seem to be the first schemes achieving this in a very efficient way and based on simple assumptions such as Factoring and RSA. To give a more concrete idea about the efficiency of our scheme, if we consider the case of messages in $\mathbb{F}_2$, then our signing algorithm is more efficient than that in [8] in the same order of magnitude as taking a square root in $\mathbb{Z}_N^*$ is more efficient than sampling a pre-image in lattice-based trapdoor functions, at comparable security levels.

2   Preliminaries

In what follows we will denote with $\lambda \in \mathbb{N}$ a security parameter. We say that a function ϵ is negligible if it vanishes faster than the inverse of any polynomial. If S is a set, we denote with $x \xleftarrow{\$} S$ the process of selecting x uniformly at random in S. Let $\mathcal{A}$ be a probabilistic algorithm. We denote with $x \xleftarrow{\$} \mathcal{A}(\cdot)$ the process of running $\mathcal{A}$ on some appropriate input and assigning its output to x.

Below we give informal definitions of verifiable computation and linearly homomorphic signatures. For more formal and precise descriptions, we defer the interested reader to the full version of this paper [11] and to relevant related work [34,17].

Verifiable Computation [34]. A Verifiable Computation scheme $\mathcal{VC}$ enables a client to outsource the computation of a function f to an untrusted worker, in such a way that the client can verify the correctness of the result returned by the worker. In order for the outsourcing to make sense, it is crucial that the cost of verification at the client must be cheaper than computing the function locally. A $\mathcal{VC}$ scheme for a class of functions $\mathcal{F}$ is defined by the following algorithms. The key generation $\mathsf{KeyGen}(1^\lambda, f)$, given a function $f \in \mathcal{F}$, produces a secret key SK_f that will be used for input delegation, a public verification key PK_f, used to verify the correctness of the delegated computation, and a public evaluation key EK_f which will be handed to the server to delegate the computation of f. The problem generation algorithm $\mathsf{ProbGen}(\mathsf{PK}_f, \mathsf{SK}_f, x) \to (\sigma_x, \mathsf{VK}_x)$ takes a value $x \in \mathsf{Dom}(f)$, and is run by the delegator to produce an encoding σ_x of x, together with a public verification key VK_x. $\mathsf{Compute}(\mathsf{EK}_f, \sigma_x) \to \sigma_y$ is run by the worker to compute an encoded version of $y = f(x)$. The verification algorithm $\mathsf{Verify}(\mathsf{PK}_f, \mathsf{VK}_x, \sigma_y) \to y \cup \bot$ takes the public information and an encoded output σ_y, and returns a value y or an error $\bot$.

Intuitively, for security, we require that any PPT worker, with oracle access to ProbGen, should not be able to cheat by producing a proof σ for $y' \neq f(x)$ that correctly verifies for $f(x)$.

Linearly-Homomorphic Signatures. Linearly-homomorphic signatures, as recently formalized in [9,8,17], extend the standard notion of digital signatures as follows. A linearly-homomorphic signature scheme consists of the following algorithms. The key generation $\mathsf{Hom.KG}(1^\lambda, m)$, given a maximum data set size m, outputs a public key PK and a secret key SK. The signing algorithm $\mathsf{Hom.Sign}(\mathsf{SK}, \tau, M, i)$ takes SK, a tag τ identifying a data set, a message M and an index $i \in \{1, 2, \ldots, m\}$, and outputs a signature σ. $\mathsf{Hom.Ver}(\mathsf{VK}, \tau, M, \sigma, f)$ checks whether σ is valid w.r.t. a tag τ, a message M and a function $f \in \mathcal{F}$. The evaluation algorithm $\mathsf{Hom.Eval}(\mathsf{VK}, \tau, f, \boldsymbol{\sigma})$, given a tag τ, a function f and a tuple of signatures $\{\sigma_i\}_{i=1}^m$ (that should be valid for $\{M_i\}_{i=1}^m$ respectively) outputs a new signature σ' that will verify correctly for $f(M_1, \ldots, M_m)$.[2]

The security notion for linearly-homomorphic signatures is an extension of the classical notion of unforgeability against chosen-message attacks. The adversary $\mathcal{A}$ can ask signatures on triples of the form (τ, M, i) (precisely, the tag is chosen by the challenger), and at the end it should not be able to produce a valid signature σ^* on (τ^*, M^*, f^*) such that: either (1) τ^* is "new", or (2) $\tau^* = \tau$ for some tag τ asked during the game and $M^* \neq f^*(M_1, \ldots, M_m)$, where $M_1, \ldots, M_m$ are the messages in the data set identified by τ. Notice that by definition of Hom.Eval, for any f^* everyone could compute a valid signature on $M = f^*(M_1, \ldots, M_m)$. Thus condition (2) makes sure that no one can do it for $M^* \neq f^*(M_1, \ldots, M_m)$.

3 Algebraic (Trapdoor) One-Way Functions

A family of one-way functions consists of two efficient algorithms (Gen, F) that work as follows. $\mathsf{Gen}(1^\lambda)$ takes as input a security parameter 1^λ and outputs a key κ. Such key κ determines a member $F_\kappa(\cdot)$ of the family, and in particular it specifies two sets $\mathcal{X}_\kappa$ and $\mathcal{Y}_\kappa$ such that $F_\kappa : \mathcal{X}_\kappa \to \mathcal{Y}_\kappa$. Given κ, for any input $x \in \mathcal{X}_\kappa$ it is efficient to compute $y \in \mathcal{Y}_\kappa$ where $y = F_\kappa(x)$. In addition, we assume that κ specifies a finite ring $\mathbb{K}$ that will be used as described below.

(Gen, F) is a family of *algebraic one-way functions* if it is:

Algebraic: $\forall \lambda \in \mathbb{N}$, and every $\kappa \xleftarrow{\$} \mathsf{Gen}(1^\lambda)$, the sets $\mathcal{X}_\kappa, \mathcal{Y}_\kappa$ are abelian cyclic groups. In our work we denote the group operation by multiplication, and we assume that given κ, sampling a (random) generator as well as computing the group operation can be done efficiently (in probabilistic polynomial time).

Homomorphic: $\forall \lambda \in \mathbb{N}$, every $\kappa \xleftarrow{\$} \mathsf{Gen}(1^\lambda)$, for any inputs $x_1, x_2 \in \mathcal{X}_\kappa$, it holds: $F_\kappa(x_1) \cdot F_\kappa(x_2) = F_\kappa(x_1 \cdot x_2)$.

Ring-homomorphic: intuitively, this property states that it is possible to evaluate inner product operations in the exponent given some "blinded" bases. Before stating the property formally, we give a high level explanation of this idea by using an example. Assume that one is given values $W_1 = h^{\omega_1}, W_2 = h^{\omega_2} \in \mathcal{X}_\kappa$, $\omega_1, \omega_2 \in \mathbb{Z}$, and wants to compute $h^{(\omega_1 \alpha_1 + \omega_2 \alpha_2 \bmod q)}$ for some integer coefficients α_1, α_2. If $q \neq |\mathcal{X}_\kappa|$ and the order of $\mathcal{X}_\kappa$ is not known, then it is not clear how to compute such a value efficiently (notice that h is not given). The ring-homomorphic property basically says that with the additional knowledge of $F_\kappa(h)$, such computation can be done efficiently. More formally, let $\kappa \xleftarrow{\$} \mathsf{Gen}(1^\lambda)$, $h_1, \ldots, h_m \in \mathcal{X}_\kappa$ be generators (for $m \geq 1$), and let $W_1, \ldots, W_\ell \in \mathcal{X}_\kappa$ be group elements, each of the form $W_i = h_1^{\omega_i^{(1)}} \cdots h_m^{\omega_i^{(m)}} \cdot R_i$, for some $R_i \in \mathcal{X}_\kappa$ and some integers $\omega_i^{(j)} \in \mathbb{Z}$ (note that this decomposition may not be unique).

---

[2] We remark that, for technical reasons, the realization given in section 5, slightly deviates from the above syntax. In particular, it requires Hom.Eval to receive, as additional inputs, the vector messages M and the functions f under which the signatures σ are supposed to verify.

We say that (Gen, F) is *ring-homomorphic* (for the ring $\mathbb{K}$ specified by κ) if there exists an efficient algorithm Eval such that for any $\kappa \xleftarrow{\$} \mathsf{Gen}(1^\lambda)$, any set of generators $h_1, \ldots, h_m \in \mathcal{X}_\kappa$, any vector of elements $\boldsymbol{W} \in \mathcal{X}_\kappa^\ell$ of the above form, and any vector of integers $\boldsymbol{\alpha} \in \mathbb{Z}^\ell$, it holds

$$\mathsf{Eval}(\kappa, \boldsymbol{A}, \boldsymbol{W}, \boldsymbol{\Omega}, \boldsymbol{\alpha}) = h_1^{\langle \boldsymbol{\omega}^{(1)}, \boldsymbol{\alpha} \rangle} \cdots h_m^{\langle \boldsymbol{\omega}^{(m)}, \boldsymbol{\alpha} \rangle} \prod_{i=1}^{\ell} R_i^{\alpha_i}$$

where $\boldsymbol{A} = (A_1, \ldots, A_m) \in \mathcal{Y}_\kappa^m$ is such that $A_i = F_\kappa(h_i)$, $\boldsymbol{\Omega} = (\omega_i^{(j)})_{i,j} \in \mathbb{Z}^{\ell \times m}$, and each product $\langle \boldsymbol{\omega}^{(j)}, \boldsymbol{\alpha} \rangle$ in the exponent is computed over the ring $\mathbb{K}$. We notice that over all the paper we often abuse notation by treating elements of the ring $\mathbb{K}$ as integers and vice versa. For this we assume a canonical interpretation of $d \in \mathbb{K}$ as an integer $[d] \in \mathbb{Z}$ between 0 and $|\mathbb{K}| - 1$, and that both d and $[d]$ are efficiently computable from one another.

We note that in the case when the ring $\mathbb{K}$ is $\mathbb{Z}_p$, where p is the order of the group $\mathcal{X}_\kappa$, then this property is trivially realized: *every* OWF where $\mathcal{X}_\kappa$ is a group of order p, is ring-homomorphic for $\mathbb{Z}_p$. To see this, observe that the following efficient algorithm trivially follows from the simple fact that $\mathcal{X}_\kappa$ is a finite group: $\overline{\mathsf{Eval}}(\kappa, \boldsymbol{A}, \boldsymbol{W}, \boldsymbol{\Omega}, \boldsymbol{\alpha}) = \prod_{i=1}^\ell W_i^{\alpha_i}$.

What makes the property non-trivial for some instantiations (in particular the RSA and Factoring-based ones shown in the next section) is that the algorithm Eval must compute the inner products $\langle \boldsymbol{\omega}^{(j)}, \boldsymbol{\alpha} \rangle$ over the ring $\mathbb{K}$, which might be different from $\mathbb{Z}_p$, where p is the order of the group $\mathcal{X}_\kappa$ over which the function is defined.

Flexibly One-way: finally, we require a family (Gen, F) to be non-invertible in a strong sense. Formally, we say that (Gen, F) is *flexibly one-way* if for any PPT adversary $\mathcal{A}$ it holds:

$$\Pr[\mathcal{A}(1^\lambda, \kappa, y) = (x', d) : d \neq 0 \wedge d \in \mathbb{K} \wedge F_\kappa(x') = y^d]$$

is negligible, where $\kappa \xleftarrow{\$} \mathsf{Gen}(1^\lambda)$, $x \xleftarrow{\$} \mathcal{X}_\kappa$ is chosen uniformly at random and $y = F_\kappa(x)$.

Our definition asks for $d \neq 0$ as we additionally require that in the case when $d = 0$ (over the ring $\mathbb{K}$) the function must be efficiently invertible. More precisely, given a value $y = F_\kappa(x) \in \mathcal{Y}_\kappa$ (for any $x \in \mathcal{X}_\kappa$) and an integer d such that $d = 0$ over the ring $\mathbb{K}$ (d may though be different from zero over the integers), there is an efficient algorithm that computes $x' \in \mathcal{X}_\kappa$ such that $F_\kappa(x') = y^d$.

Notice that flexible one-wayness is stronger than standard one-wayness (in which d is always fixed to 1). Also, our notion is closely related to the notion of *q-one wayness* for group homomorphisms given in [15]. Informally, this latter notion states that for some prime q: (1) f is one-way in the standard sense, (2) there is a polynomial-time algorithm that on input (f, z, y, i) such that $f(z) = y^i$ (for $0 < i < q$) computes x such that $f(x) = y$, and (3) y^q is efficiently invertible.

It is not hard to see that when $q = |\mathbb{K}|$ flexible one-wayness and q-one-wayness are basically equivalent, except for that we do not require the existence of an efficient algorithm that on input (F, z, y, i) such that $F(z) = y^i$ computes x such that $F(x) = y$.

We stress that even though flexible one-wayness may look non-standard, in the next section we demonstrate that our candidates satisfy it under very simple and standard assumptions.

ALGEBRAIC TRAPDOOR ONE-WAY FUNCTIONS. Our notion of algebraic one-way functions can be easily extended to the trapdoor case, in which there exists a trapdoor key that allows to efficiently invert the function. More formally, we define a family of *trapdoor one-way functions* as a set of efficient algorithms (Gen, F, Inv) that work as follows. Gen(1^λ) takes as input a security parameter 1^λ and outputs a pair (κ, td). Given κ, F_κ is the same as before. On input the trapdoor td and a value $y \in \mathcal{Y}_\kappa$, the inversion algorithm Inv computes $x \in \mathcal{X}_\kappa$ such that $F_\kappa(x) = y$. Often we will write $\mathsf{Inv}_{\mathsf{td}}(\cdot)$ as $F_\kappa^{-1}(\cdot)$. Then we say that (Gen, F, Inv) is a family of *algebraic trapdoor one-way functions* if it is algebraic, homomorphic and ring-homomorphic, in the same way as defined above.

Finally, when the input space $\mathcal{X}_\kappa$ and the output space $\mathcal{Y}_\kappa$ are the same (i.e., $\mathcal{X}_\kappa = \mathcal{Y}_\kappa$) and the function $F_\kappa : \mathcal{X}_\kappa \to \mathcal{X}_\kappa$ is a permutation, then we call (Gen, F, Inv) a family of *algebraic trapdoor permutations*.

3.1   Instantiations

We give three simple constructions of algebraic (trapdoor) one-way functions from a variety of number theoretic assumptions: CDH in bilinear groups, RSA and factoring.

CDH in Bilinear Groups

Gen(1^λ): use $\mathcal{G}(1^\lambda)$ to generate groups $\mathbb{G}_1, \mathbb{G}_2, \mathbb{G}_T$ of the same prime order p, together with an efficiently computable bilinear map $e : \mathbb{G}_1 \times \mathbb{G}_2 \to \mathbb{G}_T$. Sample two random generators $g_1 \in \mathbb{G}_1, g_2 \in \mathbb{G}_2$ and output $\kappa = (p, e, g_1, g_2)$. The finite ring $\mathbb{K}$ is $\mathbb{Z}_p$.

$F_\kappa(x)$: the function $F_\kappa : \mathbb{G}_1 \to \mathbb{G}_T$ is defined by: $F_\kappa(x) = e(x, g_2)$.

The algebraic and homomorphic properties are easy to check. Moreover, the function is trivially ring-homomorphic for $\mathbb{Z}_p$ as p is the order of $\mathbb{G}_1$.

Its security can be shown via the following Theorem. The proof is straightforward and is deferred to the full version.

Theorem 1. *If the co-CDH assumption holds for $\mathcal{G}(\cdot)$, then the above function is flexibly one-way.*

RSA (over $\mathbb{QR}_N$). This construction is an algebraic trapdoor permutation, and it allows to explicitly choose the ring $\mathbb{K}$ as $\mathbb{Z}_e$ for any prime $e \geq 3$.

Gen($1^\lambda, e$): let $e \geq 3$ be a prime number. Run $(N, p, q) \xleftarrow{\$} \mathsf{RSAGen}(1^\lambda)$ to generate a Blum integer N, product of two safe primes p and q. If $gcd(e, \phi(N)) \neq 1$, then reject the tuple (N, p, q) and try again. Output $\kappa = (N, e)$ and td $=$ (p, q).

$F_\kappa(x)$: the function $F_\kappa : \mathbb{QR}_N \to \mathbb{QR}_N$ is defined by: $F_\kappa(x) = x^e \bmod N$.

$\mathsf{Inv}_{\mathsf{td}}(y)$: the inversion algorithm computes $c = e^{-1} \bmod \phi(N)$, and then outputs: $x^c \bmod N$.

$\mathsf{Eval}(\kappa, \boldsymbol{A}, \boldsymbol{W}, \boldsymbol{\Omega}, \boldsymbol{\alpha})$: for $j = 1$ to m, compute $\omega^{(j)} = \langle \omega^{(j)}, \boldsymbol{\alpha} \rangle$ over the integers and write it as $\omega^{(j)} = \omega^{(j)'} + e \cdot \omega^{(j)''}$, for some $\omega^{(j)'}, \omega^{(j)''} \in \mathbb{Z}$. Finally, output

$$V = \frac{\prod_{i=1}^{\ell} W_i^{\alpha_i}}{\prod_{j=1}^{m} A_j^{\omega^{(j)''}}} \bmod N$$

The algebraic and homomorphic properties are easy to check. To see that the function is ring-homomorphic for $\mathbb{K} = \mathbb{Z}_e$, we show the correctness of the Eval algorithm as follows:

$$V = \frac{\prod_{i=1}^{\ell} W_i^{\alpha_i}}{\prod_{j=1}^{m} A_j^{\omega^{(j)''}}} \bmod N = \frac{\prod_{i=1}^{l} (\prod_{j=1}^{m} h_j^{\omega_i^{(j)}} \cdot R_i)^{\alpha_i}}{\prod_{j=1}^{m} h_j^{(e\omega^{(j)''} \bmod \phi(N))}} \bmod N$$

$$= \frac{\prod_{j=1}^{m} h_j^{(\langle \omega^{(j)}, \boldsymbol{\alpha} \rangle \bmod \phi(N))} \prod_{i=1}^{l} R_i^{\alpha_i}}{\prod_{j=1}^{m} h_j^{(e\omega^{(j)''} \bmod \phi(N))}} \bmod N$$

$$= \frac{\prod_{j=1}^{m} h_j^{(\omega^{(j)'} + e\omega^{(j)''} \bmod \phi(N))} \prod_{i=1}^{l} R_i^{\alpha_i}}{\prod_{j=1}^{m} h_j^{(e\omega^{(j)''} \bmod \phi(N))}} \bmod N$$

$$= h_1^{\omega^{(1)'}} \cdots h_m^{\omega^{(m)'}} \prod_{i=1}^{l} R_i^{\alpha_i} \bmod N.$$

The security of the function is shown via the following Theorem:

Theorem 2. *If the RSA assumption holds for* RSAGen, *the above function is flexibly one-way.*

To prove the theorem, we simply observe that since $d \neq 0$ and $d \in \mathbb{Z}_e$, it holds $gcd(e, d) = 1$. Therefore, it is possible to apply the well known Shamir's trick [36] to transform any adversary against the security of our OWF to an adversary which solves the RSA problem for the fixed e.

On the other hand, given $y \in \mathcal{Y}_\kappa$, in the special case when $d = 0 \bmod e$, finding a pre-image of y^d can be done efficiently by computing $y^{d'}$ where d' is the integer such that $d = e \cdot d'$.

Factoring. This construction also allows to explicitly choose the ring $\mathbb{K}$, which can be $\mathbb{Z}_{2^t}$ for any integer $t \geq 1$.

$\mathsf{Gen}(1^\lambda, t)$: run $(N, p, q) \xleftarrow{\$} \mathsf{RSAGen}(1^\lambda)$ to generate a Blum integer N product of two safe primes p and q. Output $\kappa = (N, t)$ and td $= (p, q)$.

$F_\kappa(x)$: The function $F_\kappa : \mathbb{QR}_N \to \mathbb{QR}_N$ is defined by: $F_\kappa(x) = x^{2^t} \bmod N$.

$\mathsf{Inv_{td}}(y)$: given $\mathsf{td} = (p, q)$ and on input $y \in \mathbb{QR}_N$, the inversion algorithm proceeds as follows. First, it uses the factorization of N to compute the four square roots $x, -x, x', -x' \in \mathbb{Z}_N^*$ of y, and then it outputs the only one which is in $\mathbb{QR}_N$ (recall that since N is a Blum integer exactly one of the roots of y is a quadratic residue).

$\mathsf{Eval}(\kappa, \boldsymbol{A}, \boldsymbol{W}, \boldsymbol{\omega}, \boldsymbol{\alpha})$: for $j = 1$ to m, compute $\omega^{(j)} = \langle \boldsymbol{\omega}^{(j)}, \boldsymbol{\alpha} \rangle$ over the integers and write it as $\omega^{(j)} = \omega^{(j)'} + 2^t \cdot \omega^{(j)''}$. Finally, output

$$V = \frac{\prod_{i=1}^{\ell} W_i^{\alpha_i}}{\prod_{j=1}^{m} A_j^{\omega^{(j)''}}} \bmod N$$

The algebraic and homomorphic properties are easy to check. To see that the function is ring-homomorphic for $\mathbb{Z}_{2^t}$, observe that its correctness can be checked similarly to the RSA case. We notice that this construction is an algebraic trapdoor permutation.

The security of the function can be shown via the following Theorem. For lack of space, its proof appears in the full version of this paper.

Theorem 3. *If Factoring holds for* RSAGen, *then the above function is flexibly one-way.*

4   Our Verifiable Computation Schemes

In this section we propose the construction of verifiable computation schemes for the delegation of multivariate polynomials and matrix multiplications. Our constructions make generic use of our new notion of algebraic one-way functions.

An Overview of Our Solutions. Our starting point is the protocol of [6]: assume the client has a polynomial $F(\cdot)$ of large degree d, and it wants to compute the value $F(x)$ for arbitrary inputs x. In [6] the client stores the polynomial in the clear with the server as a vector of coefficients c_i in $\mathbb{Z}_p$. The client also stores with the server a vector of group elements t_i of the form $g^{ac_i + r_i}$ where g generates a cyclic group $\mathbb{G}$ of order p, $a \in_R \mathbb{Z}_p$, and r_i is the ith-coefficient of a polynomial $R(\cdot)$ of the same degree as $F(\cdot)$. When queried on input x, the server returns $y = F(x)$ and $t = g^{aF(x) + R(x)}$, and the client accepts y iff $t = g^{ay + R(x)}$.

If $R(\cdot)$ was a random polynomial, then this is a secure way to authenticate y, however checking that $t = g^{ay + R(x)}$ would require the client to compute $R(x)$ – the exact work that we set out to avoid! The crucial point, therefore, is how to perform this verification fast, i.e., in $o(d)$ time. The fundamental tool in [6] is the introduction of pseudo-random functions (PRFs) with a special property called *closed-form efficiency*: if we define the coefficients r_i of $R(\cdot)$ as $PRF_K(i)$ (which preserves the security of the scheme), then for any input x the value $g^{R(x)}$ can be computed very efficiently (sub-linearly in d) by a party who knows the secret key K for the PRF.

Our first observation was to point out that one of the PRFs proposed in [6] was basically a variant of the Naor-Reingold PRF [32] which can be easily istantiated over RSA moduli assuming the DDH assumption holds over such groups (in particular over the subgroup of quadratic residues).

Note, however, that this approach implies a private verification algorithm by the same client who outsourced the polynomial in the first place, since it requires knowledge of the secret key K. To make verification public, Fiore and Gennaro proposed the use of Bilinear Maps together with algebraic PRFs based on the decision linear problem [16].

Our second observation was to note that the scheme in [6] is really an information-theoretic authentication of the polynomial "in the exponent". Instead of using exponentiation, we observed that any "one-way function" with the appropriate "homomorphic properties" would do. We teased out the relevant properties and defined the notion of an *Algebraic One-Way Function* and showed that it is possible to instantiate it using the RSA/Rabin functions.

If we use our algebraic one-way functions based on RSA and factoring described in Section 3.1, then we obtain new verifiable computation schemes whose security relies on these assumptions and that support polynomials over a large variety of finite rings: $\mathbb{Z}_e$ for any prime $e \geq 3$, $\mathbb{Z}_{2^t}$ for any integer $t \geq 1$. Previously known solutions [33,16] could support only polynomials over $\mathbb{Z}_p$ where p must be a *large* prime whose size strictly depends on the security parameter 1^λ (basically, p must be such that the discrete logarithm problem is hard in a group of order p).

In contrast, our factoring and RSA solutions allow for much more flexibility. Precisely, using the RSA function allows us to compute polynomials over $\mathbb{Z}_e$ for any prime $e \geq 3$, where e is the prime used by the RSA function. Using the Rabin function allows us to handle polynomials over $\mathbb{Z}_{2^t}$ for any integer $t \geq 1$.

A Solution for Polynomials of Degree d in Each Variable. In this section we propose the construction of a scheme for delegating the computation of m-variate polynomials of degree at most d in each variable. These polynomials have up to $l = (d+1)^m$ terms which we index by $(i_1, \ldots, i_m)$, for $0 \leq i_j \leq d$. Similarly to [6,16], we define the function $h : \mathbb{K}^m \to \mathbb{K}^l$ which expands the input x to the vector $(h_1(x), \ldots, h_l(x))$ of all monomials as follows: for all $1 \leq j \leq l$, use a canonical ordering to write $j = (i_1, \ldots, i_m)$ with $0 \leq i_k \leq d$, and then $h_j(x) = (x_1^{i_1} \cdots x_m^{i_m})$. So, using this notation we can write the polynomial as $f(x) = \langle f, h(x) \rangle = \sum_{j=1}^l f_j \cdot h_j(x)$ where the f_j's are its coefficients.

Our scheme uses two main building blocks: an algebraic one-way function (see definition in Section 3) (Gen, F) and a pseudorandom function with closed form efficiency for polynomials whose notion is recalled below.

CLOSED-FORM EFFICIENT PRFs. The notion of closed form efficient pseudorandom functions, firstly introduced by Benabbas et al. [6] and later refined by Fiore and Gennaro [16], is defined as follows.

The function consists of algorithms (PRF.KG, PRF.F). The key generation PRF.KG takes as input the security parameter 1^λ, and outputs a secret key K and some public parameters pp that specify domain $\mathcal{X}$ and range $\mathcal{Y}$ of the function. On input $x \in \mathcal{X}$, PRF.F$_K(x)$ uses the secret key K to compute a value $y \in \mathcal{Y}$. It must of course satisfy the usual pseudorandomness property. Namely,

(PRF.KG, PRF.F) is secure if for every PPT adversary $\mathcal{A}$, the following difference is negligible:

$$\left| \Pr[\mathcal{A}^{\mathsf{PRF.F}_K(\cdot)}(1^\lambda, \mathsf{pp}) = 1] - \Pr[\mathcal{A}^{R(\cdot)}(1^\lambda, \mathsf{pp}) = 1] \right|$$

where $(K, \mathsf{pp}) \xleftarrow{\$} \mathsf{PRF.KG}(1^\lambda)$, and $R(\cdot)$ is a random function from $\mathcal{X}$ to $\mathcal{Y}$.

In addition, it is required to satisfy the following *closed-form efficiency* property. Consider an arbitrary computation Comp that takes as input l random values $R_1, \ldots, R_l \in \mathcal{Y}$ and a vector of m arbitrary values $\boldsymbol{x} = (x_1, \ldots, x_m)$, and assume that the best algorithm to compute $\mathsf{Comp}(R_1, \ldots, R_l, x_1, \ldots, x_m)$ takes time T. Let $z = (z_1, \ldots, z_l)$ a l-tuple of arbitrary values in the domain $\mathcal{X}$ of PRF.F. We say that a PRF (PRF.KG, PRF.F) is *closed-form efficient* for (Comp, z) if there exists an algorithm $\mathsf{PRF.CFEval}_{\mathsf{Comp},z}$ such that

$$\mathsf{PRF.CFEval}_{\mathsf{Comp},z}(K, x) = \mathsf{Comp}(F_K(z_1), \ldots, F_K(z_l), x_1, \ldots, x_m)$$

and its running time is $o(T)$. For $z = (1, \ldots, l)$ we usually omit the subscript z.

Note that depending on the structure of Comp, this property may enforce some constraints on the range $\mathcal{Y}$ of the PRF. In particular in our case, $\mathcal{Y}$ will be an abelian group. We also remark that due to the pseudorandomness property the output distribution of $\mathsf{PRF.CFEval}_{\mathsf{Comp},z}(K, x)$ (over the random choice of K) is indistinguishable from the output distribution of $\mathsf{Comp}(R_1, \ldots, R_\ell, x_1, \ldots, x_m)$ (over the random choices of the R_i).

OUR SCHEME. Our verifiable computation scheme works generically for any family of functions $\mathcal{F}$ that is the set of m-variate polynomials of degree d over a finite ring $\mathbb{K}$ such that: (1) the algebraic one-way function $F_\kappa : \mathcal{X}_\kappa \to \mathcal{Y}_\kappa$ is ring-homomorphic for $\mathbb{K}$, and (2) there exists a PRF whose range is $\mathcal{X}_\kappa$, and that has closed form efficiency relative to the computation of polynomials, i.e., for the algorithm $\mathsf{Poly}(\boldsymbol{R}, \boldsymbol{x}) = \sum_{j=1}^l R_j^{h_j(\boldsymbol{x})}$.

If we instantiate these primitives with the CDH-based algebraic OWF of Section 3.1 and the PRFs based on Decision Linear described in [16], then our generic construction captures the verifiable computation scheme of Fiore and Gennaro [16]. Otherwise we can obtain new schemes by using our algebraic OWFs based on RSA and Factoring described in Section 3.1. They have input and output space $\mathcal{X}_\kappa = \mathcal{Y}_\kappa = \mathbb{QR}_N$, the subgroup of quadratic residues in $\mathbb{Z}_N^*$. So, to complete the instantiation of the scheme $\mathcal{VC}_{\mathsf{Poly}}$, we need a PRF with closed form efficiency whose range is $\mathbb{QR}_N$. For this purpose we can use the PRF constructions described in [6] that are based on the Naor-Reingold PRF. The only difference is that in our case we have to instantiate the PRFs in the group $\mathbb{QR}_N$, and thus claim their security under the hardness of DDH in the group $\mathbb{QR}_N$.

With these instantiations we obtain new verifiable computation schemes that support polynomials over a *large* variety of finite rings: $\mathbb{Z}_e$ for any prime $e \geq 3$, $\mathbb{Z}_{2^t}$ for any integer $t \geq 1$. Previously known solutions [33,16] could support only polynomials over $\mathbb{Z}_p$ where p must be a *large* prime whose size strictly depends on the security parameter 1^λ. In contrast, our factoring and RSA solutions allow for much more flexibility.

The description of our generic construction $\mathcal{VC}_{\mathsf{Poly}}$ follows.

KeyGen($1^\lambda, f$). Run $\kappa \xleftarrow{\$} \mathsf{Gen}(1^\lambda)$ to obtain a one-way function $F_\kappa : \mathcal{X}_\kappa \to \mathcal{Y}_\kappa$
that is ring-homomorphic for $\mathbb{K}$. Let f be encoded as the set of its coefficients
$(f_1, \ldots, f_l) \in \mathbb{K}^l$.
Generate the seed of a PRF, $K \xleftarrow{\$} \mathsf{PRF.KG}(1^\lambda, \lceil \log d \rceil, m)$, whose output
space is $\mathcal{X}_\kappa$, the input of the one-way function. Choose a random generator
$h \xleftarrow{\$} \mathcal{X}_\kappa$, and compute $A = F_\kappa(h)$.
For $i = 1$ to l, compute $W_i = h^{f_i} \cdot \mathsf{PRF.F}_K(i)$. Let $W = (W_1, \ldots, W_l) \in (\mathcal{X}_\kappa)^l$.
Output $\mathsf{EK}_f = (f, W, A)$, $\mathsf{PK}_f = A$, $\mathsf{SK}_f = K$.
ProbGen($\mathsf{PK}_f, \mathsf{SK}_f, x$). Output $\sigma_x = x$ and $\mathsf{VK}_x = F_\kappa(\mathsf{PRF.CFEval}_{\mathsf{Poly}}(K, h(x)))$.
Compute(EK_f, σ_x). Let $\mathsf{EK}_f = (f, W, A)$ and $\sigma_x = x$. Compute $y = f(x) = \sum_{i=1}^{l} f_i \cdot h_i(x)$ (over $\mathbb{K}$) and $V = \mathsf{Eval}(\kappa, A, W, f, h(x))$, and return $\sigma_y = (y, V)$.
Verify($\mathsf{PK}_f, \mathsf{VK}_x, \sigma_y$). Parse σ_y as (y, V). If $y \in \mathbb{K}$ and $F_\kappa(V) = A^y \cdot \mathsf{VK}_x$, then
output y, otherwise output $\perp$.

The correctness of the scheme follows from the properties of the algebraic one-way function and the correctness of $\mathsf{PRF.CFEval}$.

Theorem 4. *If* (Gen, F) *is a family of algebraic one-way functions and* $\mathsf{PRF.F}$
is a family of pseudo-random functions then any PPT adversary $\mathcal{A}$ *making at
most* $q = poly(\lambda)$ *queries has negligible advantage* $\mathbf{Adv}_{\mathcal{A}}^{\mathsf{PubVer}}(\mathcal{VC}_{\mathsf{Poly}}, \mathcal{F}, q, \lambda)$.

Proof (Sketch). Here we provide a proof sketch of Theorem 4. We defer the interested reader to the the full version of this work for the formal proof.
    Consider the following hybrid games:

Game 0: this is the real security game.
Game 1: this is the same as Game 0 except that the challenger performs a
    different evaluation of the algorithm ProbGen. Let x be the input asked by
    the adversary. The challenger computes $\mathsf{VK}_x = \prod_{i=1}^{l} \mathsf{PRF.F}_K(i)^{h_i(x)}$.
    By correctness of $\mathsf{PRF.CFEval}$, Game 1 is identically distributed as Game 0.
Game 2: this game proceeds as Game 1, except that the function $\mathsf{PRF.F}_k(i)$
    is replaced by a truly random function that on every i lazily samples a value
    $R_i \xleftarrow{\$} \mathcal{X}_\kappa$ uniformly at random.
    By the security of the pseudorandom function, it is not hard to see that
    Game 2 is negligibly-close to Game 1.

To complete the proof of the theorem it remains to show that by the flexible one-wayness of the algebraic OWF, any PPT adversary has at most negligible advantage of winning in Game 2.
    Assume by contradiction there exists a PPT adversary $\mathcal{A}$ that has non-negligible probability ϵ of winning in Game 2. We show that from such $\mathcal{A}$ it is possible to construct an efficient algorithm $\mathcal{B}$ that breaks the flexible one-wayness of the algebraic one-way function with the same probability ϵ.

$\mathcal{B}$ receives the pair (κ, A) as its input, where $A \in \mathcal{Y}_\kappa$, and proceeds as follows. It chooses l random values $W_1, \ldots, W_l \xleftarrow{\$} \mathcal{X}_\kappa$, and it sets $\mathsf{EK}_f = (f, W, A)$ and $\mathsf{PK}_f = A$. Next, for $i = 1$ to l, $\mathcal{B}$ computes $Z_i = F_\kappa(W_i) \cdot A^{-f_i}$.

$\mathcal{B}$ runs $\mathcal{A}(\mathsf{PK}_f, \mathsf{EK}_f)$ and answers each query $\boldsymbol{x}$ as follows: it computes $\mathsf{VK}_x = \prod_{i=1}^l Z_i^{h_i(\boldsymbol{x})}$ and returns VK_x. By the homomorphic property of F_κ this computation of VK_x is equivalent to the one made by the challenger in Game 2.

Finally, let $\boldsymbol{x}^*, \hat{\sigma}_y = (\hat{y}, \hat{V})$ be the output of $\mathcal{A}$ at the end of the game such that $\mathsf{Verify}(\mathsf{PK}_f, \mathsf{VK}_{x^*}, \hat{\sigma}_y) = \hat{y}$, $\hat{y} \neq \perp$ and $\hat{y} \neq f(\boldsymbol{x}^*)$. By verification, this means that $F_\kappa(\hat{V}) = A^{\hat{y}} \cdot \mathsf{VK}_{x^*}$. Let $y = f(\boldsymbol{x}^*) \in \mathbb{K}$ be the correct output of the computation, and let $V = \mathsf{Eval}(\kappa, A, W, f, h(\boldsymbol{x}))$ be the proof as obtained by honestly running Compute. By correctness of the scheme we have that $F_\kappa(V) = A^y \cdot \mathsf{VK}_{x^*}$. Hence, we can divide the two verification equations and by the homomorphic property of F_κ, we obtain $F_\kappa(\hat{V}/V) = A^\delta$ where $\delta = \hat{y} - y \neq 0$. $\mathcal{B}$ outputs $U = \hat{V}/V$ and δ as a solution for the flexible one-wayness of $F_\kappa(A)$.

Extensions of our Protocols. The techniques showed above can be further extended in order to provide efficient solutions for the class of polynomials in m variables and maximum degree d in each monomial, and for matrix multiplications. We leave the description of these extensions for the full version of this work [11].

5   Linearly-Homomorphic FDH Signatures

In this section we show a direct application of Algebraic Trapdoor One Way Permutations (TDP) to build linearly-homomorphic signatures.

An Intuitive Overview of Our Solution. Our construction can be seen as a linearly-homomorphic version of Full-Domain-Hash (FDH) signatures. Recall that a FDH signature on a message m is $F^{-1}(H(m))$ where F is any TDP and H is a hash function modeled as a random oracle. Starting from this basic scheme, we build our linearly homomorphic signatures by defining a signature on a message m, tag τ and index i as $\sigma = F^{-1}(H(\tau, i) \cdot G(m))$ where F is now an algebraic TDP, H is a classical hash function that will be modeled as a random oracle and G is a homomorphic hash function (i.e, such that $G(x) \cdot G(y) = G(x + y)$). Then, we will show that by using the special properties of algebraic TDPs (in particular, ring-homomorphicity and flexible one-wayness) both the security and the homomorphic property of the signature scheme follow immediately.

Precisely, if the algebraic TDP used in the construction is ring-homomorphic for a ring $\mathbb{K}$, then our signature scheme supports the message space $\mathbb{K}^n$ (for some integer $n \geq 1$) and all linear functions over this ring. Interestingly, by instantiating our generic construction with our two algebraic TDPs based on Factoring and RSA (see Section 3.1), we obtain schemes that are linearly-homomorphic for *arbitrary* finite rings, i.e., $\mathbb{Z}_{2^t}$ or $\mathbb{Z}_e$, for any $t \geq 1$ and any prime e. As we will detail at the end of this section, previous solutions (e.g., [7,19,3,9,8,12,13,17]) could support only large fields whose size strictly depends on the security parameter. The only exception are the lattice-based schemes of Boneh and Freeman

[9,8] that work for small fields, but are less efficient than our solution. In this sense, one of our main contributions is to propose a solution that offers a great flexibility as it can support arbitrary finite rings, both small and large, whose characteristic can be basically chosen ad-hoc (e.g., according to the desired application) at the moment of instantiating the scheme.

Our Scheme. The scheme is defined by the following algorithms.

Hom.KG($1^\lambda, m, n$) On input the security parameter λ, the maximum data set size m, and an integer $n \geq 1$ used to determine the message space $\mathcal{M}$ as we specify below, the key generation algorithm proceeds as follows.

Run $(\kappa, \mathsf{td}) \xleftarrow{\$} \mathsf{Gen}(1^\lambda)$ to obtain an algebraic TDP, $F_\kappa : \mathcal{X}_\kappa \to \mathcal{X}_\kappa$ that is ring-homomorphic for the field $\mathbb{K}$. Next, sample $n+1$ group elements $u, g_1, \ldots, g_n \xleftarrow{\$} \mathcal{X}_\kappa$ and choose a hash function $H : \{0,1\}^* \to \mathcal{X}_\kappa$.

The public key is set as $\mathsf{VK} = (\kappa, u, g_1, \ldots, g_n, H)$, while the secret key is the trapdoor $\mathsf{SK} = \mathsf{td}$.

The message space $\mathcal{M} = (\mathbb{K})^n$ is the set of n-dimensional vectors whose components are elements of $\mathbb{K}$, while the set of admissible functions $\mathcal{F}$ is all degree-1 polynomials over $\mathbb{K}$ with m variables and constant-term zero.

Hom.Sign(SK, τ, M, i) The signing algorithm takes as input the secret key SK, a tag $\tau \in \{0,1\}^\lambda$, a message $M = (M_1, \ldots, M_n) \in \mathbb{K}^n$ and an index $i \in \{1, \ldots, m\}$. To sign, choose $s \xleftarrow{\$} \mathbb{K}$ uniformly at random and use the trapdoor td to compute

$$x = F_\kappa^{-1}(H(\tau, i) \cdot u^s \cdot \prod_{j=1}^{n} g_j^{M_j})$$

and output $\sigma = (x, s)$.

Hom.Ver($\mathsf{VK}, \tau, M, \sigma, f$) To verify a signature $\sigma = (x, s)$ on a message $M \in \mathcal{M}$, w.r.t. tag τ and the function f, the verification algorithm proceeds as follows. Let f be encoded as its set of coefficients $(f_1, f_2, \ldots, f_m)$. Check that all values f_i and M_j are in $\mathbb{K}$ and then check that the following equation holds

$$F_\kappa(x) = \prod_{i=1}^{m} H(\tau, i)^{f_i} \cdot u^s \cdot \prod_{j=1}^{n} g_j^{M_j}$$

If both checks are satisfied, then output 1 (accept), otherwise output 0 (reject).

Hom.Eval($\mathsf{VK}, \tau, f, \boldsymbol{\sigma}, \boldsymbol{M}, \boldsymbol{f}$) The public evaluation algorithm takes as input the public key VK, a tag τ, a function $f \in \mathcal{F}$ encoded as $(f_1, \ldots, f_m) \in \mathbb{K}^m$, a vector of signatures $\boldsymbol{\sigma} = (\sigma_1, \ldots, \sigma_m)$ where $\sigma_i = (x_i, s_i)$, a vector of messages $\boldsymbol{M} = (M^{(1)}, \ldots, M^{(m)})$ and a vector of functions $\boldsymbol{f} = (f^{(1)}, \ldots, f^{(m)})$. If each signature σ_i is valid for the tag τ, the message $M^{(i)}$ and the function $f^{(i)}$, then the signature σ output by Hom.Eval is valid for the message $M = f(M^{(1)}, \ldots, M^{(m)})$. In order to do this, our algorithm first computes $s = f(s_1, \ldots, s_m) = \sum_{i=1}^{m} f_i \cdot s_i$ (over $\mathbb{K}$). Next, it defines:

$$\boldsymbol{A} = (H(\tau, 1), \ldots, H(\tau, m), u, g_1, \ldots, g_n) \in \mathcal{X}_\kappa^{m+n+1},$$

$$\Omega = \begin{bmatrix} f_1^{(1)} & \cdots & f_m^{(1)} & s_1 & M_1^{(1)} & \cdots & M_n^{(1)} \\ \vdots & & \vdots & \vdots & \vdots & & \vdots \\ f_1^{(m)} & \cdots & f_m^{(m)} & s_m & M_1^{(m)} & \cdots & M_n^{(m)} \end{bmatrix} \in \mathbb{Z}^{m \times m+n+1}$$

and uses the Eval algorithm of the algebraic TDP to compute $x = \mathsf{Eval}(\kappa, \boldsymbol{A}, \boldsymbol{x}, \Omega, f)$. Finally, it outputs $\sigma = (x, s)$.

We remark that our construction requires the Hom.Eval algorithm to know the messages $M^{(i)}$ for which the signatures σ_i are supposed to verify correctly. Moreover we stress that Hom.Eval needs to receive both f and $\boldsymbol{f}$ as otherwise it would not be able to correctly perform the homomorphic operations. Notice, however, that the value of the produced message does not depend on $\boldsymbol{f}$ (this is needed essentially to run the Eval algorithm correctly).

Since our scheme follows the FDH paradigm, its security holds in the random oracle model, however, following similar results for FDH signatures, in the full version we propose a variant of our scheme that can be proven secure in the standard model in the weaker security model of Q-time security, in which the adversary is restricted to query signatures on at most Q different datasets, and Q is a pre-fixed bound.

The security of our scheme follows from the following theorem. For lack of space, its proof appears in the full version.

Theorem 5. *If* (Gen, F, Inv) *is a family of algebraic trapdoor permutations and H is modeled as a random oracle, then the linearly-homomorphic signature scheme described above is secure.*

EFFICIENCY AND COMPARISONS. The most attractive feature of our proposal is that it allows for great variability of the underlying message space. In particular our scheme allows to consider finite rings of arbitrary size without sacrificing efficiency[3]. This is in sharp contrast with previous solutions which can either support only large fields (whose size directly depends on the security parameter e.g., [7,19,3,9,8,12,13,17]) or are much less efficient in practice [9,8]. Here we discuss in more details the efficiency of our scheme when instantiated with our RSA and Factoring based Algebraic TDP. Since each signature $\sigma = (x, s)$ consists of an element $x \in \mathbb{Z}_N^*$ and a value s in the field $\mathbb{K}$, i.e., its size is $|\sigma| = |N| + |S|$ where $|N|$ is the bit size of the RSA modulus and $|S|$ is the bit size of the cardinality S of $\mathbb{K}$. Ignoring the cost of hashing, both signing and verifying require one single multi-exponentiation (where all exponents have size $|S|$) and one additional exponentiation. Thus the actual efficiency of the scheme heavily depends on the size of $|S|$. For large values of $|S|$ our scheme is no better than previous schemes (such as the RSA schemes by Gennaro *et al.* [19] and by Catalano, Fiore and Warinschi [13]). For smaller $|S|$, however, our schemes allow for extremely efficient instantiations. If we consider for instance the binary field $\mathbb{F}_2$, then generating a signature costs only (again ignoring the cost of hashing)

---

[3] In fact, the exact size of the ring can be chosen ad-hoc (e.g., according to the desired application) at the moment of instantiating the scheme.

one square root extraction and a bunch of multiplications. Notice however that for the specific N (i.e. $N = pq$ where $p = 2p' + 1$, $q = 2q' + 1$ and p', q' are both primes) considered in our instantiations, extracting square root costs one single exponentiation (i.e., one just exponentiates to the power $z = 2^{-1} \bmod p'q'$). Verification is even cheaper as it requires (roughly) $m + n$ multiplications.

As mentioned above, the only known schemes supporting small fields are those by Boneh and Freeman [9,8]. Such schemes are also secure in the random oracle model, but rely on the hardness of SIS-related problems over lattices. There, a signature is a short vector σ in the lattice, whereas the basic signing operation is computing a short vector in the intersection of two integer lattices. This is done by using techniques from [22,10]. Even though the algebraic tools underlying our scheme are significantly different with respect to those used in [9,8] and it is not easy to make exact comparisons, it is reasonable to expect that taking a square root in $\mathbb{Z}_N^*$ is faster than state-of-the-art pre-image sampling for comparable security levels.

Acknowledgements. The second author did the present work while at NYU supported by NSF grant CNS-1017471. The research of the third author was sponsored by the U.S. Army Research Laboratory and the U.K. Ministry of Defence and was accomplished under Agreement Number W911NF-06-3-0001. The views and conclusions contained in this document are those of the author(s) and should not be interpreted as representing the official policies, either expressed or implied, of the U.S. Army Research Laboratory, the U.S. Government, the U.K. Ministry of Defence or the U.K. Government. The U.S. and U.K. Governments are authorized to reproduce and distribute reprints for Government purposes notwithstanding any copyright notation hereon.

References

1. Ahlswede, R., Ning-Cai, Li, S., Yeung, R.: Network information flow. IEEE Transactions on Information Theory 46(4), 1204–1216 (2000)
2. Applebaum, B., Ishai, Y., Kushilevitz, E.: From Secrecy to Soundness: Efficient Verification via Secure Computation. In: Abramsky, S., Gavoille, C., Kirchner, C., Meyer auf der Heide, F., Spirakis, P.G. (eds.) ICALP 2010, Part I. LNCS, vol. 6198, pp. 152–163. Springer, Heidelberg (2010)
3. Attrapadung, N., Libert, B.: Homomorphic Network Coding Signatures in the Standard Model. In: Catalano, D., Fazio, N., Gennaro, R., Nicolosi, A. (eds.) PKC 2011. LNCS, vol. 6571, pp. 17–34. Springer, Heidelberg (2011)
4. Babai, L.: Trading group theory for randomness. In: 17th ACM STOC, Providence, Rhode Island, USA, May 6-8, pp. 421–429. ACM Press (1985)
5. Belenkiy, M., Chase, M., Erway, C.C., Jannotti, J., Küpçü, A., Lysyanskaya, A.: Incentivizing outsourced computation. In: Workshop on Economics of Networked Systems – NetEcon, pp. 85–90 (2008)
6. Benabbas, S., Gennaro, R., Vahlis, Y.: Verifiable Delegation of Computation over Large Datasets. In: Rogaway, P. (ed.) CRYPTO 2011. LNCS, vol. 6841, pp. 111–131. Springer, Heidelberg (2011)

7. Boneh, D., Freeman, D., Katz, J., Waters, B.: Signing a Linear Subspace: Signature Schemes for Network Coding. In: Jarecki, S., Tsudik, G. (eds.) PKC 2009. LNCS, vol. 5443, pp. 68–87. Springer, Heidelberg (2009)
8. Boneh, D., Freeman, D.M.: Homomorphic Signatures for Polynomial Functions. In: Paterson, K.G. (ed.) EUROCRYPT 2011. LNCS, vol. 6632, pp. 149–168. Springer, Heidelberg (2011)
9. Boneh, D., Freeman, D.M.: Linearly Homomorphic Signatures over Binary Fields and New Tools for Lattice-Based Signatures. In: Catalano, D., Fazio, N., Gennaro, R., Nicolosi, A. (eds.) PKC 2011. LNCS, vol. 6571, pp. 1–16. Springer, Heidelberg (2011)
10. Cash, D., Hofheinz, D., Kiltz, E., Peikert, C.: Bonsai Trees, or How to Delegate a Lattice Basis. In: Gilbert, H. (ed.) EUROCRYPT 2010. LNCS, vol. 6110, pp. 523–552. Springer, Heidelberg (2010)
11. Catalano, D., Fiore, D., Gennaro, R., Vamvourellis, K.: Algebraic (trapdoor) one-way functions and their applications. Cryptology ePrint Archive, Report 2012/434 (2012); Full version
12. Catalano, D., Fiore, D., Warinschi, B.: Adaptive Pseudo-free Groups and Applications. In: Paterson, K.G. (ed.) EUROCRYPT 2011. LNCS, vol. 6632, pp. 207–223. Springer, Heidelberg (2011)
13. Catalano, D., Fiore, D., Warinschi, B.: Efficient Network Coding Signatures in the Standard Model. In: Fischlin, M., Buchmann, J., Manulis, M. (eds.) PKC 2012. LNCS, vol. 7293, pp. 680–696. Springer, Heidelberg (2012)
14. Chung, K.-M., Kalai, Y., Vadhan, S.: Improved Delegation of Computation Using Fully Homomorphic Encryption. In: Rabin, T. (ed.) CRYPTO 2010. LNCS, vol. 6223, pp. 483–501. Springer, Heidelberg (2010)
15. Cramer, R., Damgård, I.: Zero-Knowledge Proofs for Finite Field Arithmetic or: Can Zero-Knowledge Be for Free? In: Krawczyk, H. (ed.) CRYPTO 1998. LNCS, vol. 1462, pp. 424–441. Springer, Heidelberg (1998)
16. Fiore, D., Gennaro, R.: Publicly verifiable delegation of large polynomials and matrix computations, with applications. In: 2012 ACM Conference on Computer and Communication Security. ACM Press (October 2012), Full version available at http://eprint.iacr.org/2012/281
17. Freeman, D.M.: Improved Security for Linearly Homomorphic Signatures: A Generic Framework. In: Fischlin, M., Buchmann, J., Manulis, M. (eds.) PKC 2012. LNCS, vol. 7293, pp. 697–714. Springer, Heidelberg (2012)
18. Gennaro, R., Gentry, C., Parno, B.: Non-interactive Verifiable Computing: Outsourcing Computation to Untrusted Workers. In: Rabin, T. (ed.) CRYPTO 2010. LNCS, vol. 6223, pp. 465–482. Springer, Heidelberg (2010)
19. Gennaro, R., Katz, J., Krawczyk, H., Rabin, T.: Secure Network Coding over the Integers. In: Nguyen, P.Q., Pointcheval, D. (eds.) PKC 2010. LNCS, vol. 6056, pp. 142–160. Springer, Heidelberg (2010)
20. Gennaro, R., Leigh, D., Sundaram, R., Yerazunis, W.S.: Batching Schnorr Identification Scheme with Applications to Privacy-Preserving Authorization and Low-Bandwidth Communication Devices. In: Lee, P.J. (ed.) ASIACRYPT 2004. LNCS, vol. 3329, pp. 276–292. Springer, Heidelberg (2004)
21. Gentry, C.: Fully homomorphic encryption using ideal lattices. In: Mitzenmacher, M. (ed.) 41st ACM STOC, Bethesda, Maryland, USA, May 31-June 2, pp. 169–178. ACM Press (2009)
22. Gentry, C., Peikert, C., Vaikuntanathan, V.: Trapdoors for hard lattices and new cryptographic constructions. In: Ladner, R.E., Dwork, C. (eds.) 40th ACM STOC, Victoria, British Columbia, Canada, May 17-20, pp. 197–206. ACM Press (2008)

23. Goldwasser, S., Kalai, Y.T., Rothblum, G.N.: Delegating computation: interactive proofs for muggles. In: Ladner, R.E., Dwork, C. (eds.) 40th ACM STOC, Victoria, British Columbia, Canada, May 17-20, pp. 113–122. ACM Press (2008)

24. Goldwasser, S., Micali, S., Rackoff, C.: The knowledge complexity of interactive proof systems. SIAM Journal on Computing 18(1), 186–208 (1989)

25. Guillou, L.C., Quisquater, J.-J.: A Practical Zero-Knowledge Protocol Fitted to Security Microprocessor Minimizing Both Transmission and Memory. In: Günther, C.G. (ed.) EUROCRYPT 1988. LNCS, vol. 330, pp. 123–128. Springer, Heidelberg (1988)

26. Johnson, R., Molnar, D., Song, D., Wagner, D.: Homomorphic Signature Schemes. In: Preneel, B. (ed.) CT-RSA 2002. LNCS, vol. 2271, pp. 244–262. Springer, Heidelberg (2002)

27. Kilian, J.: A note on efficient zero-knowledge proofs and arguments. In: 24th ACM STOC, Victoria, British Columbia, Canada, May 4-6, pp. 723–732. ACM Press (1992)

28. Lewko, A., Waters, B.: New Proof Methods for Attribute-Based Encryption: Achieving Full Security through Selective Techniques. In: Safavi-Naini, R. (ed.) CRYPTO 2012. LNCS, vol. 7417, pp. 180–198. Springer, Heidelberg (2012)

29. Micali, S.: Cs proofs. In: 35th FOCS, Santa Fe, New Mexico, November 20-22, New (1994)

30. Mohassel, P.: Efficient and secure delegation of linear algebra. Cryptology ePrint Archive, Report 2011/605 (2011)

31. Monrose, F., Wyckoff, P., Rubin, A.D.: Distributed execution with remote audit. In: NDSS 1999, San Diego, California, USA, February 3-5. The Internet Society (1999)

32. Naor, M., Reingold, O.: Number-theoretic constructions of efficient pseudo-random functions. In: 38th FOCS, Miami Beach, Florida, October 19-22, pp. 458–467. IEEE Computer Society Press (1997)

33. Papamanthou, C., Shi, E., Tamassia, R.: Signatures of correct computation. Cryptology ePrint Archive, Report 2011/587 (2011)

34. Parno, B., Raykova, M., Vaikuntanathan, V.: How to Delegate and Verify in Public: Verifiable Computation from Attribute-Based Encryption. In: Cramer, R. (ed.) TCC 2012. LNCS, vol. 7194, pp. 422–439. Springer, Heidelberg (2012)

35. Robert-Li, S.-Y., Yeung, R.Y., Cai, N.: Linear network coding. IEEE Transactions on Information Theory 49(2), 371–381 (2003)

36. Shamir, A.: On the generation of cryptographically strong pseudorandom sequences. ACM Trans. Comput. Syst. 1(1), 38–44 (1983)

37. Smith, S.W., Weingart, S.: Building a high-performance, programmable secure coprocessor. Computer Networks 31, 831–860 (1999)

38. Yee, B.: Using Secure Coprocessors. PhD thesis, Carnegie Mellon University (1994)

Randomness-Dependent Message Security

Eleanor Birrell, Kai-Min Chung, Rafael Pass*, and Sidharth Telang

Cornell University
{eleanor,chung,rafael,sidtelang}@cs.cornell.edu

Abstract. Traditional definitions of the security of encryption schemes assume that the messages encrypted are chosen independently of the randomness used by the encryption scheme. Recent works, implicitly by Myers and Shelat (FOCS'09) and Bellare et al (AsiaCrypt'09), and explicitly by Hemmenway and Ostrovsky (ECCC'10), consider *randomness-dependent message (RDM) security* of encryption schemes, where the message to be encrypted may be selected as a function—referred to as the RDM function—of the randomness used to encrypt this particular message, or other messages, but in a circular way. We carry out a systematic study of this notion. Our main results demonstrate the following:

- *Full RDM security*—where the RDM function may be an arbitrary polynomial-size circuit—is not possible.
- Any secure encryption scheme can be slightly modified, by just performing some *pre-processing to the randomness*, to satisfy *bounded-RDM* security, where the RDM function is restricted to be a circuit of *a priori* bounded polynomial size. The scheme, however, requires the randomness r needed to encrypt a message m to be slightly longer than the length of m (i.e., $|r| > |m| + \omega(\log k)$, where k is the security parameter).
- We present a black-box provability barrier to compilations of *arbitrary* public-key encryption into RDM-secure ones using just pre-processing of the randomness, whenever $|m| > |r| + \omega(\log k)$. On the other hand, under the DDH assumption, we demonstrate the existence of bounded-RDM secure schemes that can encrypt arbitrarily "long" messages using "short" randomness.

We finally note that the existence of public-key encryption schemes imply the existence of a fully RDM-secure encryption scheme in an "ultra-weak" Random-Oracle Model—where the security reduction need not "program" the oracle, or see the queries made by the adversary to the oracle; combined with our impossibility result, this yields the first example of a cryptographic task that has a secure implementation in such a weak Random-Oracle Model, but does not have a secure implementation without random oracles.

* Pass is supported in part by a Alfred P. Sloan Fellowship, Microsoft New Faculty Fellowship, NSF Award CNS-1217821, NSF CAREER Award CCF-0746990, NSF Award CCF-1214844, AFOSR YIP Award FA9550-10-1-0093, and DARPA and AFRL under contract FA8750-11-2- 0211. The views and conclusions contained in this document are those of the authors and should not be interpreted as representing the official policies, either expressed or implied, of the Defense Advanced Research Projects Agency or the US Government.

A. Sahai (Ed.): TCC 2013, LNCS 7785, pp. 700–720, 2013.

1   Introduction

Traditional definitions of secure encryption, including semantic (or CPA) security and CCA security, address the problem of how to securely communicate a message in the presence of a polynomially-bounded adversary that observes encrypted messages. In the standard approach, it is assumed that the message, the keys, and the randomness used to encrypt the message, are all chosen independently.

More recently, new definitions have emerged that relax some of these independence assumptions. Most notably, a line of work initiated independently by Camenisch and Lysyanskaya [21] and by Black, Rogaway, and Shrimpton [14] addresses the problem of "key-dependent" messages (KDM): namely, they consider the security of a public-key encryption scheme in a setting where the message to be encrypted may (adversarially) depend on the secret-key. A variant of this notion instead considers "circular" security: here, the adversary may observe a "cycle" of q messages $\overrightarrow{m}$ encrypted using different keys $(\overrightarrow{pk}, \overrightarrow{sk})$, but where m_i may depend on the depends on the secret-key $sk_{(i+1 \mod q)}$. One motivation for studying key-dependence arises in the context of hard-drive encryption: you want to encrypt your hard-drive, on which your secret-key is also found. Circular security arises naturally in a situation when two parties want to share their secret keys with each other (but not with the rest of the world): a natural solution to the problem would be for player 1 to send an encrypted version of his secret key using player 2's public key, and vice versa. For this protocol to be secure, circular security is needed. More recently, circular security has found important applications in the context of fully-homomorphic encryptions (indeed, to date, all known FHE schemes rely on the assumption that some underlying encryption scheme is circularly secure).

We here focus on an alternative relaxation of the classic independence assumptions, first implicitly considered by Myers and Shelat [36] and Bellare et al [10], and explicitly by Hemmenway and Ostrovsky [31]: We study of the security of encryption schemes in a scenario where the message to be encrypted may be selected as a function—referred to as the *RDM function*—of the randomness used to encrypt this particular message, or other messages, but in a circular way. More precisely, in analogy with KDM security and circular security, we consider two notions of randomness dependent message security.

- *Randomness-dependent message (RDM) security*: roughly speaking, a public-key encryption scheme is said to be RDM-secure if indistinguishability of ciphertexts holds even if the encrypted messages are chosen as a function of the randomness used to encrypt *this particular* message.
- *Circular randomness-dependent (circular-RDM) security*: roughly speaking, a public-key encryption scheme is said to be circular RDM-secure if indistinguishability of ciphertexts holds even if the encrypted messages are chosen as a function of the randomness used to encrypt *other* messages, but in a circular way. More precisely, we consider a scenario where q messages $\overrightarrow{m}$ are encrypted using randomness $\overrightarrow{r}$, where m_1 is chosen as a function of r_q and

each other message m_i is chosen as a function of r_{i-1} and the "previous" ciphertext $c_{i-1} = \mathrm{Enc}_{pk}(m_{i-1}, r_{i-1})$.

Why Care about Randomness-Dependent Message Security. We consider two reasons to study RDM security:

1. *involuntary RDM attacks:* Implementations of secure protocols are prone to programming mistakes; attacks exploiting such programming mistakes (e.g., buffer overflow attacks) have been demonstrated on secure protocols. Attacks of this type may allow an attacker to see encryptions of randomness dependent messages, even if the original protocol chooses messages independently of the randomness used to encrypt it. RDM security would block such "involuntary" RDM attacks.

    To prevent against these we need to be able to handle sufficiently general classes of RDM functions that may be produced by the attackers.

2. *voluntary RDM attacks* As shown in the beautiful work by Myers and She-lat [36], the possibility of encrypting the randomness used in other encryptions, in a circular way, leads to new powerful techniques in the design of encryption schemes. This techniques was further refined in a recent work by Hohenberger, Lewko and Waters [33]. Another application is found in the work of Hemmenway and Ostrovsky [31], that explicitly considers a notion of circular randomness dependent "one-wayness" and show its usefulness for constructing injective trapdoor functions. In this context, the protocol designer is "voluntarily" creating a (circular-)RDM attack. The above-mentioned works either implicitly (as in [36] and [33]), or explicitly (as in [31]) consider and design encryption schemes that are circular-RDM secure for the specific randomness-dependent messages selected by their protocols. Although for this particular application it suffices to consider specific RDM functions, having general-purpose RDM-secure encryption schemes simplifies the design and the security analysis of protocols.

    Another motivation stems from non-black-box simulation techniques pioneered in the work by Barak [5]; in a variant of Barak's simulation technique due to [41], the simulator commits to its own code (that, in particular, contains the randomness used for the commitment, and thus circularity arises). In this particular application, the circularity could be broken, but having general techniques for dealing with RDM security may simplify future applications.

Before explaining our result, let us also point out that RDM secure encryption is very related to *hedged encryption schemes* introduced by Bellare et al [10]— encryption schemes that remain secure as long as the joint message-randomness distribution comes from a high-entropy source, that is independent of the public-key of the encryption scheme (which in turn are very related to *deterministic encryption* [8,11,15]; see [10] for more details). Hedged encryption schemes are RDM-secure if restricting the attacker to using RDM functions that do not depend on the public-key.[1] Our focus here is on notions of RDM security where the RDM function may depend also on the public-key.

1.1   Our Results

Full RDM Security. Our first result shows that if the RDM function may be an arbitrary polynomial-size circuit (chosen by the adversary), then RDM security, as defined by Hemmenway and Ostrovsky [31], is impossible to achieve.

Theorem 1 (Informal Statement). *There does not exist an encryption scheme that is (fully) RDM-secure.*

We next show that if there exists some polynomial q such that an encryption scheme is q-circular RDM secure, then the encryption scheme is also RDM secure; thus q-circular RDM security is impossible for all polynomials q.

Theorem 2 (Informal Statement). *There does not exist an encryption scheme that is (fully) q-circular RDM-secure for any polynomial q.*

Bounded RDM Security. Since "unbounded" RDM security is impossible, we consider RDM security with respect to restricted classes of RDM functions.

Our first positive result demonstrates that if the RDM function is restricted to be a circuit of *a priori* polynomially bounded size, then any secure encryption scheme can be modified to satisfy both RDM and circular-RDM security.

Theorem 3 (Informal Statement). *Assume the existence of a secure public key encryption scheme. Then, for every polynomial s, there exists an encryption scheme Π that is RDM secure when restricting the RDM function to be computed by a circuit of size at most $s(k)$ where k is the security parameter. Additionally Π is q-circular RDM secure for every polynomial q under the same restrictions on the RDM function.*

Theorem 3 is proven by modifying any secure encryption scheme to first "hash" the randomness using a t-wise independent hash-function. The same transformation was previously used by Hemmenway and Ostrovsky [31] to transform "lossy encryption schemes" [42], that can encrypt messages longer than the randomness, into schemes that satisfy a notion of circular-RDM "one-wayness"[2] (as opposed to semantic security) with respect to a particular circular-RDM function (the identity function).

---

[1] However, it is not clear in general whether hedged encryption schemes are *circular* RDM secure, even if we restrict to RDM functions that do not depend on the public-key.

[2] The notion of q-circular RDM one-wayness of Hemmenway and Ostrovsky requires that no polynomial-time attacker can recover $r_1, r_2, \ldots r_q$ given $\mathrm{Enc}_{pk}(r_q; r_1), \mathrm{Enc}_{pk}(r_1; r_2), \ldots, \mathrm{Enc}_{pk}(r_{q-1}; r_q)$ except with negligible probability, over the choice of pk and uniform $r_1, \ldots r_q$.

In order to encrypt a message m, our encryption scheme requires using $|m| + \omega(\log k)$ bits; that is, the randomness used to encrypt a message needs to be sufficiently longer than the message being encrypted (as such, the encryption scheme of Theorem 3 does not handle "the identity function" as an RDM function.) Our next positive result strictly strengthens the conclusion of Theorem 3 (but under a stronger assumption) and the results of [31]: the existence of *lossy trapdoor functions* [43] implies the existence of both bounded RDM-secure and bounded circular-RDM secure encryption schemes that can encrypt also "long" messages using "short" randomness—the ratio between the message-length and the randomness length is proportional to the lossiness of the trapdoor function. Our construction mirrors a construction of hedged encryption of Bellare et al [10]; roughly, the encryption is done by first "hashing" the message-randomness pair and then applying a lossy trapdoor function to the hashed value. The key difference is that we replace the use of univeral hashing (in the construction of [10]) with t-wise independent hashing.[3]

Theorem 4 (Informal Statement). *Assume the existence of "sufficiently" lossy trapdoor functions (the existence of which are implied e.g., by the DDH assumption). Then, for every polynomials s, l, there exists a $l(k)$-bit encryption scheme Π using only k-bits of randomness that is RDM secure (and q-circular RDM secure for every polynomial q), when restricting the RDM function to be computed by a circuit of size at most $s(k)$ where k is the security parameter.*

To prove the above two theorems we develop several new information-theoretic tools regarding t-wise independent hash functions, that may be of independent interests. For instance, with very high probability, a t-wise independent hash functions is a "good" randomness extractor for any min-entropy source with *with computationally-bounded leakage* (mirroring a lemma of Trevisan-Vadhan [44]). We also present "crooked" versions of such deterministic extraction lemmas (mirroring the "crooked left-over-hash lemma of [25]).

An interesting question is whether any encryption schemes can be modified by simply performing some pre-processing to the randomness (as in Theorem 3) to become bounded RDM secure, but still handle long messages using short randomness. At first sight, it may seem like we could use a pseudorandom generator to "stretch" a small seed into the required long random string for the construction in Theorem 3. We have no attack against this construction. However, we show that security reductions that only use the attacker and the RDM function as a black-box—following [28], we refer to such reductions as *strongly black-box*—cannot be used to demonstrate RDM security of encryption schemes with *perfect correctness* and *efficiently recognizable public-keys* that can encrypt long messages using short randomness, based on a falsifiable intractability assumption [37]; for instance, this means that the El-Gamal crypto system cannot be

---

[3] The construction of [10] actually requires universal hash *permutations*. As far as we know, constructions of t-wise independent permutations are not known, which requires us to further modify the scheme to guarantee correctness.

modified (by performing pre-processing to the randomness) to become bounded RDM secure for long messages.

Theorem 5 (Informal statement). *Assume the existence of one-way functions secure against subexponential-sized circuits. For every polynomials m and r such that $m(k) \geq r(k) + \omega(\log k)$, there exists a polynomial s such that for every $m(\cdot)$-bit encryption scheme Π with perfect correctness and efficiently recognizable public-keys that uses $r(\cdot)$ bits of randomness to encrypt a message, s-bounded security of Π cannot be based on any falsifiable assumption using a strongly black-box reduction, unless the assumption is false.*

Let us point out that the reason Theorem 5 does not contradict Theorem 4 is that in the construction used to prove Theorem 4, valid ("injective") public-keys are indistinguisbale from invalid ("lossy") public-keys, and thus the schemes does not have efficiently recognizable public-keys.

RDM Security beyond Encryption. We note that the notion of RDM security applies not only to encryption but makes sense also in the context of more general cryptographic protocols. For instance, the notion of RDM security directly extends to commitments—just as in the case of encryption, we here let the RDM function select the messages to be committed to as a function of the committer's randomness. We remark that Theorem 1 readily extends also to rule out (even computationally binding and computationally-hiding) RDM-secure commitments. Additionally, Theorem 3 extends to show that any commitment scheme in the CRS model can be turned into a bounded RDM secure commitment scheme in the CRS model. However, Theorem 5 does not extend to the setting to commitments—using a collision-resistant hash function, any RDM secure commitment for short messages can be turned into a RDM-secure commitment for long messages. The above results for commitment schemes can be found in the full version of this work.

We leave an exploration of RDM security for other tasks (e.g., zero-knowledge and witness indistinguishability—where the RDM function may select the statement and witness to the proved as a function of the prover's randomness, or secure computation—where the RDM function may select a player's input as a function of his randomness) for future work.

On the Soundness of the Random-Oracle Methodology. Starting with the work of Canetti, Goldreich and Halevi [22,23], there are several "uninstantiability results" for the random oracle model [7], showing schemes that are secure in the random oracle model, but where every instantiation of random oracle with a concrete (efficient) function leads to an insecure protocol (see e.g., [5,27,34]). Another vein of work shows *tasks* (as opposed to schemes) that can be securely implemented in the random oracle model, but for which there are no secure implementations in the standard model (see e.g., [39,40,9]). As far as we know, all these separations for tasks, however, make a relatively strong use of the random oracle model; [39,9] rely on the security reduction "programming the random oracle", and [40] relies on the security reduction "seeing all the queries to the random oracle". Thus, it is conceivable that a weaker usage of random oracles may circumvent these uninstantiability results. For instance, Unruh [45] introduced a weaker random oracle model where the adversary may get an (inefficient) non-uniform advice about the random oracle, and suggested that proofs of security in this weaker random oracle model may still be "sound". We here address this question using RDM-secure encryption as a task.

We show that in the random-oracle model the existence of public-key encryption schemes imply the existence of "fully" RDM secure encryption schemes (i.e., without restricting the RDM function); our scheme is essentially identical to the hedged encryption scheme of [10] (but the analysis is quite different given the different security goals).[4] Our use of the random oracle model is extremely weak: we do not need to "program it", or "see queries to it", and security holds even the attacker may get any inefficient non-uniform advice about it (as in the model of [45]). (The only property we need of the random oracle is that it acts as a $k^{\log k}$-wise indepedent hash function.) We refer to such a model as the "ultra-weak" Random Oracle Model.

Theorem 6 (Informal Statement). *Assume the existence of a secure public key encryption scheme. Then, there exists a encryption scheme Π that is "fully" RDM secure in the "ultra-weak" Random Oracle Model.*

Theorem 6, combined with our impossibility result (Theorem 1), thus yields an example of an arguably natural task (i.e., RDM-secure encryption) that can be securely implemented in the ultra-weak random-oracle model, but not in the standard model. Let us point out that a cruicial aspect of the security proof of our RO-based scheme is that the RDM function is not allowed to query the random oracle; in case we allow it to query the random oracle, our impossibility result still holds.

1.2 Related Work

As mentioned in the introduction, (circular) RDM security was first implicitly considered by Myers and Shelat [36] and explicitly by Hemmenway and Ostrovsky [31]. [36] [33] demonstrate semantic security of encryption schemes of a specific type of circular RDM attack, but do not formally introduce a notion of RDM security. Hemmenway and Ostrovsky [31] provide the first formal definition of RDM-secure encryption schemes, but only investigate, and provide constructions of, schemes satisfying the weaker notion of "circular-RDM one-wayness". As far as we know, we are the first to explicitly study the feasibility of satisfying (circular-)RDM *semantic* security (as opposed to one-wayness). As mentioned above, Bellare et al [10] study *hedged encryption schemes* that are closely related to RDM-secure encryption schemes; such encryption schemes are RDM secure if restricting the attacker to using RDM functions that do not depend on the

---

[4] Hedged encryption exists also in the plain model so we cannot hope to get a separation by directly appealing to the results of [10].

public-key. Nevertheless, as mentioned, the constructions of both Bellare et al and Hemmenway and Ostrovsky are very useful to us.

As mentioned in the introduction, the related notion of key-dependent message (KDM) security was first introduced by Black, Rogaway, and Shrimpton in 2002 [14], who demonstrated the possibility of achieving their definition in the random-oracle model. The related notion of circular security (in which there exists a cycle of ciphertexts where each message depends on the previous secret key) was independently and concurrently introduced by Camenisch and Lysyan-skaya [21], who also showed constructions in the random-oracle model. Follow-up work considered message-dependent PRFs [30] and symmetric encryption [32,4] in the standard model. In [29] barriers to constructing KDM secure schemes for general classes of key-dependencies. In 2008, Boneh, Halevi, Hamburg, and Ostrovsky presented the first KDM-secure public-key encryption scheme [16]; their construction was based on the DDH assumption. Subsequent work developed schemes that were KDM secure and CCA2 secure [20], KDM secure and resilient to leakage on the secret key [6], circular secure under alternative assumptions [17], and circular secure against larger classes of functions [18]. Recent work has also shown that there exist schemes that are secure under standard definitions but which are not 2-circular secure [1,24].

A separate, but related line of related work focuses on leakage-resilient encryption (see e.g., [35,26,2,3,38,19]). In a sense, RDM security can be viewed as a CPA security game where the attacker gets to see some leakage on the encryptor's randomness before selecting the messages; indeed, in our positive results, this view will be instrumental.

Overview of the Paper. Some preliminaries are found in Section 2. We provide formal definitions of RDM and circular RDM security in Section 3. Our impossibility results regarding RDM and circular RDM security are found in Section 4. Finally, in Section 5 we present our positive results. The black-box unprovability results are postponed to the full version. All full proofs are found in the full version.

2   Preliminaries

For a distribution S, $s \leftarrow S$ means that s is chosen according to distribution S. For a set S, $s \leftarrow S$ means that s is chosen uniformly from the set S. U_n denotes the uniform distribution over n-bit strings. For a probabilistic algorithm A, $A(x; r)$ denotes the output of A running on input x with randomness r; $A(x)$ denotes the output of A on input x with uniformly chosen randomness. All logarithms are base 2 unless otherwise specified. We say that a function $\varepsilon : \mathbb{N} \to [0, 1]$ is negligible if for every constant $c \in \mathbb{N}$, $\varepsilon(n) < k^{-c}$ for sufficiently large k.

The *statistical difference* between two probability distributions X, Y is defined by $\Delta(X, Y) = (1/2) \cdot \sum_x |\Pr[x \leftarrow X] - \Pr[x \leftarrow Y]|$. X and Y are ε-close if $\Delta(X, Y) \leq \varepsilon$. The *statistical difference* between two ensembles $\{X_k\}_k$ and

$\{Y_k\}_k$ is a function δ defined by $\delta(k) = \Delta(X_k, Y_k)$. Two probability ensembles are said to be *statistically close* if their statistical difference is negligible. We also say X_k and Y_k are statistically close if $\Delta(X_k, Y_k) \leq \epsilon(k)$ for some negligible function ϵ. Two ensembles $\{X_k\}, \{Y_k\}$ are *computationally indistinguishable* if for every PPT distinguisher D, there exists a negligible function μ such that for every $k \in \mathbb{N}$,

$$| \Pr[D(1^k, X_k) = 1] - \Pr[D(1^k, Y_k) = 1]| \leq \mu(k).$$

The *min-entropy* of a random variable X, denoted $H_\infty(X)$ is defined by $H_\infty(X) = -\log(max_x \Pr[x \leftarrow X])$. A random variable X is a *k-source* if $H_\infty(X) \geq k$.

A family of hash functions $\mathcal{H} = \{h : S_1 \rightarrow S_2\}$ is *t-wise independent* if the following two conditions hold:

1. $\forall x \in S_1$, the random variable $h(x)$ is uniformly distributed over S_2, where $h \leftarrow \mathcal{H}$.
2. $\forall x_1 \neq \cdots \neq x_t \in S_1$, the random variables $h(x_1), \ldots, h(x_t)$ are independent, where $h \leftarrow \mathcal{H}$.

A function $\mathrm{Ext}\{0,1\}^n \times \{0,1\}^d \rightarrow \{0,1\}^m$ is a *strong (k, ε)-extractor* if for every k-source X over $\{0,1\}^n$, $(U_d, \mathrm{Ext}(X, U_d))$ is ε-close to (U_d, U_m).

Definition 1 (Public-Key Encryption). *An l-bit public-key encryption scheme consists of a triple $\Pi = (\mathrm{Gen}, \mathrm{Enc}, \mathrm{Dec})$ of PPT algorithms where (i) Gen takes a security parameter 1^k as input and generates a pair of public and secret key $(pk, sk) \leftarrow \mathrm{Gen}(1^k)$, (ii) Enc takes a public key pk and a message m in a message space $\{0,1\}^{l(k)}$ as input and generates a ciphertext $c \leftarrow \mathrm{Enc}_{pk}(m)$, (iii) Dec is a deterministic algorithm that takes a secret key sk and a ciphertext c as input and outputs $m' = \mathrm{Dec}_{sk}(c)$, and (iv) there exists a negligible function μ such that for every $k \in \mathbb{N}$, for random $(pk, sk) \leftarrow \mathrm{Gen}(1^k)$,*

$$\Pr\left[\exists m \in \{0,1\}^{l(k)} s.t. \mathrm{Dec}_{sk}(\mathrm{Enc}_{pk}(m)) \neq m\right] \leq \mu(k),$$

where the probability is taken over the randomness of Gen and the randomness of the encryption. We say that Π has perfect correctness if the above condition holds for $\mu(k) = 0$.

Definition 2 (CPA and CCA Security). *An l-bit public-key encryption scheme $\Pi = (\mathrm{Gen}, \mathrm{Enc}, \mathrm{Dec})$ is CPA-secure if for every probabilistic polynomial time adversary $A = (A_1, A_2)$, the ensembles $\{IND_0^\Pi(A, k)\}_k$ and $\{IND_1^\Pi(A, k)\}_k$ are computationally indistinguishable, where*

$$\begin{aligned}
IND_b^\Pi(A, k) := \ & (pk, sk) \leftarrow \mathrm{Gen}(1^k) \\
& (m_0, m_1, \mathsf{state}) \leftarrow A_1(1^k, pk) \\
& c \leftarrow \mathrm{Enc}_{pk}(m_b) \\
& o \leftarrow A_2(c, \mathsf{state}) \\
& Output \ o
\end{aligned}$$

We say Π is CCA-secure *if the above holds when A_2 has access to a decryption oracle but is not allowed to query the decryption oracle with the challenge ciphertext c.*

Remark 1. In the above definition and for essentially all the results in this paper, we consider a *uniform* polynomial-time attacker A. In case security holds against also *non-uniform* polynomial-time attackers, we refer to the scheme as being non-uniformly CPA/CCA secure. As is often the case, all our constructions in uniform setting directly extend also to the case of non-uniform security (if assuming that the underlying schemes are non-uniformly secure).

Note that the above definition assumes that messages encrypted are chosen independently of the randomness used by the encryption algorithm.

3   Definition of RDM Security

In this section, we formally define two notions of randomness-dependent message security for encryption schemes.

Our first definition is essentially equivalent to the definition of RDM security due to Hemmenway and Ostrovsky [31]. In this definition, messages are adversarially chosen functions (after seeing the public key) of the randomness used for encryption: we say the encryption scheme is secure if the adversary cannot distinguish between encryptions of different functions of the randomness.

Definition 3. *[RDM-Security] An l-bit public-key encryption scheme $\Pi =$ (Gen, Enc, Dec) is* randomness-dependent message secure (RDM-secure) *if for every* PPT *adversary $A = (A_1, A_2)$, the ensembles $\{RDM_0^\Pi(A, k)\}_{k \in \mathbb{N}}$ and $\{RDM_1^\Pi(A, k)\}_{k \in \mathbb{N}}$ are computationally indistinguishable where*

$$RDM_b^\Pi(A, k) := (pk, sk) \leftarrow \text{Gen}(1^k)$$
$$(f_0, f_1, \text{state}) \leftarrow A_1(1^k, pk)$$
$$r \leftarrow U_R$$
$$c \leftarrow \text{Enc}_{pk}(f_b(r); r)$$
$$o \leftarrow A_2(c, \text{state})$$
$$Output\ o$$

and R is the encryption randomness length of Π. The RDM functions f_b are represented as circuits from $\{0, 1\}^{|r|}$ to $\{0, 1\}^{l(k)}$ We say Π is RDM-CCA-secure if the above holds when A_2 has access to a decryption oracle but is not allowed to query the decryption oracle with the challenge ciphertext c.

We remark that by a standard hybrid argument, we can assume without loss of generality that the adversary A_1 always choose f_1 to be a constant function $f_1 = 0$. As mentioned, Definition 3 is essentially identical to the notion of RDM security defined by Hemmenway and Ostrovsky [31]: the definition of [31] is a multi-message version of Definition 3 where the attacker gets to see a sequence of encrypted messages (that may depend in a correlated way on the randomness used to encrypt them), and thus the definition of [31] implies Definition 3. (Looking forward, since we are proving an impossibility result regarding Definition 3, considering a weaker definition makes our results stronger.)

Consider a sequence of encryptions where messages are functions of the previous (but most recent) encryption randomness and ciphertext. Security in this setting is guaranteed by CPA security, since encryption randomness is still independent of the messages. However if this dependency is circular, it is unclear whether or not we have security. We now formally introduce this notion of circular randomness dependent message security.

Definition 4 (q-circular RDM Security). *Let $q : \mathbb{N} \to \mathbb{N}$ be efficiently computable. An l-bit public-key encryption scheme $\Pi = (\text{Gen}, \text{Enc}, \text{Dec})$ is q-circular RDM secure if for every PPT adversary $A = (A_1, A_2)$, the following two ensembles $\{CIR_0^{\Pi}(A, k)\}_{k \in \mathbb{N}}$ and $\{CIR_1^{\Pi}(A, k)\}_{k \in \mathbb{N}}$ are computationally indistinguishable, where*

$$
\begin{aligned}
CIR_b^{\Pi}(A, k) := \ &(pk, sk) \leftarrow \text{Gen}(1^k) \\
&(f_0^1, f_0^2, \ldots, f_0^{q(k)}, f_1^1, f_1^2, \ldots, f_1^{q(k)}, \text{state}) \leftarrow A_1(1^k, pk) \\
&r^1, r^2, \ldots, r^{q(k)} \leftarrow U_R^{q(k)} \\
&c^1 \leftarrow \text{Enc}_{pk}(f_b^1(r^q); r^1) \\
&for\ i = 2, \ldots, q \\
&\quad c^i \leftarrow \text{Enc}_{pk}(f_b^i(r^{i-1}, c^{i-1}); r^i) \\
&o \leftarrow A_2(\bar{c}, \text{state}) \\
&Output\ o
\end{aligned}
$$

and R is the encryption randomness length of Π. The RDM functions f_b^i are represented as circuits as defined in Definition 3. $\bar{c}$ denotes the vector $(c^1, c^2, \ldots c^n)$. Furthermore, Π is circular RDM secure if Π is k^c-circular RDM secure for every constant c. q-circular-CCA and circular-CCA RDM security are defined in analogous way.

Remark 2. Note that by a hybrid argument, we can assume without loss of generality that A always choose $f_1^i = 0$ for every $i \in [q]$. We will use this observation later in the proof of Theorem 11.

We also define relaxations of RDM security and circular RDM security where we restrict the RDM function to be computable by circuits of *a priori* bounded size.

Definition 5. *Let $s : \mathbb{N} \to \mathbb{N}$ be efficiently computable. An l-bit public key encryption scheme Π is s-bounded RDM secure (resp., s-bounded (q-)circular RDM secure) if Π is RDM secure (resp., (q-)circular RDM secure) under the additional restriction that in the corresponding security game, the adversary A_1 can only output RDM functions computable by circuits of size bounded by $s(k)$. CCA security is defined analogously.*

4   Impossibility Results

In this section we prove that both RDM-security and q-circular security are impossible to achieve. Throughout this section, we focus on bit-encryption schemes; this only makes our results stronger. We first establish the impossibility result on the RDM-secure encryption schemes; our techniques (of using pairwise independent hashfunctions to signal a message) are similar to those used by Bellare and Keelveedhi [12] in a different context.

Theorem 7. *For every 1-bit encryption scheme* $\Pi = (\text{Gen}, \text{Enc}, \text{Dec})$, Π *is not RDM-secure.*

Proof. Let $\Pi = (\text{Gen}, \text{Enc}, \text{Dec})$ be a 1-bit encryption scheme. We construct a PPT adversary $A = (A_1, A_2)$ that breaks the RDM security of Π. The idea is to use f_b to signal the bit b in the RDM_b^{Π} experiment by pairwise independent hash functions.

Fix a security parameter $k \in \mathbb{N}$. Let C denotes the ciphertext space of Π for the corresponding security parameter k, and let $\mathcal{H} = \{h : C \to \{0,1\}\}$ be a pairwise independent hash function family that hashes ciphertexts to a bit. Our adversary A uses $h \leftarrow \mathcal{H}$ to construct functions $f_{b,h}$ for $b \in \{0,1\}$ that signals the bit b as follows.

- $A_1(1^k, pk)$: A_1 samples $h \leftarrow \mathcal{H}$ and outputs $(f_{0,h}, f_{1,h}, h)$, where for $b \in \{0,1\}$, $f_{b,h}$ on input r, outputs a message $m \in \{0,1\}$ such that $h(\text{Enc}_{pk}(m,r)) = b$ if such an m exists; otherwise $f_{b,h}$ outputs $m = 0$.
- $A_2(c, h)$: A_2 simply outputs one bit $h(c)$.

To show that A breaks the RDM security of Π, it suffices to show the following claim, which clearly implies $\text{RDM}_0^{\Pi}(A, k)$ and $\text{RDM}_1^{\Pi}(A, k)$ are distinguishable.

Claim. $\Pr[\text{RDM}_b^{\Pi}(A, k) = b] \geq 3/4 - \text{negl}(k)$ for $b \in \{0,1\}$.

Proof. Note that the output of $\text{RDM}_b^{\Pi}(A, k)$ is simply $h(\text{Enc}_{pk}(f_b(r), r))$ where $(pk, sk) \leftarrow \text{Gen}(1^k)$, $r \leftarrow U_{|r|}$, and $h \leftarrow \mathcal{H}$. The correctness of Π implies that,

$$\Pr_{pk,r}[\text{Enc}_{pk}(0,r) \neq \text{Enc}_{pk}(1,r)] \geq 1 - \text{negl}(k). \tag{1}$$

When this is the case, by the pairwise independence,

$$\Pr_h[\exists \ m \text{ s.t. } h(\text{Enc}_{pk}(m,r)) = b] = 3/4.$$

It follows by an union bound that

$$\Pr[\text{RDM}_b^{\Pi}(A, k) = b]$$
$$\geq \Pr_{pk,r,h}[(\text{Enc}_{pk}(0,r) \neq \text{Enc}_{pk}(1,r)) \wedge (\exists \ m \text{ s.t. } h(\text{Enc}_{pk}(m,r)) = b)]$$
$$\geq 3/4 - \text{negl}(k).$$

$\square$

We proceed to establish the impossibility result on the circular RDM-secure encryption schemes.

Theorem 8. *For every 1-bit encryption scheme $\Pi = (\text{Gen}, \text{Enc}, \text{Dec})$, Π is not q-circular RDM-secure for every efficiently computable and polynomially bounded q.*

We prove Theorem 8 by showing that in fact, circular RDM security implies RDM security. Theorem 8 follows by combining Theorem 7 and 9.

Theorem 9. *Let $\Pi = (\text{Gen}, \text{Enc}, \text{Dec})$ be a 1-bit encryption scheme, and $q : \mathbb{N} \to \mathbb{N}$ be efficiently computable and polynomially bounded. If Π is q-circular RDM-secure, then Π is RDM-secure.*

Proof. (Sketch) The formal proof can be found in the full version; we here just provide a proof sketch. Let us first sketch the proof for the special case that Π has perfect correctness and that $q = 2$, to illustrate the idea behind the proof. Suppose there exists a PPT adversary A that breaks the RDM security of Π, we want to construct a PPT adversary B that breaks the 2-circular security of Π.

The idea is to let B simulate the attack of A in the circular RDM security game using the second message (in general, using the last message). More precisely, recall that in the RDM security game RDM_b^{Π}, A generates RDM functions f_0 and f_1, and receives $c = \text{Enc}_{pk}(f_b(r); r)$. To simulate the attack of A in CIR_b^{π}, B generates $f_0^1, f_0^2, f_1^1, f_1^2$ in a way so that B will receive $\bar{c} = (c^1, c^2)$ with $c^2 = \text{Enc}_{pk}(f_b(r^2); r^2)$. Then B can output whatever A_2 outputs on input c^2, and break the circular RDM security with the same advantage as A.

Now, the key observation is that the RDM function $f_b^2(r^1, c^1)$ can in fact decrypt c^1 to get the message $f_b^1(r^2)$ by checking whether c^1 equals to $\text{Enc}_{pk}(0, r^1)$ or $\text{Enc}_{pk}(1, r^1)$ (the perfect correctness implies $\text{Enc}_{pk}(0, r^1) \neq \text{Enc}_{pk}(1, r^1)$ and the decryption will be always correct). Thus, B can let $f_b^1 = f_b$ and let $f_b^2(r^1, c^1) = f_b^1(r^2)$, and by doing so B will receive $c^2 = \text{Enc}_{pk}(f_b^2(r^1, c^1), r^2) = \text{Enc}_{pk}(f_b(r^2), r^2)$, as desired. This completes the proof of the special case.

We can readily extend the proof to the general q-circular RDM security, by letting B set $f_b^1 = f_b$ and $f_b^{i+1}(r^i, c^i) = f_b^i(r^{i-1}, c^{i-1})$ for $i = 1, \ldots, q-1$. On the other hand, imperfect correctness only causes negligible probability of decryption errors, and thus only reduces the advantage of B by a negligible amount. $\quad\square$

5 Positive Results

5.1 Bounded RDM Security

In the previous sections we have seen that RDM security and circular RDM security are impossible to achieve. In this section we see how we can achieve the weaker notions of bounded RDM security and bounded circular RDM security. In fact we achieve a stronger notion of RDM security which implies both of the above.

This strong RDM security is in fact security in the presence of randomness leakage (such that the leakage function size is *a priori* bounded by a polynomial) which is available to the adversary when it chooses the messages to encrypt.

Definition 6. *For every* $s, p : \mathbb{N} \to \mathbb{N}$ *an* l-*bit public-key encryption scheme* $\Pi = (\text{Gen}, \text{Enc}, \text{Dec})$ *is* s-*bounded* p-*strong RDM secure (BSRDM-secure) if for every PPT adversary* $A = (A_1, A_2)$, *the ensembles* $\{BSRDM_0^{\Pi}(A, k)\}_{k \in \mathbb{N}}$ *and* $\{BSRDM_1^{\Pi}(A, k)\}_{k \in \mathbb{N}}$ *are computationally indistinguishable where*

$$
\begin{aligned}
BSRDM_b^{\Pi}(A, k) := \ &(pk, sk) \leftarrow \text{Gen}(1^k) \\
&r \leftarrow U_R \\
&(f, \text{state}_1) \leftarrow A_1(1^k, pk) \\
&(m_0, m_1, \text{state}_2) \leftarrow A_2(f(r), \text{state}_1) \\
&c \leftarrow \text{Enc}_{pk}(m_b; r) \\
&o \leftarrow A_3(c, \text{state}_2) \\
&Output\ o,
\end{aligned}
$$

R *is the encryption randomness length of* Π *and* $f : \{0,1\}^{|r|} \to \{0,1\}^{p(k)}$ *is a function computed by a circuit of size at most* $s(k)$. *CCA security is defined analogously.*

We show that any secure encryption scheme can be compiled to a bounded strong RDM-secure encryption scheme (with "long" encryption randomness).

Theorem 10. *Assume the existence of a CPA (resp., CCA) secure public key encryption scheme. Then, there exists a* l-*bit* s-*bounded* p-*strong RDM-secure (resp., RDM-CCA-secure) encryption scheme for every polynomial* l, s *and* p.

We start by providing a construction that converts any secure encryption scheme to bounded strong RDM secure encryption scheme. The main idea is that though leakage degrades the randomness, the randomness is long enough to have enough residual min-entropy so that the random bits necessary for encryption can be extracted from it. The problem with this is that the extractor seed will have to be part of the public key, and the adversary can choose a leakage function after seeing the public key. Hence the leakage could be such that the seed always fails to extract randomness from the source. This is where we exploit the fact that the set of possible leakage functions is bounded: using a union bound, we show that if the randomness used by the encryption scheme is long enough, then with overwhelming probability a random seed can extract randomness from the source resulting from any leakage function. The following lemma captures the above idea.

Lemma 1. *[Deterministic Extraction From Bounded Leakage Sources] Let* $\mathcal{F} = \{f : \{0,1\}^n \to \{0,1\}^\ell\}$ *be a class of (leakage) functions. Let* $\mathcal{H} = \{h : \{0,1\}^n \to \{0,1\}^m\}$ *be a* t-*wise independent hash function family. If*

$$
\begin{cases}
t \geq 2(m + \ell + \log |\mathcal{F}| + \log(1/\delta) + 3), \\
m \leq n - \ell - 3\log(1/\varepsilon) - \log t - 5,
\end{cases}
$$

then with probability at least $(1 - \delta)$ *over* $h \leftarrow \mathcal{H}$, *it holds that for every* $f \in \mathcal{F}$,

$$
\Delta((f(U_n), h(U_n)), (f(U_n), U_m)) \leq \varepsilon.
$$

The proof of the lemma can be found in the full version, and relies on the ideas similar to those used by [44] to demonstrate deterministic extraction from sources computable by bounded size circuits. We now see how we can get a bounded-SRDM-secure encryption scheme from any secure encryption scheme.

The following transformation is essentially identical to the one used in [31] but using different parameters and using a different analysis.[5]

Definition 7. *For every polynomial s and p and encryption scheme Π = (Gen, Enc, Dec), define a new encryption scheme $\Pi' = (Gen', Enc', Dec')$ as follows:*

- $Gen'(1^k)$: $(pk, sk) \leftarrow Gen(1^k), h_k \leftarrow \mathcal{H}_k$ *where* $\mathcal{H}_k = \{h_k : \{0,1\}^{R'(k)} \rightarrow \{0,1\}^{R(k)}\}$ *is a $t(k)$-wise independent family of hash functions where $R(.)$ is the length of the randomness of Enc, $R'(.)$ is the length of the randomness of Enc',*

$$t(k) \geq 2(R(k) + k + s(k) + p(k) + 3)$$

and

$$R'(k) = p(k) + R(k) + 3k + \log t(k) + 5$$

Output $((pk, h_k), sk)$.
- $Enc'_{(pk,h_k)}(m)$: $r \leftarrow U_{R'(k)}$; *output* $Enc_{pk}(m; h_k(r))$.
- $Dec'_{sk}(c)$: *output* $Dec_{sk}(c)$.

In the full version we show, by appealing to Lemma 1 that the above construction transforms a CPA (resp., CCA) secure scheme to a bounded strong RDM (resp., CCA-RDM) secure scheme (thus implying Theorem 10).

Lemma 2. *Let s, p be polynomials. Let Π be a CPA (resp., CCA) secure public key encryption scheme, and Π' be the transformed encryption scheme obtained from Definition 7. Then, Π' is s-bounded p-strong RDM (resp., CCA-RDM) secure.*

It is clear that bounded strong RDM security implies RDM security. Additionally, in the full version we demonstrate that bounded strong RDM security implies also bounded circular RDM security.

Theorem 11. *For all l-bit public key encryption schemes Π = (Gen, Enc, Dec), if Π is s-bounded l-strong RDM secure (resp., CCA-RDM secure) then Π is s-bounded circular RDM secure (resp., CCA-RDM secure).*

Full RDM Security in the Random Oracle Model. In the full version of this paper, we demonstrate that the above scheme actually yeilds a fully (as opposed to bounded) RDM secure encryption scheme in the random oracle model [7], if replacing the t-wise independent hashfunction with a random oracle. Our use of

---

[5] As mentioned in Section 1.2, the results of [31] require the underlying encryption schemes to satisfy additional properties (e.g., "lossiness") and the results established about the resulting encryption scheme are very different.

the random oracle model is extremely weak: we do not need to "program it", or "see queries to it". Additionally, security holds even if the attacker may get any inefficient non-uniform advice about the random oracle (as in the model of [45]). The only property we need of the random oracle is that it acts as a $k^{\log k}$-wise indepedent hash function (to be able to apply Lemma 1).

This result, combined with Theorem 7, show the existence of a task—RDM secure encryption—that can be achieved in such an "ultra-weak" random oracle model (assuming the existence of CPA secure encryption schemes), but cannot be achieved in the plain model. As far as we know, this is the first separation between tasks achievable in such a weak random oracle model, and the plain model.

5.2   Bounded RDM Security with Short Randomness

The above construction yields strong bounded RDM-secure encryption schemes where the length of the randomness is longer than the length of the message. We now provide a construction of a bounded RDM-secure and bounded circular RDM-secure encryption scheme that can encrypt arbitrarily long messages using "short" randomness. This construction, however, relies on stronger cryptographic assumption—namely, we require the existence of "lossy" trapdoor functions.

Definition 8 ([43]). *A tuple* $(\text{GenLossy}, \text{GenInj}, F, \text{invert}))$ *is an* (n, u)-*lossy trapdoor function if the following holds:*

- *(Injection mode) For every* $k \in \mathbb{N}$, $\Pr[(pk, sk) \leftarrow \text{GenInj}(1^k) : x \leftarrow U_{n(k)} :$
  $\text{invert}_{sk}(F_{pk}(x)) = x] = 1$
- *(Lossy mode) For every* $k \in \mathbb{N}$ *and* $pk \leftarrow \text{GenLossy}(1^k)$, *the size of the range of* $F_{pk}(.)$ *(which takes as input strings of length* $n(k)$*) is at most* $2^{u(k)}$.
- *The following ensembles are computationally indistinguishable*

$$\{(pk, sk) \leftarrow \text{GenInj}(1^k) : pk\}_{k \in \mathbb{N}}$$

$$\{pk \leftarrow \text{GenLossy}(1^k) : pk\}_{k \in \mathbb{N}}$$

We turn to providing our construction of a bounded-RDM secure encryption scheme that can encrypt also "long" messages using "short" randomness—the ratio between the message-length and the randomness length is proportional to the lossiness of the trapdoor function. Formally, we establish the following theorem.

Theorem 12. *Let* l *and* R *be the message length and randomness length parameters with* $R(k) \geq k$. *Assuming the existence of* (n, u)-*lossy trapdoor functions with* $n \geq 3(l + R)$ *and* $u \leq R/8$, *then for every polynomial* s, *there exist a* l-*bit* s-*bounded circular RDM secure encryption scheme with randomness length* R.

In particular, assuming the DDH assumption holds, for every polynomial l, R, s *with* $R(k) \geq k$, *there exist a* l-*bit* s-*bounded circular RDM secure encryption scheme with randomness length* R.

We mention that the "in particular" part of the theorem follows by the DDH-based construction of lossy trapdoor functions in [43]. Our construction is closely related to the "pad-then-deterministic" construction of hedged encryption schemes of Bellare et al [10], where the encryption is done by first applying a *invertible* universal hash *permutation* h to the message-randomness pair $(m||r)$ and then applying a lossy trapdoor function F_{pk} to the hashed value. Recall that hedged encryption scheme already satisfy a notion of RDM security when restricting to RDM functions that do not depend on the public-key. To deal with RDM functions that depend on the public key, our key modification to their scheme is to replace the use of univeral hashing with t-wise independent hashing. However, since constructions of t-wise independent *permutations* are not known, to deal with arbitrary t-wise independent hash functions, we further modify the scheme to "pad" the message-randomness pair with a sufficiently long sequence of 0's.

Recall that the standard construction of t-wise independent hash functions is a degree $t-1$ univariate polynomial over a prime field, which is invertible by the Berlekamp algorithm [13].

Definition 9. *Let l, R, and s be the message length, randomness length, and size parameters with $R(k) \geq k$. Let (GenLossy, GenInj, F, invert) be an (n, u)-lossy trapdoor function with public-key length v such that $u \leq R/8$ and $n = 3(l + R)$. Let $t = 8(s + u + v + R)$ and $\mathcal{H}_n = \{h : \{0,1\}^n \to \{0,1\}^n\}$ be an invertible family of $t(\cdot)$-wise independent hash functions. Define an l-bit s-bounded (circular) RDM-secure encryption scheme $\Pi = $ (Gen, Enc, Dec) with randomness length R as follows[6]:*

- Gen(1^k) : $(pk, sk) \leftarrow$ GenInj(1^k), $h \leftarrow \mathcal{H}_n$; output $((pk, h), (sk, h))$.
- Enc$_{(pk,h)}(m)$: $r \leftarrow U_{R(k)}$; output $c = F_{pk}(h(m||r||0^{2(l+R)}))$.
- Dec$_{(sk,h)}(c)$: output the first $l(k)$ bits of $h^{-1}(\text{invert}_{sk}(c))$.

While our construction is bounded circular RDM secure, it is instructive to first focus on the bounded RDM security. Recall the security of the [10] scheme (which relies on a construction of deterministic encryption from [15]) relies on a "crooked" version of leftover hash lemma [25], which asserts that when F_{pk} has small range size (which is the case in the lossy mode) and the source $(m||r)$ has sufficient min-entropy and is independent of h, then $F_{pk}(h(m||r))$ is statistically close to the "crooked" distribution $F_{pk}(U_{|m|+|r|})$.

In our context, however, the adversary selects a s-bounded RDM function f after seeing the public key, and thus the source $(f(r)||r||0^{2(l+R)})$ may be correlated with the hash function h (and also F_{pk}). We overcome this issue by using t-wise independent hashing and proving a crooked version of the deterministic extraction lemma from computationally bounded source of Trevisan and Vadhan [44]. The lemma asserts that with overwhelming probability over

---

[6] In fact, to achieve only bounded RDM security (as opposed to circular RDM security), it suffices to, say, satisfy $u \leq R/5$ and set $t = 4(s+u+v)$. We do not optimize the parameters here.

$h \leftarrow \mathcal{H}$, the encryption $F_{pk}(f(r)\|r\|0^{2(l+R)})$ is statistically close to a corresponding crooked distribution $F_{pk}(U_n)$ for *every lossy* function F_{pk} and *every* s-bounded RDM function f. Therefore, the s-bounded RMD security follows by switching to the lossy mode and applying the crooked deterministic extraction lemma. We proceed to state the crooked deterministic extraction lemma and prove the s-bounded RDM security of our scheme. The proof of Lemma 3 can be found in the full version and follows similar techniques to those used by [44].

Lemma 3 (Crooked Deterministic Extraction). *Let* $\mathcal{H} = \{h : \{0,1\}^n \to \{0,1\}^n\}$ *be a* t-*wise independent hash function family. Let* $\mathcal{F} = \{f : \{0,1\}^n \to R_f\}$ *be a family of functions where each* $f \in \mathcal{F}$ *has range* R_f *of size* $|R_f| \leq 2^m$. *Let* $\mathcal{C}$ *be a family of distributions over* $\{0,1\}^n$ *such that every* $X \in \mathcal{C}$ *has min-entropy* $H_\infty(X) \geq k$. *If*

$$\begin{cases} t \geq 2(m + \log|\mathcal{F}| + \log|\mathcal{C}| + \log(1/\delta) + 3), \\ m \leq k - 2\log(1/\varepsilon) - \log t - 2, \end{cases}$$

then with probability at least $(1 - \delta)$ *over* $h \leftarrow \mathcal{H}$, *it holds that for every* $f \in \mathcal{F}$ *and every* $X \in \mathcal{C}$,

$$\Delta(f(h(X)), f(U_n)) \leq \varepsilon.$$

In the full version we show the following lemma, by appealing to Lemma 3.

Lemma 4. *The* l-*bit encryption scheme* $\Pi = (\text{Gen}, \text{Enc}, \text{Dec})$ *constructed in Definition 9 is correct and* s-*bounded RDM secure.*

We now turn to prove also circular RDM security of our scheme. To do this, we require the use of a generalized form of the above crooked deterministic extraction lemma that also deals with leakage (just as our "plain" deterministic extraction of leakage-source lemma, lemma 1).

Lemma 5. *Let* $\mathcal{H} = \{h : \{0,1\}^n \to \{0,1\}^n\}$ *be a* t-*wise independent hash function family. Let* $\mathcal{F} = \{f : \{0,1\}^n \to R_f\}$ *be a family of functions where each* $f \in \mathcal{F}$ *has range* R_f *of size* $|R_f| \leq 2^m$. *Let* $\mathcal{G} = \{g : \{0,1\}^n \to \{0,1\}^n\}$ *be a family of functions. Let* $\mathcal{C}$ *be a family of distributions over* $\{0,1\}^n$ *such that every* $X \in \mathcal{C}$ *has min-entropy* $H_\infty(X) \geq k$. *If*

$$\begin{cases} t \geq 2(2m + \log|\mathcal{F}| + \log|\mathcal{G}| + \log|\mathcal{C}| + \log(1/\delta) + 3), \\ m \leq (k - 3\log(1/\varepsilon) - \log t - 5)/2, \end{cases}$$

then with probability at least $(1 - \delta)$ *over* $h \leftarrow \mathcal{H}$, *it holds that for every* $f \in \mathcal{F}$, $g \in \mathcal{G}$, *and* $X \in \mathcal{C}$,

$$\Delta((f(g(X)), f(h(X))), (f(g(X)), f(U_n))) \leq \varepsilon.$$

In the full version we show the following lemma, by appealing to Lemma 5.

Lemma 6. *The* l-*bit encryption scheme* $\Pi = (\text{Gen}, \text{Enc}, \text{Dec})$ *constructed in Definition 9 is* s-*bounded circular RDM secure.*

Acknowledgments. We thank to Mihir Bellare, Rafail Ostrovsky and anonymous referees for very useful comments. We are extremely grateful and indebted to Mihir Bellare for pointing out the connection to Hedged Encryption; in particular, our construction of RDM-secure encryption schemes with short randomness was developed as a consequence of this connection. Thanks a lot!

References

1. Acar, T., Belenkiy, M., Bellare, M., Cash, D.: Cryptographic Agility and Its Relation to Circular Encryption. In: Gilbert, H. (ed.) EUROCRYPT 2010. LNCS, vol. 6110, pp. 403–422. Springer, Heidelberg (2010)
2. Akavia, A., Goldwasser, S., Vaikuntanathan, V.: Simultaneous Hardcore Bits and Cryptography against Memory Attacks. In: Reingold, O. (ed.) TCC 2009. LNCS, vol. 5444, pp. 474–495. Springer, Heidelberg (2009)
3. Alwen, J., Dodis, Y., Wichs, D.: Leakage-Resilient Public-Key Cryptography in the Bounded-Retrieval Model. In: Halevi, S. (ed.) CRYPTO 2009. LNCS, vol. 5677, pp. 36–54. Springer, Heidelberg (2009)
4. Applebaum, B., Harnik, D., Ishai, Y.: Semantic security under related-key attacks and applications. In: ICS, pp. 45–60 (2011)
5. Barak, B.: How to go beyond the black-box simulation barrier. In: FOCS, pp. 106–115 (2001)
6. Barak, B., Haitner, I., Hofheinz, D., Ishai, Y.: Bounded Key-Dependent Message Security. In: Gilbert, H. (ed.) EUROCRYPT 2010. LNCS, vol. 6110, pp. 423–444. Springer, Heidelberg (2010)
7. Bellare, M., Rompel, J.: Randomness-efficient oblivious sampling. In: Proceedings of the 35th Annual Symposium on Foundations of Computer Science, pp. 276–287 (1994)
8. Bellare, M., Boldyreva, A., O'Neill, A.: Deterministic and Efficiently Searchable Encryption. In: Menezes, A. (ed.) CRYPTO 2007. LNCS, vol. 4622, pp. 535–552. Springer, Heidelberg (2007)
9. Bellare, M., Boldyreva, A., Palacio, A.: An Uninstantiable Random-Oracle-Model Scheme for a Hybrid-Encryption Problem. In: Cachin, C., Camenisch, J.L. (eds.) EUROCRYPT 2004. LNCS, vol. 3027, pp. 171–188. Springer, Heidelberg (2004)
10. Bellare, M., Brakerski, Z., Naor, M., Ristenpart, T., Segev, G., Shacham, H., Yilek, S.: Hedged Public-Key Encryption: How to Protect against Bad Randomness. In: Matsui, M. (ed.) ASIACRYPT 2009. LNCS, vol. 5912, pp. 232–249. Springer, Heidelberg (2009)
11. Bellare, M., Fischlin, M., O'Neill, A., Ristenpart, T.: Deterministic Encryption: Definitional Equivalences and Constructions without Random Oracles. In: Wagner, D. (ed.) CRYPTO 2008. LNCS, vol. 5157, pp. 360–378. Springer, Heidelberg (2008)
12. Bellare, M., Keelveedhi, S.: Authenticated and Misuse-Resistant Encryption of Key-Dependent Data. In: Rogaway, P. (ed.) CRYPTO 2011. LNCS, vol. 6841, pp. 610–629. Springer, Heidelberg (2011)
13. Berlekamp, E.R.: Factoring polynomials over finite fields. Bell System Technical Journal 46, 1853–1859 (1967)
14. Black, J., Rogaway, P., Shrimpton, T.: Encryption-Scheme Security in the Presence of Key-Dependent Messages. In: Nyberg, K., Heys, H.M. (eds.) SAC 2002. LNCS, vol. 2595, pp. 62–75. Springer, Heidelberg (2003)

15. Boldyreva, A., Fehr, S., O'Neill, A.: On Notions of Security for Deterministic Encryption, and Efficient Constructions without Random Oracles. In: Wagner, D. (ed.) CRYPTO 2008. LNCS, vol. 5157, pp. 335–359. Springer, Heidelberg (2008)

16. Boneh, D., Halevi, S., Hamburg, M., Ostrovsky, R.: Circular-Secure Encryption from Decision Diffie-Hellman. In: Wagner, D. (ed.) CRYPTO 2008. LNCS, vol. 5157, pp. 108–125. Springer, Heidelberg (2008)

17. Brakerski, Z., Goldwasser, S.: Circular and Leakage Resilient Public-Key Encryption under Subgroup Indistinguishability. In: Rabin, T. (ed.) CRYPTO 2010. LNCS, vol. 6223, pp. 1–20. Springer, Heidelberg (2010)

18. Brakerski, Z., Goldwasser, S., Kalai, Y.T.: Black-Box Circular-Secure Encryption beyond Affine Functions. In: Ishai, Y. (ed.) TCC 2011. LNCS, vol. 6597, pp. 201–218. Springer, Heidelberg (2011)

19. Brakerski, Z., Kalai, Y.T., Katz, J., Vaikuntanathan, V.: Overcoming the hole in the bucket: Public-key cryptography resilient to continual memory leakage. In: Proceedings of the 2010 IEEE 51st Annual Symposium on Foundations of Computer Science, FOCS 2010, pp. 501–510 (2010)

20. Camenisch, J., Chandran, N., Shoup, V.: A Public Key Encryption Scheme Secure against Key Dependent Chosen Plaintext and Adaptive Chosen Ciphertext Attacks. In: Joux, A. (ed.) EUROCRYPT 2009. LNCS, vol. 5479, pp. 351–368. Springer, Heidelberg (2009)

21. Camenisch, J.L., Lysyanskaya, A.: An Efficient System for Non-transferable Anonymous Credentials with Optional Anonymity Revocation. In: Pfitzmann, B. (ed.) EUROCRYPT 2001. LNCS, vol. 2045, pp. 93–118. Springer, Heidelberg (2001)

22. Canetti, R., Goldreich, O., Halevi, S.: On the Random-Oracle Methodology as Applied to Length-Restricted Signature Schemes. In: Naor, M. (ed.) TCC 2004. LNCS, vol. 2951, pp. 40–57. Springer, Heidelberg (2004)

23. Canetti, R., Goldreich, O., Halevi, S.: The random oracle methodology, revisited. J. ACM 51(4), 557–594 (2004)

24. Cash, D., Green, M., Hohenberger, S.: New Definitions and Separations for Circular Security. In: Fischlin, M., Buchmann, J., Manulis, M. (eds.) PKC 2012. LNCS, vol. 7293, pp. 540–557. Springer, Heidelberg (2012)

25. Dodis, Y., Smith, A.: Correcting errors without leaking partial information. In: STOC, pp. 654–663 (2005)

26. Dziembowski, S., Pietrzak, K.: Leakage-resilient cryptography. In: Proceedings of the 2008 49th Annual IEEE Symposium on Foundations of Computer Science, pp. 293–302 (2008)

27. Goldwasser, S., Kalai, Y.T.: On the (in)security of the fiat-shamir paradigm. In: FOCS, pp. 102–113 (2003)

28. Haitner, I., Holenstein, T.: On the (Im)Possibility of Key Dependent Encryption. In: Reingold, O. (ed.) TCC 2009. LNCS, vol. 5444, pp. 202–219. Springer, Heidelberg (2009)

29. Haitner, I., Holenstein, T.: On the (Im)Possibility of Key Dependent Encryption. In: Reingold, O. (ed.) TCC 2009. LNCS, vol. 5444, pp. 202–219. Springer, Heidelberg (2009)

30. Halevi, S., Krawczyk, H.: Security under key-dependent inputs. In: Proceedings of the 14th ACM Conference on Computer and Communications Security, CCS 2007, pp. 466–475 (2007)

31. Hemenway, B., Ostrovsky, R.: Building injective trapdoor functions from oblivious transfer. Electronic Colloquium on Computational Complexity (ECCC) 17 (2010)

32. Hofheinz, D., Unruh, D.: Towards Key-Dependent Message Security in the Standard Model. In: Smart, N.P. (ed.) EUROCRYPT 2008. LNCS, vol. 4965, pp. 108–126. Springer, Heidelberg (2008)
33. Hohenberger, S., Lewko, A., Waters, B.: Detecting Dangerous Queries: A New Approach for Chosen Ciphertext Security. In: Pointcheval, D., Johansson, T. (eds.) EUROCRYPT 2012. LNCS, vol. 7237, pp. 663–681. Springer, Heidelberg (2012)
34. Maurer, U.M., Renner, R.S., Holenstein, C.: Indifferentiability, Impossibility Results on Reductions, and Applications to the Random Oracle Methodology. In: Naor, M. (ed.) TCC 2004. LNCS, vol. 2951, pp. 21–39. Springer, Heidelberg (2004)
35. Micali, S., Reyzin, L.: Physically Observable Cryptography (Extended Abstract). In: Naor, M. (ed.) TCC 2004. LNCS, vol. 2951, pp. 278–296. Springer, Heidelberg (2004)
36. Myers, S., Shelat, A.: Bit encryption is complete. In: FOCS, pp. 607–616 (2009)
37. Naor, M.: On Cryptographic Assumptions and Challenges. In: Boneh, D. (ed.) CRYPTO 2003. LNCS, vol. 2729, pp. 96–109. Springer, Heidelberg (2003)
38. Naor, M., Segev, G.: Public-Key Cryptosystems Resilient to Key Leakage. In: Halevi, S. (ed.) CRYPTO 2009. LNCS, vol. 5677, pp. 18–35. Springer, Heidelberg (2009)
39. Nielsen, J.B.: Separating Random Oracle Proofs from Complexity Theoretic Proofs: The Non-committing Encryption Case. In: Yung, M. (ed.) CRYPTO 2002. LNCS, vol. 2442, pp. 111–126. Springer, Heidelberg (2002)
40. Pass, R.: On Deniability in the Common Reference String and Random Oracle Model. In: Boneh, D. (ed.) CRYPTO 2003. LNCS, vol. 2729, pp. 316–337. Springer, Heidelberg (2003)
41. Pass, R., Rosen, A., Tseng, W.l.D.: Public-coin parallel zero-knowledge for np (2011)
42. Peikert, C., Vaikuntanathan, V., Waters, B.: A Framework for Efficient and Composable Oblivious Transfer. In: Wagner, D. (ed.) CRYPTO 2008. LNCS, vol. 5157, pp. 554–571. Springer, Heidelberg (2008)
43. Peikert, C., Waters, B.: Lossy trapdoor functions and their applications. SIAM J. Comput. 40(6), 1803–1844 (2011)
44. Trevisan, L., Vadhan, S.: Extracting randomness from samplable distributions. In: Proceedings of the 41st Annual Symposium on Foundations of Computer Science, pp. 32–42 (2000)
45. Unruh, D.: Random Oracles and Auxiliary Input. In: Menezes, A. (ed.) CRYPTO 2007. LNCS, vol. 4622, pp. 205–223. Springer, Heidelberg (2007)

Errata to *(Nearly) Round-Optimal Black-Box Constructions of Commitments Secure against Selective Opening Attacks*

David Xiao

LIAFA
CNRS and Université Paris Diderot - Paris 7
dxiao@liafa.univ-paris-diderot.fr

Abstract. Several proofs initially presented by the author [2] were shown to be incorrect in a recent work of Ostrovsky *et al.* [1]. In this notice we summarize the errors and summarize the current state of the art after taking into account the errors and subsequent work.

In TCC 2011 the author claimed several results about nearly round-optimal black-box constructions of commitments secure against selective opening attacks [2]. It was later shown by Ostrovsky *et al.* [1] (a proceedings version appears in the current volume), that several of the proofs in [2] contained errors. Here we restate the errors discovered by Ostrovsky *et al.* [1], and we summarize what remains true from [2], as well as the current state of the art in light of the revised theorems from [2] and subsequent work including [1].

Errors in [2]: (for details, we refer the reader to [1]

1. The proof of Theorem 1, which claimed several nearly round-optimal black-box constructions, is incorrect as presented there. This is due to problems with the hiding and binding properties of the constructions presented there.
2. Items 1 and 2 of Theorem 2, which claimed to rule out selective-opening secure black-box constructions of 3-round parallel computational binding and hiding commitments and 4-round parallel statistically binding commitments, are incorrect. This is due to an incorrect implicit assumption that the sender sends the last message in the commit phase.

Unaffected results: the proofs of the following theorems from [2] remain valid:

1. Item 3 of Theorem 2, stating that one can build constant-round stand-alone statistically hiding commitments in a black-box way using constant-round statistically binding parallel selective-opening secure commitments.
2. Corollary 1, stating that there is no black-box construction using one-way permutations to build constant-round statistically binding parallel selective-opening secure commitments.
3. Theorem 3, stating there exist no black-box constructions for constant-round receiver public-coin protocols and or perfect binding protocols.

Item 4 of Theorem 2 of [2] regarding fully concurrent selective-opening security also remains valid, but this is superseded by the results of [1] (see below).

A. Sahai (Ed.): TCC 2013, LNCS 7785, pp. 721–722, 2013.
© International Association for Cryptologic Research 2013

Revised results: The following weakened statement of Theorem 2, Items 1 and 2 of [2] holds, using the original proof except removing the incorrect implicit assumption that the sender sends the last message in the commit phase:

Theorem (Revision of Theorem 2 of [2]). *There exist no black-box constructions of commitments that are parallel selective-opening secure with 2 rounds and that are computationally binding and hiding, or with 3 rounds and that are statistically binding.*

The author was also able to give a different proof of Item 2 of Theorem 1 of [2], which claimed a black-box construction of $(t + 3)$ statistically-binding parallel selective-opening secure commitments assuming t-round stand-alone statistically hiding commitments, but this is superseded by the results of [4] (see below).

State of the art: For parallel selective opening security, Ostrovsky *et al.* [1] and subsequent work of the author [4] gave the following black-box constructions:

1. 3-round computationally binding and hiding commitments, assuming appropriate stand-alone trapdoor commitment schemes [1] (this is optimal by the revised theorem above).
2. $(t + 2)$-round statistically binding commitments, assuming the existence of stand-alone t-round statistically hiding commitments [4]. (For the case $t = 2$ this is optimal by the above revised theorem.)

Ostrovsky *et al.* [1] also give other constructions with different round complexities under weaker assumptions and/or allowing interactive decommitment.

For concurrent security, it was proved in [1] that *no* secure black-box constructions exist with fully concurrent selective-opening security, although their constructions (including their 3-round construction) are secure in a model they term concurrent-with-barrier. We refer the reader to [1] for details.

Revised Manuscript: a revised (unrefereed) manuscript [3] is available on the Cryptology ePrint archive containing the valid results from [2].

References

[1] Ostrovsky, R., Rao, V., Scafuro, A., Visconti, I.: Revisiting Lower and Upper Bounds for Selective Decommitments. Cryptology ePrint Archive, Report 2011/536 (2011), http://eprint.iacr.org/
[2] Xiao, D.: (Nearly) Round-Optimal Black-Box Constructions of Commitments Secure against Selective Opening Attacks. In: Ishai, Y. (ed.) TCC 2011. LNCS, vol. 6597, pp. 541–558. Springer, Heidelberg (2011)
[3] Xiao, D.: On the round complexity of black-box constructions of commitments secure against selective opening attacks. Technical Report 2009/513, Cryptology ePrint Archive (2012)
[4] Xiao, D.: Round-Optimal Black-Box Statistically Binding Selective-Opening Secure Commitments. In: Mitrokotsa, A., Vaudenay, S. (eds.) AFRICACRYPT 2012. LNCS, vol. 7374, pp. 395–411. Springer, Heidelberg (2012)

Author Index